Civil Procedure

Civil Procedure

Cases, Text, Notes, and Problems

THIRD EDITION

Larry L. Teply
PROFESSOR OF LAW
CREIGHTON UNIVERSITY

Ralph U. Whitten
SENATOR ALLEN A. SEKT PROFESSOR OF LAW
CREIGHTON UNIVERSITY

Denis F. McLaughlin
PROFESSOR OF LAW & WILLIAM E. GARLAND FELLOW
SETON HALL UNIVERSITY

CAROLINA ACADEMIC PRESS
Durham, North Carolina

ISBN 978-1-61163-357-3
LCCN 2013939805

Carolina Academic Press
700 Kent Street
Durham, North Carolina 27701
Telephone (919) 489-7486
Fax (919) 493-5668
www.cap-press.com

Printed in the United States of America

Contents

Table of Cases

Principal cases are listed in bolded capital typeface. References are to pages of the casebook. **Bold page numbers indicate the location of reprinted cases.** Cases cited in principal cases and within other quoted materials are not included in this Table of Cases.

Table of Short Form Citations

CHEMERINSKY = ERWIN CHEMERINSKY, FEDERAL JURISDICTION (5th ed. 2007).

CLARK = CHARLES E. CLARK, HANDBOOK OF THE LAW OF CODE PLEADING (2d ed. 1947).

[vol.] DOBBS = DAN B. DOBBS, LAW OF REMEDIES (2d practitioner's ed. 1993).

Federal Form = Federal Forms in the Appendix of Forms to the Federal Rules of Civil Procedure.

KOFFLER & REPPY = JOSEPH H. KOFFLER & ALISON REPPY, HANDBOOK OF COMMON LAW PLEADING (1969).

TEPLY & WHITTEN = LARRY L. TEPLY & RALPH U. WHITTEN, CIVIL PROCEDURE (5th ed. 2013).

[title] U.S.C. = UNITED STATES CODE (with varying dates).

WRIGHT & KANE = CHARLES A. WRIGHT & MARY K. KANE, THE LAW OF FEDERAL COURTS (7th ed. 2011).

[vol.] WRIGHT ET AL. = CHARLES A. WRIGHT, ARTHUR R. MILLER & EDWARD H. COOPER, FEDERAL PRACTICE AND PROCEDURE (3d ed., vols. 13, 15-16, 18-19, with varying dates).

[vol.] WRIGHT ET AL. = CHARLES A. WRIGHT, ARTHUR R. MILLER, EDWARD H. COOPER & JOAN E. STEINMAN, FEDERAL PRACTICE AND PROCEDURE (3d ed., vol. 14, with varying dates).

[vol.] WRIGHT ET AL. = CHARLES A. WRIGHT, ARTHUR R. MILLER & MARY KAY KANE, FEDERAL PRACTICE AND PROCEDURE (3d ed., vols. 6-7C, 10-11A, with varying dates).

[vol.] WRIGHT ET AL. = CHARLES A. WRIGHT, ARTHUR R. MILLER & RICHARD L. MARCUS, FEDERAL PRACTICE AND PROCEDURE (3d ed., vols. 8-8A, 12, with varying dates).

[vol.] WRIGHT & MILLER = CHARLES A. WRIGHT & ARTHUR R. MILLER, FEDERAL PRACTICE AND PROCEDURE (3d ed., vols. 4-5B, 9-9A, with varying dates).

Preface

This third edition of *Civil Procedure: Cases, Text, Notes, and Problems* continues the philosophy and fundamental features of the first two editions. We have updated this edition to reflect all current amendments of the Federal Rules of Civil Procedure as well as federal statutes, including the "Federal Courts Jurisdiction and Venue Clarification Act of 2011." The new edition also includes the latest decisions of the U.S. Supreme Court on subject-matter and personal jurisdiction, the Erie Doctrine, class actions, pleadings, joinder, and preclusion. The new edition also continues to cover all Federal Civil Procedure bar examination topics.

At the level of introductory Civil Procedure, law school curricula typically provide from three to six credit hours within which to cover the wide range of topics relevant to civil litigation. We have constructed this casebook to accommodate the demands and opportunities presented by "short" and "long" courses alike. It carefully integrates both basic and more complex issues of federal and state civil procedure. This material is presented in a "user friendly" format. Throughout the book, explanatory text has been interwoven with illustrative cases, notes, questions, and figures to make the presentation of the material more efficient for the professor and more understandable for the student. As an additional teaching feature, all of the chapters contain carefully drafted problems following each topic section. The problems are designed to provide maximum teaching flexibility—enabling a professor to utilize the problems in each section to teach all or part of the material.

The casebook is also organized to facilitate a variety of teaching approaches. Chapter 1 provides background and introduction to all topics germane to the civil litigation process. Professors then have the option to commence more in-depth treatment beginning with Jurisdiction and Venue in Chapters 2 through 4 or with Pleadings and Joinder in Chapters 6 and 7.

In all of the chapters, we have selected cases with regard to each topic that will optimize students' understanding of the important issues pertaining to the topic. We have included traditional cases when we believe they are the best vehicles with which to produce a clear understanding of a topic. However, we include a significant number of recent cases when they are better learning tools.

The text, notes, and questions accompanying the cases are designed to help students read the cases effectively and critically. The explanatory text also provides historical material that bears on the evolution of the procedures being studied when necessary for a clear understanding of the topic. The notes and questions accompanying the cases raise other matters related to the issues explored in the cases. The notes and questions also address other issues of real concern in the general procedural area under study, but which may be a step beyond the material directly covered by the case. This array of material thus allows individual professors to select the best way in which to achieve comprehension of the subject of Civil Procedure.

As is true with virtually all Civil Procedure casebooks, the materials primarily focus on federal practice, especially the Federal Rules of Civil Procedure. However, we have also included materials on state practice and highlighted the contrast with federal practice when it is important for a full understanding of particular procedural topics. The traditional mainstays of Civil Procedure—personal and subject-matter jurisdiction, the Erie doctrine, pleadings, and joinder—receive comprehensive treatment. Furthermore, with the ever-increasing emphasis in modern practice on pre-trial litigation, special treatment is afforded discovery, including "e-discovery."

We owe a significant debt to the people who supported and encouraged us in the preparation of this third edition. Particular mention should be made of the support provided by Creighton University School of Law and Seton Hall University School of Law. Professors Teply and Whitten wish to thank Creighton law librarian, Kay Andrus, and the staff of the Klutznick Law Library for their research support. They also wish to thank the efficient and helpful secretarial assistance provided by Pat Andersen and Pam Flint as well as the copying services provided by Colleen Kelly-Firmature.

Professor McLaughlin wishes to thank his research assistant, Nicole M. Magdziak, and Seton Hall reference librarian, Jeanne O'Connor, for their invaluable assistance.

Special thanks are also due to our Civil Procedure students at Creighton and Seton Hall for their helpful comments and suggestions. We also appreciate the excellent assistance of Joellen Craft and Tim Colton of Carolina Academic Press.

Finally, more than thanks is due to our families who have suffered through multiple editions of this casebook. Professor Teply wishes to dedicate this casebook to his grandchildren: Anna Louisa Teply, Nicholas Benjamin Teply, Lydia Beatrice Teply, and Clara Elizabeth Teply. Professor McLaughlin also wishes to dedicate this casebook in loving memory of his parents, Marie and William McLaughlin, and with heartfelt thanks to his wife, Barbara, and his children, Kathleen and Kevin.

Larry L. Teply
Ralph U. Whitten
Denis F. McLaughlin
June 2013

Civil Procedure

Chapter 1

Introduction to Civil Procedure and Practice

In Anglo-American legal systems, *civil actions* are the basic means by which parties resolve legal disputes. *Civil procedure* is the body of rules that prescribes the method of conducting those actions. This book examines the systems of civil procedure used in the state and federal courts of the United States.

Chapter 1 introduces the subject of civil procedure and provides an overview of the many topics that will be examined in greater detail in subsequent chapters. Chapter 1 consists of textual discussion with specific references to applicable statutes and rules. Problems are interwoven to provide you an opportunity to review some of the basic information explained in this chapter. Throughout the course, you should continue to view Chapter 1 as a handy reference chapter and as a glossary of the many procedural terms and concepts germane to the civil litigation process.

Section A. The Study of the Subject of "Civil Procedure" and Its Importance

Most law school courses, such as Contracts, Torts, and Property, focus on *substantive law*—the body of law governing the "primary rights and obligations" of persons relative to others. In these courses, you will learn when a breach of contract occurs, what the elements of various torts are, what laws govern the ownership of property, etc. However, few clients will enter a lawyer's office and ask, "What are the elements of promissory estoppel?" Instead, a client is much more likely to tell the lawyer, "I was fired from my job" and want to know, "Can I get it back?" Civil Procedure defines the form and method by which substantive legal rights are enforced and provides the means for securing a proper remedy if the client is entitled to one under the applicable substantive law.

The study of Civil Procedure focuses on understanding how litigation is conducted. This course will help you answer questions that lawyers must constantly ask themselves: In what court or courts can my client sue? How do I present my client's grievance? Who must be joined in the litigation? How do I present objections? Can I require the opposing party to provide me with information about the case? Is my client entitled to a jury trial? Can I take advantage of determinations made in prior litigation?

In addition, the study of Civil Procedure is concerned with strategy and tactics. Given the choices of the courts and locations for suit, which one would be most advantageous to my client? Considering the possible defendants, which one or ones should be sued? Even if my client is entitled to demand a jury trial, will this case be a good one to be decided by a judge rather than a jury? Would it be better to structure the action as a class action? Of the options available to discover needed information, which option would be the best?

Traditionally, you will learn the "substantive law" by reading and analyzing appellate court decisions. You will also be reading appellate court decisions in Civil Procedure. However, a distinctive feature of the subject of Civil Procedure is its focus on the set of rules and statutory provisions governing the conduct of civil litigation. Much of the time in this course will be spent understanding the nature and relationship of these rules, focusing on the meaning and requirements of relevant statutes, and learning how these rules and statutes are applied.

Some of the time will also be spent on learning the terminology of civil litigation. What is a "third-party complaint"? What are "Rule 11 sanctions"? What is "interpleader"? What is "judgment as a matter of law"? What is the "clean-up doctrine"? What is "supplemental jurisdiction"? Lawyers know the meaning of terms such as these without having to look them up, and you will come to understand them as this course progresses.

In sum, the subject of Civil Procedure is essential to practicing lawyers involved in civil litigation. It is used to achieve a client's legal goals by providing the means to "bridge the gap" between the client's legal rights on one side and the desired legal remedy on the other. Elements of Civil Procedure will be present in *every* litigated civil case no matter what substantive rights are involved. Furthermore, failure to master this subject may lead to the loss of a client's rights as a result of procedural errors or missteps.

Section B. Court Systems in the United States

An essential prerequisite for learning about civil actions and civil procedure is a basic understanding of the organization of court systems in the United States.

Federalism. The United States is a federal system, meaning that governing authority is divided between a central federal government and the fifty individual states. The U.S. Constitution authorizes the federal government to operate only within limited subject areas, and the fifty state governments retain authority over many subject areas within their respective geographical boundaries. The Constitution makes federal laws supreme on subjects within the scope of the authority of the federal government, but many areas of substantive law, such as contracts, torts and property, are governed by state, not federal, law. Another consequence of the federal system is the existence of dual courts in each state — federal courts created under the authority of the federal government and state courts created under the authority of each state government. Procedure in the federal courts is governed by the Federal Rules of Civil Procedure, but the states are free to adopt their own rules of procedure for application in their state courts.

State Court Systems. The typical structure of a state court system is illustrated in Figure 1-1. Civil actions are usually commenced and initially adjudicated in the trial courts. The highest court in the state reviews decisions of lower courts in the state if the lower court decisions are appealed. Many states also have intermediate appellate courts that hear appeals from the trial courts. Some states have just one intermediate appellate court. Others have multiple intermediate appellate courts that adjudicate appeals from trial courts in different locations within the state.

The most common designation of the highest court in a court system is the "Supreme Court," *e.g.*, the California Supreme Court. Some states use other designations, *e.g.*, the

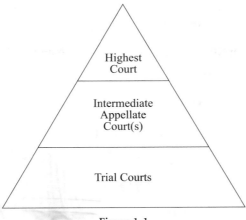

Figure 1-1

New York Court of Appeals or the Massachusetts Supreme Judicial Court. The names of intermediate appellate courts also vary. For example, in California, they are called Courts of Appeal; in Florida, they are called District Courts of Appeal; and in New York, they are called the Appellate Division of the Supreme Court. The principal trial courts are frequently called district courts, superior courts, or circuit courts. For example, in California, they are called Superior Courts; in Nebraska, they are called District Courts; and in New York, they are called Supreme Courts. Other specialized courts, variously named, also exist. These courts include county courts, probate courts, small claims courts, housing courts, and domestic relations courts.

The vast majority of civil actions are filed in state, rather than federal, courts. In 2010, for instance, nearly 19 million civil actions were filed nationwide in state courts compared to 293,352 civil actions (excluding bankruptcy filings) in the federal district courts. *See* NATIONAL CENTER FOR STATE COURTS, EXAMINING THE WORK OF STATE COURTS: AN ANALYSIS OF 2010 STATE COURT CASELOADS (2012); ADMINISTRATIVE OFFICE OF THE UNITED STATES COURTS, STATISTICAL TABLES FOR THE FEDERAL JUDICIARY, Dec. 31, 2010, Table C-2. Likewise, the number of state court judges far exceeds the number of federal judges. In California, for example, there are twice as many state court judges as there are nationwide in the entire federal court system.

The Federal Court System. The United States district courts are the principal federal trial courts. There is at least one federal district court in every state, and some states are divided into multiple districts. For example, Florida is divided into the Northern, Middle, and Southern Districts. The federal intermediate appellate courts are today called courts of appeals. Thirteen federal courts of appeals exist. Most of these courts hear appeals taken from federal district courts within a specific geographical area. For example, the U.S. Court of Appeals for the Second Circuit covers appeals from federal district courts in Vermont, New York, and Connecticut; the Fifth Circuit covers Texas, Louisiana, and Mississippi; and the Eighth Circuit covers North Dakota, South Dakota, Nebraska, Minnesota, Iowa, Missouri, and Arkansas. The Court of Appeals for the Federal Circuit hears appeals from all district courts involving patent litigation and certain claims against the federal government. Some additional specialized federal courts also exist, for example, the Court of International Trade, the Court of Federal Claims and the Tax Court. Of course, the top of the pyramid in the federal court system is the U.S. Supreme Court.

Hierarchy of Authority. State constitutions, statutes, and procedural rules define and limit the scope of state-court authority. Similarly, the U.S. Constitution, federal statutes, and federal procedural rules define, limit, and regulate the authority of the United States courts. However, while the U.S. Constitution limits the authority of the state courts in certain ways, state constitutions do not limit the authority of the federal courts.

Section C. The Role of Civil Actions in the Administration of Justice

1. The Relationship Between Civil, Criminal, and Administrative Actions

As noted above, parties commence *civil actions* to resolve disputes governed by the noncriminal substantive law. In contrast, the government usually brings *criminal actions* to enforce the substantive criminal law against persons who violate it. A criminal action may be brought even if an injured party also sues for damages—whether or not the injured party wins or loses. The punishments for violating criminal laws are usually fines or imprisonments. Thus, one fundamental division between civil and criminal law in the United States is that legal "remedies" (such as damages) redress *civil wrongs* in civil actions while the government imposes "punishments" for *criminal violations*. In addition, all American legal systems provide for administrative actions. *Administrative actions* generally involve disputes between private parties and government officials or agencies charged with the responsibility of enforcing civil or criminal laws.

Civil, criminal, and administrative proceedings can all originate from a single event, such as an auto accident. If a driver was guilty of a traffic violation leading to the accident, the accident may lead to a traffic citation. It also may lead to a civil action by the injured parties. In addition, it may lead to a proceeding to revoke one of the drivers' licenses under appropriate circumstances. The action to revoke the license may be an administrative proceeding. Furthermore, if the driver loses, the driver may have a right to obtain judicial review of that adverse decision in a civil proceeding.

The rules and principles of civil procedure govern how parties conduct civil actions. Rules of criminal procedure govern criminal actions and special rules of administrative procedure govern administrative actions. Other law school courses will address criminal and administrative procedure. Although separate systems of procedure govern civil, criminal, and administrative actions, considerable overlap and similarity exist between the systems. For example, due process clauses in the state and federal constitutions in the United States apply in similar ways to civil, criminal, and administrative proceedings. Likewise, many of the same rules govern the kinds of evidence that can be admitted in both civil and criminal actions. Analogous evidentiary rules exist in administrative proceedings.

2. Limits of Civil Actions in Resolving Disputes

Many disputes are brought to the courts for decision as "civil actions." Most of those disputes fall within traditional areas of the substantive law and routinely proceed through the court system. However, some cases fall at or near the outer limits of the kinds of cases that the courts will accept. When courts find that a civil action is not an appropriate type of case for the courts to adjudicate, the courts will rule that the case is not "*justiciable.*"

For example, in *Georgia High School Association v. Waddell,* 285 S.E.2d 7 (Ga. 1981), Osborne and Lithia Springs High Schools were playing a high school championship play-off football game. The score was 7 to 6 in favor of Osborne, with 7 minutes, 1 second, remaining in the game. Osborne had the ball on its 47-yard line, fourth down and 21 yards to go for a first down. Osborne punted, but a "roughing the kicker" penalty was called on the Lithia Springs team. The referee officiating the game assessed a 15-yard penalty, placed the ball on the 38-yard line, and declared it to be fourth down and 6 yards to go for Osborne. However, the rules clearly provided that the penalty for "roughing the kicker" was 15 yards and an automatic first down. Osborne's coaches disputed the referee's decision, but play was resumed. With fourth down and 6 yards to go at the 38-yard line, Osborne punted again. Lithia Springs received the punt, drove down the field, and scored a three-point field goal to win the game.

Osborne filed a protest with the proper State High School Association authorities, but it was denied on the ground that an "official protest" had not been made to the referee by Osborne's coaches immediately following the play in question. Osborne's coaches, however, vigorously asserted that their protest at the time should be considered sufficient to constitute an "official protest." The parents of Osborne's football players then filed a civil action in the proper Georgia trial court. They asserted that the players had a property right in the game of football being played according to the rules. In addition, they asserted that the referee had violated this property right and had denied the players equal protection of the laws by failing to apply the rules correctly. *Id.* at 8.

After a hearing in which evidence was taken, the trial court found that the referee's decision clearly violated the rules and that a sufficient protest had been made by Osborne's coaches. The court then ordered the game between the two teams to resume on an upcoming date, with 7 minutes, 1 second left in the fourth quarter, the ball at Lithia Springs' 38 yard line, and Osborne in possession with a first down. *Id.* On appeal, the Georgia Supreme Court reversed and held "that courts ... in this state are without authority to review decisions of football referees because those decisions do not present judicial controversies." *Id.* at 9; *cf. McDonald v. John P. Scripps Newspaper,* 257 Cal. Rptr. 473 (Ct. App. 1989) (error committed by national spelling bee contest officials was not justiciable, quoting *Evans v. Evans,* 161 Eng. Rep. 466, 467 (Consistory Ct. 1790): "Courts of Justice do not pretend to furnish cures for all the miseries of human life. They redress or punish gross violations of duty, but they go no farther; they cannot make [people] virtuous; and, as the happiness of the world depends upon its virtue, there may be much unhappiness in it which human laws cannot undertake to remove.").

Cudahy Junior Chamber of Commerce v. Quirk

Supreme Court of Wisconsin, 1969
41 Wis. 2d 698, 165 N.W.2d 116

In the spring election of 1966, the voters of the [C]ity of Cudahy [Wisconsin] were to decide by referendum whether the community water supply was to be fluoridated. A leading proponent of fluoridation was the Cudahy Junior Chamber of Commerce. A leading foe of fluoridating the water was James Quirk, working as or through The Greater Milwaukee Committee Against Fluoridation.

In the midst of the spirited campaign, Quirk "challenged" the Jaycees, offering to give them $1,000 " ... if a daily dose of four glasses [of fluoridated water] cannot cause 'dermatologic, gastrointestinal and neurological disorders,'" and adding, "If the Jaycees should find that we have misrepresented matters in this paper, we will then also pay the sum of $1,000." The Jaycees did some checking, so found to their satisfaction, and demanded payment by Quirk of $1,000. When payment was refused, the Jaycees brought this action, seeking (1) a court finding that Quirk did misrepresent matters in his brochure; (2) a court finding that four glasses of fluoridated water cannot cause the mentioned disorders; [and] (3) a court judgment for $1,000. [After a jury trial,] the jury found misrepresentation. Judgment was granted on the verdict. Motions after verdict were denied. Defendant Quirk appeals.

Jaycees sought

ROBERT W. HANSEN, JUSTICE.

This case revolves around a question and answer that headed up a two-page brochure that James Quirk distributed in Cudahy, urging a "No" vote in the April, 1966 election on the question of whether the public water supply should be fluoridated. Here's the question and here's the answer:

> [Question] Is it true, as Dr. Chelius has once again told the people of Cudahy that "A person would have to drink the equivalent of fifty bathtubs of water at once to get a harmful dose of fluoride?"

> [Answer] So preposterous is this statement that we shall give $1,000 to the Jaycees for fluoridation promotion if a daily dose of four glasses cannot cause "dermatologic, gastrointestinal and neurological disorders." If the Jaycees should find that we have misrepresented matters in this paper, we will then also pay the sum of $1,000.

WHAT HAVE WE HERE?

In the eyes of the law, exactly what is this sort of challenge made in the heat of an election campaign? Was it an offer that, upon acceptance, became a binding contract? Was it a reward, analogous to the sums of money offered for information leading to the arrest and conviction of the perpetrator of a crime? Was it a bet, a wagering of $1,000 against the possibility that one might be wrong?

In [the] *Restatement [of] Contracts* [§] 520, comment c, the following is stated: "A wager may relate to a trial of skill or to *proof of an actual fact* or even to a certain point that happened in the past" (emphasis supplied). The *Restatement* gives this example of a wager:

> A promises B one hundred dollars if B can give ocular demonstration of the rotundity of the earth, to the satisfaction of C; in consideration of which B promises to pay a similar amount if [B] fails. B, by sights established over a large lake, satisfies C. A does not believe when [A] enters into the transaction that B can make the proof. B knows [B] can. Though condition is not fortuitous, the transaction is a wager.

The only difference between the example given and the case before us is that the Jaycees were not required to risk their $1,000 or any other amount of money to accept the bet or take up the challenge. It can be contended that the time, effort, and expense involved in seeking to prove the defendant wrong supply the element of consideration, a something lost if the effort to prove the defendant wrong should fail. This would make the accepted challenge a contract, but would not change the nature of such contract. It would remain a wager, unenforceable as against public policy....

WHO WON THE BET?

The jury's finding, which was sustained by the trial court, was that the Jaycees won the wager. This amounted to an acceptance of the credibility of the testimony offered by the Jaycees that Quirk had "misrepresented matters" in his brochure. We do not reach the issue of fact as to who won and who lost the wager. Our holding is that the participants ~Holding~ in a wager may not use the court to settle their dispute because gambling debts cannot be established or collected in the courts.

The Question of Public Policy

In addition to the judicial reluctance to hold the stakes or decide the winner in a betting situation, there are sound reasons of public policy for not having court or jury decide whose gloved fist is to be lifted in victory in this dispute. It is clear that, while $1,000 would be a welcome addition to club coffers, the primary concern of the Jaycees is to vindicate the rightness of their position that fluoridation of the Cudahy water supply involves no harmful side effects. It is at least as clear that James Quirk's principal interest is in seeking court confirmation of his contention that fluoridation of a community's drinking water risks harmful consequences....

If disputants on the issue of the harmful effects of fluoridation can[, by] the process of challenge and acceptance[,] bring their dispute on this issue of public concern to the courts for adjudication, the list of matters in which litigants could seek determinations by the court of questions of public policy would be a long one. Dedicated crusaders for varying points of view, pro and con, by the process of challenge and response, could have courts rule on whether birth control pills have harmful side-effects, whether cigarettes cause cancer, [or] whether sugar substitutes alter chromosomes. If there are ways of bringing such controversies to court, putting up $1,000 to be paid to anyone who can prove you wrong does not make the courts the forum or the referee. Here the true controversy is as to the effects of fluoridation. We have grave doubts as to whether this is a justiciable issue—one appropriate for judicial inquiry....

The Issue of Public Debate

It is to be remembered that the brochure in which the claimed misrepresentation was printed was a part of the public debate of a public issue in a public referendum. It is pertinent that "... more than 900 referendums on fluoridation have been held in the United States since 1950.... Probably no issue of science and public policy has involved as much emotional fervor as fluoridation of public drinking water." ... This case must be considered against the background of what has been termed "... a profound national commitment to the principle that debate on public issues should be uninhibited, robust, and wide-open." ...

While there may be situations in which the courts are required to intervene, as in cases of libel or slander, it is clear that there is a wide latitude constitutionally assured to participants in the political process of persuading an electorate to vote, Yes, or, No, in a referendum election. It includes the right to be wrong, as one side almost always is in a debate of a public issue.

It is understandable that the Jaycees, a civic organization of young men with an established record for effective participation in civic enterprises, would want to have its presentation of facts found to be accurate, and that of its principal adversary found to be false, misleading and misrepresented. It is not the role or function of the judicial branch of our government to make that determination. Some may see it as a weakness, but it is the heart of the referendum law and the democratic process that, in this situation, the voters, not judge or jury, are to bring in the verdict. We can with propriety commend all individuals and all groups who participate in securing the expressed will of an informed electorate, but it is not for us to determine whose presentation had either the greatest accuracy or greatest persuasiveness. The cases, affirmative and negative, were submitted to the jury at the polls. They were not for a jury in a courtroom to affirm or reverse.

The what, why, when, and where of this case require that the judgment be reversed and the case dismissed.

    ....

Notes and Questions

1. In the *Waddell* case (which is summarized immediately before the *Cudahy* opinion), why did the Georgia Supreme Court decide that judicial review of the football referee's decision in that case did not raise a "justiciable" issue? Was it because a football referee's decision in a high school football game is not "important" enough to justify judicial intervention? If that is the touchstone of *Waddell* and similar cases, then why did the Wisconsin Supreme Court in *Cudahy* hold that the issue of whether fluoride causes neurological damage was not justiciable? Certainly, that issue is more "important" than the decision of a football referee, isn't it?

2. In *Cudahy*, the Wisconsin Supreme Court indicated that it would be inappropriate for the courts to "rule on whether birth control pills have harmful side effects, whether cigarettes cause cancer, [or] whether sugar substitutes alter chromosomes." *Cudahy*, 165 N.W.2d at 119. But haven't the courts decided all of these issues and more in many highly publicized cases in recent years? Consider, for example, the multibillion dollar liability cases that were successfully litigated against the tobacco companies over the past two decades. Didn't the courts in these cases necessarily agree to decide whether cigarettes caused a variety of health problems justifying legal compensation? If the nature of the issue, *i.e.*, a football referee's decision, is the trouble spot in *Waddell*, is the trouble spot in *Cudahy* something else? Is it that the nature of the issue is important in *Cudahy*, but the particular manner in which the issue is presented makes the case not "justiciable"?

3. If a child actually ingested fluoride or some other product and suffered neurological damage because of inadequate warnings about the dangers of the product, would this case then present a justiciable issue? Is such a case now different from *Cudahy*? If so, how?

4. Returning to the football (*Waddell*) case, suppose one of the students at Osborne High School was told by the referee that the student could not play in the game because of the student's race or ethnicity? Would this "decision" of the referee now raise a justiciable issue? What's different about this case?

5. In this regard, consider the U.S. Supreme Court's decision in professional golfer Casey Martin's suit against the PGA. Martin, a talented golfer, suffered from a progressive, degenerative circulatory disorder that eventually atrophied his right leg. As a result, Martin could no longer walk an 18-hole golf course, and he requested that PGA tour officials allow him to ride in a golf cart in PGA tournaments. When the tour officials denied Martin's request, he sued the PGA claiming that the PGA's decision unlawfully discriminated against him under the federal "Americans with Disabilities Act" because he suffered from a protected disability. The U.S. Supreme Court upheld Martin's claim under the federal act. *See PGA Tour, Inc. v. Martin*, 532 U.S. 661 (2001). Why did this "decision" by the golf officials raise a "justiciable" issue, but the "decision" by the football officials in *Waddell* did not?

6. Can you now articulate a general standard for when a case presents a justiciable issue? Is it that (a) the litigants must be "proper" litigants in the sense that they are ap-

propriate persons to present the issue for decision and (b) the issue raised must be a "proper" issue in that it is sufficiently important and appropriate for judicial decision? If "justiciability" can be explained in this two-part test, which part of the test did the *Waddell* case fail? Which part did the *Cudahy* case fail?

Case Captions. As you read cases, be aware that some appellate courts, like the U.S. Supreme Court and some state supreme courts, adjust lower court case captions to list the party advancing the appeal first. Thus, in both the *PGA Tour* and *Georgia High School Association* cases, the PGA Tour and the Georgia High School Association were listed first in the supreme court captions, even though these parties were the defendants in the trial courts. However, the appellate courts in all jurisdictions do not do this, as the *Cudahy* case illustrates. In *Cudahy,* it was the defendant Quirk who advanced the appeal, but the Wisconsin Supreme Court caption remained the same as the original lower court caption.

Section D. The Adversary System

Civil actions in the United States are conducted according to an *adversary system.*

Characteristics of the Adversary System. In an adversary system, the parties, usually through their lawyers, bear the principal burden of initiating, developing, and presenting their dispute in court. Thus, the parties must present their respective legal claims and defenses and define the issues. They must develop proof in support of their respective positions and demonstrate that proof to the court. If the case is not settled or otherwise disposed of during the pretrial stage, these activities culminate in a trial before a judge and, depending on the circumstances, maybe also a jury. The final result of the proceeding is a *judgment*, a formal determination of the controversy.

In a "pure" adversary system, the parties to a civil action would have to develop their cases without assistance from the opposing parties or the court. Such a system might produce difficulties that would distort the result on the merits in many cases. For example, if the financial resources available to one party were substantially greater than those available to the opposing party, the richer party would be in a vastly superior litigating position. Likewise, if the lawyer for one party were of significantly greater competence than the lawyer for the opposing party, the side with the more competent representation would often prevail, even if that side possessed the objectively weaker case on the merits. Similarly, if evidence needed to prove one party's case were in the exclusive possession of the other party, the party needing the evidence would lose the action in a pure adversary system.

Restraints on the Adversary System. Modern procedural systems attempt to mitigate the rigors of the adversary system in a variety of ways to prevent excessive distortion of the merits of civil actions. For example, modern procedural systems contain *discovery rules.* These rules allow each party to learn what evidence the opposing party has that bears on the claims or defenses in the action. In this way, modern systems seek to avoid the problem that occurs when essential evidence is in the exclusive possession of one of the parties. Rules of discovery also seek to avoid "unfair surprise" by forcing each of the parties to disclose the evidence they will rely on to prove their own side of the case.

Nevertheless, procedural rules cannot completely eliminate litigational advantages produced by the adversary system. For example, disparities in party resources or lawyer competence will always produce advantages that procedural rules cannot entirely eradicate. Still, at least to some extent, procedural rules can enhance the strengths and diminish the weaknesses of the adversary process.

When procedural rules, such as discovery rules, attempt to affect the adversary system, they can produce new problems that may have to be addressed by court decisions or additional procedural rules. For example, modern discovery rules are tempered by restrictions that prevent parties from engaging in excessive discovery that unduly burdens other parties. Discovery is also restricted to protect the "work product" of the parties (*i.e.*, materials prepared in anticipation of litigation or preparation for trial).

Ethical constraints also prevent lawyers from abusing the adversary process. For example, it is unethical for lawyers to bring "frivolous" lawsuits—*i.e.*, lawsuits that have no basis in fact or law. Similarly, lawyers cannot knowingly make false statements of fact or offer false evidence. Lawyers can be punished in a variety of ways for violating ethical restrictions, including disbarment and monetary sanctions payable to the court or other parties.

Costs of Litigation. Litigation involves public costs, principally the cost of maintaining the court system. At present, the taxpayers bear most of these costs. Litigation also involves private costs, including the cost of securing legal representation and the cost of investigating, preparing, and presenting the case to the court. With few exceptions, each party bears most of its own litigation costs, including attorney's fees. In most instances, the substantive law simply does not provide for their recovery.

As discussed in the next section, a system of publicly supported courts for the resolution of private civil disputes is a deeply rooted and longstanding feature of the Anglo-American litigation system. On the other hand, the rule requiring each party to pay its own litigation costs is a feature of the adversary system in the United States, but not in England.

In recent years, the increasing public and private costs of litigation have spawned a variety of reforms and proposed reforms designed to decrease or shift litigation costs in a variety of ways. However, these proposals have focused almost entirely on the heavy costs of litigation to private parties, rather than on increased public costs. For example, Chapter 9 and the discussion below will examine methods of alternative dispute resolution that shift the resolution of civil controversies from expensive and time-consuming formal litigation to less expensive and more rapid methods. Chapters 6, 8, and 9 will examine rules and proposed reforms designed to shift the private expenses of civil litigation from one party (usually the winner) to the other (usually the loser).

Section E. Historical Origins of Civil Procedure

Modern procedural rules in the United States are the result of an evolutionary process originating in England. Today, some aspects of procedural rules are entirely the result of historical accident and can only be understood as such. Other aspects reflect successive reforms in which older procedures have been updated to fit modern conditions. Even when a more modern rule has replaced an older one, however, an understanding of the purpose of the change is essential to interpreting and applying the modern rule properly. This section briefly summarizes the historical evolution of procedure, which will be helpful in understanding the modern procedures that you will study later.

1. Writs and the Forms of Action

Development of the Royal Courts. Before the Norman Conquest of England in 1066, local courts administered justice according to local custom. After the Conquest, a system of royal courts developed. These courts—the King's Bench, Exchequer, and Common Pleas—did not replace the preexisting local courts. Unlike the preexisting local courts, justice in the royal courts was not part of the public machinery of the state. Instead, the courts were available at the king's discretion and applied to those cases that "interested" the king.

The royal courts offered litigants several advantages over the preexisting local courts. First, royal justice was convenient. Judges traveled from place to place for the purpose of holding trials. The formal papers in the litigation were sent to the full courts sitting at Westminster for determination of legal questions and for entry of the judgment, but the trials were local. Second, judges and lawyers in the royal courts developed expertise and, as a result, presumably provided better justice to the parties. Third, the royal courts offered a better means of determining facts in many (but not all) types of actions than the local courts: the precursor of the modern trial by jury.

In contrast, the local courts used older modes of trial, mainly *trial by battle* or "*wager of law*" (also called *compurgation*). *Wager of law* required one of the parties to swear a formal oath to the justice of the party's claim or to the injustice of the opposing party's claim and to produce several "oath helpers," usually twelve. However, the oath helpers did not swear to the facts. Instead, the oath helpers swore that a party's oath was trustworthy. A party lost if the party was unable to get the required number of oath helpers. A party also lost if the party or any of the oath helpers made an error in the formal oath.

Original Writs. The royal courts were limited to the type of matter delegated to them by administrative orders that came to be known as *original writs*. These writs had a twofold purpose: (1) they ordered the sheriff to summon the defendant to appear in court on a specific day; and (2) they gave the court authority to hear the case. A person who wanted a writ had to purchase it from the king's secretary, the chancellor. Each writ contained a summary statement of the cause of the complaint.

Forms of Action. In the twelfth century, the English kings began to expand the authority of the royal courts by issuing original writs based on the king's traditional interest in keeping the peace and remedying defaults of justice. This process of modifying or inventing original writs led to the development of particular *forms of action*. Writs involving the same or similar types of cases came to be grouped and issued as a matter of course. These forms of action were organized into three basic categories: (1) *real actions* (focusing on property rights, primarily for the specific recovery of *seisin*—the possession of a freehold estate in land); (2) *ex contractu personal actions* (focusing on contract rights, including the actions of *debt, detinue, covenant,* and *account*); and (3) *ex delicto personal actions* (focusing on redressing wrongs and recovery of personal property, including the actions of *replevin, trespass,* and the derivatives of trespass discussed below). Each form of action had its own distinctive procedural, substantive, and remedial law.

Restriction on the Issuance of New Types of Writs. In 1285, the Statute of Westminster II, 13 Edw. 1, ch. 24, limited the issuance of new writs to cases "similar" to those in which writs had previously been granted. Subsequent development of the forms of action focused primarily on a gradual expansion of the writ of trespass. One reason that the development of the common law focused on expansion of the writ of *trespass* was that trial by jury was available in trespass. The development is sometimes analogized to the growth

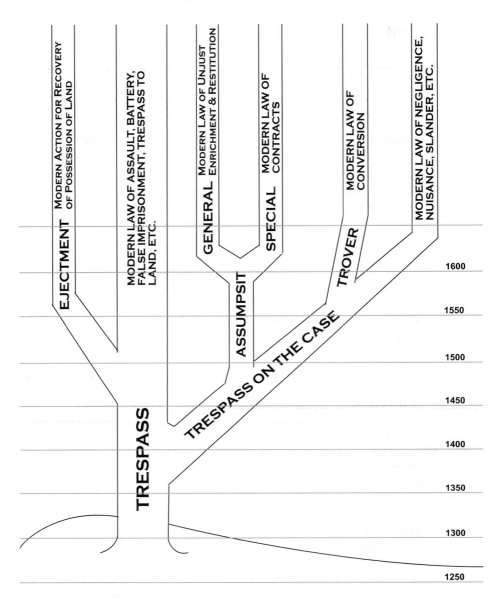

Figure 1-2

of a tree, which is summarized in Figure 1-2. Around 1250, trespass—the "trunk" of the tree—began growing in the king's courts.

Trespass covered several types of wrongs, including: (1) assault and battery; (2) injuries to personal property; (3) taking of personal property (*trespass de bonis asportatis*); (4) unlawful entry upon land (*trespass quare clausum fregit*); (5) injuries to land; and (6) false imprisonment. These actions were part criminal in nature and had a central focus: violence—a breach of the king's peace. The defendant had to have committed the injury with actual or implied force. The courts would imply force when the injury was "immediate" and "direct." When the defendant injured property, the plaintiff had to be in actual or constructive possession of the property at the time of the injury. The remedy was money damages for the harm done.

Over time, several "limbs" branched off: trespass, including "trespass on the case," which allowed recovery for "indirect" injuries. About 1500, case produced a branch called *assumpsit*. One version of this form of action, *special assumpsit*, provided most of the modern law of contracts. Another version, *general assumpsit*, provided the principles denoted today as "unjust enrichment," "quasi-contracts," and "restitution." Another branch included *trover*, which eventually came to cover any unauthorized exercise of "dominion" over personal property, including the taking, detention, destruction, or misuse of the property. The plaintiff recovered as damages the entire value of the chattel at the time and place of the wrongful act ("conversion"). Thus, trover amounted to a "forced sale." Lastly, another major limb branched off from the trespass trunk to provide a more effective remedy for the recovery of land: *ejectment*.

Effect of Choosing the "Wrong" Writ. The plaintiff had to choose the proper writ to recover. If the facts that were proved fell outside the selected writ and form of action, the plaintiff lost—even though the facts proved would have been sufficient to support a recovery under a different writ and form of action. A plaintiff who picked the wrong form of action could start over. In other words, the judgment was "not on the merits," provided that a proper form of action covered the situation and the plaintiff so desired.

Overlapping Nature of Some Forms of Action. Some forms of action overlapped. Why would a plaintiff choose one form over another? The plaintiff might choose a particular form of action based whether a jury trial was available. In addition, the plaintiff might choose a particular form of action based on the remedy available.

Influence of the Forms of Action. The influence of the forms of action (and the distinctions between them) on modern substantive law and remedies has been immense. In particular, the elements of an action that the plaintiff has to prove to recover, the nature of the remedy available, and the measurement of the remedy all originated in the development of the forms of action. *See* Teply & Whitten at 15–31 (discussing the development of the forms of action in detail).

2. Procedure in the Common-Law Courts

The Declaration. After the chancellor issued the original writ and the defendant appeared, the plaintiff had to state the claim in more detail. In the earliest days, this statement was oral. In later times, written "pleadings" developed, and the claim was set out in a document known as a *declaration*. In a common-law declaration, the plaintiff specified the facts and circumstances on which the action was based. Some declarations, such as ones based on trespasses, set forth the events in a relatively direct and straightforward manner. Others reflected elaborate fictions developed in certain common-law actions, such as ejectment, in order to extend the writ to new situations. Declarations in general assumpsit contained standard, generalized allegations known as various *common counts* (such as the common count for "money had and received"). After the plaintiff stated the claim in the declaration, the defendant was required to respond in one of the ways described below.

Pleading to a Single Issue of Law or Fact. Common-law procedure required the parties, through a series of *pleadings*, to disclose the issues between them. The end-result of the process was the definition of a single issue of law or fact. For example, an issue of law was created when a party filed a *general demurrer.* In this situation, the demurring party admitted the previously alleged facts, but asserted that the facts did not give rise to a legally recognized claim or defense. If the demurrer was sustained, the demurring party won the action. If the demurrer was overruled, judgment would be entered based on the demurring party's admission of the facts. The modern equivalent of a demurrer is still called a demurrer in some procedural systems; in others, it is called a *motion to dismiss.*

A *dilatory plea* could be used to delay or defeat the action by raising, for example, objections to the jurisdiction of the court, the location of the suit, or other matters "in abatement" that did not dispute the merits of the claim. In modern systems, such matters can be raised in various ways, most often by a *motion to dismiss.*

An issue of fact was created when a party "traversed" a prior factual allegation. A *traverse* was simply a denial of a factual allegation. The disputed factual issue raised by a traverse then had to be resolved by the trier of fact in the case (*e.g.,* the jury in trespass actions). A party could not demur and traverse at the same time. The party had to choose whether to raise an issue of law or fact. The modern counterpart of the common-law traverse is a *denial.*

A party might choose not to demur generally or traverse an allegation of fact in a prior pleading. Instead, the party might enter a plea in *confession and avoidance.* Such a plea admitted the allegations of the prior pleading and presented new matter to avoid the legal effect of those allegations, such as self-defense in an action of assault and battery. The modern version of the plea of confession and avoidance is an *affirmative defense.*

If the defendant entered a plea of confession and avoidance to the declaration, no issue of fact or law resulted, and the plaintiff had to respond. If the plaintiff believed the plea was insufficient as a matter of law, the plaintiff would demur to the plea. If not, the plaintiff filed a *replication* (reply), which either traversed a material allegation in the plea or admitted the truth of the plea and raised a new matter of confession and avoidance. If the plaintiff raised a new matter of confession and avoidance in the replication, the defendant had to either demur or file a *rejoinder* containing either a traverse or a new matter of confession and avoidance. The process continued until a single issue of law or fact was reached when one side either traversed or demurred. The initial phase of the common-law pleading process is summarized in Figure 1-3.

The common-law requirement that the pleading process produce a single issue of fact or law simplified the adjudication of cases from the standpoint of the courts. However, it posed substantial disadvantages to the litigants. A party could not assert that a fact alleged by an opposing party was both legally insufficient and untrue. The party had to choose at the party's peril. Likewise, a party who wished to deny the truth of more than one fact could not do so and had to select its strongest point upon which to present proof.

Reform of Common-Law Pleading. The stringency and complexity of common-law pleading produced piecemeal reforms in England. These reforms focused primarily on (1) limiting the time when purely formal defects could be raised and (2) lessening the single-issue requirement. The defendant was given the option of denying the legal conclusion sought to be drawn from the declaration by means of the *general issue.* It enabled the defendant to contest most of the plaintiff's factual allegations and, in some actions, to raise various issues of law. The defendant could also raise some affirmative defenses under the general issue. The form of the general issue varied according to the form of action, such as "not guilty" in trespass, case, and trover.

SUMMARY OF THE COMMON-LAW PLEADING PROCESS		
Plaintiff's Pleading	**Defendant's Possible Responses (Simplified)**	**Result or Next Step**
Declaration (Pleading) based on the appropriate writ setting out the plaintiff's claim	**1) General Demurrer** challenged the legal sufficiency of the facts alleged, *i.e.,* assuming the facts were true, is there a rule of law under the circumstances that creates a legal interest in this plaintiff against this defendant? **or**	**Ruling by the Court** If *"overruled,"* judgment for the plaintiff was entered on the defendant's tacit admission of the facts; if *"sustained,"* judgment of dismissal was entered, but the plaintiff could start over again with a new declaration
	2) Plea (Pleading) A) **Dilatory plea** raised objections to location of suit (venue), jurisdiction of the court, jurisdiction over the particular defendant, etc., **or**	**Ruling by the Court** If *"overruled,"* then the defendant had to respond with a traverse or confession and avoidance; if *"sustained,"* then plaintiff could sue in the proper location, the proper court, etc. if the plaintiff wanted to do so
	B) **Traverse** denied the facts alleged, **or**	**Trial on the Merits** to resolve disputed fact issues
	C) **Confess and Avoid** admitting the allegations of the declaration and presenting new matter (*i.e.,* defense) to avoid the legal effect of those allegations	**Plaintiff** had to either **Demurrer** (which produced a ruling by the court; if *"overruled,"* judgment for the plaintiff was entered "on the merits" or if *"sustained,"* judgment was entered "on the merits" against the defendant on the defendant's concession) **or** plead further in a **Replication (Pleading),** which either A) **Traversed** the matter raised in avoidance and created an issue of fact **or** B) **Confessed** the new matter raised by the defendant and **avoided** it with the additional new matter; the defendant would then have to respond by either demurring or pleading further in a **"Rejoinder" (Pleading).** The process continued until a single issue of law or fact was reached.

Figure 1-3

Later reforms focused on (1) allowing the plaintiff to use separate counts and the defendant to interpose several pleas in bar to the same count, (2) simplifying pleading, and (3) liberalizing the "joinder" of parties and claims. As you will see below, modern procedural systems eliminate the rigidity of the common-law pleading system and provide each party with multiple options with which to challenge the opposing party's case. For example, in modern systems, it is possible both to deny factual allegations in the opposing party's pleading and to raise affirmative defenses to the claim stated in that pleading. *See* TEPLY & WHITTEN at 573–79 (discussing common-law pleading).

3. Equity (Chancery) Courts

Development of Equity. Historically, the English court system was divided into two fundamentally different types of courts: (1) common-law courts (*law*), discussed above, and (2) the *Chancery* (*equity*), which was recognized as a separate court in about the middle of the fourteenth century. There were also other courts, such as admiralty and ecclesiastical courts, but they may be ignored for purposes of this discussion.

As the common-law courts became rigid in their procedures and remedies, individuals petitioned the king's council (made up of various officers of the state and advisors) to intervene to do justice between the parties based on the circumstances of the case. These petitions were heard in large measure by the chancellor, who eventually needed a regularly organized court and staff to deal with them. This court was called the Court of Chancery.

Pleading in Equity and Equitable Relief. As previously stated, the first pleading at common law was the declaration. The first pleading in equity was called a *bill*. The principal remedy provided by the common-law courts was a *judgment* awarding money damages. In contrast, equity often gave a different kind of relief: personal orders directing an individual to do or refrain from doing a specific act. These orders took the form of *injunctions* or *decrees of specific performance*. Equity also offered other remedies not available in the law courts, including discovery, rescission, and reformation. Equity enforced these orders by means of *contempt* sanctions — punishment by fines, imprisonment, or both. Equity orders were considered personal directives against the party, hence the maxim — "equity acts in personam." Another important difference between the common-law courts and equity was the absence of a jury in equity proceedings.

Equitable relief was available when the procedures of the common-law courts rendered common-law remedies unavailable or inadequate. Eventually, this basic rationale for intervention by the equity courts evolved into a jurisdictional rule: equity would not act unless the remedy at law was inadequate. However, this development did not mean that equity would give only "equitable relief." If equity jurisdiction was established because of the inadequacy of the remedy "at law," an equity court could also give common-law relief to avoid a multiplicity of actions under the *equitable clean-up doctrine*. For example, if the defendant were engaging in repeated trespasses on the plaintiff's land, an equity court would issue an injunction to prevent future trespasses and give damages under the clean-up doctrine for past trespasses. In this way, equity avoided a multiplicity of suits because money damages would otherwise have to be recovered in a separate common-law action. *See* Teply & Whitten at 29 (discussing equity jurisdiction and procedure).

Merger of Law and Equity. In modern procedural systems, "law" and "equity" have been "merged." The significance of a merged system is that a single court can now give both legal and equitable remedies. In England, the Judicature Act of 1873, 36 & 37 Vic., ch. 66, merged law and equity. The Act also gave rulemaking power over procedure to the judiciary. Merger of law and equity in American state and federal courts is discussed below.

Merger has not altogether eliminated the significance of the distinctions between legal and equitable claims and procedures which developed at common law. In the United States, for example, the constitutional right to a jury trial in state and federal courts is primarily based on whether a right to a jury trial would have existed in an analogous action at common law. At common law, a right to a jury trial generally existed for actions cognizable in the common-law courts, *i.e.* the "law" courts, but no right existed for actions brought in the Chancery, *i.e.* the "equity" courts. Thus, it is still necessary today to distinguish between "law" and "equity" claims and remedies in determining whether a constitutional right to a jury trial exists. As you will learn in Chapter 10, determining when a constitutional right to a jury trial exists is often difficult because in a modern merged system, the same court can now hear cases in which both legal and equitable claims are joined in ways that were not possible under the old system of separate law and equity courts. In addition, many of our modern procedural rules have been derived from the more flexible procedures available in equity, and these rules are today available in actions for purely legal relief. *See* Stephen N. Subrin, *How Equity Conquered Common Law: The Federal Rules of Civil Procedure in Historical Perspective*, 135 U. Pa. L. Rev. 909 (1987). As a result, courts have had to create tests to preserve the right to a jury trial as it would have existed at common law in cases that could not have been heard, in their entirety, by either law or equity courts.

The merger of law and equity has also produced other dilemmas that the courts have coped with haltingly at best. The basic rule separating the jurisdiction of law and equity courts was the *inadequate-remedy-at-law rule*, discussed above. This rule also controlled the availability of equitable remedies. When the legislative branches of the state and federal governments merged law and equity, they gave no direction about what rules should control equitable relief. As a result, the inadequate-remedy-at-law rule continued to control the availability of equitable remedies, even though those remedies were now being given by a court with both common-law and equitable "jurisdiction." As might be expected, the courts continued to honor the inadequate-remedy-at-law rule in name, while evolving its content to meet modern remedial needs in ways that would not have been recognized in separate courts of equity.

4. Development and Reform of Civil Procedure in the United States

Reception of English Procedure in the United States. By the nineteenth century, much of the technicality of English procedure had been adopted in the United States. In most American court systems, equity jurisprudence also became an accepted feature of the legal system, either in the form of separate law and equity courts or in formally distinct parts of the same court.

Code Pleading. The first significant reform in American procedure took place in New York around the middle of the nineteenth century. The New York Constitution of 1846 abolished the New York Court of Chancery. The New York Constitution also directed the New York Legislature, at its first session after the adoption of the constitution, to appoint three commissioners. Their task was to "revise, reform, simplify, and abridge the rules of practice, pleading, forms, and proceedings of the [New York state] courts." In accord with the commissioners' recommendations, the New York Legislature enacted the Field Code in 1848. The Field Code — so named after David Dudley Field, the most prominent commissioner — embodied numerous reforms, including (1) the merger of law and equity; (2) the simplification and limitation of pleading; (3) the broadening of claim and party joinder; and (4) the liberalization of permissible amendments and variances between pleading and subsequent proof at trial.

The Field Code established a single form of action known as a "civil action" and limited pleading to a *complaint*, an *answer*, and a *reply*. The plaintiff's complaint had to state facts constituting a *cause of action*. As at common law, the defendant could still challenge the defects on the face of the complaint by a demurrer, including the failure of the complaint to set forth facts sufficient to state a cause of action. The defendant's answer had to admit or deny the allegations of the complaint as well as assert any new matter constituting a defense. The plaintiff then had to reply to any new matter contained in the answer. After the reply, the pleadings stopped. Thus, a major difference between the Field Code and common-law pleading was that the Field Code did not attempt to achieve a single issue of fact or law. By 1900, almost thirty states had adopted some version of the Field Code, and more adopted it in the twentieth century.

Despite the laudable aims of the "codes," reform did not come easily. As Maitland aptly noted in his lectures, we have buried the forms of action, "but they still rule us from their graves." Frederic W. Maitland, The Forms of Action at Common Law 1 (1969 prtg.). In particular, as noted in the discussion of equity, above, the forms of action still play an important role in determining jury trial rights under American constitutions.

Development of Federal Procedure. Under Article III of the U.S. Constitution, the judicial power of the federal government is vested in "one [S]upreme Court, and in such inferior Courts as the Congress may from time to time ordain and establish" and extends to "all Cases, in Law and Equity" within certain limited categories. In the Judiciary Act of 1789, ch. 20, §§ 1–4, 1 Stat. 73, 73–75, Congress implemented the provisions of Article III by establishing a Supreme Court and a system of circuit and district courts. Congress maintained the traditional distinction between equity and common-law jurisdiction, even though law and equity were not administered in separate federal courts.

Process Acts. With respect to procedure in the federal courts, Congress, through a series of Process Acts, established *static conformity* to state procedural law. Originally, static conformity meant that the federal courts in common-law cases were obligated to use the procedural law of the state in which they were sitting as that procedural law appeared in 1789. This scheme of *static conformity* was altered by the Conformity Act of 1872, ch. 255, § 5, 17 Stat. 196, 197, by requiring a *dynamic conformity* to state procedures in common-law actions. Thus, in common-law cases after 1872, federal procedure conformed to state procedures that existed at the time the federal court adjudicated the case. In contrast, the process acts never required conformity to state procedure in equity cases. Instead, the U.S. Supreme Court used its rulemaking power to create rules for equity cases from time to time. (The U.S. Supreme Court and lower federal courts also had rulemaking power in common-law cases, but the courts exercised it sparingly.)

Rules Enabling Act. In 1934, Congress enacted the Rules Enabling Act, ch. 651, 48 Stat. 1064 (1934) (codified as amended at 28 U.S.C. § 2072 *et seq.*). This Act allowed the U.S. Supreme Court "to prescribe, by general rules, for the district courts of the United States and for the courts of the District of Columbia, the forms of process, writs, pleadings, and motions, and the practice and procedure in civil actions at law." *Id.* § 1, 48 Stat. 1064, 1064. The rules promulgated pursuant to this authority could not "abridge, enlarge, nor modify the substantive rights of any litigant." *Id.* The Act also allowed the Court at any time to "unite the general rules prescribed by it for cases in equity with those in actions at law so as to secure one form of civil action and procedure for both." *Id.* § 2. However, in merging law and equity, "the right of trial by jury as at common law and declared by the seventh amendment to the Constitution [had to] be preserved to the parties inviolate." *Id.*

Federal Rules of Civil Procedure. In 1935, the U.S. Supreme Court appointed an advisory committee to draft the new rules. After the legal profession examined the Advisory Committee's proposed rules, some changes were made. The Federal Rules of Civil Procedure were approved with those changes. The Rules took effect on September 16, 1938. The U.S. Supreme Court has amended the Federal Rules of Civil Procedure numerous times since 1938.

In 1958, the functions of the original Advisory Committee were replaced by the Judicial Conference, a body of federal judges. Congress directed the Judicial Conference to "carry on a continuous study of the operation and effect of the general rules of practice and procedure" and from time to time recommend to the U.S. Supreme Court changes or additions to the rules. *See* 28 U.S.C. § 331 (indicating the purpose of such changes is "to promote simplicity in procedure, fairness in administration, the just determination of litigation, and the elimination of unjustifiable expense and delay"). The Judicial Conference has a standing committee and various advisory committees, which report to the standing committee. One such advisory committee is for the civil rules. These committees are appointed by the Chief Justice of the U.S. Supreme Court. The standing committee reports to the Judicial Conference, which, in turn, advises the U.S. Supreme Court. *See* 28 U.S.C. § 2073.

New or amended rules promulgated by the U.S. Supreme Court must be transmitted to Congress by the first of May of the year in which they are to become effective. Rules so transmitted automatically become law unless Congress enacts a statute to prevent them from going into effect. Unless otherwise provided by law, the rules can be effective no earlier than the first of December of the year in which the rules were transmitted. *See* 28 U.S.C. § 2074. When a rule goes into effect, it supersedes all other rules and statutes that are in conflict with it. *See* 28 U.S.C. § 2072(b).

As noted earlier, the Federal Rules of Civil Procedure have been amended numerous times since 1938. Throughout the years, these amendments have been made on a piece-meal basis generally to effectuate some new substantive change in the operation of certain rules. For example, in 1993, the rules governing discovery were amended to add new requirements for the mandatory automatic disclosure of certain information by the parties. In 2007, however, all of the Federal Rules of Civil Procedure underwent a complete "style" revision, the first since their original enactment in 1938, in order to clarify and simplify the language and formatting of the rules. All of the Federal Rules of Civil Procedure (Rules 1–86) as well as the accompanying Appendix of Forms (Forms 1–82) were restyled. The new restyled rules were the culmination of a four-year, comprehensive textual-revision project by the Advisory Committee on the Civil Rules and the Standing Committee of the Judicial Conference. As explained in the Judicial Conference report, the restyled rules were intended to "clarify, simplify, and modernize" the presentation and language of the rules.

First among the goals of the restyling project was to eliminate long, convoluted sentences that were difficult to read and replace them with more concise sentences. For example, in determining the sufficiency of a pleading, former Rule 8(e)(2) read: "When two or more statements are made in the alternative and one of them if made independently would be sufficient, the pleading is not made insufficient by the insufficiency of one or more of the alternative statements." The restyled rule, now Rule 8(d)(2), reads: "If a party makes alternative statements, the pleading is sufficient if any one of them is sufficient." In addition, the rules were re-formatted so that nearly every rule is now subdivided into separately lettered and numbered constituent parts with progressively indented paragraphs and individual headings.

The Advisory Committee's Note accompanying the new rules specifically described the rule revisions as "stylistic only" and expressly emphasized that the revisions "are intended to make no changes in substantive meaning." Critics have noted, however, that language rephrasing, by its very nature, can create differences in substantive meaning and trigger unintended changes in the proper application of the rules. Hopefully, the restyled rules will not generate serious interpretive problems for lawyers and judges and will justify the long and tedious effort expended on the revision project.

Organization of the Federal Rules. The coverage and organization of the Federal Rules of Civil Procedure are shown in Figure 1-4. Rule 1 states that the rules govern "procedure in all civil actions and proceedings in the United States district courts." Rule 2 establishes "one form of action—the civil action." Rules 7, 8, and 12 simplify pleading and motion practice. Those rules effectively limit the pleadings to a "complaint" and an "answer" in most situations. Rule 15 permits *amendments* to be made freely and liberalizes the rules governing variances between pleading and proof. Rules 18 and 20 broaden basic claim and party joinder. Rules 26 through 37 set out a comprehensive scheme of *discovery*—a major improvement over the limited discovery provided by the codes. Rule 83(a)(1) allows each district court to adopt *local rules*, provided those rules are "consistent with" and do not "duplicate" the Federal Rules of Civil of Procedure or federal statutes. *See also*

PROVISION	ORGANIZATION AND COVERAGE OF THE FEDERAL RULES OF CIVIL PROCEDURE
Rules 1-2	Scope and Purpose; Form of Action
Rules 3-16	Commencing an Action; Service of Process; Pleadings; Motions; and Orders
Rules 17-25	Parties
Rules 26-37	Disclosures and Discovery
Rules 38-53	Trials
Rules 54-63	Judgment
Rules 64-71	Provisional and Final Remedies
Rules 71.1-76	Special Proceedings
Rules 77-80	District Courts and Clerks: Conducting Business; Recordkeeping
Rules 81-86	General Provisions
Forms 1-82	Appendix of Forms

Figure 1-4

28 U.S.C. §2071 (allowing federal courts generally "from time to time [to] prescribe rules for the conduct of their business"). These individual court rules provide the working details for practice in each particular district court and court of appeals.

Some aspects of procedure in the federal courts are not governed by the Federal Rules of Civil Procedure or local rules of the district courts. For example, you will see in Chapters 3 and 4 that Congress directly regulates the subject-matter jurisdiction and venue of the federal courts in *Title 28* of the *United States Code* (the codification of federal statutes divided into fifty "titles," each one dealing with a particular subject). Title 28 also contains many other statutory regulations of procedure.

The distinction between matters regulated directly by Congress in Title 28 and those regulated by the Supreme Court in various Federal Rules of Civil Procedure is not easy to state. Generally, Congress regulates "more important" matters of procedure in Title 28, while the Supreme Court deals with the less important "housekeeping" matters in the Federal Rules of Civil and Appellate Procedure and the Federal Rules of Evidence. However, as noted below, rules created by the Supreme Court can supersede inconsistent statutes. Thus, the Court can choose to create a rule under the Enabling Act that supersedes some provision of Title 28. There are, however, constitutional *separation-of-powers restrictions* on the Court's ability to take this action. These restrictions will be explored in Chapter 5.

The Federal Rules of Civil Procedure were designed to be both *uniform* and *trans-substantive*; that is, the same rules would govern civil actions in all federal courts throughout the United States (uniformity), and those rules would not differ according to the kinds of substantive rights being litigated in the action (trans-substantive). In recent years, this ideal of uniform, trans-substantive procedure has been subject to much debate as well as erosion through direct legislation by Congress, local rulemaking by the various district courts, and the practice of individual judges.

In addition, some amendments to the Federal Rules of Civil Procedure have aroused great controversy. Moreover, the controversy extends not only to the desirability of individual amendments, but also, more fundamentally, to the desirability of court-directed procedural rulemaking. Many aspects of this debate, as well as controversies as to the nature and substance of various rule amendments, will be encountered in subsequent chapters of this book. You should consider each procedural rule or statute that you study in later materials critically, both as to its content and as to the institutional competence of the body (court or legislature) that created the law in question.

In spite of the controversies, state rules of procedure have been substantially influenced by the Federal Rules of Civil Procedure and the number of "code pleading" states continues to dwindle. Many states pattern their rules of procedure on the Federal Rules and adopt the language of the Federal Rules, including amendments, without significant change.

Section F. An Overview of a Civil Action

Before exploring particular procedural subjects in later chapters, it will be helpful to have a broad understanding of how modern procedural rules work in a civil action. To that end, the following sections provide an overview of the procedures in the American civil action. The "stages" of such an action are shown in Figure 1-5. As specific procedural topics are examined in later chapters, you will encounter procedures and terminology that you have not yet studied in depth. This overview will provide you with a rough familiarity with these matters until you have studied them in depth. In addition, by carefully studying this section, you will learn the essential elements of Civil Procedure with which every lawyer is familiar.

1. Presuit Investigation

The first formal contact between a lawyer and a potential client is the initial client interview. This interview establishes the professional working relationship between the lawyer and the client. Typically, a client will have decided to consult a lawyer because some type of actual or potential dispute exists—ranging from the neighbor's dog barking late at night to injuries arising out of an automobile accident.

The client will typically want to know what can be done, legally and practically, about the problem that has arisen. For example, can the client get his or her job back? Does the other driver have a valid claim? Can a promise be enforced? The answers depend, in part, on what substantive legal rights or obligations, if any, are enforceable in a court of law. To determine what a client's legal rights or obligations are, the lawyer ordinarily will ask the client to describe the problem and then ask questions exploring and verifying various substantive legal theories.

During the initial interview, as well as at later times in the lawyer-client relationship, a lawyer will counsel the client about the available choices or alternatives—what can be done in the situation and what should be done. The choice most directly related to civil procedure is litigation, in which a judge or jury resolves the dispute within the court system. At the opposite end of the spectrum from litigation is the possibility of some form of informal "self help" that parties can unilaterally take to stop other parties from violating their rights. As discussed in subsection 16, below, other choices may include negotiation, arbitration, mediation, or other forms of *alternative dispute resolution* ("ADR").

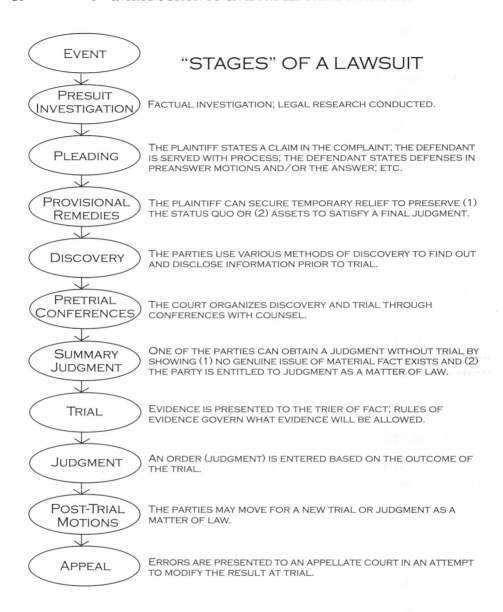

Figure 1-5

2. The Plaintiff's Initial Litigation Decisions

If the plaintiff decides to litigate, the plaintiff faces several basic decisions. In which court or courts can the action be commenced? Who should be named as defendants in the action? Is a particular choice of forum more likely to apply law favorable to the plaintiff?

At the outset, it is important to note that the plaintiff's choice of a court will be limited in at least three ways. First, the court must have proper "*subject-matter jurisdiction*" over the action. Second, the court must be one in which "*personal jurisdiction*" over the defendant may be obtained. Third, the court must be one of proper "*venue.*" All of these requirements must be met in order to sue in a particular court. Depending on the kind of case involved, the place where the facts giving rise to the case occurred, the places where the parties reside, and other factors, the plaintiff may be able to sue in a state court, a federal court, or either (at the plaintiff's option).

(a) Choosing a Court Authorized to Hear a Particular Type of Case (Subject-Matter Jurisdiction)

Subject-matter jurisdiction is the court's power to hear the *class* of cases to which the plaintiff's suit belongs. Courts in the United States are authorized by the constitution and statutes of each government. These legal sources also define and limit the courts' subject-matter jurisdiction. Two examples were given in earlier discussions: (1) the discussion of the reform of procedure in New York noted that the New York Constitution of 1846 specifically abolished the New York Court of Chancery; and (2) the discussion of federal procedure in the United States noted: (a) that Article III of the U.S. Constitution vests the judicial power of the federal government in "one Supreme Court, and in such inferior Courts as the Congress may from time to time establish"; (b) that Article III extends the judicial power to "all cases, in law and equity" within certain limited categories; and (c) that Congress implemented the provisions of Article III in 1789 by establishing a Supreme Court and a system of lower courts. Thus, to determine what courts exist in a particular jurisdiction and the extent of their authority, a lawyer must consult the statutory compilation (covering the statutes and constitution) for the jurisdiction.

Limited and General Jurisdiction. Subject-matter jurisdiction is either *general* or *limited*. Every state has at least one court of general jurisdiction. Courts of general jurisdiction possess the broadest subject-matter authority of all the courts within a state. They are sometimes referred to as *repository courts*, because if no other court within a state can be found with subject-matter jurisdiction over a case, the court of general jurisdiction will be able to hear the case. Each state also has one or more courts of limited jurisdiction. Courts of limited jurisdiction are authorized to hear only certain kinds of cases.

However, the mere fact that a court has some limits on its jurisdiction does not mean that it is a court of limited jurisdiction. The terms "general" and "limited" jurisdiction are terms of art, which describe the position of a court in the particular court system in question. To determine which court is the court of general jurisdiction in a system, therefore, one must identify the court that is the "repository court," as described above. Happily, lawmakers often assist this classification process by explicitly designating a particular court as the court of general jurisdiction within the system.

The distinction between courts of general and limited jurisdiction has resulted in somewhat different rules for pleading and establishing subject-matter jurisdiction in the two kinds of courts. Generally, the plaintiff's initial pleading must affirmatively demonstrate the existence of the subject-matter jurisdiction in courts of limited jurisdiction, whereas this special pleading rule does not exist in courts of general jurisdiction. The distinction also traditionally resulted in differences in the way the validity of judgments rendered by each kind of court was determined when the judgments were challenged in separate proceedings (so-called "collateral attacks" on judgments). However, it is questionable whether the latter difference still exists today. *See* Teply & Whitten at 49–50.

Concurrent or Exclusive Jurisdiction. In addition to being either general or limited, subject-matter jurisdiction is either *concurrent* or *exclusive*. When a court has concurrent jurisdiction with another court, the plaintiff may choose to sue in either of the courts. However, if a court has exclusive jurisdiction over a class of cases, no other court can validly exercise jurisdiction over cases within the class. If a case within the exclusive jurisdiction of a court is commenced in another court, it must be dismissed or transferred (depending on the procedure authorized by the procedural system).

Original or Appellate Jurisdiction. Subject-matter jurisdiction is also either *original* or *appellate*. Original jurisdiction is the power of a court to adjudicate cases "in the first instance." In contrast, appellate jurisdiction is the authority of a court to review and revise determinations made by other courts. Thus, *trial* courts ordinarily exercise original jurisdiction and *appellate* courts ordinarily exercise appellate jurisdiction. However, in some instances, courts that are primarily trial courts (and thus usually exercise only original jurisdiction) also have appellate jurisdiction over other trial courts. For example, in some states, the courts of general jurisdiction might exercise appellate jurisdiction over certain types of decisions made by the courts of limited jurisdiction. Likewise, some appellate courts also possess original jurisdiction over certain kinds of cases. *See, e.g.,* 28 U.S.C. § 1251(a) (providing that the U.S. "Supreme Court shall have original and exclusive jurisdiction over all controversies between two or more States").

No-Waiver or Consent Rule. In the United States, courts view restrictions on their subject-matter jurisdiction very seriously. As a result of this view, courts have created various rules prohibiting waiver of subject-matter jurisdiction objections or conferral of subject-matter jurisdiction by the consent of the parties. These prohibitions apply whether subject-matter jurisdiction is general or limited, concurrent or exclusive, or original or appellate.

When courts say that subject-matter jurisdiction is not a *waivable* objection, they mean that the inadvertent failure of the parties to raise a subject-matter jurisdiction objection will not result in it being lost or foreclosed. When the courts say that subject-matter jurisdiction cannot be conferred by consent, they mean that if a court lacks jurisdiction under applicable constitutional or statutory provisions, the parties cannot agree to have the court hear their case anyway. The upshot of this *no-waiver or consent* rule is that American courts will raise subject-matter jurisdiction objections themselves (*sua sponte*) whenever it appears that the case is beyond their competence, even if the objections are not made by any party to the action. For example, assume that the county court in State *X* has subject-matter jurisdiction over claims that do not exceed $10,000. If *P* sues *D* for $15,000 in the county court, the court would not have subject-matter jurisdiction over the action. *D* may raise a subject-matter jurisdiction objection under the procedures provided in State *X*. However, even if *D* fails to raise the objection, the county court is obligated to raise the objection on its own motion. Depending on the appropriate procedure in State *X*, the court will either dismiss the action or transfer it to a court possessing subject-matter jurisdiction.

Furthermore, subject-matter jurisdiction objections usually can be raised for the first time on appeal from a lower court's judgment (called a *direct attack* on the judgment), either by a party or by the appellate court. In addition, a judgment can sometimes be challenged on subject-matter grounds in a wholly separate proceeding (called a *collateral attack* on the judgment).

Subject-Matter Jurisdiction of the Federal Courts. Article III of the U.S. Constitution and Title 28 of the *United States Code* define and limit federal subject-matter jurisdiction. When Article III and Title 28 authorize subject-matter jurisdiction, that jurisdiction is usually concurrent with the state courts. When subject-matter jurisdiction is concurrent, the plaintiff may sue the defendant either in state or federal court. In some subject areas, however, federal subject-matter jurisdiction is exclusive, which means that the state courts may not hear cases in those areas. *See, e.g.,* 28 U.S.C. § 1338(a) (conferring exclusive jurisdiction on the U.S. District Courts over patent infringement claims, among others).

Article III establishes the outer boundaries of federal subject-matter jurisdiction. Congress may not exceed those boundaries when it confers jurisdiction on the federal courts. However, under the conventional view, Congress is not required to confer all the jurisdiction it could under Article III on the inferior federal courts it creates under Article III. It may withhold such portions of the jurisdiction as it chooses from those courts. When Congress withholds a portion of the potential Article III jurisdiction from the lower federal courts, the cases withheld must be litigated originally in the state courts.

All federal courts are courts of limited jurisdiction. Thus, the special rules of pleading applicable to the subject-matter jurisdiction of courts of limited jurisdiction, discussed above, apply to federal courts. Similarly, subject-matter jurisdiction objections in federal court are not waivable; federal subject-matter jurisdiction may not be conferred by the consent of the parties; and federal subject-matter jurisdiction objections may be raised for the first time on appeal.

Federal Question Jurisdiction. The largest branch of federal jurisdiction is *federal question* jurisdiction. Federal question jurisdiction exists when the *plaintiff's* claim "arises under the Constitution, laws, or treaties of the United States." *See* 28 U.S.C. § 1331. Original federal question jurisdiction does not exist merely because a question of federal law appears somewhere in the case, such as when the defendant raises a defense based on federal law. Normally, for federal question jurisdiction to exist, the plaintiff's claim must be created by federal law. However, a limited number of cases exist in which state law creates the plaintiff's claim for relief, but a substantial issue of federal law forms an essential element of the plaintiff's claim and thus makes federal question jurisdiction proper.

Diversity Jurisdiction. Another branch of federal subject-matter jurisdiction is jurisdiction in suits between citizens of different states — *diversity jurisdiction* — on claims arising under state law. This branch of federal subject-matter jurisdiction is concurrent with the state courts.

Diversity actions must satisfy two basic components: (1) "diversity of citizenship" between the parties must exist and (2) the amount in controversy must be satisfied. For example, if the plaintiff is a "citizen" of Texas and the defendant is a "citizen" of New York, the plaintiff can sue the defendant in a federal district court for breach of contract or negligence if the plaintiff's claim *exceeds* $75,000. *See* 28 U.S.C. § 1332(a). In general, there cannot be citizens of the same state on each side of a lawsuit. *See Strawbridge v. Curtiss,* 7 U.S. (3 Cranch) 267 (1806) ("complete diversity" required). Thus, a citizen of New York could not sue a citizen of Texas and a citizen of New York.

Furthermore, the amount claimed by the plaintiff controls in a diversity case if it is made in "good faith." A court may not dismiss a case for failure to meet the amount-in-controversy requirement unless it appears to a "legal certainty" that the plaintiff cannot recover more than $75,000. *See St. Paul Mercury Idem. Co. v. Red Cab Co.,* 303 U.S. 283, 288–89 (1938). In addition, a plaintiff is permitted to aggregate two or more claims against a single defendant to meet the amount-in-controversy requirement, no matter how unrelated the claims are.

However, for reasons explored in later chapters, whether claims by multiple plaintiffs or against multiple defendants can be combined to meet the amount-in-controversy requirement is complicated. For example, when a single plaintiff asserts claims against two or more defendants, each of which are below the required amount in controversy but added together exceed the amount-in-controversy requirement, the defendants must share a "*common undivided interest*" and a "*single title or right*" must be involved, such as when the defendants own land as joint tenants, before the claims can be aggregated to meet the amount-in-controversy requirement. However, because of a special federal statute, other "multiple party" claims are sometimes treated differently, such as when multiple plaintiffs attempt to combine claims against a single defendant or a plaintiff brings a "class action."

Supplemental Jurisdiction. In addition, the federal courts are authorized by statute to exercise *supplemental jurisdiction* over state-law claims that lack an independent basis of federal jurisdiction but are factually related to claims that are properly within federal jurisdiction. *See* 28 U.S.C. § 1367.

Removal Jurisdiction. *Removal* allows the defendant or defendants in a state court action to remove the plaintiff's action to federal district court if the plaintiff's action could have otherwise been commenced in federal court. The rationale for removal is that defendants, as well as plaintiffs, should have the right to choose the federal forum for the adjudication of claims that are properly within the original jurisdiction of the federal courts.

28 U.S.C. § 1441(a) is the general removal statute and provides for the removal by the defendant or defendants of "any civil action brought in a State court of which the district courts of the United States have original jurisdiction." As a general principle, removal jurisdiction is coextensive with original jurisdiction. Thus, if the plaintiff would have had original jurisdiction to file an action in federal court, removal jurisdiction may be invoked by the defendant. When subject-matter jurisdiction is based on diversity of citizenship, however, removal is prohibited "if any of the parties in interest properly joined and served as defendants is a citizen of the State in which the action is brought." *See* 28 U.S.C. § 1441(b)(2).

Applicable Law in Federal Court. When jurisdiction is based on federal question, the plaintiff's principal claim will ordinarily be governed by federal substantive law and federal procedural law. In diversity cases, the plaintiff's substantive claim is governed by state law, but procedural aspects are governed by the Federal Rules of Civil Procedure. This "source-of-law problem" in diversity actions is complex and cannot be explored fully here. The source-of-law problem in diversity actions is briefly examined in subsection (c), below, and is examined in detail in Chapter 5.

Appellate Review. As discussed in greater detail in subsection 14, below, decisions of the U.S. District Courts may be appealed to the federal courts of appeals, and decisions of the federal courts of appeals may be appealed to the U.S. Supreme Court. Appeals may not be taken from state courts to the U.S. Supreme Court in cases in which only *state issues* are raised; such appeals are only permitted with regard to issues of *federal law*. Nor may appeals be taken from state courts to federal district courts or federal courts of appeals.

Problems

Problem 1-1. Assume that *P*, a citizen of Wisconsin, owns a tract of land in Minnesota. There is an old cabin on the land. *P* lives in neighboring State of Wisconsin and is not able to use the cabin very often. However, *P* especially enjoys fishing in a pond on the land.

P has suspected that other people might be fishing in the pond. However, *P* had no evidence of who might be doing it until a local newspaper reported that *D-1* won a $20,000 prize in a recent fishing contest open to citizens of Minnesota by catching an extraordinarily large fish in *P's* pond. *D-1* is a citizen of Minnesota and lives near *P's* land. When *P* confronted *D-1* with the newspaper article, *D-1* admitted using the cabin and fishing in the pond. *D-1* stated that everyone has fished in the pond ever since *D-1* can remember and that *D-1* has never disturbed anything in the cabin.

The discussion developed into a heated argument, and *D-1* ended up punching *P* in the nose. Because *P* apparently suffered a broken nose, *D-1* remorsefully offered to take *P* in *D-1's* pickup truck to the nearest emergency room for treatment. On the way, *D-1's* truck collided with *D-2* who was driving a sports car. Either *D-1* and *D-2*, or both, may have been driving too fast for the conditions, and the accident appears to have aggravated *P's* prior injuries. In addition, *D-1*, and *D-2* sustained personal injuries, and both vehicles were damaged. *D-2* is a citizen of Ohio who was on vacation in Minnesota when the accident occurred. Assume that all of *P's* potential claims against *D-1* and *D-2* are created by state law. Assume also that *P* wants to sue *D-1* and *D-2* in a federal district court.

Which branch of federal subject-matter jurisdiction would *P* most likely try to meet to do so? Do you think *P* could meet the requirements of that branch? If *P* could not, in what court system(s) would *P* have to sue? Assuming that *P* could meet those requirements, how would the jurisdiction of the federal district court be described? Would it be original or appellate? Would it be concurrent or exclusive? Would it be general or limited?

Problem 1-2. On the facts of *Problem 1-1*, assume that *P* decides to commence an action against *D-1* in a U.S. District Court. The action is brought pursuant to 28 U.S.C. § 1332(a)(1). *P's* complaint demands (1) $55,000 in damages for *D-1's* trespass, battery, and negligence and (2) $20,000 — the prize for the fish. Assuming the applicable law permits *P* to recover on both claims if the facts supporting the claims are proved, does *P's* action meet the $75,000 amount-in-controversy requirement of § 1332?

(b) Choosing a Location Where the Particular Defendant May Be Required to Appear and Defend ("Personal Jurisdiction")

Personal jurisdiction is the court's power to impose its decisions on the *particular parties* in a lawsuit. Like subject-matter jurisdiction, a court derives its authority to impose its decisions on particular parties from the relevant constitution or applicable laws of the government. The court's authority to obtain personal jurisdiction over a party will often be geographically limited. For example, a county court of a state may have power to subject a party to its jurisdiction only if the party lives within the county or if the events giving rise to the suit occurred there. A state court, however, may be able to exercise personal jurisdiction over parties anywhere within the state, regardless of where the parties reside or where the events giving rise to the suit occurred. For example, assume that a state legislature has statutorily created a state district court and a county court in each county of the state. Assume that the statute allows (1) the county courts to obtain personal jurisdiction only over persons who reside within the county and (2) the state's district courts to exercise personal jurisdiction over parties residing anywhere within the state. Obviously, the plaintiff will have a much broader choice of locations if the plaintiff brings suit in a state district court rather than a county court.

Federal courts must also possess personal jurisdiction over the parties in order to render a valid judgment in a lawsuit. As a general rule, a federal district court located in a particular state acquires personal jurisdiction over the parties in the same manner as a state court would and, in the absence of an applicable federal law giving the federal district court greater personal jurisdiction authority, a federal district court's authority to exercise personal jurisdiction is the same as that of a court of general jurisdiction in that state.

Service of Process. When an action is commenced, the court in which it is commenced either does or does not have subject-matter jurisdiction. However, a court must always *acquire* personal jurisdiction over a defendant by an action called *service of process*. The proper forms and methods of service of process are defined by statute or court rule. *See, e.g.,* FED. R. CIV. P. 4 ("Summons"). These forms and methods are designed to provide proper notice of the action to the defendant. However, as discussed below, even if service of process is accomplished, the court still may not be able to exercise personal jurisdiction over the defendant if it is not authorized to do so by a proper statute, or if the constitutional guarantees of due process would be violated if it did so.

"Long-Arm" Statutes. The most traditional method of serving process is simply handing the process to the defendant within the territorial limits of the jurisdiction in which the action is commenced. If the defendant lives outside the state, state *long-arm statutes* will often authorize process to be served on the defendant where the defendant resides. Typically, a long-arm statute will authorize process to be served by mailing it to the defendant or delivering it to the defendant's agent within the state where the action is brought. The agent will then inform the defendant of the existence of the action. As a last resort, when no other method of service will work, state law may authorize a notice to be published in a newspaper for a certain length of time stating that the action has been brought.

Long-arm statutes may not be applied in a way that deprives the defendant of due process of law under the U.S. Constitution. Generally, due process requires that (1) the defendant must receive adequate notice of the action and (2) a "sufficient connection" must exist between the defendant, the claim, and the state to ensure that the state is a "fair" forum in which to adjudicate the action. However, the requirement of a sufficient connection is complex and not easily summarized. It will be examined fully in Chapter 2. For the time being, you should note that the requirement of a long-arm statute for service outside the state and the due process limits on the ability of the states to apply their long-arm statutes to nonresidents are part of the personal jurisdiction requirement.

In actions in federal court, the defendant also has a right to due process of law under the U.S. Constitution and the federal district court must acquire proper personal jurisdiction over the defendant. Sometimes, a special federal long-arm statute applies which authorizes a federal district court to exercise personal jurisdiction over a defendant who has sufficient contacts with the United States, even though the defendant may not have contacts with the particular state where the federal court is located. In the absence of an applicable federal long-arm statute, however, a federal court must use the long-arm statutes of the state where the federal court sits and may only exercise personal jurisdiction over a defendant to the same extent that a state court could.

Waiver. Unlike subject-matter jurisdiction, a defendant will lose a personal jurisdiction objection unless it is raised in a timely and proper fashion (as prescribed by each procedural system). This difference in treatment between personal jurisdiction and subject-matter jurisdiction reflects differences in policy. Subject-matter jurisdiction rules are supported by policies aimed partly at protecting general governmental interests rather than only party interests. In particular, subject-matter jurisdiction rules implicate the separation of powers between the judicial and legislative branches of government. The parties cannot always be relied on to raise objections that are aimed at protecting nonparty interests. Thus, such objections are often made nonwaivable. On the other hand, personal jurisdiction rules are based on policies of party protection. If the parties do not promptly raise objections aimed at protecting their own interests, it is proper to deem the objections waived.

Problems

Problem 1-3. On the facts of *Problem 1-1*, assume that *P* sued *D-1* and *D-2* in a U.S. District Court in Wisconsin in the judicial district where *P* resides. The action is brought pursuant to 28 U.S.C. § 1332(a)(1). *P's* complaint demanded $200,000 in damages for *D-1's* trespass, battery, and negligence as well as the $20,000 prize for the fish. *P's* complaint also demanded $100,000 from *D-2* for negligently causing an aggravation to *P's* previous injuries. *D-1* and *D-2* are served with process pursuant to a "long-arm" statute. Do you think that *D-1* and *D-2* are likely to have a "sufficient connection" to Wisconsin to make litigation there "fair" for purposes of personal jurisdiction?

Problem 1-4. On the facts of *Problem 1-3*, assume, instead, that *P* commenced the action in a U.S. District Court in Minnesota. Do you think *D-2* is likely to have a valid objection based on lack of personal jurisdiction over *D-2* in Minnesota?

(c) Choosing a Court in the Proper Location ("Venue")

In addition to determining which courts have subject-matter jurisdiction over the action and can obtain personal jurisdiction over the defendant, the plaintiff's lawyer must determine the proper *venue* for the action. Venue refers to the *geographic location* within a sovereign's territory where a particular type of action may be brought. Like personal jurisdiction but unlike subject-matter jurisdiction objections, venue objections can be waived.

Venue in State Court Actions. In state courts, statutes usually define the proper venue. For example, assume that a state has created fifty trial courts, called district courts, throughout the state. Assume further that the plaintiff's action is within the subject-matter jurisdiction of the district courts. The plaintiff's lawyer will have to determine in which of the fifty district courts the action can be brought. A state venue statute will ordinarily direct the plaintiff to one or more of these district courts. For instance, a venue statute might permit the plaintiff to bring the action in the district court where the defendant resides or the district court for the district in which the plaintiff's claim or "cause of action" arose, at the plaintiff's option. Similar to the transfer of venue provisions for the federal courts, discussed in subsection 5(c), below, state venue rules often provide that actions brought in a proper venue may be transferred by the court to a more convenient location within the state and that actions brought in an improper venue may be transferred to a proper venue.

Venue in Federal Court Actions. Venue in federal courts is also prescribed by statute. The general federal venue statute provides that the plaintiff may bring the action in a judicial district where the defendant resides, where the events giving rise to the suit occurred, or where the property that is the subject of the suit is situated. *See* 28 U.S.C. § 1391(b) (venue in general). Other federal statutes provide for venue in special kinds of cases. *See, e.g.,* 28 U.S.C. § 1397 (interpleader), § 1400 (patent and copyright suits), § 1401 (stockholder's derivative actions).

"Local Action" Rule. In addition to being aware of the venue statutes in a jurisdiction, lawyers need to be aware of the possible application of the *local action* rule in state court actions. Traditionally, English and American courts have distinguished between "transitory" and "local" actions. Transitory actions are technically actions that are based on events that could have occurred anywhere. Examples of *transitory actions* include (1) actions seeking damages for negligence, (2) actions seeking damages for an assault and battery, and (3) actions seeking damages or specific performance for breach of contract. When an action is classified as transitory, it can be brought in any one of the places provided for by the appropriate venue statute, *e.g.*, where the defendant resides.

Local actions are actions that could have occurred in only one place. Local actions always concern land in some respect, but not all actions that concern land are local actions. Examples of *local actions* include (1) actions for ejectment and (2) actions seeking damages for trespass to land. If an action is classified as "local," it can be brought only where the land is located.

The "Federal Courts Jurisdiction and Venue Clarification Act of 2011" eliminated the local action rule in federal court actions, and 28 U.S.C. § 1391(a)(2) now provides that "[e]xcept as otherwise provided by Law ... (2) the proper venue for a civil action shall be determined without regard to whether the action is local or transitory in nature."

Problem

Problem 1-5. On the facts of *Problem 1-1*, assume that *P* wants to commence an action in a Minnesota state court against *D-1* for trespassing on *P's* land. Assume that *D-1* lives in County *X*, which adjoins County *Y*, the county where *P's* land is located. Assuming the Minnesota courts follow traditional rules governing venue, in which county or counties do you think *P* will be able commence the action?

(d) Choice-of-Law Considerations

Another factor that strongly influences a plaintiff's choice of a court is the substantive law that will be applied to resolve the case. Civil disputes may arise from events that occur in different locations or between parties from different places, or both. Each location may have different substantive rules of law as well as different procedural rules. For example, assume that *P* and *D* have entered into a contract. *P* is from Alaska and *D* is from New Mexico. The parties have held preliminary discussions on the telephone; they have met at various places, including New York City, Houston, and Los Angeles; they have mailed drafts to each other; they have signed the contract in Florida; they have agreed to performances of the contract in various locations, including South Carolina and Paris, France. Assume that a dispute arises from an allegedly defective performance of the contract that took place in a manufacturing plant in Utah. As you can see from the diverse contact with several jurisdictions, many different substantive and procedural rules potentially govern the transaction and any subsequent litigation about the disputed performance. You should be aware that the substantive rules of different states might govern different aspects of the transaction.

The field of law that deals with the selection of the applicable law in the preceding note is called *conflict of laws*. The process of resolving the question is called *choice of law*. Traditionally, courts followed a "territorial" approach to choice-of-law problems: the *lex loci* (the law of the place where the right was acquired or the liability was incurred) controlled the substantive rights of the parties. The *lex fori* (the law of the forum or place where relief was sought) controlled all procedural and remedial matters. Today, most courts no longer follow this territorial approach. In the absence of controlling statutory directives and subject to constitutional limitations, modern conflict-of-laws systems or methods of analysis involve at least the following two steps. First, forum courts identify the contacts between (a) the concerned states or countries, (b) the parties, and (c) the transaction giving rise to the dispute. Second, the forum state's courts then assess the relevant policies of the concerned states or countries in light of those contacts to determine what law to apply. Beyond these two steps, however, conflict-of-laws methodology differs widely among states and cannot be easily summarized.

(e) Can the Plaintiff Join Multiple Claims in One Lawsuit?

Permissible Joinder of Claims. Suppose that an automobile accident between the plaintiff and the defendant is not the first contact between the parties. Suppose, in fact, that some time before the accident the plaintiff and the defendant had entered a binding contractual relationship and that the defendant had breached the contract. Thus, the plaintiff also has a claim for damages for breach of contract. May the plaintiff join the breach of contract claim with the negligence claim in the same action, or must the plaintiff bring a wholly separate action against the defendant on the contract claim?

Modern procedural systems differ in their response to this question. In the federal courts and many states, the plaintiff may join any number of claims against the defendant in the same action. Even though they are factually and legally unrelated to one another, the claims may be joined as long as a basis exists for the court to exercise subject-matter jurisdiction, personal jurisdiction, and venue with regard to each claim. *See* FED. R. CIV. P. 18(a). In "code pleading" systems, joinder is often more restricted. Before a typical code system will permit joinder of claims, some factual relationship must exist between the claims. Code systems also permit joinder of factually unrelated claims if they all belong to a specified legal category. For example, factually unrelated contract claims may be joined because they all fall within the "contract" category. However, with regard to the tort and unrelated contract example, above, a code-pleading system would not permit *P* to join the tort and contract claims. They lack a factual relationship and do not fall within the same legal category.

The differences between the systems are based on the harm or benefit that each system perceives in allowing joinder of multiple claims at an early stage of the proceedings. In procedural systems based on the federal model, the theory is that no harm is done, and much good may result, by allowing joinder of claims at the pleading stage. The harm, if any, would come in trying unrelated claims together. The federal model addresses such potential harm by giving the court discretion to separate the claims for trial purposes.

The Prohibition on "Splitting" Claims. Note that the federal model of claim joinder would *permit P* to join the claims against *D*, but it would not *compel* joinder of the claims. Nevertheless, certain rules governing finality of judgments might, as a practical matter, compel a plaintiff to join certain *related* claims that the plaintiff possesses against the defendant. For example, suppose that an automobile accident occurs between *P* and *D*. *P* suffers both personal injuries and property damage to *P's* automobile as a result of the accident. *P* sues *D* to recover $3,000 for the damage to *P's* automobile. After winning a favorable judgment, *P* then commences a second action in the same court for $50,000 for the personal injuries received in the accident.

In most states, the doctrine of *claim preclusion* would prevent *P* from bringing this second suit. Once a party sues on a claim, whether the party wins or loses, that party is thereafter forbidden from suing on the same claim—or any part of it—again. Normally, the elements of damage to *P's* car as well as *P's* person would be considered parts of the same claim because they result from the same factual occurrence. *P's* attempt to recover for these same elements in separate suits would be said to result in "*splitting a single claim.*" *P's* personal injury claim is said to have *merged* in the first judgment for property damage. The only thing remaining to *P* is a claim (for $3,000) on the judgment itself. If *P* had lost the first suit, the judgment in the first suit would be said to have *barred* the claim for personal injuries. Rules governing finality are examined in detail in Chapter 12.

Problem

Problem 1-6. On the facts of *Problem 1-1,* assume that *P* decides to commence an action against *D-1* in a U.S. District Court. The action is brought pursuant to 28 U.S.C. § 1332(a)(1). *P's* complaint demands (1) $125,000 in damages for *D-1's* trespass, battery, and negligence and (2) $20,000—the prize for the fish. From a procedural point of view, is it clear that *P* can join all of these claims together in this lawsuit? Is there any risk that *P* might face if *P* does not join all of these claims together?

(f) Who May (or Must) Be Named as Parties in the Lawsuit?

Every procedural system contains rules governing who may (and who must) be parties to a civil action. Modern procedural systems tend to be much more flexible in their approach to party joinder than the old common-law system. In fact, many modern procedural rules governing joinder of parties originated in the former practice in equity courts, which were much more liberal on matters of party joinder than the common-law courts. Modern reforms of party-joinder practice modeled on equity practice have enabled the parties to a dispute to resolve numerous related matters in a single proceeding.

Permissive Joinder of Parties. Assume that the plaintiff is involved in a three-car collision. The plaintiff believes that either the driver of the second or the driver of the third car, or both, were negligent. May the plaintiff sue the drivers of the second and third cars in the same action? Joinder of parties, either as additional plaintiffs or additional defendants, is restricted in all modern procedural systems. For example, Federal Rule 20(a) contains two restrictions on multiple party joinder. First, the claims asserted by multiple plaintiffs or against multiple defendants must arise out of the same transaction, occurrence, or series of transactions or occurrences. Second, at least one question of law or fact common to the multiple plaintiffs or defendants must exist in the action.

Thus, in the above situation, most modern procedural systems would permit a plaintiff to join both drivers in the same proceeding to determine their liability because of the nature of the relationship between the defendants and the claims. Furthermore, if a passenger in the plaintiff's car had been injured in the accident, the passenger would be permitted to join with the plaintiff in an action against one or both of the drivers. Under modern systems, the joinder of multiple plaintiffs or multiple defendants would be permitted but not compelled.

Required Joinder of Parties. Every modern procedural system also has certain rules of mandatory party joinder. Mandatory party joinder is important because a fundamental principle of American jurisprudence is that a person cannot be bound by a judgment unless the person, or the person's legal representative, was a party to the action. The mandatory joinder rules operate in two general circumstances. First, they operate when, in the absence of another person, "complete relief" cannot be accorded among the parties already present in the suit. In this situation, the parties need the third person brought into the lawsuit so that complete relief may be afforded among them. The public also has an interest in preventing multiple lawsuits between the persons who are parties to the action when the entire matter could be resolved in one lawsuit if the absent person were joined. Second, mandatory joinder rules operate when nonjoinder will impair an interest of a party present in the lawsuit or an interest of the absent person. This impairment may take the form of double, multiple, or otherwise inconsistent obligations. *See, e.g.,* FED. R. CIV. P. 19(a) ("Persons Required to Be Joined if Feasible").

For example, assume that *A* and *D* enter into a contract allowing *D* to remove oil and gas from a certain parcel of land for 5 years in exchange for annual royalty payments to *A*. Assume that in year 2 of the contract, *P* files an action against *D* claiming that *P* is the true owner of the land and that *D* must make all royalty payments to *P*. Assume that *P* does not join *A* as a party to this action. Assume that the court rules that *P* is the true owner of the property and that *D* must make all payments to *P*. Because *A* was not a party to this action, however, *A* would not be bound by the judgment and is free to bring his own action against *D* to enforce their contract. In this new action of *A v. D,* the second court could rule that *A* is the true owner of the property and that *D* must make all payments to *A*. *D* would thus be subject to "double" and "otherwise inconsistent" obligations based on the two conflicting judgments. Under the first judgment, *D* would be obligated to make all royalty payments to *P*, but under the second judgment, *D* would be obligated to make all royalty payments to *A*. Under the usual rules of mandatory joinder, *D* would ask the first court to require the joinder of *A* by *P* in the action of *P v. D*. In this way, one court would decide who is the true owner of the land and who is entitled to the oil and gas royalty payments and this single judgment would bind all of the affected parties.

A situation may arise in which it is impossible to join a person who ought to be joined under the mandatory joinder rules. For example, joining the absent person may destroy subject-matter jurisdiction or make venue improper, or the person who ought to be joined may not be subject to personal jurisdiction. When joining an absent party is impossible, the court will determine whether it can take some action to prevent the threatened harm that would be caused by the person's absence. If the court can prevent the harm, the court will allow the lawsuit to continue between the original parties. If the court cannot prevent the harm, it will classify the absent party as *indispensable* and will dismiss the action for filing in another jurisdiction where all of the affected parties may be properly joined. *See, e.g.,* FED. R. CIV. P. 19(b) ("When Joinder Is Not Feasible").

Special Joinder Devices—Interpleader and Class Actions. In addition to the basic rules governing joinder of parties discussed above, the plaintiff can utilize several special joinder devices at the outset of the lawsuit, including *interpleader* and *class actions. Interpleader* is a procedure that allows a party in possession of money or other property to bring all the adverse claimants to the property before the court to resolve their claims in a single proceeding. The purpose of interpleader is to eliminate the danger of double liability that would exist if the party in possession of the money or property (called the "stakeholder") were to be sued in separate actions by the claimants.

For example, assume that two claimants, *C-1* and *C-2*, both claim to own money in *P's* possession. If *P* gives the money to *C-1*, *C-2* might sue *P* and recover if the court determines that the money really belonged to *C-2*. If *P* gives the money to *C-2*, *C-1* might sue *P* and recover. Under these circumstances, *P* may *interplead C-1* and *C-2—i.e., P* may sue *C-1* and *C-2* in the same proceeding and force them to litigate their claims to the money in a single action that would bind all parties. Thus, an *interpleader* action avoids the possibility that *P* will be subjected to double liability. *See* FED. R. CIV. P. 22 ("Interpleader"—often referred to as "Rule Interpleader"); *see also* 28 U.S.C. §§ 1335, 1397 & 2361 (federal interpleader statutes—often referred to as "Statutory Interpleader").

A *class action* is a procedure that allows an action to be brought by or against a party who is a representative of a large number of persons similarly situated to the representative, but who are not formally named as parties in the action. Class actions are designed to avoid multiple lawsuits over the same basic matter and to permit the vindication of claims that would otherwise be lost due to the impracticability of bringing individual actions by or against the members of the class.

For example, assume that *R* is a member of a class of one million people who were injured by *D* in a similar way. Assume that *D* has injured each class member in only a small way. Individual damages amount to only $5.00 per class member. Because of the small amounts involved in each class member's claim, the class members are unlikely to bring separate actions to recover against *D*. If they did, a large amount of litigation would occur over the same basic matter. In addition, joining all class members in a single suit against *D* would be impossibly cumbersome. For these reasons, *R* may, under appropriate circumstances, bring a *class action*; *R* would sue for $5,000,000 on behalf of all class members. *See* FED. R. CIV. P. 23 ("Class Actions").

Problem

Problem 1-7. On the facts of *Problem 1-1*, assume that *P* sued *D-1* and *D-2* in a U.S. District Court. The action is brought pursuant to 28 U.S.C. § 1332(a)(1). *P's* complaint demanded $200,000 in damages for *D-1's* trespass, battery, and negligence as well as the $20,000 prize for the fish. *P's* complaint also demanded $100,000 from *D-2* for negligently causing an aggravation to *P's* previous injuries in the accident. From a procedural point of view, is it clear that *P* can join *D-1* and *D-2* in this lawsuit? Do you think it should be a problem that some of *P's* claims do not involve the accident and are not made against *D-2*?

(g) Is a Person Who Wants to Commence the Action the "Real Party in Interest" and Do All the Parties Have the "Capacity to Sue or Be Sued"?

In order to commence a civil action, a party must meet basic two requirements. First, the party must be the *real party in interest*. *See* FED. R. CIV. P. 17(a) ("Real Party in Interest"). The real party in interest is the person to whom the substantive law gives the right to bring and control the action. For example, assume that *D* owes *C* $100,000. *C* validly assigns the right to collect the entire debt to *P*. If *D* refuses to pay, the real party in interest is *P*, the assignee. *P*, not *C*, must bring the action.

Second, the plaintiff must have the *capacity to sue,* and every defendant must have the *capacity to be sued.* For example, a person who is *legally incapacitated* by reason of age or mental infirmity may not be named as the plaintiff (or the defendant) in a lawsuit. This requirement does not necessarily mean, however, that legally incapacitated persons cannot sue or be sued. Instead, a representative will have to sue or defend on their behalf. *See* FED. R. CIV. P. 17(b) ("Capacity to Sue or Be Sued"), (c) ("Minor or Incompetent Person"). If the court appoints a representative, the representative is called a *guardian ad litem*. In some states, a person who safeguards a minor's interests in the action is called the minor's *next friend.*

Problem

Problem 1-8. On the facts of *Problem 1-1*, assume that *D-2* was fifteen years old, and at the time *D-2* hit *D-1's* truck, *D-2* (1) was driving illegally without a license and (2) was so intoxicated that *D-2* lacked the physical and mental ability to control the sports car. In this situation, does *D-2* lack the capacity to be sued? Why or why not?

3. Commencement and Service of Process

After deciding to sue, selecting a proper court, deciding who will be joined as parties, and weighing other considerations, the plaintiff must formally commence the suit. In the federal courts and many states, the plaintiff would commence the action by filing a *complaint* (a statement of the claim or claims made against the defendant) with the court — usually with the clerk of court. *See* FED. R. CIV. P. 3 ("Commencing an Action"). Filing with the court, however, does not notify the defendant of the action. Nor does it secure personal jurisdiction over the defendant. The plaintiff provides notice and obtains personal jurisdiction by serving a *summons* and the complaint on the defendant (*"service of process"*). In some states, serving process accomplishes both the acquisition of personal jurisdiction and the commencement of the action. A summons is a paper that notifies the defendant that the action has been commenced. It also commands the defendant to appear and defend the action by a certain date or the court will enter a judgment (a *default judgment*) against the defendant for the remedy demanded by the plaintiff.

The plaintiff may deliver the summons to the defendant in a variety of ways. Sometimes, it is delivered by a public official, such as a sheriff. Private parties are also often authorized by law or by special appointment of the court to deliver the summons. Traditionally, the process server will give the summons to the defendant in person (*in-hand personal service*). Often, the statutes or rules will also authorize the process server to leave the summons at the defendant's home with someone responsible who, in turn, will be likely to deliver it to the defendant. *See, e.g.,* FED. R. CIV. P. 4(e) ("Serving an Individual Within a Judicial District of the United States"). After service of process has been accomplished, the process server must complete a *return of service.* The return of service is a statement by the process server of when and how service was accomplished. This return is written on either the lower portion or the reverse side of the original summons. In most states and in the federal courts, this return is given under oath. The return is filed with the clerk's office. *See, e.g.,* FED. R. CIV. P. 4(*l*) ("Proving Service").

4. The Plaintiff's First Pleading, Remedies, and Amendments

In all systems of pleading, the plaintiff must provide the defendant with information about the nature of the claim. This information is contained in a document called the *complaint, declaration,* or *petition.* This document is the first *pleading* in the action.

Functions of the Pleadings. The functions of the pleadings differ from system to system and directly affect the degree of detail required in the complaint. At a minimum, the plaintiff must give the defendant fair "notice" of the claim and the grounds upon which it is based. In some procedural systems, such as those governed by the Federal Rules of Civil Procedure, no greater detail would be required in the substantive statement of the claim.

Code pleading systems, however, require greater detail in pleading. "Code" systems are so-named after the New York Field Code of 1848 discussed above. Code pleading systems are sometimes also referred to as *fact pleading* systems, in contrast with the *notice pleading* standards embodied in the Federal Rules of Civil Procedure. Code (fact) pleading requires a plaintiff to state the "facts" constituting a *cause of action* and to plead the claim with substantial specificity. This kind of detailed pleading identifies and narrows the legal and factual issues in the case. One assumption of code systems is that if the pleading process allows the legal issues to be identified with sufficient clarity, the court may be able to rule on them early in the lawsuit.

For example, suppose that the plaintiff's complaint alleges that on a certain date on a certain public highway the "defendant unintentionally and in a non-negligent manner drove a motor vehicle against the plaintiff who was then crossing said highway," injuring the plaintiff in certain described ways. Such a complaint would be alleging a claim against the defendant in "strict liability," *i.e.,* a claim that the defendant is liable to the plaintiff merely because the defendant *caused* the plaintiff's injuries, even though the defendant was without fault in doing so. Assume that, under the applicable substantive law, no cause of action in damages exists unless an injury is the product of an intentional or negligent wrong. Thus, the plaintiff cannot possibly win the case on such facts. After an appropriate response by the defendant so indicating (discussed below), the court will dismiss the action.

A system of pleading that requires only general "notice" to the parties also functions to identify and narrow the issues. Nonetheless, the nature of notice pleading severely limits its ability to do so compared to fact-pleading systems. For example, assume that the applicable substantive law provides the plaintiff a right to damages against the defendant for negligent acts, but not for non-negligent acts. Assume also that the plaintiff is only required to state in the complaint that the defendant was negligent, without describing the particular *way* in which the defendant was negligent (speeding, driving while intoxicated, etc.). Under such circumstances, the feasibility of disposing of the case on the basis of the plaintiff's initial statement is drastically reduced. Yet, under notice-pleading systems, this amount of detail is all that would be required in the complaint. *See* Federal Form 11 ("Complaint For Negligence").

General-notice systems of pleading assume that, on average, the costs of requiring the plaintiff to state in detail the elements of the claim outweigh any benefits that might accrue from early disposition of the action. Notice pleading moves particularization of the case from the pleading stage of the action to a later stage, called the discovery stage, discussed below. Systems requiring greater detail in pleading are based on a different philosophy. In those systems, the costs of requiring particularized pleading in all cases are not thought to outweigh the benefit of an early disposition of some cases.

Another traditional function of the pleadings is to aid the parties in their preparation for trial by requiring a statement sufficient to identify the matters each side will attempt to prove if the action reaches the trial stage. This function aims at identifying factual, rather than legal, issues. The general-notice systems cannot perform this function as well as the more particularized fact-pleading systems. Today, however, neither general-notice nor fact-pleading systems rely exclusively on the pleadings for this purpose. Unlike the old common-law and early code-pleading systems, which lacked elaborate provisions for pretrial discovery, all modern procedural systems now contain discovery rules. These rules allow trial preparation to be conducted much more efficiently than was possible solely by use of the parties' written statements of their claims and defenses. Therefore, while the pleadings may significantly aid trial preparation in some cases, modern procedural systems do not rely heavily on the pleadings for this purpose.

An additional function of pleading in some courts of limited jurisdiction is to demonstrate to the court that it possesses subject-matter jurisdiction over the case. Courts of limited jurisdiction are presumed to lack subject-matter jurisdiction. Thus, unless the plaintiff demonstrates that subject-matter jurisdiction exists, the court will dismiss the action on its own initiative. Often, this demonstration will occur in the initial pleading. All federal courts are courts of limited jurisdiction. Jurisdictional statements are always required in pleadings in those courts. Thus, for example, a plaintiff can sue a defendant in a federal district court if the parties are citizens of different states and the plaintiff's claim exceeds $75,000; the plaintiff's complaint must have a jurisdictional statement so stating or the court will dismiss the action. *See* Federal Form 7 ("Statement of Jurisdiction"). In contrast to the federal courts, every state has at least one court of general jurisdiction. The subject-matter jurisdiction of courts of general jurisdiction is presumed to exist unless the contrary appears. Therefore, a court of general jurisdiction ordinarily will not require a jurisdictional statement.

Remedies and the Demand for Relief. As part of preparing the complaint, the plaintiff must make "a demand for the relief sought, which may include relief in the alternative or different types of relief." *See* Fed. R. Civ. P. 8(a)(3) ("Claim for Relief"). The relief demanded will reflect the remedies available under the circumstances. The four kinds of final remedies are (1) damages, (2) restitution, (3) coercive remedies, and (4) declaratory remedies. *See* 1 Dobbs § 1.1, at 2.

The *damages remedy* is a monetary award to a party designed to compensate the party for losses. Damages focus on economic losses. (A special category of damages, called *punitive damages*, is designed to punish the defendant for extreme behavior rather than to compensate. Most damage awards, however, are compensatory.)

The *restitutionary remedy* prevents the defendant's *unjust enrichment* at the plaintiff's expense. Restitution is always "restorative" in some sense. Nevertheless, restitution may not always restore the exact object or money taken from the plaintiff. For example, assume that the defendant steals $1,000 from the plaintiff. The defendant uses the $1,000 to buy a painting. If the painting rises in value to $2,000, the damage remedy would give the plaintiff $1,000 in compensation. The restitutionary remedy, however, would give the plaintiff the painting itself, or $2,000, if the defendant had sold the painting, to prevent the defendant from profiting by the wrong.

Coercive remedies are best exemplified by the *injunction*. An injunction is an *equitable* order that directs a party to do or cease doing certain things. As a form of equitable relief, an injunction is considered a personal directive against the party, hence the maxim — "equity acts in personam." When a party fails to comply with an equitable order, the court may use its contempt powers to punish the disobedient party. By contrast, a court order granting *legal* relief, typically compensatory money damages, is not enforceable by the court's contempt powers. The defendant who does not pay must suffer the consequences, which may be levy or execution on the defendant's property sufficient to satisfy the money judgment, but the defendant is not subject to contempt for failure to obey or satisfy a judgment granting only legal relief.

The contempt power of the court may also be invoked during the course of an action, irrespective of whether the action seeks legal or equitable relief, to enforce certain directives related to the litigation. For example, Rule 37(b)(2)(A)(vii) provides that the court may treat a party's violation of an order to provide or permit discovery as a contempt of court. Similarly, Rule 45(e) provides that a person who fails to obey a subpoena to testify or produce documents in an action may be held in contempt.

The punishments for contempt may be monetary fines, imprisonment, or both. Two kinds of contempt exist: *civil contempt* and *criminal contempt*.

Civil contempt is designed primarily to coerce compliance with the court's order in the future. For example, assume that the plaintiff obtains an injunction commanding the defendant to stop discharging waste water from his property onto the plaintiff's adjoining property. If the defendant continues to discharge the waste water in violation of the injunction, the court may hold the defendant in civil contempt and impose a monetary fine on the defendant for each day that the defendant continues to discharge waste water onto the plaintiff's property. Alternatively, the court may, under appropriate circumstances, impose an indefinite jail sentence ordering that the defendant remain incarcerated until the defendant agrees to comply with the court's injunction. In both instances, once the defendant complies with the court's injunction, the coercive function of civil contempt is satisfied and the order of coercive imprisonment and/or fines is lifted. Civil contempt may also serve a compensatory function for the plaintiff. In addition to the above, the court may order the defendant to pay money damages to the plaintiff for any losses caused to the plaintiff by the defendant's violation of the injunction.

The willful violation of a court injunction is also considered a criminal offense and, in addition to civil contempt, the defendant may also face separate criminal contempt proceedings. The goal of criminal contempt, as in other criminal actions, is to vindicate society's interest in punishing past unlawful conduct and to deter like actions by others. While civil contempt proceedings are conducted according to the usual rules of civil procedure, criminal contempt proceedings are conducted under the rules of criminal procedure. Unlike civil contempt, criminal contempt involves the imposition of a fixed punishment for the defendant's *past* violation of a court order. Thus, if a defendant violates an injunction, the court may jail the defendant for a fixed term or fine the defendant a fixed amount as punishment for the violation. The court may impose these criminal contempt penalties even if the defendant shows every willingness to comply with the injunction in the future and compensating the plaintiff is unnecessary. Moreover, the penalties may be imposed even if the court has also imposed civil contempt sanctions to coerce compliance with the court's decree.

Traditionally, it was not possible to defend a criminal contempt proceeding on the ground that the order disobeyed by the defendant was erroneous. Rather, the only kind of error that would constitute a defense to a criminal contempt proceeding was a lack of personal or subject-matter jurisdiction in the court that issued the injunction. Today, it may be possible to raise nonjurisdictional errors of law in defense of a contempt proceeding. *See* 1 Dobbs §§ 2.8(3), 2.8(4), 2.8(6); Teply & Whitten at 675–76.

The modern remedy of the *declaratory judgment* exemplifies *declaratory remedies*. A declaratory judgment simply declares the rights and liabilities of the parties to a dispute. Every damage, restitutionary, or coercive remedy implicitly declares the legal rights and liabilities of the parties. Thus, these remedies are, in part, declaratory remedies. Sometimes, however, the relationship between the parties has not deteriorated to the point where damage, restitutionary, or coercive remedies are available or desirable. The parties may find themselves disagreeing in good faith about the nature or extent of their legal rights, and they may be quite willing to obey a court decree determining their rights. All that is needed is a simple declaration of those rights.

Provisional Remedies. Various *provisional remedies* are also available to a party suing on a claim. Provisional remedies are, as their name suggests, remedies available to a party for a temporary period. These remedies are designed (1) to preserve the status quo, (2)

Provisional Remedies

to safeguard against the dissipation of assets that might later be needed to satisfy a final judgment in an action, or (3) to prevent other serious harm from accruing to one of the parties during the litigation. The principal provisional remedies are (1) temporary restraining orders, (2) preliminary injunctions, (3) attachment, (4) garnishment, (5) replevin, and (6) receivership.

Temporary restraining orders and *preliminary injunctions* are simply injunctive orders issued against a party during litigation. Usually, the court issues these orders against the defendant at or near the beginning of a lawsuit. The objective of the remedies is to prevent harm during the course of litigation to the party seeking the temporary restraining order or preliminary injunction.

Attachment is the seizure from the defendant of property, which is then brought into the custody of the court. *Garnishment* is a warning issued to a third party, such as a bank. The garnishment directs the third party not to pay the defendant's assets in the third party's possession to the defendant. Instead, the third party must hold them subject to further order of the court. Attachment and garnishment are both designed to ensure that property will be available with which to satisfy any judgment that the plaintiff obtains against the defendant.

Replevin is seizure of specific personal property in the defendant's possession to which the plaintiff is immediately entitled, such as when the plaintiff has a lien or ownership interest in the property. Replevin is called *sequestration* in some jurisdictions. The purpose of replevin is to prevent the deterioration, destruction, or disposition of the property during the pendency of the litigation.

Receivership is the appointment of a neutral third party to manage property that is the subject of the action. The purpose of a receivership is to preserve the property from ruin or dissipation by either party.

Two examples will suffice to illustrate how provisional remedies work. First, assume that the plaintiff sues for an injunction to prevent the defendant from trespassing on the plaintiff's land. The plaintiff will receive the injunction, if at all, only after a full hearing on the merits of the plaintiff's claim and the defendant's defenses. A considerable period may pass before this full hearing takes place. If the defendant is trespassing in the interim, the plaintiff may want the trespassing stopped immediately. The temporary restraining order (T.R.O.) and preliminary injunction may be used to stop the trespasses during the period necessary to conduct a full hearing on the merits. A T.R.O. secures the status quo until a request for a preliminary injunction may be heard. Under some circumstances, the court may issue a T.R.O. without notice or an opportunity to be heard in defense. Of course, the order must be served on the defendant before it is obligatory. *See* FED. R. CIV. P. 65(b) ("Temporary Restraining Order"). Because of due process limitations in state and federal constitutions, notice and an opportunity to be heard can be omitted only in emergencies. The plaintiff must show that serious harm would result if notice were given and a hearing were held before the court issued the T.R.O. In contrast, a preliminary injunction is issued to prevent irreparable harm or to preserve the status quo until after a full adjudication on the merits. A preliminary injunction is always preceded by notice to the defendant and an opportunity to be heard. *See* FED. R. CIV. P. 65(a) ("Preliminary Injunction"). Much like final injunctions, courts enforce T.R.O.s and preliminary injunctions by contempt proceedings.

Second, assume that *P* sues *D* for damages. *D* anticipates that the court will enter a final judgment in the action in the plaintiff's favor and wants to prevent assets from being seized to satisfy the judgment. Assume that *P's* lawyer learns that *D* is removing those assets from the state in which the action is pending. Under such circumstances, *P's* lawyer may seek an order of attachment. This order will result in seizure of *D's* assets by the sheriff in an amount sufficient to satisfy the damage judgment *P* hopes to obtain. Like a T.R.O., in true emergencies, attachment may occur without prior notice and an opportunity to be heard. If no notice or hearing is provided before seizure, due process requires a prompt post-seizure hearing.

It may seem strange that a court will grant provisional remedies without a full trial of the merits of a case. After all, the defendant may ultimately win the case. If that happens, the defendant will have been erroneously deprived of liberty or property by the provisional remedy without having had a full opportunity to litigate the merits of the plaintiff's claim. Protection is afforded to such a defendant in a variety of ways. As indicated above, provisional remedies issued without prior notice and opportunity to be heard are limited to emergency situations. In addition, a hearing is required at some early stage of the litigation. At the hearing, the moving party will not only be required to demonstrate the existence of the requisite emergency, but will also be required to show some degree of likelihood of succeeding on the merits of the claim. Furthermore, the statutes and rules governing provisional remedies usually require the moving party to post security before obtaining the remedy. This security will often be in the form of a bond. The security is supposed to be of a sufficient amount to indemnify the opposing party for any harm that accrues if the court erroneously issues the provisional remedy.

Inconsistent, Hypothetical, and Alternative Pleading. Unlike the old common-law system of pleading, modern systems of pleading usually allow inconsistent, hypothetical, and alternative pleading. For example, Federal Rule 8(d)(2) ("Alternative Statements of a Claim or Defense") permits a party stating a claim or defense to "set out 2 or more statements of a claim or defense alternately or hypothetically, either in a single count or defense or in separate ones." Federal Rule 8(d)(3) ("Inconsistent Claims or Defenses") further provides that "[a] party may state as many separate claims or defenses as it has, regardless of consistency." Allowance of alternative, hypothetical, and inconsistent pleading ensures that the parties will be able to raise multiple claims and defenses without running into the kinds of objections that could formerly be raised to that practice at common-law. In addition, as required by Federal Rule 8(d)(1), each allegation in a pleading "must be simple, concise, and direct."

Amendments. *Amendments* correct errors or seek to cure pleading omissions. In modern systems, whether of the general-notice or code-pleading type, courts readily permit amendments to avoid hardship and injustice to the parties. For example, assume that the plaintiff in an automobile negligence action mistakenly omits the allegation that the defendant "*negligently*" drove an automobile into the plaintiff. Modern systems would give the plaintiff a certain amount of time to add the allegation of negligence as a matter of right. After that time expires, courts liberally allow the plaintiff to amend upon request. *See* FED. R. CIV. P. 15(a) ("Amendments Before Trial").

Sometimes, a plaintiff will attempt to add a claim by amendment after the applicable *statute of limitations* has run. (Statutes of limitations establish the time within which a party must take judicial action to enforce a claim or be barred from enforcing it thereafter.) Whether such an amendment is permissible depends on the *doctrine of relation back* followed in the particular procedural system. Often, if the claim to be added by amendment is sufficiently related to the plaintiff's original claim, the procedural system will provide that it "relates back" to the date of the first complaint to avoid the bar of the statute of limitations. *See, e.g.,* FED. R. CIV. P. 15(c) ("Relation Back of Amendments").

Supplemental Pleadings. Federal Rule 15(d) allows a *supplemental pleading* to set forth "any transaction, occurrence, or event that happened after the date of the pleading to be supplemented." A typical use of a supplemental pleading would be to raise new damages occurring *after* commencement of the action. In this context, the plaintiff would serve a *supplemental complaint* asserting the new damages.

Problems

Problem 1-9. On the facts of *Problem 1-1*, assume that the fish caught by *D-1* had a fair market value of $25 at the time and place of taking. Which legal theory—damages or restitution—would support a recovery of $25? Which these legal theories would support a recovery of the prize won by *D-1* ($20,000)?

Problem 1-10. On the facts of *Problem 1-1*, assume *P* has properly commenced an action against *D-1* in federal district court. Shortly after the action was commenced, *P* learns that *D-1* has two freezers full of fish that had been caught in *P*'s pond prior to the commencement of the action. Can *P* add a claim for the value of those fish to *P*'s pending action? If so, how?

Problem 1-11. On the facts of *Problem 1-1*, assume *D-1* has continued to trespass repeatedly after *P* has properly commenced an action against *D-1* in federal district court. Is there some way that P could include damages for these trespasses in *P*'s action against *D-1*? If so, how?

Problem 1-12. On the facts of *Problem 1-1*, assume that *P* has properly commenced an action against *D-1* and has been awarded damages, but *D-1* still continues to trespass repeatedly on *P*'s land. Is there a remedy that *P* could seek that might more effectively discourage *D-1* from trespassing?

Problem 1-13. On the facts of *Problem 1-1*, assume that *P* wants to sue to recover for the injuries that *P* received in the accident. *P* is not completely sure whether *D-1* or *D-2*, or both, were negligent. What should *P* do? Does Federal Form 12 help you answer this question?

Problem 1-14. On the facts of *Problem 1-1*, assume that *D-3*, a neighbor, is threatening to cut certain trees on land that *P* claims to own. *D-3* claims that *P* does not own the land on which the trees are located. *P* wants to stop *D-3* from cutting the trees until the dispute over the title to the land is settled. What provisional remedy should *P* seek? If *D-3* is going to cut the trees immediately and a lengthy trial of the title issue will be necessary, what should *P* do? How would the remedy or remedies be enforced against *D-3*? What steps should be taken to protect *D-3*'s rights under these circumstances?

5. The Defendant's Response to the Plaintiff's Commencement of the Action

(a) Default

In response to the plaintiff's commencement of the action, one option for the defendant is simply to *default*. Suppose, for example, that a plaintiff commences an action against a defendant and serves the defendant with a summons and complaint. If the defendant fails to respond within the time prescribed to answer, the defendant defaults. When the plaintiff calls the attention of the clerk of the court to the default in a proper manner, the clerk will enter the default in the record. After the plaintiff takes any further steps required by the procedural system, a *default judgment* may be entered. *See* Fed. R. Civ. P. 55 ("Default; Default Judgment"). Unless the defendant can show a good reason for the default, a default judgment will mean that the defendant loses the right to defend the action on the merits. The plaintiff may enforce the default judgment to the same extent as a judgment entered after a full trial. A default can occur at various stages of an action, not simply at the beginning.

Note that a plaintiff can also default by failing to "prosecute" the action. A default by the plaintiff can result in an involuntary dismissal of the plaintiff's action, discussed below.

(b) Transfer, Forum Non Conveniens, and Removal

After the plaintiff has commenced an action in a particular court and the defendant has been served with process, it may be possible for the defendant to have the action moved to another forum. Three possibilities for doing so involve transfers, the doctrine of forum non conveniens, and removal.

Transfer. If the plaintiff commences a federal action in an improper venue, the defendant may object. If the objection is a valid one, the federal district court must dismiss or transfer the action to a proper venue. *See* 28 U.S.C. § 1406 ("Cure or waiver of defects"). Even when venue is proper, there may be a more convenient district in which the action might have been brought. In such a situation, the court has the discretion to transfer the case to the more convenient district. *See* 28 U.S.C. § 1404(a) ("Change of venue"). States also have statutes authorizing the transfer of actions from one court to another within a particular state.

Forum Non Conveniens. In addition to statutorily authorized state and federal transfer provisions, an important common-law doctrine, *forum non conveniens*, allows defendants to move for dismissal of actions brought in inconvenient locations. A dismissal based on forum non conveniens is available in state court when there is a substantially more convenient alternate forum in another state or foreign country. Some states also allow forum non conveniens dismissals when there is a more convenient forum elsewhere in the same state, although this kind of problem is ordinarily handled by a transfer statute. Forum non conveniens dismissals in federal court are, practically speaking, limited to cases in which a substantially more convenient forum exists in a foreign country.

Removal from State to Federal Court. If a plaintiff whose action fits within some grant of federal subject-matter jurisdiction elects to sue a defendant in a state court instead of a federal district court, the defendant can file a notice of removal in federal district court and request removal of the state court action to federal district court. *See* 28 U.S.C. §§ 1441, 1446; *see also* the discussion of removal in section F(2)(a), above. There is no equivalent procedure for removing a case from a federal court to a state court.

Problems

Problem 1-15. On the facts of *Problem 1-1*, assume that P sues D-2 in a U.S. District Court in Ohio in the judicial district where D-2 resides. The action is brought pursuant to 28 U.S.C. § 1332(a)(1). *P's* complaint demands $100,000 from D-2 for negligently causing an aggravation of *P's* previous injuries. D-2 is properly served with process, but D-2 fails to respond or otherwise appear in the action. In such a situation, what should P do?

Problem 1-16. On the facts of *Problem 1-1*, assume that *P* sued *D-2* in an Ohio state court. *D-2* would prefer to litigate in the federal district court rather than state court. Is there a way for *D-2* to have the case moved to the appropriate federal district court in Ohio?

Problem 1-17. On the facts of *Problem 1-1*, assume that *P* sues *D-2* in a U.S. District Court in Ohio in the judicial district where *D-2* resides. The action is brought pursuant to 28 U.S.C. §1332(a)(1). *P's* complaint demanded $100,000 from *D-2* for negligently causing an aggravation of *P's* previous injuries. Even though the action has been commenced in *D-2's* current home state, *D-2* is planning to move to Minnesota soon and feels that it would be more convenient for everyone if the action were litigated where the accident occurred—in Minnesota. Is there a way for *D-2* to seek to have the action moved to a federal district court in Minnesota?

Problem 1-18. On the facts of *Problem 1-17*, but assume that *P* had commenced the action in an Ohio state court instead of a U.S. District Court in Ohio. Is there a way for *D-2* to seek to have the action brought instead in a state or federal court in Minnesota?

(c) The Defendant's Basic Responses to the Complaint

The above subsections discussed decisions that the plaintiff had to make before commencing an action. If the plaintiff makes one or more of those decisions incorrectly, the defendant will have objections that can be raised early in the action. For example, if the plaintiff chooses a court that cannot properly assert personal jurisdiction over the defendant, the defendant will be allowed by a proper procedure to object on this ground. In addition, there are other grounds for objecting to the location of the suit.

Rule 12 of the Federal Rules of Civil Procedure regulates when and how defenses and objections are presented in a federal civil action. In general, a defendant must assert all of the defendant's defenses to the plaintiff's action in a *responsive pleading* called an *answer* (which is the principal pleading by the defendant).

Preanswer Motions. Rule 12(b), however, permits certain defenses to be raised in a *preanswer motion*, at the defendant's option. These defenses include lack of subject-matter jurisdiction, lack of personal jurisdiction, improper venue, insufficient process, and insufficient service of process. *See* FED. R. CIV. P. 12(b)(1)-(5). A *motion* is simply an application to the court requesting an order or ruling in favor of the moving party. If the court denies a defendant's preanswer motion, the defendant must then assert any remaining defenses in the answer. Similarly, in modern code-pleading states, if certain legal deficiencies appear "on the face" of the plaintiff's complaint, the defendant will be able to raise these issues by either a *motion* or *demurrer*.

Challenges to the "Legal Sufficiency" of the Complaint. Assume that (1) the plaintiff's complaint alleges that the defendant is strictly liable to the plaintiff and (2) the applicable substantive law does not give the plaintiff any right to damages from the defendant under a strict liability theory. If the action is pending in federal court, the defendant can file a motion to dismiss for "failure to state a claim upon which relief can be granted" under Federal Rule 12(b)(6). If the action is pending in a code-pleading system, the defendant will file a demurrer for failure to state facts sufficient to constitute a cause of action.

Either the motion or the demurrer will raise the issue of the "legal sufficiency" of the complaint. If the defendant's legal objection is valid, the court will dismiss the action. In both systems, the defendant's objection is *legal*, rather than factual. The court will assume the truth of the facts stated in the plaintiff's complaint for purposes of the motion or demurrer. The question for the court is whether the applicable substantive law provides the plaintiff a right to relief under the facts alleged by the plaintiff. As noted above, the rules of the particular system (like the Federal Rules of Civil Procedure) may also permit the defendant to incorporate legal objections in an *answer* to the plaintiff's initial pleading rather than make that objection the subject of a motion or demurrer.

Admissions and Denials. The answer will contain the defendant's responses to the factual allegations contained in the plaintiff's pleading. Assume, for example, the plaintiff has alleged certain facts in the complaint that the defendant cannot in good faith deny. In that situation, the defendant will either admit the facts or say nothing about them, which will result in their implicit admission for purposes of further proceedings. If other facts exist that the defendant believes in good faith to be false, the defendant will deny them. Denials help form the issues of fact that will be the subject of the trial—assuming that one of the methods of disposing of an action without trial (discussed below) cannot be used to determine the case. *See* Fed. R. Civ. P. 8(b) ("Defenses; Admissions and Denials").

Affirmative Defenses. In addition to admissions and denials, the defendant may in good faith believe that additional facts (not mentioned in the plaintiff's initial pleading) exist that provide a good defense to the action. For example, assume that a defendant in an automobile negligence action believes that the plaintiff was driving while intoxicated. Assume that this fact, if true, would make the plaintiff "contributorily negligent" under the applicable substantive law. On these assumptions, the defendant would have a complete defense to the plaintiff's claim. The defendant can plead the fact of the plaintiff's intoxication, in such detail as required, as an *affirmative defense* in the answer. *See* Fed. R. Civ. P. 8(c) ("Affirmative Defenses").

Misjoinder or Nonjoinder of Parties. Rule 12(b)(7) of the Federal Rules of Civil Procedure permits the defendant to assert in a preanswer motion that the plaintiff has failed to join an absent party as required by Rule 19 ("Required Joinder of Parties"). If this objection is not raised in a preanswer motion, it may be included in the defendant's answer or even as late as the trial on the merits.

Federal Rule 21 ("Misjoinder and Nonjoinder of Parties") permits a party to move that an improperly joined party be dropped at any stage of the action. The court may also do so on its own initiative. However, misjoinder of parties is not a ground for dismissal. Instead, any claim against a party may be severed and proceeded with separately on terms as are just.

Comparison with Common-Law Pleading. Recall that the modern responses to the plaintiff's initial pleading correspond to the system of common-law pleading discussed above. As noted there, the modern denial is the equivalent of the common-law traverse; the modern affirmative defense is the equivalent of the common-law plea in confession and avoidance; and the modern demurrer or motion to dismiss is the equivalent of the common-law demurrer.

Modern pleading systems are much more flexible than the common-law system. For example, the common-law demurrer admitted the facts alleged in the opposing pleading conclusively for purposes of the action, while the modern demurrer and motion to dismiss do not. In modern systems, the truth of the facts alleged is simply admitted for purposes of the demurrer or motion. Thus, if the demurrer or motion is overruled, the action continues and the party whose pleading was challenged must later establish the facts alleged in the pleading. At common law, if a demurrer was overruled—for example, a demurrer to the plaintiff's declaration—the action was over and the plaintiff won.

Modern systems also permit more than a single issue of fact or law to be formed by the pleadings. Thus, the defendant can deny factual allegations in the complaint, assert affirmative defenses to the claim, and raise questions about the legal sufficiency of the complaint.

Waiver. In presenting various defenses, a defendant must take care not to waive certain defenses. For example, the interaction of Federal Rules 12(g) ("Joining Motions") and (h) ("Waiving and Preserving Certain Defenses") can produce waiver of objections made on the grounds of lack of personal jurisdiction, improper venue, insufficient process, and insufficient service of process. If the defendant elects to make a preanswer motion pursuant to Rule 12 and omits one or more of the above grounds, the omitted defense will be waived if the defense was "available" at the time the defendant made the preanswer motion. If the defendant does not make a preanswer motion and fails to assert one or more of the above grounds in the defendant's answer, the omitted defenses will be waived. *See* FED. R. CIV. P. 12(g)(2), (h)(1). Rule 12(h)(2) allows certain defenses to be raised all the way up to trial on the merits, including failure to state a claim upon which relief can be granted and failure to join a required party under Rule 19. Under Rule 12(h)(3), lack of subject-matter jurisdiction may be raised at any time and the defense is never waived.

Problems

Problem 1-19. On the facts of *Problem 1-1*, assume that P sued D-1 and D-2 in a U.S. District Court in Wisconsin. In terms of the methods of asserting a personal jurisdiction objection, how can D-1 and D-2 raise the objection to personal jurisdiction under the Federal Rules of Civil Procedure?

Problem 1-20. On the facts of *Problem 1-1*, assume that P decides to commence an action against D-1 in a U.S. District Court in Minnesota. The action is brought pursuant to 28 U.S.C. § 1332(a)(1). P's complaint demands (1) $70,000 in damages for D-1's trespass, battery, and negligence and (2) $20,000 — the prize for the fish. How could D-1 raise the following defenses?

(a) D-1 wants to dispute P's allegations that D-1 had been negligent in operating D-1's truck.

(b) D-1 believes that P cannot meet the jurisdictional amount requirement for § 1332(a)(1) because the applicable law only allows P to recover the value of the fish at the time and place of taking ($25), not the prize that D-1 won for catching the fish.

(c) Even if P is able to prove everything P has alleged in P's complaint, D-1 maintains that P has waited too long to sue and P's claim is barred by the applicable statute of limitations.

(d) D-1 asserts that P has commenced the action in the wrong location.

(e) D-1 believes that P's negligence also contributed to the accident because P grabbed the steering wheel just before the collision. Assume that if D-1 is correct, D-1 would have a complete defense to P's claim.

Problem 1-21. On the facts of *Problem 1-1*, assume that P sued D-1 and D-2 in a U.S. District Court in Minnesota. The action is brought pursuant to 28 U.S.C. § 1332(a)(1). P's complaint demanded $200,000 in damages for D-1's trespass and battery as well as the $20,000 prize for the fish. P's complaint also demanded $100,000 from D-2 for negligently causing P's injuries in the auto accident. D-2 believes that D-1 and D-2 are improperly joined in this action. How could D-2 raise this objection?

Problem 1-22. Assume that *P* sued *D-1* in a U.S. District Court in Wisconsin in the judicial district where *P* resides. The action is brought pursuant to 28 U.S.C. § 1332(a)(1). Based on the facts stated in *Problem 1-1*, *P's* complaint demanded from *D-1* (1) $100,000 in damages for *D-1's* trespass, battery, and negligence, (2) $20,000 — the prize for the fish — on the basis of unjust enrichment, and (3) $5,000 in attorney's fees. Before serving an answer, *D-1* moves to have the action dismissed pursuant to Federal Rule 12(b)(7) because *D-1* believes *D-2* is an "indispensable" party who has not been joined in the action. The court denies *D-1's* motion. *D-1* then realizes for the first time that (1) *D-1* has a valid venue objection and (2) the applicable law clearly does not allow *P* to recover attorney's fees under the circumstances of this case. Can *D-1* serve a second preanswer motion based on these newly discovered defenses? Does the language of Federal Rule 12(g) help you answer this question? If not, can *D-1* assert these two defenses in *D-1's* answer? Does the language of Federal Rule 12(h) help you answer this question?

(d) Assertion of Claims by the Defendant Against Other Parties

Crossclaims. Modern pleading systems also permit, but do not require, coparties (parties aligned on the same side of the action) to assert claims against each other. Such claims are normally called *crossclaims*. For example, suppose that *P* sues *D-1* and *D-2*. *P* asserts claims against them for negligence arising out of an automobile accident. Under these circumstances, *D-1* and *D-2* are coparties — specifically, they are codefendants. Modern procedural systems would permit, but would not require, *D-1* to assert a crossclaim in *D-1's* answer against *D-2* for the injuries that *D-1* received in the automobile accident. *See* FED. R. CIV. P. 13(g) ("Crossclaim Against a Coparty"). If *D-1* does assert a crossclaim, *D-2* would be required to serve an answer to *D-1's* crossclaim.

Counterclaims. A party who is defending a claim may assert a claim against the opposing party. Such a claim is called a *counterclaim*. There are two types of counterclaims: permissive and compulsory. Suppose the defendant in an automobile negligence action possesses a factually unrelated breach of contract claim against the plaintiff at the time the plaintiff sues for the injuries received in the accident. May or must the defendant assert this claim in the answer to the plaintiff's complaint? Under the federal model, the defendant's claim would be a *permissive counterclaim*. The defendant would be permitted, but not required, to assert it in the answer as long as independent grounds of subject-matter jurisdiction existed to support it. *See* FED. R. CIV. P. 13(b) ("Permissive Counterclaim").

However, assume that the defendant asserts that the defendant was not at fault in an automobile accident. Furthermore, the defendant asserts that the plaintiff was at fault and had caused the defendant's injuries. Under the federal model, the situation is quite different from the one described in the preceding paragraph. The defendant's claim for damages against the plaintiff arising out of the accident would be a *compulsory counterclaim.* The defendant must include this counterclaim in the defendant's answer. If it is not included in the answer or in an amendment to the answer, the defendant's claim for damages will be lost — *i.e.*, the defendant cannot sue on it later in a separate action. *See* FED. R. CIV. P. 13(a) ("Compulsory Counterclaim").

A counterclaim included in the defendant's answer is set forth in the same manner that a claim is pleaded in the complaint. *See* Federal Form 30 ("Answer Presenting Defenses under Rule 12(b)"). Counterclaims can also appear in pleadings other than answers, and compulsory counterclaim rules, such as Federal Rule 13(a), are framed to operate any time a party serves a pleading on an opposing party.

Code-pleading systems are both more restrictive and more liberal with respect to counterclaims than systems based on the federal model. Ordinarily, before the defendant is *permitted* to join the counterclaim, a factual relationship must exist between the defendant's counterclaim and the plaintiff's claim. In addition, code systems allow the defendant to assert counterclaims in certain kinds of actions if the counterclaims arise out of the same legal category as the plaintiff's claim. For example, the defendant might be able to join a contract counterclaim in an action by the plaintiff for breach of a contract that is factually unrelated to the counterclaim.

On the other hand, even if the counterclaim arises out of the same events as the plaintiff's claim, code-pleading systems do not normally compel the defendant to assert a counterclaim. Thus, compulsory counterclaims do not exist in code practice. However, a caveat is in order here. The rules governing finality of judgments may effectively preclude a defendant from asserting a related claim in a separate proceeding against the plaintiff after losing in the initial action, even if no compulsory counterclaim rule operates to bar the claim.

Impleader. *Impleader,* also known as *third-party practice,* is a procedure that allows a defending party, acting as a *third-party plaintiff,* to join a person to the action who is or may be liable to the defending party for all or part of the claim asserted against the defending party. The person joined is known as a *third-party defendant.* This type of special joinder is initiated by serving a summons and *third-party complaint.* If such a complaint is served by the *third-party plaintiff,* then the *third-party defendant* must serve a *third-party answer. See* FED. R. CIV. P. 14 ("Third-Party Practice").

Impleader is often used by a defendant in a negligence action. For example, in a negligence action involving numerous potential defendants, the plaintiff may choose to sue only one of the defendants. Under the law of "contribution," a tortfeasor against whom a judgment is rendered may be entitled to recover proportional shares from other "joint tortfeasors." Such a recovery would be permitted when (1) the other joint tortfeasors' negligence contributed to the plaintiff's injury and (2) the joint tortfeasors would have been liable to the plaintiff if the plaintiff had chosen to join them in the action. Thus, in a negligence action involving two potential tortfeasors, if *P* only sued one tortfeasor, *D,* *D* would be entitled to *implead T,* the second tortfeasor, in the action. In this way, the court will determine *T's* obligations to *D* in the same proceeding in which *D's* obligation to *P* is determined.

Interpleader. *Interpleader* was discussed earlier as a special joinder device available to the plaintiff. Interpleader is also available to the defendant. Assume that both *C-1* and *C-2* claim to own an automobile in *D's* possession. If one of the claimants sues *D,* then *D* may counterclaim for interpleader, joining *C-2* in the action to force *C-1* and *C-2* to litigate their claims to the automobile in a single action. *See* FED. R. CIV. P. 22(a)(2) ("A defendant exposed to [double or multiple] liability may seek interpleader through a crossclaim or counterclaim.").

(e) Good-Faith Requirements

It should be noted that state systems of pleading impose restrictions on what is permissible in the pleading process, either through specific rules or general ethical restrictions on attorneys' behavior. Likewise, the Federal Rules of Civil Procedure place limits on what is permissible in the pleading process. Specifically, Rule 11(b)(1) prohibits a party from presenting a pleading, motion, or other paper for "any improper purpose, such as to harass, cause unnecessary delay, or needlessly increase the cost of litigation." Rule 11(b)(2) additionally prohibits presenting a pleading, motion, or other paper containing claims, defenses, or other legal contentions unless they are "warranted by existing law or by a nonfrivolous argument for extending, modifying, or reversing existing law or for establishing new law." Rule 11(b)(3) also prohibits alleging facts without existing evidentiary support or evidentiary support that is likely to be obtained after a reasonable opportunity for further investigation or discovery. In addition, Rule 11(b)(4) prohibits unwarranted denials of factual contentions.

Problems

Problem 1-23. On the facts of *Problem 1-1*, assume that *P's* complaint in a federal court action against *D-2* alleges that *D-2* negligently drove into *D-1's* truck at a particular date and time. *D-2* points out to *D-2's* attorney that *D-2* was in another city at that date and time. In framing a response to *P's* allegation, in light of Federal Rule 11, what should *D-2's* attorney do? Do you need additional information to answer this question?

Problem 1-24. On the facts of *Problem 1-23*, assume *D-2* agrees that *D-2* negligently crashed into *D-1's* truck as alleged in the complaint, but does not think *P* can prove it. In light of Federal Rule 11, can *D-2* deny *P's* allegations and require *P* to prove them?

Problem 1-25. On the facts of *Problem 1-1*, assume that *P* sues *D-1* and *D-2* in a federal action, alleging that *D-1* and *D-2* were negligent and that they caused *P* personal injuries in the accident. *D-1* wants to crossclaim against *D-2* for injuries that *D-1* received in the accident. Under the Federal Rules of Civil Procedure, what is the name of the document that *D-1* would use to assert this crossclaim? Does Federal Form 30 help you answer this question?

Problem 1-26. On the facts of *Problem 1-25*, suppose that *D-1* also possesses a claim against *D-2* that is factually and legally unrelated to the automobile accident. Do the Federal Rules of Civil Procedure permit *D-1* to join that claim with *D-1's* crossclaim for damages arising out of the automobile accident? Does Federal Rule 18(a) help you answer this question?

Problem 1-27. On the facts of *Problem 1-25*, assume that *D-1* asserts a crossclaim against *D-2* arising out of the automobile accident. Does *D-2* have to respond to this crossclaim under the Federal Rules? If so, what is the name of the document that *D-2* must serve on *D-1* to make the response? Does Federal Rule 7(a) help you answer this question? If *D-2* possesses a claim against *D-1* arising out of the automobile accident, does *D-2* have to assert it in *D-2's* response to *D-1's* crossclaim, or may *D-2* sue *D-1* on the claim in a separate action? Does Federal Rule 13(a) help you answer this question?

Problem 1-28. On the facts of *Problem 1-1*, assume that *P* subsequently unexpectedly died from *P's* injuries in the accident. Assume that *P* had a life insurance policy issued by *M* (Mega Insurance Co.) in the amount of $500,000 payable to "my spouse." It appears that *P* had secretly married two different persons, *S-1* and *S-2*, who now each claim to be *P's* "spouse." Both *S-1* and *S-2* are threatening to sue *M* for the $500,000. *M* wants to join *S-1* and *S-2* in an action to determine who should receive the policy proceeds. What special joinder device might be available to *M* for this purpose?

Problem 1-29. On the facts of *Problem 1-28*, assume that before *M* can make use of any of the joinder devices discussed above, *M* is sued by *S-1* for the $500,000. What alternatives are open to *M* to allow *M* to protect against a separate action by *S-2* against *M* for the money?

6. The Plaintiff's Possible Responses to the Defendant's Answer

Whether a plaintiff must respond to the answer depends on (1) the kind of procedural system in which the action is pending and (2) what the defendant's answer contains. In the federal courts, the plaintiff does not have to respond to the defendant's answer — assuming the answer contains only admissions, denials, and affirmative defenses. Only if the defendant's answer contains a "counterclaim" do the Federal Rules of Civil Procedure require the plaintiff to serve an answer to the defendant's counterclaim. *See* FED. R. CIV. P. 7(a)(3). Under Federal Rule 7(a)(7), however, the court may order the plaintiff to serve a *reply* to a defendant's answer which contains some new matter or issue, even though the defendant's answer does not contain a counterclaim. In a typical code-pleading state, the plaintiff would have to serve a reply to any affirmative defense or counterclaim in the answer. For example, in response to an allegation of contributory negligence, the plaintiff must serve a reply on the defendant in a code-pleading state.

Under some circumstances, the plaintiff must assert a counterclaim in response to a counterclaim asserted by the defendant against the plaintiff. For example, assume that *P* sues *D* for personal injuries received in an automobile accident and *D* then asserts an unrelated breach of contract counterclaim against *P* in *D's* answer, as permitted by Federal Rule 13(b) ("Permissive Counterclaim"). Assume further that *P's* position is that *D*, not *P*, has breached the contract and that *D* has damaged *P* by the breach. When *P* serves an answer to *D's* counterclaim denying the breach, *P must* counterclaim for breach of contract against *D* in *P's* answer under Federal Rule 13(a).

Under the Federal Rule 13(a), any time a party is required to serve a pleading on another party, the party serving the pleading *must* include any counterclaim in the pleading that *arises out of the same facts* as the opposing party's claim. *P's* answer to *D's* counterclaim is a pleading. At the time of serving the answer, *P* possesses a claim for relief against *D* that arises out of the same facts as *D's* breach-of-contract counterclaim against *P*. Therefore, under the Federal Rules, *P's* claim is a compulsory counterclaim, which must be asserted or it will be lost. Thus, even though *D's* original counterclaim for breach of contract was a permissive counterclaim because it was factually unrelated to *P's* tort claim, *P's* breach-of-contract claim is a compulsory counterclaim because it is based on the same facts as *D's* counterclaim.

In all modern pleading systems, the pleadings would not extend beyond a plaintiff's answer or reply. As discussed earlier, the philosophy of modern systems is to limit the functions performed by the pleadings. Modern systems provide more efficient procedures for matters, such as trial preparation, that had to be performed by the pleadings under the old common-law system. Therefore, even in a code-pleading system that requires the plaintiff to reply to an affirmative defense in the answer, any allegations of *new matter* in the plaintiff's reply, such as an affirmative defense to the defendant's affirmative defense, would automatically be assumed to be denied or "avoided" (met by still another affirmative defense) by the defendant. *Cf.* FED. R. CIV. P. 8(b)(6) ("Effect of Failing to Deny"). This assumption ends the pleading stage.

Problems

Problem 1-30. On the facts of *Problem 1-1*, assume that *D-1* sues *D-2* in a U.S. District Court for $100,000. *D-1* asserts that *D-2* negligently crashed into *D-1's* truck and is liable for *D-1's* personal injuries suffered as a result of the accident and for damage to *D-1's* truck. *D-2* serves an answer denying *D-2's* negligence and asserting *D-1's* contributory negligence as an affirmative defense. *D-1* vigorously disputes *D-2's* assertions that *D-1* was contributorily negligent because at the time of the accident *D-1* was in a "position of helpless peril" and *D-2* had the "last clear chance" to avoid the accident. Is *D-1* required to serve an answer to *D-2's* allegations? Does the language of Federal Rule 7(a) help you answer this question? If *D-1* is not required to answer, what is the effect of *D-1's* lack of response to *D-2's* assertion? Does the language of Federal Rule 8(b)(6) help you answer this question?

Problem 1-31. On the facts of *Problem 1-30*, assume that *D-2's* answer contains a "counterclaim" in which *D-2* asserted that *D-1's* negligence was the cause of the accident and that *D-1* is liable for *D-2's* personal injuries suffered as a result of the accident and for damage to *D-2's* sports car. Does *D-1* now have to answer?

7. Intervention by Parties Outside of the Lawsuit

Intervention is a procedure by which a person who is not a party to an action, but whose interests are affected by the action, may become a party. The object of intervention is to allow the nonparty to protect its interest without unduly disrupting the interests of the persons already parties to the action. For example, assume that a suit between *P* and *D* will, as a practical matter, affect *I's* interests. *I* may petition the court to allow *I* to *intervene* and participate in the action between *P* and *D* to protect *I's* interests. *See* FED. R. CIV. P. 24 ("Intervention").

Problem

Problem 1-32. On the facts of *Problem 1-29*, assume that *S-2* learns of *S-1's* action against *M* for the money. What should *S-2* do to protect *S-2's* interest in the money?

8. Discovery by Parties to the Action

Modern procedural systems rely upon pretrial *discovery* to identify and narrow the issues in the action. Discovery also allows parties to prepare for trial. Modern discovery rules evolved from English equity practice. (The common-law courts did not permit discovery to any significant extent.) The scope of modern discovery is often quite broad, extending to "any nonprivileged matter that is relevant to any party's claim or defense." *See* FED. R. CIV. P. 26(b)(1) ("Discovery Scope and Limits"). This standard even allows discovery of matter that will not be admissible at trial, as long as it is reasonably calculated to lead to admissible evidence. *See id.*

Modern civil actions are often managed carefully by the court. Early in many cases, judges will issue scheduling or progression orders detailing the time limits for amending pleadings and completing discovery. Such orders may also place the case on the trial calendar at a date long in the future. *See* FED. R. CIV. P. 16(b) ("Scheduling"). Unless modified, these orders will set the parameters within which the parties will conduct discovery by means of the methods discussed in the following subsections.

(a) Depositions

Of the basic types of discovery procedures, *depositions* are the most important. A deposition is simply testimony of a party or witness recorded outside of court. A deposition has several purposes. It can be used to (1) obtain information relevant to the case, (2) establish what a witness' testimony will be and preserve the witness' testimony for trial in the event the witness becomes unavailable, and (3) establish a foundation for impeaching the witness if the witness' testimony changes at trial. *See* Fed. R. Civ. P. 32(a) ("Using Depositions in Court Proceedings").

Depositions can be taken orally or by written questions. In an oral deposition, the lawyer asks questions and the deponent answers them spontaneously. In a deposition upon written questions, the parties submit questions prior to taking the deposition. The questions are read to the deponent, who answers them orally. *See* Fed. R. Civ. P. 30 ("Depositions By Oral Examination"), 31 ("Depositions By Written Questions"). Depositions may be taken before or after an action has been commenced. *See* Fed. R. Civ. P. 27 ("Depositions To Perpetuate Testimony"). Under rules like Federal Rule 27, depositions prior to the commencement of the action are strictly limited to the perpetuation of testimony that the party taking the deposition expects will be important in a future action. The deposition procedure is not available for the purpose of determining whether a basis exists for a possible future action. *See* 8A Wright et al. § 2071, at 384–85.

(b) Interrogatories

Written *interrogatories* are simply questions prepared by a party. They are then submitted to another party. The receiving party provides answers to the questions. Written interrogatories may be submitted only to parties to an action. Interrogatories are less expensive than depositions and are useful in obtaining basic information. Because they are answered with a lawyer's assistance, however, interrogatories are not as useful as oral depositions for some purposes. For example, they are less effective in making probing inquiries that will pin down the deponent's testimony for trial purposes. On the other hand, they are an inexpensive way of obtaining information from an opposing party for case preparation. *See* Fed. R. Civ. P. 33 ("Interrogatories to Parties").

(c) Requests for the Production of Documents and Tangible Things

A *request for the production of documents* allows one party to inspect and copy information in the possession of another party in the form of documents or electronically stored information. As with written interrogatories, parties may only direct such requests to other parties. The modern request for production extends far beyond documents. Such requests now include testing or sampling of tangible things as well as entry on and inspection of land. *See* Fed. R. Civ. P. 34 ("Producing Documents, Electronically Stored Information, and Tangible Things, or Entering onto Land, for Inspection and Other Purposes").

(d) Requests for Admission

Written *requests for admission* eliminate undisputed issues from the case. In a request for admission, one party requests another party to admit certain matters of fact or application of law to fact. *See* Fed. R. Civ. P. 36 ("Requests for Admission"). As a result, they eliminate the need for evidence on such issues at trial.

(e) Physical or Mental Examinations

Modern procedural systems permit a party to request a *physical or mental examination* of another party or of a person in the custody or legal control of another party. Courts allow such requests when a physical or mental condition is "in controversy" and the requesting party can show "good cause" for the examination. *See* FED. R. CIV. P. 35 ("Physical and Mental Examinations"). For example, assume that *P* sues *D* for personal injuries resulting from an automobile accident. *D* may request a physical examination of *P* to determine the true nature and extent of *P's* injuries.

(f) Mandatory Disclosures

Federal Rule 26 was amended in 1993 (and further revised in 2000) to impose on the parties a duty of *mandatory* "automatic" *disclosures*. The disclosures take place without using any of the discovery procedures described above. Early in the case, the parties must exchange basic information about potential witnesses, documentary evidence, damages, and insurance. At an appropriate time during the discovery period, the parties must also exchange information about expert witnesses and the details of their possible testimony. Finally, as the trial date approaches, the parties must identify the evidence that they may offer at trial. *See* FED. R. CIV. P. 26(a) ("Required Disclosures"). In addition to making mandatory disclosures, Rule 26 also requires the parties to have a discovery planning meeting and to prepare a proposed discovery plan. *See* FED. R. CIV. P. 26(f) ("Conference of the Parties; Planning for Discovery"). Some states also have developed mandatory disclosure requirements of their own. Other states whose rules are patterned on the Federal Rules of Civil Procedure have also adopted mandatory disclosure requirements.

(g) Sanctions

Safeguards exist to protect parties against harassment resulting from the improper use of discovery procedures. The court may issue an order protecting a party from undue burden or expense, annoyance, embarrassment, or oppression during the discovery process. *See, e.g.*, FED. R. CIV. P. 26(c) ("Protective Orders"). *Sanctions* also exist for failure to make disclosures and other discovery properly. *See* FED. R. CIV. P. 37 ("Failure to Make Disclosures or Cooperate in Discovery; Sanctions").

Problems

Problem 1-33. On the facts of *Problem 1-1*, assume that *P* has properly commenced an action against *D-1* and *D-2* in a federal district court. Suppose that *P* wants to establish the following facts, which the plaintiff believes will be undisputed by the defendant:

> (1) That on the date of the accident there was a highway designated as State Highway 8 running north and south through the city of Metropolis and that the highway was a paved, black-topped highway, which curved to the west at a point approximately 7.2 miles north of the city of Metropolis and was level and straight for the next 1.2 miles;

> (2) That on the date and at the place where the accident occurred (the place described in paragraph (1), above), the highway was dry, it was daylight, and the weather was clear.

Which of the discovery devices discussed above should *P* use to establish these facts in the least expensive way?

Problem 1-34. Suppose on the facts of *Problem 1-1* that *P* seeks an eye examination and a psychiatric examination of *D-2* pursuant to Federal Rule 35. *P* asserts that, under the circumstances of the accident, *D-2* would have to have been either blind or crazy, or both, to have collided with *D-1's* truck in which *P* was a passenger. What should *P* have to show to obtain these examinations?

Problem 1-35. Suppose on the facts of *Problem 1-1* that *P* wants to find out about the condition and maintenance of the brakes on *D-1's* truck. Which of the discovery devices discussed above could *P* use to find out this information?

9. Pretrial Conferences

During the course of a lawsuit, courts will hold a series of *pretrial conferences* designed to manage the litigation, plan discovery, sharpen the preparation and presentation of cases, eliminate surprises at trial, and improve and facilitate the settlement process. *See, e.g.,* FED. R. CIV. P. 16 ("Pretrial Conferences; Scheduling; Management").

10. Disposition of the Action Without Trial

As discussed above, the court may dispose of an action through a default judgment or a defendant's motion to dismiss or a demurrer. Other methods of disposing of an action before trial include the following: (1) judgment on the pleadings; (2) summary judgment; (3) voluntary dismissal; (4) involuntary dismissal; and (5) settlement.

(a) Judgment on the Pleadings

Motions to dismiss and demurrers test the legal sufficiency of a pleading. A *motion for judgment on the pleadings* exists in many modern procedural systems. It also tests the legal sufficiency of a pleading. *See, e.g.,* FED. R. CIV. P. 12(c) ("Motion for Judgment on the Pleadings"). Either or both of the parties may move for judgment on the pleadings after the pleadings have closed. A motion for judgment on the pleadings challenges the legal sufficiency of the other party's case, as revealed by all the pleadings in the action. In evaluating a motion for judgment on the pleadings, the court must accept as true the factual position taken in the nonmoving party's pleading.

For example, assume that a defendant (1) admits all of the allegations of the complaint and (2) asserts an affirmative defense in the answer. If the plaintiff believes the affirmative defense is insufficient as a matter of law, the plaintiff might move for judgment on the pleadings. In this situation, such a motion would raise the legal sufficiency of the affirmative defense. The court assumes that the facts alleged in the complaint are true *because the defendant's answer admits those facts.* The court also assumes that any facts alleged in support of the affirmative defense are true. Under these circumstances, if the plaintiff is correct that the affirmative defense is legally unsound, the court will enter a judgment in the plaintiff's favor.

(b) Summary Judgment 56

Summary judgment avoids the necessity of a trial in certain situations. In a *motion for summary judgment,* a party resorts to materials outside the pleadings to demonstrate that

(1) no genuine issue of material fact exists in the case and (2) the movant is entitled to a judgment as a matter of law. *See* Fed. R. Civ. P. 56 ("Summary Judgment"). For example, assume that the defendant denies all of the factual allegations of a complaint. The plaintiff believes that the defendant cannot realistically dispute the factual allegations at trial. If so, neither the plaintiff nor the court system should be burdened with the necessity of a full-blown trial of the issues formed by the pleadings. In this situation, the plaintiff may move for summary judgment.

With the motion, the plaintiff may submit affidavits or materials developed through discovery, such as depositions, interrogatories, and admissions. If these materials demonstrate that no genuine issue of fact exists for trial and that the plaintiff is entitled to a judgment as a matter of law, the court will enter summary judgment in the plaintiff's favor. A party may receive "partial" summary judgment on one or more issues. The moving party need not win on all issues. For example, summary judgment may be granted on the issue of liability, leaving the amount of damages for trial.

(c) Voluntary Dismissal

After a plaintiff has commenced an action, common sense indicates that the procedural system should not force the plaintiff to continue the action to a formal conclusion. Modern procedural systems provide plaintiffs who have second thoughts about prosecuting the action with an opportunity to obtain a *voluntary dismissal*. Such a dismissal is "without prejudice" to the right of the plaintiff to bring a later action on the claim— at least if the voluntary dismissal is only the first one that the plaintiff has obtained. Procedural systems often limit the plaintiff's right to take successive voluntary dismissals without prejudice. Furthermore, a procedural system may allow the plaintiff to take a voluntary dismissal as a matter of right within a certain time or before certain events have occurred in the action. Thereafter, the plaintiff will need the consent of the defendant or the court's permission before taking a voluntary dismissal. *See, e.g.*, Fed. R. Civ. P. 41(a)(1) & (2).

(d) Involuntary Dismissal

Modern procedural systems also provide for *involuntary dismissals*. Such dismissals are usually available on the defendant's motion when the plaintiff fails to prosecute the action in a timely fashion. They are also available when the plaintiff fails to comply with procedural rules. An involuntary dismissal is usually "with prejudice" ("on the merits"). In other words, the plaintiff cannot bring a subsequent action on the same claim against the defendant. The court, however, may have the discretion to specify that involuntary dismissals are without prejudice. *See, e.g.*, Fed. R. Civ. P. 41(b) ("Involuntary Dismissal; Effect").

(e) Settlement

The pressure, expense, and uncertain outcome of litigation often move the parties toward compromise and settlement. Indeed, less than five percent of all civil actions go to trial in the federal district courts. Most are settled at some point during the litigation process. Settlements often are embodied in *consent judgments* to prevent future litigation. A consent judgment embodies the terms and provisions to which the parties have agreed. In essence, a consent judgment is a contract of record made by the parties and entered by the court.

Some procedural systems have rules to encourage settlement. For example, it is common to find rules providing that a defendant can make a formal, written offer of settlement to the plaintiff. Typically, these rules provide that if the plaintiff decides to refuse the offer and thereafter fails to obtain a judgment that is more favorable than the offer, the plaintiff must pay the defendant's "costs" in the action. *See, e.g.,* FED. R. CIV. P. 68 ("Offer of Judgment"). "Alternative dispute resolution" methods, discussed in subsection 16 and in Chapter 9(F), can also facilitate termination of pending litigation.

68

Problem

Problem 1-36. On the facts of *Problem 1-1*, assume that *P* sued *D-1* and *D-2* in federal district court for operating their respective motor vehicles in a negligent manner and, as a result, causing injuries to *P*. *P* took *D-1's* and *D-2's* depositions in which they both admitted that they had been driving slightly in excess of the posted speed limit. *P* believes that despite their denials of negligence in their answers, *D-1* and *D-2* depositions demonstrate that there is no genuine issue of fact with regard to the issue of their negligence (*i.e.,* they both had been speeding and thus were negligent as a matter of law). In this situation, should *P* move for judgment on the pleadings? If not, what should *P* do?

11. Trial

If the case cannot be disposed of through one of the methods discussed above, a trial of the factual issues will be necessary after the pleading and discovery stages have been completed. As observed above, early in many cases judges issue progression or scheduling orders that detail time limits for amending pleadings and completing discovery and place the case on the trial calendar. If a case is not set for trial in this manner, it can be placed on the trial calendar on the clerk's initiative or at the request of the parties. *See* FED. R. CIV. P. 40 ("Scheduling Cases for Trial"). As the trial date draws near, courts hold final pretrial conferences. Such conferences facilitate the trial by simplifying the issues, limiting the number of witnesses, and dealing with other matters that will aid in disposing of the action. *See* FED. R. CIV. P. 16(e) ("Final Pretrial Conference and Orders").

40

16(e)

Right to a Jury Trial. In Anglo-American judicial systems, some cases are tried to the judge and some cases are tried to a jury. In the United States, the right to a jury trial has a constitutional dimension in both the state and federal courts. As stated earlier, cases in which a jury trial is constitutionally guaranteed are determined primarily, though not exclusively in all systems, on historical grounds. Generally, a constitutional right to a jury trial exists in cases that would have been triable to a jury in the common-law courts before the merger of law and equity. No such right exists when a jury trial would not have been available in a common-law action. Nor does such a right exist when the case would have been tried in an equity court. Even when a jury trial is available as a matter of right, however, a party who wants a jury trial must formally demand it. *See* FED. R. CIV. P. 38(b) ("Right to a Jury Trial; Demand"). Failure to demand a jury trial results in waiver of the right. In addition to the right to a jury trial under a constitutional provision, a right to a jury trial may also exist under an applicable statute.

38(b)

Selecting the Jury. When an action is to be tried to a jury, the first matter undertaken is the selection of the jurors. A panel of prospective jurors will be assembled under a method provided by the statutes or rules of the particular procedural system. The court or the parties' lawyers (or both) will then conduct a *voir dire* examination. The purpose of this examination is to determine each juror's fitness to serve in the particular case. Parties will ordinarily be able to *challenge jurors for cause* on grounds such as bias or prejudice. In addition, each party will have a certain number of *peremptory* challenges, which each party can exercise without stating a reason.

Burden of Proof. To understand the order and progression of trial, one must first understand the concept of *burden of proof*. The burden of proof determines who must produce evidence on each issue in the case and how much evidence they must produce to win on each issue. For example, the plaintiff is normally allocated the burden of proof on certain basic elements of the plaintiff's claim or cause of action; likewise, the defendant will normally have the burden of proof on affirmative defenses asserted against the plaintiff's claim. In a civil action, the party bearing the burden of proof must demonstrate by a *preponderance of the evidence* that the party is entitled to win. In contrast, in a criminal action, the government must meet a much higher standard. It must demonstrate that the defendant is guilty *beyond a reasonable doubt.*

How the burden of proof is allocated between the parties depends upon several factors. Chapter 6 will examine these factors in conjunction with allocating the burden of pleading, which involves similar considerations. Burden of proof is also examined more fully in Chapter 10. The next section examines the effect of the burden of proof on the order in which the parties present evidence and the methods of enforcing the burden of proof.

Presenting Evidence at Trial and Challenging the Sufficiency of a Party's Presentation. After the court has impaneled the jury, if there is to be one, the trial begins with the *opening statements*. The plaintiff, who has the burden of proving the principal facts necessary to establish a claim for relief under the substantive law, will make an opening statement. The defendant may then make an opening statement or reserve the right to do so until the beginning of the defendant's case. The plaintiff will then begin presenting evidence on those issues upon which the plaintiff has the burden of proof. Each witness called will be subject to *direct examination* by the plaintiff's lawyer. At the end of the direct examination, the defendant can *cross-examine* the witness to cast doubt in a variety of ways on the witness' testimony.

After the plaintiff's direct evidence has been presented, the defendant can move for a *directed verdict* in a *jury* trial, which is now called a *motion for judgment as a matter of law* in federal court. *See* Fed. R. Civ. P. 50(a) ("Judgment as a Matter of Law in a Jury Trial"). In federal court, this motion may be made after the plaintiff has been fully heard on a controlling issue or at the close of the plaintiff's direct evidence. *Id.* In a *nonjury* trial, the defendant can move for a *nonsuit* or an *involuntary dismissal.* In federal court, this motion is now called a *motion for partial findings*, which results in a *judgment as a matter of law. See* Fed. R. Civ. P. 52(c) ("Judgment on Partial Findings"). Federal courts may enter judgment any time a dispositive finding of fact on the evidence can be made, not just at the close of a party's presentation of direct evidence. *Id.*

These motions would be proper if the plaintiff failed to present adequate proof on the issues on which the plaintiff had the burden of proof. If the judge grants one of these motions, the case ends with a judgment that the plaintiff take nothing. For example, the following are the four elements for a negligence claim: (1) a duty to exercise due care; (2) the defendant's failure to conform to that duty; (3) a direct causal connection between the breach of duty and the infliction of injury; and (4) actual damage to the plaintiff. Assume that in such an action the plaintiff offers overwhelming evidence of the defendant's failure to exercise due care. Assume, however, that the plaintiff does not offer any proof that the defendant's failure to exercise due care caused the plaintiff's injuries.

Under such circumstances, the judge would grant the defendant's motion for a directed verdict in a jury trial or an involuntary dismissal in a nonjury trial. Granting such a motion does not infringe the plaintiff's right to a jury trial because the jury could not have properly decided in the plaintiff's favor. "Reasonable minds" could not have differed on the outcome because no proof existed on an essential element of the claim. Other circumstances may also justify granting directed verdicts. For example, assume that the plaintiff offers some slight evidence on causation. The judge may direct a verdict against the plaintiff if, viewing only the evidence favorable to the plaintiff, a "reasonable" jury would not be justified in finding causation.

If a motion for a directed verdict is not made, or is made but denied, the defendant will attempt to rebut the plaintiff's proof. The defendant will also present evidence on those matters upon which the defendant has the burden of proof, such as affirmative defenses. At the close of the defendant's case in chief, the plaintiff will be given an opportunity to rebut the defendant's evidence. After the plaintiff's *rebuttal,* the defendant may present *surrebuttal* evidence, and so forth, until each party rests.

Before the case is submitted to the jury, each party may move for a directed verdict in a jury trial (now called a motion for judgment as a matter of law in federal court). Such a motion is appropriate when the opposing party has failed to meet the burden of proof allotted to the opposing party. If the judge grants the motion, the court will enter a judgment for the moving party. Of course, if the motion is granted, the jury will not decide the case. If such a motion is not made, or is made but denied, the court will submit the case to the jury.

Rules of Evidence. In presenting proof at trial, the parties are aided and limited by *rules of evidence.* In the federal courts, the Federal Rules of Evidence, which took effect on July 1, 1975, govern the admission and exclusion of evidence. Each state also has its own rules of evidence. Many states, however, have adopted rules substantially like the Federal Rules of Evidence.

The rules of evidence prohibit, *inter alia,* (1) *irrelevant evidence* and (2) *hearsay.* Relevant evidence is evidence having any tendency to make a fact of consequence to the action to be more or less probable. *See* FED. R. EVID. 401 ("Test for Relevant Evidence"). Relevant evidence is admissible unless some other evidentiary rule, such as the hearsay rule, makes it inadmissible. *See* FED. R. EVID. 402 ("General Admissibility of Relevant Evidence"). For example, in an automobile negligence action, assume that the plaintiff attempts to introduce testimony that the defendant gambles. Such evidence will be inadmissible as irrelevant because the defendant's gambling has no bearing on any fact of consequence to the action, such as negligence or proximate cause. Relevant evidence can also be excluded if its probative value is substantially outweighed by the danger of unfair prejudice, confusing the issues, misleading the jury, undue delay, waste of time, or needlessly presenting cumulative evidence. *See* FED. R. EVID. 403 ("Excluding Relevant Evidence for Prejudice, Confusion, Waste of Time, or Other Reasons").

Hearsay is a previously made statement offered in court to prove the truth of the matter contained in the statement. Hearsay evidence is inadmissible unless it fits within one of many hearsay exceptions. For example, assume that X, a witness to an automobile accident, tells W several days after the accident that D was speeding. W's testimony regarding X's statement would be hearsay if offered to prove that D was speeding. However, even inadmissible evidence will not be excluded unless the party opposing its admission raises a proper objection. Thus, if the plaintiff places W on the stand and asks about X's statement and D does not object to the testimony, W's testimony will be admitted. The trier of fact may rely on it fully when deciding the case.

Jury Instructions, Findings, and Verdicts. Before submitting the case to the jury, the judge will instruct the jurors on the legal principles that they must follow in deciding the case. Previously, the parties' lawyers will have had an opportunity to request that particular *jury instructions* be given by the judge. *See* FED. R. CIV. P. 51 ("Instructions to the Jury; Objections; Preserving a Claim of Error"). In addition, the lawyers for both sides will have made *closing arguments* to the jury. The jury then retires, deliberates, and returns its verdict for one side or the other.

When a judge decides a case without a jury, the judge will make *findings of fact and conclusions of law*. *See* FED. R. CIV. P. 52(a)(1) ("In an action tried on the facts without a jury or with an advisory jury, the court must find the facts specially and state its conclusions of law separately."). A jury also can be required to make specific findings of fact (without declaring the ultimate winner) through use of a device known as the *special verdict*. *See* FED. R. CIV. P. 49 ("Special Verdict; General Verdict and Questions"). However, special verdicts are less common than *general verdicts*. In a general verdict, the jury simply finds for one party or the other without indicating the reasons for the verdict.

Problems

Problem 1-37. On the facts of *Problem 1-1*, assume *D-1* has trespassed repeatedly on *P*'s land and *D-1* is threatening to continue to do so in the future.

(a) If *P* sues *D-1* to obtain an injunction to prevent *D-1* from trespassing on *P*'s land in the future, would there be a constitutional right to a jury trial in the action in most American procedural systems?

(b) If *P* sues *D-1* to recover damages that *D-1*'s past trespasses have inflicted on *P*'s land, would there be a constitutional right to a jury trial in most American procedural systems?

Problem 1-38. On the facts of *Problem 1-1*, assume *D-1* calls *P* a thief in the presence of *W*. *P* sues *D-1* for damages for slander. At trial, *P* calls *W* to testify that *D-1* made the statement. *D-1* objects that *W*'s testimony is hearsay. Is *D-1*'s objection valid?

Problem 1-39. On the facts of *Problem 1-38*, suppose *W* is allowed to testify. How should *D-1* be allowed to show that *W* is lying? For example, could *D-1* introduce evidence during *D-1*'s cross-examination of *W* that *W* had been convicted of a serious crime? If *D-1* attempted to do so and the judge asked *D-1* how the evidence tended to prove that *W* was lying, what argument could *D-1* make that the evidence has probative value on the issue of *W*'s credibility? If such evidence is admissible, should there be any conditions or restrictions on its use?

12. Post-Trial Motions

After the trial has been completed, three *post-trial motions* may be available: (1) a motion for judgment notwithstanding the verdict (judgment as a matter of law); (2) a motion for a new trial; and (3) a motion to alter or amend the judgment. Under some circumstances, a party may also seek "extraordinary relief" from the judgment through a motion to reopen the judgment.

Motions for Judgment Notwithstanding the Verdict or Judgment as a Matter of Law. After the jury returns its verdict in a jury trial, the losing party may move for *judgment notwithstanding the verdict* (now called a *judgment as a matter of law* in federal court). *See* FED. R. CIV. P. 50(b) ("Renewing Motion After Trial; Alternative Motion for a New

Trial"). This motion requests the court not to enter judgment on the verdict in favor of the winning side. Instead, the motion asks the court to enter judgment for the losing party. This motion raises the same issue as a motion for a directed verdict: that the party opposing the motion has not satisfied the applicable burden of proof. Assume, for example, in a negligence action that the plaintiff either (1) failed to offer any proof that the injuries complained of were caused by the accident or (2) offered so little evidence that a reasonable jury could not find in the plaintiff's favor. Assume the trial judge decides not to grant the defendant's motion for a directed verdict at the close of the plaintiff's evidence. If the jury returns a verdict for the plaintiff under these circumstances, the judge could still properly grant the defendant's motion for judgment notwithstanding the verdict.

In many jurisdictions, the moving party must have asked for a directed verdict at the close of all the evidence in order to later move for judgment notwithstanding the verdict. Otherwise, the court will deny the motion. In federal court, a party is now permitted under Rule 50(b) to renew its motion for judgment as a matter of law after the jury verdict provided the party made a motion for judgment as a matter of law under Rule 50(a) *50(a)* at any time prior to the submission of the case to the jury, even though the motion was not made at the literal close of all the evidence.

Motions for a New Trial. A losing party in a jury or nonjury case may also move for a *new trial*. In a jury action, the moving party may combine the motion for a new trial with a motion for a judgment notwithstanding the verdict. The motion for a new trial allows the trial judge to correct errors that occurred during the trial. For example, the judge may have erred in admitting or excluding evidence or in instructing the jury. When the judge grants a motion for new trial in a case tried to a jury, an entirely new trial before a second jury will occur. When the judge grants a new trial in a nonjury case, however, the judge may simply reopen the case and take new testimony, make new findings, or otherwise correct the error. *See* FED. R. CIV. P. 59(a) ("New Trial; Altering or Amending *59(a)* a Judgment").

Motions to Alter or Amend a Judgment. A clerical error in a judgment may be corrected by a motion under Federal Rule 59(e), if the motion is filed no later than 28 days *59(e)* after the entry of the judgment. After 28 days, such relief can be obtained under Rule *60(a)* 60(a) ("Corrections Based on Clerical Mistakes; Oversights and Omissions").

Extraordinary Relief from Judgments. After a judgment has been entered and becomes final in the sense that the time for making post-trial motions and appealing has passed, a party may still move to reopen the judgment. This motion is available only for extraordinary reasons, such as newly discovered evidence or fraud in procuring the judgment. *See* FED. R. CIV. P. 60(b) ("Grounds for Relief from a Final Judgment, Order, or Proceeding"). *60(b)* After the court has entered a final judgment, however, many matters that might have been raised earlier are foreclosed from further consideration. Thus, the court rarely will grant a motion to reopen a judgment; it will do so only when compelling circumstances exist.

Problems

Problem 1-40. On the facts of *Problem 1-1*, assume that after a trial to a jury in *P*'s personal injury action against *D-1*, the jury returns a verdict in favor of *D-1*. *P* believes that the judge erred during the trial when the judge excluded certain evidence offered by *P* after *D-1* objected. Which post-trial motion is appropriate to bring this error to the trial court's attention?

Problem 1-41. On the facts of *Problem 1-40*, but after a trial to a jury, the jury returns a verdict in favor of *P*. *D-1* believes that *P* has failed to introduce evidence on an essential element of the case on which *P* has the burden of proof. Which post-trial motion is appropriate to bring this error to the trial court's attention? Are there any conditions on *D-1's* ability to make the motion?

13. Judgments and Final Remedies

Judgments. A *judgment* is simply the official decision of a court on the parties' respective rights. As indicated in the preceding subsections, a court may enter a judgment with or without extensive litigation over the merits of the case. When the court renders a judgment in favor of a party defending against a claim, the judgment will direct that the party suing on the claim take nothing. *See* Federal Form 70 ("Judgment on a Jury Verdict"); Federal Form 71 ("Judgment by the Court Without a Jury").

Final Remedies. "[R]emedies are means of carrying into effect the substantive right." 1 DOBBS § 1.7, at 22. Thus, "the remedy should reflect the right or the policy behind that right as precisely as possible," and before a remedy is requested or selected, it is important to know the substantive policies being enforced. *See id.* When the court renders a judgment in favor of the plaintiff, the judgment will embody the remedy to which the plaintiff is entitled, as found by the court or jury. The judgment will include recoverable costs.

A judgment based upon a damage or restitutionary remedy can be executed against the losing party's property. Execution simply means that if the defendant does not pay a judgment (say, for damages) voluntarily within a certain time, a public official, such as the sheriff, will be authorized by a *writ of execution* to seize property of the defendant not exempt from execution by law and to sell it at public auction to satisfy the judgment. If necessary, the plaintiff can utilize the discovery devices discussed earlier, such as the deposition, to learn the location and extent of the defendant's assets.

Unlike a damage or restitutionary remedy, a declaratory judgment is not subject to execution. Nor is violating a declaratory judgment punishable by contempt. However, after an appropriate proceeding, refusing to obey a declaratory judgment may result in one of the other remedies being issued against a party, such as an injunction. *See* 28 U.S.C. § 2201 ("Creation of Remedy"), § 2202 ("Further Relief").

14. Appeals

Appeals. Every system has at least one *appellate court*. The function of appellate courts is to correct errors committed in trial court proceedings that have not been rectified by one of the post-trial motions discussed previously. But reversals on appeal are not routine. In the federal system, less than 15% of appeals filed in the courts of appeals result in reversal. This is because the scope of appellate review is very limited. Only legal rulings by the trial court ("issues of law") are reviewed "de novo," meaning that the appellate court gives no deference to the trial court's ruling and decides the matter "fresh." By contrast, rulings on matters entrusted to the discretion of the trial court are not reversed unless an "abuse of discretion" is shown. Similarly, findings of fact are not set aside on appeal unless they are "clearly erroneous." Furthermore, even if error by the trial court is established, the error must have potentially affected the result in the action, known as *prejudicial or reversible error*. Appellate courts will not reverse trial court judgments on the basis of *harmless* error.

The party seeking review is called either the *appellant* or *petitioner*, and the defending party is called the *appellee* or *respondent*. In older opinions, the appellant or petitioner is sometimes called the *plaintiff-in-error*, and the appellee or respondent is called the *defendant-in-error*.

Appellate Courts. Some states have both an intermediate court of appeals and an appellate court of last resort. However, do not assume that appeals may only be taken from courts of original jurisdiction to "pure" appellate courts. Many states provide for appeals from courts of "inferior" original jurisdiction to other courts of original jurisdiction. For example, some states provide for appeals to the state courts of general jurisdiction in some civil cases originally tried in other state courts of limited jurisdiction. These appeals may be subject to a jurisdictional amount in controversy or other limitations. Often, such appeals result in *trials de novo*—*i.e.*, the court of general jurisdiction tries the case over rather than simply reviewing errors of law committed by the court of limited jurisdiction. In certain types of cases, the losing party may even choose between an appeal to another court of original jurisdiction or an appeal to an appellate court.

In the federal system, appeals are ordinarily taken from the federal district courts to the federal courts of appeals. Appeals from the courts of appeals are taken to the United States Supreme Court. *See* 28 U.S.C. § 1254 ("Courts of appeals; certiorari; certified questions"), § 1291 ("Final decisions of district courts"). In addition to reviewing the decisions of lower federal courts on all matters, the U.S. Supreme Court may review a decision that has been made "by the highest court of a State in which a decision could be had" on issues of *federal law* in the state case. *See* 28 U.S.C. § 1257 ("State courts; certiorari"). The party seeking review in the U.S. Supreme Court does so in most cases by requesting a *writ of certiorari*. This writ is derived from English practice. It commands an inferior court to submit the record of a proceeding to a higher court for purposes of judicial review of the inferior court's decision. Figure 1-6 summarizes (in general terms) the jurisdiction and relationship of the state and federal courts.

Appellate Subject-Matter Jurisdiction. Most appeals can be taken only from final judgments. This *final judgment rule* usually, but not always, requires that a case be entirely completed at the trial level before an appeal will be permitted. The purpose of the rule is to prevent the constant disruption of the pretrial and trial process by appeals from various orders or rulings of the trial judge.

Nevertheless, an *interlocutory appeal* is sometimes allowed. Such an appeal takes place during the course of the litigation in the trial court. For example, some orders during litigation are considered important enough to justify an immediate appeal. Usually such an order must threaten serious and unjustifiable injury to a party if the order is issued erroneously. An interlocutory appeal is sometimes also appropriate to resolve important legal issues. Such issues must usually be ones that, if settled authoritatively, would be likely to terminate the case without the need for trial. *See* 28 U.S.C. § 1292 ("Interlocutory decisions").

Appellate Procedure. Appellate procedure varies from jurisdiction to jurisdiction, but some common elements exist. To commence an appeal, a party must ordinarily file a *notice of appeal* with the trial court or the appellate court. The party must file this notice within a fixed period of time after the entry of the judgment or order from which the party appeals. *See, e.g.*, Fed. R. App. P. 3(a) ("Appeals as of Right—How Taken"), 4 ("Appeals as of Right—When Taken").

Every jurisdiction provides means for suspending the winning party's ability to enforce the judgment while the losing party appeals. *See, e.g.*, Fed. R. Civ. P. 62 ("Stay of Pro-

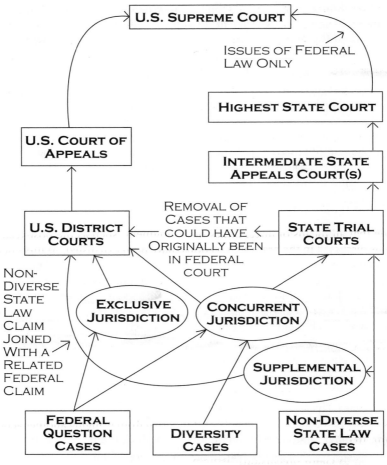

Figure 1-6

ceedings to Enforce a Judgment"). The trial court will transmit a *record on appeal* to the appellate court. Typically, this record will consist of (1) the original papers and exhibits filed in the district court, (2) those portions of the trial transcript necessary for the appeal, and (3) the docket entries prepared by the clerk of the trial court. *See, e.g.*, FED. R. APP. P. 10(a) ("The Record on Appeal"). The parties will then file *appellate briefs* on the issues appealed. In addition to the briefs, the appellate court will often hear *oral arguments*.

Problems

Problem 1-42. On the facts of *Problem 1-1*, assume that *P* sues *D-2* in a state court of State of Minnesota. *P* seeks $100,000 in damages for personal injuries received in the automobile accident. At the end of the trial, *D-2* moves for a directed verdict. This motion is granted by the trial court on the ground that *P* has not proved an essential element of *P*'s case under the applicable substantive law of the State of Minnesota. *P* appeals to the Minnesota Supreme Court. *P* asserts that the trial court erred in granting the directed verdict because Minnesota law does not require proof of the element found necessary by the trial court. After this appeal is rejected by the Minnesota Supreme Court, *P* petitions the U.S. Supreme Court for a writ of certiorari to review the Minnesota Supreme Court's decision on the issue of Minnesota law. Does the U.S. Supreme Court have jurisdiction to review the decision of the Minnesota Supreme Court on the issue raised by P? Would your answer differ if the issue had been whether the assertion of personal jurisdiction over D-2 comports with due process of law?

Problem 1-43. On the facts of *Problem 1-1*, assume that P, as part of P's claims against D-1, P seeks a permanent injunction to prevent D-1 from trespassing on P's land. P also seeks a preliminary injunction to prevent D-1 from violating P's rights during the time necessary to adjudicate P's claim, but the U.S. District Court refuses to issue the preliminary injunction. May P appeal the court's refusal to issue the preliminary injunction?

15. Finality in Litigation

Assume that all means of *direct attack* on a judgment, such as the post-trial motions and appeals discussed in the preceding sections, have been exhausted. Matters determined by the judgment may not be relitigated in a subsequent action. Furthermore, matters that *might* have been determined but were not — for example, because the parties failed to raise them — may also precluded. Such matters are *res judicata*, or "a thing adjudicated."

Traditionally, courts have expressed rules of "claim preclusion" in terms of *merger* and *bar*. When a court has rendered a valid and final personal judgment in favor of the plaintiff, the plaintiff's entire "claim" or cause of action *merges* into the judgment. Thereafter, the plaintiff is limited to executing the judgment itself against the defendant's property or bringing a second action on the judgment itself. No new action may be brought on any part of the "claim" or cause of action. Similarly, the defendant cannot use any defenses that the defendant raised or could have raised in the plaintiff's initial action. On the other hand, if the defendant wins the first action, then the plaintiff is *barred* from bringing another action on the same claim. In other words, a party may not "split" a "claim" or "cause of action."

In addition to claim preclusion, "issue preclusion" is another important part of the doctrine of res judicata. Suppose that an automobile accident occurs between P and D. P suffers both personal injuries and property damage to P's automobile as a result of the accident. P sues D to recover $3,000 for the damage to P's automobile and P wins. In the course of the litigation, the issues of D's negligence and P's contributory negligence were litigated and determined against D. Subsequently, D brings an action to recover for personal injuries that D received in the same accident. The doctrine of claim preclusion does not apply because D is suing on a *different* claim than was involved in P's suit. (D is a different party, and each party to a factual occurrence like the one described is ordinarily deemed to have a separate claim from all other parties to the occurrence.) Furthermore, assume that D is not barred from asserting the claim in a subsequent action because the procedural system in which the first action was brought does not have a compulsory counterclaim rule.

Nevertheless, D's suit would fail because of the doctrine of issue preclusion (sometimes called *collateral estoppel*). Once a factual or legal issue has been fully and fairly litigated and determined against a party, the issue may not thereafter be relitigated in a subsequent proceeding on a different claim. D litigated and lost both on the issue of D's own negligence and on the issue of P's negligence. D may not *collaterally attack* the first judgment. In other words, D cannot relitigate these identical issues in a second action.

The rules of claim and issue preclusion are subject to numerous exceptions. A basic policy at the core of most of the exceptions is that the party to be bound by the judgment must have had a full and fair opportunity to litigate the merits of the matter in question in the first proceeding.

Problems

Problem 1-44. On the facts of *Problem 1-1*, assume that *P* sues *D-1* for $1,000 in medical expenses incurred as a result of an automobile accident in a state court. *P* alleges that *D-1's* negligence caused the accident and resulting injuries to *P*. After a trial, *P* wins. *P* then sues *D-1* for $125,000 for (1) pain and suffering and (2) future lost earning capacity caused by the same accident. Should *P's* second suit succeed? Why or why not?

Problem 1-45. On the facts of *Problem 1-44*, assume that in *P's* action for medical expenses, a jury specifically has found *D-1* to have been negligent. Subsequently, *D-1* sues *P* for $250,000 for personal injuries received in the same accident. Should the doctrine of either claim or issue preclusion prevent *D-1's* action? Do you need further information to answer this question? Are you concerned that *P's* action involved a claim for only $1,000 and that *D-1's* action is for a much greater amount? What problems might this difference produce for *D-1*?

16. Alternative Dispute Resolution

As noted at the outset of this section, the parties will often have alternatives to litigation. These alternatives principally involve negotiation, mediation, and arbitration.

Negotiation. In a *negotiation*, the parties or their representatives submit and consider offers to arrive at a satisfactory settlement of their dispute. A negotiated settlement avoids the uncertainties and vagaries, the substantial economic expenses, and the social and psychological costs of litigation. Compared to litigation, the parties retain a much greater degree of autonomy and can shape creative solutions that serve the interests of both parties — as opposed to the "winner-take-all" nature of most remedies awarded by a court. However, negotiation is a voluntary process. One party may not be willing to negotiate at all with the opposing party. Likewise, the parties may not be able to reach a mutually satisfactory agreement even if they negotiate in good faith.

Mediation. In *mediation*, a neutral third party (a "mediator") helps the disputants reach mutually satisfactory agreement. A mediation usually begins with the mediator describing the process and ground rules. Next, the disputants tell their respective stories in a face-to-face negotiation. Mediators typically help (1) frame the issues, (2) facilitate communication and information exchange, (3) isolate points of agreement and disagreement, (4) generate options, and (5) encourage compromise. Mediators may caucus privately with each of the parties to the mediation.

Mediation can be thought of as a facilitated negotiation. Like negotiation, mediation is usually much less expensive and more expeditious than litigation in court. The mediator can assist the parties in unveiling hidden agendas and emotional issues that would be irrelevant in litigation. In this way, the mediator can help the parties adjust their conflicting perspectives and view their concerns in a broader framework than just the legal issues. Because they participate in the process and help shape solutions, the parties may be more willing to comply with any agreement reached. However, both mediation and negotiation usually lack procedural, evidentiary, and constitutional protections inherent in litigation because they ordinarily operate independently of the judicial system. Mediation especially depends on the willingness of the parties to participate in the process in good faith. Serious questions may be raised about the "fairness" of some mediated outcomes, particularly when one of the parties has a dominant personality, is more articulate, has a better grasp of the facts or the law, or has substantial emotional or economic power.

Arbitration. *Arbitration* is the most formalized alternative to litigation of a dispute in court. In arbitration, the disputing parties present their "case" to a neutral third person or persons who are empowered to render a decision. Arbitration may result from a contractual agreement in which the parties have agreed to arbitrate future disputes. After a dispute has arisen, arbitration may result from either an *ad hoc* agreement to arbitrate in lieu of formal judicial proceedings or a court rule or statute that requires arbitration of certain disputes. An arbitration hearing is similar to a trial in some respects. Like negotiation and mediation, arbitration is usually more expeditious, less costly, and more flexible than litigation in court. Furthermore, the parties choose the arbitrators, who may have more expertise in the specific subject matter of the dispute than judges in court. On the other hand, the parties may feel that the difficulty of appealing an arbitral award may give arbitrators too much leeway.

Alternative Dispute Resolution During Litigation. Even after full-scale litigation has commenced, alternative means of dispute resolution may still come into play. Negotiated settlements are often eventually reached in litigated cases. Furthermore, "court-annexed" (court-administered) dispute resolution processes are becoming widespread, in which various forms of arbitration, mediation, findings by special masters, neutral experts, and summary jury trials are used. In addition, the parties may hold private "mini-trials" or adopt some hybrid of mediation and arbitration to settle the litigation. These processes are discussed in Chapter 9(F), below.

17. The Path for Studying Civil Procedure

This chapter has presented an overview of the entire course of Civil Procedure. The remaining chapters provide you with greater detail and insights about the many topics of Civil Procedure. You are likely to follow one of two paths. You may be directed to proceed next to Chapter 2 and subsequent chapters, which take up matters that should be considered before a lawsuit is commenced — where can personal jurisdiction be obtained, where is venue proper, which courts have subject-matter jurisdiction, and what law will be applied, particularly if the action is commenced in a federal court. On the other hand, you may be directed to proceed first to Chapter 6 and following chapters, which deal with the internal mechanics of a commenced lawsuit — pleadings, amendments, joinder of claims and parties, discovery, etc. — before addressing the topics of Chapters 2–5. This book is designed to accommodate either of these teaching approaches.

Chapter 2

Personal Jurisdiction and Related Matters

As explained in Chapter 1, personal jurisdiction is the court's power to impose its decisions on the particular parties in a lawsuit. As the party commencing the lawsuit and selecting the forum, the plaintiff is deemed to have voluntarily submitted to personal jurisdiction in the chosen forum. The defendant, however, as the party summoned to appear in the lawsuit, must be subject to personal jurisdiction in the chosen court. A judgment entered without valid personal jurisdiction over the defendant violates the defendant's U.S. Constitutional right to *due process of law* and is not enforceable against the defendant in that court or in any other court. As a consequence, issues of personal jurisdiction arise constantly, both in purely intrastate actions and those involving interstate (or international) elements. Consider this simple example: D, a citizen of New York, and P, a citizen of California, are involved in a car accident while vacationing in Florida. P was injured and wants to sue D. In which state(s) would personal jurisdiction exist over D? New York, where the defendant lives? California, where the plaintiff lives? Florida, where the accident occurred?

Overview. Currently, there are four constitutionally valid bases for acquiring personal jurisdiction over a defendant—personal service of process upon the defendant within the forum state; consent by the defendant either before the lawsuit or by appearing in the action without making a proper and timely objection to personal jurisdiction; domicile by the defendant in the forum state; and "minimum contacts" with the forum state by the defendant. Satisfying one of the above bases is necessary to acquire personal jurisdiction over the defendant.

The formal acquisition of personal jurisdiction over the defendant, however, requires an additional step. The defendant must also be properly served with *process* (the complaint together with a summons to appear) in order to complete the court's acquisition of personal jurisdiction over the defendant. Service of process upon the defendant also satisfies another U.S. Constitutional requirement of due process—that the defendant be given *notice of the action* and the *opportunity to be heard.*

Section A. "Territorial" Rules of Jurisdiction

1. Personal Jurisdiction Prior to the Adoption of the Fourteenth Amendment

In the United States, the modern law of personal jurisdiction is dominated by rules derived from the Due Process Clause of the Fourteenth Amendment, which forbids states from depriving persons of "life, liberty, or property, without due process of law." However, the Fourteenth Amendment was not ratified until 1868. Before that date, the rules governing the power of the states to adjudicate cases involving nonresidents were "territorial" in nature.

These territorial rules were based on the idea that governments had sovereign power only over persons and things within their territorial boundaries. Thus, state courts had authority over nonresident defendants who were served with process while within the state. The rules also permitted a nonresident's property within the state to be seized and used as the basis of jurisdiction to adjudicate a claim against the nonresident up to the limits of the property. This kind of "in rem" jurisdiction could be used as the basis of adjudicating an action even when the underlying controversy between the parties had nothing to do with the property itself. In addition, states had power over nonresidents who consented to suit within the state.

The rules described in the preceding paragraph were not constitutional rules, but were derived from international law, the law governing the relationships between independent sovereign nations. The states had retained their sovereignty except as they had delegated a portion of it to the national government in the Constitution. To the extent that they retained the status of independent sovereigns, they were regulated by the same rules that pertained to relationships between different countries. Thus, the territorial rules reflected the concepts of sovereignty prevailing in the late eighteenth and early nineteenth centuries.

Nonetheless, the U.S. Constitution was relevant to the enforcement of the territorial rules of jurisdiction. The Full Faith and Credit Clause of Article IV, § 1 of the Constitution stated that "Full Faith and Credit shall be given in each State to the public Acts, Records, and judicial Proceedings of every other State. And the Congress may by general Laws prescribe the Manner in which such Acts, Records and Proceedings shall be proved, and the Effect thereof." In 1790, Congress enacted a statute designed to implement the Full Faith and Credit Clause in part. This statute provided as follows:

> That the acts of the legislatures of the several states shall be authenticated by having the seal of their respective states affixed thereto: That the records and judicial proceedings of the courts of any state, shall be proved or admitted in any other court within the United States, by the attestation of the clerk, and the seal of the court annexed, if there be a seal, together with a certificate of the judge, chief justice, or presiding magistrate, as the case may be, that the said attestation is in due form. And the said records and judicial proceedings authenticated as aforesaid, shall have *such faith and credit* given to them in every court within the United States, as they have by law or usage in the courts of the state from whence the said records are or shall be taken.

Act of May 26, 1790, ch. 11, 1 Stat. 122 (now codified as 28 U.S.C. § 1738) (emphasis added).

In 1813, the U.S. Supreme Court interpreted the "such faith and credit" language of this statute as designed to declare that judgments rendered by the courts of one state had to be given the same "effect" in other states that they would receive in the state where they were rendered. *See Mills v. Duryee*, 11 U.S (7 Cranch) 481 (1813). Thus, when a judgment was rendered against a nonresident defendant in a state court, it could be enforced in the courts of other states, such as the state of the defendant's residence; the plaintiff could require the other state to give effect to the judgment as a matter of federal law. Refusal to enforce the judgment without adequate cause would violate the implementing statute and could be reversed by the U.S. Supreme Court.

In 1851, however, the U.S. Supreme Court in *D'Arcy v. Ketchum*, 52 U.S. (11 How.) 165 (1851), held that neither the Constitution nor the implementing statute was intended to override the territorial rules of international jurisdiction that controlled the relationships between the states when the Constitution and statute were formed. Thus, violation of one of these territorial rules would constitute sufficient justification for a state to refuse to give effect to another state's judgment.

2. Incorporation of the Traditional Territorial Rules into the Due Process Clause of the Fourteenth Amendment

As noted above, the Fourteenth Amendment to the U.S. Constitution was ratified in 1868. The following case, *Pennoyer v. Neff*, 95 U.S. 714 (1878), was the first case in which the U.S. Supreme Court considered the limitations the Due Process Clause of the Fourteenth Amendment imposed on the power of a state court to assert jurisdiction over a defendant. Technically, the Court's statements as to the effect of the Fourteenth Amendment were *dicta* because the seizure of Mr. Neff's property and the initial judgment in favor of Mr. Mitchell both took place prior to ratification of the Fourteenth Amendment. Nonetheless, the *Pennoyer* case was—and remains—an important decision regarding the traditional territorial limits on personal jurisdiction, which were based on concepts of international law and which, the *Pennoyer* Court made clear, now had a constitutional foundation as well through the Due Process Clause of the Fourteenth Amendment.

Pennoyer v. Neff

Full Faith in Credit Case

United States Supreme Court, 1878
95 U.S. 714, 24 L. Ed. 565

Error to the Circuit Court of the United States for the District of Oregon.

Justice FIELD delivered the opinion of the Court.

This is an action to recover the possession of a tract of land, of the alleged value of $15,000, situated in the State of Oregon. The plaintiff asserts title to the premises by a patent of the United States issued to him in [March,] 1866, under the Act of Congress of Sept. 27, 1850, usually known as the Donation Law of Oregon. The defendant claims to have acquired the premises under a sheriff's deed, made upon a sale of the property on execution issued upon a judgment recovered against the plaintiff in one of the circuit courts of the State. The case turns upon the validity of this judgment.

It appears from the record that the judgment was rendered in February, 1866, in favor of J.H. Mitchell, for less than $300, including costs, in an action brought by him upon a demand for services as an attorney; that, at the time the action was commenced and the judgment rendered, the defendant therein, the plaintiff here, was a non-resident of the

State; that he was not personally served with process, and did not appear therein; and that the judgment was entered upon his default in not answering the complaint, upon a constructive service of summons by publication.

The Code of Oregon provides for such service when an action is brought against a non-resident and absent defendant, who has property within the State. It also provides, where the action is for the recovery of money or damages, for the attachment of the property of the non-resident. And it also declares that no natural person is subject to the jurisdiction of a court of the State, "unless he appear in the court, or be found within the State, or be a resident thereof, or have property therein; and, in the last case, only to the extent of such property at the time the jurisdiction attached." Construing this latter provision to mean, that, in an action for money or damages where a defendant does not appear in the court, and is not found within the State, and is not a resident thereof, but has property therein, the jurisdiction of the court extends only over such property, the declaration expresses a principle of general, if not universal, law. The authority of every tribunal is necessarily restricted by the territorial limits of the State in which it is established. Any attempt to exercise authority beyond those limits would be deemed in every other forum, as has been said by this court, an illegitimate assumption of power, and be resisted as mere abuse. *D'Arcy v. Ketchum*, 52 U.S. (11 How.) 165 (1851). In the case against the plaintiff, the property here in controversy sold under the judgment rendered was not attached, nor in any way brought under the jurisdiction of the court. Its first connection with the case was caused by a levy of the execution. It was not, therefore, disposed of pursuant to any adjudication, but only in enforcement of a personal judgment, having no relation to the property, rendered against a non-resident without service of process upon him in the action, or his appearance therein. The court below did not consider that an attachment of the property was essential to its jurisdiction or to the validity of the sale, but held that the judgment was invalid from defects in the affidavit upon which the order of publication was obtained, and in the affidavit by which the publication was proved.

There is some difference of opinion among the members of this court as to the rulings upon these alleged defects. The majority are of opinion that inasmuch as the statute requires, for an order of publication, that certain facts shall appear by affidavit *to the satisfaction of the court or judge*, defects in such affidavit can only be taken advantage of on appeal, or by some other direct proceeding, and cannot be urged to impeach the judgment collaterally....

If, therefore, we were confined to the rulings of the court below upon the defects in the affidavits mentioned, we should be unable to uphold its decision. But it was also contended in that court, and is insisted upon here, that the judgment in the State court against the plaintiff was void for want of personal service of process on him, or of his appearance in the action in which it was rendered, and that the premises in controversy could not be subjected to the payment of the demand of a resident creditor except by a proceeding *in rem*; that is, by a direct proceeding against the property for that purpose. If these positions are sound, the ruling of the Circuit Court as to the invalidity of that judgment must be sustained, notwithstanding our dissent from the reasons upon which it was made. And that they are sound would seem to follow from two well-established principles of public law respecting the jurisdiction of an independent State over persons and property. The several States of the Union are not, it is true, in every respect independent, many of the rights and powers which originally belonged to them being now vested in the government created by the Constitution. But, except as restrained and limited by that instrument,

[handwritten margin note: When Code of Oregon Finds person subject to jurisdiction of court of state]

they possess and exercise the authority of independent States, and the principles of public law to which we have referred are applicable to them. One of these principles is, that every State possesses exclusive jurisdiction and sovereignty over persons and property within its territory. As a consequence, every State has the power to determine for itself the civil *status* and capacities of its inhabitants; to prescribe the subjects upon which they may contract, the forms and solemnities with which their contracts shall be executed, the rights and obligations arising from them, and the mode in which their validity shall be determined and their obligations enforced; and also to regulate the manner and conditions upon which property situated within such territory, both personal and real, may be acquired, enjoyed, and transferred. The other principle of public law referred to follows from the one mentioned; that is, that no State can exercise direct jurisdiction and authority over persons or property without its territory. Story, Confl. Laws, ch. 2; Wheat. Int. Law, pt. 2, ch. 2. The several States are of equal dignity and authority, and the independence of one implies the exclusion of power from all others. And so it is laid down by jurists, as an elementary principle, that the laws of one State have no operation outside of its territory, except so far as is allowed by comity; and that no tribunal established by it can extend its process beyond that territory so as to subject either persons or property to its decisions. "Any exertion of authority of this sort beyond this limit," says Story, "is a mere nullity, and incapable of binding such persons or property in any other tribunals." Story, Confl. Laws, § 539.

But as contracts made in one State may be enforceable only in another State, and property may be held by non-residents, the exercise of the jurisdiction which every State is admitted to possess over persons and property within its own territory will often affect persons and property without it. To any influence exerted in this way by a State affecting persons resident or property situated elsewhere, no objection can be justly taken; whilst any direct exertion of authority upon them, in an attempt to give ex-territorial operation to its laws, or to enforce an ex-territorial jurisdiction by its tribunals, would be deemed an encroachment upon the independence of the State in which the persons are domiciled or the property is situated, and be resisted as usurpation.

Thus the State, through its tribunals, may compel persons domiciled within its limits to execute, in pursuance of their contracts respecting property elsewhere situated, instruments in such form and with such solemnities as to transfer the title, so far as such formalities can be complied with; and the exercise of this jurisdiction in no manner interferes with the supreme control over the property by the State within which it is situated....

So the State, through its tribunals, may subject property situated within its limits owned by non-residents to the payment of the demand of its own citizens against them; and the exercise of this jurisdiction in no respect infringes upon the sovereignty of the State where the owners are domiciled. Every State owes protection to its own citizens; and, when non-residents deal with them, it is a legitimate and just exercise of authority to hold and appropriate any property owned by such non-residents to satisfy the claims of its citizens. It is in virtue of the State's jurisdiction over the property of the non-resident situated within its limits that its tribunals can inquire into that non-resident's obligations to its own citizens, and the inquiry can then be carried only to the extent necessary to control the disposition of the property. If the non-resident [has] no property in the State, there is nothing upon which the tribunals can adjudicate.

These views are not new. They have been frequently expressed, with more or less distinctness, in opinions of eminent judges, and have been carried into adjudications in numerous cases....

. . . .

Substituted service by publication, or in any other authorized form, may be sufficient to inform parties of the object of proceedings taken where property is once brought under the control of the court by seizure or some equivalent act. The law assumes that property is always in the possession of its owner, in person or by agent; and it proceeds upon the theory that its seizure will inform him, not only that it is taken into the custody of the court, but that he must look to any proceedings authorized by law upon such seizure for its condemnation and sale. Such service may also be sufficient in cases where the object of the action is to reach and dispose of property in the State, or of some interest therein, by enforcing a contract or a lien respecting the same, or to partition it among different owners, or, when the public is a party, to condemn and appropriate it for a public purpose. In other words, such service may answer in all actions which are substantially proceedings *in rem*. But where the entire object of the action is to determine the personal rights and obligations of the defendants, that is, where the suit is merely *in personam*, constructive service in this form upon a non-resident is ineffectual for any purpose. Process from the tribunals of one State cannot run into another State, and summon parties there domiciled to leave its territory and respond to proceedings against them. Publication of process or notice within the State where the tribunal sits cannot create any greater obligation upon the non-resident to appear. Process sent to him out of the State, and process published within it, are equally unavailing in proceedings to establish his personal liability.

The want of authority of the tribunals of a State to adjudicate upon the obligations of non-residents, where they have no property within its limits, is not denied by the court below: but the position is assumed, that, where they have property within the State, it is immaterial whether the property is in the first instance brought under the control of the court by attachment or some other equivalent act, and afterwards applied by its judgment to the satisfaction of demands against its owner; or such demands be first established in a personal action, and the property of the non-resident be afterwards seized and sold on execution. But the answer to this position has already been given in the statement, that the jurisdiction of the court to inquire into and determine his obligations at all is only incidental to its jurisdiction over the property. Its jurisdiction in that respect cannot be made to depend upon facts to be ascertained after it has tried the cause and rendered the judgment. If the judgment be previously void, it will not become valid by the subsequent discovery of property of the defendant, or by his subsequent acquisition of it. The judgment, if void when rendered, will always remain void: it cannot occupy the doubtful position of being valid if property be found, and void if there be none. Even if the position assumed were confined to cases where the non-resident defendant possessed property in the State at the commencement of the action, it would still make the validity of the proceedings and judgment depend upon the question whether, before the levy of the execution, the defendant had or had not disposed of the property. If before the levy the property should be sold, then, according to this position, the judgment would not be binding. This doctrine would introduce a new element of uncertainty in judicial proceedings. The contrary is the law: the validity of every judgment depends upon the jurisdiction of the court before it is rendered, not upon what may occur subsequently. . . .

The force and effect of judgments rendered against non-residents without personal service of process upon them, or their voluntary appearance, have been the subject of frequent consideration in the courts of the United States and of the several States, as attempts have been made to enforce such judgments in States other than those in which they were rendered, under the provision of the [Full Faith and Credit Clause of the] Constitution [and the implementing statute]. In the earlier cases, it was supposed that the act gave to all judgments the same effect in other States which they had by law in the State where rendered. But this view was afterwards qualified so as to make the act applicable only when the court rendering the judgment had jurisdiction of the parties and of the subject-matter, and not to preclude an inquiry into the jurisdiction of the court in which the judgment was rendered, or the right of the State itself to exercise authority over the person or the subject-matter.... In the case of *D'Arcy v. Ketchum*, ... this view is stated with great clearness...." The international law," said the court, "as it existed among the States in 1790, was that a judgment rendered in one State, assuming to bind the person of a citizen of another, was void within the foreign State, when the defendant had not been served with process or voluntarily made defence; because neither the legislative jurisdiction nor that of courts of justice had binding force." And the court held that the act of Congress did not intend to declare a new rule, or to embrace judicial records of this description. As was stated in a subsequent case, the doctrine of this court is, that the act "was not designed to displace that principle of natural justice which requires a person to have notice of a suit before he can be conclusively bound by its result, nor those rules of public law which protect persons and property within one State from the exercise of jurisdiction over them by another." *Lafayette Ins. Co. v. French*, 59 U.S. (18 How.) 404 (1856).

. . . .

Since the adoption of the Fourteenth Amendment to the Federal Constitution, the validity of such judgments may be directly questioned, and their enforcement in the State resisted, on the ground that proceedings in a court of justice to determine the personal rights and obligations of parties over whom that court has no jurisdiction do not constitute due process of law. Whatever difficulty may be experienced in giving to those terms a definition which will embrace every permissible exertion of power affecting private rights, and exclude such as is forbidden, there can be no doubt of their meaning when applied to judicial proceedings. They then mean a course of legal proceedings according to those rules and principles which have been established in our systems of jurisprudence for the protection and enforcement of private rights. To give such proceedings any validity, there must be a tribunal competent by its constitution—that is, by the law of its creation—to pass upon the subject-matter of the suit; and, if that involves merely a determination of the personal liability of the defendant, he must be brought within its jurisdiction by service of process within the State, or his voluntary appearance.

Except in cases affecting the personal *status* of the plaintiff, and cases in which that mode of service may be considered to have been assented to in advance, as hereinafter mentioned, the substituted service of process by publication, allowed by the law of Oregon and by similar laws in other States, where actions are brought against non-residents, is effectual only where, in connection with process against the person for commencing the action, property in the State is brought under the control of the court, and subjected to its disposition by process adapted to that purpose, or where the judgment is sought as a means of reaching such property or affecting some interest therein; in other words, where the action is in the nature of a proceeding *in rem*. As stated by Cooley in his Treatise on Constitutional Limitations, 405, for any other purpose than to subject the property of a non-resident to valid claims against him in the State, "due process of law would require appearance or personal service before the defendant could be personally bound by any judgment rendered."

It is true that, in a strict sense, a proceeding *in rem* is one taken directly against property, and has for its object the disposition of the property, without reference to the title of individual claimants; but, in a larger and more general sense, the terms are applied to actions between parties, where the direct object is to reach and dispose of property owned by them, or of some interest therein. Such are cases commenced by attachment against the property of debtors, or instituted to partition real estate, foreclose a mortgage, or enforce a lien. So far as they affect property in the State, they are substantially proceedings *in rem* in the broader sense which we have mentioned.

It is hardly necessary to observe, that in all we have said we have had reference to proceedings in courts of first instance, and to their jurisdiction, and not to proceedings in an appellate tribunal to review the action of such courts. The latter may be taken upon such notice, personal or constructive, as the State creating the tribunal may provide. They are considered as rather a continuation of the original litigation than the commencement of a new action....

It follows from the views expressed that the personal judgment recovered in the State court of Oregon against the plaintiff herein, then a non-resident of the State, was without any validity, and did not authorize a sale of the property in controversy.

To prevent any misapplication of the views expressed in this opinion, it is proper to observe that we do not mean to assert, by any thing we have said, that a State may not authorize proceedings to determine the *status* of one of its citizens towards a non-resident, which would be binding within the State, though made without service of process or personal notice to the non-resident. The jurisdiction which every State possesses to determine the civil *status* and capacities of all its inhabitants involve authority to prescribe the conditions on which proceedings affecting them may be commenced and carried on within its territory. The State, for example, has absolute right to prescribe the conditions upon which the marriage relation between its own citizens shall be created, and the causes for which it may be dissolved. One of the parties guilty of acts for which, by the law of the State, a dissolution may be granted, may have removed to a State where no dissolution is permitted. The complaining party would, therefore, fail if a divorce were sought in the State of the defendant; and if application could not be made to the tribunals of the complainant's domicile in such case, and proceedings be there instituted without personal service of process or personal notice to the offending party, the injured citizen would be without redress....

Neither do we mean to assert that a State may not require a non-resident entering into a partnership or association within its limits, or making contracts enforceable there, to appoint an agent or representative in the State to receive service of process and notice in legal proceedings instituted with respect to such partnership, association, or contracts, or to designate a place where such service may be made and notice given, and provide, upon their failure, to make such appointment or to designate such place that service may be made upon a public officer designated for that purpose, or in some other prescribed way, and that judgments rendered upon such service may not be binding upon the non-residents both within and without the State.... Nor do we doubt that a State, on creating corporations or other institutions for pecuniary or charitable purposes, may provide a mode in which their conduct may be investigated, their obligations enforced, or their charters revoked, which shall require other than personal service upon their officers or members. Parties becoming members of such corporations or institutions would hold their interest subject to the conditions prescribed by law....

In the present case, there is no feature of this kind, and, consequently, no consideration of what would be the effect of such legislation in enforcing the contract of a non-resident can arise. The question here respects only the validity of a money judgment rendered in one State, in an action upon a simple contract against the resident of another, without service of process upon him, or his appearance therein.

Judgment affirmed.

[The dissenting opinion of JUSTICE HUNT is omitted.]

Notes and Questions

1. *Pennoyer v. Neff* involved many colorful characters. Marcus Neff was a young, illiterate homesteader who was one of the first group of settlers to claim land under the Oregon Donations Act. Apparently, he encountered difficulties with processing his land "patent." Around that time, he consulted J.H. Mitchell, an attorney specializing in land matters. Although it is not clear if Mitchell represented Neff in his efforts to obtain the land, it appears likely. Regardless, Neff had not chosen his attorney well. Mitchell was the alias of John Hipple, an attorney who had absconded from Pennsylvania with his clients' money. He was also a bigamist and had been involved in at least one fraud scheme. Nonetheless, he was elected to the U.S. Senate several times. *See* Wendy Collins Perdue, *Sin, Scandal, and Substantive Due Process: Personal Jurisdiction and* Pennoyer *Reconsidered*, 62 Wash. L. Rev. 479, 481–85, 489 (1987).

Mitchell waited several years to sue Neff for money allegedly owed him. When he received a default judgment, Mitchell did not execute it immediately. Rather, he waited until the title to Neff's property was delivered in Oregon several months later. Even though "Mitchell had alleged that Neff could not be found, the Oregon land office apparently had no difficulty delivering the patent [title] to Neff." *Id.* at 485.

The property was sold in execution of the default judgment for $341.60, just enough to cover the amount of the judgment and the sheriff's fees. The purchaser was not Sylvester Pennoyer, but J.H. Mitchell, who then transferred the property to Pennoyer three days later. Pennoyer held the property for eight years, paying taxes, cutting timber, and even selling a portion of the land. Then, Neff reappeared to reclaim the property. As you know, Neff was successful in evicting Pennoyer. Pennoyer, it appears, never recovered for his loss. *Id.* at 486–87.

Pennoyer later became the governor of Oregon. In his inaugural address, Pennoyer bitterly criticized the decision in his case as a usurpation of states' rights. He remained a vociferous critic of the U.S. Supreme Court, calling it a judicial oligarchy and urging impeachment of all of its members. *See id.* at 488–89.

2. In *Pennoyer*, the U.S. Supreme Court held that the international, territorial rules of jurisdiction required that an attachment of property had to be accomplished at the outset of an action, or at least prior to judgment. As Justice Hunt's dissent in *Pennoyer* pointed out, however, the timing of the seizure of property had always been considered to be a matter of municipal choice by the states, unaffected by the international rules. *See* Ralph U. Whitten, *The Constitutional Limitations on State-Court Jurisdiction: A Historical Interpretative Reexamination of the Full Faith and Credit and Due Process Clauses (pt. 1)*, 14 Creighton L. Rev. 499, 507 n.30 (1981); *id. (pt. 2)* at 826; *see also* James Weinstein, *The Federal Common Law Origins of Judicial Jurisdiction: Implications for Modern Doctrine*, 90 Va. L. Rev. 169 (2004) (arguing that the current unsatisfactory state of personal jurisdiction doctrine can be traced to *Pennoyer's* mismatch between the source of authority for federal restrictions on state court jurisdiction and the content of the rules). Why do you suppose that the Court created a rule that attachment before judgment was necessary to satisfy the international rules?

3. *Pennoyer's* prospective incorporation of the international territorial rules of jurisdiction into the Due Process Clause of the Fourteenth Amendment has been defended on the ground that "the restriction on state sovereign power [imposed by the international rules] is a function of the individual liberty interest preserved by the due process clause." John N. Drobak, *The Federalism Theme in Personal Jurisdiction*, 68 Iowa L. Rev. 1015, 1033 (1983). How did the international territorial rules protect "individual liberty"? For exam-

ple, if the international rules (as interpreted by the Court) had been fully complied with in *Pennoyer,* would the rights of the defendant in the state action, Neff, have been adequately protected?

3. The Operation of the Territorial Rules

For almost a century after *Pennoyer,* the traditional territorial rules dominated the law of personal jurisdiction. After *Pennoyer,* these rules were enforceable in the state where the judgment was rendered by virtue of the Due Process Clause of the Fourteenth Amendment. Over a long time, the rules evolved considerably from their original configuration. In addition, the states developed procedures governing personal jurisdiction that depended on the notion of territorial power reflected in the constitutional rules.

As you will see in later subsections, the concepts governing personal jurisdiction today differ in many respects from the territorial concepts that prevailed under *Pennoyer.* However, under the U.S. Supreme Court decision in *Burnham v. Superior Court,* 495 U.S. 604 (1990), reprinted in section C, below, it appears that at least some of the territorial rules have survived modern developments. Similarly, procedures still existing in the states continue to reflect the territorial heritage of the law of personal jurisdiction. Consequently, it is necessary to understand the scope of the territorial rules (as they had evolved to the point when the Court began to develop the modern approach to personal jurisdiction with the decision in *International Shoe,* reprinted in section B(1), below, as well as the reaction of the states to the modern rules, discussed in section B(2), below.

(a) In Rem and Quasi in Rem Jurisdiction

In Rem Jurisdiction. *Pennoyer's* concepts of in rem jurisdiction (jurisdiction over the thing) were highly dependent on the theory of state territorial power. The states had power over property located within their borders. Consequently, the states could, by a proper procedure, adjudicate the rights of nonresidents to that property. For example, in an action to determine title to property, the court of the state in which the property was located would have jurisdiction to determine ownership, regardless of where potential claimants resided. *See, e.g., Tyler v. Judges of the Court of Registration,* 55 N.E. 812, 813 (Mass. 1900) ("Looked at either from the point of view of history or of the necessary requirements of justice, a proceeding in rem, dealing with a tangible res, may be instituted and carried to judgment without personal service upon claimants within the state, or notice by name to those outside of it.... Jurisdiction is secured by the power of the court over the res.").

Conversely, the states had no direct power to affect property outside their borders, but they could do so indirectly. These principles produced curious decisions that sometimes allowed expansive power to be exercised over nonresidents. On other occasions, the decisions seemed to restrict state power unduly. In both instances, what the states could and could not do turned on distinctions of dubious practical utility.

In describing the operation of the territorial rules of jurisdiction that determined whether state judgments had to be enforced in other states under the 1790 implementing act to the Full Faith and Credit Clause, the Supreme Court stated that the act was only applicable

> when the court rendering the judgment had jurisdiction of the parties and of the subject matter, and not to preclude an inquiry into the jurisdiction of the court in which the judgment was rendered, *or the right of the State itself to exercise authority over the person or the subject matter.*

See Pennoyer, 95 U.S. at 733 (emphasis added). The Court's statement about the power of a state over the subject matter was clearly a reference to cases in which out-of-state land was involved in an action. In the next paragraph of its opinion, the Court stated that

> since the adoption of the Fourteenth Amendment ... the validity of *such judg-ments* may be directly questioned ... on the grounds that ... [they] do not con-stitute due process of law.

See id. (emphasis added). The reference to "such judgments" seemingly included all the judgments described in the preceding paragraph, including judgments in land cases in which the forum state lacked "jurisdiction over the subject matter." If this is a correct reading, then *Pennoyer* prospectively incorporated not only a rule of territorial subject-matter ju-risdiction into the Due Process Clause, but also a rule that was indisputably designed to protect the sovereignty of the state where the land was located rather than the rights of the parties before the non-situs forum court. As we will see later in this chapter, this ques-tion of whether the Due Process Clause incorporates sovereignty policies or only policies designed to assure the protection of individual rights continues to crop up in modern due process decisions. Note that one of the practical effects of incorporation of such a rule of subject-matter jurisdiction into the Due Process Clause would be that the issue could be raised before the non-situs forum court as a means of obtaining dismissal of the ac-tion, even when the forum is a perfectly acceptable place to adjudicate the action but for the fact that land is located outside the state. *See* Robert L. Felix & Ralph U. Whitten, American Conflicts Law § 44 (6th ed. 2011) (discussing this problem more completely).

Interestingly, none of the cases to arise after *Pennoyer* involving the question of the power of a state court to enter a judgment affecting land located in another state have ever again mentioned the Due Process Clause of the Fourteenth Amendment. Instead, all of the cases involve collateral attack on the judgment of the non-situs court in the courts of the state where the land is located. All of the cases stated that the situs state need not give full faith and credit to the judgments of non-situs courts that "directly af-fected" the land.

For example, in *Clarke v. Clarke*, 178 U.S. 186 (1900), a South Carolina testatrix died being survived by her husband and two infant daughters, and leaving land located in, among other places, Connecticut. Shortly afterward, one of the infant daughters also died intestate. Under the intestate distribution law of South Carolina, the surviving hus-band and daughter would inherit the share of the Connecticut real property left to the de-ceased daughter by the testatrix in equal shares. However, under the intestate distribution law of Connecticut, the surviving daughter would inherit all of the land. The South Car-olina probate court interpreted the will of the testatrix to work an "equitable conversion" of all of the testatrix's land into personalty, which meant that the administrator of the South Carolina estate could sell it, thus converting it into money, for purposes of dis-tributing the now converted money in accordance with South Carolina law.

The administrator of the estate (the surviving husband) then commenced an action in a Connecticut state court to dispose of the land there located. The Connecticut trial court entered an order finding that the surviving daughter was the sole heir of her deceased sis-ter, and the Supreme Court of Errors of Connecticut affirmed. The latter court held that under Connecticut law, the will did not work an equitable conversion of the land into personalty (though the court admitted that if the will had contained a clause explicitly doing this it would have been given effect by Connecticut). This meant that the property re-mained realty, and the Connecticut court held that South Carolina did not have the power to enter a decree directly affecting the title to the land. The U.S. Supreme Court affirmed, holding that Connecticut did not have to give full faith and credit to the South Carolina judgment. The Court's opinion contains statements clearly indicating concern that South Carolina's action allowed it to apply its law to affect the Connecticut land title in a way not permissible under Connecticut law. However, for our purposes, the important feature of the case is that the Court held the South Carolina court did not have subject-matter jurisdiction to directly affect the title to the land because it was located in Connecticut.

A second famous case, decided after *Clarke*, is *Fall v. Eastin*, 215 U.S. 1 (1909). In *Fall*, a Washington state court awarded real property located in Nebraska to a wife in a divorce action. However, the husband refused to deed the land to her. The court then appointed a commissioner pursuant to a Washington statute, and the commissioner issued a deed to the wife. The wife went into possession of the land under this deed. Subsequently, the husband conveyed the same land to his sister in repayment of a debt. The wife then sued the sister in a quiet title action in Nebraska. The wife requested that the commissioner's deed issued pursuant to the Washington state court judgment be given effect.

The U.S. Supreme Court held the Full Faith and Credit Clause did not require Nebraska to accept the deed. The Court indicated that Washington's attempt to convey the land directly to the wife through the statutory commissioner's procedure was an invalid infringement of Nebraska's sovereign power over the land. However, the Court also made it clear that Washington could have, by an appropriate proceeding in that state, compelled the husband to make out a valid deed to the Nebraska land. For example, the Washington court might have ordered the husband to convey the land and imprisoned him for contempt until he agreed to do so. Furthermore, even if the Washington court merely entered an order against the husband to convey the land, a Nebraska court would consider itself obligated by the doctrine of issue preclusion to enforce the order in an appropriate Nebraska proceeding. Therefore, the problem with the order in *Fall* was a narrow one: it attempted to directly accomplish the official act of transferring the title to the Nebraska land (through the commissioner's deed).

Note that the land title restriction, both at the conflict-of-laws level and at the jurisdictional level is a particularly sterile one. It does not really forbid a state from effectively disposing of land located in another state, as long as the state proceeds in a procedurally circumspect manner. If a state wishes to award out-of-state land belonging to one spouse to another in a divorce proceeding, all it has to do is order the spouse who owns that land to convey the land by a deed valid under the law of the situs state and imprison the owner for contempt if he or she refuses; the recalcitrant spouse can then be held in jail until the deed is executed.

Quasi in Rem Jurisdiction. Quasi in rem jurisdiction was commonly exercised in cases in which the defendant could not be served personally within the state. If the absent defendant owned property in the state, that property could be seized or attached, even if it were unrelated to the subject matter of the proceeding. Thus, in the original suit by Mitchell against Neff, quasi in rem jurisdiction could have properly been asserted, Justice Field concluded, if Mr. Neff's property had been seized at the outset of the lawsuit. (Prior attachment was not possible in that case, it appears, as Mr. Neff's title to the property had not yet been delivered at the time that Mr. Mitchell commenced the original suit for recovery of his fees in Oregon state court.)

Justice Field's assertion that the principles of international law required attachment at the outset of the lawsuit was incorrect as a matter of existing precedent, but it was essential to his decision and became the law of the nation. Attachment of a non-resident's property at the commencement of the action served the dual purpose of establishing the basis for the court's assertion of jurisdiction and providing constructive notice of the lawsuit to the absent defendant. (Notice of the pending lawsuit, a requirement of due process separate from the requirement of personal jurisdiction, is considered separately, in section F, below.)

This type of quasi in rem jurisdiction is constitutionally the most troubling, as you shall see when you study the case of *Shaffer v. Heitner*, 433 U.S. 186 (1977), reprinted in section B(3), below. In *Shaffer*, the Supreme Court held that a plaintiff can no longer simply attach property of the defendant located in the state and use the property to establish quasi in rem jurisdiction to adjudicate a claim against the defendant, unless there is also a constitutionally valid basis for asserting *personal* jurisdiction over the defendant.

Quasi in Rem Jurisdiction over Intangible Property: *Harris v. Balk* (1905) and *New York Life Insurance Co. v. Dunlevy* (1911). In *Harris v. Balk*, 198 U.S. 215 (1905), Harris, a resident of North Carolina, owed $180 to Balk, who was also a North Carolina resident. Balk, in turn, allegedly owed Epstein, a Maryland resident, $300. While Harris was in Maryland, Epstein garnished the $180 that Harris owed to Balk. Harris consented to the garnishment and paid the $180 to Epstein, notifying Balk of the garnishment. On the same day that Harris paid the $180 to Epstein, Balk sued Harris for the $180 in a North Carolina state court. Harris defended by pleading the Maryland garnishment judgment. The North Carolina courts held that the Maryland courts lacked jurisdiction to garnish the $180 debt because Harris was only temporarily in Maryland and the situs of the debt was in North Carolina.

The U.S. Supreme Court reversed. The Court held the Maryland judgment was valid and had to be given effect in North Carolina. The Court concluded that a debt followed the debtor even on temporary trips into other states. That debt could be "seized" in other states as long as the creditor would be able to sue the debtor there. Proper notice of the garnishment had to be given to the creditor, but that had been done in the Maryland proceeding. The Court observed that Balk had the right under Maryland law to litigate the question of liability to Epstein in the Maryland courts within a year and a day after entry of judgment in the garnishment proceeding, but Balk had not done so. Whether due process required such an opportunity was unclear from the Court's opinion.

Eleven years after *Harris v. Balk*, the Court decided *New York Life Insurance Co. v. Dunlevy*, 241 U.S. 518 (1916). In *Dunlevy*, Boggs & Buhl recovered a judgment against Dunlevy in a Pennsylvania state court. Two years later, New York Life became liable to Gould, Dunlevy's father, for $2,479.70 under a life insurance policy. Dunlevy contended that Gould had assigned the right to the policy proceeds to her, but Gould contested the validity of the assignment. Boggs & Buhl garnished the debt allegedly owed by New York Life to Dunlevy in a proceeding in a Pennsylvania state court, summoning both Gould and New York Life as garnishees. A short time later, Dunlevy sued New York Life in California, where she had moved, to recover the policy proceeds. Both New York Life and Gould were properly served with process in the California action. After the commencement of the California action, New York Life answered Boggs & Buhl's garnishment action in Pennsylvania by setting up the conflicting claims to the policy proceeds and requesting interpleader. Interpleader is discussed in Chapter 1(F)(2)(f) and Chapter 7(G).

Accordingly, New York Life admitted owing the debt to someone and paid the policy proceeds into court in Pennsylvania. Dunlevy was notified of this action, but she did not appear or plead in the proceeding. The Pennsylvania proceeding determined the assignment to be invalid and awarded the proceeds to Gould. New York Life then pleaded the Pennsylvania judgment in defense in the California proceeding. The California court rejected this defense, and the U.S. Supreme Court affirmed. The Court's opinion indicated that if New York life had simply let the Pennsylvania garnishment proceeding continue to its conclusion without requesting interpleader, it would have been protected by the resulting judgment in the California proceeding. The reason was that the garnishment would have been considered simply a continuation of the original proceeding by Boggs & Buhl against Dunlevy, in which there was personal jurisdiction over Dunlevy. However, by requesting interpleader, the company initiated a new proceeding that required a new acquisition of personal jurisdiction over Dunlevy in Pennsylvania. This new acquisition was impossible because Dunlevy had moved to California and was beyond the territorial reach of Pennsylvania process.

Notes and Questions

1. Why didn't the U.S. Supreme Court in *Dunlevy* sustain jurisdiction in the Pennsylvania interpleader action on the in rem theory of *Harris v. Balk*? New York Life, Dunlevy's debtor, was "present" in Pennsylvania, so the property was present there, wasn't it? Likewise, Dunlevy was properly notified of the proceeding. What was the difference between *Dunlevy* and *Harris*?

2. Was the practical effect of the interpleader proceeding on Dunlevy's rights any different from the practical effect of the garnishment proceeding? If not, why would the Court consider the interpleader proceeding invalid while indicating the garnishment would have been valid if it had been allowed to continue?

———————

Limited Appearance Procedures. A separate problem in the quasi in rem cases concerned the dilemma posed for a defendant whose property was attached when value of the property was worth less than the amount of the plaintiff's claim. (Remember that, under *Pennoyer*, the claim need have nothing to do with the attached property.) If the defendant did not appear and defend the action, a default judgment would be rendered and the property would be sold to satisfy the judgment. If the judgment was for more than the value of the property, the excess judgment could not be enforced against the defendant. Under *Pennoyer*, the judgment was only valid to the extent of the property that was the basis of the court's jurisdiction. Nevertheless, the property itself would be lost without the defendant ever having a chance to contest the merits. On the other hand, if the defendant appeared and defended the action, the appearance would be "general," and the court would acquire in personam jurisdiction over the defendant. Such jurisdiction could, in turn, result in a valid judgment for the full amount of the plaintiff's claim against the defendant—a judgment that could be taken to other states and enforced against the defendant's assets there.

Some states responded to this dilemma by providing *limited appearance* procedures. When available, these procedures allowed the defendant to appear for the limited purpose of defending the property. In effect, the defendant could litigate the merits of the case without fear of a judgment for the full amount of the claim being entered against the defendant. If the defendant won the action, the property would be saved. If the defendant lost the action, the property would be lost. However, the judgment would not be enforceable in another state for any amount in excess of the value of the property. To satisfy any amount of the claim unsatisfied by the property, the plaintiff would have to sue the defendant again in a state in which the defendant could be subjected to personal jurisdiction (or had other property). It should be emphasized, however, that the Due Process

Clause did not require a state to provide a limited appearance procedure. Whether a state did so was purely a matter of domestic policy.

(b) In Personam Jurisdiction: Physical Presence—Personal Service Upon the Defendant Within the Forum State

Jurisdiction Based on Transient Presence. Under *Pennoyer*, personal service of process on a defendant who was physically present in the forum state was sufficient to subject the defendant to personal jurisdiction consistent with the Due Process Clause. (Recall that in *Pennoyer*, Mr. Neff had not been personally served in the forum state.) Even if the defendant were only temporarily in the state, service based on physical presence at the time of service would be valid. Such jurisdiction could produce obvious litigational burdens to the defendant, especially given that the claim asserted by the plaintiff did not have to have any relationship to the state. Some relief might be available under a venue doctrine known as *forum non conveniens* (if the forum state followed the doctrine), but relief under that doctrine is discretionary with the courts. *See* Chapter 3(D). In the ordinary case, therefore, the defendant would have to bear the burdens.

As you will see when you study the case of *Burnham v. Superior Court*, 495 U.S. 186 (1990), reprinted in section D, below, the Supreme Court reconfirmed the concept of transient presence jurisdiction. Thus, personal service of process upon a defendant while the defendant is physically present in the forum state remains a constitutionally valid basis for the exercise of personal jurisdiction, even though the defendant is only temporarily in the state and the lawsuit is unrelated to the defendant's in-state activities.

Immunity from Service of Process. In certain cases, the states developed rules to mitigate the rigors of this *transitory presence*, or *tag* jurisdiction. The states would often provide immunity from service of process when nonresident parties, nonresident attorneys, or nonresident witnesses needed to enter the forum to participate in litigation there. The immunity would last only as long as necessary for the nonresident to attend the litigation and for a reasonable time in transit. The grant of immunity was predicated on the notion that the needs of the administration of justice required it.

Fraud-and-Force Rules. In addition, the states had rules prohibiting the acquisition of jurisdiction over a nonresident by fraud or force. The fraud-and-force rules only prohibited acquisition of jurisdiction over nonresidents, as opposed to residents, by fraud or force. They were based on the policy of preventing the plaintiff from profiting from inequitable conduct. *See, e.g., Wyman v. Newhouse*, 93 F.2d 313 (2d Cir. 1937) (in-state personal service on defendant not valid in acquiring personal jurisdiction where plaintiff lied to defendant about her love for him and her mother's illness to trick defendant into entering the state).

It should be emphasized that both the immunity rules and the fraud-and-force rules were discretionary with the states. The Due Process Clause did not require them.

(c) In Personam Jurisdiction: Consent, Appearance, and Waiver

Consent. As explained in Chapter 1, the fundamental policy underlying the requirement of personal jurisdiction is party protection. It has long been recognized, therefore, that consent to jurisdiction by a party in a particular forum is a constitutionally valid basis for asserting personal jurisdiction. A party can consent to personal jurisdiction even before a controversy ever arises. For example, in a commercial context, the parties may agree by contract, as a condition of doing business with each other, to submit to the jurisdiction of the courts of a particular state in the event a lawsuit is filed. A party may also consent to personal jurisdiction by appointing an agent within the state to receive service.

Waiver; General and Special Appearances. Conduct of the parties after the commencement of the action can also form the basis for the valid exercise of personal jurisdiction. As explained in Chapter 1, after the action is commenced any objection to personal jurisdiction must be properly and timely raised or the objection is *waived*. If a defendant responds to the plaintiff's complaint but fails to assert a personal jurisdiction defense, the defendant is said to have *generally appeared* in the action. By generally appearing, the defendant has *consented* to jurisdiction in the forum court and *waived* any personal jurisdiction objection that the defendant may have.

Traditionally, a defendant who wanted to object to personal jurisdiction had to *specially appear* in the action for that purpose only. Usually, a special appearance had to be made before any other action was taken, and the defendant could not request any relief in a special appearance procedure other than dismissal for lack of personal jurisdiction. In the federal courts and states adopting rules similar to the Federal Rules of Civil Procedure, the special appearance procedure is replaced by a process of raising jurisdictional and other objections by preanswer motion or in the answer. *See* Fed. R. Civ. P. 12(b). Thus, the consolidation of personal jurisdiction objections with other objections in a preanswer motion or in the answer will not result in waiver of those objections. *See* Fed. R. Civ. P. (12)(g)(2), (h)(1)(A).

Direct vs. Collateral Attacks. Once a defendant has appeared in an action and litigated a jurisdictional objection, the defendant is bound by the determination of the jurisdictional issue in the original action and the defendant's only recourse for review is an appeal of the ruling in the appellate courts of the forum state. This is known as a *direct attack* on the judgment because it occurs in a continuation of the same proceeding in which the judgment was rendered. The defendant is prohibited from *collaterally attacking* the ruling in some other proceeding. For example, if the defendant appears in an action and the plaintiff seeks to enforce the resulting judgment in another court, most likely in the defendant's home state or some other state where the defendant has assets, the defendant is precluded from arguing in that second court that the judgment is unenforceable because the original court lacked personal jurisdiction.

The defendant's appearance in the original action is the key. If the defendant appeared in the original action and failed to assert lack of personal jurisdiction, then the original court had valid personal jurisdiction because the defendant's *general appearance* constitutes a waiver of the personal jurisdiction defense. If the defendant appeared and asserted the personal jurisdiction defense, then the defendant was bound to appeal the original court's ruling in the appellate courts of the forum state and cannot collaterally attack the judgment in another proceeding.

It is only when the defendant makes no appearance whatsoever in the original action that a collateral attack of a judgment for lack of personal jurisdiction is allowed in another proceeding. Recall also from the discussion in Chapter 1 that after service, the defendant may simply refuse to appear in the action. In the normal course of events, a default judgment will be entered against the defendant. At that point, if the defendant has no assets in the jurisdiction where the default judgment is rendered, then the plaintiff will have to take the judgment to a state where the defendant has assets and request that the judgment be enforced. Because the defendant made no appearance whatsoever in the original action, however, the defendant will be permitted to argue in the second action that the judgment is unenforceable because the original court lacked personal jurisdiction. In addition, a non-appearing defendant may sometimes collaterally attack the judgment by initiating his own independent action separate from the one in which the judgment was obtained. In *Pennoyer*, for example, Neff commenced his own action in the U.S. Circuit Court in Oregon to recover possession of his land and "collaterally attack" the validity of the prior Oregon state court judgment based on lack of personal jurisdiction. Do you now see why Neff was able to challenge the first court's judgment in the second action?

This option of making no appearance in the first action, however, comes with great risk. If the second court finds the original judgment invalid because of lack of personal jurisdiction, the court will refuse to enforce it. However, if the judgment is valid, the full faith and credit implementing statute, 28 U.S.C. § 1738, will obligate the court of the judgment-enforcing state to give the same effect to the judgment that it would receive in the state where it was rendered. Under such circumstances, the defendant loses the right to defend the action on the merits. Thus, before a defendant selects the option of making no appearance whatsoever, a defendant who has a good defense on the merits must be certain the jurisdictional objection is valid.

Notes and Questions

1. The U.S. Supreme Court has never held that a state is constitutionally obligated to provide a special appearance procedure, or its equivalent, that will allow a nonresident defendant to challenge an assertion of personal jurisdiction by the state's courts. The ability of the defendant to default and collaterally attack the judgment in the courts of another state is deemed constitutionally sufficient. *See York v. Texas*, 137 U.S. 15, 21 (1890). However, this lack of a constitutional obligation to provide a special appearance procedure or its equivalent presents no problem today because every state either offers a special appearance procedure or a motion procedure like the one available under Federal Rule 12(b).

2. As noted in the above discussion on "direct vs. collateral attacks," after a defendant asserts a personal jurisdiction objection and the objection is denied by the court, the defendant must appeal the adverse ruling in the appellate courts of the forum state. But when does this appeal occur? In some jurisdictions, an immediate appeal on the personal jurisdiction issue is allowed, known as an "interlocutory appeal," before any further action is taken in the trial court as to the substantive merits of the plaintiff's claim. The *World-Wide* and *Asahi* cases, reprinted in this chapter, are examples of such interlocutory appeals. Other jurisdictions require the defendant to wait until the case has fully concluded in the trial court and a final judgment rendered on the merits of the plaintiff's claim before appealing the jurisdictional issue. The *Burger King* and *Helicopteros* cases, also reprinted below, are examples of this latter approach. After reading those cases, think about which approach you feel is better in terms of fairness to the litigants and judicial efficiency.

3. Do you think that a state can provide a special appearance procedure and require the defendant, after losing at the trial level in such a procedure, to choose whether to litigate the jurisdictional issue on appeal or to litigate the merits of the case? In other words, can a state provide either (a) that the defendant can only appeal the jurisdictional question by waiving the right to litigate the merits or (b) that the defendant can, after losing on the jurisdictional issue at the trial level, litigate the merits, but only on pain of not being able to litigate the jurisdictional issue on appeal if the defendant loses on the merits at trial? *Cf.* RESTATEMENT (SECOND) OF CONFLICT OF LAWS § 81 cmt. c (1971) (indicating that the states have wide latitude in structuring their schemes of special appearance).

4. In the federal courts and in most states, a defendant, after properly, but unsuccessfully, challenging the forum court's assertion of personal jurisdiction, may, if an interlocutory appeal is not allowed, fully litigate the merits of the action while fully preserving the right to later appeal the jurisdictional ruling. If the defendant loses on the merits, the defendant may assert on appeal in the appellate courts of the forum state any errors committed in adjudicating the jurisdictional question as well as any errors committed in adjudicating the merits of the action.

(d) In Personam Jurisdiction: Domicile in the Forum State

Domicile as a Basis for Personal Jurisdiction. The requirements of domicile are discussed more fully in Chapter 4 on subject-matter jurisdiction. For present purposes, it is sufficient to understand that domicile refers to the place where a person resides and considers home. A person can have only one domicile and once a person acquires a domicile, that domicile continues until the person acquires a new one. After *Pennoyer*, the U.S. Supreme Court recognized that nationality and domicile were valid bases for asserting personal jurisdiction over defendants. Thus, United States citizens residing abroad could be validly served with process outside the United States and subjected to the jurisdiction of United States courts on the basis of their citizenship. *See Blackmer v. United States*, 284 U.S. 421, 437–38 (1932) ("Nor can it be doubted that the United States possesses the power inherent in sovereignty to require the return to this country of a citizen, resident elsewhere, whenever the public interest requires it, and to penalize him in case of refusal.").

Similarly, a person domiciled in, but absent from, the forum state could be validly subjected to personal jurisdiction under an appropriately drafted long-arm statute authorizing service of process on the defendant outside of the state. *See Milliken v. Meyer*, 311 U.S. 457, 463–64 (1940) ("Domicile in the state is alone sufficient to bring an absent defendant within the reach of the state's jurisdiction for purposes of a personal judgment by means of appropriate substituted service.... The state which accords him privileges and affords protection to him and his property by virtue of his domicile may also exact reciprocal duties.... The attendant duties, like the rights and privileges incident to domicile, are not dependent on continuous presence in the state").

The theory of these cases rested upon the inherent "power" that a government had over its citizens. The theory was broad enough to allow a state to exercise personal jurisdiction over a defendant who merely possessed a "technical" domicile in the state—*i.e.*, a person (1) who was domiciled in the state, (2) who was no longer present in the state, (3) who no longer had a substantial relationship with the state, but (4) who had never acquired a new domicile in another state. In addition, these cases refer to the theory that citizens of a state enjoy the benefits and protection of that state's laws, and thus have a reciprocal obligation to answer suits in the state. You shall see that this latter point—the duty to answer suits in those states where a defendant has received the benefits and protections of the forum state's laws—will provide the basis of the "minimum contacts" theory of personal jurisdiction originating with the *International Shoe* case, reprinted in section B(1), below.

Issues of "Personal Status." In addition to the power of the state to exercise jurisdiction over absent domiciliaries, domicile also provided the basis for a state to exercise jurisdiction to alter status. Recall that in *Pennoyer*, the U.S. Supreme Court recognized that the states had the power to alter the "civil *status* and capacities of all its inhabitants." The Court gave as an example the power of the states to prescribe the conditions upon which the marriage relationships between its "citizens" could be created and dissolved. Specifically, the

Court pointed to the necessity of the states having power to exercise divorce jurisdiction on the basis of a plaintiff's residence when the defendant had "removed to a State where no dissolution is permitted." The power of the states to alter the status of their domiciliaries was, like jurisdiction over property, considered to be a species of in rem jurisdiction.

Under the rule that ultimately evolved after *Pennoyer*, the states were broadly permitted to exercise divorce jurisdiction. They were permitted to exercise jurisdiction based on the domicile of the plaintiff alone when the plaintiff had moved to a state where divorce was permitted. Due process, of course, requires that the absent spouse be given proper notice of the action (see section F, below). This ex parte divorce jurisdiction was permitted even though the defendant in the divorce action had never been associated with the divorcing state and, in fact, remained in the state of the original marital domicile, which would not permit the divorce. However, this ex parte divorce jurisdiction does not extend to jurisdiction to adjudicate related matters, such as alimony or child custody issues. *See* TEPLY & WHITTEN at 318. Unlike the original power over status discussed in *Pennoyer*, this power to divorce based on the domicile of a peripatetic plaintiff is of relatively recent origin. The traditional approach was that the domicile of one spouse alone was insufficient to satisfy due process. *See* RESTATEMENT (FIRST) OF CONFLICT OF LAWS §113 cmt. a (1934).

Section B. The "Minimum Contacts" Test

1. Development of Modern Restrictions on State Court Jurisdiction in *International Shoe*

After *Pennoyer*, many of the due process cases concerning the reach of state court jurisdiction involved corporations. In these cases, the U.S. Supreme Court adapted the "consent" and "presence" tests to determine when corporations could be subjected to the adjudicatory power of a state. Generally, the states were allowed to require foreign corporations doing intrastate business in a state to appoint agents to receive service of process. In default of an actual appointment, the states were allowed to appoint an agent by operation of law—*i.e.*, by means of a statute. The theory that justified this exercise of state power was that the states could exclude foreign corporations from doing intrastate business in the state if they so chose. Having the power to exclude, it followed that they had the power to condition the doing of intrastate business upon the appointment, actual or by operation of law, of an agent to receive service. This "implied consent" was held to comport with due process.

When a corporation was doing purely interstate business, the consent theory would not work. Under the U.S. Constitution, the states did not have the power to prevent foreign corporations from engaging in interstate commerce within the state. In such cases, the presence theory was adapted to allow the states to assert jurisdiction over foreign corporations that were doing sufficient business to warrant the conclusion that they were "present" in the state. Like the consent theory, the presence theory depended upon whether the corporation was "doing business" within the state. Thus, in each case, the question became whether the corporation was doing sufficient business to subject it to jurisdiction under the theory on which the assertion of jurisdiction was based.

The implied consent theory was also extended to cases involving individuals. Whenever a state had the power to prevent an individual from conducting a certain activity within the state, it was held that the state could, instead, condition the activity upon the appointment of an agent to receive service of process in actions arising out of the activity. For example, the states were held to have the power to prevent nonresidents from operating automobiles within the state—a dangerous activity. Instead of preventing nonresidents from driving in the state, however, the state could enact a statute providing that when a nonresident operated an automobile within the state, the nonresident consented to the appointment of a state official, such as the state registrar of motor vehicles, as agent for the receipt of process in actions that might be brought arising out of the operation of the automobile in the state. *See Hess v. Pawloski*, 274 U.S. 352, 355–56 (1927) (upholding the Massachusetts statute). This theory was broad enough to allow the state to enact an implied-consent type of statute any time it possessed the power to regulate, and thus to place conditions on, the defendant's activity within the state.

The fictional nature of the implied consent theory (as well as the presence theory as applied to corporations) cried out for more rational principles to govern the due process limits on state-court jurisdiction. The U.S. Supreme Court began to develop these principles in *International Shoe Co. v. Washington*, below, with the establishment of the "minimum contacts" theory for acquiring personal jurisdiction over a defendant. However, the task of developing these principles has not been easy and is far from complete. In reading the cases and materials that follow, you should ask whether the Court has gone too far or not far enough in its search for a more rational basis to define the limits of state-court authority over nonresident defendants.

International Shoe Co. v. Washington

United States Supreme Court, 1945
326 U.S. 310, 66 S. Ct. 154, 90 L. Ed. 95

CHIEF JUSTICE STONE delivered the opinion of the Court.

The questions for decision are (1) whether, within the limitations of the Due Process Clause of the Fourteenth Amendment, appellant, a Delaware corporation, has by its activities in the State of Washington rendered itself amenable to proceedings in the courts of that state to recover unpaid contributions to the state unemployment compensation fund exacted by state statutes, Washington Unemployment Compensation Act..., and (2) whether the state can exact those contributions consistently with the Due Process Clause of the Fourteenth Amendment.

The statutes in question set up a comprehensive scheme of unemployment compensation, the costs of which are defrayed by contributions required to be made by employers to a state unemployment compensation fund. The contributions are a specified percentage of the wages payable annually by each employer for his employees' services in the state. The assessment and collection of the contributions and the fund are administered by appellees. Section 14(c) of the Act ... authorizes appellee Commissioner to issue an order and notice of assessment of delinquent contributions upon prescribed personal service of the notice upon the employer if found within the state, or, if not so found, by mailing the notice to the employer by registered mail at his last known address. That section also authorizes the Commissioner to collect the assessment by distraint if it is not paid within ten days after service of the notice. By §§ 14e and 6b the order of assessment may be administratively reviewed by an appeal tribunal within the office of unemployment upon petition of the employer, and this determination is by § 6i made subject to judicial review on questions of law by the state Superior Court, with further right of appeal in the state Supreme Court as in other civil cases.

In this case notice of assessment for the years in question was personally served upon a sales solicitor employed by appellant in the State of Washington, and a copy of the notice was mailed by registered mail to appellant at its address in St. Louis, Missouri. Appellant appeared specially before the office of unemployment and moved to set aside the order and notice of assessment on the ground that the service upon appellant's salesman was not proper service upon appellant; that appellant was not a corporation of the State of Washington and was not doing business within the state; that it had no agent within the state upon whom service could be made; and that appellant is not an employer and does not furnish employment within the meaning of the statute.

[margin note: special Appearance]

[margin note: Intnl. Shoe's Motion]

The motion was heard on evidence and a stipulation of facts by the appeal tribunal which denied the motion and ruled that appellee Commissioner was entitled to recover the unpaid contributions. That action was affirmed by the Commissioner; both the Superior Court and the Supreme Court affirmed.... Appellant in each of these courts assailed the statute as applied, as a violation of the Due Process Clause of the Fourteenth Amendment, and as imposing a constitutionally prohibited burden on interstate commerce. The cause comes here on appeal [with the] appellant assigning as error that the challenged statutes as applied infringe the Due Process Clause of the Fourteenth Amendment and the Commerce Clause.

[margin note: Issue in supreme Court]

The facts as found by the appeal tribunal and accepted by the state Superior Court and Supreme Court, are not in dispute. Appellant is a Delaware corporation, having its principal place of business in St. Louis, Missouri, and is engaged in the manufacture and sale of shoes and other footwear. It maintains places of business in several states, other than Washington, at which its manufacturing is carried on and from which its merchandise is distributed interstate through several sales units or branches located outside the State of Washington.

Appellant has no office in Washington and makes no contracts either for sale or purchase of merchandise there. It maintains no stock of merchandise in that state and makes there no deliveries of goods in intrastate commerce. During the years from 1937 to 1940, now in question, appellant employed eleven to thirteen salesmen under direct supervision and control of sales managers located in St. Louis. These salesmen resided in Washington; their principal activities were confined to that state; and they were compensated by commissions based upon the amount of their sales. The commissions for each year totaled more than $31,000. Appellant supplies its salesmen with a line of samples, each consisting of one shoe of a pair, which they display to prospective purchasers. On occasion they rent permanent sample rooms, for exhibiting samples, in business buildings, or rent rooms in hotels or business buildings temporarily for that purpose. The cost of such rentals is reimbursed by appellant.

[margin note: Facts]

The authority of the salesmen is limited to exhibiting their samples and soliciting orders from prospective buyers, at prices and on terms fixed by appellant. The salesmen transmit the orders to appellant's office in St. Louis for acceptance or rejection, and when accepted the merchandise for filling the orders is shipped f.o.b. from points outside Washington to the purchasers within the state. All the merchandise shipped into Washington is invoiced at the place of shipment from which collections are made. No salesman has authority to enter into contracts or to make collections.

[margin note: see on bottom]

The Supreme Court of Washington was of opinion that the regular and systematic solicitation of orders in the state by appellant's salesmen, resulting in a continuous flow of appellant's product into the state, was sufficient to constitute doing business in the state so as to make appellant amenable to suit in its courts. But it was also of opinion that

[margin note: Washington Supreme Court's Opinion]

there were sufficient additional activities shown to bring the case within the rule frequently stated, that solicitation within a state by the agents of a foreign corporation plus some additional activities there are sufficient to render the corporation amenable to suit brought in the courts of the state to enforce an obligation arising out of its activities there.... The court found such additional activities in the salesmen's display of samples sometimes in permanent display rooms, and the salesmen's residence within the state, continued over a period of years, all resulting in a substantial volume of merchandise regularly shipped by appellant to purchasers within the state. The court also held that the statute as applied did not invade the constitutional power of Congress to regulate interstate commerce and did not impose a prohibited burden on such commerce.

....

Appellant ... insists that its activities within the state were not sufficient to manifest its "presence" there and that in its absence the state courts were without jurisdiction, that consequently it was a denial of due process for the state to subject appellant to suit. It refers to those cases in which it was said that the mere solicitation of orders for the purchase of goods within a state, to be accepted without the state and filled by shipment of the purchased goods interstate, does not render the corporation seller amenable to suit within the state.... And appellant further argues that since it was not present within the state, it is a denial of due process to subject it to taxation or other money exaction. It thus denies the power of the state to lay the tax or to subject appellant to a suit for its collection.

Historically the jurisdiction of courts to render judgment *in personam* is grounded on their de facto power over the defendant's person. Hence his presence within the territorial jurisdiction of a court was prerequisite to its rendition of a judgment personally binding him. *Pennoyer v. Neff*, 95 U.S. at 733. But now that the *capias ad respondendum* has given way to personal service of summons or other form of notice, due process requires only that in order to subject a defendant to a judgment *in personam*, if he be not present within the territory of the forum, he have certain minimum contacts with it such that the maintenance of the suit does not offend "traditional notions of fair play and substantial justice."...

Since the corporate personality is a fiction, although a fiction intended to be acted upon as though it were a fact ... it is clear that unlike an individual its "presence" without, as well as within, the state of its origin can be manifested only by activities carried on in its behalf by those who are authorized to act for it. To say that the corporation is so far "present" there as to satisfy due process requirements, for purposes of taxation or the maintenance of suits against it in the courts of the state, is to beg the question to be decided. For the terms "present" or "presence" are used merely to symbolize those activities of the corporation's agent within the state which courts will deem to be sufficient to satisfy the demands of due process. L. Hand, J., in *Hutchinson v. Chase & Gilbert, Inc.*, 45 F.2d 139, 141 (2d Cir. 1930). Those demands may be met by such contacts of the corporation with the state of the forum as make it reasonable, in the context of our federal system of government, to require the corporation to defend the particular suit which is brought there. An "estimate of the inconveniences" which would result to the corporation from a trial away from its "home" or principal place of business is relevant in this connection. *Id.*

"Presence" in the state in this sense has never been doubted when the activities of the corporation there have not only been continuous and systematic, but also give rise to the liabilities sued on, even though no consent to be sued or authorization to an agent to accept service of process has been given.... Conversely it has been generally recognized that the casual presence of the corporate agent or even his conduct of single or isolated items of activities in a state in the corporation's behalf are not enough to subject it to suit on causes of action unconnected with the activities there.... To require the corporation in such circumstances to defend the suit away from its home or other jurisdiction where it carries on more substantial activities has been thought to lay too great and unreasonable a burden on the corporation to comport with due process.

While it has been held, in cases on which appellant relies, that continuous activity of some sorts within a state is not enough to support the demand that the corporation be amenable to suits unrelated to that activity, ... there have been instances in which the continuous corporate operations within a state were thought so substantial and of such a nature as to justify suit against it on causes of action arising from dealings entirely distinct from those activities....

Finally, although the commission of some single or occasional acts of the corporate agent in a state sufficient to impose an obligation or liability on the corporation has not been thought to confer upon the state authority to enforce it, ... other such acts, because of their nature and quality and the circumstances of their commission, may be deemed sufficient to render the corporation liable to suit.... True, some of the decisions holding the corporation amenable to suit have been supported by resort to the legal fiction that it has given its consent to service and suit, consent being implied from its presence in the state through the acts of its authorized agents.... But more realistically it may be said that those authorized acts were of such a nature as to justify the fiction....

It is evident that the criteria by which we mark the boundary line between those activities which justify the subjection of a corporation to suit, and those which do not, cannot be simply mechanical or quantitative. The test is not merely, as has sometimes been suggested, whether the activity, which the corporation has seen fit to procure through its agents in another state, is a little more or a little less.... Whether due process is satisfied must depend rather upon the quality and nature of the activity in relation to the fair and orderly administration of the laws which it was the purpose of the due process clause to insure. That clause does not contemplate that a state may make binding a judgment *in personam* against an individual or corporate defendant with which the state has no contacts, ties, or relations....

But to the extent that a corporation exercises the privilege of conducting activities within a state, it enjoys the benefits and protection of the laws of that state. The exercise of that privilege may give rise to obligations, and, so far as those obligations arise out of or are connected with the activities within the state, a procedure which requires the corporation to respond to a suit brought to enforce them can, in most instances, hardly be said to be undue. (That is Due process)

Applying these standards, the activities carried on in behalf of appellant in the State of Washington were neither irregular nor casual. They were systematic and continuous throughout the years in question. They resulted in a large volume of interstate business, in the course of which appellant received the benefits and protection of the laws of the state, including the right to resort to the courts for the enforcement of its rights. The obligation which is here sued upon arose out of those very activities. It is evident that these operations establish sufficient contacts or ties with the state of the forum to make it reasonable and just, according to our traditional conception of fair play and substantial justice, to permit the state to enforce the obligations which appellant has incurred there. Hence we cannot say that the maintenance of the present suit in the State of Washington involves an unreasonable or undue procedure.

We are likewise unable to conclude that the service of the process within the state upon an agent whose activities establish appellant's "presence" there was not sufficient notice of the suit, or that the suit was so unrelated to those activities as to make the agent an inappropriate vehicle for communicating the notice. It is enough that appellant has established such contacts with the state that the particular form of substituted service adopted there gives reasonable assurance that the notice will be actual.... Nor can we say that the mailing of the notice of suit to appellant by registered mail at its home office was not reasonably calculated to apprise appellant of the suit....

....

Affirmed.

Justice Jackson took no part in the consideration or decision of this case. [The dissenting opinion of Justice Black is omitted.]

Notes and Questions

1. In *International Shoe*, could the U.S. Supreme Court have sustained the State of Washington's assertion of jurisdiction over International Shoe under the traditional consent or presence tests?

2. Does the Court's opinion in *International Shoe* indicate whether the "minimum contacts" test applies only to corporate defendants or also to individual defendants?

3. Based on the Court's opinion in *International Shoe*, can you describe when a defendant will be held *not* to have sufficient "contacts" with the state to satisfy due process?

2. Reaction of the States to the "Minimum Contacts" Test: Enactment of "Long-Arm" Statutes

Recall that before *International Shoe* the states had enacted statutes designed to satisfy the "territorial power" tests articulated by the U.S. Supreme Court—*e.g.,* implied consent nonresident motorist statutes. Similarly, after *International Shoe* the states began to enact "long-arm" statutes designed to meet the requirements of the "minimum contacts" test. Illinois led the way in 1955. Its statute provided that the state's courts could assert jurisdiction over a nonresident defendant on a "cause of action" arising from any one of four kinds of acts performed within the state: (1) transacting any business within the state; (2) committing a tortious act within the state; (3) owning, using, or possessing any real estate in the state; or (4) contracting to insure any person, property, or risk located within the state at the time the contract was made. 1955 Ill. Laws 2283, § 1; *see* Smith-Hurd Ill. Comp. Stat. Ann. ch. 735, § 5/2-209 (West Supp. 2012).

Seven years after the enactment of the Illinois statute, the National Conference of Commissioners on Uniform State Laws approved a Uniform "Long-Arm" Act. Numerous states have adopted this Act:

> (a) A court may exercise personal jurisdiction over a person, who acts directly or by an agent, as to a [cause of action] [claim for relief] arising from the person's
>
> (1) transacting any business in this state;

Jnifolm
Long'
Arm
Act

(2) contracting to supply services or things in this state;

(3) causing [a] tortious injury by an act or omission in this state;

(4) causing [a] tortious injury in this state by an act or omission outside this state if [that person] regularly does or solicits business, or engages in any other persistent course of conduct, or derives substantial revenue from goods used or consumed or services rendered, in this state; [or]

(5) having an interest in, using, or possessing real property in this state[; or

(6) contracting to insure any person, property, or risk located within this state at the time of contracting].

UNIF. INTERSTATE & INT'L PROC. ACT § 1.03 (1962) (withdrawn 1977), 13 U.L.A. 355, 361–62 (1986).

In contrast to the approach of the Illinois and Uniform Acts, California has simply authorized its courts to "exercise jurisdiction on any basis not inconsistent with the Constitution of this state or of the United States." CAL. CIV. PROC. CODE § 410.10 (West 2004). Under the Illinois and Uniform Acts, the first step in analyzing a state's assertion of jurisdiction over a nonresident is finding a section of the long-arm statute that fits the facts of the case. Once a section of the statute is found to apply, the next question is whether the pertinent section of the statute is constitutional as applied to the facts. In contrast, under the California statute, the statutory and constitutional tests are collapsed into each other. However, this distinction between different kinds of long-arm statutes should not be overemphasized. Many states having "specific" long-arm statutes like the Uniform Act have construed their statutes to extend "as far as due process permits." For example, Oklahoma courts interpreted the long-arm provision in the *World-Wide Volkswagen* case, reprinted below, as conferring jurisdiction to the limits of due process. Thus, by judicial construction, these states have effectively converted their statutes into the general kind of statute enacted by California and some other states.

Notes and Questions

1. How should the original Illinois statute be applied to a claim in tort arising out of a component negligently manufactured outside the state, incorporated into a finished product outside the state and sent into the state, where the component malfunctions, injuring a consumer? *See Gray v. American Radiator & Standard Sanitary Corp.*, 176 N.E.2d 761 (Ill. 1961) (tort was committed when the last act necessary to its existence, the injury, occurred).

2. Does the Uniform Act solve any problems of interpretation involved with the Illinois statute? For example, which statute best deals with the problem of the defective component, described in Note 1, above?

3. A state would never combine the approach of the Uniform Act with the California approach, would it? What would such a combination accomplish? *See, e.g.*, NEB. REV. STAT. § 25-536 (2008).

4. Is there any reason to believe the approach of the Uniform Act is more likely to pass constitutional muster than the approach of the California statute?

5. You should note that the advent of modern long-arm statutes has not necessarily eliminated the ability of states to assert jurisdiction through service in one of the older ways. *See, e.g.*, *State ex rel. K-Mart Corp. v. Holliger*, 986 S.W.2d 165 (Mo. 1999) (rejecting an

argument that jurisdiction must be asserted under a long-arm statute and could not be asserted over a foreign corporation by serving its registered agent in that state).

3. Developing the Content of the "Minimum Contacts" Test

In the early years after *International Shoe*, the U.S. Supreme Court decisions demonstrate the difficulty of refining a workable test for "minimum contacts" that was capable of consistent and principled application. The following cases, however, provide the "building blocks," in addition to *International Shoe* itself, for the construction of the current framework for analyzing personal jurisdiction based on minimum contacts.

The *Mullane* Case (1950). In *Mullane v. Central Hanover Bank & Trust Co.*, 339 U.S. 306 (1950), discussed further in section E, below, New York enacted "common trust fund" legislation. This legislation permitted small trust estates to pool their assets in a single fund for purposes of investment administration. Periodic accountings were required after a bank established such a fund. In the accounting proceedings brought to comply with the legislation, the resulting judicial decree was made binding and conclusive on all persons having any interest in the common fund or any participating estate, trust, or fund. Central Hanover Bank & Trust established a common trust fund in January 1946. It petitioned in March 1947, for settlement of its first account as common trustee. In this proceeding, the representative of the trust beneficiaries questioned the power of New York to bind nonresident beneficiaries of the trust without personal service of process on them in the state. The U.S. Supreme Court stated that whether the proceedings were classified as in personam or in rem, New York had power to adjudicate the claims of nonresidents due to its strong interests in providing the means to close trusts that were established under its laws and administered under the supervision of its courts.

The *Perkins* Case (1952). In *Perkins v. Benguet Consolidated Mining Co.*, 342 U.S. 437 (1952), the defendant was a mining corporation whose operations in the Philippines had been suspended due to the Japanese occupation during World War II. The plaintiff sued to recover damages due to the failure of the corporation to issue certain shares of stock to her. The action was brought in Ohio because the president of the company had returned there to live and was conducting the activities of the corporation there during the suspension of mining activities. The U.S. Supreme Court held that due process would not be offended by an assertion of jurisdiction over the corporation under these circumstances. *Id.* at 446 (noting that "no requirement of federal due process ... either *prohibits* Ohio from opening its courts to the cause of action ... presented or *compels* Ohio to do so."). The Court characterized the activities of the corporation in Ohio as "continuous and systematic." *Id.* at 445. According to the Court, this high level activity made it valid under the minimum contacts test for Ohio to assert jurisdiction over the corporation, even though the claim against the corporation did not arise out of the activities of the corporation in the state. *Id.* at 445–46.

The *McGee* Case (1957). In *McGee v. International Life Insurance Co.*, 355 U.S. 220 (1957), a California statute subjected foreign insurance companies to suit in California on insurance contracts with residents of California, even though the companies could not be served within the state. A resident of California purchased an insurance policy from an Arizona insurance company, Empire Mutual, in 1944. In 1946, the defendant, a Texas corporation, assumed all of the Arizona company's insurance obligations. The defendant mailed a reinsurance certificate to the California insured, offering to reinsure him in accord with the policy he held with the Arizona company. The offer was accepted. The insured paid premiums on the policy by mailing them from California to Texas until his death in 1950. The defendant refused to pay the proceeds of the policy on the ground that the insured had committed suicide. The beneficiary sued the company in a California state court, asserting personal jurisdiction under the statute described above. The defendant did not appear in the action.

After a default judgment was entered against the defendant, the plaintiff sued on the judgment in Texas to enforce it there. The defendant challenged the validity of the judgment on the ground that California's assertion of jurisdiction violated the Due Process Clause of the Fourteenth Amendment. The U.S. Supreme Court sustained the validity of the California judgment. The Court held that

> [i]t is sufficient for purposes of due process that the suit was based on a contract which had substantial connection with that State.... The contract was delivered in California, the premiums were mailed from there and the insured was a resident of that State when he died. It cannot be denied that California has a manifest interest in providing effective means of redress for its residents when their insurers refuse to pay claims. These residents would be at a severe disadvantage if they were forced to follow the insurance company to a distant State in order to hold it legally accountable. When claims were small or moderate individual claimants frequently could not afford the cost of bringing an action in a foreign forum—thus in effect making the company judgment proof. Often the crucial witnesses—as here on the company's defense of suicide—will be found in the insured's locality. Of course there may be inconvenience to the insurer if it is held amenable to suit in California where it had this contract but certainly nothing which amounts to a denial of due process.

Id. at 223–24.

Significantly, the Court upheld jurisdiction on the basis of the *single* contract of reinsurance issued by the defendant. The Court expressly noted that "[i]t appears that neither Empire Mutual nor respondent has ever had any office or agent in California. And so far as the record before us shows, respondent has never solicited or done any insurance business in California apart from the policy involved here." *Id.* at 223.

The *Hanson* Case (1958). In *Hanson v. Denckla,* 357 U.S. 235 (1958), Mrs. Dora Donner, a Pennsylvania resident, established a financial trust for certain of her assets in 1935. She named the Wilmington Trust Co., of Wilmington, Delaware, as trustee. Under the terms of the trust, Mrs. Donner was to receive the income from the trust assets during her lifetime. Upon her death, the trust assets were to pass to whomever she specified—either by "appointment" during her lifetime or by her will at death. Mrs. Donner subsequently moved to Florida in 1944 and became domiciled there. She executed a will in Florida in 1949 and died there in 1952.

Mrs. Donner had three daughters. At the time the will was executed, Mrs. Donner also executed two powers of appointment from the Delaware trust for $200,000 each to two children of one her daughters, Elizabeth Hanson, effective upon Mrs. Donner's death. Mrs. Donner allowed the remainder of the trust (about one million dollars) to pass through the "residuary clause" of her will to her two other daughters, Katherine Denckla and Dorothy Stewart. If the powers of appointment executed by Mrs. Donner were void, however, Katherine Denckla and Dorothy Stewart would receive all of the assets of trust under the "residuary clause" of Mrs. Donner's will.

Katherine Denckla and Dorothy Stewart sought a declaratory judgment from a Florida court that the powers of appointment were testamentary in nature and, therefore, void because they had been not executed with the necessary formalities under Florida law. The defendants in this action moved to dismiss on the ground that the court lacked personal jurisdiction over certain nonresident indispensable parties, including the Wilmington Trust Co., the Delaware trustee. The Florida trial court held that it lacked personal jurisdiction over these parties. Nevertheless, the court held the powers of appointment void as to the parties before it. The Florida Supreme Court agreed the powers of appointment were void, but held the court did have personal jurisdiction over the nonresidents based on its power to construe the will. This judgment was appealed to the U.S. Supreme Court.

After the Florida litigation had commenced, but before the lower Florida court rendered its decree, a declaratory judgment action was instituted in Delaware to determine who was entitled to participate in the trust assets located in that state. The parties were essentially the same as in the Florida litigation, but were reversed, with the Florida defendants as the plaintiffs in the Delaware action. The Delaware trial court held the trust and the powers of appointment valid under Delaware law. The Delaware action was on appeal when the Florida Supreme Court made its decision. The defendants in the Delaware action moved the Delaware Supreme Court to remand the action on the ground that the Florida decree had to be given full faith and credit. The Delaware Supreme Court rejected this conclusion on the ground that the Florida courts did not have personal jurisdiction over the nonresident defendants, including the Delaware trustee.

The U.S. Supreme Court granted certiorari to review the decision and consolidated the Florida and Delaware cases. Ultimately, the Court held that the Florida judgment was void because the Florida courts did not have personal jurisdiction over the Delaware trustee consistent with the Due Process Clause of the Fourteenth Amendment. Under the applicable law, the Wilmington Trust Co., as trustee, was considered an indispensable party to any litigation involving the validity of the trust. Without jurisdiction over the Delaware trustee, therefore, the Florida court was without jurisdiction to determine the validity of the trust. The Court first rejected the ability of Florida to exercise jurisdiction on an in rem basis because the trust assets were located in Delaware. *See id.* at 246–50. Then the Court turned to the question of in personam jurisdiction over the Delaware trustee. The Court seemed to hold the "minimum contacts" test was only relevant to the in personam category of jurisdiction:

> Appellees' stronger argument is for *in personam* jurisdiction over the Delaware trustee. They urge that the circumstances of this case amount to sufficient affiliation with the State of Florida to empower its courts to exercise personal jurisdiction over this nonresident defendant. Principal reliance is placed upon *McGee v. International Life Insurance Co....* In *McGee* the Court noted the trend of expanding personal jurisdiction over nonresidents. As technological progress has increased the flow of commerce between States, the need for jurisdiction over nonresidents has undergone a similar increase. At the same time, progress in communications and transportation has made the defense of a suit in a foreign tribunal less burdensome. In response to these changes, the requirements for personal jurisdiction over nonresidents have evolved from the rigid rule of *Pennoyer* ... to the flexible standard of *International Shoe....* But it is a mistake to assume that this trend heralds the eventual demise of all restrictions on the personal jurisdiction of state courts.... Those restrictions are more than a guarantee of immunity from inconvenient or distant litigation. They are a consequence of territorial limitations on the power of the respective States. However minimal the burden of defending in a foreign tribunal, a defendant may not be called

upon to do so unless he has had the "minimal contacts" with that State that are a prerequisite to its exercise of power over him.…

We fail to find such contacts in the circumstances of this case.… The cause of action in this case is not one that arises out of an act done or transaction consummated in the forum State.… From Florida Mrs. Donner carried on several bits of trust administration that may be compared to the mailing of premiums in *McGee.* But the record discloses no instance in which the *trustee* performed any acts in Florida that bear the same relationship to the agreement as the solicitation in *McGee.* Consequently, this suit cannot be said to be one to enforce an obligation that arose from a privilege the defendant exercised in Florida.…

The execution in Florida of the powers of appointment under which the beneficiaries and appointees claim does not give Florida a substantial connection with the contract on which this suit is based.… The unilateral activity of those who claim some relationship with a nonresident defendant cannot satisfy the requirement of contact with the forum State. The application of that rule will vary with the quality and nature of the defendant's activity, but it is essential in each case that there be some act by which the defendant purposefully avails itself of the privilege of conducting activities within the forum State, thus invoking the benefits and protections of its laws.… The settlor's execution in Florida of her power of appointment cannot remedy the absence of such an act in this case.

Notes and Questions

1. The structure and language of the opinion in the *Hanson* case are clearly different from that of *Mullane* and *McGee.* In *Mullane,* especially, the Court rejected the use of the in rem and in personam categories as analytical tools. On the other hand, *Hanson* seems to suggest that the presence of property within a state would still be a proper basis for exercising jurisdiction to adjudicate.

2. In both *Mullane* and *McGee,* the U.S. Supreme Court emphasized the state's interest in asserting jurisdiction over nonresidents under the circumstances of the cases. However, the Due Process Clause is designed to protect the defendant's opportunity to be heard in defense. How does evaluating the state's interest as part of the due process inquiry contribute to that goal?

3. Given that all activities that were possible for the corporation to carry on were being conducted in Ohio, could there be any doubt that Ohio could constitutionally assert personal jurisdiction over the corporation in the *Perkins* case?

4. In Rem and Quasi in Rem Jurisdiction after *International Shoe*

As explained in *Pennoyer v. Neff* and the material in section A(3)(a), above, the traditional territorial rules of jurisdiction distinguished between *in rem* and *in personam* jurisdiction. In order for a court to validly adjudicate a claim against a defendant, the court needed either jurisdiction over the defendant's property (*in rem*) or jurisdiction over the defendant's person (*in personam*). Under this long-established view, a court could properly adjudicate a claim involving the defendant's property under *in rem* jurisdiction, even

Important

though the court did not have any constitutionally valid basis for exercising *in personam* jurisdiction over the defendant. This long-held view came under attack in *Shaffer*.

Shaffer v. Heitner

United States Supreme Court, 1977
433 U.S. 186, 97 S. Ct. 2569, 53 L. Ed. 2d 683

JUSTICE MARSHALL delivered the opinion of the Court.

The controversy in this case concerns the constitutionality of a Delaware statute that allows a court of that State to take jurisdiction of a lawsuit by sequestering any property of the defendant that happens to be located in Delaware. Appellants contend that the sequestration statute as applied in this case violates the Due Process Clause of the Fourteenth Amendment both because it permits the state courts to exercise jurisdiction despite the absence of sufficient contacts among the defendants, the litigation, and the State of Delaware and because it authorizes the deprivation of defendants' property without providing adequate procedural safeguards. We find it necessary to consider only the first of these contentions.

. . . .

Appellee Heitner, a nonresident of Delaware, is the owner of one share of stock in the Greyhound Corp., a business incorporated under the laws of Delaware with its principal place of business in Phoenix, Ariz. On May 22, 1974, he filed a shareholder's derivative suit in the Court of Chancery for New Castle County, Del., in which he named as defendants Greyhound, its wholly owned subsidiary Greyhound Lines, Inc.,[1] and 28 present or former officers or directors of one or both of the corporations. In essence, Heitner alleged that the individual defendants had violated their duties to Greyhound by causing it and its subsidiary to engage in actions that resulted in the corporations being held liable for substantial damages in a private antitrust suit and a large fine in a criminal contempt action. The activities which led to these penalties took place in Oregon.

Simultaneously with his complaint, Heitner filed a motion for an order of sequestration of the Delaware property of the individual defendants pursuant to Del. Code Ann., tit. 10, § 366 (1975).[2] This motion was accompanied by a supporting affidavit of counsel which stated that the individual defendants were nonresidents of Delaware. The affidavit identified the property to be sequestered as

---

1. Greyhound Lines, Inc., is incorporated in California and has its principal place of business in Phoenix, Ariz.
2. Section 366 provides:

(a) If it appears in any complaint filed in the Court of Chancery that the defendant or any one or more of the defendants is a nonresident of the State, the Court may make an order directing such nonresident defendant or defendants to appear by a day certain to be designated. Such order shall be served on such nonresident defendant or defendants by mail or otherwise, if practicable, and shall be published in such manner as the Court directs, not less than once a week for 3 consecutive weeks. The Court may compel the appearance of the defendant by the seizure of all or any part of his property, which property may be sold under the order of the Court to pay the demand of the plaintiff, if the defendant does not appear, or otherwise defaults. Any defendant whose property shall have been so seized and who shall have entered a general appearance in the cause may, upon notice to the plaintiff, petition the Court for an order releasing such property or any part thereof from the seizure. The Court shall release such property unless the plaintiff shall satisfy the Court that because of other circumstances there is a reasonable possibility that such release may render it substantially less likely that plaintiff will obtain satisfaction of any judgment secured. . . .

. . . .

common stock, 3% Second Cumulative Preferred Stock and stock unit credits of the Defendant Greyhound Corporation, a Delaware corporation, as well as all options and all warrants to purchase said stock issued to said individual Defendants and all contractual [*sic*] obligations, all rights, debts or credits due or accrued to or for the benefit of any of the said Defendants under any type of written agreement, contract or other legal instrument of any kind whatever between any of the individual Defendants and said corporation.

The requested sequestration order was signed the day the motion was filed. Pursuant to that order, the sequestrator "seized" approximately 82,000 shares of Greyhound common stock belonging to 19 of the defendants, and options belonging to another 2 defendants. These seizures were accomplished by placing "stop transfer" orders or their equivalents on the books of the Greyhound Corp. So far as the record shows, none of the certificates representing the seized property was physically present in Delaware. The stock was considered to be in Delaware, and so subject to seizure, by virtue of Del. Code Ann., tit. 8, § 169 (1975), which makes Delaware the situs of ownership of all stock in Delaware corporations.[9]

All 28 defendants were notified of the initiation of the suit by certified mail directed to their last known addresses and by publication in a New Castle County newspaper. The 21 defendants whose property was seized (hereafter referred to as appellants) responded by entering a special appearance for the purpose of moving to quash service of process and to vacate the sequestration order.... [A]ppellants asserted that under the rule of *International Shoe Co. v. Washington*..., they did not have sufficient contacts with Delaware to sustain the jurisdiction of that State's courts.

The Court of Chancery rejected [this argument] in a letter opinion which emphasized the purpose of the Delaware sequestration procedure:

> The primary purpose of "sequestration" as authorized by 10 *Del. Ch.* § 366 is not to secure possession of property pending a trial between resident debtors and creditors on the issue of who has the right to retain it. On the contrary, as here employed, "sequestration" is a process used to compel the personal appearance of a nonresident defendant to answer and defend a suit brought against him in a court of equity.... It is accomplished by the appointment of a sequestrator by this Court to seize and hold property of the nonresident located in this State subject to further Court order. If the defendant enters a general appearance, the sequestered property is routinely released, unless the plaintiff makes special application to continue its seizure, in which event the plaintiff has the burden of proof and persuasion.... ... [T]he court held that the statutory Delaware situs of the stock provided a sufficient basis for the exercise of *quasi in rem* jurisdiction by a Delaware court....

On appeal, the Delaware Supreme Court affirmed the judgment of the Court of Chancery....

Appellants' claim that the Delaware courts did not have jurisdiction to adjudicate this action received ... cursory treatment. The court's analysis of the jurisdictional issue is contained in two paragraphs:

---

9. Section 169 provides:
   For all purposes of title, action, attachment, garnishment and jurisdiction of all courts held in this State, but not for the purpose of taxation, the situs of the ownership of the capital stock of all corporations existing under the laws of this State, whether organized under this chapter or otherwise, shall be regarded as in this State.

There are significant constitutional questions at issue here but we say at once that we do not deem the rule of *International Shoe* to be one of them.... The reason, of course, is that jurisdiction under § 366 remains ... *quasi in rem* founded on the presence of capital stock here, not on prior contact by defendants with this forum. Under 8 Del. C. § 169 the "situs of the ownership of the capital stock of all corporations existing under the laws of this State ... [is] in this State," and that provides the initial basis for jurisdiction. Delaware may constitutionally establish situs of such shares here, ... it has done so and the presence thereof provides the foundation for § 366 in this case....

We hold that seizure of the Greyhound shares is not invalid because plaintiff has failed to meet the prior contacts tests of *International Shoe*....

Supreme Court [We noted probable jurisdiction.... We reverse.]

....

The Delaware courts rejected appellants' jurisdictional challenge by noting that this suit was brought as a *quasi in rem* proceeding. Since *quasi in rem* jurisdiction is traditionally based on attachment or seizure of property present in the jurisdiction, not on contacts between the defendant and the State, the courts considered appellants' claimed lack of contacts with Delaware to be unimportant. This categorical analysis assumes the continued soundness of the conceptual structure founded on the century-old case of *Pennoyer v. Neff*, 95 U.S. 714 (1878).

....

From our perspective, the importance of *Pennoyer* is not its result, but the fact that its principles and corollaries derived from them became the basic elements of the constitutional doctrine governing state-court jurisdiction.... As we have noted, under *Pennoyer* state authority to adjudicate was based on the jurisdiction's power over either persons or property. This fundamental concept is embodied in the very vocabulary which we use to describe judgments. If a court's jurisdiction is based on its authority over the defendant's person, the action and judgment are denominated "*in personam*" and can impose a personal obligation on the defendant in favor of the plaintiff. If jurisdiction is based on the court's power over property within its territory, the action is called "*in rem*" or "*quasi in rem*." The effect of a judgment in such a case is limited to the property that supports jurisdiction and does not impose a personal liability on the property owner, since he is not before the court.[17] In *Pennoyer's* terms, the owner is affected only "indirectly" by an *in rem* judgment adverse to his interest in the property subject to the court's disposition.

By concluding that "[t]he authority of every tribunal is necessarily restricted by the territorial limits of the State in which it is established," ... *Pennoyer* sharply limited the availability of *in personam* jurisdiction over defendants not resident in the forum State. If a nonresident defendant could not be found in a State, he could not be sued there. On the other hand, since the State in which property was located was considered to

---

17. A judgment *in rem* affects the interests of all persons in designated property. A judgment *quasi in rem* affects the interests of particular persons in designated property. The latter is of two types. In one the plaintiff is seeking to secure a pre-existing claim in the subject property and to extinguish or establish the nonexistence of similar interests of particular persons. In the other the plaintiff seeks to apply what he concedes to be the property of the defendant to the satisfaction of a claim against him. Restatement, Judgments, 5–9. *Hanson v. Denckla*, 357 U.S. 235, 246 n.12 (1958). As did the Court in *Hanson*, we will for convenience generally use the term "*in rem*" in place of "*in rem* and *quasi in rem*."

have exclusive sovereignty over that property, *in rem* actions could proceed regardless of the owner's location. Indeed, since a State's process could not reach beyond its borders, this Court held after *Pennoyer* that due process did not require any effort to give a property owner personal notice that his property was involved in an *in rem* proceeding....

The *Pennoyer* rules generally favored nonresident defendants by making them harder to sue. This advantage was reduced, however, by the ability of a resident plaintiff to satisfy a claim against a nonresident defendant by bringing into court any property of the defendant located in the plaintiff's State....

Pennoyer itself recognized that its rigid categories, ... could not accommodate some necessary litigation. Accordingly, Justice Field's opinion carefully noted that cases involving the personal status of the plaintiff, such as divorce actions, could be adjudicated in the plaintiff's home State even though the defendant could not be served within that State.... Similarly, the opinion approved the practice of considering a foreign corporation doing business in a State to have consented to being sued in that State.... This basis for *in personam* jurisdiction over foreign corporations was later supplemented by the doctrine that a corporation doing business in a State could be deemed "present" in the State, and so subject to service of process under the rule of *Pennoyer*....

The advent of automobiles, with the concomitant increase in the incidence of individuals causing injury in States where they were not subject to *in personam* actions under *Pennoyer*, required further moderation of the territorial limits on jurisdictional power. This modification, like the accommodation to the realities of interstate corporate activities, was accomplished by use of a legal fiction that left the conceptual structure established in *Pennoyer* theoretically unaltered.... The fiction used was that the out-of-state motorist, who it was assumed could be excluded altogether from the State's highways, had by using those highways appointed a designated state official as his agent to accept process.... Since the motorist's "agent" could be personally served within the State, the state courts could obtain *in personam* jurisdiction over the nonresident driver.

The motorists' consent theory was easy to administer since it required only a finding that the out-of-state driver had used the State's roads. By contrast, both the fictions of implied consent to service on the part of a foreign corporation and of corporate presence required a finding that the corporation was "doing business" in the forum State. Defining the criteria for making that finding and deciding whether they were met absorbed much judicial energy.... While the essentially quantitative tests which emerged from these cases purported simply to identify circumstances under which presence or consent could be attributed to the corporation, it became clear that they were in fact attempting to ascertain "what dealings make it just to subject a foreign corporation to local suit." ... In *International Shoe*, we acknowledged that fact.

....

[T]he relationship among the defendant, the forum, and the litigation, rather than the mutually exclusive sovereignty of the States on which the rules of *Pennoyer* rest, became the central concern of the inquiry into personal jurisdiction.[20] The immediate ef-

---

20. Nothing in *Hanson v. Denckla*, 357 U.S. 235 (1958), is to the contrary. The *Hanson* Court's statement that restrictions on state jurisdiction "are a consequence of territorial limitations on the power of the respective States," ... simply makes the point that the States are defined by their geographical territory. After making this point, the Court in *Hanson* determined that the defendant over which personal jurisdiction was claimed had not committed any acts sufficiently connected to the State to justify jurisdiction under the *International Shoe* standard.

fect of this departure from *Pennoyer's* conceptual apparatus was to increase the ability of the state courts to obtain personal jurisdiction over nonresident defendants....

No equally dramatic change has occurred in the law governing jurisdiction *in rem*. There have, however, been intimations that the collapse of the *in personam* wing of *Pennoyer* has not left that decision unweakened as a foundation for *in rem* jurisdiction. Well-reasoned lower court opinions have questioned the proposition that the presence of property in a State gives that State jurisdiction to adjudicate rights to the property regardless of the relationship of the underlying dispute and the property owner to the forum.... The overwhelming majority of commentators have also rejected *Pennoyer's* premise that a proceeding "against" property is not a proceeding against the owners of that property. Accordingly, they urge that the "traditional notions of fair play and substantial justice" that govern a State's power to adjudicate *in personam* should also govern its power to adjudicate personal rights to property located in the State....

Although this Court has not addressed this argument directly, we have held that property cannot be subjected to a court's judgment unless reasonable and appropriate efforts have been made to give the property owners actual notice of the action.... This conclusion recognizes, contrary to *Pennoyer*, that an adverse judgment *in rem* directly affects the property owner by divesting him of his rights in the property before the court.... Moreover, ... we [have] held that Fourteenth Amendment rights cannot depend on the classification of an action as *in rem* or *in personam*, since that is

> a classification for which the standards are so elusive and confused generally and which, being primarily for state courts to define, may and do vary from state to state....

It is clear, therefore, that the law of state-court jurisdiction no longer stands securely on the foundation established in *Pennoyer*. We think that the time is ripe to consider whether the standard of fairness and substantial justice set forth in *International Shoe* should be held to govern actions *in rem* as well as *in personam*.

....

The case for applying to jurisdiction *in rem* the same test of "fair play and substantial justice" as governs assertions of jurisdiction *in personam* is simple and straightforward. It is premised on recognition that "[t]he phrase, 'judicial jurisdiction over a thing,' is a customary elliptical way of referring to jurisdiction over the interests of persons in a thing." Restatement (Second) of Conflict of Laws § 56, Introductory Note (1971) (hereinafter Restatement). This recognition leads to the conclusion that in order to justify an exercise of jurisdiction *in rem*, the basis for jurisdiction must be sufficient to justify exercising "jurisdiction over the interests of persons in a thing." The standard for determining whether an exercise of jurisdiction over the interests of persons is consistent with the Due Process Clause is the minimum-contacts standard elucidated in *International Shoe*.

This argument, of course, does not ignore the fact that the presence of property in a State may bear on the existence of jurisdiction by providing contacts among the forum State, the defendant, and the litigation. For example, when claims to the property itself are the source of the underlying controversy between the plaintiff and the defendant,[24] it would be unusual for the State where the property is located not to have jurisdiction. In such cases, the defendant's claim to property located in the State would normally[25] indi-

---

24. This category includes true *in rem* actions and the first type of *quasi in rem* proceedings....

25. In some circumstances the presence of property in the forum State will not support the inference suggested in text. *Cf., e.g., Restatement (Second) of Conflict of Laws* § 60, cmt. c ["*Limitations upon exercise of jurisdiction—chattel brought into state by fraud or for use in judicial proceedings. A state will*

In Rem change?

cate that he expected to benefit from the State's protection of his interest. The State's strong interests in assuring the marketability of property within its borders and in providing a procedure for peaceful resolution of disputes about the possession of that property would also support jurisdiction, as would the likelihood that important records and witnesses will be found in the State. The presence of property may also favor jurisdiction in cases, such as suits for injury suffered on the land of an absentee owner, where the defendant's ownership of the property is conceded but the cause of action is otherwise related to rights and duties growing out of that ownership.

It appears, therefore, that jurisdiction over many types of actions which now are or might be brought *in rem* would not be affected by a holding that any assertion of state-court jurisdiction must satisfy the *International Shoe* standard.[30] For the type of *quasi in rem* action typified by *Harris v. Balk* and the present case, however, accepting the proposed analysis would result in significant change. These are cases where the property which now serves as the basis for state-court jurisdiction is completely unrelated to the plaintiff's cause of action. Thus, although the presence of the defendant's property in a State might suggest the existence of other ties among the defendant, the State, and the litigation, the presence of the property alone would not support the State's jurisdiction. If those other ties did not exist, cases over which the State is now thought to have jurisdiction could not be brought in that forum.

Since acceptance of the *International Shoe* test would most affect this class of cases, we examine the arguments against adopting that standard as they relate to this category of litigation. Before doing so, however, we note that this type of case also presents the clearest illustration of the argument in favor of assessing assertions of jurisdiction by a single standard. For in cases such as *Harris* and this one, the only role played by the property is to provide the basis for bringing the defendant into court. Indeed, the express purpose of the Delaware sequestration procedure is to compel the defendant to enter a personal appearance. In such cases, if a direct assertion of personal jurisdiction over the defendant would violate the Constitution, it would seem that an indirect assertion of that jurisdiction should be equally impermissible.

The primary rationale for treating the presence of property as a sufficient basis for jurisdiction to adjudicate claims over which the State would not have jurisdiction if *International Shoe* applied is that a wrongdoer

> should not be able to avoid payment of his obligations by the expedient of removing his assets to a place where he is not subject to an in personam suit....

... This justification, however, does not explain why jurisdiction should be recognized without regard to whether the property is present in the State because of an effort to avoid

---

not usually exercise judicial jurisdiction to affect interests in a chattel which the owner has been induced by fraud of the plaintiff to send into the state, or which the owner has allowed to be sent into the state to be used as evidence in a judicial proceeding, unless and until the owner has had a reasonable opportunity to remove the chattel, or has otherwise waived the exemption...."] & cmt. d ["*Limitations upon exercise of jurisdiction—chattel brought into state without consent of owner*. A state will not usually exercise judicial jurisdiction to affect interests in a chattel brought into its territory without the consent of the owner unless and until the owner has had a reasonable opportunity to remove the chattel, or has otherwise waived the exemption...."] (1971); Note, *The Power of a State to Affect Title in a Chattel Atypically Removed to It*, 47 Colum. L. Rev. 767 (1947).

30. *Cf.* Smit, *The Enduring Utility of In Rem Rules: A Lasting Legacy of* Pennoyer v. Neff, 43 Brook. L. Rev. 600 (1977). We do not suggest that jurisdictional doctrines other than those discussed in text, such as the particularized rules governing adjudications of status, are inconsistent with the standard of fairness....

the owner's obligations. Nor does it support jurisdiction to adjudicate the underlying claim. At most, it suggests that a State in which property is located should have jurisdiction to attach that property, by use of proper procedures, as security for a judgment being sought in a forum where the litigation can be maintained consistently with *International Shoe....* Moreover, we know of nothing to justify the assumption that a debtor can avoid paying his obligations by removing his property to a State in which his creditor cannot obtain personal jurisdiction over him. The Full Faith and Credit Clause, after all, makes the valid *in personam* judgment of one State enforceable in all other States.[36]

It might also be suggested that allowing *in rem* jurisdiction avoids the uncertainty inherent in the *International Shoe* standard and assures a plaintiff of a forum.[37] ... We believe, however, that the fairness standard of *International Shoe* can be easily applied in the vast majority of cases. Moreover, when the existence of jurisdiction in a particular forum under *International Shoe* is unclear, the cost of simplifying the litigation by avoiding the jurisdictional question may be the sacrifice of "fair play and substantial justice." That cost is too high.

We are left, then, to consider the significance of the long history of jurisdiction based solely on the presence of property in a State. Although the theory that territorial power is both essential to and sufficient for jurisdiction has been undermined, we have never held that the presence of property in a State does not automatically confer jurisdiction over the owner's interest in that property. This history must be considered as supporting the proposition that jurisdiction based solely on the presence of property satisfies the demands of due process, ... but it is not decisive. "[T]raditional notions of fair play and substantial justice" can be as readily offended by the perpetuation of ancient forms that are no longer justified as by the adoption of new procedures that are inconsistent with the basic values of our constitutional heritage.... The fiction that an assertion of jurisdiction over property is anything but an assertion of jurisdiction over the owner of the property supports an ancient form without substantial modern justification. Its continued acceptance would serve only to allow state-court jurisdiction that is fundamentally unfair to the defendant.

We therefore conclude that all assertions of state-court jurisdiction must be evaluated according to the standards set forth in *International Shoe* and its progeny.[39]

....

The Delaware courts based their assertion of jurisdiction in this case solely on the statutory presence of appellants' property in Delaware. Yet that property is not the subject matter of this litigation, nor is the underlying cause of action related to the property. Appellants' holdings in Greyhound do not, therefore, provide contacts with Delaware sufficient to support the jurisdiction of that State's courts over appellants. If it exists, that jurisdiction must have some other foundation.

---

36. Once it has been determined by a court of competent jurisdiction that the defendant is a debtor of the plaintiff, there would seem to be no unfairness in allowing an action to realize on that debt in a State where the defendant has property, whether or not that State would have jurisdiction to determine the existence of the debt as an original matter....

37. This case does not raise, and we therefore do not consider, the question whether the presence of a defendant's property in a State is a sufficient basis for jurisdiction when no other forum is available to the plaintiff.

39. It would not be fruitful for us to re-examine the facts of cases decided on the rationales of *Pennoyer* and *Harris* to determine whether jurisdiction might have been sustained under the standard we adopt today. To the extent that prior decisions are inconsistent with this standard, they are overruled.

Appellee Heitner did not allege and does not now claim that appellants have ever set foot in Delaware. Nor does he identify any act related to his cause of action as having taken place in Delaware. Nevertheless, he contends that appellants' positions as directors and officers of a corporation chartered in Delaware provide sufficient "contacts, ties, or relations" ... with that State to give its courts jurisdiction over appellants in this stockholder's derivative action. This argument is based primarily on what Heitner asserts to be the strong interest of Delaware in supervising the management of a Delaware corporation. That interest is said to derive from the role of Delaware law in establishing the corporation and defining the obligations owed to it by its officers and directors. In order to protect this interest, appellee concludes, Delaware's courts must have jurisdiction over corporate fiduciaries such as appellants.

This argument is undercut by the failure of the Delaware Legislature to assert the state interest appellee finds so compelling. Delaware law bases jurisdiction, not on appellants' status as corporate fiduciaries, but rather on the presence of their property in the State. Although the sequestration procedure used here may be most frequently used in derivative suits against officers and directors ... the authorizing statute evinces no specific concern with such actions. Sequestration can be used in any suit against a nonresident ... and reaches corporate fiduciaries only if they happen to own interests in a Delaware corporation, or other property in the State. But as Heitner's failure to secure jurisdiction over seven of the defendants named in his complaint demonstrates, there is no necessary relationship between holding a position as a corporate fiduciary and owning stock or other interests in the corporation.[43] If Delaware perceived its interest in securing jurisdiction over corporate fiduciaries to be as great as Heitner suggests, we would expect it to have enacted a statute more clearly designed to protect that interest.

Moreover, even if Heitner's assessment of the importance of Delaware's interest is accepted, his argument fails to demonstrate that Delaware is a fair forum for this litigation. The interest appellee has identified may support the application of Delaware law to resolve any controversy over appellants' actions in their capacities as officers and directors. But we have rejected the argument that if a State's law can properly be applied to a dispute, its courts necessarily have jurisdiction over the parties to that dispute....

Appellee suggests that by accepting positions as officers or directors of a Delaware corporation, appellants performed the acts required by *Hanson v. Denckla*. He notes that Delaware law provides substantial benefits to corporate officers and directors, and that these benefits were at least in part the incentive for appellants to assume their positions. It is, he says, "only fair and just" to require appellants, in return for these benefits, to respond in the State of Delaware when they are accused of misusing their power....

But like Heitner's first argument, this line of reasoning establishes only that it is appropriate for Delaware law to govern the obligations of appellants to Greyhound and its stockholders. It does not demonstrate that appellants have "purposefully avail[ed themselves] of the privilege of conducting activities within the forum State" ... in a way that would justify bringing them before a Delaware tribunal. Appellants have simply had nothing to do with the State of Delaware. Moreover, appellants had no reason to expect to be haled before a Delaware court. Delaware, unlike some States,[47] has not enacted a statute

---

43. Delaware does not require directors to own stock. Del. Code Ann., tit. 8, §141(b) (Supp. 1976).

47. *See, e.g.,* Conn. Gen. Stat. Rev. §33-322 (1976); N.C. Gen. Stat. §55-33 (1975); S.C. Code Ann. §33-5-70 (1977).

that treats acceptance of a directorship as consent to jurisdiction in the State. And "[i]t strains reason ... to suggest that anyone buying securities in a corporation formed in Delaware 'impliedly consents' to subject himself to Delaware's ... jurisdiction on any cause of action." ... Appellants, who were not required to acquire interests in Greyhound in order to hold their positions, did not by acquiring those interests surrender their right to be brought to judgment only in States with which they had had "minimum contacts."

> The Due Process Clause
>
> does not contemplate that a state may make binding a judgment ... against an individual or corporate defendant with which the state has no contacts, ties, or relations.

International Shoe Co. v. Washington. ... Delaware's assertion of jurisdiction over appellants in this case is inconsistent with that constitutional limitation on state power. The judgment of the Delaware Supreme Court must, therefore, be reversed.

> *It is so ordered.*

Justice Rehnquist took no part in the consideration or decision of this case.

[Justice Powell's concurring opinion is omitted. Justice Brennan's opinion, in which he concurred in part and dissented in part, is also omitted. Justice Stevens' concurring opinion is also omitted.]

Notes and Questions

1. With respect to the constitutional power of a state to adjudicate claims *directly relating* to property located within its borders, *Shaffer* was careful to emphasize that "it would be unusual for the State where the property is located not to have jurisdiction." In such cases, even if the defendant has no contacts with the state other than the assertion of a claim to the property, wouldn't that claim alone normally suffice to satisfy any due process concerns?

2. With respect to the state's power to adjudicate claims that are *unrelated* to the defendant's property, however, the Court was clear that attachment of the property alone can no longer establish quasi in rem jurisdiction to adjudicate an unrelated claim against the defendant, unless there is also a constitutionally valid basis for asserting *personal* jurisdiction over the defendant with respect to that claim. As a practical matter, though, if the plaintiff can acquire personal jurisdiction over the defendant, then there is no need to seek quasi in rem jurisdiction because the plaintiff can now recover a full judgment against the defendant, and not one that would be limited solely to the value of the attached property, as allowed under quasi in rem jurisdiction. Of course, as the Court noted, the plaintiff could still attach the defendant's property as security for enforcing the judgment being sought.

3. Could a state's quasi in rem statute ever be useful in acquiring jurisdiction after *Shaffer*? Recall from the discussion of state long-arm statutes in section B(2), above, that while some state statutes provide for long-arm jurisdiction to the fullest extent allowed under the U.S. Constitution, other states have specifically defined long-arm statutes. Suppose that a defendant's contacts with a state are sufficient to provide a *constitutional* basis for asserting personal jurisdiction, but the state's long-arm statute does not reach the defendant's actions, thus preventing the court's assertion of personal jurisdiction over the defendant. Because a *constitutional* basis for asserting personal jurisdiction over the defendant exists, however, if the defendant owns property in the state and the state has a statute

[handwritten note in margin:] Exam

[handwritten note at bottom:] you need const basis to state's long arm statute

that allows for quasi in rem jurisdiction based on the attachment of in-state property, then quasi in rem jurisdiction could be asserted in this case consistent with *Shaffer*.✻

4. (a) Before *Shaffer*, some states, following the lead of the New York case, *Seider v. Roth*, 216 N.E.2d 312 (N.Y. 1966), had approved of a form of quasi in rem jurisdiction in automobile accident cases against insured defendants. In states permitting it, plaintiffs would garnish the obligation of the defendant's insurance company to defend and indemnify the defendant. In this way, the plaintiff could bring the action in any state in which the insurance company was doing business and, as a consequence, subject to personal jurisdiction. The theory of the cases was based on *Harris v. Balk*, discussed in section A(3)*(a)*, above. The states approving of *Seider*-type jurisdiction obviously assumed that *Harris* survived *International Shoe*. *Seider* jurisdiction was limited in important ways to assure its constitutionality. The judgment in a *Seider* action was limited to the face amount of the insurance policy, the defendant had the right to a limited appearance, and the plaintiff either had to live in the forum state or the claim had to arise there. These restrictions made *Seider* jurisdiction look much like a direct action against the insurance company, which some states have authorized by statute. Thus, even after *Shaffer*, there was reason to believe that *Seider* jurisdiction would be held valid.

(b) In 1980, however, the U.S. Supreme Court held in *Rush v. Savchuk*, 444 U.S. 320 (1980), that *Seider* actions were not the equivalent of direct actions against insurers. The Court held the state's ability to exercise jurisdiction over the insured was "analytically prerequisite" to the insurer's entry into the case. In addition, the Court held an assumption that the insured did not have a real stake in the case was "far from self-evident," citing (i) the potential impact on the insured when multiple plaintiffs sued in different states for an aggregate amount in excess of the policy limits; (ii) the potential impact an adverse decision might have on the defendant's insurability; and (iii) the potential noneconomic impact that might occur in professional malpractice actions in which the insured's professional competence and integrity are questioned. *See id.* at 331 n.20. Note, however, that none of these "impacts" on the insured were present in *Rush*.

5. *Shaffer* and *Rush* do not exhaust the constitutional restrictions on a state's ability to authorize provisional remedies against a defendant. Those cases concern only due process restrictions on state power to use the remedies as jurisdictional substitutes for contacts between the defendant and the state. Other due process limitations on provisional remedies also exist in the form of restrictions on the state's ability to authorize seizure of property without a hearing. These restrictions are discussed in section E, below.

6. After *Rush*, can you make an argument that a state direct action statute that allows a plaintiff to sue an insurance company for a tort committed by its insured in another state would be unconstitutional? Assume for the purposes of this problem the insured has no contacts with the forum other than the fact that its insurance company is doing business there.

7. After *Shaffer* was decided, Delaware enacted a statute providing that acceptance of a directorship in a Delaware corporation or the continuance in such a directorship would be deemed consent to appointment of the corporation's registered agent as the director's agent for service of process in an action like *Shaffer*. *See* Del. Code Ann. tit. 10, § 3114 (Supp. 2012). Assume that a suit exactly like *Shaffer* arises after the effective date of this statute. Should an assertion of jurisdiction by a Delaware court under the statute be constitutional?

5. Further Refinement of the "Minimum Contacts" Test

Following *Shaffer*, the U.S. Supreme Court decided a series of cases from 1978 to 1984 that further defined how the "minimum contacts" test should be applied in various contexts from child support actions to products liability and defamation.

The *Kulko* Case (1978). In *Kulko v. Superior Court*, 436 U.S. 84 (1978), Ezra and Sharon Kulko, who were living in New York, decided to divorce. The couple entered into a separation agreement, which provided that the couple's two children, Darwin and Ilsa, would live with the father a in New York during the school year, but would spend Christmas, Easter, and summer vacations with the mother in California, where she had relocated. The agreement provided that the father would pay $3,000 per year in child support for the time the children lived with the mother in California. The mother acquired a Haitian divorce which incorporated the terms of this separation agreement. Subsequently, each of the children expressed a desire to live with the mother permanently in California, and the father acquiesced.

The mother sued the father in a California state court to establish the Haitian divorce as a California judgment, to modify the judgment to award her custody, and to increase the support obligations of the father. The father was served with long-arm process under the general California long-arm statute described in section B(2), above. The father specially appeared to challenge the jurisdiction of the California courts under the Due Process Clause. The California Supreme Court upheld the assertion of personal jurisdiction. *Id.* at 86–90.

The U.S. Supreme Court reversed. The Court held California could not constitutionally assert jurisdiction over the father on the basis of the acts he had performed. The Court began its analysis by reiterating the core holding of *Hanson v. Denckla* that "[t]he unilateral activity of those who claim some relationship with a nonresident defendant cannot satisfy the requirements of contact with the forum State.... [I]t is essential in each case that there be some act by which the defendant purposefully avails [him]self of the privilege of conducting activities within the forum State...." *Id.* at 93–94. In this regard, the Court stated that

> We cannot accept the proposition that [the father's] acquiescence in [his daughter's] desire to live with her mother conferred jurisdiction over [the father] in the California courts in this action. A father who agrees, in the interests of family harmony and his children's preferences, to allow them to spend more time in California than was required under a separation agreement can hardly be said to have "purposefully availed himself" of the "benefits and protections" of California's laws. *See Shaffer v. Heitner....*[7]

> Nor can we agree with the assertion of the court below that the exercise of *in personam* jurisdiction here was warranted by the financial benefit [the father] derived from his daughter's presence in California for nine months of the year. This argument rests on the premise that, while [the father's] liability for sup-

---

7. The court below stated that the presence in California of [the father's] daughter gave appellant the benefit of California's "police and fire protection, its school system, its hospital services, its recreational facilities, its libraries and museums...." But, in the circumstances presented here, these services provided by the State were essentially benefits to the child, not the father, and in any event were not benefits that appellant purposefully sought for himself.

port payments remained unchanged, his yearly expenses for supporting the child in New York decreased. But this circumstance, even if true, does not support California's assertion of jurisdiction here. Any diminution in [his] household costs resulted, not from the child's presence in California, but rather from her absence from [his] home. Moreover, an action by [the mother] to increase support payments could now be brought, and could have been brought when [his daughter] first moved to California, in the State of New York; a New York court would clearly have personal jurisdiction over appellant and, if a judgment were entered by a New York court increasing [his] child-support obligations, it could properly be enforced against him in both New York and California. Any ultimate financial advantage to [the father] thus results not from the child's presence in California, but from [the mother's] failure earlier to seek an increase in payments under the separation agreement. The argument below to the contrary, in our view, confuses the question of [the father's] liability with that of the proper forum in which to determine that liability.

....

In seeking to justify the burden that would be imposed on appellant were the exercise of *in personam* jurisdiction in California sustained, [the mother] argues that California has substantial interests in protecting the welfare of its minor residents and in promoting to the fullest extent possible a healthy and supportive family environment in which the children of the State are to be raised. These interests are unquestionably important. But while the presence of the children and one parent in California arguably might favor application of California law in a lawsuit in New York, the fact that California may be the "center of gravity" for choice-of-law purposes does not mean that California has personal jurisdiction over the defendant. *Hanson v. Denckla....* And California has not attempted to assert any particularized interest in trying such cases in its courts by, *e.g.*, enacting a special jurisdictional statute. *Cf. McGee v. International Life Ins. Co....* California's legitimate interest in ensuring the support of children resident in California without unduly disrupting the children's lives, moreover, is already being served by the State's participation in the Revised Uniform Reciprocal Enforcement of Support Act of 1968. This statute provides a mechanism for communication between court systems in different States, in order to facilitate the procurement and enforcement of child-support decrees where the dependent children reside in a State that cannot obtain personal jurisdiction over the defendant. California's version of the Act essentially permits a California resident claiming support from a nonresident to file a petition in California and have its merits adjudicated in the State of the alleged obligor's residence, without either party's having to leave his or her own State.... New York State is a signatory to a similar Act.

In light of our conclusion that appellant did not purposefully derive benefit from any activities relating to the State of California, it is apparent that the California Supreme Court's reliance on appellant's having caused an "effect" in California was misplaced.... This "effects" test is derived from the American Law Institute's *Restatement (Second) of Conflict of Laws* § 37 (1971), which provides: "A state has power to exercise judicial jurisdiction over an individual who causes effects in the state by an act done elsewhere with respect to any cause of action arising from these effects unless the nature of the effects and of the individual's relationship to the state make the exercise of such jurisdiction unreasonable."

While this provision is not binding on this Court, it does not in any event support the decision below. As is apparent from the examples accompanying § 37 in the *Restatement*, this section was intended to reach wrongful activity outside of the State causing injury within the State, *see, e.g.*, cmt. *a* (shooting bullet from one State into another), or commercial activity affecting state residents, *id.* Even in such situations, moreover, the *Restatement* recognizes that there might be circumstances that would render "unreasonable" the assertion of jurisdiction over the nonresident defendant.

The circumstances in this case clearly render "unreasonable" California's assertion of personal jurisdiction. There is no claim that appellant has visited physical injury on either property or persons within the State of California....

Id. at 94–97.

Notes and Questions

1. Justice Brennan, with whom Justices White and Powell joined dissenting in *Kulko*, indicated that "I cannot say that the Court's determination against state-court *in personam* jurisdiction is implausible, but, though the issue is close, my independent weighing of the facts leads me to conclude, in agreement with the analysis and determination of the California Supreme Court, that appellant's connection with the State of California was not too attenuated, under the standards of reasonableness and fairness implicit in the Due Process Clause, to require him to conduct his defense in the California courts." *Id.* at 102. In what way, if any, does Justice Brennan's observation highlight the weakness of the "minimum contacts" standard articulated in *International Shoe* and subsequent cases?

2. In *Kulko*, the Court pointed out that in reaching its result, the California Supreme Court did not rely on the father's prior "glancing presence" in California. The father had been in California on only two occasions, once in 1959 for a three-day military stopover on his way to Korea and again in 1960 for a 24-hour stopover on his return from Korean service. The visits were approximately thirteen years before the subsequent controversy. In this regard, the Court commented as follows:

To hold such temporary visits to a State a basis for the assertion of *in personam* jurisdiction over unrelated actions arising in the future would make a mockery of the limitations on state jurisdiction imposed by the Fourteenth Amendment. Nor did the California court rely on the fact that appellant was actually married in California on one of his two brief visits. We agree that where two New York domiciliaries, for reasons of convenience, marry in the State of California and thereafter spend their entire married life in New York, the fact of their California marriage by itself cannot support a California court's exercise of jurisdiction over a spouse who remains a New York resident in an action relating to child support.

Id. at 92–93.

The *World-Wide* Case (1980). In *World-Wide Volkswagen Corp. v. Woodson*, the Supreme Court first addressed the application of the "minimum contacts" test in the context of a products liability action involving the so-called "stream of commerce." Unlike the situation in *International Shoe*, in which the same defendant manufactured, sold and directly shipped its product to the forum state, the "stream of commerce" refers to the flow of products through a series of multiple participants in a structured chain of distribution from manufacture to distribution to retail sale. As you read *World-Wide,* be careful to note the Court's different treatment of local distributors and retailers in contrast to manufacturers and multistate distributors. Personal jurisdiction based on the "stream of commerce" was again addressed by the Supreme Court in the *Asahi* and *McIntyre* cases, which are reprinted in section C, below.

World-Wide Volkswagen Corp. v. Woodson

United States Supreme Court, 1980
444 U.S. 286, 100 S. Ct. 559, 62 L. Ed. 2d 490

JUSTICE WHITE delivered the opinion of the court.

The issue before us is whether, consistently with the Due Process Clause of the Fourteenth Amendment, an Oklahoma court may exercise *in personam* jurisdiction over a nonresident automobile retailer and its wholesale distributor in a products-liability action, when the defendants' only connection with Oklahoma is the fact that an automobile sold in New York to New York residents became involved in an accident in Oklahoma.

    ....

Respondents Harry and Kay Robinson purchased a new Audi automobile from petitioner Seaway Volkswagen, Inc. (Seaway), in Massena, N. Y., in 1976. The following year the Robinson family, who resided in New York, left that State for a new home in Arizona. As they passed through the State of Oklahoma, another car struck their Audi in the rear, causing a fire which severely burned Kay Robinson and her two children.

The Robinsons subsequently brought a products-liability action in the District Court for Creek County, Okla., claiming that their injuries resulted from defective design and placement of the Audi's gas tank and fuel system. They joined as defendants the automobile's manufacturer, Audi NSU Auto Union Aktiengesellschaft (Audi); its importer Volkswagen of America, Inc. (Volkswagen); its regional distributor, petitioner World-Wide Volkswagen Corp. (World-Wide); and its retail dealer, petitioner Seaway. Seaway and World-Wide entered special appearances, claiming that Oklahoma's exercise of jurisdiction over them would offend the limitations on the State's jurisdiction imposed by the Due Process Clause of the Fourteenth Amendment.

The facts presented to the District Court showed that World-Wide is incorporated and has its business office in New York. It distributes vehicles, parts, and accessories, under contract with Volkswagen, to retail dealers in New York, New Jersey, and Connecticut. Seaway, one of these retail dealers, is incorporated and has its place of business in New York. Insofar as the record reveals, Seaway and World-Wide are fully independent corporations whose relations with each other and with Volkswagen and Audi are contractual only. Respondents adduced no evidence that either World-Wide or Seaway does any business in Oklahoma, ships or sells any products to or in that State, has an agent to receive process there, or purchases advertisements in any media calculated to reach Oklahoma. In fact, as respondents' counsel conceded at oral argument, ... there was no showing that any automobile sold by World-Wide or Seaway has ever entered Oklahoma with the single exception of the vehicle involved in the present case.

Despite the apparent paucity of contacts between petitioners and Oklahoma, the District Court rejected their constitutional claim and reaffirmed that ruling in denying petitioners' motion for reconsideration. Petitioners then sought a writ of prohibition in the Supreme Court of Oklahoma to restrain the District Judge, respondent Charles S. Woodson, from exercising in personam jurisdiction over them. They renewed their contention that, because they had no "minimal contacts," with the State of Oklahoma, the actions of the District Judge were in violation of their rights under the Due Process Clause.

The Supreme Court of Oklahoma denied the writ ... holding that personal jurisdiction over petitioners was authorized by Oklahoma's "long-arm" statute Okla. Stat., tit. 12, §1701.03(a)(4) (1971). Although the court noted that the proper approach was to test jurisdiction against both statutory and constitutional standards, its analysis did not distinguish these questions, probably because §1701.03(a)(4) has been interpreted as conferring jurisdiction to the limits permitted by the United States Constitution....

We granted certiorari ... to consider an important constitutional question with respect to state-court jurisdiction and to resolve a conflict between the Supreme Court of Oklahoma and the highest courts of at least four other States. We reverse.

....

The Due Process Clause of the Fourteenth Amendment limits the power of a state court to render a valid personal judgment against a nonresident defendant. *Kulko v. Superior Court*, 436 U.S. 84, 91 (1978). A judgment rendered in violation of due process is void in the rendering State and is not entitled to full faith and credit elsewhere. *Pennoyer v. Neff*, 95 U.S. 714 (1878). Due process requires that the defendant be given adequate notice of the suit, *Mullane v. Central Hanover Trust Co.*, 339 U.S. 306, 313–14 (1950), and be subject to the personal jurisdiction of the court, *International Shoe Co. v. Washington*, 326 U.S. 310 (1945). In the present case, it is not contended that notice was inadequate; the only question is whether these particular petitioners were subject to the jurisdiction of the Oklahoma courts.

As has long been settled, and as we reaffirm today, a state court may exercise personal jurisdiction over a nonresident defendant only so long as there exist "minimum contacts" between the defendant and the forum State. Id. at 316. The concept of minimum contacts, in turn, can be seen to perform two related, but distinguishable, functions. It protects the defendant against the burdens of litigating in a distant or inconvenient forum. And it acts to ensure that the States through their courts, do not reach out beyond the limits imposed on them by their status as coequal sovereigns in a federal system.

The protection against inconvenient litigation is typically described in terms of "reasonableness" or "fairness." We have said that the defendant's contacts with the forum State must be such that maintenance of the suit "does not offend 'traditional notions of fair play and substantial justice.'" *Id.* at 316, quoting *Milliken v. Meyer*, 311 U.S. 457 (1940). The relationship between the defendant and the forum must be such that it is "reasonable ... to require the corporation to defend the particular suit which is brought there." 326 U.S. at 317. Implicit in this emphasis on reasonableness is the understanding that the burden on the defendant, while always a primary concern, will in an appropriate case be considered in light of other relevant factors, including the forum State's interest in adjudicating the dispute, *see McGee v. International Life Ins. Co.*, 355 U.S. 220, 223 (1957); the plaintiff's interest in obtaining convenient and effective relief, *see Kulko v. Superior Court*, 436 U.S. 84, 92 (1977), at least when that interest is not adequately protected by the plaintiff's power to choose the forum, *cf. Shaffer v. Heitner*, 433 U.S. 186, 211, n.37 (1977); the interstate judicial system's interest in obtaining the most efficient resolution of controversies; and the shared interest of the several States in furthering fundamental substantive social policies, *see Kulko v. Superior Court*, 436 U.S. at 93.

The limits imposed on state jurisdiction by the Due Process Clause, in its role as a guarantor against inconvenient litigation, have been substantially relaxed over the years.... Nevertheless, we have never accepted the proposition that state lines are irrelevant for jurisdictional purposes, nor could we, and remain faithful to the principles of interstate federalism embodied in the Constitution....

Hence, even while abandoning the shibboleth that "[t]he authority of every tribunal is necessarily restricted by the territorial limits of the State in which it is established," *Pennoyer v. Neff*, 95 U.S. at 720, we emphasized that the reasonableness of asserting jurisdiction over the defendant must be assessed "in the context of our federal system of government," *International Shoe Co. v. Washington*, 326 U.S. at 317, and stressed that the Due Process Clause ensures not only fairness, but also the "orderly administration of the laws," *id*. at 319. As we noted in *Hanson v. Denckla*, 357 U.S. 235, 250–51 (1958):

> As technological progress has increased the flow of commerce between the States, the need for jurisdiction over nonresidents has undergone a similar increase. At the same time, progress in communications and transportation has made the defense of a suit in a foreign tribunal less burdensome. In response to these changes, the requirements for personal jurisdiction over nonresidents have evolved from the rigid rule of *Pennoyer v. Neff* ... to the flexible standard of *International Shoe Co. v. Washington*.... But it is a mistake to assume that this trend heralds the eventual demise of all restrictions on the personal jurisdiction of state courts.... Those restrictions are more than a guarantee of immunity from inconvenient or distant litigation. They are a consequence of territorial limitations on the power of the respective States.

[handwritten: Read in Class]

Thus, the Due Process Clause "does not contemplate that a state may make binding a judgment *in personam* against an individual or corporate defendant with which the state has no contacts, ties, or relations." *International Shoe Co. v. Washington*, 326 U.S. at 319. Even if the defendant would suffer minimal or no inconvenience from being forced to litigate before the tribunals of another State; even if the forum State has a strong interest in applying its law to the controversy; even if the forum State is the most convenient location for litigation, the Due Process Clause, acting as an instrument of interstate federalism, may sometimes act to divest the State of its power to render a valid judgment. *Hanson v. Denckla*, 357 U.S. at 251, 254.

. . . .

[handwritten margin: Why min. contacts doesn't exist here]

Applying these principles to the case at hand, we find in the record before us a total absence of those affiliating circumstances that are a necessary predicate to any exercise of state-court jurisdiction. Petitioners carry on no activity whatsoever in Oklahoma. They close no sales and perform no services there. They avail themselves of none of the privileges and benefits of Oklahoma law. They solicit no business there either through salespersons or through advertising reasonably calculated to reach the State. Nor does the record show that they regularly sell cars at wholesale or retail to Oklahoma customers or residents or that they indirectly, through others, serve or seek to serve the Oklahoma market. In short, respondents seek to base jurisdiction on one, isolated occurrence and whatever inferences can be drawn therefrom: the fortuitous circumstance that a single Audi automobile, sold in New York to New York residents, happened to suffer an accident while passing through Oklahoma.

It is argued, however, that because an automobile is mobile by its very design and purpose it was "foreseeable" that the Robinsons' Audi would cause injury in Oklahoma. Yet "foreseeability" alone has never been a sufficient benchmark for personal jurisdiction under the Due Process Clause. In *Hanson v. Denckla*, … it was no doubt foreseeable that the settlor of a Delaware trust would subsequently move to Florida and seek to exercise a power of appointment there; yet we held that Florida courts could not constitutionally exercise jurisdiction over a Delaware trustee that had no other contacts with the forum State. In *Kulko v. Superior Court*, 436 U.S. 84 (1978), it was surely "foreseeable" that a divorced wife would move to California from New York, the domicile of the marriage, and that a minor daughter would live with the mother. Yet we held that California could not exercise jurisdiction in a child-support action over the former husband who had remained in New York.

If foreseeability were the criterion, a local California tire retailer could be forced to defend in Pennsylvania when a blowout occurs there, …; a Wisconsin seller of a defective automobile jack could be haled before a distant court for damage caused in New Jersey, …; or a Florida soft-drink concessionaire could be summoned to Alaska to account for injuries happening there…. Every seller of chattels would in effect appoint the chattel his agent for service of process. His amenability to suit would travel with the chattel.…

This is not to say, of course, that foreseeability is wholly irrelevant. But the foreseeability that is critical to due process analysis is not the mere likelihood that a product will find its way into the forum State. Rather, it is that the defendant's conduct and connection with the forum State are such that he should reasonably anticipate being haled into court there…. The Due Process Clause, by ensuring the "orderly administration of the laws," *International Shoe Co. v. Washington*, 326 U.S. at 319, gives a degree of predictability to the legal system that allows potential defendants to structure their primary conduct with some minimum assurance as to where that conduct will and will not render them liable to suit.

When a corporation "purposefully avails itself of the privilege of conducting activities within the forum State," *Hanson v. Denckla*, 357 U.S. at 253, it has clear notice that it is subject to suit there, and can act to alleviate the risk of burdensome litigation by procuring insurance, passing the expected costs on to customers, or, if the risks are too great, severing its connection with the State. Hence if the sale of a product of a manufacturer or distributor such as Audi or Volkswagen is not simply an isolated occurrence, but arises from the efforts of the manufacturer or distributor to serve directly or indirectly, the market for its product in other States, it is not unreasonable to subject it to suit in one of those States if its allegedly defective merchandise has there been the source of injury to its owner or to others. The forum State does not exceed its powers under the Due Process Clause if it asserts personal jurisdiction over a corporation that delivers its products into the stream of commerce with the expectation that they will be purchased by consumers in the forum State. *Cf. Gray v. American Radiator & Standard Sanitary Corp.*, 176 N.E.2d 761 (Ill. 1961).

But there is no such or similar basis for Oklahoma jurisdiction over World-Wide or Seaway in this case. Seaway's sales are made in Massena, N. Y. World-Wide's market, although substantially larger, is limited to dealers in New York, New Jersey, and Connecticut. There is no evidence of record that any automobiles distributed by World-Wide are sold to retail customers outside this tristate area. It is foreseeable that the purchasers of automobiles sold by World-Wide and Seaway may take them to Oklahoma. But the mere "unilateral activity of those who claim some relationship with a nonresident defendant cannot satisfy the requirement of contact with the forum State." *Hanson v. Denckla*, 357 U.S. at 253.

In a variant on the previous argument, it is contended that jurisdiction can be supported by the fact that petitioners earn substantial revenue from goods used in Oklahoma. The

Oklahoma Supreme Court so found ... drawing the inference that because one automobile sold by petitioners had been used in Oklahoma, others might have been used there also....

This argument seems to make the point that the purchase of automobiles in New York, from which the petitioners earn substantial revenue, would not occur *but for* the fact that the automobiles are capable of use in distant States like Oklahoma. Respondents observe that the very purpose of an automobile is to travel, and that travel of automobiles sold by petitioners is facilitated by an extensive chain of Volkswagen service centers throughout the country, including some in Oklahoma. However, financial benefits accruing to the defendant from a collateral relation to the forum State will not support jurisdiction if they do not stem from a constitutionally cognizable contact with that State. *See Kulko v. Superior Court*, 436 U.S. at 94–95. In our view, whatever marginal revenues [World-Wide and Seaway] may receive by virtue of the fact that their products are capable of use in Oklahoma is far too attenuated a contact to justify that State's exercise of in personam jurisdiction over them.

Because we find that [World-Wide and Seaway] have no "contacts, ties, or relations" with the State of Oklahoma, ... the judgment of the Supreme Court of Oklahoma is *reversed*.

[The dissenting opinions of Justices Marshall, Blackmun, and Brennan are omitted.]

The *Insurance Corp. of Ireland* Case (1982). Two years after *World-Wide Volkswagen*, the Court withdrew from its description of the function of the "minimum contacts" test in *Insurance Corp. of Ireland, Ltd. v. Compagnie des Bauxites de Guinee*, 456 U.S. 694 (1982):

> The restriction on state sovereign power described in *World-Wide Volkswagen Corp....* must be seen as ultimately a function of the individual liberty interest preserved by the Due Process Clause. That Clause is the only source of the personal jurisdiction requirement and the Clause itself makes no mention of federalism concerns. Furthermore, if the federalism concept operated as an independent restriction on the sovereign power of the court, it would not be possible to waive the personal jurisdiction requirement: Individual actions cannot change the powers of sovereignty, although the individual can subject himself to powers from which he may otherwise be protected.

Id. at 702–03 n.10.

Notes and Questions

1. Considering that Audi and Volkswagen of America would have had sufficient assets to pay any judgment awarded to the Robinsons and that they did not even challenge personal jurisdiction on appeal, why do you think the plaintiffs wanted to sue World-Wide and Seaway, in addition to Audi and Volkswagen, and thus raise difficult questions of personal jurisdiction? The Robinsons were technically still citizens of New York at the time of the suit and, as discussed in Chapter 4, the joinder of World-Wide and Seaway, who were also citizens of New York, prevented any of the defendants from removing the case to federal court. The location where the action was brought (state court in Creek County, Oklahoma) was regarded as "one of the best venues" in the United States for personal injury plaintiffs in terms of high jury-verdict awards. *See* Charles W. Adams, World-Wide Volkswagen v. Woodson — *The Rest of the Story*, 72 Neb. L. Rev. 1122, 1128–30 (1993).

2. Despite the fact that the U.S. Supreme Court withdrew from the description of the Due Process Clause as an instrument of interstate federalism in *Insurance Corp. of Ireland*, some courts surprisingly still continue to treat the statement as good law. *See, e.g., Williams v. Lakeview Co.*, 13 P.3d 280, 285 (Ariz. 2000).

The *Keeton* and *Calder* Cases (1984). After *World-Wide*, the Court's approach was loose and unstructured, as it had largely been before *World-Wide*. In *Keeton v. Hustler Magazine, Inc.*, 465 U.S. 770 (1984), Kathy Keeton, a nonresident plaintiff, brought a libel action against Hustler Magazine in New Hampshire. The defendant's contacts with New Hampshire consisted of the sale of 10,000 to 15,000 copies of its magazines in the state each month. The plaintiff sued in New Hampshire because the statutes of limitation of all other states had run on the libel claim. However, the plaintiff was seeking to recover damages done by the libel nationwide, not just in New Hampshire. Such an action was permissible under a rule known as the "single publication rule," followed by New Hampshire as well as other states.

The U.S. Supreme Court sustained New Hampshire's exercise of jurisdiction in the case. Among other things, the Court stated that New Hampshire's interests were enhanced by two features of its statutory scheme. First, the state had not limited its criminal defamation statute (which was not applicable to the case) to libels aimed at the state's residents. Second, some time before the action, the state had amended its long-arm statute to eliminate a requirement that torts falling within the statute be committed against residents of the state.

In *Calder v. Jones*, 465 U.S. 783 (1984), another libel case decided the same day as *Keeton*, Shirley Jones, a professional entertainer who lived and worked in California, sued the *National Enquirer*, the California distributor of the *Enquirer*, Iain Calder (the president and editor of the *Enquirer*), and John South (a reporter for the *Enquirer*) in California state court. The *National Enquirer*, which was headquartered in Florida, had a weekly circulation of over 5 million copies with about 600,000 sold in California. Neither the National Enquirer nor the California distributor challenged personal jurisdiction. Defendants Calder and South, however, who were both residents of Florida, objected to California's assertion of personal jurisdiction. Calder, the editor, had been to California twice, once for pleasure and once to testify in an unrelated case. South, the reporter, frequently traveled to California, but did most, if not all, of the research on the allegedly libelous article in Florida.

Nevertheless, the U.S. Supreme Court concluded the relationship between the editor and reporter and California was sufficient to satisfy the due process. Particularly important in the Court's analysis was the fact that California was the focal point for the article as well as the location of the harm suffered by the plaintiff. As the Court stated,

> [t]he allegedly libelous story concerned the California activities of a California resident. It impugned the professionalism of an entertainer whose television career was centered in California. The article was drawn from California sources, and the brunt of the harm, in terms both of respondent's emotional distress and the injury to her professional reputation, was suffered in California. In sum, California is the focal point both of the story and of the harm suffered. Jurisdiction over petitioners is therefore proper in California based on the "effects" of their Florida conduct in California.

....

[Petitioners'] intentional, and allegedly tortious, actions were expressly aimed at California. Petitioner South wrote and petitioner Calder edited an article that they knew would have a potentially devastating impact upon respondent. And they knew that the brunt of that injury would be felt by respondent in the State in which she lives and works and in which the *National Enquirer* has its largest circulation. Under the circumstances, petitioners must "reasonably anticipate being haled into court there" to answer for the truth of the statements made in their article.... An individual injured in California need not go to Florida to seek redress from persons who, though remaining in Florida, knowingly cause the injury in California.

Id. at 788–90.

The Court also rejected an argument that the First Amendment should be interpreted to contain special jurisdictional limits on libel cases. Note, however, that California's assertion of jurisdiction was accomplished under its very general long-arm statute, discussed in section B(2), above. The Court did not find that this very general statute detracted from the state's interest in *Calder*.

Notes and Questions

1. Does it make sense for the state's interest in *Keeton* to be considered stronger because of the absence of a limitation in an inapplicable statute? Does it make sense for the state's interest to be considered stronger because of the removal of a limitation in a statute? Are there other things about the facts of *Keeton* that might more rationally be said to produce a strong state interest in adjudicating the suit?

2. Assume that a defendant commits an intentional tort that has an impact in the forum state, but the defendant's actions were not specifically directed at the forum state. Could *Calder's* "effects" test justify an assertion of jurisdiction over the defendant in the forum under such circumstances? *See* TEPLY & WHITTEN at 303–04 (suggesting that the connection of the defendant's actions to the forum might be too tenuous to justify personal jurisdiction under *Calder*).

Section C. The Concepts of Specific and General Jurisdiction

In 1984, in a significant development, the U.S. Supreme Court first adopted the terms *specific jurisdiction* and *general jurisdiction* in *Helicopteros Nacionales de Colombia, S.A. v. Hall*, 466 U.S. 408 (1984), which is reprinted in the section C(2), below. The origin of these concepts was a pathbreaking article in the *Harvard Law Review* by Professors von Mehren and Trautman in 1966. They argued that the traditional terminology (*in personam, in rem,* and *quasi in rem*) used to discuss multistate jurisdiction was not helpful. *See* Arthur T. von Mehren & Donald T. Trautman, *Jurisdiction to Adjudicate: A Suggested Analysis*, 79 HARV. L. REV. 1121, 1135–36 (1966). They recommended the expression "jurisdiction to adjudicate" be substituted for the traditional categories of jurisdiction.

They also suggested the term "specific jurisdiction" be used to describe power to adjudicate issues arising out of "the very controversy that establishes jurisdiction to adjudicate"— for example, an automobile accident in a state gives the state power to adjudicate a negligence action arising out of the accident. *Id.* at 1136. They suggested the term "general jurisdiction" be used to describe "power to adjudicate any kind of controversy when jurisdiction is based on relationships, direct or indirect, between the forum and the person or persons whose legal rights are to be affected." *Id.* Thus, a defendant who lives in the forum state has sufficient relationships with the state to give it jurisdiction to adjudicate a claim that arises from events occurring outside the state and having nothing to do with the state. The distinction between general and specific jurisdiction is important because the standards for analyzing and judging the validity of an assertion of personal jurisdiction differ for each category.

1. Specific Jurisdiction

As noted above, the U.S. Supreme Court has divided the universe of cases under the "minimum contacts" test into two categories: *specific jurisdiction* and *general jurisdiction*. In *Burger King Corp. v. Rudzewicz*, reprinted below, the Court addressed specific jurisdiction and returned to the more structured "two-step" minimum contacts test first used in the *World-Wide* case. However, the Court described the functions of the test in a very different manner than in *World-Wide*. "Sovereignty protection" is not a function of either part of the test, unless it is covertly included in the "state interest" factor of the reasonableness part of the test.

Burger King Corp. v. Rudzewicz
United States Supreme Court, 1985
471 U.S. 462, 105 S. Ct. 2174, 85 L. Ed. 2d 528

JUSTICE BRENNAN delivered the opinion of the Court.

The State of Florida's long-arm statute extends jurisdiction to "[a]ny person, whether or not a citizen or resident of this state," who, *inter alia*, "[b]reach[es] a contract in this state by failing to perform acts required by the contract to be performed in this state," so long as the cause of action arises from the alleged contractual breach. Fla. Stat. § 48.193(1)(g) (Supp. 1984). The United States District Court for the Southern District of Florida, sitting in diversity, relied on this provision in exercising personal jurisdiction over a Michigan resident who allegedly had breached a franchise agreement with a Florida corporation by failing to make required payments in Florida. The question presented is whether this exercise of long-arm jurisdiction offended "traditional conception[s] of fair play and substantial justice" embodied in the Due Process Clause of the Fourteenth Amendment....

....

Burger King Corporation is a Florida corporation whose principal offices are in Miami. It is one of the world's largest restaurant organizations, with over 3,000 outlets in the 50 States, the Commonwealth of Puerto Rico, and 8 foreign nations. Burger King conducts approximately 80% of its business through a franchise operation that the company styles the "Burger King System"—"a comprehensive restaurant format and operating system for the sale of uniform and quality food products."... Burger King licenses its franchisees to use its trademarks and service marks for a period of 20 years and leases standardized restaurant facilities to them for the same term. In addition, franchisees acquire a variety of proprietary information concerning the "standards, specifications, procedures and methods for operating a Burger King Restaurant."... They also receive market research and advertising assistance; ongoing training in restaurant management;[3] and account-

---

3. Mandatory training seminars are conducted at Burger King University in Miami and at Whopper College Regional Training Centers around the country....

ing, cost-control, and inventory-control guidance. By permitting franchisees to tap into Burger King's established national reputation and to benefit from proven procedures for dispensing standardized fare, this system enables them to go into the restaurant business with significantly lowered barriers to entry.

In exchange for these benefits, franchisees pay Burger King an initial $40,000 franchise fee and commit themselves to payment of monthly royalties, advertising and sales promotion fees, and rent computed in part from monthly gross sales. Franchisees also agree to submit to the national organization's exacting regulation of virtually every conceivable aspect of their operations. Burger King imposes these standards and undertakes its rigid regulation out of conviction that "[u]niformity of service, appearance, and quality of product is essential to the preservation of the Burger King image and the benefits accruing therefrom to both Franchisee and Franchisor." ...

Burger King oversees its franchise system through a two-tiered administrative structure. The governing contracts provide that the franchise relationship is established in Miami and governed by Florida law, and call for payment of all required fees and forwarding of all relevant notices to the Miami headquarters. The Miami headquarters sets policy and works directly with its franchisees in attempting to resolve major problems.... Day-to-day monitoring of franchisees, however, is conducted through a network of 10 district offices which in turn report to the Miami headquarters.

The instant litigation grows out of Burger King's termination of one of its franchisees, and is aptly described by the franchisee as "a divorce proceeding among commercial partners." ... The appellee John Rudzewicz, a Michigan citizen and resident, is the senior partner in a Detroit accounting firm. In 1978, he was approached by Brian MacShara, the son of a business acquaintance, who suggested that they jointly apply to Burger King for a franchise in the Detroit area. MacShara proposed to serve as the manager of the restaurant if Rudzewicz would put up the investment capital; in exchange, the two would evenly share the profits. Believing that MacShara's idea offered attractive investment and tax-deferral opportunities, Rudzewicz agreed to the venture....

Rudzewicz and MacShara jointly applied for a franchise to Burger King's Birmingham, Michigan, district office in the autumn of 1978. Their application was forwarded to Burger King's Miami headquarters, which entered into a preliminary agreement with them in February 1979. During the ensuing four months it was agreed that Rudzewicz and Mac-Shara would assume operation of an existing facility in Drayton Plains, Michigan. Mac-Shara attended the prescribed management courses in Miami during this period, ... and the franchisees purchased $165,000 worth of restaurant equipment from Burger King's Davmor Industries division in Miami. Even before the final agreements were signed, however, the parties began to disagree over site-development fees, building design, computation of monthly rent, and whether the franchisees would be able to assign their liabilities to a corporation they had formed. During these disputes Rudzewicz and MacShara negotiated both with the Birmingham district office and with the Miami headquarters.[7] With some misgivings, Rudzewicz and MacShara finally obtained limited concessions from the Miami headquarters, signed the final agreements, and commenced operations in June 1979. By signing the final agreements, Rudzewicz obligated himself personally to payments exceeding $1 million over the 20-year franchise relationship.

---

7. Although Rudzewicz and MacShara dealt with the Birmingham district office on a regular basis, they communicated directly with the Miami headquarters in forming the contracts; moreover, they learned that the district office had "very little" decisionmaking authority and accordingly turned directly to headquarters in seeking to resolve their disputes....

The Drayton Plains facility apparently enjoyed steady business during the summer of 1979, but patronage declined after a recession began later that year. Rudzewicz and Mac-Shara soon fell far behind in their monthly payments to Miami. Headquarters sent notices of default, and an extended period of negotiations began among the franchisees, the Birmingham district office, and the Miami headquarters. After several Burger King officials in Miami had engaged in prolonged but ultimately unsuccessful negotiations with the franchisees by mail and by telephone,[9] headquarters terminated the franchise and ordered Rudzewicz and MacShara to vacate the premises. They refused and continued to occupy and operate the facility as a Burger King restaurant.

. . . .

Burger King commenced the instant action in the United States District Court for the Southern District of Florida in May 1981, invoking that court's diversity jurisdiction pursuant to 28 U.S.C. § 1332(a) and its original jurisdiction over federal trademark disputes pursuant to § 1338(a). Burger King alleged that Rudzewicz and MacShara had breached their franchise obligations "within [the jurisdiction of] this district court" by failing to make the required payments "at plaintiff's place of business in Miami, Dade County, Florida," . . . and also charged that they were tortiously infringing its trademarks and service marks through their continued, unauthorized operation as a Burger King restaurant. . . . Burger King sought damages, injunctive relief, and costs and attorney's fees. Rudzewicz and Mac-Shara entered special appearances and argued, inter alia, that because they were Michigan residents and because Burger King's claim did not "arise" within the Southern District of Florida, the District Court lacked personal jurisdiction over them. The District Court denied their motions after a hearing, holding that, pursuant to Florida's long-arm statute, "a non-resident Burger King franchisee is subject to the personal jurisdiction of this Court in actions arising out of its franchise agreements." . . . Rudzewicz and MacShara then filed an answer and a counterclaim seeking damages for alleged violations by Burger King of Michigan's Franchise Investment Law, Mich. Comp. Laws § 445.1501 *et seq.* (1979).

After a 3-day bench trial, the court again concluded that it had "jurisdiction over the subject matter and the parties to this cause." . . . Finding that Rudzewicz and MacShara had breached their franchise agreements with Burger King and had infringed Burger King's trademarks and service marks, the court entered judgment against them, jointly and severally, for $228,875 in contract damages. The court also ordered them "to immediately close Burger King Restaurant Number 775 from continued operation or to immediately give the keys and possession of said restaurant to Burger King Corporation," . . . found that they had failed to prove any of the required elements of their counterclaim, and awarded costs and attorney's fees to Burger King.

Rudzewicz appealed to the Court of Appeals for the Eleventh Circuit.[11] A divided panel of that Circuit reversed the judgment, concluding that the District Court could not properly exercise personal jurisdiction over Rudzewicz pursuant to Fla. Stat. § 48.193(1)(g)

---

9. Miami's policy was to "deal directly" with franchisees when they began to encounter financial difficulties, and to involve district office personnel only when necessary. . . . In the instant case, for example, the Miami office handled all credit problems, ordered cost-cutting measures, negotiated for a partial refinancing of the franchisees' debts, communicated directly with the franchisees in attempting to resolve the dispute, and was responsible for all termination matters. . . .

11. MacShara did not appeal his judgment. . . . In addition, Rudzewicz entered into a compromise with Burger King and waived his right to appeal the District Court's finding of trademark infringement and its entry of injunctive relief. . . . Accordingly, we need not address the extent to which the tortious act provisions of Florida's long-arm statute, *see* Fla. Stat. § 48.193(1)(b) (Supp. 1984), may constitutionally extend to out-of-state trademark infringement. *Cf. Calder v. Jones,* 465 U.S. 783,

(Supp. 1984) because "the circumstances of the Drayton Plains franchise and the negotiations which led to it left Rudzewicz bereft of reasonable notice and financially unprepared for the prospect of franchise litigation in Florida." ... Accordingly, the panel majority
concluded that "[j]urisdiction under these circumstances would offend the fundamental
fairness which is the touchstone of due process." ...

Burger King appealed the Eleventh Circuit's judgment to this Court.... [W]e now
reverse.

....

The Due Process Clause protects an individual's liberty interest in not being subject to
the binding judgments of a forum with which he has established no meaningful "contacts, ties, or relations." *International Shoe Co. v. Washington*, 326 U.S. at 319.[13] By requiring that individuals have "fair warning that a particular activity may subject [them]
to the jurisdiction of a foreign sovereign," *Shaffer v. Heitner*, 433 U.S. 186 (1977) (STEVENS,
J., concurring in judgment), the Due Process Clause "gives a degree of predictability to
the legal system that allows potential defendants to structure their primary conduct with
some minimum assurance as to where that conduct will and will not render them liable
to suit," *World-Wide Volkswagen Corp. v. Woodson*, 444 U.S. 286, 297 (1980).

Where a forum seeks to assert specific jurisdiction over an out-of-state defendant who
has not consented to suit there,[14] this "fair warning" requirement is satisfied if the defendant has "purposefully directed" his activities at residents of the forum, *Keeton v. Hustler Magazine, Inc.*, 465 U.S. 770, 774 (1984), and the litigation results from alleged injuries
that "arise out of or relate to" those activities, *Helicopteros Nacionales de Colombia, S.A.
v. Hall*, 466 U.S. 408, 414 (1984).[15] Thus "[t]he forum State does not exceed its powers
under the Due Process Clause if it asserts personal jurisdiction over a corporation that delivers its products into the stream of commerce with the expectation that they will be
purchased by consumers in the forum State" and those products subsequently injure
forum consumers. *World-Wide Volkswagen Corp. v. Woodson*, 444 U.S. at 297–98. Similarly, a publisher who distributes magazines in a distant State may fairly be held accountable in that forum for damages resulting there from an allegedly defamatory story.
Keeton v. Hustler Magazine, Inc., 465 U.S. 770 (1984); *see also Calder v. Jones*, 465 U.S. 783
(1984) (suit against author and editor). And with respect to interstate contractual obligations, we have emphasized that parties who "reach out beyond one state and create continuing relationships and obligations with citizens of another state" are subject to regulation

---

788–89 (1984) (tortious out-of-state conduct); *Keeton v. Hustler Magazine, Inc.*, 465 U.S. 770, 776 (1984)
(same).

13. Although this protection operates to restrict state power, it "must be seen as ultimately a function of the individual liberty interest preserved by the Due Process Clause" rather than as a function
"of federalism concerns." *Insurance Corp. of Ireland v. Compagnie des Bauxites de Guinee*, 456 U.S.
694, 702–03, n.10 (1982).

14. We have noted that, because the personal jurisdiction requirement is a waivable right, there
are a "variety of legal arrangements" by which a litigant may give "express or implied consent to the
personal jurisdiction of the court." ... For example, particularly in the commercial context, parties frequently stipulate in advance to submit their controversies for resolution within a particular jurisdiction. *See National Equip. Rental, Ltd. v. Szukhent*, 375 U.S. 311 (1964). Where such forum-selection
provisions have been obtained through "freely negotiated" agreements and are not "unreasonable and
unjust," *M/S Bremen v. Zapata Off-Shore Co.*, 407 U.S. 1, 15 (1972), their enforcement does not offend due process.

15. "Specific" jurisdiction contrasts with "general" jurisdiction, pursuant to which "a State exercises personal jurisdiction over a defendant in a suit not arising out of or related to the defendant's
contacts with the forum." ...

and sanctions in the other State for the consequences of their activities. *Travelers Health Ass'n v. Virginia*, 339 U.S. 643, 647 (1950); *see also McGee v. International Life Ins. Co.*, 355 U.S. 220, 222–23 (1957).

We have noted several reasons why a forum legitimately may exercise personal jurisdiction over a nonresident who "purposefully directs" his activities toward forum residents. A State generally has a "manifest interest" in providing its residents with a convenient forum for redressing injuries inflicted by out-of-state actors. *Id.* at 223.... Moreover, where individuals "purposefully derive benefit" from their interstate activities, *Kulko v. Superior Court*, 436 U.S. 84, 96 (1978), it may well be unfair to allow them to escape having to account in other States for consequences that arise proximately from such activities; the Due Process Clause may not readily be wielded as a territorial shield to avoid interstate obligations that have been voluntarily assumed. And because "modern transportation and communications have made it much less burdensome for a party sued to defend himself in a State where he engages in economic activity," it usually will not be unfair to subject him to the burdens of litigating in another forum for disputes relating to such activity. *McGee v. International Life Ins. Co.*, 355 U.S. at 223.

Notwithstanding these considerations, the constitutional touchstone remains whether the defendant purposefully established "minimum contacts" in the forum State. *International Shoe Co. v. Washington*, 326 U.S. at 31. Although it has been argued that foreseeability of causing *injury* in another State should be sufficient to establish such contacts there when policy considerations so require, the Court has consistently held that this kind of foreseeability is not a "sufficient benchmark" for exercising personal jurisdiction. *World-Wide Volkswagen Corp. v. Woodson*, 444 U.S. at 295. Instead, "the foreseeability that is critical to due process analysis ... is that the defendant's conduct and connection with the forum State are such that he should reasonably anticipate being haled into court there." *Id.* at 297. In defining when it is that a potential defendant should "reasonably anticipate" out-of-state litigation, the Court frequently has drawn from the reasoning of *Hanson v. Denckla* ...:

> The unilateral activity of those who claim some relationship with a nonresident defendant cannot satisfy the requirement of contact with the forum State. The application of that rule will vary with the quality and nature of the defendant's activity, but it is essential in each case that there be some act by which the defendant purposefully avails itself of the privilege of conducting activities within the forum State, thus invoking the benefits and protections of its laws.

This "purposeful availment" requirement ensures that a defendant will not be haled into a jurisdiction solely as a result of "random," "fortuitous," or "attenuated" contacts, *Keeton v. Hustler Magazine, Inc.*, 465 U.S. at 774; *World-Wide Volkswagen Corp. v. Woodson*, 444 U.S. at 299, or of the "unilateral activity of another party or a third person," *Helicopteros Nacionales de Colombia, S.A. v. Hall*, 466 U.S. at 417. Jurisdiction is proper, however, where the contacts proximately result from actions by the defendant himself that create a "substantial connection" with the forum State. *McGee v. International Life Ins. Co.*, 355 U.S. at 223; *see also Kulko v. Superior Court*, 436 U.S. at 94, n.7.[18] Thus where the defendant "de-

---

18. So long as it creates a "substantial connection" with the forum, even a single act can support jurisdiction. *McGee v. International Life Ins. Co.*, 355 U.S. at 223. The Court has noted, however, that "some single or occasional acts" related to the forum may not be sufficient to establish jurisdiction if "their nature and quality and the circumstances of their commission" create only an "attenuated" affiliation with the forum. *International Shoe Co. v. Washington*, 326 U.S. 310, 318 (1945); *World-Wide Volkswagen Corp. v. Woodson*, 444 U.S. at 299. This distinction derives from the belief that, with re-

liberately" has engaged in significant activities within a State, *Keeton v. Hustler Magazine, Inc.*, 465 U.S. at 781, or has created "continuing obligations" between himself and residents of the forum, *Travelers Health Ass'n v. Virginia*, 339 U.S. at 648, he manifestly has availed himself of the privilege of conducting business there, and because his activities are shielded by "the benefits and protections" of the forum's laws it is presumptively not unreasonable to require him to submit to the burdens of litigation in that forum as well.

Jurisdiction in these circumstances may not be avoided merely because the defendant did not *physically* enter the forum State. Although territorial presence frequently will enhance a potential defendant's affiliation with a State and reinforce the reasonable foreseeability of suit there, it is an inescapable fact of modern commercial life that a substantial amount of business is transacted solely by mail and wire communications across state lines, thus obviating the need for physical presence within a State in which business is conducted. So long as a commercial actor's efforts are "purposefully directed" toward residents of another State, we have consistently rejected the notion that an absence of physical contacts can defeat personal jurisdiction there....

Once it has been decided that a defendant purposefully established minimum contacts within the forum State, these contacts may be considered in light of other factors to determine whether the assertion of personal jurisdiction would comport with "fair play and substantial justice." ... Thus courts in "appropriate case[s]" may evaluate the burden on the defendant," the forum State's interest in adjudicating the dispute," the plaintiff's interest in obtaining convenient and effective relief," the interstate judicial system's interest in obtaining the most efficient resolution of controversies," and the "shared interest of the several States in furthering fundamental substantive social policies." *World-Wide Volkswagen Corp. v. Woodson*, 444 U.S. at 292. These considerations sometimes serve to establish the reasonableness of jurisdiction upon a lesser showing of minimum contacts than would otherwise be required. *See, e.g., Keeton v. Hustler Magazine, Inc.*, 465 U.S. at 780; *Calder v. Jones*, 465 U.S. at 788–89; *McGee v. International Life Ins. Co.*, 355 U.S. at 223–24. On the other hand, where a defendant who purposefully has directed his activities at forum residents seeks to defeat jurisdiction, he must present a compelling case that the presence of some other considerations would render jurisdiction unreasonable. Most such considerations usually may be accommodated through means short of finding jurisdiction unconstitutional. For example, the potential clash of the forum's law with the "fundamental substantive social policies" of another State may be accommodated through application of the forum's choice-of-law rules. Similarly, a defendant claiming substantial inconvenience may seek a change of venue.[20] Nevertheless, minimum requirements inherent in the concept of "fair play and substantial justice" may defeat the reasonableness of jurisdiction even if the defendant has purposefully engaged in forum activities.... As we previously have noted, jurisdictional rules may not be employed in such a way as to make litigation "so gravely difficult and inconvenient" that a party unfairly is at a "severe disadvantage" in comparison to his opponent....

....

---

spect to this category of "isolated" acts, *id.* at 297, the reasonable foreseeability of litigation in the forum is substantially diminished.

20. *See, e.g.,* 28 U.S.C. §1404(a) ("For the convenience of parties and witnesses, in the interest of justice, a district court may transfer any civil action to any other district or division where it might have been brought."). This provision embodies in an expanded version the common-law doctrine of *forum non conveniens*, under which a court in appropriate circumstances may decline to exercise its jurisdiction in the interest of the "easy, expeditious and inexpensive" resolution of a controversy in another forum....

Analysis

Applying these principles to the case at hand, we believe there is substantial record evidence supporting the District Court's conclusion that the assertion of personal jurisdiction over Rudzewicz in Florida for the alleged breach of his franchise agreement did not offend due process. At the outset, we note a continued division among lower courts respecting whether and to what extent a contract can constitute a "contact" for purposes of due process analysis. If the question is whether an individual's contract with an out-of-state party *alone* can automatically establish sufficient minimum contacts in the other party's home forum, we believe the answer clearly is that it cannot. The Court long ago rejected the notion that personal jurisdiction might turn on "mechanical" tests ... or on "conceptualistic ... theories of the place of contracting or of performance." ... Instead, we have emphasized the need for a "highly realistic" approach that recognizes that a "contract" is "ordinarily but an intermediate step serving to tie up prior business negotiations with future consequences which themselves are the real object of the business transaction." ... It is these factors— prior negotiations and contemplated future consequences, along with the terms of the contract and the parties' actual course of dealing—that must be evaluated in determining whether the defendant purposefully established minimum contacts within the forum.

In this case, no physical ties to Florida can be attributed to Rudzewicz other than MacShara's brief training course in Miami.[22] Rudzewicz did not maintain offices in Florida and, for all that appears from the record, has never even visited there. Yet this franchise dispute grew directly out of "a contract which had a *substantial* connection with that State." ... Eschewing the option of operating an independent local enterprise, Rudzewicz deliberately "reach[ed] out beyond" Michigan and negotiated with a Florida corporation for the purchase of a long-term franchise and the manifold benefits that would derive from affiliation with a nationwide organization.... Upon approval, he entered into a carefully structured 20-year relationship that envisioned continuing and wide-reaching contacts with Burger King in Florida. In light of Rudzewicz' voluntary acceptance of the long-term and exacting regulation of his business from Burger King's Miami headquarters, the "quality and nature" of his relationship to the company in Florida can in no sense be viewed as "random," "fortuitous," or "attenuated." ... Rudzewicz' refusal to make the contractually required payments in Miami, and his continued use of Burger King's trademarks and confidential business information after his termination, caused foreseeable injuries to the corporation in Florida. For these reasons it was, at the very least, presumptively reasonable for Rudzewicz to be called to account there for such injuries.

The Court of Appeals concluded, however, that in light of the supervision emanating from Burger King's district office in Birmingham, Rudzewicz reasonably believed that "the Michigan office was for all intents and purposes the embodiment of Burger King" and that he therefore had no "reason to anticipate a Burger King suit outside of Michigan." ... This reasoning overlooks substantial record evidence indicating that Rudzewicz most cer-

---

22. The Eleventh Circuit held that MacShara's presence in Florida was irrelevant to the question of Rudzewicz' minimum contacts with that forum, reasoning that "Rudzewicz and MacShara never formed a partnership" and "signed the agreements in their individual capacities." 724 F.2d at 1513, n.14. The two did jointly form a corporation through which they were seeking to conduct the franchise, however.... They were required to decide which one of them would travel to Florida to satisfy the training requirements so that they could commence business, and Rudzewicz participated in the decision that MacShara would go there. We have previously noted that when commercial activities are "carried on in behalf of" an out-of-state party those activities may sometimes be ascribed to the party, ... at least where he is a "primary participan[t]" in the enterprise and has acted purposefully in directing those activities, *Calder v. Jones*, 465 U.S. at 790. Because MacShara's matriculation at Burger King University is not pivotal to the disposition of this case, we need not resolve the permissible bounds of such attribution.

tainly knew that he was affiliating himself with an enterprise based primarily in Florida. The contract documents themselves emphasize that Burger King's operations are conducted and supervised from the Miami headquarters, that all relevant notices and payments must be sent there, and that the agreements were made in and enforced from Miami.... Moreover, the parties' actual course of dealing repeatedly confirmed that decisionmaking authority was vested in the Miami headquarters and that the district office served largely as an intermediate link between the headquarters and the franchisees. When problems arose over building design, site-development fees, rent computation, and the defaulted payments, Rudzewicz and MacShara learned that the Michigan office was powerless to resolve their disputes and could only channel their communications to Miami. Throughout these disputes, the Miami headquarters and the Michigan franchisees carried on a continuous course of direct communications by mail and by telephone, and it was the Miami headquarters that made the key negotiating decisions out of which the instant litigation arose....

Moreover, we believe the Court of Appeals gave insufficient weight to provisions in the various franchise documents providing that all disputes would be governed by Florida law. The franchise agreement, for example, stated:

> This Agreement shall become valid when executed and accepted by BKC at Miami, Florida; it shall be deemed made and entered into in the State of Florida and shall be governed and construed under and in accordance with the laws of the State of Florida. The choice of law designation does not require that all suits concerning this Agreement be filed in Florida....

... The Court of Appeals reasoned that choice-of-law provisions are irrelevant to the question of personal jurisdiction, relying on *Hanson v. Denckla* for the proposition that "the center of gravity for choice-of-law purposes does not necessarily confer the sovereign prerogative to assert jurisdiction." ... This reasoning misperceives the import of the quoted proposition. The Court in *Hanson* and subsequent cases has emphasized that choice-of-law *analysis*—which focuses on all elements of a transaction, and not simply on the defendant's conduct—is distinct from minimum-contacts jurisdictional analysis—which focuses at the threshold solely on the defendant's purposeful connection to the forum. Nothing in our cases, however, suggests that a choice-of-law *provision* should be ignored in considering whether a defendant has "purposefully invoked the benefits and protections of a State's laws" for jurisdictional purposes. Although such a provision standing alone would be insufficient to confer jurisdiction, we believe that, when combined with the 20-year interdependent relationship Rudzewicz established with Burger King's Miami headquarters, it reinforced his deliberate affiliation with the forum State and the reasonable foreseeability of possible litigation there. As Judge Johnson argued in his dissent below, Rudzewicz "purposefully availed himself of the benefits and protections of Florida's laws" by entering into contracts expressly providing that those laws would govern franchise disputes....[24]

    ....

---

24. In addition, the franchise agreement's disclaimer that the "choice of law designation does not *require* that all suits concerning this Agreement be filed in Florida," ... reasonably should have suggested to Rudzewicz that by negative implication such suits *could* be filed there. The lease also provided for binding arbitration in Miami of certain condemnation disputes, ... and Rudzewicz conceded the validity of this provision at oral argument.... Although it does not govern the instant dispute, this provision also should have made it apparent to the franchisees that they were dealing directly with the Miami headquarters and that the Birmingham district office was *not* "for all intents and purposes the embodiment of Burger King." ...

Nor has Rudzewicz pointed to other factors that can be said persuasively to outweigh the considerations discussed above and to establish the *unconstitutionality* of Florida's assertion of jurisdiction. We cannot conclude that Florida had no "legitimate interest in holding [Rudzewicz] answerable on a claim related to" the contacts he had established in that State. *Keeton v. Hustler Magazine, Inc.*, 465 U.S. at 776; *see also McGee v. International Life Ins. Co.*, 355 U.S. at 223 (noting that State frequently will have a "manifest interest in providing effective means of redress for its residents").[25] Moreover, although Rudzewicz has argued at some length that Michigan's Franchise Investment Law, Mich. Comp. Laws § 445.1501 *et seq.* (1979), governs many aspects of this franchise relationship, he has not demonstrated how Michigan's acknowledged interest might possibly render jurisdiction in Florida *unconstitutional.*[26] Finally, the Court of Appeals' assertion that the Florida litigation "severely impaired [Rudzewicz'] ability to call Michigan witnesses who might be essential to his defense and counterclaim" ... is wholly without support in the record.[27] And even to the extent that it is inconvenient for a party who has minimum contacts with a forum to litigate there, such considerations most frequently can be accommodated through a change of venue.... Although the Court has suggested that inconvenience may at some point become so substantial as to achieve *constitutional* magnitude, *McGee v. International Life Ins. Co.*, 355 U.S. at 223, this is not such a case.

The Court of Appeals also concluded, however, that the parties' dealings involved "a characteristic disparity of bargaining power" and "elements of surprise," and that Rudzewicz "lacked fair notice" of the potential for litigation in Florida because the contractual provisions suggesting to the contrary were merely "boilerplate declarations in a lengthy printed contract." ... Rudzewicz presented many of these arguments to the District Court, contending that Burger King was guilty of misrepresentation, fraud, and duress; that it gave insufficient notice in its dealings with him; and that the contract was one of adhesion.... After a 3-day bench trial, the District Court found that Burger King had made no misrepresentations, that Rudzewicz and MacShara "were and are experienced and sophisticated businessmen," and that "at no time" did they "ac[t] under economic duress or disadvantage imposed by" Burger King.... Federal Rule of Civil Procedure 52(a) requires that "[f]indings of fact shall not be set aside unless clearly erroneous," and neither Rudzewicz nor the Court of Appeals has pointed to record evidence that would support a "definite and firm conviction" that the District Court's findings are mistaken.... To the contrary, Rudzewicz was represented by counsel throughout these complex transactions and, as

---

25. Complaining that "when Burger King is the plaintiff, you won't 'have it your way' because it sues all franchisees in Miami," ... Rudzewicz contends that Florida's interest in providing a convenient forum is negligible given the company's size and ability to conduct litigation anywhere in the country. We disagree. Absent compelling considerations, *cf. McGee v. International Life Ins. Co.*, 355 U.S. at 223, a defendant who has purposefully derived commercial benefit from his affiliations in a forum may not defeat jurisdiction there simply because of his adversary's greater net wealth.

26. Rudzewicz has failed to show how the District Court's exercise of jurisdiction in this case might have been at all inconsistent with Michigan's interests. To the contrary, the court found that Burger King had fully complied with Michigan law, ... and there is nothing in Michigan's franchise Act suggesting that Michigan would attempt to assert exclusive jurisdiction to resolve franchise disputes affecting its residents. In any event, minimum-contacts analysis presupposes that two or more States may be interested in the outcome of a dispute, and the process of resolving potentially conflicting "fundamental substantive social policies" ... can usually be accommodated through choice-of-law rules rather than through outright preclusion of jurisdiction in one forum....

27. The only arguable instance of trial inconvenience occurred when Rudzewicz had difficulty in authenticating some corporate records; the court offered him as much time as would be necessary to secure the requisite authentication from the Birmingham district office, and Burger King ultimately stipulated to their authenticity rather than delay the trial....

Judge Johnson observed in dissent below, was himself an experienced accountant "who for five months conducted negotiations with Burger King over the terms of the franchise and lease agreements, and who obligated himself personally to contracts requiring over time payments that exceeded $1 million." ... Rudzewicz was able to secure a modest reduction in rent and other concessions from Miami headquarters ...; moreover, to the extent that Burger King's terms were inflexible, Rudzewicz presumably decided that the advantages of affiliating with a national organization provided sufficient commercial benefits to offset the detriments.[28]

....

Notwithstanding these considerations, the Court of Appeals apparently believed that it was necessary to reject jurisdiction in this case as a prophylactic measure, reasoning that an affirmance of the District Court's judgment would result in the exercise of jurisdiction over "out-of-state consumers to collect payments due on modest personal purchases" and would "sow the seeds of default judgments against franchisees owing smaller debts." ... We share the Court of Appeals' broader concerns and therefore reject any talismanic jurisdictional formulas; "the facts of each case must [always] be weighed" in determining whether personal jurisdiction would comport with "fair play and substantial justice." ... The "quality and nature" of an interstate transaction may sometimes be so "random," "fortuitous," or "attenuated" that it cannot fairly be said that the potential defendant "should reasonably anticipate being haled into court" in another jurisdiction. *World-Wide Volkswagen Corp. v. Woodson*, 444 U.S. at 297.... We also have emphasized that jurisdiction may not be grounded on a contract whose terms have been obtained through "fraud, undue influence, or overweening bargaining power" and whose application would render litigation "so gravely difficult and inconvenient that [a party] will for all practical purposes be deprived of his day in court." ... Just as the Due Process Clause allows flexibility in ensuring that commercial actors are not effectively "judgment proof" for the consequences of obligations they voluntarily assume in other States, *McGee v. International Life Ins. Co.*, ... so too does it prevent rules that would unfairly enable them to obtain default judgments against unwitting customers....

For the reasons set forth above, however, these dangers are not present in the instant case. Because Rudzewicz established a substantial and continuing relationship with Burger King's Miami headquarters, received fair notice from the contract documents and the course of dealing that he might be subject to suit in Florida, and has failed to demonstrate how jurisdiction in that forum would otherwise be fundamentally unfair, we conclude that the District Court's exercise of jurisdiction pursuant to Fla. Stat. §48.193(1)(g) (Supp. 1984) did not offend due process. The judgment of the Court of Appeals is accordingly reversed, and the case is remanded for further proceedings consistent with this opinion.

It is so ordered.

JUSTICE POWELL took no part in the consideration or decision of this case.

---

28. We do not mean to suggest that the jurisdictional outcome will always be the same in franchise cases. Some franchises may be primarily intrastate in character or involve different decision-making structures, such that a franchisee should not reasonably anticipate out-of-state litigation. Moreover, commentators have argued that franchise relationships may sometimes involve unfair business practices in their inception and operation.... For these reasons, we reject Burger King's suggestion for "a general rule, or at least a presumption, that participation in an interstate franchise relationship" represents consent to the jurisdiction of the franchisor's principal place of business....

[The dissenting opinion of Justice Stevens, with whom Justice White joined, is omitted.]

Notes and Questions

1. In *Burger King*, the Court made clear that the "minimum contacts" test in specific jurisdiction cases requires a two-step analysis. First, the defendant must have "*purposefully availed*" itself of the privilege of conducting activities in the forum state, thus invoking the benefits and protections of the forum state's laws. The Court referred to this requirement of *purposeful availment* as the "constitutional touchstone" of the minimum contacts analysis. Second, if purposeful contacts are present, the contacts are then considered in light of other "reasonableness" or "fairness" factors to determine whether the exercise of personal jurisdiction would comport with "fair play and substantial justice." Under this second prong of the "minimum contacts" analysis, the defendant can only invalidate the state's assertion of jurisdiction with great difficulty—by demonstrating that the state is a substantially unfair forum making the exercise of jurisdiction "unreasonable." In this second prong of the analysis, the Court identified five "reasonableness" factors to be considered and balanced:

(1) the burdens on the defendant of a suit within the forum;

(2) the forum state's interest in adjudicating the dispute;

(3) the plaintiff's interest in obtaining convenient and effective relief;

(4) the interstate judicial system's interest in the most efficient resolution of controversies; and

(5) the shared interests of the several states in furthering fundamental substantive social policies.

The Court in *Burger King* described the "purposeful availment" prong of the "minimum contacts" test as the provision of "fair warning" to the defendant that its activities will subject it to suit in the forum. The goal of the "reasonableness" prong was described as the assurance that the forum is "fair" to the defendant. Does this scheme make sense? Why is the second step in the test necessary?

2. In *Burger King*, the Court indicated that the "reasonableness" factors may sometimes serve to validate an assertion of specific jurisdiction "upon a lesser showing of minimum contacts than would otherwise be required." Can you think of a case in which the reasonableness test could be used in this fashion? Did the Court provide any guidance on this question in *Burger King*?

3. Is personal jurisdiction in contract cases doctrinally different from tort cases? If not, does *Burger King* give you a solid basis for determining how to ascertain the constitutionality of assertions of jurisdiction in contract actions, given the variety of factual variations that can be expected in such cases?

4. The contract in *Burger King* contained a "choice-of-law clause." As explained in Chapter 1(F)(2)(d), choice-of-law rules vary widely among the states. Parties therefore insert choice-of-law provisions in contracts to avoid difficult choice-of-law questions in determining which state's substantive law governs the contract in the event of a dispute. A choice-of-law clause, however, is not the equivalent of a "consent to jurisdiction" clause, which, as explained in section A(3)(c) above, confers personal jurisdiction in the selected forum by its express terms. But does a choice-of-law clause have any personal jurisdiction significance? As the Court held in *Burger King*, a choice-of-law clause "standing alone would be insufficient to confer jurisdiction," but can be considered, along with other con-

tacts, in determining whether a defendant has "purposefully availed" itself of the benefits and protections of the forum state's laws. If Burger King wanted to avoid the kind of
jurisdictional challenge it faced in this case, what language should it have inserted in its
franchise contracts?

Asahi Metal Industry Co. v. Superior Court

United States Supreme Court, 1987
480 U.S. 102, 107 S. Ct. 1026, 94 L. Ed. 2d 92

[JUSTICE O'CONNOR announced the Court's judgment and delivered the Court's unan-
imous opinion with respect to Part I, the Court's opinion with respect to Part II-B, in which
THE CHIEF JUSTICE, JUSTICE BRENNAN, JUSTICE WHITE, JUSTICE MARSHALL, JUSTICE
BLACKMUN, JUSTICE POWELL, and JUSTICE STEVENS join, and an opinion with respect to Parts
II-A and III, in which THE CHIEF JUSTICE, JUSTICE POWELL, and JUSTICE SCALIA join.]

This case presents the question whether the mere awareness on the part of a foreign
defendant that the components it manufactured, sold, and delivered outside the United
States would reach the forum State in the stream of commerce constitutes "minimum
contacts" between the defendant and the forum State such that the exercise of jurisdiction "does not offend 'traditional notions of fair play and substantial justice.'" ...

[handwritten: ISSUE]
[handwritten: (purposeful Availment)]

I *[handwritten: Unanimous Opinion]*

On September 23, 1978, on Interstate Highway 80 in Solano County, California, Gary Zurcher
lost control of his Honda motorcycle and collided with a tractor. Zurcher was severely injured, and his passenger and wife, Ruth Ann Moreno, was killed. In September 1979, Zurcher
filed a product liability action in the Superior Court of the State of California in and for the
County of Solano. Zurcher alleged that the 1978 accident was caused by a sudden loss of air
and an explosion in the rear tire of the motorcycle, and alleged that the motorcycle tire,
tube, and sealant were defective. Zurcher's complaint named, *inter alia*, Cheng Shin Rubber Industrial Co., Ltd. (Cheng Shin), the Taiwanese manufacturer of the tube. Cheng Shin
in turn filed a cross-complaint seeking indemnification from its co-defendants and from petitioner, Asahi Metal Industry Co., Ltd. (Asahi), the manufacturer of the tube's valve as-
sembly. Zurcher's claims against Cheng Shin and the other defendants were eventually settled
and dismissed, leaving only Cheng Shin's indemnity action against Asahi.

[handwritten: inter alia: Among other things]

California's long-arm statute authorizes the exercise of jurisdiction "on any basis not
inconsistent with the Constitution of this state or of the United States." Cal. Civ. Proc. Code
Ann. § 410.10 (West 1973). Asahi moved to quash Cheng Shin's service of summons, arguing the State could not exert jurisdiction over it consistent with the Due Process Clause
of the Fourteenth Amendment.

In relation to the motion, the following information was submitted by Asahi and Cheng
Shin. Asahi is a Japanese corporation. It manufactures tire valve assemblies in Japan and
sells the assemblies to Cheng Shin, and to several other tire manufacturers, for use as components in finished tire tubes. Asahi's sales to Cheng Shin took place in Taiwan. The ship-
ments from Asahi to Cheng Shin were sent from Japan to Taiwan. Cheng Shin bought and
incorporated into its tire tubes 150,000 Asahi valve assemblies in 1978; 500,000 in 1979;
500,000 in 1980; 100,000 in 1981; and 100,000 in 1982. Sales to Cheng Shin accounted for
1.24 percent of Asahi's income in 1981 and 0.44 percent in 1982. Cheng Shin alleged that approximately 20 percent of its sales in the United States are in California. Cheng Shin purchases
valve assemblies from other suppliers as well, and sells finished tubes throughout the world.

In 1983 an attorney for Cheng Shin conducted an informal examination of the valve stems of the tire tubes sold in one cycle store in Solano County. The attorney declared that of the approximately 115 tire tubes in the store, 97 were purportedly manufactured in Japan or Taiwan, and of those 97, 21 valve stems were marked with the circled letter "A," apparently Asahi's trademark. Of the 21 Asahi valve stems, 12 were incorporated into Cheng Shin tire tubes. The store contained 41 other Cheng Shin tubes that incorporated the valve assemblies of other manufacturers.... An affidavit of a manager of Cheng Shin whose duties included the purchasing of component parts stated: "'In discussions with Asahi regarding the purchase of valve stem assemblies the fact that my Company sells tubes throughout the world and specifically the United States has been discussed. I am informed and believe that Asahi was fully aware that valve stem assemblies sold to my Company and to others would end up throughout the United States and in California.'"... An affidavit of the president of Asahi, on the other hand, declared that Asahi "'has never contemplated that its limited sales of tire valves to Cheng Shin in Taiwan would subject it to lawsuits in California.'"... The record does not include any contract between Cheng Shin and Asahi....

Primarily on the basis of the above information, the Superior Court denied the motion to quash summons, stating that "Asahi obviously does business on an international scale. It is not unreasonable that they defend claims of defect in their product on an international scale."...

The Court of Appeal of the State of California issued a peremptory writ of mandate commanding the Superior Court to quash service of summons. The court concluded that "it would be unreasonable to require Asahi to respond in California solely on the basis of ultimately realized foreseeability that the product into which its component was embodied would be sold all over the world including California."...

The Supreme Court of the State of California reversed and discharged the writ issued by the Court of Appeal.... The court observed that "Asahi has no offices, property or agents in California. It solicits no business in California and has made no direct sales [in California]."... Moreover, "Asahi did not design or control the system of distribution that carried its valve assemblies into California."... Nevertheless, the court found the exercise of jurisdiction over Asahi to be consistent with the Due Process Clause. It concluded that Asahi knew that some of the valve assemblies sold to Cheng Shin would be incorporated into tire tubes sold in California, and that Asahi benefitted indirectly from the sale in California of products incorporating its components. The court considered Asahi's intentional act of placing its components into the stream of commerce—that is, by delivering the components to Cheng Shin in Taiwan—coupled with Asahi's awareness that some of the components would eventually find their way into California, sufficient to form the basis for state court jurisdiction under the Due Process Clause.

We granted certiorari ... and now reverse.

II
A

The Due Process Clause of the Fourteenth Amendment limits the power of a state court to exert personal jurisdiction over a nonresident defendant. "[T]he constitutional touchstone" of the determination whether an exercise of personal jurisdiction comports with due process "remains whether the defendant purposefully established 'minimum contacts' in the forum State."... Most recently we have reaffirmed the oft-quoted reasoning of *Hanson v. Denckla* ... that minimum contacts must have a basis in "some act by which the defendant purposefully avails itself of the privilege of conducting activities within the forum State, thus invoking the benefits and protections of its laws." *Burger King*, 471 U.S. at 475. "Jurisdiction is proper ... where the contacts proximately result from actions by the defendant *himself* that create a 'substantial connection' with the forum State." ...

Applying the principle that minimum contacts must be based on an act of the defendant, the Court in *World-Wide Volkswagen Corp. v. Woodson* ... rejected the assertion that a *consumer's* unilateral act of bringing the defendant's product into the forum State was a sufficient constitutional basis for personal jurisdiction over the defendant. It had been argued in *World-Wide Volkswagen* that because an automobile retailer and its wholesale distributor sold a product mobile by design and purpose, they could foresee being haled into court in the distant States into which their customers might drive. The Court rejected this concept of foreseeability as an insufficient basis for jurisdiction under the Due Process Clause.... The Court disclaimed, however, the idea that "foreseeability is wholly irrelevant" to personal jurisdiction, concluding that "[t]he forum State does not exceed its powers under the Due Process Clause if it asserts personal jurisdiction over a corporation that delivers its products into the stream of commerce with the expectation that they will be purchased by consumers in the forum State." ... The Court reasoned:

> When a corporation "purposefully avails itself of the privilege of conducting activities within the forum State," ... it has clear notice that it is subject to suit there, and can act to alleviate the risk of burdensome litigation by procuring insurance, passing the expected costs on to customers, or, if the risks are too great, severing its connection with the State. Hence if the sale of a product of a manufacturer or distributor ... is not simply an isolated occurrence, but arises from the efforts of the manufacturer or distributor to serve, directly or indirectly, the market for its product in other States, it is not unreasonable to subject it to suit in one of those States if its allegedly defective merchandise has there been the source of injury to its owners or to others....

In *World-Wide Volkswagen* itself, the state court sought to base jurisdiction not on any act of the defendant, but on the foreseeable unilateral actions of the consumer. Since *World-Wide Volkswagen*, lower courts have been confronted with cases in which the defendant acted by placing a product in the stream of commerce, and the stream eventually swept defendant's product into the forum State, but the defendant did nothing else to purposefully avail itself of the market in the forum State. Some courts have understood the Due Process Clause, as interpreted in *World-Wide Volkswagen*, to allow an exercise of personal jurisdiction to be based on no more than the defendant's act of placing the product in the stream of commerce. Other courts have understood the Due Process Clause and the above-quoted language in *World-Wide Volkswagen* to require the action of the defendant to be more purposefully directed at the forum State than the mere act of placing a product in the stream of commerce.

The reasoning of the Supreme Court of California in the present case illustrates the former interpretation of *World-Wide Volkswagen*. The Supreme Court of California held that, because the stream of commerce eventually brought some valves Asahi sold Cheng Shin into California, Asahi's awareness that its valves would be sold in California was sufficient to permit California to exercise jurisdiction over Asahi consistent with the requirements of the Due Process Clause. The Supreme Court of California's position was consistent with those courts that have held that mere foreseeability or awareness was a constitutionally sufficient basis for personal jurisdiction if the defendant's product made its way into the forum State while still in the stream of commerce....

Other courts, however, have understood the Due Process Clause to require something more than that the defendant was aware of its product's entry into the forum State through the stream of commerce in order for the State to exert jurisdiction over the defendant. In the present case, for example, the State Court of Appeal did not read the Due Process Clause, as interpreted by *World-Wide Volkswagen*, to allow "mere foreseeability that the product will enter the forum state [to] be enough by itself to establish jurisdiction over the distributor and retailer." ...

We now find this latter position to be consonant with the requirements of due process. The "substantial connection" ... between the defendant and the forum State necessary for a finding of minimum contacts must come about by *an action of the defendant purposefully directed toward the forum State.* ... The placement of a product into the stream of commerce, without more, is not an act of the defendant purposefully directed toward the forum State. Additional conduct of the defendant may indicate an intent or purpose to serve the market in the forum State, for example, designing the product for the market in the forum State, advertising in the forum State, establishing channels for providing regular advice to customers in the forum State, or marketing the product through a distributor who has agreed to serve as the sales agent in the forum State. But a defendant's awareness that the stream of commerce may or will sweep the product into the forum State does not convert the mere act of placing the product into the stream into an act purposefully directed toward the forum State.

Assuming, *arguendo*, that respondents have established Asahi's awareness that some of the valves sold to Cheng Shin would be incorporated into tire tubes sold in California, respondents have not demonstrated any action by Asahi to purposefully avail itself of the California market. Asahi does not do business in California. It has no office, agents, employees, or property in California. It does not advertise or otherwise solicit business in California. It did not create, control, or employ the distribution system that brought its valves to California.... There is no evidence that Asahi designed its product in anticipation of sales in California.... On the basis of these facts, the exertion of personal jurisdiction over Asahi by the Superior Court of California* exceeds the limits of due process.

B **8/9 Justices join**   **8-0 vote**

The strictures of the Due Process Clause forbid a state court from exercising personal jurisdiction over Asahi under circumstances that would offend "'traditional notions of fair play and substantial justice.'" ...

We have previously explained that the determination of the reasonableness of the exercise of jurisdiction in each case will depend on an evaluation of several factors. A court must consider the burden on the defendant, the interests of the forum State, and the plaintiff's interest in obtaining relief. It must also weigh in its determination "the interstate judicial system's interest in obtaining the most efficient resolution of controversies; and the shared interest of the several States in furthering fundamental substantive social policies." ...

A consideration of these factors in the present case clearly reveals the unreasonableness of the assertion of jurisdiction over Asahi, even apart from the question of the placement of goods in the stream of commerce.

---

* We have no occasion here to determine whether Congress could, consistent with the Due Process Clause of the Fifth Amendment, authorize federal court personal jurisdiction over alien defendants based on the aggregate of *national* contacts, rather than on the contacts between the defendant and the State in which the federal court sits....

Certainly the burden on the defendant in this case is severe. Asahi has been commanded by the Supreme Court of California not only to traverse the distance between Asahi's headquarters in Japan and the Superior Court of California in and for the County of Solano, but also to submit its dispute with Cheng Shin to a foreign nation's judicial system. The unique burdens placed upon one who must defend oneself in a foreign legal system should have significant weight in assessing the reasonableness of stretching the long arm of personal jurisdiction over national borders.

When minimum contacts have been established, often the interests of the plaintiff and the forum in the exercise of jurisdiction will justify even the serious burdens placed on the alien defendant. In the present case, however, the interests of the plaintiff and the forum in California's assertion of jurisdiction over Asahi are slight. All that remains is a claim for indemnification asserted by Cheng Shin, a Tawainese corporation, against Asahi. The transaction on which the indemnification claim is based took place in Taiwan; Asahi's components were shipped from Japan to Taiwan. Cheng Shin has not demonstrated that it is more convenient for it to litigate its indemnification claim against Asahi in California rather than in Taiwan or Japan.

Because the plaintiff is not a California resident, California's legitimate interests in the dispute have considerably diminished. The Supreme Court of California argued that the State had an interest in "protecting its consumers by ensuring that foreign manufacturers comply with the state's safety standards."... The State Supreme Court's definition of California's interest, however, was overly broad. The dispute between Cheng Shin and Asahi is primarily about indemnification rather than safety standards. Moreover, it is not at all clear at this point that California law should govern the question whether a Japanese corporation should indemnify a Taiwanese corporation on the basis of a sale made in Taiwan and a shipment of goods from Japan to Taiwan. *Phillips Petroleum Co. v. Shutts*, 472 U.S. 797, 821–22 (1985); *Allstate Ins. Co. v. Hague*, 449 U.S. 302, 312–13 (1981). The possibility of being haled into a California court as a result of an accident involving Asahi's components undoubtedly creates an additional deterrent to the manufacture of unsafe components; however, similar pressures will be placed on Asahi by the purchasers of its components as long as those who use Asahi components in their final products, and sell those products in California, are subject to the application of California tort law.

World-Wide Volkswagen also admonished courts to take into consideration the interests of the "several States," in addition to the forum State, in the efficient judicial resolution of the dispute and the advancement of substantive policies. In the present case, this advice calls for a court to consider the procedural and substantive policies of other *nations* whose interests are affected by the assertion of jurisdiction by the California court. The procedural and substantive interests of other nations in a state court's assertion of jurisdiction over an alien defendant will differ from case to case. In every case, however, those interests, as well as the federal interest in its foreign relations policies, will be best served by a careful inquiry into the reasonableness of the assertion of jurisdiction in the particular case, and an unwillingness to find the serious burdens on an alien defendant outweighed by minimal interests on the part of the plaintiff or the forum State. "Great care and reserve should be exercised when extending our notions of personal jurisdiction into the international field." ...

Considering the international context, the heavy burden on the alien defendant, and the slight interests of the plaintiff and the forum State, the exercise of personal jurisdiction by a California court over Asahi in this instance would be unreasonable and unfair.

III *opinion of chief Justice, Justice Powell, & Justice Scalia & Justice O Connor*

Because the facts of this case do not establish minimum contacts such that the exercise of personal jurisdiction is consistent with fair play and substantial justice, the judgment of the Supreme Court of California is reversed, and the case is remanded for further proceedings not inconsistent with this opinion.

It is so ordered.

Concurring JUSTICE BRENNAN, with whom JUSTICE WHITE, JUSTICE MARSHALL, and JUSTICE BLACKMUN join, concurring in part and concurring in the judgment.

I do not agree with the interpretation in Part II-A of the stream-of-commerce theory, nor with the conclusion that Asahi did not "purposely avail itself of the California market." ... I do agree, however, with the Court's conclusion in Part II-B that the exercise of personal jurisdiction over Asahi in this case would not comport with "fair play and substantial justice".... This is one of those rare cases in which "minimum requirements inherent in the concept of 'fair play and substantial justice'... defeat the reasonableness of jurisdiction even [though] the defendant has purposefully engaged in forum activities." *Burger King Corp. v. Rudzewicz*.... I therefore join Parts I and II-B of the Court's opinion, and write separately to explain my disagreement with Part II-A.

Part II-A states that "a defendant's awareness that the stream of commerce may or will sweep the product into the forum State does not convert the mere act of placing the product into the stream into an act purposefully directed toward the forum State." ... Under this view, a plaintiff would be required to show "[a]dditional conduct" directed toward the forum before finding the exercise of jurisdiction over the defendant to be consistent with the Due Process Clause.... I see no need for such a showing, however. The stream of commerce refers not to unpredictable currents or eddies, but to the regular and anticipated flow of products from manufacture to distribution to retail sale. As long as a participant in this process is aware that the final product is being marketed in the forum State, the possibility of a lawsuit there cannot come as a surprise. Nor will the litigation present a burden for which there is no corresponding benefit. A defendant who has placed goods in the stream of commerce benefits economically from the retail sale of the final product in the forum State, and indirectly benefits from the State's laws that regulate and facilitate commercial activity. These benefits accrue regardless of whether that participant directly conducts business in the forum State, or engages in additional conduct directed toward that State. Accordingly, most courts and commentators have found that jurisdiction premised on the placement of a product into the stream of commerce is consistent with the Due Process Clause, and have not required a showing of additional conduct.

The endorsement in Part II-A of what appears to be the minority view among Federal Courts of Appeals represents a marked retreat from the analysis in *World-Wide Volkswagen v. Woodson*.... In that case, "respondents [sought] to base jurisdiction on one, isolated occurrence and whatever inferences can be drawn therefrom: the fortuitous circumstance that a single Audi automobile, sold in New York to New York residents, happened to suffer an accident while passing through Oklahoma." ... The Court held that the possibility of an accident in Oklahoma, while to some extent foreseeable in light of the inherent mobility of the automobile, was not enough to establish minimum contacts between the forum State and the retailer or distributor.... The Court then carefully explained:

> [T]his is not to say, of course, that foreseeability is wholly irrelevant. But the foreseeability that is critical to due process analysis is not the mere likelihood that a product will find its way into the forum State. Rather, it is that the de-

fendant's conduct and connection with the forum State are such that he should reasonably anticipate being haled into Court there....

The Court reasoned that when a corporation may reasonably anticipate litigation in a particular forum, it cannot claim that such litigation is unjust or unfair, because it "can act to alleviate the risk of burdensome litigation by procuring insurance, passing the expected costs on to consumers, or, if the risks are too great, severing its connection with the State."...

To illustrate the point, the Court contrasted the foreseeability of litigation in a State to which a consumer fortuitously transports a defendant's product (insufficient contacts) with the foreseeability of litigation in a State where the defendant's product was regularly *sold* (sufficient contacts). The Court stated:

> Hence if the *sale* of a product of a manufacturer or distributor such as Audi or Volkswagen is not simply an isolated occurrence, but arises from the efforts of the manufacturer or distributor to serve, *directly or indirectly*, the market for its product in other States, it is not unreasonable to subject it to suit in one of those States if its allegedly defective merchandise has there been the source of injury to its owner or to others. The forum State does not exceed its powers under the Due Process Clause if it asserts personal jurisdiction over a corporation that delivers its products into the stream of commerce *with the expectation that they will be purchased by consumers* in the forum State.... (emphasis added).

The Court concluded its illustration by referring to *Gray v. American Radiator & Standard Sanitary Corp.*, 22 Ill. 2d 432, 176 N.E.2d 761 (1961), a well-known stream-of-commerce case in which the Illinois Supreme Court applied the theory to assert jurisdiction over a component-parts manufacturer that sold no components directly in Illinois, but did sell them to a manufacturer who incorporated them into a final product that was sold in Illinois....

The Court in *World-Wide Volkswagen* thus took great care to distinguish "between a case involving goods which reach a distant State through a chain of distribution and a case involving goods which reach the same State because a consumer ... took them there."... The California Supreme Court took note of this distinction, and correctly concluded that our holding in *World-Wide Volkswagen* preserved the stream-of-commerce theory....

In this case, the facts found by the California Supreme Court support its finding of minimum contacts. The court found that "[a]lthough Asahi did not design or control the system of distribution that carried its valve assemblies into California, Asahi was aware of the distribution system's operation, and it knew that it would benefit economically from the sale in California of products incorporating its components."... Accordingly, I cannot join the determination in Part II-A that Asahi's regular and extensive sales of component parts to a manufacturer it knew was making regular sales of the final product in California is insufficient to establish minimum contacts with California.

JUSTICE STEVENS, with whom JUSTICE WHITE and JUSTICE BLACKMUN join, concurring in part and concurring in the judgment.

The judgment of the Supreme Court of California should be reversed for the reasons stated in Part II-B of the Court's opinion. While I join Parts I and II-B, I do not join Part II-A for two reasons. First, it is not necessary to the Court's decision. An examination of minimum contacts is not always necessary to determine whether a state court's assertion of personal jurisdiction is constitutional.... Part II-B establishes, after considering the factors set forth in *World-Wide Volkswagen Corp. v. Woodson* ... that California's exercise of jurisdiction over Asahi in this case would be "unreasonable and unfair." ... This finding alone requires reversal; this case fits within the rule that "minimum requirements inherent in the concept of 'fair play and substantial justice' may defeat the reasonableness of jurisdiction even if the defendant has purposefully engaged in forum activities." ... Accordingly, I see no reason in this case for the Court to articulate "purposeful direction" or any other test as the nexus between an act of a defendant and the forum State that is necessary to establish minimum contacts.

Second, even assuming that the test ought to be formulated here, Part II-A misapplies it to the facts of this case. The Court seems to assume that an unwavering line can be drawn between "mere awareness" that a component will find its way into the forum State and "purposeful availment" of the forum's market.... Over the course of its dealings with Cheng Shin, Asahi has arguably engaged in a higher quantum of conduct than "[t]he placement of a product into the stream of commerce, without more...." Whether or not this conduct rises to the level of purposeful availment requires a constitutional determination that is affected by the volume, the value, and the hazardous character of the components. In most circumstances I would be inclined to conclude that a regular course of dealing that results in deliveries of over 100,000 units annually over a period of several years would constitute "purposeful availment" even though the item delivered to the forum State was a standard product marketed throughout the world.

Notes and Questions

1. The Court in *Asahi* applied the same two-step "minimum contacts" analysis for specific jurisdiction that the Court did in *Burger King*. The dispute among the Justices in *Asahi* centered on defining the proper constitutional standard for determining "purposeful availment" in a "stream of commerce" case. On this question, the Justices issued three separate opinions with no majority (controlling) holding or rationale. Four Justices, led by Justice O'Connor, believed that placing a product into the "stream of commerce" with the awareness that the product will reach the forum state is insufficient to establish "purposeful availment" and additional conduct by the defendant directed toward the forum state is required. These four Justices endorsing the "O'Connor" test found that Asahi did not meet the requirement of purposeful availment because Asahi did not engage in any "additional conduct" directed towards California.

Four other Justices, led by Justice Brennan, believed that additional conduct is not required and that placing a product into the stream of commerce with the awareness that it will be purchased by consumers in the forum state is sufficient to constitute "purposeful availment." These four Justices endorsing the "Brennan" test found that Asahi did meet the requirement of purposeful availment because Asahi placed its product into the stream of commerce with the awareness that the final product incorporating its component part would be sold in California.

Justice Stevens, who did not join the opinions of either Justice O'Connor or Justice Brennan, believed that the determination of "purposeful availment" in a case such as this must be measured "by the volume, the value, and the hazardous character of the components." Based on this test, Justice Stevens stated that he "would be inclined to conclude" that Asahi's actions constituted "purposeful availment." Justices White and Blackmun joined in the opinions of both Justice Brennan and Justice Stevens, thus resulting in a 4–4–3 division of support for the Justices' three "purposeful availment" opinions.

2. As noted in *Asahi*, the lower courts were divided on the question of what constituted "purposeful availment" in a "stream of commerce" case and remained so afterwards as the *Asahi* Court issued no majority ruling on this issue. The only controlling rationale in *Asahi* is on the second prong of the minimum contacts analysis, the "reasonableness" test. Even though on the requirement of "purposeful availment" five Justices (Justice Brennan's four, plus Justice Stevens) would have found Asahi's contacts sufficient, the Justices voted 8–0 on Part II-B of Justice O'Connor's opinion in holding that the exercise of personal jurisdiction over Asahi was unreasonable.

3. *Asahi* is the only case in which the U.S. Supreme Court has applied the reasonableness test to defeat jurisdiction. As noted by Justice Brennan, this was "one of those rare cases" in which the reasonableness factors rendered personal jurisdiction unconstitutional. This is because, as Justice O'Connor explained, "often the interests of the plaintiff and the forum ... will justify even the serious burdens placed on an alien defendant." Assume that a case on all fours with *Asahi* arises again, except the injured plaintiff joins *Asahi* as an original defendant in the tort action. Would the result in the case be the same? What factors in the reasonableness test might weigh more strongly in favor of jurisdiction under these changed circumstances?

4. In *Burger King,* the Court indicated that the reasonableness factors may sometimes serve to validate an assertion of specific jurisdiction "upon a *lesser* showing of minimum contacts than would otherwise be required." Note, however, that the Court has never applied the reasonableness test to create jurisdiction in a situation in which purposeful contacts were absent from a case. As stated in *Burger King,* purposeful availment remains the "constitutional touchstone" of minimum contacts jurisdiction.

5. Consider the role of the "state interest" factor in the reasonableness test, which has been mentioned in many Supreme Court cases over the years.

(a) Recall, for example, that in *Shaffer v. Heitner*, discussed in section B(4), above, for example, the Court rejected an argument that Delaware's interest in adjudicating the action was high. The Court stated that the argument was undercut by the failure of Delaware's Legislature to assert the state's interest in a statute. This statement suggests that the "state interest" factor of the reasonableness test can be enhanced by legislative action. Should this be a valid consideration?

(b) Recall that in *Keeton v. Hustler Magazine, Inc.*, discussed in section B(5), above, the Court stated that New Hampshire's interests were enhanced by two features of its statutory scheme. First, the state had not limited its criminal defamation statute (which was not applicable to the case) to libels aimed at the state's residents. Second, some time before the action, the state had amended its long-arm statute to eliminate a requirement that torts falling within the statute be committed against residents of the state.

(c) Recall that in *Calder v. Jones*, another libel case decided the same day as *Keeton*, California's assertion of jurisdiction was accomplished under its very general long-arm statute, discussed in section B(2), above. The Court did not find that this very general statute detracted from the state's interest in *Calder*. What do *Keeton* and *Calder*, taken together, indicate about how a statute can affect the "state interest" factor in the reasonableness test? Recall the Court's citation of these cases in *Burger King*. Does the proposition for which the cases were cited give you any other basis for determining how the "state interest" factor operates?

6. Recall the discussion in Justice O'Connor's opinion in *Asahi* of how advertising in the forum state might provide the "additional conduct" by the defendant which Justice O'Connor believed to be necessary to establish purposeful availment. Is it possible for

advertising alone in the forum to establish the constitutional prerequisites for personal jurisdiction over a nonresident defendant? Should it matter what kind of service or product the defendant is advertising? *See, e.g., Mastondrea v. Occidental Hotels Mgmt. S.A.,* 918 A.2d. 27, 35–36 (N.J. App. Div. 2007) ("targeted advertising" and solicitation of New Jersey residents by independent tour operators and marketing company on behalf of Mexican resort sufficient to establish specific jurisdiction over Mexican resort in New Jersey in action by resident injured at resort).

J. McIntyre Machinery, Ltd. v. Nicastro

Supreme Court of the United States, 2011

564 U.S. ___, 131 S. Ct. 2780, 180 L. Ed. 2d 765

JUSTICE KENNEDY announced the judgment of the Court and delivered an opinion, in which THE CHIEF JUSTICE, JUSTICE SCALIA, and JUSTICE THOMAS join.

Whether a person or entity is subject to the jurisdiction of a state court despite not having been present in the State either at the time of suit or at the time of the alleged injury, and despite not having consented to the exercise of jurisdiction, is a question that arises with great frequency in the routine course of litigation. The rules and standards for determining when a State does or does not have jurisdiction over an absent party have been unclear because of decades-old questions left open in *Asahi Metal Industry Co.* v. *Superior Court*, 480 U.S. 102 (1987).

Here, the Supreme Court of New Jersey, relying in part on *Asahi*, held that New Jersey's courts can exercise jurisdiction over a foreign manufacturer of a product so long as the manufacturer "knows or reasonably should know that its products are distributed through a nationwide distribution system that might lead to those products being sold in any of the fifty states." *Nicastro* v. *McIntyre Mach. Am., Ltd.*, 201 N.J. 48, 76, 77, 987 A.2d 575, 591, 592 (2010). Applying that test, the court concluded that a British manufacturer of scrap metal machines was subject to jurisdiction in New Jersey, even though at no time had it advertised in, sent goods to, or in any relevant sense targeted the State.

That decision cannot be sustained. Although the New Jersey Supreme Court issued an extensive opinion with careful attention to this Court's cases and to its own precedent, the "stream of commerce" metaphor carried the decision far afield. Due process protects the defendant's right not to be coerced except by lawful judicial power. As a general rule, the exercise of judicial power is not lawful unless the defendant "purposefully avails itself of the privilege of conducting activities within the forum State, thus invoking the benefits and protections of its laws." *Hanson* v. *Denckla,* 357 U.S. 235, 253 (1958). There may be exceptions, say, for instance, in cases involving an intentional tort. But the general rule is applicable in this products-liability case, and the so-called "stream-of-commerce" doctrine cannot displace it.

I

This case arises from a products-liability suit filed in New Jersey state court. Robert Nicastro seriously injured his hand while using a metal-shearing machine manufactured by J. McIntyre Machinery, Ltd. (J. McIntyre). The accident occurred in New Jersey, but the machine was manufactured in England, where J. McIntyre is incorporated and operates. The question here is whether the New Jersey courts have jurisdiction over J. McIntyre, notwithstanding the fact that the company at no time either marketed goods in the State or shipped them there. Nicastro was a plaintiff in the New Jersey trial court and is the respondent here; J. McIntyre was a defendant and is now the petitioner.

At oral argument in this Court, Nicastro's counsel stressed three primary facts in defense of New Jersey's assertion of jurisdiction over J. McIntyre....

First, an independent company agreed to sell J. McIntyre's machines in the United States. J. McIntyre itself did not sell its machines to buyers in this country beyond the U.S. distributor, and there is no allegation that the distributor was under J. McIntyre's control.

Second, J. McIntyre officials attended annual conventions for the scrap recycling industry to advertise J. McIntyre's machines alongside the distributor. The conventions took place in various States, but never in New Jersey.

Third, no more than four machines (the record suggests only one ...), including the machine that caused the injuries that are the basis for this suit, ended up in New Jersey....

In light of these facts, the New Jersey Supreme Court concluded that New Jersey courts could exercise jurisdiction over petitioner without contravention of the Due Process Clause. Jurisdiction was proper, in that court's view, because the injury occurred in New Jersey; because petitioner knew or reasonably should have known "that its products are distributed through a nationwide distribution system that might lead to those products being sold in any of the fifty states"; and because petitioner failed to "take some reasonable step to prevent the distribution of its products in this State." 201 N.J. at 77, 987 A.2d at 592.

Both the New Jersey Supreme Court's holding and its account of what it called "[t]he stream-of-commerce doctrine of jurisdiction," *id.* at 80, 987 A.2d at 594, were incorrect, however. This Court's *Asahi* decision may be responsible in part for that court's error regarding the stream of commerce, and this case presents an opportunity to provide greater clarity.

II

The Due Process Clause protects an individual's right to be deprived of life, liberty, or property only by the exercise of lawful power. *Cf. Giaccio* v. *Pennsylvania*, 382 U.S. 399, 403 (1966) (The Clause "protect[s] a person against having the Government impose burdens upon him except in accordance with the valid laws of the land"). This is no less true with respect to the power of a sovereign to resolve disputes through judicial process than with respect to the power of a sovereign to prescribe rules of conduct for those within its sphere. *See Steel Co.* v. *Citizens for Better Env't*, 523 U.S. 83, 94 (1998) ("Jurisdiction is power to declare the law"). As a general rule, neither statute nor judicial decree may bind strangers to the State. *Cf. Burnham* v. *Superior Court*, 495 U.S. 604, 608–09 (1990) (opinion of Scalia, J.) (invoking "the phrase *coram non judice,* 'before a person not a judge' — meaning, in effect, that the proceeding in question was not a *judicial* proceeding because lawful judicial authority was not present, and could therefore not yield a *judgment*").

A court may subject a defendant to judgment only when the defendant has sufficient contacts with the sovereign "such that the maintenance of the suit does not offend 'traditional notions of fair play and substantial justice.'" *International Shoe Co.* v. *Washington*, 326 U.S. 310, 316 (1945) (quoting *Milliken* v. *Meyer*, 311 U.S. 457, 463 (1940)). Freeform notions of fundamental fairness divorced from traditional practice cannot transform a judgment rendered in the absence of authority into law. As a general rule, the sovereign's exercise of power requires some act by which the defendant "purposefully avails itself of the privilege of conducting activities within the forum State, thus invoking the benefits and protections of its laws," *Hanson*, 357 U.S. at 253, though in some cases, as with an intentional tort, the defendant might well fall within the State's authority by reason of his attempt to obstruct its laws. In products-liability cases like this one, it is the defendant's purposeful availment that makes jurisdiction consistent with "traditional notions of fair play and substantial justice."

A person may submit to a State's authority in a number of ways. There is, of course, explicit consent. *E.g.*, *Insurance Corp. of Ireland* v. *Compagnie des Bauxites de Guinee*, 456 U.S. 694, 703 (1982). Presence within a State at the time suit commences through service of process is another example. *See Burnham, supra.* Citizenship or domicile—or, by analogy, incorporation or principal place of business for corporations—also indicates general submission to a State's powers.... Each of these examples reveals circumstances, or a course of conduct, from which it is proper to infer an intention to benefit from and thus an intention to submit to the laws of the forum State. *Cf. Burger King Corp.* v. *Rudzewicz*, 471 U.S. 462, 476 (1985). These examples support exercise of the general jurisdiction of the State's courts and allow the State to resolve both matters that originate within the State and those based on activities and events elsewhere. *Helicopteros Nacionales de Colombia, S.A.* v. *Hall*, 466 U.S. 408, 414 & n.9 (1984). By contrast, those who live or operate primarily outside a State have a due process right not to be subjected to judgment in its courts as a general matter.

There is also a more limited form of submission to a State's authority for disputes that "arise out of or are connected with the activities within the state." *International Shoe Co.*, 311 U.S. at 319. Where a defendant "purposefully avails itself of the privilege of conducting activities within the forum State, thus invoking the benefits and protections of its laws," *Hanson*, 357 U.S. at 253, it submits to the judicial power of an otherwise foreign sovereign to the extent that power is exercised in connection with the defendant's activities touching on the State. In other words, submission through contact with and activity directed at a sovereign may justify specific jurisdiction "in a suit arising out of or related to the defendant's contacts with the forum." *Helicopteros*, 466 U.S. at 414, n.8....

The imprecision arising from *Asahi*, for the most part, results from its statement of the relation between jurisdiction and the "stream of commerce." The stream of commerce, like other metaphors, has its deficiencies as well as its utility. It refers to the movement of goods from manufacturers through distributors to consumers, yet beyond that descriptive purpose its meaning is far from exact. This Court has stated that a defendant's placing goods into the stream of commerce "with the expectation that they will be purchased by consumers within the forum State" may indicate purposeful availment. *World-Wide Volkswagen Corp.* v. *Woodson*, 444 U.S. 286, 298 (1980) (finding that expectation lacking). But that statement does not amend the general rule of personal jurisdiction. It merely observes that a defendant may in an appropriate case be subject to jurisdiction without entering the forum—itself an unexceptional proposition—as where manufacturers or distributors "seek to serve" a given State's market. *Id.* at 295. The principal inquiry in cases of this sort is whether the defendant's activities manifest an intention to submit to the power of a sovereign. In other words, the defendant must "purposefully avai[l] itself of the privilege of conducting activities within the forum State, thus invoking the benefits and protections of its laws." *Hanson*, 357 U.S. at 253; *Insurance Corp.*, 456 U.S. at 704–05 ("[A]ctions of the defendant may amount to a legal submission to the jurisdiction of the court"). Sometimes a defendant does so by sending its goods rather than its agents. The defendant's transmission of goods permits the exercise of jurisdiction only where the defendant can be said to have targeted the forum; as a general rule, it is not enough that the defendant might have predicted that its goods will reach the forum State.

In *Asahi*, an opinion by Justice Brennan for four Justices outlined a different approach. It discarded the central concept of sovereign authority in favor of considerations of fairness and foreseeability. As that concurrence contended, "jurisdiction premised on the placement of a product into the stream of commerce [without more] is consistent with the Due Process Clause," for "[a]s long as a participant in this process is aware that the final product is being marketed in the forum State, the possibility of a lawsuit there cannot come as a surprise." 480 U.S. at 117 (opinion concurring in part and concurring in judgment). It was the premise of the concurring opinion that the defendant's ability to anticipate suit renders the assertion of jurisdiction fair. In this way, the opinion made foreseeability the touchstone of jurisdiction.

The standard set forth in Justice Brennan's concurrence was rejected in an opinion written by Justice O'Connor; but the relevant part of that opinion, too, commanded the assent of only four Justices, not a majority of the Court. That opinion stated: "The 'substantial connection' between the defendant and the forum State necessary for a finding of minimum contacts must come about by an action of the defendant purposefully directed toward the forum State. The placement of a product into the stream of commerce, without more, is not an act of the defendant purposefully directed toward the forum State." *Id.* at 112 (emphasis deleted; citations omitted).

Since *Asahi* was decided, the courts have sought to reconcile the competing opinions. But Justice Brennan's concurrence, advocating a rule based on general notions of fairness and foreseeability, is inconsistent with the premises of lawful judicial power. This Court's precedents make clear that it is the defendant's actions, not his expectations, that empower a State's courts to subject him to judgment.

The conclusion that jurisdiction is in the first instance a question of authority rather than fairness explains, for example, why the principal opinion in *Burnham* "conducted no independent inquiry into the desirability or fairness" of the rule that service of process within a State suffices to establish jurisdiction over an otherwise foreign defendant. 495 U.S. at 621. As that opinion explained, "[t]he view developed early that each State had the power to hale before its courts any individual who could be found within its borders." *Id.* at 610. Furthermore, were general fairness considerations the touchstone of jurisdiction, a lack of purposeful availment might be excused where carefully crafted judicial procedures could otherwise protect the defendant's interests, or where the plaintiff would suffer substantial hardship if forced to litigate in a foreign forum. That such considerations have not been deemed controlling is instructive....

Two principles are implicit in the foregoing. First, personal jurisdiction requires a forum-by-forum, or sovereign-by-sovereign, analysis. The question is whether a defendant has followed a course of conduct directed at the society or economy existing within the jurisdiction of a given sovereign, so that the sovereign has the power to subject the defendant to judgment concerning that conduct. Personal jurisdiction, of course, restricts "judicial power not as a matter of sovereignty, but as a matter of individual liberty," for due process protects the individual's right to be subject only to lawful power. *Insurance Corp.*, 456 U.S. at 702. But whether a judicial judgment is lawful depends on whether the sovereign has authority to render it.

The second principle is a corollary of the first. Because the United States is a distinct sovereign, a defendant may in principle be subject to the jurisdiction of the courts of the United States but not of any particular State.... For jurisdiction, a litigant may have the requisite relationship with the United States Government but not with the government of any individual State. That would be an exceptional case, however. If the defendant is a domestic domiciliary, the courts of its home State are available and can exercise general jurisdiction. And if another State were to assert jurisdiction in an inappropriate case, it would upset the federal balance, which posits that each State has a sovereignty that is not subject to unlawful intrusion by other States. Furthermore, foreign corporations will often target or concentrate on particular States, subjecting them to specific jurisdiction in those forums.

It must be remembered, however, that although this case and *Asahi* both involve foreign manufacturers, the undesirable consequences of Justice Brennan's approach are no less significant for domestic producers. The owner of a small Florida farm might sell crops to a large nearby distributor, for example, who might then distribute them to grocers across the country. If foreseeability were the controlling criterion, the farmer could be sued in Alaska or any number of other States' courts without ever leaving town. And the issue of foreseeability may itself be contested so that significant expenses are incurred just on the preliminary issue of jurisdiction. Jurisdictional rules should avoid these costs whenever possible.

The conclusion that the authority to subject a defendant to judgment depends on purposeful availment, consistent with Justice O'Connor's opinion in *Asahi*, does not by itself resolve many difficult questions of jurisdiction that will arise in particular cases. The defendant's conduct and the economic realities of the market the defendant seeks to serve will differ across cases, and judicial exposition will, in common-law fashion, clarify the contours of that principle.

III

In this case, petitioner directed marketing and sales efforts at the United States. It may be that, assuming it were otherwise empowered to legislate on the subject, the Congress could authorize the exercise of jurisdiction in appropriate courts. That circumstance is not presented in this case, however, and it is neither necessary nor appropriate to address here any constitutional concerns that might be attendant to that exercise of power....

Respondent has not established that J. McIntyre engaged in conduct purposefully directed at New Jersey. Recall that respondent's claim of jurisdiction centers on three facts: The distributor agreed to sell J. McIntyre's machines in the United States; J. McIntyre officials attended trade shows in several States but not in New Jersey; and up to four machines ended up in New Jersey. The British manufacturer had no office in New Jersey; it neither paid taxes nor owned property there; and it neither advertised in, nor sent any employees to, the State. Indeed, after discovery the trial court found that the "defendant does not have a single contact with New Jersey short of the machine in question ending up in this state." ... These facts may reveal an intent to serve the U.S. market, but they do not show that J. McIntyre purposefully availed itself of the New Jersey market.

It is notable that the New Jersey Supreme Court appears to agree, for it could "not find that J. McIntyre had a presence or minimum contacts in this State—in any jurisprudential sense—that would justify a New Jersey court to exercise jurisdiction in this case." 987 A.2d at 582. The court nonetheless held that petitioner could be sued in New Jersey based on a "stream-of-commerce theory of jurisdiction." *Id.* As discussed, however, the stream-of-commerce metaphor cannot supersede either the mandate of the Due Process Clause or the limits on judicial authority that Clause ensures. The New Jersey Supreme Court also cited "significant policy reasons" to justify its holding, including the State's "strong interest in protecting its citizens from defective products." *Id.* at 590. That interest is doubtless strong, but the Constitution commands restraint before discarding liberty in the name of expediency.

....

Due process protects petitioner's right to be subject only to lawful authority. At no time did petitioner engage in any activities in New Jersey that reveal an intent to invoke or benefit from the protection of its laws. New Jersey is without power to adjudge the rights and liabilities of J. McIntyre, and its exercise of jurisdiction would violate due process. The contrary judgment of the New Jersey Supreme Court is *[r]eversed*.

JUSTICE BREYER, with whom JUSTICE ALITO joins, concurring in the judgment.

The Supreme Court of New Jersey adopted a broad understanding of the scope of personal jurisdiction based on its view that "[t]he increasingly fast-paced globalization of the world economy has removed national borders as barriers to trade." *Nicastro* v. *McIntyre Mach. Am., Ltd.*, 987 A.2d 575, 577 (N.J. 2010). I do not doubt that there have been many recent changes in commerce and communication, many of which are not anticipated by our precedents. But this case does not present any of those issues. So I think it unwise to announce a rule of broad applicability without full consideration of the modern-day consequences.

In my view, the outcome of this case is determined by our precedents. Based on the facts found by the New Jersey courts, respondent Robert Nicastro failed to meet his burden to demonstrate that it was constitutionally proper to exercise jurisdiction over petitioner J. McIntyre Machinery, Ltd. (British Manufacturer), a British firm that manufactures scrap-metal machines in Great Britain and sells them through an independent distributor in the United States (American Distributor). On that basis, I agree with the plurality that the contrary judgment of the Supreme Court of New Jersey should be reversed.

I

In asserting jurisdiction over the British Manufacturer, the Supreme Court of New Jersey relied most heavily on three primary facts as providing constitutionally sufficient "contacts" with New Jersey, thereby making it fundamentally fair to hale the British Manufacturer before its courts: (1) The American Distributor on one occasion sold and shipped one machine to a New Jersey customer, namely, Mr. Nicastro's employer, Mr. Curcio; (2) the British Manufacturer permitted, indeed wanted, its independent American Distributor to sell its machines to anyone in America willing to buy them; and (3) representatives of the British Manufacturer attended trade shows in "such cities as Chicago, Las Vegas, New Orleans, Orlando, San Diego, and San Francisco." *Id.* at 54–55, 987 A.2d at 578–79. In my view, these facts do not provide contacts between the British firm and the State of New Jersey constitutionally sufficient to support New Jersey's assertion of jurisdiction in this case.

None of our precedents finds that a single isolated sale, even if accompanied by the kind of sales effort indicated here, is sufficient. Rather, this Court's previous holdings suggest the contrary. The Court has held that a single sale to a customer who takes an accident-causing product to a different State (where the accident takes place) is not a sufficient basis for asserting jurisdiction. *See World-Wide Volkswagen Corp.* v. *Woodson*, 444 U.S. 286 (1980). And the Court, in separate opinions, has strongly suggested that a single sale of a product in a State does not constitute an adequate basis for asserting jurisdiction over an out-of-state defendant, even if that defendant places his goods in the stream of commerce, fully aware (and hoping) that such a sale will take place. *See Asahi Metal Industry Co.* v. *Superior Court*, 480 U.S. 102, 111, 112 (1987) (opinion of O'Connor, J.) (requiring "something more" than simply placing "a product into the stream of commerce," even if defendant is "awar[e]" that the stream "may or will sweep the product into the forum State"); *id.* at 117 (Brennan, J., concurring in part and concurring in judgment) (jurisdiction should lie where a sale in a State is part of "the regular and anticipated flow" of commerce into the State, but not where that sale is only an "edd[y]," *i.e.*, an isolated occurrence); *id.* at 122 (Stevens, J., concurring in part and concurring in judgment) (indicating that "the volume, the value, and the hazardous character" of a good may affect the jurisdictional inquiry and emphasizing Asahi's "regular course of dealing").

Here, the relevant facts found by the New Jersey Supreme Court show no "regular … flow" or "regular course" of sales in New Jersey; and there is no "something more," such as special state-related design, advertising, advice, marketing, or anything else. Mr. Nicastro, who here bears the burden of proving jurisdiction, has shown no specific effort by the British Manufacturer to sell in New Jersey. He has introduced no list of potential New Jersey customers who might, for example, have regularly attended trade shows. And he has not otherwise shown that the British Manufacturer "purposefully avail[ed] itself of the privilege of conducting activities" within New Jersey, or that it delivered its goods in the stream of commerce "with the expectation that they will be purchased" by New Jersey users. *World-Wide Volkswagen,* 444 U.S. at 297–98 (internal quotation marks omitted).

There may well have been other facts that Mr. Nicastro could have demonstrated in support of jurisdiction. And the dissent considers some of those facts. See [infra] (opinion of Ginsberg, J.) (describing the size and scope of New Jersey's scrap-metal business). But the plaintiff bears the burden of establishing jurisdiction, and here I would take the facts precisely as the New Jersey Supreme Court stated them.…

Accordingly, on the record present here, resolving this case requires no more than adhering to our precedents.

II

I would not go further. Because the incident at issue in this case does not implicate modern concerns, and because the factual record leaves many open questions, this is an unsuitable vehicle for making broad pronouncements that refashion basic jurisdictional rules.

A

The plurality seems to state strict rules that limit jurisdiction where a defendant does not "inten[d] to submit to the power of a sovereign" and cannot "be said to have targeted the forum." … But what do those standards mean when a company targets the world by selling products from its Web site? And does it matter if, instead of shipping the products directly, a company consigns the products through an intermediary (say, Amazon.com) who then receives and fulfills the orders? And what if the company markets its products through popup advertisements that it knows will be viewed in a forum? Those issues have serious commercial consequences but are totally absent in this case.

B

But though I do not agree with the plurality's seemingly strict no-jurisdiction rule, I am not persuaded by the absolute approach adopted by the New Jersey Supreme Court and urged by respondent and his *amici.* Under that view, a producer is subject to jurisdiction for a products-liability action so long as it "knows or reasonably should know that its products are distributed through a nationwide distribution system that *might* lead to those products being sold in any of the fifty states." 987 A.2d at 592 (emphasis added). In the context of this case, I cannot agree.

For one thing, to adopt this view would abandon the heretofore accepted inquiry of whether, focusing upon the relationship between "the defendant, the *forum,* and the litigation," it is fair, in light of the defendant's contacts *with that forum,* to subject the defendant to suit there. *Shaffer* v. *Heitner,* 433 U.S. 186, 204 (1977) (emphasis added). It would ordinarily rest jurisdiction instead upon no more than the occurrence of a product-based accident in the forum State. But this Court has rejected the notion that a defendant's amenability to suit "travel[s] with the chattel." *World-Wide Volkswagen*, 444 U.S. at 296.

For another, I cannot reconcile so automatic a rule with the constitutional demand for "minimum contacts" and "purposefu[l] avail[ment]," each of which rest upon a particular notion of defendant-focused fairness. *Id.* at 291, 297 (internal quotation marks omitted). A rule like the New Jersey Supreme Court's would permit every State to assert jurisdiction in a products-liability suit against any domestic manufacturer who sells its products (made anywhere in the United States) to a national distributor, no matter how large or small the manufacturer, no matter how distant the forum, and no matter how few the number of items that end up in the particular forum at issue. What might appear fair in the case of a large manufacturer which specifically seeks, or expects, an equal-sized distributor to sell its product in a distant State might seem unfair in the case of a small manufacturer (say, an Appalachian potter) who sells his product (cups and saucers) exclusively to a large distributor, who resells a single item (a coffee mug) to a buyer from a distant State (Hawaii). I know too little about the range of these or in-between possibilities to abandon in favor of the more absolute rule what has previously been this Court's less absolute approach.

Further, the fact that the defendant is a foreign, rather than a domestic, manufacturer makes the basic fairness of an absolute rule yet more uncertain. I am again less certain than is the New Jersey Supreme Court that the nature of international commerce has changed so significantly as to require a new approach to personal jurisdiction.

It may be that a larger firm can readily "alleviate the risk of burdensome litigation by procuring insurance, passing the expected costs on to customers, or, if the risks are too great, severing its connection with the State." *World-Wide Volkswagen*, 444 U.S. at 297. But manufacturers come in many shapes and sizes. It may be fundamentally unfair to require a small Egyptian shirt maker, a Brazilian manufacturing cooperative, or a Kenyan coffee farmer, selling its products through international distributors, to respond to products-liability tort suits in virtually every State in the United States, even those in respect to which the foreign firm has no connection at all but the sale of a single (allegedly defective) good. And a rule like the New Jersey Supreme Court suggests would require every product manufacturer, large or small, selling to American distributors to understand not only the tort law of every State, but also the wide variance in the way courts within different States apply that law....

C

At a minimum, I would not work such a change to the law in the way either the plurality or the New Jersey Supreme Court suggests without a better understanding of the relevant contemporary commercial circumstances....

This case presents no such occasion, and so I again reiterate that I would adhere strictly to our precedents and the limited facts found by the New Jersey Supreme Court. And on those grounds, I do not think we can find jurisdiction in this case. Accordingly, though I agree with the plurality as to the outcome of this case, I concur only in the judgment of that opinion and not its reasoning.

Justice Ginsburg, with whom Justice Sotomayor and Justice Kagan join, dissenting.

A foreign industrialist seeks to develop a market in the United States for machines it manufactures. It hopes to derive substantial revenue from sales it makes to United States purchasers. Where in the United States buyers reside does not matter to this manufacturer. Its goal is simply to sell as much as it can, wherever it can. It excludes no region or State from the market it wishes to reach. But, all things considered, it prefers to avoid products liability litigation in the United States. To that end, it engages a U.S. distributor to ship its machines stateside. Has it succeeded in escaping personal jurisdiction in a State where one of its products is sold and causes injury or even death to a local user?

Under this Court's pathmarking precedent in *International Shoe Co.* v. *Washington*, 326 U.S. 310 (1945), and subsequent decisions, one would expect the answer to be unequivocally, "No." But instead, six Justices of this Court, in divergent opinions, tell us that the manufacturer has avoided the jurisdiction of our state courts, except perhaps in States where its products are sold in sizeable quantities. Inconceivable as it may have seemed yesterday, the splintered majority today "turn[s] the clock back to the days before modern long-arm statutes when a manufacturer, to avoid being haled into court where a user is injured, need only Pilate-like wash its hands of a product by having independent distributors market it." Weintraub, *A Map Out of the Personal Jurisdiction Labyrinth*, 28 U. C. Davis L. Rev. 531, 555 (1995).

I

. . . .

The machine that injured Nicastro, a "McIntyre Model 640 Shear," sold in the United States for $24,900 in 1995 ... and features a "massive cutting capacity".... According to McIntyre UK's product brochure, the machine is "use[d] throughout the [w]orld." *Id.* McIntyre UK represented in the brochure that, by "incorporat[ing] off-the-shelf hydraulic parts from suppliers with international sales outlets," the 640 Shear's design guarantees serviceability "wherever [its customers] may be based." ... The instruction manual advises "owner[s] and operators of a 640 Shear [to] make themselves aware of [applicable health and safety regulations]," including "the American National Standards Institute Regulations (USA) for the use of Scrap Metal Processing Equipment." ...

Nicastro operated the 640 Shear in the course of his employment at Curcio Scrap Metal (CSM) in Saddle Brook, New Jersey...."New Jersey has long been a hotbed of scrap-metal businesses." *See* Drake, *The Scrap-Heap Rollup Hits New Jersey, Business News New Jersey*, June 1, 1998, at 1. In 2008, New Jersey recycling facilities processed 2,013,730 tons of scrap iron, steel, aluminum, and other metals—more than any other State—outpacing Kentucky, its nearest competitor, by nearly 30 percent. Von Haaren, Themelis, & Goldstein, *The State of Garbage in America*, BioCycle, Oct. 2010, at 19.

CSM's owner, Frank Curcio, "first heard of [McIntyre UK's] machine while attending an Institute of Scrap Metal Industries [(ISRI)] convention in Las Vegas in 1994 or 1995, where [McIntyre UK] was an exhibitor." ... ISRI "presents the world's largest scrap recycling industry trade show each year." ... The event attracts "owners [and] managers of scrap processing companies" and others "interested in seeing—and purchasing—new equipment." ... According to ISRI, more than 3,000 potential buyers of scrap processing and recycling equipment attend its annual conventions, "primarily because th[e] exposition provides them with the most comprehensive industry-related shopping experience concentrated in a single, convenient location."....

McIntyre UK representatives attended every ISRI convention from 1990 through 2005.... These annual expositions were held in diverse venues across the United States; in addition to Las Vegas, conventions were held 1990–2005 in New Orleans, Orlando, San Antonio, and San Francisco.... McIntyre UK's president, Michael Pownall, regularly attended ISRI conventions.... He attended ISRI's Las Vegas convention the year CSM's owner first learned of, and saw, the 640 Shear.... McIntyre UK exhibited its products at ISRI trade shows, the company acknowledged, hoping to reach "anyone interested in the machine from anywhere in the United States." ...

Although McIntyre UK's U.S. sales figures are not in the record, it appears that for several years in the 1990's, earnings from sales of McIntyre UK products in the United States "ha[d] been good" in comparison to "the rest of the world." ... In response to interrogatories, McIntyre UK stated that its commissioning engineer had installed the company's equipment in several States—Illinois, Iowa, Kentucky, Virginia, and Washington....

From at least 1995 until 2001, McIntyre UK retained an Ohio-based company, McIntyre Machinery America, Ltd. (McIntyre America), "as its exclusive distributor for the entire United States." ... Though similarly named, the two companies were separate and independent entities with "no commonality of ownership or management." ... In invoices and other written communications, McIntyre America described itself as McIntyre UK's national distributor, "America's Link" to "Quality Metal Processing Equipment" from England....

In a November 23, 1999 letter to McIntyre America, McIntyre UK's president spoke plainly about the manufacturer's objective in authorizing the exclusive distributorship: "All we wish to do is sell our products in the [United] States and get paid!" ... Notably, McIntyre America was concerned about U.S. litigation involving McIntyre UK products, in which the distributor had been named as a defendant. McIntyre UK counseled McIntyre America to respond personally to the litigation, but reassured its distributor that "the product was built and designed by McIntyre Machinery in the UK and the buck stops here—if there's something wrong with the machine." ... Answering jurisdictional interrogatories, McIntyre UK stated that it had been named as a defendant in lawsuits in Illinois, Kentucky, Massachusetts, and West Virginia.... And in correspondence with McIntyre America, McIntyre UK noted that the manufacturer had products liability insurance coverage....

Over the years, McIntyre America distributed several McIntyre UK products to U.S. customers, including, in addition to the 640 Shear, McIntyre UK's "Niagara" and "Tardis" systems, wire strippers, and can machines.... In promoting McIntyre UK's products at conventions and demonstration sites and in trade journal advertisements, McIntyre America looked to McIntyre UK for direction and guidance.... To achieve McIntyre UK's objective, *i.e.*, "to sell [its] machines to customers throughout the United States," ..."the two companies [were acting] closely in concert with each other," ... McIntyre UK never instructed its distributor to avoid certain States or regions of the country; rather, as just noted, the manufacturer engaged McIntyre America to attract customers "from anywhere in the United States." ...

In sum, McIntyre UK's regular attendance and exhibitions at ISRI conventions was surely a purposeful step to reach customers for its products "anywhere in the United States." At least as purposeful was McIntyre UK's engagement of McIntyre America as the conduit for sales of McIntyre UK's machines to buyers "throughout the United States." Given McIntyre UK's endeavors to reach and profit from the United States market as a whole, Nicastro's suit, I would hold, has been brought in a forum entirely appropriate for the adjudication of his claim. He alleges that McIntyre UK's shear machine was defectively designed or manufactured and, as a result, caused injury to him at his workplace. The machine arrived in Nicastro's New Jersey workplace not randomly or fortuitously, but as a result of the U.S. connections and distribution system that McIntyre UK deliberately arranged.[3] On what sensible view of the allocation of adjudicatory au-

---

3. McIntyre UK resisted Nicastro's efforts to determine whether other McIntyre machines had been sold to New Jersey customers.... McIntyre did allow that McIntyre America "may have resold products it purchased from [McIntyre UK] to a buyer in New Jersey," ... but said it kept no record of the ultimate destination of machines it shipped to its distributor.... A private investigator engaged by Nicastro found at least one McIntyre UK machine, of unspecified type, in use in New Jersey.... But McIntyre UK objected that the investigator's report was "unsworn and based upon hearsay." ... More-

thority could the place of Nicastro's injury within the United States be deemed off limits for his products liability claim against a foreign manufacturer who targeted the United States (including all the States that constitute the Nation) as the territory it sought to develop?

II

A few points on which there should be no genuine debate bear statement at the outset. First, all agree, McIntyre UK surely is not subject to general (all-purpose) jurisdiction in New Jersey courts, for that foreign-country corporation is hardly "at home" in New Jersey....

Second, no issue of the fair and reasonable allocation of adjudicatory authority among States of the United States is present in this case. New Jersey's exercise of personal jurisdiction over a foreign manufacturer whose dangerous product caused a workplace injury in New Jersey does not tread on the domain, or diminish the sovereignty, of any sister State....

Third, the constitutional limits on a state court's adjudicatory authority derive from considerations of due process, not state sovereignty [quoting *Insurance Corp. of Ireland* v. *Compagnie des Bauxites de Guinee*, 456 U.S. 694, 703 n.10 (1982)].... *See also Shaffer* v. *Heitner*, 433 U.S. 186, 204 & n.20 (1977) (recognizing that "the mutually exclusive sovereignty of the States [is not] the central concern of the inquiry into personal jurisdiction"). *But see* ... (plurality opinion) (asserting that "sovereign authority," not "fairness," is the "central concept" in determining personal jurisdiction).

Finally, in *International Shoe* itself, and decisions thereafter, the Court has made plain that legal fictions, notably "presence" and "implied consent," should be discarded, for they conceal the actual bases on which jurisdiction rests....

Whatever the state of academic debate over the role of consent in modern jurisdictional doctrines, the plurality's notion that consent is the animating concept draws no support from controlling decisions of this Court. Quite the contrary, the Court has explained, a forum can exercise jurisdiction when its contacts with the controversy are sufficient; invocation of a fictitious consent, the Court has repeatedly said, is unnecessary and unhelpful. *See, e.g., Burger King Corp.* v. *Rudzewicz*, 471 U.S. 462, 472 (1985) (Due Process Clause permits "forum" to assert specific jurisdiction over an out-of-state defendant who has not consented to suit there); *McGee* v. *International Life Ins. Co.*, 355 U.S. 220, 222 (1957) ("[T]his Court [has] abandoned 'consent,' 'doing business,' and 'presence' as the standard for measuring the extent of state judicial power over [out-of-state] corporations.").[5]

III

This case is illustrative of marketing arrangements for sales in the United States common in today's commercial world. A foreign-country manufacturer engages a U.S. company to promote and distribute the manufacturer's products, not in any particular State, but anywhere and everywhere in the United States the distributor can attract purchasers. The product proves defective and injures a user in the State where the user lives or works. Often, as here, the manufacturer will have liability insurance covering personal injuries caused by its products....

---

over, McIntyre UK maintained, no evidence showed that the machine the investigator found in New Jersey had been "sold into [that State]."...

5. *But see* ... (plurality opinion) (maintaining that a forum may be fair and reasonable, based on its links to the episode in suit, yet off limits because the defendant has not submitted to the State's authority). The plurality's notion that jurisdiction over foreign corporations depends upon the defendant's "submission," ... seems scarcely different from the long-discredited fiction of implied consent. It bears emphasis that a majority of this Court's members do not share the plurality's view.

When industrial accidents happen, a long-arm statute in the State where the injury occurs generally permits assertion of jurisdiction, upon giving proper notice, over the foreign manufacturer. For example, the State's statute might provide, as does New York's long-arm statute, for the "exercise [of] personal jurisdiction over any non-domiciliary ... who ... commits a tortious act without the state causing injury to person or property within the state, ... if he ... expects or should reasonably expect the act to have consequences in the state and derives substantial revenue from interstate or international commerce." N.Y. Civ. Prac. Law Ann. § 302(a)(3)(ii) (West 2008).[7] Or, the State might simply provide, as New Jersey does, for the exercise of jurisdiction "consistent with due process of law." N.J. Ct. Rule 4:4-4(b)(1) (2011).

The modern approach to jurisdiction over corporations and other legal entities, ushered in by *International Shoe*, gave prime place to reason and fairness. Is it not fair and reasonable, given the mode of trading of which this case is an example, to require the international seller to defend at the place its products cause injury? Do not litigational convenience and choice-of-law considerations point in that direction? On what measure of reason and fairness can it be considered undue to require McIntyre UK to defend in New Jersey as an incident of its efforts to develop a market for its industrial machines anywhere and everywhere in the United States?[12] Is not the burden on McIntyre UK to defend in New Jersey fair, *i.e.*, a reasonable cost of transacting business internationally, in comparison to the burden on Nicastro to go to Nottingham, England to gain recompense for an injury he sustained using McIntyre's product at his workplace in Saddle Brook, New Jersey?

McIntyre UK dealt with the United States as a single market. Like most foreign manufacturers, it was concerned not with the prospect of suit in State X as opposed to State Y, but rather with its subjection to suit anywhere in the United States.... If McIntyre UK is answerable in the United States at all, is it not "perfectly appropriate to permit the exercise of that jurisdiction ... at the place of injury"? ...

In sum, McIntyre UK, by engaging McIntyre America to promote and sell its machines in the United States, "purposefully availed itself" of the United States market nationwide, not a market in a single State or a discrete collection of States. McIntyre UK thereby availed itself of the market of all States in which its products were sold by its exclusive distributor. "Th[e] 'purposeful availment' requirement," this Court has explained, simply "ensures that a defendant will not be haled into a jurisdiction solely as a result of 'random,' 'fortuitous,' or 'attenuated' contacts." *Burger King*, 471 U.S. at 475. Adjudicatory authority is appropriately exercised where "actions by the defendant *himself*" give rise to the affiliation with the forum. *Id.* How could McIntyre UK not have intended, by its actions targeting a national market, to sell products in the fourth largest destination for imports among all States of the United States and the largest scrap metal market? ...

Courts, both state and federal, confronting facts similar to those here, have rightly rejected the conclusion that a manufacturer selling its products across the USA may evade

---

7. This provision was modeled in part on the Uniform Interstate and International Procedure Act. *See* N. Y. Legislative Doc. 90, Judicial Conference of the State of New York, 11th Annual Report 132–-47 (1966). Connecticut's long-arm statute also uses the "derives substantial revenue from interstate or international commerce" formulation. *See* Conn. Gen. Stat. § 52-59b(a) (2011).

12. The plurality suggests that the Due Process Clause might permit a federal district court in New Jersey, sitting in diversity and applying New Jersey law, to adjudicate McIntyre UK's liability to Nicastro.... In other words, McIntyre UK might be compelled to bear the burden of traveling to New Jersey and defending itself there under New Jersey's products liability law, but would be entitled to federal adjudication of Nicastro's state-law claim. I see no basis in the Due Process Clause for such a curious limitation.

jurisdiction in any and all States, including the State where its defective product is distributed and causes injury. They have held, instead, that it would undermine principles of fundamental fairness to insulate the foreign manufacturer from accountability in court at the place within the United States where the manufacturer's products caused injury. *See, e.g., Tobin v. Astra Pharm. Prods., Inc.*, 993 F.2d 528, 544 (6th Cir. 1993); *A. Uberti & C. v. Leonardo*, 181 Ariz. 565, 573, 892 P.2d 1354, 1362 (1995).

. . . .

V

. . . .

... I would hold McIntyre UK answerable in New Jersey for the harm Nicastro suffered at his workplace in that State using McIntyre UK's shearing machine. While I dissent from the Court's judgment, I take heart that the plurality opinion does not speak for the Court, for that opinion would take a giant step away from the "notions of fair play and substantial justice" underlying *International Shoe.* 326 U.S. at 316 (internal quotation marks omitted).

[An Appendix of cases by Justice Ginsburg in which the courts have upheld exercises of personal jurisdiction over an alien or out-of-state corporation that used a distributor to target a national market is omitted.]

Notes and Questions

1. Consider the cases of *Pennoyer v. Neff* and *International Shoe v. Washington* after *McIntyre*. Does Justice Kennedy's analysis comport better with *Pennoyer* or *International Shoe*? Why do you suppose some members of the Court continue to insist that the Due Process Clauses of the Constitution are designed to embody sovereignty policies? The core principle embodied in the due process concept is that a person is entitled to a reasonable opportunity to be heard in an unbiased judicial proceeding before life, liberty, or property may be taken from the person. What does sovereignty have to do with that principle?

2. McIntyre sold all of its machines in the United States through an independent distributor located outside New Jersey, where the accident occurred. What argument could be made in favor of personal jurisdiction by the injured plaintiff over J. McIntyre in a state court where the independent distributor was located? Or did the Court mean to say that J. McIntyre wasn't subject to jurisdiction in any state in the United States? The answer to this question might be especially important if the independent distributor had become insolvent after the sale or lacked products liability coverage.

3. Recall that the *Burger King* case indicated that the "reasonableness" factors of the second prong of the minimum contacts test could be used in specific jurisdiction cases to enhance the validity of an assertion of specific jurisdiction "upon a lesser showing of minimum contacts than would otherwise be required," and not simply to defeat jurisdiction. The cases cited in *Burger King* in support of this suggestion seemed to indicate that the "state's interest" factor in the reasonableness test might be the most important factor in the ability to validate an assertion of specific jurisdiction.

In finding that jurisdiction did not exist in this case, neither the opinion of Justice Kennedy nor Justice Breyer discussed the possible application of the "reasonableness" factors in assessing the validity of jurisdiction. Do you think that *McIntyre* is the kind of case that should justify jurisdiction on a lesser showing of minimum contacts due to the strong interests of the plaintiff and the State of New Jersey in having the case litigated there? Can you identify what those strong interests were?

4. In an omitted portion of the dissent, the dissenters opined that *McIntyre* should not be controlled by *Asahi* and to hold otherwise was "dead wrong." 131 S. Ct. at 2803. The dissent noted that in *Asahi,* the California plaintiff had settled before trial, leaving only an indemnity dispute between two foreign litigants. Moreover, in contrast to J. McIntyre, the Court in *Asahi* was dealing with a component manufacturer, not the manufacturer of the final product, and unlike J. McIntyre, Asahi did not itself seek out customers for its product in the United States or engage a distributor to promote its product here. Do you agree with the dissent that the factual circumstances of *McIntyre* presented a different case for personal jurisdiction than *Asahi*?

5. Given the splintered majority in *McIntyre,* there unfortunately remains no clear jurisdictional standard as to the type of conduct required by a defendant in a stream-of-commerce case to satisfy the "purposeful availment" prong of the minimum contacts test. Because none of the various stream-of-commerce tests espoused by the different groups of Justices in *Asahi* (the separate tests of Justices O'Connor, Brennan, and Stevens, respectively) and *McIntyre* (the separate tests of Justices Kennedy and Ginsburg, respectively) were endorsed by a majority of the Justices, there is no superior position in law as to any of these tests. As a result, the divided views of *Asahi* and *McIntyre* will likely continue to generate uncertainty and conflicting opinions in the lower courts.

6. (a) In this regard, consider the concurring opinion of Justices Breyer and Alito, who represented the deciding swing votes in *McIntyre.* In the concurring opinion, Justice Breyer emphasized that he concurred "only in the judgment of [Justice Kennedy's] opinion and not its reasoning." Justice Breyer narrowly tailored his finding of no jurisdiction to the facts found by the New Jersey Supreme Court, which noted only one sale of defendant's product in New Jersey. Based on this finding, Justice Breyer stated that under any reading of the existing precedents, "a single isolated sale, even if accompanied by the kind of sales effort indicated here," is not sufficient. Do you agree with Justice Breyer that any reading of existing Supreme Court precedent demonstrates that a "single isolated sale" is insufficient for jurisdiction? What about *McGee v. International Life Ins. Co.,* 355 U.S. 220 (1957), which is discussed in section B(3), above? In *McGee,* the defendant insurer's only contact with the forum state was the *single* sale of a certificate of reinsurance to the decedent. In upholding jurisdiction, the Court expressly noted that "so far as the record before us shows, [the defendant insurer] has never solicited or done any insurance business in California apart from the policy involved here." *Id.* at 222.

(b) Irrespective of the issue of precedent, do you agree with Justice Breyer that the number of sales in this case should be the deciding factor in determining "purposeful availment"? In a case of specific jurisdiction, as in *McIntyre,* why should it matter whether a defendant sold only one product in the forum state or 1,000? In a case of specific jurisdiction, as opposed to general jurisdiction, the defendant is only required to defend an action arising out of or related to the specific product or products sold. If a defendant only sold one product in the forum state, then the defendant is only required to defend that one action. Is that unfair? Couldn't any special circumstance of unfairness in a particular case be resolved, as it was in *Asahi,* through the application of the "reasonableness" factors of the second prong of the minimum contacts analysis?

7. Justice Breyer further noted that "there may well have been other facts that Mr. Nicastro could have demonstrated in support of jurisdiction, ... [but] here I would take the facts precisely as the New Jersey Supreme Court stated them." Do you think that Justice Breyer's comments expressly basing his decision on the "single isolated sale" scenario presented in *McIntyre* suggest that if evidence of more regular sales had been shown, Jus-

tices Breyer and Alito would have upheld jurisdiction in this case? In a future case with more regular sales, do you think Justices Breyer and Alito would agree with Justice Ginsburg's view that purposeful availment can occur based on national marketing, even without any specific targeting or additional conduct directed towards the forum state? How many machines should have to be sold in the state over what period of time to satisfy Justice Breyer that the purposeful availment requirement is satisfied?

Problems

Problem 2-1. *P*, a citizen and resident of State *X*, is a collector of Civil War memorabilia. *P* purchased a rare Confederate battle flag from *A*, a citizen and resident of State *Z*, in State *Z*. Subsequently, *D*, a citizen of State *Y*, asserted that the flag had belonged to *D* and had been stolen from *D* at a date long prior to the time *P* had purchased it from *A*. *D's* assertions were made outside State *X* to a number of collectors attending events concerning Civil War memorabilia. However, some collectors in State *X* also learned of the assertions indirectly. *P* contends the assertions are false and that *D* sold the flag, along with several other Civil War artifacts, to a person unknown, who later sold them to *A*. *P* commences an action against *D* in a state court of State *X*. *P* seeks damages for slander of *P's* title to the flag. *D* is served with process in State *Y* under the provisions of the State *X* long-arm statute. The statute extends the jurisdiction of the State *X* courts as far as due process permits. *D* properly objects to State *X's* assertion of jurisdiction on the ground that it violates the Due Process Clause of the Fourteenth Amendment. Which of the U.S. Supreme Court's modern decisions is the best authority for sustaining the assertion of jurisdiction by State *X*? Are there factual distinctions between that case and the facts of this problem that would dictate that State *X's* assertion of jurisdiction should be held unconstitutional?

Problem 2-2. *D*, a physician, is a citizen and resident of State *Y*. *D* owns a clinic located in State *Y*. *D's* practice is territorially limited to State *Y*. However, *D* advertises in a newspaper published in State *Y*, but circulated in states adjoining State *Y*, including State *X*. The newspaper advertisements include a toll-free number for prospective patients to call in order to make appointments at *D's* clinic. *P*, a citizen of State *X*, reads one of the advertisements, calls the 800 number, and makes an appointment with *D* at *D's* clinic. *D* treats *P* at the clinic on several occasions. Contending the treatment was negligent and caused *P* certain permanent injuries, *P* sued *D* in a state court of State *X* to recover damages for the injuries. *D* was served with process in State *Y* pursuant to the State *X* long-arm statute. The statute extends the jurisdiction of the State *X* courts as far as the Due Process Clause permits. *D* properly objects to State *X's* assertion of jurisdiction on the ground that it violates due process. What should the result be and why?

2. General Jurisdiction

When a court asserts jurisdiction to adjudicate a claim that does not "arise out of or relate to the defendant's contacts with the forum state," the assertion of jurisdiction is labeled "general" rather than "specific." The level of the defendant's forum activity required for general jurisdiction is far greater than that specific jurisdiction. This is because when general jurisdiction is exercised, the defendant may be sued in that state on *any* cause of action. As noted in *International Shoe,* the defendant's continuous activities in the forum state must be "so substantial and of such a nature as to justify suit against it on causes of action arising from dealings entirely distinct from those activities."

The following cases and accompanying materials explore the concept of general jurisdiction. Among other questions, you should ask yourself why the Supreme Court has found it necessary to divide the universe of personal jurisdiction into two categories — specific and general — and why separate tests for the validity of each kind of jurisdictional assertion are necessary. In addition, you should consider whether it is possible to synthesize a single test for all kinds of jurisdictional assertions that would make more sense than the existing tests.

Helicopteros Nacionales de Colombia, S.A. v. Hall

United States Supreme Court, 1984
466 U.S. 408, 104 S. Ct. 1868, 80 L. Ed. 2d 404

Justice Blackmun delivered the opinion of the Court.

We granted certiorari in this case ... to decide whether the Supreme Court of Texas correctly ruled that the contacts of a foreign corporation with the State of Texas were sufficient to allow a Texas state court to assert jurisdiction over the corporation in a cause of action not arising out of or related to the corporation's activities within the State.

....

Petitioner Helicopteros Nacionales de Colombia, S.A. (Helicol), is a Colombian corporation with its principal place of business in the city of Bogota in that county. It is engaged in the business of providing helicopter transportation for oil and construction companies in South America. On January 26, 1976, a helicopter owned by Helicol crashed in Peru. Four United States citizens were among those who lost their lives in the accident. Respondents are the survivors and representatives of the four decedents.

At the time of the crash, respondents' decedents were employed by Consorcio, a Peruvian consortium, and were working on a pipeline in Peru. Consorcio is the alter ego of a joint venture named Williams-Sedco-Horn (WSH).[1] The venture had its headquarters in Houston, Tex. Consorcio had been formed to enable the venturers to enter into a contract with Petro Peru, the Peruvian state-owned oil company. Consorcio was to construct a pipeline for Petro Peru running from the interior of Peru westward to the Pacific Ocean. Peruvian law forbade construction of the pipeline by any non-Peruvian entity.

Consorcio/WSH[2] needed helicopters to move personnel, materials, and equipment into and out of the construction area. In 1974, upon request of Consorcio/WSH, the chief executive officer of Helicol, Francisco Restrepo, flew to the United States and conferred in Houston with representatives of the three joint venturers. At that meeting, there was a discussion of prices, availability, working conditions, fuel, supplies, and housing. Restrepo represented that Helicol could have the first helicopter on the job in 15 days. The Consorcio/WSH representatives decided to accept the contract proposed by Restrepo. Helicol began performing before the agreement was formally signed in Peru on November 11, 1974. The contract was written in Spanish on official gov-

---

1. The participants in the joint venture were Williams International Sudamericana, Ltd., a Delaware corporation; Sedco Construction Corporation, a Texas corporation; and Horn International, Inc., a Texas corporation.

2. Throughout the record in this case the entity is referred to both as Consorcio and as WSH. We refer to it hereinafter as Consorcio/WSH.

ernment stationery and provided that the residence of all the parties would be Lima, Peru. It further stated that controversies arising out of the contract would be submitted to the jurisdiction of Peruvian courts. In addition, it provided that Consorcio/ WSH would make payments to Helicol's account with the Bank of America in New York City....

Aside from the negotiation session in Houston between Restrepo and the representatives of Consorcio/WSH, Helicol had other contacts with Texas. During the years 1970–1977, it purchased helicopters (approximately 80% of its fleet), spare parts, and accessories for more than $4 million from Bell Helicopter Company in Fort Worth. In that period, Helicol sent prospective pilots to Fort Worth for training and to ferry the aircraft to South America. It also sent management and maintenance personnel to visit Bell Helicopter in Fort Worth during the same period in order to receive "plant familiarization" and for technical consultation. Helicol received into its New York City and Panama City, Fla., bank accounts over $5 million in payments from Consorcio/WSH drawn upon First City National Bank of Houston.

Beyond the foregoing, there have been no other business contacts between Helicol and the State of Texas. Helicol never has been authorized to do business in Texas and never has had an agent for the service of process within the State. It never has performed helicopter operations in Texas or sold any product that reached Texas, never solicited business in Texas, never signed any contract in Texas, never had any employee based there, and never recruited an employee in Texas. In addition, Helicol never has owned real or personal property in Texas and never has maintained an office or establishment there. Helicol has maintained no records in Texas and has no shareholders in that State. None of the respondents or their decedents were domiciled in Texas,[5] ... but all of the decedents were hired in Houston by Consorcio/WSH to work on the Petro Peru pipeline project.

Respondents instituted wrongful-death actions in the District Court of Harris County, Tex., against Consorcio/WSH, Bell Helicopter Company, and Helicol. Helicol filed special appearances and moved to dismiss the actions for lack of *in personam* jurisdiction over it. The motion was denied. After a consolidated jury trial, judgment was entered against Helicol on a jury verdict of $1,141,200 in favor of respondents.[6] ...

The Texas Court of Civil Appeals ... reversed the judgment of the District Court, holding that in personam jurisdiction over Helicol was lacking.... The Supreme Court of Texas, with three justices dissenting, initially affirmed the judgment of the Court of Civil Appeals.... Seven months later, however, on motion for rehearing, the court withdrew its prior opinions and, again with three justices dissenting, reversed the judgment of the intermediate court.... In ruling that the Texas courts had *in personam* jurisdiction, the Texas Supreme Court first held that the State's long-arm statute reaches as far as the Due Process Clause of the Fourteenth Amendment permits.... Thus, the only question re-

ISSUE

---

5. Respondents' lack of residential or other contacts with Texas of itself does not defeat otherwise proper jurisdiction. *Keeton v. Hustler Magazine, Inc.*, 465 U.S. 770, 780 (1984); *Calder v. Jones*, 465 U.S. 783, 788 (1984). We mention respondents' lack of contacts merely to show that nothing in the nature of the relationship between respondents and Helicol could possibly enhance Helicol's contacts with Texas. The harm suffered by respondents did not occur in Texas. Nor is it alleged that any negligence on the part of Helicol took place in Texas.

6. Defendants Consorcio/WSH and Bell Helicopter Company were granted directed verdicts with respect to respondents' claims against them. Bell Helicopter was granted a directed verdict on Helicol's cross-claim against it.... Consorcio/WSH, as cross-plaintiff in a claim against Helicol, obtained a judgment in the amount of $70,000....

maining for the court to decide was whether it was consistent with the Due Process Clause for Texas courts to assert *in personam* jurisdiction over Helicol....

....

The Due Process Clause of the Fourteenth Amendment operates to limit the power of a State to assert *in personam* jurisdiction over a nonresident defendant.... Due process requirements are satisfied when *in personam* jurisdiction is asserted over a nonresident corporate defendant that has "certain minimum contacts with [the forum] such that the maintenance of the suit does not offend 'traditional notions of fair play and substantial justice.'" ... When a controversy is related to or "arises out of" a defendant's contacts with the forum, the Court has said that a "relationship among the defendant, the forum, and the litigation" is the essential foundation of in personam jurisdiction....[8]

Even when the cause of action does not arise out of or relate to the foreign corporation's activities in the forum State,[9] due process is not offended by a State's subjecting the corporation to its *in personam* jurisdiction when there are sufficient contacts between the State and the foreign corporation. *Perkins v. Benguet Consolidated Mining Co.*, 342 U.S. 437 (1952)....

All parties to the present case concede that respondents' claims against Helicol did not "arise out of," and are not related to, Helicol's activities within Texas.[10] We thus must explore the nature of Helicol's contacts with the State of Texas to determine whether they constitute the kind of continuous and systematic general business contacts the Court found to exist in *Perkins*. We hold that they do not.

It is undisputed that Helicol does not have a place of business in Texas and never has been licensed to do business in the State. Basically, Helicol's contacts with Texas consisted

---

8. It has been said that when a State exercises personal jurisdiction over a defendant in a suit arising out of or related to the defendant's contacts with the forum, the State is exercising "specific jurisdiction" over the defendant. *See* Von Mehren & Trautman, *Jurisdiction to Adjudicate: A Suggested Analysis*, 79 Harv. L. Rev. 1121, 1144–64 (1966).

9. When a State exercises personal jurisdiction over a defendant in a suit not arising out of or related to the defendant's contacts with the forum, the State has been said to be exercising "general jurisdiction" over the defendant. *See* Brilmayer, *How Contacts Count: Due Process Limitations on State Court Jurisdiction*, 1980 Sup. Ct. Rev. 77, 80–81; Von Mehren & Trautman, 79 Harv. L. Rev. at 1136–44....

10. Because the parties have not argued any relationship between the cause of action and Helicol's contacts with the State of Texas, we, contrary to the dissent's implication, assert no "view" with respect to that issue.

The dissent suggests that we have erred in drawing no distinction between controversies that "relate to" a defendant's contacts with a forum and those that "arise out of" such contacts. This criticism is somewhat puzzling, for the dissent goes on to urge that, for purposes of determining the constitutional validity of an assertion of specific jurisdiction, there really should be no distinction between the two.

We do not address the validity or consequences of such a distinction because the issue has not been presented in this case. Respondents have made no argument that their cause of action either arose out of or is related to Helicol's contacts with the State of Texas. Absent any briefing on the issue, we decline to reach the questions (1) whether the terms "arising out of" and "related to" describe different connections between a cause of action and a defendant's contacts with a forum, and (2) what sort of tie between a cause of action and a defendant's contacts with a forum is necessary to a determination that either connection exists. Nor do we reach the question whether, if the two types of relationship differ, a forum's exercise of personal jurisdiction in a situation where the cause of action "relates to," but does not "arise out of," the defendant's contacts with the forum should be analyzed as an assertion of specific jurisdiction.

of sending its chief executive officer to Houston for a contract-negotiation session; accepting into its New York bank account checks drawn on a Houston bank; purchasing helicopters, equipment, and training services from Bell Helicopter for substantial sums; and sending personnel to Bell's facilities in Fort Worth for training.

The one trip to Houston by Helicol's chief executive officer for the purpose of negotiating the transportation-services contract with Consorcio/WSH cannot be described or regarded as a contact of a "continuous and systematic" nature, as *Perkins* described it ... and thus cannot support an assertion of *in personam* jurisdiction over Helicol by a Texas court. Similarly, Helicol's acceptance from Consorcio/WSH of checks drawn on a Texas bank is of negligible significance for purposes of determining whether Helicol had sufficient contacts in Texas. There is no indication that Helicol ever requested that the checks be drawn on a Texas bank or that there was any negotiation between Helicol and Consorcio/WSH with respect to the location or identity of the bank on which checks would be drawn. Common sense and everyday experience suggest that, absent unusual circumstances, the bank on which a check is drawn is generally of little consequence to the payee and is a matter left to the discretion of the drawer. Such unilateral activity of another party or a third person is not an appropriate consideration when determining whether a defendant has sufficient contacts with a forum State to justify an assertion of jurisdiction. *See Kulko v. Superior Court* ...; *Hanson v. Denckla*. ...

The Texas Supreme Court focused on the purchases and the related training trips in finding contacts sufficient to support an assertion of jurisdiction. We do not agree with that assessment, for the Court's opinion in *Rosenberg Bros. & Co. v. Curtis Brown Co.*, 260 U.S. 516 (1923) (Brandeis, J., for a unanimous tribunal), makes clear that purchases and related trips, standing alone, are not a sufficient basis for a State's assertion of jurisdiction.

The defendant in *Rosenberg* was a small retailer in Tulsa, Okla., who dealt in men's clothing and furnishings. It never had applied for a license to do business in New York, nor had it at any time authorized suit to be brought against it there. It never had an established place of business in New York and never regularly carried on business in that State. Its only connection with New York was that it purchased from New York wholesalers a large portion of the merchandise sold in its Tulsa store. The purchases sometimes were made by correspondence and sometimes through visits to New York by an officer of the defendant. The Court concluded: "Visits on such business, even if occurring at regular intervals, would not warrant the inference that the corporation was present within the jurisdiction of [New York]." ...

This Court in *International Shoe* acknowledged and did not repudiate its holding in *Rosenberg*. ... In accordance with *Rosenberg*, we hold that mere purchases, even if occurring at regular intervals, are not enough to warrant a State's assertion of *in personam* jurisdiction over a nonresident corporation in a cause of action not related to those purchase transactions.[12] Nor can we conclude that the fact that Helicol sent personnel into Texas for training in con-

---

12. This Court in *International Shoe* cited *Rosenberg* for the proposition that "the commission of some single or occasional acts of the corporate agent in a state sufficient to impose an obligation or liability on the corporation has not been thought to confer upon the state authority to enforce it." ... Arguably, therefore, *Rosenberg* also stands for the proposition that mere purchases are not a sufficient basis for either general or specific jurisdiction. Because the case before us is one in which there has been an assertion of general jurisdiction over a foreign defendant, we need not decide the continuing validity of *Rosenberg* with respect to an assertion of specific jurisdiction, *i.e.*, where the cause of action arises out of or relates to the purchases by the defendant in the forum State.

nection with the purchase of helicopters and equipment in that State in any way enhanced the nature of Helicol's contacts with Texas. The training was a part of the package of goods and services purchased by Helicol from Bell Helicopter. The brief presence of Helicol employees in Texas for the purpose of attending the training sessions is no~~more~~ a significant contact than were the trips to New York made by the buyer for the retail store in *Rosenberg*....

....

Holding

We hold that Helicol's contacts with the State of Texas were insufficient to satisfy the requirements of the Due Process Clause of the Fourteenth Amendment.[13] Accordingly, we reverse the judgment of the Supreme Court of Texas.

It is so ordered.

Dissent

JUSTICE BRENNAN, dissenting.

Decisions applying the Due Process Clause of the Fourteenth Amendment to determine whether a State may constitutionally assert *in personam* jurisdiction over a particular defendant for a particular cause of action most often turn on a weighing of facts.... To a large extent, today's decision follows the usual pattern. Based on essentially undisputed facts, the Court concludes that petitioner Helicol's contacts with the State of Texas were insufficient to allow the Texas state courts constitutionally to assert "general jurisdiction" over all claims filed against this foreign corporation. Although my independent weighing of the facts leads me to a different conclusion, the Court's holding on this issue is neither implausible nor unexpected.

What is troubling about the Court's opinion, however, are the implications that might be drawn from the way in which the Court approaches the constitutional issue it addresses. First, the Court limits its discussion to an assertion of general jurisdiction of the Texas courts because, in its view, the underlying cause of action does "not aris[e] out of or relat[e] to the corporation's activities within the State." Then, the Court relies on a 1923 decision in *Rosenberg Bros. & Co. v. Curtis Brown Co.*... without considering whether that case retains any validity after our more recent pronouncements concerning the permissible reach of a State's jurisdiction. By posing and deciding the question presented in this manner, I fear that the Court is saying more than it realizes about constitutional limitations on the potential reach of *in personam* jurisdiction. In particular, by relying on a precedent whose premises have long been discarded, and by refusing to consider any distinction between controversies that "relate to" a defendant's contacts with the forum and causes of action that "arise out of" such contacts, the Court may be placing severe limitations on the type and amount of contacts that will satisfy the constitutional minimum.

In contrast, I believe that the undisputed contacts in this case between petitioner Helicol and the State of Texas are sufficiently important, and sufficiently related to the underlying cause of action, to make it fair and reasonable for the State to assert personal jurisdiction over Helicol for the wrongful-death actions filed by the respondents. Given that Helicol has purposefully availed itself of the benefits and obligations of the forum,

---

13. As an alternative to traditional minimum-contacts analysis, respondents suggest that the Court hold that the State of Texas had personal jurisdiction over Helicol under a doctrine of "jurisdiction by necessity." *See Shaffer v. Heitner*, 433 U.S. 186, 211, n.37 (1977). We conclude, however, that respondents failed to carry their burden of showing that all three defendants could not be sued together in a single forum. It is not clear from the record, for example, whether suit could have been brought against all three defendants in either Colombia or Peru. We decline to consider adoption of a doctrine of jurisdiction by necessity—a potentially far-reaching modification of existing law—in the absence of a more complete record.

and given the direct relationship between the underlying cause of action and Helicol's contacts with the forum, maintenance of this suit in the Texas courts "does not offend [the] 'traditional notions of fair play and substantial justice'"... that are the touchstone of jurisdictional analysis under the Due Process Clause. I therefore dissent.

....

The Court expressly limits its decision in this case to "an assertion of general jurisdiction over a foreign defendant."...

....

The Court also fails to distinguish the legal principles that controlled our prior decisions in *Perkins* and *Rosenberg*. In particular, the contacts between petitioner Helicol and the State of Texas, unlike the contacts between the defendant and the forum in each of those cases, are significantly related to the cause of action alleged in the original suit filed by the respondents. Accordingly, in my view, it is both fair and reasonable for the Texas courts to assert specific jurisdiction over Helicol in this case.

By asserting that the present case does not implicate the specific jurisdiction of the Texas courts, ... the Court necessarily removes its decision from the reality of the actual facts presented for our consideration.[3] Moreover, the Court refuses to consider any distinction between contacts that are "related to" the underlying cause of action and contacts that "give rise" to the underlying cause of action. In my view, however, there is a substantial difference between these two standards for asserting specific jurisdiction. Thus, although I agree that the respondents' cause of action did not formally "arise out of" specific activities initiated by Helicol in the State of Texas, I believe that the wrongful-death claim filed by the respondents is significantly related to the undisputed contacts between Helicol and the forum. On that basis, I would conclude that the Due Process Clause allows the Texas courts to assert specific jurisdiction over this particular action.

The wrongful-death actions filed by the respondents were premised on a fatal helicopter crash that occurred in Peru. Helicol was joined as a defendant in the lawsuits because it provided transportation services, including the particular helicopter and pilot involved in the crash, to the joint venture that employed the decedents. Specifically, the respondent Hall claimed in her original complaint that "Helicol is ... legally responsible for its own negligence through its pilot employee."... Viewed in light of these allegations,

---

3. Nor do I agree with the Court that the respondents have conceded that their claims are not related to Helicol's activities within the State of Texas. Although parts of their written and oral arguments before the Court proceed on the assumption that no such relationship exists, other portions suggest just the opposite:

> If it is the concern of the Solicitor General [appearing as *amicus curiae*] that a holding for Respondents here will cause foreign companies to refrain from purchasing in the United States for fear of exposure to general jurisdiction on unrelated causes of action, such concern is not well founded.
>
> Respondents' cause is not dependent on a ruling that mere purchases in a state, together with incidental training for operating and maintaining the merchandise purchased can constitute the ties, contacts and relations necessary to justify jurisdiction over an unrelated cause of action. However, regular purchases and training coupled with other contacts, ties and relations may form the basis for jurisdiction.

Brief for Respondents 13–14.

Thus, while the respondents' position before this Court is admittedly less than clear, I believe it is preferable to address the specific jurisdiction of the Texas courts because Helicol's contacts with Texas are in fact related to the underlying cause of action.

the contacts between Helicol and the State of Texas are directly and significantly related to the underlying claim filed by the respondents. The negotiations that took place in Texas led to the contract in which Helicol agreed to provide the precise transportation services that were being used at the time of the crash. Moreover, the helicopter involved in the crash was purchased by Helicol in Texas, and the pilot whose negligence was alleged to have caused the crash was actually trained in Texas.... This is simply not a case, therefore, in which a state court has asserted jurisdiction over a nonresident defendant on the basis of wholly unrelated contacts with the forum. Rather, the contacts between Helicol and the forum are directly related to the negligence that was alleged in the respondent Hall's original complaint. Because Helicol should have expected to be amenable to suit in the Texas courts for claims directly related to these contacts, it is fair and reasonable to allow the assertion of jurisdiction in this case.

Despite this substantial relationship between the contacts and the cause of action, the Court declines to consider whether the courts of Texas may assert specific jurisdiction over this suit. Apparently, this simply reflects a narrow interpretation of the question presented for review.... It is nonetheless possible that the Court's opinion may be read to imply that the specific jurisdiction of the Texas courts is inapplicable because the cause of action did not formally "arise out of" the contacts between Helicol and the forum. In my view, however, such a rule would place unjustifiable limits on the bases under which Texas may assert its jurisdictional power.

Limiting the specific jurisdiction of a forum to cases in which the cause of action formally arose out of the defendant's contacts with the State would subject constitutional standards under the Due Process Clause to the vagaries of the substantive law or pleading requirements of each State. For example, the complaint filed against Helicol in this case alleged negligence based on pilot error. Even though the pilot was trained in Texas, the Court assumes that the Texas courts may not assert jurisdiction over the suit because the cause of action "did not 'arise out of,' and [is] not related to," that training.... If, however, the applicable substantive law required that negligent training of the pilot was a necessary element of a cause of action for pilot error, or if the respondents had simply added an allegation of negligence in the training provided for the Helicol pilot, then presumably the Court would concede that the specific jurisdiction of the Texas courts was applicable.

Our interpretation of the Due Process Clause has never been so dependent upon the applicable substantive law or the State's formal pleading requirement. At least since *International Shoe Co. v. Washington*, ... the principal focus when determining whether a forum may constitutionally assert jurisdiction over a nonresident defendant has been on fairness and reasonableness to the defendant. To this extent, a court's specific jurisdiction should be applicable whenever the cause of action arises out of *or* relates to the contacts between the defendant and the forum. It is eminently fair and reasonable, in my view, to subject a defendant to suit in a forum with which it has significant contacts directly related to the underlying cause of action. Because Helicol's contacts with the State of Texas meet this standard, I would affirm the judgment of the Supreme Court of Texas.

Notes and Questions

1. As described in *Helicopteros*, for a case to be one of specific jurisdiction, the claim must either "arise out of" the defendant's contacts with the state or be "related to" the de-

fendant's contacts with the state. A claim arising out of the defendant's contacts with the state is easy enough to comprehend. For example, if the defendant drives an automobile into the forum and has an accident there giving rise to a negligence claim by the plaintiff, the claim certainly "arises out of" the defendant's contacts with the state.

2. But what does it mean for a claim to "relate to" the defendant's contacts with the state? The U.S. Supreme Court has not yet said. Presumably, the claim will arise from events that occur entirely outside the forum state. However, it is difficult to see what events must occur in the forum state for the claim to be deemed "related to" the defendant's contacts with the state. Justice Brennan's dissenting opinion in the *Helicopteros* decision argued the claim in that case should be considered "related to" the defendant's contacts with the forum. However, the defendant's contacts in *Helicopteros* were not liability-producing activities. The defendant engaged in acts in the forum in preparation for other acts outside the forum that eventually gave rise to the claim for relief. Is there any problem with considering such preparatory activities sufficient to give rise to a case of specific jurisdiction?

Goodyear Dunlap Tire Operations, S.A. v. Brown

Supreme Court of the United States, 2011
564 U.S. ___, 131 S. Ct. 2846, 180 L. Ed. 2d 796

JUSTICE GINSBURG delivered the opinion of the Court.

This case concerns the jurisdiction of state courts over corporations organized and operating abroad. We address, in particular, this question: Are foreign subsidiaries of a *Issue* United States parent corporation amenable to suit in state court on claims unrelated to any activity of the subsidiaries in the forum State?

A bus accident outside Paris that took the lives of two 13-year-old boys from North Carolina gave rise to the litigation we here consider. Attributing the accident to a defective tire manufactured in Turkey at the plant of a foreign subsidiary of The Goodyear Tire and Rubber Company (Goodyear USA), the boys' parents commenced an action for damages in a North Carolina state court; they named as defendants Goodyear USA, an Ohio corporation, and three of its subsidiaries, organized and operating, respectively, in Turkey, France, and Luxembourg. Goodyear USA, which had plants in North Carolina and regularly engaged in commercial activity there, did not contest the North Carolina court's jurisdiction over it; Goodyear USA's foreign subsidiaries, however, maintained that North Carolina lacked adjudicatory authority over them.

A state court's assertion of jurisdiction exposes defendants to the State's coercive power, and is therefore subject to review for compatibility with the Fourteenth Amendment's Due Process Clause. *International Shoe* Co. v. *Washington*, 326 U.S. 310, 316 (1945) (assertion of jurisdiction over out-of-state corporation must comply with "'traditional notions of fair play and substantial justice'" (quoting *Milliken* v. *Meyer*, 311 U.S. 457, 463 (1940)). Opinions in the wake of the pathmarking *International Shoe* decision have differentiated between general or all-purpose jurisdiction, and specific or case-linked jurisdiction. *Helicopteros Nacionales de Colombia, S.A.* v. *Hall*, 466 U.S. 408, 414, nn. 8, 9 (1984).

A court may assert general jurisdiction over foreign (sister-state or foreign-country) corporations to hear any and all claims against them when their affiliations with the State are so "continuous and systematic" as to render them essentially at home in the forum State.

See International Shoe, 326 U.S. at 317. Specific jurisdiction, on the other hand, depends on an "affiliatio[n] between the forum and the underlying controversy," principally, activity or an occurrence that takes place in the forum State and is therefore subject to the State's regulation. von Mehren & Trautman, *Jurisdiction to Adjudicate: A Suggested Analysis*, 79 Harv. L. Rev. 1121, 1136 (1966) (hereinafter von Mehren & Trautman); *see* Brilmayer et al., *A General Look at General Jurisdiction*, 66 Texas L. Rev. 721, 782 (1988) (hereinafter Brilmayer). In contrast to general, all-purpose jurisdiction, specific jurisdiction is confined to adjudication of "issues deriving from, or connected with, the very controversy that establishes jurisdiction." von Mehren & Trautman at 1136.

Because the episode-in-suit, the bus accident, occurred in France, and the tire alleged to have caused the accident was manufactured and sold abroad, North Carolina courts lacked specific jurisdiction to adjudicate the controversy. The North Carolina Court of Appeals so acknowledged. *Brown v. Meter*, 199 N.C. App. 50, 57–58, 681 S.E.2d 382, 388 (2009). Were the foreign subsidiaries nonetheless amenable to general jurisdiction in North Carolina courts? Confusing or blending general and specific jurisdictional inquiries, the North Carolina courts answered yes. Some of the tires made abroad by Goodyear's foreign subsidiaries, the North Carolina Court of Appeals stressed, had reached North Carolina through "the stream of commerce"; that connection, the Court of Appeals believed, gave North Carolina courts the handle needed for the exercise of general jurisdiction over the foreign corporations. *Id.* at 67–68, 681 S.E.2d at 394–95.

Supreme Court's holding A connection so limited between the forum and the foreign corporation, we hold, is an inadequate basis for the exercise of general jurisdiction. Such a connection does not establish the "continuous and systematic" affiliation necessary to empower North Carolina courts to entertain claims unrelated to the foreign corporation's contacts with the State.

I

On April 18, 2004, a bus destined for Charles de Gaulle Airport overturned on a road outside Paris, France. Passengers on the bus were young soccer players from North Carolina beginning their journey home. Two 13-year-olds, Julian Brown and Matthew Helms, sustained fatal injuries. The boys' parents, respondents in this Court, filed a suit for wrongful-death damages in the Superior Court of Onslow County, North Carolina, in their capacity as administrators of the boys' estates. Attributing the accident to a tire that failed when its plies separated, the parents alleged negligence in the "design, construction, testing, and inspection" of the tire. 199 N.C. App. at 51, 681 S.E.2d, at 384 (internal quotation marks omitted).

Goodyear Luxembourg Tires, SA (Goodyear Luxembourg), Goodyear Lastikleri T. A. S. (Goodyear Turkey), and Goodyear Dunlop Tires France, SA (Goodyear France), petitioners here, were named as defendants. Incorporated in Luxembourg, Turkey, and France, respectively, petitioners are indirect subsidiaries of Goodyear USA, an Ohio corporation also named as a defendant in the suit. Petitioners manufacture tires primarily for sale in European and Asian markets. Their tires differ in size and construction from tires ordinarily sold in the United States. They are designed to carry significantly heavier loads, and to serve under road conditions and speed limits in the manufacturers' primary markets.[1]

---

1. Respondents portray Goodyear USA's structure as a reprehensible effort to "outsource" all manufacturing, and correspondingly, tort litigation, to foreign jurisdictions. *See* Brief for Respondents at 51–53. Yet Turkey, where the tire alleged to have caused the accident-in-suit was made, is hardly a strange location for a facility that primarily supplies markets in Europe and Asia.

In contrast to the parent company, Goodyear USA, which does not contest the North Carolina courts' personal jurisdiction over it, petitioners are not registered to do business in North Carolina. They have no place of business, employees, or bank accounts in North Carolina. They do not design, manufacture, or advertise their products in North Carolina. And they do not solicit business in North Carolina or themselves sell or ship tires to North Carolina customers. Even so, a small percentage of petitioners' tires (tens of thousands out of tens of millions manufactured between 2004 and 2007) were distributed within North Carolina by other Goodyear USA affiliates. These tires were typically custom ordered to equip specialized vehicles such as cement mixers, waste haulers, and boat and horse trailers. Petitioners state, and respondents do not here deny, that the type of tire involved in the accident, a Goodyear Regional RHS tire manufactured by Goodyear Turkey, was never distributed in North Carolina.

Petitioners moved to dismiss the claims against them for want of personal jurisdiction. The trial court denied the motion, and the North Carolina Court of Appeals affirmed. Acknowledging that the claims neither "related to, nor ... ar[o]se from, [petitioners'] contacts with North Carolina," the Court of Appeals confined its analysis to "general rather than specific jurisdiction," which the court recognized required a "higher threshold" showing: A defendant must have "continuous and systematic contacts" with the forum. *Id.* at 58, 681 S.E.2d at 388 (internal quotation marks omitted). That threshold was crossed, the court determined, when petitioners placed their tires "in the stream of interstate commerce without any limitation on the extent to which those tires could be sold in North Carolina." *Id.* at 67, 681 S.E.2d at 394.

Nothing in the record, the court observed, indicated that petitioners "took any affirmative action to cause tires which they had manufactured to be shipped into North Carolina." *Id.* at 64, 681 S.E.2d at 392. The court found, however, that tires made by petitioners reached North Carolina as a consequence of a "highly-organized distribution process" involving other Goodyear USA subsidiaries. *Id.* at 67, 681 S.E.2d at 394. Petitioners, the court noted, made "no attempt to keep these tires from reaching the North Carolina market." *Id.* at 66, 681 S.E.2d at 393. Indeed, the very tire involved in the accident, the court observed, conformed to tire standards established by the U.S. Department of Transportation and bore markings required for sale in the United States. *Id.*[2] As further support, the court invoked North Carolina's "interest in providing a forum in which its citizens are able to seek redress for [their] injuries," and noted the hardship North Carolina plaintiffs would experience "[were they] required to litigate their claims in France," a country to which they have no ties. *Id.* at 68, 681 S.E.2d, at 394. The North Carolina Supreme Court denied discretionary review....

We granted certiorari to decide whether the general jurisdiction the North Carolina courts asserted over petitioners is consistent with the Due Process Clause of the Fourteenth Amendment....

---

2. Such markings do not necessarily show that any of the tires were destined for sale in the United States. To facilitate trade, the Solicitor General explained, the United States encourages other countries to "treat compliance with [Department of Transportation] standards, including through use of DOT markings, as evidence that the products are safely manufactured." Brief for United States as *Amicus Curiae* at 32.

II

A

The Due Process Clause of the Fourteenth Amendment sets the outer boundaries of a state tribunal's authority to proceed against a defendant. *Shaffer* v. *Heitner*, 433 U.S. 186, 207 (1977). The canonical opinion in this area remains *International Shoe*, 326 U.S. 310, in which we held that a State may authorize its courts to exercise personal jurisdiction over an out-of-state defendant if the defendant has "certain minimum contacts with [the State] such that the maintenance of the suit does not offend 'traditional notions of fair play and substantial justice.'" *Id.* at 316 (quoting *Meyer*, 311 U.S. at 463).

Endeavoring to give specific content to the "fair play and substantial justice" concept, the Court in *International Shoe* classified cases involving out-of-state corporate defendants. First, as in *International Shoe* itself, jurisdiction unquestionably could be asserted where the corporation's in-state activity is "continuous and systematic" and *that activity gave rise to the episode-in-suit.* 326 U.S. at 317. Further, the Court observed, the commission of certain "single or occasional acts" in a State may be sufficient to render a corporation answerable in that State with respect to those acts, though not with respect to matters unrelated to the forum connections. *Id.* at 318. The heading courts today use to encompass these two *International Shoe* categories is "specific jurisdiction." *See* von Mehren & Trautman at 1144–63. Adjudicatory authority is "specific" when the suit "aris[es] out of or relate[s] to the defendant's contacts with the forum." *Helicopteros*, 466 U.S. at 414, n.8.

International Shoe distinguished from cases that fit within the "specific jurisdiction" categories, "instances in which the continuous corporate operations within a state [are] so substantial and of such a nature as to justify suit against it on causes of action arising from dealings entirely distinct from those activities." 326 U.S. at 318. Adjudicatory authority so grounded is today called "general jurisdiction." *Helicopteros*, 466 U.S. at 414, n.9. For an individual, the paradigm forum for the exercise of general jurisdiction is the individual's domicile; for a corporation, it is an equivalent place, one in which the corporation is fairly regarded as at home. *See* Brilmayer 728 (identifying domicile, place of incorporation, and principal place of business as "paradig[m]" bases for the exercise of general jurisdiction).

Since *International Shoe*, this Court's decisions have elaborated primarily on circumstances that warrant the exercise of specific jurisdiction, particularly in cases involving "single or occasional acts" occurring or having their impact within the forum State....

In only two decisions postdating *International Shoe* ... has this Court considered whether an out-of-state corporate defendant's in-state contacts were sufficiently "continuous and systematic" to justify the exercise of general jurisdiction over claims unrelated to those contacts: *Perkins* v. *Benguet Consol. Mining Co.*, 342 U.S. 437 (1952) (general jurisdiction appropriately exercised over Philippine corporation sued in Ohio, where the company's affairs were overseen during World War II); and *Helicopteros*, 466 U.S. 408 (helicopter owned by Colombian corporation crashed in Peru; survivors of U.S. citizens who died in the crash, the Court held, could not maintain wrongful-death actions against the Colombian corporation in Texas, for the corporation's helicopter purchases and purchase-linked activity in Texas were insufficient to subject it to Texas court's general jurisdiction).

B

To justify the exercise of general jurisdiction over petitioners, the North Carolina courts relied on the petitioners' placement of their tires in the "stream of commerce." ... The stream-of-commerce metaphor has been invoked frequently in lower court decisions permitting "jurisdiction in products liability cases in which the product has traveled through an extensive chain of distribution before reaching the ultimate consumer." ... Typically, in such cases, a nonresident defendant, acting *outside* the forum, places in the stream of commerce a product that ultimately causes harm *inside* the forum....

Many States have enacted long-arm statutes authorizing courts to exercise specific jurisdiction over manufacturers when the events in suit, or some of them, occurred within the forum state. For example, the "Local Injury; Foreign Act" subsection of North Carolina's long-arm statute authorizes North Carolina courts to exercise personal jurisdiction in "any action claiming injury to person or property within this State arising out of [the defendant's] act or omission outside this State," if, "in addition[,] at or about the time of the injury," "[p]roducts ... manufactured by the defendant were used or consumed, within this State in the ordinary course of trade." N.C. Gen. Stat. Ann. § 1-75.4(4)(b) (Lexis 2009). As the North Carolina Court of Appeals recognized, this provision of the State's long-arm statute "does not apply to this case," for both the act alleged to have caused injury (the fabrication of the allegedly defective tire) and its impact (the accident) occurred outside the forum....[4]

The North Carolina court's stream-of-commerce analysis elided the essential difference between case-specific and all-purpose (general) jurisdiction. Flow of a manufacturer's products into the forum, we have explained, may bolster an affiliation germane to *specific* jurisdiction. *See, e.g., World-Wide Volkswagen [v. Woodson]*, 444 U.S. [286,] 297 (where "the sale of a product ... is not simply an isolated occurrence, but arises from the efforts of the manufacturer or distributor to serve ... the market for its product in [several] States, it is not unreasonable to subject it to suit in one of those States if its allegedly defective merchandise *has there been the source of injury to its owner or to others*" (emphasis added)). But ties serving to bolster the exercise of specific jurisdiction do not warrant a determination that, based on those ties, the forum has *general* jurisdiction over a defendant. *See, e.g., Stabilisierungsfonds Fur Wein v. Kaiser Stuhl Wine Distributors Pty. Ltd.*, 647 F.2d 200, 203, n.5 (D.C. Cir. 1981) (defendants' marketing arrangements, although "adequate to permit litigation of claims relating to [their] introduction of ... wine into the United States stream of commerce, ... would not be adequate to support general, 'all purpose' adjudicatory authority").

A corporation's "continuous activity of some sorts within a state," *International Shoe* instructed, "is not enough to support the demand that the corporation be amenable to suits unrelated to that activity." 326 U.S. at 318. Our 1952 decision in *Perkins* v. *Benguet Consol. Mining Co.* remains "[t]he textbook case of general jurisdiction appropriately exercised over a foreign corporation that has not consented to suit in the forum." *Donahue* v. *Far Eastern Air Transp. Corp.*, 652 F.2d 1032, 1037 (D.C. Cir. 1981).

Sued in Ohio, the defendant in *Perkins* was a Philippine mining corporation that had ceased activities in the Philippines during World War II. To the extent that the company was conducting any business during and immediately after the Japanese occupation of the Philippines, it was doing so in Ohio: the corporation's president maintained his office there, kept the company files in that office, and supervised from the Ohio office "the

---

4. The court instead relied on N.C. Gen. Stat. Ann. § 1-75.4(1)(d), *see* 199 N.C. App. at 57, 681 S.E.2d at 388, which provides for jurisdiction, "whether the claim arises within or without [the] State," when the defendant "[i]s engaged in substantial activity within this State, whether such activity is wholly interstate, intrastate, or otherwise." This provision, the North Carolina Supreme Court has held, was "intended to make available to the North Carolina courts the full jurisdictional powers permissible under federal due process." *Dillon* v. *Numismatic Funding Corp.*, 291 N.C. 674, 676, 231 S.E.2d 629, 630 (1977).

necessarily limited wartime activities of the company." *Perkins*, 342 U.S. at 447–48. Although the claim-in-suit did not arise in Ohio, this Court ruled that it would not violate due process for Ohio to adjudicate the controversy. *Id.*; *see Keeton* v. *Hustler Magazine, Inc.*, 465 U.S. 770, 779–80, n.11 (1984) (Ohio's exercise of general jurisdiction was permissible in *Perkins* because "Ohio was the corporation's principal, if temporary, place of business").

We next addressed the exercise of general jurisdiction over an out-of-state corporation over three decades later, in *Helicopteros*. In that case, survivors of United States citizens who died in a helicopter crash in Peru instituted wrongful-death actions in a Texas state court against the owner and operator of the helicopter, a Colombian corporation. The Colombian corporation had no place of business in Texas and was not licensed to do business there. "Basically, [the company's] contacts with Texas consisted of sending its chief executive officer to Houston for a contract-negotiation session; accepting into its New York bank account checks drawn on a Houston bank; purchasing helicopters, equipment, and training services from [a Texas enterprise] for substantial sums; and sending personnel to [Texas] for training." 466 U.S. at 416. These links to Texas, we determined, did not "constitute the kind of continuous and systematic general business contacts ... found to exist in *Perkins*," and were insufficient to support the exercise of jurisdiction over a claim that neither "ar[o]se out of ... no[r] related to" the defendant's activities in Texas. *Id.* at 415–16 (internal quotation marks omitted).

Helicopteros concluded that "mere purchases [made in the forum State], even if occurring at regular intervals, are not enough to warrant a State's assertion of [general] jurisdiction over a nonresident corporation in a cause of action not related to those purchase transactions." *Id.* at 418. We see no reason to differentiate from the ties to Texas held insufficient in *Helicopteros*, the sales of petitioners' tires sporadically made in North Carolina through intermediaries. Under the sprawling view of general jurisdiction urged by respondents and embraced by the North Carolina Court of Appeals, any substantial manufacturer or seller of goods would be amenable to suit, on any claim for relief, wherever its products are distributed. *But cf. World-Wide Volkswagen*, 444 U.S. at 296 (every seller of chattels does not, by virtue of the sale, "appoint the chattel his agent for service of process").

Measured against *Helicopteros* and *Perkins*, North Carolina is not a forum in which it would be permissible to subject petitioners to general jurisdiction. Unlike the defendant in *Perkins*, whose sole wartime business activity was conducted in Ohio, petitioners are in no sense at home in North Carolina. Their attenuated connections to the State ... fall far short of the "the continuous and systematic general business contacts" necessary to em-

---

5. As earlier noted ... the North Carolina Court of Appeals invoked the State's "well-recognized interest in providing a forum in which its citizens are able to seek redress for injuries that they have sustained." 199 N.C. App. at 68, 681 S.E.2d at 394. But "[g]eneral jurisdiction to adjudicate has in [United States] practice never been based on the plaintiff's relationship to the forum. There is nothing in [our] law comparable to ... article 14 of the Civil Code of France (1804) under which the French nationality of the plaintiff is a sufficient ground for jurisdiction." von Mehren & Trautman at 1137; *see* Clermont & Palmer, *Exorbitant Jurisdiction*, 58 Me. L. Rev. 474, 492–95 (2006) (French law permitting plaintiff-based jurisdiction is rarely invoked in the absence of other supporting factors). When a defendant's act outside the forum causes injury in the forum, by contrast, a plaintiff's residence in the forum may strengthen the case for the exercise of *specific jurisdiction*. *See Calder* v. *Jones*, 465 U.S. 783, 788 (1984); von Mehren & Trautman 1167–73.

power North Carolina to entertain suit against them on claims unrelated to anything that connects them to the State. *Helicopteros*, 466 U.S. at 416.[5]

C

Respondents belatedly assert a "single enterprise" theory, asking us to consolidate petitioners' ties to North Carolina with those of Goodyear USA and other Goodyear entities.... In effect, respondents would have us pierce Goodyear corporate veils, at least for jurisdictional purposes. *See* Brilmayer & Paisley, *Personal Jurisdiction and Substantive Legal Relations: Corporations, Conspiracies, and Agency*, 74 Cal. L. Rev. 1, 14, 29–30 (1986) (merging parent and subsidiary for jurisdictional purposes requires an inquiry "comparable to the corporate law question of piercing the corporate veil"). *But see* 199 N.C. App. at 64, 681 S.E.2d at 392 (North Carolina Court of Appeals understood that petitioners are "separate corporate entities ... not directly responsible for the presence in North Carolina of tires that they had manufactured"). Neither below nor in their brief in opposition to the petition for certiorari did respondents urge disregard of petitioners' discrete status as subsidiaries and treatment of all Goodyear entities as a "unitary business," so that jurisdiction over the parent would draw in the subsidiaries as well.... Respondents have therefore forfeited this contention, and we do not address it....

. . . .

For the reasons stated, the judgment of the North Carolina Court of Appeals is [r]eversed.

Notes and Questions

1. To qualify for general jurisdiction, the Court states that the defendant's contacts with the forum state must be "so continuous and systematic as to render [the defendant] essentially at home in the forum State." The Court indicates that for an individual, the "paradigm forum" for general jurisdiction is the individual's "domicile." As noted in section A(3)(d), above, and as you will learn in Chapter 4, a person may have residences in more than one state, but a person can have only one legal domicile and that is the place where the person's permanent home is. But the Court only identified a person's domicile as the "paradigm forum" for general jurisdiction, and thus a person's residence in another state could qualify for general jurisdiction in that state, in addition to the person's state of domicile, if the court determined that the person was also "essentially at home" at this other residence.

2. For corporations, the Court indicates in its cited parenthetical, at page 163, above, that the "paradigm forums" for general jurisdiction are the state or states where the corporation is incorporated and the state where the corporation has its principal place of business. As you will learn in Chapter 4, a corporation is deemed to have only one principal place of business and, for purposes of subject-matter jurisdiction in diversity-of-citizenship cases, that is the location of the corporation's headquarters. But these are only "paradigm forums" for general jurisdiction, and a corporation with manufacturing or service locations in other states could be subject to general jurisdiction in those states if the court determined that the corporation was "fairly regarded as at home" there. For example, a corporation that is incorporated in Delaware, with its corporate headquarters in New York, and its main manufacturing plant in Michigan would likely be subject to general jurisdiction in all three states.

Beyond this, however, the Court makes clear in both *Helicopteros* and *Goodyear*, respectively, that neither purchases nor sales of goods by the defendant in a state, even if occurring at regular intervals, can alone justify the exercise of general jurisdiction.

3. With the threshold for general jurisdiction so much higher than for specific jurisdiction, do you think it is important for the Court to clearly define what it means for a cause of action to "arise out of or *relate to*" a defendant's forum state activities? Recall that in footnote 10 in *Helicopteros*, the Court expressly declined to decide what, if any, distinction existed between a claim that "arises out of" the defendant's contacts and one that "relates to" those contacts. Does the Court's opinion in *Goodyear* clarify what these terms mean? Do you think Justice Brennan's dissent in *Helicopteros* is useful in this analysis?

4. If the plaintiff-respondents had not "forfeited" their contention that all Goodyear entities should be treated as a "unitary business," do you think the Court might have upheld an assertion of general jurisdiction over Goodyear USA's foreign subsidiaries?

5. In a general jurisdiction case, after deciding that the defendant's contacts are "so continuous and systematic as to render [the defendant] essentially at home in the forum State," is it permissible for the court to employ the "reasonableness" factors to defeat jurisdiction, as was done in *Asahi* in the context of a specific jurisdiction case? Prior to *Goodyear,* some courts so held, even though existing U.S. Supreme Court authority did not indicate whether such an analysis was required, or even permissible. Should the very high threshold of contacts required for general jurisdiction render such an assertion of jurisdiction reasonable per se?

6. Aside from the question of whether the reasonableness factors could be used to defeat jurisdiction, could a court employ the reasonableness factors to enhance the case for general jurisdiction in a situation in which the defendant's "continuous and systematic" contacts are almost, but not quite, substantial enough to render the defendant "essentially at home"? Recall that in *Burger King,* the Court indicated that the reasonableness factors might sometimes serve to validate an assertion of specific jurisdiction on a lesser showing of minimum contacts than would otherwise be required. Does the fact that the Court in *Goodyear* found the assertion of general jurisdiction in that case invalid, but did not inquire into the reasonableness factors, mean that those factors should not be used at all in general jurisdiction cases? Or does it just mean the factors cannot be used to enhance the case for the validity of an assertion of general jurisdiction? Does footnote 5 in the opinion cast any light on this question?

Problems

Problem 2-3. D is a citizen and resident of State *Y. D* operates a delivery service, which delivers packages to customers in States *X, Y,* and *Z.* While driving a delivery truck in State *Z, D* collided with *P,* a citizen and resident of State *X. P* sued *D* in a state court of State *X* to recover for personal injuries received in the accident. *D* was served under the State *X* long-arm statute. The statute extends jurisdiction of State *X* courts as far as the Due Process Clause of the Fourteenth Amendment permits. *D* specially appears in the action, objecting that State *X's* assertion of personal jurisdiction violates the Due Process Clause. Analyze this problem under the cases you have studied dealing with specific and general jurisdiction. Under those cases, what determines whether *D's* objection is valid?

Problem 2-4. P and *A,* residents of State *X,* decided to travel into State *Y,* a state adjacent to State *X,* with *A* driving and *P* riding as passenger in *A's* automobile. While *P* and *A* were in State *Y,* they decided to visit *D Casino. D* is incorporated in State *Y* and has its sole place of business there. *D* advertises in State *X* and has made special offers to bus companies in State *X* to persuade them to stop at *D Casino* when they are conducting tours in State *Y*. However, *P* and *A* were not responding to any advertising by *D* in State *X* or any other incentive or communication made by *D* into State *X* when they stopped at the *D Casino*. *P* and *A* did not know about the existence of the *D Casino*, but happened to see the casino while they were in State *Y* and stopped there. While in *D Casino*, *A* was served too much liquor by employees of *D*. As a result, when *A* and *P* left *D* and drove back into State *X*, they had an accident in State *X* because of *A's* intoxication. *P* was injured in the accident and sued *D* in a State *X* court, asserting jurisdiction over *D* under *X's* long-arm statute, which extends the jurisdiction of the State *X* courts as far as the U.S. Constitution permits. *D* moved to dismiss the action, arguing that the assertion of jurisdiction violated due process. Who should win and why?

3. Application of the "Minimum Contacts" Test to Internet Activities

As a practical matter, internet activities do not involve territorial boundaries in a traditional sense. Internet sites can be accessed from virtually any jurisdiction around the world. Harmful effects can be felt in distant locations, including unexpected ones. It is difficult, if not impossible, to limit internet access to local markets. E-mail contacts and exchanges can play a critical role in transactions. These activities and disputes related to them have forced the courts to attempt to adapt existing principles of personal jurisdiction to new circumstances — in some ways just like the courts did in the years leading up to the Supreme Court's decision in *International Shoe Co. v. Washington*.

The lower court decisions, with a few exceptions, have attempted to apply the standards of the "minimum contacts" test to specific contexts involving internet activities. This approach has been taken, in part, because the "minimum contacts" test is essentially "technology neutral." In applying these standards, the courts have struggled with basic questions like: How do "traditional notions of fair play and justice" operate in an internet environment? To what extent has a defendant purposefully availed itself of the privilege of acting in a state through its internet website? In the course of a contract initiated by email contacts, should it make a difference who made the first contact? What constitutes "substantial connection" with a forum when the only contacts are electronic? How should the burdens and inconveniences be balanced in the context of internet activities? How do "stream of commerce" concepts apply to internet activities? How does the "effects" test of *Calder v. Jones* apply to internet activities?

The following leading cases highlight some of the issues and contexts. *See Dudnikov v. Chalk & Vermilion Fine Arts, Inc.*, 514 F.3d 1063 (10th Cir. 2008) (upholding jurisdiction in a declaratory judgment noninfringement action commenced in Colorado by a Colorado-based eBay seller against the British copyright holder and its Delaware agent; finding targeted "effects" in Colorado based on defendants' use of eBay's notice-of-infringement procedure that stopped plaintiffs' auction in Colorado and a subsequent email threatening suit sent to plaintiffs in Colorado); *Jennings v. AC Hydraulic A/S*, 383 F.3d 546 (7th Cir. 2004) (assertion of long-arm jurisdiction based solely on "passive" website that only provided information about the manufacturer and products insufficient to satisfy due process); *Cybersell, Inc. v. Cybersell, Inc.*, 130 F.3d 414 (9th Cir. 1997) (specific jurisdiction in a distant forum not allowed in a trademark infringement case based on the use of the plaintiff's mark on the defendant's home page because the contacts with the distant forum were not "purposeful" and there was no evidence that the defendant had done business or had contacts with anyone in the distant forum); *Maritz, Inc. v. CyberGold, Inc.*, 947 F. Supp. 1328

(E.D. Mo. 1996) (specific jurisdiction in a distant forum proper under the "tortious act" provision of a long-arm statute based on advertising accessible from anywhere around the world on the website); *Zippo Mfg. Co. v. Zippo Dot Com, Inc.*, 952 F. Supp. 1119 (W.D. Pa. 1997) (suggesting "the likelihood that personal jurisdiction can be constitutionally exercised is directly proportionate to the nature and quality of commercial activity that an entity conducts over the Internet," which is essentially a "sliding scale" approach).

To date, the Supreme Court has not provided specific guidance to the lower courts on these issues, but there is a wealth of academic literature and numerous lower court decisions related to this subject that can be accessed. *See* TEPLY & WHITTEN at 322–28.

Section D. Personal Service in the Forum State — Transient Presence Jurisdiction after *Shaffer*

In its 1977 opinion in *Shaffer v. Heitner*, reprinted in section B(4), the Supreme Court used broad language in its holding that "[w]e therefore conclude that all assertions of state-court jurisdiction must be evaluated according to the standards set forth in *International Shoe* and its progeny." Although *Shaffer* was concerned with the continued validity of the traditional rules of *in rem* and *quasi in rem* jurisdiction, the Court's language raised a question as to the continued validity of the traditional rule authorizing jurisdiction over a defendant who is personally served in the forum state while only temporarily in the state, *i.e.*, transient presence jurisdiction. See the discussion of transient presence jurisdiction in section A(3)(b), above.

In *Burnham*, reprinted below, the Court answered this question. In reading *Burnham*, note that under the doctrine of "divisible divorce," which is discussed in section A(3)(d), above, and in Notes 3–5 following *Burnham*, the California court would have had jurisdiction to enter a divorce decree in the case based solely on the domicile of Mrs. Burnham in California. Mrs. Burnham, however, also sought additional relief against Mr. Burnham and to grant any relief beyond the divorce itself, the California court needed personal jurisdiction over Mr. Burnham.

Burnham v. Superior Court

United States Supreme Court, 1990
495 U.S. 604, 110 S. Ct. 2105, 109 L. Ed. 2d 631

[JUSTICE SCALIA announced the judgment of the Court and delivered an opinion in which CHIEF JUSTICE REHNQUIST and JUSTICE KENNEDY joined, and in which JUSTICE WHITE joined as to Parts I, II-A, II-B, and II-C.]

The question presented is whether the Due Process Clause of the Fourteenth Amendment denies California courts jurisdiction over a nonresident, who was personally served with process while temporarily in that State, in a suit unrelated to his activities in the State.

I 4|9

Petitioner Dennis Burnham married Francie Burnham in 1976, in West Virginia. In 1977 the couple moved to New Jersey, where their two children were born. In July 1987 the

Burnhams decided to separate. They agreed that Mrs. Burnham, who intended to move to California, would take custody of the children. Shortly before Mrs. Burnham departed for California that same month, she and petitioner agreed that she would file for divorce on grounds of "irreconcilable differences."

In October 1987, petitioner filed for divorce in New Jersey state court on grounds of "desertion." Petitioner did not, however, obtain an issuance of summons against his wife, and did not attempt to serve her with process. Mrs. Burnham, after unsuccessfully demanding that petitioner adhere to their prior agreement to submit to an "irreconcilable differences" divorce, brought suit for divorce in California state court in early January 1988.

In late January, petitioner visited southern California on business, after which he went north to visit his children in the San Francisco Bay area, where his wife resided. He took the older child to San Francisco for the weekend. Upon returning the child to Mrs. Burnham's home on January 24, 1988, petitioner was served with a California court summons and a copy of Mrs. Burnham's divorce petition. He then returned to New Jersey.

Later that year, petitioner made a special appearance in the California Superior Court, moving to quash the service of process on the ground that the court lacked personal jurisdiction over him because his only contacts with California were a few short visits to the State for the purpose of conducting business and visiting his children. The Superior Court denied the motion, and the California Court of Appeal denied mandamus relief, rejecting petitioner's contention that the Due Process Clause prohibited California courts from asserting jurisdiction over him because he lacked "minimum contacts" with the State. The court held it to be "a valid jurisdictional predicate for *in personam* jurisdiction" that the "defendant [was] present in the forum state and personally served with process." ... We granted certiorari....

II
A 4|9

. . . .

To determine whether the assertion of personal jurisdiction is consistent with due process, we have long relied on the principles traditionally followed by American courts in marking out the territorial limits of each State's authority. That criterion was first announced in *Pennoyer v. Neff*, ... in which we stated that due process "mean[s] a course of legal proceedings according to those rules and principles which have been established in our systems of jurisprudence for the protection and enforcement of private rights," ... including the "well-established principles of public law respecting the jurisdiction of an independent State over persons and property." ... In what has become the classic expression of the criterion, we said in *International Shoe Co. v. Washington*, ... that a State court's assertion of personal jurisdiction satisfies the Due Process Clause if it does not violate "'traditional notions of fair play and substantial justice.'" ... Since *International Shoe*, we have only been called upon to decide whether these "traditional notions" permit States to exercise jurisdiction over absent defendants in a manner that deviates from the rules of jurisdiction applied in the 19th century. We have held such deviations permissible, but only with respect to suits arising out of the absent defendant's contacts with the State. ... The question we must decide today is whether due process requires a similar connection between the litigation and the defendant's contacts with the State in cases where the defendant is physically present in the State at the time process is served upon him.

B 4|9

Among the most firmly established principles of personal jurisdiction in American tradition is that the courts of a State have jurisdiction over nonresidents who are physically present in the State. The view developed early that each State had the power to hale before its courts any individual who could be found within its borders, and that once having acquired jurisdiction over such a person by properly serving him with process, the State could retain jurisdiction to enter judgment against him, no matter how fleeting his visit.... That view had antecedents in English common-law practice, which sometimes allowed "transitory" actions, arising out of events outside the country, to be maintained against seemingly nonresident defendants who were present in England.... Justice Story believed the principle, which he traced to Roman origins, to be firmly grounded in English tradition: "[B]y the common law[,] personal actions, being transitory, may be brought in any place, where the party defendant may be found," for "every nation may ... rightfully exercise jurisdiction over all persons within its domains." J. Story, Commentaries on the Conflict of Laws §§ 554, 543 (1846)....

Recent scholarship has suggested that English tradition was not as clear as Story thought, *see* Hazard, *A General Theory of State-Court Jurisdiction*, 1965 Sup. Ct. Rev. 241, 253–60; Ehrenzweig, *The Transient Rule of Personal Jurisdiction: The "Power" Myth and Forum Conveniens*, 65 Yale L.J. 289 (1956). Accurate or not, however, judging by the evidence of contemporaneous or near-contemporaneous decisions one must conclude that Story's understanding was shared by American courts at the crucial time for present purposes: 1868, when the Fourteenth Amendment was adopted....

....

Decisions in the courts of many States in the 19th and early 20th centuries held that personal service upon a physically present defendant sufficed to confer jurisdiction, without regard to whether the defendant was only briefly in the State or whether the cause of action was related to his activities there.... Although research has not revealed a case deciding the issue in every State's courts, that appears to be because the issue was so well settled that it went unlitigated.... Opinions from the courts of other States announced the rule in dictum.... Most States, moreover, had statutes or common-law rules that exempted from service of process individuals who were brought into the forum by force or fraud ... or who were there as a party or witness in unrelated judicial proceedings.... These exceptions obviously rested upon the premise that service of process conferred jurisdiction.... Particularly striking is the fact that, as far as we have been able to determine, *not one* American case from the period (or, for that matter, not one American case until 1978) held, or even suggested, that in-state personal service on an individual was insufficient to confer personal jurisdiction. Commentators were also seemingly unanimous on the rule....

This American jurisdictional practice is, moreover, not merely old; it is continuing. It remains the practice of, not only a substantial number of the States, but as far as we are aware *all* the States and the federal government—if one disregards (as one must for this purpose) the few opinions since 1978 that have erroneously said, on grounds similar to those that petitioner presses here, that this Court's due-process decisions render the practice unconstitutional.... We do not know of a single State or federal statute, or a single judicial decision resting upon State law, that has abandoned in-State service as a basis of jurisdiction. Many recent cases reaffirm it....

C 4/9

Despite this formidable body of precedent, petitioner contends, in reliance on our decisions applying the *International Shoe* standard, that in the absence of "continuous and systematic" contacts with the forum, ... a nonresident defendant can be subjected to judgment only as to matters that arise out of or relate to his contacts with the forum. This argument rests on a thorough misunderstanding of our cases.

The view of most courts in the 19th century was that a court simply could not exercise *in personam* jurisdiction over a nonresident who had not been personally served with process in the forum.... *Pennoyer v. Neff*, while renowned for its statement of the principle that the Fourteenth Amendment prohibits such an exercise of jurisdiction, in fact set that forth only as dictum, and decided the case (which involved a judgment rendered more than two years before the Fourteenth Amendment's ratification) under "well-established principles of public law." ... Those principles, embodied in the Due Process Clause, required (we said) that when proceedings "involv[e] merely a determination of the personal liability of the defendant, he must be brought within [the court's] jurisdiction by service of process within the State, or his voluntary appearance." ... We invoked that rule in a series of subsequent cases, as either a matter of due process or a "fundamental principl[e] of jurisprudence." ...

Later years, however, saw the weakening of the *Pennoyer* rule. In the late 19th and early 20th centuries, changes in the technology of transportation and communication, and the tremendous growth of interstate business activity, led to an "inevitable relaxation of the strict limits on state jurisdiction" over nonresident individuals and corporations.... States required, for example, that nonresident corporations appoint an in-state agent upon whom process could be served as a condition of transacting business within their borders ... and provided in-state "substituted service" for nonresident motorists who caused injury in the State and left before personal service could be accomplished.... We initially upheld these laws under the Due Process Clause on grounds that they complied with *Pennoyer's* rigid requirement of either "consent," ... or "presence,".... As many observed, however, the consent and presence were purely fictional.... Our opinion in *International Shoe* cast those fictions aside, and made explicit the underlying basis of these decisions: due process does not necessarily *require* the States to adhere to the unbending territorial limits on jurisdiction set forth in *Pennoyer*. The validity of assertion of jurisdiction over a nonconsenting defendant who is not present in the forum depends upon whether "the quality and nature of [his] activity" in relation to the forum ... renders such jurisdiction consistent with " 'traditional notions of fair play and substantial justice.' " ... Subsequent cases have derived from the *International Shoe* standard the general rule that a State may dispense with in-forum personal service on nonresident defendants in suits arising out of their activities in the State.... As *International Shoe* suggests, the defendant's litigation-related "minimum contacts" may take the place of physical presence as the basis for jurisdiction....

Nothing in *International Shoe* or the cases that have followed it, however, offers support for the very different proposition petitioner seeks to establish today: that a defendant's presence in the forum is not only unnecessary to validate novel, nontraditional assertions of jurisdiction, but is itself no longer sufficient to establish jurisdiction. That proposition is unfaithful to both elementary logic and the foundations of our due process jurisprudence. The distinction between what is needed to support novel procedures and what is needed to sustain traditional ones is fundamental.... The short of the matter is that jurisdiction based on physical presence alone constitutes due process because it is one of the continuing traditions of our legal system that define the due process standard of "traditional notions of fair play and substantial justice." That standard was developed by *analogy* to "physical presence," and it would be perverse to say it could now be turned against that touchstone of jurisdiction.

D 3|9

Petitioner's strongest argument, though we ultimately reject it, relies upon our decision in *Shaffer v. Heitner*.... Reasoning that Delaware's sequestration procedure was simply a mechanism to compel the absent defendants to appear in a suit to determine their personal rights and obligations, we concluded that the normal rules we had developed under *International Shoe* for jurisdiction over suits against absent defendants should apply — *viz.*, Delaware could not hear the suit because the defendants' sole contact with the State (ownership of property there) was unrelated to the lawsuit....

It goes too far to say, as petitioner contends, that *Shaffer* compels the conclusion that a State lacks jurisdiction over an individual unless the litigation arises out of his activities in the State. *Shaffer*, like *International Shoe*, involved jurisdiction over an *absent defendant*, and it stands for nothing more than the proposition that when the "minimum contact" that is a substitute for physical presence consists of property ownership it must, like other minimum contacts, be related to the litigation. Petitioner wrenches out of its context our statement in *Shaffer* that "all assertions of state-court jurisdiction must be evaluated according to the standards set forth in *International Shoe* and its progeny." ... When read together with the two sentences that preceded it, the meaning of this statement becomes clear:

> The fiction that an assertion of jurisdiction over property is anything but an assertion of jurisdiction over the owner of the property supports an ancient form without substantial modern justification. Its continued acceptance would serve only to allow state-court jurisdiction that is fundamentally unfair to the defendant.

> We *therefore conclude* that all assertions of state-court jurisdiction must be evaluated according to the standards set forth in *International Shoe* and its progeny.

[*Shaffer*, 433 U.S. at 212] (emphasis added). *Shaffer* was saying, in other words, not that all bases for the assertion of *in personam* jurisdiction (including, presumably, in-state service) must be treated alike and subjected to the "minimum contacts" analysis of *International Shoe*; but rather that *quasi in rem* jurisdiction, that fictional "ancient form," and *in personam* jurisdiction, are really one and the same and must be treated alike — leading to the conclusion that *quasi in rem* jurisdiction, *i.e.*, that form of *in personam* jurisdiction based upon a "property ownership" contact and by definition unaccompanied by personal, in-state service, must satisfy the litigation-relatedness requirement of *International Shoe*. The logic of *Shaffer's* holding — which places all suits against absent nonresidents on the same constitutional footing, regardless of whether a separate Latin label is attached to one particular basis of contact — does not compel the conclusion that physically present defendants must be treated identically to absent ones. As we have demonstrated at length, our tradition has treated the two classes of defendants quite differently, and it is unreasonable to read *Shaffer* as casually obliterating that distinction. *International Shoe* confined its "minimum contacts" requirement to situations in which the defendant "be not present within the territory of the forum," ... and nothing in *Shaffer* expands that requirement beyond that.

It is fair to say, however, that while our holding today does not contradict *Shaffer*, our basic approach to the due process question is different. We have conducted no independent inquiry into the desirability or fairness of the prevailing in-state service rule, leaving that judgment to the legislatures that are free to amend it; for our purposes, its validation is its pedigree, as the phrase "*traditional notions* of fair play and substantial justice" makes clear. *Shaffer* did conduct such an independent inquiry, asserting that "'traditional notions of fair play and substantial justice' can be as readily offended by the perpetuation of ancient forms that are no longer justified as by the adoption of new procedures that are inconsistent with the basic values of our constitutional heritage." ... Perhaps that assertion can be sustained when the "perpetuation of ancient forms" is engaged in by only a very small minority of the States. Where, however, as in the present case, a jurisdictional principle is both firmly approved by tradition and still favored, it is impossible to imagine what standard we could appeal to for the judgment that it is "no longer justified." While in no way receding from or casting doubt upon the holding of *Shaffer* or any other case, we reaffirm today our time-honored approach.... For new procedures, hitherto unknown, the Due Process clause requires analysis to determine whether "traditional notions of fair play and substantial justice" have been offended.... But a doctrine of personal jurisdiction that dates back to the adoption of the Fourteenth Amendment and is still generally observed unquestionably meets that standard.

III

A few words in response to Justice Brennan's opinion concurring in the judgment: It insists that we apply "contemporary notions of due process" to determine the constitutionality of California's assertion of jurisdiction.... But our analysis today comports with that prescription, at least if we give it the only sense allowed by our precedents. The "contemporary notions of due process" applicable to personal jurisdiction are the enduring "*traditional* notions of fair play and substantial justice" established as the test by *International Shoe*. By its very language, that test is satisfied if a state court adheres to jurisdictional rules that are generally applied and have always been applied in the United States.

But the concurrence's proposed standard of "contemporary notions of due process" requires more: it measures state-court jurisdiction not only against traditional doctrines in this country, including current state-court practice, but against each Justice's subjective assessment of what is fair and just. Authority for that seductive standard is not to be found in any of our personal jurisdiction cases. It is, indeed, an outright break with the test of "traditional notions of fair play and substantial justice," which would have to be reformulated "*our* notions of fair play and substantial justice."

The subjectivity, and hence inadequacy, of this approach becomes apparent when the concurrence tries to explain *why* the assertion of jurisdiction in the present case meets its standard of continuing-American-tradition-*plus*-innate-fairness. Justice Brennan lists the "benefits" Mr. Burnham derived from the State of California—the fact that, during the few days he was there, "[h]is health and safety [were] guaranteed by the State's police, fire, and emergency medical services; he [was] free to travel on the State's roads and waterways; he likely enjoy[ed] the fruits of the State's economy." ... Three days' worth of these benefits strike us as powerfully inadequate to establish, as an abstract matter, that it is "fair" for California to decree the ownership of all Mr. Burnham's worldly goods acquired during the ten years of his marriage, and the custody over his children. We daresay a contractual exchange swapping those benefits for that power would not survive the "unconscionability" provision of the Uniform Commercial Code. Even less persuasive are the other "fairness" factors alluded to by Justice Brennan. It would create "an asymmetry," we are told, if Burnham were *permitted* (as he is) to appear in California courts as a plaintiff, but were not *compelled* to appear in California courts as defendant; and travel being as easy as it is nowadays, and modern procedural devices being so convenient, it is no great hardship to appear in California courts.... The problem with these assertions is that they justify the exercise of jurisdiction over *everyone, whether or not* he ever comes to California. The only "fairness" elements setting Mr. Burnham apart from the rest of the world are the three-days' "benefits" referred to above—and even those, do not set him apart from many other people who have enjoyed three days in the Golden State (savoring the fruits of its economy, the availability of its roads and police services) but who were fortunate enough not to be served with process while they were there and thus are not (simply by reason of that savoring) subject to the general jurisdiction of California's courts.... In other words, even if one agreed with Justice Brennan's conception of an equitable bargain, the "benefits" we have been discussing would explain why it is "fair" to assert general jurisdiction over Burnham-returned-to-New-Jersey-after-service only at the expense of proving that it is also "fair" to assert general jurisdiction over Burnham-returned-to-New-Jersey-*without*-service—which we *know* does not conform with "contemporary notions of due process."

There is, we must acknowledge, one factor mentioned by Justice Brennan that *both* relates distinctively to the assertion of jurisdiction on the basis of personal in-state service *and* is fully persuasive—namely, the fact that a defendant voluntarily present in a particular State has a "reasonable expectatio[n]" that he is subject to suit there.... By formulating it as a "reasonable expectation" Justice Brennan makes that seem like a "fairness" factor; but in reality, of course, it is just tradition masquerading as "fairness." The only reason for charging Mr. Burnham with the reasonable expectation of being subject to suit is that the States of the Union assert adjudicatory jurisdiction over the person, and have always asserted adjudicatory jurisdiction over the person, by serving him with process during his temporary physical presence in their territory. That continuing tradition, which anyone entering California should have known about, renders it "fair" to Mr. Burnham, who voluntarily entered California, to be sued there for divorce—at least "fair" in the limited sense that he has no one but himself to blame. Justice Brennan's long journey is a circular one, leaving him, at the end of the day, in complete reliance upon the very factor he sought to avoid: The existence of a continuing tradition is not enough, fairness also must be considered; fairness exists here because there is a continuing tradition.

While Justice Brennan's concurrence is unwilling to confess that the Justices of this Court can possibly be bound by a continuing American tradition that a particular procedure is fair, neither is it willing to embrace the logical consequences of that refusal—or even to be clear about what consequences (logical or otherwise) it does embrace. Justice Brennan says that "[f]or these reasons [*i.e.*, because of the reasonableness factors enumerated above], as a rule the exercise of personal jurisdiction over a defendant based on his voluntary presence in the forum will satisfy the requirements of due process."... The use of the word "rule" conveys the reassuring feeling that he is establishing a principle of law one can rely upon—but of course he is not. Since Justice Brennan's only criterion of constitutionality is "fairness," the phrase "as a rule" represents nothing more than his estimation that, *usually*, all the elements of "fairness" he discusses in the present case will exist. But what if they do not? Suppose, for example, that a defendant in Mr. Burnham's situation enjoys not three days' worth of California's "benefits," but 15 minutes' worth. Or suppose we remove one of those "benefits"—"enjoy[ment of] the fruits of the State's economy"—by positing that Mr. Burnham had not come to California on business, but only to visit his children. Or suppose that Mr. Burnham were demonstrably so impecunious as to be unable to take advantage of the modern means of transportation and communication that Justice Brennan finds so relevant. Or suppose, finally, that the California courts lacked the "variety of procedural devices,"... that Justice Brennan says can reduce the burden upon out-of-state litigants. One may also make additional suppositions, relating not to the absence of the factors that Justice Brennan discusses, but to the presence of additional factors bearing upon the ultimate criterion of "fairness." What if, for example, Mr. Burnham were visiting a sick child? Or a dying child? ... Since, so far as one can tell, Justice Brennan's approval of applying the in-state service rule in the present case rests on the presence of *all* the factors he lists, and on the absence of any others, every different case will present a different litigable issue. Thus, despite the fact that he manages to work the word "rule" into his formulation, Justice Brennan's approach does not establish a rule of law at all, but only a "totality of the circumstances" test, guaranteeing what traditional territorial rules of jurisdiction were designed precisely to avoid: uncertainty and litigation over the preliminary issue of the forum's competence. It may be that those evils, necessarily accompanying a freestanding "reasonableness" inquiry, must be accepted at the margins, when we evaluate *non*traditional forms of jurisdiction newly adopted by the states.... But that is no reason for injecting them into the core of our American practice, exposing to such a "reasonableness" inquiry the ground of jurisdiction that has hitherto been considered the very *baseline* of reasonableness, physical presence.

The difference between us and Justice Brennan has nothing to do with whether "further progress [is] to be made" in the "evolution of our legal system." ... It has to do with whether changes are to be adopted as progressive by the American people or decreed as progressive by the Justices of this Court. Nothing we say today prevents individual States from limiting or entirely abandoning the in-state-service basis of jurisdiction. And nothing prevents an overwhelming majority of them from doing so, with the consequence that the "traditional notions of fairness" that this Court applies may change. But the states have overwhelmingly declined to adopt such limitation or abandonment, evidently not considering it to be progress. The question is whether, armed with no authority other than individual Justices' perceptions of fairness that conflict with both past and current practice, this Court can compel the states to make such a change on the ground that "due process" requires it. We hold that it cannot.

Because the Due Process Clause does not prohibit the California courts from exercising jurisdiction over petitioner based on the fact of in-state service of process, the judgment is

Affirmed.

JUSTICE WHITE, concurring in part and concurring in the judgment.

I join Part I and Parts II-A, II-B, and II-C of Justice Scalia's opinion and concur in the judgment of affirmance. The rule allowing jurisdiction to be obtained over a non-resident by personal service in the forum state, without more, has been and is so widely accepted throughout this country that I could not possibly strike it down, either on its face or as applied in this case, on the ground that it denies due process of law guaranteed by the Fourteenth Amendment. Although the Court has the authority under the Amendment to examine even traditionally accepted procedures and declare them invalid, *e.g.*, *Shaffer v. Heitner*, 433 U.S. 186 (1977), there has been no showing here or elsewhere that as a general proposition the rule is so arbitrary and lacking in common sense in so many instances that it should be held violative of Due Process in every case. Furthermore, until such a showing is made, which would be difficult indeed, claims in individual cases that the rule would operate unfairly as applied to the particular non-resident involved need not be entertained. At least this would be the case where presence in the forum state is intentional, which would almost always be the fact. Otherwise, there would be endless, fact-specific litigation in the trial and appellate courts, including this one. Here, personal service in California, without more, is enough, and I agree that the judgment should be affirmed.

JUSTICE BRENNAN, with whom JUSTICE MARSHALL, JUSTICE BLACKMUN, and JUSTICE O'CONNOR join, concurring in the judgment.

I agree with Justice Scalia that the Due Process Clause of the Fourteenth Amendment generally permits a state court to exercise jurisdiction over a defendant if he is served with process while voluntarily present in the forum State. I do not perceive the need, however, to decide that a jurisdictional rule that "'has been immemorially the actual law of the land'" ... automatically comports with due process simply by virtue of its "pedigree." Although I agree that history is an important factor in establishing whether a jurisdictional rule satisfies due process requirements, I cannot agree that it is the *only* factor such that all traditional rules of jurisdiction are, *ipso facto*, forever constitutional. Unlike Justice Scalia, I would undertake an "independent inquiry into the ... fairness of the prevailing in-state service rule." ... I therefore concur in the judgment.

I

I believe that the approach adopted by Justice Scalia's opinion today—reliance solely on historical pedigree—is foreclosed by our decisions in *International Shoe Co. v. Washington* ... and *Shaffer v. Heitner*.... In *International Shoe*, we held that a state court's assertion of personal jurisdiction does not violate the Due Process Clause if it is consistent with "'traditional notions of fair play and substantial justice.'" ...

While our *holding* in *Shaffer* may have been limited to *quasi in rem* jurisdiction, our mode of analysis was not. Indeed, that we were willing in *Shaffer* to examine anew the appropriateness of the *quasi in rem* rule—until that time dutifully accepted by American courts for at least a century—demonstrates that we did not believe that the "pedigree" of a jurisdictional practice was dispositive in deciding whether it was consistent with due process....

II

Tradition, though alone not dispositive, is of course *relevant* to the question whether the rule of transient jurisdiction is consistent with due process.[7] ...

... I find the historical background relevant because, however murky the jurisprudential origins of transient jurisdiction, the fact that American courts have announced the rule for perhaps a century (first in dicta, more recently in holdings) provides a defendant voluntarily present in a particular State *today* "clear notice that [he] is subject to suit" in the forum.... Regardless of whether Justice Story's account of the rule's genesis is mythical, our common understanding *now*, fortified by a century of judicial practice, is that jurisdiction is often a function of geography. The transient rule is consistent with reasonable expectations and is entitled to a strong presumption that it comports with due process. "If I visit another State, ... I knowingly assume some risk that the State will exercise its power over my property or my person while there. My contact with the State, though minimal, gives rise to predictable risks." ...

By visiting the forum State, a transient defendant actually "avail[s]" himself ... of significant benefits provided by the State. His health and safety are guaranteed by the State's police, fire, and emergency medical services; he is free to travel on the State's roads and waterways; he likely enjoys the fruits of the State's economy as well. Moreover, the Privileges and Immunities Clause of Article IV prevents a state government from discriminating against a transient defendant by denying him the protections of its law or the right of access to its courts.... Subject only to the doctrine of *forum non conveniens*, an out-of-state plaintiff may use state courts in all circumstances in which those courts would be available to state citizens. Without transient jurisdiction, an asymmetry would arise: a transient would have the full benefit of the power of the forum State's courts as a plaintiff while retaining immunity from their authority as a defendant....

---

7. I do not propose that the "contemporary notions of due process" to be applied are no more than "each Justice's subjective assessment of what is fair and just." ... Rather, the inquiry is guided by our decisions beginning with *International Shoe Co. v. Washington*, ... and the specific factors that we have developed to ascertain whether a jurisdictional rule comports with "traditional notions of fair play and substantial justice." ... Our experience with this approach demonstrates that it is well within our competence to employ.

The potential burdens on a transient defendant are slight. "'[M]odern transportation and communications have made it much less burdensome for a party sued to defend himself'" in a State outside his place of residence.... That the defendant has already journeyed at least once before to the forum—as evidenced by the fact that he was served with process there—is an indication that suit in the forum likely would not be prohibitively inconvenient. Finally, any burdens that do arise can be ameliorated by a variety of procedural devices.[13] For these reasons, as a rule the exercise of personal jurisdiction over a defendant based on his voluntary presence in the forum will satisfy the requirements of due process....

In this case, it is undisputed that petitioner was served with process while voluntarily and knowingly in the State of California. I therefore concur in the judgment.

JUSTICE STEVENS, concurring in the judgment.

As I explained in my separate writing, I did not join the Court's opinion in *Shaffer v. Heitner* ... because I was concerned by its unnecessarily broad reach.... The same concern prevents me from joining either Justice Scalia's or Justice Brennan's opinion in this case. For me, it is sufficient to note that the historical evidence and consensus identified by Justice Scalia, the considerations of fairness identified by Justice Brennan, and the common sense displayed by Justice White, all combine to demonstrate that this is, indeed, a very easy case. Accordingly, I agree that the judgment should be affirmed.

Notes and Questions

1. Although the Justices in *Burnham* produced four separate opinions outlining their respective rationales for upholding jurisdiction based on in-state personal service, with no opinion commanding a majority, the ultimate judgment of the Court was unanimous in holding that jurisdiction based on personal service within the forum state is constitutionally valid even though the defendant is only temporarily in the state and even though the suit is unrelated to the defendant's activities in the state. Even Justice Brennan, who presented his analysis in a "minimum contacts" framework, ultimately concluded that "as a *rule* the exercise of personal jurisdiction over a defendant based on his voluntary presence in the forum will satisfy the requirements of due process."

2. Transient presence jurisdiction does not apply to corporations. In *James-Dickinson Farm Mortgage Co. v. Harry*, 273 U.S. 119, 122 (1927), the Supreme Court held that "[j]urisdiction over a corporation of one State cannot be acquired in another State or district in which it has no place of business and is not found, merely by serving process upon an executive officer temporarily therein, even if he is there on business of the company."

States, however, uniformly require out-of-state corporations doing business within the state to register and appoint an in-state agent to accept service of process. When in-state service is made on the registered agent, personal jurisdiction over the corporation has been upheld on the theory of "consent." The lower courts are split, however, on whether this

---

13. For example, in the federal system, a transient defendant can avoid protracted litigation of a spurious suit through a motion to dismiss for failure to state a claim or through a motion for summary judgment. Fed. R. Civ. P. 12(b)(6) and 56. He can use relatively inexpensive methods of discovery, such as oral deposition by telephone (Rule 30(b)([4])), deposition upon written questions (Rule 31), interrogatories (Rule 33), and requests for admission (Rule 36), while enjoying protection from harassment (Rule 26(c)), and possibly obtaining costs and attorney's fees for some of the work involved (Rule 37(a)([5]), (b)–(d)). Moreover, a change of venue may be possible. 28 U.S.C. § 1404. In state court, many of the same procedural protections are available, as is the doctrine of *forum non conveniens*, under which the suit may be dismissed....

"consent" is limited solely to claims arising from the corporation's in-state activities or may properly encompass consent to general jurisdiction.

3. Even before *Burnham*, it was clear that all the territorial rules were not necessarily rendered defunct by the statement in *Shaffer* that "all assertions of state-court jurisdiction must be evaluated according to the standards set forth in *International Shoe* and its progeny." In footnote 30 in *Shaffer*, the Court had attempted to prevent invalidation of ex parte divorce jurisdiction based on plaintiff's domicile. The Court stated it was not suggesting that "the particularized rules governing the adjudication of status are inconsistent with the [*International Shoe*] standard of fairness." Can you make an argument that divorce jurisdiction based on the domicile of the plaintiff alone would be constitutional under the "minimum contacts" test? Are there any potential constitutional limitations on the power of a state to divorce a plaintiff from a defendant who has no connections whatsoever with the state?

4. The burdens of ex parte divorce jurisdiction are mitigated by the concept of "divisible divorce" developed by the U.S. Supreme Court after *International Shoe*. Under the "divisible divorce" concept, a defendant spouse's right to support cannot be cut off by a judgment of divorce unless the divorcing state has personal jurisdiction under ordinary standards over the defendant. Thus, while the domicile of the plaintiff alone will allow a state to divorce the plaintiff and the defendant, it will not allow a state to cut off most other important rights of the defendant. *See* Luther L. McDougal, III, Robert L. Felix & Ralph U. Whitten, American Conflicts Law § 183 (6th ed. 2011). Does the "divisible divorce" concept help answer the questions at the end of the preceding note?

5. In *Abernathy v. Abernathy*, 482 S.E.2d 265 (Ga. 1997), the concept of "divisible divorce" collided with the language in *Shaffer* indicating that a state would normally have the constitutional power to adjudicate claims to property located within the state, discussed in Note 1, following *Shaffer*. In *Abernathy*, a couple was married in Florida and lived in Louisiana until their separation. Upon separation, the husband moved to Georgia and purchased real property there, apparently with assets accumulated during the marriage. After about a year, the husband commenced a divorce action against the wife in Georgia. As part of the divorce proceeding, the husband requested that the property located in Georgia be awarded to him.

The wife objected to personal jurisdiction, but a Georgia trial court asserted jurisdiction over the "res of the marriage relationship" and "in rem jurisdiction with respect to [the] property located within this State." *Id.* at 266. The Georgia Supreme Court affirmed. According to the court, the Georgia courts had jurisdiction to divorce based on the plaintiff's domicile in Georgia and that the assertion of in rem jurisdiction over the property did not violate the "minimum contacts" test because of the language in *Shaffer* with respect to the power of state courts to adjudicate claims directly related to property located within the state. Presiding Judge Fletcher dissented on the ground that the "divisible divorce" cases required the opposite result:

> The majority's opinion opens the doors of Georgia's courts to any citizen of this country who wants to divorce and to obtain an unfair advantage over his or her spouse in the division of marital property. All any citizen need do is leave his or her marital home, take any or all assets of the couple, move to Georgia and file for divorce.... The non-resident spouse is then forced to litigate his or her claim to those marital assets in a foreign jurisdiction.

Id. at 269.

Justice Sears also dissented, observing that the Georgia Legislature had, in the Georgia long-arm statute, specifically required personal jurisdiction over a non-resident spouse in actions for division of marital property. *See id.* at 270–71. (The majority had held the

Georgia long-arm statute irrelevant because the trial court was exercising in rem jurisdiction over the property.) Justice Sears also argued, in the alternative, that the "minimum contacts" test was violated by Georgia's assertion of jurisdiction over the wife. Justice Sears pointed to language in *Shaffer* in which the U.S. Supreme Court had given an example of when property located in the state would not support jurisdiction to adjudicate a claim directly related to the property.

That example was taken from comment c to the RESTATEMENT (SECOND) OF CONFLICT OF LAWS § 60 (1971), which provides that a state will not *usually* exercise jurisdiction over personal property brought into its territory without the owner's consent. Section 60 is the "property equivalent" of state rules prohibiting the acquisition of personal jurisdiction by force. The rules prohibiting acquisition of jurisdiction by fraud and force were previously examined in section A(3)(b), above. The specific language of comments c and d on § 60 are set out in footnote 25 in Justice Marshall's opinion in *Shaffer*, which is reprinted in this section. Justice Sears further argued that the wife did not have the necessary "purposeful contacts" to satisfy the constitutional test for specific jurisdiction. Who has the best of this argument?

6. *Kulko*, discussed in section B(4), above, obviously posed an obstacle to the ability of the wife in *Burnham* to assert long-arm jurisdiction over the husband. However, can you make an argument that *Kulko* and *Burnham* are distinguishable and that the husband in *Burnham* did, in fact, have sufficient contacts with California to satisfy due process?

7. Assume a basis other than physical presence within the state is available to acquire personal jurisdiction over the defendant. However, the plaintiff chooses to serve the defendant on the basis of physical presence. Should either the immunity rules or the fraud-and-force rules discussed in section A(3)*(b)*, above, have any application? *See* TEPLY & WHITTEN at 231–32 (discussing this issue and concluding that these rules should have no application when a nonresident is otherwise constitutionally subject to personal jurisdiction pursuant to, for example, a state long-arm statute).

Problems

Problem 2-5. P and D are both citizens of State X. Each claims title to the same land located in State Y. P sues D in a state court of State X. P seeks a declaration that P, not D, has title to the land. D is personally served with process in State X. However, D objects to the jurisdiction of the State X court on the ground that an assertion of jurisdiction to adjudicate the title to land located in another state violates the Due Process Clause of the Fourteenth Amendment. After *Shaffer* and *Burnham*, is D's objection sound?

Problem 2-6. P and D are both citizens of State X married to each other. P and D separate, and P moves to State Y, taking (without D's consent) a portion of the parties' marital property that belonged to them jointly. After fulfilling the statutory period of residency in State Y, P commences an action for divorce against D. P also requests that the State Y court award P all of the marital property that P brought to State Y. Does the State Y court have the constitutional power to divorce P and *ain* D and to award the property to P?

Section E. Jurisdiction by Necessity ← No such Thing

The U.S. Supreme Court has reserved decision on whether "jurisdiction by necessity" could exist in a case if the ordinary requirements of due process are not satisfied by a state's assertion of personal jurisdiction. The basic idea of jurisdiction by necessity is that there must be at least one forum somewhere with power to adjudicate every case. Thus, even if a defendant lacks minimum contacts with every state, jurisdiction by necessity would nevertheless allow some state to adjudicate the plaintiff's claim against the defendant. *See, e.g.*, Arthur T. von Mehren & Donald T. Trautman, *Jurisdiction to Adjudicate: A Suggested Analysis*, 79 HARV. L. REV. 1121 (1966).

Within the doctrine of jurisdiction by necessity, however, there are at least two distinguishable kinds of cases. One potential kind of jurisdiction-by-necessity case is represented by *Mullane v. Central Hanover Bank & Trust Co.*, discussed in section B(4), above and discussed in section E, below. In *Mullane*, strong practical considerations pointed to New York as the only realistic forum in which to settle trust accounts established in New York under New York law. If absent defendant-beneficiaries of the trust could defeat the accounting proceeding by refusing to consent to jurisdiction in New York, they could paralyze the ability of others also interested in the subject matter of the action to settle their own claims to the assets located within the state. Individual accounting actions in every state where beneficiaries of New York trusts resided, in addition to being expensive and inefficient, posed a danger of conflicting judgments to the assets that would not bind claimants in other states. As a practical matter, this would have prevented the settlement of the trust accounts and would have defeated the ability to establish trusts of the sort in *Mullane* in which nonresident beneficiaries could participate. The same reasons point to the need for jurisdiction in the state where real property is located when nonresidents assert claims to the property. Unless the situs state is allowed to adjudicate all the claims to the land, it might be impossible to settle the title to the land at all.

Another kind of jurisdiction-by-necessity case could be described as a "pure" one. It involves a situation in which there is no jurisdiction in which the "minimum contacts" test is satisfied as to all the defendants joined in the action. In footnote 37 of the Court's opinion in *Shaffer v. Heitner*, discussed in section B(3), above, the Court reserved decision on whether jurisdiction would exist in the state where the defendant owned property if no other state existed in which the plaintiff could obtain personal jurisdiction over the defendant. In addition, in footnote 13 of the Court's opinion in *Helicopteros Nacionales de Colombia, S.A. v. Hall*, reprinted in section C(2), above, the Court refused to decide whether a doctrine of jurisdiction by necessity exists because the plaintiff had not demonstrated that all three of the defendants in *Helicopteros* could not be sued in a single forum — e.g., Colombia or Peru. Thus, if jurisdiction by necessity is a viable doctrine, it may not be appropriate when the plaintiff can sue all defendants in a single forum, even if the single forum is in a foreign country. In addition, because none of the defendants in *Helicopteros* were indispensable parties to actions against the others, the Court's statement implies that the concept of jurisdiction by necessity might apply when they cannot all be sued in a single forum but could be sued individually in different fora, which would extend the doctrine to a very broad category of cases.

Notes and Questions

1. The *Mullane* kind of jurisdiction-by-necessity case is undisturbing. Indeed, it is questionable whether it is a "real" jurisdiction-by-necessity case at all. For it is arguable that the ordinary requirements of due process are satisfied in cases like *Mullane* as well as in cases in which real property is located within the state. Do you understand why?

2. Even if jurisdiction by necessity is a viable concept, shouldn't it be limited to cases in which all of the defendants are indispensable parties to a suit against the other defendants? (In *Helicopteros*, the plaintiff could have sued all defendants individually in separate fora. The only problem the plaintiff would have faced in doing so is that the defendants might have separately defended different actions by pointing to the other defendants as solely responsible for the plaintiff's injuries.)

3. In *Phillips Petroleum Co. v. Shutts*, 472 U.S. 797 (1985), the plaintiffs commenced a class action in Kansas state court to recover interest on certain royalty payments that had been withheld from the plaintiff class members. The defendants objected that the Kansas courts did not have sufficient contacts with nonresident members of the *plaintiff's* class to justify adjudicating their claims as part of the class action. The Supreme Court rejected this argument. The Court held that absent members of the plaintiff's class did not face the same burdens as nonresident defendants, given the protections afforded to them by the Kansas class action rule, which included the right to "opt-out," required court certification of the class, the necessity of court approval for any settlement, etc. In *Phillips*, many of the claims of the absent members of the class were so small that individual actions by each member of the class would have been economically unfeasible. Can you make an argument that *Phillips* was a jurisdiction-by-necessity case?

4. In a later phase of the *Phillips* litigation, the U.S. Supreme Court held in *Sun Oil Co. v. Wortman*, 486 U.S. 717 (1988), that it was constitutional for Kansas to apply its longer statute of limitations to interest claims that arose in other states and were barred by the statutes of limitation of those states. In that case, Kansas did have some contact with the events giving rise to the suit. However, should a state with no contacts with the parties or events giving rise to the action be allowed to exercise jurisdiction by necessity merely because it was the only state whose statute of limitations had not run?

5. Assuming the U.S. Supreme Court will someday approve of a doctrine of jurisdiction by necessity, how should the Court determine in which of all the universe of fora the defendant(s) can be sued? Should the plaintiff be allowed to choose any forum the plaintiff wishes or should there be limitations on the choice? If there should be limitations on the choice, what should they be? Does the difficulty in answering these questions indicate that the whole idea of jurisdiction by necessity should be discarded? After all, the idea is predicated on the notion that the ordinary due process rights of the defendant should give way to the right of the plaintiff to prosecute a claim. What in the U.S. Constitution gives the right to a plaintiff to prosecute a claim even if the defendant would have to be deprived of the ordinary protections of the Due Process Clause for the plaintiff to do so?

Problems

Problem 2-7. P, a citizen and resident of State *X*, sues *D*, a citizen and resident of a foreign nation, in State *Y*, by attaching property in State *Y* owned by *D*. Other than the ownership of the property, *D* has no contacts with State *Y*. *P's* claim is based on an automobile accident that occurred in Canada between *P* and *D*. *D* has returned to *D's* home country, which would not permit its courts to entertain an action by *P* and would not enforce a judgment against *D* obtained in any court within the United States or any court of any other nation. Is this situation for a valid jurisdiction-by-necessity case in State *Y*? Should *P* be forced to proceed against *D* first in Canada and then, if a judgment is obtained against *D* there, take the judgment to State *Y* for enforcement? Would such a procedure accomplish anything as a practical matter?

Problem 2-8. On the facts of *Problem 2-7*, but assuming that *D* is a citizen of Great Britain, is there any argument that can be made in favor of jurisdiction by necessity in State *Y*? Would it matter whether the property in State *Y* is the only asset *D* owns?

Section F. Due Process Requirements of Notice and Opportunity to Be Heard

In addition to the requirement of personal jurisdiction over the defendant, another fundamental requirement of the Due Process Clause is that the defendant be provided with adequate *notice* of the commencement of the action and the *opportunity to be heard*.

1. The Constitutional Requirement of Notice

The modern due process standard of notice is basically the same as the standard followed by the state courts under the due process clauses of their constitutions before the Fourteenth Amendment existed: given the options available to the lawmaker (ordinarily a legislature), the form of notice provided must be reasonably likely to provide the defendant with actual notice that the action has been commenced. However, this test must be applied today in a procedural world vastly different from the one existing before the Fourteenth Amendment.

The *Mullane* Case. In the landmark case of *Mullane v. Central Hanover Bank & Trust Co.*, 339 U.S. 306 (1950), which is discussed in section B(4) & E, above, the Court announced the constitutional standard for notice under the Due Process Clause. In *Mullane*, New York had enacted "common trust fund" legislation that permitted small trust estates to pool their assets in a single fund for purposes of investment administration in New York. Periodic judicial accounting proceedings were required under the statute for any institution establishing such a fund. The statute provided that the resulting judicial decree was binding and conclusive on all beneficiaries, resident or nonresident, having any interest in the common fund or any participating estate, trust, or fund. The only notice of the judicial accounting required under the statute to beneficiaries was by publication in a newspaper.

The Central Hanover Bank & Trust Co. established such a common trust fund under the statute and filed for a judicial accounting, as required under the statute. Notice of the judicial accounting was given to all beneficiaries, as authorized under the statute, by publication in a local New York newspaper. The specially appointed guardian and attorney for the beneficiaries challenged the adequacy of this statutory notice by publication as a violation of due process under the Fourteenth Amendment. The Court held that notice by publication violated due process as to beneficiaries whose identities and location were known, but that such notice satisfied due process as to beneficiaries whose identities and location were not known. *[handwritten: Could's Holding]*

The Court held that to satisfy due process, the notice must be "reasonably calculated, under all the circumstances, to apprise interested parties of the pendency of the action" and "must be such as one desirous of actually informing the absentee might reasonably adopt to accomplish it." Applying this "reasonably calculated" standard, the Court held that notice by personal service was not constitutionally required and that notice by ordinary mail to known beneficiaries was sufficient to meet the due process standard. The Court held, however, that notice by publication was constitutionally sufficient as to beneficiaries whose identities and location were not known because this was the best practicable notice under the circumstances.

As the Court held,

[a]n elementary and fundamental requirement of due process in any proceeding which is to be accorded finality is notice reasonably calculated, under all the circumstances, to apprise interested parties of the pendency of the action and afford them an opportunity to present their objections.... The notice must be of such nature as reasonably to convey the required information, and it must afford a reasonable time for those interested to make their appearance.... But if with due regard for the practicalities and peculiarities of the case these conditions are reasonably met the constitutional requirements are satisfied....

But when notice is a person's due, process which is a mere gesture is not due process. The means employed must be such as one desirous of actually informing the absentee might reasonably adopt to accomplish it. The reasonableness and hence the constitutional validity of any chosen method may be defended on the ground that it is in itself reasonably certain to inform those affected ... or, where conditions do not reasonably permit such notice, that the form chosen is not substantially less likely to bring home notice than other of the feasible and customary substitutes.

It would be idle to pretend that publication alone as prescribed here, is a reliable means of acquainting interested parties of the fact that their rights are before the courts.

. . . .

This Court has not hesitated to approve of resort to publication as a customary substitute in another class of cases where it is not reasonably possible or practicable to give more adequate warning. Thus it has been recognized that, in the case of persons missing or unknown, employment of an indirect and even a probably futile means of notification is all that the situation permits and creates no constitutional bar to a final decree foreclosing their rights....

Those beneficiaries represented by appellant whose interests or whereabouts could not with due diligence be ascertained come clearly within this category. As to them the statutory notice is sufficient. However great the odds that publication will never reach the eyes of such unknown parties, it is not in the typical case much more likely to fail than any of the choices open to legislators endeavoring to prescribe the best notice practicable.

. . . .

As to known present beneficiaries of known place of residence, however, notice by publication stands on a different footing. Exceptions in the name of necessity do not sweep away the rule that within the limits of practicability notice must be such as is reasonably calculated to reach interested parties. Where the names and post office addresses of those affected by a proceeding are at hand, the reasons disappear for resort to means less likely than the mails to apprise them of its pendency.

The trustee has on its books the names and addresses of the income beneficiaries represented by appellant, and we find no tenable ground for dispensing with a serious effort to inform them personally of the accounting, at least by ordinary mail to the record addresses.

. . . .

We need not weigh contentions that a requirement of personal service of citation on even the large number of known resident or nonresident beneficiaries would, by reasons of delay if not of expense, seriously interfere with the proper administration of the fund. Of course personal service even without the jurisdiction of the issuing authority serves the end of actual and personal notice, whatever power of compulsion it might lack. However, no such service is required under the circumstances. This type of trust presupposes a large number of small interests. The individual interest does not stand alone but is identical with that of a class. The rights of each in the integrity of the fund and the fidelity of the trustee are shared by many other beneficiaries. Therefore notice reasonably certain to reach most of those interested in objecting is likely to safeguard the interests of all, since any objections sustained would inure to the benefit of all. We think that under such circumstances reasonable risks that notice might not actually reach every beneficiary are justifiable. . . .

The statutory notice to known beneficiaries is inadequate, not because in fact it fails to reach everyone, but because under the circumstances it is not reasonably calculated to reach those who could easily be informed by other means at hand.

Id. at 314–19.

The *Jones* Case. In *Jones v. Flowers*, 547 U.S. 220 (2006), the Court addressed the operation of the *Mullane* test in a situation where the plaintiff knew the defendant had not received notice sent. In *Jones*, Gary Jones purchased a house in Little Rock, Arkansas. He lived in the house with his wife until they separated. Jones then moved into an apartment in Little Rock, and his wife continued to live in the house. Jones paid his mortgage each month for 30 years, and the mortgage company paid Jones' property taxes. After Jones paid off his mortgage, the property taxes went unpaid, and the property was certified as delinquent. Subsequently, the Commissioner of State Lands attempted to notify Jones of his tax delinquency, and his right to redeem the property, by mailing a certified letter addressed to Jones at the house. The letter indicated that unless Jones redeemed the property, it would be subject to public sale two years later. Nobody was home to sign for the letter, and nobody appeared at the post office to retrieve the letter within the next 15 days. The post office returned the letter to the Commissioner marked "unclaimed."

Two years later, and just a few weeks before the public sale, the Commissioner published a notice of public sale in a local newspaper. No bids were submitted, which permitted the State to negotiate a private sale of the property. Several months later, Linda Flowers submitted a purchase offer. The Commissioner mailed another certified letter addressed to Jones at the house, attempting to notify him that his house would be sold to Flowers if he did not pay his taxes. Like the first letter, the second was also returned "unclaimed." Flowers purchased the house, which the parties stipulated in the trial court had a fair market value of $80,000, for $21,042.15. Immediately after the 30-day period for post-sale redemption passed, Flowers had an unlawful detainer notice delivered to the property. The notice was served on Jones' daughter, who contacted Jones and notified him of the tax sale.

Jones filed a lawsuit in Arkansas state court against the Commissioner and Flowers, alleging that the Commissioner's failure to provide notice of the tax sale and of Jones' right to redeem resulted in the taking of his property without due process. The Commissioner and Flowers moved for summary judgment on the ground that the two unclaimed letters sent by the Commissioner were a constitutionally adequate attempt at notice. The trial court granted summary judgment. It concluded that the Arkansas tax sale statute, which set forth the notice procedure followed by the Commissioner, complied with constitutional due process requirements. Jones appealed, and the Arkansas Supreme Court affirmed the trial court's judgment. The Supreme Court granted certiorari and reversed.

The Commissioner argued that once the State provided notice reasonably calculated to apprise Jones of the impending tax sale by mailing him a certified letter, due process was satisfied. In response, the Court stated:

> We do not think that a person who actually desired to inform a real property owner of an impending tax sale of a house he owns would do nothing when a certified letter sent to the owner is returned unclaimed. If the Commissioner prepared a stack of letters to mail to delinquent taxpayers, handed them to the postman, and then watched as the departing postman accidentally dropped the letters down a storm drain, one would certainly expect the Commissioner's office to prepare a new stack of letters and send them again. No one "desirous of actually informing" the owners would simply shrug his shoulders as the letters disappeared and say "I tried." Failure to follow up would be unreasonable, despite the fact that the letters were reasonably calculated to reach their intended recipients when delivered to the postman.
>
> By the same token, when a letter is returned by the post office, the sender will ordinarily attempt to resend it, if it is practicable to do so.... This is especially true when, as here, the subject matter of the letter concerns such an important and irreversible prospect as the loss of a house. Although the State may have made a reasonable calculation of how to reach Jones, it had good reason to suspect when the notice was returned that Jones was "no better off than if the notice had never been sent." ... Deciding to take no further action is not what someone "desirous of actually informing" Jones would do; such a person would take further reasonable steps if any were available.
>
> It is certainly true ... the failure of notice in a specific case does not establish the inadequacy of the attempted notice; in that sense, the constitutionality of a particular procedure for notice is assessed *ex ante*, rather than *post hoc*. But if a feature of the State's chosen procedure is that it promptly provides additional information to the government about the effectiveness of notice, it does not contravene the *ex ante* principle to consider what the government does with that information in assessing the adequacy of the chosen procedure....

Id. at 229–31.

After concluding that the state should have taken additional reasonable steps to notify Jones, if practicable to do so, the Court then addressed the question whether there were any such available steps. In this regard, the Court indicated that one reasonable step would be for the State to resend the notice by regular mail, so that a signature was not required. The Court pointed out the use of certified mail might make actual notice less likely in some cases because the letter cannot be left like regular mail to be examined at the end of the day and can only be retrieved from the post office for a specified period of time. In the Court's view, doing so would have increased the chances of actual notice to Jones if—as it turned out—he had moved.

Furthermore, even occupants who ignored certified mail notice slips addressed to the owner might add the owner's new address on the notice packet and leave it for the postman to retrieve, or notify Jones directly. Another reasonable step would have been to post notice on the front door or to address otherwise undeliverable mail to "occupant," which would have increased the likelihood that the owner would be notified. In fact, in this case, Jones first learned of the state's effort to sell his house when he was alerted by his daughter, one of the occupants, after she was served with the unlawful detainer notice. On the other hand, the Court indicated that the Commissioner did not have to engage in a search for his new address in the Little Rock phonebook and other government records such as income tax rolls.

Justice Thomas, with whom joined by Justices Scalia and Kennedy joined, dissented. Based on the Court's prior precedents, Justice Thomas asserted that (1) whether the method of notice is reasonably calculated to notify the interested party should be only determined *ex ante*, *i.e.*, from the viewpoint of the government agency at the time its notice is sent and (2) the government should not be required to take additional steps to ensure that notice has been received.

Notes and Questions

1. The *Mullane* case remains the primary modern authority on the due process requirements of notice. Does *Jones* appear to alter the *Mullane* test in any way? Can an argument be made that *Jones* now requires that a plaintiff take multiple steps to provide for notice to the defendant in every case when the plaintiff knows that an initial attempt at notice has been unsuccessful? How would such a requirement be applied in other factual circumstances? For example, suppose a state service of process provision allows service on a defendant at the defendant's home by leaving the process with someone of suitable age and discretion. Pursuant to such a provision, a process server hired by the plaintiff serves the defendant by leaving the process with the defendant's spouse at the defendant's home, but as the process server is leaving, she sees the defendant's spouse stuff the process into a garbage can. The process server makes out a proper return indicating how and when process was served, but informs the plaintiff's attorney what she saw. Does the plaintiff have to take further steps to notify the defendant of the action to satisfy due process under these circumstances? Does the answer in any way depend on what provisions the state has for allowing the defendant to seek vacation of a default judgment when the defendant has not received proper notice of the action?

2. Due process has never required that the defendant actually receive the notice provided, so long as the state prescribes a form of service that is reasonably calculated to get to the defendant. Does it make sense to you that a reasonable form of notice that does not reach the defendant will be satisfactory, as long as the plaintiff does not know that the notice has not reached the defendant, but that a form of notice that is not allowed by the relevant statutes and rules that does reach the defendant will still be subject to an insufficient-service-of-process objection under state law (as is usually the case)? If the due process validity of otherwise proper notice depends on whether the plaintiff knows that the process has not reached the defendant, will plaintiffs simply be encouraged to use forms of notice that are, judged *ex ante*, reasonable, but which will not bring any lack of actual notice to their attention—for example, ordinary mail, which will be adequate in many instances under the *Mullane* test?

3. Do you think that service of process over the internet should satisfy the notice requirements of the Due Process Clause?

Problem

Problem 2-9. *P* sues *D* in a court of proper subject-matter jurisdiction and venue in the state where *P* and *D* live. The relevant statutes in the state provide that the normal method of serving process on the defendant in a civil action is by delivering a copy of the process to the defendant personally. This method is unsuccessful in *P's* action against *D* because *D*, aware that *P* has commenced an action against *D*, is successfully able to evade numerous attempts to serve *D* personally. A state statute also authorizes service of process on defendants by publication in a newspaper for several successive weeks when ordinary means of serving process on the defendant fail or the plaintiff is able to demonstrate that the whereabouts of the defendant is unknown. *P* uses this statute to serve *D* with notice by publication. After notice by publication is made for the prescribed period, *P* obtains a default judgment against *D*. Is the judgment valid under the *Mullane* test?

2. Notice and Opportunity to Be Heard in the Context of Provisional Remedies

Chapter 1 examined the various provisional remedies that are available under state law. Provisional remedy statutes and rules often allow a particular remedy to be issued without prior notice and an opportunity to be heard. In this context, the central question is, what kinds of protections must state provisional remedies statutes and rules contain to satisfy the minimum requirements of the Due Process Clause of the Fourteenth Amendment?

The U.S. Supreme Court has decided a series of cases (mostly) answering this question. In *Sniadach v. Family Finance Corp.,* 395 U.S. 337 (1969), the Court invalidated a Wisconsin statute providing for garnishment of wages on the ground that it failed to provide notice and opportunity to be heard prior to the seizure in violation of the Due Process Clause. Three years later, in *Fuentes v. Shevin,* 407 U.S. 67 (1972), the Court invalidated a Florida statue providing for prejudgment replevin of consumer goods without notice and opportunity to be heard after the consumer had stopped making payments on the goods, even though the plaintiff was required to post a bond in an amount double the value of the property.

In contrast, two years later, in *Mitchell v. W.T. Grant Co.,* 416 U.S. 600 (1974), the Court upheld a Louisiana sequestration procedure that did not provide for notice and opportunity to be heard before the writ of sequestration was issued. In *Mitchell,* a creditor had used the sequestration procedure to repossess consumer goods in which the creditor had a vendor's lien. The Louisiana statutes permitted a person who "claims the ownership or right to possession of property, or a mortgage, lien, or privilege thereon ... if it is within the power of the defendant to conceal, dispose of or waste the property or the revenues therefrom, or remove the property from the parish, during the pendency of the action" to use the procedure.

The statues also required the party seeking sequestration to show "the nature of the claim and the amount thereof, if any, and the grounds relied upon for the issuance of the writ clearly appear from specific facts" shown by a verified petition or affidavit. Such showing had been made to a judge, and the writ was issued only upon the judge's authorization and only after the creditor has filed a sufficient bond to protect the vendee against all damages if the writ of sequestration turns out to have been improvidently issued. The sheriff served the writ upon the debtor and became responsible for the safekeeping of the property. The plaintiff-creditor could then take possession of the goods if the defendant did not secure possession of the goods by posting his own bond within ten days, but the plaintiff-creditor had no right to sell the goods until final judgment on the merits.

The statutes entitled the debtor to seek immediate dissolution of the writ. If the plaintiff-creditor failed to prove the grounds upon which the writ was issued and the existence of the debt, lien, and delinquency, the court could order return of the property and assess damages in favor of the debtor, including attorney's fees. The damages obtained compensated for the period during which the buyer was deprived of the use of the property, but are not restricted to pecuniary loss. They could also include compensation for injury to social standing, reputation, humiliation, and mortification. The debtor, with or without moving to dissolve the sequestration, could also regain possession by filing a bond to protect the plaintiff-creditor against interim damage should the plaintiff-creditor ultimately obtain a judgment against the debtor for the unpaid balance of the purchase price. The statutes also provided that the debtor's bond necessary to repossess the property could not exceed by one-fourth the value of the property as determined by the court, or by one-fourth the amount of the claim, whichever was less. The Court also pointed out that the procedure was simple and largely involved documentary proof.

One year later, in *North Georgia Finishing, Inc. v. Di-Chem, Inc.,* 419 U.S. 601 (1975), the Court again invalidated a garnishment statute because it permitted a writ of garnishment to be issued in pending suits by court clerk without participation by judge based on an affidavit of plaintiff or the plaintiff's attorney containing only conclusory allegations. The statute also prescribed the filing of bond by the defendant as the only method of dissolving garnishment and which made no provision for early hearing.

Sixteen years later, in *Connecticut v. Doehr,* 501 U.S. 1 (1991), the Court invalidated a Connecticut statute that authorized prejudgment attachment of real estate without prior notice or hearing, without a showing of extraordinary circumstances, and without a requirement that the person seeking the attachment post a bond. In doing so, the Court considered (1) the private interest that affected by the prejudgment measure; (2) the risk of erroneous deprivation through the procedures under attack and the probable value of additional or alternative safeguards; and (3) the interest of the party seeking the prejudgment remedy, with, nonetheless, due regard for any ancillary interest the government may have in providing the procedure or forgoing the added burden of providing greater protections. In *Doehr,* the plaintiff had sought a prejudgment attachment of the defendant's home in a civil action for assault and battery. This action did not involve the defendant's real estate; nor did the plaintiff have any pre-existing interest either in defendant's home or any other property. In holding the Connecticut statute invalid, the Court emphasized the lack of a requirement of a showing of exigent circumstances in order to justify an ex part seizure. Four Justices also strongly argued that a bond should be a constitutional requirement, but a majority did not reach that issue.

Two years later, in *United States v. James Daniel Good Real Property,* 510 U.S. 43 (1993), the Court held it unconstitutional under the Fifth Amendment of the U.S. Constitution to seize the defendant's realty in an ex parte proceeding. The action in which the seizure occurred was brought for the ultimate purpose of forfeiting the property because it had been used to facilitate the commission of a federal drug offense. The Court's opinion emphasized that real property was the subject of the seizure. The fact that the real property could not "abscond" impaired the government's interest in prompt seizure of the property. Also, the facts that individual freedom finds tangible expression in property rights and that the security and privacy of the home are often involved when real property is seized enhanced the defendant's interest in a hearing before seizure is allowed. Furthermore, the United States had left the defendant's tenants in possession of the property, thus dispelling any apparent fear that the property would be destroyed. The Court may also have been influenced by the fact that there was a four-year period between the defendant's drug conviction and the commencement of the forfeiture proceeding, which clouded the government's asserted need for a prompt seizure.

In sum, based on the Courts decisions from *Sniadach* through *Good,* the constitutional standard, derived appears to require: (1) exigent circumstances; (2) the provision of facts by the plaintiff (through an affidavit or other sworn testimony by someone with personal knowledge) showing that the grounds for issuing the provisional remedy exist; (3) the examination of the plaintiff's application by a judge, as opposed to some other kind of official (such as the court clerk), for the purpose of determining whether the grounds for issuing the provisional remedy exist; and (4) the provision of a prompt postseizure hearing in which the plaintiff will bear the burden of proving that the grounds for the provisional remedy exist. In addition, it is likely that the judicial officer must scrutinize the plaintiff's complaint or other statement of the plantiff's claim to determine that the substantive law affords the plaintiff at least a possibility of succeeding on the merits if the facts alleged are proved. There would be no justification for depriving the defendant of property for even a short time if the plaintiff has not chance of winning.

While the above elements are indispensable to the constitutionality of a provisional remedy scheme, a provision for a bond and/or the existence of an interest in the property seized on the part of the plaintiff will enhance the case for the validity of a provisional remedy, all other things being equal. Conversely, the fact that real property is the subject of the seizure will make it more difficult to demonstrate exigent circumstances and cause the Court to scrutinize the case carefully for alternative ways to protect the plaintiff's interests.

Notes and Questions

1. Assume that a state enacts a provisional remedies scheme that allows seizure of the defendant's property as security for a judgment and provides that there must be prior notice and an opportunity to be heard in every case before seizure is allowed. In the hearing on the issuance of the provisional remedy, the court is permitted to allow the seizure only on a showing that the plaintiff's complaint states a claim and upon testimony the plaintiff, if believed, would establish the claim at trial. No exigent circumstances are required by the scheme. Assume further that an assault and battery claim like that in *Doehr* has occurred. Could the court constitutionally allow seizure of the defendant's property under the scheme on a record that contained only a complaint that stated a claim and testimony of the plaintiff that would establish the claim at trial, if believed? If so, what real good is prior notice and opportunity to be heard to the defendant? If not, shouldn't the Supreme Court drop the rhetoric about due process necessitating protections such as an "exigency requirement" *only in the absence of prior notice and an opportunity to be heard*?

2. How well does the constitutional test apply to Federal Rule 65 governing the issuance of temporary restraining orders. Do the elements of Rule 65 pass constitutional muster? Are there other elements that should also be required before a temporary restraining order can issue without notice and a prior opportunity to be heard being given to the defendant?

3. (a) The bond requirement in provisional remedies cases is an important protection for the defendant. When a plaintiff obtains a bond, the surety on the bond will be liable for the defendant's losses, but the surety will have a claim against the plaintiff for the amount that the surety must pay. Most courts hold that the plaintiff's liability is limited to the amount of the bond, although a few have held the plaintiff individually liable to the defendant for losses caused by the erroneous issuance of a provisional remedy. *See* 1 DOBBS § 2.11(3), at 197–98. In addition, there are rare cases in which the plaintiff may be liable in tort for malicious abuse of civil process, under a rule such as Rule 11, or, in a case where the plaintiff has gained something of value through the issuance of the provisional remedy, for restitution based on unjust enrichment. *See id.* at 199.

(b) Nevertheless, the bond usually provides the only basis upon which the defendant can recover money amounts based on the erroneous issuance of a provisional remedy. In this regard, you should note that a provisional remedy is usually considered "erroneously" issued for purposes of the bond requirement only if the defendant wins the action on the merits, not if the defendant loses but the court, *e.g.,* followed the wrong standard in granting the provisional remedy. However, a few courts have deviated from this restriction and allowed recovery for reasons not going to the merits, such as lack of jurisdiction in the court issuing the provisional remedy. *See id.* at 202–03. Note also that the damages the defendant can recover are only those caused by the erroneous issuance of the provisional remedy, and these must be proved in the ordinary way damages are proved in any other kind of case. In other words, the defendant does not automatically get the face amount of the bond. *See id.* at 203–04.

(c) Given the description of the bond requirement in the preceding note, should the Supreme Court hold a bond to be constitutionally required in a provisional remedies cases?

4. In determining whether to issue a preliminary injunction, courts generally take into account four factors: (1) the injury that would result to the applicant if the injunction is denied; (2) the likelihood of the applicant's success on the merits; (3) whether the threatened injury to the applicant outweighs the possible injury to the opposing party; and (4) whether the public interest would be harmed by issuing the injunction. In *Gonzales v. Centro Espirita Beneficente Uniao Do Vegetal*, 546 U.S. 418 (2006), which involved the second of these factors, the Supreme Court considered the relative burden of proof that the plaintiff and the defendant must carry on the probability-of-success-on-the-merits element of the test for obtaining a preliminary injunction. In *Gonzales,* the plaintiff sued under the Religious Freedom Restoration Act, 42 U.S.C. § 2000bb-1(a) ("RIFRA"), to invalidate a prohibition on the plaintiffs' use of a hallucinogenic substance in religious ceremonies. RIFRA prohibits the federal government from substantially burdening a person's exercise of religion, even under a rule of general applicability, unless the government can demonstrate a compelling governmental interest and that the burden is the least restrictive means of furthering that interest. The prohibition on the use of the substance was conceded to impose a substantial burden on the plaintiffs' religious freedom.

However, the government, which would have the burden of proof at trial on the other two issues because they were affirmative defenses, contended that the plaintiff, in order to demonstrate the probability of success necessary to obtain a preliminary injunction, had to bear the burden of showing no compelling state interest and that the means employed by the government was not the least restrictive alternative. The Supreme Court rejected this contention, holding that the burden of proof at the preliminary injunction stage mirrors the burden of proof at trial. Thus, the plaintiff bears the burden on elements of the plaintiff's claim, and the defendant bears the burden of proof on affirmative defenses that it would have to establish at trial. Because the evidence on the two affirmative defenses was in equipoise, this meant that the government lost and the plaintiff was entitled to the preliminary injunction. *Gonzales* is an important clarification of preliminary injunction practice that has potentially far-reaching effects in other kinds of cases.

Does the reasoning in *Gonzales* apply to nonequitable provisional remedies in federal court? Does it matter that Federal Rule 64 provides for use of state provisional remedies statutes in cases involving nonequitable provisional remedies?

Section G. Statutory and Rule Requirements for Notice and Service of Process

As explained in section F(1), above, the constitutional standard for notice under the due process clause requires only that the notice be "reasonably calculated, under all the circumstances, to apprise interested parties of the pendency of the action." Although this general "reasonably calculated" constitutional standard may be satisfied in a case, statutes and court rules typically prescribe more specific requirements for notice and service of process, and these separate statutory and rule requirements must also be followed in order to properly serve the defendant.

For example, even though the Court in *Mullane* held that service by ordinary mail upon the known beneficiaries satisfied the due process requirement of notice, if an applicable service of process statute or rule required personal service upon the defendant or service by certified mail, then service by ordinary mail, while constitutionally valid, would be invalid under the applicable statute or rule.

Conversely, even though an applicable statute or rule may authorize service in a particular manner, the manner of service must still satisfy the constitutional requirement of notice. For example, in *Mullane*, even though the applicable New York statute only required that notice of the judicial accounting be given by newspaper publication, the Court held that notice by publication, while statutorily authorized, was constitutionally invalid as to known beneficiaries.

The following material reviews the requirements for notice and service of process under the Federal Rules as well as under state statutes and rules.

1. Methods and Manner of Service

Service of Process. As stated in the introduction of this chapter, before a court may exercise personal jurisdiction over a defendant, the defendant must be served with *process*. Under Federal Rule 4(c)(1), process consists of a copy of the complaint and a summons to appear in the action. Service of process serves the dual functions of notifying the defendant of the action and formally asserting personal jurisdiction over the defendant. The traditional method of serving process on a defendant was for a process server to physically hand the defendant a copy of the plaintiff's complaint and a summons to appear in the action, *i.e., personal service*. However, other ways of serving process also exist in modern practice. For example, it is commonplace today for statutes or rules of court to provide that process may be left at the defendant's home or usual place of abode with

BASIC METHODS OF SERVICE OF PROCESS ON INDIVIDUALS, CORPORATIONS, OR ASSOCIATIONS UNDER THE FEDERAL RULES OF CIVIL PROCEDURE		
Type of Defendant/Service	**Rule**	**Method of Service of Process**
Individuals within a judicial district of the United States	4(e)	**(1) following state law for serving a summons in an action brought in courts** of general jurisdiction in the state where the distict court is located or where service is made; **or** **(2) (A) delivering a copy of the summons and the complaint to the individual personally; or** **(B) leaving a copy of the summons and the complaint at the individual's dwelling or usual place of abode** with someone of suitable age and discretion who resides there; **or** **(C) delivering a copy of the summons and the complaint to an agent** authorized by appointment or by law to receive service of process
Minors and Incompetent Persons within a judicial district of the United States	4(g)	**Must be served by following state law** for serving a summons or like process on such a defendant in an action brought in the courts of general jurisdiction of the state where service is made
A **domestic or foreign corporation or a partnership or other unincorporated association** within a judicial district of the United States	4(h)	**(1) in the manner prescribed by Rule 4(e)(1) (set out above) for serving an individual; or** **(2) by delivering a copy of the summons and the complaint to an officer, a managing or general agent, or any other agent authorized by appointment or by law to receive service of process** and, if the agent is one authorized by statute to receive service and the statute so requires, by also mailing a copy of each to the defendant

Figure 2-1

someone of suitable age and discretion. When a form of process other than in-hand service is authorized, it is called *substituted service*.

Service of process statutes and rules in the states, while containing many common features, vary widely in detail. The common theme of such statutes and rules is to provide methods of service that are calculated to give actual notice of the action to the defendant. This theme is, of course, derived from the due process requirements of notice examined in section F, above. The methods of service for various types of defendants under Federal Rule 4 are summarized in Figure 2-1.

Insufficient Service of Process and Insufficient Process. Because the statutes and rules governing service of process are tailored to achieve actual notice, the courts usually insist on strict adherence to their terms. Thus, even if service achieves actual notice, many courts hold, upon proper objection, that service of process is insufficient and personal jurisdiction has not been properly acquired over the defendant if service is made in a way or on a person not authorized by the statute or rule. *See* FED. R. CIV. P. 12(b)(5). Statutes or rules of court also prescribe how the process must be prepared and what information the summons must contain. *See, e.g.,* FED. R. CIV. P. 4(a); Federal Form 3 ("Summons"). If the process is deficient in form, the defendant has an "insufficient process" objection rather than an "insufficient service of process" objection. *See* FED. R. CIV. P. 12(b)(4). Both objections, however, must be raised in timely fashion by the defendant or the objections are waived. *See* FED. R. CIV. P. 12(b)(4), (5), 12(h)(1).

Ordinarily, if either the process or service is insufficient, the plaintiff can simply serve the defendant again in the proper manner. Sometimes, however, if the process or service is insufficient and the action is dismissed as a result, the consequences may be serious if the statute of limitations expires before proper service can be effectuated. In some court systems, the consequences of insufficient service might not be severe even if the statute of limitations has run between the commencement of the action and the ruling on the defendant's insufficiency objection. For example, the federal courts have the discretion to "quash" service of process when it is insufficient rather than dismiss the action. *See* 5B WRIGHT

& MILLER § 1354. When service is quashed, the plaintiff needs only to serve the defendant properly and the action will continue.

Notes and Questions

1. Federal Rule 4 provides a typical example of service provisions generally. Read Federal Rule 4 carefully and answer the following questions:

(a) Whose responsibility is it to prepare the summons? *JT*

(b) What must be served with the summons? *a copy of the complaint*

(c) May a sixteen-year-old plaintiff serve the defendant with process under Rule 4? *NO. 18*

(d) Assume a nonresident individual defendant could be validly served with process under a long-arm statute of the state in which the district court is located and constitutionally subjected to personal jurisdiction in the courts of the state. The plaintiff has the defendant served by leaving a copy of the summons and complaint with the defendant's spouse at the defendant's home in another state. Does the service confer jurisdiction on the U.S. District Court? If the plaintiff used a method of service provided for in the long-arm statute of the state in which the district court is located, would the U.S. District Court acquire personal jurisdiction over the defendant?

2. Provisions like Rule 4(e)(2) allow service to be made on an individual by "delivering a copy of the summons and of the complaint to the individual personally." What constitutes delivery "personally" within the meaning of this kind of provision? Do you think that something less than placing the process in the defendant's hands will satisfy this requirement?

3. Rule 4(m) provides that if service is not made on a defendant within 120 days after the filing of the complaint, the court "must dismiss the action without prejudice" or direct that service be effected within a specified time — unless the plaintiff shows good cause for the failure to serve.

2. Waiver of Service

In recent times, reform of service of process has focused on methods of notifying the defendant that are less burdensome than the traditional method of in-hand service of process on the defendant. For example, it is common in the states to find statutes or rules authorizing mail service in a variety of circumstances. The 1993 amendments to Rule 4 of the Federal Rules of Civil Procedure established a system for "waiver of service" to avoid the expense and burden of ordinary service of process. Rule 4 provides a good example of typical provisions governing service of process as well as the direction that future reforms may take in the states.

Rule 4(d) is designed to reduce the costs of service of process by encouraging certain classes of defendants to waive the service of the summons. The waiver provisions apply only to defendants who are competent adult individuals or that are corporations, partnerships, or unincorporated associations. The waiver provisions do not apply to defendants who are minors or incompetent persons, or to the United States, its agencies, corporations, officers, or employees, or to foreign, state, or local governments. These defendants must, instead, be served as prescribed in Rule 4(g), (i), and (j).

As to those defendants to whom the waiver process applies, Rule 4(d) permits a plaintiff to notify a defendant in writing by first class mail that the action has been commenced and to request that the defendant waive the service of a summons. Rule 4(d) contains various provisions detailing what must accompany the waiver request and the form in which the waiver must appear. *See* Federal Forms 5 and 6 in the appendix of forms. The defendant must be given a reasonable time within which to return the waiver, which cannot be less than thirty days from the date on which the waiver was sent, or sixty days if the defendant is outside the United States.

If the defendant returns the waiver as requested, the normal twenty-day period within which to answer the complaint does not apply and the defendant's answer is due sixty days, or ninety days if the defendant is outside the United States, from the date on which the request for waiver was sent. Under Rule 4(d)(5), a defendant who waives service of the summons does not thereby waive any objection to personal jurisdiction or venue. The defendant would, however, waive any objection to insufficient process or service of process.

If the defendant does not return the waiver, the plaintiff must have the defendant served in the ordinary way provided for the class of defendant in question under Rule 4. The plaintiff may request that the court impose the full costs of the alternative service on the defendant unless the defendant shows good cause for the failure to return the waiver. These costs include a reasonable attorney's fee for any motion that must be filed to collect the costs.

Problems

Problem 2-10. *P*, a citizen of State *X*, sues *D*, a citizen of State *Y*, for $500,000 in a U.S. District Court in State *X*. *P*'s claim is for personal injuries received in an automobile accident with *D* in State *Z*. *D* has no contacts, ties, or relations with State *X*. After commencement of the action, *P*'s attorney sends a notice and request for waiver of service prescribed by Rule 4(d) to *D*. *D* wants to move to dismiss *P*'s action for lack of personal jurisdiction and improper venue. If *D* returns the form waiving service of process, will *D* also waive the personal jurisdiction and venue objections that *D* possesses to *P*'s action?

Problem 2-11. Assume on the facts of *Problem 2-10* that *D* returns the waiver of service as requested by *P*. Thereafter, *D* does not appear and defend the action. As a result, a default judgment is entered against *D*. When *P* attempts to enforce the default judgment against *D* in State *Y* where *D* lives, may *D* collaterally attack the default judgment on the ground that it is void for lack of personal jurisdiction? If *D*'s only valid objection had been an objection for lack of proper venue in the U.S. District Court in State *X*, could *D* collaterally attack the default judgment for lack of venue when it is brought to State *Y* for enforcement there?

Problem 2-12. On the facts of *Problem 2-10*, assume *D* did not return the waiver of service as requested by *P*. Subsequently, *P* has *D* served with the summons and complaint personally under the law of State *Y* where *D* lives. *D* then appears in the action in the U.S. District Court in State *X* and moves to dismiss for lack of personal jurisdiction, improper venue, and insufficient service of process. Assume the court finds one or more of the objections valid. Nevertheless, *P* moves to have *D* pay the costs of alternative service of process as prescribed by Rule 4(d). Should the court require *D* to pay the costs of service?

Problem 2-13. On the facts of *Problem 2-10*, assume the statute of limitations of State *X* where the action is commenced requires that an action be commenced by personal service of summons on the defendant within the statutory period. At the time *D* receives the notice and request for waiver of service of process under Rule 4, the statute of limitations has not yet run. However, by the time *D* returns the waiver of process and it is filed by *P*, the statute has run. *D*'s answer contains, among other defenses, the affirmative defense of the statute of limitations. Is the defense good?

Section H. Special Issues of Amenability to Process and Personal Jurisdiction in Federal Court

With the exception of the *Burger King* case, all of the Supreme Court personal jurisdiction cases reviewed in this chapter originated in *state court* and presented the issue of whether a *state court* could properly exercise personal jurisdiction over a defendant consistent with the Due Process Clause of the Fourteenth Amendment. This is why *International Shoe* and the subsequent cases defined the "minimum contacts" test in terms of the defendant's contacts with the particular *state* seeking to assert personal jurisdiction. The Fourteenth Amendment, however, prohibits only the *states,* not the federal government, from depriving persons of "life, liberty, or property, without due process of law." When a civil action is filed in federal, rather than state court, it is the federal government, acting through its federal courts, that is affecting a person's rights. The Due Process Clause of the Fifth Amendment, however, applies to the federal government and provides, similarly to the Fourteenth Amendment, that no person shall be "deprived of life, liberty, or property, without due process of law."

But questions exist over the proper constitutional standard that should apply in determining the validity of federal court personal jurisdiction. Just as the states have the right, consistent with Fourteenth Amendment due process, to enact long-arm statutes and rules to authorize state courts to exercise of personal jurisdiction over nonresident defendants, so too does the federal government have the right, consistent with Fifth Amendment due process, to enact long-arm statutes and rules to authorize the federal courts to exercise personal jurisdiction over defendants. But this raises two questions. First, what is the proper standard under Fifth Amendment due process when a federal court asserts personal jurisdiction under a federal long-arm statute or rule? Second, how does a federal court assert personal jurisdiction, and what constitutional standard applies, when there is no federal long-arm statute or rule?

Part of the reason for the continued uncertainty over the proper standard of Fifth Amendment due process is that Congress has rarely exercised its power to enact nationwide long-arm statutes or rules for the federal courts. Instead, Congress has generally directed the federal courts, as reflected in Rule 4(k)(1)(A), to use *state* long-arm statutes in acquiring personal jurisdiction over defendants. As a consequence, in the absence of an applicable federal long-arm statute or rule authorizing greater personal jurisdiction, the federal courts are limited to using the long-arm statutes of the state in which they are located and thus have no greater personal jurisdiction authority than "a court of general jurisdiction in the state where the district court is located." Fed. R. Civ. P. 4(k)(1)(A).

This is why in the *Burger King* case, reprinted in section C(1), above, the Supreme Court analyzed the propriety of exercising personal jurisdiction over the Michigan defendants under the Florida state long-arm statute and under Fourteenth Amendment due process, even though the action was filed in federal district court in Florida. In the absence of a federal long-arm statute or rule, the federal district court could exercise personal jurisdiction over the Michigan defendants only if a Florida *state* court could do so consistent with Fourteenth Amendment due process and the applicable state long-arm statute. In the vast majority of cases, therefore, the personal jurisdiction analysis will be identical whether the action is filed in state or federal court.

Federal Long-Arm Statutes. In those instances in which Congress has enacted a federal long-arm statute or rule, however, as illustrated in the *Republic of Panama* case discussed below, it is clear that the issue is governed by the Fifth Amendment Due Process Clause. The lower federal courts are divided on the proper scope of this constitutional standard.

The traditional view is that Congress has the absolute power to extend long-arm jurisdiction to all persons throughout the United States. However, this view originated when *Pennoyer v. Neff's* understanding of the Due Process Clause of the Fourteenth Amendment prevailed. Under *Pennoyer*, the Due Process Clause of the Fourteenth Amendment limited the power of the states to assert personal jurisdiction only when the states reached outside their borders to summon nonresidents to defend suits in their courts. It followed from this territorial view that the Due Process Clause of the Fifth Amendment only limited the power of the federal government when Congress authorized the federal courts to reach outside the borders of the United States to summon nonresidents to defend suits within the country. Thus, in theory, a resident of a state could be summoned to defend a suit in a federal court anywhere within the United States consistent with Fifth Amendment due process irrespective of the burdens placed on the defendant in defending the suit in the chosen locale.

Should this strict territorial view of Congress's power still control today? If, as *International Shoe* and its progeny indicate, Fourteenth Amendment due process requires consideration of the litigational burdens placed on a defendant by the location of suit, there seems to be no good reason why such burdens should be irrelevant under the Fifth Amendment. However, the *Burnham* case, examined in section D, above, suggests that the historical pedigree of the traditional view of the Fifth Amendment limits on federal long-arm jurisdiction may sustain the old territorial limits on Congress's power. *But cf.* the *Insurance Corp. of Ireland* decision, discussed in section B(3), above, stating that the purpose of the Due Process Clause of the Fourteenth Amendment is to protect the individual liberty interests of defendants rather than the sovereign interests of the states.

Defendants Residing Outside the United States. The discussion in the preceding paragraph focused on defendants residing in the United States. However, if the defendant in question resides outside the United States—for example, a citizen or subject of a foreign state—and is not subject to service of process within the United States, it would seem that even under the traditional territorial view of Congress's power, there must be some due process restrictions on the ability to confer long-arm jurisdiction on federal courts. In this situation, the question becomes what the test should be to determine whether the Due Process Clause of the Fifth Amendment is violated. For example, should a "minimum contacts" test of some sort be used? If so, should the test be whether the defendant has minimum contacts with a particular state or with the United States as a whole? Should the concepts of specific and general jurisdiction be imported into the Due Process Clause of the Fifth Amendment?

Fifth Amendment Due Process Limits on Personal Jurisdiction. The U.S. Supreme Court has not yet addressed the Fifth Amendment Due Process Clause limits on the exercise of personal jurisdiction by the federal courts. As a result, the law has developed largely in the lower federal courts as the Republic of Panama case illustrates. In *Republic of Panama v. BCCI Holdings (Luxembourg) S.A.*, 119 F.3d 935 (11th Cir. 1997), an action was brought in the U.S. District Court for the Southern District of Florida, asserting federal law claims under the "Racketeer Influenced and Corrupt Organizations Act" (RICO), 18 U.S.C. § 1961 et seq., and supplemental state claims against American and foreign defendants. The district court dismissed the claims against the two American defendants for lack of personal jurisdiction. On appeal, the Eleventh Circuit Court of Appeals reversed the personal jurisdiction ruling.

Section 1965(d) of the RICO statute provides for nationwide service of process in any judicial district in which a defendant is found, thus making it a federal long-arm statute. Accordingly, the court held that the validity of the exercise of personal jurisdiction under the RICO statute was governed by the Fifth Amendment Due Process Clause, and not the Fourteenth Amendment Due Process Clause. The court held that Fifth Amendment due process inquiry must examine the defendant's "aggregate contacts with the nation as a whole rather than his contacts with the forum state." Because the two American defendants clearly had minimum contacts with the United States as a whole, this part of the court's analysis was straightforward.

The difficulty came in deciding whether the reasonableness factors developed under the Fourteenth Amendment Due Process Clause should apply under the Fifth Amendment Due Process Clause analysis after a finding of "national" minimum contacts. The court concluded that there was no reason to discard a reasonableness inquiry when jurisdiction is being asserted under a federal long-arm statute rather than a state long-arm statute. Although this approach required consideration of the same reasonableness factors as under the Fourteenth Amendment analysis, the court observed that the Fifth and Fourteenth Amendment concerns were not "precisely parallel." In particular, the court stated that a defendant's contacts with the forum state play no "magical role" in the Fifth Amendment analysis, because there is "nothing inherently burdensome about crossing state lines." Thus, it is the defendant's aggregate contacts with the United States as a whole that count, rather than its contacts with the forum state.

The court held that after minimum contacts with the United States have been established, a reasonableness inquiry should be performed to determine whether the assertion of jurisdiction is nevertheless unfair. The defendant must demonstrate that an assertion of jurisdiction over it in the particular place within the United States where the action was brought will make litigation so gravely difficult that it unfairly disadvantages the defendant in comparison to its opponent. In this regard, the court stated as follows:

> In order to evaluate whether the Fifth Amendment requirements of fairness and reasonableness have been satisfied, courts should balance the burdens imposed on the individual defendant against the federal interest involved in the litigation.... As in other due process inquiries, the balancing seeks to determine if the infringement on individual liberty has been justified sufficiently by reference to important governmental interests.

> We note, however, that courts must engage in this balancing only if a defendant has established that his liberty interests actually have been infringed.... Only when a defendant challenging jurisdiction has "present[ed] a compelling case that ... would render jurisdiction unreasonable," ... should courts weigh the federal interests favoring the exercise of jurisdiction.

> In determining whether the defendant has met his burden of establishing constitutionally significant inconvenience, courts should consider the factors used in determining fairness under the Fourteenth Amendment. Courts should not, however, apply these factors mechanically in cases involving federal statutes....

119 F.3d at 946.

Importantly, when the court undertook to apply this standard to the facts of the case, it observed that the defendants had widespread business all across the eastern seaboard, and that because discovery would be conducted throughout the world, Florida would not be significantly more inconvenient as a forum than any other district in the country. Citing *Burger King,* however, the court also observed that inconvenience can ordinarily be accommodated through a change of venue.

Because the defendants had failed to demonstrate the requisite burdens, the court found it unnecessary to balance the federal interest in maintaining the suit in Florida against the defendants' interests.

Notes and Questions

1. In *Republic of Panama,* the court did not discuss the implications of the *Burnham* case for Fifth Amendment due process analysis. Should it have?

2. The *Republic of Panama* case dealt with the federal long-arm statute contained in the Racketeer Influenced and Corrupt Organizations Act ("RICO"), 18 U. S.C. § 1965(d). As noted in the introductory text, Congress has not chosen to enact a general long-arm statute applicable in all federal court actions and has only done so in connection with specific federal statutes. In addition to RICO, some other federal long-arm provisions include nationwide service of process in statutory interpleader actions, *see* 28 U.S.C. § 2361; antitrust actions, *see* 15 U.S.C. § 22; bankruptcy actions, *see* Bankr. R. 7004(d); and ERISA (Employee Retirement Income Security Act) actions, *see* 29 U.S.C. § 1132(e)(2). Federal Rule 4(k)(1)(B) and (k)(2), discussed in the following notes, are other examples of federal long-arm provisions.

3. Rule 4(k)(2) is a federal long-arm rule that extends the long-arm jurisdiction of the federal courts to a small category of cases in which jurisdiction is not authorized by any federal or state statute. As previously noted, the constitutionality of an assertion of jurisdiction under Rule 4(k)(2) is tested under the Fifth Amendment.

4. For Rule 4(k)(2) to apply, (i) the plaintiff's claim must be based on federal law; (ii) jurisdiction cannot be asserted over the defendant in any state court of general jurisdiction; and (iii) the exercise of jurisdiction by the federal court must be consistent with Fifth Amendment due process. In effect, the second requirement means that if jurisdiction is possible in a state under Rule 4(k)(1)(A), Rule 4(k)(2) cannot be used by the plaintiff. Who has the burden of showing whether the defendant is subject to jurisdiction in a state court of general jurisdiction? The leading case is *United States v. Swiss American Bank, Ltd.,* 191 F.3d 30 (1st Cir. 1999), in which the First Circuit Court of Appeals held that a plaintiff seeking to invoke Rule 4(k)(2) must show that (i) the claim asserted arises under federal law; (ii) personal jurisdiction is not available under any applicable federal long-arm statute; and (iii) the defendant's contacts with the United States as a whole suffice to satisfy constitutional requirements. In addition, the plaintiff must "certify" that, based on the information readily available to the plaintiff, the defendant is not subject to suit in the courts of general jurisdiction of any state. Once this showing has been made, the burden shifts to the defendant to produce evidence that one or more specific states exist in which it can be sued or that its contacts with the United States make an assertion of jurisdiction over it constitutionally insufficient. If the defendant produces evidence that it is subject to personal jurisdiction in one or more states and the plaintiff chooses to contest that matter further, the defendant will be deemed to have waived any claim that it is subject to personal jurisdiction in states other than the ones it has identified.

5. Rule 4(k)(1)(B) contains the so-called "100-mile bulge" provision authorizing jurisdiction over a defendant who is joined under Rule 14 or 19 and is served within 100 miles of the federal district court where the action is pending. Rule 4(k)(1)(B) thus provides an additional form of long-arm jurisdiction for the federal courts, but only as to de-

fendants joined under Rule 14 or 19. Party joinder under Rules 14 and 19 is limited and Rule 4(k)(1)(B) does not apply to defendants joined under Rule 20, which is the rule under which the vast majority of defendants are joined to the action by the plaintiff. Party joinder is examined in depth in Chapter 7

Problems

Problem 2-14. S, a citizen of State X, is in possession of property claimed by C-1, a citizen of State Y, and C-2, a citizen of State Z. S commences an action of interpleader under 28 U.S.C. § 1335 against C-1 and C-2 in State Y. (Review the procedure of interpleader examined in Chapter 1.) C-2 is served in this action in the district in State Z where C-2 resides pursuant to 28 U.S.C. § 2361, a nationwide federal long-arm statute applicable to interpleader actions under § 1335. (Note that venue is proper in this action under 28 U.S.C. § 1397.) C-2 has no contacts whatever with State Y. If C-2 moves to dismiss the action on the ground that it violates the Due Process Clause of the Fifth Amendment, what should the result be and why?

Problem 2-15. P, a citizen of State X, sues D, a citizen of State Y, in a U.S. District Court in the Western District of State Y, where D resides. P seeks to recover $1,000,000 for personal injuries received in an automobile accident in State Z. The automobile accident was a three-car collision between cars driven by P, D, and T. T is a citizen of State Q who resides in the Eastern District of State Q. State Q is adjacent to State Y. T's residence in the Eastern District of Q is thirty miles from the city in State Y where P commenced the action against D. D impleads T in the action by P under Federal Rule 14. D asserts that if D is liable to P, T is liable to D for one half of any damages D must pay to P. T is served under Rule 4(k)(1)(B). T has never been to State Y and has no contacts, ties, or relations whatsoever with the state. If T moves to dismiss the impleader claim on the ground that it violates the Due Process Clause of the Fifth Amendment, what should the result be and why?

Chapter 3

Venue and Related Matters

As explained in Chapter 1(F)(2), the plaintiff's selection of a forum is limited in at least three ways. First, the court must have proper *subject-matter jurisdiction* over the action. Second, the court must be one in which *personal jurisdiction* over the defendant exists. Third, the court must be one of proper *venue*. All of these requirements must be met in order to sue in a particular court. Venue, however, must be carefully distinguished from jurisdiction. Jurisdiction refers to the *power* of a court to hear and decide a particular case. A judgment entered without proper subject-matter or personal jurisdiction is void. Venue, on the other hand, is of lesser significance and refers only to the *geographic location within a particular court system* where the case may be brought, assuming proper jurisdiction exists in that court system.

Venue rules are designed to ensure that an action is brought in an appropriate location within a court system having some connection to the parties or the claim. Venue rules are based on considerations of party and witness convenience and judicial efficiency. In this respect, venue restrictions overlap with personal jurisdiction restrictions, but serve an additional function. As you learned in Chapter 2, personal jurisdiction under the Fourteenth Amendment is defined in terms of the power of a particular *state* to exercise jurisdiction over a defendant. The constitutional requirements of personal jurisdiction do not define where *within* that state the action should be brought. Thus, if a defendant is found to have "minimum contacts" with the state of Texas, it would be constitutionally permissible for *any court* within the state of Texas to exercise personal jurisdiction over the defendant. But where *within the Texas court system* should the case be heard? This is what venue rules determine.

Like personal jurisdiction (but unlike subject-matter jurisdiction), the parties can normally waive venue restrictions. However, unlike personal jurisdiction, venue is not constitutionally required, and neither the venue restrictions of the forum state nor the U.S. Constitution will ordinarily render a judgment void and subject to *collateral attack* for improper venue. For example, in an action involving a nonresident defendant, assume that venue is improper in the court within the forum state in which the action is brought. Ordinarily, the defendant cannot fail to appear and then collaterally attack a default judgment in a proceeding in another state on the ground of improper venue, as the defendant could do in the case of lack of personal jurisdiction.

This chapter examines venue in the federal courts under the general federal venue statute, 28 U.S.C. §1391. In addition, it examines related matters, including the traditional venue distinction between "transitory" and "local" actions; the transfer of venue within and between judicial systems; the doctrine of forum non conveniens; the enforceability of forum-selection clauses; the ability to obtain an injunction in one forum to prevent litigation in another; and the use of a stay of proceedings in one court in deference to out-of-state litigation.

Venue in State Court Actions. All state court systems have venue requirements, usually established by statute or rule, that define where an action may be brought within the state court system. Typically, these provisions provide that an action shall be brought in the county, or other geographic location, where the cause of action arose or one of the parties to the action resides or does business. As noted in section A, below, actions involving real property generally must be brought in the location where the property is situated. Similar to the federal transfer of venue provisions discussed in section C, below, state venue rules often provide that actions brought in a proper venue may be transferred to a more convenient location within the state and that actions brought in an improper venue may be transferred to a proper venue.

Section A. Transitory and Local Actions

As discussed in Chapter 1(F)(2)(c), the courts have traditionally distinguished between "transitory" and "local" actions. A transitory action is one that can be adjudicated anywhere. However, local actions always involve land and can be adjudicated only where the land is located. Administration of the "local action" rule is complicated because not all actions involving land are classified as local actions. Also, the "local action" rule, when it is applicable, overrides general venue provisions, such as provisions allowing suit in the district where the defendant resides—even though the venue statutes in a jurisdiction often do not indicate that local actions are an exception to their provisions and even when the statutes make no mention of the "local action" rule at all.

The "local action" rule has been under attack by commentators in the United States for many years. *See, e.g.*, ROBERT L. FELIX & RALPH U. WHITTEN, AMERICAN CONFLICTS LAW § 31 (6th ed. 2011); RUSSELL J. WEINTRAUB, COMMENTARY ON THE CONFLICT OF LAWS § 4.39, at 331 (6th ed. 2010). In response, the "Federal Courts Jurisdiction and Venue Clarification Act of 2011" eliminated the local action rule in federal court actions, and 28 U.S.C. § 1391(a)(2) now provides that "[e]xcept as otherwise provided by Law ... (2) the proper venue for a civil action shall be determined without regard to whether the action is local or transitory in nature." However, the "local action" rule remains of significance in state court actions.

The "local action" rule was a byproduct of the evolution of jury trial in English practice. Originally, English juries based their decisions on their own knowledge of the case gained as neighbors of the litigants or by searching out evidence before trial. *See* W.H. Wicker, *The Development of the Distinction Between Local and Transitory Actions*, 4 TENN. L. REV. 55 (1926). This practice made it important to be able to obtain jurors from the locality in which the facts occurred. Later, the jury's function evolved into one of determining the truth of facts based on testimony produced at trial. After this development, it was unnecessary to draw a jury from the locality in which the facts occurred, and the courts generally relaxed the venue rules in most actions. However, there was no relaxation of the rules in actions involving real property. Thus, the "local action" rule continued in actions for the recovery of land, to establish or enforce a right arising out of land, and for damages for trespass to land.

The "local action" rule did not apply in equity because equity courts did not use juries. Therefore, as long as the defendant was before the court and an equity court had power to enforce any decree it might render, the fact that land was involved would not restrict the venue of the action. This difference accounts for the fact that certain kinds of equitable actions involving land, such as an action for specific performance of a contract to convey land, are not subject to the "local action" rule. *See, e.g., Bergeron v. Boyle*, 838 A.2d 918,

924 (Vt. 2003) (action for declaratory relief and specific performance of contract for sale of a farm property was not a local action with state's statutory local action rule).

In spite of the attacks on the "local action" rule, the rule has shown great resilience. Only a few states, either by statute or by judicial decision, have abolished the rule in the category of cases in which it is most questionable—actions for damages to land located in another state. *See, e.g., Reasor-Hill Corp. v. Harrison,* 249 S.W.2d 994, 996 (Ark. 1952) (asserting that the "local action" rule has "no basis in logic or equity and rests solely on English cases that were decided before America was discovered and in circumstances not even comparable to those existing in our Union" and abandoning the "local action" rule in an action for injuries to real property situated in another state); *Candlewood Timber Group, LLC v. Pan Am. Energy,* LLC, 859 A.2d 989, 1004–05 (Del. 2004) (action for damages to land in foreign country is transitory). In other kinds of actions "directly" involving foreign land and in actions involving land located within the state, but outside the county in which the action is brought, the rule has been generally retained. However, modern venue schemes preserving the local action concept vary widely in the kinds of cases that are considered local.

Notes and Questions

1. Some courts treat the "local action" rule itself as a subject-matter jurisdiction objection and, therefore, as nonwaivable. *See* TEPLY & WHITTEN at 376–77. Assuming that the "local action" rule itself is otherwise sound, is this "jurisdictional" approach also justifiable?

2. What is the difference between (a) the "local action" rule and (b) a venue statute in an action not involving land limiting the venue of the action to one court? Assuming that local actions are, like other venue objections, waivable, there may be no difference. In that circumstance, even if a "local action" were brought in an improper place, venue would be proper if the defendant did not object. However, if the rule is treated as a rule of subject-matter jurisdiction, it might differ from a transitory single venue rule in that the latter could be waivable while a local action objection would not be.

3. Chapter 2, above, discussed a possible constitutional restriction on the power of state courts over actions directly affecting *title* to land located outside the state. At least some such cases will also be local actions. There is doubt whether this restriction, assuming that it still exists today, is a remnant of the old international, territorial rules of jurisdiction enforced prior to the Fourteenth Amendment, or is imposed by the Due Process Clause of that Amendment. There is no question that the rule, even after the Fourteenth Amendment was ratified, was treated as a *subject-matter jurisdiction* limitation. Assuming that the restriction still exists, would it still be justifiable to treat it as a subject-matter jurisdiction rule today?

4. For what it is worth, even in the cases in which situs states have been allowed to refuse effect to foreign judgments "directly affecting" the title to land, the courts have recognized that a foreign judgment ordering the conveyance of land (for example, in a divorce proceeding) can have a conclusive effect between the parties to an action and be enforced in other states. *See, e.g., Tobjy v. Tobjy,* 581 N.Y.S.2d 403 (App. Div. 1992) (Oklahoma divorce decree awarding party New York land entitled to enforcement in New York; defendant's resistance to the New York enforcement action no more than an attempt to relitigate the merits of the Oklahoma divorce action); *McElreath v. McElreath,* 345 S.W.2d 722, 724–25, 732 (Tex. 1961) (Oklahoma divorce decree ordering Oklahoma husband to convey Texas land to Oklahoma wife was valid and enforceable in Texas as a

matter of comity); *Weesner v. Weesner*, 95 N.W.2d 682 (Neb. 1959) (Wyoming divorce decree between Wyoming parties ordered husband to execute a deed to wife of Nebraska land; decree was a valid in personam order binding the husband and enforceable in Nebraska). Under these authorities, the only kind of decree that will not be enforced in the situs state is one that somehow directly transfers the title, or adjudicates directly that the title is in one party rather than another—*i.e.*, a decree that has an "in rem" effect. Any other order will be considered "in personam" and have a preclusive effect between the parties in another state.

Problems

Problem 3-1. P, a citizen of State X, enters into a contract with D, a citizen of State Y. The contract provides for P's purchase of D's land located in State Y. D subsequently refuses to convey the land to P. P sues D in a state court of State X. P seeks a decree of specific performance that would require D to convey the land. D is personally served with process in State X while D is there on business. Assume that such service validly subjects D to the personal jurisdiction of the State X court in P's action. D defends the State X proceeding on the ground that P's action is a local action that must be brought in State Y, where the land is located. Assuming that State X follows the traditional "local action" rule, is D's "local action" objection valid?

Problem 3-2. On the facts of *Problem 3-1*, assume that the State X court issues a decree of specific performance against D, but that D refuses to convey the land. Assume further that a statute of State X gives the State X courts the option of either (1) imprisoning parties who disobey specific performance decrees until they comply with the decrees or (2) entering an order that would directly vest the title to the land in P. Is there any reason to conclude that the statutory options are *not* both available to the court under these circumstances?

Section B. Venue in the Federal Courts

1. The General Venue Statute: 28 U.S.C. § 1391

Although there are various *special* venue statutes which govern venue in particular types of federal court actions, *see, e.g.*, 28 U.S.C. § 1397 defining venue in interpleader actions, most actions are governed by the *general* venue statute, 28 U.S.C. § 1391. As § 1391(a)(1) expressly provides, "[e]xcept as otherwise provided by law—(1) this section shall govern the venue of all civil actions brought in district courts of the United States."

The general venue statute has a long history tracing its origins to the first Judiciary Act of 1789. Not surprisingly, this statute has been amended several times over the years, most recently in 2011 as part of the "Federal Courts Jurisdiction and Venue Clarification Act of 2011." In researching any venue issue, therefore, it is important to remember that the current provisions of § 1391 may be different from the provisions being applied by a court in an earlier case. It is also important to note that federal venue statutes are framed in terms of which federal *judicial district* an action may be brought in, and not which state. Some states (*e.g.*, Maine, Nebraska, and New Jersey) are single district states and thus the venue decision under § 1391 would be the same statewide. Other more populous states (*e.g.*, California, Florida, and New York) are divided into multiple districts, and in such cases, venue may be proper under § 1391 in one judicial district within the state, but not in another.

General Venue Provisions. Newly amended § 1391(b) sets forth the general venue provisions and provides:

A civil action may be brought in—

(1) a judicial district in which any defendant resides, if all defendants are residents of the State in which the district is located;

(2) a judicial district in which a substantial part of the events or omissions giving rise to the claim occurred, or a substantial part of property that is the subject of the action is situated; or

(3) if there is no district in which an action may otherwise be brought as provided in this section, any judicial district in which any defendant is subject to the court's personal jurisdiction with respect to such action.

The above provisions of § 1391(b) were enacted as part of the "Federal Courts Jurisdiction and Venue Clarification Act of 2011." Although new § 1391(b) merges the former separate venue subsections of § 1391, new § 1391(b) carries forward the main provisions for venue under the prior law—(1) where the defendant(s) reside ("*residency*" based venue), or (2) where a substantial part of the events occurred ("*events*" based venue) or where a substantial part of the property is situated ("*property*" based venue, or (3) pursuant to the "*fallback*" provision. Significantly, the 2011 Act eliminates the former separate venue subsections of § 1391, one which governed venue in diversity of citizenship actions and one which governed venue in non-diversity actions. Section 1391 now establishes, in the absence of an applicable *special* venue provision, a single, unitary *general* venue standard applicable to all civil actions whether founded on diversity of citizenship, federal question, or any other jurisdictional basis.

Section 1391(b)(3) carries forward the "fallback" provision of former § 1391(a)(3), but eliminates this former subsection's qualifying phrase that personal jurisdiction exist "at the time the action is commenced." Section 1391(b)(3) now simply provides that the defendant be "subject to the court's personal jurisdiction with respect to such action." No explanation is given in the legislative history of the Act for this language change, but it would arguably now allow for "fallback" venue under § 1391(b)(3) when a defendant later waives or consents to personal jurisdiction in a situation where personal jurisdiction did not otherwise exist at the time the action was commenced.

Residence for Venue Purposes. The 2011 Act also creates an entirely new § 1391(c) which now expressly defines residence for "all venue purposes" for natural persons and entities, whether incorporated or not. The provisions of § 1391(c) clarify certain issues and make several changes from the former law.

Section 1391(c)(1) provides that "a natural person, including an alien lawfully admitted for permanent residence in the United States, shall be deemed to reside in the judicial district in which that person is domiciled." This provision now clarifies that the "residence" of a natural person for all venue purposes is the place where the person is legally "domiciled." As you will learn in Chapter 4, a person's legal domicile is the place where a person physically resides and considers his or her permanent home. A person may have several residences, but a person may have only one legal domicile. Section 1391(c)(1) resolves a former split among the lower federal courts as to the proper definition of "residence" for a natural person under the venue statutes.

In addition, under § 1391(c)(1), in combination with § 1391(c)(3), permanent resident alien defendants lawfully domiciled in the United States may now assert a defense to the propriety of venue under § 1391. Former § 1391(d), which is repealed by the 2011 Act, provided that "[a]n alien may be sued in any district." This provision effectively denied an alien defendant the right to raise an objection to the propriety of venue under § 1391. In contrast, § 1391(c)(3) shifts the focus from a defendant's status as an alien to a defendant's status as a nonresident of the United States. Section 1391(c)(3) now provides that "a defendant not resident in the United States may be sued in any judicial district." Thus, if a defendant lawfully resides in the United States, even though an alien, that defendant is no longer one who "may be sued in any judicial district." As stated in the legislative history, this provision would not apply to aliens who are not lawfully in the United States because "an alien can obtain a 'lawful domicile' in the United States only if he or she has the ability under the immigration laws to form the intent to remain in the country indefinitely." H.R. REP. No. 112-10, 112th Cong., 1st Sess., at 23, n.16 (2011).

With respect to defendants who are nonresidents of the United States, § 1391(c)(3) further provides that "the joinder of such a defendant shall be disregarded in determining where the action may be brought with respect to other defendants." This provision would be significant in determining venue in a multiple-defendant case under § 1391(b)(1). Do you see why?

Finally, it is important to note that § 1391(c)(3)'s provision that a nonresident of the United States may be sued in any judicial district is *only* for purposes of determining venue under § 1391. Section § 1391(c)(3) does not prevent a nonresident defendant from asserting lack of personal jurisdiction, seeking a transfer of venue under § 1404(a), or seeking dismissal of the action under the doctrine of *forum non conveniens*. Transfers under § 1404(a) and dismissals for *forum non conveniens* are discussed in sections C and D, below.

Residence of Entities. With respect to entities, the provisions of former § 1391(c) expressly defined the "residence" of a corporation for venue purposes as "any judicial district in which it is subject to personal jurisdiction at the time the action is commenced." The former statute, however, never specified the appropriate "residence" for unincorporated associations, such as partnerships, limited liability companies, nonprofit organizations, or labor unions. However, in *Denver & Rio Grande Western Railroad Co. v. Brotherhood of Railroad Trainmen*, 387 U.S. 556 (1967), the Supreme Court held that unincorporated associations should be treated the same as corporate defendants in determining residence under the then-existing venue statutes. New § 1391(c)(2) now defines the venue standard for determining the "residence" of all entities, whether or not incorporated. The standard is different, however, if the entity is a plaintiff or a defendant. Section 1391(c)(2) now provides:

> an entity with the capacity to sue and be sued in its common name under applicable law, whether or not incorporated, shall be deemed to reside, if a defendant, in any judicial district in which such defendant is subject to the court's personal jurisdiction with respect to the civil action in question and, if a plaintiff, only in the judicial district in which it maintains its principal place of business.

Although the general venue provisions of § 1391(b) do not provide for venue based on the residency of a plaintiff, some special venue statutes so provide and thus § 1391(c)(2) includes a definition of residency for a plaintiff-entity.

For a defendant-entity, the standard of residence under § 1391(c)(2) equates with personal jurisdiction, and means that a defendant-entity, subject to the special limit of

§ 1391(d), is a "resident" for venue purposes of *every* judicial district in *every* state where the defendant-entity is subject to personal jurisdiction. In contrast, under § 1391(c)(1), a natural person can have only *one* residence for venue purposes, *i.e.,* where the person is legally domiciled, and simply because a natural person may be subject to personal jurisdiction in another jurisdiction does not make that person a resident of that jurisdiction under § 1391(c).

Corporate Residency in Multidistrict States. With respect to corporate defendants, the 2011 Act relocated, in identical language, the second sentence of the former § 1391(c) to new § 1391(d) entitled "Residency of Corporations." This provision narrows the residency of corporate defendants in multidistrict states. Section § 1391(d) provides:

> For purposes of venue under this chapter, in a State which has more than one judicial district and in which a defendant that is a corporation is subject to personal jurisdiction at the time an action is commenced, such corporation shall be deemed to reside in any district in that State within which its contacts would be sufficient to subject it to personal jurisdiction if that district were a separate State, and, if there is no such district, the corporation shall be deemed to reside in the district within which it has the most significant contacts.

Under § 1391(d), a corporate defendant sued in a multidistrict state will only be deemed a "resident" for venue purposes of those individual districts in which it would be subject to personal jurisdiction if that district, hypothetically, were a separate state. For example, assume that a California corporation ships its products only into Philadelphia, Pennsylvania for use and sale only in Philadelphia. Assume that one of its products causes injury in Philadelphia. In terms of personal jurisdiction, assuming a Pennsylvania long-arm statute properly applied, there would be statewide personal jurisdiction over the California corporation in all Pennsylvania state courts, and also, pursuant to Rule 4(k)(1)(A), in all Pennsylvania federal district courts.

However, even though the California defendant would be subject to statewide personal jurisdiction throughout Pennsylvania, because the federal district courts in Pennsylvania are divided into the Eastern, Middle and Western Districts, the California defendant, pursuant to § 1391(d), would only be deemed a "resident" for venue purposes of the Eastern District of Pennsylvania, where Philadelphia is located, and would not be deemed a "resident" of the Middle and Western Districts of Pennsylvania. Do you see why?

Note that the multidistrict residency limitation of § 1391(d) only applies to corporate defendants and not to non-corporate defendants [entity]. In the example above, if the California defendant were an unincorporated association, § 1391(d) would not apply, and only § 1391(c)(2) would apply. Under § 1391(c)(2), the California defendant would now be deemed a "resident" for venue purposes in all three Pennsylvania federal districts. Do you see why?

The legislative history of the Act does not explain why this limiting provision § 1391(d) only applies to corporate defendants and not to all defendant-entities as in § 1391(c)(2). The legislative silence on this disparate treatment in § 1391(d) is surprising given that the legislative history of § 1391(c)(2) expressly states that its purpose was to "restore the parity of treatment contemplated in *Denver & Rio Grande*" in treating unincorporated associations the same as corporations for venue purposes. H.R. Rep. No. 112-10, 112th Cong., 1st Sess., at 21 (2011). The legislative history also does not explain why § 1391(d) retains the qualifying phrase "subject to personal jurisdiction *at the time an action is commenced*," whereas the corresponding language of new § 1391(c)(2) simply states that the defendant-entity be "subject to the court's personal jurisdiction with respect to the civil action in question." It is unclear, therefore, whether § 1391(c)(2) is intended to cover more situations than § 1391(d) and to apply when a defendant later waives or consents to personal jurisdiction, even though personal jurisdiction did not otherwise exist at the time the action was commenced.

Venue in Removed Actions. Venue in actions removed to federal court is not determined by the general venue statutes. Instead, 28 U.S.C. § 1441(a) provides that civil actions may be removed "to the district court of the United States for the district and division embracing the place where [the state] action is pending." This language makes venue proper in the district court to which the action is removed, even if venue would not have been proper in that district court had the action been commenced there originally.

The 2011 Act clarifies and reaffirms in newly created § 1390 that "[t]his chapter shall not determine the district court to which a civil action pending in a State court may be removed." Section 1390 provides, however, that once an action is removed to federal district court, the transfer of venue to another district or division is governed by the venue statutes. Transfer of venue from one federal district court to another under the venue statutes is discussed section C, below.

When Venue Is Determined. In general, venue is determined at the outset of the original action and subsequent additions of parties by means of certain procedural rules, such as intervention by a party under Rule 24 or joinder of a third-party defendant under Rule 14, do not make original venue improper. For example, venue of third-party proceedings under Rule 14 follow that of the original proceeding and, thus, third-party defendants may be brought in without regard to venue.

However, when a *plaintiff* seeks to join an additional defendant to the complaint under Rule 20, or is directed to do so by the court under Rule 19, venue in the action may be affected. When venue is based on the provisions of § 1391(b)(1) (all defendants residing in the same state), and the defendant proposed to be joined would not meet this venue provision, then the joinder of this additional defendant would not be permitted, unless some other venue provision applied or the additional defendant waived the objection to improper venue. The above rules of party joinder were reviewed in Chapter 1 and are examined in depth in Chapter 7.

Multiple Venue Choices. In many cases, several judicial districts may properly qualify for venue under the applicable venue provisions. In such situations, the choice rests with the *plaintiff* to select among the various proper venues in filing the action. As noted below, the defendant may object when the plaintiff selects an improper venue, but when the plaintiff selects a *proper* venue, the defendant's only recourse is to demonstrate that trial in the plaintiff's chosen venue is inconvenient and, "in the interest of justice," should be transferred under 28 U.S.C. § 1404(a) to another judicial district with proper venue. Transfers of venue are examined in section C, below.

Challenging Improper Venue and Venue Waiver. When the plaintiff selects an improper venue, the defendant has the right to object. Similar to objections for lack of personal jurisdiction, however, objections for improper venue must be timely made or they are waived. The defense of improper venue must be raised by a preanswer motion to dismiss under Federal Rule 12(b)(3) or asserted in the defendant's answer. Otherwise, the objection is waived under Rule 12(h)(1), in the same manner as lack of personal jurisdiction. Furthermore, 28 U.S.C. § 1406(b) expressly provides that "[n]othing in this chapter shall impair the jurisdiction of a district court of any matter involving a party who does not interpose timely and sufficient objection to the venue." Thus, in the absence of a proper and timely objection, the ensuing judgment is fully valid, even though venue may have been improper.

If a venue objection is made and upheld by the court, the court must, under 28 U.S.C. § 1406(a), either dismiss the action or "if it be in the interest of justice, transfer such case to any district or division in which it could have been brought." Courts generally conclude that the interests of justice are better served by transferring the action under § 1406(a) rather than dismissing the action. The *Pfeiffer* case, reprinted below, illustrates this judicial preference.

The following sections 2–4 demonstrate the operation of venue determinations under § 1391. Note that statutory citations in the cases were adjusted where necessary to comport with the 2011 amendments to § 1391.

2. Interaction of § 1391(b)(1), (2), and (3)

Pfeiffer v. Insty Prints

United States District Court, Northern District of Illinois, Oct. 29, 1993
No. 93 C 2937, 1993 WL 443403, 1993 U.S. Dist. LEXIS 15317

HART, DISTRICT JUDGE.

Plaintiff Jules Pfeiffer filed suit against defendants Insty Prints; Michelle M. Wojciuk ("Wojciuk"); Computer Processing Corp.; Performing Arts Center of Milwaukee ("MCWM"); and Joseph Ahern ("Ahern"). Presently pending are defendants MCWM's, Ahern's, Wojciuk's, and Insty Prints' motions to dismiss. Defendants argue that this court lacks personal jurisdiction over them and that the Northern District of Illinois is an improper venue for plaintiff's claims. Alternatively, defendants argue the case should be transferred to another venue. This court has jurisdiction over this action pursuant to 28 U.S.C. § 1332(a)(1) because there is complete diversity of citizenship and the amount in controversy is in excess of [the required jurisdictional amount].

. . . .

The first issue to be addressed is the question of venue. Plaintiff bears the burden of proving that venue is proper in the forum state. . . .

Plaintiff, an Illinois resident, alleges that he entered into two distinct contracts. Plaintiff alleges that he contracted with MCWM to perform a play at one of MCWM's theaters. Ahern was to oversee the production of the play and supervise the theater. MCWM is a theater corporation incorporated in Wisconsin and having its primary place of business in Milwaukee. Ahern is a Wisconsin resident and the associate managing director of a division of MCWM. The second contract was with Insty Prints for the printing and mailing of tickets in connection with the aforementioned performance. Insty Prints is a Minnesota corporation with its principal place of business in Minnesota. Insty Prints is licensed to do business in Wisconsin. Wojciuk, a Milwaukee resident, managed the Milwaukee Insty Prints location with which plaintiff contracted.

Plaintiff alleges that all defendants breached their contractual agreements. Plaintiff contends that the theater was not properly supervised, nor was proper supervision of ticket sales provided, resulting in theft of ticket proceeds. Additionally, tickets were mailed late or not at all, inhibiting the success of the performance. The final week of the performance had to be canceled due to the failure of the performance during the first three weeks. Defendant Ahern failed to procure television and radio advertising according to plaintiff's specifications. Plaintiff also contends that MCWM and Ahern had a duty to inform him that he should find a new printer when the original manager of Insty Print resigned and was replaced by Wojciuk. The breaches allegedly resulted in the play's financial and critical failure, caused plaintiff to suffer financial losses and physical injury, and damaged the reputation of the play.

Federal Rule of Civil Procedure 12(b)(3) allows for a motion to dismiss due to improper venue. Defendants contend that venue is not proper in the Northern District of Illinois. In this diversity case, venue is governed by 28 U.S.C. § 1391([b]).... The facts of this case do not support venue in this district.

According to both the allegations of the complaint and the individual defendants' affidavits, Ahern and Wojciuk are residents of Milwaukee, Wisconsin. Pursuant to 28 U.S.C. § 1391([d]), a corporation is considered to be a resident of any [judicial district] in which it is subject to personal jurisdiction at the time the action commences. The corporate defendants are incorporated in Wisconsin and/or do business in the Eastern District of Wisconsin. They acknowledge that they are subject to personal jurisdiction in that district. Pursuant to § 1391([b])(1), venue would be proper in the Eastern District of Wisconsin because all defendants are residents of that district.

Still at issue is whether venue would be proper in the Northern District of Illinois. Since neither Wojciuk nor Ahern reside in Illinois, § 1391([b])(1) does not provide for venue in Illinois.

Section 1391([b])(2) provides that venue is proper in a district where a substantial part of the events or omissions giving rise to the claim occurred. The test is not whether a majority of the activities pertaining to the case were performed in a particular district, but whether a substantial portion of the activities giving rise to the claim occurred in the particular district....

The performance of this contract occurred in Milwaukee [WI] and no defendant ever entered Illinois in regards to the contract. The theater at issue is located in Milwaukee; the play was produced and performed in Milwaukee; the tickets were printed in Milwaukee; the tickets were mailed in Milwaukee; and all defendants performing the contract were located in Milwaukee. Clearly a substantial part of the activities giving rise to this claim occurred in Milwaukee.

Plaintiff contends that he received correspondence and telephone calls in Illinois pertaining to this contract which constituted a substantial part of the events which gave rise to his cause of action. In *Merchants National Bank v. Safrabank*, 776 F. Supp. 538, 541 (D. Kan. 1991), plaintiff was solicited by defendants in Kansas. In addition, defendants conducted much of their business with plaintiff through mailing and phone calls to plaintiff in Kansas. These contacts rendered Kansas a proper venue for the case. This case can be distinguished from *Merchants*. The facts alleged in the complaint and the documents submitted by plaintiff only support that the phone calls and correspondence relied upon informed plaintiff about ongoing contractual activities in Milwaukee, and did not constitute the performance of those contractual obligations. More importantly, unlike the situation in *Merchants*, plaintiff solicited business from defendants; defendants did not seek out plaintiff or solicit him in Illinois.

. . . .

The second prong of § 1391([b])(2) provides for venue in the district where property that is the subject of the claim is situated. Plaintiff contends that the property that is the subject of this claim is his documentation of ownership of the play. His ownership papers are located in Illinois. However, the subject of plaintiff's claim is the production of his play in Wisconsin and breaches of contracts related to that production. Plaintiff's ownership of the play does not establish venue in Illinois under 28 U.S.C. § 1391([b])(2).[4]

Finally, § 1391([b])(3) allows a plaintiff to bring a claim in a venue where [any defendant is] subject to personal jurisdiction at the time the action is commenced. However, this subsection only applies if there are no districts in which the action may otherwise be brought. As previously indicated, venue would be proper in the Eastern District of Wisconsin pursuant to § 1391([b])(1). It would also be proper under § 1391([b])(2) since a substantial part of the events underlying plaintiff's claim occurred in the Eastern District of Wisconsin. Since venue is otherwise proper in the Eastern District of Wisconsin, § 1391([b])(3) does not apply to establish venue in the Northern District of Illinois.

Having determined that the Northern District of Illinois is an improper venue for this claim, 28 U.S.C. § 1406(a) provides that, in the interest of justice, a court may transfer a case to another proper forum even if venue and personal jurisdiction were not proper in the transferor forum.... Given that most of the witnesses, documents, and defendants are located in Wisconsin and that the Eastern District of Wisconsin appears to be the only proper venue, in the interest of justice, this case will be transferred to the Eastern District of Wisconsin.

. . . .

IT IS THEREFORE ORDERED that:

. . . .

(3) Defendants' motions to dismiss or for change of venue are granted in part and denied in part.

(4) Ten days after the entry of today's order, the Clerk of the Court is directed to transfer this case to the Eastern District of Wisconsin pursuant to 28 U.S.C. § 1406(a).

Problems

Problem 3-3. P, a citizen of State X, is injured in a three-car accident with D-1, a citizen and resident of the Northern District of State Y, and D-2, a citizen and resident of the Southern District of State Y. The accident occurred in the Western District of State Q. Jurisdiction is based solely on diversity of citizenship. Where is federal venue proper in a personal injury action by P against D-1 and D-2?

Problem 3-4. Assume the same facts as *Problem 3-3*, except that D-2 is a citizen and resident of the Southern District of State R. Where is federal venue proper?

Problem 3-5. (a) Assume the same facts as *Problem 3-4*, except that the accident occurred in the United Kingdom. Where is federal venue proper? Do you need additional information to answer this question?

(b) Assume (again under the same facts as *Problem 3-4*) that P sues D-1 and D-2 in a state court of State X, and D-1 and D-2 remove the action to the U.S. District Court of State X. D-1 and D-2 then move to dismiss the action on the ground of improper venue. Is this venue objection sound?

---

4. In addition, there is doubt as to whether intangible property can satisfy the "substantial property" requirement of 28 U.S.C. § 1391([b])(2). *See* D. Siegel, Commentary on 1990 Revision of Subdivisions (a), (b) and (e).

Problem 3-6. Assume the same facts as *Problem 3-5(a)*, with the following additional information: *P* sues *D-1* and *D-2* in the Northern District of State *Q*. Twenty days after the action is commenced, *D-1* and *D-2* enter the Northern District of State *Q*, not knowing about the existence of the action that has been brought by *P*. While *D-1* and *D-2* are in the Northern District of State *Q*, *P* has them personally served with process. Assume that this personal service validly subjects *D-1* and *D-2* to personal jurisdiction in the Northern District of State *Q*. Is federal venue proper? Would venue be proper if *D-1* and *D-2* had been served in the Southern District of State *Q*?

Problem 3-7. *P*, a citizen of State *X*, wants to sue *D*, a citizen and resident of the Northern District of State *Y*, and *D Corp.*, which is incorporated and has its principal place of business in State *Z*. *D Corp.* does extensive business in the Southern District of State *Y*. Based on that business, *D Corp.* is subject to personal jurisdiction throughout State *Y*. However, *D Corp.* does not do any business in the Northern District of State *Y*. *P's* claim is based on an automobile accident with *D* and an agent of *D Corp.* in the Western District of State *Q*. Jurisdiction is based solely on diversity. Identify all the places where federal venue is proper.

3. Venue Based on Substantial Events Within the District

Bates v. C & S Adjusters, Inc.

United States Court of Appeals, Second Circuit, 1992
980 F.2d 865

JON O. NEWMAN, Circuit Judge:

This appeal concerns venue in an action brought under the Fair Debt Collection Practices Act, 15 U.S.C. §§ 1692–1692o (1988). Specifically, the issue is whether venue exists in a district in which the debtor resides and to which a bill collector's demand for payment was forwarded. The issue arises on an appeal by Phillip E. Bates from the May 21, 1992, judgment of the District Court for the Western District of New York (William M. Skretny, Judge), dismissing his complaint because of improper venue. We conclude that venue was proper under 28 U.S.C. § 1391(b)(2) and therefore reverse and remand.

. . . .

Bates commenced this action in the Western District of New York upon receipt of a collection notice from C & S Adjusters, Inc. ("C & S"). Bates alleged violations of the Fair Debt Collection Practices Act, and demanded statutory damages, costs, and attorney's fees. The facts relevant to venue are not in dispute. Bates incurred the debt in question while he was a resident of the Western District of Pennsylvania. The creditor, a corporation with its principal place of business in that District, referred the account to C & S, a local collection agency which transacts no regular business in New York. Bates had meanwhile moved to the Western District of New York. When C & S mailed a collection notice to Bates at his Pennsylvania address, the Postal Service forwarded the notice to Bates' new address in New York.

In its answer, C & S asserted two affirmative defenses and also counterclaimed for costs, alleging that the action was instituted in bad faith and for purposes of harassment. C & S subsequently filed a motion to dismiss for improper venue, which the District Court granted.

....

Bates concedes that the only plausible venue provision for this action is 28 U.S.C. § 1391(b)(2), which allows an action to be brought in "a judicial district in which a substantial part of the events or omissions giving rise to the claim occurred." Prior to 1990, section 1391 allowed for venue in "the judicial district ... in which the claim arose." 28 U.S.C. § 1391(b) (1988). This case represents our first opportunity to consider the significance of the 1990 amendments.

Prior to 1966, venue was proper in federal question cases, absent a special venue statute, only in the defendant's state of citizenship. If a plaintiff sought to sue multiple defendants who were citizens of different states, there might be no district where the entire action could be brought.... Congress closed this "venue gap" by adding a provision allowing suit in the district "in which the claim arose." This phrase gave rise to a variety of conflicting interpretations. Some courts thought it meant that there could be only one such district; others believed there could be several. Different tests developed, with courts looking for "substantial contacts," the "weight of contacts," the place of injury or performance, or even to the boundaries of personal jurisdiction under state law.... District courts within the Second Circuit used at least three of these approaches....

The Supreme Court gave detailed attention to section 1391(b) in *Leroy v. Great Western United Corp.*, 443 U.S. 173 (1979). The specific holding of *Leroy* was that Great Western, a Texas corporation, which had attempted to take over an Idaho corporation, could not bring suit in Texas against Idaho officials who sought to enforce a state anti-takeover law. Although the effect of the Idaho officials' action might be felt in Texas, the Court rejected this factor as a basis for venue, since it would allow the Idaho officials to be sued anywhere a shareholder of the target corporation could allege that he wanted to accept Great Western's tender offer.... The Court made several further observations: (1) the purpose of the 1966 statute was to close venue gaps and should not be read more broadly than necessary to close those gaps ... ; (2) the general purpose of the venue statute was to protect defendants against an unfair or inconvenient trial location ...; (3) location of evidence and witnesses was a relevant factor ...; (4) familiarity of the Idaho federal judges with the Idaho anti-takeover statute was a relevant factor ...; (5) plaintiff's convenience was not a relevant factor ...; and (6) in only rare cases should there be more than one district in which a claim can be said to arise....

Subsequent to *Leroy* and prior to the 1990 amendment to section 1391(b), most courts have applied at least a form of the "weight of contacts" test.... Courts continued to have difficulty in determining whether more than one district could be proper....

Against this background, we understand Congress' 1990 amendment to be at most a marginal expansion of the venue provision. The House Report indicates that the new language was first proposed by the American Law Institute in a 1969 Study, and observes:

> The great advantage of referring to the place where things happened ... is that it avoids the litigation breeding phrase "in which the claim arose." It also avoids the problem created by the frequent cases in which substantial parts of the underlying events have occurred in several districts.

... Thus it seems clear that *Leroy's* strong admonition against recognizing multiple venues has been disapproved. Many of the factors in *Leroy*—for instance, the convenience of defendants and the location of evidence and witnesses—are most useful in distinguishing between two or more plausible venues. Since the new statute does not, as a general matter, require the District Court to determine the best venue, these factors will be of less significance.... Apart from this point, however, *Leroy* and other precedents remain important sources of guidance....

. . . .

Under the version of the venue statute in force from 1966 to 1990, at least three District Courts held that venue was proper under the Fair Debt Collection Practices Act in the plaintiff's home district if a collection agency had mailed a collection notice to an address in that district or placed a phone call to a number in that district. . . . None of these cases involved the unusual fact, present in this case, that the defendant did not deliberately direct a communication to the plaintiff's district.

We conclude, however, that this difference is inconsequential, at least under the current venue statute. The statutory standard for venue focuses not on whether a defendant has made a deliberate contact — a factor relevant in the analysis of personal jurisdiction — but on the location where events occurred. Under the new version of section 1391(b)(2), we must determine only whether a "substantial part of the events . . . giving rise to the claim" occurred in the Western District of New York.

In adopting this statute, Congress was concerned about the harmful effect of abusive debt practices on consumers. . . . This harm does not occur until receipt of the collection notice. Indeed, if the notice were lost in the mail, it is unlikely that a violation of the Act would have occurred. Moreover, a debt collection agency sends its dunning letters so that they will be received. Forwarding such letters to the district to which a debtor has moved is an important step in the collection process. If the bill collector prefers not to be challenged for its collection practices outside the district of a debtor's original residence, the envelope can be marked "do not forward." We conclude that receipt of a collection notice is a substantial part of the events giving rise to a claim under the Fair Debt Collection Practices Act.

The relevant factors identified in *Leroy* add support to our conclusion. Although "bona fide error" can be a defense to liability under the Act . . . the alleged violations of the Act turn largely not on the collection agency's intent, but on the content of the collection notice. The most relevant evidence — the collection notice — is located in the Western District of New York. Because the collection agency appears not to have marked the notice with instructions not to forward, and has not objected to the assertion of personal jurisdiction, trial in the Western District of New York would not be unfair.

. . . .

The judgment of the District Court is reversed, and the matter is remanded for further proceedings consistent with this decision.

Notes and Questions

1. In *Daniel v. American Board of Emergency Medicine*, 428 F.3d 408 (2d Cir. 2005), emergency medicine physicians brought suit in the U.S. District Court for the Western District of New York. The defendants were a medical specialty certification board for emergency medicine and hospitals operating residency programs in emergency medicine. The complaint alleged that the defendants conspired to restrict competition in the market for emergency medicine physicians in violation of the Sherman and Clayton Antitrust Acts. The Second Circuit Court of Appeals held that venue was improper in the district.

According to the court, an "events based" venue inquiry under § 1391(b)(2) requires a two-step analysis. First, the court should identify the nature of the claims and the acts and omissions that the plaintiff alleges give rise to those claims. Second, the court should determine whether a substantial part of those acts and omissions occurred in the district where suit was filed. The court described the substantiality inquiry as "more a qualitative than a quantitative inquiry." *Id.* at 432–33. The vast majority of the acts giving rise to the claims of the plaintiffs occurred outside the State of New York. The plaintiffs were able to point to only six of the numerous plaintiffs who had been notified of adverse certification decisions in the Western District of New York. In addition, of the hospitals sued, none were located in the Western District of New York. Thus, the court stated as follows:

> Viewed in this context, [the certification board's] transmittal into the Western District of New York of a half-dozen letters rejecting applications to sit for its certification examination outside New York constitutes only an insignificant and certainly not "a substantial part of the events or omissions giving rise to the [plaintiff's antitrust] claims[s]." We conclude that these incidental contacts are insufficient to afford venue in the Western District of New York pursuant to § 1391(b)(2).

Id. at 434.

Note, however, that the individual plaintiffs who had received rejection notices in the Western District of New York could probably have subjected the board defendant to personal jurisdiction there, if not also the hospital defendants. Does this mean that *Daniel* overruled *Bates*, or did the multiple-plaintiff, multiple-defendant nature of the case require the court to take a different approach to the "substantial events" test?

2. In *Bates*, the defendant, C & S, was a corporation and the action was filed in the Western District of New York. As a multidistrict state, § 1391(d) would therefore apply in determining the judicial districts in which C & S is deemed a "resident" for venue purposes. The court held that C & S waived any personal jurisdiction objection that it might have had by failing to raise it by preanswer motion or in the answer. But establishment of personal jurisdiction by the defendant's post-commencement waiver would not establish "residence" under the language of § 1391(d), would it? Suppose that C & S were an unincorporated association. Now the "residence" of C & S for venue purposes would be governed by § 1391(c)(2). Would your answer as to the effect of personal jurisdiction by waiver be the same?

3. Do you think the defendant in *Bates* made all of the proper motions to dismiss? The only motion the defendant filed was a motion to dismiss for improper venue under Rule 12(b)(3). As noted in the court's opinion, the plaintiff "concede[d] that the only plausible venue provision for this action is 28 U.S.C. § 1391(b)(2) [events-based venue]." In terms of the possible bases for venue under § 1391(b), what does the plaintiff's concession indicate? Based on this, what motion do you think the defendant should have joined with its motion to dismiss for improper venue? Can the defendant file this motion now? What does Rule 12(g)(2) and (h)(1)(A) provide? If the defendant had properly filed this other motion, how do you think the court in *Bates* would have ruled given the court's findings in its opinion?

4. How should it be determined whether the events occurring within a district are "substantial" under § 1391(b)(2)? To date, no consistent approach to this question has emerged in the lower federal courts. It is clear that a majority of the events giving rise to the claim do not have to take place in the district. However, beyond this, very little is clear. Should the courts establish some minimum percentage of activity that is necessary to be "substantial"? Is the question whether the defendant is subject to personal jurisdiction within the district relevant to this issue?

5. Some courts have held that if venue would be proper under § 1391(b)(1) in the state where all the defendants reside, the plaintiff cannot use § 1391(b)(2) to establish an alternative venue in the district where a substantial part of the events giving rise to the claim occurred. These holdings are clearly incorrect, are they not? When Congress wanted

to make the applicability of a subsection of the venue statute depend upon the inapplicability of other subsections of the statute, it showed in § 1391(b)(3) that it knew how to do so, didn't it?

6. If a substantial part of the total events giving rise to the plaintiff's claims occurred within the district, but the specific acts alleged against some of the defendants occurred entirely outside the district, is venue proper with regard to the latter defendants in the district under § 1391(b)(2)?

7. The drafters of § 1391(b)(3) generally envisioned that the sections could only be used in cases in which the events giving rise to suit occurred outside the United States. This assumption was that if the events giving rise to suit occurred inside the United States, the plaintiff would always be able to find some district in which a substantial part of the events giving rise to the claim occurred and thus predicate venue in that district under § 1391(b)(2), even if there were multiple defendants in the action residing in different districts in different states. Is it ever possible in a situation in which the claim arises inside the United States for the events giving rise to the claim to be so spread out that no district contains a substantial part of the events? One district court so held. *See Telamerica Media, Inc. v. AMN Television Mktg.*, No. 99-25-72, 1999 WL 1244423, 1999 U.S. Dist. LEXIS 19423 (E.D. Pa. Dec. 21, 1999). But if this is so, would it be possible to obtain personal jurisdiction over multiple defendants in any one place in the United States, even if venue is proper under § 1391(b)(3)? If it would be possible, why shouldn't the court conclude that a substantial part of the events giving rise to the claim occurred in that place?

Problems

Problem 3-8. P, a citizen and resident of State X, sued D, a citizen and resident of State Y. P's action is brought in the U.S. District Court for the District of State Z. P seeks $2,000,000 damages resulting from a libel of P in a national magazine published by D. P brought the action in State Z because State Z was the only state whose statute of limitations had not yet run on P's claim. Nevertheless, P seeks damages from D for the harm caused by the libel throughout the United States. D sells 10,000 to 15,000 copies of the magazine per month in State Z, but sells many more copies in most other states. For example, D sells 50,000 copies per month in each of States X and Y. What argument could be made that venue is proper under § 1391(b)(2) in the District of State Z? 10-15K substantial part of property

Problem 3-9. P, a citizen of State X, is a building contractor licensed in State Y. P is a plaintiff in a lawsuit in State X. Upon the request of the defendant in P's lawsuit, D, a citizen of State Y, sent confidential information from P's licensing file to the defendant in violation of State Y law. P sued D in U.S. District Court in State X (a single district state) for $100,000 in damages resulting from the disclosure. Is venue proper in State X? If venue is held improper on these facts, can the result be reconciled with *Bates*?

Problem 3-10. P, a citizen of State X, sued D, a citizen of State Y, in the U.S. District Court for the District of State X. P seeks $500,000 in damages for personal injuries and property damage received in an automobile accident that occurred in State Y between P and D. P argues that venue is proper under 28 U.S.C. § 1391(b)(2) in the District of State X because P underwent substantial medical treatment in that district and P's automobile was repaired in that district. Evaluate P's argument.

Problem 3-11. P is a citizen and resident of State X, which is a single district state. P sues D, a citizen and resident of the Southern District of State Y, in the U.S. District Court for State X. P's claim is for federal trademark infringement. The infringement allegedly occurred when D sold a product that infringed P's trademark. D had sales in all fifty states. Five percent of the infringing sales occurred in State X. Is federal venue proper in State X? What additional information, if any, would be helpful in formulating an answer to this question?

4. The "Local Action" Rule and Property-Based Venue in Federal Court

As noted in section A, above, the "Federal Courts Jurisdiction and Venue Clarification Act of 2011" eliminated the local action rule in federal court actions, and § 1391(a)(2) now provides that "[e]xcept as otherwise provided by Law ... (2) the proper venue for a civil action shall be determined without regard to whether the action is local or transitory in nature." This amendment, however, does not necessarily affect cases holding that states do not have jurisdiction to enter judgments directly affecting title to land in other states. As discussed in Chapter 2 and section A of this chapter, these cases may have constitutional stature.

Irrespective of the elimination of the "local action" rule in federal court actions, questions of interpretation still exist in determining "property-based" venue under § 1391(b)(2), which authorizes venue in a judicial district in which "a substantial part of property that is the subject of the action is situated. For example, how should the courts determine whether property is the "subject of the action" within the meaning of § 1391(b)(2)? In addition, when property is located in different districts, how should the courts determine whether the part of the property located in the district where the action is brought is "substantial"? Should the courts make this determination in the same manner that they determine whether the claim-producing events in a district are substantial? When the property in question is personalty, which can be moved from district to district, what standards should the courts use to prevent the property from being moved to manufacture venue artificially?

Problem

Problem 3-12. P is a citizen and resident of the Northern District of State X. D is a citizen and resident of the District of State Y. P sues D in the U.S. District Court for the Northern District of State X. P seeks $150,000 for damage to P's valuable antique automobile. The damage resulted from an automobile accident in the Southern District of State Z. After the accident, the automobile was towed to the Northern District of State X, where it has remained in a repair shop specializing in repair of antique automobiles ever since. Is venue proper in the Northern District of State X? If the repair shop had been in the District of State Q would venue be proper there?

Section C. Transfers of Venue
Within a Judicial System

This section explores the process of transfers between U.S. District Courts under the federal transfer statutes.

Transfers of Venue for the Convenience of the Parties and Witnesses — § 1404(a). As noted in section B, when several venue choices are proper under the applicable venue provisions, the plaintiff has the right to choose where to file the action. Even though venue may be proper, however, 28 U.S.C. § 1404(a) provides that "[f]or the convenience of parties and witnesses, in the interest of justice, a district court may transfer any civil action to any other district or division where it might have been brought or to any district or division to which all parties have consented." The "Federal Courts Jurisdiction and Venue Clarification Act of 2011" amended § 1404(a) to add the final phrase "or to any district or division to which all parties have consented." This language was added in response to the Supreme Court's holding in *Hoffman v. Blaski*, 363 U.S. 335 (1960), that the "where it might have been brought" language in § 1404(a) limited transfer to only those districts where the plaintiff *originally* had the right to bring the action. The Court held that transfer to a district where venue or personal jurisdiction would have been improper as an original matter was not authorized, even though the defendant was willing to waive those defenses in the transferee court. The newly added phrase now authorizes a district court to transfer an action to a more convenient district, even though personal jurisdiction or venue would not have been proper in that district if the plaintiff had filed there originally, provided all parties consent to the transfer.

The district court is given wide discretion in deciding whether to transfer a case under § 1404(a) and the statute does not enumerate specific factors for the court to consider other than the "convenience of parties and witnesses" and "the interest of justice." The burden is on the party seeking transfer, however, to demonstrate that transfer is justified, otherwise the action remains in the plaintiff's properly chosen venue. Although rare, a plaintiff is also entitled to seek a transfer of venue under § 1404(a) and must meet the same burden to justify transfer. *Ferens v. John Deere Co.*, 494 U.S. 516 (1990), discussed in Chapter 5, is such an example.

Although the *Piper Aircraft* case, reprinted in section D below, concerns a dismissal for *forum non conveniens*, the same public and private factors reviewed in *Piper Aircraft* would also be considered by the court on a § 1404(a) transfer. A transfer under § 1404(a), however, would require a lesser showing of inconvenience than a dismissal for *forum non conveniens*. See *Norwood v. Kirkpatrick*, 349 U.S. 29 (1955) ("we believe that Congress, by the term 'for the convenience of parties and witnesses, in the interest of justice,' intended to permit courts to grant transfers upon a lesser showing of inconvenience [than under the doctrine of *forum non conveniens*]. This is not to say that the relevant factors have changed or that the plaintiff's choice of forum is not to be considered, but only that the discretion to be exercised is broader."). A transfer under § 1404(a) would require a lesser showing of inconvenience because the action is only being transferred from one federal district court to another. On a *forum non conveniens* dismissal, the case is dismissed entirely for refiling in a foreign judicial system which will often result in a change in the substantive and procedural laws governing the case.

Transfers When Venue in the Forum Is Improper — § 1406(a). When an action has been commenced in a federal district court where venue is *improper*, the burden on the moving party is different than under § 1404(a). A defendant objecting to improper venue need not demonstrate inconvenience or any other factor justifying transfer other than to show that under the applicable venue provisions, venue is improper. If the court upholds the defendant's objection, the court must, under 28 U.S.C. § 1406(a), either dismiss the action or "if it be in the interest of justice, transfer such case to any district or division in which it could have been brought." As illustrated by the *Pfeiffer* case, reprinted above, the preference of the courts is to transfer the action rather than dismissing it. Under § 1406(a), an action may be transferred even if the transferor court lacks personal jurisdiction over the defendant, provided venue would be proper and personal jurisdiction would be obtainable over the defendant in the district where the action will be transferred. *See Goldlawr, Inc. v. Heiman*, 369 U.S. 463 (1962).

Note three important distinctions between the choices available to the court under § 1404(a) and § 1406(a). First, under § 1404(a), because the plaintiff's chosen venue is *proper*, the court has no discretion to dismiss the action and must *keep* the case unless a transfer is ordered. In contrast, under § 1406(a), because the plaintiff's chosen venue is *improper*, the court has no discretion to keep the action and must *dismiss* the case unless a transfer is ordered. Second, an objection for *improper* venue must be timely made at the inception of the case or the objection is waived under Rule 12(h)(1), thus eliminating the option to seek transfer under § 1406(a). In contrast, a motion to transfer an action with proper venue under § 1404(a) may be made at any time, although delay would certainly be a factor in the court's analysis. Finally, under the 2011 amendment to § 1404(a), a transfer under § 1404(a) may now be made to a district where the action could not have been brought originally provided all parties consent to the transfer. No corresponding change, however, was made to the language of § 1406(a), which continues to provide that the court may only transfer the action to "any district or division in which it could have been brought."

Transfers for Pretrial Purposes—§ 1407. Transfer is available under 28 U.S.C. § 1407 of civil actions pending in different districts "to *any* district for coordinated or consolidated *pretrial* proceedings." Transfer is made by a judicial panel on multidistrict litigation, consisting of seven circuit and district judges appointed by the Chief Justice of the United States. Often, transferred cases involve complex litigation, such as antitrust or securities actions. After the pretrial proceedings are completed, the cases are supposed to be transferred back to the districts from which they came, but they are often settled. The American Law Institute has proposed a more comprehensive scheme for transfer and consolidation of complex litigation. *See* ALI, Complex Litigation: Statutory Recommendations and Analysis With Reporter's Study (1994).

Transfers Between Different Judicial Systems. Transfers are not ordinarily available between courts in different judicial systems. However, in 1991, the National Conference of Commissioners on Uniform State Laws approved the Uniform Transfer of Litigation Act. If adopted by the states, this Act would permit transfers between state courts in different states. The American Law Institute complex litigation proposal cited in the preceding subsection also contains recommendations for transfer and consolidation from federal to state courts and transfer and consolidation between state courts. *See* ALI, Complex Litigation: Statutory Recommendations and Analysis with Reporter's Study 177–216, 455–546, 547–84 (1994).

Notes and Questions

1. Which statute—§ 1404(a) or § 1406—governs if venue is proper but personal jurisdiction is improper in the transferor district? Some courts have held transfer can be made in this situation under § 1404(a). *If all parties consented*

2. In *Lexecon, Inc. v. Milberg Weiss Bershad Hynes & Lerach*, 523 U.S. 26 (1998), the Supreme Court held that after transfer of a case under § 1407 for pretrial proceedings, the transferee court could not permanently transfer the case to itself for trial under § 1404(a). Does the text of § 1407 support the Court's decision? *Yes "pretrial proceedings"*

3. As noted in Chapter 5, state substantive law must be applied by a federal district court when the court is adjudicating a claim based on state, rather than federal, law. But which state's law applies when a case is transferred? As explained in Chapter 5, the state law of the transferor court applies on a § 1404(a) transfer, but the state law of the transferee court applies on a § 1406(a) transfer. Why do you think this would be so? See also the discussion of this issue in footnote 8 in the *Piper Aircraft* case, reprinted below.

Section D. The Doctrine of Forum Non Conveniens

The doctrine of forum non conveniens is a common-law doctrine that is ordinarily applied only when there is a court in *another judicial system* that is substantially more convenient than the court where the plaintiff has commenced the action. As previously noted, transfers are not ordinarily available between courts in different judicial systems. Under these circumstances, the only option of the court in the place where the action was commenced is to dismiss the action thus forcing the plaintiff to bring it in the more convenient forum. Thus, if an accident occurred in Great Britain and the plaintiff sues the defendant in Illinois, an Illinois court might dismiss the action under the doctrine of forum non conveniens in preference to a court in Great Britain if it would be substantially more convenient to try the action there. As noted in the preceding subsection, within a judicial system statutory transfer is usually employed to obtain a more convenient venue rather than forum non conveniens. However, some states follow a "common-law" doctrine of intrastate forum non conveniens that also permits transfer. *See, e.g., Peile v. Skelgas, Inc.*, 645 N.E.2d 184 (Ill. 1994); *Stevens v. Blevins*, 890 P.2d 936 (Okla. 1995).

In the state courts that recognize the doctrine, forum non conveniens can be employed to dismiss an action in preference to a more convenient court in another state or in a foreign country. However, in the federal courts, forum non conveniens is, as a practical matter, available only in preference to a more convenient court in a foreign nation. Transfer under § 1404(a) has replaced the doctrine of forum non conveniens when the more convenient forum is a U.S. District Court in another district. The standards employed by the state and federal courts to determine whether an action may be dismissed under the doctrine of forum non conveniens are similar. They are explored in the following case and accompanying materials.

Piper Aircraft Co. v. Reyno

United States Supreme Court, 1981
454 U.S. 235, 102 S. Ct. 252, 70 L. Ed. 2d 419

JUSTICE MARSHALL delivered the opinion of the Court.

These cases arise out of an air crash that took place in Scotland. Respondent, acting as representative of the estates of several Scottish citizens killed in the accident, brought wrongful-death actions against petitioners that were ultimately transferred to the United States District Court for the Middle District of Pennsylvania. Petitioners moved to dismiss on the ground of *forum non conveniens*. After noting that an alternative forum existed in Scotland, the District Court granted their motions.... The United States Court of Appeals for the Third Circuit reversed.... The Court of Appeals based its decision, at least in part, on the ground that dismissal is automatically barred where the law of the alternative forum is less favorable to the plaintiff than the law of the forum chosen by the plaintiff. Because we conclude that the possibility of an unfavorable change in law should not, by itself, bar dismissal, and because we conclude that the District Court did not otherwise abuse its discretion, we reverse.

I

....

In July 1976, a small commercial aircraft crashed in the Scottish highlands during the course of a charter flight from Blackpool to Perth. The pilot and five passengers were killed instantly. The decedents were all Scottish subjects and residents, as are their heirs and next of kin. There were no eyewitnesses to the accident. At the time of the crash the plane was subject to Scottish air traffic control.

The aircraft, a twin-engine Piper Aztec, was manufactured in Pennsylvania by petitioner Piper Aircraft Co. (Piper). The propellers were manufactured in Ohio by petitioner Hartzell Propeller, Inc. (Hartzell). At the time of the crash the aircraft was registered in Great Britain and was owned and maintained by Air Navigation and Trading Co., Ltd. (Air Navigation). It was operated by McDonald Aviation, Ltd. (McDonald), a Scottish air taxi service. Both Air Navigation and McDonald were organized in the United Kingdom. The wreckage of the plane is now in a hangar in Farnsborough, England.

The British Department of Trade investigated the accident shortly after it occurred. A preliminary report found that the plane crashed after developing a spin, and suggested that mechanical failure in the plane or the propeller was responsible. At Hartzell's request, this report was reviewed by a three-member Review Board, which held a 9-day adversary hearing attended by all interested parties. The Review Board found no evidence of defective equipment and indicated that pilot error may have contributed to the accident. The pilot, who had obtained his commercial pilot's license only three months earlier, was flying over high ground at an altitude considerably lower than the minimum height required by his company's operations manual.

In July 1977, a California probate court appointed respondent Gaynell Reyno administratrix of the estates of the five passengers. Reyno is not related to and does not know any of the decedents or their survivors; she was a legal secretary to the attorney who filed this lawsuit. Several days after her appointment, Reyno commenced separate wrongful-death actions against Piper and Hartzell in the Superior Court of California, claiming negligence and strict liability. Air Navigation, McDonald, and the estate of the pilot are not parties to this litigation. The survivors of the five passengers whose estates are represented by Reyno filed a separate action in the United Kingdom against Air Navigation,

McDonald, and the pilot's estate.[2] Reyno candidly admits that the action against Piper and Hartzell was filed in the United States because its laws regarding liability, capacity to sue, and damages are more favorable to her position than are those of Scotland. Scottish law does not recognize strict liability in tort. Moreover, it permits wrongful-death actions only when brought by a decedent's relatives. The relatives may sue only for "loss of support and society."

On petitioners' motion, the suit was removed to the United States District Court for the Central District of California. Piper then moved for transfer to the United States District Court for the Middle District of Pennsylvania, pursuant to 28 U.S.C. § 1404(a). Hartzell moved to dismiss for lack of personal jurisdiction, or in the alternative, to transfer.[5] In December 1977, the District Court quashed service on Hartzell and transferred the case to the Middle District of Pennsylvania. Respondent then properly served process on Hartzell.

. . . .

In May 1978, after the suit had been transferred, both Hartzell and Piper moved to dismiss the action on the ground of *forum non conveniens*. The District Court granted these motions in October 1979. It relied on the balancing test set forth by this Court in *Gulf Oil Corp. v. Gilbert,* 330 U.S. 501 (1947) and its companion case *Koster v. Lumbermens Mut. Cas. Co,* 330 U.S. 518 (1947). In those decisions, the Court stated that a plaintiff's choice of forum should rarely be disturbed. However, when an alternative forum has jurisdiction to hear the case, and when trial in the chosen forum would "establish . . . oppressiveness and vexation to a defendant . . . out of all proportion to plaintiff's convenience," or when the "chosen forum [is] inappropriate because of considerations affecting the court's own administrative and legal problems," the court may, in the exercise of its sound discretion, dismiss the case. . . . To guide trial court discretion, the Court provided a list of "private interest factors" affecting the convenience of the litigants, and a list of "public interest factors" affecting the convenience of the forum. . . .[6]

After describing our decisions in *Gilbert* and *Koster*, the District Court analyzed the facts of these cases. It began by observing that an alternative forum existed in Scotland; Piper and Hartzell had agreed to submit to the jurisdiction of the Scottish courts and to waive any statute of limitations defense that might be available. It then stated that plaintiff's choice of forum was entitled to little weight. The court recognized that a plaintiff's choice ordinarily deserves substantial deference. It noted, however, that Reyno "is a representative of foreign citizens and residents seeking a forum in the United States because of the more liberal rules concerning products liability law," and that "the courts have been less

---

2. The pilot's estate has also filed suit in the United Kingdom against Air Navigation, McDonald, Piper, and Hartzell.

5. The District Court concluded that it could not assert personal jurisdiction over Hartzell consistent with due process. However, it decided not to dismiss Hartzell because the corporation would be amenable to process in Pennsylvania.

6. The factors pertaining to the private interests of the litigants included the "relative ease of access to sources of proof; availability of compulsory process for attendance of unwilling, and the cost of obtaining attendance of willing, witnesses; possibility of view of premises, if view would be appropriate to the action; and all other practical problems that make trial of a case easy, expeditious and inexpensive." *Gilbert*, 330 U.S. at 508. The public factors bearing on the question included the administrative difficulties flowing from court congestion; the "local interest in having localized controversies decided at home"; the interest in having the trial of a diversity case in a forum that is at home with the law that must govern the action; the avoidance of unnecessary problems in conflict of laws, or in the application of foreign law; and the unfairness of burdening citizens in an unrelated forum with jury duty. *Id.* at 509.

solicitous when the plaintiff is not an American citizen or resident, and particularly when the foreign citizens seek to benefit from the more liberal tort rules provided for the protection of citizens and residents of the United States." ...

The District Court next examined several factors relating to the private interests of the litigants, and determined that these factors strongly pointed towards Scotland as the appropriate forum. Although evidence concerning the design, manufacture, and testing of the plane and propeller is located in the United States, the connections with Scotland are otherwise "overwhelming." ... The real parties in interest are citizens of Scotland, as were all the decedents. Witnesses who could testify regarding the maintenance of the aircraft, the training of the pilot, and the investigation of the accident — all essential to the defense — are in Great Britain. Moreover, all witnesses to damages are located in Scotland. Trial would be aided by familiarity with Scottish topography, and by easy access to the wreckage.

private

The District Court reasoned that because crucial witnesses and evidence were beyond the reach of compulsory process, and because the defendants would not be able to implead potential Scottish third-party defendants, it would be "unfair to make Piper and Hartzell proceed to trial in this forum." ... The survivors had brought separate actions in Scotland against the pilot, McDonald, and Air Navigation. "[I]t would be fairer to all parties and less costly if the entire case was presented to one jury with available testimony from all relevant witnesses." ... Although the court recognized that if trial were held in the United States, Piper and Hartzell could file indemnity or contribution actions against the Scottish defendants, it believed that there was a significant risk of inconsistent verdicts.[7]

The District Court concluded that the relevant public interests also pointed strongly towards dismissal. The court determined that Pennsylvania law would apply to Piper and Scottish law to Hartzell if the case were tried in the Middle District of Pennsylvania.[8] As a result, "trial in this forum would be hopelessly complex and confusing for a jury." ... In addition, the court noted that it was unfamiliar with Scottish law and thus would have to rely upon experts from that country. The court also found that the trial would be enormously costly and time-consuming; that it would be unfair to burden citizens with jury duty when the Middle District of Pennsylvania has little connection with the controversy; and that Scotland has a substantial interest in the outcome of the litigation.

In opposing the motions to dismiss, respondent contended that dismissal would be unfair because Scottish law was less favorable. The District Court explicitly rejected this claim. It reasoned that the possibility that dismissal might lead to an unfavorable change in the law did not deserve significant weight; any deficiency in the foreign law was a "matter to be dealt with in the foreign forum". ...

---

7. The District Court explained that inconsistent verdicts might result if petitioners were held liable on the basis of strict liability here, and then required to prove negligence in an indemnity action in Scotland. Moreover, even if the same standard of liability applied, there was a danger that different juries would find different facts and produce inconsistent results.

8. Under *Klaxon Co. v. Stentor Electric Manufacturing Co.*, 313 U.S. 487 (1941), a court ordinarily must apply the choice-of-law rules of the State in which it sits. However, where a case is transferred pursuant to 28 U.S.C. § 1404(a), it must apply the choice-of-law rules of the State from which the case was transferred. *Van Dusen v. Barrack.* ... Relying on these two cases, the District Court concluded that California choice-of-law rules would apply to Piper, and Pennsylvania choice-of-law rules would apply to Hartzell. It further concluded that California applied a "governmental interests" analysis in resolving choice-of-law problems, and that Pennsylvania employed a "significant contacts" analysis. The court used the "governmental interests" analysis to determine that Pennsylvania liability rules would apply to Piper, and the "significant contacts" analysis to determine that Scottish liability rules would apply to Hartzell.

....

On appeal, the United States Court of Appeals for the Third Circuit reversed and remanded for trial. The decision to reverse appears to be based on two alternative grounds. First, the Court held that the District Court abused its discretion in conducting the *Gilbert* analysis. Second, the Court held that dismissal is never appropriate where the law of the alternative forum is less favorable to the plaintiff.

Reasons Appeals Ct. Reverse

....

II

The Court of Appeals erred in holding that plaintiffs may defeat a motion to dismiss on the ground of *forum non conveniens* merely by showing that the substantive law that would be applied in the alternative forum is less favorable to the plaintiffs than that of the present forum. The possibility of a change in substantive law should ordinarily not be given conclusive or even substantial weight in the *forum non conveniens* inquiry.

We expressly rejected the position adopted by the Court of Appeals in our decision in *Canada Malting Co. v. Paterson S.S., Ltd.*, 285 U.S. 413 (1932). That case arose out of a collision between two vessels in American waters. The Canadian owners of cargo lost in the accident sued the Canadian owners of one of the vessels in Federal District Court. The cargo owners chose an American court in large part because the relevant American liability rules were more favorable than the Canadian rules. The District Court dismissed on grounds of *forum non conveniens*. The plaintiffs argued that dismissal was inappropriate because Canadian laws were less favorable to them. This Court nonetheless affirmed:

> We have no occasion to enquire by what law the rights of the parties are governed, as we are of the opinion that, under any view of that question, it lay within the discretion of the District Court to decline to assume jurisdiction over the controversy...."[T]he court will not take cognizance of the case if justice would be as well done by remitting the parties to their home forum." ...

The Court further stated that "[t]here was no basis for the contention that the District Court abused its discretion." ...

It is true that *Canada Malting* was decided before *Gilbert*, and that the doctrine of *forum non conveniens* was not fully crystallized until our decision in that case.[13] However, *Gilbert* in no way affects the validity of *Canada Malting*. Indeed, by holding that the central focus of the *forum non conveniens* inquiry is convenience, *Gilbert* implicitly recognized that dis-

---

13. The doctrine of *forum non conveniens* has a long history. It originated in Scotland, *see* Braucher, *The Inconvenient Federal Forum*, 60 Harv. L. Rev. 908, 909–11 (1947), and became part of the common law of many States, *see id.* at 911–12; Blair, *The Doctrine of Forum Non Conveniens in Anglo-American Law*, 29 Colum. L. Rev. 1 (1929). The doctrine was also frequently applied in federal admiralty actions. *See, e.g., Canada Malting Co. v. Paterson S.S., Ltd.; see also* Bickel, *The Doctrine of Forum Non Conveniens As Applied in the Federal Courts in Matters of Admiralty*, 35 Cornell L.Q. 12 (1949). In *Williams v. Green Bay & W.R.R.*, 326 U.S. 549 (1946), the Court first indicated that motions to dismiss on grounds of *forum non conveniens* could be made in federal diversity actions. The doctrine became firmly established when *Gilbert* and *Koster* were decided one year later.

In previous *forum non conveniens* decisions, the Court has left unresolved the question whether under *Erie R.R. v. Tompkins*, 304 U.S. 64 1188 (1938), state or federal law of *forum non conveniens* applies in a diversity case. *Gilbert*, 330 U.S. at 509; *Koster*, 330 U.S. at 529; *Williams v. Green Bay & W.R.R.*, 326 U.S. at 551, 558–59. The Court did not decide this issue because the same result would have been reached in each case under federal or state law. The lower courts in these cases reached the same conclusion: Pennsylvania and California law on *forum non conveniens* dismissals are virtually identical to federal law. *See* 630 F.2d at 158. Thus, here also, we need not resolve the *Erie* question.

missal may not be barred solely because of the possibility of an unfavorable change in law. Under *Gilbert*, dismissal will ordinarily be appropriate where trial in the plaintiff's chosen forum imposes a heavy burden on the defendant or the court, and where the plaintiff is unable to offer any specific reasons of convenience supporting his choice.[15] If substantial weight were given to the possibility of an unfavorable change in law, however, dismissal might be barred even where trial in the chosen forum was plainly inconvenient.

The Court of Appeals' decision is inconsistent with this Court's earlier *forum non conveniens* decisions in another respect. Those decisions have repeatedly emphasized the need to retain flexibility. In *Gilbert*, the Court refused to identify specific circumstances "which will justify or require either grant or denial of remedy." ... Similarly, in *Koster*, the Court rejected the contention that where a trial would involve inquiry into the internal affairs of a foreign corporation, dismissal was always appropriate. "That is one, but only one, factor which may show convenience." ... And in *Williams v. Green Bay & Western R.R. Co.*, 326 U.S. 549, 557 (1946), we stated that we would not lay down a rigid rule to govern discretion, and that "[e]ach case turns on its facts." If central emphasis were placed on any one factor, the *forum non conveniens* doctrine would lose much of the very flexibility that makes it so valuable.

In fact, if conclusive or substantial weight were given to the possibility of a change in law, the *forum non conveniens* doctrine would become virtually useless. Jurisdiction and venue requirements are often easily satisfied. As a result, many plaintiffs are able to choose from among several forums. Ordinarily, these plaintiffs will select that forum whose choice-of-law rules are most advantageous. Thus, if the possibility of an unfavorable change in substantive law is given substantial weight in the *forum non conveniens* inquiry, dismissal would rarely be proper....

....

The Court of Appeals' approach is not only inconsistent with the purpose of the *forum non conveniens* doctrine, but also poses substantial practical problems. If the possibility of a change in law were given substantial weight, deciding motions to dismiss on the ground of *forum non conveniens* would become quite difficult. Choice-of-law analysis would become extremely important, and the courts would frequently be required to interpret the law of foreign jurisdictions. First, the trial court would have to determine what law would apply if the case were tried in the chosen forum, and what law would apply if the case were tried in the alternative forum. It would then have to compare the rights, remedies, and procedures available under the law that would be applied in each forum. Dismissal would be appropriate only if the court concluded that the law applied by the alternative forum is as favorable to the plaintiff as that of the chosen forum. The doctrine of *forum non conveniens*, however, is designed in part to help courts avoid conducting complex exercises in comparative law. As we stated in *Gilbert*, the public interest factors point towards dismissal where the court would be required to "untangle problems in conflict of laws, and in law foreign to itself." ...

Upholding the decision of the Court of Appeals would result in other practical problems. At least where the foreign plaintiff named an American manufacturer as defendant,[17] a court could not dismiss the case on grounds of *forum non conveniens* where

---

15. In other words, *Gilbert* held that dismissal may be warranted where a plaintiff chooses a particular forum, not because it is convenient, but solely in order to harass the defendant or take advantage of favorable law. This is precisely the situation in which the Court of Appeals' rule would bar dismissal.

17. In fact, the defendant might not even have to be American. A foreign plaintiff seeking damages for an accident that occurred abroad might be able to obtain service of process on a foreign de-

dismissal might lead to an unfavorable change in law. The American courts, which are already extremely attractive to foreign plaintiffs,[18] would become even more attractive. The flow of litigation into the United States would increase and further congest already crowded courts.[19]

The Court of Appeals based its decision, at least in part, on an analogy between dismissals on grounds of *forum non conveniens* and transfers between federal courts pursuant to § 1404(a). In *Van Dusen v. Barrack*, 376 U.S. 612 (1964), this Court ruled that a § 1404(a) transfer should not result in a change in the applicable law. Relying on dictum in an earlier Third Circuit opinion interpreting *Van Dusen*, the court below held that that principle is also applicable to a dismissal on *forum non conveniens* grounds.... However, § 1404(a) transfers are different than dismissals on the ground of *forum non conveniens*.

Congress enacted § 1404(a) to permit change of venue between federal courts. Although the statute was drafted in accordance with the doctrine of *forum non conveniens* ... it was intended to be a revision rather than a codification of the common law.... District courts were given more discretion to transfer under § 1404(a) than they had to dismiss on grounds of *forum non conveniens*....

The reasoning employed in *Van Dusen v. Barrack* is simply inapplicable to dismissals on grounds of *forum non conveniens*. That case did not discuss the common-law doctrine. Rather, it focused on "the construction and application" of § 1404(a).... Emphasizing the remedial purpose of the statute, *Barrack* concluded that Congress could not have intended a transfer to be accompanied by a change in law.... The statute was designed as a "federal housekeeping measure," allowing easy change of venue within a unified federal system.... The Court feared that if a change in venue were accompanied by a change in law, forum-shopping parties would take unfair advantage of the relaxed standards for transfer. The rule was necessary to ensure the just and efficient operation of the statute.

---

fendant who does business in the United States. Under the Court of Appeals' holding, dismissal would be barred if the law in the alternative forum were less favorable to the plaintiff — even though none of the parties are American, and even though there is absolutely no nexus between the subject matter of the litigation and the United States.

18. First, all but 6 of the 50 American States — Delaware, Massachusetts, Michigan, North Carolina, Virginia, and Wyoming — offer strict liability.... Rules roughly equivalent to American strict liability are effective in France, Belgium, and Luxembourg. West Germany and Japan have a strict liability statute for pharmaceuticals. However, strict liability remains primarily an American innovation. Second, the tort plaintiff may choose, at least potentially, from among 50 jurisdictions if he decides to file suit in the United States. Each of these jurisdictions applies its own set of malleable choice-of-law rules. Third, jury trials are almost always available in the United States, while they are never provided in civil law jurisdictions.... Even in the United Kingdom, most civil actions are not tried before a jury.... Fourth, unlike most foreign jurisdictions, American courts allow contingent attorney's fees, and do not tax losing parties with their opponents' attorney's fees.... Fifth, discovery is more extensive in American than in foreign courts....

19. In holding that the possibility of a change in law unfavorable to the plaintiff should not be given substantial weight, we also necessarily hold that the possibility of a change in law favorable to defendant should not be considered. Respondent suggests that Piper and Hartzell filed the motion to dismiss, not simply because trial in the United States would be inconvenient, but also because they believe the laws of Scotland are more favorable. She argues that this should be taken into account in the analysis of the private interests. We recognize, of course, that Piper and Hartzell may be engaged in reverse forum-shopping. However, this possibility ordinarily should not enter into a trial court's analysis of the private interests. If the defendant is able to overcome the presumption in favor of plaintiff by showing that trial in the chosen forum would be unnecessarily burdensome, dismissal is appropriate — regardless of the fact that defendant may also be motivated by a desire to obtain a more favorable forum....

We do not hold that the possibility of an unfavorable change in law should *never* be a relevant consideration in a *forum non conveniens* inquiry. Of course, if the remedy provided by the alternative forum is so clearly inadequate or unsatisfactory that it is no remedy at all, the unfavorable change in law may be given substantial weight; the district court may conclude that dismissal would not be in the interests of justice.[22] In these cases, however, the remedies that would be provided by the Scottish courts do not fall within this category. Although the relatives of the decedents may not be able to rely on a strict liability theory, and although their potential damages award may be smaller, there is no danger that they will be deprived of any remedy or treated unfairly.

III

The Court of Appeals also erred in rejecting the District Court's *Gilbert* analysis. The Court of Appeals stated that more weight should have been given to the plaintiff's choice of forum, and criticized the District Court's analysis of the private and public interests. However, the District Court's decision regarding the deference due plaintiff's choice of forum was appropriate. Furthermore, we do not believe that the District Court abused its discretion in weighing the private and public interests.

....

The District Court acknowledged that there is ordinarily a strong presumption in favor of the plaintiff's choice of forum, which may be overcome only when the private and public interest factors clearly point towards trial in the alternative forum. It held, however, that the presumption applies with less force when the plaintiff or real parties in interest are foreign.

The District Court's distinction between resident or citizen plaintiffs and foreign plaintiffs is fully justified. In *Koster*, the Court indicated that a plaintiff's choice of forum is entitled to greater deference when the plaintiff has chosen the home forum....[23] When the home forum has been chosen, it is reasonable to assume that this choice is convenient. When the plaintiff is foreign, however, this assumption is much less reasonable. Because the central purpose of any *forum non conveniens* inquiry is to ensure that the trial is convenient, a foreign plaintiff's choice deserves less deference.[24]

---

22. At the outset of any *forum non conveniens* inquiry, the court must determine whether there exists an alternative forum. Ordinarily, this requirement will be satisfied when the defendant is "amenable to process" in the other jurisdiction.... In rare circumstances, however, where the remedy offered by the other forum is clearly unsatisfactory, the other forum may not be an adequate alternative, and the initial requirement may not be satisfied. Thus, for example, dismissal would not be appropriate where the alternative forum does not permit litigation of the subject matter of the dispute....

23. In *Koster*, we stated that "[i]n any balancing of conveniences, a real showing of convenience by a plaintiff who has sued in his home forum will normally outweigh the inconvenience the defendant may have shown."...

As the District Court correctly noted in its opinion, ... the lower federal courts have routinely given less weight to a foreign plaintiff's choice of forum....

A citizen's forum choice should not be given dispositive weight, however.... Citizens or residents deserve somewhat more deference than foreign plaintiffs, but dismissal should not be automatically barred when a plaintiff has filed suit in his home forum. As always, if the balance of conveniences suggests that trial in the chosen forum would be unnecessarily burdensome for the defendant or the court, dismissal is proper.

24. ....

Respondent argues that since plaintiffs will ordinarily file suit in the jurisdiction that offers the most favorable law, establishing a strong presumption in favor of both home and foreign plaintiffs will ensure that defendants will always be held to the highest possible standard of accountability for their

. . . .

The *forum non conveniens* determination is committed to the sound discretion of the trial court. It may be reversed only when there has been a clear abuse of discretion; where the court has considered all relevant public and private interest factors, and where its balancing of these factors is reasonable, its decision deserves substantial deference. . . . Here, the Court of Appeals expressly acknowledged that the standard of review was one of abuse of discretion. In examining the District Court's analysis of the public and private interests, however, the Court of Appeals seems to have lost sight of this rule, and substituted its own judgment for that of the District Court.

. . . .

In analyzing the private interest factors, the District Court stated that the connections with Scotland are "overwhelming." . . . This characterization may be somewhat exaggerated. Particularly with respect to the question of relative ease of access to sources of proof, the private interests point in both directions. As respondent emphasizes, records concerning the design, manufacture, and testing of the propeller and plane are located in the United States. She would have greater access to sources of proof relevant to her strict liability and negligence theories if trial were held here.[25] However, the District Court did not act unreasonably in concluding that fewer evidentiary problems would be posed if the trial were held in Scotland. A large proportion of the relevant evidence is located in Great Britain.

The Court of Appeals found that the problems of proof could not be given any weight because Piper and Hartzell failed to describe with specificity the evidence they would not be able to obtain if trial were held in the United States. It suggested that defendants seeking *forum non conveniens* dismissal must submit affidavits identifying the witnesses they would call and the testimony these witnesses would provide if the trial were held in the alternative forum. Such detail is not necessary. Piper and Hartzell have moved for dismissal precisely because many crucial witnesses are located beyond the reach of compulsory process, and thus are difficult to identify or interview. Requiring extensive investigation would defeat the purpose of their motion. Of course, defendants must provide enough information to enable the District Court to balance the parties' interests. Our examination of the record convinces us that sufficient information was provided here. Both Piper and Hartzell submitted affidavits describing the evidentiary problems they would face if the trial were held in the United States.

The District Court correctly concluded that the problems posed by the inability to implead potential third-party defendants clearly supported holding the trial in Scotland. Joinder of the pilot's estate, Air Navigation, and McDonald is crucial to the presentation of petitioners' defense. If Piper and Hartzell can show that the accident was caused not by a design defect, but rather by the negligence of the pilot, the plane's owners, or the charter company, they will be relieved of all liability. It is true, of course, that if Hartzell and Piper were found liable after a trial in the United States, they could institute an action for indemnity or contribution against these parties in Scotland. It would be far more convenient, however, to resolve all claims in one trial. The Court of Appeals rejected this argument. Forcing petitioners to rely on actions for indemnity or contributions would be "burdensome"

---

purported wrongdoing. However, the deference accorded a plaintiff's choice of forum has never been intended to guarantee that the plaintiff will be able to select the law that will govern the case. . . .

25. In the future, where similar problems are presented, district courts might dismiss subject to the condition that defendant corporations agree to provide the records relevant to the plaintiff's claims.

but not "unfair." ... Finding that trial in the plaintiff's chosen forum would be burdensome, however, is sufficient to support dismissal on grounds of *forum non conveniens.*

....

The District Court's review of the factors relating to the public interest was also reasonable. On the basis of its choice-of-law analysis, it concluded that if the case were tried in the Middle District of Pennsylvania, Pennsylvania law would apply to Piper and Scottish law to Hartzell. It stated that a trial involving two sets of laws would be confusing to the jury. It also noted its own lack of familiarity with Scottish law. Consideration of these problems was clearly appropriate under *Gilbert*; in that case we explicitly held that the need to apply foreign law pointed towards dismissal.[29] The Court of Appeals found that the District Court's choice-of-law analysis was incorrect, and that American law would apply to both Hartzell and Piper. Thus, lack of familiarity with foreign law would not be a problem. Even if the Court of Appeals' conclusion is correct, however, all other public interest factors favored trial in Scotland.

Scotland has a very strong interest in this litigation. The accident occurred in its airspace. All of the decedents were Scottish. Apart from Piper and Hartzell, all potential plaintiffs and defendants are either Scottish or English. As we stated in *Gilbert*, there is "a local interest in having localized controversies decided at home." ... Respondent argues that American citizens have an interest in ensuring that American manufacturers are deterred from producing defective products, and that additional deterrence might be obtained if Piper and Hartzell were tried in the United States, where they could be sued on the basis of both negligence and strict liability. However, the incremental deterrence that would be gained if this trial were held in an American court is likely to be insignificant. The American interest in this accident is simply not sufficient to justify the enormous commitment of judicial time and resources that would inevitably be required if the case were to be tried here.

IV

The Court of Appeals erred in holding that the possibility of an unfavorable change in law bars dismissal on the ground of *forum non conveniens.* It also erred in rejecting the District Court's *Gilbert* analysis. The District Court properly decided that the presumption in favor of the respondent's forum choice applied with less than maximum force because the real parties in interest are foreign. It did not act unreasonably in deciding that the private interests pointed towards trial in Scotland. Nor did it act unreasonably in deciding that the public interests favored trial in Scotland. Thus, the judgment of the Court of Appeals is

Reversed.

[The opinion of JUSTICE WHITE, who concurred in part and dissented in part, is omitted.]

Notes and Questions

1. As noted in *Piper Aircraft*, the doctrine of forum non conveniens presupposes that another court exists in which the action may be brought. Therefore, a court will not dismiss on forum non conveniens grounds if, for example, no other court can obtain personal jurisdiction over the defendant. Similarly, a court will not dismiss on forum non conveniens grounds if the action will be barred by limitations in the alternative forum.

---

29. Many *forum non conveniens* decisions have held that the need to apply foreign law favors dismissal.... Of course, this factor alone is not sufficient to warrant dismissal when a balancing of all relevant factors shows that the plaintiff's chosen forum is appropriate....

A forum non conveniens dismissal can be conditioned on the defendant's agreement to submit to personal jurisdiction or waive statute-of-limitations objections in the alternative forum. As noted in the procedural history in *Piper Aircraft,* for instance, both Piper and Hartzell, as part of their motion, agreed to submit to the jurisdiction of the Scottish courts and waive any statute-of-limitations defense.

2. The doctrine of forum non conveniens is an exception to the usual preference given to the plaintiff's choice of a forum. Ordinarily, as long as the plaintiff complies with subject-matter jurisdiction, personal jurisdiction, and venue requirements, the plaintiff's choice of forum is respected. As indicated in *Piper Aircraft*, the burden is on the defendant to justify a dismissal based on forum non conveniens. Note, however, the statement in *Piper Aircraft* that the plaintiff's choice will be given less deference when the plaintiff chooses a foreign court.

3. It is clear, is it not, that the plaintiff's choice of forum may be heavily influenced by a desire to obtain a favorable applicable substantive law? It is equally clear that a defendant will not move for a dismissal based on forum non conveniens unless the substantive law that will be applied by the alternative forum is at least as favorable to the defendant as the substantive law that would be applied by the forum. These calculations require both the plaintiff and the defendant to consider not only the substantive rules of the forum and the alternative forum, but also the conflict-of-laws rules that would be applied by those jurisdictions. Thus, the battle over the forum non conveniens issue will, in many cases, be waged for the purpose of obtaining a favorable result on the merits under different applicable substantive laws in the forum and the alternative forum.

4. *Piper Aircraft* speaks with two voices on the issue discussed in the preceding note. On one hand, the Court states that an unfavorable change in the substantive law applicable to the plaintiff's claim should not ordinarily be given substantial weight in determining whether to dismiss on forum non conveniens grounds. On the other hand, the Court noted that a change in the applicable substantive law may be given substantial weight when the remedy in the alternative forum "is so clearly inadequate or unsatisfactory that it is no remedy at all." Such a result may be a feature of the principle that a dismissal based on forum non conveniens is not available unless there is an alternative forum. However, suppose the alternative forum is (a) a jurisdiction where the events giving rise to the claim occurred, (b) is the plaintiff's home state or nation, and (c) would not give the plaintiff a remedy under the circumstances of the case. Why should a court considering a forum non conveniens dismissal give any weight to the fact that dismissal will deprive the plaintiff of a remedy? Instead, why should the plaintiff not be made to live with the result that would be reached by the plaintiff's home state or nation?

5. In *Piper Aircraft*, the U.S. Supreme Court discouraged forum non conveniens inquiries that would involve complex choice-of-law determinations. How can it be determined whether the plaintiff will totally be deprived of a remedy in the alternative forum unless the court undertakes a choice-of-law inquiry? Furthermore, in evaluating the public interest factors pertinent to the forum non conveniens decision, it is relevant to determine whether the forum will have to apply foreign law if the case is not dismissed and whether the alternative forum will have to apply the forum's law if the case is dismissed. This is because the law that must be applied by the respective courts is also relevant to the convenience of adjudicating the case one place rather than another. The necessity of applying unfamiliar and perhaps complicated substantive law will increase the burden of litigation on whichever court adjudicates the action. Therefore, since choice-of-law analysis is an inevitable part of every forum non conveniens determination, how does the Supreme Court expect the lower courts to avoid a complex choice-of-law inquiry?

6. In *Piper Aircraft*, the Court states that forum non conveniens dismissals are within the discretion of the trial court and are to be reviewed accordingly. What might a trial court do or fail to do in a forum non conveniens analysis that would constitute an abuse of discretion?

7. Recall from Chapter 2 that the minimum contacts test limits the location of suit to reasonably nonburdensome fora. Should convenient forum decisions be made through the Due Process Clause or through the doctrine of forum non conveniens?

Problems

Problem 3-13. P, a citizen of Country *X*, is the administrator of the estate of *A*, a citizen of Country *X* who died in an aircraft crash in Country *X*. *P* sues *D*, a corporation incorporated in and with its principal place of business in State *Y* of the United States. *P* seeks $1,000,000 in damages for the wrongful death of *A*. *D* is the manufacturer of the aircraft in which *A* was a passenger at the time of his death. *P* brings the action in the U.S. District Court for the District of State *Y*. *D* moves to dismiss on the ground of forum non conveniens. State the information that you would like to have to determine whether *D's* motion should be granted.

Problem 3-14. On the facts of *Problem 3-13*, assume that Country *X* does not recognize actions for wrongful death and would apply its own substantive law to the action if the case were filed there. State the arguments that would be made by *D* to overcome the *Piper Aircraft* dictum, discussed in Note 4, above, and prevent the trial court from giving substantial weight to the absence of a remedy in Country *X*. State the arguments that would be made by *P* to refute *D's* arguments.

Problem 3-15. P, a citizen of State *X*, and *D*, a citizen of State *Y*, have a car accident in Quebec, Canada. *P* sues *D* in the U.S. District Court for the District of State *Y* to recover $1,000,000 for personal injuries inflicted due to *D's* negligence in causing the accident. Quebec does not recognize common-law actions for negligence. Instead, Quebec provides a statutory scheme of no-fault compensation for victims of accidents and places a statutory cap on the amount that victims can receive—a cap that is far less than the amount *P* seeks to recover. *D* moves to dismiss the action on the ground of forum non conveniens. *P* argues that the Quebec scheme of compensation meets the qualification in *Piper Aircraft* and "is so clearly inadequate and unsatisfactory that it is no remedy at all." Therefore, *P* argues that the unfavorable change in law that would result from a forum non conveniens dismissal should be given substantial weight in this case. Evaluate the plaintiff's argument. Besides the adequacy or inadequacy of Quebec's remedy, is any other part of the *Piper Aircraft* analysis relevant to the question whether a forum non conveniens dismissal would be appropriate on the facts of this problem?

Section E. Forum-Selection Clauses

Like personal jurisdiction, venue is a waivable objection. As previously explained, a defendant in federal court can waive a venue objection by failing to raise the defense in proper and timely fashion under Rule 12(h)(1). As with personal jurisdiction, waiver can also occur through contractual provisions entered into before a dispute arises. Many contracts include a "forum-selection" clause. A forum-selection clause will usually provide that suit on the contract may be brought only in the courts of the chosen forum. In terms of personal jurisdiction, a forum-selection clause also means that the parties have consented to personal jurisdiction in the chosen forum. A forum-selection clause thus has dual significance. As a plaintiff, the party has waived any choice in selecting the forum and as a defendant, the party has waived any challenge to personal jurisdiction in the selected forum. The wording of the forum-selection clause appearing in the *Carnival Cruise Lines* case, below, is typical.

Validity of "Forum-Selection" Clauses. Traditionally, American courts almost unanimously held forum-selection clauses to be invalid against public policy. The traditional notion was that parties should not be able to oust a court of jurisdiction through a contract clause. More recently, however, such clauses have come to be generally, although not universally, enforced. For example, in *M/S Bremen v. Zapata Off-Shore Co.*, 407 U.S. 1 (1972), the Supreme Court, as a matter of federal law, held a clause providing for disputes to be resolved before the London Court of Justice to be valid. In *Bremen*, a tug owner had contracted to tow a barge from Louisiana to Italy. The Court pointed out that (1) the American company had special expertise and had contracted with a foreign company, (2) the parties were experienced and sophisticated, and (3) the towing contract had been entered into after "arms' length" negotiations. *Id.* at 9, 12. In such circumstances, the Court held the forum-selection clause to be prima facie valid and was to be honored by the parties and enforced by courts in absence of some compelling and countervailing reason making enforcement unreasonable. *Id.* at 10–19.

Unlike the situation in *Bremen* in which the forum-selection clause was freely negotiated by equally positioned parties, the issue in *Carnival Cruise Lines* was the enforceability of such a clause against a consumer in a form contract.

Carnival Cruise Lines, Inc. v. Shute

United States Supreme Court, 1991
499 U.S. 585, 111 S. Ct. 1522, 113 L. Ed. 2d 622

JUSTICE BLACKMUN delivered the opinion of the Court.

In this admiralty case we primarily consider whether the United States Court of Appeals for the Ninth Circuit correctly refused to enforce a forum-selection clause contained in tickets issued by petitioner Carnival Cruise Lines, Inc., to respondents Eulala and Russel Shute.

. . . .

The Shutes, through an Arlington, Washington, travel agent, purchased passage for a 7-day cruise on petitioner's ship, the *Tropicale*. Respondents paid the fare to the agent who forwarded the payment to petitioner's headquarters in Miami, Fla. Petitioner then prepared the tickets and sent them to respondents in the State of Washington. The face of each ticket, at its left-hand lower corner, contained this admonition: "SUBJECT TO CONDITIONS OF CONTRACT ON LAST PAGES **IMPORTANT!** PLEASE READ CONTRACT—ON LAST PAGES 1, 2, 3". . . . [*words on Ticket*]

The following appeared on "contract page 1" of each ticket:

TERMS AND CONDITIONS OF PASSAGE CONTRACT TICKET

. . . .

3. (a) The acceptance of this ticket by the person or persons named hereon as passengers shall be deemed to be an acceptance and agreement by each of them of all of the terms and conditions of this Passage Contract Ticket.

....

8. It is agreed by and between the passenger and the Carrier that all disputes and matters whatsoever arising under, in connection with or incident to this Contract shall be litigated, if at all, in and before a Court located in the State of Florida, U.S.A., to the exclusion of the Courts of any other state or country.

The last quoted paragraph is the forum-selection clause at issue.

....

Respondents boarded the *Tropicale* in Los Angeles, Cal. The ship sailed to Puerto Vallarta, Mexico, and then returned to Los Angeles. While the ship was in international waters off the Mexican coast, respondent Eulala Shute was injured when she slipped on a deck mat during a guided tour of the ship's galley. Respondents filed suit against petitioner in the United States District Court for the Western District of Washington, claiming that Mrs. Shute's injuries had been caused by the negligence of Carnival Cruise Lines and its employees....

Petitioner moved for summary judgment, contending that the forum clause in respondents' tickets required the Shutes to bring their suit against petitioner in a court in the State of Florida....

....

We begin by noting the boundaries of our inquiry. First, this is a case in admiralty, and federal law governs the enforceability of the forum-selection clause we scrutinize.... Second, we do not address the question whether respondents had sufficient notice of the forum clause before entering the contract for passage. Respondents essentially have conceded that they had notice of the forum-selection provision. Brief for Respondents 26 ("The respondents do not contest the incorporation of the provisions nor [*sic*] that the forum[-]selection clause was reasonably communicated to the respondents, as much as three pages of fine print can be communicated").... Within this context, respondents urge that the forum clause should not be enforced because, contrary to this Court's teachings in *The Bremen*, the clause was not the product of negotiation, and enforcement effectively would deprive respondents of their day in court. Additionally, respondents contend that the clause violates the Limitation of Vessel Owner's Liability Act, 46 U.S.C. App. § 183c. We consider these arguments in turn.

....

[R]espondents' passage contract was purely routine and doubtless nearly identical to every commercial passage contract issued by petitioner and most other cruise lines.... In this context, it would be entirely unreasonable for us to assume that respondents—or any other cruise passenger—would negotiate with petitioner the terms of a forum-selection clause in an ordinary commercial cruise ticket. Common sense dictates that a ticket of this kind will be a form contract the terms of which are not subject to negotiation, and that an individual purchasing the ticket will not have bargaining parity with the cruise line....

.... First, a cruise line has a special interest in limiting the fora in which it potentially could be subject to suit. Because a cruise ship typically carries passengers from many locales, it is not unlikely that a mishap on a cruise could subject the cruise line to litigation in several different fora.... Additionally, a clause establishing *ex ante* the forum for dispute resolution has the salutary effect of dispelling any confusion about where suits arising from the contract must be brought and defended, sparing litigants the time and expense of pretrial motions to determine the correct forum and conserving judicial resources that otherwise would be devoted to deciding those motions.... Finally, it stands to reason that passengers who purchase tickets containing a forum clause like that at issue in this case benefit in the form of reduced fares reflecting the savings that the cruise line enjoys by limiting the fora in which it may be sued....

. . . .

It bears emphasis that forum-selection clauses contained in form passage contracts are subject to judicial scrutiny for fundamental fairness. In this case, there is no indication that petitioner set Florida as the forum in which disputes were to be resolved as a means of discouraging cruise passengers from pursuing legitimate claims. Any suggestion of such a bad-faith motive is belied by two facts: Petitioner has its principal place of business in Florida, and many of its cruises depart from and return to Florida ports. Similarly, there is no evidence that petitioner obtained respondents' accession to the forum clause by fraud or overreaching. Finally, respondents have conceded that they were given notice of the forum provision and, therefore, presumably retained the option of rejecting the contract with impunity. In the case before us, therefore, we conclude that the Court of Appeals erred in refusing to enforce the forum-selection clause.

. . . .

The judgment of the Court of Appeals is reversed.

It is so ordered.

Justice Stevens, with whom Justice Marshall joins, dissenting.

. . . .

Forum-selection clauses in passenger tickets involve the intersection of two strands of traditional contract law that qualify the general rule that courts will enforce the terms of a contract as written. Pursuant to the first strand, courts traditionally have reviewed with heightened scrutiny the terms of contracts of adhesion, form contracts offered on a take-or-leave basis by a party with stronger bargaining power to a party with weaker power. Some commentators have questioned whether contracts of adhesion can justifiably be enforced at all under traditional contract theory because the adhering party generally enters into them without manifesting knowing and voluntary consent to all their terms....

. . . .

The second doctrinal principle implicated by forum-selection clauses is the traditional rule that "contractual provisions, which seek to limit the place or court in which an action may ... be brought, are invalid as contrary to public policy." ... Although adherence to this general rule has declined in recent years, particularly following our decision in *The Bremen v. Zapata Off-Shore Co.*, 407 U.S. 1 (1972), the prevailing rule is still that forum-selection clauses are not enforceable if they were not freely bargained for, create additional expense for one party, or deny one party a remedy....

. . . .

Notes and Questions

1. *Carnival Cruise Lines* was a case based on federal admiralty jurisdiction. The Court's reasoning, however, is applicable with respect to the general enforceability of forum-selection clauses as a matter of federal common law and in other areas controlled by federal law. Do you agree with the Court's reasoning on this issue? Do the reasons given for holding the forum-selection clause enforceable place any real restrictions on the enforcement of such clauses? For example, in what kind of circumstances might "fundamental fairness" provide a significant restriction?

2. The reasoning in *Carnival Cruise Lines* is not binding in the determination of venue in state court action; and a number of state courts, contra to the analysis in *Carnival Cruise Lines,* have refused to enforce forum-selection clauses based on unequal bargaining power in "contracts of adhesion." *See, e.g., America Online, Inc. v. Superior Court*, 108 Cal. Rptr. 2d 699 (Ct. App. 2001), in which the court refused to enforce a forum-selection clause and a choice-of-law clause in a contract between AOL and its online consumer subscribers. The contract required that all actions be filed in Virginia and be governed by Virginia substantive law. AOL subscribers filed a class action against AOL in California under various California consumer protection laws. AOL, similar to Carnival Cruise Lines, filed a motion to dismiss the class action in California based on the contract provisions.

The court refused to enforce these provisions, noting that "[o]ur law favors forum selection agreements only so long as they are procured freely and voluntarily, with the place chosen having some logical nexus to one of the parties or the dispute, and so long as California consumers will not find their substantial legal rights significantly impaired by their enforcement." *Id.* at 707. The court found that the contract was not freely negotiated, that Virginia substantive law was "ostensibl[y] hostile to [consumer] class actions" and that the many protections afforded to California consumers under California substantive law would be eviscerated if the plaintiffs were forced to proceed with their case in Virginia and required to sue under Virginia substantive law. *Id.* at 708–20.

Forum-Selection Clauses and Transfer. Forum-selection clauses are also relevant in cases of transfer under § 1404(a). In *Stewart Organization v. Ricoh Corp.*, 487 U.S. 22 (1988), the Supreme Court held that the existence of a forum-selection clause would not absolutely control the question whether a case should be transferred under § 1404(a). Instead, such a clause would be weighed in the balance along with all other factors to determine whether transfer is appropriate. *Stewart Organization* has proved to be a controversial decision. In particular, the Court's determination that federal law in the form of § 1404(a) controlled the effect of a forum-selection clause, rather than the state law of contracts, has been criticized. This aspect of the decision will be examined in Chapter 5.

Notes and Questions

1. Do you think *Stewart Organization v. Ricoh* was correctly decided as a simple matter of statutory interpretation? When a procedural statute such as § 1404(a) does not say anything about a particular subject (such as forum-selection clauses), is it the "plain meaning" of the statute that it controls the unmentioned subject? Or is it the "plain meaning" of the statute that it does not control the unmentioned subject?

2. (a) Should a case like *Stewart Organization* be treated as one in which venue is proper in the transferor district as long as the general federal venue statutes are satisfied? Or should it be treated as one in which venue is improper because it was commenced in a place prohibited by the forum-selection clause? Doesn't this issue have an important bearing on whether transfer should be under § 1404(a) or under § 1406? The U.S. Supreme Court did not discuss this issue in *Stewart Organization*. *But see In re Atlantic Marine Constr. Co.*, 701 F.3d 736 (5th Cir. 2012) (proper procedural mechanism for raising an issue involving a forum-selection clause is a motion to transfer under § 1404(a), not a motion for improper venue under Rule 12(b)(3) and § 1406).

(b) Is it possible to argue that *neither* § 1404(a) *nor* § 1406 was applicable to the issue in *Stewart Organization*?

3. If federal statutory venue is proper and personal jurisdiction exists over the defendant, but the action has been brought in federal court contrary to a forum-selection clause limiting the venue to a particular state court, can the federal court dismiss the action after *Stewart Organization*? *See International Software Sys., Inc. v. Amplicon, Inc.*, 77 F.3d 112 (5th Cir. 1996) (yes).

Section F. Injunctions Against Extrastate Litigation and Stays of Forum Proceedings

In addition to the mechanisms discussed in the previous sections, American courts sometimes employ two other means of controlling the location of suit: injunctions against suits pending in another forum and stay of forum proceedings in deference to litigation pending in another forum.

Injunctions Against Extrastate Litigation. The general rule is that parallel actions in different jurisdictions are allowed to proceed until a judgment is rendered in one place that can be pleaded as res judicata in another state. However, under certain circumstances, American courts will grant injunctions to restrain one of the parties from proceeding in another forum. The injunction is not issued against the foreign court, only against the party. If the party refuses to discontinue the foreign action, the injunction must be enforced through contempt proceedings against the party in the injunction-rendering court.

There are two general approaches to injunctions against foreign litigation. One approach permits injunctions only to protect the jurisdiction of the forum court or to prevent evasion of important public policies of the forum that would be undermined by the foreign litigation. The other approach also permits injunctions to protect the forum court's jurisdiction and prevent undermining of the forum's important public policies, but it also allows injunctions against foreign suits in order to (1) prevent "vexation and oppression" and (2) on the basis of "other equitable considerations." Although the grounds articulated under both approaches may seem broad enough to cover any conceivable case, the cases under both approaches actually administer the standards quite conservatively, with the result that injunctions against foreign litigation are relatively rare.

An example of a successful case is *Churchill Corp. v. Third Century, Inc.*, 578 A.2d 532 (Pa. Super. Ct. 1990). In this case, a small Pennsylvania corporation entered into a short-term lease of a single piece of office equipment from a large and established Missouri corporation doing business in Pennsylvania. After the item failed to operate, the Pennsylvania lessee stopped payments. The lessor then filed a collection action against the lessee in a rural Missouri county pursuant to a forum-selection clause in the lease requiring suit there. Rather than incurring the substantial expense of traveling to Missouri to challenge the action, the lessee filed the instant action in Pennsylvania seeking an injunction against the lessor from proceeding with the Missouri action. The Pennsylvania court refused to enforce the forum-selection clause and granted the injunction. The court found the clause "unfair and arguably unconscionable" noting that it was a "boilerplate" provision in a form contract drafted by the lessor which possessed superior bargaining power and resources. The court further found that the transportation and witness expenses for the lessees to travel to the designated rural Missouri county would render access to the court impractical and that the Missouri courts did not otherwise possess personal jurisdiction over the lessee. *Id.* at 535–40.

Stay of Forum Proceedings. Many state courts will abate a proceeding involving the same parties and subject matter in favor of a prior pending action in the same state. Usually, courts will not abate proceedings in favor of actions in other states, but a few state courts exercise discretion to stay (as opposed to abate or dismiss) an action in favor of an action in another jurisdiction. The main reason courts grant such stays is to prevent vexation of defendants when there is no apparent reason for the plaintiff to bring two identical actions in different states. When an action in the forum is stayed in favor of another action in a different state, a judgment in the latter action will control the forum action under the ordinary principles of res judicata because the full-faith-and-credit implementing statute, 28 U.S.C. § 1738, requires the courts in each state to give the same effect to the judgments of other states as those judgments would receive in the state where they are rendered.

Chapter 4

Subject-Matter Jurisdiction

The concept of subject-matter jurisdiction in the state and federal courts of the United States was introduced in Chapter 1. This chapter examines subject-matter jurisdiction in greater depth by focusing primarily on the federal court system because it provides a convenient model for the study of subject-matter jurisdiction generally. Federal courts exist within every state, and the practice in the federal courts is the same, or very similar, everywhere. Thus, study of the basic jurisdictional grants to these courts is useful to practitioners throughout the country.

In addition, the business of the federal courts, particularly their role in interpreting the U.S. Constitution and federal laws, is of increasing importance in our national life. Study of the federal courts is also essential in providing a foundation for understanding the relationship between the state and federal judicial systems, which you will later study in courses on Federal Courts and Conflict of Laws, among other subjects. Furthermore, although the subject-matter rules of the state and federal courts differ, some overlap exists between federal and state subject-matter jurisdiction concepts. Therefore, study of federal subject-matter jurisdiction has utility in understanding state practice as well.

Section A. Overview of the Subject-Matter Jurisdiction of the Federal Courts

1. The Federal Judicial System

Judicial Power Under Article III. Article III, § 1 of the U.S. Constitution provides that "[t]he judicial Power of the United States shall be vested in one [S]upreme Court, and in such inferior Courts as the Congress may from time to time ordain and establish." Although the establishment of a Supreme Court is constitutionally mandated under Article III, the Constitution does not explicitly require the establishment of the lower federal courts, but gives Congress discretion whether to create such courts. This provision represented a compromise at the Constitutional Convention (called the "Madisonian compromise") between those framers who felt that the creation of the lower federal courts should be constitutionally required and those who felt that only a Supreme Court was necessary with original jurisdiction over certain matters and appellate jurisdiction over state court decisions.

Structure and Organization of the Federal Courts. In the Judicial Code, Congress has provided for the organization of the U.S. Supreme Court, which consists of nine Justices and sits atop the federal judicial system. Under the current judicial structure, Congress has also created two layers of lower federal courts inferior to the Supreme Court. The

U.S. District Courts comprise the bottom layer and are the principal federal trial courts of original jurisdiction. Currently, eighty-nine federal "judicial districts" are located throughout the fifty states in addition to one each for the District of Columbia and Puerto Rico. Each state has at least one judicial district, and some of the larger states have more than one. New York, for instance, is divided into Eastern, Southern, Northern, and Western Districts. Many judicial districts are also further divided into "divisions." The Northern District of Alabama, for instance, is divided into seven divisions.

The U.S. Courts of Appeals constitute the intermediate layer and are courts of appellate jurisdiction. Of the current thirteen federal courts of appeals, eleven are numbered federal judicial circuits. They are located throughout the United States and are identified as the U.S. Court of Appeals for the First, Second, etc. Circuit. The twelfth is the U.S. Court of Appeals for the District of Columbia Circuit. These courts review decisions of the U.S. District Courts located within their geographic regions. The thirteenth court of appeals is the U.S. Court of Appeals for the Federal Circuit, which hears appeals from all district courts involving patents, certain claims against the federal government, and other specialized cases.

Congress has also created several specialized lower federal tribunals. The Court of International Trade has jurisdiction over claims involving various tariffs and other federal trade agreements. It is created under Congress' Article III power. Other specialized courts include the Court of Federal Claims, the Tax Court, and the District Courts for the United States Territories, *e.g.*, Guam and the Virgin Islands. The Court of Federal Claims has jurisdiction over certain damage claims against the United States.

The District Courts for U.S. Territories are created pursuant to Congress' legislative powers to regulate the Territories under Article I of the Constitution. Similarly, the Tax Court is created pursuant to Congress' Article I power to "lay and collect Taxes." The exact ability of these Article I courts to exercise Article III judicial powers is subject to debate. For our purposes, though, it is only essential that you are aware of the existence of these additional specialized courts. Judgments from the specialized courts are reviewed by the appropriate U.S. Court of Appeals, with appeals from the Courts of International Trade and Federal Claims heard by the Federal Circuit Court of Appeals.

The Bankruptcy Courts and the Magistrate Judges, also created under Article I, serve as adjuncts to the district courts. Congress has also established a separate court system for the District of Columbia with jurisdiction over local matters, but these courts are distinct from and should not be confused with the U.S. District Court and U.S. Court of Appeals for the D.C. Circuit.

2. Federal Courts as Courts of Limited Jurisdiction

Although it may seem from your observation of modern society that the federal government is an entity with all-encompassing authority, the U.S. Constitution actually created a national government with limited powers. A fundamental principle of United States constitutional law is that all three branches of government—legislative, executive, and judicial—possess only those powers that are expressly or impliedly granted to them in the U.S. Constitution. Under the original constitutional scheme, reiterated by the Tenth Amendment of the Constitution, all other powers are reserved to the States or to the people. Under this constitutional structure, therefore, all federal courts, including the Supreme Court, are courts of limited subject-matter jurisdiction.

Article III, § 2 of the Constitution defines the outer limits of federal court jurisdiction and expressly enumerates nine categories of cases and controversies to which federal judicial power extends:

(1) "all Cases, in Law and Equity, arising under this Constitution, the Laws of the United States, and Treaties made, or which shall be made, under their Authority";

(2) "all Cases affecting Ambassadors, other public Ministers and Consuls";

(3) "all Cases of admiralty and maritime jurisdiction";

(4) "Controversies to which the United States shall be a Party";

(5) "Controversies between two or more States";

(6) Controversies "between a State and Citizens of another State";

(7) Controversies "between Citizens of different States";

(8) Controversies "between Citizens of the same State claiming Lands under Grants of different States"; and

(9) Controversies "between a State, or the Citizens thereof, and foreign States, Citizens or Subjects."

Despite the wording of Article III that federal judicial power "shall be vested" and "shall extend," the U.S. Supreme Court has repeatedly held (with certain limited exceptions concerning the jurisdiction of the U.S. Supreme Court) that (1) Article III does not directly grant subject-matter jurisdiction to the federal courts and (2) such jurisdiction "lies dormant" until brought to life by a jurisdictional statute enacted by Congress.

3. Subject-Matter Jurisdiction of the U.S. Supreme Court

Although Article III, § 2 of the Constitution defines the scope of federal subject-matter jurisdiction, the second paragraph of § 2 expressly grants *original* jurisdiction only to the U.S. Supreme Court and only in specified cases (*i.e.*, "[i]n all Cases affecting Ambassadors, other public Ministers and Counsels, and those in which a State shall be [a] Party"). This grant of original jurisdiction to the Supreme Court is the one jurisdictional grant in Article III that is traditionally considered to be both "self-executing" and free from limitation by Congress. Although Article III grants original jurisdiction directly to the Supreme Court in these cases without the need for a jurisdictional statute, the Constitution is silent as to whether the Supreme Court's jurisdiction in these cases is *exclusive*. This question is answered by 28 U.S.C. § 1251, which defines the kinds of cases in which the Court's original jurisdiction is exclusive.

Article III, § 2 also establishes the appellate jurisdiction of the Supreme Court, but this constitutional grant is expressly subject to "such Exceptions, and under such Regulations as the Congress shall make" and thus is not completely immune from limitation by Congress. Sections 1253–1259 of Title 28 of the United States Code currently define the appellate jurisdiction of the Supreme Court. By affirmatively defining the kinds of cases in which the appellate jurisdiction exists, but leaving out others in which jurisdiction is authorized by Article III, it has traditionally been understood that Congress has made "exceptions" to the constitutional scope of the appellate jurisdiction in the cases omitted from the statutory grant of appellate jurisdiction. For example, as you will learn in section C, Article III, § 2 (seventh clause) provides constitutional authority for the federal courts to hear all controversies "between Citizens of different States" even though the controversies may involve purely state law issues. Under 28 U.S.C. § 1257, however, Congress expressly limits the Supreme Court's appellate jurisdiction to review a decision by a State's highest court to cases involving a United States treaty, law or Constitutional provision.

4. Subject-Matter Jurisdiction of the Lower Federal Courts and the Need for Both Constitutional and Statutory Authority

With respect to the lower federal courts, all grants of subject-matter jurisdiction, whether appellate or original, must be affirmatively authorized by Congress. Moreover, the U.S. Supreme Court has consistently held that in enacting a jurisdictional statute, Congress is not obligated to grant to the federal courts the full scope of the judicial power potentially authorized in Article III, § 2. The theory underlying this principle is that Congress has the constitutional authority to create the lower federal courts or not to create them, in its discretion; thus, Congress has the corresponding authority to define, within the ultimate boundaries of Article III, the actual scope of the subject-matter jurisdiction that the federal courts shall be permitted to exercise. Congress, of course, may not expand the jurisdiction of the federal courts beyond the boundaries established by the Constitution (the nine categories of cases and controversies enumerated in Article III, § 2).

From the first Judiciary Act in 1789 to the present, Congress has never granted to the lower federal courts the full scope of the judicial power that is possible under Article III. The two main jurisdictional statutes that you will study, 28 U.S.C. §§ 1331–1332, illustrate this point. These sections grant subject-matter jurisdiction to the federal district courts in "federal question" and "diversity" cases, respectively. Currently, the original jurisdiction of the district courts is defined in 28 U.S.C. §§ 1330–1368, and the appellate jurisdiction of the courts of appeals is defined in 28 U.S.C. §§ 1291–1296. As observed in Chapter 1, Congress has also generally authorized "removal" jurisdiction from the state courts to the federal district courts in certain kinds of cases.

Therefore, subject-matter jurisdiction in the lower federal courts does not properly exist in any case unless *both* constitutional and statutory authorization are present. A case must fit within one of the nine categories of Article III, § 2. In addition, Congress must have enacted a statute to confer on the lower federal courts jurisdiction within the Article III category. A case need not satisfy all or more than one of the constitutional categories or all or more than one of the jurisdictional statutes for subject-matter jurisdiction to exist. With respect to the jurisdiction of the district courts, for instance, if a case "arises under" federal law as defined by Article III, § 2, and "arises under" federal law as defined by 28 U.S.C. § 1331, full subject-matter jurisdiction exists over the case even though the case would not satisfy 28 U.S.C. § 1332 because it is between citizens of the same state or is for less than $75,000.01.

5. Principal Jurisdictional Categories of Article III

Although Article III, § 2 creates nine categories of federal court subject-matter jurisdiction set out above, the principal jurisdictional categories of civil cases commenced by private litigants are set out in Figure 4-1. As you study the following materials, you should remember that the general grants of federal question jurisdiction under 28 U.S.C. § 1331

PRINCIPAL CATEGORIES OF CIVIL CASES COMMENCED BY PRIVATE PARTIES AUTHORIZED BY ARTICLE III	
"Federal Question" Jurisdiction	Cases "arising under" the • U.S. Constitution • Laws of the United States • Treaties
"Diversity" Jurisdiction	Controversies between • Citizens of different states • Citizens of a state and foreign citizens or subjects

Figure 4-1

and diversity jurisdiction under 28 U.S.C. § 1332 are *concurrent* with the jurisdiction of the state courts. Thus, even though federal question or diversity jurisdiction may properly exist in an action, the action may be filed in either federal or state court, at the option of the plaintiff. In certain actions, however, Congress has conferred *exclusive* subject-matter jurisdiction on the federal courts, and these actions must be filed in federal court. Some examples of exclusive federal jurisdiction statutes are 28 U.S.C. § 1333 (admiralty), § 1334 (bankruptcy), and § 1338 (patent and copyright).

6. Seriousness of a Subject-Matter Jurisdiction Defect

As discussed in Chapter 1, subject-matter jurisdiction requirements are treated very seriously in all judicial systems, both state and federal. The parties may not waive subject-matter jurisdiction deficiencies or confer subject-matter jurisdiction on an American court by consent. If the parties do not raise a subject-matter jurisdiction objection, the court in which the action is commenced is obligated to raise the objection on its own initiative, "*sua sponte.*" In the federal system, for instance, Rule 12(h)(3) expressly provides that "[i]f the court determines at any time that it lacks subject-matter jurisdiction, the court must dismiss the action." If neither the parties nor the trial court raises a subject-matter jurisdiction objection, an appellate court before which the case is brought is obligated to raise the objection on its own initiative and reverse the judgment for lack of subject-matter jurisdiction if the objection is valid.

The seriousness with which American courts view questions of subject-matter jurisdiction is attributable to the constitutional doctrine of separation of powers existing in every American jurisdiction. That doctrine presupposes that the fundamental authority of courts is defined and limited by a constitution of the government of which the courts are a part. To the extent that a constitution gives authority to the legislative branch of government to create, define, and limit the powers of the judiciary, the judiciary is supposed to defer to the legislative limits so prescribed.

7. Hierarchical Order of Consideration

The seriousness with which courts treat subject-matter jurisdiction questions also results in hierarchical rules governing the order in which certain kinds of questions should be considered. Generally, subject-matter jurisdiction appears first in the hierarchy of decision-making on "threshold" questions. For example, in *Steel Co. v. Citizens for a Better*

Environment, 523 U.S. 83 (1998), the Supreme Court held that federal courts must first decide whether they have subject-matter jurisdiction over an action before deciding whether the complaint states a claim upon which relief can be granted. *Id.* at 94–95. However, the order is sometimes modified in some circumstances. For example, in *Ruhrgas AG v. Marathon Oil Co.*, 526 U.S. 574 (1999), the Court held that in actions removed from state to federal court, no absolute jurisdictional hierarchy requires the federal courts to consider and dispose of subject-matter jurisdiction objections before considering a challenge to personal jurisdiction. *Id.* at 584–85.

8. Effect of a Dismissal for Lack of Subject-Matter Jurisdiction

Dismissal of a claim for lack of subject-matter jurisdiction in the federal courts is not considered an adjudication on the merits of the claim and, therefore, such claims may be refiled in any state court where subject matter jurisdiction is proper. Dismissals for lack of subject-matter jurisdiction over a claim can sometimes be difficult to distinguish from dismissals based on factual or legal deficiencies in the substantive merits of a claim. As you will see in section B, this difficulty is especially true in federal question cases in which the subject-matter jurisdiction of the federal courts is based on the existence of a substantive claim "arising under" federal law.

You may wonder what difference it makes whether a dismissal is based on failure of the substantive merits of the claim or on lack of subject-matter jurisdiction. Insofar as the plaintiff's ability to reassert the same claim in federal court is concerned, it would make no difference because in both situations the plaintiff's claim cannot be refiled in federal court. However, as noted above, dismissal of a claim for lack of subject-matter jurisdiction is not considered an adjudication on the merits and, therefore, such claims may be refiled in any state court where subject-matter jurisdiction is proper. In contrast, as you will learn in Chapter 12, if the dismissal is based on the failure of the substantive merits of the claim, the claim cannot be refiled in state court under the doctrine of claim preclusion. This doctrine precludes relitigation of a claim that has already been adjudicated on the merits in any court, state or federal.

9. Refiling in State Court — Statute of Limitations Tolling

One difficulty a litigant may face in bringing an action in state court after a dismissal in federal court for lack of subject-matter jurisdiction is the expiration of the applicable statute of limitations. Statutes of limitations provide that actions must be commenced within a specified period of time after the accrual of a substantive cause of action. As noted in the above section, if a plaintiff's claim is dismissed by the federal court for lack of subject-matter jurisdiction, and not on the merits, the plaintiff may refile the action in state court. But what if the applicable statute of limitations period has since expired? This limitations problem is sometimes alleviated by special statutory provisions or rules.

Many states provide for the "tolling" of any applicable statute of limitations while an action is pending in federal court if the action is thereafter dismissed for lack of jurisdiction. Tolling means that the statute of limitations will not bar a claim when the action that "tolls" the limitations period is commenced before the expiration of the limitations period. These so-called "tolling" or "savings" provisions permit the dismissed party to refile the action in state court, generally within a specified period of time, even though the statute of limitations on the claim would have otherwise expired during the pendency of the federal action. *See, e.g.,* N.Y. C.P.L.R. § 205(a) (West 2003) (tolling the statute of limitations for lack of subject-matter jurisdiction dismissals and allowing a six-month grace period for refiling in state court). A federal tolling provision also exists in cases in which a federal court dismisses a state law claim that has been brought within its "supplemental" jurisdiction. *See* 28 U.S.C. § 1367(d) (discussed in section E(5), below).

Problem

Problem 4-1. P and D are citizens of the State of New York. They entered into a complex contract which involves multiple, future performances by both of the parties. The contract contains a provision stating that the contract is governed by the law of the State of New York. The contract also contains a provision requiring all disputes concerning the contract to be litigated in a U.S. District Court in the Southern District of New York. When a dispute subsequently arises under the contract, P commences an action in that court. Does this action appear to be one that the U.S. District Court should handle? Why or why not?

Section B. Federal Question Jurisdiction

Article III, § 2 (first clause) of the U.S. Constitution states that the "judicial power shall extend to all Cases, in Law and Equity, arising under this Constitution, the Laws of the United States, and Treaties made, or which shall be made, under their Authority." This "arising under" (or "federal question") jurisdiction allows Congress to confer on the federal courts power to adjudicate cases involving federal law. However, as discussed in the preceding section, Congress need not confer all the power on federal courts that Article III authorizes, and Congress has not done so. Thus, in federal question cases, it is important to distinguish between the subject-matter jurisdiction that Article III authorizes and the jurisdiction that Congress has actually conferred on the lower federal courts.

The touchstone of both Article III and 28 U.S.C. § 1331 is the phrase "arising under." The proper interpretation of this phrase has been the source of great debate. Although Article III, § 2 and § 1331 are virtually identical in extending jurisdiction over all cases "arising under" the Constitution, laws, or treaties of the United States, the Supreme Court has long construed the "arising under" language of Article III as broader and more inclusive than the "arising under" language of § 1331. As discussed below, the statutory grant is limited to cases in which the *plaintiff's claim* is, in some way, based on federal law. Thus, it is insufficient under § 1331 that federal law is relevant to the case because the defendant relies on it defensively or the plaintiff relies on it to rebut a defense.

1. The Scope of the Constitutional Grant

Osborn's "Ingredient" Theory. The seminal case defining the permissible constitutional scope of federal question jurisdiction under Article III is *Osborn v. Bank of the United States*, 22 U.S. (9 Wheat.) 738 (1824). In *Osborn*, the Supreme Court held that Article III of the Constitution permits Congress to confer jurisdiction on the federal courts pursuant to the "arising under" language of Article III whenever federal law forms an "ingredient" in the case. As stated by Chief Justice Marshall,

> ... [i]f it be a sufficient foundation for jurisdiction, that the title or right set up by the party, may be defeated by one construction of the constitution or law of the United States, and sustained by the opposite construction ... then all the other questions must be decided as incidental to this, which gives that jurisdiction....

> [W]hen a question to which the judicial power of the Union is extended by the constitution, forms an ingredient of the original cause, it is in the power of Congress to give the Circuit Courts jurisdiction of that cause, although other questions of fact or law may be involved in it.

Id. at 822–23.

Based on the Supreme Court's analysis in the *Osborn* case, federal question jurisdiction is considered proper under Article III whenever federal law forms an "ingredient" of any part of the case, irrespective of whether the federal law is technically part of the plaintiff's initial claim, the defendant's defense, or the plaintiff's reply to a defense. Because the wording of Article III expressly extends jurisdiction over "all *cases* arising under," the theory is that the Constitution authorizes Congress to grant jurisdiction over an entire case and not just over an individual claim, and that a "case" consists of not only what the plaintiff asserts but also what the defendant asserts.

Relationship Between the Constitutional Grant and Federal Statutory Grants of Jurisdiction. The general federal question jurisdiction statute, 28 U.S.C. § 1331, states that the U.S. District Courts have subject-matter jurisdiction over "all civil actions arising under the Constitution, laws, or treaties of the United States." The Supreme Court has held that, even though this statute is worded almost identically to the "arising under" language of Article III of the Constitution, § 1331 does not grant the full scope of the constitutionally permissible federal question jurisdiction to the district courts. This means that under § 1331, it is not statutorily permissible for the district courts to exercise subject-matter jurisdiction over all cases in which federal law forms an "ingredient" of the case, even though it would be constitutionally permissible under Article III and *Osborn*. Instead, as you will see in subsection 2, below, § 1331 requires that the *plaintiff's* claim be properly based on federal law, and that federal law claims or defenses asserted by the defendant cannot provide the basis for jurisdiction under § 1331.

Nevertheless, the Court's broad interpretation of the "arising under" language of Article III in *Osborn* is important because it provides Congress with needed constitutional flexibility to extend federal question jurisdiction in appropriate cases as circumstances may dictate. In several instances, Congress has made use of this flexibility by enacting special federal question jurisdictional statutes in which jurisdiction is based not on the plaintiff's claim, but on a federal law issue that the *defendant* raises either as a defense or a counterclaim. For example, under 28 U.S.C. § 1442(a), removal to federal district court is authorized of any state court action against a federal officer if a federal law defense is asserted by the federal officer. Thus, even if the plaintiff's claim is based entirely on state law and would not otherwise qualify for federal jurisdiction, removal in this instance is both constitutionally and statutorily authorized solely on the basis of the *defendant's* federal law defense.

Similarly, in 28 U.S.C. § 1454, enacted in 2011, removal to federal district court is authorized of any state court action in which any party, including the defendant, asserts a claim under federal patent, plant variety protection, or copyright laws. Thus, even if the plaintiff's claim is based entirely on state law and would not otherwise qualify for federal jurisdiction, removal is both constitutionally and statutorily authorized solely on the basis of the *defendant's* patent, plant variety protection, or copyright counterclaim. Significantly, *Osborn's* "ingredient" theory also provides the constitutional authority for the Supreme Court's appellate jurisdiction under 28 U.S.C. § 1257 to review decisions of a state's highest court on federal law questions that may not have been statutorily cognizable in the federal districts courts in terms of original jurisdiction under § 1331. A prime example would be the *Mottley II* case, discussed in notes 5 and 6 in section B(2)(b), below.

In addition, the "ingredient" of federal law that *Osborn* relied on for subject-matter jurisdiction was the act incorporating the Bank of the United States. According to Marshall, the federal statute incorporating the Bank formed an original "ingredient" in every action in which the Bank was a party, even if no question of the validity or interpretation of the incorporating statute was ever raised in the case. *See also Bank of the United States v. Planters' Bank*, 22 U.S. (9 Wheat.) 904 (1824) (federal charter of Bank of the United States confers the right to sue the Bank's debtors on a state law contract claim in federal court). This holding survives today and allows Congress to create federal question jurisdiction in any case in which a federally chartered corporation is a party. For example, in *American National Red Cross v. S.G.*, 505 U.S. 247 (1992), the Supreme Court reaffirmed *Osborn* by holding that "Article III's 'arising under' jurisdiction is broad enough to authorize Congress to confer federal court jurisdiction over actions involving federally chartered corporations." *Id*. at 264. The Court ruled that the Red Cross charter, which authorizes the Red Cross "to sue and be sued in courts of law and equity, State or Federal, within the jurisdiction of the United States," properly granted statutory federal question jurisdiction in actions involving the Red Cross, even those actions are entirely controlled by state substantive law. *Id* at 264–65.

In addition to its federal question significance, *Osborn's* definition of a "case" for purposes of Article III (as including other "incidental" questions of fact or law involved in the action) also provides the necessary constitutional foundation for the supplemental jurisdiction statute, 28 U.S.C. § 1367, which extends jurisdiction over nonfederal claims based on their relationship to jurisdictionally sufficient federal claims appearing in the same case. The idea is that the presence of the federal claim allows Congress to authorize the federal courts to hear an entire case, and that the case may include nonfederal as well as federal issues. Obviously, under this reasoning, it becomes very important to define the scope of a constitutional "case." This matter is examined further in conjunction with the topic of supplemental jurisdiction in Section E, below.

2. The Scope of the Statutory Grant

For purposes of the *statutory* grant of federal question jurisdiction under 28 U.S.C. § 1331, the *plaintiff's* claim must "arise under" federal law before *statutory* federal question jurisdiction will exist. Deciding when the plaintiff's claim properly arises under federal law, however, can be a difficult task. Figure 4-2 shows the two main types of federal question cases identified by the U.S. Supreme Court that satisfy § 1331's statutory "arising under" test.

TWO TYPES OF CASES THAT SATISFY THE "ARISING UNDER" REQUIREMENT OF § 1331	
"Category 1"	Cases in which **federal law** creates the plaintiff's claim for relief based on • Claims **expressly created** by federal law **or** • Claims **impliedly created** by federal law
"Category 2"	Cases in which **state law** creates the plaintiff's claim for relief, but **federal law is an essential element** of the plaintiff's state law claim

Figure 4-2

(a) Cases in Which Federal Law Creates the Plaintiff's Claim for Relief

The vast majority of cases qualifying for federal question jurisdiction under § 1331 are those in which federal law creates the plaintiff's claim for relief. This first type of federal question case is derived from Justice Holmes' statement in *American Well Works Co. v. Layne & Bowler Co.*, 241 U.S. 257, 260 (1916), that "[a] suit arises under the law that creates the cause of action." To qualify under this first type of statutory federal question jurisdiction (which we will refer to as "Category 1" statutory federal question cases), the plaintiff's claim for relief must be created by federal law either expressly or impliedly.

Claims Expressly Created by Federal Law. Many federal laws, such as federal civil rights laws, consumer protection laws, antitrust laws, patent laws, copyright laws, and environmental laws, expressly authorize a private claim for damages and/or injunctive relief for violation of the federal law. In such cases, federal question jurisdiction is taken as a matter of course.

Claims Impliedly Created by Federal Law. Federal question jurisdiction also exists when the federal law creates a duty and the courts interpret the law impliedly to create a remedy for private litigants for violation of the law. For example, the Fourth Amendment to the U.S. Constitution imposes a duty on federal officers not to engage in unreasonable searches and seizures. The Fourth Amendment, however, does not expressly create any private remedy for the breach of this duty. Nevertheless, in *Bivens v. Six Unknown Named Agents of Fed. Bureau of Narcotics*, 403 U.S. 388 (1971), the Supreme Court was willing to imply a remedy of damages against federal officers for breach of the duty. Thus, an action to recover damages for a violation of an individual's Fourth Amendment rights by a federal officer arises under federal law for purposes of § 1331. *Id.* at 395–97.

Similarly, in enacting a federal statute, Congress may impose statutory obligations but not expressly authorize a private suit for violation of the statute. At times, enforcement of the statute is effectuated through criminal or administrative action and the statute is silent as to remedies for private litigants. In recent years, the courts have been very reluctant to find an implied private cause of action under such substantive laws. *See, e.g., Alexander v. Sandoval*, 532 U.S. 1049 (2001) (no private cause of action under Title VI of Civil Rights Act of 1964); *Karahalios v. National Fed'n of Fed. Employees*, 489 U.S. 527 (1989) (no private cause of action for breach of union's duty of fair representation under the Civil Service Reform Act). Nevertheless, if the court finds that an implied private cause of action is appropriate under a federal law, federal question jurisdiction is established. *See, e.g., Cannon v. University of Chicago*, 441 U.S. 677 (1979) (federal Title IX prohibiting sex discrimination in federally funded educational programs created implied private cause of action for affected individual); *Jackson v. Birmingham Bd. of Educ.*, 544 U.S. 167 (2005) (implied private cause of action under Title IX, as found in *Cannon v. University of Chicago*, encompasses coach's claim of retaliation after complaining about discrimination against girls' basketball team).

(b) Cases in Which Federal Law Is an Essential Element of the Plaintiff's State Law Claim

In this second type of statutory federal question jurisdiction under § 1331 (which we will refer to as "Category 2" statutory federal question cases), jurisdiction will sometimes exist even though *state* law, rather than federal law, creates the plaintiff's claim for relief. However, jurisdiction will exist only if a substantial question of federal law is an *essential element* of the plaintiff's state law claim. Although recognized by the Supreme Court as a valid basis for establishing federal question jurisdiction, this second type of federal question jurisdiction is actually very narrow in application. Category 2 federal question cases must survive not only the requirement of the "well-pleaded complaint" rule, examined in subsection (c), below, but must also meet the additional requirements set out in the *Grable* and *Gunn* cases, reprinted in subsection (d), below.

(c) The "Well-Pleaded Complaint" Rule

The "well-pleaded complaint" rule is a long-established requirement of satisfying § 1331's statutory test of federal question jurisdiction. This rule requires that federal law be an essential element of the *plaintiff's* claim. Federal law that is only properly asserted as a defense by the defendant does not count for jurisdictional purposes. Although, as explained in section B(1), a case "arises under" federal law for purposes of Article III if federal law forms an "ingredient" of any part of either the plaintiff's or the defendant's case, for purposes of § 1331 an action only "arises under" federal law if federal law is an essential element of the *plaintiff's* claim.

Under the "well pleaded complaint" rule, the claims and defenses of the defendant do not qualify for federal question jurisdiction, and the plaintiff may not properly raise an issue of federal law in the plaintiff's complaint solely in anticipation of or in reply to a defense or claim of the defendant. Because the "well-pleaded complaint" rule bars jurisdiction under § 1331 if the federal issue arises solely as a defense, the rule can result in situations, like *Mottley,* in which a substantial and disputed "federal issue" clearly exists in the case, yet a § 1331 "federal question" does not.

Louisville & Nashville Railroad Co. v. Mottley

United States Supreme Court, 1908

211 U.S. 149, 29 S. Ct. 42, 53 L. Ed. 126

Statement by JUSTICE MOODY:

The appellees (husband and wife), being residents and citizens of Kentucky, brought this suit in equity in the circuit court of the United States for the western district of Kentucky against the appellant, a railroad company and a citizen of the same state. The object of the suit was to compel the specific performance of the following contract:

"Louisville, Ky., Oct. 2nd, 1871.

The Louisville & Nashville Railroad Company in consideration that E. L. Mottley and wife, Annie E. Mottley, have this day released Company from all damages or claims for damages for injuries received by them on the 7th of September, 1871, in consequence of a collision of trains on the railroad of said Company at Randolph's Station, Jefferson County, Ky., hereby agrees to issue free passes on said Railroad and branches now existing or to exist, to said E. L. & Annie E. Mottley for the remainder of the present year, and thereafter, to renew said passes annually during the lives of said Mottley and wife or either of them."

The bill alleged that in September, 1871, plaintiffs, while passengers upon the defendant railroad, were injured by the defendant's negligence, and released their respective claims for damages in consideration of the agreement for transportation during their lives, expressed in the contract. It is alleged that the contract was performed by the defendant up to January 1, 1907, when the defendant declined to renew the passes. The bill then alleges that the refusal to comply with the contract was based solely upon that part of the [A]ct of Congress of June 29, 1906, 34 Stat. 584, ... which forbids the giving of free passes or free transportation. The bill further alleges: First, that the [A]ct of Congress referred to does not prohibit the giving of passes under the circumstances of this case; and, second, that if the law is to be construed as prohibiting such passes, it is in conflict with the Fifth Amendment of the Constitution, because it deprives the plaintiffs of their property without due process of law. The defendant demurred to the bill. The judge of the Circuit Court overruled the demurrer, entered a decree for the relief prayed for, and the defendant appealed directly to this court.

    ....

JUSTICE MOODY, after making the foregoing statement, delivered the opinion of the Court:

Two questions of law were raised by the demurrer to the bill, were brought here by appeal, and have been argued before us. They are, first, whether that part of the [A]ct of Congress of June 29, 1906 [ch. 3591, 34 Stat. 584], which forbids the giving of free passes or the collection of any different compensation for transportation of passengers than that specified in the tariff filed, makes it unlawful to perform a contract for transportation of persons, who in good faith, before the passage of the [A]ct, had accepted such contract in satisfaction of a valid cause of action against the railroad; and, second, whether the statute, if it should be construed to render such a contract unlawful, is in violation of the Fifth Amendment of the Constitution of the United States. We do not deem it necessary, however, to consider either of these questions, because, in our opinion, the court below was without jurisdiction of the cause. Neither party has questioned that jurisdiction, but it is the duty of this court to see to it that the jurisdiction of the Circuit Court, which is defined and limited by statute, is not exceeded. This duty we have frequently performed of our own motion....

There was no diversity of citizenship and it is not and cannot be suggested that there was any ground of jurisdiction, except that the case was a "suit ... arising under the Constitution and laws of the United States." Act of Aug. 13, 1888, ch. 866, 25 Stat. 433, 434. It is the settled interpretation of these words, as used in this statute, conferring jurisdiction, that a suit arises under the Constitution and laws of the United States only when the plaintiff's statement of his own cause of action shows that it is based upon those laws or that Constitution. It is not enough that the plaintiff alleges some anticipated defense to his cause of action and asserts that the defense is invalidated by some provision of the Constitution of the United States. Although such allegations show that very likely, in the course of the litigation, a question under the Constitution would arise, they do not show that the suit, that is, the plaintiff's original cause of action, arises under the Constitution.... [I]n *Boston & Montana Consolidated Copper Co. v. Montana Ore Purchasing Co.*, 188 U.S. 632 (1903), the plaintiff brought suit in the Circuit Court of the United States for the conversion of copper ore and for an injunction against its continuance. The plaintiff then alleged, for the purpose of showing jurisdiction, in substance, that the defendant would set up in defense certain laws of the United States. The cause was held to be beyond the jurisdiction of the Circuit Court, the court saying, by Justice Peckham....

> It would be wholly unnecessary and improper in order to prove complainant's cause of action to go into any matters of defense which the defendants might possibly set up, and then attempt to reply to such defense, and thus, if possible, to show that a Federal question might or probably would arise in the course of the trial of the case. To allege such defense and then make an answer to it before the defendant has the opportunity to itself plead or prove its own defense is inconsistent with any known rule of pleading, so far as we are aware, and is improper.

> The rule is a reasonable and just one that the complainant in the first instance shall be confined to a statement of its cause of action, leaving to the defendant to set up in his answer what his defense is, and, if anything more than a denial of complainant's cause of action, imposing upon the defendant the burden of proving such defense.

> Conforming itself to that rule, the complainant would not, in the assertion or proof of its cause of action, bring up a single Federal question. The presentation of its cause of action would not show that it was one arising under the Constitution or laws of the United States.

> The only way in which it might be claimed that a Federal question was presented would be in the complainant's statement of what the defense of defendants would be and complainant's answer to such defense....

The interpretation of the [A]ct which we have stated was first announced in *Metcalf v. City of Watertown*, 128 U.S. 586 (1888), and has since been repeated and applied in [17 Supreme Court decisions]. The application of this rule to the case at bar is decisive against the jurisdiction of the circuit court.

It is ordered that the judgment be reversed and the case remitted to the circuit court with instructions to dismiss the suit for want of jurisdiction.

Notes and Questions

1. What are the purposes of federal question jurisdiction? Given the fact that Congress does not have to give the lower federal courts jurisdiction over any particular category of cases listed in Article III, § 2, why has it chosen to give the federal courts jurisdiction

over "arising under" cases? As limited by the "well-pleaded complaint" rule of *Mottley*, can the grant of general federal question jurisdiction in § 1331 effectively accomplish those purposes? Remember that any case that violates the "well-pleaded complaint" rule must be litigated in state court. Remember also that jurisdiction of the federal courts under § 1331 is concurrent with the state courts.

2. How would *Mottley* have been decided under the "ingredient" test of *Osborn*? Under this test, was there constitutional federal question jurisdiction under the "arising under" language of Article III?

3. (a) Precisely why did the Mottleys' action fail to satisfy statutory federal question jurisdiction under the "well-pleaded complaint" rule? Understanding the proper application of the rule can be difficult. The confusion is partially caused by the fact that the rule is typically stated as requiring that "it must be clear from the *face* of the plaintiff's complaint that there is a federal question." CHEMERINSKEY at 283. (emphasis added). This statement of the rule, although entirely accurate, mistakenly leads some to believe that the rule is satisfied whenever the plaintiff physically incorporates a reference to federal law somewhere in the body (*i.e.*, "on the face") of the plaintiff's complaint. But you know from *Mottley* that this is not the proper test because the Mottleys expressly included the federal law issues in the body of their complaint. Nor could the Mottleys have somehow "rephrased" their complaint to comply with the rule. Nor does it matter that the Mottleys' *ultimate* right to win against the railroad necessarily depended upon the court's resolution of the federal statutory and constitutional issues presented in the case. (The Mottleys' right to enforce the contract ultimately depended on whether or not the federal law invalidated the contract and, if so, whether such invalidation was a violation of the Mottleys' Fifth Amendment rights under the U.S. Constitution. If the court were to rule against the Mottleys on these issues, the Mottleys would lose their case against the railroad.)

(b) Rather, the determination of whether federal law is an essential element of a plaintiff's claim sufficient to meet the "well-pleaded complaint" rule requires an analysis of how federal law contributes to the case. The Mottleys' substantive claim against the railroad for breach of contract was created by state contract law. In order to initially establish a prima facie case for breach of contract against the railroad, the Mottleys only needed to establish the existence of a contract between the railroad and themselves and that the railroad had breached its terms. If they were able to do that, state law created a right of action on their behalf. The Mottleys were not required to plead or prove any element of federal law in order to establish their initial claim for breach of contract against the railroad. Federal law was, therefore, not an essential element of their state law claim. While federal law was certainly relevant to the ultimate resolution of the case, the assertion that a federal statute invalidated the contract contributed to the case solely as a defense that the railroad would want to raise to the Mottleys' complaint. In addition, the Mottleys' assertion that the Fifth Amendment invalidated the federal statute only arises once the railroad raises the defense — *i.e.*, as a reply to the statutory defense by the railroad.

4. Category 1 federal question cases, *i.e.*, cases in which federal law either expressly or impliedly creates the plaintiff's claim for relief, will clearly satisfy the "well-pleaded complaint" rule. Do you understand why? The "well-pleaded complaint" rule, however, severely limits the number of cases that may potentially qualify for federal question jurisdiction under Category 2, *i.e.*, cases in which federal law is an essential element of a state law claim. After studying *Mottley*, do you now see why?

5. As noted earlier, dismissals for lack of subject-matter jurisdiction are not considered adjudications on the merits and do not preclude the refiling of the dismissed claim in a

state court possessing proper subject-matter jurisdiction. Indeed, the Mottleys refiled their identical claim for specific performance against the railroad in Kentucky state court. As in the first litigation, the Mottleys were successful in the lower courts. The Kentucky state court held that the new federal Act did not invalidate the Mottleys' contract with the railroad and the Mottleys were granted a judgment specifically enforcing the contract. *Mottley v. Louisville & Nashville R.R. Co.*, 118 S.W. 982 (Ky. 1909). The railroad again appealed to the U.S. Supreme Court, and this time the Court addressed the merits of the federal issues. Unfortunately for the Mottleys, the Court again reversed. The Court in *Mottley II* held that the federal law invalidated the Mottleys' contract and that this result did not constitute an unconstitutional violation of the Mottleys' Fifth Amendment rights. *Louisville & Nashville R.R. Co. v. Mottley*, 219 U.S. 467 (1911) (*Mottley II*).

6. Do you understand why the U.S. Supreme Court had jurisdiction to decide the merits of the federal issues in *Mottley II* when the U.S. Circuit Court had no jurisdiction to do so in *Mottley I*? Review the material in section B(1), above.

(d) Meeting the Requirements for "Arising Under" Jurisdiction in "Category 2" Federal Question Cases

As noted earlier, federal question jurisdiction in Category 2 cases, *i.e.*, cases in which federal law is an essential element of the plaintiff's state law claim, is very narrow and restricted. Category 2 federal question cases must satisfy not only the requirement of the "well-pleaded complaint" rule, examined above, but must also meet the additional requirements set forth in *Grable*.

Grable & Son's Metal Products, Inc. v. Darue Engineering & Manufacturing

United States Supreme Court, 2005
545 U.S. 308, 125 S. Ct. 2363, 162 L. Ed. 2d 257

JUSTICE SOUTER delivered the opinion of the Court.

Issue

The question is whether want of a federal cause of action to try claims of title to land obtained at a federal tax sale precludes removal to federal court of a state action with non-diverse parties raising a disputed issue of federal title law. We answer no, and hold that the national interest in providing a federal forum for federal tax litigation is sufficiently substantial to support the exercise of federal question jurisdiction over the disputed issue on removal, which would not distort any division of labor between the state and federal courts, provided or assumed by Congress.

Holding

In 1994, the Internal Revenue Service seized Michigan real property belonging to petitioner Grable & Sons Metal Products, Inc., to satisfy Grable's federal tax delinquency. Title 26 U.S.C. § 6335 required the IRS to give notice of the seizure, and there is no dispute that Grable received actual notice by certified mail before the IRS sold the property to respondent Darue Engineering & Manufacturing. Although Grable also received notice of the sale itself, it did not exercise its statutory right to redeem the property within 180 days of the sale, 26 U.S.C. § 6337(b)(1), and after that period had passed, the Government gave Darue a quitclaim deed. 26 U.S.C. § 6339.

Five years later, Grable brought a quiet title action in state court, claiming that Darue's record title was invalid because the IRS had failed to notify Grable of its seizure of the property in the exact manner required by § 6335(a), which provides that written notice must be "given by the Secretary to the owner of the property [or] left at his usual place of abode or business." Grable said that the statute required personal service, not service by certified mail.

Darue removed the case to Federal District Court as presenting a federal question, because the claim of title depended on the interpretation of the notice statute in the federal tax law. The District Court declined to remand the case at Grable's behest after finding that the "claim does pose a significant question of federal law," ... and ruling that Grable's lack of a federal right of action to enforce its claim against Darue did not bar the exercise of federal jurisdiction. On the merits, the court granted summary judgment to Darue, holding that although § 6335 by its terms required personal service, substantial compliance with the statute was enough....

The Court of Appeals for the Sixth Circuit affirmed.... On the jurisdictional question, the panel thought it sufficed that the title claim raised an issue of federal law that had to be resolved, and implicated a substantial federal interest (in construing federal tax law). The court went on to affirm the District Courts judgment on the merits. We granted certiorari on the jurisdictional question alone ... to resolve a split within the Courts of Appeals on whether *Merrell Dow Pharmaceuticals Inc. v. Thompson*, 478 U.S. 804 (1986) always requires a federal cause of action as a condition for exercising federal question jurisdiction. We now affirm.

II

Darue was entitled to remove the quiet title action if Grable could have brought it in federal district court originally, 28 U.S.C. § 1441(a), as a civil action "arising under the Constitution, laws, or treaties of the United States," 28 U.S.C. § 1331. This provision for federal question jurisdiction is invoked by and large by plaintiffs pleading a cause of action created by federal law (*e.g.,* claims under 42 U.S.C. § 1983). There is, however, another longstanding, if less frequently encountered, variety of federal "arising under" jurisdiction, this Court having recognized for nearly 100 years that in certain cases federal question jurisdiction will lie over state-law claims that implicate significant federal issues. *E.g., Hopkins v. Walker*, 244 U.S. 486, 490–91 (1917). The doctrine captures the common-sense notion that a federal court ought to be able to hear claims recognized under state law that nonetheless turn on substantial questions of federal law, and thus justify resort to the experience, solicitude, and hope of uniformity that a federal forum offers on federal issues, see ALI, *Study of the Division of Jurisdiction Between State and Federal Courts* 164–66 (1968).

The classic example is *Smith v. Kansas City Title & Trust Co.*, 255 U.S. 180 (1921), a suit by a shareholder claiming that the defendant corporation could not lawfully buy certain bonds of the National Government because their issuance was unconstitutional. Although Missouri law provided the cause of action, the Court recognized federal question jurisdiction because the principal issue in the case was the federal constitutionality of the bond issue. *Smith* thus held, in a somewhat generous statement of the scope of the doctrine, that a state-law claim could give rise to federal question jurisdiction so long as it "appears from the [complaint] that the right to relief depends upon the construction or application of [federal law]." *Id.* at 199.

The *Smith* statement has been subject to some trimming to fit earlier and later cases recognizing the vitality of the basic doctrine, but shying away from the expansive view that mere need to apply federal law in a state-law claim will suffice to open the "arising under" door. As early as 1912, this Court had confined federal question jurisdiction over state-law claims to those that "really and substantially involv[e] a dispute or controversy respecting the validity, construction or effect of [federal] law." *Shulthis v. McDougal*, 225 U.S. 561 (1912). This limitation was the ancestor of Justice Cardozo's later explanation that a request to exercise federal question jurisdiction over a state action calls for a "common-sense accommodation of judgment to [the] kaleidoscopic situations" that present a federal issue, in "a selective process which picks the substantial causes out of the web and lays the other ones aside." ... It has in fact become a constant refrain in such cases that federal jurisdiction demands not only a contested federal issue, but a substantial one, indicating a serious federal interest in claiming the advantages thought to be inherent in a federal forum.... *Franchise Tax Bd. v. Construction Laborers Vacation Trust*, 463 U.S. 1, 28 (1983).

But even when the state action discloses a contested and substantial federal question, the exercise of federal jurisdiction is subject to a possible veto. For the federal issue will ultimately qualify for a federal forum only if federal jurisdiction is consistent with congressional judgment about the sound division of labor between state and federal courts governing the application of §1331. Thus, *Franchise Tax Board* explained that the appropriateness of a federal forum to hear an embedded issue could be evaluated only after considering the "welter of issues regarding the interrelation of federal and state authority and the proper management of the federal judicial system." *Id.* at 8. Because arising-under jurisdiction to hear a state-law claim always raises the possibility of upsetting the state-federal line drawn (or at least assumed) by Congress, the presence of a disputed federal issue and the ostensible importance of a federal forum are never necessarily dispositive; there must always be an assessment of any disruptive portent in exercising federal jurisdiction. *See also Merrell Dow* at 810.

These considerations have kept us from stating a "single, precise, all-embracing" test for jurisdiction over federal issues embedded in state-law claims between nondiverse parties.... We have not kept them out simply because they appeared in state raiment, as Justice Holmes would have done, ... *see Smith* at 214 (dissenting opinion), but neither have we treated "federal issue" as a password opening federal courts to any state action embracing a point of federal law. Instead, the question is, does a state-law claim necessarily raise a stated federal issue, actually disputed and substantial, which a federal forum may entertain without disturbing any congressionally approved balance of federal and state judicial responsibilities.

III
A

This case warrants federal jurisdiction. Grable's state complaint must specify "the facts establishing the superiority of [its] claim," Mich. Ct. Rule 3.411(B)(2)(c) (West 2005), and Grable has premised its superior title claim on a failure by the IRS to give it adequate notice, as defined by federal law. Whether Grable was given notice within the meaning of the federal statute is thus an essential element of its quiet title claim, and the meaning of the federal statute is actually in dispute; it appears to be the only legal or factual issue contested in the case. The meaning of the federal tax provision is an important issue of federal law that sensibly belongs in a federal court. The Government has a strong interest in the "prompt and certain collection of delinquent taxes" ... and the ability of the IRS to satisfy its claims from the property of delinquents requires clear terms of notice to allow buyers like Darue to satisfy themselves that the Service has touched the bases necessary for good title. The Government thus has a direct interest in the availability of a federal forum to vindicate its own administrative action, and buyers (as well as tax delinquents) may find it valuable to come before judges used to federal tax matters. Finally, because it will be the rare state title case that raises a contested matter of federal law, federal jurisdiction to resolve genuine disagreement over federal tax title provisions will portend only a microscopic effect on the federal-state division of labor....

This conclusion puts us in venerable company, quiet title actions having been the subject of some of the earliest exercises of federal question jurisdiction over state-law claims. In *Hopkins*, 244 U.S. at 490–91, the question was federal jurisdiction over a quiet title action based on the plaintiffs' allegation that federal mining law gave them the superior claim. Just as in this case, "the facts showing the plaintiffs' title and the existence and invalidity of the instrument or record sought to be eliminated as a cloud upon the title are essential parts of the plaintiffs' cause of action."[3] *Id.* at 490. As in this case again, "it is plain that a controversy respecting the construction and effect of the [federal] laws is involved and is sufficiently real and substantial." *Id.* at 489. This Court therefore upheld federal jurisdiction in *Hopkins*, as well as in the similar quiet title [cases].... Consistent with those cases, the recognition of federal jurisdiction is in order here.

B

Merrell Dow Pharmaceuticals Inc. v. Thompson, 478 U.S. 804 (1986), on which Grable rests its position, is not to the contrary. *Merrell Dow* considered a state tort claim resting in part on the allegation that the defendant drug company had violated a federal misbranding prohibition, and was thus presumptively negligent under Ohio law.... The Court assumed that federal law would have to be applied to resolve the claim, but after closely examining the strength of the federal interest at stake and the implications of opening the federal forum, held federal jurisdiction unavailable. Congress had not provided a private federal cause of action for violation of the federal branding requirement, and the Court found "it would ... flout, or at least undermine, congressional intent to conclude that federal courts might nevertheless exercise federal question jurisdiction and provide remedies for violations of that federal statute solely because the violation ... is said to be a ...'proximate cause' under state law." *Id.* at 812.

Because federal law provides for no quiet title action that could be brought against Darue,[4] Grable argues that there can be no federal jurisdiction here, stressing some broad language in *Merrell Dow* (including the passage just quoted) that on its face supports Grable's position.... But an opinion is to be read as a whole, and *Merrell Dow* cannot be read whole as overturning decades of precedent, as it would have done by effectively adopting the Holmes dissent in *Smith*, ... and converting a federal cause of action from a sufficient condition for federal question jurisdiction[5] into a necessary one.

In the first place, *Merrell Dow* disclaimed the adoption of any bright-line rule, as when the Court reiterated that "in exploring the outer reaches of § 1331, determinations about

---

3. The quiet title cases also show the limiting effect of the requirement that the federal issue in a state-law claim must actually be in dispute to justify federal question jurisdiction. In *Shulthis v. McDougal*, 225 U.S. 561 (1912), this Court found that there was no federal question jurisdiction to hear a plaintiffs quiet title claim in part because the federal statutes on which title depended were not subject to "any controversy respecting their validity, construction, or effect." *Id.* at 570. As the Court put it, the requirement of an actual dispute about federal law was "especially" important in "suit[s] involving rights to land acquired under a law of the United States," because otherwise "every suit to establish title to land in the central and western states would so arise [under federal law], as all titles in those States are traceable back to those laws." *Id.* at 569–70.

4. Federal law does provide a quiet title cause of action against the Federal Government. 28 U.S.C. § 2410. That right of action is not relevant here, however, because the federal government no longer has any interest in the property, having transferred its interest to Darue through the quitclaim deed.

5. For an extremely rare exception to the sufficiency of a federal right of action, *see Shoshone Mining Co. v. Rutter*, 177 U.S. 505, 507 (1900).

federal jurisdiction require sensitive judgments about congressional intent, judicial power, and the federal system." 478 U.S. at 810. The opinion included a lengthy footnote explaining that questions of jurisdiction over state-law claims require "careful judgments," *id.* at 814, about the "nature of the federal interest at stake," *id.* at 814, n.12 (emphasis deleted). And as a final indication that it did not mean to make a federal right of action mandatory, it expressly approved the exercise of jurisdiction sustained in *Smith*, despite the want of any federal cause of action available to *Smith's* shareholder plaintiff. 478 U.S. at 814, n.12. *Merrell Dow* then, did not toss out, but specifically retained the contextual enquiry that had been *Smith's* hallmark for over 60 years. At the end of *Merrell Dow*, Justice Holmes was still dissenting.

Accordingly, *Merrell Dow* should be read in its entirety as treating the absence of a federal private right of action as evidence relevant to, but not dispositive of, the "sensitive judgments about congressional intent" that § 1331 requires. The absence of any federal cause of action affected *Merrell Dow's* result two ways. The Court saw the fact as worth some consideration in the assessment of substantiality. But its primary importance emerged when the Court treated the combination of no federal cause of action and no preemption of state remedies for misbranding as an important clue to Congress's conception of the scope of jurisdiction to be exercised under § 1331. The Court saw the missing cause of action not as a missing federal door key, always required, but as a missing welcome mat, required in the circumstances, when exercising federal jurisdiction over a state misbranding action would have attracted a horde of original filings and removal cases raising other state claims with embedded federal issues. For if the federal labeling standard without a federal cause of action could get a state claim into federal court, so could any other federal standard without a federal cause of action. And that would have meant a tremendous number of cases.

One only needed to consider the treatment of federal violations generally in garden variety state tort law. "The violation of federal statutes and regulations is commonly given negligence per se effect in state tort proceedings." *Restatement (Third) of Torts* (proposed final draft) § 14, cmt. *a; see also* W. Keeton et al., *Prosser and Keeton on Torts*, § 36, at 221, n.9 (5th ed.1984) ("[T]he breach of a federal statute may support a negligence per se claim as a matter of state law" (collecting authority)). A general rule of exercising federal jurisdiction over state claims resting on federal mislabeling and other statutory violations would thus have heralded a potentially enormous shift of traditionally state cases into federal courts. Expressing concern over the "increased volume of federal litigation," and noting the importance of adhering to "legislative intent," *Merrell Dow* thought it improbable that the Congress, having made no provision for a federal cause of action, would have meant to welcome any state-law tort case implicating federal law "solely because the violation of the federal statute is said to [create] a rebuttable presumption [of negligence] ... under state law." 478 U.S. at 811–12 (internal quotation marks omitted). In this situation, no welcome mat meant keep out. *Merrell Dow's* analysis thus fits within the framework of examining the importance of having a federal forum for the issue, and the consistency of such a forum with Congress's intended division of labor between state and federal courts.

As already indicated, however, a comparable analysis yields a different jurisdictional conclusion in this case. Although Congress also indicated ambivalence in this case by providing no private right of action to Grable, it is the rare state quiet title action that involves contested issues of federal law.... Consequently, jurisdiction over actions like Grable's would not materially affect, or threaten to affect, the normal currents of litigation. Given the absence of threatening structural consequences and the clear interest the Government, its buyers, and its delinquents have in the availability of a federal forum, there is no good reason to shirk from federal jurisdiction over the dispositive and contested federal issue at the heart of the state-law title claim.[7]

IV

The judgment of the Court of Appeals, upholding federal jurisdiction over Grable's quiet title action, is affirmed.

It is so ordered.

Concurring JUSTICE THOMAS, concurring.

The Court faithfully applies our precedents interpreting 28 U.S.C. § 1331 to authorize federal court jurisdiction over some cases in which state law creates the cause of action but requires determination of an issue of federal law.... In this case, no one has asked us to overrule those precedents and adopt the rule Justice Holmes set forth in *American Well Works Co. v. Layne & Bowler Co.,* 241 U.S. 257 (1916), limiting § 1331 jurisdiction to cases in which federal law creates the cause of action pleaded on the face of the plaintiffs complaint.... In an appropriate case, and perhaps with the benefit of better evidence as to the original meaning of § 1331's text, I would be willing to consider that course.

Jurisdictional rules should be clear. Whatever the virtues of the *Smith* standard, it is anything but clear....

Whatever the vices of the *American Well Works* rule, it is clear. Moreover, it accounts for the "vast majority" of cases that come within § 1331 under our current case law ... — further indication that trying to sort out which cases fall within the smaller *Smith* category may not be worth the effort it entails.... Accordingly, I would be willing in appropriate circumstances to reconsider our interpretation of § 1331.

Notes and Questions

1. Prior to *Grable,* the lower federal courts were divided about how to determine when an action comprised a proper federal question case in the Category 2 situation. This division was caused by the Supreme Court's 5–4 opinion in the *Merrell Dow* case, discussed in *Grable,* which was susceptible to a number of interpretations, each of which would produce a different scope for Category 2 cases. The *Grable* Court, however, clarified two main points of uncertainty following *Merrell Dow.*

(a) First, the *Grable* Court made clear that it was a mistake to interpret *Merrell Dow* as requiring the existence of a federal cause of action as a necessary prerequisite for federal question jurisdiction in all cases. The Court rejected this view and expressly reaffirmed its tradition of "nearly 100 years" of Category 2 federal question jurisdiction over state law claims that raise disputed and substantial questions of federal law, even though the federal law in question provides no cause of action to the plaintiff.

(b) Second, the *Grable* Court made clear, in footnote 7 reprinted above that a plaintiff need not raise a federal constitutional issue, as the plaintiff had in *Smith v. Kansas*

---

7. At oral argument Grable's counsel espoused the position that after *Merrell Dow,* federal question jurisdiction over state-law claims absent a federal right of action, could be recognized only where a constitutional issue was at stake. There is, however, no reason in text or otherwise to draw such a rough line. As *Merrell Dow* itself suggested, constitutional questions may be the more likely ones to reach the level of substantiality that can justify federal jurisdiction. 478 U.S. at 814, n.12. But a flat ban on statutory questions would mechanically exclude significant questions of federal law like the one this case presents.

City Title & Trust Co., discussed in *Grable,* in order to properly invoke federal question jurisdiction in a Category 2 case. The Court held that a state law claim involving a purely statutory question of federal law, as in *Grable,* may properly qualify under Category 2 jurisdiction. The confusion on this issue was also caused by the *Merrell Dow* opinion which, in rejecting Category 2 jurisdiction in that case, distinguished the Court's landmark Category 2 decision in *Smith* by noting that *Smith* involved "the constitutionality of an important federal statute." 478 U.S. 808, 814, n.12 (1986). This language in *Merrell Dow* suggested that Category 2 jurisdiction was perhaps only proper when a federal constitutional issue was at stake.

2. Apart from its clarification of certain points from *Merrell Dow,* does *Grable* articulate a test for Category 2 federal question jurisdiction that will be easier to administer by the lower federal courts? The *Grable* Court continued to caution that the exercise of jurisdiction for this second type of federal question case requires "careful" and "sensitive" analysis and articulated a four-part test to determine the propriety of jurisdiction in such cases:

first, an issue of federal law must be an "essential element" of the plaintiff's state law claim (*i.e.* the requirement of the "well-pleaded complaint" rule);

second, the federal law issue must be "actually in dispute" in the case;

third, the federal interest at stake in the determination of the federal issue must be sufficiently "substantial" to justify resort to the federal forum; and

fourth, federal jurisdiction must be "consistent with congressional judgment about the sound division of labor between state and federal courts governing the application of 1331."

[handwritten margin notes: "Cat. 2 Fed. Q. Grable Test" with numbers 1, 2, 3, 4 marking the four parts]

3. (a) With respect to the first requirement that federal law must be an "essential element" of the plaintiff's state law claim and thus satisfy the "well-pleaded complaint" rule, do you understand why this requirement was met in *Grable* and *Smith,* but not in *Mottley*? In all three cases, the plaintiffs' substantive claim was based on *state* law. But unlike the Mottleys, the plaintiffs in *Smith* and *Grable* had to establish an issue of federal law as an *essential element* of their state law claims. In *Smith,* for example, state substantive law prohibited the defendant corporation from investing in illegally issued bonds and provided shareholders of the corporation a remedy against the corporation for breach of this duty. A plaintiff-shareholder sued under this state law to prevent the corporation from investing in certain federal bonds. The plaintiff argued that the state law was violated because the federal bonds had been illegally issued in violation of the U.S. Constitution. Thus, state law created the plaintiff's substantive claim, but federal law was an essential element of that claim because it was the U.S. Constitution that allegedly made the bonds illegal. If the plaintiff failed to establish that the bonds were illegal, the plaintiff would not have established a prima facie case against the defendant under state law.

(b) Similarly in *Grable,* state substantive law allowed the plaintiff to sue the defendant to quiet title to the property, but the only way the plaintiff could prove its superior title to the property was to prove that the IRS failed to give the plaintiff adequate notice of the tax sale as required under federal law. If the IRS failed to give the plaintiff proper notice, then the defendant's title acquired from the tax sale would have been invalid. If the plaintiff failed to establish that the notice was invalid under federal law, the plaintiff would not have established a prima facie case against the defendant to quiet title under state law. By contrast, the Mottleys did not have to rely on any element of federal law in order to initially establish their breach-of-contract claim against the railroad and the federal issue only arose as a defense to the action.

4. (a) In *Grable*, the Court retained the requirement from *Merrell Dow* that the federal issue involved in a Category 2 case must be sufficiently "substantial" to warrant adjudication by a federal court. The *Grable* Court noted that Category 2 jurisdiction rests on "the commonsense notion that a federal court ought to be able to hear claims recognized under state law that nonetheless turn on substantial questions of federal law, and thus justify resort to the experience, solicitude, and hope of uniformity that a federal forum offers on federal issues." Following *Grable*, the Court addressed this issue in two cases and held in both that the substantial federal issue requirement was not met.

(b) In *Empire HealthChoice Assurance, Inc. v. McVeigh*, 547 U.S. 677 (2006), the Court reconfirmed that Category 2 federal question jurisdiction remains a "special and small category." In a 5–4 decision, the Court held that federal question jurisdiction was lacking in an insurer's suit for reimbursement of medical benefits paid to an insured federal employee. Reimbursement was sought after the employee recovered damages for his injuries in a state court tort action against the tortfeasors. The Federal Employees Health Benefit Act authorized the insurance contract, but the claim for reimbursement was held to be based on state law. The Court held that this case was "poles apart" from *Grable* and although the federal government had a strong interest in the welfare of its workers, this did not justify converting "an insurer's contract-derived claim" into a federal question case. The Court noted that "*Grable* presented a nearly 'pure question of law' …'that could be settled once and for all and thereafter would govern numerous tax sale cases'… [whereas] Empire's reimbursement claim … is fact-bound and situation-specific…. In sum, *Grable* emphasized that it takes more than a federal element to 'open the "arising under" door'.… This case cannot be squeezed into the slim category *Grable* exemplifies." *Id.* at 701.

In *Gunn,* the Court again addressed the requirements for Category 2 jurisdiction.

Gunn v. Minton

United States Supreme Court, 2013
___ U.S. ___, 133 S. Ct. 1059, 185 L. Ed. 2d 72

CHIEF JUSTICE ROBERTS delivered the opinion of the Court.

Federal courts have exclusive jurisdiction over cases "arising under any Act of Congress relating to patents." 28 U.S.C. § 1338(a). The question presented is whether a state law claim alleging legal malpractice in the handling of a patent case must be brought in federal court.

I

In the early 1990s, respondent Vernon Minton developed a computer program and telecommunications network designed to facilitate securities trading. In March 1995, he leased the system—known as the Texas Computer Exchange Network, or TEXCEN—to R.M. Stark & Co., a securities brokerage. A little over a year later, he applied for a patent for an interactive securities trading system that was based substantially on TEXCEN. The U.S. Patent and Trademark Office issued the patent in January 2000.

Patent in hand, Minton filed a patent infringement suit in Federal District Court against the National Association of Securities Dealers, Inc. (NASD) and the NASDAQ Stock Market, Inc. He was represented by Jerry Gunn and the other petitioners. NASD and NASDAQ moved for summary judgment on the ground that Minton's patent was invalid under the "on sale" bar, 35 U.S.C. § 102(b). That provision specifies that an inventor is not entitled to a patent if "the invention was … on sale in [the United States], more than one year prior to the date of the application," and Minton had leased TEXCEN to Stark more than one year prior to filing his patent application. Rejecting Minton's argument that there were differences between TEXCEN and the patented system that precluded application of the on-sale bar, the District Court granted the summary judgment motion and declared Minton's patent invalid....

Minton then filed a motion for reconsideration in the District Court, arguing for the first time that the lease agreement with Stark was part of ongoing testing of TEXCEN and therefore fell within the "experimental use" exception to the on-sale bar. The District Court denied the motion....

Minton appealed to the U.S. Court of Appeals for the Federal Circuit. That court affirmed, concluding that the District Court had appropriately held Minton's experimental-use argument waived....

Minton, convinced that his attorneys' failure to raise the experimental-use argument earlier had cost him the lawsuit and led to invalidation of his patent, brought this malpractice action in Texas state court. His former lawyers defended on the ground that the lease to Stark was not, in fact, for an experimental use, and that therefore Minton's patent infringement claims would have failed even if the experimental-use argument had been timely raised. The trial court agreed, holding that Minton had put forward "less than a scintilla of proof" that the lease had been for an experimental purpose. It accordingly granted summary judgment to Gunn and the other lawyer defendants.

On appeal, Minton raised a new argument: Because his legal malpractice claim was based on an alleged error in a patent case, it "aris[es] under" federal patent law for purposes of 28 U.S.C. § 1338(a). And because, under § 1338(a), "[n]o State court shall have jurisdiction over any claim for relief arising under any Act of Congress relating to patents," the Texas court— where Minton had originally brought his malpractice claim—lacked subject matter jurisdiction to decide the case. Accordingly, Minton argued, the trial court's order should be vacated and the case dismissed, leaving Minton free to start over in the Federal District Court.

A divided panel of the Court of Appeals of Texas rejected Minton's argument. Applying the test we articulated in *Grable & Sons Metal Products, Inc. v. Darue Engineering & Mfg.*, 545 U.S. 308, 314 (2005), it held that the federal interests implicated by Minton's state law claim were not sufficiently substantial to trigger § 1338 "arising under" jurisdiction. It also held that finding exclusive federal jurisdiction over state legal malpractice actions would, contrary to *Grable*'s commands, disturb the balance of federal and state judicial responsibilities. Proceeding to the merits of Minton's malpractice claim, the Court of Appeals affirmed the trial court's determination that Minton had failed to establish experimental use and that arguments on that ground therefore would not have saved his infringement suit.

The Supreme Court of Texas reversed. 355 S.W.3d 634 (2011). The Court concluded that Minton's claim involved "a substantial federal issue" within the meaning of *Grable* "because the success of Minton's malpractice claim is reliant upon the viability of the experimental use exception as a defense to the on-sale bar." *Id.* at 644. Adjudication of Minton's claim in federal court was consistent with the appropriate balance between federal and state judicial responsibilities, it held, because "the federal government and patent litigants have an interest in the uniform application of patent law by courts well-versed in that subject matter." *Id.* at 646.

Justice Guzman, joined by Justices Medina and Willett, dissented. The dissenting justices would have held that the federal issue was neither substantial nor disputed, and that maintaining the proper balance of responsibility between state and federal courts precluded relegating state legal malpractice claims to federal court.

We granted certiorari....

II

"Federal courts are courts of limited jurisdiction," possessing "only that power authorized by Constitution and statute." *Kokkonen v. Guardian Life Ins. Co. of America*, 511 U.S. 375, 377 (1994). There is no dispute that the Constitution permits Congress to extend federal court jurisdiction to a case such as this one, *see Osborn v. Bank of United States*, 22 U.S. (9 Wheat.) 738, 823–24 (1824); the question is whether Congress has done so.

As relevant here, Congress has authorized the federal district courts to exercise original jurisdiction in "all civil actions arising under the Constitution, laws, or treaties of the United States," 28 U.S.C. § 1331, and, more particularly, over "any civil action arising under any Act of Congress relating to patents," § 1338(a). Adhering to the demands of "[l]inguistic consistency," we have interpreted the phrase "arising under" in both sections identically, applying our § 1331 and § 1338(a) precedents interchangeably. *See Christianson v. Colt Indus. Operating Corp.*, 486 U.S. 800, 808–09 (1988). For cases falling within the patent-specific arising under jurisdiction of § 1338(a), however, Congress has not only provided for federal jurisdiction but also eliminated state jurisdiction, decreeing that "[n]o State court shall have jurisdiction over any claim for relief arising under any Act of Congress relating to patents." § 1338(a). To determine whether jurisdiction was proper in the Texas courts, therefore, we must determine whether it would have been proper in a federal district court—whether, that is, the case "aris[es] under any Act of Congress relating to patents."

For statutory purposes, a case can "aris[e] under" federal law in two ways. Most directly, a case arises under federal law when federal law creates the cause of action asserted. *See American Well Works Co. v. Layne & Bowler Co.*, 241 U.S. 257, 260 (1916) ("A suit arises under the law that creates the cause of action"). As a rule of inclusion, this "creation" test admits of only extremely rare exceptions, *see, e.g., Shoshone Mining Co. v. Rutter*, 177 U.S. 505 (1900), and accounts for the vast bulk of suits that arise under federal law.... Minton's original patent infringement suit against NASD and NASDAQ, for example, arose under federal law in this manner because it was authorized by 35 U.S.C. §§ 271, 281.

But even where a claim finds its origins in state rather than federal law—as Minton's legal malpractice claim indisputably does—we have identified a "special and small category" of cases in which arising under jurisdiction still lies. *Empire Healthchoice Assurance, Inc. v. McVeigh*, 547 U.S. 677, 699 (2006). In outlining the contours of this slim category, we do not paint on a blank canvas. Unfortunately, the canvas looks like one that Jackson Pollock got to first....

In an effort to bring some order to this unruly doctrine several Terms ago, we condensed our prior cases into the following inquiry: Does the "state-law claim necessarily raise a stated federal issue, actually disputed and substantial, which a federal forum may entertain without disturbing any congressionally approved balance of federal and state judicial responsibilities"? *Grable*, 545 U.S. at 314. That is, federal jurisdiction over a state law claim will lie if a federal issue is: (1) necessarily raised, (2) actually disputed, (3) substantial, and (4) capable of resolution in federal court without disrupting the federal-state balance approved by Congress. Where all four of these requirements are met, we held, jurisdiction is proper because there is a "serious federal interest in claiming the advantages thought to be inherent in a federal forum," which can be vindicated without disrupting Congress's intended division of labor between state and federal courts. *Id.* at 313–14.

III

Applying *Grable*'s inquiry here, it is clear that Minton's legal malpractice claim does not arise under federal patent law. Indeed, for the reasons we discuss, we are comfortable concluding that state legal malpractice claims based on underlying patent matters will rarely, if ever, arise under federal patent law for purposes of § 1338(a). Although such cases may necessarily raise disputed questions of patent law, those cases are by their nature unlikely to have the sort of significance for the federal system necessary to establish jurisdiction.

A

To begin, we acknowledge that resolution of a federal patent question is "necessary" to Minton's case. Under Texas law, a plaintiff alleging legal malpractice must establish four elements: (1) that the defendant attorney owed the plaintiff a duty; (2) that the attorney breached that duty; (3) that the breach was the proximate cause of the plaintiff's injury; and (4) that damages occurred.... In cases like this one, in which the attorney's alleged error came in failing to make a particular argument, the causation element requires a "case within a case" analysis of whether, had the argument been made, the outcome of the earlier litigation would have been different.... To prevail on his legal malpractice claim, therefore, Minton must show that he would have prevailed in his federal patent infringement case if only petitioners had timely made an experimental-use argument on his behalf. That will necessarily require application of patent law to the facts of Minton's case.

B

The federal issue is also "actually disputed" here—indeed, on the merits, it is the central point of dispute. Minton argues that the experimental-use exception properly applied to his lease to Stark, saving his patent from the on-sale bar; petitioners argue that it did not. This is just the sort of "'dispute ... respecting the ... effect of [federal] law'" that *Grable* envisioned. 545 U.S. at 313 (quoting *Shulthis v. McDougal*, 225 U.S. 561, 569 (1912)).

C

Minton's argument founders on *Grable*'s next requirement, however, for the federal issue in this case is not substantial in the relevant sense. In reaching the opposite conclusion, the Supreme Court of Texas focused on the importance of the issue to the plaintiff's case and to the parties before it. 355 S.W.3d at 644 ("because the success of Minton's malpractice claim is reliant upon the viability of the experimental use exception as a defense to the on-sale bar, we hold that it is a substantial federal issue"). As our past cases show, however, it is not enough that the federal issue be significant to the particular parties in the immediate suit; that will always be true when the state claim "necessarily raise[s]" a disputed federal issue, as *Grable* separately requires. The substantiality inquiry under *Grable* looks instead to the importance of the issue to the federal system as a whole.

In *Grable* itself, for example, the Internal Revenue Service had seized property from the plaintiff and sold it to satisfy the plaintiff's federal tax delinquency. 545 U.S. at 310–11. Five years later, the plaintiff filed a state law quiet title action against the third party that had purchased the property, alleging that the IRS had failed to comply with certain federally imposed notice requirements, so that the seizure and sale were invalid. *Id.* In holding that the case arose under federal law, we primarily focused not on the interests of the litigants themselves, but rather on the broader significance of the notice question for the Federal Government. We emphasized the Government's "strong interest" in being able to recover delinquent taxes through seizure and sale of property, which in turn "require[d] clear terms of notice to allow buyers ... to satisfy themselves that the Service has touched the bases necessary for good title." *Id.* at 315. The Government's "direct interest in the availability of a federal forum to vindicate its own administrative action" made the question "an important issue of federal law that sensibly belong[ed] in a federal court." *Id.*

A second illustration of the sort of substantiality we require comes from *Smith v. Kansas City Title & Trust Co.*, 255 U.S. 180 (1921), which *Grable* described as "[t]he classic example" of a state claim arising under federal law. 545 U.S. at 312. In *Smith*, the plaintiff argued that the defendant bank could not purchase certain bonds issued by the Federal Government because the Government had acted unconstitutionally in issuing them. 255 U.S. at 198. We held that the case arose under federal law, because the "decision depends upon the determination" of "the constitutional validity of an act of Congress which is directly drawn in question." *Id.* at 201. Again, the relevant point was not the importance of the question to the parties alone but rather the importance more generally of a determination that the Government "securities were issued under an unconstitutional law, and hence of no validity." *Id.*

Here, the federal issue carries no such significance. Because of the backward-looking nature of a legal malpractice claim, the question is posed in a merely hypothetical sense: If Minton's lawyers had raised a timely experimental-use argument, would the result in the patent infringement proceeding have been different? No matter how the state courts resolve that hypothetical "case within a case," it will not change the real-world result of the prior federal patent litigation. Minton's patent will remain invalid.

Nor will allowing state courts to resolve these cases undermine "the development of a uniform body of [patent] law." *Bonito Boats, Inc. v. Thunder Craft Boats, Inc.*, 489 U.S. 141, 162 (1989). Congress ensured such uniformity by vesting exclusive jurisdiction over actual patent cases in the federal district courts and exclusive appellate jurisdiction in the Federal Circuit. *See* 28 U.S.C. §§ 1338(a), 1295(a)(1). In resolving the nonhypothetical patent questions those cases present, the federal courts are of course not bound by state court case-within-a-case patent rulings. *See Tafflin v. Levitt*, 493 U.S. 455, 465 (1990). In any event, the state court case-within-a-case inquiry asks what would have happened in the prior federal proceeding if a particular argument had been made. In answering that question, state courts can be expected to hew closely to the pertinent federal precedents. It is those precedents, after all, that would have applied had the argument been made....

As for more novel questions of patent law that may arise for the first time in a state court "case within a case," they will at some point be decided by a federal court in the context of an actual patent case, with review in the Federal Circuit. If the question arises frequently, it will soon be resolved within the federal system, laying to rest any contrary state court precedent; if it does not arise frequently, it is unlikely to implicate substantial federal interests. The present case is "poles apart from *Grable*," in which a state court's resolution of the federal question "would be controlling in numerous other cases." *Empire Healthchoice Assurance, Inc.*, 547 U.S. at 700.

. . . .

Nor can we accept the suggestion that the federal courts' greater familiarity with patent law means that legal malpractice cases like this one belong in federal court.... It is true that a similar interest was among those we considered in *Grable*, 545 U.S. at 314. But the possibility that a state court will incorrectly resolve a state claim is not, by itself, enough to trigger the federal courts' exclusive patent jurisdiction, even if the potential error finds its root in a misunderstanding of patent law.

There is no doubt that resolution of a patent issue in the context of a state legal malpractice action can be vitally important to the particular parties in that case. But something more, demonstrating that the question is significant to the federal system as a whole, is needed. That is missing here.

D

It follows from the foregoing that *Grable*'s fourth requirement is also not met. That requirement is concerned with the appropriate "balance of federal and state judicial responsibilities." *Id.* We have already explained the absence of a substantial federal issue within the meaning of *Grable*. The States, on the other hand, have "a special responsibility for maintaining standards among members of the licensed professions." *Ohralik v. Ohio State Bar Ass'n*, 436 U.S. 447, 460 (1978). Their "interest ... in regulating lawyers is especially great since lawyers are essential to the primary governmental function of administering justice, and have historically been officers of the courts." *Goldfarb v. Virginia State Bar*, 421 U.S. 773, 792 (1975) (internal quotation marks omitted). We have no reason to suppose that Congress—in establishing exclusive federal jurisdiction over patent cases—meant to bar from state courts state legal malpractice claims simply because they require resolution of a hypothetical patent issue.

As we recognized a century ago, "[t]he Federal courts have exclusive jurisdiction of all cases arising under the patent laws, but not of all questions in which a patent may be the subject-matter of the controversy." *New Marshall Engine Co. v. Marshall Engine Co.*, 223 U.S. 473, 478 (1912). In this case, although the state courts must answer a question of patent law to resolve Minton's legal malpractice claim, their answer will have no broader effects. It will not stand as binding precedent for any future patent claim; it will not even affect the validity of Minton's patent. Accordingly, there is no "serious federal interest in claiming the advantages thought to be inherent in a federal forum," *Grable*, 545 U.S. at 313. Section 1338(a) does not deprive the state courts of subject matter jurisdiction.

The judgment of the Supreme Court of Texas is reversed, and the case is remanded for further proceedings not inconsistent with this opinion.

It is so ordered.

Notes and Questions

1. (a) Based on the Court's analysis in *Grable* and *Gunn*, can you now articulate a standard for determining the type of federal interest necessary to satisfy the "substantial federal issue" requirement for Category 2 federal question jurisdiction? Why was the federal interest deemed "substantial" in *Smith* and *Grable*, and not substantial in *Merrell Dow* and *Gunn*?

(b) As you will recall, the plaintiffs in *Merrell Dow* filed a state law negligence action against the defendant drug company alleging that it had misbranded one of its drugs in violation of the Federal Food, Drug, and Cosmetic Act (FDCA). Because the FDCA did not create, either expressly or impliedly, a private cause of action for persons injured as a result of violations of the FDCA, the plaintiffs' claim did not qualify for Category 1 federal question jurisdiction. Under state tort law, however, a violation of the FDCA constituted a rebuttable presumption of negligence and, in the absence of an effective rebuttal, would be sufficient under state law to establish the defendant's negligence and entitle the plaintiffs to recover on their state law claim.

(c) Although the Court in *Merrell Dow* held that the plaintiffs' state law claim satisfied the "well-pleaded complaint" rule, and thus potentially qualified for Category 2 federal question jurisdiction, the Court held that the plaintiffs' claim case did not raise a "substantial federal issue." Based on the Court's analysis in *Gunn*, would the result in *Merrell Dow*, a 1986 decision, be the same today? In determining whether a "substantial federal issue" exists, should you weigh whether the federal interest in protecting the public from misbranded drugs would be seriously undermined if a state court erroneously held that the defendant's drug was not misbranded under the FDCA? As you will learn in Chapter 12, any state court decision would not be binding on the Federal Food and Drug Administration because it would not be party to the state court action, and the Federal Food and Drug Administration could still enforce the provisions of the FDCA against the defendant in its own action. In this sense, is *Merrell Dow* more like *Smith* and *Grable* or more like *Gunn*?

2. In properly understanding the Court's denial of federal question jurisdiction in *Merrell Dow* and *Gunn*, it is important to distinguish the Court's denial of federal question jurisdiction in *Mottley*. Although the plaintiffs in all three cases were asserting *state* law claims, jurisdiction was denied in *Mottley* because the plaintiffs' claim failed to satisfy the "well-pleaded complaint" rule, which is the first requirement for Category 2 federal question jurisdiction. By contrast, jurisdiction was denied in *Merrell Dow* and *Gunn* because the plaintiffs' claims failed the separate third and fourth requirements for Category 2 jurisdiction, *i.e.,* substantial federal issue and proper federal/state court balance. The plaintiffs' claims in both *Merrell Dow* and *Gunn* fully satisfied the "well-pleaded complaint" rule. Do you understand why?

Problem

Problem 4-2. P is manufacturing an item which D believes infringes a patent owned by D. D threatens to sue P and all persons purchasing the item from P for patent infringement under the federal patent laws. If D actually brought such a suit, D would have to bring it in a U.S. District Court because the patent laws are federal and the U.S. District Courts have exclusive jurisdiction over patent infringement actions under 28 U.S.C. § 1338. However, D never actually brings a patent infringement action, but continues to threaten P and P's customers. P believes that D's patent is invalid under the federal patent laws and, therefore, that P has a perfect right to manufacture the item purportedly covered by the patent. Furthermore, P believes that D's threats to sue and allegations that P did not own the right to manufacture the item were false and have damaged P's business.

If P is correct, the threats and allegations give rise to a claim for "slander of title" under state law, which would entitle P to damages from D. A claim for slander of title under state law arises when a person makes a false statement disparaging another person's title to real or personal property. Thus, the plaintiff must allege ownership of the property, a false statement by the defendant that the plaintiff did not own the property, and damages. P sues D in a U.S. District Court for damages for slander of title. P's complaint contains a jurisdictional statement alleging that the case arises under the federal patent laws. In addition to the allegations of ownership and damages, the complaint alleges that D's patent is invalid under the federal patent laws and, therefore, that D's assertions about having a valid patent on the item manufactured by P are false and slanderous. Is there federal question jurisdiction over P's action?

3. Distinguishing Proper Subject-Matter Jurisdiction in a Federal Question Case from Ultimate Success on the Merits

As explained in the previous sections, subject-matter jurisdiction in a federal question case is based on the existence of a substantive claim that properly "arises under" federal law within the meaning of Article III, §2 (first clause) and §1331. It is not necessary, however, that a plaintiff ultimately succeed on the substantive merits of the claim giving rise to federal question jurisdiction for subject-matter jurisdiction to properly exist in the action. Even though the plaintiff fails to succeed on its substantive claim and loses the case on the merits, the court is not divested of jurisdiction and the action need not be dismissed for lack of subject-matter jurisdiction. As the Supreme Court explained in *Bell v. Hood*, 327 U.S. 678 (1946),

> Jurisdiction ... is not defeated ... by the possibility that the averments might fail to state a cause of action on which the [plaintiff] could actually recover. For it is well settled that the failure to state a proper cause of action calls for a judgment on the merits and not for a dismissal for want of jurisdiction.

Id. at 682. It is only when the alleged federal law claim "clearly appears to be immaterial and made solely for the purpose of obtaining jurisdiction or where such a claim is wholly insubstantial and frivolous [and] so patently without merit" that a dismissal for lack of subject-matter jurisdiction is warranted. *Id.* at 682–83.

Grable is an excellent illustration of this principle. In *Grable*, the federal district court held, and the court of appeals affirmed, that the challenged IRS notice did not violate federal law as the plaintiff had alleged and that the plaintiff's substantive claim should be dismissed on the merits. The Supreme Court, nevertheless, unanimously affirmed the lower courts' exercise of federal question jurisdiction to adjudicate the substantive merits of the plaintiff's claim and render a valid judgment as to whether or not the IRS notice violated federal law.

4. Scope of the Statutory Grant in Declaratory Judgment Actions

Nature of the Declaratory Judgment Remedy. Recall from Chapter 1 that an action for a declaratory judgment seeks a judicial declaration of the parties' legal rights and obligations as applied to an actual controversy between the parties. Declaratory relief is distinct from the two traditional forms of judicial relief—legal relief, typically money damages, and equitable relief, such as an injunction. Declaratory relief may be requested independently of any request for legal or equitable relief. It is especially useful in cases in which the parties need an authoritative statement from a court to settle a dispute over their legal rights, but the dispute has not yet reached the stage at which either party possesses a claim for legal or equitable relief or the party possessing such a claim chooses not to sue on it at the time.

Suppose, for example, that *P* begins marketing a new product, but is informed by *D* that the new product is in violation of *D*'s federal patent. *D* threatens to sue *P* for patent infringement if *P* does not stop marketing the product. *P* believes that *P*'s product does not infringe *D*'s patent, but in the absence of a judicial determination of this issue, *P* is faced with a difficult choice. *P* must either accede to *D*'s demand and discontinue marketing the product or continue marketing the product at the risk of incurring substantial damages if *P*'s position is not later upheld in a subsequent patent infringement suit by *D*. An action for declaratory relief would be particularly advantageous to *P* in this case, as it would allow *P* to resolve the issue of infringement without incurring the cost of ceasing profitable activity or the risk of incurring damages if *P*'s legal position is incorrect.

The Federal Declaratory Judgment Act. Actions for declaratory relief, however, are of relatively recent origin in American jurisprudence. One serious impediment to declaratory judgments in the federal system was the hallowed principle of constitutional law that federal courts have no constitutional authority to render "advisory opinions" because such actions do not constitute "cases or controversies" within the meaning of Article III, §2 of the Constitution. In 1933, however, the Supreme Court held that actions for declaratory relief can qualify constitutionally as "cases or controversies" within the meaning of Article III. *Nashville, Chattanooga & St. Louis Ry. v. Wallace*, 288 U.S. 249 (1933). In 1934, Congress responded with the Federal Declaratory Judgment Act, now codified in 28 U.S.C. §§ 2201–2202. Section 2201 provides as follows:

> In a case of *actual controversy within its jurisdiction* ... any court of the United States, upon the filing of an appropriate pleading, may declare the rights and other legal relations of any interested party seeking such declaration, whether or not further relief is or could be sought.

28 U.S.C. § 2201(a) (emphasis added).

Determining when a declaratory judgment action is "within [their] jurisdiction," however, has been a source of difficulty for the federal courts. Fortunately, these jurisdictional complexities are limited to declaratory judgment actions based on federal question jurisdiction. As you will learn in section C, federal subject-matter jurisdiction based on diversity of citizenship exists whenever the parties are of diverse citizenship and the amount in controversy exceeds $75,000, irrespective of the federal or non-federal nature of the plaintiff's substantive claim.

Essentially, the Supreme Court has held that in evaluating whether a declaratory judgment action is suitable for federal question jurisdiction, the first question that must be asked is whether either party to the declaratory judgment action (the declaratory plaintiff or the declaratory defendant) could have commenced a traditional action for legal or equitable relief in federal court based on federal question jurisdiction. *See Skelly Oil Co. v. Phillips Petroleum Co.*, 339 U.S. 667 (1950). The claims of both sides are examined in the jurisdictional analysis because in a declaratory judgment action, the position of the parties is often the exact reverse of what it would be in a traditional action for legal or equitable relief. Typically, the party who would be the defendant in an action for legal or equitable relief is the plaintiff in the declaratory judgment action. In *Skelly Oil*, however, the Court made clear that federal question jurisdiction is still improper in a declaratory judgment action if the issue of federal law would only have been raised as a defense to a state law claim in a traditional suit for legal or equitable relief. Under *Skelly Oil*, it is how federal law would have been raised in a traditional non-declaratory judgment action that is critical to the jurisdictional analysis.

Consider the earlier example of the patent infringement dispute. The federal patent laws expressly create a right of action for patent infringement, and the federal courts have exclusive federal question jurisdiction of such actions under 28 U.S.C. § 1338. Suppose, however, that *D*, the party with the patent infringement claim, does not sue on the infringement claim, but simply threatens *P*, the alleged patent infringer, with suit. Assume *P* now commences a declaratory judgment action in federal court to obtain a declaration of non-infringement. Under these circumstances, the *Skelly Oil* test is met. Although *P* has no non-declaratory claim for relief suitable for federal question jurisdiction, *D* does have such a claim—a patent infringement claim. Because *D* can bring a non-declaratory judgment action within federal question jurisdiction, the alleged infringer, *P*, can bring a declaratory judgment action for non-infringement in federal court.

Would a declaratory judgment action have been possible in the *Mottley* case? Certainly, the Mottleys' claim, which failed the "well-pleaded complaint" rule, could not provide the basis for federal question jurisdiction in a declaratory judgment action. But what about the railroad? Suppose the applicable state substantive law allowed either party to a contract to sue for rescission of the contract based on illegality. If the railroad could sue the Mottleys for rescission alleging that the contract was illegal under the new federal Act, would such a claim by the railroad contain an "essential element" of federal law and be within federal question jurisdiction? If so, would this claim have made an action for declaratory relief proper?

The *Franchise Tax Board* Qualification. However, satisfaction of the above test is not the end of the story. A plaintiff cannot always sue in federal court for a declaratory judgment just because the defendant could have sued within the federal question jurisdiction for a nondeclaratory remedy. In *Franchise Tax Board v. Construction Laborers Vacation Trust*, 463 U.S. 1 (1983), the Supreme Court held that even if one of the parties in the declaratory judgment action could sue within the federal question jurisdiction for nondeclaratory relief, that fact alone was not sufficient to sustain jurisdiction. In addition, the Court held that the declaratory judgment plaintiff must also have a "clear interest" in a swift *federal* resolution of the issue of federal law upon which the parties disagree. *See* 463 U.S. at 21 n.23. In the patent case described in the preceding paragraph, such an interest exists because "[p]arties subject to conflicting state and federal regulatory schemes ... have a clear interest in sorting out the scope of each government's authority, especially [when] they face a threat of liability if the application of federal law is not quickly made clear." *Id.* The steps in analyzing whether a declaratory judgment action qualifies for federal question jurisdiction are summarized in Figure 4-3.

STEPS IN ANALYZING WHETHER A DECLARATORY JUDGMENT ACTION QUALIFIES FOR "FEDERAL QUESTION" JURISDICTION	
Step 1	Could either party to the declaratory judgment action (the declaratory plaintiff or the declaratory defendant) have commenced a non-declaratory federal question action in federal court based on federal question jurisdiction? • **If yes, go to Step 2.** • **If no, then the court is not authorized to hear the declaratory judgment action on the basis of federal question jurisdiction.**
Step 2	Does the declaratory plaintiff have a "clear interest" in a swift *federal* resolution of the issue of federal law upon which the parties disagree? • **If yes, the declaratory judgment action is within the federal question jurisdiction of the federal courts.** • **If no, then the court is not authorized to hear the declaratory judgment action on the basis of federal question jurisdiction.**

Figure 4-3

In *Franchise Tax Board* itself, however, the strength of the interest was not strong enough to allow the declaratory judgment action to be brought within the federal question jurisdiction. One of the parties (the declaratory judgment defendant in the action brought by the Franchise Tax Board) could have sued in federal court for an injunction under federal law. However, the state tax board seeking the declaratory judgment could not show a sufficiently strong interest in obtaining federal declaratory relief in the case because the state had a variety of means by which it could enforce its own laws in its own courts, in which the federal issues could also be satisfactorily adjudicated. *See id.* at 21.

To understand the *Franchise Tax Board* qualification of federal question jurisdiction in declaratory judgment cases, one must appreciate the difference between the dilemma of the alleged patent infringer and the dilemma of a plaintiff like the California Franchise Tax Board. The alleged patent infringer is faced with two unpalatable choices in the absence of an authoritative declaration of its federal rights. If it continues to manufacture and sell the alleged infringing product in the fact of threats to sue by the patent holder, it might be subjecting itself to large monetary damages for each item sold if its view of federal law turns out to be wrong.

On the other hand, if it ceases the alleged infringing activity to avoid suit, it may be giving up substantial profits that it is entitled to earn by manufacturing and selling the product if its view of federal law is correct. Only an authoritative declaration of its federal rights will eliminate this dilemma and tell it what the correct course of action is. In contrast, the California Franchise Tax Board simply wants to collect taxes that it alleges are due to the state. It can accomplish that by an action against the taxpayer in state court in which the taxpayer's federal defenses can be litigated fully. Alternatively, if the taxpayer sues it in state or federal court for an injunction, the federal issues can be litigated there. In either case, it is not in danger of losing valuable rights if it does not obtain a declaratory judgment from a federal court. It is this difference in the dilemma faced by the two kinds of litigants that justifies the declaratory judgment suit by the patent infringer, but not by the Franchise Tax Board.

Problems

Problem 4-3. *D* believes that *P* is infringing a patent owned by *D* by manufacturing an item covered by the patent. *D* threatens to sue *P* and all persons purchasing the item from *P* for patent infringement under the federal patent laws. If *D* actually brought such an action, *D* would have to bring it in U.S. District Court because the patent laws are federal and the U.S. District Courts have exclusive jurisdiction over patent infringement actions under 28 U.S.C. § 1338. However, *D* never brings a patent infringement action, but *D* continues to threaten *P* and *P's* customers with suit. *P* believes that *D's* patent is invalid and would like to stop the threats. Therefore, *P* sues *D* in a U.S. District Court for a declaratory judgment that *D's* patent is invalid. Is there federal question jurisdiction over *P's* action?

Problem 4-4. *D* has threatened to sue *P*, an F.B.I. agent, for damages resulting from a single past search of *D* by *P* that allegedly violated the Fourth Amendment. *P* disputes that the Fourth Amendment was violated. Before *D* sues *P*, *P* sues *D* in a U.S. District Court to obtain a declaratory judgment that the search did not violate the Fourth Amendment. *D* moves to dismiss the action for lack of subject-matter jurisdiction. What should the result be? Would the result be different if *P* had been conducting an ongoing investigation of *D* that required periodic searches of the same kind for which *D* is threatening to sue *P*?

Problem 4-5. *D* threatened to sue *P* for damages for libel if *P*, a television broadcaster, did not retract allegedly defamatory remarks that *P* made during a news broadcast. Libel claims are created by state law. *P* sues *D* in a U.S. District Court for a declaratory judgment that the remarks are protected by the First Amendment. *D* moves to dismiss the action for lack of subject-matter jurisdiction. What should the result be?

Section C. Diversity and Alienage Jurisdiction

After federal question cases, the second largest category of federal court civil cases involving private litigants is diversity-of-citizenship cases, which currently comprise about one-third of the civil docket of the federal district courts. As discussed in section A, above, in order for a case to qualify for subject-matter jurisdiction in the federal courts, there must be both constitutional and statutory authorization for the exercise of jurisdiction. Diversity-of-citizenship cases are constitutionally authorized under Article III, §2 (seventh clause), which extends the federal judicial power to "Controversies between Citizens of different States."

Relationship Between the Constitutional and Statutory Grants of Diversity Jurisdiction. Ever since the first Judiciary Act of 1789, Congress has continuously authorized the federal courts to exercise diversity jurisdiction. By comparison, it was not until 1875 that Congress first enacted a general federal question jurisdiction statute. Statutory authorization for general diversity cases is currently contained in 28 U.S.C. §1332(a). Section 1332(a)(1) provides for original jurisdiction over all civil actions between citizens of different states when the amount in controversy exceeds $75,000. In subsections (a)(2)–(4), §1332 also provides for jurisdiction over cases between state citizens and foreign nationals, commonly referred to as "alienage jurisdiction." Alienage jurisdiction is constitutionally authorized by Article III, §2 (ninth clause), which extends the federal judicial power to controversies "between a State, or the Citizens thereof, and foreign States, Citizens or Subjects." Interpleader actions, which are statutorily authorized under 28 U.S.C. §1335, are also based on the same constitutional provision authorizing diversity jurisdiction. Jurisdiction in all diversity cases is *concurrent* with the state courts, and such actions do not have to be filed in federal court.

As you know from studying federal question jurisdiction, Congress is not required in enacting a jurisdictional statute to grant to the federal courts the full scope of the judicial power authorized in Article III, §2. Congress can choose to give the federal courts less than the full constitutional power permitted by Article III. Such is the case with diversity jurisdiction. In the same way that the constitutional scope of "arising under" is broader than the statutory scope of "arising under" in federal question jurisdiction, the constitutional scope of diversity jurisdiction is broader than the statutory scope of §1332.

The Supreme Court has held that the constitutional grant of diversity jurisdiction under Article III requires only "minimal diversity," *i.e.*, at least one party must be diverse from at least one opposing party. *See State Farm Fire & Cas. Co. v. Tashire*, 386 U.S. 523, 530–31 (1967). In contrast, the Supreme Court in *Strawbridge v. Curtiss*, 7 U.S. (3 Cranch) 267 (1806), held that the grant of jurisdiction under the diversity statute requires "complete diversity of citizenship," *i.e.*, every plaintiff must be diverse from every defendant. In addition, Article III imposes no amount-in-controversy requirement, while §1332(a) requires that the amount in controversy exceed $75,000. The interplay of these statutory requirements under §1332(a) and their relationship to the constitutional grant are shown in Figure 4-4 on the next page.

Purposes of Diversity Jurisdiction. Unlike federal question jurisdiction, which is based on the plaintiff's claim arising under federal law, diversity jurisdiction is based solely on the citizenship of the litigants, irrespective of the substantive nature of the plaintiff's claim. Diversity jurisdiction, therefore, provides a basis for the assertion of purely state law claims in federal court simply because the litigants are citizens of different states. Pure diversity actions are, by definition, always based on state law because if the case arose under federal law, the litigants would simply invoke §1331 and avoid §1332's additional requirements for complete diversity and amount in controversy.

The traditional justification for diversity jurisdiction is that, even though diversity cases are not based on federal law, a neutral federal forum is necessary to protect against bias in state courts in cases involving out-of-state litigants. Some scholars question whether this bias still exists today, at least to a degree justifying the additional strain on the federal docket, especially considering that the federal courts have no particular expertise in

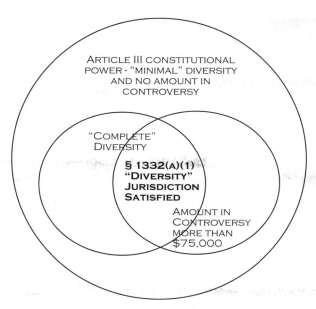

Figure 4-4

deciding claims based on state law. Not surprisingly, various proposals have been made over the years to curtail or eliminate diversity jurisdiction. In fact, the 1990 Report of the congressionally appointed Federal Courts Study Committee, concluded that "no other class of cases has a weaker claim on federal judicial resources" and recommended that diversity jurisdiction be virtually eliminated, except in cases of complex multistate litigation, interpleader, and suits involving aliens. Despite such proposals, Congress has repeatedly chosen to retain general diversity jurisdiction in its current form.

A Litigant's Perspective. Because jurisdiction in diversity cases is concurrent with the state courts, why would a plaintiff want to file (or in the case of a defendant remove) a state law diversity case in federal court? As you will learn in Chapter 5, a doctrine known as the "*Erie* doctrine" requires a federal court adjudicating a state law claim to apply the same substantive law that a state court would have applied if the case had been commenced in the state court in which the federal court is sitting. Thus, in theory, the litigants will not receive any substantive law advantage by filing a diversity case in federal court. Rather, litigants choose federal court because they perceive some procedural or tactical advantage in federal court. Empirical studies show that lawyers representing out-of-state clients do consider possible state court bias, whether actual or imagined, as a factor in choosing the federal forum. *See, e.g.,* Victor E. Flango, *Attorneys' Perspectives on Choice of Forum in Diversity Cases*, 25 AKRON L. REV. 41, 105 (1991). Even though federal court juries are chosen from the state in which the federal court is located, the jury pool will be district-wide and not county-wide as in state court. Thus, the federal jury may be less parochial in its viewpoint than a state court jury. Similarly, although federal judges are ordinarily selected from local state bar membership, they are appointed by the President and possess life tenure. They are thus (arguably) more insulated from local political pressures than a state court judge.

In addition, although the *Erie* doctrine requires the federal courts to apply state substantive law in adjudicating state law issues, the federal courts are free to apply their own

not on Exam

rules of procedure in adjudicating a diversity case. Depending on the corresponding procedures in the state courts, therefore, litigants may choose a federal over a state forum because of procedural considerations, such as more favorable evidentiary standards for proving their cases under the Federal Rules of Evidence or more favorable rules for service of process, pleading, joinder of claims, discovery, jury trials, judgment execution and docketing, or other provisions under the Federal Rules of Civil Procedure or federal procedural statutes. Litigants also consider other factors, such as docket backlog, location and convenience of the courthouses, quality of the judges, and individual familiarity and comfort with the different court systems.

Special Diversity Statutes—(a) **The Multiparty, Multiforum Trial Jurisdiction Act of 2002, 28 U.S.C. §1369.** In 2002, Congress conferred jurisdiction on the district courts under 28 U.S.C. §1369 in certain mass tort civil actions where at least 75 "natural persons" have died in an accident "at a discrete location." *See* 28 U.S.C. §1369(a). The Act requires only "minimal diversity," which is satisfied if any party is diverse from any other adverse party. 28 U.S.C. §1369(c)(1). The purpose of the Act is to "streamline the process" for the adjudication of multidistrict litigation involving mass tort disasters. *See* H.R. Conf. Rep. No. 107-685, at 199 (2002).

(b) **The Class Action Fairness Act of 2005, 28 U.S.C. §1332(d).** In 2005, Congress broadened federal jurisdiction, also on the basis of "minimal diversity," with respect to certain nationwide class actions. The purpose of the Act, codified in 28 U.S.C. §1332(d)(1)–(11), is to prevent the perceived abuses that have occurred in some state courts in these actions. Specifically, Congress provided complex provisions for jurisdiction in certain class actions in which "(A) any member of a class of plaintiffs is a citizen of a State different from any defendant; (B) any member of a class of plaintiffs is a foreign state or a citizen or subject of a foreign state and any defendant is a citizen of a State; or (C) any member of a class of plaintiffs is a citizen of a State and any defendant is a foreign state or a citizen or subject of a foreign state." *See* 28 U.S.C. §1332(d)(2)(A)-(C). Under §1332(d)(2), the amount in controversy must exceed $5,000,000, but the claims of the individual class members are aggregated in determining if the jurisdictional amount is met. *See* 28 U.S.C. §1332(d)(6).

1. Suits between Citizens of Different States

Definition of a "Citizen of a State." The fundamental requirement of diversity jurisdiction under both Article III and 28 U.S.C. §1332 is a controversy "between citizens of different states." Neither Article III nor §1332, however, defines what elements qualify a natural person as a "citizen of a state." The Fourteenth Amendment to the U.S. Constitution, adopted in 1868, provides that "[a]ll persons born or naturalized in the United States, and subject to the jurisdiction thereof, are citizens of the United States and of the State wherein they reside." The federal courts, however, have long interpreted the diversity statute as defining state citizenship in terms of *domicile* and not residence. To be a "citizen of a state" within the meaning of §1332, a natural person must be (1) legally domiciled in that state and (2) a citizen of the United States.

Note that §1332(e) provides that the word "States," as used in §1332, "includes the Territories, the District of Columbia, and the Commonwealth of Puerto Rico," and this statutory extension of diversity jurisdiction has been upheld against constitutional challenge.

Domicile of Individuals. Although the concept of domicile embraces residence, the terms are not synonymous. Domicile is a common-law concept derived from "conflict-of-laws" principles and is more or less equivalent with the concept of a person's permanent home. People may have several residences, but they can have only one legal domicile. People retain their existing domiciles until they acquire new ones. A new domicile can only be acquired by being physically present in a new state and *simultaneously* having the intent to make the new state home. To effectuate a change in domicile, the factors of physical presence and intent *must* coincide. In addition, the intent must be a *present* intention to make the new place home, not an intent to make the new place home in the future.

One of the consequences of the rule defining "state citizenship" in terms of domicile is that a U.S. citizen domiciled abroad may not sue or be sued under the diversity statute. This rule may seem curious, but it is based on the notion that a United States citizen domiciled abroad is neither a citizen of a state (because the person is not domiciled in any state) nor a citizen or subject of a foreign state (because the person is a citizen of the United States).

The courts have developed a number of rules for determining the propriety of jurisdiction in a diversity case and the domicile of an individual, all of which are highlighted in the text and footnotes of the *Walls* case. As you read *Walls,* focus on identifying each of these separate rules.

Walls v. Ahmed

United States District Court, Eastern District of Pennsylvania, 1993
832 F. Supp. 940

Katz, District Judge.

Defendant, Khalil Ahmed, contends in his trial brief that there is no subject-matter jurisdiction in this case. This is a wrongful death, 42 Pa. Cons. Stat. Ann. § 8301, and survival action, 42 Pa. Cons. Stat. Ann. § 8302, that arises out of a multi-vehicle accident (the "Accident") that occurred on August 3, 1992 in Pennsylvania. This Accident resulted in the death of Teresa Lynn Bastiand (the "Decedent"). The Decedent was traveling from her former home in New Jersey to her new home in Florida when the Accident occurred. Jurisdiction is premised on diversity of citizenship, 28 U.S.C. § 1332(a).

The plaintiffs'[1] assertion that the Decedent was a citizen of Florida is essential to diversity jurisdiction since the defendants[2] are citizens of New Jersey and Pennsylvania. 28 U.S.C. § 1332(a)(1). The issue is whether the fact that the Decedent had not completed moving to her new home precludes her from being a citizen of the state she considered her permanent home.

The case is presently on trial and I have heard the evidence pertaining to jurisdiction.

....

Lack of subject-matter jurisdiction is a ground for dismissal and may be raised at any time by the parties or by the court *sua sponte.*[3] ... "In order to sustain jurisdiction based on

---

1. The plaintiffs in this action are Yvonne Walls, as executrix of the Estate of the Decedent, and the Decedent's child, Jacque Ramon Ahmadi, a minor and citizen of Virginia, by his guardian, Said Mohammad Ahmadi.

2. The defendants in this action are Khalil Ahmed, a New Jersey citizen, William R. White, a Pennsylvania citizen, and Matsinger Enterprises, Inc., a Pennsylvania corporation with its principal place of business in Pennsylvania.

3. "The burden of persuasion as to diversity jurisdiction remains at all time on the proponent of jurisdiction." *Liakakos v. Cigna Corp.,* 704 F. Supp. 583, 586 (E.D. Pa. 1988)....

complete diversity rule

diversity of the parties, there must exist an actual, substantial controversy between citizens of different states, all of whom on one side of the controversy are citizens of different states from all parties on the other side." ... If one of the defendants is a citizen of the same state as any of the plaintiffs, complete diversity is lacking.... [The legal representative of a decedent's estate is deemed to be a citizen of the same state as the decedent. 28 U.S.C. § 1332(c)(2).[4]] *Rule*

Rule Mere residence in a state is not sufficient to establish citizenship for purposes of diversity.... *rule* The concept of "domicile" is controlling.... The test for determining domicile centers on two factors: (1) the intent of the person in question to make a particular location their permanent home, and (2) physical presence.... In other words, "[a] person's domicile is that place where he has his true fixed and permanent home and principal establishment, and to which he ... has the intention of returning whenever he is absent therefrom." ... Moreover, a person may be a domiciliary of only one state....*Rule*

Domicile Test

[Where a person changes his state of residence, a presumption in favor of the original domicile arises.][5] *Rule* [However, no minimum residence time period exists before a person can establish a new domicile.][6] With these principles in mind the court makes the following findings of fact and conclusions of law.

....

The defendants were citizens of New Jersey and Pennsylvania, and plaintiff Jacque Ahmadi was a citizen of Virginia at the time the Complaint was filed.[8]

At the time of the Accident, the Decedent was in the final phase of moving her personal property from New Jersey to Florida.

The court finds clear evidence that the Decedent intended Pt. St. Lucie, Florida to be her permanent home. Florida was the center of the Decedent's domestic, social and civil life. For example:

1. Decedent purchased a lot in Pt. St. Lucie in August 1991;

2. In November 1991, Decedent executed an agreement of sale, a mortgage, and arranged to have a home built on this lot;

3. Decedent oversaw the construction of this home;

4. Decedent inspected the homesite during construction;

5. She enrolled her son in school in Florida;

6. She arranged for telephone service and obtained an operating phone number;

7. The van Decedent rented to transfer her personal property to Florida was rented on one-way terms;

Evidence FL was intended to be permanent home & proof of physical presence

---

4. 28 U.S.C. § 1332(c)(2) provides:
   [T]he legal representative of the estate of a decedent shall be deemed to be a citizen only of the same State as the decedent, and the legal representative of an infant or incompetent shall be deemed to be a citizen of only the same State as the infant or incompetent.

5. "Where the proponent of diversity contends that there has been a change of citizenship of one of the litigants, the effect of the presumption in favor of the former domicile is to raise the standard of proof that the proponent must bear." ... The proponent must then prove that the change of citizenship by clear and convincing proof.... *Rule*

6. The presumption in favor of the former or original domicile has been alternatively described as, "the presumption that a domicile, once established, continues until it is changed." ...

8. For purposes of diversity jurisdiction, the relevant date for determining domicile and thus citizenship is the date on which the complaint is filed.... *Rule*

8. The Decedent expressed her belief that Florida was her permanent home;[9] and,

9. The Decedent obtained employment in Florida.

In addition to the substantial step of purchasing a home in Florida, she spent a significant amount of time in Florida. She made a considerable physical and emotional commitment to Florida. The court finds that the Decedent established a significant and lasting physical presence in Florida and abandoned her home in New Jersey.

. . . .

After finding that (1) the Decedent intended that Florida be her permanent home, (2) the Decedent had a physical presence in Florida, and (3) the Decedent abandoned her former domicile, the court concludes the Decedent was a citizen of Florida at the time of her death. Therefore, her personal representative is deemed to be a citizen of Florida, 28 U.S.C. § 1332(c)(2), and the necessary conditions for diversity exist. . . .

In support of the position that the decedent should be adjudged a citizen of New Jersey, defendant Ahmed makes two points. First, he notes the presumption in favor of the original or former domicile. . . . Here, the uncontroverted facts establishing the Decedent's intent to make her permanent home in Florida and her physical presence in Florida are sufficient to overcome this presumption. . . .

Second, defendant Ahmed asserts that Restatement (Second) of Conflict of Laws § 19 cmt. a, illus. 4 (1969), which reads:

> 4. *A*, having a domicil in state *X*, decides to make his home in state *Y*. He leaves *X* and is on his way to *Y* but has not yet reached *Y*. His domicil is in *X*.

is identical to the issue in this case and dictates that the Decedent should be considered a citizen of New Jersey. This assertion is unpersuasive.

The situation here is not identical to . . . Illustration 4. Here, contrary to the assumption implicit in Illustration 4, the Decedent had established a "home" in Florida, and had "reached" Florida on many prior occasions.[10] Additionally, the Restatement notes "As between two homes, a person's principal home is that to which he is more closely related, or stated in other words, that which is *more nearly the center of his domestic, social and civil life.*" Restatement (Second) of Conflict of Laws § 20 cmt. b (1969) (emphasis added). Here, the Decedent's domestic, social and civil life [was] centered in Florida.

. . . .

The court finds the diversity requirements [of] § 1332 to be satisfied. Each of the plaintiffs is a citizen of a different state from all of the defendants.

Notes and Questions

1. As stated in footnote 8 in the *Walls* opinion, the time for determining the citizenship of the parties for purposes of establishing diversity is the date on which the complaint is filed. Thus, provided the parties are completely diverse at the time the action is commenced, diversity is not destroyed if the parties later change their citizenship during the pendency of the action or were non-diverse at the time the cause of

---

9. Ms. Walls testified that the Decedent stated that she had given up on New Jersey and that Ms. Walls should move to Florida so the two of them could be together.

10. Additionally, when Illustration 4 of § 19 is read in the context of Illustrations 1–3, it becomes clear that Illustration 4 is intended as an example of the principle that a person must exhibit a physical presence in a state to become a domiciliary of that state.

action accrued. In *Grupo Dataflux v. Atlas Global Group, L.P.*, 541 U.S. 567 (2004), the Supreme Court held that a lack of diversity at the commencement of the action cannot be cured by a party's post-commencement change in citizenship. In *Grupo Dataflux*, the Court distinguished a prior case, *Caterpillar Inc. v. Lewis*, 519 U.S. 61 (1996), which was a removal case, on the ground that the jurisdictional defects in *Caterpillar* had been cured by dismissal of a party rather than a change in citizenship. 541 U.S. at 571–74.

2. As will be further examined in Chapter 7, the plaintiff may seek to join additional parties to the action after the commencement of the action under Rule 20 or may be directed to do so by the court under Rule 19. In a diversity action, these additional parties must also satisfy the requirements of subject-matter jurisdiction at the time of joinder or the new parties may not be joined to the action.

3. (a) One of the parties in the *Walls* case was the legal representative of the estate of the decedent in the case. In a diversity action, whose citizenship matters, the citizenship of the decedent or the citizenship of the legal representative who brings the action? *See* 28 U.S.C. § 1332(c)(2).

(b) Sometimes, it is difficult to determine when a person qualifies as a "legal representative of an estate" within the meaning of § 1332(c)(2). Ordinarily, when a person dies due to the wrongful conduct of another person, a statutory claim for "wrongful death" results. Any damage recovery is distributed to the persons designated by the wrongful death statute to compensate them for the losses they have suffered due to the decedent's death. In *Tank v. Chronister*, 160 F.3d 597 (10th Cir. 1998), Kansas law authorized any heir at law to bring a wrongful death action for the benefit of all the heirs at law. The district court held that the phrase "legal representative of an estate" in § 1332(c)(2) meant one who is appointed by a court to bring an action. Because the plaintiff derived the right to bring the action from a relationship with the decedent rather than a court appointment, the court held that § 1332(c)(2) did not apply. The court of appeals affirmed, holding that § 1332(c)(2) excludes from its coverage one who is not representing the estate of a decedent, even if the individual in question is appointed pursuant to a statute conferring authority to bring a wrongful death action. Do you agree with this result? *See also Steinlage v. Mayo Clinic Rochester*, 434 F.3d 1070 (8th Cir. 2006) (Minnesota wrongful death trustee is not a representative of a decedent's estate as required by § 1332(c)(2); therefore, trustee's own citizenship controls for purposes of diversity).

4. Federal Form 7(a) demonstrates how to plead jurisdiction "founded on diversity of citizenship and amount." Even when diversity of citizenship exists between the parties in an objective sense, a party may fail to allege that it exists in the jurisdictional paragraph of the complaint, or a party may allege it improperly, such as when the plaintiff alleges that someone is a "resident" rather than a "citizen" of a particular state. It is possible to correct defective allegations of jurisdiction by amendment. *See* 28 U.S.C. § 1653 providing that "[d]efective allegations of jurisdiction may be amended, upon terms, in the trial or appellate courts." However, if the allegations are not corrected by amendment, the action will be dismissed.

· 2. Citizenship of Corporations

A corporation is a distinct legal entity with a status and capacity of its own separate from its shareholders, who own the corporation, and its directors and officers, who manage the corporation. Corporations are created through a formal process known as "incorporation." All fifty states have procedures for incorporation, and most corporations are incorporated under state law. As noted in section B(1) on federal question jurisdiction, though, some corporations, such as the American Red Cross, are incorporated under federal law.

When a corporation sues or is sued in federal court and the basis for subject-matter jurisdiction is diversity of citizenship, a question arises whether a corporation qualifies as a "citizen of a state." Article III, § 2 expressly authorizes jurisdiction over controversies "between Citizens of different States," but it is silent as to corporations. Although the Supreme Court has held that a corporation is not a "state citizen" for all constitutional purposes, *see, e.g., Ashbury Hosp. v. Cass County,* 326 U.S. 207 (1945) (a corporation is not a "citizen of a state" for purposes of the privileges and immunities clause of Article IV), it is now well settled, despite early Supreme Court challenges, that Congress has the power under Article III of the Constitution to make a corporation a "state citizen" for purposes of diversity jurisdiction.

Section § 1332(c)(1) provides that "a corporation shall be deemed to be a citizen of every State and foreign state by which it has been incorporated and of the State or foreign state where it has its principal place of business." Corporations thus have dual citizenship for purposes of diversity jurisdiction. Be careful not to misinterpret this provision. It is not an "either/or" definition and does not allow the parties to choose the state of corporate citizenship which best suits the requirements of complete diversity. Thus, if P is a citizen of California and D is a corporation, incorporated in New York with its principal place of business in California, complete diversity does not exist because both P and D are citizens of California, even though D's New York citizenship is diverse from P. Be careful also not to confuse this definition of corporate "citizenship" for subject-matter jurisdiction purposes with the distinct definition of corporate "residence" for venue purposes under § 1391(c) & (d), reviewed in Chapter 3(B)(1).

The first definition of corporate citizenship under § 1332(c)(1), *i.e,* every state of incorporation, refers only to the state or states or foreign state in which a corporation is formally incorporated. A corporation that transacts business in other states may be required to register and be licensed to do business in those states, but registering and being licensed to do business in a state is not the same as formal incorporation and does not make the corporation a citizen of that state for purposes of § 1332(c)(1).

Although certain public corporations may be incorporated in more than one state, private corporations are generally incorporated in only one state thus making determination of a corporation's state of citizenship under the first part of § 1332(c)(1) straightforward. If a corporation does formally incorporate in more than one state, however, the corporation is also deemed a citizen of these additional states under § 1332(c)(1).

By contrast, under the second part of § 1332(c)(1), a corporation can only have *one* principal place of business. Section 1332(c)(1) has never defined the standard for determining a corporation's principal place of business, and for years, the lower federal courts struggled in articulating a uniform test for determining *the* principal place of business of a corporation for purposes of § 1332(c)(1). In *Hertz Corp. v. Friend,* the Supreme Court resolved this question of statutory interpretation and adopted the so-called "nerve center" test.

Hertz Corp. v. Friend

Supreme Court of the United States, 2010
559 U.S. 77, 130 S. Ct. 1181, 175 L. Ed. 2d 1029

JUSTICE BREYER delivered the opinion of the Court.

The federal diversity jurisdiction statute provides that "a corporation shall be deemed to be a citizen of [every] State [and foreign state] by which it has been incorporated *and of the State* [or foreign state] *where it has its principal place of business.*" 28 U.S.C. § 1332(c)(1) (emphasis added). We seek here to resolve different interpretations that the Circuits have given this phrase. In doing so, we place primary weight upon the need for judicial administration of a jurisdictional statute to remain as simple as possible. . . .

. . . .

. . . We conclude that "principal place of business" is best read as referring to the place where a corporation's officers direct, control, and coordinate the corporation's activities. It is the place that Courts of Appeals have called the corporation's "nerve center." And in practice it should normally be the place where the corporation maintains its headquarters—provided that the headquarters is the actual center of direction, control, and coordination, *i.e.,* the "nerve center," and not simply an office where the corporation holds its board meetings (for example, attended by directors and officers who have traveled there for the occasion).

Three sets of considerations, taken together, convince us that this approach, while imperfect, is superior to other possibilities. First, the statute's language supports the approach. The statute's text deems a corporation a citizen of the "State where it has its principal place of business." 28 U.S.C. § 1332(c)(1). The word "place" is in the singular, not the plural. . . .

[handwritten margin note: 3 reasons for nerve center]

A corporation's "nerve center," usually its main headquarters, is a single place. . . . By contrast, the application of a more general business activities test has led some courts, as in the present case, to look, not at a particular place within a State, but incorrectly at the State itself, measuring the total amount of business activities that the corporation conducts there and determining whether they are "significantly larger" than in the next-ranking State. . . .

. . . .

Second, administrative simplicity is a major virtue in a jurisdictional statute. . . . Complex jurisdictional tests complicate a case, eating up time and money as the parties litigate, not the merits of their claims, but which court is the right court to decide those claims. . . . Complex tests produce appeals and reversals, encourage gamesmanship, and, again, diminish the likelihood that results and settlements will reflect a claim's legal and factual merits. Judicial resources too are at stake. Courts have an independent obligation to determine whether subject-matter jurisdiction exists, even when no party challenges it. . . . So courts benefit from straightforward rules under which they can readily assure themselves of their power to hear a case. . . .

Simple jurisdictional rules also promote greater predictability. Predictability is valuable to corporations making business and investment decisions. . . . Predictability also benefits plaintiffs deciding whether to file suit in a state or federal court.

A "nerve center" approach, which ordinarily equates that "center" with a corporation's headquarters, is simple to apply *comparatively speaking.* . . .

Third, the statute's legislative history, for those who accept it, offers a simplicity-related interpretive benchmark. The Judicial Conference provided an initial version of its proposal that suggested a numerical test. A corporation would be deemed a citizen of the State that accounted for more than half of its gross income.... The Conference changed its mind in light of criticism that such a test would prove too complex and impractical to apply.... That history suggests that the words "principal place of business" should be interpreted to be no more complex than the initial "half of gross income" test. A "nerve center" test offers such a possibility. A general business activities test does not.

We recognize that there may be no perfect test that satisfies all administrative and purposive criteria. We recognize as well that, under the "nerve center" test we adopt today, there will be hard cases. For example, in this era of telecommuting, some corporations may divide their command and coordinating functions among officers who work at several different locations, perhaps communicating over the Internet. That said, our test nonetheless points courts in a single direction, towards the center of overall direction, control, and coordination. Courts do not have to try to weigh corporate functions, assets, or revenues different in kind, one from the other. Our approach provides a sensible test that is relatively easier to apply, not a test that will, in all instances, automatically generate a result.

We also recognize that the use of a "nerve center" test may in some cases produce results that seem to cut against the basic rationale for 28 U.S.C. § 1332(c)(1).... For example, if the bulk of a company's business activities visible to the public take place in New Jersey, while its top officers direct those activities just across the river in New York, the "principal place of business" is New York. One could argue that members of the public in New Jersey would be *less* likely to be prejudiced against the corporation than persons in New York-yet the corporation will still be entitled to remove a New Jersey state case to federal court. And note too that the same corporation would be unable to remove a New York state case to federal court, despite the New York public's presumed prejudice against the corporation.

We understand that such seeming anomalies will arise. However, in view of the necessity of having a clearer rule, we must accept them. Accepting occasionally counterintuitive results is the price the legal system must pay to avoid overly complex jurisdictional administration while producing the benefits that accompany a more uniform legal system.

....

It is so ordered.

Notes and Questions on Additional Diversity Jurisdiction Issues

1. How should the citizenship of an unincorporated association be determined? Generally speaking, such an association is a citizen of every state where one of its members is a citizen. *See, e.g., Carden v. Arkoma Assocs.*, 494 U.S. 185 (1990) (limited partnership is a citizen of every state where one of partners is citizen); *United Steelworkers of Am. v. R.H. Bouligny, Inc.*, 382 U.S. 145 (1965) (labor union is a citizen of every state where one of its members is a citizen).

2. Parties sometimes try to create diversity jurisdiction by assigning all or part of their claims to persons of diverse citizenship to the opposing party in the action. When claims are assigned to diverse parties, 28 U.S.C. § 1359 determines whether the assignment will result in the creation of diversity jurisdiction. Section 1359 deprives the district courts of subject-matter jurisdiction whenever "any party, by assignment or otherwise, has been

improperly or collusively made or joined to invoke the jurisdiction of such court." The U.S. Supreme Court has held that a colorable rather than a real assignment will not be effective to create diversity jurisdiction under § 1359. *See Kramer v. Caribbean Mills, Inc.*, 394 U.S. 823 (1969) (Texas resident who took assignment, for one dollar consideration, of Panama corporation's interest in contract with Haitian corporation and immediately reassigned 95% of that interest to the Panama corporation was "improperly or collusively made" a party to invoke jurisdiction).

3. Similarly, the federal courts have generally held that if the primary motive for making an assignment is to create diversity, the motive can be taken into account as a negative factor in determining whether jurisdiction exists. *See* 14 WRIGHT ET AL § 3639. In addition, the courts have developed presumptions against certain kinds of assignments creating diversity jurisdiction. For example, a presumption exists against the legitimacy of assignments between principal and subsidiary corporations that create diversity jurisdiction. Of course, the assignment is only ineffective to create diversity, not necessarily ineffective in other respects. The existence of a plausible business motive for the assignment is important to the assignee's ability to rebut the presumption that the assignment is illegitimate. If evidence of a jurisdictional motive for the assignment exists, however, it may make it more difficult for the assignee to rebut the presumption, even if there is also a legitimate business reason for the assignment. *See, e.g., Nike, Inc. v. Comercial Iberica de Exclusivas Deportivas, S.A.*, 20 F.3d 987 (9th Cir. 1994) (when evidence of a jurisdictional motive for the assignment exists, a heightened presumption is employed; assignee cannot simply show a plausible business reason, but must show a business reason so compelling that the assignment would have been made absent the purpose of obtaining a federal forum).

4. The doctrine of realignment states that in determining the existence of diversity of citizenship, the court is not bound by the alignment of the parties in the pleadings. Instead, the court must look beyond the pleadings and arrange the parties according to their true interests in the action. In theory, this rule applies to all diversity cases, even though there is no question of proper party alignment in most cases. *See* TEPLY & WHITTEN at 762–63. The lower federal courts follow two general approaches to realignment questions. Some courts follow the "principal purpose" test. This test requires the courts to identify the primary issue in dispute in the case and then align the parties in accord with their positions on that primary issue. *See, e.g., United States Fidelity & Guar. Co. v. A & S Mfg. Co.*, 48 F.3d 131 (4th Cir. 1995). Other courts follow the "collision-of-interests" test. This test only requires an actual, substantial controversy, or collision of interests between opposing parties, though the conflict may concern an issue other than the principal issue in the case. *See, e.g., Maryland Cas. Co. v. W.R. Grace & Co.*, 23 F.3d 617 (2d Cir. 1993). A third test may be emerging that would require a court to align the parties according to the primary purpose of the suit and then investigate any other conflicts that might justify aligning them differently. *See, e.g., U.S.I. Props. Corp. v. M.D. Constr. Co.*, 860 F.2d 1, 4 (1st Cir. 1988). Realignment has its most important functions in Rule 19 cases involving "indispensable" parties and in cases of intervention under Rule 24. These Rules are examined in depth in Chapter 7.

Problems

Problem 4-6. P, a citizen of State *X*, sues *D*, a citizen of State *Y*, in a U.S. District Court in State *X* for $150,000. Under § 1332(a), does diversity jurisdiction exist? As a matter of policy, should *P* be allowed to invoke diversity jurisdiction in *P's* home state?

Problem 4-7. D, who was born in State Y, abandons D's home in State Y and moves to Paris, France, intending to live in Paris forever. However, D does not become a naturalized citizen of France, but retains United States citizenship. Subsequently, P, a citizen of State X, sues D in a U.S. District Court in State Y for $150,000. Does diversity of citizenship exist between P and D?

Problem 4-8. D, a citizen of State Y, abandons D's home in State Y and sets out for State X, where D intends to live permanently. Before reaching State X, which is a state to which D has never been before, D is sued by P, a citizen of State X, in a U.S. District Court in State X for $150,000. Does diversity jurisdiction exist under § 1332? If so, does it continue to exist when D arrives in State X?

Problem 4-9. D, a citizen of State X, abandons D's home in State X and begins roaming from place to place around the world. D never intends to make any of the places to which D travels home, nor does D ever intend to remain in any of the places indefinitely or permanently. While D is traveling, D is sued by P, a citizen of State X in a U.S. District Court in State X for $150,000. Does diversity jurisdiction exist?

Problem 4-10. P-1, a citizen of State X, and P-2, a citizen of State X, sue D-1, a citizen of State Y, and D-2, a citizen of State Z, in a U.S. District Court in State Q for $250,000. Does diversity jurisdiction exist?

Problem 4-11. P, a citizen of State X, sued D Corp. in a federal court in State Y. D is incorporated in State Z. D moved to dismiss the action on the ground that D's principal place of business is in State X. D had a plant in State X that employed over 9,000 employees. However, D's activities were spread over several states, and some of D's operations in other states generated more income for D than its operations in State X. D's home office is in State Q. Where is D's principal place of business for diversity purposes?

Problem 4-12. P, a citizen of the United States, is domiciled in State Y. P moves from State Y to State X to attend law school. However, P lives in State X only during the school year. Each summer P returns to State Y to live with P's parents and work. P retains a State Y driver's license and automobile registration and is registered to vote in State Y. While in State Y during the summer following P's second year of law school, D, a citizen of State Y, allegedly assaulted P in a bar. P sued D in the U.S. District Court for the District of State Y to recover damages for the assault. P asserted jurisdiction based on diversity of citizenship. D moved to dismiss the action for lack of subject-matter jurisdiction. What should the result be?

3. Alienage Jurisdiction

As noted earlier, Article III, § 2 (ninth clause) of the U.S. Constitution authorizes Congress to confer jurisdiction on the federal courts over controversies "between a State, or the Citizens thereof, and foreign States, Citizens, or Subjects." Based on this provision, Congress has granted jurisdiction to the federal courts in § 1332(a)(2)-(4). All of these grants of jurisdiction are generally referred to under the label "alienage jurisdiction."

Section 1332(a)(2) authorizes jurisdiction in actions between "citizens of a State and citizens or subjects of a foreign state...." The statute's use of the terms "citizens" or "subjects" of a State or foreign state does not mean that more than one citizen or subject must sue or be sued to establish alienage jurisdiction. An action between a citizen of Texas and a citizen of France is within § 1332(a)(2). Nor does the phrase citizens/subjects "of *a* State" or "of *a* foreign state" mean that in cases involving multiple parties, all plaintiffs or defendants must be from the same state or country. Thus, an action by citizens of New York and Ohio against citizens of Canada and Mexico would be within § 1332(a)(2).

As with § 1332(a)(1), § 1332(a)(2) requires "complete diversity" between the adverse parties. This means that all of the state citizens and all of the foreign citizens must be on separate sides of the litigation for jurisdiction to exist under § 1332(a)(2). Actions involving a mixture of state and foreign citizens on the same side of the litigation are governed by § 1332(a)(3), which authorizes jurisdiction in actions between "citizens of different States and in which citizens or subjects of a foreign state are additional parties."

Based on its express wording, therefore, § 1332(a)(3) first requires a valid diversity action between citizens of different states and then foreign citizens or subjects may be included as additional parties on either side or both sides of the litigation. Thus, actions in which a state citizen and a foreign citizen are on one side of the litigation and a foreign citizen is on the other side are not within § 1332(a)(3). Nor would such an action be within § 1332(a)(2). Do you see why?

Finally, § 1332(a)(4) authorizes jurisdiction in actions between "a foreign state … as plaintiff and citizens of a State or of different States." This section is expressly limited to actions *by* a foreign state as plaintiff. Actions *against* a foreign state are governed by the Foreign Sovereign Immunities Act, 28 U.S.C. § 1330, cited below. As with § 1332(a)(1), § 1332(a)(4) requires "complete" diversity between the adverse parties. Thus, there may not be aliens on both sides of the suit. For jurisdiction to exist in cases in which aliens are on both sides of the action, there must also be citizens of different states on each side of the action, thus qualifying the case under § 1332(a)(3).

The grant of alienage jurisdiction under Article III, § 2 (ninth clause) does not authorize, and § 1332 does not attempt to confer, jurisdiction in a suit solely between foreign states or citizens or subjects of foreign states. In 1809, the Supreme Court held that it would be unconstitutional under this provision of Article III, § 2 for Congress to attempt to confer such jurisdiction on the federal courts. *See Hodgson v. Bowerbank*, 9 U.S. (5 Cranch) 303 (1809). In addition, the lower federal courts have held that a person who is neither a citizen of the United States nor a citizen or subject of a foreign state—a so-called "stateless alien"—cannot sue or be sued under alienage jurisdiction.

Purposes of Alienage Jurisdiction. The purposes of alienage jurisdiction are generally the same as those of the grant of jurisdiction in suits between citizens of different states: to prevent bias and prejudice from operating in state courts against persons from foreign countries. However, unlike diversity jurisdiction under § 1332(a)(1), there seems to be general agreement that a real danger of prejudice may exist in suits in which aliens and citizens of states are parties. If such prejudice were allowed to operate in state courts, it could create a significant problem for the foreign relations of the United States.

Difference Between Alienage Jurisdiction and Other Actions Involving Foreign States or Citizens. Alienage jurisdiction under § 1332(a)(2)-(4) is considered a part of diversity jurisdiction and should not be confused with other jurisdictional statutes that also provide original jurisdiction in certain actions involving foreign states or citizens. For example, the Foreign Sovereign Immunities Act, 28 U.S.C. § 1330, authorizes original jurisdiction, under certain circumstances, in civil actions against foreign states and their agencies and instrumentalities in accordance with the provisions of 28 U.S.C. §§ 1605–1607. The Alien Tort Statute, 28 U.S.C. § 1350, authorizes original jurisdiction of "any civil action by an alien for a tort only, committed in violation of the law of nations or a treaty of the United States." Sections 1330 and 1350 are partly based on federal question jurisdiction and derive their constitutional authority from the "arising under" language of Article III, § 2 (first clause). In addition, 28 U.S.C. § 1351 authorizes original and exclusive jurisdiction of "all civil actions and proceedings against (1) consuls or vice consuls of foreign states; or (2) members of a mission or members of their families." Section 1351 derives its constitutional authority from the provision of Article III, § 2 (second clause) which authorizes jurisdiction "over all Cases affecting Ambassadors, other public Ministers and Consuls."

Finally, if an action by or against a foreign state or citizen fully satisfies the requirements for federal question jurisdiction under § 1331, jurisdiction would be proper under that section, unless jurisdiction were otherwise precluded by a special immunity provision. *See, e.g.,* 28 U.S.C. § 1604 (providing that "a foreign state shall be immune from the jurisdiction of the courts of the United States and of the States except as provided" under the Foreign Sovereign Immunities Act). Although, as noted earlier, an action entirely between foreign states or citizens or subjects of foreign states would be unconstitutional under Article III, § 2 (ninth clause), such an action would not be unconstitutional under the "arising under" jurisdiction of Article III, § 2 (first clause). As explained in section B, "arising under" jurisdiction is based on the federal nature of the plaintiff's substantive claim, and not on the citizenship or nationality of the parties.

For example, assume that a German corporation with an office in New York terminated a Japanese citizen employed at its New York office in violation of federal employment discrimination laws. In this case, the Japanese citizen could properly file a federal court action against the German corporation under § 1331 for discrimination under federal law, even though both parties are foreign citizens. Similarly, under the Foreign Sovereign Immunities Act, 28 U.S.C. § 1330, which is also a federal question/"arising under" jurisdictional statute, a plaintiff filing an action against a foreign state may also be a citizen of a foreign state. *See Verlinden B.V. v. Central Bank of Nigeria,* 461 U.S. 480 (1983) (jurisdiction proper under § 1330 in action by Dutch plaintiff against instrumentality of Nigeria).

Section 1332(a)(2) Restriction for Permanent Resident Aliens. In 1988, Congress amended § 1332(a) to provide that "[a]n alien admitted to the United States for permanent residence shall be deemed a citizen of the State in which such alien is domiciled." This provision was added to restrict the availability of "alienage jurisdiction" for foreign citizens who are domiciled in the United States and admitted as permanent residents. Before the 1988 amendment, if a citizen of a foreign state were admitted to the United States as a permanent resident and became domiciled in New York, for instance, alienage jurisdiction would still exist under § 1332(a)(2) in an action between the permanent resident and a New York citizen because the permanent resident would still qualify as a "citizen of a foreign state" and the action would be against a "citizen of a State."

By deeming a permanent resident a citizen of his/her state of domicile, alienage jurisdiction was no longer permissible in the above situation because the action was now between "citizens" of the same state. Although the purpose of the 1988 amendment was clearly to restrict alienage jurisdiction in cases involving permanent resident aliens, an unintended consequence of the amendment was to potentially expand jurisdiction in situations that raised a significant constitutional issue. As noted earlier, under Article III, § 2, (ninth clause), alienage jurisdiction cannot constitutionally extend to actions entirely between foreign citizens. Under the 1988 amendment, however, if a permanent resident domiciled in New

York filed an action either against another permanent resident alien domiciled in a different state or against a foreign citizen, jurisdiction would technically be proper under § 1332(a)(1) or (2), respectively, even though the action was actually between two foreign citizens.

The "Federal Courts Jurisdiction and Venue Clarification Act of 2011" eliminated this constitutional problem by deleting the 1988 language which deemed a permanent resident a "citizen" of the state of his/her domicile, and amending § 1332(a)(2) to provide that "the district courts shall not have original jurisdiction under this subsection of an action between citizens of a State and citizens or subjects of a foreign state who are lawfully admitted for permanent residence in the United States and are domiciled in the same State." This amendment thus preserves the objective of the 1988 amendment, *i.e.*, to destroy alienage jurisdiction under § 1332(a)(2) when a permanent resident is domiciled in the same state as an opposing state citizen.

Problems

Problem 4-13. P, a citizen of State *X*, and *D*, a citizen of France admitted to permanent residence in the United States and domiciled in State *X*, have an automobile accident in State *X*. *P* sues *D* in a U.S. District Court in State *X*. *P* asserts jurisdiction under 28 U.S.C. § 1332(a)(2). Does jurisdiction exist? Is there any constitutional problem with § 1332(a) in this case? Why or why not?

Problem 4-14. P, a Cuban refugee, lost *P's* original Cuban citizenship when *P* fled Cuba. *P* is now admitted to permanent residence in the United States and is domiciled in State *X*. *P* sues *D*, a citizen of State *Y*, in a U.S. District Court in State *Y*. *P* asserts jurisdiction under 28 U.S.C. § 1332(a)(1). Does jurisdiction exist? Is there any constitutional problem with § 1332(a) in this case? Why or why not?

4. Determining the Amount in Controversy

Relationship Between the Constitution and the Statutory Restriction. Article III, § 2 imposes no amount-in-controversy requirement as a prerequisite for subject-matter jurisdiction with respect to any of the nine jurisdictional categories. Similar to the requirement of "complete diversity," the amount-in-controversy requirement is a purely statutory limitation imposed by Congress on federal court jurisdiction. With respect to diversity jurisdiction, Congress has always required a minimum amount in controversy ever since the first Judiciary Act of 1789.

Originally set at $500, the amount has been raised over the years to adjust for inflation and to prevent cases of limited value from clogging the federal courts. In 1958, Congress raised the limit from $3,000 to $10,000 and in 1988 to $50,000. In 1996, Congress raised the limit to its current level. Section 1332(a) now confers diversity and alienage jurisdiction under (a)(1)-(4) only when "the matter in controversy exceeds the sum or value of $75,000." The interpleader statute, § 1335, which is also based on diversity of citizenship, maintains a nominal amount-in-controversy requirement of $500.

Federal Question Cases. From its enactment in 1875, the general federal question statute also had an amount-in-controversy requirement, but Congress abolished this requirement in 1980. Thus, there is no amount-in-controversy requirement for federal question cases, except in the rare instances that such a requirement is imposed by one of the particular federal question statutes. *See, e.g.,* 28 U.S.C. § 1337(a) (requiring that certain interstate commerce freight damage claims exceed $10,000). Under the current jurisdictional statutes, therefore, the amount-in-controversy requirement is essentially only relevant in diversity cases.

(a) Cases in Which the Plaintiff Requests Money Damages

General Rules. Determining the proper amount in controversy is not always easy and certain principles need to be kept in mind. First, like any requirement of subject-matter jurisdiction, the jurisdictional amount is nonwaivable. Thus, this defect may be raised by the parties or the court at any time. Second, the requirement is *not* that the plaintiff actually be awarded an amount in excess of $75,000, but rather that such an amount be *in controversy*. It is rarely predictable how the merits of a plaintiff's claim will be ultimately decided by a judge or jury. In fact, the uncertainty of outcome inherent in all litigation is one of the reasons why so many cases settle during the litigation process. Even though the plaintiff may have a reasonable basis for asserting a claim in excess of $75,000, the judge or jury may not be entirely persuaded by the plaintiff's evidence and the plaintiff may be awarded less than $75,000 or perhaps nothing at all. Such a result does not automatically mean that a sum in excess of $75,000 was not legitimately in controversy and that the action must be dismissed for lack of subject-matter jurisdiction.

As explained in section A(8), a dismissal for lack of subject-matter jurisdiction means that the federal court never had any authority to decide the merits of the case and that the entire proceeding is void. In such a situation, even though the case may have been fully litigated and the defendant may have prevailed on the merits, the plaintiff would be free to refile the action against the defendant in state court and start the process all over again, provided the statute of limitations has not expired. Similarly, for a partially victorious plaintiff who recovers a money judgment, but for less than $75,000, the judgment in the plaintiff's favor would also have to be voided, forcing the plaintiff to relitigate its claim in state court. Thus, automatic dismissal for lack of subject-matter jurisdiction every time the plaintiff fails to recover a judgment in excess of $75,000 would be problematic. Other sanctions are, therefore, more appropriate than dismissal for lack of subject-matter jurisdiction in this situation. *See* 28 U.S.C. § 1332(b) (denial or imposition of costs).

Development of the "Legal Certainty" Test. Recognizing these considerations, the U.S. Supreme Court in *St. Paul Mercury Indemnity Co. v. Red Cab Co.*, 303 U.S. 283 (1938), established a very generous test for judging compliance with the amount-in-controversy requirement. The Court held that "[i]t must appear to a *legal certainty* that the [plaintiff's] claim is really for less than the jurisdictional amount to justify dismissal" of the action for lack of subject-matter jurisdiction. *Id.* at 289 (emphasis added). Furthermore, although a court has the right to review compliance with the amount-in-controversy requirement at all stages of the litigation, even on appeal, the temporal context in which the claim is evaluated remains the same, *i.e.*, the date of the commencement of the action. Thus, to dismiss a claim because of failure to satisfy the jurisdictional amount, it must appear to a "legal certainty" that, as of the commencement of the action, the plaintiff never had a claim meeting the jurisdictional amount. Finally, if the amount in controversy properly exists at the time of the commencement of the action, jurisdiction is not ousted by subsequent events reducing the amount or by the presentation of a valid defense to the claim. *Id.* at 289–90.

Given these standards, it is not surprising that jurisdictional dismissals for failure to meet the amount-in-controversy requirement are unusual. Nevertheless, certain cases do meet the "legal certainty" test for dismissal. Although the courts have not been entirely consistent in applying the standards for dismissal, dismissed cases generally fall into three categories:

(1) "legal certainty" based on the applicable substantive law; (2) "legal certainty" based on a contractual limit of liability; and (3) "legal certainty" based on undisputed objective facts.

"Legal Certainty" Based on the Applicable Substantive Law. At times, it may appear to a "legal certainty" that the plaintiff cannot recover an amount in excess of $75,000 because the applicable substantive law under which the plaintiff is suing either does not allow for certain damages claimed by the plaintiff or places a clear limit on such damages that are below the jurisdictional amount. For example, under the substantive law of most states, punitive damages are generally not recoverable in contract actions. 3 DOBBS § 12.5[1], [2]. Assume that a plaintiff sues for breach of contract. The plaintiff claims $25,000 in actual damages and $100,000 in punitive damages. If the applicable substantive law clearly prohibits recovery for punitive damages for breach of contract, dismissal for lack of subject-matter jurisdiction would be justified. Similarly, the applicable substantive law under which the plaintiff is suing sometimes specifically limits the amount of damages that are recoverable. If it is undisputed that the monetary limit applies to the plaintiff's claim and the limit is below the jurisdictional amount, dismissal would also be warranted.

"Legal Certainty" Based on a Contractual Limit of Liability. Similar to a limitation of damages imposed by law, if a legally enforceable contract provision clearly limits plaintiff's damages to an amount below the jurisdictional amount, dismissal is appropriate. If the application of the limitation clause is disputed, however, dismissal is not appropriate.

"Legal Certainty" Based on Undisputed Objective Facts. Assume that the substantive law allows for the plaintiff's damage claim and that damages are not statutorily or contractually limited. However, the undisputed facts clearly show from the time the plaintiff filed the complaint that the plaintiff never could have recovered an amount in excess of the jurisdictional amount. A court is more likely to dismiss for this reason when the plaintiff's claim is for specified and easily quantifiable damages, such as a suit on a promissory note. However, in cases in which the plaintiff is suing for non-specific, unliquidated damages, such as pain and suffering, emotional distress, loss of future earning capacity, or loss of business good will, it is difficult to conclude to a "legal certainty" that the plaintiff could not recover in excess of the jurisdictional amount. In such cases, the plaintiff's good faith allegations generally control.

An example of the operation of the good faith-legal certainty test in a contract damages case occurred in *Tongkook America, Inc. v. Shipton Sportswear Co.*, 14 F.3d 781 (2d Cir. 1994). In *Tongkook*, the plaintiff sued the defendant for breach of contract claiming damages of $117,621.05, plus interest,. The amount demanded represented a balance that both parties believed was due on a sale of goods by the plaintiff to the defendant. However, during discovery, the parties learned that prior to the commencement of the action the plaintiff had drawn $80,760.00 on a letter of credit that had been provided by the defendant to the plaintiff. The result was that the actual amount of the plaintiff's claim at commencement of the action was $36,861.05, which was below the amount-in-controversy requirement. The defendant amended its answer to raise the defense of partial payment after this discovery. Subsequently, the district court raised the issue of subject-matter jurisdiction, and the defendant in response sought dismissal on this ground. However, the district court retained jurisdiction and ultimately entered judgment for the plaintiff in the amount of $36,861.05. The Second Circuit Court of Appeals reversed, holding that the good-faith legal certainty rule had been violated. The court acknowledged that the amount in controversy had to be determined as of commencement of the action, that events subsequent to commencement could not destroy jurisdiction, and that a valid defense also could not defeat jurisdiction. Nevertheless, the court held that the objective facts existing at the time that the action was commenced demonstrated that the amount-in-controversy requirement was not satisfied.

Tongkook should be compared with *Coventry Sewage Associates v. Dworkin Realty Co.*, 71 F.3d 1 (1st Cir. 1995). In *Coventry Sewage*, a mistaken calculation by a third party, upon whom the plaintiff and defendant had no choice but to rely, resulted in inflation of the amount in controversy above the required minimum. The First Circuit Court of Appeals upheld jurisdiction. The court distinguished *Tongkook* on the ground that the plaintiff in *Tongkook* should have discovered before commencement that its claim did not meet the amount requirement. In contrast, the third party's error in *Coventry Sewage* could not have been discovered by either of the parties prior to the action. Nevertheless, the two cases are impossible to reconcile under the traditional statement of the amount-in-controversy rules, because in both cases the objective facts in existence at the time of commencement demonstrated that the amount requirement was not satisfied. A comparison of the cases suggests the courts may be applying a rule that they have not fully articulated that focuses on whether the amount requirement has been inflated by the negligence or manipulative behavior of the plaintiff. If so, the case should be dismissed. If not, the good faith-legal certainty test should be deemed satisfied. *See* Teply & Whitten at 102–05.

Notes and Questions

1. How should the amount in controversy be determined when the amount the plaintiff can recover will be determined by future events, such as future installment payments, future taxes that would be levied if the suit is not successful, and so forth? To say the least, the courts have not adopted a coherent approach to these problems. In cases involving periodic (installment) payments, Professors Wright and Kane suggested that the amount in controversy "is the amount involved as a direct legal effect of the judgment," which depends on the applicable substantive law. Thus, if the substantive law allows recovery only for the amount of payments due at the time of suit, the amount in controversy would be less than if the law permits recovery for amounts not yet due. *See* Wright & Kane § 33, at 204–05. Unfortunately, this test does not seem to reconcile all the cases. The major problem in this area is determining when the amount in controversy can include future payments on the ground that the effect of the judgment obligates the defendant to make those payments, even though the right to the payments may be cut off by the occurrence of future events, such as the death of the plaintiff. *See* 14B Wright et al. § 3710, at 203.

2. Suppose the plaintiff claims $51,000 in damages plus $25,000 in attorney's fees. The amount of the fees is based on the plaintiff's estimate of how much the plaintiff's attorney will have to be paid after full litigation of the suit. Assuming that the attorney's fees would be recoverable under the applicable substantive law, should they be counted in determining whether the amount-in-controversy requirement has been satisfied? *See Gardynski-Leschuck v. Ford Motor Co.*, 142 F.3d 955 (7th Cir. 1998) (attorney's fees may not be counted; amount in controversy is calculated as of commencement of the action, on which date the attorney's fees had not yet been incurred; fees could be avoided by defendant's prompt payment of the plaintiff's claim).

Problems

Problem 4-15. P, a citizen of State *X*, sues *D*, a citizen of State *Y*, in a U.S. District Court in State Y. *P* seeks $5,000 in actual damages and $75,000 in punitive damages for an assault and battery committed by *D* against *P*. Under the substantive law applicable to *P's* claim, punitive damages are not recoverable. Assuming that *P* was unaware of the unavailability of punitive damages when the action was commenced, should the amount-in-controversy requirement be deemed satisfied? *NO. objective test*

Problem 4-16. P, a citizen of State X, sues D, a citizen of State Y, in a U.S. District Court in State Y. P seeks $80,000 from D for the conversion by D of personal property owned by P. Under the applicable substantive law, a plaintiff may recover damages for conversion of personal property measured by the value of the personal property at the time of the conversion. However, if the defendant returns the personal property, the plaintiff's damages are limited to any amount by which the plaintiff has been damaged by the detention of the property. Assume that the value of the personal property at the time of the conversion was $80,000, as alleged by P, but that by the time the action was commenced D had returned the property and the damages for detention were only $2,000. Is the jurisdictional amount requirement satisfied by P's request for $80,000, assuming that P said nothing about return of the property in the complaint and the return had to be alleged by D as a matter of defense? *No. $ was not in controversy at time of complaint* Suppose the personal property had not been returned at the time the action was commenced, but was returned shortly thereafter and the damages for detention are still only $2,000. Should the amount-in-controversy requirement be deemed satisfied under these circumstances? *yes at time of complaint Amt was satisfied*

(b) Aggregation of Claims

Claims Against the Same Party. Under Federal Rule 18(a), it is procedurally permissible for a plaintiff to join as many claims as the plaintiff possesses against a defendant, irrespective of whether the claims are factually or legally related. However, this rule does not establish subject-matter jurisdiction over the claims. Nevertheless, the aggregation rules developed under the jurisdictional statute allow all claims between the same two parties to be aggregated. Thus, all claims that a plaintiff has against a defendant may be aggregated to meet the jurisdictional amount as to that defendant, even if the claims are unrelated and even if no one claim against the defendant is in excess of the jurisdictional amount. For example, assume that P sues D. P asserts both a $40,000 negligence claim and a factually and legally unrelated $40,000 breach-of-contract claim. The amount-in-controversy requirement is satisfied in this case, even though neither claim of P on its own would be cognizable in federal court. If the negligence claim were for $80,000 and the contract claim were for $40,000, aggregation would similarly be permitted as to the breach-of-contract claim, and jurisdiction would be proper as to both claims.

Notes and Questions

1. Even though a party may aggregate as many claims as the party possesses against an opposing party, what happens under the "good faith-legal certainty test" if some of the claims are eliminated on a motion for summary judgment and their elimination reduces the amount below the required jurisdictional level? Recall from Chapter 1 that to win on a motion for summary judgment, the defendant would have to show that there is no genuine issue of material fact and that the defendant is entitled to a judgment as a matter of law. Wouldn't this mean that, on the objective facts existing at the commencement of the lawsuit, the required amount in controversy was not present? Apparently, the courts do not think so. *See Wolde-Meskel v. Vocational Instruction Project Cmty. Servs., Inc.*, 166 F.3d 59 (2d Cir. 1999); *Herremans v. Carrera Designs, Inc.*, 157 F.3d 1118 (7th Cir. 1998).

2. If the plaintiff's claim does not exceed $75,000, but the defendant asserts a compulsory counterclaim, *i.e.,* a counterclaim that arises out of the same transaction or occurrence as the plaintiff's claim, that meets the jurisdictional amount, should the amount-in-controversy

requirement be deemed satisfied? Some courts have said yes, reasoning that the plaintiff's claim is not the totality of the "controversy" and that when a defendant decides not to move to dismiss for lack of subject matter jurisdiction, but asserts a compulsory counterclaim instead, the defendant thereby places the amount of the counterclaim into controversy and the court must consider that amount in determining if it has jurisdiction under § 1332. *See Spectator Mgmt. Group v. Brown,* 131 F.3d 120, 122–25 (3rd Cir. 1997); *see also* Teply & Whitten at 113–14, 725–27. If such cases permitting aggregation of counterclaims are correct, can't the defendant who does not want to be in federal court still just move to dismiss for lack of subject-matter jurisdiction rather than serving an answer asserting the counterclaim?

Claims By or Against Multiple Parties. Under Federal Rule 20(a), it is procedurally permissible for claims by multiple parties or against multiple defendants to be joined if the claims share a common question of law or fact and arise out of the same transaction or series of transactions. However, traditionally, special aggregation rules have applied in multiple plaintiff or multiple defendant cases to determine when amounts asserted by or against the multiple parties can be added together to meet the amount-in-controversy requirement. Under these special aggregation rules, aggregation is not permitted based on compliance with Rule 20(a) alone, and each claim must individually meet the amount-in-controversy requirement.

A simple way of viewing the issue is to ask whether each plaintiff, if suing alone, would independently meet the amount-in-controversy requirement against each defendant. For example, if two passengers in a car each have a $40,000 personal injury negligence claim against a defendant driver arising out of the same automobile accident, the passengers cannot aggregate their claims to meet the amount-in-controversy requirement. This rule of nonaggregation traditionally applied even though one or more of the claims satisfied the jurisdictional amount. Thus, even if one passenger had a claim for $80,000 and the other had a claim for $40,000, the $40,000 could not be aggregated with the $80,000 claim and subject-matter jurisdiction would only exist over the $80,000 claim. Similarly, if a single plaintiff sued multiple defendants, the plaintiff would have to independently satisfy the amount-in-controversy requirement against each defendant, and aggregation of the claims against the defendants was not allowed.

"Common and Undivided Interest" Test. The only exception permitting aggregation for claims by or against multiple parties under the traditional rule existed when the claims derived from a "common undivided interest and a single title or right was involved." Wright & Kane § 36, at 213. Applying this "common and undivided interest" test has been a source of perpetual confusion for the courts because except in certain contexts, the term has no clear meaning under modern procedural rules. The test is not satisfied simply because the claims may be factually or legally related. Rather, the test requires a careful analysis in each case under the applicable substantive law to determine if the claims are truly "common and undivided" and involve a "single title or right."

Not only is the traditional aggregation test difficult to apply conceptually, it is very narrow in scope. Outside of the area of property and partnership law, "common and undivided" claims are unusual, and the typical breach-of-contract or tort claim asserted in a diversity case generally does not qualify. For instance, in the example of the negligence claims by the two passengers, although the claims are factually and legally related, they are separate claims that each passenger possesses under the substantive law of torts for individual injuries that each has suffered. Each passenger can sue individually for his or her injuries, and recovery by one for those injuries is separate and distinct from the injuries suffered by the other. Thus, only if both passengers suffered individual damages exceeding $75,000 would the amount-in-controversy requirement be satisfied as to both plaintiffs.

By comparison, assume four children are equal share beneficiaries in a trust worth $100,000. The trust funds are converted by the trustee. Even though each child will ultimately receive only one-fourth of the trust funds, under the substantive law of property each of the children would have a "common and undivided" right to seek restoration of the full $100,000 amount. Thus, if the four children join in an action against the trustee, the case would not be viewed as four individual claims for $25,000, but rather as a "common and undivided" claim based on a single right for $100,000. Similarly, assume two plaintiffs each own a one-half interest in an item of property worth $80,000. If the property is destroyed by *D*, the plaintiffs would have a single right to recovery under the substantive law of property for $80,000. Based on their "common and undivided" interest, the amount in controversy would be satisfied as to both plaintiffs. It cannot be said that the cases demonstrate a coherent approach outside the property area.

Joint and Several Liability. At times, multiple defendants may combine to cause a single injury to a plaintiff—thus giving rise to "joint and several" liability. Assume, for example, that *P* is injured in an automobile accident and suffers damages of $100,000. *P* alleges that the accident was caused by the negligence of either *D-1* or *D-2*, or both jointly. Under these circumstances, the amount in controversy is satisfied as to *P's* claim against both *D-1* and *D-2*. Under the substantive law, either *D-1* or *D-2* could be found completely responsible for the accident and liable to *P* for $100,000. If *D-1* and *D-2* are held jointly liable, under the traditional law of joint and several liability, *P* may recover the full $100,000 from either *D-1* or *D-2*, with *D-1* or *D-2* then having a right of contribution against the other. Because *P* has a valid claim for $100,000 against each defendant, the amount in controversy is satisfied as to both *D-1* and *D-2*.

It is important to distinguish joint-and-several-liability cases from aggregation cases. Joint-and-several-liability situations do not involve the application of the special aggregation rules discussed above because they are cases in which each defendant is liable to the plaintiff for the entire amount of the plaintiff's damages. The fact that one of the defendants may be absolved from liability altogether after trial does not change the fact that at the commencement of the action, total liability for all the damages may attach to both defendants.

Supplemental Jurisdiction and the Aggregation Rules. The aggregation rules discussed above are the traditional rules administered under the diversity jurisdiction statute. However, the ability to aggregate claims in class actions and in multiple plaintiff cases has been affected by the supplemental jurisdiction statute, 28 U.S.C. §1367, discussed in section E, below. As you will learn there, supplemental jurisdiction sometimes extends to jurisdictionally inadequate claims involving multiple parties and in class actions if those claims are sufficiently related to another claim in the action over which the court has original jurisdiction.

(c) Relief Other Than Monetary Damages

When the plaintiff requests relief other than monetary damages, such as an injunction, the rules discussed in the preceding subsections are not applicable. Instead, a special rule, known generally as the "value of the object of the suit" rule determines whether the amount-in-controversy requirement is satisfied. Basically, this rule states that when nonmonetary relief is requested, the value of the object of the suit governs. However, there is a serious ambiguity in this statement of the rule that the U.S. Supreme Court has never resolved. The ambiguity concerns the "viewpoint" from which the object of the suit should be measured. Sometimes, the value of the relief to the plaintiff is different from the cost of the relief to the defendant. In that situation, the question is from whose viewpoint should the amount in controversy be measured. Most courts agree that jurisdiction exists if the value to the plaintiff exceeds $75,000. When the value to the plaintiff does not exceed $75,000, the courts are divided as to whether jurisdiction can be sustained if the cost to the defendant exceeds $75,000.

Problems

Problem 4-17. P, a citizen of State *X*, sues *D*, a citizen of State *Y*. *P* seeks an order that would require *D* to remove a building that *D* constructed by mistake partly on *P's* land. The encroachment decreases the value of *P's* land by $36,000. It will cost *D* $350,000 to remove the encroachment. What arguments can you make that the amount-in-controversy requirement is satisfied by *P's* claim? That it is not satisfied? In framing these arguments, consider the possible purposes of the amount-in-controversy requirement of § 1332.   P's claim only 36k

Problem 4-18. *A*, a citizen of State *X*, sold land to *D*, a citizen of State *Y*. *A* took two separate notes, each for $38,000, in return for the land. *A* also reserved a vendor's lien on the land. Subsequently, *A* validly assigned one of the notes to *P-1* and the other to *P-2*. Both *P-1* and *P-2* are citizens of State *X*. *D* failed to pay the notes on maturity. *P-1* and *P-2* sue *D* in a U.S. District Court in State *Y* to enforce the vendor's lien. May *P-1* and *P-2* aggregate their claims to meet the jurisdictional amount requirement? If *A* had not reserved a vendor's lien and *P-1* and *P-2* had simply sued on the notes, would they be able to aggregate their claims to meet the amount-in-controversy requirement? No   yes B/c lien?

Problem 4-19. *D Corp.* is incorporated with its principal place of business in State *Y*. It operates a manufacturing plant in State *X*. The plant emits fumes that are damaging land owned by *P-1* and *P-2*, who are both citizens of State *X*. This "nuisance" is reducing the value of *P-1's* land by $38,000. It is also reducing the value of *P-2's* land by the same amount. *P-1* and *P-2* sue *D Corp.* in a U.S. District Court in State *X*. *P-1* and *P-2* seek an order requiring the defendant to abate the nuisance. May *P-1* and *P-2* aggregate their claims to meet the jurisdictional amount? Does the answer to this question involve any other issue than the operation of the aggregation rules?   P's   No

Section D. Judicial Exceptions to Federal Jurisdiction

Neither the constitutional nor the statutory grants of federal court jurisdiction make any express exception for domestic relations or probate cases. Nevertheless, both exceptions have been long recognized under federal case law.

1. Domestic Relations Cases

In *Ankenbrandt v. Richards*, 504 U.S. 689 (1992), the Supreme Court noted that although the so-called "domestic relations" exception was not compelled by Article III nor explicitly stated in § 1332, the federal courts had for more than 100 years interpreted the diversity statute as including such an exception. The corresponding acquiescence of Congress in that interpretation despite its subsequent amendments of the statute justified the conclusion that Congress intended this exception as the proper construction of § 1332. The Court also noted that sound policy supported the Court's holding as the state courts were "eminently more suited" to handle delicate domestic matters that often require ongoing supervision and support services beyond the capability and expertise of the federal courts.

The Court, however, clarified the scope of the exception and narrowed it, at least as it had been applied by some lower federal courts. *Ankenbrandt* held that the exception applies only to claims seeking a grant or modification of a divorce, alimony, or child custody decree and does not bar diversity jurisdiction over other claims even though they may arise in a domestic relations context. *See id.* at 694–97. In *Ankenbrandt,* for instance, the Court upheld diversity jurisdiction over the plaintiff's tort complaint for money damages filed on behalf of her two children, which alleged that her ex-husband and his female companion had sexually and physically abused the children.

Unfortunately, *Ankenbrandt* has not settled all the questions about the scope of the domestic relations exception. Part of the difficulty that courts have with determining which kinds of cases do, and which do not, fit within the exception is caused by the ingenuity of parties who wish to sue in federal court in developing devices with which to evade the exception. The lower federal courts have been reluctant to allow litigants to place the labels "tort" or "contract" on controversies that the courts view as being essentially domestic relations disputes. It is arguable that these decisions are inconsistent with either *Ankenbrandt* or the other Supreme Court decisions interpreting the scope of the exception. *See, e.g., Barber v. Barber,* 62 U.S. (21 How.) 582 (1859) (refusing to apply the exception in an action seeking to enforce the judgment of a state court ordering the defendant to pay alimony to the plaintiff).

The courts have held that the domestic relations exception does not bar federal question jurisdiction over legitimate constitutional and other federal law claims even though they may arise in a domestic relations setting. The highly publicized case in 2000 of Elian Gonzalez, a young Cuban boy who was found floating in the waters off Florida after fleeing with his mother from Cuba, illustrates this distinction. After Elian's mother died at sea, Elian's Miami relatives filed a federal court action challenging the U.S. Government's order to return Elian to his natural father in Cuba. Although arising out of the custody dispute between Elian's father and Miami relatives, the federal court action filed by Elian's relatives did not seek custody or support, but only challenged the government's action under federal constitutional, statutory, and regulatory provisions in refusing to consider Elian's petition for asylum. Jurisdiction was thus properly upheld under federal question jurisdiction. *Gonzalez v. Reno,* 86 F. Supp. 2d 1167 (S.D. Fla. 2000), *aff'd,* 212 F.3d 1338 (11th Cir. 2000). Although the Miami relatives did not seek an original award of custody or support, such a request presumably would have fallen within the domestic relations exception, even though the main relief requested was properly within federal question jurisdiction.

The Court's decision in *Troxel v. Granville,* 530 U.S. 57 (2000), also illustrates how federal question issues can arise in a domestic relations context. In *Troxel,* the Court accepted appellate jurisdiction over a state court action concerning the constitutionality of a state statute authorizing grandparent visitation despite the natural parent's wishes. Although the Court would not decide what amount of visitation was appropriate, it properly exercised appellate jurisdiction to decide the constitutional question of whether the state statute violated the due process rights of the natural parent.

2. Probate Cases

Similar to the "domestic relations" exception, the so-called "probate" exception is neither constitutionally nor statutorily mandated or expressed, but is rather a longstanding judicial interpretation of the jurisdictional statutes. Under the probate exception, a federal court may not exercise jurisdiction to probate the will of a decedent or administer an estate. However, this restriction does not mean that the federal courts lack subject-matter jurisdiction over every matter that may concern a decedent's estate. Federal courts may entertain claims against administrators, executors, and others that are otherwise within federal jurisdiction provided the federal court does not assume control of property that is in the custody of a state probate court.

The Supreme Court's most recent analysis of the "probate" exception is *Marshall v. Marshall*, 547 U.S. 293 (2006). In this case, the Supreme Court addressed the scope of the probate exception in a bankruptcy proceeding otherwise governed by the federal bankruptcy laws. The decedent, J. Howard Marshall, died without making provisions for his wife, Vickie Lynn Marshall, also known as Anna Nicole Smith, in his will. Vickie contended that J. Howard had intended to provide for her through a gift in the form of a "catch-all" trust. While J. Howard's estate was being probated in a Texas state court, Vickie instituted federal bankruptcy proceedings in California. J. Howard's son, E. Pierce Marshall, who was the beneficiary of J. Howard's estate under the will, filed a proof of claim in the federal bankruptcy proceeding. Pierce alleged that Vickie had defamed him by telling the press after J. Howard's death that Pierce had engaged in forgery, fraud, and overreaching to gain control of his father's assets. Vickie asserted truth as a defense to this claim and also counterclaimed in the bankruptcy proceeding, alleging that Pierce had tortiously interfered with a gift that she expected from J. Howard.

The federal bankruptcy court granted summary judgment to Vickie on Pierce's claim against her and, after a trial on the merits, entered judgment for Vickie on her counterclaim. Pierce then filed a post-trial motion to dismiss for lack of subject-matter jurisdiction, asserting that Vickie's claim could only be asserted in the Texas state probate proceeding. This motion was denied by the bankruptcy court, which held that a federal court has jurisdiction to adjudicate rights in probate property, as long as the final judgment in the federal proceeding does not interfere with the state court's possession of the property. The U.S. District Court, on review of the bankruptcy court's judgment, agreed that the probate exception did not prevent adjudication of Vickie's counterclaim. In further review of the bankruptcy judgment, the District Court agreed that Vickie's tortious interference claim was sound and awarded Vickie $44.3 million in actual damages and another $44.3 million in punitive damages. On review of the district court's judgment, however, the Ninth Circuit Court of Appeals reversed the judgment, holding that the probate exception to federal jurisdiction barred federal jurisdiction. The U.S. Supreme Court, in turn, granted certiorari and reversed the Ninth Circuit, holding that the case did not fall within the probate exception.

Following its analysis in *Ankenbrandt* limiting the scope of the "domestic relations" exception (discussed above), the Court similarly construed the probate exception narrowly. The Court reaffirmed that while the probate exception prevents federal courts from probating a will or administering an estate, it does not prevent federal courts from adjudicating other claims that are properly within federal jurisdiction, so long as the federal court is not "endeavoring to dispose of property that is in the custody of a state probate court." Finding no such situation here, the Court held that Vickie's tortious interference claim was not jurisdictionally barred by the probate exception. *See* 547 U.S. at 308–14.

Problems

Problem 4-20. P, a citizen of State *X*, sued *D*, a citizen of State *Y*, in a U.S. District Court. *P* seeks enforcement of the judgment of a state court ordering *D* to pay alimony to *P*. *P* seeks payment of $100,000 of back alimony awarded but unpaid under the state judgment. Should the U.S. District Court have diversity jurisdiction over this action? *No, alimony exception* [handwritten]

Problem 4-21. P, a citizen of State *X*, suffered personal injuries in an automobile accident with *A*, a citizen of State *Y*. *A* was killed in the accident. *D*, a citizen of State *X*, was appointed administrator of *A's* estate. *P* sues *D* in a U.S. District Court in State *Y* to recover $100,000 for the personal injuries *P* received in the accident. If *P* wins, the damages will be paid out of *D's* estate. Should the district court have diversity jurisdiction over this action? *Yes, not probating a will* [handwritten]

Section E. Supplemental Jurisdiction

1. Overview

As you have learned, the requirements for subject-matter jurisdiction in the lower federal courts are very strict. Jurisdiction must be both constitutionally authorized under Article III and statutorily authorized by Congress. Moreover, under the jurisdictional statutes you have studied thus far, proper jurisdiction must exist over *all* claims asserted in a federal court action. When one plaintiff sues only one defendant on a single claim, the jurisdictional inquiry can be easily resolved by applying the subject-matter jurisdiction requirements for original jurisdiction to the plaintiff's single claim. Many cases, however, involve multiple claims and multiple parties, and proper jurisdiction must exist over these additional claims as well. When these additional claims independently satisfy the requirements of subject-matter jurisdiction, jurisdiction fully exists over these claims as it would over any other federal claim. Thus, if *P*, a citizen of State *X*, sued *D*, a citizen of State *X*, alleging violation of a federal age discrimination law, and also joined a claim against *D* under a federal sex discrimination law, full subject-matter jurisdiction would exist over both claims under § 1331.

Suppose, though, that *P's* additional claim against *D* is for violation of a state employment discrimination law and both *P* and *D* are citizens of the same state. *P's* additional state law claim would now independently fail to satisfy the jurisdictional requirements of either § 1331 or § 1332. The state law claim is not a claim arising under the Constitution or laws of the United States, and there is no diversity of citizenship between the parties. However, the supplemental jurisdiction statute, 28 U.S.C. § 1367, was enacted in 1990. Under that statute, the federal courts may exercise subject-matter jurisdiction over *P's* state law claim against *D* if *P's* state law claim is sufficiently related to *P's* federal claim. Under § 1367(a), supplemental jurisdiction extends to any claims asserted by a party that are "so related" to another claim within the original jurisdiction of the district courts as to "form part of the same case or controversy under Article III of the United States Constitution."

Osborn v. Bank of the United States, discussed in section B, provides the constitutional underpinnings of the doctrine of supplemental jurisdiction. The theory of *Osborn* is that Congress may give to the federal courts jurisdiction over entire "cases," not just those portions of the "cases" that are "federal." Thus, as long as Article III would allow any part of the case to be adjudicated by a federal court, Congress can give jurisdiction to the federal courts to adjudicate the entire case, including those parts over which there would be no federal subject-matter jurisdiction if they were presented alone. For example, if *P's* federal and state discrimination claims are sufficiently related to form part of the same "case or controversy" for purposes of Article III, Congress can authorize the federal courts to adjudicate both claims, even though there would be no constitutional or statutory authority to hear the *P's* state law claim if it were asserted by itself. Obviously, it is very important under *Osborn* to determine what is the proper scope of an Article III "case or controversy." The accepted view is that all claims must "derive from a common nucleus of operative fact" to constitute the same "case or controversy" for purposes of Article III. The Supreme Court employed this test in the landmark case of *United Mine Workers v. Gibbs*, 383 U.S. 715, 725 (1966).

[handwritten margin note: Scope of Case or Controversy]

As you study supplemental jurisdiction, it is important to keep certain fundamental concepts in mind. All assertions of supplemental jurisdiction under §1367(a) are expressly premised on the fact that the federal court already has full and proper *original* subject-matter jurisdiction in the action under §1331, §1332, or one of the other jurisdictional statutes. ("[I]n any civil action of which the district courts have original jurisdiction, the district courts shall have supplemental jurisdiction over all other claims that … form part of the same case or controversy…."). In *Exxon Mobil Corp. v. Allapattah Services, Inc.*, 545 U.S. 546 (2005), reprinted below, the Supreme Court interpreted the language in §1367(a) requiring that there be a "civil action over which the district courts have original jurisdiction." Despite the fact that this language could literally be read to require that independent original jurisdiction exist over every claim in the action, the Court held that, with the exception of the requirement of complete diversity in §1332 actions, the existence of one claim over which there is original jurisdiction is sufficient to satisfy the "civil action" prerequisite of the statute.

It is helpful to view this claim that vests original subject-matter jurisdiction in the action as the "freestanding" or "anchor" claim. If the necessary relationship exists between the freestanding and supplemental claims to make them part of the same Article III "case or controversy," the supplemental claims are then permitted to "ride the coattails" of the freestanding claim, even though, on their own, the supplemental claims would not independently satisfy the requirements for original subject-matter jurisdiction. By definition, therefore, supplemental jurisdiction cannot exist in the absence of a valid freestanding claim.

For example, recall the *Mottley* case in section B, above. Supplemental jurisdiction would not have been available to save the Mottleys' case against the railroad because there was no freestanding claim in the action within the original jurisdiction of the federal courts. The federal issues in the case arose as defenses and replies to defenses and thus did not contribute to the plaintiff's claim, which is necessary for original jurisdiction to exist under the federal question statute (§1331). Because there was also no diversity of citizenship between the Mottleys and the railroad, there was no freestanding claim within diversity jurisdiction under §1332. Suppose, however, that the Mottleys sued the appropriate federal agency to enjoin enforcement of the new federal law claiming that the law violated their constitutional rights. If this claim against the federal agency now properly qualified as a federal question claim under §1331, the Mottleys would have been able to join the railroad to the action as an additional party and assert their state law breach-of-contract claim against the railroad under supplemental jurisdiction. *See* the final sentence of 28 U.S.C. §1367(a) which extends supplemental jurisdiction to "claims that involve the joinder or intervention of additional parties."

Notes and Questions

1. Prior to the enactment of the supplemental jurisdiction statute in 1990, the federal courts exercised supplemental jurisdiction for many years without express congressional authorization under the judicially created doctrines of "pendent" and "ancillary" jurisdiction. As a general rule, "pendent" jurisdiction applied to supplemental claims by plaintiffs in federal question cases and "ancillary" jurisdiction applied to supplemental claims by defendants and intervenors in federal question and diversity cases. In order to avoid confusion with the standards of these former doctrines, § 1367 adopted the new, all-encompassing term "supplemental jurisdiction." The provisions of § 1367 fully apply to all supplemental claims, irrespective of whether those claims would have been characterized as "pendent" or "ancillary" under these former judicial doctrines.

2. What policy reasons do you think support the exercise supplemental jurisdiction? In answering this question, consider what the consequences would be to a plaintiff who possessed both federal and state law claims arising from the same transaction if the plaintiff *could not* litigate the state claim with the federal claim in a single action in federal court.   ↑ ch. cost w/ separate litigation & + time

3. As explained in Note 1 above, supplemental jurisdiction exists over claims asserted by defendants (such as counterclaims), assuming that the defendant's claims are sufficiently related to the plaintiff's freestanding claim that confers original jurisdiction. Are the policy reasons the same for allowing supplemental jurisdiction over defendants' claims as for permitting supplemental jurisdiction over plaintiffs' claims? If not, are the policies for allowing supplemental jurisdiction over defendants' claims stronger or weaker than for allowing supplemental jurisdiction over plaintiffs' claims?

2. Meeting the Requirements of § 1367(a)

(a) Determining When Claims Are Part of the Same Article III "Case or Controversy"

Section 1367(a) extends supplemental jurisdiction to all claims that are "*so related* to claims in the action within ... original jurisdiction that they form part of the *same case or controversy* under Article III" (emphasis added). The most important issue under § 1367(a), therefore, is determining the degree of relatedness required between the claims to constitute the "same case or controversy" for purposes of Article III.

As explained in the preceding subsection, existing Supreme Court precedent, in particular the decision of *United Mine Workers v. Gibbs*, 383 U.S. 715 (1966), indicates that for federal and state claims to be part of the same constitutional case or controversy, they must be factually related. As stated in *Gibbs*, the claims must "derive from a common nucleus of operative fact." *Id.* at 725. However, the lower federal court decisions are in disagreement about how close the factual relationship between the claims must be to satisfy the Supreme Court's test. Some decisions hold that only a "loose factual relationship" must exist to satisfy Article III. Other decisions require a close factual relationship.

For example, assume that *P-1* sues *D-1*, the company for which *P-1* works, asserting sexual harassment and sexual discrimination claims against the company under federal law. Assume that *P-1's* claims arise out of the treatment of *P-1* by *D-2*, *P-1's* supervisor in the company. *P-1's* fiancé, *P-2*, joins with *P-1* as a plaintiff in the action to assert a state law claim against *D-2* for slander. *P-2's* slander claim is based on remarks made by *D-2* to *P-1* to the effect that *P-2*, an attorney, was a cheat and a liar, like all lawyers. Assume that these slanderous remarks were part of the ongoing harassment of *P-1* that gave rise to *P-1's* federal law claims. A court requiring a close factual relationship to satisfy Article III would hold that no supplemental jurisdiction exists over *P-2's* state law claim. On the other hand, a court finding a loose factual relationship sufficient to satisfy Article III would likely uphold supplemental jurisdiction on the facts given. *See* TEPLY & WHITTEN at 145–48 (discussing the close and loose factual relationship tests).

It is important to recognize that although the Supreme Court's decisions to date, including the *Gibbs* case, all state that some sort of factual relationship is necessary between federal and state claims to satisfy Article III, the Court has never had before it a case in which Congress has specifically authorized the federal courts to exercise supplemental jurisdiction over factually unrelated federal and state claims. Only when such a case arises will the Court be able to make an authoritative statement about the factual relationship that is necessary between federal and state claims to satisfy Article III. Until such a case arises, you should be aware that there are both historical and precedential reasons to believe that, under appropriate circumstances, Congress may have the authority to authorize the federal courts to exercise jurisdiction over state claims that have no factual relationship at all to the freestanding federal claims that provide the basis for federal jurisdiction. *See* TEPLY & WHITTEN at 125–28 (discussing this problem).

Notes and Questions

1. Assuming that a factual relationship between federal and state claims is necessary to satisfy Article III, are there policy reasons to prefer either a close factual relationship test or a loose factual relationship test? *See* Denis F. McLaughlin, *The Federal Supplemental Jurisdiction Statute—A Constitutional and Statutory Analysis*, 24 ARIZ. ST. L.J. 849, 907–13 (1992) ("case or controversy" standard of Article III should be interpreted broadly to maximize judicial and party efficiency in resolving all aspects of an entire controversy in a single proceeding).

2. Are there policy reasons for preferring a test under Article III that would require no factual relationship between claims? (Renew this question after studying separate and independent claim removal under 28 U.S.C. § 1441(c) in section F, below.) If Article III does not require any factual relationship between claims, what kind of test would be applied to determine when a multiple claim/multiple party case with both federal and state claims satisfies or does not satisfy Article III requirements?

Problem

Problem 4-22. *P* was employed by *D*, a municipality. *P* received a thirty-day suspension because *P's* supervisor had a reasonable suspicion that *P* had been under the influence of alcohol while on the job. *P* also received an additional fifteen day suspension for verbally harassing *P's* supervisor. In addition, *P* was required to enter an alcohol rehabilitation program and to consent to random drug and alcohol testing during work hours for one year. If *P* tested positive, *P's* employment could be terminated immediately. Furthermore, *P* was required to attend counseling sessions through an Employee Assistance Program. While serving the suspension, *P* enrolled in an outpatient alcohol rehabilitation program. *P* then returned to work and has not had a drinking problem since that time. After returning to work, *P's* immediate supervisor gave satisfactory evaluations. Had *D* followed its standard practice of giving performance ratings only on the basis of *P's* work on an annual basis, *P* would have received a satisfactory rating. However, *P* was given a rating of "poor" on *P's* performance evaluation by combining two years of evaluation into one report.

As a result of this combination, *D* was able to evaluate *P* on the basis of performance and other related problems that occurred prior to *P's* completion of rehabilitation. As a consequence, *P* was again put on probation. *P* informed *D* that this action constituted employment discrimination on the basis of *P's* age and former alcohol-related handicap. *P* was then demoted. As a result, *P* filed charges of discrimination with the appropriate governmental agency. Immediately thereafter, *P* was fired for "a pattern of unsafe practices." *P* then commenced an action against *D* in U.S. District Court. *P's* complaint alleged violations of three federal statutes: the American with Disabilities Act, the Age Discrimination in Employment Act, and the Rehabilitation Act of 1973. *P's* complaint alleged, in effect, discrimination, retaliation, and adverse employment action. *P* sought damages and reinstatement.

After taking the depositions of *D's* current employees, *P* sought leave to amend *P's* complaint to add two additional claims. First, *P* sought to add a claim for intentional infliction of emotional distress based on the events giving rise to *P's* termination. This claim is a state tort law claim. Second, *P* sought to add a claim asserting that the therapist employed in *D's* Employee Assistance Program disclosed confidential information regarding *P* to a number of *D's* employees in violation of a state Mental Health and Developmental Disabilities Confidential Act. These disclosures took place after *P* was terminated. *P* was particularly upset about these post-termination disclosures. Specifically, *P* feels that if *P* were to be reinstated, the disclosures to *P's* co-workers concerning *P's* condition and the therapist's opinion about *P's* mental health and stability will negatively affect *P's* ability to return to *P's* former position successfully.

D objected on the ground that the claims in the proposed amendment are not within the supplemental jurisdiction of the court under § 1367(a). How should the court rule on *D's* objections?

(b) Supplemental Jurisdiction for Claims Involving Additional Parties

As further discussed in the *Exxon Mobil* case, reprinted in subsection 3, below, § 1367(a) was aimed, in part, at overruling the result in the U.S. Supreme Court's decision in *Finley v. United States*, 490 U.S. 545 (1989). In *Finley*, the plaintiff asserted a federal law claim against one defendant and joined with that claim a state law claim arising out of the same facts against a second nondiverse defendant. The Supreme Court held that supplemental jurisdiction over the plaintiff's state law claim against the additional nondiverse party was improper absent an affirmative statutory grant of such jurisdiction to the federal courts by Congress.

The final sentence of § 1367(a) providing that "supplemental jurisdiction shall include claims that involve the joinder or intervention of additional parties" was specifically designed to overrule the result in *Finley* and provide the affirmative congressional authorization that the *Finley* Court deemed necessary. Of course, all supplemental claims, whether involving the joinder of additional claims by or against existing or additional parties, must meet the "same case or controversy" test of § 1367(a), as examined in subsection (a), to be within the supplemental jurisdiction of the federal courts.

Problem

Problem 4-23. P, a citizen of State *X*, sued *D-1*, a citizen of State *X*, on a federal claim in a U.S. District Court. *P* joined a state tort law claim against *D-2*, a citizen of State *X*, which also arose out of the same facts giving rise to *P's* federal claim against *D-1*. Applying the language of § 1367(a) and (b), is there supplemental jurisdiction over *P's* claim against *D-2*?

3. Restrictions Imposed by § 1367(b) in Actions Founded Solely on Diversity of Citizenship

Section 1367(a) authorizes the broadest possible scope of supplemental jurisdiction in all federal actions. Under § 1367(a), provided the supplemental claims are sufficiently related to the freestanding claim to satisfy the constitutional "case or controversy" requirement of Article III, full supplemental jurisdiction exists for all claims asserted by or against *any* party irrespective of whether the party is a plaintiff, defendant, third-party defendant, intervenor, or Rule 19 party.

In actions in which original jurisdiction is founded *solely* on § 1332, however, supplemental jurisdiction is substantially restricted for claims by *plaintiffs* and any additional parties joining or intervening as *plaintiffs*. The rationale for this restriction stated in the legislative history of the statute is to prevent easy evasion of the jurisdictional requirements of § 1332 by plaintiffs through "the simple expedient of naming initially only those defendants whose joinder satisfies section 1332's requirements and later adding claims not within original jurisdiction against other defendants who have intervened or been joined on a supplemental basis." H.R. Rep. No. 734, 101st Cong., 2d Sess., at 29 (1990). Specifically, § 1367(b) restricts supplemental jurisdiction

> over claims by plaintiffs against persons made parties under Rule 14, 19, 20, or 24 of the Federal Rules of Civil Procedure, or over claims by persons proposed to be joined as plaintiffs under Rule 19 of such rules, or seeking to intervene as plaintiffs under Rule 24 of such rules, when exercising supplemental jurisdiction over such claims would be inconsistent with the jurisdictional requirements of section 1332.

Note carefully that § 1367(b) imposes no supplemental jurisdiction restrictions on claims asserted by *defendants* or those intervening or joining as *defendants*. For claims by defendants in diversity cases, full supplemental jurisdiction continues to apply to the same extent as in federal question cases and other nondiversity cases.

Procedural Joinder of Multiple Claims and Parties Under the Federal Rules. To properly understand the application of § 1367(b), you need to familiarize yourself with the various procedural rules for the party joinder referred to in § 1367(b). These rules of party joinder were reviewed in Chapter 1(F) and will be examined in depth in Chapter 7.

Specifically, under Rule 20(a), the plaintiff is permitted to join with additional plaintiffs or join additional defendants to the action if the claims are properly related under the rule. Rule 20 is the basic rule under which multiple plaintiffs and multiple defendants are joined in all types of civil actions. Under Rule 14(a) impleader, the defendant is permitted to join ("implead") an additional party to the action, known as a third-party defendant, when that person is or may be liable to the defendant for all or part of the plaintiff's claim against the defendant. Under Rule 24, non-parties having an interest in the litigation are permitted to intervene in the action under appropriate circumstances in order to protect their interests. Finally, a non-party is sometimes considered essential to the adjudication of the action and a motion is made requiring the joinder of this nonparty. Such parties are joined under Rule 19.

These are the four party joinder rules which expressly trigger the restrictions § 1367(b). One rule of party joinder not listed in § 1367(b) is Rule 23. Rule 23 permits parties to join in a class action when the parties are too numerous to join individually under Rule 20. As you will see, the absence of Rule 23 from the enumerated listing of § 1367(b) was critical to the Court's holding in the *Exxon Mobil* case, reprinted below.

Procedural Versus Jurisdictional Requirements for Joinder. The Federal Rules of Civil Procedure, summarized above, only establish when it is procedurally permissible to join an additional party. The rules do not provide the jurisdictional authority for the joinder of these additional claims or parties. Proper constitutional and statutory authority for subject-matter jurisdiction must still exist as to every joined claim and party. In fact, Rule 82 expressly provides that "[t]hese rules do not extend or limit the jurisdiction of the district courts." As the Court stated in *Owen Equipment & Erection Co. v. Kroger*, 437 U.S. 365 (1978), "although [Rule] 14(a) permits a plaintiff to assert a claim against a third-party defendant, it does not purport to say whether or not such a claim requires an independent basis of federal jurisdiction. Indeed, it could not determine that question because it is axiomatic that the Federal Rules of Civil Procedure do not create or withdraw federal jurisdiction." *Id.* at 370.

The *"Kroger"* Rationale Restricting Claims by Plaintiffs. Under the former doctrines of pendent and ancillary jurisdiction, which the courts used prior to the enactment of § 1367, supplemental jurisdiction was similarly restricted, as it is now under § 1367(b), for claims by plaintiffs in diversity cases. The leading case establishing such a restriction was *Owen Equipment & Erection Co. v. Kroger*, 437 U.S. 365 (1978), decided by the Supreme Court in 1978. In fact, the legislative history of § 1367 states that "[t]he net effect of subsection (b) is to implement the principal rationale of *Owen Equipment & Erection Co. v. Kroger*." H.R. Rep. No. 734, 101st Cong., 2d Sess., at 29, n.16 (1990).

In *Kroger*, the plaintiff's husband, James Kroger, had been electrocuted when a steel crane came too close to a high tension electric power line. The plaintiff, a citizen of Iowa, initially filed a diversity action for wrongful death against the Omaha Public Power District (OPPD), a citizen of Nebraska. OPPD then filed a third-party claim under Rule 14(a) against Owen Equipment & Erection Co. (Owen), a citizen of both Iowa and Nebraska. After Owen was joined to the action by OPPD under Rule 14, the plaintiff then amended her complaint to assert a direct claim against Owen. Under the "complete diversity" rule of *Strawbridge v. Curtiss*, discussed above, Owen could not have been joined originally in the action by the plaintiff. However, because the claim arose from the same facts as the plaintiff's original claim against OPPD and because the claim was asserted in the action after the assertion of the original claim and in response to events over which the plaintiff had no control (the impleader of Owen by OPPD), the plaintiff argued that the former doctrine of ancillary jurisdiction should apply to the plaintiff's claim.

The Supreme Court, however, rejected the application of ancillary jurisdiction to the claim by Kroger against Owen. The Court held that to extend ancillary jurisdiction to a plaintiff's claim against a nondiverse defendant "would simply flout the congressional command" of complete diversity. 437 U.S. at 377. Despite the fact that it was the defendant OPPD and not the plaintiff who had joined Owen to the action, the Court feared that if ancillary jurisdiction applied to such claims, a plaintiff could easily evade the requirement of complete diversity "by the simple expedient of suing only those defendants who were of diverse citizenship and waiting for them to implead nondiverse defendants." *Id.* at 374.

The Court distinguished the traditional application of ancillary jurisdiction in diversity cases to state law counterclaims, crossclaims, and impleader claims by defendants and state law claims by intervenors of right when such claims, viewed independently, failed to satisfy the requirements of § 1332. The Court emphasized that

> the context in which the nonfederal claim is asserted is crucial ... [and] the nonfederal claim here was asserted by the plaintiff, who voluntarily chose to bring suit upon a state-law claim in a federal court. By contrast, ancillary jurisdiction typically involves claims by a defending party haled into court against his will, or by another person whose rights might be irretrievably lost unless he could assert them in an ongoing action in a federal court. A plaintiff cannot complain if ancillary jurisdiction does not encompass all of his possible claims in a case such as this one, since it is he who has chosen the federal rather than the state forum and must thus accept its limitations.

Id. at 375–76. The essence of the *Kroger* rationale, therefore, is that the "context" in which a claim is asserted is crucial in determining whether supplemental jurisdiction should apply to it. A plaintiff in a diversity case should not be allowed to use supplemental jurisdiction as a means of circumventing and evading the jurisdictional requirements of § 1332. It is this rationale that was carried forward in § 1367(b).

Supplemental Claims by Defendants. As noted earlier, the restrictions of § 1367(b) do not apply to claims by defendants. Even though a defendant "acts as a plaintiff" in asserting a claim for relief as a counterclaim, cross-claim, third-party impleader claim, or an intervenor's claim, a defendant does not convert into a "plaintiff" for purposes of § 1367(b) by asserting such claims. With respect to defendants, therefore, it does not matter if original jurisdiction in the action is founded on § 1332 or any other jurisdictional statute. In *all* federal actions, there is full supplemental jurisdiction for all defendants, irrespective of the restrictions of § 1367(b).

The Rule 20 Gap. As noted earlier, the restrictions of § 1367(b) are expressed in terms of the particular Federal Rules under which persons are made parties to the action. Although you will not fully understand all of the procedural requirements of these rules until you study Chapter 7, it is only necessary at this point that you understand the *jurisdictional* significance of being joined under these rules. Generally, if the person asserting a jurisdictionally insufficient claim is a *plaintiff* and jurisdiction in the action is founded *solely* on § 1332, then supplemental jurisdiction will not exist for the claim if it is asserted against a person joined under one of the rules listed in § 1367(b).

One of the most troublesome statutory issues in applying § 1367(b) is the section's so-called "Rule 20 gap." Read carefully the three restricting clauses of § 1367(b). The first clause prohibits supplemental jurisdiction over claims "by plaintiffs against persons made parties under Rule 14, 19, 20, or 24." The second and third clauses prohibit supplemental jurisdiction over claims by plaintiffs joined under Rule 19 or intervening under Rule 24. These three clauses were intended to cover all possible claims by plaintiffs for which supplemental jurisdiction was to be denied in a diversity-only case. As written, however, § 1367(b) does not prohibit supplemental jurisdiction over claims by plaintiffs joined under *Rule 20* in an action against a *single defendant.*

This is because an action against a single defendant does not require any special rule of joinder, and thus none of the prohibited joinder rules of the first clause of

§ 1367(b) are implicated. Because a single defendant is not a person made a party under Rules 14, 19, 20, or 24, and because the second and third clauses of § 1367(b) only apply to plaintiffs joining or intervening under Rules 19 or 24, and not to plaintiffs joining under Rule 20, there is a "gap" in § 1367(b) when a Rule 20 plaintiff asserts a supplemental claim against a single defendant. The plain language of § 1367(b) does not prohibit supplemental jurisdiction over an otherwise jurisdictionally insufficient claim by a plaintiff joined under Rule 20 in an action against a single defendant. This is the so-called "Rule 20 gap," and the resolution of this statutory oversight sharply divided the courts of appeals prior to the Supreme Court's decision in *Exxon Mobil,* reprinted below.

Effect of § 1367(b) on Class Action Cases—The Rule 23 Gap. Under Federal Rule 23, one or more members of a class may sue or be sued as representative parties on behalf of all when the class is too numerous for individual joinder and there are questions of law or fact common to the class. In *Supreme Tribe of Ben-Hur v. Cauble*, 255 U.S. 356 (1921), the Supreme Court held that only the citizenship of the named class representatives is considered in determining whether complete diversity exists. Thus, even though other members of the class may be nondiverse to the defendant, subject-matter jurisdiction is proper as to the claims of all class members provided the named class representatives are completely diverse from the opposing party. *Id.* at 365–66. With respect to the amount-in-controversy requirement, however, the Supreme Court in *Snyder v. Harris*, 394 U.S. 332 (1969), held that the normal multiple party aggregation rules applied and that in the absence of a "common and undivided interest," the members of the class could not aggregate their individual claims to meet the amount-in-controversy requirement.

In *Snyder*, no class member had a claim for the requisite amount. In *Zahn v. International Paper Co.*, 414 U.S. 291 (1973), however, the claims of the named representatives were jurisdictionally sufficient, but the claims of the other class members were not. The Supreme Court, nevertheless, extended the ruling in *Synder* and held that in the absence of a "common and undivided" interest, the insufficient claims of the general class members could not be aggregated with the jurisdictionally sufficient claims of the named class representatives. *Id.* at 301. In diversity class actions in federal court, therefore, unless the "common and undivided interest" test is satisfied, the holding in *Zahn* meant that every member of the class must have a claim that exceeds $75,000 for diversity jurisdiction to be proper for all members of the class. The *Zahn* case creates the jurisdictional anomaly of allowing complete diversity to be judged only as to the named class representatives, but assessing the amount in controversy as to every member of the class.

Section 1367(b) does not, however, mention Rule 23. Literally, therefore, the section does not exclude from supplemental jurisdiction claims of class members in the *Zahn* kind of case. Thus, if the claims of some representative parties meet the amount requirement and the claims of other representative parties or the absent members of the class do not, but the latter claims are part of the same Article III "case or controversy" as the freestanding claims, supplemental jurisdiction exists over the non-freestanding claims under § 1367(a) and it is not literally withdrawn by § 1367(b).

The *Exxon Mobil* Decision. Both the Rule 20 gap and the omission of Rule 23 from § 1367(b) were apparently the result of drafting errors. The lower federal courts were sharply split on whether to apply the exclusions of § 1367(b) to both Rule 20 multiple plaintiff and Rule 23 cases. The issue also sharply divided the U.S. Supreme Court, 5–4, in the *Exxon Mobil* case.

Exxon Mobil Corp. v. Allapattah Services, Inc.

Supreme Court of the United States, 2005
545 U.S. 546, 125 S. Ct. 2611, 162 L. Ed. 2d 502

JUSTICE KENNEDY delivered the opinion of the Court.

These consolidated cases present the question whether a federal court in a diversity action may exercise supplemental jurisdiction over additional plaintiffs whose claims do not satisfy the minimum amount-in-controversy requirement, provided the claims are part of the same case or controversy as the claims of plaintiffs who do allege a sufficient amount in controversy. Our decision turns on the correct interpretation of 28 U.S.C. § 1367. The question has divided the Courts of Appeals, and we granted certiorari to resolve the conflict....

We hold that, where the other elements of jurisdiction are present and at least one named plaintiff in the action satisfies the amount-in-controversy requirement, § 1367 does authorize supplemental jurisdiction over the claims of other plaintiffs in the same Article III case or controversy, even if those claims are for less than the jurisdictional amount specified in the statute setting forth the requirements for diversity jurisdiction. We affirm the judgment of the Court of Appeals for the Eleventh Circuit ... and we reverse the judgment of the Court of Appeals for the First Circuit....

I

In 1991, about 10,000 Exxon dealers filed a class-action suit against the Exxon Corporation in the United States District Court for the Northern District of Florida. The dealers alleged an intentional and systematic scheme by Exxon under which they were overcharged for fuel purchased from Exxon. The plaintiffs invoked the District Court's § 1332(a) diversity jurisdiction. After a unanimous jury verdict in favor of the plaintiffs, the District Court certified the case for interlocutory review, asking whether it had properly exercised § 1367 supplemental jurisdiction over the claims of class members who did not meet the jurisdictional minimum amount in controversy.

The Court of Appeals for the Eleventh Circuit upheld the District Court's extension of supplemental jurisdiction to these class members...."[W]e find," the court held, "that § 1367 clearly and unambiguously provides district courts with the authority in diversity class actions to exercise supplemental jurisdiction over the claims of class members who do not meet the minimum amount in controversy as long as the district court has original jurisdiction over the claims of at least one of the class representatives." ... This decision accords with the views of the Courts of Appeals for the Fourth, Sixth, and Seventh Circuits.... The Courts of Appeals for the Fifth and Ninth Circuits, adopting a similar analysis of the statute, have held that in a diversity class action the unnamed class members need not meet the amount-in-controversy requirement, provided the named class members do. These decisions, however, are unclear on whether all the named plaintiffs must satisfy this requirement....

In the other case now before us the Court of Appeals for the First Circuit took a different position on the meaning of § 1367(a).... In that case, a 9-year-old girl sued Star-Kist in a diversity action in the United States District Court for the District of Puerto Rico, seeking damages for unusually severe injuries she received when she sliced her finger on a tuna can. Her family joined in the suit, seeking damages for emotional distress and certain medical expenses. The District Court granted summary judgment to Star-Kist, finding that none of the plaintiffs met the minimum amount-in-controversy requirement. The Court of Appeals for the First Circuit, however, ruled that the injured girl, but not her family members, had made allegations of damages in the requisite amount.

The Court of Appeals then addressed whether, in light of the fact that one plaintiff met the requirements for original jurisdiction, supplemental jurisdiction over the remaining plaintiffs' claims was proper under § 1367. The court held that § 1367 authorizes supplemental jurisdiction only when the district court has original jurisdiction over the action, and that in a diversity case original jurisdiction is lacking if one plaintiff fails to satisfy the amount-in-controversy requirement. Although the Court of Appeals claimed to "express no view" on whether the result would be the same in a class action, ... its analysis is inconsistent with that of the Court of Appeals for the Eleventh Circuit. The Court of Appeals for the First Circuit's view of § 1367 is, however, shared by the Courts of Appeal for the Third, Eighth, and Tenth Circuits, and the latter two Courts of Appeals have expressly applied this rule to class actions.

II

A

[In this part of the opinion, the Court traced the history of supplemental jurisdiction up to the enactment of the supplemental jurisdiction statute. The Court also reviewed the existing precedents at issue in this case, specifically *Clark v. Paul Gray, Inc.*, 306 U.S. 583 (1939) and *Zahn v. International Paper Co.*, 414 U.S. 291 (1973). *Clark* held that each plaintiff joined in a federal court action must independently meet any applicable jurisdictional amount requirement. *Zahn* confirmed that rule in class actions holding that each class member must independently satisfy the jurisdictional amount.

Significantly, the Court drew a distinction between defects in diversity of citizenship between the parties and defects in the amount-in-controversy requirement in terms of establishing original jurisdiction in the action. The Court stated that defects in diversity contaminated the entire case and thus destroyed original jurisdiction over "all claims" in the action. In effect, this means that there can be no supplemental jurisdiction over the joinder by a plaintiff of a non-diverse party under § 1367(a) in violation of the complete diversity requirement. However, the Court stated that defects in amount in controversy could be analyzed "claim by claim," thus allowing original jurisdiction to be properly established if at least one claim by a plaintiff meets the amount-in-controversy requirement. Supplemental jurisdiction would then be permissible under § 1367(a) over claims that do not meet the amount-in-controversy requirement of 28 U.S.C. § 1332, as long as those claims are related to at least one claim in the action that does meet the amount requirement.]

B

....

All parties to this litigation and all courts to consider the question agree that § 1367 overturned the result in *Finley*. There is no warrant, however, for assuming that § 1367 did no more than to overrule *Finley* and otherwise to codify the existing state of the law of supplemental jurisdiction. We must not give jurisdictional statutes a more expansive interpretation than their text warrants, ...; but it is just as important not to adopt an artificial construction that is narrower than what the text provides. No sound canon of interpretation requires Congress to speak with extraordinary clarity in order to modify the rules of federal jurisdiction within appropriate constitutional bounds. Ordinary principles of statutory construction apply. In order to determine the scope of supplemental jurisdiction authorized by § 1367, then, we must examine the statute's text in light of context, structure, and related statutory provisions.

Section 1367(a) is a broad grant of supplemental jurisdiction over other claims within the same case or controversy, as long as the action is one in which the district courts would have original jurisdiction. The last sentence of § 1367(a) makes it clear that the grant of supplemental jurisdiction extends to claims involving joinder or intervention of additional parties. The single question before us, therefore, is whether a diversity case in which the claims of some plaintiffs satisfy the amount-in-controversy requirement, but the claims of others plaintiffs do not, presents a "civil action of which the district courts have original jurisdiction." If the answer is yes, § 1367(a) confers supplemental jurisdiction over all claims, including those that do not independently satisfy the amount-in-controversy requirement, if the claims are part of the same Article III case or controversy. If the answer is no, § 1367(a) is inapplicable and, in light of our holdings in *Clark* and *Zahn*, the district court has no statutory basis for exercising supplemental jurisdiction over the additional claims.

We now conclude the answer must be yes. When the well-pleaded complaint contains at least one claim that satisfies the amount-in-controversy requirement, and there are no other relevant jurisdictional defects, the district court, beyond all question, has original jurisdiction over that claim. The presence of other claims in the complaint, over which the district court may lack original jurisdiction, is of no moment. If the court has original jurisdiction over a single claim in the complaint, it has original jurisdiction over a "civil action" within the meaning of § 1367(a), even if the civil action over which it has jurisdiction comprises fewer claims than were included in the complaint. Once the court determines it has original jurisdiction over the civil action, it can turn to the question whether it has a constitutional and statutory basis for exercising supplemental jurisdiction over the other claims in the action.

Section 1367(a) commences with the direction that §§ 1367(b) and (c), or other relevant statutes, may provide specific exceptions, but otherwise § 1367(a) is a broad jurisdictional grant, with no distinction drawn between pendent-claim and pendent-party cases.... The terms of § 1367 do not acknowledge any distinction between pendent jurisdiction and the doctrine of so-called ancillary jurisdiction. Though the doctrines of pendent and ancillary jurisdiction developed separately as a historical matter, the Court has recognized that the doctrines are "two species of the same generic problem,".....

If § 1367(a) were the sum total of the relevant statutory language, our holding would rest on that language alone. The statute, of course, instructs us to examine § 1367(b) to determine if any of its exceptions apply, so we proceed to that section. While § 1367(b) qualifies the broad rule of § 1367(a), it does not withdraw supplemental jurisdiction over the claims of the additional parties at issue here. The specific exceptions to § 1367(a) contained in § 1367(b), moreover, provide additional support for our conclusion that § 1367(a) confers supplemental jurisdiction over these claims. Section 1367(b), which applies only to diversity cases, withholds supplemental jurisdiction over the claims of plaintiffs proposed to be joined as indispensable parties under Federal Rule of Civil Procedure 19 or who seek to intervene pursuant to Rule 24. Nothing in the text of § 1367(b), however, withholds supplemental jurisdiction over the claims of plaintiffs permissively joined under Rule 20 ... or certified as class-action members pursuant to Rule 23.... The natural, indeed the necessary, inference is that § 1367 confers supplemental jurisdiction over claims by Rule 20 and Rule 23 plaintiffs. This inference, at least with respect to Rule 20 plaintiffs, is strengthened by the fact that § 1367(b) explicitly excludes supplemental jurisdiction over claims against defendants joined under Rule 20.

We cannot accept the view, urged by some of the parties, commentators, and Courts of Appeals, that a district court lacks original jurisdiction over a civil action unless the court has original jurisdiction over every claim in the complaint. As we understand this position, it requires assuming either that all claims in the complaint must stand or fall as a single, indivisible "civil action" as a matter of definitional necessity—what we will refer to as the "indivisibility theory"—or else that the inclusion of a claim or party falling outside the district court's original jurisdiction somehow contaminates every other claim in the complaint, depriving the court of original jurisdiction over any of these claims—what we will refer to as the "contamination theory."

The indivisibility theory is easily dismissed, as it is inconsistent with the whole notion of supplemental jurisdiction. If a district court must have original jurisdiction over every claim in the complaint in order to have "original jurisdiction" over a "civil action," then in *Gibbs* there was no civil action of which the district court could assume original jurisdiction under § 1331, and so no basis for exercising supplemental jurisdiction over any of the claims. The indivisibility theory is further belied by our practice—in both federal-question and diversity cases—of allowing federal courts to cure jurisdictional defects by dismissing the offending parties rather than dismissing the entire action....

We also find it unconvincing to say that the definitional indivisibility theory applies in the context of diversity cases but not in the context of federal-question cases. The broad and general language of the statute does not permit this result. The contention is premised on the notion that the phrase "original jurisdiction of all civil actions" means different things in § 1331 and § 1332. It is implausible, however, to say that the identical phrase means one thing (original jurisdiction in all actions where at least one claim in the complaint meets the following requirements) in § 1331 and something else (original jurisdiction in all actions where every claim in the complaint meets the following requirements) in § 1332.

The contamination theory, as we have noted, can make some sense in the special context of the complete diversity requirement because the presence of nondiverse parties on both sides of a lawsuit eliminates the justification for providing a federal forum. The theory, however, makes little sense with respect to the amount-in-controversy requirement, which is meant to ensure that a dispute is sufficiently important to warrant federal-court attention. The presence of a single nondiverse party may eliminate the fear of bias with respect to all claims, but the presence of a claim that falls short of the minimum amount in controversy does nothing to reduce the importance of the claims that do meet this requirement.

It is fallacious to suppose, simply from the proposition that § 1332 imposes both the diversity requirement and the amount-in-controversy requirement, that the contamination theory germane to the former is also relevant to the latter. There is no inherent logical connection between the amount-in-controversy requirement and § 1332 diversity jurisdiction. After all, federal-question jurisdiction once had an amount-in-controversy requirement as well. If such a requirement were revived under § 1331, it is clear beyond peradventure that § 1367(a) provides supplemental jurisdiction over federal-question cases where some, but not all, of the federal-law claims involve a sufficient amount in controversy....

  ....

Finally, it is suggested that our interpretation of § 1367(a) creates an anomaly regarding the exceptions listed in § 1367(b): It is not immediately obvious why Congress would withhold supplemental jurisdiction over plaintiffs joined as parties "needed for just adjudication" under Rule 19 but would allow supplemental jurisdiction over plaintiffs permissively joined under Rule 20. The omission of Rule 20 plaintiffs from the list of exceptions in § 1367(b) may have been an "unintentional drafting gap,".... If that is the case, it is up to Congress rather than the courts to fix it....

C

The proponents of the alternative view of § 1367 insist that the statute is at least ambiguous and that we should look to other interpretive tools, including the legislative history of § 1367, which supposedly demonstrate Congress did not intend § 1367 to overrule *Zahn*. We can reject this argument at the very outset simply because § 1367 is not ambiguous....

Those who urge that the legislative history refutes our interpretation rely primarily on the House Judiciary Committee Report on the Judicial Improvements Act. H.R. Rep. No. 101-734 (1990) (House Report or Report). This Report explained that § 1367 would "authorize jurisdiction in a case like *Finley*, as well as essentially restore the pre-*Finley* understandings of the authorization for and limits on other forms of supplemental jurisdiction." House Report, at 28. The Report stated that § 1367(a) "generally authorizes the district court to exercise jurisdiction over a supplemental claim whenever it forms part of the same constitutional case or controversy as the claim or claims that provide the basis of the district court's original jurisdiction," and in so doing codifies *Gibbs* and fills the statutory gap recognized in *Finley*. House Report, at 28–29, and n.15. The Report then remarked that § 1367(b) "is not intended to affect the jurisdictional requirements of [§ 1332] in diversity-only class actions, as those requirements were interpreted prior to *Finley*," citing, without further elaboration, *Zahn* and *Supreme Tribe of Ben-Hur v. Cauble*, 255 U.S. 356 (1921). House Report, at 29 & n.17. The Report noted that the "net effect" of § 1367(b) was to implement the "principal rationale" of *Kroger*. House Report, at 29 & n.16, effecting only "one small change" in pre-*Finley* practice with respect to diversity actions: § 1367(b) would exclude "Rule 23(a) plaintiff-intervenors to the same extent as those sought to be joined as plaintiffs under Rule 19." House Report, at 29. (It is evident that the report here meant to refer to Rule 24, not Rule 23.)

As we have repeatedly held, the authoritative statement is the statutory text, not the legislative history or any other extrinsic material. Extrinsic materials have a role in statutory interpretation only to the extent they shed a reliable light on the enacting Legislature's understanding of otherwise ambiguous terms. Not all extrinsic materials are reliable sources of insight into legislative understandings, however, and legislative history in particular is vulnerable to two serious criticisms. First, legislative history is itself often murky, ambiguous, and contradictory.... Second, judicial reliance on legislative materials like committee reports, which are not themselves subject to the requirements of Article I, may give unrepresentative committee members — or, worse yet, unelected staffers and lobbyists — both the power and the incentive to attempt strategic manipulations of legislative history to secure results they were unable to achieve through the statutory text....

First of all, the legislative history of § 1367 is far murkier than selective quotation from the House Report would suggest. The text of § 1367 is based substantially on a draft proposal contained in a Federal Court Study Committee working paper, which was drafted by a Subcommittee chaired by Judge Posner.... While the Subcommittee explained, in language echoed by the House Report, that its proposal "basically restores the law as it existed prior to *Finley*," Subcommittee Working Paper, at 561, it observed in a footnote that its proposal would overrule *Zahn* and that this would be a good idea.... Therefore, even if the House Report could fairly be read to reflect an understanding that the text of § 1367 did not overrule *Zahn*, the Subcommittee Working Paper on which § 1367 was based reflected the opposite understanding. The House Report is no more authoritative than the Subcommittee Working Paper....

Second, the worst fears of critics who argue legislative history will be used to circumvent the Article I process were realized in this case. The telltale evidence is the statement, by three law professors who participated in drafting § 1367, see House Report, at 27, n. 13, that § 1367 "on its face" permits "supplemental jurisdiction over claims of class members that do not satisfy section 1332's jurisdictional amount requirement, which would overrule [*Zahn*]. [There is] a disclaimer of intent to accomplish this result in the legislative history.... It would have been better had the statute dealt explicitly with this problem, and the legislative history was an attempt to correct the oversight." Rowe, Burbank, & Mengler, *Compounding or Creating Confusion About Supplemental Jurisdiction? A Reply to Professor Freer,* 40 Emory L.J. 943, 960 n.90 (1991). The professors were frank to concede that if one refuses to consider the legislative history, one has no choice but to "conclude that section 1367 has wiped *Zahn* off the books."... One need not subscribe to the wholesale condemnation of legislative history to refuse to give any effect to such a deliberate effort to amend a statute through a committee report.

In sum, even if we believed resort to legislative history were appropriate in these cases—a point we do not concede—we would not give significant weight to the House Report....

....

The judgment of the Court of Appeals for the Eleventh Circuit is affirmed. The judgment of the Court of Appeals for the First Circuit is reversed, and the case is remanded for proceedings consistent with this opinion.

It is so ordered.

Dissent JUSTICE STEVENS, with whom JUSTICE BREYER joins, dissenting.

Justice Ginsburg's carefully reasoned opinion ... demonstrates the error in the Court's rather ambitious reading of this opaque jurisdictional statute. She also has demonstrated that "ambiguity" is a term that may have different meanings for different judges, for the Court has made the remarkable declaration that its reading of the statute is so obviously correct—and Justice Ginsburg's so obviously wrong—that the text does not even qualify as "ambiguous." ... Because ambiguity is apparently in the eye of the beholder, I remain convinced that it is unwise to treat the ambiguity *vel non* of a statute as determinative of whether legislative history is consulted. Indeed, I believe that we as judges are more, rather than less, constrained when we make ourselves accountable to *all* reliable evidence of legislative intent....

Dissent #2 JUSTICE GINSBURG with whom JUSTICE STEVENS, JUSTICE O'CONNOR, and JUSTICE BREYER join, dissenting.

These cases present the question whether Congress, by enacting 28 U.S.C. § 1367, overruled this Court's decisions in *Clark v. Paul Gray, Inc.,* 306 U.S. 583, 589 (1939) ... and *Zahn v. International Paper Co.,* 414 U.S. 291 (1973). *Clark* held that, when federal-court jurisdiction is predicated on a specified amount in controversy, each plaintiff joined in the litigation must independently meet the jurisdictional amount requirement. *Zahn* confirmed that in class actions governed by *Federal Rule of Civil Procedure 23(b)(3)*, "[e]ach [class member] ... must satisfy the jurisdictional amount, and any [class member] who does not must be dismissed from the case." 414 U.S. at 301.

Section 1367, all agree, was designed to overturn this Court's decision in *Finley....* *Finley* concerned not diversity-of-citizenship jurisdiction..., but original federal-court jurisdiction in cases arising under federal law.... This Court held ... that the District Court lacked jurisdiction over the "pendent-party" state-law claims.... In so holding, the Court stressed that Congress held the control rein.... Congress could reverse the result in *Finley* and permit pendent jurisdiction over state-law claims against additional defendants, if it so chose.... Congress did so in § 1367.

What more § 1367 wrought is an issue on which courts of appeals have sharply divided.... The Court adopts a plausibly broad reading of § 1367, a measure that is hardly a model of the careful drafter's art. There is another plausible reading, however, one less disruptive of our jurisprudence regarding supplemental jurisdiction. If one reads § 1367(a) to instruct, as the statute's text suggests, that the district court must first have "original jurisdiction" over a "civil action" before supplemental jurisdiction can attach, [and that the requirements of both the complete diversity rule and the nonaggregation rules of *Clark* and *Zahn* must be satisfied before there is "original jurisdiction" over a "civil action"], then *Clark* and *Zahn* are preserved, and supplemental jurisdiction does not open the way for joinder of plaintiffs, or inclusion of class members, who do not independently meet the amount-in-controversy requirement.... I conclude that this narrower construction is the better reading of § 1367.

....

Notes and Questions

1. The *Exxon Mobil* holding applies to aggregation problems under § 1367(a) and (b) in the two categories of cases addressed in the opinion. However, all other things equal, under the Court's interpretation of § 1367(a), supplemental jurisdiction would also exist over multiple plaintiff cases in which one plaintiff was diverse with the defendant and another plaintiff or plaintiffs were not. Furthermore, § 1367(b) would not withdraw the supplemental jurisdiction so conferred. To avoid overruling the complete diversity restriction of *Strawbridge v. Curtis* in multiple plaintiff cases, the majority opinion attempts to distinguish incomplete diversity defects in supplemental claims from jurisdictional amount defects. Can such a distinction be justified under the language of the statute?

2. (a) Did the Court in *Exxon Mobil* finally resolve the Rule 20/Rule 23 gap or did it just create another anomaly in the statute? In both *Exxon Mobil* and the companion case, *Star-Kist*, only a single defendant was sued and it is unclear from the Court's opinion whether its ruling as to § 1367's extension of supplemental jurisdiction to below-limit claims by Rule 20 and 23 plaintiffs also applies in diversity actions involving multiple defendants joined under Rule 20. The Court held that because § 1367(b) in clauses 2 and 3 only expressly prohibits supplemental jurisdiction for claims by Rule 19 and 24 plaintiffs and is silent as to supplemental claims by Rule 20 or 23 plaintiffs, supplemental jurisdiction could properly extend to below-limit claims by Rule 20 and 23 plaintiffs, thus overruling the prior holdings of *Zahn* and *Clark*.

(b) But this reading of § 1367(b) as overruling *Zahn* and *Clark* is only correct with respect to actions involving a single defendant, isn't it? When multiple defendants are sued, either in a general diversity action or a class action, the defendants would be joined under Rule 20. As such, the plain language of the first clause of § 1367(b) would still prohibit supplemental jurisdiction for claims by plaintiffs *against* defendants joined under Rule 20. In ruling that the plain language of § 1367(b) overruled *Zahn* and *Clark*, did the Court in *Exxon Mobil* adequately address this distinction between single defendant and multiple defendant cases?

3. As noted in section C on "Special Diversity Statutes," the "Class Action Fairness Act of 2005," codified in 28 U.S.C. § 1332(d), expressly provides, for nationwide class actions within its provisions, that "the claims of the individual class members *shall be aggregated* to determine whether the matter in controversy exceeds the sum or value of $5,000,000."

28 U.S.C. § 1332(d)(6) (emphasis added). Thus, as to class actions covered by § 1332(d), the aggregation problems of *Zahn* and *Synder* and the effect of § 1367(b) are statutorily obviated. Do you think Congress should have similarly resolved, through express statutory language in § 1367(b), the propriety of aggregation for other diversity actions as well, rather than leaving this issue for the courts to decipher?

––––––––––

Effect of § 1367(b) on Joinder of "Required" Parties Under Rule 19. Section 1367(b) also expressly restricts supplemental jurisdiction over claims by plaintiffs *against* persons made parties under Rule 19 and over claims *by* persons proposed to be joined as plaintiffs under Rule 19. With respect to Rule 19 parties, the statute is worded awkwardly and must be parsed carefully to avoid untoward results.

Literally, the language prohibiting claims against persons "made parties" under Rule 19 suggests that a person can be joined as a party under Rule 19, even though the person's joinder as an original matter would have destroyed subject-matter jurisdiction as long as the plaintiff does not assert a claim against the person once that person has been joined. For example, assume *P*, a citizen of State *X*, could sue *D-1*, a citizen of State *Y*, for $100,000, and join *D-2*, a citizen of State *X*, as a defendant with *D-1* within the supplemental jurisdiction of the district court. The claim between *P* and *D-1* would confer jurisdiction under § 1332, and the claim against *D-2* would be within the supplemental jurisdiction of the district court (assuming that it fell within the same Article III case or controversy as the claim between *P* and *D-1*), because § 1367(a) extends supplemental jurisdiction to "claims that involve the joinder or intervention of additional parties." Assume that *D-2* is a Rule 19(a) party.

Under the literal language of § 1367(b), *D-2* could be joined in the action, but *P* could not assert a claim against *D-2* once *D-2* had been joined. The drafters of § 1367(b) state that this interpretation of the section is correct because there are certain kinds of cases in which the plaintiff has no claim against the absent party, but the party is, nevertheless, a Rule 19(a) party because the party could be adversely affected by the action. However, others disagree that a person can be joined as a defendant in a case when the plaintiff possesses no claim against the person. *See* Teply & Whitten at 764–68 (discussing this issue and citing authorities).

Effect of § 1367(b) on Intervention Under Rule 24. The language of § 1367(b) prohibits not only claims by plaintiffs against persons who intervene on the defendant's side of the action, but also claims by intervening plaintiffs that would violate the policies of the diversity jurisdiction. However, the statute does not explicitly prohibit claims by intervening defendants. Note that, as in Rule 19 situations, the court is not bound by the alignment of the parties in the pleadings in determining whether complete diversity of citizenship exists and may realign them in accord with their interests.

Note

To date, there have been few cases concerning supplemental jurisdiction and Rule 19. What case law exists is not encouraging about the courts' understanding of how § 1367(b) should operate in Rule 19 cases. *See* Teply & Whitten at 768–69 (discussing the cases).

Problems

Problem 4-24. *P*, a citizen of State *X*, sues *D-1* and *D-2* in a U.S. District Court for the District of State *Y*. Both *D-1* and *D-2* are citizens of State *Y*. *P's* complaint alleges *P* was injured as a result of *D-1* and *D-2's* negligent conduct. *P's* claim against *D-1* is for $100,000. *P's* claim against *D-2* is for $50,000. Under § 1367(a) & (b), is there federal jurisdiction over this action?

Problem 4-25. *P-1*, a citizen of State *X*, and *P-2*, a citizen of State *Y,* sue *D*, a citizen of State *Y*, in the U.S. District Court for the District of State *Y. P-1* and *P-2* assert a joint claim against *D* for breach of contract for $200,000. (Both *P-1* and *P-2* are parties to the contract with *D* and are both injured by the breach in the same way.) Under § 1367(a) & (b), is there federal jurisdiction over this action?

Problem 4-26. *R-1*, a citizen of State *X*, and *R-2*, a citizen of State *Y* sue *D*, a citizen of State *Y,* in the U.S. District Court for the District of State *Y* in a class action under Federal Rule 23(b)(3). *R-1* and *R-2* seek $50,000,000 for tortious activity conducted by *D* that has injured the members of the class that *R-1* and *R-2* are representing. *R-1's* claim against *D* is for $80,000, and *R-2's* claim is for $100,000. However, no other member of the class has a claim that exceeds $75,000. Under § 1367(a) & (b), is there federal jurisdiction over this action?

Problem 4-27. *P*, a citizen of State *X*, sues *D*, a citizen of State *Y*, in the U.S. District Court for the District of State *Y. P* asserts a state claim against *D* for $100,000. *D* impleads *T*, a citizen of State *X*, under Federal Rule 14. *D* asserts that, under state law, if *D* is liable to *P, T* is liable to *D* for any amount that *D* is obligated to pay to *P*. After *T* is joined in the action, *T* asserts a state claim directly against *P* for $80,000 arising out of the same facts as *P's* claim against *D*, as permitted by Rule 14. After *T* asserts this claim against *P*, *P* asserts a state-law counterclaim against *T* for $100,000 arising out of the same facts as *T's* claim against *P*. In light of § 1367(a) & (b), does federal jurisdiction exist over all the claims asserted in this action?

Problem 4-28. *P*, a citizen of State *X*, sues *D*, a citizen of State *Y*, in the U.S. District Court for the District of State *Y. P* asserts a state claim against *D* for $100,000. *D's* answer contains a permissive counterclaim against *P* for $80,000. *P* impleads *T,* a citizen of State *X*, under Federal Rule 14. *P* asserts that if *P* is liable to *D* on the counterclaim, *T* is liable to *P* for the entire $80,000 that *P* will have to pay *D*. Under the language of § 1367(a) & (b), does federal jurisdiction exist over all the claims asserted in this action?

Problem 4-29. *D-1*, a citizen of State *Y*, leases store space in a mall to *P*, a citizen of State *X*. The lease agreement provides that *D-1* will not lease store space in the mall to any of *P's* competitors. Subsequently, *D-1* leases store space in the mall to *D-2*, a citizen of State *X*, who is allegedly a competitor of *P*. *P* sues *D-1* in a U.S. District Court in State *Y*, to enjoin enforcement of the lease between *D-1* and *D-2*. Should *D-2* be joined in the action under Rule 19(a)? If so, are *D-2's* interests aligned with, *P's* or *D-1's*? Do §§ 1332 & 1367 permit *D-2's* joinder in the action?

Problem 4-30. *D*, a citizen of State *Y*, leases store space in a mall to *P*, a citizen of State *X*. The lease agreement provides that *D* will not lease store space to any of *P's* competitors. Subsequently, *D* leases store space in the mall to *I*, a citizen of State *X*, who is a competitor of *P*. *P* sues *D* in a U.S. District Court to enjoin enforcement of the lease between *D* and *I*. *I* applies to intervene in the action under Federal Rule 24(a)(2). Does supplemental jurisdiction exist over *I's* application for intervention?

4. Discretionary Dismissals Under § 1367(c)

Prior to the enactment of § 1367, the former doctrines of pendent and ancillary jurisdiction permitted the courts a certain amount of discretion to dismiss supplemental claims that otherwise met the standards of pendent or ancillary jurisdiction. In *United Mine Workers v. Gibbs*, 383 U.S. 715 (1966), the Supreme Court articulated five factors that would point to dismissal of a supplemental claim in a federal question case: (1) the absence of judicial economy, convenience, and fairness to litigants; (2) the avoidance of needless decisions of state law; (3) the dismissal of federal claims (upon which jurisdiction is based) before trial; (4) the predominance of state issues in terms of proof, scope of the issues raised, or comprehensiveness of the remedy sought; and (5) the likelihood of jury confusion in treating divergent legal theories. In addition, the Court stated that if the state claim is closely tied to federal policy, retaining jurisdiction over the claim would be justified. *See id.* at 726–27.

In § 1367(c), Congress authorized the discretionary dismissal of supplemental claims on the basis of a number of the factors that the Supreme Court previously recognized as legitimate <u>bases</u> for discretionary dismissal in *Gibbs*. The factors stated in § 1367(c) are summarized in Figure 4-5.

BASES FOR DECLINING TO EXERCISE SUPPLEMENTAL JURISDICTION OVER A CLAIM AS STATED IN § 1367(c)	
§ 1367(c)(1)	The claim raises a **novel or complex issue of state law**
§ 1367(c)(2)	The claim **substantially predominates** over the claim or claims over which the district court has original jurisdiction
§ 1367(c)(3)	The district court has **dismissed all claims** over which it has original jurisdiction
§ 1367(c)(4)	**Exceptional circumstances** provide other **compelling reasons** for declining supplemental jurisdiction

Figure 4-5

The lower federal courts are divided on whether § 1367(c) should be interpreted as an attempt by Congress to restrict the discretion of the district courts to the four factors listed in § 1367(c), or should be read as a codification of the formerly open-ended discretion of the *Gibbs* case. In *Executive Software North America, Inc. v. United States District Court*, 24 F.3d 1545 (9th Cir. 1994), the Ninth Circuit Court of Appeals held that the factors listed in § 1367(c) were the exclusive bases for discretionary dismissals of supplemental claims:

> It is clear that, once it is determined that the assertion of supplemental jurisdiction is permissible under sections 1367(a) and (b), section 1367(c) provides the only valid basis upon which the district court may decline jurisdiction.... Moreover, we conclude that although subsections (c)(1)–(3) appear to codify most preexisting applications of the *Gibbs* doctrine, subsection (c)(4), which also permits a court to decline jurisdiction when, "in exceptional circumstances, there are other compelling reasons," channels the district court's discretion to identify new grounds for declining jurisdiction more particularly than did preexisting doctrine. Accordingly, we conclude that the district court erred to the extent that it relied on a basis for [declining jurisdiction over supplemental] claims not permitted under section 1367(c).

24 F.3d at 1551–52. Other federal courts have disagreed with the *Executive Software* approach and concluded that the *Gibbs* open-ended discretionary approach has been codified by § 1367(c). *See, e.g., Edmondson & Gallagher v. Alban Towers Tenants Ass'n*, 48 F.3d 1260, 1266 (D.C. Cir. 1995) (*Gibbs* determines the framework within which § 1367(c) factors are to be considered). Presumably, this question will ultimately have to be resolved by the Supreme Court (or by amendment of the statute).

The following notes and questions explore other interpretive problems with § 1367(c).

Notes and Questions

1. The four factors listed in § 1367(c) are technically applicable to both diversity and federal question cases. However, the factors were at least partially drawn from the *Gibbs* case, which involved supplemental jurisdiction by a plaintiff in a federal question case. The *Gibbs* test for discretionary dismissal and those of the § 1367(c) factors that mimic the test were thus devised in the context of a federal question case, not a diversity case. This raises the question whether the § 1367(c) factors are all suitable for use in diversity actions. For example, would it be permissible in a diversity case to dismiss a claim otherwise within supplemental jurisdiction on the ground that it raises novel and complex issues of state law? Isn't it the function of federal courts in diversity actions to adjudicate issues of state law, no matter how novel and complex they are? What about dismissal of a supplemental claim in a diversity case on the ground that it substantially predominates over the claim that confers jurisdiction? For example, could a compulsory counterclaim on which a nondiverse party is added by the defendant be dismissed on this ground?

2. Since the enactment of § 1367(c), the vast majority of discretionary dismissals have been under § 1367(c)(3) after dismissal of the "freestanding" federal claim. In this regard, however, there is a critical distinction between a dismissal of the freestanding claim on the merits and a dismissal of the freestanding claim for lack of subject-matter jurisdiction. If the freestanding claim is dismissed for lack of subject-matter jurisdiction, all supplemental claims *must* be dismissed as well and the question of discretionary dismissal under § 1367(c)(3) is never reached. Without a freestanding claim, the first requirement of § 1367(a) that original jurisdiction exist in the action is not met. If there is no original jurisdiction, by definition, there can be no supplemental jurisdiction and mandatory, rather than discretionary, dismissal of all claims is required, irrespective of how much judicial time and effort has been expended in the case.

3. The provision for discretionary dismissal under § 1367(c)(3) is, therefore, only applicable when the freestanding claim has been dismissed on a nonjurisdictional basis. If original jurisdiction properly exists in an action, the dismissal of the freestanding claim on a nonjurisdictional basis does not divest the court of subject-matter jurisdiction and the court retains jurisdiction, in its discretion, to adjudicate the supplemental claims. Note, however, that the courts do not always dismiss supplemental claims under § 1367(c)(3) after the freestanding claim has been dismissed. Under what circumstances would it be justifiable for a district court to retain a supplemental claim after a nonjurisdictional dismissal of the freestanding claim? *See* Teply & Whitten at 155–56.

4. The American Law Institute has proposed revision of § 1367(c) as part of its general revision of the supplemental jurisdiction statute. *See* ALI Federal Judicial Code Revision Project § 1367(d) at 14 (2004). The revision narrows the discretion of the district courts to dismiss supplemental claims. Proposed § 1367(d)(1) permits dismissal of supplemental claims only when the freestanding federal claims have been dismissed "prior to trial," a restriction that does not textually appear in the current statute. Proposed § 1367(d)(2) would make it impermissible to dismiss state claims on the ground that they present novel or complex issues if the district courts would still have to decide these issues as freestanding claims in diversity actions. Proposed § 1367(d)(3) would allow dismissal on the ground that state claims predominate only if they predominate in a manner that would alter the character of the litigation. Finally, proposed § 1367(d)(4) makes it clear that "compelling reasons" and "exceptional circumstances" can only justify declining supplemental jurisdiction, not jurisdiction over freestanding claims. Would these revisions better define the proper scope of discretionary dismissal under § 1367(c)? *See* Teply & Whitten at 158–59.

5. Tolling of the State Statute of Limitations Under § 1367(d)

If a party asserts a supplemental claim under § 1367, but the claim is dismissed without prejudice by the court and not adjudicated on the merits, the party would be entitled to refile the claim in state court. A problem may exist, however, for the party under the applicable state statute of limitations. If no provision has been made to the contrary, the claim may be barred because the claim had not been commenced in a state court of proper jurisdiction before the limitations period expired and the state might not consider the limitations period tolled by the federal action. Section 1367(d) is designed to deal with this problem by providing that the state limitations period will be tolled while the federal action is pending and for 30 days after the state claim is dismissed from the federal action, unless state law provides a longer period. The same tolling period is provided for any other claim that is voluntarily dismissed at the same time the supplemental claim is dismissed by the federal court.

Notes and Questions

1. In *Jinks v. Richland County*, 538 U.S. 456 (2003), the Supreme Court held § 1367(d) constitutional in a case in which the plaintiff had sued the county and other defendants in an action under 42 U.S.C. § 1983 and also asserted claims against the defendants under state law. The § 1983 action was dismissed on summary judgment, and the state claims were dismissed under § 1367(c)(3). The plaintiff refiled the state claims in state court within the tolling period provided in § 1367(d). The Supreme Court reversed the decision of the South Carolina Supreme Court, which had held that § 1367(d) was unconstitutional and that the state claims were time-barred under South Carolina state law. The U.S. Supreme Court held that § 1367(d) is constitutional because it is a necessary and proper exercise of congressional authority under Article III of the Constitution as it eliminates "a serious impediment to access to the federal courts on the part of plaintiffs pursuing federal-law and state-law claims" arising from the same facts.

2. In *Raygor v. Regents of University of Minnesota*, 534 U.S. 533 (2002), the Supreme Court held that § 1367(a) did not provide jurisdiction over supplemental state claims against a state that had not consented to be sued. The Court also held that § 1367(d) did not toll the state statute of limitations applicable to the claims against the state. Both interpretations were designed in part to avoid a potential collision with the Eleventh Amendment, which generally prohibits suits in federal court against a state without the state's consent.

3. Should § 1367(d) be interpreted as tolling a state statute of limitations both when a state claim is dismissed under § 1367(c) in the court's discretion and when a state claim is dismissed for lack of jurisdiction under § 1367(a)?

Problems

Problem 4-31. Reconsider the *Jinks* decision described briefly in Note 1, above. Can you explain how a federal tolling provision for state claims eliminates a serious impediment to access to the federal courts on the part of plaintiffs pursuing federal and state claims arising from the same facts?

Problem 4-32. What does the word "tolled" mean in § 1367(d)? For example, suppose a state statute of limitations is two years and the plaintiff commences a federal action after one year of the two-year period has run. The federal action remains pending for another year, at which time the federal claim is dismissed on the merits and the state claim is dismissed under § 1367(c). Should the plaintiff have thirty days, one-year and thirty days, or some other period within which to refile the state claims in state court?

Section F. Removal Jurisdiction

Removal of Cases to Federal Court. The traditional rule in American jurisprudence is that plaintiffs have the right to select the forum, either state or federal, in which to litigate their claims, provided proper subject-matter jurisdiction, personal jurisdiction, and venue exist in the chosen forum. Removal is an exception to this general principle and allows the defendant or defendants to "trump" the plaintiff's choice of a state court forum and "remove" the plaintiff's state court action to federal district court if the plaintiff's action could otherwise have been commenced in federal court. The rationale for removal is that defendants, as well as plaintiffs, should have the right to choose the federal forum for the adjudication of claims that are properly within the original jurisdiction of the federal courts.

Although the authority for removal jurisdiction is not expressly stated in Article III, the Supreme Court has long held that Congress has the constitutional power to authorize removal, and Congress has so provided for removal continuously since the first Judiciary Act of 1789. As a creature of statute, however, the federal courts have long held that the statutory procedures and requirements for removal are to be strictly construed and uncertainties are resolved in favor of remand to state court. Nevertheless, if the jurisdictional and procedural requirements of the removal statutes are fully satisfied, the defendant has the absolute right to remove the plaintiff's action to federal court, despite any objection by the plaintiff.

The removal statutes are currently codified in 28 U.S.C. §§ 1441–1454. The removal provisions empower only a federal court to "remove" an action from state court. There is no procedure for a state court to "remove" an action from federal court. If the federal court determines that an action was improperly removed from state court, the federal court "remands" the case to state court. Removal only applies "vertically" in removing an action from state court to federal court and should not be confused with "transfer of venue," examined in Chapter 3, which is the "horizontal" transfer of an action pending in one federal district court to another federal district court.

Removal and Original Jurisdiction Compared. Section 1441 is the general removal statute. Subsection (a) authorizes, except as otherwise provided, the removal of "any civil action brought in a State court of which the district courts of the United States have original jurisdiction." As a general principle, removal jurisdiction is coextensive with original jurisdiction. Thus, if the plaintiff would have had original jurisdiction to file the action in federal court, removal jurisdiction exists. However, this principle is not universally true. Removal jurisdiction does not exist in certain actions even though original jurisdiction would have existed if the plaintiff had filed the action in federal court. In certain actions, therefore, removal jurisdiction is narrower than original jurisdiction.

For example, § 1441(b)(2) provides that "[a] civil action otherwise removable on the basis of the jurisdiction under section 1332(a) [diversity and alienage jurisdiction] of this title may not be removed if any of the parties in interest properly joined and served as defendants is a citizen of the State in which such action is brought." Thus, if a citizen of

New York sued a citizen of Pennsylvania, a citizen of Delaware, and a citizen of New Jersey on a state law claim in New Jersey state court, the action could not be removed by any of the defendants, despite the existence of complete diversity because one of the defendants would be a citizen of the forum state.

The rationale for this restriction is that the primary purpose of diversity jurisdiction is to provide a federal forum for out-of-state litigants to protect them from local bias. The presence of a resident defendant in the action arguably eliminates such danger and justifies the denial of removal jurisdiction. As previously noted in section C, this restriction, despite numerous proposals, has never been applied to the invocation of original diversity jurisdiction, and a resident plaintiff is not barred under § 1332 from invoking diversity jurisdiction in the plaintiff's home state. Note that the citizenship restriction in § 1441(b)(2) does *not* apply to federal question cases or any other non-§ 1332(a) cases, and such cases are fully removable without regard to the citizenship of the parties.

In addition to the limitation of § 1441(b)(2), certain actions are expressly made non-removable. 28 U.S.C. § 1445, for instance, expressly prohibits removal of certain actions, such as Federal Employers' Liability Act actions against railroads and state workers' compensation cases, even though original jurisdiction may have existed in the case if the plaintiff had initially filed in federal court.

In certain limited situations, removal is available even though original jurisdiction would not have existed over the plaintiff's action. For example, in *Mesa v. California*, 489 U.S. 121 (1989), the Supreme Court held that federal officers can remove cases under 28 U.S.C. § 1442(a) solely on the basis of a federal defense to a state law claim even though under the "well-pleaded complaint" rule, original jurisdiction would not exist over such a case. Similarly, in 28 U.S.C. § 1454, enacted in 2011, Congress authorized the removal to federal district court of any state court action in which any party, including the defendant, asserts a claim under federal patent, plant variety protection, or copyright laws. Thus, even if the plaintiff's claim is based entirely on state law and would not otherwise qualify for original jurisdiction, the defendant may remove the plaintiff's action to federal district court based solely on the defendant's patent, plant variety protection, or copyright counterclaim.

The "Complete Preemption" Doctrine. As discussed in section B, above, the propriety of federal question jurisdiction under § 1331 is based on the plaintiff's claim. Essential in the jurisdictional inquiry, therefore, is an analysis of the plaintiff's complaint to see if the plaintiff is asserting a claim that properly arises under federal law. For example, suppose *P* is the victim of employment discrimination and that the employer's action would violate both federal and state employment discrimination laws. For tactical or other reasons, *P* may decide to sue the employer only for violation of the state employment discrimination laws and make no claim under the federal law. In such a case, federal question jurisdiction would not exist even though *P* also possessed a potential cause of action under federal employment discrimination laws.

As noted earlier, a defendant generally cannot remove a case from state to federal court if the plaintiff's complaint does not establish a claim within federal court jurisdiction. Thus, in the above example, the employer could not remove *P's* action to federal court on the basis of federal question jurisdiction. However, one important exception to this rule that has been recognized by the Supreme Court is the doctrine of "complete preemption." Under certain limited circumstances, the courts may conclude that an area of law has been so regulated by federal law that, under the Supremacy Clause of U.S. Constitution, federal law "completely preempts" any otherwise applicable state law. As noted by the Supreme Court, "[o]nce an area of state law has been completely preempted, any claim purportedly based on that pre-empted state law claim is considered, from its inception, a federal claim, and therefore arises under federal law." *Caterpillar, Inc. v. Williams*, 482 U.S. 386, 393 (1987). In such a case, therefore, proper federal question jurisdiction exists because the plaintiff's claim is considered purely federal, and the defendant may remove the case to federal court even though the plaintiff's complaint only alleges a claim based entirely on state law.

Note that this exception is very limited, however, and thus far the Supreme Court has only recognized three areas of "complete preemption." *See Beneficial Nat'l Bank v. Anderson*, 539 U.S. 1 (2003) (holding federal removal of a usury action against a national bank proper on the grounds that the National Bank Act provided the exclusive basis for usury claims against national banks and that despite the plaintiffs' attempt to frame the claim as one under state law, the claims could only arise under federal law); *Metropolitan Life Ins. Co. v. Taylor*, 481 U.S. 58, 65–66 (1987) (upholding removal based on preemptive effect of § 502 of Employee Retirement Income Security Act); *Avco Corp. v. Aero Lodge No. 735*, 390 U.S. 557, 560 (1968) (upholding removal based on preemptive effect of § 301 of the Labor Management Relations Act). Aside from these areas, the lower federal courts have not been uniform in their application of the "complete preemption" doctrine. *Compare, e.g., Railway Labor Executives Ass'n v. Pittsburgh & Lake Erie R.R. Co.*, 858 F.2d 936, 939–43 (3d Cir. 1988) (finding no complete preemption under the Railway Labor Act) *with Deford v. Soo Line R.R. Co.*, 867 F.2d 1080, 1084–86 (8th Cir. 1989) (Railway Labor Act completely preempts state law). *See* TEPLY & WHITTEN at 165–66.

Who Has the Right to Remove? Although a special removal statute may grant the right to remove to any party, including the plaintiff, *see, e.g.,* 28 U.S.C. § 1452 (removal of claims within bankruptcy jurisdiction), the general removal statute, § 1441(a), expressly limits the right to remove to "the defendant or the defendants." Under § 1441(a), plaintiffs are not granted any right to remove a state court action to federal court.

In cases removed solely under § 1441(a) and involving multiple defendants, all defendants must join in or consent to removal. Section 1446(b)(2)(A), enacted in 2011, codifies this long-established, judicially created "rule of unanimity," and provides that "[w]hen a civil action is removed solely under section 1441(a), all defendants who have been properly joined and served must join in or consent to the removal of the action." Consistent with prior law, the new provision is limited to cases removed solely under § 1441(a), and has no application to other provisions authorizing removal. Thus, if a defendant has a right of removal under another provision, such as federal agencies and officers under the special removal provisions of § 1442(a), a defendant may remove the action without the consent of the other defendants. In addition, as established under prior law, the federal courts recognize an exception to the unanimity requirement when a nondiverse defendant has been "fraudulently joined" with a diverse defendant, the diverse defendant may remove alone by demonstrating the fraudulent joinder. The doctrine of "fraudulent joinder," however, is quite narrow and can be demonstrated only if the plaintiff has no valid claim for relief against the nondiverse defendant.

Effect of Counterclaims. What happens if the plaintiff files an action in state court and the defendant files a counterclaim against the plaintiff within original federal jurisdiction? In defending the counterclaim, does the plaintiff now qualify as a "defendant" for purposes of the removal statutes allowing the plaintiff to seek removal on the basis of the defendant's counterclaim? In *Shamrock Oil & Gas Corp. v. Sheets*, 313 U.S. 100 (1941), the Supreme Court answered no. The Court held that a plaintiff does not convert to a "defendant" for purposes of the removal statutes, even though the defendant files a counterclaim against the plaintiff and even though under state law the plaintiff would be characterized as a "defendant" on the counterclaim. In *Shamrock,* the defendant's counterclaim satisfied the requirements of diversity jurisdiction, but the rule of *Shamrock* fully applies to counterclaims within federal question jurisdiction. In either case, removal by the plaintiff on the basis of the defendant's counterclaim is not permitted.

Could the defendant, nevertheless, remove on the basis of the defendant's counterclaim if it independently meets the requirements for federal subject-matter jurisdiction? Again, the answer is no. Although defendants are granted the right to remove under § 1441(a), removal jurisdiction under § 1441(a) is based on whether original jurisdiction would have existed in the action. As explained throughout this chapter, original jurisdiction is determined on the basis of the plaintiff's claim and counterclaims are disregarded. One minor exception is that some federal courts have permitted a defendant to remove the plaintiff's action when the plaintiff's claim is for less than the jurisdictional amount, but the defendant has a counterclaim exceeding $75,000 that is compulsory under state law. Most courts, however, prohibit removal on this basis. *See, e.g., Conference Am., Inc. v. Q.E.D. Int'l, Inc.,* 50 F. Supp. 2d 1239, 1242 (M.D. Ala. 1999) ("[D]istrict courts in the Fifth Circuit ... and the majority of courts in other circuits have held that the amount in controversy for removal purposes is to be determined solely by referring to the plaintiff's complaint and without regard to any subsequently filed counterclaims.").

Separate and Independent Claim Removal Under § 1441(c). In 28 U.S.C. § 1441(c), Congress provided (in the 1948 revision of the Judicial Code) that when a separate and independent removable claim was joined with an otherwise nonremovable claim, the entire action could be removed. Prior to 1990, § 1441(c) applied to both federal question and diversity cases. In 1990, Congress amended the statute to eliminate diversity cases from its scope. The 1990 amendments gave rise to a serious constitutional question. If a "separate and independent"—*i.e.* factually unrelated—state law claim was joined with an otherwise removable federal law claim, the statute made the entire case removable, even though the conventional interpretation of the supplemental jurisdiction statute, 28 U.S.C. § 1367, is that federal and state law claims must be factually related in order to be part of the same case or controversy under Article III. Thus, it appeared that § 1441(c) might be unconstitutional. Congress addressed this problem in the "Federal Courts Jurisdiction and Venue Clarification Act of 2011" by amending § 1441(c) as follows:

(c) Joinder of Federal Law Claims and State Law Claims. —

(1) If a civil action includes—

(A) a claim arising under the Constitution, laws, or treaties of the United States (within the meaning of [§] 1331 of this title), and

(B) a claim not within the original or supplemental jurisdiction of the district court or a claim that has been made nonremovable by statute,

the entire action may be removed if the action would be removable without the claim described in subparagraph (B).

(2) Upon removal of an action described in paragraph (1), the district court shall sever from the action all claims described in paragraph (1)(B) and shall remand the severed claims to the State court from which the action was re-

moved. Only defendants against whom a claim described in paragraph (1)(A) has been asserted are required to join in or consent to the removal under paragraph (1).

The legislative history accompanying this amendment states that it was designed to eliminate the constitutional questions about removal under § 1441(c). *See* H.R. Rep. No. 112-10, 112th Cong., 1st Sess., at 8 (2011). This goal seems to have been achieved.

Removal Procedure and Effect. Section § 1441(a) provides that a state court action may be removed to the federal district court "for the district and division embracing the place where such action is pending." This means that an action filed in state court in Chicago, Illinois must be removed to the federal district court for the Northern District of Illinois, Eastern Division, and not to the federal district court in another federal district or division either in Illinois or in another state.

Under § 1446(a), the defendant or defendants must initiate the removal process by filing a "notice of removal" in the federal district court for the district and division in which the state action is pending. The notice of removal must comply with Federal Rule 11 and contain a proper jurisdictional statement indicating the basis for removal. Under § 1446(d), after the notice of removal is filed with the federal district court, notice must "promptly" be given to all other parties and the notice must be filed with the state court. These steps effectuate removal, and the state court is directed to proceed no further unless and until the case is remanded. If at any time before final judgment the federal district court determines that it lacks subject-matter jurisdiction, the court must remand the case under § 1447(c) to the state court from which it was removed. A motion to remand the case to state court on the basis of any other defect must be made within 30 days after the filing of the notice of removal. *See* 28 U.S.C. § 1447(c).

Removal Based on Diversity of Citizenship and the One-Year Time Limit. When the basis of original jurisdiction is diversity of citizenship, removal is restricted by § 1441(b)(2) to cases in which none of the defendants properly joined and served is a citizen of the state in which the action is brought. Also, when removal is based on diversity of citizenship, diversity must exist at the time the action is commenced in state court and at the time removal is sought. This requirement only means that a party cannot change domiciles after commencement of the state action in order to create diverse citizenship and thus removal jurisdiction. However, diversity jurisdiction can be created after commencement in other ways. For example, the elimination of a nondiverse party from a state action after commencement (as by voluntary dismissal of a defending nondiverse party by the plaintiff) can sometimes result in the creation of removal jurisdiction. Note that an action can also become removable if the plaintiff initially asserts only state law claims against a nondiverse defendant, but later amends the complaint to add one or more federal law claims.

In cases that become removable on the basis of diversity after commencement, Congress has placed a one-year time limit on removal. Under § 1446(b)(3), if a civil action is not removable when it is commenced in the state court, but later becomes removable, a notice of removal may be filed within 30 days after receipt by the defendant, by service or otherwise, of a "copy of an amended pleading, motion, order or other paper from which it may first be ascertained that the case is one which is or has become removable." In 1988, Congress provided in § 1446(b) that when the basis of original jurisdiction is diversity of citizenship, an action that becomes removable after commencement may not be removed more than one-year after commencement. This change gave rise to significant attempts by plaintiffs to prevent removal by joining nondiverse parties and dropping them after one-year and by other devices.

Know there is a time limit

Congress addressed this manipulation in the "Federal Courts Jurisdiction and Venue Clarification Act of 2011" and § 1446(c)(1) now provides that the district court may allow removal after one year if it "finds that the plaintiff has acted in bad faith in order to prevent a defendant from removing the action." In addition, Congress provided in § 1446(c)(3)(B) that the district court may allow removal beyond the one-year limit if it finds that the plaintiff deliberately failed to disclose the actual amount in controversy to prevent removal, classifying this as bad faith. Congress also enacted special provisions in § 1446(c)(2) for determining the jurisdictional amount when the plaintiff in the state action seeks non-monetary relief or the state procedural requirements do not allow the plaintiff to demand a specific amount in a damages action or permits a recovery in excess of the amount demanded by the plaintiff.

It should be noted that traditionally when a nondiverse defendant was not voluntarily dismissed by the plaintiff, but was dismissed by order of the court, the case did not "become removable" because of fear that the dismissal could be reversed by a higher state court, thus making the case nonremovable again. Furthermore, when a nondiverse defendant was fraudulently joined in the action to prevent removal, the citizenship of that defendant could be disregarded in determining removal. Thus, the case was removable from the outset. It is not clear at this time whether the new power in the district courts to allow removal when the plaintiff has acted in bad faith will affect these traditional rules.

The 30-Day Time Limit for Removal. Under § 1446(b)(1), a defendant desiring to remove a state action must file the notice of removal within 30 days after receipt "through service or otherwise" of the initial pleading setting forth the claim for relief upon which the action is based, or within 30 days after the service of summons if the initial pleading has been filed in court and is not required to be served on the defendant, whichever period is shorter. In _Murphy Brothers v. Michetti Pipe Stringing, Inc.,_ 526 U.S. 344 (1999), the U.S. Supreme Court held that formal service of process is essential to trigger the running of the 30-day removal period. It is not sufficient that the plaintiff transmit the complaint to the defendant by some means without effectuating formal service. This decision ended the questionable practice of providing the defendant with a "courtesy copy" of the complaint prior to formal service, which some lower courts had held would start the running of the 30-day period.

Under the 2011 amendments to § 1446(b), it is made explicit that each defendant has 30 days after service on that defendant of the initial pleading or summons to file a notice of removal, thus making it clear that the time period does not begin to run on some defendants by service on others. In addition, the 2011 amendments now provide in § 1446(b)(2)(B) & (C) that if defendants are served at different times and a later served defendant files a notice of removal, any earlier served defendant may consent to the removal, even though that defendant did not previously initiate or consent to removal. These amendments, of course, clarify how the "unanimous consent" requirement of § 1446(b)(2)(A) applies in cases in which service on multiple defendants takes place at different times and in which the notice of removal is filed by one defendant served earlier or later than others.

Waiver of the Right to Remove. The right to remove an action can be waived. For example, the defendant can waive the right to remove by taking substantial defensive action in the state court before seeking to remove. In addition, a party can waive the right to remove by entering into a "forum selection clause" in a contract mandating that any suit arising out of the contract must be conducted in state court.

Remand of Improperly Removed Actions. Under § 1447(c), the proper procedure for dealing with an improperly removed action is a motion to remand. Section 1447(c) states that a motion to remand a case "on the basis of any defect other than lack of subject-matter jurisdiction" must be made within 30 days after the filing of the notice of removal under § 1446(a). However, § 1447(c) also states that "[i]f at any time before final judgment it appears that the district court lacks subject-matter jurisdiction, the case shall be remanded." Thus, the language of the statute draws a distinction between defects in subject-matter jurisdiction, which cannot be waived, and defects other than subject-matter jurisdiction, which can be waived. In addition, this language suggests that a defect other than lack of subject-matter jurisdiction must be raised by a motion to remand by the plaintiff, whereas a subject-matter jurisdiction defect can be raised by the district court on its own motion. The difficulty is in determining what is a subject-matter jurisdiction defect and what is merely a procedural defect.

Clearly, a violation of one of the requirements of original jurisdiction, such as the "complete diversity" rule or the "well-pleaded complaint" rule would be a jurisdictional defect. However, numerous other restrictions on removal range, in a policy sense, from the very mundane to the very serious. As one approaches the more serious end of the policy spectrum, it becomes problematic to classify a defect as merely "procedural."

However, even a case that is improperly removed without subject-matter jurisdiction will not necessarily have to be remanded. In *Caterpillar Inc. v. Lewis*, 519 U.S. 61 (1996), a defendant removed an action to federal court on the basis of diversity of citizenship, even though another defendant was joined in the action who was nondiverse to the plaintiff. The district court erroneously refused to remand on the plaintiff's motion, but the nondiverse defendant was dismissed prior to trial, thus making diversity complete at the time of judgment. The U.S. Supreme Court held that the district court's error was not fatal to the validity of the judgment because the requisites of original jurisdiction existed at the time of the judgment. Although it might seem as if the *Caterpillar* case has the potential to produce wholesale evasions of jurisdictional restrictions in removal cases, the lower federal courts have generally interpreted it narrowly. *See* TEPLY & WHITTEN at 197–98 (discussing *Caterpillar*). Remember that the *Caterpillar* rule can be applied only if, despite the jurisdictionally improper removal, original jurisdiction exists at the time of judgment.

Problems

Problem 4-33. P, a citizen of State X, sues D, a citizen of State Y, in a state court in State Y. P seeks $100,000 for breach of contract under the law of State Y. Two days after being served with the summons and complaint, D files a notice of removal in the U.S. District Court for State Y. Is the action removable? Would the action be removable if D changed domiciles to State Q immediately after the commencement of the action and then sought removal?

Problem 4-34. Assume the same facts as *Problem 4-33*, except that *P's* claim against D is based on a federal statute. Is the action removable?

Problem 4-35. Assume the same facts as *Problem 4-34*, except that D does not file the notice of removal until one year and a day after commencement of the action in state court. Is the action removable?

Problem 4-36. P, a citizen of State X, sues D-1, a citizen of State Y, and D-2, a citizen of State X, in a state court in State X. P seeks $100,000 for breach of contract under the law of State X. D-1 files a notice of removal in the U.S. District Court for State X two days after receiving copies of the summons and complaint. Is the action removable? Do you need additional information to answer this question?

NO | X – state
     | NO DIV.
D2: X

Problem 4-37. P, a citizen of State X, sues D, a citizen of State Y, in a state court in State X. P seeks $100,000 for an assault and battery committed under the law of State X. The complaint reveals the citizenship of both parties and the amount in controversy. Thirteen months after commencement of the action, P amends the complaint to drop the state assault and battery claim and assert instead a claim against D under a federal statute. The federal claim is based on the same facts as the assault and battery claim. Forty days after receiving the amended complaint, D files a notice of removal in the U.S. District Court for State X. Forty days after D files the notice of removal, P moves to remand the action to state court. Should the action be remanded?

Chapter 5

Sources of Law

Chapter 1 briefly described the general choice-of-law process. In addition, the discussion of federal civil actions based on diversity of citizenship in Chapter 4 pointed out that the federal courts ordinarily apply state substantive law and federal procedural law. However, beneath these simple descriptions are a complex history and body of law concerning proper sources of law for federal courts whenever a federal court is adjudicating a claim derived from *state*, rather than *federal*, substantive law. Furthermore, as discussed in Chapter 4, federal courts adjudicate state law claims when exercising diversity and supplemental jurisdiction. This body of law, which is an important component of the general choice-of-law process in American law, is known today as the "*Erie* doctrine," deriving its name from the 1938 Supreme Court decision in *Erie Railroad Co. v. Tompkins*, reprinted in section A(4), below. This chapter examines the history and contemporary authorities governing this "source-of-law" problem.

The *Erie* doctrine involves both separation-of-powers and federalism policies. The separation-of-powers policies concern the proper allocation of lawmaking power *between the federal courts and Congress*. The federalism policies concern the proper allocation of authority *between federal and state courts*. As you study the materials in this chapter, you should consider which of these policies provides the better basis for the doctrines announced in the cases.

Section A. Overview of the *Erie* Doctrine

1. Introduction to Source-of-Law Issues in United States Law

Sources of Law in the United States. The United States is a federal system. That is, the country is comprised of fifty different state governments and a national government. The national government is limited to those powers delegated to it by the United States Constitution. The Tenth Amendment provides that all powers not delegated to the national government in the Constitution "are reserved to the states respectively, or to the people." This division of power has meant, as a practical matter, that the bulk of the laws governing the day-to-day activities of people within the country are created by the states. This traditional picture of law within the United States has changed somewhat since the country was formed. Today, the national ("federal") government exercises much more extensive lawmaking power than it did when the country was formed and for the first century and a half of its existence. Nevertheless, it is still true, though less so, that the states create most of the laws that govern the day-to-day activities of the average person.

The Separation-of-Powers Doctrine. Within each state and the federal government, lawmaking power is divided between the legislative, executive, and judicial branches of government. Although the legislature of each state and the U.S. Congress are, respectively, the primary lawmaking branches of the state and national governments, the executive and judicial branches also create law in a more limited fashion within their respective areas of operation. However, the doctrine of separation of powers restricts the law-creating power of the judicial and executive branches of the state and federal governments. Traditionally, the job of the executive was to enforce the laws enacted by the legislative branch, and this enforcement was to take place only within the context of judicial proceedings in which the laws would be neutrally interpreted and enforced. The actual administration of law in the twenty-first century is much more complex than this discussion indicates, but it still describes the basic distribution of powers between the different branches of government today.

Relations Between State and Federal Courts. The federal system and the separation-of-powers doctrine that operates within each government have an important bearing on actions in both state and federal courts. As indicated in Chapter 4, most cases within the jurisdiction of the federal courts are also within the "concurrent jurisdiction" of the state courts. If a plaintiff commences an action in a state court with proper subject-matter jurisdiction, venue, and personal jurisdiction over the defendant, the state court will apply whatever law is pertinent to the dispute revealed by the parties' pleadings. This will often be state law, but state courts also have the authority to hear claims based on federal law that are not within the exclusive subject-matter jurisdiction of the federal courts. State courts also have the authority to hear federal defenses to state and federal claims.

State Law Claims in Federal Court. Federal courts, of course, have subject-matter jurisdiction over cases arising under federal law, which includes the power to hear both claims and defenses created by that law. As we have learned, however, federal courts also have jurisdiction to adjudicate state law claims when diversity of citizenship is established under 28 U.S.C. § 1332 and when supplemental jurisdiction exists under 28 U.S.C. § 1367. By definition, the substantive claim in both of these instances is based on state, rather than federal, law because if the claim were based on federal law, it would independently satisfy the requirements of federal question jurisdiction under 28 U.S.C. § 1331 and neither diversity nor supplemental jurisdiction would be needed. Federal courts also adjudicate state law claims under 28 U.S.C. § 1335 (interpleader) and § 1369 (mass disaster tort actions), both of which are based on minimal diversity. A federal court would also be adjudicating a state law claim under federal question jurisdiction in cases in which state law creates the substantive claim, but an essential element of the claim is based on federal law — the so-called Category 2 federal question cases examined in Chapter 4(B)(2)(b) & (d). In these situations, the *Erie* doctrine would apply to the *state law* aspect of the claim.

2. The *Erie* Doctrine — Basic Rule

Once it is determined that the case is one in which a federal court is adjudicating a state law claim, the *Erie* doctrine applies and basically commands that the federal court apply state substantive law but federal procedural law in adjudicating the state law claim, as illustrated in Figure 5-1.

The line of demarcation between what is properly an aspect of state substantive law and what is properly an aspect of federal procedural law, however, has traditionally been a point of confusion for the courts and continues to be so as the Supreme Court's most re-

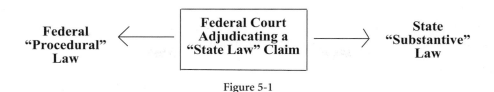

Figure 5-1

cent decision in the *Shady Grove* case illustrates, reprinted in section C, below. The explanation of how the *Erie* doctrine came to be and its current parameters is best understood in a historical context.

3. The Rules of Decision Act and the *Swift* Doctrine

The Rules of Decision Act. The explanation (and history) must begin with § 34 of the Judiciary Act of 1789, which was known as the Rules of Decision Act. It provided "[t]hat the laws of the several states, except where the Constitution, treaties, or statutes of the United States shall otherwise require or provide, shall be regarded as rules of decision in trials at common law in the Courts of the United States, in cases where they apply." § 34, 1 Stat. 73, 92, codified as amended, 28 U.S.C. § 1652. The modern interpretation of this provision is derived from the 1938 decision by the U.S. Supreme Court in *Erie Railroad Co. v. Tompkins.* However, to understand the Rules of Decision Act and the *Erie* decision, one must begin with *Swift v. Tyson*, 41 U.S. (16 Pet.) 1 (1842). The *Swift* case and the body of doctrine that was known as the "*Swift* doctrine" controlled the administration of state law in federal courts from the beginning of the Constitution until *Erie* was decided.

Swift v. Tyson. *Swift v. Tyson* concerned a commercial transaction involving a bill of exchange. A bill of exchange is an unconditional order in writing addressed by one person to another, signed by the person giving it, requiring the person to whom it was addressed to pay on demand or at a fixed future date a certain sum of money. To be effective, a bill of exchange must be "accepted" by the person to whom it is addressed. The addressee accepts by "endorsing" the bill. In *Swift*, Norton and Keith purported to convey land located in Maine to Tyson in return for Tyson "accepting" the bill of exchange, which was "drawn by" Norton and Keith. By accepting the bill, Tyson agreed to pay $1,540.30 to Norton six months later.

One of the useful aspects of bills of exchange is their negotiability. They can be transferred, or "negotiated," to a third party by the holder of the bill. When the transfer takes place before the bill is due, without notice of any illegality in the original transaction giving rise to the bill, and in exchange for a valuable consideration, the person to whom the bill is negotiated becomes a "bona fide purchaser for value" (today called a "holder in due course"). A bona fide purchaser for value is insulated from defenses that may exist between the original parties to the bill. In *Swift*, Norton endorsed the bill to Swift before the bill was due to Swift. In return, Swift canceled a preexisting debt (promissory note) owed to him by Norton. This transaction is summarized in Figure 5-2.

When Swift presented the bill for payment to Tyson, Tyson refused to pay. Tyson alleged fraud in the original transaction with Norton and Keith. Swift then sued Tyson in a federal court in New York. Tyson asserted the fraud defense in the action by Swift on the bill, and Swift countered that he was a bona fide purchaser for value and, as such, was not subject to the fraud defense. Tyson replied that Swift was not a bona fide purchaser

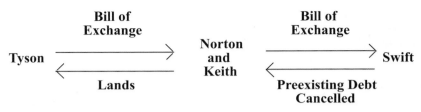

Figure 5-2

for value because cancellation of a preexisting debt did not constitute "valuable consideration" within the meaning of the applicable negotiable instruments law.

The issue in *Swift*—and the one for which the decision is famous—involved the proper source of law with which to determine whether Swift was a bona fide purchaser. Under prevailing conflict-of-laws rules, the law of the place where the bill of exchange was "accepted" was universally regarded as governing the transaction. A bill of exchange is a contract, and the conflict-of-laws rule governing contracts provided that the law of the place where the contract was "made" governed the scope and validity of the contract. The contract was made where the "last act" necessary to bring it into existence occurred. In this instance, Tyson had accepted the bill in New York. Acceptance was the last act necessary to create a contract. Thus, the law of New York applied because the contract was "made" there. In contrast, had the bill been accepted in Maine, the law of Maine would have applied because the contract would have been "made" there.

Although the prevailing conflict-of-laws rules were generally followed by all courts, it had long been established by the time that *Swift* was decided that the "in cases where they apply" language of the Rules of Decision Act commanded the federal courts to make a conflict-of-laws decision about which state's law should apply in a diversity action independent of anything that the states would decide about the same matter. Thus, even though the federal and state courts generally followed the same conflict-of-laws rules, if the state courts deviated from the generally accepted conflicts doctrines that were thought to regulate the authority of independent sovereigns relative to each other, the federal courts were not obligated to parrot what the state courts would do. This independent conflict-of-laws authority was an important feature of the justice afforded to litigants in diversity actions.

However, even though it was conceded that New York law was to govern the contract in *Swift*, the source-of-law issue was complicated by the fact that the decisions in New York were unsettled on the commercial law question involved in the case. Tyson asserted that under "the law of New York, as ... expounded by its Courts, a pre-existing debt does not constitute, in the sense of the general rule, a valuable consideration applicable to negotiable instruments." *See Swift*, 41 U.S. at 16. Thus, Tyson argued that the law reflected in the New York court decisions was the "law" of the state that had to be regarded as the "rule of decision" by the federal court under the Rules of Decision Act. *See id.* Justice Story, for the Court, concluded that the New York decisions were unsettled on the question at issue in the case, which under the ordinary doctrine of stare decisis meant that the federal courts would have had to make an independent judgment about what the rule of New York law was in the action. However, Justice Story went on to reason that even if the New York decisions had been settled in favor of Tyson, they would not bind the federal courts in diversity actions. Justice Story's conclusion in this latter regard is the controversial part of *Swift*. His conclusion turned in part on the nature of court decisions and whether they should be deemed to be "law."

Importantly, Justice Story prefaced his reasoning by pointing out that "the Courts of New York [did] not [base] their decisions upon this point [of commercial law] upon any local statute...." *Id.* at 18. In other words, New York did not have a statute resolving the commercial law issue. If there had existed a New York statute providing that a preexisting debt was not the valuable consideration necessary to give Swift the status of a bona fide purchaser for value, Justice Story's opinion implies that the statute would have to be applied under the Rules of Decision Act. Thus, the statute would have constituted an applicable state law and been binding on the federal court as a state rule of decision under the Act. Because the prevailing conflict-of-laws rules controlled decisions of the federal courts under the "in cases where they apply" language of the Act, the New York statute would have applied to the case because the bill of exchange had been accepted in New York. Under accepted rules of stare decisis, the settled decisions of New York's courts interpreting the statute would have applied in a federal diversity action. *See* Teply & Whitten at 450–54.

Justice Story's opinion also observed that "the Courts of New York do not [base] their decisions [on this issue of commercial law] upon any ... positive, fixed, or ancient local usage." *See Swift*, 41 U.S. at 18. Again, this implies that if the New York court decisions had been based on a "positive, fixed, or ancient local usage" they would have been binding on the federal courts under the Rules of Decision Act. The controlling conflict of laws principles, binding under the "in cases where they apply" language of the Act, would have required the federal courts to follow any authoritative local custom of New York on commercial law matters because the bill of exchange had been accepted in New York. Because the settled decisions of the New York courts would have constituted the highest evidence of the content of any such local custom, those decisions would also have been binding on the federal courts under prevailing concepts of stare decisis.

Thus, settled state court decisions on "local" matters were binding on the federal courts under the Rules of Decision Act, but what types of matters were regarded as "local" in nature for this purpose? According to Justice Story, such matters included "the positive statutes of the state, and the construction thereof adopted by the local tribunals, and to rights and titles to things having a permanent locality, such as the rights and titles to real estate, and other matters immovable and intraterritorial in their nature and character." *See id.*

However, Justice Story pointed out that, rather than being based on an interpretation of "local" law, the New York courts "deduce[d] the doctrine from the general principles of commercial law." *Id.* The reference to "general principles of commercial law" was to the body of customary law that merchants throughout the world had developed over a long period while trading between seafaring countries. The English courts had incorporated this body of custom into the common law by the time the United States was formed. *See* Teply & Whitten at 438–41. By deciding to follow the general commercial law, New York had made a significant policy choice. General commercial law was not regarded as being the law of any one sovereign because it was understood to be based on the practices, customs, and expectations of private parties developed over centuries throughout the world. Once New York had decided to follow the general commercial law, the functions performed by the New York state courts and the federal courts were viewed to be the same. As Justice Story stated, "state tribunals are called upon to perform the like functions as ourselves, that is, to ascertain upon general reasoning and legal analogies, what is the true exposition of the contract or instrument, or what is the just rule furnished by the principles of commercial law to govern the case." *See Swift*, 41 U.S. at 19. Thus, Justice Story held that the federal courts had a right to make a judgment on the content of the "general commercial law" that was independent of what the state courts might hold the content of that law to be. *Cf.* Anthony J. Bell, Jr. & Bradford R. Clark, *General Law in Federal Court*, 54 Wm. & Mary L. Rev. 655, 660 (2013) ("Because no sovereign had unilateral authority to prescribe the content of general law, the courts of each sovereign exercised independent judgment to determine its content and expected the courts of other sovereigns to do likewise.").

Swift's **Critics.** This last aspect of *Swift* has been highly criticized. The argument of the critics is that if state court decisions are to be considered "law" under the Rules of Decision Act on "local" issues, it is inconsistent not to consider them law on general commercial law issues. *See, e.g.*, John C. Gray, The Nature and Sources of the Law 255 (2d rev. ed. 1921; Peter Smith reprint 1972). Despite Justice Story's critics, however, recent scholarship tends to confirm that Justice Story's view of law was widely shared at the time *Swift* was decided. *See, e.g.*, Wilfred J. Ritz, Rewriting the History of the Judiciary Act of 1789 at 28–30 (Wythe Holt & L.H. LaRue eds., 1989) (discussing the eighteenth century function of judges to "find" rather than "make" law); William A. Fletcher, *The General Common Law and Section 34 of the Judiciary Act of 1789: The Example of Marine Insurance*, 97 Harv. L. Rev. 1513 (1984) (finding the *Swift* holding to be a restatement of settled law). Furthermore, although the doctrine under which the federal courts made an independent decision on both conflict-of-laws matters and upon general commercial law matters is referred to today as the "*Swift* doctrine," the doctrine was well-settled in the federal courts by the time *Swift* was decided in 1842.

Federal Common Law Versus General Commercial Law. It is also commonplace today to read descriptions of *Swift* which state that the Court was authorizing the creation of "federal common law" in the case. *See, e.g.*, Chemerinsky, § 5.3.5, at 321. However, this does not accurately describe what was going on in *Swift*. For example, assume that immediately after the Supreme Court's decision in *Swift*, an identical case had arisen between a citizen of New York and a citizen of Maine, but that the suit was brought in a New York state court. After a trial and appeal, the highest court of New York holds the general commercial law rule to be that cancellation of a preexisting debt does *not* constitute valuable consideration for the transfer of a bill of exchange. It is clear that the holder of the bill of exchange could not appeal this decision to the Supreme Court of the United States under a statute allowing appeals from the state's highest court to the Supreme Court when a state court renders a decision on an issue of federal law that conflicts with a prior decision of the Supreme Court on the same issue. The reason was that the U.S. Supreme Court made it clear that the body of law being applied in *Swift* and like cases was not "federal" in nature, but general. *See* Teply & Whitten 468–69 (citing cases in which the Court refused to review state court decisions on general law matters under § 25 of the Judiciary Act of 1789 because no federal question was involved); Ernest A. Young, *The Last Brooding Omnipresence:* Erie Railroad v. Tompkins *and the Unconstitutionality of Preemptive Federal Maritime Law*, 43 St. Louis L.J. 1349, 1359 (1999) (abundant research shows that the law merchant was not viewed as federal in nature).

Given the persistent misdescription of *Swift* as involving the creation and application of "federal common law," it is ironic that after *Erie* overruled *Swift*, the U.S. Supreme Court recognized that it was legitimate for the federal courts to develop true federal common law under certain circumstances. By "true" federal common law, we mean pure "substantive" common law that preempts state law and controls decisions in both state and federal courts in cases in which it is applicable. Section F examines this "new" federal common law.

Admiralty and Equity Cases. At the time *Swift* was decided, the Rules of Decision Act, by its terms, applied only to "trials at common law." Federal courts had exclusive jurisdiction of most admiralty cases and applied "general maritime law" in such cases. General maritime law, like general commercial law, was considered to be a body of worldwide customary law, subject (also like general commercial law) to alteration by local custom or statute as conditions in different nations demanded. *See* TEPLY & WHITTEN at 460–62.

In "equity" cases, the pattern was more complicated, but federal diversity courts generally enforced primary rights created by state law, while recognizing an independent equitable "remedial" power. *See id.* This "equitable remedial rights" doctrine will be important when you study the *Erie* doctrine, below, especially in conjunction with the Supreme Court's decision in the case of *Guaranty Trust Co. v. York*, which is reprinted in section B, below. The issue there will be whether, and if so to what extent, an independent equity power has survived the *Erie* decision.

The *Swift* Doctrine Changes. As the materials above have indicated, the *Swift* decision was part of a complex body of doctrine that controlled the power of federal courts to choose and apply law in actions within their subject-matter jurisdiction. Although the doctrine took its name from *Swift*, it originated long prior to that case and continued to develop long after it. Unsurprisingly, as the doctrine developed, it changed in certain respects. Some aspects of the change would not have been deemed acceptable under the doctrine as it was configured at the time *Swift* was decided and, indeed, are not deemed to be acceptable today. In addition, in the late nineteenth and, especially, the early twentieth centuries, the way in which judges and others viewed judge-made law began to change. These changes in jurisprudential philosophy, together with the ways in which the *Swift* doctrine itself had changed, made Justice Story's opinion seem increasingly illegitimate. *See id.* at 462–63.

4. The *Erie Railroad Co. v. Tompkins* Decision

In 1938, the developments described in the preceding subsection produced the Supreme Court's decision in *Erie Railroad Co. v. Tompkins*. In reading *Erie*, you should pay particular attention to the Court's description of the different viewpoints about the nature of law that controlled at the times when *Swift* and *Erie* were decided. You should ask yourself whether these differences were just alternative ways of looking at the same judicial behavior, or whether, after *Swift*, federal (and, perhaps, state) judges had altered their behavior in ways that produced a different view of the nature of law. In addition, although the Court in *Erie* attributes certain illegitimate practices in diversity actions to *Swift*, you should ask yourself whether these practices were really part of the "pure" *Swift* doctrine, or were practices that developed later in the name of *Swift*. *Cf.* Anthony J. Bellia Jr. & Bradford R. Clark, *General Law in Federal Court*, 54 WM. & MARY L. REV. 655, 658 (2013) (*Swift* and *Erie* represent compatible concepts of federal law when each is understood in its full historical context).

Finally, you should note that another major change occurred in 1938 in addition to *Erie*. Recall from Chapter 1 that in 1938 the U.S. Supreme Court promulgated the Federal Rules of Civil Procedure under the authority granted by Congress to the Court in the Rules Enabling Act of 1934. *See* 28 U.S.C. § 2072 *et seq.* The Federal Rules of Civil Procedure ended federal conformity to state law in matters of procedure, subject to a restriction in the Act that provided the rules could not "abridge, enlarge, nor modify the substantive rights of any litigant." In reading *Erie*, you should ask yourself how the doctrine announced by the Court applies, if at all, to issues concerning the validity of Federal Rules of Civil Procedure under the Rules Enabling Act's "substantive rights" restriction. As the materials following *Erie* indicate, the answer to this question has differed at different points in the development of the *Erie* doctrine. Until recently, it was thought to be settled that the test announced in *Erie* itself does not govern whether a Federal Rule of Civil Procedure that conflicts with state law may be validly applied in a diversity action. Instead, that question is governed by a different test developed under the Enabling Act.

Erie Railroad Co. v. Tompkins

United States Supreme Court, 1938
304 U.S. 64, 58 S. Ct. 817, 82 L. Ed. 1188

JUSTICE BRANDEIS delivered the opinion of the Court.

The question for decision is whether the oft-challenged doctrine of *Swift v. Tyson* shall now be disapproved.

Tompkins, a citizen of Pennsylvania, was injured on a dark night by a passing freight train of the Erie Railroad Company while walking along its right of way at Hughestown in that State. He claimed that the accident occurred through negligence in the operation, or maintenance, of the train; that he was rightfully on the premises as licensee because [he was] on a commonly used beaten footpath which ran for a short distance alongside the tracks; and that he was struck by something which looked like a door projecting from one of the moving cars. To enforce that claim he brought an action in the federal court for southern New York, which had jurisdiction because the company is a corporation of that State. It denied liability; and the case was tried by a jury.

The Erie insisted that its duty to Tompkins was no greater than that owed to a trespasser. It contended, among other things, that its duty to Tompkins, and hence its liability, should be determined in accordance with the Pennsylvania law; that under the law of Pennsylvania, as declared by its highest court, persons who use pathways along the railroad right of way — that is a longitudinal pathway as distinguished from a crossing — are to be deemed trespassers; and that the railroad is not liable for injuries to undiscovered trespassers resulting from its negligence, unless it be wanton or wilful. Tompkins denied that any such rule had been established by the decisions of the Pennsylvania courts; and contended that, since there was no statute of the State on the subject, the railroad's duty and liability is to be determined in federal courts as a matter of general law.

The trial judge refused to rule that the applicable law precluded recovery. The jury brought in a verdict of $30,000; and the judgment entered thereon was affirmed by the Circuit Court of Appeals, which held ... that it was unnecessary to consider whether the law of Pennsylvania was as contended, because the question was one not of local, but of general, law and that "upon questions of general law the federal courts are free, in the absence of a local statute, to exercise their independent judgment as to what the law is; and it is well settled that the question of the responsibility of a railroad for injuries caused by its servants is one of general law.... Where the public has made open and notorious use of a railroad right of way for a long period of time and without objection, the company owes to persons on such permissive pathway a duty of care in the operation of its trains.... It is likewise generally recognized law that a jury may find that negligence exists toward a pedestrian using a permissive path on the railroad right of way if he is hit by some object projecting from the side of the train."

The Erie had contended that application of the Pennsylvania rule was required, among other things, by § 34 of the Federal Judiciary Act of September 24, 1789, ch. 20, 28 U.S.C. § 725, which provides:

"The laws of the several States, except where the Constitution, treaties, or statutes of the United States otherwise require or provide, shall be regarded as rules of decision in trials at common law, in the courts of the United States, in cases where they apply."

Because of the importance of the question whether the federal court was free to disregard the alleged rule of the Pennsylvania common law, we granted certiorari.

First. Swift v. Tyson ... held that federal courts exercising jurisdiction on the ground of diversity of citizenship need not, in matters of general jurisprudence, apply the unwritten law of the State as declared by its highest court; that they are free to exercise an independent judgment as to what the common law of the State is—or should be....

The Court in applying the rule of § 34 to equity cases, in *Mason v. United States*, 260 U.S. 545, 559 (1923), said: "The statute, however, is merely declarative of the rule which would exist in the absence of the statute."[2] The federal courts assumed, in the broad field of "general law," the power to declare rules of decision which Congress was confessedly without power to enact as statutes. Doubt was repeatedly expressed as to the correctness of the construction given § 34, and as to the soundness of the rule which it introduced. But it was the more recent research of a competent scholar, who examined the original document, which established that the construction given to it by the Court was erroneous; and that the purpose of the section was merely to make certain that, in all matters except those in which some federal law is controlling, the federal courts exercising jurisdiction in diversity of citizenship cases would apply as their rules of decision the law of the State, unwritten as well as written.[5]

Criticism of the doctrine became widespread after the decision of *Black & White Taxicab Co. v. Brown & Yellow Taxicab Co.*, 276 U.S. 518 (1928). There, Brown and Yellow, a Kentucky corporation owned by Kentuckians, and the Louisville and Nashville Railroad, also a Kentucky corporation, wished that the former should have the exclusive privilege of soliciting passenger and baggage transportation at the Bowling Green, Kentucky, railroad station; and that the Black and White, a competing Kentucky corporation, should be prevented from interfering with that privilege. Knowing that such a contract would be void under the common law of Kentucky, it was arranged that the Brown and Yellow reincorporate under the law of Tennessee, and that the contract with the railroad should be executed there. The suit was then brought by the Tennessee corporation in the federal court for western Kentucky to enjoin competition by the Black and White; an injunction issued by the District Court was sustained by the Court of Appeals; and this Court, citing many decisions in which the doctrine of *Swift v. Tyson* had been applied, affirmed the decree.

Second. Experience in applying the doctrine of *Swift v. Tyson*, had revealed its defects, political and social; and the benefits expected to flow from the rule did not accrue. Per-

---

2. In *Hawkins v. Barney's Lessee*, 30 U.S. (5 Pet.) 457, 464 (1831), it was stated that § 34 "has been uniformly held to be no more than a declaration of what the law would have been without it: to wit, that the lex loci must be the governing rule of private right, under whatever jurisdiction private right comes to be examined." *See also Bank of Hamilton v. Dudley's Lessee*, 27 U.S. (2 Pet.) 492, 525 (1829); *cf. Jackson v. Chew*, 25 U.S. (12 Wheat.) 153, 162, 168 (1827); *Livingston v. Moore*, 32 U.S. (7 Pet.) 469, 542 (1833).

5. Charles Warren, *New Light on the History of the Federal Judiciary Act of 1789*, 37 Harv. L. Rev. 49, 51–52, 81–88, 108 (1923).

sistence of state courts in their own opinions on questions of common law prevented uniformity; and the impossibility of discovering a satisfactory line of demarcation between the province of general law and that of local law developed a new well of uncertainties.

On the other hand, the mischievous results of the doctrine had become apparent. Diversity of citizenship jurisdiction was conferred in order to prevent apprehended discrimination in state courts against those not citizens of the State. *Swift v. Tyson* introduced grave discrimination by non-citizens against citizens. It made rights enjoyed under the unwritten "general law" vary according to whether enforcement was sought in the state or in the federal court; and the privilege of selecting the court in which the right should be determined was conferred upon the non-citizen. Thus, the doctrine rendered impossible equal protection of the law. In attempting to promote uniformity of law throughout the United States, the doctrine had prevented uniformity in the administration of the law of the State.

The discrimination resulting became in practice far-reaching. This resulted in part from the broad province accorded to the so-called "general law" as to which federal courts exercised an independent judgment. In addition to questions of purely commercial law, "general law" was held to include the obligations under contracts entered into and to be performed within the State, the extent to which a carrier operating within a State may stipulate for exemption from liability for his own negligence or that of his employee; the liability for torts committed within the State upon persons resident or property located there, even where the question of liability depended upon the scope of a property right conferred by the State; and the right to exemplary or punitive damages. Furthermore, state decisions construing local deeds, mineral conveyances, and even devises of real estate were disregarded.

In part the discrimination resulted from the wide range of persons held entitled to avail themselves of the federal rule by resort to the diversity of citizenship jurisdiction. Through this jurisdiction individual citizens willing to remove from their own State and become citizens of another might avail themselves of the federal rule. And, without even change of residence, a corporate citizen of the State could avail itself of the federal rule by reincorporating under the laws of another State, as was done in the *Taxicab* case.

The injustice and confusion incident to the doctrine of *Swift v. Tyson* have been repeatedly urged as reasons for abolishing or limiting diversity of citizenship jurisdiction. Other legislative relief has been proposed. If only a question of statutory construction were involved, we should not be prepared to abandon a doctrine so widely applied throughout nearly a century. But the unconstitutionality of the course pursued has now been made clear and compels us to do so.

Third. Except in matters governed by the Federal Constitution or by Acts of Congress, the law to be applied in any case is the law of the State. And whether the law of the State shall be declared by its Legislature in a statute or by its highest court in a decision is not a matter of federal concern. There is no federal general common law. Congress has no power to declare substantive rules of common law applicable in a State whether they be local in their nature or "general," be they commercial law or a part of the law of torts. And no clause in the Constitution purports to confer such a power upon the federal courts....

The fallacy underlying the rule declared in *Swift v. Tyson* is made clear by Justice Holmes. The doctrine rests upon the assumption that there is "a transcendental body of law outside of any particular State but obligatory within it unless and until changed by statute," that federal courts have the power to use their judgment as to what the rules of common law are; and that in the federal courts "the parties are entitled to an independent judgment on matters of general law":

But law in the sense in which courts speak of it today does not exist without some definite authority behind it. The common law so far as it is enforced in a State, whether called common law or not, is not the common law generally but the law of that State existing by the authority of that State without regard to what it may have been in England or anywhere else....

... [T]he authority and only authority is the State, and if that be so, the voice adopted by the State as its own [whether it be of its Legislature or of its Supreme Court] should utter the last word.

Thus the doctrine of *Swift v. Tyson* is, as Justice Holmes said, "an unconstitutional assumption of powers by courts of the United States which no lapse of time or respectable array of opinion should make us hesitate to correct." In disapproving that doctrine we do not hold unconstitutional § 34 of the Federal Judiciary Act of 1789 or any other Act of Congress. We merely declare that in applying the doctrine this Court and the lower courts have invaded rights which in our opinion are reserved by the Constitution to the several States.

Fourth. The defendant contended that by the common law of Pennsylvania as declared by its highest court in *Falchetti v. Pennsylvania Railroad Co.*, 160 A. 859 (Pa. 1932), the only duty owed to the plaintiff was to refrain from wilful or wanton injury. The plaintiff denied that such is the Pennsylvania law. In support of their respective contentions the parties discussed and cited many decisions of the Supreme Court of the State. The Circuit Court of Appeals ruled that the question of liability is one of general law; and on that ground declined to decide the issue of state law. As we hold this was error, the judgment is reversed and the case remanded to it for further proceedings in conformity with our opinion.

Reversed.

JUSTICE CARDOZO took no part in the consideration or decision of this case. [The concurring opinion of JUSTICE BUTLER, in which JUSTICE McREYNOLDS joined, is omitted. The concurring opinion of JUSTICE REED is also omitted.]

Notes and Questions

1. In *Erie*, the Court described changes that had taken place in the *Swift* doctrine between *Swift* and *Erie*. These changes did indeed involve the extension of the area of "general law" to subjects that it did not originally cover. For example, "general law" was held to extend to many types of issues in tort. *Erie's* criticism of *Swift* aside, were these changes justifiable?

2. In *Erie*, the Court stated: "There is no federal general common law." Did *Swift* hold that there was such law?

3. In *Erie*, the Court stated: "Congress has no power to declare substantive rules of common law applicable in a state whether they be local in their nature or general." Can you make sense of this statement? Congress never declares common-law rules, does it? It enacts statutes. What is the Court saying about the power of Congress to legislate rules of decision? Consider the constitutionality of the following hypothetical statutes:

(a) Congress enacts a statute regulating the tort liabilities of interstate railroads. The statute is preemptive—it prevents the operation of state law to determine such tort liabilities and is applicable in both state and federal courts. Did the Court mean to suggest in *Erie* that such a statute would be unconstitutional?

(b) Congress enacts a statute regulating the tort liabilities of all persons in the states under all circumstances, without regard to whether such persons are operating in, or affecting by their actions, interstate commerce. The statute is preemptive. That is, it applies in both state and federal courts, and inconsistent state law is of no further effect. Is this the kind of legislation the Court in *Erie* was suggesting would be unconstitutional? If so, the Court's suggestion is unexceptional and trivial, isn't it?

(c) Congress enacts a statute regulating the tort liabilities of railroads that are sued within the federal diversity jurisdiction. The statute only applies in federal court in diversity cases. If a railroad is sued in state court, the statute is inapplicable. Is this the kind of legislation the Court in *Erie* believed would be unconstitutional? Such a statute, in application, would be quite close to the result reached under the Rules of Decision Act by the lower court in *Erie*. Can you make an argument that this sort of statute would be constitutional? Can you formulate a persuasive argument that this kind of statute would be unconstitutional? Is the latter argument based on federalism or separation-of-powers restrictions in the Constitution?

4. The Court in *Erie* purported not to find anything that Congress had done unconstitutional, but rather to find the federal courts' application of the *Swift* doctrine unconstitutional. What was unconstitutional about it? Under what provision of the Constitution? Some parts of the Court's opinion seem to suggest that the only problem with what the federal courts were doing under *Swift* was a federalism problem—that is, the federal government did not have the power to make law in certain areas reserved to the states. *See, e.g.,* the statement quoted in Note 3, above, about the power of Congress. However, if federalism is the only problem with what was happening in *Swift*, then whenever the federal government does have the power to make law in a particular area, there would be no objection to the federal courts making that law. Do you believe this is correct? If not, is it incorrect because federalism was not the only problem with *Swift*, or is it incorrect for some other reason?

5. The Court in *Erie* distinguished between substantive rules of law and procedural rules, suggesting that federal courts in diversity cases are bound by state substantive rules, but not state procedural rules. Does this distinction between "substance" and "procedure" provide an adequate guide to the kinds of issues upon which federal courts must follow state law?

5. *Klaxon* and the Application of *Erie* to Conflict-of-Laws Issues

Although the *Erie* decision resolved the question of whether a decision of a state's highest court could qualify as a state substantive law, the Supreme Court did not answer the question of *which* state's substantive law controlled in an *Erie* situation. Three years later in *Klaxon Co. v. Stentor Electric Manufacturing Co.,* 313 U.S. 487 (1941), the Court answered the question and held that the federal district court must apply the same conflict-of-laws rules that would be applied by a state court judge in the state in which the federal district court sits. As discussed in Chapter 1, a state always applies its own conflict-of-laws rules to decide which state's substantive laws it should apply to a particular dispute.

In *Erie*, the action was brought originally in a *New York* federal district court. Yet the Supreme Court assumed that *Pennsylvania* substantive tort law should be applied to resolve the case. It was not clear from the decision whether this was because the Court was making its own independent conflict-of-laws decision that Pennsylvania law was applicable, as it had previously done under *Swift,* or whether it was because the New York courts would choose Pennsylvania law under a state conflict-of-laws analysis. In *Klaxon,* the Court resolved the issue in holding:

> *very.* We are of opinion that the prohibition declared in *Erie Railroad Co. v. Tompkins* ... against such independent determinations by the federal courts extends to the field of conflict of laws. The conflict of laws rules to be applied by the federal court ... must conform to those prevailing in ... state courts [in which the federal court is sitting]. Otherwise, the accident of diversity of citizenship would constantly disturb equal administration of justice in coordinate state and federal courts sitting side by side.... Any other ruling would do violence to the principle of uniformity within a state upon which the [*Erie*] decision is based. Whatever lack of uniformity this may produce between federal courts in different states is attributable to our federal system, which leaves to a state, within the limits permitted by the Constitution, the right to pursue local policies diverging from those of its neighbors. It is not for the federal courts to thwart such local policies by enforcing an independent "general law" of conflict of laws.

Id. at 496.

[handwritten margin note: Uniformity w/in a state]
[handwritten margin note: holding]

Even though *Erie* was correct to reject what the *Swift* doctrine had become, a strong argument can be made that *Klaxon* is wrong. The "in cases where they apply" language of the Rules of Decision Act was uniformly interpreted before and after *Swift* to be a command to the federal courts that they make conflict-of-laws decisions independent of state law. Arguably, the expansion of the substantive areas in which federal courts would apply "general law" after *Swift* should not have affected the Court's interpretation of this command in the Act. Even if all state substantive law is to be treated as "local" after *Erie,* the conflict-of-laws command of the Act could operate independently of this holding to allow federal courts to make their own selection of which state's local law should be applied. Furthermore, under *Swift,* the independent conflict-of-laws authority of federal courts provided a valuable protection against biased selection of a state's own law over that of another state through the application of conflict-of-laws rules. After *Klaxon,* this valuable protection has been lost at a time when conflict-of-laws doctrine within the states is particularly confused. The elimination of independent conflict-of-laws authority has tended to diminish the value of the diversity jurisdiction as it is presently configured. If *Klaxon* had been decided differently the existence of independent conflicts authority in the federal courts might have diminished criticisms and calls for the elimination of the diversity jurisdiction.

Furthermore, *Klaxon* has been applied to a case in which subject-matter jurisdiction is based on diversity of citizenship, but personal jurisdiction is acquired under a federal long-arm statute providing for nationwide service. *See Griffin v. McCoach,* 313 U.S. 498 (1941). It has also been applied to a case in which the state conflict-of-laws rules would select the substantive law of a foreign nation to apply to an action between American citizens when the foreign nation does not have any conceivable interest in having its law applied. *See Day & Zimmermann, Inc. v. Challoner,* 423 U.S. 3 (1975). These cases indicate that the Supreme Court is intent upon applying the *Klaxon* doctrine across the board to all kinds of cases, even ones in which the state in which the federal district court is sitting may not be able to obtain jurisdiction to hear an action in its own courts, or in which it is difficult to see how the state has any policy basis for applying its conflict-of-laws rules to the case. *See also* Caleb Nelson, *A Critical Guide to* Erie Railroad Co. v. Tompkins, 54 WM. & MARY L. REV. 921, 963 (2013) ("unless [the state in which the district court is sitting] has achieved clarity in conflict-of-laws analysis, [*Klaxon*] does not eliminate the need for federal courts to draw murky lines; it simply tells federal courts to try to apply the same murky lines that the state courts would use").

Notes and Questions

1. In *Coca-Cola Co. v. Harmar Bottling Co.*, 218 S.W.3d 671 (Tex. 2006), the plaintiffs sued Coca-Cola in Texas state court under the Texas antitrust statute. Some of the behavior alleged to have violated the statute occurred in Arkansas, Louisiana, and Oklahoma. Therefore, the plaintiffs alleged in the alternative that (1) Texas law governed all behavior wherever it occurred, and (2) that the law of the other states where the behavior occurred was identical to Texas law. The Texas Supreme Court held that the Texas antitrust statute did not authorize the Texas courts to adjudicate and remedy anticompetitive injury occurring in another state. The court further held that Texas courts, as a matter of interstate "comity," would not decide how another state's antitrust laws apply to injuries confined to that state. According to the court, the content of antitrust law was so dependent on the "social needs and values" of each state and so heavily dependent on the policy determinations of other states that it would unduly intrude on the other states' prerogatives to try to interpret their law. Although Coca-Cola had not denied that Texas law and the law of the other states were identical, the court refused to presume that the other states' laws were the same (as it would have done in other cases) for similar reasons.

2. What should a federal diversity court in Texas do with a case identical to *Harmar*? Is it conceivable that *Klaxon* should be interpreted to disable a federal court from applying another state's law because the Texas Supreme Court finds the interpretive difficulties of doing so too great? Or is the Texas Supreme Court's decision in effect announcing a kind of conflict-of-laws rule that federal diversity courts in Texas are obliged to follow?

Section B. Initial Developments after the *Erie* Decision

The *Erie* decision initiated a complicated doctrinal evolution concerning the power of federal courts to create and apply law in a variety of circumstances. Ultimately, the *Erie* doctrine split into two branches. One branch is governed by the Rules of Decision Act, which was the subject of the *Erie* decision. The other branch is governed by the Rules Enabling Act, under which the Federal Rules of Civil Procedure are created. Both branches require the federal courts to draw a distinction between substantive rules of law and procedural rules. Peculiar as it may seem, however, the substantive-procedure distinction may be different under each Act. However, for many years it was unclear that there were two branches of the doctrine. During these years, cases involving the validity of Federal Rules of Civil Procedure were decided interchangeably with cases decided under the Rules of Decision Act and appeared to be governed by the general *Erie* standard. As a result, statements appearing in some older cases involving the validity of Federal Rules of Civil Procedure may actually announce standards that are more pertinent to cases under the Rules of Decision Act.

This section examines the development of the *Erie* doctrine prior to the split, the case that clarified that there were two branches to the doctrine, and the subsequent development of the doctrine within each of its branches. Subsection 1 explores the evolution of the *Erie* doctrine before it split in the case of *Hanna v. Plumer. Hanna* itself is examined in subsection 2, below.

1. Early Post-*Erie* Decisions

Cities Service. In *Cities Service Oil Co. v. Dunlap*, 308 U.S. 208 (1939), decided one year after the *Erie* decision, the Fifth Circuit Court of Appeals held that a federal court in a diversity case was not bound by *Erie* to follow a state burden-of-proof rule in a suit to remove a cloud from a land title, but could instead follow the general equitable rule on burden of proof. The Fifth Circuit considered this a matter of "practice and procedure ... not a matter of substantive law," and thus not controlled by *Erie*. The Supreme Court disagreed, holding that the state burden-of-proof rule involved in the case related "to a substantial right upon which the holder of recorded legal title to Texas land may confidently rely." *See id.* at 212. Thus, the Court seemed to consider the burden of proof rule in the case to be more than a "pure" rule of procedure because it was intertwined with and supported the rights of the legal title holder of land in Texas.

Sibbach. In *Sibbach v. Wilson & Co.*, 312 U.S. 1 (1941), an action was commenced in the U.S. District Court for the Northern District of Illinois in which the plaintiff sought damages for personal injuries received in an automobile accident in Indiana. The district court ordered the plaintiff to submit to a physical examination under Federal Rule 35 to determine the extent of her injuries. The plaintiff refused, and the district court held her in contempt of court and ordered her imprisoned until she complied with the order. The court of appeals affirmed, but the U.S. Supreme Court granted certiorari and reversed.

The Court held that the lower courts had erred in concluding that contempt was an appropriate sanction for refusal to submit to a physical examination, but rejected the plaintiff's challenges to the validity of Rule 35 under the Rules Enabling Act. The Court stated that "substantive rights," within the meaning of the Act, included "rights conferred by the law to be protected and enforced by the adjective law of judicial procedure." *Id.* at 13. "The test" for whether a Federal Rule was valid under the Enabling Act was "whether a rule really regulates procedure — the judicial process for enforcing rights and duties recognized by substantive law and for justly administering remedy and redress for disregard or infraction of them." *Id.* at 14. In effect, the Court in *Sibbach* seemed to divide the universe of laws into two mutually exclusive categories of "substantive rules" and "procedural rules" and imply that if a rule fit into one category it could not also fit within the other.

Palmer. In *Palmer v. Hoffman*, 318 U.S. 109 (1943), in a diversity action for personal injuries, the district court charged the jury that the burden of proof on the issue of contributory negligence was on the defendant. This charge was contrary to state law, which placed the burden of proving freedom from contributory negligence on the plaintiff. On appeal, the plaintiff argued that this charge was correct because Federal Rule 8(c) made contributory negligence a defense. The Supreme Court rejected this argument because Rule 8(c) "concerns only the manner of pleading," not the burden of proof. Citing *Erie* and *Cities Service* as authority, the Court held that "the burden of establishing contributory negligence is a question of local law which federal courts in diversity cases ... must apply." *Id.* at 117.

Guaranty Trust Co. v. York

United States Supreme Court, 1945
326 U.S. 99, 65 S. Ct. 1464, 89 L. Ed. 2d 2079

JUSTICE FRANKFURTER delivered the opinion of the Court.

[Plaintiff filed a class action against Guaranty Trust in federal district court based on diversity of citizenship jurisdiction. Plaintiff's complaint alleged an equitable claim of breach of trust under state law. The federal district court granted summary judgment in favor of the defendant. The court of appeals reversed, holding that in a suit brought on the equity side of a federal court, the court was not obliged to apply the statute of limitations that would govern in the state courts of the same state, even though federal jurisdiction was based exclusively on diversity of citizenship. The Supreme Court reversed. In doing so, Justice Frankfurter announced the so-called "outcome determination" test.]

In exercising their jurisdiction on the ground of diversity of citizenship, the federal courts, in the long course of their history, have not differentiated in their regard for State law between actions at law and suits in equity. Although § 34 of the Judiciary Act of 1789 ... directed that the "laws of the several states ... shall be regarded as rules of decision in trials at common law ..." this was deemed, consistently for over a hundred years, to be merely declaratory of what would in any event have governed the federal courts and therefore was equally applicable to equity suits....

... In giving federal courts "cognizance" of equity suits in cases of diversity jurisdiction, Congress never gave, nor did the federal courts ever claim, the power to deny substantive rights created by State law or to create substantive rights denied by State law.

This does not mean that whatever equitable remedy is available in a State court must be available in a diversity suit in a federal court, or conversely, that a federal court may not afford an equitable remedy not available in a State court. Equitable relief in a federal court is of course subject to restrictions: the suit must be within the traditional scope of equity as historically evolved in the English Court of Chancery ...; a plain, adequate and complete remedy at law must be wanting, § 16, 1 Stat. 73, 82, 28 U.S.C. § 384; explicit Congressional curtailment of equity powers must be respected, *see, e.g.,* Norris-LaGuardia Act, 47 Stat. 70, 29 U.S.C. § 101 *et seq.*; the constitutional right to trial by jury cannot be evaded.... That a State may authorize its courts to give equitable relief unhampered by any or all such restrictions cannot remove these fetters from the federal courts.... State law cannot define the remedies which a federal court must give simply because a federal court in diversity jurisdiction is available as an alternative tribunal to the State's courts. Contrariwise, a federal court may afford an equitable remedy for a substantive right recognized by a State even though a State court cannot give it. Whatever contradiction or confusion may be produced by a medley of judicial phrases severed from their environment, the body of adjudications concerning equitable relief in diversity cases leaves no doubt that the federal courts enforced State-created substantive rights if the mode of proceeding and remedy were consonant with the traditional body of equitable remedies, practice and procedure, and in so doing they were enforcing rights created by the States and not arising under any inherent or statutory federal law.

....

Our starting point [in this case] must be the policy of federal jurisdiction which *Erie Railroad Co. v. Tompkins* ... embodies. In overruling *Swift v. Tyson,* ... *Erie Railroad Co. v. Tompkins* did not merely overrule a venerable case. It overruled a particular way of looking at law which dominated the judicial process long after its inadequacies had been laid bare.... Law was conceived as a "brooding omnipresence" of Reason, of which decisions were merely evidence and not themselves the controlling formulations. Accordingly, federal courts deemed themselves free to ascertain what Reason, and therefore Law, required wholly independent of authoritatively declared State law, even in cases where a legal right as the basis for relief was created by State authority and could not be created by federal authority and the case got into a federal court merely because it was "between Citizens of different States" under Art. III, §2 of the Constitution of the United States.

. . . .

And so this case reduces itself to the narrow question whether, when no recovery could be had in a State court because the action is barred by the statute of limitations, a federal court in equity can take cognizance of the suit because there is diversity of citizenship between the parties. Is the outlawry, according to State law, of a claim created by the States a matter of "substantive rights" to be respected by a federal court of equity when that court's jurisdiction is dependent on the fact that there is a State-created right, or is such statute of "a mere remedial character," ... which a federal court may disregard?

. . . .

Here we are dealing with a right to recover derived not from the United States but from one of the States. When, because the plaintiff happens to be a non-resident, such a right is enforceable in a federal as well as in a State court, the forms and mode of enforcing the right may at times, naturally enough, vary because the two judicial systems are not identic. But since a federal court adjudicating a State-created right solely because of the diversity of citizenship of the parties is for that purpose, in effect, only another court of the State, it cannot afford recovery if the right to recover is made unavailable by the State nor can it substantially affect the enforcement of the right as given by the State.

And so the question is not whether a statute of limitations is deemed a matter of "procedure" in some sense. The question is whether such a statute concerns merely the manner and the means by which a right to recover, as recognized by the State, is enforced, or whether such statutory limitation is a matter of substance in the aspect that alone is relevant to our problem, namely, does it significantly affect the result of a litigation for a federal court to disregard a law of a State that would be controlling in an action upon the same claim by the same parties in a State court?

It is therefore immaterial whether statutes of limitation are characterized either as "substantive" or "procedural" in State court opinions in any use of those terms unrelated to the specific issue before us. *Erie Railroad Co. v. Tompkins* was not an endeavor to formulate scientific legal terminology. It expressed a policy that touches vitally the proper distribution of judicial power between State and federal courts. In essence, the intent of that decision was to insure that, in all cases where a federal court is exercising jurisdiction solely because of the diversity of citizenship of the parties, the outcome of the litigation in the federal court should be substantially the same, so far as legal rules determine the outcome of a litigation, as it would be if tried in a State court. The nub of the policy that underlies *Erie Railroad Co. v. Tompkins* is that for the same transaction the accident of a suit by a non-resident litigant in a federal court instead of in a State court a block away should not lead to a substantially different result. And so, putting to one side abstractions regarding "substance" and "procedure," we have held that in diversity cases the federal courts must follow the law of the State as to burden of proof, *Cities Service Oil Co. v. Dunlap*, ... as to conflict of laws, ... *Klaxon Co. v. Stentor Elec. Mfg. Co.*, ... as to contributory negligence, *Palmer v. Hoffman*, ... *Erie Railroad Co. v. Tompkins* has been applied with an eye alert to essentials in avoiding disregard of State law in diversity cases in the federal courts. A policy so important to our federalism must be kept free from entanglements with analytical or terminological niceties.

Plainly enough, a statute that would completely bar recovery in a suit if brought in a State court bears on a State-created right vitally and not merely formally or negligibly. As to consequences that so intimately affect recovery or non-recovery a federal court in a diversity case should follow State law.... The fact that under New York law a statute of limitations might be lengthened or shortened, that a security may be foreclosed though the debt be barred, that a barred debt may be used as a set-off, are all matters of local law properly to be respected by federal courts sitting in New York when their incidence comes into play there. Such particular rules of local law, however, do not in the slightest change the crucial consideration that if a plea of the statute of limitations would bar recovery in a State court, a federal court ought not to afford recovery.

Prior to *Erie Railroad Co. v. Tompkins* it was not necessary, as we have indicated, to make the critical analysis required by the doctrine of that case of the nature of jurisdiction of the federal courts in diversity cases. But even before *Erie Railroad Co. v. Tompkins*, federal courts relied on statutes of limitations of the States in which they sat. In suits at law State limitations statutes were held to be "rules of decision" within § 34 of the Judiciary Act of 1789 and as such applied in "trials at common law." ... While there was talk of freedom of equity from such State statutes of limitations, the cases generally refused recovery where suit was barred in a like situation in the State courts, even if only by way of analogy.... However in *Kirby v. Lake Shore & M.S. Railroad Co.*, 120 U.S. 130 (1887), the Court disregarded a State statute of limitations where the Court deemed it inequitable to apply it.

To make an exception to *Erie Railroad Co. v. Tompkins* on the equity side of a federal court is to reject the considerations of policy which, after long travail, led to that decision. Judge Augustus N. Hand thus summarized below the fatal objection to such inroad upon *Erie Railroad Co. v. Tompkins*: "In my opinion it would be a mischievous practice to disregard state statutes of limitation whenever federal courts think that the result of adopting them may be inequitable. Such procedure would promote the choice of United States rather than of state courts in order to gain the advantage of different laws. The main foundation for the criticism of *Swift v. Tyson* was that a litigant in cases where federal jurisdiction is based only on diverse citizenship may obtain a more favorable decision by suing in the United States courts." ...

Diversity jurisdiction is founded on assurance to nonresident litigants of courts free from susceptibility to potential local bias. The Framers of the Constitution, according to Marshall, entertained "apprehensions" lest distant suitors be subjected to local bias in State courts, or, at least, viewed with "indulgence the possible fears and apprehensions" of such suitors.... And so Congress afforded out-of-State litigants another tribunal, not another body of law. The operation of a double system of conflicting laws in the same State is plainly hostile to the reign of law. Certainly, the fortuitous circumstance of residence out of a State of one of the parties to a litigation ought not to give rise to a discrimination against others equally concerned but locally resident. The source of substantive rights enforced by a federal court under diversity jurisdiction, it cannot be said too often, is the law of the States. Whenever that law is authoritatively declared by a State, whether its voice be the legislature or its highest court, such law ought to govern in litigation founded on that law, whether the forum of application is a State or a federal court and whether the remedies be sought at law or may be had in equity.

Dicta may be cited characterizing equity as an independent body of law. To the extent that we have indicated, it is. But insofar as these general observations go beyond that, they merely reflect notions that have been replaced by a sharper analysis of what federal courts do when they enforce rights that have no federal origin. And so, before the true source of law that is applied by the federal courts under diversity jurisdiction was fully explored, some things were said that would not now be said. But nothing that was decided, unless it be the *Kirby* case, needs to be rejected.

The judgment is reversed and the case is remanded for proceedings not inconsistent with this opinion.

So ordered.

Justice Roberts and Justice Douglas took no part in the consideration or decision of this case. [The dissenting opinion of Justice Rutledge, with whom Justice Murphy joined, is omitted.]

Notes and Questions

1. Consider Justice Frankfurter's statement in *Guaranty Trust* concerning the equitable powers of the federal courts after *Erie*. That statement indicates not only that federal courts are restricted in exercising their equitable powers by valid exercises of congressional power, but also that the exercise of their power "must be within the traditional scope of equity as historically evolved in the English Court of Chancery." Is this a constitutional restriction ingrained in Article III of the Constitution? In addition, the opinion states that a federal court may sometimes afford equitable remedies not available in a state court, *Erie* notwithstanding. How does this last statement square with the rest of the opinion and the policies supporting the *Erie* doctrine? Does it square with the modern understanding of the relationship between rights and remedies? *See* Teply & Whitten at 480–83.

2. Since *Guaranty Trust*, the Supreme Court has not clarified the statements about federal equity power in the preceding note. However, in *Grupo Mexicano de Desarrollo, S.A. v. Alliance Bond Fund, Inc.*, 527 U.S. 308 (1999), the Supreme Court held that federal district courts do not have the power under Rule 65 of the Federal Rules of Civil Procedure to issue preliminary injunctions to prevent a defendant from disposing of its assets before the plaintiff has obtained a judgment from the defendant "fixing the debt." The Court noted that this was not historically part of the power possessed by equity at the time the federal courts first obtained jurisdiction over equity cases in the Judiciary Act of 1789. The merger of law and equity by the Federal Rules of Civil Procedure had not enlarged the equity power, the Court reasoned, because the historical restriction on equity's power to issue this type of injunction, while partly procedural, was also partly substantive, and the Rules Enabling Act preserved substantive rights from abridgement or enlargement by the Federal Rules. Later, the Court indicated that whether the federal courts should have this power should be decided by Congress. *See id.* at 333.

3. Does the Court's statement in *Grupo* about the power of Congress indicate that the dictum in *Erie* about the power of Congress is now dead? That is, the contract rights in *Grupo* were substantive rights conferred by state or foreign law, not by federal law. Any restriction on the ability to enjoin the defendant would have to be part of those rights, as the Court described them, would it not? If the *Erie* dictum about Congress's inability to declare "substantive rules of common law within a state" means anything, how could Congress modify the rights in *Grupo* with a federal procedural rule, even an equitable

one? What source of authority would Congress have to enact such a rule, assuming that it would only apply in federal court?

4. Compare Justice Frankfurter's discussion of the limits of the federal equity power in *Guaranty Trust* with the Court's statement in *Grupo* that the power to issue the preliminary injunction requested there was not historically part of the power of equity in 1789. Is this the same as Justice Frankfurter's statement that to be valid "the suit must be within the traditional scope of equity as historically evolved in the English Court of Chancery"? Do either or both of these statements mean that if an equitable remedy was not within the traditional equity power when the Constitution was adopted, it would be unconstitutional for federal courts to issue the remedy today? If so, how could Congress authorize the remedy as the Court in *Grupo* suggested?

Problems

Problem 5-1. *P*, a citizen of State *X*, sues *D*, a citizen of State *Y*, in a U.S. District Court in State *Y*. *P* seeks to enjoin *D* from trespassing on *P's* land in State *Y*. Under the law of State *Y*, an injunction would not be available under the circumstances of *P's* case because the State *Y* Legislature has forbidden such injunctions by statute. Under general equitable principles followed by the federal courts prior to *Erie* and the merger of law and equity by the Federal Rules of Civil Procedure, an injunction would be available. In addition, these "federal" equitable principles would still be followed today if *P's* case were based on federal law. However, assume that *P's* substantive property rights are governed exclusively by state law and that *P's* claim does not "arise under federal law" for purposes of the federal question jurisdiction of the district courts. In *P's* diversity action, does *Erie* require the U.S. District Court to follow the state statute forbidding the injunction, or can the court apply general federal equitable principles to the case and grant the injunction? In answering this question, be sure to consider whether the disregard of the state statute would cause forum shopping or discrimination against a citizen of the forum state.

Problem 5-2. On the facts of *Problem 5-1*, assume that federal equitable principles would forbid the injunction, while state law would require that it be granted. Should the U.S. District Court follow federal equitable principles or state law under these circumstances? Assume that you conclude that the *Erie* doctrine does not require the application of state law on these facts. Should any other federal policies forbid the U.S. District Court from disregarding state law?

Murphree. In *Mississippi Publishing Corp. v. Murphree*, 326 U.S. 438 (1946), the defendant challenged the validity of original Federal Rule 4(f) under the "substantive rights" restriction of the Rules Enabling Act. Rule 4(f) expanded the ability of the district court to serve process from only within the limits of the district to the entire state in which the district court was sitting. The Court upheld the validity of Rule 4(f), stating that the substantive rights restriction was not aimed at "such incidental effects as necessarily attend the adoption of the prescribed new rules of procedure upon the rights of litigants who, agreeably to rules of practice and procedure, have been brought before a court authorized to determine their rights." *Id.* at 445. The effect of Rule 4(f) was to allow a district court sitting in one district of a state to serve process on a defendant located in another district of the same state. Consequently, a court that would have been powerless to adjudicate before Rule 4(f) came into existence could now adjudicate the defendant's rights. However, the Supreme Court stated that this expansion would "not operate to abridge, enlarge, or modify the rules of decision by which [the district court] will adjudicate" the defendant's rights. Thus, the rule related only to the manner and means by which a right to recover was enforced. *See id.* at 446. The Court cited *Guaranty Trust* as authority for sustaining Rule 4(f).[a]

Ragan. In *Ragan v. Merchants Transfer & Warehouse Co.*, 337 U.S. 530 (1949), the Court confronted an apparent conflict between Rule 3 of the Federal Rules of Civil Procedure, which provides that an action is commenced by filing a complaint with the court, and a Kansas statute that required commencement of an action by service of process in order to toll the statute of limitations. The Court held that the Kansas statute had to be applied in a federal diversity action. Without ever specifying whether Federal Rule 3 was or was not applicable to the case, the Court resorted to the *Erie-Guaranty Trust* line of cases to analyze the issue before it. *See id.* at 532–34.

Woods. In *Woods v. Interstate Realty Co.*, 337 U.S. 535 (1949), the Supreme Court was confronted with a Mississippi statute that closed the doors of the state's courts to foreign corporations that failed to qualify under state law to do business within the state. The Court held that such statutes were obligatory on the federal courts after *Erie* and *Guaranty Trust*.

Cohen. In *Cohen v. Beneficial Industrial Loan Corp.*, 337 U.S. 541 (1949), a state statute provided that, in stockholder derivative actions, a plaintiff owning less than 5% of the par value of the corporation's outstanding shares had to provide security for the reasonable expenses, including attorney's fees, that the corporation might incur in its successful defense of the action. The plaintiff contended that Rule 23 of the Federal Rules of Civil Procedure (current Rule 23.1) governed and contained no such security-for-expenses requirement. The Court specifically held that Rule 23, which did not address security for expenses, was not in conflict with the state law. *See id.* at 556. However, the dissenters considered Federal Rule 23 to be applicable to the case. *See id.* at 557–61 (Douglas, J. & Frankfurter, J., dissenting). Both the majority and the dissenters seemed to consider the *Erie-Guaranty Trust* line of cases to be the only relevant precedents.

Bernhardt. In *Bernhardt v. Polygraphic Co. of America*, 350 U.S. 198 (1956), the Court applied the outcome determinative test to a contract provision requiring arbitration of disputes under the contract. It held that the outcome might be substantially changed if the clause would be held invalid and arbitration disallowed by a state court but ordered by a federal court in a diversity action. *Id.* at 202–04.

Byrd. In *Byrd v. Blue Ridge Rural Electric Cooperative, Inc.*, 356 U.S. 525 (1958), the Supreme Court appeared to mitigate the effect of the "outcome determination test" announced by Justice Frankfurter in *Guaranty Trust Co. v. York*, 326 U.S. 99 (1945).

Byrd v. Blue Ridge Rural Electric Cooperative, Inc.

United States Supreme Court, 1958
356 U.S. 525, 78 S. Ct. 893, 2 L. Ed. 2d 953

Justice Brennan delivered the opinion of the Court.

[The plaintiff was employed as a lineman in the construction crew of a construction contractor. The plaintiff was injured while connecting power lines. The plaintiff commenced a diversity action in federal district court in South Carolina for damages for in-

---

a. [Eds. Note. The provisions governing the territorial limits of effective service are now contained in current Rule 4(k).]

juries allegedly caused by the defendant's negligence. One of defendant's affirmative defenses was that, under the South Carolina Workmen's Compensation Act, the plaintiff had the status of a "statutory employee" and was, therefore, barred from suing the respondent at law because the plaintiff was obliged to accept statutory compensation benefits as the exclusive remedy for the plaintiff's injuries. The plaintiff obtained judgment on a jury verdict. The Court of Appeals for the Fourth Circuit reversed and directed the entry of judgment for the defendant. One issue on review before the U.S. Supreme Court was whether the plaintiff, state practice notwithstanding, was entitled to a jury determination of the factual issues raised by the "statutory employee" defense.]

A question is ... presented as to whether on remand the factual issue is to be decided by the judge or by the jury. The respondent argues on the basis of the decision of the Supreme Court of South Carolina in *Adams v. Davison-Paxon Co.*, 96 S.E.2d 566 (S.C. 1957), that the issue of immunity should be decided by the judge and not by the jury. That was a negligence action brought in the state trial court against a store owner by an employee of an independent contractor who operated the store's millinery department. The trial judge denied the store owner's motion for a directed verdict made upon the ground that §72-111 barred the plaintiff's action. The jury returned a verdict for the plaintiff. The South Carolina Supreme Court reversed, holding that it was for the judge and not the jury to decide on the evidence whether the owner was a statutory employer, and that the store owner had sustained his defense....

....

First. It was decided in *Erie Railroad Co. v. Tompkins* that the federal courts in diversity cases must respect the definition of state-created rights and obligations by the state courts. We must, therefore, first examine the rule in *Adams v. Davison-Paxon Co.* to determine whether it is bound up with these rights and obligations in such a way that its application in the federal court is required. *Cities Service Oil Co. v. Dunlap....*

The Workmen's Compensation Act is administered in South Carolina by its Industrial Commission. The South Carolina courts hold that, on judicial review of actions of the Commission under §72-111, the question whether the claim of an injured workman is within the Commission's jurisdiction is a matter of law for decision by the court, which makes its own findings of fact relating to that jurisdiction. The South Carolina Supreme Court states no reasons in *Adams v. Davison-Paxon Co.* why, although the jury decides all other factual issues raised by the cause of action and defenses, the jury is displaced as to the factual issue raised by the affirmative defense under §72-111.... A State may, of course, distribute the functions of its judicial machinery as it sees fit. The decisions relied upon, however, furnish no reason for selecting the judge rather than the jury to decide this single affirmative defense in the negligence action. They simply reflect a policy ... that administrative determination of "jurisdictional facts" should not be final but subject to judicial review. The conclusion is inescapable that the *Adams* holding is grounded in the practical consideration that the question had theretofore come before the South Carolina courts from the Industrial Commission and the courts had become accustomed to deciding the factual issue of immunity without the aid of juries. We find nothing to suggest that this rule was announced as an integral part of the special relationship created by the statute. Thus the requirement appears to be merely a form and mode of enforcing the immunity, *Guaranty Trust Co. v. York* ... and not a rule intended to be bound up with the definition of the rights and obligations of the parties....

Second. But cases following *Erie* have evinced a broader policy to the effect that the federal courts should conform as near as may be — in the absence of other considerations—to state rules even of form and mode where the state rules may bear substantially on the question whether the litigation would come out one way in the federal court and another way in the state court if the federal court failed to apply a particular local rule. *E.g., Guaranty Trust Co. v. York*.... Concededly the nature of the tribunal which tries issues may be important in the enforcement of the parcel of rights making up a cause of action or defense, and bear significantly upon achievement of uniform enforcement of the right. It may well be that in the instant personal-injury case the outcome would be substantially affected by whether the issue of immunity is decided by a judge or a jury. Therefore, were "outcome" the only consideration, a strong case might appear for saying that the federal court should follow the state practice.

But there are affirmative countervailing considerations at work here. The federal system is an independent system for administering justice to litigants who properly invoke its jurisdiction. An essential characteristic of that system is the manner in which, in civil common-law actions, it distributes trial functions between judge and jury and, under the influence—if not the command[10]—of the Seventh Amendment, assigns the decisions of disputed questions of fact to the jury.... The policy of uniform enforcement of state-created rights and obligations ... cannot in every case exact compliance with a state rule[12]—not bound up with rights and obligations—which disrupts the federal system of allocating functions between judge and jury.... Thus the inquiry here is whether the federal policy favoring jury decisions of disputed fact questions should yield to the state rule in the interest of furthering the objective that the litigation should not come out one way in the federal court and another way in the state court.

We think that in the circumstances of this case the federal court should not follow the state rule. It cannot be gainsaid that there is a strong federal policy against allowing state rules to disrupt the judge-jury relationship in the federal courts. In *Herron v. Southern Pacific Co.*, 283 U.S. 91 (1931), the trial judge in a personal-injury negligence action brought in the District Court for Arizona on diversity grounds directed a verdict for the defendant when it appeared as a matter of law that the plaintiff was guilty of contributory negligence. The federal judge refused to be bound by a provision of the Arizona Constitution which made the jury the sole arbiter of the question of contributory negligence. This Court sustained the action of the trial judge, holding that "state laws cannot alter the essential character or function of a federal court" because that function "is not in any sense a local matter, and state statutes which would interfere with the appropriate performance of that function are not binding upon the federal court under either the Conformity Act or the 'rules of decision' Act." ... Perhaps even more clearly in light of the influence of the Seventh Amendment, the function assigned to the jury "is an essential factor in the process for which the Federal Constitution provides." ... Concededly the *Herron* case was decided before *Erie Railroad Co. v. Tompkins*, but even when *Swift v. Tyson* ... was governing law and allowed federal courts sitting in diversity cases to disregard state decisional law, it was never thought that state statutes or constitutions were similarly to be disregarded.... Yet *Herron* held that state statutes and constitutional provisions could not disrupt or alter the essential character or function of a federal court.

---

10. Our conclusion makes unnecessary the consideration of—and we intimate no view upon—the constitutional question whether the right of jury trial protected in federal courts by the Seventh Amendment embraces the factual issue of statutory immunity when asserted, as here, as an affirmative defense in a common-law negligence action.

12. This Court held in *Sibbach v. Wilson & Co.*, 312 U.S. 1 (1941), that Federal Rule of Civil Procedure 35 should prevail over a contrary state rule.

Third. We have discussed the problem upon the assumption that the outcome of the litigation may be substantially affected by whether the issue of immunity is decided by a judge or a jury. But clearly there is not present here the certainty that a different result would follow ... or even the strong possibility that this would be the case.... There are factors present here which might reduce that possibility. The trial judge in the federal system has powers denied the judges of many States to comment on the weight of evidence and credibility of witnesses, and discretion to grant a new trial if the verdict appears to him to be against the weight of the evidence. We do not think the likelihood of a different result is so strong as to require the federal practice of jury determination of disputed factual issues to yield to the state rule in the interest of uniformity of outcome.

The Court of Appeals did not consider other grounds of appeal raised by the respondent because the ground taken disposed of the case. We accordingly remand the case to the Court of Appeals for the decision of the other questions, with instructions that, if not made unnecessary by the decision of such questions, the Court of Appeals shall remand the case to the District Court for a new trial of such issues as the Court of Appeals may direct.

Reversed and remanded.

[The dissenting opinions of Justices WHITTAKER, FRANKFURTER, and HARLAN are omitted.]

Van Dusen. In 1964, in *Van Dusen v. Barrack*, 376 U.S. 612 (1964), the Court held that when a transfer of venue under § 1404(a) is made on the defendant's motion, the transferee district court must apply the conflict-of-laws rules of the transferor state in determining which state's substantive law should be applied in the case. This decision purported to be based, in part, on a desire to establish a rule that would not undermine the *Erie* policies. In *Van Dusen*, the Court stated:

> Although we deal here with a congressional statute apportioning the business of the federal courts, our interpretation of that statute fully accords with and is supported by the policy underlying *Erie Railroad Co. v. Tompkins*.... This Court has often formulated the *Erie* doctrine by stating that it establishes "the principle of uniformity within a state," *Klaxon Co. v. Stentor Elec. Mfg. Co*.... and declaring that federal courts in diversity of citizenship cases are to apply the laws "of the state in which they sit," *Griffin v. McCoach*.... A superficial reading of these formulations might suggest that a transferee federal court should apply the law of the State in which it sits rather than the law of the transferor State. Such a reading, however, directly contradicts the fundamental *Erie* doctrine which the quoted formulations were designed to express. As this Court said in *Guaranty Trust v. York*, ... The nub of the policy that underlies *Erie Railroad Co. v. Tompkins* ... is that for the same transaction the accident of a suit by a non-resident litigant in a federal court instead of in a State court a block away should not lead to a substantially different result.

> Applying this analysis to § 1404(a), we should ensure that the "accident" of federal diversity jurisdiction does not enable a party to utilize a transfer to achieve a result in federal court which could not have been achieved in the courts of the State where the action was filed. This purpose would be defeated in cases such as the present if nonresident defendants, properly subjected to suit in the transferor State (Pennsylvania) could invoke § 1404(a) to gain the benefits of the laws of another jurisdiction (Massachusetts)....

Id. at 637–38.

However, the Court made it clear that the applicable law after transfer can be taken into account in determining whether transfer will be convenient. For example, if the transferor state's choice-of-law rules would dictate that the transferee state's substantive law be applied to the dispute, that is one factor weighing in favor of transferring the case, since the transferee court will presumably be more familiar with the transferee state's substantive law than the transferor court. On the other hand, if the transferor state's choice-of-law rules dictate that the transferor state's substantive law should be applied to the case, that is one factor weighing against transfer because the transferee court will presumably be less familiar with that law than the transferor court. Note, however, that the simplicity or complexity of the applicable substantive law, as well as whether it is settled or unsettled, will have an important impact on how strongly the choice-of-law issue bears on the transfer decision.

2. The Branching of the *Erie* Doctrine

Hanna v. Plumer

United States Supreme Court, 1965
380 U.S. 460, 85 S. Ct. 1136, 14 L. Ed. 2d 8

CHIEF JUSTICE WARREN delivered the opinion of the Court.

The question to be decided is whether, in a civil action where the jurisdiction of the United States district court is based upon diversity of citizenship between the parties, service of process shall be made in the manner prescribed by state law or that set forth in Rule 4(d)(1) of the Federal Rules of Civil Procedure.

On February 6, 1963, petitioner, a citizen of Ohio, filed her complaint in the District Court for the District of Massachusetts, claiming damages in excess of $10,000 for personal injuries resulting from an automobile accident in South Carolina, allegedly caused by the negligence of one Louise Plumer Osgood, a Massachusetts citizen deceased at the time of the filing of the complaint. Respondent, Mrs. Osgood's executor and also a Massachusetts citizen, was named as defendant. On February 8, service was made by leaving copies of the summons and the complaint with respondent's wife at his residence, concededly in compliance with Rule 4(d)(1), which provides:

> The summons and complaint shall be served together. The plaintiff shall furnish the person making service with such copies as are necessary. Service shall be made as follows:
>
> (1) Upon an individual other than an infant or an incompetent person, by delivering a copy of the summons and of the complaint to him personally or by leaving copies thereof at his dwelling house or usual place of abode with some person of suitable age and discretion then residing therein....[a]

Respondent filed his answer on February 26, alleging, *inter alia*, that the action could not be maintained because it had been brought "contrary to and in violation of the provisions of Massachusetts General Laws (Ter. Ed.) Chapter 197, Section 9." That section provides:

> Except as provided in this chapter, an executor or administrator shall not be held to answer to an action by a creditor of the deceased which is not commenced

---

a. [Eds. Note. The service provision quoted above, which at the time of the *Hanna* decision was set forth in Rule 4(d)(1), is now set forth in current Rule 4(e)(2)(A) and (B).]

within one year from the time of his giving bond for the performance of his trust, or to such an action which is commenced within said year unless before the expiration thereof the writ in such action has been served by delivery in hand upon such executor or administrator or service thereof accepted by him or a notice stating the name of the estate, the name and address of the creditor, the amount of the claim and the court in which the action has been brought has been filed in the proper registry of probate....

Mass. Gen. Laws Ann., ch. 197, §9 (1958). On October 17, 1963, the District Court granted respondent's motion for summary judgment, citing *Ragan v. Merchants Transfer Co.*... and *Guaranty Trust Co. v. York* ... in support of its conclusion that the adequacy of the service was to be measured by §9, with which, the court held, petitioner had not complied. On appeal, petitioner admitted noncompliance with §9, but argued that Rule 4(d)(1) defines the method by which service of process is to be effected in diversity actions. The Court of Appeals for the First Circuit, finding that "[r]elatively recent amendments [to §9] evince a clear legislative purpose to require personal notification within the year,"[1] concluded that the conflict of state and federal rules was over "a substantive rather than a procedural matter," and unanimously affirmed.... Because of the threat to the goal of uniformity of federal procedure posed by the decision below, we granted certiorari....

We conclude that the adoption of Rule 4(d)(1), designed to control service of process in diversity actions, neither exceeded the congressional mandate embodied in the Rules Enabling Act nor transgressed constitutional bounds, and that the Rule is therefore the standard against which the District Court should have measured the adequacy of the service. Accordingly, we reverse the decision of the Court of Appeals.

The Rules Enabling Act, 28 U.S.C. §2072 (1958 ed.), provides, in pertinent part:

> The Supreme Court shall have the power to prescribe, by general rules, the forms of process, writs, pleadings, and motions, and the practice and procedure of the district courts of the United States in civil actions.

> Such rules shall not abridge, enlarge or modify any substantive right and shall preserve the right of trial by jury....

Under the cases construing the scope of the Enabling Act, Rule 4(d)(1) clearly passes muster. Prescribing the manner in which a defendant is to be notified that a suit has been instituted against him, it relates to the "practice and procedure of the district courts." ...

---

1. Section 9 is in part a statute of limitations, providing that an executor need not "answer to an action ... which is not commenced within one year from the time of his giving bond...." This part of the statute, the purpose of which is to speed the settlement of estates ... is not involved in this case, since the action clearly was timely commenced. (Respondent filed bond on March 1, 1962; the complaint was filed February 6, 1963; and the service — the propriety of which is in dispute — was made on February 8, 1963.) ...

Section 9 also provides for the manner of service. Generally, service of process must be made by "delivery in hand," although there are two alternatives: acceptance of service by the executor, or filing of a notice of claim, the components of which are set out in the statute, in the appropriate probate court. The purpose of this part of the statute, which is involved here, is, as the court below noted, to insure that executors will receive actual notice of claims.... Actual notice is of course also the goal of Rule 4(d)(1); however, the Federal Rule reflects a determination that this goal can be achieved by a method less cumbersome than that prescribed in §9. In this case the goal seems to have been achieved; although the affidavit filed by respondent in the District Court asserts that he had not been served in hand nor had he accepted service, it does not allege lack of actual notice.

The test must be whether a rule really regulates procedure, — the judicial process for enforcing rights and duties recognized by substantive law and for justly administering remedy and redress for disregard or infraction of them.

Sibbach v. Wilson & Co.... In *Mississippi Publishing Corp. v. Murphree* ... this Court upheld Rule 4(f), which permits service of a summons anywhere within the State (and not merely the district) in which a district court sits:

> We think that Rule 4(f) is in harmony with the Enabling Act.... Undoubtedly most alterations of the rules of practice and procedure may and often do affect the rights of litigants. Congress' prohibition of any alteration of substantive rights of litigants was obviously not addressed to such incidental effects as necessarily attend the adoption of the prescribed new rules of procedure upon the rights of litigants who, agreeably to rules of practice and procedure, have been brought before a court authorized to determine their rights. *Sibbach v. Wilson & Co.*... The fact that the application of Rule 4(f) will operate to subject petitioner's rights to adjudication by the district court for northern Mississippi will undoubtedly affect those rights. But it does not operate to abridge, enlarge or modify the rules of decision by which that court will adjudicate its rights....

Thus were there no conflicting state procedure, Rule 4(d)(1) would clearly control.... However, respondent, focusing on the contrary Massachusetts rule, calls to the Court's attention another line of cases, a line which — like the Federal Rules — had its birth in 1938. *Erie Railroad Co. v. Tompkins* ... held that federal courts sitting in diversity cases, when deciding questions of "substantive" law, are bound by state court decisions as well as state statutes. The broad command of *Erie* was therefore identical to that of the Enabling Act: federal courts are to apply state substantive law and federal procedural law. However, as subsequent cases sharpened the distinction between substance and procedure, the line of cases following *Erie* diverged markedly from the line construing the Enabling Act. *Guaranty Trust Co. v. York* ... made it clear that *Erie*-type problems were not to be solved by reference to any traditional or common-sense substance-procedure distinction:

> And so the question is not whether a statute of limitations is deemed a matter of "procedure" in some sense. The question is ... does it significantly affect the result of a litigation for a federal court to disregard a law of a State that would be controlling in an action upon the same claim by the same parties in a State court? ...[5]

Respondent, by placing primary reliance on *York* and *Ragan*, suggests that the *Erie* doctrine acts as a check on the Federal Rules of Civil Procedure, that despite the clear command of Rule 4(d)(1), *Erie* and its progeny demand the application of the Massachusetts rule. Reduced to essentials, the argument is: (1) *Erie*, as refined in *York*, demands that federal courts apply state law whenever application of federal law in its stead will alter the outcome of the case. (2) In this case, a determination that the Massachusetts service requirements obtain will result in immediate victory for respondent. If, on the other hand, it should be held that Rule 4(d)(1) is applicable, the litigation will continue, with possible victory for petitioner. (3) Therefore, *Erie* demands application of the Massachusetts rule. The syllogism possesses an appealing simplicity, but is for several reasons invalid.

In the first place, it is doubtful that, even if there were no Federal Rule making it clear that in-hand service is not required in diversity actions, the *Erie* rule would have oblig-

---

5. *See also Ragan v. Merchants Transfer Co.* ...; *Woods v. Interstate Realty Co.* ...; *Bernhardt v. Polygraphic Co. of Am.* ...; *cf. Byrd v. Blue Ridge Rural Elec. Cooperative.* ...

ated the District Court to follow the Massachusetts procedure. "Outcome-determination" analysis was never intended to serve as a talisman.... Indeed, the message of *York* itself is that choices between state and federal law are to be made not by application of any automatic, "litmus paper" criterion, but rather by reference to the policies underlying the *Erie* rule....

The *Erie* rule is rooted in part in a realization that it would be unfair for the character or result of a litigation materially to differ because the suit had been brought in a federal court.... The [*Erie*] decision was also in part a reaction to the practice of "forum-shopping" which had grown up in response to the rule of *Swift v. Tyson*.... That the *York* test was an attempt to effectuate these policies is demonstrated by the fact that the opinion framed the inquiry in terms of "substantial" variations between state and federal litigation.... Not only are nonsubstantial, or trivial, variations not likely to raise the sort of equal protection problems which troubled the Court in *Erie*; they are also unlikely to influence the choice of a forum. The "outcome-determination" test therefore cannot be read without reference to the twin aims of the *Erie* rule: discouragement of forum-shopping and avoidance of inequitable administration of the laws.[9]

The difference between the conclusion that the Massachusetts rule is applicable, and the conclusion that it is not, is of course at this point "outcome-determinative" in the sense that if we hold the state rule to apply, respondent prevails, whereas if we hold that Rule 4(d)(1) governs, the litigation will continue. But in this sense *every* procedural variation is "outcome-determinative." For example, having brought suit in a federal court, a plaintiff cannot then insist on the right to file subsequent pleadings in accord with the time limits applicable in the state courts, even though enforcement of the federal timetable will, if he continues to insist that he must meet only the state time limit, result in determination of the controversy against him. So it is here. Though choice of the federal or state rule will at this point have a marked effect upon the outcome of the litigation, the difference between the two rules would be of scant, if any, relevance to the choice of a forum. Petitioner, in choosing her forum, was not presented with a situation where application of the state rule would wholly bar recovery;[10] rather, adherence to the state rule would have resulted only in altering the way in which process was served. Moreover, it is difficult to argue that permitting service of defendant's wife to take the place of in-hand service of defendant himself alters the mode of enforcement of state-created rights in a fashion suf-

---

9. The Court of Appeals seemed to frame the inquiry in terms of how "important" §9 is to the State. In support of its suggestion that §9 serves some interest the State regards as vital to its citizens, the court noted that something like §9 has been on the books in Massachusetts a long time, that §9 has been amended a number of times, and that §9 is designed to make sure that executors receive actual notice. *See* note 1, *supra.* The apparent lack of relation among these three observations is not surprising, because it is not clear to what sort of question the Court of Appeals was addressing itself. One cannot meaningfully ask how important something is without first asking "important for what purpose?" *Erie* and its progeny make clear that when a federal court sitting in a diversity case is faced with a question of whether or not to apply state law, the importance of a state rule is indeed relevant, but only in the context of asking whether application of the rule would make so important a difference to the character or result of the litigation that failure to enforce it would unfairly discriminate against citizens of the forum State, or whether application of the rule would have so important an effect upon the fortunes of one or both of the litigants that failure to enforce it would be likely to cause a plaintiff to choose the federal court.

10. *See Guaranty Trust Co. v. York* ...; *Ragan v. Merchants Transfer Co.* ...; *Woods v. Interstate Realty Co.* ...

Similarly, a federal court's refusal to enforce the New Jersey rule involved in *Cohen v. Beneficial Indus. Loan Corp.* ... requiring the posting of security by plaintiffs in stockholders' derivative actions, might well impel a stockholder to choose to bring suit in the federal, rather than the state, court.

ficiently "substantial" to raise the sort of equal protection problems to which the *Erie* opinion alluded.

There is, however, a more fundamental flaw in respondent's syllogism: the incorrect assumption that the rule of *Erie Railroad Co. v. Tompkins* constitutes the appropriate test of the validity and therefore the applicability of a Federal Rule of Civil Procedure. The *Erie* rule has never been invoked to void a Federal Rule. It is true that there have been cases where this Court has held applicable a state rule in the face of an argument that the situation was governed by one of the Federal Rules. But the holding of each such case was not that *Erie* commanded displacement of a Federal Rule by an inconsistent state rule, but rather that the scope of the Federal Rule was not as broad as the losing party urged, and therefore, there being no Federal Rule which covered the point in dispute, *Erie* commanded the enforcement of state law.

> Respondent contends, in the first place, that the charge was correct because of the fact that Rule 8(c) of the Rules of Civil Procedure makes contributory negligence an affirmative defense. We do not agree. Rule 8(c) covers only the manner of pleading. The question of the burden of establishing contributory negligence is a question of local law which federal courts in diversity of citizenship cases ... must apply.

Palmer v. Hoffman....[12] (Here, of course, the clash is unavoidable; Rule 4(d)(1) says — implicitly, but with unmistakable clarity — that in-hand service is not required in federal courts.) At the same time, in cases adjudicating the validity of Federal Rules, we have not applied the *York* rule or other refinements of *Erie*, but have to this day continued to decide questions concerning the scope of the Enabling Act and the constitutionality of specific Federal Rules in light of the distinction set forth in *Sibbach....*

Nor has the development of two separate lines of cases been inadvertent. The line between "substance" and "procedure" shifts as the legal context changes. "Each implies different variables depending upon the particular problem for which it is used." ... It is true that both the Enabling Act and the *Erie* rule say, roughly, that federal courts are to apply state "substantive" law and federal "procedural" law, but from that it need not follow that the tests are identical. For they were designed to control very different sorts of decisions. When a situation is covered by one of the Federal Rules, the question facing the court is a far cry from the typical, relatively unguided *Erie* choice: the court has been instructed to apply the Federal Rule, and can refuse to do so only if the Advisory Committee, this Court, and Congress erred in their prima facie judgment that the Rule in question transgresses neither the terms of the Enabling Act nor constitutional restrictions.

We are reminded by the *Erie* opinion that neither Congress nor the federal courts can, under the guise of formulating rules of decision for federal courts, fashion rules which are not supported by a grant of federal authority contained in Article I or some other section of the Constitution; in such areas state law must govern because there can be no other law. But the opinion in *Erie*, which involved no Federal Rule and dealt with a question which was "substantive" in every traditional sense (whether the railroad owed a duty of care to Tompkins as a trespasser or a licensee), surely neither said nor implied that measures like Rule 4(d)(1) are unconstitutional. For the constitutional provision for a federal court system (augmented by the Necessary and Proper Clause) carries with it congressional power to make rules governing the practice and pleading in those courts, which

---

12. To the same effect, see *Ragan v. Merchants Transfer Co....*; *Cohen v. Beneficial Indus. Loan Corp....*; *cf. Bernhardt v. Polygraphic Co....*

in turn includes a power to regulate matters which, though falling within the uncertain area between substance and procedure, are rationally capable of classification as either.... Neither *York* nor the cases following it ever suggested that the rule there laid down for coping with situations where no Federal Rule applies is coextensive with the limitation on Congress to which *Erie* had adverted. Although this Court has never before been confronted with a case where the applicable Federal Rule is in direct collision with the law of the relevant State,[15] courts of appeals faced with such clashes have rightly discerned the implications of our decisions.

....

Erie and its offspring cast no doubt on the long-recognized power of Congress to prescribe housekeeping rules for federal courts even though some of those rules will inevitably differ from comparable state rules...." When, because the plaintiff happens to be a non-resident, such a right is enforceable in a federal as well as in a State court, the forms and mode of enforcing the right may at times, naturally enough, vary because the two judicial systems are not identic." ... Thus, though a court, in measuring a Federal Rule against the standards contained in the Enabling Act and the Constitution, need not wholly blind itself to the degree to which the Rule makes the character and result of the federal litigation stray from the course it would follow in state courts, *Sibbach v. Wilson & Co.*, 312 U.S. at 13–14, it cannot be forgotten that the *Erie* rule, and the guidelines suggested in *York*, were created to serve another purpose altogether. To hold that a Federal Rule of Civil Procedure must cease to function whenever it alters the mode of enforcing state-created rights would be to disembowel either the Constitution's grant of power over federal procedure or Congress' attempt to exercise that power in the Enabling Act. Rule 4(d)(1) is valid and controls the instant case.

Reversed.

Justice Harlan, concurring.

It is unquestionably true that up to now *Erie* and the cases following it have not succeeded in articulating a workable doctrine governing choice of law in diversity actions. I respect the Court's effort to clarify the situation in today's opinion. However, in doing so I think it has misconceived the constitutional premises of *Erie* and has failed to deal adequately with those past decisions upon which the courts below relied.

Erie was something more than an opinion which worried about "forum-shopping and avoidance of inequitable administration of the laws," ... although to be sure these were important elements of the decision. I have always regarded that decision as one of the modern cornerstones of our federalism, expressing policies that profoundly touch the allocation of judicial power between the state and federal systems. *Erie* recognized that there should not be two conflicting systems of law controlling the primary activity of citizens, for such alternative governing authority must necessarily give rise to a debilitating uncertainty in the planning of everyday affairs.[1] And it recognized that the scheme of our Constitution envisions an allocation of law-making functions between state and federal legislative processes which is undercut if the federal judiciary can make substantive law

---

15. In *Sibbach v. Wilson & Co.*, ... the law of the forum State (Illinois) forbade the sort of order authorized by Rule 35. However, *Sibbach* was decided before *Klaxon Co. v. Stentor Co.*... and the *Sibbach* opinion makes clear that the Court was proceeding on the assumption that if the law of any State was relevant, it was the law of the State where the tort occurred (Indiana), which, like Rule 35, made provision for such orders....

1. Since the rules involved in the present case are parallel rather than conflicting, this first rationale does not come into play here.

affecting state affairs beyond the bounds of congressional legislative powers in this regard. Thus, in diversity cases *Erie* commands that it be the state law governing primary private activity which prevails.

The shorthand formulations which have appeared in some past decisions are prone to carry untoward results that frequently arise from oversimplification. The Court is quite right in stating that the "outcome-determinative" test of *Guaranty Trust Co. v. York*, ... if taken literally, proves too much, for any rule, no matter how clearly "procedural," can affect the outcome of litigation if it is not obeyed. In turning from the "outcome" test of *York* back to the unadorned forum-shopping rationale of *Erie*, however, the Court falls prey to like oversimplification, for a simple forum-shopping rule also proves too much; litigants often choose a federal forum merely to obtain what they consider the advantages of the Federal Rules of Civil Procedure or to try their cases before a supposedly more favorable judge. To my mind the proper line of approach in determining whether to apply a state or a federal rule, whether "substantive" or "procedural," is to stay close to basic principles by inquiring if the choice of rule would substantially affect those primary decisions respecting human conduct which our constitutional system leaves to state regulation.[2] If so, *Erie* and the Constitution require that the state rule prevail, even in the face of a conflicting federal rule.

The Court weakens, if indeed it does not submerge, this basic principle by finding, in effect, a grant of substantive legislative power in the constitutional provision for a federal court system (*cf. Swift v. Tyson*, ... and through it, setting up the Federal Rules as a body of law inviolate.... So long as a reasonable man could characterize any duly adopted federal rule as "procedural," the Court, unless I misapprehend what is said, would have it apply no matter how seriously it frustrated a State's substantive regulation of the primary conduct and affairs of its citizens. Since the members of the Advisory Committee, the Judicial Conference, and this Court who formulated the Federal Rules are presumably reasonable men, it follows that the integrity of the Federal Rules is absolute. Whereas the unadulterated outcome and forum-shopping tests may err too far toward honoring state rules, I submit that the Court's "arguably procedural, *ergo* constitutional" test moves too fast and far in the other direction.

The courts below relied upon this Court's decisions in *Ragan v. Merchants Transfer & Warehouse Co.*... and *Cohen v. Beneficial Industrial Loan Corp.*... Those cases deserve more attention than this Court has given them, particularly *Ragan* which, if still good law, would in my opinion call for affirmance of the result reached by the Court of Appeals. Further, a discussion of these two cases will serve to illuminate the "diversity" thesis I am advocating.

In *Ragan*, a Kansas statute of limitations provided that an action was deemed commenced when service was made on the defendant. Despite Federal Rule 3 which provides that an action commences with the filing of the complaint, the Court held that for purposes of the Kansas statute of limitations a diversity tort action commenced only when service was made upon the defendant. The effect of this holding was that although the plaintiff had filed his federal complaint within the state period of limitations, his action was barred because the federal marshal did not serve a summons on the defendant until after the limitations period had run. I think that the decision was wrong. At most, applica-

---

2. *See* Hart & Wechsler, *The Federal Court and the Federal System* 678. *Byrd v. Blue Ridge Rural Elec. Cooperative, Inc.*... indicated that state procedures would apply if the State had manifested a particularly strong interest in their employment. *Cf. Dice v. Akron, C. & Y.R.R. Co.*, 342 U.S. 359 (1952). However, this approach may not be of constitutional proportions.

tion of the Federal Rule would have meant that potential Kansas tort defendants would have to defer for a few days the satisfaction of knowing that they had not been sued within the limitations period. The choice of the Federal Rule would have had no effect on the primary stages of private activity from which torts arise, and only the most minimal effect on behavior following the commission of the tort. In such circumstances the interest of the federal system in proceeding under its own rules should have prevailed.

Cohen v. Beneficial Indus. Loan Corp. held that a federal diversity court must apply a state statute requiring a small stockholder in a stockholder derivative suit to post a bond securing payment of defense costs as a condition to prosecuting an action. Such a statute is not "outcome determinative"; the plaintiff can win with or without it. The Court now rationalizes the case on the ground that the statute might affect the plaintiff's choice of forum..., but as has been pointed out, a simple forum-shopping test proves too much. The proper view of *Cohen* is in my opinion, that the statute was meant to inhibit small stockholders from instituting "strike suits," and thus it was designed and could be expected to have a substantial impact on private primary activity. Anyone who was at the trial bar during the period when *Cohen* arose can appreciate the strong state policy reflected in the statute. I think it wholly legitimate to view Federal Rule 23 as not purporting to deal with the problem. But even had the Federal Rules purported to do so, and in so doing provided a substantially less effective deterrent to strike suits, I think the state rule should still have prevailed. That is where I believe the Court's view differs from mine; for the Court attributes such overriding force to the Federal Rules that it is hard to think of a case where a conflicting state rule would be allowed to operate, even though the state rule reflected policy considerations which, under *Erie*, would lie within the realm of state legislative authority.

It remains to apply what has been said to the present case. The Massachusetts rule provides that an executor need not answer suits unless in-hand service was made upon him or notice of the action was filed in the proper registry of probate within one year of his giving bond. The evident intent of this statute is to permit an executor to distribute the estate which he is administering without fear that further liabilities may be outstanding for which he could be held personally liable. If the Federal District Court in Massachusetts applies Rule 4(d)(1) of the Federal Rules of Civil Procedure instead of the Massachusetts service rule, what effect would that have on the speed and assurance with which estates are distributed? As I see it, the effect would not be substantial. It would mean simply that an executor would have to check at his own house or the federal courthouse as well as the registry of probate before he could distribute the estate with impunity. As this does not seem enough to give rise to any real impingement on the vitality of the state policy which the Massachusetts rule is intended to serve, I concur in the judgment of the Court.

Notes and Questions

1. *Hanna* made it clear, at least for a time, that the *Erie-Guaranty Trust-Byrd* test is not applicable to determine the validity of Federal Rules of Civil Procedure promulgated under the Rules Enabling Act. Does the opinion make it equally clear what test is to be applied to determine when a Federal Rule invalidly affects substantive rights? How would you state the test? Note that the Court relied heavily on the case of *Sibbach v. Wilson & Co.*, 312 U.S. 1 (1941). *Sibbach* is discussed in section B(1), above.

2. In *Hanna*, the Court stated that there was a conflict between the Federal Rule and state law. Do you agree? If, as the Court also stated, the purpose of the state statute was to insure that actual notice of claims would be received within the statutory limitations

period and that purpose had been accomplished by the form of service used under Rule 4, how could there be a conflict between the Federal Rule and state law?

3. Consider Justice Harlan's concurring opinion in *Hanna*.

(a) It is clear, is it not, that Justice Harlan would apply the same test to cases (I) involving conflicts between Federal Rules of Civil Procedure and state law and (ii) cases in which no Federal Rule is applicable, but a federal court is faced with a "general" *Erie* problem of the sort involved in *Guaranty Trust*, *Byrd*, and the other Rules of Decision Act cases? Do you think that Justice Harlan or the majority has the better of the argument on this point? That is, should the same test be applied under both the Rules of Decision Act and the Rules Enabling Act to determine whether state law should control in a federal diversity case?

(b) Consider Justice Harlan's evaluation of the *Ragan* case. First, Justice Harlan is correct, isn't he, that the majority should have paid more attention to the applicability of *Ragan* as a controlling precedent in *Hanna*? However, was he also correct that *Ragan* was wrongly decided under the test he prefers? Suppose a state statute of limitations is supported by repose policies, as such statutes often are. Suppose further that the state courts enforce the time limits and service requirements rigorously. Would it really be appropriate for a federal court to conclude, as Justice Harlan states, that "[a]t most, application of the Federal Rule would have meant that potential Kansas tort defendants would have to defer for a few days the satisfaction of knowing that they had not been sued within the limitations period"? Isn't it for the state through its courts to say how flexibly the repose policies supporting a statute of limitations should be treated?

4. The process of conflict avoidance described in *Hanna* requires, as a first step, the analysis of a Federal Rule of Civil Procedure to determine whether it is broad enough to cover the case before the court. Should there be a second step that involves interpretation of the purposes of state law? That is, should the federal courts ask whether state lawmakers intended the state rule to be applicable outside the state court system? Consider the example that the Court discussed in *Hanna* in the portion of the opinion dealing with the Rules of Decision Act. Is it plausible to conclude that a conflict exists between state time limits for filing or serving pleadings and different time limits under the Federal Rules of Civil Procedure? To be sure, even if such a conflict existed, the federal time limits would control under the Rules Enabling Act because they are purely procedural. But isn't it more plausible to conclude that state and federal time limits do not conflict in the first place because the state time limits are designed to operate only within the state court system? Doesn't this example illustrate that a second step in the conflict avoidance process should exist in Rules Enabling Act cases?

5. After *Hanna*, how would you distinguish between the power of Congress to regulate the practice and procedure of the federal courts and the power of the Court to do so under the Rules Enabling Act? Does *Hanna* suggest that Congress has delegated all the power that it has to the Court to regulate procedure? If so, are there restrictions outside the Rules Enabling Act on the power of the Court to prescribe procedural rules—restrictions that do not apply to Congress?

6. With regard to the Court's refinement of the Rules of Decision Act side of the *Erie* doctrine in *Hanna*, the Court's dictum raised several interesting questions about the application of the "outcome determination" test.

(a) Does the test apply to outcome differences *other than* ultimate outcome differences on the merits of an action? Note that *Erie*, *Guaranty Trust*, and *Byrd* all involved such potential ultimate outcome differences. Does the *Hanna* dictum suggest that "lesser" outcome differences will also violate the test? Can you think of a case in which such a "lesser" outcome difference might be involved if a federal court disregarded a state law? For example, in *McKenzie v. Hawaii Permanente Medical Group, Inc.*, 29 F. Supp. 2d 1174 (D. Haw. 1998), the federal district court considered whether the plaintiffs were obligated to proceed through a state medical claims conciliation requirement that they would have had to follow before commencing an action in state court. The court held that the state requirement was "procedural," and, therefore, not obligatory in a federal diversity action because it would not affect the ultimate outcome of the case on the merits. Was the court's reasoning consistent with the directions of the Supreme Court from *Guaranty Trust* through *Hanna* about how Rules of Decision Act cases are to be analyzed? Isn't it clear that plaintiffs will forum shop for federal court to avoid the state medical claim conciliation requirement when they wish, for any reason, to commence an action without jumping through the hoop that the requirement imposes?

(b) *Hanna* also continued to emphasize the *Erie* policy against "discrimination against citizens of the forum state," calling this "inequitable administration of the laws." This policy was expressed along with the forum-shopping policy in the alternative—*i.e.*, it appears that *either* the likelihood of forum shopping *or* the likelihood of inequitable administration of the laws will violate the Rules of Decision Act. Do you understand how there could be a case in which one of the policies would be offended but the other would not? Does the policy also prohibit disregard of state law when a non-citizen would be hurt?

(c) After *Hanna's* refinement of the Rules of Decision Act side of *Erie*, what is left of *Byrd*? For example, is it still absolutely obligatory on the federal courts to apply state rules that are "bound up" with the definition of state rights and obligations? Does the outcome determination test still only apply to state rules of "form and mode"? In determining whether a state rule can be disregarded, is it still permissible to weigh federal countervailing considerations against the policy of duplicate outcomes?

(d) Note that the second "conflict avoidance" step discussed in Note 5, above, would not be permissible under the Rules of Decision Act when considering how to resolve a potential conflict between state law and a federal rule of practice not embodied in a Federal Rule of Civil Procedure. Do you understand why the second step would be improper under the *Erie-Guaranty Trust-Byrd* analysis, but might be proper under the Rules Enabling Act analysis? *See* Teply & Whitten at 512–13. At least one federal court has found that a state procedure was limited in its operation to state courts, thus making an *Erie* analysis under the Rules of Decision Act unnecessary. In *Swaim v. Fogle*, 68 F. Supp. 2d 703 (E.D. Va. 1999), a Virginia procedure in medical malpractice cases allowed either party to request review by a medical malpractice review panel after commencement of a malpractice action. The law limited the right to a review panel to actions in state court. As a result, the federal district court held that federal courts did not have to apply the procedure. (However, the court noted that one other federal court had reached a contrary conclusion.) Assuming that the state procedure in *Swain* would be classified as a rule of "form and mode" and that disregard of the procedure would affect the outcome in a way that would cause *Erie*-prohibited forum shopping or discrimination against citizens of the forum state, why should it matter that the state procedure makes no provision for use in federal actions? Shouldn't the federal courts nevertheless attempt to use the procedure in the same manner that it would be used by the state courts?

Problems

Problem 5-3. P, a citizen of Scotland, sues D, a citizen of State X, U.S.A., in a U.S. District Court in State X. Jurisdiction is based solely on the fact that the action is between a citizen of a state and a citizen or subject of a foreign state. D moves to dismiss the action under the doctrine of forum non conveniens on the ground that Scotland is a substantially more convenient forum than State X. The State X Supreme Court has interpreted the State X Constitution as forbidding the State X courts to apply a doctrine of forum non conveniens, because the constitution requires the state courts always to be open to all litigants. This is understood in State X to prohibit the state courts from declining to exercise subject-matter jurisdiction that has been conferred upon them. The U.S. Supreme Court has held that the common-law doctrine of forum non conveniens applies in federal court. Given the contours of the Rules of Decision Act side of the *Erie* doctrine established under the decisions in *Guaranty Trust*, *Byrd*, and *Hanna*, may the U.S. District Court in State X dismiss the action under the federal doctrine of forum non conveniens? If the *Erie-Guaranty Trust-Byrd-Hanna* doctrine does not prohibit dismissal under these circumstances, are there any other policies that should arguably prohibit dismissal?

Problem 5-4. Assume on the facts of *Problem 5-3* that the citizenship of the parties is reversed, with P being a citizen of State X and D being a citizen of Scotland. Under these circumstances, would the *Erie-Guaranty Trust-Byrd-Hanna* doctrine prohibit dismissal of the action under the federal doctrine of forum non conveniens?

Problem 5-5. P, a citizen of State X, is injured in an automobile accident with a truck owned by *D Corp.*, which is incorporated and has its principal place of business in State Y. The accident occurs in State Z. P sues D in a U.S. District Court in State Q to recover damages for personal injuries received by P in the accident. D is subject to personal jurisdiction in State Q because it does extensive business there. However, State Q has a statute that requires dismissal of actions on the motion of a nonresident defendant sued by a nonresident plaintiff on a claim for relief arising outside State Q. D moves to dismiss the action in federal court under this statute. Under the *Erie-Guaranty Trust-Byrd-Hanna* doctrine, should the district court disregard the state statute?

Problem 5-6. P, a citizen of State X, sues D, a citizen of State Y, in a U.S. District Court for State Y. P seeks to recover $1,000,000 from D for personal injuries received by P from a product manufactured by D. P's original complaint states a single claim based on negligence. After the State Y statute of limitations runs, P moves to amend the complaint to change the claim to one based on strict liability. Under the law of State Y, such an amendment would not relate back to the beginning of the action and would thus be barred by the statute of limitations. Under Rule 15(c)(2) of the Federal Rules of Civil Procedure, the amendment would relate back because the claim in the amended complaint arises from the same transaction or occurrence as the claim in the original complaint. Can the relation back standard of Rule 15(c)(2) be applied to allow relation back after *Hanna*? Do you need further information to answer this question?

Section C. The Evolution of the *Erie* "Branches" and the Search for Standards

In the years after the Court's decision in *Hanna*, the Supreme Court has attempted to decide a wide variety of cases in both of "branches" of the *Erie* Doctrine. In examining these cases in this section, consider whether the Court has succeeded in developing a consistent and workable approach. Have individual Justices themselves even been able to do so?

Walker. In *Walker v. Armco Steel Corp.*, 446 U.S. 740 (1980), an Oklahoma U.S. District Court rejected an argument that *Hanna* had undermined *Ragan*. The Court of Appeals for the Tenth Circuit affirmed, finding Federal Rule 3 to be in direct conflict with an Oklahoma statute of limitations that required commencement of an action by service of process, but also finding that *Ragan* was still good law. The Supreme Court affirmed, but held that Rule 3 did not conflict with the state statute. The Court observed that *Hanna* viewed *Ragan* as holding that Rule 3 is not broad enough to cover commencement for purposes of state limitations periods. The Court did not explain why Rule 3 was construed narrowly in *Ragan* and *Walker* while Rule 4 was construed broadly in *Hanna*.

Question

In footnote 9 of its opinion in *Walker*, the Court stated that the Federal Rules of Civil Procedure are not necessarily to be construed narrowly to avoid conflicts with state law, but are to be given their "plain meaning." Is its statement in footnote 9 consistent with *Hanna*? Is it consistent with what the Court did in *Ragan* and *Walker*?

Burlington Northern Railroad Co. v. Woods
United States Supreme Court, 1987
480 U.S. 1, 107 S. Ct. 967, 94 L. Ed. 2d 1

JUSTICE MARSHALL delivered the opinion of the Court.

This case presents the issue whether, in diversity actions, federal courts must apply a state statute that imposes a fixed penalty on appellants who obtain stays of judgment pending unsuccessful appeals.

. . . .

Respondents brought this tort action in Alabama state court to recover damages for injuries sustained in a motorcycle accident. Petitioner removed the case to a Federal District Court having diversity jurisdiction. A jury trial resulted in a judgment of $300,000 for respondent Alan Woods and $5,000 for respondent Cara Woods. Petitioner posted bond to stay the judgment pending appeal, and the Court of Appeals affirmed without modification. . . .

Respondents then moved in the Court of Appeals, pursuant to § 12-22-72 of the Code of Alabama (1986), for imposition of that State's mandatory affirmance penalty of 10% of the amount of judgment. Petitioner challenged the application of this statute as violative of the equal protection and due process guarantees of the Fourteenth Amendment and as "a procedural rule . . . inapplicable in federal court under the doctrine of *Erie Railroad Co. v. Tompkins* . . . and its progeny." . . . The Court of Appeals summarily granted respondents' motion to assess the penalty and subsequently denied a petition for rehearing. The parties have stipulated that the final judgment has been paid, except for the $30,500 statutory affirmance penalty, which petitioner has withheld pending proceedings in this Court.

We granted certiorari to consider the equal protection and due process challenges as well as the *Erie* claim.... Because we conclude that the Alabama statute imposing a mandatory affirmance penalty has no application in federal diversity actions, we decline to reach the Fourteenth Amendment issues.

....

The Alabama statute provides in relevant part:

> When a judgment or decree is entered or rendered for money, whether debt or damages, and the same has been stayed on appeal by the execution of bond, with surety, if the appellate court affirms the judgment of the court below, it must also enter judgment against all or any of the obligors on the bond for the amount of the affirmed judgment, 10 percent damages thereon and the costs of the appellate court....

Ala. Code § 12-22-72 (1986). As set forth in the statute, then, a combination of three conditions will automatically trigger the 10% penalty: (1) the trial court must enter a money judgment or decree, (2) the judgment or decree must be stayed by the requisite bond,[2] and (3) the judgment or decree must be affirmed without substantial modification.... The purposes of the mandatory affirmance penalty are to penalize frivolous appeals and appeals interposed for delay ... and to provide "additional damages" as compensation to the appellees for having to suffer the ordeal of defending the judgments on appeal....

Petitioner contends that the statute's underlying purposes and mandatory mode of operation conflict with the purposes and operation of Rule 38 of the Federal Rules of Appellate Procedure, and therefore that the statute should not be applied by federal courts sitting in diversity. Entitled "Damages for delay," Rule 38 provides: "If the court of appeals shall determine that an appeal is frivolous, it may award just damages and single or double costs to the appellee."[a] *See also* 28 U.S.C. § 1912. Under this Rule, "damages are awarded by the court in its discretion in the case of a frivolous appeal as a matter of justice to the appellee and as a penalty against the appellant." ...

In *Hanna v. Plumer* ... we set forth the appropriate test for resolving conflicts between state law and the Federal Rules. The initial step is to determine whether, when fairly construed, the scope of Federal Rule 38 is "sufficiently broad" to cause a "direct collision" with the state law or, implicitly, to "control the issue" before the court, thereby leaving no room for the operation of that law.... The Rule must then be applied if it represents a valid exercise of Congress' rulemaking authority, which originates in the Constitution and has been bestowed on this Court by the Rules Enabling Act, 28 U.S.C. § 2072.[3] ...

---

2. Under Alabama law, an appellant may obtain a stay of judgment pending appeal by providing an acceptable surety bond of a set amount, which in this case would have been 125% of the trial court's judgment had the case been tried in state court. Ala. R. App. P. 8(a)(1).

a. [Eds. Note. Rule 38 is now entitled "Frivolous Appeal—Damages and Costs" and currently provides: "If a court of appeals determines that an appeal is frivolous, it may, after a separately filed motion or notice from the court and reasonable opportunity to respond, award just damages and single or double costs to the appellee." The provision as to notice and opportunity to respond was added in 1994 and does not affect Rule 38's main provision for the award of damages and costs in the discretion of the court, which was the issue in *Burlington*.]

3. Article III of the Constitution, augmented by the Necessary and Proper Clause of Article I, § 8, cl. 18, empowers Congress to establish a system of federal district and appellate courts and, impliedly, to establish procedural Rules governing litigation in these courts. In the Rules Enabling Act, Con-

The constitutional constraints on the exercise of this rulemaking authority define a test of reasonableness. Rules regulating matters indisputably procedural are *a priori* constitutional. Rules regulating matters "which, though falling within the uncertain area between substance and procedure, are rationally capable of classification as either," also satisfy this constitutional standard.... The Rules Enabling Act, however, contains an additional requirement. The Federal Rule must not "abridge, enlarge or modify any substantive right...." 28 U.S.C. § 2072. The cardinal purpose of Congress in authorizing the development of a uniform and consistent system of rules governing federal practice and procedure suggests that Rules which incidentally affect litigants' substantive rights do not violate this provision if reasonably necessary to maintain the integrity of that system of rules.... Moreover, the study and approval given each proposed Rule by the Advisory Committee, the Judicial Conference, and this Court, and the statutory requirement that the Rule be reported to Congress for a period of review before taking effect ... give the Rules presumptive validity under both the constitutional and statutory constraints....

Applying the *Hanna* analysis to an analogous Mississippi statute which provides for a mandatory affirmance penalty, the United States Court of Appeals for the Fifth Circuit concluded in *Affholder, Inc. v. Southern Rock, Inc.*, 746 F.2d 305 (5th Cir. 1984), that the statute conflicted with Rule 38 and thus was not applicable in federal diversity actions. The Fifth Circuit discussed two aspects of the conflict: (1) the discretionary mode of operation of the Federal Rule, compared to the mandatory operation of the Mississippi statute, and (2) the limited effect of the Rule in penalizing only frivolous appeals or appeals interposed for purposes of delay, compared to the effect of the Mississippi statute in penalizing every unsuccessful appeal regardless of merit....

We find the Fifth Circuit's analysis persuasive. Rule 38 affords a court of appeals plenary discretion to assess "just damages" in order to penalize an appellant who takes a frivolous appeal and to compensate the injured appellee for the delay and added expense of defending the district court's judgment. Thus, the Rule's discretionary mode of operation unmistakably conflicts with the mandatory provision of Alabama's affirmance penalty statute. Moreover, the purposes underlying the Rule are sufficiently coextensive with the asserted purposes of the Alabama statute to indicate that the Rule occupies the statute's field of operation so as to preclude its application in federal diversity actions.[5]

Respondents argue that, because Alabama has a similar Appellate Rule which may be applied in state court alongside the affirmance penalty statute, see Ala. Rule App. Proc.

---

gress authorized this Court to prescribe uniform Rules to govern the "practice and procedure" of the Federal District Courts and Courts of Appeals. 28 U.S.C. § 2072. Though *Hanna v. Plumer* ... involved a conflict between state law and a Federal Rule of Civil Procedure, its analytical framework provides the test for the validity of Federal Rules of Appellate Procedure as well, since these Rules were also prescribed pursuant to the Rules Enabling Act....

5. Rule 37 of the Federal Rules of Appellate Procedure provides further indication that the Rules occupy the Alabama statute's field of operation so as to preclude its application in diversity actions. Since the affirmance penalty only applies if a trial court's judgment is stayed pending appeal, *see* Ala. Code § 12-22-72 (1986), it operates to compensate a victorious appellee for the lost use of the judgment proceeds during the period of appeal. Federal Rule 37, however, already serves this purpose by providing for an award of postjudgment interest following an unsuccessful appeal. *See also* 28 U.S.C. § 1961.

In addition, we note that federal provisions governing the availability of a stay of judgment pending appeal do not condition the procurement of a stay on exposure to payment of any additional damages in the event the appeal is unsuccessful and, unlike the state provision in this case, allow the federal courts to set the amount of security in their discretion. *Compare* Fed. R. Civ. P. 62(d) & 62(g) *and* Fed. R. App. P. 8(b) *with* Ala. R. App. P. 8(b). *See also* 28 U.S.C. § 1651.

38 ... a federal court sitting in diversity could impose the mandatory penalty and likewise remain free to exercise its discretionary authority under Federal Rule 38. This argument, however, ignores the significant possibility that a court of appeals may, in any given case, find a limited justification for imposing penalties in an amount *less than* 10% of the lower court's judgment. Federal Rule 38 adopts a case-by-case approach to identifying and deterring frivolous appeals; the Alabama statute precludes any exercise of discretion within its scope of operation. Whatever circumscriptive effect the mandatory affirmance penalty statute may have on the state court's exercise of discretion under Alabama's Rule 38, that Rule provides no authority for defining the scope of discretion allowed under Federal Rule 38.

Federal Rule 38 regulates matters which can reasonably be classified as procedural, thereby satisfying the constitutional standard for validity. Its displacement of the Alabama statute also satisfies the statutory constraints of the Rules Enabling Act. The choice made by the drafters of the Federal Rules in favor of a discretionary procedure affects only the process of enforcing litigants' rights and not the rights themselves.

. . . .

We therefore hold that the Alabama mandatory affirmance penalty statute has no application to judgments entered by federal courts sitting in diversity.

Reversed.

Notes and Questions

1. Do you agree with the Court that Federal Appellate Rule 38 was broad enough to encompass the situation in *Burlington Northern*? Isn't *Burlington Northern* a more grievous example of overbroad Rule interpretation than *Hanna*? At least in *Hanna*, Federal Rule 4 applied on its face to service of process. In *Burlington Northern*, Federal Appellate Rule 38 applied only to frivolous appeals, and there was no indication that the appeal involved in the case was frivolous. How could the Court have concluded Rule 38 was applicable? How can other courts and practitioners predict when the Court will interpret a rule in this fashion?

2. (a) Having determined that Rule 38 of the Federal Rules of Appellate Procedure was broad enough to cover the case before it, should the Court have engaged in any other method of conflict avoidance before considering the validity of Rule 38 under the Enabling Act? Note 5 following *Hanna* in section B(2), above, discussed the possibility that if a Federal Rule is found applicable to a case, the federal court should next consider whether the state rule in the case was designed to operate only in the state's own courts, as in the case of rules providing for time limits governing the filing of responsive pleadings.

(b) In *Mace v. Van Ru Credit Corp.*, 109 F.3d 338 (7th Cir. 1997), the Wisconsin Consumer Act required thirty days notice prior to commencement of an action. The plaintiff argued that this notice requirement was merely procedural and thus inapplicable in federal court. The Seventh Circuit agreed, holding that the notice requirement was a matter of procedure and inapplicable in federal court in a class action brought under Federal Rule 23. The court did not appear to hold that Rule 23, which contains no such notice requirement, conflicted with the state statute, but simply seemed to be saying that the state statute was inapplicable altogether in federal court because it was procedural. Was the court adopting the analysis suggested here and in the notes following *Hanna*, or was it just confused?

3. *Burlington Northern's* test for Federal Rule validity under the Enabling Act focuses in part on the nature of the state rule involved in a case and in part on the extent to which a Federal Rule affects the operation of the state rule. The Court seems to say that a Federal Rule can wholly supplant state procedural rights. However, a Federal Rule, to be valid, can-

not affect state "substantive rights" more than "incidentally," and even then to be valid the Federal Rule must be reasonably necessary to maintain the integrity of the uniform system of procedure that it was the purpose of the Rules Enabling Act to establish. Assuming that this is a correct statement of the *Burlington Northern* test, consider the following questions:

(a) How is it determined whether a Federal Rule impacts on state "procedural" or state "substantive" rights? Does the state law with which the Federal Rule conflicts have to embody "substantive" rights, or is it sufficient that application of the Federal Rule instead of the conflicting state rule will impact on "substantive" rights in some other respect, such as by changing the outcome of the case on the merits? (Would this last be plausible given the rejection in *Hanna* of the idea that the outcome determinative analysis of *Guaranty Trust* determines the validity of Federal Rules of Civil Procedure? On the other hand, recall the Supreme Court's statement in *Hanna* that "a court, in measuring a Federal Rule against the standards contained in the Enabling Act and the Constitution, need not wholly blind itself to the degree to which the Rule makes the character and result of the federal litigation stray from the course it would follow in state courts....") What kind of rights did the Alabama statute in *Burlington Northern* confer?

(b) Assuming that a Federal Rule impacts on substantive rights in the relevant respect, how much of an effect can a Federal Rule have on the substantive rights before the effect will be considered more than "incidental"? How much of an effect did Rule 38 have on the operation of the Alabama statute in *Burlington Northern*?

(c) Assuming that a Federal Rule has only an "incidental effect" on state substantive rights, how is one to determine whether the Rule is reasonably necessary to maintain the integrity of the uniform system of procedure that it was the purpose of the Rules Enabling Act to establish? Is Rule 38, as interpreted by the Court in *Burlington Northern*, reasonably necessary to the uniform scheme?

4. Assume that the Court had, at the beginning of its analysis, found that Rule 38 was not broad enough to encompass the case before it in *Burlington Northern*. Under such circumstances, there would be no applicable Federal Rule created under the Rules Enabling Act that conflicted with the Alabama statute. Nevertheless, this would not end the question of the Alabama statute's applicability in federal court, would it? Under such circumstances, wouldn't the issue arise whether the federal courts were obligated under the Rules of Decision Act to apply the Alabama statute in diversity actions? Apply the *Erie-Guaranty Trust-Byrd* test (as refined in *Hanna*) to this issue. Are the federal courts obligated to apply the Alabama statute under that test? Does any aspect of the test cast light on any aspect of the Court's Rules Enabling Act test?

Stewart Organization. Although technically not decided under the Rules Enabling Act, in *Stewart Organization v. Ricoh Corp.*, 487 U.S. 22 (1988), the Supreme Court applied the *Burlington Northern* approach to rule interpretation to a federal procedural statute, 28 U.S.C. § 1404(a). In *Stewart Organization*, the issue was the weight to be given to a forum selection clause in a contract when a transfer of venue was sought under § 1404(a) to the forum specified by the clause. The controlling state law would arguably have rendered the forum selection clause invalid and thus of no weight at all. Despite the fact that § 1404(a) says nothing about forum selection clauses, the Court held that § 1404(a) controlled the effect of the clause in the case. *Id.* at 28–31.

In dissent, Justice Scalia challenged the Court's conclusion that § 1404(a) controlled the situation or occupied the field. Justice Scalia asserted that

> § 1404(a) was enacted against a background that issues of contract, including a contract's validity, are nearly always governed by state law. It is simply contrary

to the practice of our system that such an issue should be wrenched from state control in absence of a clear conflict with federal law or explicit statutory provision. It is particularly instructive in this regard to compare § 1404(a) with [§ 2 of the Federal Arbitration Act, 9 U.S.C. § 2], enacted by the same Congress a year earlier, that did pre-empt state contract law, and in precisely the same field of agreement regarding forum selection....

Section 1404(a) is simply a venue provision that nowhere mentions contracts or agreements, much less that the validity of certain contracts or agreements will be matters of federal law. It is difficult to believe that state contract law was meant to be pre-empted by this provision that we have said "should be regarded as a federal judicial housekeeping measure," *Van Dusen v. Barrack*,.... that we have said did not change "the relevant factors" which federal courts used to consider under the doctrine of forum non conveniens, *Norwood v. Kirkpatrick*, 349 U.S. 29, 32 (1955), and that we have held can be applied retroactively because it is procedural.... It seems to me the generality of its language—"[f]or the convenience of parties and witnesses, in the interest of justice"—is plainly insufficient to work the great change in law asserted here.

Id. at 36.

Notes and Questions

1. With regard to the validity of a forum-selection clause, would the application of a federal judge-made determination, rather than state law, under the Court's decision in *Stewart Organization* be likely to produce forum shopping or discrimination against a citizen of the forum state who would be deprived of the benefit of a valuable rule that would have been applied by the state courts?

2. The majority in *Stewart Organization* did not explain why § 1404(a) was the controlling federal statute. At the district court level, the defendant had moved in the alternative to transfer under § 1404(a) or to dismiss under § 1406, (which controls dismissal and transfer when an action is commenced in an incorrect venue). What explanation could the Court have given, if any? Should it have made any difference? *Cf. In re* Atlantic Marine Constr. Co., 701 F.3d 736 (5th Cir. 2012) (holding that the proper procedural method is a § 1404(a) motion to transfer).

3. Reconsider the 1993 amendments to Federal Rule 4, examined in Chapter 2. Assume that a state statute of limitations requires commencement within the statutory period by service of a summons. Rule 4 provides for waiver of service and allows service of a summons at any time within 120 days of the filing of a complaint. Apply the method of rule and statute interpretation established in *Burlington Northern* and *Stewart Organization* to Rule 4 and the state statute-of-limitations commencement provision. Rule 4(d)(4) states that if a defendant returns a waiver and the plaintiff files it, "these rules apply as if a summons and complaint had been served at the time of filing the waiver." Is Rule 4 broad enough to encompass commencement for purposes of the state statute? If you were representing a plaintiff in a case in which the state statute of limitations was about to expire, would you feel safe in filing the waiver within the statutory period without serving a summons on the defendant on the assumption that Rule 4(d)(4) would protect you?

Ferens. As discussed in section B, the Supreme Court decided *Van Dusen v. Barrack*, 376 U.S. 612 (1964), one year before the *Hanna* case. Recall that in *Van Dusen*, the Court held that after transfer on the *defendant's* motion under 28 U.S.C. § 1404(a), the conflict-of-laws rules of the transferor state must be applied in determining which state's substantive law should be applied in the case. The *Van Dusen* holding was based on the policy of preventing the defendant from moving for transfer to obtain a different applicable law rather than simply a more convenient forum. *Van Dusen* effectively means that the transferee court must attempt to duplicate the substantive legal result that would have been reached in the transferor state.

In *Ferens v. John Deere Co., 494 U.S. 516* (1990), the Supreme Court held that the *Van Dusen* rule should apply even when the *plaintiff* makes a transfer motion under § 1404(a). Moreover, the Court indicated that the *Van Dusen* rule would apply to transfers made (a) on motion of both plaintiff and defendant, (b) on the district court's own motion, (c) on the motion of the plaintiff after the defendant removes the action, (d) when only one of several plaintiffs moves for transfer, and (e) when, through no fault of the plaintiff, circumstances change, making a once desirable forum inconvenient.

Ferens was a classic case of forum shopping by the plaintiff. The plaintiff lived in Pennsylvania, where he was injured. After the Pennsylvania statute of limitations ran on one of his claims, he commenced an action in a U.S. District Court in Mississippi, where the statute of limitations had not yet run. The plaintiff then moved to transfer the action to Pennsylvania under § 1404(a). The action was transferred and then dismissed under the Pennsylvania statute of limitations. The Third Circuit Court of Appeals affirmed the dismissal, but the U.S. Supreme Court held it to be erroneous. The Court's opinion in *Ferens* indicated that application of the *Van Dusen* rule to transfers on plaintiffs' motions would not enhance the opportunities for forum shopping that plaintiffs already possessed and would support the *Van Dusen* policy of assuring that transfers were made when litigational convenience so dictated.

Like *Van Dusen*, *Ferens* purported to be based in part on *Erie* policies, which the Court indicated would be undermined if the applicable law changed after a transfer granted on the plaintiff's motion. The Court stated as follows:

> The *Erie* policy had a clear implication for *Van Dusen*. The existence of diversity jurisdiction gave the defendants the opportunity to make a motion to transfer venue under § 1404(a), and if the applicable law were to change after transfer, the plaintiff's venue privilege and resulting state-law advantages could be defeated at the defendant's option. . . .
>
> Transfers initiated by a plaintiff involve some different considerations, but lead to the same result. Applying the transferor law, of course, will not deprive the plaintiff of any state-law advantages. A defendant, in one sense, also will lose no legal advantage if the transferor law controls after a transfer initiated by the plaintiff; the same law, after all, would have applied if the plaintiff had not made the motion. In another sense, however, a defendant may lose a nonlegal advantage. Deere, for example, would lose whatever advantage inheres in not having to litigate in Pennsylvania, or, put another way, in forcing the Ferenses to litigate in Mississippi or not at all.
>
> We, nonetheless, find the advantage that the defendant loses slight. A plaintiff always can sue in the favorable state court or sue in diversity and not seek a transfer. By asking for application of the Mississippi statute of limitations following a transfer to Pennsylvania on grounds of convenience, the Ferenses are seeking to deprive Deere only of the advantage of using against them the inconvenience of litigating in Mississippi. The text of § 1404(a) may not say anything about choice of law, but we think it not the purpose of the section to protect a party's ability to use inconvenience as a shield to discourage or hinder litigation other-

wise proper.... By creating an opportunity to have venue transferred between courts in different States on the basis of convenience, an option that does not exist absent federal jurisdiction, Congress, with respect to diversity, retained the *Erie* policy while diminishing the incidents of inconvenience.

Applying the transferee law, by contrast, would undermine the *Erie* rule in a serious way. It would mean that initiating a transfer under § 1404(a) changes the state law applicable to a diversity case....

Id. at 524–26.

Notes and Questions

1. With regard to the *Ferens* case, do you think that a plaintiff should be rewarded with a choice-of-law advantage by intentionally selecting an inconvenient forum and then seeking a transfer to a more convenient forum?

2. *Ferens* was decided 25 years after *Hanna*. Is *Ferens* consistent with *Hanna's* refinement of the outcome determination test? Note that the Court in *Ferens* stated that application of the transferee state's law after transfer on a plaintiff's motion would undermine *Erie* because it would change the state law applicable to a diversity case. Is this consistent with *Hanna's* view of the *Erie* policies? Wasn't the whole point of *Hanna* that a federal court's departure from state law in a diversity case did *not* violate the *Erie* policies *unless* forum shopping for a federal over a state court or discrimination against a citizen of the forum state would result? If, in cases like *Ferens*, the Court had held that the transferee state's law would apply after a transfer on a plaintiff's motion, would anyone have been tempted to shop for a federal over a state court? Would there have been discrimination against a citizen of the forum state? Indeed, can you make an argument that the *Ferens* rule will result in a kind of forum shopping similar to that which *Erie* was designed to prevent?

3. Should the Court's description of the *Erie* policies in *Ferens* be interpreted as broadening them? Thus, should we now conclude that *Erie* is violated any time a federal court takes action that results in a change in the applicable state law, even if forum shopping or inequitable administration of the law would not occur as a result of the action?

4. Even if plaintiffs are able to obtain a choice-of-law advantage by selecting an inconvenient (though proper) forum in which to commence the action, there is empirical evidence that transfer counterbalances the forum shopping and diminishes the plaintiff's chances of winning the action. Does this also suggest that some or all of the burden of pretrial litigation over transfer motions may be outweighed by the diminution of inaccurate results that transfer produces?

5. The holdings of *Van Dusen* and *Ferens* should not apply to a § 1406(a) transfer for *improper* venue. In such a case, lower federal courts have held that the normal rule of *Klaxon* should govern and the transferee federal district court should apply the same conflict-of-law rules that its state courts would have applied. *See, e.g., Adam v. J.B. Hunt Transp., Inc.,* 130 F.3d 219, 230 (6th Cir. 1997). If the holdings of *Van Dusen* and *Ferens* applied to § 1406(a) transfers, do you see the problem that approach would create?

Chambers. In *Chambers v. NASCO, Inc.,* 501 U.S. 32 (1991), the plaintiff brought a federal diversity action to obtain specific performance of a contract. The defendant engaged in a substantial amount of bad-faith conduct before and during the course of the litigation. Some of the conduct violated Federal Rule 11, but some did not. The district court sanctioned the defendant under its "inherent powers" for the conduct that did not violate Rule 11. Rejecting an argument that *Erie* required a federal court with diversity jurisdiction to look to state law to determine what conduct should be sanctioned in the absence of an applicable Federal Rule, the court of appeals affirmed. The Supreme Court agreed. The state law in question did not recognize a bad-faith exception to the general American Rule against fee-shifting in civil actions.

Using *Hanna's* refinement of the outcome determination test, the Court confirmed that application of a federal rule of practice over conflicting state law does not violate *Erie* unless forum shopping or inequitable administration of the law (*i.e.,* discrimination against citizens of the forum state) results. No danger of forum shopping existed in *Chambers* because the imposition of sanctions under the district court's inherent powers did not depend upon who wins the litigation, but on how the parties conduct themselves during litigation. No danger of inequitable administration of the law existed because the Court did not consider it inequitable for the district courts to use their inherent power to impose sanctions on citizens and noncitizens alike who had the power by controlling their conduct to determine whether sanctions would be assessed.

Notes and Questions

1. According to *Byrd*, the outcome determination test is only supposed to be applied when the potentially applicable state rule is a rule of form and mode. If the rule is one defining state rights and obligations or bound up with the definition of state rights and obligations, the rule is absolutely obligatory on the federal courts. Note that this formulation, if it is still good law, took on added importance after *Byrd* held that federal countervailing considerations could be balanced against the outcome determinative policies and *Hanna* held that only outcome differences that encouraged forum shopping or inequitable administration of the law violated *Erie*. If a rule defines state rights or is bound up with the definition of state rights, it is not necessary to ask whether disregard of the rule would produce forum shopping, etc. Nor is it necessary to balance federal countervailing considerations against the outcome determinative policies because those policies are only applicable to rules of form and mode. In any event, rules defining state rights and obligations and rules bound up with state rights and obligations are absolutely obligatory in federal courts, whether or not their disregard would produce forum shopping or inequitable administration of the laws.

2. Why didn't the Court in *Chambers* consider what category of state rules was involved in the action? Was it clear that the rule was a rule of form and mode? At one point in its opinion the Court stated:

> Only when there is a conflict between state and federal substantive law are the concerns of *Erie* ... at issue. As we explained in *Hanna* ..., the "outcome determinative" test of *Erie* and *Guaranty Trust* ..."cannot be read without reference to the twin aims of the *Erie* rule: discouragement of forum shopping and avoidance of inequitable administration of the laws." ...

501 U.S. at 52. Do you understand this passage? Wasn't the *Byrd* tripartite categorization process part of the *way* in which we determine what rules are "substantive" for *Erie* purposes, just like the *Guaranty Trust* outcome determination test?

3. Does *Chambers* indicate that the *Byrd* categorization process is dead? If so, does that mean that deviation from rules bound up with the definition of state rights must now be judged by *Hanna's* refined outcome determination test? Does it mean that federal diversity courts should balance federal countervailing considerations against the out-

come determinative polices when a state rule bound up with state rights is involved? (The question whether federal policies allow deviation from state rules defining state rights is examined below in the section on federal substantive common law.)

4. Even assuming that the state rule in *Chambers* was a rule of form and mode, was the Court correct that disregard of the rule would not produce forum shopping? Was it correct that disregard of the state rule would not produce inequitable administration of the law?

5. Assume that the state rule in *Chambers* was not only a rule of form and mode, but that disregard of the rule would produce an outcome difference that would either result in forum shopping or inequitable administration of the laws, or both. Are there federal countervailing considerations present that would outweigh the outcome determinative policies?

6. Are the answers to any of the questions asked in the preceding notes affected by the fact that *Chambers* involved the use of the district court's inherent powers to sanction conduct occurring *after* litigation had commenced? For *Erie* purposes, does sanctioning of post-commencement conduct differ from the application of a general federal rule of practice, such as a rule of equity jurisprudence, whose application the parties can anticipate before commencement and that they cannot avoid once the action has been commenced in a federal court?

Problem

Problem 5-7. Assume that a state possesses a statute providing that in any case in which an insurance company denies the payment of a claim under a policy issued by the company, the insured may recover reasonable attorney's fees in any action successfully brought to recover on the policy. If an insured brings a successful federal diversity action to recover on a policy under the circumstances covered by the state statute, can the federal court disregard the statute and refuse to award attorney's fees to the plaintiff? If not, how do you distinguish this case from *Chambers*?

Business Guides. In *Business Guides, Inc. v. Chromatic Communications Enterprises, Inc.*, 498 U.S. 533 (1991), the Court considered a challenge to the validity of Federal Rule 11 under the Enabling Act. The issue was whether Rule 11 could validly be applied to sanction a represented party who had signed a litigation document in violation of the rule, but in good faith. The Court held that Rule 11's requirement of reasonable inquiry applied to represented parties as well as attorneys. The sanctioned party argued that sanctions against represented parties violated the Rules Enabling Act in two ways: (i) by authorizing fee shifting in a manner not approved by Congress, and (ii) by creating a federal tort of malicious prosecution that encroached on various state causes of action. The Court rejected both these arguments. In its Rules Enabling Act analysis, the Court repeated the statement, first made in *Hanna*, that the Federal Rules are to be considered "prima facie" valid because of the participation by the Supreme Court, Congress, and the Advisory Committee in the rulemaking process.

To overcome this presumptive validity, a party aggrieved by a rule must demonstrate that the *Burlington Northern* test has been violated. According to the Court, the version of Rule 11 then in effect did not violate the test because "[t]here is little doubt that Rule 11 is reasonably necessary to maintain the integrity of the system of federal practice and procedure and that any effect on substantive rights is incidental." *Id.* at 552. Rule 11 did not inappropriately shift fees because (i) Rule 11 sanctions are not keyed to the outcome of litigation, but to specific filings within litigation, (ii) Rule 11 sanctions do not shift the entire cost of litigation, but only the cost of a discrete litigational event, and (iii) Rule 11 only mandates an appropriate sanction,[a] not necessarily attorney's fees. Rule 11 did not create a federal tort of malicious civil prosecution because the main objective of the rule is not to compensate parties victimized by unwarranted litigation, but to deter baseless filings and abuses. Monetary sanctions imposed on a party that benefit other litigants impose merely an incidental effect on substantive rights. *See id*.

Four Justices dissented in *Business Guides*. However, the dissenters were reluctant to draw the conclusion that the majority's interpretation of Rule 11 produced a Rules Enabling Act violation. Instead, they argued that the Rules Enabling Act concerns raised by the sanctioned party in *Business Guides* counseled strongly against the majority's interpretation of Rule 11. *See id*. at 564–66 (Justice Kennedy, with whom Justices Marshall and Stevens joined, and with whom Justice Scalia joined in part).

Business Guides added little to the *Burlington Northern* analysis. It seems important that the Court stuck to the analysis and continued to indicate that the Enabling Act imposed something more on the Court's power to make rules than the Constitution imposes on the power of Congress to do so. In addition, you should note that the Court's reference to the fact that Rule 11 sanctions are not keyed to the outcome of litigation on the merits could be interpreted as saying that an "impact on substantive rights" within the meaning of *Burlington Northern* means that a Federal Rule must somehow change the outcome on the merits to be invalid. However, the ambiguity of the Court's opinion precludes saying this for sure.

Notes and Questions

1. What do you suppose the Court means in cases like *Hanna*, *Burlington Northern*, and *Business Guides* by saying that the Federal Rules are "prima facie" valid, or "presumptively valid" because of the scrutiny they are given? Presumptions are normally matters that pertain to proof of facts at trial. Is the "presumption" that the Federal Rules are valid a factual presumption? In any event, is it really true that the Federal Rules go through exacting scrutiny by the Court and Congress before they become law? Consider Justice Frankfurter's warning in *Sibbach* that the participation by Congress in the rulemaking process cannot be given significant weight:

> Plainly the Rules are not acts of Congress and cannot be treated as such. Having due regard to the mechanics of legislation and the practical conditions surrounding the business of Congress ... to draw any inference of tacit approval from non-action by Congress is to appeal to unreality.

Sibbach, 312 U.S. at 18 (Frankfurter, J., dissenting).

2. Federal Rule 4(m) prescribes that if service of process is not made within 120 days after filing of the complaint, the court "must dismiss the action" unless the plaintiff "shows good cause for the failure." By negative implication, service is timely if made within 120 days. However, suppose a federal statute enacted before the 120-day time limit of Rule 4(m) became law provides that service must be sooner than 120 days. Can Rule 4 supersede the statute consistently with the Rules Enabling Act and other restrictions on the rule making power, such as Rule 82? *Cf. Henderson v. United States*, 517 U.S. 654 (1996) (yes).

---

a. [Eds. Note. Current Rule 11(c) now provides that sanctions are discretionary.]

3. Procedural regulation in the federal courts is divided between Congress, acting directly in Title 28 to regulate many matters of procedure, and the Supreme Court, acting under the Rules Enabling Act to provide "housekeeping" rules for the lower federal courts. Should there be limitations on the power of the Court outside the Rules Enabling Act to create purely procedural rules when Congress has extensively regulated an area? *See* Teply & Whitten at 533–40.

Problems

Problem 5-8. Reevaluate *Problem 5-6* on the basis of *Burlington Northern* and *Business Guides*.

Problem 5-9. Consider Rule 4(k)(2) of the Federal Rules of Civil Procedure, added to the Federal Rules by the 1993 amendments to Rule 4. Is Rule 4(k)(2) valid under the Rules Enabling Act? If so, is there any other law or doctrine that might invalidate the rule?

Gasperini v. Center for Humanities, Inc.

United States Supreme Court, 1996
518 U.S.415, 116 S. Ct. 2211, 135 L. Ed. 2d 659

Justice Ginsburg delivered the opinion of the Court.

[Gasperini, a photo-journalist, lent 300 color transparencies to the Center for Humanities for use in an educational videotape. The Center subsequently lost the color transparencies. Gasperini commenced a diversity action in the Southern District of New York for state-law claims of negligence, breach of contract, and conversion. A jury awarded Gasperini $450,000 in compensatory damages. This amount was based on testimony offered by Gasperini's expert who valued each of the 300 transparencies at $1,500. The Center moved for a new trial on several grounds, including the verdict was excessive, in part, because Gasperini had earned only a total of approximately $10,000 from his photography work in the prior ten years. The district court denied the Center's motion. The Court of Appeals for the Second Circuit reversed on the ground that the verdict materially deviated from what is reasonable compensation and ordered a new trial unless Gasperini agreed to an award of $100,000. The U.S. Supreme Court reversed.]

In 1986, as part of a series of tort reform measures, New York codified a standard for judicial review of the size of jury awards. Placed in [N.Y. Civ. Prac. Law & Rules (CPLR) § 5501(c) (McKinney 1995], the prescription reads:

> In reviewing a money judgment ... in which it is contended that the award is excessive or inadequate and that a new trial should have been granted unless a stipulation is entered to a different award, the appellate division shall determine that an award is excessive or inadequate if it deviates materially from what would be reasonable compensation.

As stated in Legislative Findings and Declarations accompanying New York's adoption of the "deviates materially" formulation, the lawmakers found the "shock the conscience" test an insufficient check on damage awards; the legislature therefore installed a standard "inviting more careful appellate scrutiny." ... At the same time, the legislature instructed the Appellate Division, in amended § 5522, to state the reasons for the court's rulings on the size of verdicts, and the factors the court considered in complying with § 5501(c)....

New York state-court opinions confirm that § 5501(c)'s "deviates materially" standard calls for closer surveillance than "shock the conscience" oversight....

Although phrased as a direction to New York's intermediate appellate courts, § 5501(c)'s "deviates materially" standard, as construed by New York's courts, instructs state trial judges as well.... Application of § 5501(c) at the trial level is key to this case.

To determine whether an award "deviates materially from what would be reasonable compensation," New York state courts look to awards approved in similar cases.... The "deviates materially" standard, however, in design and operation, influences outcomes by tightening the range of tolerable awards....

. . . .

In cases like Gasperini's, in which New York law governs the claims for relief, does New York law also supply the test for federal court review of the size of the verdict? The Center answers yes. The "deviates materially" standard, it argues, is a substantive standard that must be applied by federal appellate courts in diversity cases. The Second Circuit agreed.... Gasperini, emphasizing that § 5501(c) trains on the New York Appellate Division, characterizes the provision as procedural, an allocation of decisionmaking authority regarding damages, not a hard cap on the amount recoverable. Correctly comprehended, Gasperini urges, § 5501(c)'s direction to the Appellate Division cannot be given effect by federal appellate courts without violating the Seventh Amendment's re-examination clause.

As the parties' arguments suggest, CPLR § 5501(c), appraised under *Erie Railroad Co. v. Tompkins* ... and decisions in *Erie's* path, is both "substantive" and "procedural": "substantive" in that § 5501(c)'s "deviates materially" standard controls how much a plaintiff can be awarded; "procedural" in that § 5501(c) assigns decisionmaking authority to New York's Appellate Division. Parallel application of § 5501(c) at the federal appellate level would be out of sync with the federal system's division of trial and appellate court functions, an allocation weighted by the Seventh Amendment. The dispositive question, therefore, is whether federal courts can give effect to the substantive thrust of § 5501(c) without untoward alteration of the federal scheme for the trial and decision of civil cases.

. . . .

Federal diversity jurisdiction provides an alternative forum for the adjudication of state-created rights, but it does not carry with it generation of rules of substantive law. As *Erie* read the Rules of Decision Act: "Except in matters governed by the Federal Constitution or by Acts of Congress, the law to be applied in any case is the law of the State."... Under the *Erie* doctrine, federal courts sitting in diversity apply state substantive law and federal procedural law.

Classification of a law as "substantive" or "procedural" for *Erie* purposes is sometimes a challenging endeavor.[7] *Guaranty Trust Co. v. York*.... an early interpretation of *Erie*, propounded an "outcome determination" test: "[D]oes it significantly affect the result of a litigation for a federal court to disregard a law of a State that would be controlling in an action upon the same claim by the same parties in a State court?"... Ordering

---

7. Concerning matters covered by the Federal Rules of Civil Procedure, the characterization question is usually unproblematic: It is settled that if the Rule in point is consonant with the Rules Enabling Act, 28 U.S.C. § 2072, and the Constitution, the Federal Rule applies regardless of contrary state law. *See Hanna v. Plumer* ...; *Burlington N.R.R. v. Woods*.... Federal courts have interpreted the Federal Rules, however, with sensitivity to important state interests and regulatory policies. *See, e.g., Walker v. Armco Steel Corp.*....

application of a state statute of limitations to an equity proceeding in federal court, the Court said in *Guaranty Trust*: "[W]here a federal court is exercising jurisdiction solely because of the diversity of citizenship of the parties, the outcome of the litigation in the federal court should be substantially the same, so far as legal rules determine the outcome of a litigation, as it would be if tried in a State court." ... A later pathmarking case, qualifying *Guaranty Trust*, explained that the "outcome-determination" test must not be applied mechanically to sweep in all manner of variations; instead, its application must be guided by "the twin aims of the *Erie* rule: discouragement of forum-shopping and avoidance of inequitable administration of the laws." *Hanna v. Plumer*....

Informed by these decisions, we address the question whether New York's "deviates materially" standard, codified in CPLR § 5501(c), is outcome-affective in this sense: Would "application of the [standard] ... have so important an effect upon the fortunes of one or both of the litigants that failure to [apply] it would [unfairly discriminate against citizens of the forum State, or] be likely to cause a plaintiff to choose the federal court"?[8] ...

We start from a point the parties do not debate. Gasperini acknowledges that a statutory cap on damages would supply substantive law for *Erie* purposes.... Although CPLR § 5501(c) is less readily classified, it was designed to provide an analogous control.

New York's Legislature codified in § 5501(c) a new standard, one that requires closer court review than the common law "shock the conscience" test.... More rigorous comparative evaluations attend application of § 5501(c)'s "deviates materially" standard.... To foster predictability, the legislature required the reviewing court, when overturning a verdict under § 5501(c), to state its reasons, including the factors it considered relevant.... We think it a fair conclusion that CPLR § 5501(c) differs from a statutory cap principally "in that the maximum amount recoverable is not set by statute, but rather is determined by case law." ... In sum, § 5501(c) contains a procedural instruction ... but the State's objective is manifestly substantive....

It thus appears that if federal courts ignore the change in the New York standard and persist in applying the "shock the conscience" test to damage awards on claims governed by New York law,[10] "'substantial' variations between state and federal money judgments" may be expected. *See Hanna*, 380 U.S. at 467–68.[11] We therefore agree with the Second Circuit that New York's check on excessive damages implicates what we have called *Erie's*

---

8. *Hanna* keyed the question to *Erie's* "twin aim"; in full, *Hanna* instructed federal courts to ask "whether application of the state's rule would make so important a difference to the character or result of the litigation that failure to enforce it would unfairly discriminate against citizens of the forum State, or whether application of the rule would have so important an effect upon the fortunes of one or both of the litigants that failure to enforce it would be likely to cause a plaintiff to choose the federal court." ...

10. Justice Scalia questions whether federal *district* courts in New York "actually apply" or "*ought*" to apply the "shock the conscience" test in assessing a jury's award for excessiveness.... If there is a federal district court standard, it must come from the Court of Appeals, not from the over 40 district court judges in the Southern District of New York, each of whom sits alone and renders decisions not binding on the others. Indeed, in *Ismail v. Cohen*, ... the authority upon which Justice Scalia relies, the Second Circuit stated that district courts test damage awards for excessiveness under the "shock the conscience" standard....

11. Justice Scalia questions whether application of CPLR § 5501(c), in lieu of the standard generally used by federal courts within the Second Circuit ... will in fact yield consistent outcome differentials.... The numbers, as the Second Circuit believed, are revealing.... Is the difference between an award of $450,000 and $100,000 ... or between $1,500 per transparency and $500 ... fairly described as insubstantial? We do not see how that can be so.

"twin aims." ...[12] Just as the *Erie* principle precludes a federal court from giving a state-created claim "longer life ... than the claim would have had in the state court," ... so *Erie* precludes a recovery in federal court significantly larger than the recovery that would have been tolerated in state court.

....

CPLR § 5501(c), as earlier noted ... is phrased as a direction to the New York Appellate Division. Acting essentially as a surrogate for a New York appellate forum, the Court of Appeals reviewed Gasperini's award to determine if it "deviated materially" from damage awards the Appellate Division permitted in similar circumstances. The Court of Appeals performed this task without benefit of an opinion from the District Court, which had denied "without comment" the Center's Rule 59 motion.... Concentrating on the authority § 5501(c) gives to the Appellate Division, Gasperini urges that the provision shifts factfinding responsibility from the jury and the trial judge to the appellate court. Assigning such responsibility to an appellate court, he maintains, is incompatible with the Seventh Amendment's re-examination clause, and therefore, Gasperini concludes, § 5501(c) cannot be given effect in federal court.... Although we reach a different conclusion than Gasperini, we agree that the Second Circuit did not attend to "an essential characteristic of the federal-court system," *Byrd v. Blue Ridge Rural Elec. Cooperative, Inc.*, ... when it used § 5501(c) as "the standard for federal appellate review"....

That "essential characteristic" was described in *Byrd*, a diversity suit for negligence in which a pivotal issue of fact would have been tried by a judge were the case in state court. The *Byrd* Court held that, despite the state practice, the plaintiff was entitled to a jury trial in federal court. In so ruling, the Court said that the *Guaranty Trust* "outcome-determination" test was an insufficient guide in cases presenting countervailing federal interests.... The Court described the countervailing federal interests present in *Byrd* this way:

> The federal system is an independent system for administering justice to litigants who properly invoke its jurisdiction. An essential characteristic of that system is the manner in which, in civil common-law actions, it distributes trial functions between judge and jury and, under the influence — if not the command — of the Seventh Amendment, assigns the decisions of disputed questions of fact to the jury....

The Seventh Amendment, which governs proceedings in federal court, but not in state court, bears not only on the allocation of trial functions between judge and jury, the issue in *Byrd*; it also controls the allocation of authority to review verdicts, the issue of concern here. The Amendment reads:

> In Suits at common law, where the value in controversy shall exceed twenty dollars, the right of trial by jury shall be preserved, and no fact tried by a jury, shall be otherwise re-examined in any Court of the United States, than according to the rules of the common law....

Byrd involved the first clause of the Amendment, the "trial by jury" clause. This case involves the second, the "Reexamination" Clause. In keeping with the historic understanding, the re-examination clause does not inhibit the authority of trial judges to grant new trials "for any of the reasons for which new trials have heretofore been granted in actions

---

12. For rights that are state-created, state law governs the amount properly awarded as punitive damages, subject to an ultimate federal constitutional check for exorbitancy.... An evenhanded approach would require federal court deference to endeavors like New York's to control compensatory damages for excessiveness....

at law in the courts of the United States." Fed. R. Civ. P. 59(a).[a] That authority is large...."The trial judge in the federal system," we have reaffirmed, "has ... discretion to grant a new trial if the verdict appears to the judge to be against the weight of the evidence."... This discretion includes overturning verdicts for excessiveness and ordering a new trial without qualification, or conditioned on the verdict winner's refusal to agree to a reduction (remittitur)....

In contrast, appellate review of a federal trial court's denial of a motion to set aside a jury's verdict as excessive is a relatively late, and less secure, development. Such review was once deemed inconsonant with the Seventh Amendment's Reexamination Clause.... We subsequently recognized that, even in cases in which the *Erie* doctrine was not in play— cases arising wholly under federal law—the question was not settled....

Before today, we have not "expressly held that the Seventh Amendment allows appellate review of a district court's denial of a motion to set aside an award as excessive."... But in successive reminders that the question was worthy of this Court's attention, we noted, without disapproval, that courts of appeals engage in review of district court excessiveness determinations, applying "abuse of discretion" as their standard....

As the Second Circuit explained, appellate review for abuse of discretion is reconcilable with the Seventh Amendment as a control necessary and proper to the fair administration of justice: "We must give the benefit of every doubt to the judgment of the trial judge; but surely there must be an upper limit, and whether that has been surpassed is not a question of fact with respect to which reasonable men may differ, but a question of law."... We now approve this line of decisions...."Nothing in the Seventh Amendment ... precludes appellate review of the trial judge's denial of a motion to set aside a jury verdict as excessive."...

....

In *Byrd*, the Court faced a one-or-the-other choice: trial by judge as in state court, or trial by jury according to the federal practice.[21] In the case before us, a choice of that order is not required, for the principal state and federal interests can be accommodated. The Second Circuit correctly recognized that when New York substantive law governs a claim for relief, New York law and decisions guide the allowable damages.... But that court did not take into account the characteristic of the federal-court system that caused us to reaffirm: "The proper role of the trial and appellate courts in the federal system in reviewing the size of jury verdicts is ... a matter of federal law."...

New York's dominant interest can be respected, without disrupting the federal system, once it is recognized that the federal district court is capable of performing the checking function, *i.e.*, that court can apply the State's "deviates materially" standard in line with New York case law evolving under CPLR § 5501(c).[22] We recall, in this regard, that the

---

a. [Eds. Note. Following the 2007 "restyling" of the Federal Rules, the quoted portion of Rule 59(a) now reads, "for any reason for which a new trial has heretofore been granted in an action at law in federal court."]

21. The two-trial rule posited by Justice Scalia ... surely would be incompatible with the existence of "the federal system as an independent system for administering justice."... We discern no disagreement on such examples among the many federal judges who have considered this case.

22. Justice Scalia finds in Federal Rule of Civil Procedure 59 a "federal standard" for new trial motions in "'direct collision'" with, and "'leaving no room for the operation of,'" a state law like CPLR § 5501(c).... The relevant prescription, Rule 59(a), has remained unchanged since the adoption of the Federal Rules by this Court in 1937.... Rule 59(a) is as encompassing as it is uncontroversial. It is indeed "Hornbook" law that a most usual ground for a Rule 59 motion is that "the damages are excessive."... Whether damages are excessive for the claim-in-suit must be governed by some law. And there is no candidate for that governance other than the law that gives rise to the claim for relief— here, the law of New York....

"deviates materially" standard serves as the guide to be applied in trial as well as appellate courts in New York....

Within the federal system, practical reasons combine with Seventh Amendment constraints to lodge in the district court, not the court of appeals, primary responsibility for application of § 5501(c)'s "deviates materially" check. Trial judges have the "unique opportunity to consider the evidence in the living courtroom context," ... while appellate judges see only the "cold paper record"....

District court applications of the "deviates materially" standard would be subject to appellate review under the standard the Circuits now employ when inadequacy or excessiveness is asserted on appeal: abuse of discretion.... In light of *Erie's* doctrine, the federal appeals court must be guided by the damage-control standard state law supplies,[23] but as the Second Circuit itself has said: "If we reverse, it must be because of an abuse of discretion.... The very nature of the problem counsels restraint.... We must give the benefit of every doubt to the judgment of the trial judge." ...

....

It does not appear that the District Court checked the jury's verdict against the relevant New York decisions demanding more than "industry standard" testimony to support an award of the size the jury returned in this case. As the Court of Appeals recognized ... the uniqueness of the photographs and the plaintiff's earnings as photographer — past and reasonably projected — are factors relevant to appraisal of the award.... Accordingly, we vacate the judgment of the Court of Appeals and instruct that court to remand the case to the District Court so that the trial judge, revisiting his ruling on the new trial motion, may test the jury's verdict against CLPR § 5501(c)'s "deviates materially" standard.

It is so ordered.

[The dissenting opinion of JUSTICE STEVENS is omitted.]

JUSTICE SCALIA, with whom the CHIEF JUSTICE and JUSTICE THOMAS join, dissenting.

Today the Court overrules a longstanding and well-reasoned line of precedent that has for years prohibited federal appellate courts from reviewing refusals by district courts to set aside civil jury awards as contrary to the weight of the evidence. One reason is given for overruling these cases: that the courts of appeals have, for some time now, decided to ignore them. Such unreasoned capitulation to the nullification of what was long regarded as a core component of the Bill of Rights — the Seventh Amendment's prohibition on appellate reexamination of civil jury awards — is wrong. It is not for us, much less for the courts of appeals, to decide that the Seventh Amendment's restriction on federal-court review of jury findings has outlived its usefulness.

The Court also holds today that a state practice that relates to the division of duties between state judges and juries must be followed by federal courts in diversity cases. On this issue, too, our prior cases are directly to the contrary.

As I would reverse the judgment of the Court of Appeals, I respectfully dissent.

---

23. If liability and damage-control rules are split apart here, as Justice Scalia says they must be to save the Seventh Amendment, then Gasperini's claim and others like it would be governed by a most curious "law." The sphinx-like, damage-determining law he would apply to this controversy has a state forepart, but a federal hindquarter. The beast may not be brutish, but there is little judgment in its creation.

[Justice Scalia first concluded that appellate review of district court refusals to set-aside jury awards as contrary to the weight of the evidence violates the "re-examination clause" of the Seventh Amendment.]

The Court's holding that federal courts of appeals may review district court denials of motions for new trials for error of fact is not the only novel aspect of today's decision. The Court also directs that the case be remanded to the District Court, so that it may "test the jury's verdict against CPLR § 5501(c)'s 'deviates materially' standard".... This disposition contradicts the principle that "the proper role of the trial and appellate courts in the federal system in reviewing the size of jury verdicts is ... a matter of federal law." ...

The Court acknowledges that state procedural rules cannot, as a general matter, be permitted to interfere with the allocation of functions in the federal court system.... Indeed, it is at least partly for this reason that the Court rejects direct application of § 5501(c) at the appellate level as inconsistent with an "essential characteristic" of the federal court system — by which the Court presumably means abuse-of-discretion review of denials of motions for new trials.... But the scope of the Court's concern is oddly circumscribed. The "essential characteristic" of the federal jury, and, more specifically, the role of the federal trial court in reviewing jury judgments, apparently counts for little. The Court approves the "accommodat[ion]" achieved by having district courts review jury verdicts under the "deviates materially" standard, because it regards that as a means of giving effect to the State's purposes "without disrupting the federal system".... But changing the standard by which trial judges review jury verdicts *does* disrupt the federal system, and is plainly inconsistent with "the strong federal policy against allowing state rules to disrupt the judge-jury relationship in federal court." *Byrd*....[9] The Court's opinion does not even acknowledge, let alone address, this dislocation.

We discussed precisely the point at issue here in *Browning-Ferris Industries, Inc. v. Kelco Disposal, Inc.,* 492 U.S. 257 (1989), and gave an answer altogether contrary to the one provided today. *Browning-Ferris* rejected a request to fashion a federal common-law rule limiting the size of punitive-damages awards in federal courts, reaffirming the principle of *Erie Railroad Co. v. Tompkins* ... that "in a diversity action, or in any other lawsuit where state law provides the basis of decision, the propriety of an award of punitive damages ... and the factors the jury may consider in determining their amount, are questions of state law." ... But the opinion expressly stated that "[f]ederal law ... will control on those issues involving the proper review of the jury award by a federal district court and court of appeals." ..."In reviewing an award of punitive damages," it said, "the role of the district court is to determine whether the jury's verdict is within the confines of state law, and to determine, by reference to federal standards developed under Rule 59, whether a new trial or remittitur should be ordered." The same distinction necessarily applies where the judgment under review is for compensatory damages: State substantive law controls what injuries are compensable and in what amount; but federal standards determine whether the award exceeds what is lawful to such degree that it may be set aside by order for new trial or remittitur.[10]

---

9. Since I reject application of the New York standard on other grounds, I need not consider whether it constitutes "reexamination" of a jury's verdict in a manner "otherwise ... than according to the rules of the common law."

10. Justice Stevens thinks that if an award "exceeds what is lawful," the result is "legal error" that "may be corrected" by the appellate court.... But the sort of "legal error" involved here is the imposition of legal consequences (in this case, damages) in light of *facts* that, under the law, may not war-

The Court does not disavow those statements in *Browning-Ferris* (indeed, it does not even discuss them), but it presumably overrules them, at least where the state rule that governs "whether a new trial or remittitur should be ordered" is characterized as "substantive" in nature. That, at any rate, is the reason the Court asserts for giving § 5501(c) dispositive effect. The objective of that provision, the Court states, "is manifestly substantive," ... since it operates to "control how much a plaintiff can be awarded" by "tightening the range of tolerable awards".... Although "less readily classified" as substantive than "a statutory cap on damages," it nonetheless "was designed to provide an analogous contro[l]," ... by making a new trial mandatory when the award "deviat[es] materially" from what is reasonable....

I do not see how this can be so. It seems to me quite wrong to regard this provision as a "substantive" rule for *Erie* purposes. The "analog[y]" to "a statutory cap on damages" ... fails utterly. There is an absolutely fundamental distinction between a *rule of law* such as that, which would ordinarily be imposed upon the jury in the trial court's instructions, and a *rule of review*, which simply determines how closely the jury verdict will be scrutinized for compliance with the instructions. A tighter standard for reviewing jury determinations can no more plausibly be called a "substantive" disposition than can a tighter appellate standard for reviewing trial-court determinations. The one, like the other, provides additional assurance *that the law has been complied with*; but the other, like the one, *leaves the law unchanged*.

The Court commits the classic *Erie* mistake of regarding whatever changes the outcome as substantive.... That is not the only factor to be considered. *See Byrd* ... ("[W]ere 'outcome' the only consideration, a strong case might appear for saying that the federal court should follow the state practice. But there are affirmative countervailing considerations at work here"). Outcome-determination "was never intended to serve as a talisman," *Hanna v. Plumer* ..., and does not have the power to convert the most classic elements of the *process* of assuring that the law is observed into the substantive law itself. The right to have a jury make the findings of fact, for example, is generally thought to favor plaintiffs, and that advantage is often thought significant enough to be the basis for forum selection. But no one would argue that *Erie* confers a right to a jury in federal court wherever state courts would provide it; or that, were it not for the Seventh Amendment, *Erie* would require federal courts to dispense with the jury whenever state courts do so.

In any event, the Court exaggerates the difference that the state standard will make. It concludes that different outcomes are likely to ensue depending on whether the law being applied is the state "deviates materially" standard of § 5501(c) or the "shocks the conscience" standard.... Of course it is not the federal *appellate* standard but the federal *district-court* standard for granting new trials that must be compared with the New York standard to determine whether substantially different results will obtain—and it is far from clear that the district-court standard *ought* to be "shocks the conscience." Indeed, it is not even clear (as the Court asserts) that "shocks the conscience" *is* the standard (erroneous or not) actually applied by the district courts of the Second Circuit. The Second Circuit's test for reversing a grant of a new trial for an excessive verdict is whether the award was "*clearly* within the maximum limit of a reasonable range," *Ismail v. Cohen* ... so any district court that uses that standard will be affirmed. And while many district-court decisions express the "shocks the conscience" criterion ... some have used a standard of "indisputably egregious," ... or have adopted the inverse of the Second Circuit's test for oftlinereversing a grant of new trial,

---

rant them. To suggest that every fact may be reviewed, because what may ensue from an erroneous factual determination is a "legal error," is to destroy the notion that there is a factfinding function reserved to the jury.

namely, "*clearly* outside the maximum limit of a reasonable range." ... Moreover, some decisions that *say* "shocks the conscience" in fact apply a rule much less stringent. One case, for example, says that any award that would not be sustained under the New York "deviates materially" rule "shocks the conscience." ... In sum, it is at least highly questionable whether the consistent outcome differential claimed by the Court even exists. What seems to me far more likely to produce forum shopping is the consistent difference between the state and federal *appellate* standards, which the Court leaves untouched. Under the Court's disposition, the Second Circuit reviews only for abuse of discretion, whereas New York's appellate courts engage in a *de novo* review for material deviation, giving the defendant a double shot at getting the damages award set aside. The only result that would produce the conformity the Court erroneously believes *Erie* requires is the one adopted by the Second Circuit and rejected by the Court: *de novo* federal appellate review under the § 5501(c) standard.

To say that application of § 5501(c) in place of the federal standard will not consistently produce disparate results is not to suggest that the decision the Court has made today is not a momentous one. The *principle* that the state standard governs is of great importance, since it bears the potential to destroy the uniformity of federal practice and the integrity of the federal court system. Under the Court's view, a state rule that directed courts "to determine that an award is excessive or inadequate if it deviates *in any degree* from *the proper measure of compensation*" would have to be applied in federal courts, effectively requiring federal judges to determine the amount of damages *de novo*, and effectively taking the matter away from the jury entirely.... Or consider a state rule that allowed the defendant a second trial on damages, with judgment ultimately in the amount of the lesser of two jury awards.... Under the reasoning of the Court's opinion, even such a rule as that would have to be applied in the federal courts.

The foregoing describes why I think the Court's *Erie* ~~analysis~~ [NEW YORK] is flawed. But in my view, one does not even reach the *Erie* question in this case. The standard to be applied by a district court in ruling on a motion for a new trial is set forth in Rule 59 of the Federal Rules of Civil Procedure, which provides that "a new trial may be granted ... for any of the reasons for which new trials have heretofore been granted in actions at law *in the courts of the United States*" (emphasis added). That is undeniably a federal standard.[12] Federal district courts in the Second Circuit have interpreted that standard to permit the granting of new trials where "'it is quite clear that the jury has reached a seriously erroneous result'" and letting the verdict stand would result in a "'miscarriage of justice.'" ... Assuming ... that this is a correct interpretation of what Rule 59 requires, it is undeniable that the federal rule is "'sufficiently broad' to cause a 'direct collision' with the state law or, implicitly, to 'control the issue' before the court, thereby leaving no room for the operation of that law." *Burlington N.R.R. Co. v. Woods*.... It is simply not possible to give controlling effect both to the federal standard and the state standard in reviewing the jury's award. That being so, the court has no choice but to apply the Federal Rule, which is an exercise of what we have called Congress's "power to regulate matters which, though falling within the uncertain area between substance and procedure, are rationally capable of classification as either," *Hanna*....

[handwritten margin note: Materially deviate tougher than shock the conscience]

---

12. I agree with the Court's entire progression of reasoning ... leading to the conclusion that state law must determine "[w]hether damages are excessive." But the question of whether damages are excessive is quite separate from the question of when a jury award may be set aside for excessiveness.... It is the latter that is governed by Rule 59; as *Browning-Ferris* said, district courts are "to determine, by reference to federal standards developed under Rule 59, whether a new trial or remittitur should be ordered." ...

....

When there is added to the revision of the Seventh Amendment the Court's precedent-setting disregard of Congress's instructions in Rule 59, one must conclude that this is a bad day for the Constitution's distinctive Article III courts in general, and for the role of the jury in those courts in particular. I respectfully dissent.

Notes and Questions

1. On remand in *Gasperini*, the district court stated:

> The Supreme Court decision in this case represents an extension of *Erie* ... or more likely a reversion by the Supreme Court to prior *Erie* doctrine since abandoned, of which *Guaranty Trust* ... is the outstanding example. The Supreme Court in *Guaranty Trust* and again in *Gasperini* seems to have endorsed the outcome-determinative test to determine whether a disputed point of law is *procedural*, and therefore governed by the Federal Rules of Civil Procedure and case law developed thereunder, or *substantive* so as to be governed by state law.

Gasperini v. Center for Humanities, Inc., 972 F. Supp. 765, 767 (S.D.N.Y. 1997). Based on the description of the case above, do you agree that the Supreme Court held that the outcome determination test should be used to determine whether a disputed point is substantive or procedural for purposes of determining whether the point is governed by the Federal Rules of Civil Procedure?

2. Consider, first, Justice Scalia's argument that Federal Rule 59(a) was applicable to the case and left no room for the operation of state law. Given the Court's prior methodology of rule interpretation in *Hanna* and *Burlington Northern*, was his approach or the majority's "correct." What is the soundest approach? Consider the following questions:

(a) As Justice Scalia observes, Rule 59 states that new trials may be granted when a jury has returned a verdict "for any of the reasons for which new trials have heretofore been granted in actions at law in the Courts of the United States." Does this establish an independent standard by Federal Rule, or does it just refer to standards existing outside the Federal Rules for determining when new trials should be granted? Consider the following description of Rule 59(a):

> Rule 59 does not list the grounds for which a new trial may be granted, but says only that this action may be taken for any of the reasons for which new trials have "heretofore been granted" in actions at law in federal courts. The usual grounds for a new trial are that the verdict is against the weight of the evidence, that the damages are excessive, or that, for other reasons, the trial was not fair....

Wʀɪɢʜᴛ & Kᴀɴᴇ § 95, at 676.

(b) If the seemingly broad interpretive process used in *Hanna* and *Burlington Northern* is employed to determine whether Rule 59 is broad enough to cover the case, what would the result be? Note that the majority in *Gasperini* stated that federal courts had interpreted the Federal Rules with sensitivity to state interests, citing *Walker. See* 518 U.S. at 427 n.7. Did this mean the majority was approving of the narrow interpretive methodology used in *Walker* and disapproving of the broad methodology of *Hanna* and *Burlington Northern*? Is this why the majority did not consider Rule 59(a) applicable?

(c) Even if Justice Scalia was correct that Rule 59(a) was broad enough to cover the case, shouldn't he have applied the Rules Enabling Act test to determine whether the rule was valid? If that test (as elaborated in *Burlington Northern*) is applied to Rule 59 (construed broadly), what would the result be in *Gasperini*?

3. Both the majority and the dissent in *Gasperini* paid lip service to the *Hanna* refinement of the Rules of Decision Act portion of the *Erie* doctrine. However, neither the majority nor the dissenting opinion adequately analyzed the case to determine whether the Rules of Decision Act was violated. Consider the following questions:

(a) Why was there no discussion of whether the state rule was a rule bound up with state rights or a rule of form and mode? Is the failure of the majority or dissent to consider this question evidence that the *Byrd* categorization process is dead? In *Kampa v. White Consolidated Industries, Inc.*, 115 F.3d 585 (8th Cir. 1997), the court was faced with a potential conflict between the Minnesota Human Rights Act, which specifically provided that claims brought under the Act were to be decided by a judge without a jury. The court explicitly acknowledged that under *Byrd* state law that is bound up with the substantive claim should be applied by federal diversity courts. The court found "no clear evidence" that the Minnesota prohibition on jury trials was bound up with the substantive claim created by the Human Rights Act, but held, in any event, that the Seventh Amendment required a jury trial in federal court. Does *Kampa* provide some evidence that the *Byrd* categorization process is still alive?

(b) Assuming it was proper to apply the outcome determination test in *Gasperini* to determine whether state law could be disregarded, did the majority do an adequate job of analyzing the case? The majority simply stated that disregard of the New York standard would produce "substantial variations" in state and federal money judgments by allowing larger recoveries in federal courts than would be possible in state courts. Would this cause a noncitizen plaintiff to shop for a federal court, or do plaintiffs consider such matters when selecting a forum? If noncitizen plaintiffs would not forum shop, would a noncitizen defendant remove a case to federal court if the federal courts are allowed to disregard the state standard? If you think forum shopping is not a danger in cases like *Gasperini*, would discrimination against citizens of the forum state occur if federal courts are allowed to disregard state law? Regardless of how you have answered these questions, shouldn't the majority have discussed them? Or are the answers obvious to everyone but Civil Procedure teachers?

(c) Was Justice Scalia's analysis of the general *Erie* problem better than that of the majority? Justice Scalia stated that it was "wrong" to consider the state law as a "substantive" rule for *Erie* purposes. In discussing whether disregard of New York law would cause a prohibited outcome difference, he first argued that the various verbalizations of the standard for granting new trials on the grounds that the verdict was excessive really would not produce differences in outcome at the district court level. Is this plausible? Justice Scalia also argued that forum shopping was much more likely to occur because of the differences in the federal and state appellate standards. However, this really *is* implausible, isn't it? Doesn't this presuppose that plaintiffs will go to federal rather than state courts because they are aware that if a jury awards them too much and a federal district court (following a state standard) fails to grant a new trial, a federal appellate court is more likely than a state appellate court to sustain the (erroneous) trial court determination? Do plaintiffs plan litigation on bases like this in real life?

4. Consider the majority's application of the *Byrd* "countervailing considerations" test. In *Byrd*, the Court balanced federal countervailing considerations against the federal

outcome determination policies. In *Gasperini*, the Court appeared to measure the federal countervailing considerations against "state interests." Is this a change in doctrine for future cases, or is it somehow explained by the fact that the majority "accommodated" the state and federal interests in the case? On the other hand, Justice Scalia argued that federal countervailing considerations of the same sort involved in *Byrd* were present. Was this correct? Would reviewing a jury's verdict by a more stringent standard disrupt the federal judge-jury relationship as much as shifting the question from the jury to the judge altogether (as under the state law in *Byrd*)? If not, how should one determine how to weigh the degree of disruption involved against the outcome determinative policies (or against state interests, if that is to be the counterbalancing factor)? Does either the majority or dissent give any additional guidance about (a) the legitimate sources of federal countervailing considerations or (b) how to attach weight to them?

Problems

Problem 5-10. Reevaluate *Problems 5-3* and *5-4* on the basis of the Court's decisions through *Gasperini*. Has your evaluation changed because of the later cases?

Problem 5-11. As part of a tort reform effort, the State *Y* legislature enacted a "certificate of merit" requirement applicable to all products liability actions. The statute contained three requirements: a plaintiff commencing a products liability action must file with the complaint an affidavit verifying that (a) a qualified expert in product manufacturing and design was consulted and that the expert drafted a report concerning the merits of the plaintiff's claim; (b) the expert retained for the purpose of producing the report has reviewed the facts of the case with the plaintiff or the plaintiff's attorney; and (c) the expert has examined the product or literature pertaining to the product before reaching conclusions. In addition, in a product liability action based on negligence, the expert's report must identify the specific act or omission or other fault that caused the plaintiff's injuries and must conclude that the alleged negligence was a proximate cause of the harm resulting to the plaintiff. Failure to comply with the statutory requirements results in dismissal of the action on the merits.

After the effective date of this statute, *P*, a citizen of State *X*, was injured by a product manufactured by *D*, a citizen of State *Y*. *P* purchased the product in State *Y* and was injured by it there. *P* commenced an action against *D* in the U.S. District Court for the District of State *X* (obtaining "general" personal jurisdiction over *D* under the State *X* long-arm statute). *P* seeks $1,000,000 for the injuries received from the product. *P's* complaint alleged that the product was negligently manufactured by *D*, but the complaint was not accompanied by the affidavit required by the law of State *Y*. *D* moves to dismiss the action with prejudice on the grounds that the State *Y* affidavit requirement is a substantive law that must be applied by the U.S. District Court in State *X*. Does the *Erie* doctrine require the federal court in State *X* to apply the State *Y* affidavit requirement?

Semtek. In *Semtek International Inc. v. Lockheed Martin Corp.*, 531 U.S. 497 (2001), the plaintiff commenced an action in California state court. The complaint alleged a breach of contract and various business torts. The defendant removed the action to a California federal district court on the basis of diversity of citizenship. The defendant then moved to dismiss the plaintiff's claims on the ground that they were barred by California's two-year statute of limitations. The court ordered the plaintiff's claims dismissed "in [their] entirety on the merits and with prejudice." Without contesting the court's designation of the dismissal as one "on the merits," the plaintiff appealed to the Ninth Circuit Court of Appeals. The Ninth Circuit affirmed the district court's order. *Id.* at 499.

In addition to the appeal, the plaintiff commenced an action in Maryland state court against the defendant. The plaintiff alleged the same causes of action, which were not barred under Maryland's three-year statute of limitations. The defendant moved to dismiss the Maryland action on the ground of res judicata arguing that the California federal court dismissal was on the merits and claim preclusive as a matter of federal law. (The doctrine of claim preclusion, which is covered in Chapter 12, generally prohibits a party from refiling a claim in another court after it has been dismissed on the merits in an earlier action.) The plaintiff contended that the scope of the California federal judgment should be controlled by California state law, which provided that a judgment of dismissal on statute-of-limitations grounds is without prejudice and, therefore, not claim preclusive. The Maryland Court of Special Appeals affirmed the trial court's conclusion that the action should be dismissed on the basis of res judicata. The Maryland Court of Special Appeals held that federal law controlled the scope of the federal judgment and precluded the new action. *Id.* at 500.

The U.S. Supreme Court reversed. In an opinion by Justice Scalia, the Court initially confronted the applicability of Federal Rule 41(b), which provides that all dismissals in federal court are on the merits unless the court specifies otherwise or they are within one of three specified categories—dismissals for lack of jurisdiction, improper venue, or failure to join a required party under Federal Rule 19. In reaching the conclusion that Rule 41(b) did not apply, the Court first stated that the expression "on the merits" originally meant an adjudication that actually passes directly on the substance of a particular claim. It then observed that the meaning of "judgment on the merits" had changed over the years and had "come to be applied to some judgments ... that do *not* pass upon the substantive merits of the claim and hence do *not* (in many jurisdictions) entail claim-preclusive effect."

The Court next concluded that Rule 41(b) sets forth "nothing more than a default rule for determining the import of a dismissal." The Court reasoned that a default rule like Rule 41(b) would be a peculiar context in which to announce a federally prescribed rule on the complex question of claim preclusion and it would be peculiar to find a rule governing the effect that must be accorded to federal judgments by "other courts" in rules governing the internal procedures of the federal courts. Later, the Court indicated that the effect of Rule 41(b) was simply to prevent the refiling of the action in the U.S. District Court in California by which it was dismissed. Furthermore, according to the Court, to interpret Rule 41(b) to require the California federal judgment to be entitled to a claim preclusive effect in other states would "seem" to violate the substantive rights restriction of the Rules Enabling Act. Thus, the Court indicated that the rule should be interpreted in a way that would avoid this possibility.

Thus, the Court ultimately held (1) Rule 41(b) inapplicable to the case, (2) that the scope of federal diversity judgments is controlled by federal common law, but (3) that federal common law would normally adopt the res judicata law of the state where the federal diversity judgment was rendered. In reaching the latter conclusion, the Court relied on the *Erie* doctrine only in passing. In discussing the general *Erie* policies, however, the Court stated that providing a claim-preclusive effect on the *Semtek* facts would encourage forum shopping in the initial action in order to get a statute-of-limitations dismissal that would bar suit everywhere. This statement clearly indicates that forum shopping by a defendant through removal violates the *Erie* policies, a question technically left open by the Court's prior decisions. It is also a statement that it is forum shopping in the first action that matters, rather than forum shopping in the second action in which the res judicata effect of the judgment is being determined. The Court's further holding that the res judicata effect of federal diversity judgments is to be determined by reference to state law unless state res judicata rules are "incompatible with federal interests" is examined further in Chapter 12.

Notes and Questions

1. Read Federal Rule 41(b). Do you understand what the Court meant when it indicated that the last sentence of Rule 41(b) was a "default provision"? Examine the second sentence of Rule 41(b) carefully. To what does the language "[u]nless the dismissal order states otherwise" refer? Should a "default provision" have had any application at all when the district court specifically stated that its dismissal was "on the merits"? Recall that the federal district court ordered the plaintiff's claims dismissed "in [their] entirety on the merits and with prejudice." Was the real problem not with Rule 41(b) but with the court's order?

2. In the U.S. Supreme Court, the defendant argued that Federal Rule 41(b) controlled the outcome of the case because the dismissal order by the California federal district court did not state otherwise and did not pertain to the excepted subjects of jurisdiction, venue, or joinder. Thus, as a result of the operation of Rule 41(b) making all other dismissals operate "as an adjudication on the merits," the defendant asserted that the dismissal by the California federal district court was entitled to claim preclusive effect. *Semtek*, 531 U.S. at 500. In response, the Court held that the use of the words "on the merits" in Rule 41(b), and in the California district court's order, did not automatically produce a claim-preclusive effect. *Id.* at 503. Apart from the Rules Enabling Act and *Erie* considerations, the Court offered three principal "interpretative" reasons for its conclusion that "on the merits" language in Rule 41(b) did not dictate the result in the case. First, as observed above, the Court asserted that Rule 41(b) was merely a "default rule for determining the import of a dismissal" and was not designed to announce a federally prescribed rule on the complex question of claim preclusion. *Id.*

Second, the Court concluded that the phrase "without prejudice" as used in Rule 41(a) meant that the defendant could return later to the same court with the same underlying claim. It then concluded an "adjudication on the merits," as used in Rule 41(b), was simply meant to establish the opposite of a "dismissal without prejudice," *i.e.*, that the plaintiff could not return to the same court with the same underlying claim when there had been an "adjudication on the merits." *Id.* at 505. Third, because Rule 41(b) was a rule "governing the internal procedures of the rendering court itself," *id.* at 503, the Court concluded the "'adjudication-on-the-merits' default provision of Rule 41(b) — and, presumably, of the explicit order in the present case that used the language of that default provision — [means] simply that, unlike a dismissal 'without prejudice,' the dismissal in the present case barred refiling of the same claim in the United States District Court for the Central District of California." *Id.* at 506. Do you think the Court construed Rule 41(b) correctly?

3. Immediately following its discussion about possible violation of the Rules Enabling Act, the Court indicated that if Rule 41(b) were interpreted to mandate a claim-preclusive effect in *Semtek*, it would violate the outcome determination test evolved under the Rules of Decision Act in *Erie* and *Guaranty Trust*. The clear implication of this statement is that the outcome determination test evolved under the Rules of Decision Act is somehow relevant to the validity of Federal Rules of Civil Procedure. What is left of *Hanna* after this statement? What is now the test for determining whether a Federal Rule of Civil Procedure is valid? As you will see in the *Shady Grove* decision, below, these implications of the statement are not true. Nevertheless, this is unfortunate sloppiness on the Court's part, is it not?

Problems

Problem 5-12. *P*, a citizen of State *X*, sues *D*, a citizen of State *Y*, in a U.S. District Court in State *Y* for $100,000. *D* moves to dismiss *P's* complaint under Federal Rule 12(b)(6), and the court grants *D's* motion with leave to *P* to amend within a certain period of time. *P* does not amend, and the Court enters a final judgment against *P* without specifying whether the judgment is or is not "on the merits." *P* recommences the action with a corrected complaint in a state court in State *Y*. *D* pleads the federal judgment as res judicata. Assume that under State *Y* law a judgment of dismissal for failure to state a claim is not on the merits and has no claim-preclusive effect. Is the federal judgment res judicata after *Semtek*?

Problem 5-13. *P*, a citizen of State *X*, sues *D*, a citizen of State *Y*, in a U.S. District Court in State *X* for $100,000. *D* answers the complaint, denying *P's* allegations and raising certain affirmative defenses to *P's* claim. After a trial, *D* wins a judgment that *P* take nothing. Subsequently, *D* sues *P* in a state court of State *X*, asserting a claim against *P* that arose out of the same occurrence as *P's* claim against *D* in the federal action. *P* pleads res judicata as a defense against this claim, contending that it was a compulsory counterclaim in the federal action and that as a result, Rule 13(a) prohibits *D* from asserting it in a second proceeding. Assume that the counterclaim was indeed a compulsory counterclaim in the federal action, but that State *X* does not have a compulsory counterclaim rule. Thus, if the first action had been in a State *X* court, *D's* claim would not be precluded. After *Semtek*, is *D* precluded from asserting the claim in the state action?

Shady Grove Orthopedic Associates v. Allstate Insurance Co.

United States Supreme Court, 2010
559 U.S. ___, 130 S. Ct. 1431, 176 L. Ed. 2d 311

JUSTICE SCALIA announced the judgment of the Court and delivered the opinion of the Court with respect to Parts I and II-A, an opinion with respect to Parts II-B and II-D, in which THE CHIEF JUSTICE, JUSTICE THOMAS, and JUSTICE SOTOMAYOR joined, and an opinion with respect to Part II-C, in which THE CHIEF JUSTICE and JUSTICE THOMAS joined.

New York law prohibits class actions in suits seeking penalties or statutory minimum damages.[1] We consider whether this precludes a federal district court sitting in diversity from entertaining a class action under Federal Rule of Civil Procedure 23.

---

1. N.Y. Civ. Prac. Law Ann. § 901 (West 2006) provides:
"(a) One or more members of a class may sue or be sued as representative parties on behalf of all if:"
"1. the class is so numerous that joinder of all members, whether otherwise required or permitted, is impracticable;"
"2. there are questions of law or fact common to the class which predominate over any questions affecting only individual members;"
"3. the claims or defenses of the representative parties are typical of the claims or defenses of the class;"
"4. the representative parties will fairly and adequately protect the interests of the class; and"
"5. a class action is superior to other available methods for the fair and efficient adjudication of the controversy."
"(b) Unless a statute creating or imposing a penalty, or a minimum measure of recovery specifically authorizes the recovery thereof in a class action, an action to recover a penalty, or minimum measure of recovery created or imposed by statute may not be maintained as a class action."

NY wouldn't proceed as class action

I

The petitioner's complaint alleged the following: Shady Grove Orthopedic Associates, P.A., provided medical care to Sonia E. Galvez for injuries she suffered in an automobile accident. As partial payment for that care, Galvez assigned to Shady Grove her rights to insurance benefits under a policy issued in New York by Allstate Insurance Co. Shady Grove tendered a claim for the assigned benefits to Allstate, which under New York law had 30 days to pay the claim or deny it. *See* N.Y. Ins. Law Ann. § 5106(a) (West 2009). All-state apparently paid, but not on time, and it refused to pay the statutory interest that accrued on the overdue benefits (at two percent per month), *see id.* Shady Grove filed this diversity suit in the Eastern District of New York to recover the unpaid statutory interest. Alleging that Allstate routinely refuses to pay interest on overdue benefits, Shady Grove sought relief on behalf of itself and a class of all others to whom Allstate owes interest. The District Court dismissed the suit for lack of jurisdiction.... It reasoned that N.Y. Civ. Prac. Law Ann. § 901(b), which precludes a suit to recover a "penalty" from proceeding as a class action, applies in diversity suits in federal court, despite Federal Rule of Civil Procedure 23. Concluding that statutory interest is a "penalty" under New York law, it held that § 901(b) prohibited the proposed class action. And, since Shady Grove conceded that its individual claim (worth roughly $500) fell far short of the amount-in-controversy requirement for individual suits under 28 U.S.C. § 1332(a), the suit did not belong in federal court.[3]

The Second Circuit affirmed.... The court did not dispute that a federal rule adopted in compliance with the Rules Enabling Act, 28 U.S.C. § 2072, would control if it conflicted with § 901(b). But there was no conflict because (as we will describe in more detail below) the Second Circuit concluded that Rule 23 and § 901(b) address different issues. Finding no federal rule on point, the Court of Appeals held that § 901(b) is "substantive" within the meaning of *Erie R.R. Co. v. Tompkins,* 304 U.S. 64 (1938), and thus must be applied by federal courts sitting in diversity.

We granted certiorari....

II

The framework for our decision is familiar. We must first determine whether Rule 23 answers the question in dispute. *Burlington Northern R.R. Co. v. Woods,* 480 U.S. 1, 4–5 (1987). If it does, it governs—New York's law notwithstanding—unless it exceeds statutory authorization or Congress's rulemaking power. *Id.* at 5; *see Hanna v. Plumer,* 380 U.S. 460, 463–64 (1965). We do not wade into *Erie's* murky waters unless the federal rule is inapplicable or invalid. *See* 380 U.S. at 469–71.

A

The question in dispute is whether Shady Grove's suit may proceed as a class action. Rule 23 provides an answer. It states that "[a] class action may be maintained" if two conditions are met: The suit must satisfy the criteria set forth in subdivision (a) (*i.e.,* numerosity, commonality, typicality, and adequacy of representation), and it also must fit into one of the three categories described in subdivision (b). Fed. R. Civ. P. 23(b). By its terms this creates a categorical rule entitling a plaintiff whose suit meets the specified criteria to pursue his claim as a class action. (The Federal Rules regularly use "may" to con-

---

3. Shady Grove had asserted jurisdiction under 28 U.S.C. § 1332(d)(2), which relaxes, for class actions seeking at least $5 million, the rule against aggregating separate claims for calculation of the amount in controversy. *See Exxon Mobil Corp. v. Allapattah Servs., Inc.,* 545 U.S. 546, 571 (2005).

fer categorical permission, *see, e.g.,* Fed. R. Civ. P. 8(d)(2)-(3), 14(a)(1), 18(a)-(b), 20(a)(1)-(2), 27(a)(1), 30(a)(1), as do federal statutes that establish procedural entitlements, *see, e.g.,* 29 U.S.C. §626(c)(1); 42 U.S.C. §2000e-5(f)(1).) Thus, Rule 23 provides a one-size-fits-all formula for deciding the class-action question. Because §901(b) attempts to answer the same question—*i.e.,* it states that Shady Grove's suit "may *not* be maintained as a class action" (emphasis added) because of the relief it seeks—[§901(b)] cannot apply in diversity suits unless Rule 23 is ultra vires.

(NY)

The Second Circuit believed that §901(b) and Rule 23 do not conflict because they address different issues. Rule 23, it said, concerns only the criteria for determining whether a given class can and should be certified; section 901(b), on the other hand, addresses an antecedent question: whether the particular type of claim is eligible for class treatment in the first place—a question on which Rule 23 is silent.... Allstate embraces this analysis....

We disagree. To begin with, the line between eligibility and certifiability is entirely artificial. Both are preconditions for maintaining a class action. Allstate suggests that eligibility must depend on the "particular cause of action" asserted, instead of some other attribute of the suit.... But that is not so. Congress could, for example, provide that only claims involving more than a certain number of plaintiffs are "eligible" for class treatment in federal court. In other words, relabeling Rule 23(a)'s prerequisites "eligibility criteria" would obviate Allstate's objection—a sure sign that its eligibility—certifiability distinction is made-to-order.

There is no reason, in any event, to read Rule 23 as addressing only whether claims made eligible for class treatment by some *other* law should be certified as class actions. Allstate asserts that Rule 23 neither explicitly nor implicitly empowers a federal court "to certify a class in each and every case" where the Rule's criteria are met.... But that is *exactly* what Rule 23 does: It says that if the prescribed preconditions are satisfied "[a] class action *may be maintained*" (emphasis added)—not "*a class action may be permitted.*" Courts do not maintain actions; litigants do. The discretion suggested by Rule 23's "may" is discretion residing in the plaintiff: He may bring his claim in a class action if he wishes. And like the rest of the Federal Rules of Civil Procedure, Rule 23 *automatically* applies "in all civil actions and proceedings in the United States district courts," Fed. R. Civ. P. 1....

    ....

The dissent argues that §901(b) has nothing to do with whether Shady Grove may maintain its suit as a class action, but affects only the *remedy* it may obtain if it wins.... Whereas "Rule 23 governs procedural aspects of class litigation" by "prescrib[ing] the considerations relevant to class certification and postcertification proceedings," §901(b) addresses only "the size of a monetary award a class plaintiff may pursue."... Accordingly, the dissent says, Rule 23 and New York's law may coexist in peace.

We need not decide whether a state law that limits the remedies available in an existing class action would conflict with Rule 23; that is not what §901(b) does. By its terms, the provision precludes a plaintiff from "maintain[ing]" a class action seeking statutory penalties. Unlike a law that sets a ceiling on damages (or puts other remedies out of reach) in properly filed class actions, §901(b) says nothing about what remedies a court may award; it prevents the class actions it covers from coming into existence at all.[4]....

---

4. Contrary to the dissent's implication ... we express no view as to whether state laws that set a ceiling on damages recoverable in a single suit ... are pre-empted. Whether or not those laws conflict with Rule 23, §901(b) does conflict because it addresses not the remedy, but the procedural right to maintain a class action. As Allstate and the dissent note, several federal statutes also limit the recovery available in class actions. *See, e.g.,* 12 U.S.C. §2605(f)(2)(B); 15 U.S.C. §1640(a)(2)(B); 29 U.S.C.

The dissent asserts that a plaintiff can avoid § 901(b)'s barrier by omitting from his complaint (or removing) a request for statutory penalties.... Even assuming all statutory penalties are waivable, the fact that a complaint omitting them could be brought as a class action would not at all prove that § 901(b) is addressed only to remedies. If the state law instead banned class actions for fraud claims, a would-be class-action plaintiff could drop the fraud counts from his complaint and proceed with the remainder in a class action. Yet that would not mean the law provides no remedy for fraud; the ban would affect only the procedural means by which the remedy may be pursued. In short, although the dissent correctly abandons Allstate's eligibility—certifiability distinction, the alternative it offers fares no better.

The dissent all but admits that the literal terms of § 901(b) address the same subject as Rule 23—*i.e.,* whether a class action may be maintained—but insists the provision's *purpose* is to restrict only remedies....

This evidence of the New York Legislature's purpose is pretty sparse. But even accepting the dissent's account of the Legislature's objective at face value, it cannot override the statute's clear text. Even if its aim is to restrict the remedy a plaintiff can obtain, § 901(b) achieves that end by limiting a plaintiff's power to maintain a class action. The manner in which the law "could have been written," ... has no bearing; what matters is the law the Legislature *did* enact. We cannot rewrite that to reflect our perception of legislative purpose.... The dissent's concern for state prerogatives is frustrated rather than furthered by revising state laws when a potential conflict with a Federal Rule arises; the state-friendly approach would be to accept the law as written and test the validity of the Federal Rule.

. . . .

But while the dissent does indeed artificially narrow the scope of § 901(b) by finding that it pursues only substantive policies, that is not the central difficulty of the dissent's position. The central difficulty is that even artificial narrowing cannot render § 901(b) compatible with Rule 23. *Whatever* the policies they pursue, they flatly contradict each other. Allstate asserts (and the dissent implies ...) that we can (and must) *interpret* Rule 23 in a manner that avoids overstepping its authorizing statute. If the Rule were susceptible of two meanings—one that would violate § 2072(b) and another that would not—we would agree. *See Ortiz v. Fibreboard Corp.,* 527 U.S. 815, 842, 845 (1999); *cf. Semtek Int'l Inc. v. Lockheed Martin Corp.,* 531 U.S. 497, 503–04 (2001). But it is not. Rule 23 unambiguously authorizes *any* plaintiff, in *any* federal civil proceeding, to maintain a class action if the Rule's prerequisites are met. We cannot contort its text, even to avert a collision with state law that might render it invalid. *See Walker v. Armco Steel Corp.,* 446 U.S. 740, 750, n.9 (1980). What the dissent's approach achieves is not the avoiding of a "conflict between Rule 23 and § 901(b)," ... but rather the invalidation of Rule 23 (pursuant to § 2072(b) of the Rules Enabling Act) to the extent that it conflicts with the substantive policies of § 901. There is no other way to reach the dissent's destination. We must therefore confront head-on whether Rule 23 falls within the statutory authorization.

B

Erie involved the constitutional power of federal courts to supplant state law with judge-made rules. In that context, it made no difference whether the rule was technically

---

§ 1854(c)(1). But Congress has plenary power to override the Federal Rules, so its enactments, unlike those of the States, prevail even in case of a conflict.

one of substance or procedure; the touchstone was whether it "significantly affect[s] the result of a litigation." *Guaranty Trust Co. v. York*, 326 U.S. 99, 109 (1945). That is not the test for either the constitutionality or the statutory validity of a Federal Rule of Procedure. Congress has undoubted power to supplant state law, and undoubted power to prescribe rules for the courts it has created, so long as those rules regulate matters "rationally capable of classification" as procedure. *Hanna*, 380 U.S. at 472. In the Rules Enabling Act, Congress authorized this Court to promulgate rules of procedure subject to its review, 28 U.S.C. § 2072(a), but with the limitation that those rules "shall not abridge, enlarge or modify any substantive right," § 2072(b).

We have long held that this limitation means that the Rule must "really regulat[e] procedure—the judicial process for enforcing rights and duties recognized by substantive law and for justly administering remedy and redress for disregard or infraction of them," *Sibbach*, 312 U.S. at 14; *see Hanna*, 380 U.S. at 464; *Burlington*, 480 U.S. at 8. The test is not whether the rule affects a litigant's substantive rights; most procedural rules do. *Mississippi Publishing Corp. v. Murphree*, 326 U.S. 438, 445 (1946). What matters is what the rule itself regulates: If it governs only "the manner and the means" by which the litigants' rights are "enforced," it is valid; if it alters "the rules of decision by which [the] court will adjudicate [those] rights," it is not. *Id.* at 446 (internal quotation marks omitted).

Applying that test, we have rejected every statutory challenge to a Federal Rule that has come before us. We have found to be in compliance with § 2072(b) rules prescribing methods for serving process, *see id.* at 445–46 (Fed. R. Civ. P. 4(f)); *Hanna*, 380 U.S. at 463–65 (Fed. R. Civ. P. 4(d)(1)), and requiring litigants whose mental or physical condition is in dispute to submit to examinations, *see Sibbach*, 312 U.S. at 14–16 (Fed. R. Civ. P. 35); *Schlagenhauf v. Holder*, 379 U.S. 104, 113–14 (1964) (same). Likewise, we have upheld rules authorizing imposition of sanctions upon those who file frivolous appeals, *see Burlington*, 480 U.S. at 8 (Fed. R. App. P. 38), or who sign court papers without a reasonable inquiry into the facts asserted, *see Business Guides, Inc. v. Chromatic Communications Enters., Inc.*, 498 U.S. 533, 551–54 (1991) (Fed. R. Civ. P. 11). Each of these rules had some practical effect on the parties' rights, but each undeniably regulated only the process for enforcing those rights; none altered the rights themselves, the available remedies, or the rules of decision by which the court adjudicated either.

Applying that criterion, we think it obvious that rules allowing multiple claims (and claims by or against multiple parties) to be litigated together are also valid. *See, e.g.*, Fed. R. Civ. P. 18 (joinder of claims), 20 (joinder of parties), 42(a) (consolidation of actions). Such rules neither change plaintiffs' separate entitlements to relief nor abridge defendants' rights; they alter only how the claims are processed. For the same reason, Rule 23—at least insofar as it allows willing plaintiffs to join their separate claims against the same defendants in a class action—falls within § 2072(b)'s authorization. A class action, no less than traditional joinder (of which it is a species), merely enables a federal court to adjudicate claims of multiple parties at once, instead of in separate suits. And like traditional joinder, it leaves the parties' legal rights and duties intact and the rules of decision unchanged.

. . . .

Allstate contends that the authorization of class actions is not substantively neutral: Allowing Shady Grove to sue on behalf of a class "transform[s] [the] dispute over a five *hundred* dollar penalty into a dispute over a five *million* dollar penalty." . . .

. . . .

Allstate [also] argues that Rule 23 violates §2072(b) because the state law it displaces, §901(b), creates a right that the Federal Rule abridges—namely, a "substantive right ... not to be subjected to aggregated class-action liability" in a single suit....

The fundamental difficulty with both these arguments is that the substantive nature of New York's law, or its substantive purpose, *makes no difference.* A Federal Rule of Procedure is not valid in some jurisdictions and invalid in others—or valid in some cases and invalid in others—depending upon whether its effect is to frustrate a state substantive law (or a state procedural law enacted for substantive purposes). That could not be clearer in *Sibbach*:

> The petitioner says the phrase ["substantive rights" in the Rules Enabling Act] connotes more; that by its use Congress intended that in regulating procedure this Court should not deal with important and substantial rights theretofore recognized. Recognized where and by whom? The state courts are divided as to the power in the absence of statute to order a physical examination. In a number such an order is authorized by statute or rule....

> The asserted right, moreover, is no more important than many others enjoyed by litigants in District Courts sitting in the several states before the Federal Rules of Civil Procedure altered and abolished old rights or privileges and created new ones in connection with the conduct of litigation.... If we were to adopt the suggested criterion of the importance of the alleged right we should invite endless litigation and confusion worse confounded. The test must be whether a rule really regulates procedure....

312 U.S. at 13–14 (footnotes omitted).

Hanna unmistakably expressed the same understanding that compliance of a Federal Rule with the Enabling Act is to be assessed by consulting the Rule itself, and not its effects in individual applications:

> [T]he court has been instructed to apply the Federal Rule, and can refuse to do so only if the Advisory Committee, this Court, and Congress erred in their prima facie judgment that the Rule in question transgresses neither the terms of the Enabling Act nor constitutional restrictions.

380 U.S. at 471.

In sum, it is not the substantive or procedural nature or purpose of the affected state law that matters, but the substantive or procedural nature of the Federal Rule. We have held since *Sibbach,* and reaffirmed repeatedly, that the validity of a Federal Rule depends entirely upon whether it regulates procedure. *See Sibbach*, 312 U.S. at 14; *Hanna*, 380 U.S. at 464; *Burlington*, 480 U.S. at 8. If it does, it is authorized by §2072 and is valid in all jurisdictions, with respect to all claims, regardless of its incidental effect upon state-created rights.

C

A few words in response to the concurrence. We understand it to accept the framework we apply—which requires first, determining whether the federal and state rules can be reconciled (because they answer different questions), and second, if they cannot, determining whether the Federal Rule runs afoul of §2072(b).... The concurrence agrees with us that Rule 23 and §901(b) conflict, ... and departs from us only with respect to the second part of the test, *i.e.,* whether application of the Federal Rule violates §2072(b).... Like us, it answers no, but for a reason different from ours....

The concurrence would decide this case on the basis, not that Rule 23 is procedural, but that the state law it displaces is procedural, in the sense that it does not "function as a part of the State's definition of substantive rights and remedies." ... A state procedural rule is not preempted, according to the concurrence, so long as it is [not] "so bound up with," or "sufficiently intertwined with," a substantive state-law right or remedy "that it defines the scope of that substantive right or remedy"....

This analysis squarely conflicts with *Sibbach*, which established the rule we apply....

In reality, the concurrence seeks not to apply *Sibbach*, but to overrule it (or, what is the same, to rewrite it). Its approach, the concurrence insists, gives short shrift to the statutory text forbidding the Federal Rules from "abridg[ing], enlarg[ing], or modify[ing] any substantive right," § 2072(b).... There is something to that. It is possible to understand how it can be determined whether a Federal Rule "enlarges" substantive rights without consulting State law: If the Rule creates a substantive right, even one that duplicates some state-created rights, it establishes a new *federal* right. But it is hard to understand how it can be determined whether a Federal Rule "abridges" or "modifies" substantive rights without knowing what state-created rights would obtain if the Federal Rule did not exist. *Sibbach's* exclusive focus on the challenged Federal Rule—driven by the very real concern that Federal Rules which vary from State to State would be chaos, *see* 312 U.S. at 13–14—is hard to square with § 2072(b)'s terms.

Sibbach has been settled law, however, for nearly seven decades. Setting aside any precedent requires a "special justification" beyond a bare belief that it was wrong. *Patterson v. McLean Credit Union*, 491 U.S. 164, 172 (1989) (internal quotation marks omitted). And a party seeking to overturn a *statutory* precedent bears an even greater burden, since Congress remains free to correct us, *id.*, and adhering to our precedent enables it do so, *see, e.g., Finley v. United States*, 490 U.S. 545, 556; 28 U.S.C. § 1367; *Exxon Mobil Corp. v. Allapattah Servs., Inc.*, 545 U.S. 546, 558 (2005). We do Congress no service by presenting it a moving target....

D

We must acknowledge the reality that keeping the federal-court door open to class actions that cannot proceed in state court will produce forum shopping. That is unacceptable when it comes as the consequence of judge-made rules created to fill supposed "gaps" in positive federal law. *See Hanna*, 380 U.S. at 471–72. For where neither the Constitution, a treaty, nor a statute provides the rule of decision or authorizes a federal court to supply one, "state law must govern because there can be no other law." *Id.; see* Clark, Erie's *Constitutional Source*, 95 Cal. L. Rev. 1289, 1302, 1311 (2007). But divergence from state law, with the attendant consequence of forum shopping, is the inevitable (indeed, one might say the intended) result of a uniform system of federal procedure. Congress itself has created the possibility that the same case may follow a different course if filed in federal instead of state court. *Cf. Hanna*, 380 U.S. at 472–73. The short of the matter is that a Federal Rule governing procedure is valid whether or not it alters the outcome of the case in a way that induces forum shopping. To hold otherwise would be to "disembowel either the Constitution's grant of power over federal procedure" or Congress's exercise of it. *Id.* at 473–74.

    ....

The judgment of the Court of Appeals is reversed, and the case is remanded for further proceedings.

It is so ordered.

says conflicts w/ Fed. Rule 23? (handwritten)

JUSTICE STEVENS, concurring in part and concurring in the judgment.

The New York law at issue, N.Y. Civ. Prac. Law Ann. (CPLR) § 901(b) (West 2006), is a procedural rule that is not part of New York's substantive law. Accordingly, I agree with Justice Scalia that Federal Rule of Civil Procedure 23 must apply in this case and join Parts I and II-A of the Court's opinion. But I also agree with Justice Ginsburg that there are some state procedural rules that federal courts must apply in diversity cases because they function as a part of the State's definition of substantive rights and remedies.

I

It is a long-recognized principle that federal courts sitting in diversity "apply state substantive law and federal procedural law." *Hanna v. Plumer,* 380 U.S. 460, 465 (1965). This principle is governed by a statutory framework, and the way that it is administered varies depending upon whether there is a federal rule addressed to the matter. *See id.* at 469–72. If no federal rule applies, a federal court must follow the Rules of Decision Act, 28 U.S.C. § 1652, and make the "relatively unguided *Erie* choice," *Hanna,* 380 U.S. at 471, to determine whether the state law is the "rule of decision." But when a situation is covered by a federal rule, the Rules of Decision Act inquiry by its own terms does not apply. *See* 28 U.S.C. § 1652; *Hanna,* 380 U.S. at 471. Instead, the Rules Enabling Act (Enabling Act) controls. *See* 28 U.S.C. § 2072.

That does not mean, however, that the federal rule always governs. Congress has provided for a system of uniform federal rules, *see id.,* under which federal courts sitting in diversity operate as "an independent system for administering justice to litigants who properly invoke its jurisdiction," *Byrd v. Blue Ridge Rural Elec. Cooperative, Inc.,* 356 U.S. 525, 537 (1958), and not as state-court clones that assume all aspects of state tribunals but are managed by Article III judges. *See Hanna,* 380 U.S. at 473–74. But while Congress may have the constitutional power to prescribe procedural rules that interfere with state substantive law in any number of respects, that is not what Congress has done. Instead, it has provided in the Enabling Act that although "[t]he Supreme Court" may "prescribe general rules of practice and procedure," § 2072(a), those rules "shall not abridge, enlarge or modify any substantive right," § 2072(b). Therefore, "[w]hen a situation is covered by one of the Federal Rules, ... the court has been instructed to apply the Federal Rule" unless doing so would violate the Act or the Constitution. *Hanna,* 380 U.S. at 471.

Although the Enabling Act and the Rules of Decision Act "say, roughly, that federal courts are to apply state 'substantive' law and federal 'procedural' law," the inquiries are not the same. *Id.; see also id.* at 469–70. The Enabling Act does not invite federal courts to engage in the "relatively unguided *Erie* choice," *id.* at 471, but instead instructs only that federal rules cannot "abridge, enlarge or modify any substantive right," § 2072(b). The Enabling Act's limitation does not mean that federal rules cannot displace state policy judgments; it means only that federal rules cannot displace a State's definition of its own rights or remedies. *See Sibbach v. Wilson & Co.,* 312 U.S. 1, 13–14 (1941) (reasoning that "the phrase 'substantive rights'" embraces only those state rights that are sought to be enforced in the judicial proceedings).

. . . .

It is important to observe that the balance Congress has struck turns, in part, on the nature of the state law that is being displaced by a federal rule. And in my view, the application of that balance does not necessarily turn on whether the state law at issue takes the *form* of what is traditionally described as substantive or procedural. Rather, it turns on whether the state law actually is part of a State's framework of substantive rights or remedies. *See* 28 U.S.C. § 2072(b); *cf. Hanna,* 380 U.S. at 471 ("The line between 'substance' and 'procedure' shifts as the legal context changes"); *Guaranty Trust Co. v. York,* 326 U.S.

99, 108 (1945) (noting that the words "'substance'" and "'procedure'" "[e]ach impl[y] different variables depending upon the particular problem for which [they] are used").

....

II

When both a federal rule and a state law appear to govern a question before a federal court sitting in diversity, our precedents have set out a two-step framework for federal courts to negotiate this thorny area. At both steps of the inquiry, there is a critical question about what the state law and the federal rule mean.

The court must first determine whether the scope of the federal rule is "'sufficiently broad'" to "'control the issue'" before the court, "thereby leaving no room for the operation" of seemingly conflicting state law.... *From Burlington*

If ... the federal rule is "sufficiently broad to control the issue before the Court," such that there is a "direct collision," *Walker,* 446 U.S. at 749–50, the court must decide whether application of the federal rule "represents a valid exercise" of the "rulemaking authority ... bestowed on this Court by the Rules Enabling Act." *Burlington Northern R.R. Co.,* 480 U.S. at 5; *see also Gasperini,* 518 U.S. at 427, n.7; *Hanna,* 380 U.S. at 471–74. That Act requires, *inter alia,* that federal rules "not abridge, enlarge or modify *any* substantive right." 28 U.S.C. § 2072(b) (emphasis added). Unlike Justice Scalia, I believe that an application of a federal rule that effectively abridges, enlarges, or modifies a state-created right or remedy violates this command. Congress may have the constitutional power "to supplant state law" with rules that are "rationally capable of classification as procedure," ... but we should generally presume that it has not done so.... Indeed, the mandate that federal rules "shall not abridge, enlarge or modify any substantive right" evinces the opposite intent, as does Congress' decision to delegate the creation of rules to this Court rather than to a political branch....

Thus, the second step of the inquiry may well bleed back into the first. When a federal rule appears to abridge, enlarge, or modify a substantive right, federal courts must consider whether the rule can reasonably be interpreted to avoid that impermissible result. *See, e.g., Semtek Int'l Inc. v. Lockheed Martin Corp.,* 531 U.S. 497, 503 (2001) (avoiding an interpretation of Federal Rule of Civil Procedure 41(b) that "would arguably violate the jurisdictional limitation of the Rules Enabling Act" contained in § 2072(b)). And when such a "saving" construction is not possible and the rule would violate the Enabling Act, federal courts cannot apply the rule. *See* 28 U.S.C. § 2072(b) (mandating that federal rules "shall not" alter "*any* substantive right" (emphasis added)); *Hanna,* 380 U.S. at 473 ("[A] court, in measuring a Federal Rule against the standards contained in the Enabling Act ... need not wholly blind itself to the degree to which the Rule makes the character and result of the federal litigation stray from the course it would follow in state courts"); *see also Semtek Int'l Inc.,* 531 U.S. at 503–04 (noting that if state law granted a particular right, "the federal court's extinguishment of that right ... would seem to violate [§ 2072(b)]") ... A federal rule, therefore, cannot govern a particular case in which the rule would displace a state law that is procedural in the ordinary use of the term but is so intertwined with a state right or remedy that it functions to define the scope of the state-created right. And absent a governing federal rule, a federal court must engage in the traditional Rules of Decision Act inquiry, under the *Erie* line of cases. This application of the Enabling Act shows "sensitivity to important state interests," ... and "regulatory policies," ... but it does so as Congress authorized, by ensuring that federal rules that ordinarily "prescribe general rules of practice and procedure," § 2072(a), do "not abridge, enlarge or modify any substantive right," § 2072(b).

Justice Scalia believes that the sole Enabling Act question is whether the federal rule "really regulates procedure," ... which means, apparently, whether it regulates "the manner and the means by which the litigants' rights are enforced," ... I respectfully disagree. This interpretation of the Enabling Act is consonant with the Act's first limitation to "general rules of practice and procedure," § 2072(a). But it ignores the second limitation that such rules also "not abridge, enlarge or modify *any* substantive right," § 2072(b) (emphasis added),[8] and in so doing ignores the balance that Congress struck between uniform rules of federal procedure and respect for a State's construction of its own rights and remedies. It also ignores the separation-of-powers presumption ... and federalism presumption, ... that counsel against judicially created rules displacing state substantive law.[9]

....

Although the plurality appears to agree with much of my interpretation of § 2072, ... it nonetheless rejects that approach for two reasons, both of which are mistaken. First, Justice Scalia worries that if federal courts inquire into the effect of federal rules on state law, it will enmesh federal courts in difficult determinations about whether application of a given rule would displace a state determination about substantive rights.... I do not see why an Enabling Act inquiry that looks to state law necessarily is more taxing than Justice Scalia's. But in any event, that inquiry is what the Enabling Act requires: While it may not be easy to decide what is actually a "substantive right," "the designations substantive and procedural become important, for the Enabling Act has made them so." ... The question, therefore, is not what rule *we* think would be easiest on federal courts. The question is what rule Congress established. Although Justice Scalia may generally prefer easily administrable, bright-line rules, his preference does not give us license to adopt a second-best interpretation of the Rules Enabling Act. Courts cannot ignore text and context in the service of simplicity.

Second, the plurality argues that its interpretation of the Enabling Act is dictated by this Court's decision in *Sibbach,* which applied a Federal Rule about when parties must

---

8. Justice Scalia concedes as much ... but argues that insofar as I allow for the possibility that a federal rule might violate the Enabling Act when it displaces a seemingly procedural state rule, my approach is itself "unfaithful to the statute's terms," which cover "substantive rights" but not "procedural rules,".... This is not an objection to my interpretation of the Enabling Act—that courts must look to whether a federal rule alters substantive rights in a given case—but simply to the way I would apply it, allowing for the possibility that a state rule that regulates something traditionally considered to be procedural might actually define a substantive right. Justice Scalia's objection, moreover, misses the key point: In some instances, a state rule that appears procedural really is not. A rule about how damages are reviewed on appeal may really be a damages cap. See *Gasperini,* 518 U.S. at 427. A rule that a plaintiff can bring a claim for only three years may really be a limit on the existence of the right to seek redress. A rule that a claim must be proved beyond a reasonable doubt may really be a definition of the scope of the claim. These are the sorts of rules that one might describe as "procedural," but they nonetheless define substantive rights. Thus, if a federal rule displaced such a state rule, the federal rule would have altered the State's "substantive rights."

9. The plurality's interpretation of the Enabling Act appears to mean that no matter how bound up a state provision is with the State's own rights or remedies, any contrary federal rule that happens to regulate "the manner and the means by which the litigants' rights are enforced," ... must govern. There are many ways in which seemingly procedural rules may displace a State's formulation of its substantive law. For example, statutes of limitations, although in some sense procedural rules, can also be understood as a temporal limitation on legally created rights; if this Court were to promulgate a federal limitations period, federal courts would still, in some instances, be required to apply state limitations periods. Similarly, if the federal rules altered the burden of proof in a case, this could eviscerate a critical aspect—albeit one that deals with *how* a right is enforced—of a State's framework of rights and remedies. Or if a federal rule about appellate review displaced a state rule about how damages are reviewed on appeal, the federal rule might be pre-empting a state damages cap. Cf. *Gasperini,* 518 U.S. at 427.

submit to medical examinations. But the plurality misreads that opinion. As Justice Harlan observed in *Hanna*, "shorthand formulations which have appeared in earlier opinions are prone to carry untoward results that frequently arise from oversimplification." 380 U.S. at 475 (concurring opinion). To understand *Sibbach*, it is first necessary to understand the issue that was before the Court. The petitioner raised only the facial question whether "Rules 35 and 37 [of the Federal Rules of Civil Procedure] are ... within the mandate of Congress to this court" and not the specific question of "the obligation of federal courts to apply the substantive law of a state." 312 U.S. at 9. The Court, therefore, had no occasion to consider whether the particular application of the Federal Rules in question would offend the Enabling Act.

Nor, in *Sibbach*, was any further analysis necessary to the resolution of the case because the matter at issue, requiring medical exams for litigants, did not pertain to "substantive rights" under the Enabling Act. Although most state rules bearing on the litigation process are adopted for some policy reason, few seemingly "procedural" rules define the scope of a substantive right or remedy. The matter at issue in *Sibbach* reflected competing federal and state judgments about privacy interests. Those privacy concerns may have been weighty and in some sense substantive; but they did not pertain to the scope of any state right or remedy at issue in the litigation. Thus, in response to the petitioner's argument in *Sibbach* that "substantive rights" include not only "rights sought to be adjudicated by the litigants" but also "general principle[s]" or "question[s] of public policy that the legislature is able to pass upon," *id.* at 2–3, we held that "the phrase 'substantive rights'" embraces only state rights, such as the tort law in that case, that are sought to be enforced in the judicial proceedings. *Id.* at 13–14. If the Federal Rule had in fact displaced a state rule that was sufficiently intertwined with a state right or remedy, then perhaps the Enabling Act analysis would have been different. Our subsequent cases are not to the contrary.

III

Justice Ginsburg views the basic issue in this case as whether and how to apply a federal rule that dictates an answer to a traditionally procedural question (whether to join plaintiffs together as a class), when a state law that "defines the dimensions" of a state-created claim dictates the opposite answer.... As explained above, I readily acknowledge that if a federal rule displaces a state rule that is "'procedural' in the ordinary sense of the term," *S.A. Healy Co.*, 60 F.3d at 310, but sufficiently interwoven with the scope of a substantive right or remedy, there would be an Enabling Act problem, and the federal rule would have to give way. In my view, however, this is not such a case.

. . . .

The text of CPLR § 901(b) expressly and unambiguously applies not only to claims based on New York law but also to claims based on federal law or the law of any other State. And there is no interpretation from New York courts to the contrary. It is therefore hard to see how § 901(b) could be understood as a rule that, though procedural in form, serves the function of defining New York's rights or remedies....

. . . .

Accordingly, I concur in part and concur in the judgment.

JUSTICE GINSBURG, with whom JUSTICE KENNEDY, JUSTICE BREYER, and JUSTICE ALITO join, dissenting.

. . . .

The Court reads Rule 23 relentlessly to override New York's restriction on the availability of statutory damages. Our decisions, however, caution us to ask, before undermining state legislation: Is this conflict really necessary? *Cf.* Traynor, *Is This Conflict Really Necessary?* 37 Tex. L. Rev. 657 (1959). Had the Court engaged in that inquiry, it would not have read Rule 23 to collide with New York's legitimate interest in keeping certain monetary awards reasonably bounded. I would continue to interpret Federal Rules with awareness of, and sensitivity to, important state regulatory policies. Because today's judgment radically departs from that course, I dissent.

I

....

[handwritten: Ginsburg — doesn't see direct collision]

B

In our prior decisions in point, many of them not mentioned in the Court's opinion, we have avoided immoderate interpretations of the Federal Rules that would trench on state prerogatives without serving any countervailing federal interest. "Application of the *Hanna* analysis," we have said, "is premised on a 'direct collision' between the Federal Rule and the state law." *Walker v. Armco Steel Corp.*, 446 U.S. 740, 749–50 (1980) (quoting *Hanna*, 380 U.S. at 472). To displace state law, a Federal Rule, "when fairly construed," must be " 'sufficiently broad' " so as "to 'control the issue' before the court, thereby leaving *no room* for the operation of that law." *Burlington Northern R. Co. v. Woods*, 480 U.S. 1, 4–5 (1987) (quoting *Walker*, 446 U.S. at 749–50 & n.9) (emphasis added); *cf. Stewart Organization, Inc. v. Ricoh Corp.*, 487 U.S. 22, 37–38 (1988) (Scalia, J., dissenting) ("[I]n deciding whether a federal ... Rule of Procedure encompasses a particular issue, a broad reading that would create significant disuniformity between state and federal courts should be avoided if the text permits.").

In pre-*Hanna* decisions, the Court vigilantly read the Federal Rules to avoid conflict with state laws. In *Palmer v. Hoffman*, 318 U.S. 109, 117 (1943), for example, the Court read Federal Rule 8(c), which lists affirmative defenses, to control only the manner of pleading the listed defenses in diversity cases; as to the burden of proof in such cases, *Palmer* held, state law controls.

Six years later, in *Ragan v. Merchants Transfer & Warehouse Co.*, 337 U.S. 530 (1949), the Court ruled that state law determines when a diversity suit commences for purposes of tolling the state limitations period. Although Federal Rule 3 specified that "[a] civil action is commenced by filing a complaint with the court," we held that the Rule did not displace a state law that tied an action's commencement to service of the summons. *Id.* at 531–33. The "cause of action [wa]s created by local law," the Court explained, therefore "the measure of it [wa]s to be found only in local law." *Id.* at 533.

Similarly in *Cohen v. Beneficial Industrial Loan Corp.*, 337 U.S. 541 (1949), the Court held applicable in a diversity action a state statute requiring plaintiffs, as a prerequisite to pursuit of a stockholder's derivative action, to post a bond as security for costs. At the time of the litigation, Rule 23, now Rule 23.1, addressed a plaintiff's institution of a derivative action in federal court. Although the Federal Rule specified prerequisites to a stockholder's maintenance of a derivative action, the Court found no conflict between the Rule and the state statute in question; the requirements of both could be enforced, the Court observed. *See id.* at 556. Burdensome as the security-for-costs requirement may be, *Cohen* made plain, suitors could not escape the upfront outlay by resorting to the federal court's diversity jurisdiction.

In all of these cases, the Court stated in *Hanna*, "the scope of the Federal Rule was not as broad as the losing party urged, and therefore, there being no Federal Rule which covered the point in dispute, *Erie* commanded the enforcement of state law." 380 U.S. at 470.

In *Hanna* itself, the Court found the clash "unavoidable," *id.*; the petitioner had effected service of process as prescribed by Federal Rule 4(d)(1), but that "how-to" method did not satisfy the special Massachusetts law applicable to service on an executor or administrator. Even as it rejected the Massachusetts prescription in favor of the federal procedure, however, "[t]he majority in Hanna recognized ... that federal rules ... must be interpreted by the courts applying them, and that the process of interpretation can and should reflect an awareness of legitimate state interests." R. Fallon, J. Manning, D. Meltzer, & D. Shapiro, *Hart and Wechsler's The Federal Courts and the Federal System* 593 (6th ed. 2009) (hereinafter Hart & Wechsler).

Following *Hanna,* we continued to "interpre[t] the federal rules to avoid conflict with important state regulatory policies." Hart & Wechsler 593. In *Walker,* the Court took up the question whether *Ragan* should be overruled; we held, once again, that Federal Rule 3 does not directly conflict with state rules governing the time when an action commences for purposes of tolling a limitations period. 446 U.S. at 749–52. Rule 3, we said, addresses only "the date from which various timing requirements of the Federal Rules begin to run," *id.* at 751 and does not "purpor[t] to displace state tolling rules," *id.* at 750–51. Significant state policy interests would be frustrated, we observed, were we to read Rule 3 as superseding the state rule, which required actual service on the defendant to stop the clock on the statute of limitations. *Id.* at 750–52.

We were similarly attentive to a State's regulatory policy in *Gasperini*. That diversity case concerned the standard for determining when the large size of a jury verdict warrants a new trial. Federal and state courts alike had generally employed a "shock the conscience" test in reviewing jury awards for excessiveness. *See* 518 U.S. at 422. Federal courts did so pursuant to Federal Rule 59(a) which, as worded at the time of *Gasperini,* instructed that a trial court could grant a new trial "for any of the reasons for which new trials have heretofore been granted in actions at law in the courts of the United States." Fed. R. Civ. P. 59(a). In an effort to provide greater control, New York prescribed procedures under which jury verdicts would be examined to determine whether they "deviate[d] materially from what would be reasonable compensation." *See Gasperini,* 518 U.S. at 423–25 (quoting CPLR § 5501(c)). This Court held that Rule 59(a) did not inhibit federal-court accommodation of New York's invigorated test.

Most recently, in *Semtek,* we addressed the claim-preclusive effect of a federal-court judgment dismissing a diversity action on the basis of a California statute of limitations. The case came to us after the same plaintiff renewed the same fray against the same defendant in a Maryland state court. (Plaintiff chose Maryland because that State's limitations period had not yet run.) We held that Federal Rule 41(b), which provided that an involuntary dismissal "operate[d] as an adjudication on the merits," did not bar maintenance of the renewed action in Maryland. To hold that Rule 41(b) precluded the Maryland courts from entertaining the case, we said, "would arguably violate the jurisdictional limitation of the Rules Enabling Act," 531 U.S. at 503 and "would in many cases violate [*Erie's*] federalism principle," *id.* at 504.

In sum, both before and after *Hanna,* the above-described decisions show, federal courts have been cautioned by this Court to "interpre[t] the Federal Rules ... with sensitivity to important state interests," *Gasperini,* 518 U.S. at 427, n.7, and a will "to avoid conflict with important state regulatory policies," *id.* at 438, n.22 (internal quotation marks omitted).[2] The Court veers away from that approach—and conspicuously, its most

---

2. Justice Stevens stakes out common ground on this point: "[F]ederal rules," he observes, "must be interpreted with some degree of 'sensitivity to important state interests and regulatory policies,'... and applied to diversity cases against the background of Congress' command that such rules not alter

recent reiteration in *Gasperini*—in favor of a mechanical reading of Federal Rules, insensitive to state interests and productive of discord.

C

Our decisions instruct over and over again that, in the adjudication of diversity cases, state interests—whether advanced in a statute, *e.g.,* *Cohen,* or a procedural rule, *e.g., Gasperini*—warrant our respectful consideration. Yet today, the Court gives no quarter to New York's limitation on statutory damages and requires the lower courts to thwart the regulatory policy at stake: To prevent excessive damages, New York's law controls the penalty to which a defendant may be exposed in a single suit. The story behind § 901(b)'s enactment deserves telling.

In 1975, the Judicial Conference of the State of New York proposed a new class-action statute designed "to set up a flexible, functional scheme" that would provide "an effective, but controlled group remedy." Judicial Conference Report on CPLR, *reprinted in* 1975 N.Y. Laws pp. 1477, 1493 (McKinney). As originally drafted, the legislation addressed only the procedural aspects of class actions; it specified, for example, five prerequisites for certification, eventually codified at § 901(a), that closely tracked those listed in Rule 23. *See* CPLR § 901(a) (requiring, for class certification, numerosity, predominance, typicality, adequacy of representation, and superiority).

While the Judicial Conference proposal was in the New York Legislature's hopper, "various groups advocated for the addition of a provision that would prohibit class action plaintiffs from being awarded a statutorily-created penalty ... except when expressly authorized in the pertinent statute." *Sperry v. Crompton Corp.,* 863 N.E.2d 1012, 1015 (N.Y. 2007). These constituents "feared that recoveries beyond actual damages could lead to excessively harsh results." *Id.* "They also argued that there was no need to permit class actions ... [because] statutory penalties ... provided an aggrieved party with a sufficient economic incentive to pursue a claim." *Id.* Such penalties, constituents observed, often far exceed a plaintiff's actual damages. "When lumped together," they argued, "penalties and class actions produce overkill." Attachment to Letter from G. Perkinson, New York State Council of Retail Merchants, Inc., to J. Gribetz, Executive Chamber (June 4, 1975) (Legislative Report), Bill Jacket, L. 1975, Ch. 207.

Aiming to avoid "annihilating punishment of the defendant," the New York Legislature amended the proposed statute to bar the recovery of statutory damages in class actions. V. Alexander, Practice Commentaries, C901:11, *reprinted in* 7B McKinney's Consolidated Laws of New York Ann., p. 104 (2006) (internal quotation marks omitted). In his signing statement, Governor Hugh Carey stated that the new statute "empowers the court to prevent abuse of the class action device and provides *a controlled remedy.*" Memorandum on Approving L. 1975, Ch. 207, *reprinted in* 1975 N.Y. Laws at 1748 (emphasis added).

. . . .

D

Shady Grove contends—and the Court today agrees—that Rule 23 unavoidably preempts New York's prohibition on the recovery of statutory damages in class actions. The Federal Rule, the Court emphasizes, states that Shady Grove's suit "may be" maintained

---

substantive rights and with consideration of 'the degree to which the Rule makes the character and result of the federal litigation stray from the course it would follow in state courts,' [*Hanna v. Plumer*], 380 U.S. [460, 473 (1965)]." ... But a majority of this Court, it bears emphasis, agrees that Federal Rules should be read with moderation in diversity suits to accommodate important state concerns....

as a class action, which conflicts with § 901(b)'s instruction that it "may not" so proceed.... Accordingly, the Court insists, § 901(b) "cannot apply in diversity suits unless Rule 23 is ultra vires." *Id.* Concluding that Rule 23 does not violate the Rules Enabling Act, the Court holds that the federal provision controls Shady Grove's ability to seek, on behalf of a class, a statutory penalty of over $5,000,000....

The Court, I am convinced, finds conflict where none is necessary. Mindful of the history behind § 901(b)'s enactment, the thrust of our precedent, and the substantive-rights limitation in the Rules Enabling Act, I conclude, as did the Second Circuit and every District Court to have considered the question in any detail, that Rule 23 does not collide with § 901(b). As the Second Circuit well understood, Rule 23 prescribes the considerations relevant to class certification and postcertification proceedings — but it does not command that a particular remedy be available when a party sues in a representative capacity. *See* 549 F.3d 137, 143 (2008). Section 901(b), in contrast, trains on that latter issue. Sensibly read, Rule 23 governs procedural aspects of class litigation, but allows state law to control the size of a monetary award a class plaintiff may pursue.

In other words, Rule 23 describes a method of enforcing a claim for relief, while § 901(b) defines the dimensions of the claim itself. In this regard, it is immaterial that § 901(b) bars statutory penalties in wholesale, rather than retail, fashion. The New York Legislature could have embedded the limitation in every provision creating a cause of action for which a penalty is authorized; § 901(b) operates as shorthand to the same effect. It is as much a part of the delineation of the claim for relief as it would be were it included claim by claim in the New York Code.

....

Any doubt whether Rule 23 leaves § 901(b) in control of the remedial issue at the core of this case should be dispelled by our *Erie* jurisprudence, including *Hanna,* which counsels us to read Federal Rules moderately and cautions against stretching a rule to cover every situation it could conceivably reach. The Court states that "[t]here is no reason ... to read Rule 23 as addressing only whether claims made eligible for class treatment by some *other* law should be certified as class actions." ... To the contrary, *Palmer, Ragan, Cohen, Walker, Gasperini,* and *Semtek* provide good reason to look to the law that creates the right to recover.... That is plainly so on a more accurate statement of what is at stake: Is there any reason to read Rule 23 as authorizing a claim for relief when the State that created the remedy disallows its pursuit on behalf of a class? None at all is the answer our federal system should give.

....

II

Because I perceive no unavoidable conflict between Rule 23 and § 901(b), I would decide this case by inquiring "whether application of the [state] rule would have so important an effect upon the fortunes of one or both of the litigants that failure to [apply] it would be likely to cause a plaintiff to choose the federal court." *Hanna,* 380 U.S. at 468, n.9. *See Gasperini,* 518 U.S. at 428.

....

.... When no federal law or rule is dispositive of an issue, and a state statute is outcome affective in the sense our cases on *Erie* (pre and post-*Hanna*) develop, the Rules of Decision Act commands application of the State's law in diversity suits. *Gasperini,* 518 U.S. at 428; *Hanna,* 380 U.S. at 468, n.9; *York,* 326 U.S. at 109. As this case starkly demonstrates, if federal courts exercising diversity jurisdiction are compelled by Rule 23 to award statutory penalties in class actions while New York courts are bound by § 901(b)'s proscription, "substantial variations between state and federal [money judgments] may be expected." *Gasperini,* 518 U.S. at 430 (quoting *Hanna,* 380 U.S. at 467–68 (internal quotation marks omitted)). The "variation" here is indeed "substantial." Shady Grove seeks class relief that is *ten thousand times* greater than the individual remedy available to it in state court. As the plurality acknowledges, ... forum shopping will undoubtedly result if a plaintiff need only file in federal instead of state court to seek a massive monetary award explicitly barred by state law. *See Gasperini,* 518 U.S. at 431 ("*Erie* precludes a recovery in federal court significantly larger than the recovery that would have been tolerated in state court.").[13] The "accident of diversity of citizenship," *Klaxon Co. v. Stentor Elec. Mfg. Co.,* 313 U.S. 487, 496 (1941), should not subject a defendant to such augmented liability. *See Hanna,* 380 U.S. at 467 ("The *Erie* rule is rooted in part in a realization that it would be unfair for the character or result of a litigation materially to differ because the suit had been brought in a federal court.").

....

We have long recognized the impropriety of displacing, in a diversity action, state-law limitations on state-created remedies. *See Woods,* 337 U.S. at 538 (in a diversity case, a plaintiff "barred from recovery in the state court ... should likewise be barred in the federal court"); *York,* 326 U.S. at 108–09 (federal court sitting in diversity "cannot afford recovery if the right to recover is made unavailable by the State nor can it substantively affect the enforcement of the right as given by the State"). Just as *Erie* precludes a federal court from entering a deficiency judgment when a State has "authoritatively announced that [such] judgments cannot be secured within its borders," *Angel v. Bullington,* 330 U.S. 183, 191 (1947), so too *Erie* should prevent a federal court from awarding statutory penalties aggregated through a class action when New York prohibits this recovery. *See also Ragan,* 337 U.S. at 533 ("Where local law qualifies or abridges [a claim], the federal court must follow suit. Otherwise there is a different measure of the cause of action in one court than in the other, and the principle of *Erie* ... is transgressed."). In sum, because "New York substantive law governs [this] claim for relief, New York law ... guide[s] the allowable damages." *Gasperini,* 518 U.S. at 437.

III

The Court's erosion of *Erie's* federalism grounding impels me to point out the large irony in today's judgment. Shady Grove is able to pursue its claim in federal court only by virtue of the recent enactment of the Class Action Fairness Act of 2005 (CAFA), 28 U.S.C. § 1332(d). In CAFA, Congress opened federal-court doors to state-law-based class actions so long as there is minimal diversity, at least 100 class members, and at least $5,000,000 in controversy. *Id.* By providing a federal forum, Congress sought to check what it considered to be the overreadiness of some state courts to certify class actions....

---

13. In contrast, many "state rules ostensibly addressed to procedure," ... (majority opinion) — including pleading standards and rules governing summary judgment, pretrial discovery, and the admissibility of certain evidence — would not so hugely impact forum choices. It is difficult to imagine a scenario that would promote more forum shopping than one in which the difference between filing in state and federal court is the difference between a potential award of $500 and one of $5,000,000.

....

I would continue to approach *Erie* questions in a manner mindful of the purposes underlying the Rules of Decision Act and the Rules Enabling Act, faithful to precedent, and respectful of important state interests. I would therefore hold that the New York Legislature's limitation on the recovery of statutory damages applies in this case, and would affirm the Second Circuit's judgment.

Notes and Questions

1. (a) In *Semtek*, described earlier in this section, the Court, in an opinion authored by Justice Scalia, interpreted Rule 41(b) narrowly to provide a preclusive effect only in a second action in the same court in which the first dismissal occurred. Given what you concluded about the *Semtek* Court's interpretive methodology in response to prior questions in this section, is Justice Scalia's conclusion in *Shady Grove* that Rule 23 is applicable consistent with the interpretive methodology employed in *Semtek*? If not, what accounts for the difference in his approach?

(b) Reconsider the *Cohen* case, described in section B(1). Why did that case not control the issue of rule interpretation in *Shady Grove*? Shouldn't Justice Scalia at least explained the distinction between *Shady Grove* and *Cohen*? In analyzing the difference between the cases, consider also Justice Harlan's view of *Cohen* in his concurring opinion in *Hanna* set out in section B(2). If Justice Harlan's view of the case is accurate, can there be a significant difference between *Cohen* and *Shady Grove*?

2. What is the status of the *Burlington Northern* test for rule validity under the Rules Enabling Act after *Shady Grove*? If it is intact, do you have confidence that it will be after the next decision of the Court in this area?

3. (a) Consider Justice Stevens' opinion in *Shady Grove*. While he agrees with Justice Scalia that Rule 23 is applicable and valid, Justice Stevens does not agree that in determining a Federal Rule's validity under the Rules Enabling Act, a court should focus only on the character of the Federal Rule and not on state law. To the contrary, Justice Stevens argues that Federal Rules may have to give way when they conflict with state procedural rules supported by substantive policies, or that are "intertwined" with state substantive policies. Is it clear to you when a state rule will be sufficiently "substantive" in this sense to prevent a Federal Rule from displacing it in an *Erie* situation?

(b) Note also that Justice Stevens goes on to conclude that the New York law in question is not (or not clearly) supported by substantive policies, with the result that the case only involves a conflict between two procedural rules. Do you agree with this conclusion or with Justice Ginsburg's conclusion in dissent that the New York law is supported by substantive policies because it is designed to prevent ruinous liability to a defendant in a single action?

4. Note that Justice Ginsburg interprets Federal Rule 23 with "sensitivity to state interests" as she interpreted Rule 59 in *Gasperini*. This interpretive methodology involves not just focusing on the Federal Rule, as the majority does, but also on the state rule. Thus, Justice Ginsburg concludes that Rule 23 does not mandate that a party is entitled to use the class action procedure just because the party is able to meet the certification criteria of the rule, and she does this to accommodate the state prohibition on class actions. After this, Justice Ginsburg analyzes the case under the Rules of Decision Act and resorts to the forum shopping inquiry that had previously evolved under that Act. Does it make sense to engage in the latter inquiry in this kind of case? That is, after con-

cluding that Rule 23 does not control the issue involved in the case and doing so precisely to accommodate the New York prohibition on class actions, does it then make sense to ask whether it is possible to disregard the New York law? Does it make sense to ask whether disregard of the New York law would produce forum shopping? Forum shopping to get what?

Problem

Problem 5-14. P, a citizen of State X, was injured in an automobile accident with D, a citizen of State X, in State X. P sued D in a state court of State X for $500,000 in damages for personal injuries. I is D's insurer. I is incorporated in State Y with its principal place of business there. I refused to defend and indemnify D in the action by P because I contends that the accident was of a sort that was not covered by D's policy with I. P obtained a judgment against D in the state action for $500,000, but the judgment was unsatisfied because D had no assets but the insurance policy.

P then sued I in the United States District Court for the District of State X, seeking a judgment against I that the policy between D and I did cover the accident and entitled P to $250,000, which was the coverage limit of the policy. Personal jurisdiction was properly asserted over D under the State X long arm statute. During the pretrial stage of this federal action, P made a written offer to settle the case for $250,000 under a state statute governing actions against insurance companies. The state statute provided that if an offer to settle a case against an insurance company within the policy limits is made by the plaintiff and rejected by the insurance company, and if the plaintiff recovers at least the amount of the offer in the action, the insurance company shall be liable for twice the amount of the offer (here $500,000) plus attorney's fees of up to $100,000. The legislative history of this statute indicates that the State X legislature enacted the statute to deter insurance companies from rejecting valid settlement offers by creating a substantial penalty for doing so.

I rejected the offer of settlement by P ultimately was awarded the full $250,000 under the policy. P moved under the state statute to have the award increased to $600,000 under the state statute described above. I contended that the state statute was not applicable in a federal diversity action for the following reasons:

First, I argued that Federal Rule 68 covered the subject of settlements in federal courts and precluded the operation of the state law. Rule 68 allows offers of settlements to be made by defendants, but makes no provision for offers of settlement by plaintiffs. In addition, Federal Rule 68 provides that if an offer of settlement is made by a defendant and rejected by a plaintiff, and the plaintiff does not recover more than the amount of the offer, the defendant must be awarded costs of the action, which do not include attorney's fees unless a statute providing for costs specifically defines costs as including fees, which is usually not the case. I's argument is that Rule 68 occupies the field of offers of settlement in federal court and precludes the application of state statutes that are inconsistent with its provisions. Furthermore, I also argues that as so construed, Rule 68 is a valid exercise of the rulemaking power under the Rules Enabling Act because the rule does not abridge, enlarge, or modify substantive rights.

Second, I argues that if Rule 68 is not broad enough to cover the case, the state statute is not the sort of provision that must be applied under the Rules of Decision Act under the interpretation of that Act in the *Erie* case and subsequent decisions by the U.S. Supreme Court under the Act.

Evaluate I's arguments under the cases you have studied in this chapter.

Section E. Determination of State Law

Under *Swift v. Tyson*, 41 U.S. (16 Pet.) 1 (1842), the federal courts had to follow state court decisions on all matters of local law. As the discussion of *Swift* indicated, the courts determined the content of state law by following the doctrine of stare decisis prevailing in the early nineteenth century. That doctrine did not require the federal courts to follow state decisions on matters of general law. Nor did it require them to follow unsettled state decisions on matters of local law. *Erie*, of course, abolished the distinction between general and local law that existed under *Swift*. Under *Erie*, federal courts are bound by state court decisions on all matters of state law. However, even though the federal courts are bound to follow state precedents on all state law issues, the courts still must grapple with the problem of how to determine the content of state law.

In determining the content of state law, the federal courts apply several principles. As explained by the court in *Gilstrap v. Amtrak*, 998 F.2d 559 (8th Cir. 1993):

> In a diversity case, decisions of the state's highest court are to be accepted as defining state law unless the state court has later given clear and persuasive indication that its pronouncement will be modified, limited, or restricted. Where neither the legislature nor the highest court in a state has addressed an issue, the federal court must determine what the highest state court would probably hold were it called upon to decide the issue. In making this determination, a federal court may consider relevant state precedents, analogous decisions, considered dicta, scholarly works, and any other reliable data tending convincingly to show how the highest court in the state would decide the issue at hand. Reliable data that a federal court may consider include scholarly treatises, the Restatement of Law, and germane law review articles.

Id. at 560 (internal quotation marks and citations omitted).

The problem of determining state law is especially difficult when, because of some uncertainty in the law, the federal court must attempt to predict how the state's highest court would rule if it were to decide the issue. This process of prediction is often referred to as the "*Erie* guess," as illustrated in *Gilstrap*.

In this case, the plaintiff sued Amtrak in the U.S. District Court for the District of North Dakota, alleging that an employee of Amtrak had committed a sexual assault against the plaintiff on an Amtrak train while she was traveling from California to North Dakota. Under the *Klaxon* decision, the district court applied the choice-of-law rules of North Dakota to select Washington state tort law, where the tort occurred, as the applicable substantive law to govern plaintiff's claim. The substantive issue in the case was whether Amtrak was liable for the intentional torts of its employee. The district court granted summary judgment for Amtrak and the plaintiff appealed.

On appeal, the question was whether a 1912 decision of the Washington Supreme Court holding common carriers liable for the intentional torts of their employees was still controlling law. As noted above, the decisions of a state's highest court are to be accepted as defining state law "unless the state court has later given clear and persuasive indication that its pronouncement will be modified, limited, or restricted." Amtrak contended that the 1912 decision had been undermined by more recent state court cases. However, the Court of Appeals for the Eighth Circuit noted that these cases cited by Amtrak did not deal with the special relationship between common carriers and their passengers, as did the 1912 decision. In addition, the Eighth Circuit cited Washington pattern jury instructions, the *Restatement of Agency*, and a favorable citation of the 1912 decision by the Ninth Circuit Court of Appeals to conclude that the case would still be followed by the Washington Supreme Court. Because Amtrak failed to provide "clear and persuasive" evidence that the Washington Supreme Court would overrule the 1912 decision, the federal court was obliged to follow that decision in this case.

Notes and Questions

1. In *Mason v. American Emery Wheel Works*, 241 F.2d 906 (1st Cir. 1957), the court of appeals refused to follow an old state precedent that had not been overruled, but which the court felt had been undermined by modern developments. Cases from other states establishing the modern trend had been cited with approval in a more recent decision by the state supreme court that had decided the older precedent, and the court of appeals based its decision on the belief that the state supreme court would follow the modern trend when it next had the occasion to rule on the question involved in the case. Is the approach to determining state law in *Mason* consistent with the approach in *Gilstrap*? If not, which approach is correct?

2. What happens if a federal district court decides an issue of state law based upon an existing decision of the state's highest court, the loser in the district court appeals to the appropriate court of appeals, and, while the case is on appeal, the state's highest court overrules the decision on which the district court judgment was based? Although it may seem anomalous, a court of appeals is obligated to reverse a district court decision that was "correct" at the time that it was made based on the latest accurate authority. *See Vandenbark v. Owens-Illinois Glass Co.*, 311 U.S. 538 (1941).

3. The obligation to follow the latest correct state decision has limits. In *Cincinnati Insurance Co. v. Flanders Electric Motor Service, Inc.*, 131 F.3d 625 (7th Cir. 1997), the appellant moved to stay proceedings before the court of appeals until the Indiana Supreme Court had decided a case before it involving the identical issue in the federal action. The court of appeals denied the stay and affirmed the judgment of the district court. A year and a half later, the Indiana Supreme Court decided the case before it in a way that demonstrated that the court of appeals' interpretation of Indiana law was incorrect. The federal appellant moved in the district court for relief from the final judgment under Federal Rule 60(b). The district court denied the motion, and the court of appeals affirmed, holding that the use of Rule 60(b) to obtain relief in diversity actions from erroneous interpretations of state law would unduly undermine the principle of finality in litigation. Do you agree? Should an exception to the principle of finality be recognized when a party like the appellant in *Flanders* did all it could to get the court of appeals to avoid the error by staying its proceedings and the court of appeals refused?

4. Many states have adopted some form of a *certification* process that allows federal courts to obtain an answer to an unsettled question of state law directly from the state's highest court. *See, e.g.*, UNIF. CERTIFICATION OF QUESTIONS OF LAW ACT (1967), 12 U.L.A. 45 (2008). The U.S. Supreme Court has approved the use of these certification procedures in diversity actions when the procedures exist. *See Lehman Bros. v. Schein*, 416 U.S. 386 (1974). However, the decision to certify a question is discretionary with the federal courts. What factors should guide the federal courts' discretion in determining whether to certify a question?

5. Note that the state courts will not automatically answer a certified question. For example, in *Bradbury v. GMAC Mortgage, LLC*, 58 A.3d 1054 (Me. 2012), the Maine Supreme

Court indicated that it would answer certified questions only when there is no dispute as to the material facts upon which the claim depends, when there is no clear controlling precedent, and when the answer to the question would be determinative of the case.

6. There also exist several doctrines known as *abstention* doctrines. Using abstention, federal courts can either postpone the decision of a case until the litigants obtain an answer to an issue of state law from a state court or can send the entire case to a state court for decision. However, the U.S. Supreme Court has disapproved of abstention in ordinary diversity cases just to obtain an answer to an unsettled issue of state law. *See Meredith v. City of Winter Haven*, 320 U.S. 228 (1943). Thus, to be proper for abstention, a case must have some special characteristics other than a need to decide a diversity action by resolving an unsettled issue of state law. Do you understand why the U.S. Supreme Court would approve of certification under some circumstances to obtain an answer to an unsettled question of state law in a simple diversity action, but would not approve of abstention?

7. In *Gilstrap*, the court of appeals relied on old decisions of the Washington Supreme Court to determine Washington law. Suppose the only authority on point is the decision of a state intermediate court of appeals or a state trial court. What weight should a federal court give to such a decision? *See Kurczi v. Eli Lilly & Co.*, 113 F.3d 1426 (6th Cir. 1997) (in the absence of a decision by the state's highest court, lower state court opinions, although not dispositive, are evidence from which state law may be determined and such decisions should not be disregarded by a federal court in the absence of other persuasive evidence that the state's highest court would decide otherwise).

8. Several questions exist concerning the effect that should be given by federal courts to other federal court decisions on issues of state law.

(a) In *Salve Regina College v. Russell*, 499 U.S. 225 (1991), the Supreme Court held that litigants in diversity actions are entitled to have federal courts of appeals review district courts' determinations of law de novo. (Under a de novo standard of review, the appellate court gives no deference to the trial court's determination and decides the matter anew.) This was contrary to the doctrine followed by a majority of the courts of appeals prior to *Salve Regina*. Those courts had held that the decisions of district courts on matters of state law in the state in which the district court was sitting were entitled to special deference due to the presumptively greater expertise of the district judges in administering that law. The Supreme Court disagreed, holding that deferential appellate review was inconsistent with the aims of the *Erie* doctrine, because it invited divergent development of state law among the federal courts within a single state and created a dual system for enforcing state-created rights in which the substantive rule applied to a dispute might depend upon the choice of a federal or state court. Do you agree? Although *Erie* clearly obligates federal courts to follow state law, does it really have any implications for the standard of appellate review employed by courts of appeals to review district court decisions on matters of state law? Would a litigant really forum shop for a federal court to obtain a deferential standard of review on state issues from a court of appeals?

(b) After a court of appeals has predicted the way in which the state's highest court will decide an issue of state law, what effect should the decision have in subsequent diversity litigation involving the issue? Does it matter whether the issue is presented to (I) a district court in the circuit of (ii) to another panel of the court of appeals of the circuit? Would a rigid doctrine of stare decisis that compels either a district court or another panel of the court of appeals to follow the initial decision violate any of the policies of the *Erie* doctrine?

(c) What effect should a federal court in one circuit give to a court of appeals opinion from another circuit on an issue of state law arising within the latter circuit. In *Fac-*

tors Etc., Inc. v. Pro Arts, Inc., 652 F.2d 278 (2d Cir. 1981), diversity litigation in the Second Circuit concerned the issue of whether Elvis Presley's persona (the right to use Presley's name and likeness for commercial purposes) was inheritable. In previous litigation, the Sixth Circuit Court of Appeals had held that Presley's persona was not inheritable as a matter of Tennessee law. Tennessee is encompassed by the Sixth Circuit. The Second Circuit treated the Sixth Circuit decision on the issue as binding. The court reasoned that while courts of appeals in one circuit are not absolutely bound to follow the decisions of other courts of appeals on issues of state law within the other circuit, they should do so in the absence of a clear basis in the law of the state for predicting that the state courts would reach a different result. The court stated that this approach was necessary in order to prevent conflicting court of appeals' decisions on the same issue of state law, thus disrupting the orderly development of state law. Has the *Factors* holding survived *Salve Regina*? That is, if a federal court of appeals cannot defer to the decision of a U.S. District Court on a matter of state law of the state in which the district court is sitting, how can it defer to the decision of a panel of the federal court of appeals covering the relevant state—a panel that may not even be comprised of any judges drawn from the state whose law is being administered, on a matter of state law within the circuit?

(d) It has been suggested that "the critical question that should be asked in a case like *Factors* is what weight New York's highest court would have given to the Sixth Circuit's construction of Tennessee common law." This suggestion carries the *Klaxon* doctrine too far, doesn't it? Are the courts of the state in which a U.S. District Court is sitting in any better position to determine the *content* of another state's law than the district court itself? *See* TEPLY & WHITTEN at 559–61.

(e) What deference, if any, are district courts in one circuit obligated to give to district court decisions in another circuit on an issue of *federal* law? *See Northwest Forest Res. Council v. Dombeck*, 107 F.3d 897 (D.C. Cir. 1997) (error to give stare decisis effect to decision of a district court in another circuit on an issue of federal law).

(f) Some state courts have held that they are *bound* by the determination of federal constitutional and statutory issues by the U.S. District Courts of the state and the U.S. Courts of Appeals encompassing the state. *See, e.g., City of Minneapolis v. Fisher*, 504 N.W.2d 520, 525 (Minn. Ct. App. 1993). These holdings are clearly incorrect. Do you understand why?

Section F. Federal Common Law

1. "Substantive" Federal Common Law

Introduction. Although *Erie* purported to hold that there was no "federal general common law," there is, nevertheless, still a substantive "federal common law" after *Erie*. On the same day the Supreme Court decided *Erie*, it held in *Hinderlider v. La Plata River & Cherry Creek Ditch Co.*, 304 U.S. 92 (1938), that "federal common law" governed the question whether the water of an interstate stream must be apportioned between two states. This "new federal common law," *see* Henry J. Friendly, *In Praise of* Erie—*And of the New Federal Common Law*, 39 N.Y.U. L. REV. 383 (1964), has provoked continuing controversy. There are both separation-of-powers and federalism difficulties involved when federal courts undertake to create federal common law. *See* TEPLY & WHITTEN at 563–66; WRIGHT & KANE § 60, at 414. In addition, as Professor Chemerinsky has stated "federal common law has developed in an ad hoc fashion in a number of different areas. The Court has devoted little attention to developing general principles for when federal common law may or may not be created." CHEMERINSKY, §6.1, at 368. Thus, it is difficult to predict when the federal courts will create federal common law to govern a particular area. This section explores some of the issues involved in the creation of substantive federal common law.

Definition of Federal Common Law. The first problem with "federal common law" is to define what it is. There is a tendency, when the phrase "common law" is used, to assume that the body of law represented by the phrase is different from the body of law represented by "statutory (or constitutional) interpretation." *See, e.g.*, Thomas W. Merrill, *The Common Law Powers of Federal Courts*, 52 U. CHI. L. REV. 1, 4–5 (1985) (discussing cases). However, it is generally agreed today that there is no bright line between common-law decision making and statutory or constitutional interpretation. Under this view, federal common law is a broad subject indeed. Nevertheless, assuming this approach to be the most commonly accepted one, Professor Merrill's definition of federal common law seems as good as any: "'Federal common law'... means *any* federal rule of decision that is not mandated on the face of some authoritative federal text—whether or not that rule can be described as the product of 'interpretation' in either a conventional or an unconventional sense." *See id.* at 5 (citations omitted).

Legitimacy of Federal Common Law. The second, and most fundamental problem, with federal common law is to determine whether it is legitimate. That is, given the premises of *Erie* and the text of the Rules of Decision Act, is it appropriate for federal courts to create federal common law at all? If the broad definition of federal common law described in the previous paragraph is accepted, the answer to this question must be, "yes, sometimes." At least when the courts are operating on the end of the federal common-law spectrum that has traditionally been classified as statutory (or constitutional) interpretation, the creation of federal common law must be permissible. Otherwise, federal courts could not effectively function as courts. Thus, questions about the legitimacy of federal common law tend to focus on the other end of the spectrum—*i.e.*, when the courts are creating rules of decision that are not supported by, or are only tenuously supported by, policies clearly articulated by democratically elected lawmaking institutions.

In fact, federal courts have created federal common law at both ends of the spectrum, without articulating clear limits on their power:

> Commentators and casebooks have often differentiated between cases governed by *Erie* and cases in which federal common law remains appropriate by simply listing areas of law or categories of cases in which federal common law is permissible ... without supplying any overriding principle or test.... What is needed is a standard by which both to judge the legitimacy of generally accepted categories of federal common law and to ascertain what other categories of cases are appropriate for federal common law.

Martha A. Field, *Sources of Law: The Scope of Federal Common Law*, 99 HARV. L. REV. 881, 911–12 (1986).

Standards for the Creation of Federal Common Law. Although no universal unifying principles have been developed to determine when it is legitimate to create federal common law, it is possible to describe some of the factors that courts have used in determining whether creation of such law is appropriate. In general, it can be said that there must be a significant conflict between some federal policy or interest and the use of state law. If such a conflict is present, the court should, in determining whether to create federal common law, consider additional factors such as the strength of the state interest in having its own rules govern the issue in question and the feasibility of creating a judicial substitute for state law. *See Wallis v. Pan Am. Petroleum Corp.*, 384 U.S. 63 (1966). In the absence of a significant conflict between state law and some federal policy or interest, a mere federal interest in uniformity will generally be insufficient to justify displacing state law with a federal common-law rule.

The Relationship Between the Power of Congress and Federal Common Law. It is clear that Congress, acting within its delegated powers, can override federal common law in any case in which the federal common law rule is not grounded in the Constitution. However, it is clear that Congress cannot overrule a federal common law rule that the Supreme Court determines is required by the Constitution. The difficulty in this kind of case is in determining whether a particular federal common law rule that the Court has created to remedy a constitutional violation is required by the Constitution or has simply been provided by the Court until Congress creates a better statutory substitute. The hardest of this category of cases is presented when Congress eliminates the only available remedy for the violation of a constitutional right in a particular kind of case.

You should keep in mind that the debate over the power of Congress to regulate remedies for the violation of constitutional rights is chiefly of modern origin. For example, the Court has, in modern times, been active in recognizing remedies against federal officers for the violation of constitutional rights. *See, e.g., Bivens v. Six Unknown Named Agents of Fed. Bureau of Narcotics*, 403 U.S. 388 (1971) (recognizing a remedy of damages against federal officers who violate the plaintiff's constitutional rights). Historically, it would have been inconceivable that this sort of issue would be presented, and state law would provide all relevant remedies for the officer's misbehavior in the absence of an express federal statute creating a remedy against the officer.

Conceptually, the Constitution is a document that limits the powers of government, not the powers of private parties. Thus, in the nineteenth century, if a plaintiff sued a federal officer seeking damages for the violation of the plaintiff's Fourth Amendment rights, the action would have been dismissed for failure to state a proper cause of action, because the Fourth Amendment would not have been understood as creating a right of action against a federal officer as a private individual. (Of course, if the plaintiff had sued the government directly for the Fourth Amendment violation, the action would have been barred by the doctrine of sovereign immunity, assuming that the government had not waived the immunity defense.) Instead, what a plaintiff would have done is bring an ordinary action of trespass against the officer under state law, and the officer would plead, as a defense, that he had been acting in his official capacity. The plaintiff would reply that the defense of official authority was not valid because the Constitution had been violated. In effect, the constitutional issue of the Fourth Amendment would enter the case as a reply to a defense, not as a claim for relief. The recognition of rights to remedies against the officer as an individual that originate directly in the Constitution is, therefore, purely a creature of modern constitutional jurisprudence.

A separate question is how far Congress can go in delegating to the federal courts the authority to create federal common-law rules without providing more or less precise standards to guide them in the process of creation. In *Textile Workers Union of America v. Lincoln Mills*, 353 U.S. 448 (1957), Congress gave the federal courts jurisdiction to determine disputes between employers and labor organizations representing employees in industries affecting commerce, but did not provide any substantive rules with which to determine the disputes that would arise within the jurisdictional grant. The Supreme Court concluded that the jurisdictional grant authorized the federal courts to create a federal common law of labor-management contracts. In dissent, Justice Frankfurter objected that it violated the separation-of-powers doctrine for Congress to confer "upon the federal courts, with no guides except 'judicial inventiveness,' the task of applying a whole industrial code that is as yet in the bosom of the judiciary. For the vice of the statute here lies in the impossibility of ascertaining, by any reasonable test, that the legislature meant one thing rather than another...." *Id.* at 464–65 (Frankfurter, J., dissenting). It seems clear that Justice Frankfurter's concerns were substantial ones and that *Lincoln Mills* may have crossed the separation-of-powers line in delegating federal common law powers to the federal courts.

State Law as Federal Common Law. From time to time, the Supreme Court has indicated that when federal courts have the power to create federal common law, they may use state law as the "federal common law" rule of decision. Thus, it is commonplace for Congress to enact statutory rights of action without providing statutes of limitation to cut the rights of action off after the expiration of a certain period of time. When Congress has done so, federal courts often adopt the statute of limitations of the state in which they are sitting governing the most analogous state right of action to the federal statutory right. In the statute-of-limitations situation, it is clear what it means when the federal courts say they are adopting state law as federal common law. In other situations, however, the significance of the statement that federal courts are adopting state law as federal common law is unclear.

Admiralty and Customary International Law. Under *Swift v. Tyson*, 41 U.S. (16 Pet.) 1 (1842), admiralty law was not "federal" law, but was part of the general law. Today, admiralty law is generally considered to be federal common law.

Effect of Characterizing Law as "Federal." You should keep in mind that one of the practical reasons why discussions like this makes a difference is that when the "new federal common law" after *Erie* results in the creation of a claim for relief, the claim "arises under federal law" for purposes of the federal question jurisdiction. Recall that the general law of *Swift v. Tyson* did not produce a federal issue of law for purposes of federal jurisdiction. Furthermore, the ingenuity of parties attempting to invoke federal jurisdiction is vast. For example, if the parties to a contract insert a choice-of-law clause in the contract which provides that federal common law will control the agreement, will the choice of law by agreement of the parties to the contract suffice to produce a case "arising under the laws of the United States" for purposes of jurisdiction under 28 U.S.C. § 1331, assuming that the choice of law provision is otherwise valid under applicable state conflict-of-laws rules?

2. Federal Procedural Common Law in State Courts

Sections B, C, and D, above, explored circumstances in which federal courts are compelled to apply state law that is procedural in at least some sense in federal diversity actions. Section F(1), above, examined substantive federal common law, which must be applied by state and federal courts when it exists and governs a case. This subsection examines situations in which the Supreme Court has held that federal procedural law must be applied in state courts when those courts are enforcing federal rights of action. This topic will also be important when you study state and federal pleading in Chapter 6.

In general, the U.S. Supreme Court has recognized two broad situations in which state courts may not apply their own procedures and, arguably, must apply federal procedures instead. First, when Congress enacts a federal substantive law and provides for a particular procedure to litigants as part of the substantive right of action, the states must also provide the procedure when they enforce the federal right of action.

An example of this first kind of case is *Dice v. Akron, Canton & Youngstown Railroad Co.*, 342 U.S. 359 (1952). In *Dice*, the plaintiff sued a railroad in state court under the Federal Employer's Liability Act ("F.E.L.A."). The railroad defended on the ground that the plaintiff had released all of the claims that the plaintiff possessed against the railroad. The plaintiff contended that the release was void because it was procured by fraud. Under the practice in the forum state's courts, the issue of fraud would be split between the judge and the jury, with the judge deciding some parts and the jury deciding others. The procedure in federal court would be to submit the entire issue to the jury. The Supreme Court held that federal common law governed the issue of fraud and that the fraud issue must be submitted entirely to the jury because a jury trial of this issue, as well as others, was part of the remedy that Congress afforded to plaintiffs suing under the F.E.L.A.

Second, when state courts are enforcing a federal right of action, the Court has held that they may not employ procedures that unnecessarily burden the right. In this category of cases, sometimes the states must simply refrain from using their own procedures, but are not obligated to apply any particular federal procedure in lieu of the (unreasonably burdensome) state procedure. In other situations, however, abandoning the state procedure may mean as a practical matter, that the states must apply federal procedure as an alternative because, in the circumstances of the case, they must have some alternative procedure and the only one available is the federal procedure.

An example of the second kind of case is *Brown v. Western Ry. Co.*, 338 U.S. 294 (1949). In *Brown*, the plaintiff sued a railroad under the F.E.L.A. in state court. The railroad demurred to the plaintiff's complaint on ground that it failed to state facts sufficient to constitute a cause of action, and the state court sustained the demurrer and dismissed the action. The U.S. Supreme Court held that it was impermissible for the state to use its strict pleading rules in F.E.L.A. actions, because those rules unnecessarily burdened the federal right of action given by the statute. In this situation, the state must have some rules to determine whether the plaintiff's pleading is legally sufficient. If it cannot use its own rules, the only plausible alternative would seem to be to use the notice pleading system of the Federal Rules of Civil Procedure. Thus, the prohibition on using the state's own rules practically forces the state to adopt federal procedure, or something very similar to it, as an alternative.

An example of the first kind of case is *Felder v. Casey*, 487 U.S. 131 (1988). In *Felder*, the plaintiff brought an action in state court under 42 U.S.C. § 1983 against a city and certain of its police officers. The state had a "notice of claim" statute, which provided that plaintiffs wishing to sue state or local governments or their officers had to notify the defendant of the claim and the intent to hold the defendant liable for it within 120 days after the occurrence of the event giving rise to the claim or the claim would be barred, unless the defendant had actual notice of the claim and the plaintiff could show that the defendant was not prejudiced by failure to provide the notice. Failure to comply with the "notice of claim" statute constituted grounds for dismissal. The state court dismissed the action because the plaintiff had not complied with the statute. The U.S. Supreme Court held the statute could not be applied in federal civil rights actions because it unnecessarily burdened the right of recovery afforded by federal law. Note that *Felder* means neither state nor federal courts could apply the state statute in a § 1983 action.

The Supreme Court further explained its ruling in *Felder* in *Johnson v. Fankell*, 520 U.S. 911 (1997). In *Johnson*, a terminated employee of a state liquor store sued state officials under § 1983 on the ground that the employee had been deprived of property without due process of law in an Idaho state court. The state court denied summary judgment on the officials qualified immunity defense. The officials appealed and the Idaho Supreme Court dismissed the appeal. On certiorari, the U.S. Supreme held that no federal right to an interlocutory appeal exists from a denial of qualified immunity. The Court stated, in part, as follows:

> Petitioners ... contend that, to the extent that Idaho Appellate Rule 11(a)(1) does not allow an interlocutory appeal, it is pre-empted by § 1983. Relying heavily on *Felder v. Casey*, 487 U.S. 131 (1988), petitioners first assert that pre-emption is necessary to avoid "different outcomes in § 1983 litigation based solely on whether the claim is asserted in state or federal court," *id*, at 138. Second, they argue that the state procedure "impermissibly burden[s]" the federal immunity from suit because it does not adequately protect their right to prevail on the immunity question in advance of trial.

> For two reasons, petitioners have a heavy burden of persuasion in making this argument. First, our normal presumption against pre-emption is buttressed by the fact that the Idaho Supreme Court's dismissal of the appeal rested squarely on a neutral state Rule regarding the administration of the state courts....

> A second barrier to petitioners' argument arises from the nature of the interest protected by the defense of qualified immunity. Petitioners' argument for pre-emption is bottomed on their claims that the Idaho rules are interfering with their federal rights. While it is true that the defense has its source in a federal statute (§ 1983), the ultimate purpose of qualified immunity is to protect the State and its officials from overenforcement of federal rights. The Idaho Supreme Court's application of the State's procedural rules in this context is thus less an interference with *federal* interests than a judgment about how best to balance the competing *state* interests of limiting interlocutory appeals and providing state officials with immediate review of the merits of their defense.

> Petitioners' arguments for pre-emption are not strong enough to overcome these considerable hurdles. Contrary to petitioners' assertions, Idaho's decision not to provide appellate review for the vast majority of interlocutory orders—including denials of qualified immunity in § 1983 cases—is not "outcome determinative" in the sense that we used that term when we held that Wisconsin's notice-of-claim statute could not be applied to defeat a federal civil rights action brought in state courts under § 1983. *Felder*, 487 U.S. at 153. The failure to comply with the Wisconsin statute in *Felder* resulted in a judgment dismissing a complaint that would not have been dismissed—at least not without a judicial determination of the merits of the claim—if the case had been filed in a federal court. One of the primary grounds for our decision was that, because the notice-of-claim requirement would "frequently and predictably produce different outcomes" depending on whether § 1983 claims were brought in state or federal court, it was inconsistent with the federal interest in uniformity. *Id*. at 138.

> Petitioners' reliance on *Felder* is misplaced because "outcome," as we used the term there, referred to the ultimate disposition of the case. If petitioners' claim to qualified immunity is meritorious, there is no suggestion that the application

of the Idaho rules of procedure will produce a final result different from what a federal ruling would produce. Petitioners were able to argue their immunity from suit claim to the trial court, just as they would to a federal court. And the claim will be reviewable by the Idaho Supreme Court after the trial court enters a final judgment, thus providing petitioners with a further chance to urge their immunity. Consequently, the postponement of the appeal until after final judgment will not affect the ultimate outcome of the case.

Petitioners' second argument for pre-emption of the state procedural Rule is that the Rule does not adequately protect their right to prevail in advance of trial. In evaluating this contention, it is important to focus on the precise source and scope of the federal right at issue. The right to have the trial court rule on the merits of the qualified immunity defense presumably has its source in § 1983, but the right to immediate appellate review of that ruling in a federal case has its source in § 1291. The former right is fully protected by Idaho. The latter right, however, is a federal procedural right that simply does not apply in a non-federal forum.

Id. at 918–21.

Notes and Questions

1. In *Dice* and *Brown*, discussed above, the plaintiffs could have sued on their claims in federal court. Given this fact, how can the decisions in any of the cases be justified? Why shouldn't the plaintiff be required to take the state courts as the plaintiff finds them? Can you find any congressional policy anywhere that would dictate that the state courts should have to give up their procedural practices in actions based on federal statutes when the federal courts are open to the plaintiff's claims? *Cf.* 28 U.S.C. § 1445.

2. Could Congress provide that in any action on a federal claim brought in a state court, the state courts have to use *all* the Federal Rules of Civil Procedure in adjudicating the claim? If there are restrictions on the power of Congress to require the states to use federal procedures, do these restrictions also prevent the Supreme Court from requiring the states to use them?

3. In *Johnson*, the Court interpreted *Brown* and *Felder* as cases in which the "ultimate outcome" of the state actions would have been affected by use of the state procedures in question. The Court interpreted *Dice* as a case in which Congress had provided that the jury trial procedure was to be a part of the claims brought under the F.E.L.A. Does *Fankell* mean that the states can apply their own procedures to cases involving federal claims, even if the procedures make the vindication of those claims more difficult, as long as the ultimate outcome will not *necessarily* be changed by use of the state procedures and Congress has not validly provided for substitution of a different procedure? Is it significant that *Johnson* involved a burden placed on a federal defense to a federal claim, whereas *Dice*, *Brown*, and *Felder* all involved direct burdens placed by state procedures on vindication of the federal claims themselves?

4. Is the "ultimate outcome" test sensitive enough to the immunity questions that were the subject of *Johnson*? If, as the Court stated, the immunity doctrines are designed in part to prevent officials from having to endure the burdens of trial, focusing on whether the state procedure will affect the "ultimate outcome" of the case does nothing to alleviate those burdens, does it? Are you satisfied with the Court's explanation regarding this point that the locus of the interlocutory appeal right is § 1291, which is inapplicable in state court?

5. If Congress provides a particular procedure for use in an action on a federal statutory claim and a state court considers the procedure too burdensome or alien to the state's normal processes, can it dismiss the action without prejudice and force the plaintiff to take the claim to a federal court? Can a state court do so in a case like *Brown* (in which the Supreme Court held the state procedure excessively burdensome to the federal right of action) on the theory that the only alternative to its own burdensome state procedure is an alien federal procedure that it is unaccustomed to using?

Chapter 6

Pleading and Related Matters

Pleadings define and shape the issues in a lawsuit. They also furnish a basis for the evidence and provide a foundation for application of the doctrine of res judicata. Recall from Chapter 1 that the pleading process in effect today is the result of evolution and reform. Chapter 1 described common-law pleading, which is still reflected in many aspects of pleading today. It also described the basic nature of the pleading process in state and federal courts in the United States. This chapter examines pleading in greater detail, especially the intricacies of modern pleading systems modeled after the Federal Rules of Civil Procedure.

Section A. Background and Overview

Common-Law Pleading. As described in Chapter 1, common-law pleading relied on a series of pleadings to formulate a *single issue of law or fact* based on the *forms of action*. The plaintiff's first pleading was a *declaration*. An issue of fact was created when a party *traversed* a prior factual allegation, which was simply a denial of a factual allegation. The disputed factual issue raised by a traverse then had to be resolved by the trier of fact in the case. An issue of law was created when a party filed a *demurrer*. In this situation, the demurring party admitted the previously alleged facts, but asserted (in the case of a "general" demurrer) that the facts did not give rise to a legally recognized claim or defense. If the demurrer was sustained, the demurring party won the action. If the demurrer was overruled, judgment would be entered based on the demurring party's admission of the facts.

Recall that a party might choose not to demur generally or traverse an allegation of fact in a prior pleading. Instead, the party might enter a plea in *confession and avoidance*. Such a plea admitted the allegations of the prior pleading and presented new matter to avoid the legal effect of those allegations, such as the defense of consent in an action for false imprisonment. If the defendant entered a plea of confession and avoidance to the declaration, no issue of fact or law resulted, and the plaintiff had to respond. If the plaintiff believed the plea was insufficient as a matter of law, the plaintiff would demur to the plea. If not, the plaintiff filed a *replication*, which either traversed a material allegation in the plea or admitted the truth of the plea and raised a new matter of confession and avoidance. If the plaintiff raised a new matter of confession and avoidance in the replication, the defendant had to either demur or file a *rejoinder* containing either a traverse or a new matter of confession and avoidance. The process continued until a single issue of law or fact was reached when one party either traversed or demurred.

Common-law pleading prohibited "*argumentative denials*." For example, assume that *P* alleged that *D* was in State *X* on a particular day. If *D* tried to deny (traverse) this allegation by alleging that "*D* was in State *Y*," on the date in question, the denial would be ineffective because it was "argumentative." The proper form of denial was simply to deny that D was in State X on that day.

Common-law pleading also prohibited "*negative pregnants*," which are negatives that implied an admission. Negative pregnants occurred when a denial was framed in the same language as the plaintiff's allegation. Assume, for example, that P alleged that D hit P with a baseball bat. If D responded by stating, "D denies that D hit P with a baseball bat," the response would be taken to have admitted the fact that D hit P. The denial was "pregnant" with the admission that D hit P with something.

Equity. In contrast to actions at law, the plaintiff's first pleading in an equity action was a *bill of complaint*. The bill petitioned the chancellor for relief when legal remedies were inadequate or nonexistent. Relief was in the discretion of the chancellor, so the plaintiff had to make it apparent at the outset that grounds for the relief existed. The bill enabled the chancellor to make this determination before the chancellor compelled the defendant to appear by means of a subpoena. Typically, bills in equity consisted of three parts: (1) the stating part (stating the grounds for relief); (2) the charging part (stating the evidence in detail); and (3) the interrogative part (propounding interrogatories designed to obtain admissions and discover evidence from the opposing party).

After the defendant appeared, the chancellor required the defendant to answer the bill. The evidence was largely documentary, contained in or attached to the pleadings. Pleading in equity cases never achieved the rigidity of common-law pleading. For example, the plaintiff could file a pleading called a supplemental bill in addition to the original bill. A supplemental bill remedied either some defect or omission in the original bill or introduced related matters happening since the commencement of the suit.

Code Pleading. As discussed out in Chapter 1, the New York Field Code of 1848 significantly reformed common-law pleading. By 1900, almost thirty states had adopted some version of the Field Code, and more adopted it in the twentieth century. The Field Code established a single form of action known as a *civil action* (merging law and equity), and limited pleading to a *complaint*, an *answer*, and a *reply*. The plaintiff's complaint had to state "facts" constituting a *cause of action*, which, if proven, would entitle the plaintiff to legal relief. In contrast to a statement of these "ultimate" facts, the plaintiff was not permitted to plead "evidence" nor was the plaintiff permitted to plead "legal conclusions." Recall also that code pleading allowed the parties to raise multiple issues of law and fact.

As at common law, the defendant could still challenge the defects on the face of the complaint by a demurrer, including the failure of the complaint to set forth facts sufficient to state a cause of action. The defendant's answer had to admit or deny the allegations of the complaint as well as assert any new matter constituting a defense. The plaintiff then had to reply to any new matter contained in the answer. After the reply, the pleading stage ended.

The codes typically permitted the various defenses to be raised by *demurrer* prior to serving a pleading. These defenses included (1) the court did not have (a) personal jurisdiction over the defendant or (b) subject-matter jurisdiction over the action; (2) the plaintiff lacked the legal capacity to sue; (3) a defect of parties, either plaintiff or defendant, existed; (4) the plaintiff had improperly united several causes of action; (5) another action was pending between the parties for the same cause; and (6) the complaint failed to state facts sufficient to constitute a cause of action. Today, in code-pleading states, improper venue is typically handled by a motion to transfer. If one of the defenses that could be raised by demurrer did not appear on the face of the complaint, the codes required it to be raised in the answer.

Some code-pleading states followed a doctrine known as the "theory of the pleadings." This doctrine allowed the defendant to challenge a complaint as legally insufficient if the plaintiff did not follow a consistent legal theory in the complaint. However, most code-pleading states repudiated this doctrine as inconsistent with the code plan that only facts should be pleaded, leaving the court to draw the legal conclusions about the facts. Needless to say, the Federal Rules of Civil Procedure do not require that the complaint state a consistent legal theory. *See* FED. R. CIV. P. 8(d)(3) ("Inconsistent Claims or Defenses").

Despite the seeming technicality of code pleading today when compared with Federal Rules pleading, you should remember that the code-pleading system was considered a major improvement over the common-law system that preceded it. The Field Code abolished the forms of action, limited the pleading process, merged law and equity, and liberalized the amendment process and the rules governing claim and party joinder. These reforms were truly revolutionary in their day. They were resisted by many lawyers trained under the common-law system, much like the adoption of the Federal Rules was resisted by lawyers in code states. However, do not think that resistance to reform is limited to code-state lawyers. Reform of the Federal Rules brings just as much resistance and controversy.

Federal Rules of Civil Procedure. Recall from Chapter 1 that the Federal Rules of Civil Procedure, which took effect in 1938, effectively limit the pleadings to a *complaint* and an *answer* in most situations. Federal Rules pleading is often called *notice pleading*, which, as a practical matter, does not identify and narrow the legal and factual issues as much as the more detailed "fact" pleading required by the codes. Instead, Federal Rules pleading moves particularization of the case from the pleading stage of the action to the discovery stage and relies heavily on summary judgment as a means of disposing of cases prior to trial.

The Federal Rules governing pleading are contained in Rules 7 through 15. Rule 7(a) specifies the pleadings allowed in federal court, and Rule 10(a) requires that each pleading contain a caption listing the name of the court, the title of the action, the file number, and the appropriate designation of the pleading (*e.g.*, "Complaint"). The general rules of pleading are contained in Federal Rule 8. Rule 8(a) requires that all pleadings that state a claim for relief must provide three things: "(1) a short and plain statement of the grounds for the court's jurisdiction, unless the court already has jurisdiction and the claim needs no new jurisdictional support; (2) a short and plain statement of the claim showing that the pleader is entitled to relief; and (3) a demand for the relief sought, which may include relief in the alternative or different types of relief."

Some of the Federal Rules are specifically designed to alter past pleading practices. For example, Rule 8(d)(2) permits the parties to plead alternative or hypothetical theories. Rule 8(d)(3) also permits the parties to plead inconsistent claims or defenses. Rule 10(b) requires that a pleading be divided into separate, numbered paragraphs. Furthermore, each claim founded on a single transaction or occurrence, as well as each defense other than a denial, "must be stated in a separate count or defense" whenever it "would promote clarity." The Federal Rules liberally permit amendments to pleadings under Rule 15. They also impose "good-faith" pleading requirements under Rule 11.

Section B. Stating a "Claim for Relief" in the Complaint and Pleading Special Matters

1. Degree of Detail Required in the Complaint

As discussed in Chapter 1, the plaintiff must provide the defendant with information about the nature of the claim in the plaintiff's first pleading. This pleading is called the complaint, declaration, or petition, depending upon the nomenclature employed by the procedural system in which the plaintiff is operating. As observed in Chapter 1 and in the preceding section, procedural systems differ in the extent to which they emphasize the pleading stage of the litigation. This differing emphasis directly affects the degree of detail with which the plaintiff must state the claim for relief or cause of action.

Code ("fact") pleading systems require the plaintiff to state the "facts constituting a cause of action" and to plead the claim with substantial specificity. As noted in the preceding section, "code pleading" was intended as a major improvement over the pitfalls of common-law pleading. Over the years, however, the chosen standard, "facts constituting a cause of action," spawned its own pitfalls. That standard triggered numerous pleading battles over whether a complaint properly contained "ultimate facts" as opposed to merely the "evidence" whereby the facts would be proved or "legal conclusions" to be drawn from the facts. Furthermore, the use of the term "cause of action" in the pleading standard was interpreted to require a specific fact to cover every substantive element of the cause of action, otherwise the pleading was defective.

Under the Federal Rules of Civil Procedure and in procedural systems patterned on them, so-called "notice pleading" jurisdictions, the plaintiff's complaint need only contain a "short and plain statement of the claim showing that the pleader is entitled to relief." *See* FED. R. CIV. P. 8(a)(2). The goal of "notice pleading" is precisely that — to give the defendant "fair notice" of the plaintiff's claim and the grounds upon which it rests — and represents a shift in emphasis from the stricter requirements of common-law and code pleading.

Conley v. Gibson. The leading case defining what is required by Federal Rule 8(a)(2) was, for many years, the Supreme Court's decision in *Conley v. Gibson*, 355 U.S. 41 (1957). In *Conley*, the plaintiffs were minority railroad employees who brought a class action in federal district court on behalf of themselves and other minority employees against the Union representing them. A contract between the Union and the Railroad gave the employees certain protection from discharge and loss of seniority. Thereafter, the Railroad purported to abolish 45 jobs that resulted in discharge or demotion of the minority employees. The 45 jobs, however, were not abolished at all but instead were filled by white employees.

The complaint alleged that despite repeated pleas, the Union did nothing to protect the plaintiffs against these discriminatory discharges and refused to give them protection comparable to that given white employees. The complaint also alleged that the Union had failed in general to represent all employees equally and in good faith. The complaint concluded that such discrimination constituted a violation of the Railway Labor Act to fair representation from their bargaining agent and requested relief in the nature of declaratory judgment, injunction and damages. *Id.* at 42–43.

The Union raised several defenses, including that the complaint failed to state a claim upon which relief can be granted pursuant to Rule 12(b)(6). In rejecting this defense, the Court stated as follows:

[W]e hold that under the general principles laid down in [three Railway Labor Act Supreme Court] cases the complaint adequately set forth a claim upon which relief could be granted. In appraising the sufficiency of the complaint we follow, of course, the accepted rule that a complaint should not be dismissed for failure to state a claim unless it appears beyond doubt that the plaintiff can prove no set of facts in support of his claim which would entitle him to relief. Here, the complaint alleged, in part, that petitioners were discharged wrongfully by the Railroad and that the Union, acting according to plan, refused to protect their jobs as it did those of white employees or to help them with their grievances all because they were [not white employees]. If these allegations are proven there has been a manifest breach of the Union's statutory duty to represent fairly and without hostile discrimination all of the employees in the bargaining unit. This Court squarely held ... that discrimination in representation because of race is prohibited by the Railway Labor Act. The bargaining representative's duty not to draw "irrelevant and invidious" distinctions among those it represents does not come to an abrupt end, as the respondents seem to contend, with the making of an agreement between union and employer. Collective bargaining is a continuing process. Among other things, it involves day-to-day adjustments in the contract and other working rules, resolution of new problems not covered by existing agreements, and the protection of employee rights already secured by contract. The bargaining representative can no more unfairly discriminate in carrying out these functions than it can in negotiating a collective agreement. A contract may be fair and impartial on its face yet administered in such a way, with the active or tacit consent of the union, as to be flagrantly discriminatory against some members of the bargaining unit.

....

The respondents ... argue that the complaint failed to set forth specific facts to support its general allegations of discrimination and that its dismissal is therefore proper. The decisive answer to this is that the Federal Rules of Civil Procedure do not require a claimant to set out in detail the facts upon which he bases his claim. To the contrary, all the Rules require is "a short and plain statement of the claim" that will give the defendant fair notice of what the plaintiff's claim is and the grounds upon which it rests. The illustrative forms appended to the Rules plainly demonstrate this. Such simplified "notice pleading" is made possible by the liberal opportunity for discovery and the other pretrial procedures established by the Rules to disclose more precisely the basis of both claim and defense and to define more narrowly the disputed facts and issues. Following the simple guide of Rule 8(f) that "all pleadings shall be so construed as to do substantial justice,"[a] we have no doubt that petitioners' complaint adequately set forth a claim and gave the respondents fair notice of its basis. The Federal Rules reject the approach that pleading is a game of skill in which one misstep by counsel may be decisive to the outcome and accept the principle that the purpose of pleading is to facilitate a proper decision on the merits.

Id. at 45–48.

---

a. [Eds. Note. In 2007, Rule 8(f) was restyled as Rule 8(e) and now reads: "Pleadings must be construed so as to do justice."]

Despite the Court's pronouncement in *Conley* that the pleading standard under Rule 8(a)(2) requires only "'a short and plain statement of the claim' that will give the defendant fair notice of what the plaintiff's claim is and the grounds upon which it rests," over the years the lower federal courts have attempted to impose "heightened pleading" standards in certain types of cases. As illustrated in the *Leatherman* and *Swierkiewicz* cases, reprinted below, the Supreme Court has consistently rejected these attempts.

Leatherman v. Tarrant County Narcotics Intelligence & Coordination Unit

United States Supreme Court, 1993
507 U.S. 163, 113 S. Ct. 1160, 122 L. Ed. 2d 517

CHIEF JUSTICE REHNQUIST delivered the opinion of the Court.

We granted certiorari to decide whether a federal court may apply a "heightened pleading standard"—more stringent than the usual pleading requirements of Rule 8(a) of the Federal Rules of Civil Procedure—in ... civil rights cases alleging municipal liability under ... 42 U.S.C. § 1983. We hold it may not.

We review here a decision granting a motion to dismiss, and therefore must accept as true all the factual allegations in the complaint.... This action arose out of two separate incidents involving the execution of search warrants by local law enforcement officers. Each involved the forcible entry into a home based on the detection of odors associated with the manufacture of narcotics. One homeowner claimed that he was assaulted by the officers after they had entered; another claimed that the police had entered her home in her absence and killed her two dogs. Plaintiffs sued several local officials in their official capacity and the county and two municipal corporations that employed the police officers involved in the incidents, asserting that the police conduct had violated the Fourth Amendment to the United States Constitution. The stated basis for municipal liability under *Monell v. New York City Department of Social Services*, 436 U.S. 658 (1978), was the failure of these bodies adequately to train the police officers involved....

The United States District Court for the Northern District of Texas ordered the complaints dismissed, because they failed to meet the "heightened pleading standard" required by the decisional law of the Court of Appeals for the Fifth Circuit.... The Fifth Circuit, in turn, affirmed the judgment of dismissal ... and we granted certiorari ... to resolve a conflict among the Courts of Appeals concerning the applicability of a heightened pleading standard to § 1983 actions alleging municipal liability.... We now reverse.

Respondents seek to defend the Fifth Circuit's application of a more rigorous pleading standard on two grounds. First, respondents claim that municipalities' freedom from *respondeat superior* liability ... necessarily includes immunity from suit. In this sense, respondents assert, municipalities are no different from state or local officials sued in their individual capacity. Respondents reason that a more relaxed pleading requirement would subject municipalities to expensive and time consuming discovery in every § 1983 case, eviscerating their immunity from suit and disrupting municipal functions.

This argument wrongly equates freedom from liability with immunity from suit. To be sure, we reaffirmed in *Monell* that "a municipality cannot be held liable under § 1983 on a *respondeat superior* theory." ... But, contrary to respondents' assertions, this protection against liability does not encompass immunity from suit. Indeed, this argument is flatly contradicted by *Monell* and our later decisions involving municipal liability under

§ 1983.... In short, a municipality can be sued under § 1983, but it cannot be held liable unless a municipal policy or custom caused the constitutional injury. We thus have no occasion to consider whether our qualified immunity jurisprudence would require a heightened pleading in cases involving individual government officials [who are sometimes immune from suit].

Second, respondents contend that the Fifth Circuit's heightened pleading standard is not really that at all.... According to respondents, the degree of factual specificity required of a complaint by the Federal Rules of Civil Procedure varies according to the complexity of the underlying substantive law. To establish municipal liability under § 1983, respondents argue, a plaintiff must do more than plead a single instance of misconduct. This requirement, respondents insist, is consistent with a plaintiff's Rule 11 obligation to make a reasonable pre-filing inquiry into the facts.

But examination of the Fifth Circuit's decision in this case makes it quite evident that the "heightened pleading standard" is just what it purports to be: a more demanding rule for pleading a complaint under § 1983 than for pleading other kinds of claims for relief....

We think that it is impossible to square the "heightened pleading standard" applied by the Fifth Circuit in this case with the liberal system of "notice pleading" set up by the Federal Rules. Rule 8(a)(2) requires that a complaint include only "a short and plain statement of the claim showing that the pleader is entitled to relief." In *Conley v. Gibson*, 355 U.S. 41 (1957), we said in effect that the Rule meant what it said:

> [T]he Federal Rules of Civil Procedure do not require a claimant to set out in detail the facts upon which he bases his claim. To the contrary, all the Rules require is "a short and plain statement of the claim" that will give the defendant fair notice of what the plaintiff's claim is and the grounds upon which it rests....

Rule 9(b) does impose a particularity requirement in two specific instances. It provides that "[i]n all averments of fraud or mistake, the circumstances constituting fraud or mistake shall be stated with particularity."[a] Thus, the Federal Rules do address in Rule 9(b) the question of the need for greater particularity in pleading certain actions, but do not include among the enumerated actions any reference to complaints alleging municipal liability under § 1983. *Expressio unius est exclusio alterius.*

... Perhaps if Rules 8 and 9 were rewritten today, claims against municipalities under § 1983 might be subjected to the added specificity requirement of Rule 9(b). But that is a result which must be obtained by the process of amending the Federal Rules, and not by judicial interpretation. In the absence of such an amendment, federal courts and litigants must rely on summary judgment and control of discovery to weed out unmeritorious claims sooner rather than later.

The judgment of the Court of Appeals is reversed, and the case remanded for further proceedings consistent with this opinion.

It is so ordered.

---

a. [Eds. Note. Restyled Rule 9(b) now reads: "In alleging fraud or mistake, a party must state with particularity the circumstances constituting fraud or mistake."]

Notes and Questions

1. In contrast to Rule 8(a)(2), which is the general pleading standard, Rule 9 enumerates several specific situations in which greater particularity is required in a pleading. These special pleading provisions of Rule 9 are examined in section B(2).

2. The Court uses the Latin expression, *expressio unius est exclusio alterius* ("expression of the one is the exclusion of the other"). How does this maxim apply to this case? In *Swierkiewicz v. Sorema N. A.*, reprinted below, the Court again cited this maxim from *Leatherman* in rejecting a "heightened pleading" standard in federal employment discrimination actions.

Swierkiewicz v. Sorema N. A.

United States Supreme Court, 2002
534 U.S. 506, 122 S. Ct. 992, 152 L. Ed. 2d 1

JUSTICE THOMAS delivered the opinion of the Court.

This case presents the question whether a complaint in an employment discrimination lawsuit must contain specific facts establishing a prima facie case of discrimination under the framework set forth by this Court in *McDonnell Douglas Corp. v. Green,* 411 U.S. 792 (1973). We hold that an employment discrimination complaint need not include such facts and instead must contain only "a short and plain statement of the claim showing that the pleader is entitled to relief." Fed. Rule Civ. Proc. 8(a)(2).

I

Petitioner Akos Swierkiewicz is a native of Hungary, who at the time of his complaint was 53 years old.[1] In April 1989, petitioner began working for respondent Sorema N. A., a reinsurance company headquartered in New York and principally owned and controlled by a French parent corporation. Petitioner was initially employed in the position of senior vice president and chief underwriting officer (CUO). Nearly six years later, François M. Chavel, respondent's Chief Executive Officer, demoted petitioner to a marketing and services position and transferred the bulk of his underwriting responsibilities to Nicholas Papadopoulo, a 32-year-old who, like Mr. Chavel, is a French national. About a year later, Mr. Chavel stated that he wanted to "energize" the underwriting department and appointed Mr. Papadopoulo as CUO. Petitioner claims that Mr. Papadopoulo had only one year of underwriting experience at the time he was promoted, and therefore was less experienced and less qualified to be CUO than he, since at that point he had 26 years of experience in the insurance industry.

Following his demotion, petitioner contends that he "was isolated by Mr. Chavel ... excluded from business decisions and meetings and denied the opportunity to reach his true potential at SOREMA." Petitioner unsuccessfully attempted to meet with Mr. Chavel to discuss his discontent. Finally, in April 1997, petitioner sent a memo to Mr. Chavel outlining his grievances and requesting a severance package. Two weeks later, respondent's general counsel presented petitioner with two options: He could either resign without a severance package or be dismissed. Mr. Chavel fired petitioner after he refused to resign.

---

1. Because we review here a decision granting respondent's motion to dismiss, we must accept as true all of the factual allegations contained in the complaint. *See, e.g., Leatherman v. Tarrant County Narcotics Intelligence & Coordination Unit,* 507 U.S. 163, 164 (1993).

Petitioner filed a lawsuit alleging that he had been terminated on account of his national origin in violation of Title VII of the Civil Rights Act of 1964, 42 U.S.C. §2000e *et seq.*, and on account of his age in violation of the Age Discrimination in Employment Act of 1967 (ADEA), 29 U.S.C. §621 *et seq.* The United States District Court for the Southern District of New York dismissed petitioner's complaint because it found that he "ha[d] not adequately alleged a prima facie case, in that he ha[d] not adequately alleged circumstances that support an inference of discrimination." The United States Court of Appeals for the Second Circuit affirmed the dismissal, relying on its settled precedent, which requires a plaintiff in an employment discrimination complaint to allege facts constituting a prima facie case of discrimination under the framework set forth by this Court in *McDonnell Douglas*, 411 U.S. at 802.... The Court of Appeals held that petitioner had failed to meet his burden because his allegations were "insufficient as a matter of law to raise an inference of discrimination." We granted certiorari ... to resolve a split among the Courts of Appeals concerning the proper pleading standard for employment discrimination cases, and now reverse.

II

Applying Circuit precedent, the Court of Appeals required petitioner to plead a prima facie case of discrimination in order to survive respondent's motion to dismiss. In the Court of Appeals' view, petitioner was thus required to allege in his complaint: (1) membership in a protected group; (2) qualification for the job in question; (3) an adverse employment action; and (4) circumstances that support an inference of discrimination....

The prima facie case under *McDonnell Douglas*, however, is an evidentiary standard, not a pleading requirement. In *McDonnell Douglas*, this Court made clear that "[t]he critical issue before us concern[ed] the order and allocation *of proof* in a private, non-class action challenging employment discrimination." 411 U.S. at 800 (emphasis added). In subsequent cases, this Court has reiterated that the prima facie case relates to the employee's burden of presenting evidence that raises an inference of discrimination....

This Court has never indicated that the requirements for establishing a prima facie case under *McDonnell Douglas* also apply to the pleading standard that plaintiffs must satisfy in order to survive a motion to dismiss. For instance, we have rejected the argument that a Title VII complaint requires greater "particularity," because this would "too narrowly constric[t] the role of the pleadings." *McDonald v. Santa Fe Trail Transp. Co.*, 427 U.S. 273, 283, n.11 (1976). Consequently, the ordinary rules for assessing the sufficiency of a complaint apply. *See, e.g.*, *Scheuer v. Rhodes*, 416 U.S. 232, 236 (1974) ("When a federal court reviews the sufficiency of a complaint, before the reception of any evidence either by affidavit or admissions, its task is necessarily a limited one. The issue is not whether a plaintiff will ultimately prevail but whether the claimant is entitled to offer evidence to support the claims").

In addition, under a notice pleading system, it is not appropriate to require a plaintiff to plead facts establishing a prima facie case because the *McDonnell Douglas* framework does not apply in every employment discrimination case. For instance, if a plaintiff is able to produce direct evidence of discrimination, he may prevail without proving all the elements of a prima facie case. *See Trans World Airlines, Inc. v. Thurston*, 469 U.S. 111, 121 (1985) ("[T]he *McDonnell Douglas* test is inapplicable where the plaintiff presents direct evidence of discrimination"). Under the Second Circuit's heightened pleading standard, a plaintiff without direct evidence of discrimination at the time of his complaint must plead a prima facie case of discrimination, even though discovery might uncover such direct evidence. It thus seems incongruous to require a plaintiff, in order to survive a motion to dismiss, to plead more facts than he may ultimately need to prove to succeed on the merits if direct evidence of discrimination is discovered.

Moreover, the precise requirements of a prima facie case can vary depending on the context and were "never intended to be rigid, mechanized, or ritualistic." ... Before discovery has unearthed relevant facts and evidence, it may be difficult to define the precise formulation of the required prima facie case in a particular case. Given that the prima facie case operates as a flexible evidentiary standard, it should not be transposed into a rigid pleading standard for discrimination cases.

Furthermore, imposing the Court of Appeals' heightened pleading standard in employment discrimination cases conflicts with Federal Rule of Civil Procedure 8(a)(2), which provides that a complaint must include only "a short and plain statement of the claim showing that the pleader is entitled to relief." Such a statement must simply "give the defendant fair notice of what the plaintiff's claim is and the grounds upon which it rests." *Conley v. Gibson,* 355 U.S. 41, 47 (1957). This simplified notice pleading standard relies on liberal discovery rules and summary judgment motions to define disputed facts and issues and to dispose of unmeritorious claims. *See id.* at 47–48; *Leatherman v. Tarrant County Narcotics Intelligence and Coordination Unit,* 507 U.S. 163, 168–69 (1993)....

Rule 8(a)'s simplified pleading standard applies to all civil actions, with limited exceptions. Rule 9(b), for example, provides for greater particularity in all averments of fraud or mistake. This Court, however, has declined to extend such exceptions to other contexts. In *Leatherman* we stated: "[T]he Federal Rules do address in Rule 9(b) the question of the need for greater particularity in pleading certain actions, but do not include among the enumerated actions any reference to complaints alleging municipal liability under § 1983. *Expressio unius est exclusio alterius.*" 507 U.S. at 168. Just as Rule 9(b) makes no mention of municipal liability under 42 U.S.C. § 1983, neither does it refer to employment discrimination. Thus, complaints in these cases, as in most others, must satisfy only the simple requirements of Rule 8(a).[4]

Other provisions of the Federal Rules of Civil Procedure are inextricably linked to Rule 8(a)'s simplified notice pleading standard. Rule 8(e)(1) states that "[n]o technical forms of pleading or motions are required,"[a] and Rule 8(f) provides that "[a]ll pleadings shall be so construed as to do substantial justice."[b] Given the Federal Rules' simplified standard for pleading, "[a] court may dismiss a complaint only if it is clear that no relief could be granted under any set of facts that could be proved consistent with the allegations." *Hishon v. King & Spalding,* 467 U.S. 69, 73 (1984). If a pleading fails to specify the allegations in a manner that provides sufficient notice, a defendant can move for a more definite statement under Rule 12(e) before responding. Moreover, claims lacking merit may be dealt with through summary judgment under Rule 56. The liberal notice pleading of Rule 8(a) is the starting point of a simplified pleading system, which was adopted to focus litigation on the merits of a claim. *See Conley,* 355 U.S. at 48 ("The Federal Rules reject the approach that pleading is a game of skill in which one misstep by counsel may be decisive to the outcome and accept the principle that the purpose of pleading is to facilitate a proper decision on the merits").

---

4. These requirements are exemplified by the Federal Rules of Civil Procedure Forms, which "are sufficient under the rules and are intended to indicate the simplicity and brevity of statement which the rules contemplate." Fed. Rule Civ. Proc. 84. [The Court then cited Form 9 ("Complaint for Negligence"), now restyled as Form 11, as an example.]

a. [Eds. Note. In 2007, Rule 8(e)(1) was restyled as Rule 8(d)(1) and now reads in relevant part: "No technical form is required."]

b. [Eds. Note. In 2007, Rule 8(f) was restyled as Rule 8(e) and now reads: "Pleadings must be construed so as to do justice."]

Applying the relevant standard, petitioner's complaint easily satisfies the requirements of Rule 8(a) because it gives respondent fair notice of the basis for petitioner's claims. Petitioner alleged that he had been terminated on account of his national origin in violation of Title VII and on account of his age in violation of the ADEA. His complaint detailed the events leading to his termination, provided relevant dates, and included the ages and nationalities of at least some of the relevant persons involved with his termination. These allegations give respondent fair notice of what petitioner's claims are and the grounds upon which they rest. *See Conley,* 355 U.S. at 47. In addition, they state claims upon which relief could be granted under Title VII and the ADEA.

Respondent argues that allowing lawsuits based on conclusory allegations of discrimination to go forward will burden the courts and encourage disgruntled employees to bring unsubstantiated suits. Whatever the practical merits of this argument, the Federal Rules do not contain a heightened pleading standard for employment discrimination suits. A requirement of greater specificity for particular claims is a result that "must be obtained by the process of amending the Federal Rules, and not by judicial interpretation." *Leatherman,* 507 U.S. at 168. Furthermore, Rule 8(a) establishes a pleading standard without regard to whether a claim will succeed on the merits. "Indeed it may appear on the face of the pleadings that a recovery is very remote and unlikely but that is not the test." *Scheuer,* 416 U.S. at 236.

For the foregoing reasons, we hold that an employment discrimination plaintiff need not plead a prima facie case of discrimination and that petitioner's complaint is sufficient to survive respondent's motion to dismiss. Accordingly, the judgment of the Court of Appeals is reversed, and the case is remanded for further proceedings consistent with this opinion.

It is so ordered.

Jones v. Bock. The Supreme Court again rejected the imposition of a heightened pleading standard in *Jones v. Bock,* 549 U.S. 199 (2007). The Court held that complaints by prisoners against prison officials, which are subject to the Prison Litigation Reform Act of 1995 (PLRA), 42 U.S.C. § 1997e *et seq.,* are governed by the normal "short and plain statement of the claim" pleading standard of Rule 8(a)(2). The PLRA mandates early judicial screening of prisoner complaints and requires prisoners to exhaust prison grievance procedures before filing suit. The lower federal courts were divided on whether a heightened pleading standard applied in such cases requiring the prisoner to specially plead and demonstrate compliance with the PLRA in the complaint.

Citing *Leatherman* and *Swierkiewicz,* the Court unanimously held that although exhaustion of prison grievance procedures is mandatory under the PLRA, Rule 8(a)(2) only requires a "short and plain statement of the claim," *id.* at 212, and "[g]iven that the PLRA does not itself require plaintiffs to plead exhaustion, such a result 'must be obtained by the process of amending the Federal Rules, and not by judicial interpretation.'" *Id.* at 217. The Court held that the burden was on the defendant to plead lack of exhaustion as an affirmative defense. Affirmative defenses are examined in section C(5).

Twombly* and *Iqbal. The preceding cases set out the prevailing view of what was required to satisfy Rule 8(a)(2)'s requirement of a "short and plain statement of the claim showing that the pleader is entitled to relief." However, the issue was complicated by the 2007 and 2009 Supreme Court decisions in *Bell Atlantic Corp. v. Twombly* and *Ashcroft v. Iqbal,* reprinted below. As you read these cases, consider the practical effect of the Court's "clarification" of the Rule 8(a)(2) standard and its consistency with prior cases.

Bell Atlantic Corp. v. Twombly

United States Supreme Court, 2007
550 U.S. 544, 127 S. Ct. 1955, 167 L. Ed. 2d 929

JUSTICE SOUTER delivered the opinion of the Court.

Liability under § 1 of the Sherman Act, 15 U.S.C. § 1, requires a "contract, combination..., or conspiracy, in restraint of trade or commerce." The question in this putative class action is whether a § 1 complaint can survive a motion to dismiss when it alleges that major telecommunications providers engaged in certain parallel conduct unfavorable to competition, absent some factual context suggesting agreement, as distinct from identical, independent action. We hold that such a complaint should be dismissed.

I

The upshot of the 1984 divestiture of the American Telephone & Telegraph Company's (AT & T) local telephone business was a system of regional service monopolies (variously called "Regional Bell Operating Companies," "Baby Bells," or "Incumbent Local Exchange Carriers" (ILECs)), and a separate, competitive market for long-distance service from which the ILECs were excluded. More than a decade later, Congress withdrew approval of the ILECs' monopolies by enacting the Telecommunications Act of 1996 (1996 Act), ... which "fundamentally restructure[d] local telephone markets" and "subject[ed] [ILECs] to a host of duties intended to facilitate market entry." ... In recompense, the 1996 Act set conditions for authorizing ILECs to enter the long-distance market.

. . . .

Respondents William Twombly and Lawrence Marcus (hereinafter plaintiffs) represent a putative class consisting of all "subscribers of local telephone and/or high speed internet services ... from February 8, 1996 to present." Amended Complaint in No. 02 CIV. 10220(GEL) (S.D.N.Y.) ¶ 53, App. 28 (hereinafter Complaint). In this action against petitioners, a group of ILECs,[3] plaintiffs seek treble damages and declaratory and injunctive relief for claimed violations of § 1 of the Sherman Act, ch. 647, 26 Stat. 209, as amended, 15 U.S.C. § 1, which prohibits "[e]very contract, combination in the form of trust or otherwise, or conspiracy, in restraint of trade or commerce among the several States, or with foreign nations."

The complaint alleges that the ILECs conspired to restrain trade in two ways, each supposedly inflating charges for local telephone and high-speed Internet services. Plaintiffs say, first, that the ILECs "engaged in parallel conduct" in their respective service areas to inhibit the growth of upstart CLECs ["Competitive Local Exchange Carriers"].... Their actions allegedly included making unfair agreements with the CLECs for access to ILEC networks, providing inferior connections to the networks, overcharging, and billing in ways designed to sabotage the CLECs' relations with their own customers. According to the complaint, the ILECs' "compelling common motivatio[n]" to thwart the CLECs' competitive efforts naturally led them to form a conspiracy; "[h]ad any one [ILEC] not sought to prevent CLECs ... from competing effectively..., the resulting greater competitive inroads into that [ILEC's] territory would have revealed the degree to which competitive entry by CLECs would have been successful in the other territories in the absence of such conduct."

---

3. The 1984 divestiture of AT&T's local telephone service created seven Regional Bell Operating Companies. Through a series of mergers and acquisitions, those seven companies were consolidated into the four ILECs named in this suit: BellSouth Corporation, Qwest Communications International, Inc., SBC Communications, Inc., and Verizon Communications, Inc. (successor-in-interest to Bell Atlantic Corporation).... Together, these ILECs allegedly control 90 percent or more of the market for local telephone service in the 48 contiguous States.

Second, the complaint charges agreements by the ILECs to refrain from competing against one another. These are to be inferred from the ILECs' common failure "meaningfully [to] pursu[e]" "attractive business opportunit[ies]" in contiguous markets where they possessed "substantial competitive advantages," ... and from a statement of [the] chief executive officer (CEO) of the ILEC Qwest, that competing in the territory of another ILEC "'might be a good way to turn a quick dollar but that doesn't make it right.'" ...

The complaint couches its ultimate allegations this way:

"In the absence of any meaningful competition between the [ILECs] in one another's markets, and in light of the parallel course of conduct that each engaged in to prevent competition from CLECs within their respective local telephone and/or high speed internet services markets and the other facts and market circumstances alleged above, Plaintiffs allege upon information and belief that [the ILECs] have entered into a contract, combination or conspiracy to prevent competitive entry in their respective local telephone and/or high speed internet services markets and have agreed not to compete with one another and otherwise allocated customers and markets to one another."

The United States District Court for the Southern District of New York dismissed the complaint for failure to state a claim upon which relief can be granted. The District Court acknowledged that "plaintiffs may allege a conspiracy by citing instances of parallel business behavior that suggest an agreement," but emphasized that "while '[c]ircumstantial evidence of consciously parallel behavior may have made heavy inroads into the traditional judicial attitude toward conspiracy[, ...] "conscious parallelism" has not yet read conspiracy out of the Sherman Act entirely.'" ... Thus, the District Court understood that allegations of parallel business conduct, taken alone, do not state a claim under § 1; plaintiffs must allege additional facts that "ten[d] to exclude independent self-interested conduct as an explanation for defendants' parallel behavior." ... The District Court found plaintiffs' allegations of parallel ILEC actions to discourage competition inadequate because "the behavior of each ILEC in resisting the incursion of CLECs is fully explained by the ILEC's own interests in defending its individual territory." ... As to the ILECs' supposed agreement against competing with each other, the District Court found that the complaint does not "alleg[e] facts ... suggesting that refraining from competing in other territories as CLECs was contrary to [the ILECs'] apparent economic interests, and consequently [does] not rais[e] an inference that [the ILECs'] actions were the result of a conspiracy."

The Court of Appeals for the Second Circuit reversed, holding that the District Court tested the complaint by the wrong standard. It held that "plus factors are not *required* to be pleaded to permit an antitrust claim based on parallel conduct to survive dismissal." ...

We granted certiorari to address the proper standard for pleading an antitrust conspiracy through allegations of parallel conduct ... and now reverse.

II

A

[Quoting from Supreme Court decisions in prior antitrust cases, the Court pointed out that] "§ 1 of the Sherman Act 'does not prohibit [all] unreasonable restraints of trade ... but only restraints effected by a contract, combination, or conspiracy,' ... '[t]he crucial question' is whether the challenged anticompetitive conduct 'stem[s] from independent decision or from an agreement, tacit or express'.... While a showing of parallel 'business behavior is admissible circumstantial evidence from which the fact finder may infer agreement,' it falls short of 'conclusively establish[ing] agreement or ... itself constitut[ing] a Sherman Act offense.'... Even 'conscious parallelism,' a common reaction of 'firms in a

concentrated market [that] recogniz[e] their shared economic interests and their interdependence with respect to price and output decisions' is 'not in itself unlawful.' ..."

....

B

This case presents the antecedent question of what a plaintiff must plead in order to
state a claim under § 1 of the Sherman Act. Federal Rule of Civil Procedure 8(a)(2) requires
only "a short and plain statement of the claim showing that the pleader is entitled to relief," in order to "give the defendant fair notice of what the ... claim is and the grounds
upon which it rests," *Conley v. Gibson,* 355 U.S. 41 (1957). While a complaint attacked by
a Rule 12(b)(6) motion to dismiss does not need detailed factual allegations, ... a plaintiff's obligation to provide the "grounds" of his "entitle[ment] to relief" requires more
than labels and conclusions, and a formulaic recitation of the elements of a cause of action will not do, see *Papasan v. Allain,* 478 U.S. 265, 286 (1986) (on a motion to dismiss,
courts "are not bound to accept as true a legal conclusion couched as a factual allegation"). Factual allegations must be enough to raise a right to relief above the speculative
level, see 5 C. Wright & A. Miller, *Federal Practice and Procedure* § 1216, at 235–36 (3d
ed. 2004) ("[T]he pleading must contain something more ... than ... a statement of facts
that merely creates a suspicion [of] a legally cognizable right of action"),[3] on the assumption that all the allegations in the complaint are true (even if doubtful in fact), *see,
e.g., Swierkiewicz v. Sorema N.A.,* 534 U.S. 506, 508, n.1 (2002); *Neitzke v. Williams,* 490
U.S. 319, 327 (1989) ("Rule 12(b)(6) does not countenance ... dismissals based on a
judge's disbelief of a complaint's factual allegations"); *Scheuer v. Rhodes,* 416 U.S. 232,
236 (1974) (a well-pleaded complaint may proceed even if it appears "that a recovery is
very remote and unlikely").

In applying these general standards to a § 1 claim, we hold that stating such a claim requires a complaint with enough factual matter (taken as true) to suggest that an agreement was made. Asking for plausible grounds to infer an agreement does not impose a
probability requirement at the pleading stage; it simply calls for enough fact to raise a
reasonable expectation that discovery will reveal evidence of illegal agreement.[4] And, of
course, a well-pleaded complaint may proceed even if it strikes a savvy judge that actual
proof of those facts is improbable, and "that a recovery is very remote and unlikely." *Id.*
In identifying facts that are suggestive enough to render a § 1 conspiracy plausible, we
have the benefit of the prior rulings and considered views of leading commentators, al-

---

3. The dissent greatly oversimplifies matters by suggesting that the Federal Rules somehow dispensed
with the pleading of facts altogether.... (opinion of Stevens, J.) (pleading standard of Federal Rules
"does not require, or even invite, the pleading of facts"). While, for most types of cases, the Federal
Rules eliminated the cumbersome requirement that a claimant "set out *in detail* the facts upon which
he bases his claim," *Conley v. Gibson,* 355 U.S. 41, 47 (1957) (emphasis added), Rule 8(a)(2) still requires a "showing," rather than a blanket assertion, of entitlement to relief. Without some factual allegation in the complaint, it is hard to see how a claimant could satisfy the requirement of providing
not only "fair notice" of the nature of the claim, but also "grounds" on which the claim rests. *See* 5
Wright & Miller § 1202, at 94, 95 (Rule 8(a) "contemplate[s] the statement of circumstances, occurrences, and events in support of the claim presented" and does not authorize a pleader's "bare averment that he wants relief and is entitled to it").

4. Commentators have offered several examples of parallel conduct allegations that would state a
§ 1 claim under this standard [such as] "parallel behavior that would probably not result from chance,
coincidence, independent responses to common stimuli, or mere interdependence unaided by an advance understanding among the parties"); ... The parties in this case agree that "complex and historically
unprecedented changes in pricing structure made at the very same time by multiple competitors, and
made for no other discernible reason" would support a plausible inference of conspiracy.

ready quoted, that lawful parallel conduct fails to bespeak unlawful agreement. It makes sense to say, therefore, that an allegation of parallel conduct and a bare assertion of conspiracy will not suffice. Without more, parallel conduct does not suggest conspiracy, and a conclusory allegation of agreement at some unidentified point does not supply facts adequate to show illegality. Hence, when allegations of parallel conduct are set out in order to make a § 1 claim, they must be placed in a context that raises a suggestion of a preceding agreement, not merely parallel conduct that could just as well be independent action.

The need at the pleading stage for allegations plausibly suggesting (not merely consistent with) agreement reflects the threshold requirement of Rule 8(a)(2) that the "plain statement" possess enough heft to "sho[w] that the pleader is entitled to relief." A statement of parallel conduct, even conduct consciously undertaken, needs some setting suggesting the agreement necessary to make out a § 1 claim; without that further circumstance pointing toward a meeting of the minds, an account of a defendant's commercial efforts stays in neutral territory. An allegation of parallel conduct is thus much like a naked assertion of conspiracy in a § 1 complaint: it gets the complaint close to stating a claim, but without some further factual enhancement it stops short of the line between possibility and plausibility of "entitle[ment] to relief."

. . . .

It is no answer to say that a claim just shy of a plausible entitlement to relief can, if groundless, be weeded out early in the discovery process through "careful case management," . . . , given the common lament that the success of judicial supervision in checking discovery abuse has been on the modest side. . . . And it is self-evident that the problem of discovery abuse cannot be solved by "careful scrutiny of evidence at the summary judgment stage," much less "lucid instructions to juries," . . . ; the threat of discovery expense will push cost-conscious defendants to settle even anemic cases before reaching those proceedings. Probably, then, it is only by taking care to require allegations that reach the level suggesting conspiracy that we can hope to avoid the potentially enormous expense of discovery in cases with no "'reasonably founded hope that the [discovery] process will reveal relevant evidence'" to support a § 1 claim. . . .

. . . .

Plaintiffs['] . . . main argument against the plausibility standard at the pleading stage is its ostensible conflict with an early statement of ours construing Rule 8. Justice Black's opinion for the Court in *Conley v. Gibson* spoke not only of the need for fair notice of the grounds for entitlement to relief but of "the accepted rule that a complaint should not be dismissed for failure to state a claim unless it appears beyond doubt that the plaintiff can prove no set of facts in support of his claim which would entitle him to relief." . . . This "no set of facts" language can be read in isolation as saying that any statement revealing the theory of the claim will suffice unless its factual impossibility may be shown from the face of the pleadings; and the Court of Appeals appears to have read *Conley* in some such way when formulating its understanding of the proper pleading standard. . . .

On such a focused and literal reading of *Conley's* "no set of facts," a wholly conclusory statement of claim would survive a motion to dismiss whenever the pleadings left open the possibility that a plaintiff might later establish some "set of [undisclosed] facts" to support recovery. So here, the Court of Appeals specifically found the prospect of unearthing direct evidence of conspiracy sufficient to preclude dismissal, even though the complaint does not set forth a single fact in a context that suggests an agreement. . . .

Seeing this, a good many judges and commentators have balked at taking the literal terms of the *Conley* passage as a pleading standard. [citations omitted]

We could go on, but there is no need to pile up further citations to show that *Conley's* "no set of facts" language has been questioned, criticized, and explained away long enough. To be fair to the *Conley* Court, the passage should be understood in light of the opinion's preceding summary of the complaint's concrete allegations, which the Court quite reasonably understood as amply stating a claim for relief. But the passage so often quoted fails to mention this understanding on the part of the Court, and after puzzling the profession for 50 years, this famous observation has earned its retirement. The phrase is best forgotten as an incomplete, negative gloss on an accepted pleading standard: once a claim has been stated adequately, it may be supported by showing any set of facts consistent with the allegations in the complaint.... *Conley,* then, described the breadth of opportunity to prove what an adequate complaint claims, not the minimum standard of adequate pleading to govern a complaint's survival.

III

When we look for plausibility in this complaint, we agree with the District Court that plaintiffs' claim of conspiracy in restraint of trade comes up short. To begin with, the complaint leaves no doubt that plaintiffs rest their § 1 claim on descriptions of parallel conduct and not on any independent allegation of actual agreement among the ILECs.... Although in form a few stray statements speak directly of agreement, on fair reading these are merely legal conclusions resting on the prior allegations. Thus, the complaint first takes account of the alleged "absence of any meaningful competition between [the ILECs] in one another's markets," "the parallel course of conduct that each [ILEC] engaged in to prevent competition from CLECs," "and the other facts and market circumstances alleged [earlier]"; "in light of" these, the complaint concludes "that [the ILECs] have entered into a contract, combination or conspiracy to prevent competitive entry into their ... markets and have agreed not to compete with one another."[10] ... The nub of the complaint, then, is the ILECs' parallel behavior, consisting of steps to keep the CLECs out and manifest disinterest in becoming CLECs themselves, and its sufficiency turns on the suggestions raised by this conduct when viewed in light of common economic experience.

We think that nothing contained in the complaint invests either the action or inaction alleged with a plausible suggestion of conspiracy.... [W]e agree with the District Court that nothing in the complaint intimates that the resistance to the upstarts was anything more than the natural, unilateral reaction of each ILEC intent on keeping its regional dominance.... [T]here is no reason to infer that the companies had agreed among themselves to do what was only natural anyway; so natural, in fact, that if alleging parallel decisions to resist competition were enough to imply an antitrust conspiracy, pleading a § 1 violation against almost any group of competing businesses would be a sure thing.

---

10. If the complaint had not explained that the claim of agreement rested on the parallel conduct described, we doubt that the complaint's references to an agreement among the ILECs would have given the notice required by Rule 8.... This lack of notice contrasts sharply with the model form for pleading negligence, Form 9, [now restyled as Form 11] which the dissent says exemplifies the kind of "bare allegation" that survives a motion to dismiss.... Whereas the model form alleges that the defendant struck the plaintiff with his car while plaintiff was crossing a particular highway at a specified date and time, the complaint here furnishes no clue as to which of the four ILECs (much less which of their employees) supposedly agreed, or when and where the illicit agreement took place. A defendant wishing to prepare an answer in the simple fact pattern laid out in Form 9 would know what to answer; a defendant seeking to respond to plaintiffs' conclusory allegations in the § 1 context would have little idea where to begin.

....

We agree with the District Court's assessment that antitrust conspiracy was not suggested by the facts adduced under either theory of the complaint, which thus fails to state a valid § 1 claim.[14]

Plaintiffs say that our analysis runs counter to *Swierkiewicz v. Sorema N. A.*, 534 U.S. 506, 508 (2002).... They argue that just as the prima facie case is a "flexible evidentiary standard" that "should not be transposed into a rigid pleading standard for discrimination cases," ... "transpos[ing] 'plus factor' summary judgment analysis woodenly into a rigid Rule 12(b)(6) pleading standard ... would be unwise." Brief for Respondents 39. As the District Court correctly understood, however, "*Swierkiewicz* did not change the law of pleading, but simply re-emphasized ... that the Second Circuit's use of a heightened pleading standard for Title VII cases was contrary to the Federal Rules' structure of liberal pleading requirements.".... Even though Swierkiewicz's pleadings "detailed the events leading to his termination, provided relevant dates, and included the ages and nationalities of at least some of the relevant persons involved with his termination," the Court of Appeals dismissed his complaint for failing to allege certain additional facts that Swierkiewicz would need at the trial stage to support his claim in the absence of direct evidence of discrimination.... We reversed on the ground that the Court of Appeals had impermissibly applied what amounted to a heightened pleading requirement by insisting that Swierkiewicz allege "specific facts" beyond those necessary to state his claim and the grounds showing entitlement to relief....

Here, in contrast, we do not require heightened fact pleading of specifics, but only enough facts to state a claim to relief that is plausible on its face. Because the plaintiffs here have not nudged their claims across the line from conceivable to plausible, their complaint must be dismissed.

The judgment of the Court of Appeals for the Second Circuit is reversed, and the cause is remanded for further proceedings consistent with this opinion.

It is so ordered.

JUSTICE STEVENS, with whom JUSTICE GINSBURG joins except as to Part IV [commenting on statutory interpretation being affected by underlying congressional policy concerns as in antitrust cases], dissenting.

....

Respondents' amended complaint describes a variety of circumstantial evidence and makes the straightforward allegation that petitioners "entered into a contract, combination or conspiracy to prevent competitive entry in their respective local telephone and/or high speed internet services markets and have agreed not to compete with one another and otherwise allocated customers and markets to one another." ...

---

14. In reaching this conclusion, we do not apply any "heightened" pleading standard, nor do we seek to broaden the scope of Federal Rule of Civil Procedure 9, which can only be accomplished " 'by the process of amending the Federal Rules, and not by judicial interpretation.' " *Swierkiewicz v. Sorema N. A.*, 534 U.S. 506, 515 (2002) (quoting *Leatherman v. Tarrant County Narcotics Intelligence and Coordination Unit*, 507 U.S. 163, 168 (1993)). On certain subjects understood to raise a high risk of abusive litigation, a plaintiff must state factual allegations with greater particularity than Rule 8 requires. Fed. R. Civ. P. 9(b)-(c). Here, our concern is not that the allegations in the complaint were insufficiently "particular[ized]" ...; rather, the complaint warranted dismissal because it failed *in toto* to render plaintiffs' entitlement to relief plausible.

The complaint explains that, contrary to Congress' expectation when it enacted the 1996 Telecommunications Act, and consistent with their own economic self-interests, petitioner Incumbent Local Exchange Carriers (ILECs) have assiduously avoided infringing upon each other's markets and have refused to permit nonincumbent competitors to access their networks. The complaint quotes ... the former CEO of one such ILEC, as saying that competing in a neighboring ILEC's territory "might be a good way to turn a quick dollar but that doesn't make it right." ... Moreover, respondents allege that petitioners "communicate amongst themselves" through numerous industry associations.... In sum, respondents allege that petitioners entered into an agreement that has long been recognized as a classic *per se* violation of the Sherman Act.

Under [well-settled] rules of procedure..., a judge ruling on a defendant's motion to dismiss a complaint, "must accept as true all of the factual allegations contained in the complaint." *Swierkiewicz v. Sorema N.A.,* 534 U.S. 506, 508, n.1 (2002).... But instead of requiring knowledgeable executives ... to respond to these allegations by way of sworn depositions or other limited discovery—and indeed without so much as requiring petitioners to file an answer denying that they entered into any agreement—the majority permits immediate dismissal based on the assurances of company lawyers that nothing untoward was afoot. The Court embraces the argument of those lawyers that "there is no reason to infer that the companies had agreed among themselves to do what was only natural anyway" ...; that "there was just no need for joint encouragement to resist the 1996 Act" ...; and that the "natural explanation for the noncompetition alleged is that the former Government-sanctioned monopolists were sitting tight, expecting their neighbors to do the same thing." ...

The Court and petitioners' legal team are no doubt correct that the parallel conduct alleged is consistent with the absence of any contract, combination, or conspiracy. But that conduct is also entirely consistent with the *presence* of the illegal agreement alleged in the complaint. And the charge that petitioners "agreed not to compete with one another" is not just one of "a few stray statements" ...; it is an allegation describing unlawful conduct. As such, the Federal Rules of Civil Procedure, our longstanding precedent, and sound practice mandate that the District Court at least require some sort of response from petitioners before dismissing the case.

Two practical concerns presumably explain the Court's dramatic departure from settled procedural law. Private antitrust litigation can be enormously expensive, and there is a risk that jurors may mistakenly conclude that evidence of parallel conduct has proved that the parties acted pursuant to an agreement when they in fact merely made similar independent decisions. Those concerns merit careful case management, including strict control of discovery, careful scrutiny of evidence at the summary judgment stage, and lucid instructions to juries; they do not, however, justify the dismissal of an adequately pleaded complaint without even requiring the defendants to file answers denying a charge that they in fact engaged in collective decisionmaking. More importantly, they do not justify an interpretation of Federal Rule of Civil Procedure 12(b)(6) that seems to be driven by the majority's appraisal of the plausibility of the ultimate factual allegation rather than its legal sufficiency.

I

....

The pleading paradigm under the ... Federal Rules [is] well illustrated by the inclusion in the appendix of Form 9, a complaint for negligence [now restyled as Form 11]. As relevant, the Form 9 complaint states only: "On June 1, 1936, in a public highway called

Boylston Street in Boston, Massachusetts, defendant negligently drove a motor vehicle against plaintiff who was then crossing said highway." ...[1] The complaint then describes the plaintiff's injuries and demands judgment. The asserted ground for relief-namely, the defendant's negligent driving-would have been called a "conclusion of law" under the code pleading of old.... But that bare allegation suffices under a system that "restrict[s] the pleadings to the task of general notice-giving and invest[s] the deposition-discovery process with a vital role in the preparation for trial."[3] ...

II

It is in the context of this history that *Conley v. Gibson*, 355 U.S. 41 (1957), must be understood....

Consistent with the design of the Federal Rules, *Conley's* "no set of facts" formulation permits outright dismissal only when proceeding to discovery or beyond would be futile. Once it is clear that a plaintiff has stated a claim that, if true, would entitle him to relief, matters of proof are appropriately relegated to other stages of the trial process. Today, however, in its explanation of a decision to dismiss a complaint that it regards as a fishing expedition, the Court scraps *Conley's* "no set of facts" language. Concluding that the phrase has been "questioned, criticized, and explained away long enough," ... the Court dismisses it as careless composition.

....

Today's majority calls *Conley's* "no set of facts" language "an incomplete, negative gloss on an accepted pleading standard: once a claim has been stated adequately, it may be supported by showing any set of facts consistent with the allegations in the complaint." ... This is not and cannot be what the *Conley* Court meant. First, as I have explained, and as the *Conley* Court well knew, the pleading standard the Federal Rules meant to codify does not require, or even invite, the pleading of facts.[7] The "pleading standard" label the majority gives to what it reads into the *Conley* opinion—a statement of the permissible factual support for an adequately pleaded complaint—would not, therefore, have impressed the *Conley* Court itself. Rather, that Court would have understood the majority's remodeling of its language to express an *evidentiary* standard, which the *Conley* Court had neither need nor want to explicate. Second, it is pellucidly clear that the *Conley* Court was interested in what a complaint *must* contain, not what it *may* contain. In fact, the Court said without qualification that it was "appraising the *sufficiency*

---

1. [Eds. Note. Restyled Form 11 now reads: "On *date*, at *place*, the defendant negligently drove a motor vehicle against the plaintiff"; the allegation now omits what the plaintiff was doing at the time of the accident, *i.e.*, crossing the highway.]

3. The Federal Rules do impose a "particularity" requirement on "all averments of fraud or mistake," Fed. R. Civ. P. 9(b), neither of which has been alleged in this case.... [Eds. Note. Restyled Rule 9(b) now reads in relevant part: "In alleging fraud or mistake, a party must state with particularity the circumstances constituting fraud or mistake."]

7. The majority is correct to say that what the Federal Rules require is a "'showing'" of entitlement to relief.... Whether and to what extent that "showing" requires allegations of fact will depend on the particulars of the claim. For example, had the amended complaint in this case alleged *only* parallel conduct, it would not have made the required "showing." ... Similarly, had the pleadings contained *only* an allegation of agreement, without specifying the nature or object of that agreement, they would have been susceptible to the charge that they did not provide sufficient notice that the defendants may answer intelligently. Omissions of that sort instance the type of "bareness" with which the Federal Rules are concerned. A plaintiff's inability to persuade a district court that the allegations actually included in her complaint are "plausible" is an altogether different kind of failing, and one that should not be fatal at the pleading stage.

of the complaint." 355 U.S. at 45 (emphasis added). It was, to paraphrase today's majority, describing "the minimum standard of adequate pleading to govern a complaint's survival"....

. . . .

... *Conley's* statement that a complaint is not to be dismissed unless "no set of facts" in support thereof would entitle the plaintiff to relief is hardly "puzzling," ... It reflects a philosophy that, unlike in the days of code pleading, separating the wheat from the chaff is a task assigned to the pretrial and trial process. *Conley's* language, in short, captures the policy choice embodied in the Federal Rules and binding on the federal courts.

We have consistently reaffirmed that basic understanding of the Federal Rules in the half century since *Conley*. For example, in *Scheuer v. Rhodes,* 416 U.S. 232 (1974), ... we emphasized that "[w]hen a federal court reviews the sufficiency of a complaint, before the reception of any evidence either by affidavit or admissions, its task is necessarily a limited one. The issue is not whether a plaintiff will ultimately prevail but whether the claimant is entitled to offer evidence to support the claims. *Indeed it may appear on the face of the pleadings that a recovery is very remote and unlikely but that is not the test." Id.* at 236 (emphasis added).... We again spoke with one voice against efforts to expand pleading requirements beyond their appointed limits in *Leatherman v. Tarrant County Narcotics Intelligence and Coordination Unit*, 507 U.S. 163 (1993)....

Most recently, in *Swierkiewicz,* ... we were faced with a case more similar to the present one than the majority will allow.... We reversed in another unanimous opinion ... [holding that] the "simplified notice pleading standard" of the Federal Rules "relies on liberal discovery rules and summary judgment motions to define disputed facts and issues and to dispose of unmeritorious claims."

. . . .

Everything today's majority says would therefore make perfect sense if it were ruling on a Rule 56 motion for summary judgment and the evidence included nothing more than the Court has described....

In this"Big Case," the Court succumbs to the temptation that previous Courts have steadfastly resisted. While the majority assures us that it is not applying any "heightened" pleading standard, ... I have a difficult time understanding its opinion any other way.

. . . .

Accordingly, I respectfully dissent.

Notes and Questions

1. (a) Given the forceful dissent of Justice Stevens, it is not surprising that the *Twombly* opinion generated an immediate stir in the lower federal courts. As the Second Circuit noted three weeks after the opinion, "[c]onsiderable uncertainty concerning the standard for assessing the adequacy of pleadings has recently been created by the Supreme Court's decision in [*Twombly*].... The nature and extent of [the] alteration [to traditional notice pleading standards] is not clear because the Court's explanation contains several, not entirely consistent, signals...." *Iqbal v. Hasty*, 490 F.3d 143, 155 (2d Cir. 2007). In fact, in then applying the *Twombly* standard to the plaintiff's complaint in *Iqbal*, the Second Circuit held that the complaint was sufficient, only to have the Second Circuit's decision later reversed by the Supreme Court in *Ashcroft v. Iqbal*, reprinted below.

(b) Reflective of the difficulty in the proper application of the pleading standard of *Twombly*, is the fact that Justice Souter, who authored the Court's opinion in *Twombly*, disagreed with the majority's application of that standard in *Ashcroft v. Iqbal* and authored the dissenting opinion, which concluded that the plaintiff's complaint did in fact meet the pleading standard of *Twombly*. The *Twombly* opinion thus requires careful reading in understanding the Court's standard and determining the extent to which it alters traditional notice pleading standards under the Federal Rules.

2. The *Twombly* opinion effected no change in the pleading standard of Rule (8)(a)(2), which remains "a short plain statement of the claim showing that the pleader is entitled to relief." Furthermore, in beginning its analysis, the *Twombly* Court expressly quoted and reaffirmed the oft-cited language from *Conley* that the goal of notice pleading is "to give the defendant fair notice of what the ... claim is and the grounds upon which it rests." The Court also expressly reaffirmed that "detailed factual allegations" are not required under Rule 8(a)(2) and explicitly disclaimed that it was imposing "any 'heightened' pleading standard" or broadening the scope of Rule 9, expressly citing *Swierkiewicz* and *Leatherman*.

In fact, two weeks after *Twombly*, the Court in *Erickson v. Pardus*, 551 U.S. 89 (2007) overruled the dismissal of a prisoner's complaint in a § 1983 civil rights action and reaffirmed, with direct citation to *Twombly*, that "specific facts are not necessary" under Rule 8(a)(2) and that a complaint "need only 'give the defendant fair notice of what the ... claim is and the grounds upon which it rests.'" In *Erickson*, the Court reversed a finding by the Court of Appeals that the plaintiff's complaint for denial of medical treatment made "only conclusory allegations" in alleging that plaintiff had suffered a "cognizable independent harm." Under the applicable substantive law, such a harm is necessary to give rise to an actionable claim. The plaintiff alleged that the defendants' denial of prescribed medication and treatment for his hepatitis C was "endangering [his] life." The Court held that "this alone" was sufficient to state a claim under Rule 8(a)(2).

3. So how does *Twombly* change or clarify traditional notice pleading standards under the Federal Rules? First, the Court explicitly disavowed and "retired" the oft-cited language from *Conley* "that a complaint should not be dismissed for failure to state a claim unless it appears beyond doubt that the plaintiff can prove no set of facts in support of his claim which would entitle him to relief." The Court correctly rephrased this accepted pleading standard as meaning that "once a claim has been stated adequately, it may be supported by showing any set of facts consistent with the allegations in the complaint."

Second, while reaffirming the language from *Conley* that a complaint need only "give the defendant fair notice of what the ... claim is and the grounds upon which it rests," the Court refocused this analysis by emphasizing that a proper pleading must provide not only fair notice of the claim, but must also state the *grounds* upon which the claim rests. It is on this point that the *Twombly* opinion raises the greatest difficulty. How much and what kind of detail must be alleged to properly show that the pleader is entitled to relief? The Court gave various formulations: "Factual allegations must be enough to raise a right to relief above the speculative level"; "more than labels and conclusions" are required; "a formulaic recitation of the elements of a cause of action will not do"; the statement must "possess enough heft" to show the pleader is entitled to relief; "we do not require heightened fact pleading of specifics, but only enough facts to state a claim to relief that is *plausible* on its face"; the allegations must "nudge" the claims "across the line from conceivable to *plausible*" and must not stop "short of the line between possibility and *plausibility*."

4. In establishing its "plausibility" standard, the Court stated that "asking for plausible grounds does not impose a probability requirement at the pleading stage." Thus, while it is insufficient to show only that entitlement to relief is conceivable or possible, a showing of probability is not required. Do you think it is difficult to decide when the allegations in a pleading cross the line from possible to plausible, even though they are not necessarily probable? Consider this passage from the Tenth Circuit.

> The most difficult question in interpreting *Twombly* is what the Court means by "plausibility." The Court states that the complaint must contain "enough facts to state a claim to relief that is plausible on its face." But it reiterates the bedrock principle that a judge ruling on a motion to dismiss must accept all allegations as true and may not dismiss on the ground that it appears unlikely the allegations can be proven. "[A] well-pleaded complaint may proceed even if it strikes a savvy judge that actual proof of those facts is improbable, and 'that a recovery is very remote and unlikely.'" 127 S. Ct. at 1965 (quoting *Scheuer v. Rhodes,* 416 U.S. 232, 236 (1974)). Thus, "plausible" cannot mean "likely to be true." Rather, "plausibility" in this context must refer to the scope of the allegations in a complaint: if they are so general that they encompass a wide swath of conduct, much of it innocent, then the plaintiffs "have not nudged their claims across the line from conceivable to plausible." The allegations must be enough that, if assumed to be true, the plaintiff plausibly (not just speculatively) has a claim for relief.

Robbins v. Oklahoma, 519 F.3d 1242, 1247 (10th Cir. 2008). Does this explanation help to clarify the Court's standard?

5. The plaintiffs' action in *Twombly* involved a complex antitrust action and the Court explained that the imposition of a "plausibility" standard was necessary "to avoid the potentially enormous expense of discovery in cases with no 'reasonably founded hope that the [discovery] process will reveal relevant evidence' to support a § 1 [antitrust] claim." Following *Twombly*, one question of debate was whether the Court intended its "plausibility" standard to apply only in antitrust and other complex cases involving expensive discovery. Another question was how the "plausibility" standard was to be applied in determining whether the allegations of a complaint properly pled a claim for relief.

As you read the Court's opinion in *Ashcroft v. Iqbal*, look to see how the Court answers these questions.

Ashcroft v. Iqbal

United States Supreme Court, 2009
556 U.S. 662, 129 S. Ct. 1937, 173 L. Ed. 2d 868

JUSTICE KENNEDY delivered the opinion of the Court.

[After the September 11, 2001 terrorist attacks, respondent Javaid Iqbal, a citizen of Pakistan and a Muslim, was arrested in the United States on criminal charges for fraud related to identification documents and conspiracy to defraud the United States. He pleaded guilty to the charges and was deported. Subsequently, he filed a civil action claiming he was deprived of various constitutional protections while in federal custody. Iqbal's substantive claim for constitutional violations was based on the Supreme Court decision in *Bivens v. Six Unknown Fed. Narcotics Agents,* 403 U.S. 388 (1971). Such actions are known as *Bivens* actions.

Iqbal's action was brought against numerous federal officials, including petitioners John Ashcroft, the former Attorney General of the United States, and Robert Mueller, the Director of the Federal Bureau of Investigation ("FBI"). With regard to Ashcroft and Mueller, the complaint alleged that they adopted an unconstitutional policy that subjected Iqbal to harsh conditions of confinement on account of his race, religion, or national origin. The petitioners raised the defense of qualified immunity in the district court and moved to dismiss the suit on the ground that the complaint was not sufficient to state a claim against them. The district court denied the motion to dismiss, concluding the complaint was sufficient to state a claim despite petitioners' official status at the times in question. Petitioners brought an interlocutory appeal in the Court of Appeals for the Second Circuit which then affirmed the district court's denial of the motion to dismiss. The Supreme Court granted certiorari.]

Respondent's account of his prison ordeal could, if proved, demonstrate unconstitutional misconduct by some governmental actors. But the allegations and pleadings with respect to these actors are not before us here. This case instead turns on a narrower question: Did respondent, as the plaintiff in the District Court, plead factual matter that, if taken as true, states a claim that petitioners deprived him of his clearly established constitutional rights. We hold respondent's pleadings are insufficient.

I

....

The 21-cause-of-action complaint does not challenge respondent's arrest or his confinement in the ... general prison population. Rather, it concentrates on his treatment while confined to [an Administrative Maximum Special Housing Unit ("ADMAX SHU")]. The complaint sets forth various claims against defendants who are not before us. For instance, the complaint alleges that respondent's jailers "kicked him in the stomach, punched him in the face, and dragged him across" his cell without justification, ... subjected him to serial strip and body-cavity searches when he posed no safety risk to himself or others, ... and refused to let him and other Muslims pray because there would be "[n]o prayers for terrorists...."

The allegations against petitioners are the only ones relevant here.... The complaint alleges that "the [FBI], under the direction of Defendant MUELLER, arrested and detained thousands of Arab Muslim men ... as part of its investigation of the events of September 11." ... It further alleges that "[t]he policy of holding post-September-11th detainees in highly restrictive conditions of confinement until they were 'cleared' by the FBI was approved by Defendants ASHCROFT and MUELLER in discussions in the weeks after September 11, 2001." ... Lastly, the complaint posits that petitioners "each knew of, condoned, and willfully and maliciously agreed to subject" respondent to harsh conditions of confinement "as a matter of policy, solely on account of [his] religion, race, and/or national origin and for no legitimate penological interest." ... The pleading names Ashcroft as the "principal architect" of the policy ... and identifies Mueller as "instrumental in [its] adoption, promulgation, and implementation." ...

Petitioners moved to dismiss the complaint for failure to state sufficient allegations to show their own involvement in clearly established unconstitutional conduct. The District Court denied their motion. Accepting all of the allegations in respondent's complaint as true, the court held that "it cannot be said that there [is] no set of facts on which [respondent] would be entitled to relief as against" petitioners ... (relying on *Conley v. Gibson,* 355 U.S. 41 (1957)). Invoking the collateral-order doctrine petitioners filed an interlocutory appeal in the United States Court of Appeals for the Second Circuit. While that appeal was pending, this Court decided *Bell Atlantic Corp. v. Twombly*, 550 U.S. 544 (2007), which discussed the standard for evaluating whether a complaint is sufficient to survive a motion to dismiss.

The Court of Appeals considered *Twombly*'s applicability to this case. Acknowledging that *Twombly* retired the *Conley* no-set-of-facts test relied upon by the District Court, the Court of Appeals' opinion discussed at length how to apply this Court's "standard for assessing the adequacy of pleadings." ... It concluded that *Twombly* called for a "flexible 'plausibility standard,' which obliges a pleader to amplify a claim with some factual allegations in those contexts where such amplification is needed to render the claim *plausible*." ... The court found that petitioners' appeal did not present one of "those contexts" requiring amplification. As a consequence, it held respondent's pleading adequate to allege petitioners' personal involvement in discriminatory decisions which, if true, violated clearly established constitutional law....

....

III

In *Twombly*, ... the Court found it necessary first to discuss the antitrust principles implicated by the complaint. Here too we begin by taking note of the elements a plaintiff must plead to state a claim of unconstitutional discrimination against officials entitled to assert the defense of qualified immunity.

In *Bivens*—proceeding on the theory that a right suggests a remedy—this Court "recognized for the first time an implied private action for damages against federal officers alleged to have violated a citizen's constitutional rights." ... Because implied causes of action are disfavored, the Court has been reluctant to extend *Bivens* liability "to any new context or new category of defendants." ...

In the limited settings where *Bivens* does apply, the implied cause of action is the "federal analog to suits brought against state officials under ... 42 U.S.C. § 1983." ... Based on the rules our precedents establish, respondent correctly concedes that Government officials may not be held liable for the unconstitutional conduct of their subordinates under a theory of *respondeat superior*.... Because vicarious liability is inapplicable to *Bivens* and § 1983 suits, a plaintiff must plead that each Government-official defendant, through the official's own individual actions, has violated the Constitution.

The factors necessary to establish a *Bivens* violation will vary with the constitutional provision at issue. Where the claim is invidious discrimination in contravention of the First and Fifth Amendments, our decisions make clear that the plaintiff must plead and prove that the defendant acted with discriminatory purpose.... Under extant precedent purposeful discrimination requires more than "intent as volition or intent as awareness of consequences." ... It follows that, to state a claim based on a violation of a clearly established right, respondent must plead sufficient factual matter to show that petitioners adopted and implemented the detention policies at issue not for a neutral, investigative reason but for the purpose of discriminating on account of race, religion, or national origin.

... Absent vicarious liability, each Government official, his or her title notwithstanding, is only liable for his or her own misconduct. In the context of determining whether there is a violation of clearly established right to overcome qualified immunity, purpose rather than knowledge is required to impose *Bivens* liability on the subordinate for unconstitutional discrimination; the same holds true for an official charged with violations arising from his or her superintendent responsibilities.

IV

A

We turn to respondent's complaint. Under Federal Rule of Civil Procedure 8(a)(2), a pleading must contain a "short and plain statement of the claim showing that the pleader is entitled to relief." As the Court held in *Twombly*, 550 U.S. 544 [(2007)], the pleading standard Rule 8 announces does not require "detailed factual allegations," but it demands more than an unadorned, the-defendant-unlawfully-harmed-me accusation. *Id.* at 555. A pleading that offers "labels and conclusions" or "a formulaic recitation of the elements of a cause of action will not do." *Id.* Nor does a complaint suffice if it tenders "naked assertion[s]" devoid of "further factual enhancement." *Id.* at 557.

To survive a motion to dismiss, a complaint must contain sufficient factual matter, accepted as true, to "state a claim to relief that is plausible on its face." *Id.* at 570. A claim has facial plausibility when the plaintiff pleads factual content that allows the court to draw the reasonable inference that the defendant is liable for the misconduct alleged. *Id.* at 556. The plausibility standard is not akin to a "probability requirement," but it asks for more than a sheer possibility that a defendant has acted unlawfully. *Id.* Where a complaint pleads facts that are "merely consistent with" a defendant's liability, it "stops short of the line between possibility and plausibility of 'entitlement to relief.'" *Id.* at 557.

Two working principles underlie our decision in *Twombly*. First, the tenet that a court must accept as true all of the allegations contained in a complaint is inapplicable to legal conclusions. Threadbare recitals of the elements of a cause of action, supported by mere conclusory statements, do not suffice. *Id.* at 555. Rule 8 marks a notable and generous departure from the hyper-technical, code-pleading regime of a prior era, but it does not unlock the doors of discovery for a plaintiff armed with nothing more than conclusions. Second, only a complaint that states a plausible claim for relief survives a motion to dismiss. *Id.* at 556. Determining whether a complaint states a plausible claim for relief will, as the Court of Appeals observed, be a context-specific task that requires the reviewing court to draw on its judicial experience and common sense.... But where the well-pleaded facts do not permit the court to infer more than the mere possibility of misconduct, the complaint has alleged—but it has not "show[n]"—"that the pleader is entitled to relief." Fed. R. Civ. P. 8(a)(2).

In keeping with these principles a court considering a motion to dismiss can choose to begin by identifying pleadings that, because they are no more than conclusions, are not entitled to the assumption of truth. While legal conclusions can provide the framework of a complaint, they must be supported by factual allegations. When there are well-pleaded factual allegations, a court should assume their veracity and then determine whether they plausibly give rise to an entitlement to relief.

Our decision in *Twombly* illustrates the two-pronged approach. There, we considered the sufficiency of a complaint alleging that incumbent telecommunications providers had entered an agreement not to compete and to forestall competitive entry, in violation of the Sherman Act, 15 U.S.C. § 1. Recognizing that § 1 enjoins only anticompetitive conduct "effected by a contract, combination, or conspiracy," ... the plaintiffs in *Twombly* flatly pleaded that the defendants "ha[d] entered into a contract, combination or conspiracy to prevent competitive entry ... and ha[d] agreed not to compete with one another." [*Twombly*,] 550 U.S. at 551. The complaint also alleged that the defendants' "parallel course of conduct ... to prevent competition" and inflate prices was indicative of the unlawful agreement alleged. *Id.*

The Court held the plaintiffs' complaint deficient under Rule 8. In doing so it first noted that the plaintiffs' assertion of an unlawful agreement was a "'legal conclusion'" and, as such, was not entitled to the assumption of truth. *Id.* at 555. Had the Court simply credited the allegation of a conspiracy, the plaintiffs would have stated a claim for relief and been entitled to proceed perforce. The Court next addressed the "nub" of the plaintiffs' complaint—the well-pleaded, nonconclusory factual allegation of parallel behavior—to determine whether it gave rise to a "plausible suggestion of conspiracy." *Id.* at 565–66. Acknowledging that parallel conduct was consistent with an unlawful agreement, the Court nevertheless concluded that it did not plausibly suggest an illicit accord because it was not only compatible with, but indeed was more likely explained by, lawful, unchoreographed free-market behavior. *Id.* at 567. Because the well-pleaded fact of parallel conduct, accepted as true, did not plausibly suggest an unlawful agreement, the Court held the plaintiffs' complaint must be dismissed. *Id.* at 570.

B

Under *Twombly*'s construction of Rule 8, we conclude that respondent's complaint has not "nudged [his] claims" of invidious discrimination "across the line from conceivable to plausible." ...

We begin our analysis by identifying the allegations in the complaint that are not entitled to the assumption of truth. Respondent pleads that petitioners "knew of, condoned, and willfully and maliciously agreed to subject [him]" to harsh conditions of confinement "as a matter of policy, solely on account of [his] religion, race, and/or national origin and for no legitimate penological interest." ... The complaint alleges that Ashcroft was the "principal architect" of this invidious policy ... and that Mueller was "instrumental" in adopting and executing it.... These bare assertions, much like the pleading of conspiracy in *Twombly,* amount to nothing more than a "formulaic recitation of the elements" of a constitutional discrimination claim, ... namely, that petitioners adopted a policy "'because of,' not merely 'in spite of,' its adverse effects upon an identifiable group." ... As such, the allegations are conclusory and not entitled to be assumed true.... To be clear, we do not reject these bald allegations on the ground that they are unrealistic or nonsensical. We do not so characterize them any more than the Court in *Twombly* rejected the plaintiffs' express allegation of a "'contract, combination or conspiracy to prevent competitive entry,'" ... because it thought that claim too chimerical to be maintained. It is the conclusory nature of respondent's allegations, rather than their extravagantly fanciful nature, that disentitles them to the presumption of truth.

We next consider the factual allegations in respondent's complaint to determine if they plausibly suggest an entitlement to relief. The complaint alleges that "the [FBI], under the direction of Defendant MUELLER, arrested and detained thousands of Arab Muslim men ... as part of its investigation of the events of September 11." ... It further claims that "[t]he policy of holding post-September-11th detainees in highly restrictive conditions of confinement until they were 'cleared' by the FBI was approved by Defendants ASHCROFT and MUELLER in discussions in the weeks after September 11, 2001." ... Taken as true, these allegations are consistent with petitioners' purposefully designating detainees "of high interest" because of their race, religion, or national origin. But given more likely explanations, they do not plausibly establish this purpose.

The September 11 attacks were perpetrated by 19 Arab Muslim hijackers who counted themselves members in good standing of al Qaeda, an Islamic fundamentalist group. Al Qaeda was headed by another Arab Muslim—Osama bin Laden—and composed in large part of his Arab Muslim disciples. It should come as no surprise that a legitimate policy directing law enforcement to arrest and detain individuals because of their suspected link to the attacks would produce a disparate, incidental impact on Arab Muslims, even though the purpose of the policy was to target neither Arabs nor Muslims. On the facts respondent alleges the arrests Mueller oversaw were likely lawful and justified by his nondiscriminatory intent to detain aliens who were illegally present in the United States and who had potential connections to those who committed terrorist acts. As between that "obvious alternative explanation" for the arrests … and the purposeful, invidious discrimination respondent asks us to infer, discrimination is not a plausible conclusion.

But even if the complaint's well-pleaded facts give rise to a plausible inference that respondent's arrest was the result of unconstitutional discrimination, that inference alone would not entitle respondent to relief. It is important to recall that respondent's complaint challenges neither the constitutionality of his arrest nor his initial detention in the MDC. Respondent's constitutional claims against petitioners rest solely on their ostensible "policy of holding post-September-11th detainees" in the ADMAX SHU once they were categorized as "of high interest." … To prevail on that theory, the complaint must contain facts plausibly showing that petitioners purposefully adopted a policy of classifying post-September-11 detainees as "of high interest" because of their race, religion, or national origin.

This the complaint fails to do. Though respondent alleges that various other defendants, who are not before us, may have labeled him a person of "of high interest" for impermissible reasons, his only factual allegation against petitioners accuses them of adopting a policy approving "restrictive conditions of confinement" for post-September-11 detainees until they were "'cleared' by the FBI." … Accepting the truth of that allegation, the complaint does not show, or even intimate, that petitioners purposefully housed detainees in the ADMAX SHU due to their race, religion, or national origin. All it plausibly suggests is that the Nation's top law enforcement officers, in the aftermath of a devastating terrorist attack, sought to keep suspected terrorists in the most secure conditions available until the suspects could be cleared of terrorist activity. Respondent does not argue, nor can he, that such a motive would violate petitioners' constitutional obligations. He would need to allege more by way of factual content to "nudg[e]" his claim of purposeful discrimination "across the line from conceivable to plausible." …

To be sure, respondent can attempt to draw certain contrasts between the pleadings the Court considered in *Twombly* and the pleadings at issue here. In *Twombly,* the complaint alleged general wrongdoing that extended over a period of years, … whereas here the complaint alleges discrete wrongs—for instance, beatings—by lower level Government actors. The allegations here, if true, and if condoned by petitioners, could be the basis for some inference of wrongful intent on petitioners' part. Despite these distinctions, respondent's pleadings do not suffice to state a claim. Unlike in *Twombly,* where the doctrine of *respondeat superior* could bind the corporate defendant, here, as we have noted, petitioners cannot be held liable unless they themselves acted on account of a constitutionally protected characteristic. Yet respondent's complaint does not contain any factual allegation sufficient to plausibly suggest petitioners' discriminatory state of mind. His pleadings thus do not meet the standard necessary to comply with Rule 8.

    . . . .

C

Respondent offers three arguments that bear on our disposition of his case, but none is persuasive.

1

Respondent [argues] that our decision in *Twombly* should be limited to pleadings made in the context of an antitrust dispute.… This argument is not supported by *Twombly* and is incompatible with the Federal Rules of Civil Procedure. Though *Twombly* determined the sufficiency of a complaint sounding in antitrust, the decision was based on our interpretation and application of Rule 8.... That Rule in turn governs the pleading standard "in all civil actions and proceedings in the United States district courts." Fed. R. Civ. P. 1. Our decision in *Twombly* expounded the pleading standard for "all civil actions," ... and it applies to antitrust and discrimination suits alike....

2

Respondent next implies that our construction of Rule 8 should be tempered where, as here, the Court of Appeals has "instructed the district court to cabin discovery in such a way as to preserve" petitioners' defense of qualified immunity "as much as possible in anticipation of a summary judgment motion." ... We have held, however, that the question presented by a motion to dismiss a complaint for insufficient pleadings does not turn on the controls placed upon the discovery process. *Twombly*, 550 U.S. at 559 ("It is no answer to say that a claim just shy of a plausible entitlement to relief can, if groundless, be weeded out early in the discovery process through careful case management given the common lament that the success of judicial supervision in checking discovery abuse has been on the modest side." ...).

Our rejection of the careful-case-management approach is especially important in suits where Government-official defendants are entitled to assert the defense of qualified immunity. The basic thrust of the qualified-immunity doctrine is to free officials from the concerns of litigation, including "avoidance of disruptive discovery." ... There are serious and legitimate reasons for this. If a Government official is to devote time to his or her duties, and to the formulation of sound and responsible policies, it is counterproductive to require the substantial diversion that is attendant to participating in litigation and making informed decisions as to how it should proceed. Litigation, though necessary to ensure that officials comply with the law, exacts heavy costs in terms of efficiency and expenditure of valuable time and resources that might otherwise be directed to the proper execution of the work of the Government....

It is no answer to these concerns to say that discovery for petitioners can be deferred while pretrial proceedings continue for other defendants. It is quite likely that, when discovery as to the other parties proceeds, it would prove necessary for petitioners and their counsel to participate in the process to ensure the case does not develop in a misleading or slanted way that causes prejudice to their position. Even if petitioners are not yet themselves subject to discovery orders, then, they would not be free from the burdens of discovery.

We [thus] decline respondent's invitation to relax the pleading requirements on the ground that the Court of Appeals promises petitioners minimally intrusive discovery. That promise provides especially cold comfort in this pleading context, where we are impelled to give real content to the concept of qualified immunity for high-level officials who must be neither deterred nor detracted from the vigorous performance of their duties. Because respondent's complaint is deficient under Rule 8, he is not entitled to discovery, cabined or otherwise.

3

Respondent finally maintains that the Federal Rules expressly allow him to allege petitioners' discriminatory intent "generally," which he equates with a conclusory allegation.... It follows, respondent says, that his complaint is sufficiently well pleaded because it claims that petitioners discriminated against him "on account of [his] religion, race, and/or national origin and for no legitimate penological interest." ... Were we required to accept this allegation as true, respondent's complaint would survive petitioners' motion to dismiss. But the Federal Rules do not require courts to credit a complaint's conclusory statements without reference to its factual context.

It is true that Rule 9(b) requires particularity when pleading "fraud or mistake," while allowing "[m]alice, intent, knowledge, and other conditions of a person's mind [to] be alleged generally." But "generally" is a relative term. In the context of Rule 9, it is to be compared to the particularity requirement applicable to fraud or mistake. Rule 9 merely excuses a party from pleading discriminatory intent under an elevated pleading standard. It does not give him license to evade the less rigid—though still operative—strictures of Rule 8.... And Rule 8 does not empower respondent to plead the bare elements of his cause of action, affix the label "general allegation," and expect his complaint to survive a motion to dismiss.

V

We hold that respondent's complaint fails to plead sufficient facts to state a claim for purposeful and unlawful discrimination against petitioners. The Court of Appeals should decide in the first instance whether to remand to the District Court so that respondent can seek leave to amend his deficient complaint.

The judgment of the Court of Appeals is reversed, and the case is remanded for further proceedings consistent with this opinion.

It is so ordered.

Justice Souter, with whom Justice Stevens, Justice Ginsburg and Justice Breyer join, dissenting.

....

Under *Twombly,* the relevant question is whether, assuming the factual allegations are true, the plaintiff has stated a ground for relief that is plausible. That is, in *Twombly's* words, a plaintiff must "allege facts" that, taken as true, are "suggestive of illegal conduct." ... In *Twombly,* we were faced with allegations of a conspiracy to violate § 1 of the Sherman Act through parallel conduct. The difficulty was that the conduct alleged was "consistent with conspiracy, but just as much in line with a wide swath of rational and competitive business strategy unilaterally prompted by common perceptions of the market." ... We held that in that sort of circumstance, "[a]n allegation of parallel conduct is ... much like a naked assertion of conspiracy in a § 1 complaint: it gets the complaint close to stating a claim, but without some further factual enhancement it stops short of the line between possibility and plausibility of 'entitlement to relief.'" ... Here, by contrast, the allegations in the complaint are neither confined to naked legal conclusions nor consistent with legal conduct. The complaint alleges that FBI officials discriminated against Iqbal solely on account of his race, religion, and national origin, and it alleges the knowledge and deliberate indifference that, by Ashcroft and Mueller's own admission, are sufficient to make them liable for the illegal action. Iqbal's complaint therefore contains "enough facts to state a claim to relief that is plausible on its face." ...

I do not understand the majority to disagree with this understanding of "plausibility" under *Twombly.* Rather, the majority discards the allegations discussed above with regard to Ashcroft and Mueller as conclusory, and is left considering only two statements in the complaint: that "the [FBI], under the direction of Defendant MUELLER, arrested and detained thousands of Arab Muslim men ... as part of its investigation of the events of September 11" ... and that "[t]he policy of holding post-September-11th detainees in highly restrictive conditions of confinement until they were 'cleared' by the FBI was approved by Defendants ASHCROFT and MUELLER in discussions in the weeks after September 11, 2001." ... I think the majority is right in saying that these allegations suggest only that Ashcroft and Mueller "sought to keep suspected terrorists in the most secure conditions available until the suspects could be cleared of terrorist activity," ... and that this produced "a disparate, incidental impact on Arab Muslims." ... And I agree that the two allegations selected by the majority, standing alone, do not state a plausible entitlement to relief for unconstitutional discrimination.

But these allegations do not stand alone as the only significant, nonconclusory statements in the complaint, for the complaint contains many allegations linking Ashcroft and Mueller to the discriminatory practices of their subordinates....

The majority says that these are "bare assertions" that, "much like the pleading of conspiracy in *Twombly,* amount to nothing more than a 'formulaic recitation of the elements' of a constitutional discrimination claim" and therefore are "not entitled to be assumed true." ... The fallacy of the majority's position, however, lies in looking at the relevant assertions in isolation. The complaint contains specific allegations that, in the aftermath of the September 11 attacks, the Chief of the FBI's International Terrorism Operations Section and the Assistant Special Agent in Charge for the FBI's New York Field Office implemented a policy that discriminated against Arab Muslim men, including Iqbal, solely on account of their race, religion, or national origin.... Viewed in light of these subsidiary allegations, the allegations singled out by the majority as "conclusory" are no such thing. Iqbal's claim is not that Ashcroft and Mueller "knew of, condoned, and willfully and maliciously agreed to subject" him to a discriminatory practice that is left undefined; his allegation is that "they knew of, condoned, and willfully and maliciously agreed to subject" him to a particular, discrete, discriminatory policy detailed in the complaint. Iqbal does not say merely that Ashcroft was the architect of some amorphous discrimination, or that Mueller was instrumental in an ill-defined constitutional violation; he alleges that they helped to create the discriminatory policy he has described. Taking the complaint as a whole, it gives Ashcroft and Mueller "'fair notice of what the ... claim is and the grounds upon which it rests.'" ...

That aside, the majority's holding that the statements it selects are conclusory cannot be squared with its treatment of certain other allegations in the complaint as nonconclusory. For example, the majority takes as true the statement that "[t]he policy of holding post-September-11th detainees in highly restrictive conditions of confinement until they were 'cleared' by the FBI was approved by Defendants ASHCROFT and MUELLER in discussions in the weeks after September 11, 2001." ... This statement makes two points: (1) after September 11, the FBI held certain detainees in highly restrictive conditions, and (2) Ashcroft and Mueller discussed and approved these conditions. If, as the majority says, these allegations are not conclusory, then I cannot see why the majority deems it merely conclusory when Iqbal alleges that (1) after September 11, the FBI designated Arab Muslim detainees as being of "'high interest'" "because of the race, religion, and national origin of the detainees, and not because of any evidence of the detainees' involvement in supporting terrorist activity," ... and (2) Ashcroft and Mueller "knew of, condoned, and willfully and maliciously agreed" to that discrimination.... By my lights, there is no principled basis for the majority's disregard of the allegations linking Ashcroft and Mueller to their subordinates' discrimination.

....

[JUSTICE BREYER's separate dissenting opinion is omitted.]

Notes and Questions

1. Recall the questions posed in Note 5 following *Twombly*. How does the Court in *Iqbal* resolve the question of whether the *Twombly* standard applies only in antitrust and other complex cases? Does the *Iqbal* Court affirm the statement in *Twombly*, reviewed in Note 2 following *Twombly*, that Rule 8 does not require "detailed factual allegations"? How does the Court clarify the application of the *Twombly* standard as a "two-pronged" process?

2. Do you think it is telling that in setting forth the requirements for properly pleading a claim for relief in *Iqbal*, the Justices themselves could not agree on whether Iqbal's complaint satisfied the Court's standard and divided 5–4 on the issue? Do you think that the lower federal courts will have difficulty applying the *Twombly/Iqbal* standard? Do you think it can be hard to properly distinguish between "factual allegations" vs. "legal conclusions" and "plausible" claims vs. "possible" claims?

3. Consider, for example, Form 11 ("Complaint for Negligence") in the Appendix of Forms of the Federal Rules of Civil Procedure. In footnote 10 of the *Twombly* opinion, the Court makes positive reference to this form as providing proper notice of the claim under Rule 8, in contrast to the plaintiffs' deficient complaint in *Twombly*. Rule 84 provides that "[t]he forms in this Appendix suffice under these rules and illustrate the simplicity and brevity that the rules contemplate." Do you think that Form 11 meets the two-pronged pleading standard of *Twombly* and *Iqbal*?

4. Consider further the plaintiff's discrimination complaint in *Swierkiewicz*. At the conclusion of its opinion in *Twombly*, the Court expressly rejected the plaintiffs' argument that the Court's analysis "runs counter" to its holding in *Swierkiewicz*. In his dissent in *Twombly*, Justice Stevens stated that the Court's pleading standard was "irreconcilable with Rule 8 and with … governing precedents," including *Swierkiewicz*. Do you think that the plaintiff's complaint in *Swierkiewicz* meets the two-pronged pleading standard of *Twombly* and *Iqbal*? *Cf. Fowler v. UPMC Shadyside*, 578 F.3d 203, 211 (3d Cir. 2009) ("We have to conclude … that because *Conley* has been specifically repudiated by both *Twombly* and *Iqbal*, so too has *Swierkiewicz*, at least insofar as it concerns pleading requirements and relies on *Conley*").

5. The Court's decisions in *Twombly* and *Iqbal* generated an enormous amount of controversy and debate. *See, e.g.,* Edward A. Hartnett, *Taming* Twombly, *Even After* Iqbal, 158 U. Pa. L. Rev. 473 (2010) (reviewing numerous articles published on the topic and presenting a less critical view); Luke Meier, *Why* Twombly *Is Good Law (But Poorly Drafted) and* Iqbal *Will Be Overturned*, 87 Ind. L.J. 709 (2012). In fact, two congressional bills were quickly introduced in the House and the Senate to overturn these decisions and restore pleading standards to the pre-*Twombly/Iqbal* practice. Neither bill was enacted.

6.(a) As it turned out, careful study was the better course, rather than overreaction, and in the ensuing years since *Twombly* and *Iqbal*, pleading practice in the lower federal courts has not changed significantly. Both the Federal Rules Advisory Committee and the Standing Committee of the Judicial Conference have consistently cautioned against premature action and continue to carefully study the issue of possible changes to the pleading rules based on evolving practice. As noted by the Standing Committee in its September 2012 report, "[i]t appears that there is no urgent need for a rules response. Much remains to be learned about what pleading standards will be when practices are better settled." Report of the Judicial Conference Committee on Rules of Practice and Procedure, Sept. 2012, at 26.

(b) A detailed study of pleading practices is also being conducted by the Federal Judicial Center and a follow-up study is underway. As reported by the Standing Committee, the first phase of this study found that motions to dismiss for failure to state a claim were being made more frequently after *Twombly* and *Iqbal*, but that there "was no statistically significant increase in the rate of granting motions to dismiss." REPORT OF THE JUDICIAL CONFERENCE COMMITTEE ON RULES OF PRACTICE AND PROCEDURE, Mar. 2012, at 6. A second phase of the study is examining what happens when a motion to dismiss is granted with leave to amend. The initial conclusion of the second phase has been that there "was no statistically significant increase in plaintiffs excluded by motions to dismiss for failure to state a claim or in cases terminated by such motions, but the work in this stage is still in progress...." *Id.*

(c) The Chief Counsel to the Advisory and Standing Committees also conducted an exhaustive study of the lower court cases following *Twombly* and *Iqbal* and came to a similar conclusion. As stated in the Chief Counsel's November 2011 Report to the Committees,

> [t]he cases recognize that *Twombly* and *Iqbal* require that pleadings contain more than legal conclusions and enough detail to allow the court to infer more than the mere possibility of misconduct. But the case law to date does not appear to indicate that *Iqbal* has dramatically changed the application of the standards used to determine pleading sufficiency. Instead, the appellate courts are taking a context-specific approach to applying *Twombly* and *Iqbal* and are instructing the district courts to be careful in determining whether to dismiss a complaint ... The approach taken by many courts may suggest that *Twombly* and *Iqbal* are providing a new framework in which to analyze familiar pleading concepts, rather than an entirely new pleading standard. Even after *Twombly* and *Iqbal*, many appellate court decisions instruct the district courts to use caution in dismissing complaints and have reversed dismissals where the district courts failed to presume the facts to be true or required the plaintiff to plead with too much particularity....

> Many of the circuit court cases emphasize that the *Iqbal* analysis is context-specific. Under this context-specific approach, courts appear to apply the analysis more leniently in cases where pleading with more detail may be difficult. For example, courts have continued to emphasize that *pro se* pleadings are evaluated more leniently than others, and courts continue to find pleading on "information and belief" to be appropriate when permitted under the rules and cases. Courts also continue frequently to grant leave to amend if the complaint's allegations are initially deemed insufficient.

CHEIF COUNSEL'S REPORT TO THE ADVISORY AND STANDING COMMITTEES, Nov. 2011, at 4–5.

7. As you know, the Federal Rules of Civil Procedure apply only to proceedings in the federal district courts. *See* FED. R. CIV. P. 1. However, as noted in Chapter 1, many states have patterned their state rules of civil procedure on the federal rules with many states adopting the language of the federal rules either verbatim or without significant change.

The reaction of the states to *Twombly* and *Iqbal* has been mixed. Some state courts have embraced the Supreme Court's holdings. *See, e.g., Iannacchio v. Ford Motor Co.*, 888 N.E. 2d 879, 890 (Mass. 2008) (choosing to "follow the Court's lead" in retiring the language of *Conley* and adopting the Court's "plausibility" standard as the standard for Massachusetts). Other state courts have rejected the Court's approach. *See, e.g., McCurry v. Chevy Chase Bank*, 233 P.3d 861, 863 (Wash. 2010) (specifically rejecting the plausibility approach because it "adds a determination of the likelihood of success on the merits, so that a trial judge can dismiss a claim, even where the law does provide a remedy for the conduct alleged by the plaintiff, if that judge does not believe it is plausible the claim will ultimately succeed"); *Colby v. Umbrella*, 955 A.2d 1082, 1087, n.1 (Vt. 2008) ("[W]e have relied on the *Conley* standard for over twenty years, and are in no way bound by federal jurisprudence in interpreting our state pleading rules.... We recently reaffirmed our minimal notice pleading standard ... and are unpersuaded by the dissent's argument that we should now abandon it for a heightened standard."); *Cullen v. Auto-Owners Ins. Co.*, 189 P.3d 344, 345–48 (Ariz. 2008) (traditional Arizona notice pleading standards continue as before *Twombly*).

8. In applying its pleading standard to the plaintiffs' complaint in *Twombly*, the Court stated that the standard "simply calls for enough fact to raise a reasonable expectation that discovery will reveal evidence of illegal agreement." Under Federal Rule 11, which is examined in Section G in the Casebook, a party presenting a pleading may certify that "to the best of the person's knowledge, information, and belief, formed after an inquiry reasonable under the circumstances: ... (3) the factual contentions have evidentiary support or, if specifically so identified, will likely have evidentiary support after a reasonable opportunity for further investigation or discovery." Given the Court's statement above, do you think this provision may have been helpful to the plaintiffs in *Twombly* or *Iqbal*?

Problem

Problem 6-1. Recall from *Problem 1-1* in Chapter 1(F)(2)(*a*) the controversy between *P*, *D-1*, and *D-2* in which *D-1* trespassed on *P's* land, had an altercation with *P*, and then had an accident with *D-2*. *P's* lawyer wants to sue *D-2* to recover damages for substantially aggravating *P's* prior injuries. Assume that *P* alleges the following in *P's* complaint: "On [date and specific location], *D-2* drove *D-2's* motor vehicle into another vehicle. As a result, *P* suffered injuries, was prevented from transacting *P's* business, suffered great pain of body and mind, and incurred expenses for medical attention and hospitalization in the sum of $55,000. Wherefore *P* demands judgment against *D-2* in the sum of $200,000 and costs." In an action in federal court, would this allegation meet Rules 8(a)'s requirement that the complaint contain a short and plain statement of the claim showing that the pleader is entitled to relief? Has the plaintiff alleged "enough facts to state a claim to relief that is plausible on its face" as required by *Twombly* and *Iqbal*?

2. Pleading Special Matters

Rule 9 of the Federal Rules of Civil Procedure expressly addresses the pleading of various "special" matters, including, *inter alia*, fraud and mistake, special damages, conditions of the mind, and conditions precedent. This subsection examines these special pleading provisions.

(a) Fraud and Mistake   9 (b)

Even in procedural systems governed by the Federal Rules, some special pleading requirements persist that require more particularity in pleading. For example, Federal Rule 9(b) requires the circumstances constituting fraud or mistake to be stated "with particularity." This requirement is a continuation of similar common-law and code-pleading requirements. One of the main purposes of Rule 9(b) is to apprise the defendant of fraudulent claims and of the acts that form the basis for the claim. This restriction, in turn, prevents the pleader from filing suit first and then searching for a claim through discovery. Note, however, that the requirement of Rule 9(b) expressly applies to all averments of fraud or mistake, whether set forth as part of a claim or a defense or whether asserted in the complaint or in any other pleading, including the defendant's answer.

Notes and Questions

1. What does a pleader have to do in order to plead fraud "with particularity"? According to the court in *Williams v. WMX Techs.*, 112 F.3d 175 (5th Cir. 1997), to plead fraud with particularity, the plaintiff must specify the statements that were fraudulent and why they were fraudulent, identify who made the statements, identify when the statements were made, and identify where the statements were made. The difficulty, of course, is that all this must be done before the plaintiff has access to discovery.

2. Averments of mistake must similarly be stated "with particularity" under Rule 9(b). Why do think mistake is also included with fraud for special pleading treatment? As you will learn in your course in Contracts, mistake can form the basis for reforming or avoiding an otherwise enforceable contractual obligation. It is understandable that greater pleading specificity would be required under such circumstances, because contracts, as well as other similar legal documents (deeds, trusts, etc.), are usually executed only after careful drafting and review and mistakes in drafting would not be the norm.

Problem

Problem 6-2. Assume that *P Bank* has loaned $500,000 to *D*. Assume that *D* fails to repay *P* as promised. *D's* only significant, unencumbered asset is a tract of land in Minnesota. Anticipating that *P* will sue for repayment, *D* conveys the land to *F*, a friend, as a "gift." In an action in federal court to recover the money loaned and to set aside the conveyance, *P* includes the following allegation in the complaint: "On November 1, 20xx, Defendant *D* conveyed all of *D's* real property to Defendant *F* for the purpose of defrauding the plaintiff and hindering or delaying the collection of the debt." No other allegations concerning the transfer are made. Has *P* alleged the circumstances of the "fraudulent conveyance" with sufficient particularity in light of Rule 9(b)? Does Federal Form 21 help you answer this question?

(b) Special Damages

Federal Rule 9(g) provides that "[i]f an item of special damage is claimed, it must be specifically stated." This requirement incorporates a distinction in the law of remedies between general and special damages.

General Damages. General damages are usually defined as "all actual damages which naturally and necessarily flow from the wrongful act." For example, in a personal injury case, "pain and suffering" would be a naturally expected consequence from an injury. In other contexts, general damages are often based on market measures. Thus, if *P's* car is damaged as a result of *D's* negligence, the general damage formula would provide *P* with the difference between the value of the car (a) immediately before the accident and (b) immediately after the accident. Similarly, assume *D* agrees to sell a house to *P* for $275,000. *D* then refuses to convey the house. The general damage measure would provide *P* damages based on the difference between the contract price and the market price. Thus, if the house was worth $300,000, *P* would recover $25,000. *See* 1 DOBBS § 3.2, at 216.

General damage measures often allow recovery of "paper" losses, even when no real loss is actually realized. For instance, in the example of the contract to sell the house, assume that after the breach P finds another house that P likes even better and is able to buy it for $250,000, even though its market value is $300,000. Obviously, P has realized no actual loss at all under these circumstances, but P can recover $25,000 in general damages from D with respect to the first house. *See id.* § 3.3(3), at 224.

Special or "Consequential" Damages. Sometimes general damage measures do not cover all the elements of the plaintiff's loss. In such circumstances, special or "consequential" damages may be awarded in addition to or instead of general damages. Special or consequential damages are usually subject to strict limitations that often inhibit their recovery. For example, courts require that such damages be actually realized (which is not always the case with general damages) and proven with reasonable certainty. Courts also impose "proximate cause" limits on special damages in tort cases and require that special damages be within the "contemplation of the parties" in contract cases.

In addition, pleading rules, such as Federal Rule 9(g) have long required a specific statement of special damages. The dividing line between general and special damages is not always clear. For example, in personal injury actions, pain and suffering are considered general damages, but damages such as lost wages or the value of any lost time or earning capacity must be specially pleaded. *See id.* § 3.2, at 216, § 3.3(1), at 220, § 8.1(1), at 647. In a breach of contract action, lost profits are treated as special damages, but ordinary loss of the benefit of the bargain is considered general damages. *See id.* § 3.2, at 217. The concept of special damages also arises in slander and certain other tort actions that require specific proof of harm to a person's reputation to have an actionable claim.

Notes and Questions

1. Considering that the goal of "notice pleading" under the Federal Rules is to give the defendant "fair notice" of the plaintiff's claim, why do you think Federal Rule 9(g) requires that special damages be "specifically stated"?

2. Is the level of specificity that is required in pleading special damages the same as the level of particularity required for pleading fraud under Federal Rule 9(b)? Under a plain reading of the two provisions, Rule 9(b) clearly requires greater detail, doesn't it? Federal Forms 11, 14, & 19 illustrate various allegations of special damages.

Problems

Problem 6-3. On the facts of *Problem 1-1*, assume that P sued D-2 in federal court for damages for P's injuries that result from the accident between D-1 and D-2. P alleged that D-2's sports car had been driven in a negligent manner. P incurred $35,000 for medical treatment at the emergency room of a hospital and P's subsequent stay in the hospital. P also lost $8,000 in wages because of P was unable to work for two months after the accident. P also maintains that the injuries caused substantial pain and suffering. What must P allege to comply with the requirements of Rule 9(g)? Do Federal Forms 11 and 12 and Rule 84 help you answer this question?

Problem 6-4. On the facts of *Problem 6-3*, assume that P did not request punitive damages in P's complaint. At trial, P seeks to offer evidence that is relevant only to the recovery of punitive damages from D-2. If D-2 objects to this evidence, should it be admitted?

(c) Other Special Pleading Requirements

In addition to requiring that fraud and mistake be alleged with particularity and that special damages be specifically stated, Rule 9 contains several other special pleading requirements, which are examined in the following notes and questions.

Notes and Questions

1. After requiring that a party state "with particularity the circumstances constituting fraud or mistake," Rule 9(b) then states that "[m]alice, intent, knowledge, and other conditions of a person's mind may be alleged generally." But wouldn't this general pleading standard flow naturally from Rule 8(a)(2), even without this special reference? Why did the drafters' of Rule 9(b) then include this additional reference? The provision was placed in the rule so that the requirement of pleading fraud and mistake with particularity would not be interpreted more broadly to also include these additional matters — for example, to require a pleader to allege specifically the circumstances from which *knowledge* of falsity of a fraudulent misrepresentation could be inferred. *See* 5A WRIGHT & MILLER § 1301, at 292.

2. (a) Prior to the 2007 restyling of Rule 9(a), that rule stated that it is unnecessary to allege the capacity or authority of a party to sue or be sued or the legal existence of an entity, but if a party desired to raise such an issue, the party had to do so "by specific negative averment, which shall include such supporting particulars as are peculiarly within the pleader's knowledge." Considering that such matters are rarely at issue, it makes sense, doesn't it, that the special pleading requirement of Rule 9(a) is only imposed upon a party that specifically raises the issue?

(b) Restyled Rule 9(a)(2) states that capacity issues are now to be raised "by a specific denial, which must state any supporting facts that are peculiarly within the party's knowledge" (as opposed to a specific negative averment). As indicated in Chapter 1, a denial is a defendant's response that controverts the facts that the plaintiff has alleged in the complaint. A denial can be general or specific. *See* FED. R. CIV. P. 8(b)(3) ("A party that intends in good faith to deny all the allegations of a pleading ... may do so by a general denial. A party that does not intend to deny all the allegations must either specifically deny designated allegations or generally deny all except those specifically admitted."). A general denial puts in issue all material facts alleged in the complaint. In contrast, a specific denial is a separate response directed at specific allegations in the complaint. Assuming that the plaintiff follows Rule 9(a) and does not allege capacity to sue in the complaint, the complaint is likely not to contain "designated allegations" to which a specific denial can be directed. In restyling Rule 9(a), the Advisory Committee obviously thought that a "specific negative averment" is the same as a "specific denial." As noted above, however, these terms have distinct meanings. Given the directive in the restyled rule to raise the issue of capacity by a specific denial, what is a defendant who wants to raise capacity supposed to do when the plaintiff has not alleged capacity in the complaint? *See* Note 2 in Section C(5), below.

3. Rule 9(c) similarly imposes a special pleading requirement only when the performance or occurrence of a condition precedent is denied. Rule 9(c) states that "[i]n pleading conditions precedent, it suffices to allege generally that all conditions precedent have occurred or been performed," but "when denying that a condition precedent has occurred or been performed, a party must do so with particularity." Why aren't conditions precedent treated in the same manner as capacity to sue and be sued under Rule 9(a)? Is there

any significant reason for making the plaintiff plead the performance of conditions precedent at all? *See* 5A WRIGHT & MILLER § 1302, at 324 ("[i]t seems doubtful that even the usual perfunctory allegation of performance … serves any significantly useful function").

4. Rule 9(f) states that "[a]n allegation of time or place is material when testing the sufficiency of a pleading." What type of challenge to the plaintiff's claim would be most likely facilitated by making allegations of time material? Rule 9(f) does not by its terms require pleading of time or place, but such averments are considered material for purposes of testing the sufficiency of a pleading. When do you think the failure to make a specific allegation of time and place could render a pleading "insufficient" under the "notice pleading" standard of the Federal Rules? Suppose two parties have engaged in ongoing business transactions over an extended period of time and one party now sues the other. Without specific averment as to the time and place of the alleged breach, can the other party have "fair notice" of which transaction(s) the complaint covers?

5. Other special pleading requirements are found in Federal Rules 9(d) ("Official Document or Act"), Rule 9(e) ("Judgment"), and Rule 9(h) ("Admiralty or Maritime Claim").

3. Alternative, Hypothetical, and Inconsistent Pleading

The provisions of Federal Rule 8(d)(2) and (3) modify the common-law and traditional code-pleading practice of prohibiting alternative, hypothetical, or inconsistent pleading. Rule 8(d)(2) specifically permits a party to set out two or more statements of a claim or defense alternatively or hypothetically. Rule 8(d)(3) further provides that a party may state as many separate claims or defenses as it has, "regardless of consistency." This approach contrasts with the requirements of common-law pleading as well as pleading in some code-pleading states that followed a doctrine known as the "theory of the pleadings." This doctrine allowed the defendant to challenge a complaint as legally insufficient if the plaintiff did not follow a consistent legal theory in the complaint. However, most code-pleading states repudiated this doctrine as inconsistent with the code plan that only facts should be pleaded, leaving the court to draw the legal conclusions about the facts.

Notes and Questions

1. Assume that the plaintiff is unable to determine for sure whether one or more parties were responsible for an accident. Furthermore, assume that the evidence might justify an action based on several different legal theories. How should the plaintiff plead? *See* Federal Form 12 (illustrating alternative pleading in federal court). Hypothetical pleadings are also allowed, which are really another form of an alternative pleading. How would the wording of a hypothetical pleading differ from the wording of an alternative pleading? Note that Rule 8(d)(2) provides that "[i]f a party makes alternative statements, the pleading is sufficient if any one of them is sufficient."

2. All pleadings, including alternative, hypothetical, and inconsistent pleadings, are subject to the good-faith pleading requirements of Federal Rule 11. After reviewing the situation in Form 12, do you understand how a party could plead inconsistently and still comply with the requirements of Rule 11? This subject is taken up more extensively in conjunction with the requirements of good-faith pleading in section G, below.

4. Allocating the Burden of Pleading

This subsection focuses on how the burden of pleading is allocated. To understand the general process of allocating this burden, consider the following "dog-bite" example given by Professor Cleary. *See* Edward W. Cleary, *Presuming and Pleading: An Essay on Juristic Immaturity*, 12 STAN. L. REV. 5 (1959). The starting point is the substantive law. At common law, every dog was entitled to "one bite" before the dog's owner became liable. Presumably, after one bite the owner would know of the dog's dangerous inclination to bite. Professor Cleary thus indicates the following to be the essential elements of dog bite liability: + *ownership* + *notice of dangerous character* + *biting*. Assume, however, that the legislature decides that owners of dogs should be absolutely liable for bites and eliminates notice of the propensity to bite from the liability formula. At the same time, dog owners convince the legislature to relieve them of liability if the dog is being tormented or the person bitten is unlawfully on the owner's premises. Thus, reflecting the substantive elements that the legislature deems to be material, the formula under the statute becomes as follows: + *ownership* + *biting* − *not being tormented* − *no unlawful presence on the premises*. *See id.* at 5–6.

Assume that the plaintiff is required to plead and prove every substantive element in Professor Cleary's dog-bite example. The plaintiff would have to plead and prove that the defendant owned the dog, that the dog bit the plaintiff, that the plaintiff was not tormenting the dog, and that the plaintiff was not unlawfully on the defendant's premises. *See id.* at 7–8. In this simple example, requiring the plaintiff to assume the burden of pleading and proving all the elements of liability would not be excessive. In a more complex case, however, the plaintiff's burden might become unreasonable if the plaintiff had to demonstrate every possible substantive element that might be relevant to the plaintiff's ultimate recovery on the claim. The resulting suit also might encompass a lot of "unnecessary territory" if the plaintiff had to plead and prove elements of liability that are rarely involved in the class of cases in question. For example, if the issue of lawful presence is rarely involved in dog-bite cases, requiring the plaintiff to plead and prove in every dog-bite case that the plaintiff was not unlawfully on the defendant's premises would be inefficient. Therefore, to avoid the hardship and inefficiency that would be involved in placing the burden of pleading and proof entirely on the plaintiff, some of the elements relevant to liability are usually allocated to the defendant as "defenses."

What remains becomes the elements of the plaintiff's "prima facie case." If proved, these elements allow the plaintiff to recover if no defenses are raised by the defendant. For example, ownership and biting might be allocated to the plaintiff's prima facie case, and the other elements might be allocated to the defendant as defenses. Under these circumstances, the plaintiff would have to plead and prove ownership and biting to win if the defendant raised no defenses. The defendant would be obliged to plead and prove that the plaintiff was tormenting the dog or was on the defendant's premises illegally (if those defenses were pertinent to the case). *See id.*

In Professor Cleary's example, nothing inherent in the nature of the elements of liability would prevent any one of them from being allocated to either the plaintiff or defendant. Thus, although it may seem curious, if the plaintiff were bitten by a dog on the defendant's premises, the element of the dog's ownership might be allocated to the defendant's side of the case. Such an allocation might be made, for example, if it is considered likely that most of the time when a dog bites someone who is present on the land of another, the dog belongs to the landowner. The burden of pleading and proving that the dog did not belong to the defendant would thus be placed on the defendant rather than the plaintiff. In this example, the policy reasons for allocating the burden to the defendant would be probability (and maybe also efficiency, if ownership of the dog is rarely disputed in dog-bite cases).

Of course, other reasons also exist for allocating the burden of pleading to one side or the other in a case. For example, a policy maker may decide to disfavor certain claims by allocating the burden of pleading and proof on more elements of the claim to the plaintiff—Professor Cleary gives the example of a policy maker discouraging actions of defamation by allocating the burden of pleading and proving the untruthfulness of a statement to the plaintiff, rather than allocating the burden of pleading and proving the truth of the statement to the defendant. *See id.* at 11–12.

Section C. Responding to the Complaint

1. Preanswer Motions

Motions to Dismiss Under the Federal Rules. As discussed in Chapter 1, procedural systems based on the Federal Rules permit the defendant to raise certain defenses by preanswer motion, at the option of the defendant, before otherwise responding to the plaintiff's complaint. Federal Rule 12(b) lists seven defenses that can be raised by a preanswer motion to dismiss: "(1) lack of subject-matter jurisdiction; (2) lack of personal jurisdiction; (3) improper venue; (4) insufficient process; (5) insufficient service of process; (6) failure to state a claim upon which relief can be granted; and (7) failure to join a party under Rule 19." Note that these matters may be raised at the option of the pleader, which means that they do not have to be raised by motion at all; instead, they can be asserted (along with other defenses) in the defendant's answer.

The motions to dismiss under Rule 12(b)(1)-(5) are reviewed in Chapters 2, 3, and 4 on personal jurisdiction, venue, and subject-matter jurisdiction, respectively, and the motion to dismiss under Rule 12(b)(7) is reviewed in Chapter 7 in the section on Rule 19. The remaining Rule 12(b) preanswer motion, a motion to dismiss under Rule 12(b)(6) for failure to state a claim upon which relief may be granted, is the only one of the Rule 12(b) motions that challenges the legal sufficiency of the plaintiff's complaint. As explained in the *Twombly* case, the standard for granting a motion to dismiss under Rule 12(b)(6) is tied to the pleading requirements of Rules 8 and 9. The question presented on a Rule 12(b)(6) motion is whether the facts alleged in the complaint are sufficient to show that the plaintiff is entitled to relief under the applicable substantive law.

In general, in deciding this motion, the court is required to assume the truth of all the well-pleaded facts in the plaintiff's complaint. However, the court is not obligated to accept statements in the complaint that are conclusions of law rather than factual allegations. This aspect of practice under Rule 12(b)(6) is similar to practice in the code states when the defendant demurs to the complaint on the ground that it does not state facts sufficient to constitute a cause of action. Normally, on a Rule 12(b)(6) motion to dismiss, the court may not take into account matters outside the complaint in determining the motion, unless the procedure for conversion of the motion into a summary judgment motion is followed. *See* Rule 12(d) ("Result of Presenting Matters Outside the Pleadings"). However, the court is allowed to take into account exhibits to the complaint and matters of public record.

Motions for a More Definite Statement. In addition, a party can move for a more definite statement pursuant to Federal Rule 12(e) when a pleading "is so vague or ambiguous that the party cannot reasonably prepare a response." This use of the motion to make more definite is identical to a device known as a "bill of particulars." Bills of particulars were common under code practice and required the opposing party to provide greater detail about the claim in order to limit the issues, prevent surprise, and allow the moving party to prepare for trial.

The motion for a more definite statement under Rule 12(e) is, today, much more limited. Before its amendment in 1948, Rule 12(e) permitted bills of particulars in addition to motions to make more definite. The 1948 amendment to Rule 12(e) eliminated bills of particulars from federal practice. The Advisory Committee stated that original Rule 12(e) was subject to more judicial rulings than any other provision. Today, a motion for a more definite statement under Rule 12(e) can only be granted if it is impossible for the moving party to frame a responsive pleading because of unintelligibility; the motion is not available simply to obtain greater detail about the opposing party's case.

Motions to Strike. Another motion under Federal Rule 12 is a motion to strike under Rule 12(f). Motions to strike can be used to force the deletion of "any redundant, immaterial, impertinent, or scandalous matter" from a pleading. Motions to strike are also available under Rule 12(f) against insufficient defenses.

Timing of Preanswer Motions. The mechanics of motion practice can be important under the Federal Rules. Rule 5 contains provisions governing service of papers after the original summons and complaint. Rule 6 contains important provisions governing computation of time limits. In addition, Rule 12(a)(4) provides that service of a motion under Rule 12 alters the time limits under Rule 12(a)(1)-(3) for serving responsive pleadings. Rule 6(b) permits the court to allow an extension of time periods. The basic options for possible preanswer motions under Federal Rule 12 are summarized in Figure 6-1 on the next page.

Notes and Questions

1. Given the options available to pleaders under Federal Rule 8, do you think that motions for a more definite statement under Rule 12(e) are often granted? Can you think of a case in which a motion for a more definite statement would be proper, but in which a motion to dismiss for failure to state a claim upon which relief can be granted under Rule 12(b)(6) would not be proper?

2. Federal Rule 12 allows a defense of failure to state a claim to be raised by preanswer motion or in the answer. What advantage is there, if any, in raising a failure to state a claim defense in a Rule 12(b)(6) motion rather than in the answer?

3. Read Federal Rules 5, 6, and 12(a) carefully and answer the following questions:

(a) Assume that the defendant wants to file a motion for a more definite statement. Must the motion be served on the plaintiff? If so, how may it be served if the plaintiff is represented by an attorney? How would this motion be filed with the court? When must it be filed?

(b) Assume that the defendant moves under Rule 12(b)(6) to dismiss the action on the ground that the plaintiff's complaint does not state a claim for relief. How much time does the defendant have to serve an answer if the motion is denied, assuming that the order denying the motion does not specify a time for answering?

BASIC PREANSWER MOTIONS UNDER FEDERAL RULE 12		
ACTION REQUESTED	**BASIS**	**PURPOSE**
"More Definite Statement" of the Plaintiff's Complaint	Rule 12(e)	To request complaint be redone before the defendant has to respond when the complaint "is so vague or ambiguous" that the defendant "cannot be reasonably required to frame" an answer to the complaint
Dismissal of the Action	Rule 12(b)(1)	To challenge the subject-matter jurisdiction of the court (*i.e.*, the action is not one that the court has been authorized to hear)
	Rule12(b)(2)	To challenge personal jurisdiction over the defendant
	Rule 12(b)(3)	To challenge the location of the suit based on improper venue
	Rule 12(b)(4)	To challenge the contents of the process
	Rule 12(b)(5)	To challenge the manner of service of process
	Rule 12(b)(6)	To assert that the plaintiff has failed to state a claim upon which relief may be granted (*i.e.*, even if the plaintiff proves everything that has been alleged in the complaint, the law does not provide a right of action under the applicable law)
	Rule 12(b)(7)	To assert that a "required party" has not been joined and that the action cannot continue without joining that party
Striking of Allegations in the Complaint	Rule 12(f)	To force the removal of "redundant, immaterial, impertinent, or scandalous matter" from the complaint

Figure 6-1

(c) When must the defendant's answer be served (i) if a motion for a more definite statement under Rule 12(e) is denied or (ii) if the motion is granted?

(d) Assume that a defendant moves under Rule 12(f) to strike scandalous matter in a complaint prior to answering. How much time does the defendant have to serve an answer (i) if the motion is denied or (ii) if the motion is granted?

2. What Does an "Answer" Contain?

Under the Federal Rules of Civil Procedure, the "responsive pleading" to the complaint is the defendant's "answer." *See* FED. R. CIV. P. 7(a). The defendant serves an answer when no preanswer motion has been made under Rule 12(b), (e), or (f), or when a preanswer motion has been made under Rule 12, after the motion has been ruled upon by the court. As stated in Rule 12(b), the answer must contain "[e]very defense to a claim for relief." In addition to the defendant's answer to the plaintiff's complaint, an answer must also be filed by any party against whom a claim for relief has been asserted. Thus, Rule 7(a)(3) provides for "an answer to a counterclaim designated as a counterclaim;" (a)(4) "an answer to a crossclaim;" and (a)(6) "an answer to a third-party complaint." Counterclaims, crossclaims, and third-party claims are examined in Chapter 7.

Figure 6-2 summarizes the possible contents of the defendant's answer to the plaintiff's complaint.

POSSIBLE CONTENTS OF AN ANSWER UNDER THE FEDERAL RULES OF CIVIL PROCEDURE	
Admissions or Denials	The answer must admit or deny the factual allegations in the plaintiff's complaint
Defenses	The answer must raise any defenses that the defendant has, including (a) defenses under Rule 12(b) that could have been raised by preanswer motion but were not (assuming they have not been waived), and (b) affirmative defenses, such as contributory negligence, res judicata, release, etc.
Counterclaims	The answer may contain counterclaims against the plaintiff under Rule 13(a) and (b)
Crossclaims	The answer may contain crossclaims against codefendants under Rule 13(g)

Figure 6-2

3. The Answer: Admissions and Denials

Rule 8(b)(1) provides that "[i]n responding to a pleading, a party must: (A) state in short and plain terms its defenses to each claim asserted against it; and (B) admit or deny the allegations asserted against it by an opposing party." Matters admitted by the defendant are taken as true for purposes of the remainder of the litigation. In contrast, denials create issues of fact that will have to be resolved by a trial, assuming that one of the devices for disposing of the action without trial, such as a motion for summary judgment, cannot be used to avoid a trial. Rule 8(b)(2) requires that a denial must "fairly respond to the substance of the allegation" denied. Under Rule 8(b)(4), a party that intends to deny only part of an allegation "must admit the part that is true and deny the rest." If a responsive pleading is required, Rule 8(b)(6) provides that any allegations that a party fails to deny in the responsive pleading, other than as to the amount of damages, are deemed admitted.

Under Rule 8(b)(5), parties are permitted to allege that they lack "knowledge or information sufficient to form a belief about the truth of an allegation." Such an allegation has the same effect as a denial. A denial on the ground that the pleader is without knowledge or information may appear to create a large loophole for defendants. However, this form of denial is not unrestricted. Generally, matters concerning the pleader's own conduct, matters of public record, and matters of general knowledge in the community are presumed to be within the knowledge of the pleader.

Notes and Questions

1. Could a pleader use the "without knowledge" form of denial with respect to the following allegations?

(a) whether the pleader was negligent;

(b) whether the pleader is married;

(c) whether a foreign corporation has qualified to do business in the state (by registration); or

(d) whether a street became a one-way street in a certain direction at a particular time of day.

2. As discussed in section A, common-law pleading also prohibited "*argumentative denials*" and "*negative pregnants*." Do the provisions of Federal Rule 8(b) prohibit argumentative denials or denials containing a negative pregnant? Do Federal Rules 1 and 8(e) help answer this question? Does it matter that a responsive pleading does not ordinarily have to be served to an answer that does not contain a counterclaim under the Federal Rules?

4. Waiver of Defenses by Failing to Include Them in a Preanswer Motion or the Answer

Federal Rule 12(h) expressly provides for the waiver of certain defenses that are not asserted in proper and timely fashion. Rule 12(h)(1) states that "[a] party waives any defense listed in Rule 12(b)(2)-(5) [*i.e.*, lack of personal jurisdiction, improper venue, insufficient process, and insufficient service of process] by: (A) omitting it from a motion in the circumstances described in Rule 12(g)(2); or (B) failing to either: (i) make it by motion under [Rule 12]; or (ii) include it in a responsive pleading or in an amendment allowed by Rule 15(a)(1) as a matter of course." Rule 12(g)(2) provides that if a party makes a motion under one of the provisions of Rule 12 and omits any other then available defense or objection that the party is permitted to raise by motion under Rule 12, the party is thereafter precluded from raising the omitted defense or objection by motion. In combination with Rule 12(h)(1)(A), however, the failure to include in a Rule 12 motion one of the listed defenses in Rule 12(h)(1) results in a permanent waiver of the omitted defense. For example, if a party files a Rule 12(b)(3) motion to dismiss for improper venue and fails to also assert lack of personal jurisdiction under Rule 12(b)(2), the party's personal jurisdiction defense is waived by virtue of Rule 12(h)(1)(A) in combination with Rule 12(g)(2).

Despite the provisions of Rule 12(g)(2), however, Rule 12(h)(2) expressly preserves three defenses from waiver even if they are omitted from a Rule 12 motion or a responsive pleading: (a) failure to state a claim upon which relief can be granted; (b) failure to join a party required by Rule 19; and (c) failure to state a legal defense to a claim. These defenses may be raised in any pleading allowed or ordered by Rule 7(a), by a motion for judgment on the pleadings under Rule 12(c), or at the trial. After trial, however, these defenses are waived.

The defense of lack of subject-matter jurisdiction receives special treatment under Rule 12(h)(3). Such an objection is never waived and may be raised "at any time" during the proceeding.

Waiver by Conduct. As discussed above, Rule 12(h) specifies the circumstances under which waiver of defenses will take place. Rule 12(h) does not include "waiver by conduct," other than the conduct described in the rule. Are there some situations in which waiver should be found even when the requirements of Rule 12 have been followed by the defendant? Some lower federal courts have found such a waiver when the defendant has failed to press for a ruling on a properly raised personal jurisdiction defense. For example, in *Continental Bank, N.A. v. Meyer*, 10 F.3d 1293 (7th Cir. 1993), the Seventh Circuit held that, although the defendants had raised their objection to personal jurisdiction in their answer, this defense had been waived by the defendants' participation in the action for over two and one-half years without actively contesting the lack of personal jurisdiction.

Notes and Questions

1. Assuming that waiver by conduct should occur in some cases, can you articulate a principle that would produce waiver in the appropriate kinds of cases while preserving the defendant's objection in all other cases? Should the principle focus (a) on the conduct of the defendant in accepting the benefits of court action, (b) on the propriety of the court in delaying a ruling on the defendant's personal jurisdiction defense, or (c) on all of these (plus, perhaps, other factors)?

2. Some jurisdictions address waiver by conduct by expressly requiring that the defenses of lack of personal jurisdiction, insufficient process, and insufficient service of process be raised by the defendant by motion within a specified time period, even though they are otherwise properly asserted in the defendant's answer. *See, e.g.*, N.J. Ct. R. 4:6-3 (above defenses, if asserted in answer, must be raised by motion within 90 days after service of answer).

3. The American Law Institute (ALI) proposes to codify the doctrine of waiver by conduct with regard to venue objections. *See* ALI Federal Judicial Code Revision Project § 1406(c) (2004). Given the lack of standards in the cases explaining when and how this judicially created doctrine is administered, wouldn't it be better, if this doctrine is to be adopted, for it to be expressly set forth in the Federal Rules with specific enumerated standards?

4. Some lower federal courts have held that waiver of personal jurisdiction and venue defenses can occur if the defenses are not raised by a preanswer motion under Rule 12(b), but instead are asserted in the defendant's answer and the defendant asserts a counterclaim in the case. Do you understand the rationale for such decisions? Do you think these decisions are correct? Rule 12(h)(1) explicitly provides that venue and personal jurisdiction defenses are waived only by omitting them from a preanswer motion or by failing to include them in a responsive pleading. Waiver by assertion of a counterclaim is not among the listed circumstances for waiver of these defenses. Do you think it is proper to nevertheless impose waiver under these circumstances? *See Rates Tech. Inc. v. Nortel Networks Corp.*, 399 F.3d 1302, 1308 (Fed. Cir. 2005) (provided the requirements of Rule 12(h)(1) are satisfied, no waiver by assertion of a counterclaim; "[H]olding to the contrary would effectively eliminate the unqualified right provided by Rule 12(b) of raising jurisdiction defenses either by motion or answer").

5. The Answer: Affirmative Defenses

"Affirmative Defenses" Under the Federal Rules. In addition to the requirement under Rule 8(b)(1)(B) that a party must admit or deny in its answer the specific allegations asserted against it by an opposing party, Rule 8(c) further requires that in responding to a pleading, "a party must affirmatively state any avoidance or affirmative defense." An affirmative defense is any defense that would create a partial or total avoidance of liability for the responding party, even if the allegations of the party asserting the claim are true. For example, assume that the plaintiff asserts a claim against the defendant for breach of contract. Irrespective of whether the defendant did or did not breach the contract, if the statute of limitations has expired on the plaintiff's claim, the plaintiff's claim is time barred and the defendant's liability on the contract is thus avoided. The defense of the statute of limitations is therefore considered an "affirmative defense" and the defendant must affirmatively state this defense in its answer.

Rule 8(c) lists nineteen specific defenses that fall under this special pleading requirement: accord and satisfaction; arbitration and award; assumption of risk; contributory negligence; discharge in bankruptcy; duress; estoppel; failure of consideration; fraud; illegality; injury by fellow servant; laches; license; payment; release; res judicata; statute of frauds; statute of limitations; and waiver. In addition to the listed defenses, a party is also required to state any other matter that would constitute an avoidance or affirmative defense. Examples of such unlisted affirmative defenses include prematurity of the action, mitigation of damages, and election of remedies.

Waiver of Affirmative Defenses. The potential consequence of omitting an affirmative defense from the answer is waiver of that defense, both under the codes and the Federal Rules. However, an omitted affirmative defense can be later added through an amendment of the answer under Federal Rule 15. Amendments are examined in section E, below.

Notes and Questions

1. Federal courts sometimes allow affirmative defenses to be raised by motion rather than requiring them to be raised in the answer. *See, e.g., Brinkley v. Harbour Recreation Club*, 180 F.3d 598 (4th Cir. 1999) (permitting the defendant in a motion for summary judgment to raise an affirmative defense omitted from the defendant's answer when the plaintiff was not unfairly surprised or prejudiced by the defendant's action). Is this practice proper? In *Harris v. Secretary*, 126 F.3d 339 (D.C. Cir. 1997), the court held it improper for a defendant to raise a statute of limitations defense in a dispositive motion after not raising the defense in its answer. The court stated that Rule 8(c) means what it says and that a defendant must amend its answer under Rule 15 to raise the defense previously omitted if the defendant wishes to rely on it.

2. As noted earlier, Federal Rule 9(a) does not require the plaintiff to allege the capacity or authority of a party to sue or be sued nor the legal existence of a party. Thus, if these matters are to be raised, "a party must do so by a specific denial, which must state any supporting facts that are peculiarly within the party's knowledge." Does this requirement effectively make lack of capacity an affirmative defense by use of the term "denial" in the restyled rule?

3. Affirmative defenses will be waived if omitted from the defendant's answer. However, affirmative defenses are treated much more leniently under the Federal Rules than the waivable defenses listed in Rule 12(h)(1). Under the terms of Rule 12(g)(2) & (h)(1)(A), these latter defenses can be waived even before the defendant files an answer if the defendant files a preanswer motion and omits one of the listed defenses from the motion.

Problems

Problem 6-5. Consider the following positions a defendant might wish to take in response to a complaint. How should they be raised under the Federal Rules of Civil Procedure?

(a) The defendant believes that the plaintiff's negligence contributed to the accident.

(b) Assume that a plaintiff has alleged that defendant's negligent conduct caused the plaintiff's injuries. The defendant, however, wants to show that the defendant was out of town on the date of the accident.

(c) The defendant wants to show that the plaintiff is an infant and thus lacks capacity to sue.

(d) The defendant believes that the plaintiff has omitted an allegation in stating the plaintiff's claim that is essential under the substantive law for the plaintiff to be able to recover against the defendant.

(e) The defendant believes that the allegations in the complaint show that the court lacks subject-matter jurisdiction.

(f) The defendant wants to ask for dismissal because there is another pending action between the same parties for the same cause. This prior pending action is not apparent on the face of the complaint.

(g) The defendant believes that the plaintiff's action is a local action; thus, the action should be brought where the property is located.

(h) Assume that a process server hands the defendant the summons. The defendant wants to raise the fact that the defendant is misnamed in the summons.

Problem 6-6. Absent an amendment, would a waiver of a defense occur under the Federal Rules of Civil Procedure in any of the following situations?

(a) Defendant moves before answer to dismiss the complaint for failure to state a claim upon which relief may be granted. The motion is denied. The defendant then moves to dismiss on the ground that venue is improper.

(b) Defendant omits the statute-of-limitations defense from the answer; at trial, the defendant attempts to show the action is time-barred.

(c) Defendant moves before answer to dismiss on the ground that the court lacks subject-matter jurisdiction. The motion is denied. The defendant then answers, claiming the court lacks personal jurisdiction.

(d) Defendant omits the objection that a party has failed to join a party as required by Rule 19 from the answer; at trial the defendant attempts to show that such a party has not been joined.

(e) Defendant moves to strike redundant and impertinent matter from the complaint. The motion is granted. The defendant answers challenging venue and personal jurisdiction.

Problem 6-7. Would the following actions by the defendant be proper in federal court?

(a) Defendant moves in a preanswer motion to dismiss the complaint on the ground that the court lacks personal jurisdiction over the defendant. The motion is denied. Defendant then moves in another preanswer motion to dismiss the complaint on the ground that the court lacks subject-matter jurisdiction.

(b) Defendant moves for a more definite statement of the claim. The motion is granted. Plaintiff then serves a more definite statement, showing for the first time possible grounds for a challenge that the complaint fails to state a claim upon which relief may be granted. Defendant then moves under Federal Rule 12(b)(6) to dismiss the complaint.

(c) Defendant moves before answering to dismiss the action on the ground that the contents of the summons are defective—an insufficient process objection. The motion is denied. The defendant then moves for a more definite statement under Federal Rule 12(e) on the ground that the complaint is so vague that the defendant cannot reasonably be required to frame an answer.

(d) Defendant moves before answering to dismiss the complaint on the ground that venue is improper. The motion is denied. The defendant then moves to dismiss the complaint on the ground that a party has not been joined as required by Rule 19.

(e) Defendant moves before answering to drop a misjoined party pursuant to Rule 21 of the Federal Rules of Civil Procedure. The motion is granted. Defendant then moves to dismiss the complaint on the ground that the court lacks personal jurisdiction over the defendant.

(f) The defendant answers the complaint by a general denial. The defendant then moves to strike scandalous matter from the complaint.

Problem 6-8. P sues D in federal court using allegations identical to those in Federal Form 10(c) (Complaint "For Goods Sold and Delivered"). D serves an answer by denying the allegations of the complaint other than those relating to subject-matter jurisdiction. At trial, can D offer proof that the goods delivered by P were defective and thus worthless?

Section D. Responding to the Answer

Limits on Pleading: The Reply. The philosophy of notice pleading under the Federal Rules developed through reform of the more elaborate pleading system that existed at common law and, to a lesser extent, under the codes. The common-law system placed great emphasis on the pleadings. It required the pleadings to continue until only a single issue of either law or fact remained. In theory, the common-law pleading process could proceed indefinitely—as long as each party responded to the opposing party's pleading by alleging new matter. However, modern pleading terminates the pleadings artificially before the true positions of the parties are known on all factual and legal issues. This approach reflects a belief that the pleading process is a less efficient means of narrowing the legal and factual issues than other procedures, such as discovery.

Code pleading requires a "reply" to any "new matter" in the answer. Under the Federal Rules, a party is not required to file a reply to an answer, unless the court orders a reply under Rule 7(a)(7). As previously explained in section C(2), if the answer contains a counterclaim, the party is required to file an "answer to the counterclaim" under Rule 7(a)(3). Thus, under the federal rules, unless the court orders a reply to an answer or the answer contains a counterclaim, the final pleading in the federal pleading process is an answer. No other forms of pleadings are allowed. Pleadings, of course, may be amended under Federal Rule 15, which is examined in the following section. Figure 6-3, on the next page, summarizes the pleading process under the Federal Rules of Civil Procedure.

Labeling Mistakes. Assume that P sued D in a U.S. District Court to recover $100,000 in damages for personal injuries received in an automobile accident. D's answer contained a counterclaim against P for injuries received by D in the same accident. However, D mistakenly labeled the counterclaim an "affirmative defense." P does not have to reply to this

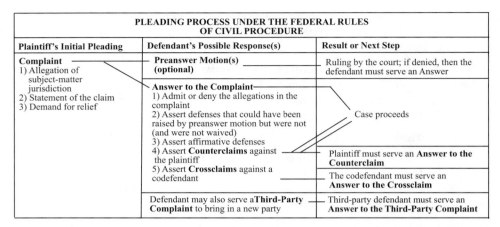

Figure 6-3

mislabeled counterclaim. Federal Rule 7(a)(3) provides that "an answer to a counterclaim" is due only when the counterclaim is "designated as a counterclaim." Furthermore, if *D's* answer had contained an affirmative defense mistakenly labeled a "counterclaim," *P* also would not have to file an answer to the mislabeled "counterclaim." The matter must not only be designated as a counterclaim, but it also must actually qualify as a "counterclaim." Both of these results are prescribed by the rules in order to prevent default when affirmative defenses and counterclaims may be very similar, or when a pleader unartfully makes them so. Federal Rule 8(c)(2) specifically provides that "[i]f a party mistakenly designates a defense as a counterclaim, or a counterclaim as a defense, the court must, if justice requires, treat the pleading as though it were correctly designated, and may impose terms for doing so."

Anticipating Defenses. Under the Federal Rules, the plaintiff is normally not *required* to anticipate defenses. Nevertheless, the courts have generally *permitted* plaintiffs to do so. When plaintiffs anticipate defenses, however, they must take care that they do not make the complaint subject to dismissal under Rule 12(b). As indicated in the preceding subsection, the courts have allowed at least some affirmative defenses to be raised by preanswer motion, and the danger is real that if the plaintiff anticipates an affirmative defense, the complaint might be legally defective. This danger can be avoided if the plaintiff also provides a response to the defense in the complaint.

Problem

Problem 6-9. Assume that the plaintiff in an action in federal court has filed and served a complaint identical to Federal Form 21. The defendant then serves an answer admitting the execution of the note, denying that the defendant owed the amount of the note to the plaintiff, and admitting that the defendant conveyed the property, but denying the conveyance was fraudulent. The defendant also asserts as an affirmative defense that the plaintiff released the claim on the promissory note for a valuable consideration. Determine what issues are in dispute. Would this be a good case for the court to order a reply to the answer? Why or why not? What position(s) would the plaintiff be free to take at trial with respect to the defendant's affirmative defense in the absence of a court-ordered reply?

Section E. Amendments

1. Amendments Pursuant to Rule 15(a)

Federal Rule 15 is the basic rule governing amendments to pleadings in federal court. The 2009 amendments to the Federal Rules of Civil Procedure changed the standard and timing for a party to amend its pleading "as a matter of course." Under revised Rule 15(a)(1)(A) and (B), a party may only amend its pleading "as a matter of course" once, but if a responsive pleading is required, the filing by the adversary of either a responsive pleading or a motion challenging the pleading under Rules 12(b), (e), or (f) now triggers a termination period for an amendment as a matter of course of twenty-one days.

Under former Rule 15(a)(1), only the filing of a responsive pleading, not a Rule 12 motion challenging the pleading, terminated the opponent's right to amend the pleading as a matter of course. Under the former Rule, serving a motion challenging a pleading did not affect the opponent's right to amend its pleading as a matter of course because a motion is not a "pleading" as defined by Rule 7.

The purpose of this amendment is to force a pleader to carefully evaluate an adversary's challenge to its pleading and to promptly decide whether an amendment as a matter of course may obviate the challenge. In addition, under revised Rule 15(a)(1), unlike former Rule 15(a)(1), the right to amend once as a matter of course is no longer terminated by the service of a responsive pleading by the adversary. Now, a party may amend its pleading once as a matter of course within twenty-one days after service of a responsive pleading by the adversary.

Finally, under revised Rule 15(a)(1)(A), if a pleading is one to which no responsive pleading is required, the party may amend its pleading once as a matter of course within twenty-one days of serving it. The time period under former Rule 15(a)(1) was twenty days.

The following case explores the standards for granting and denying leave to amend.

Hill v. Equitable Bank, N.A.

United States District Court, District of Delaware, 1985
109 F.R.D. 109

CALEB M. WRIGHT, Senior District Judge.

This litigation stems from an alleged scheme to defraud plaintiffs in relation to the sale of interests in two limited partnerships. Plaintiffs, investors in the partnerships, originally asserted claims against the defendant, Equitable Bank, N.A., under the Securities Act of 1933, the Securities Exchange Act of 1934, and the common law of Maryland and Delaware. Plaintiffs now seek to amend their complaint to assert an additional claim against defendant under the Racketeer Influenced and Corrupt Organizations Act ("RICO"), 18 U.S.C. § 1961. Defendant vigorously opposes this amendment.

The Court has chronicled the substantive facts giving rise to this litigation in two lengthy opinions ... and will not repeat them here. It is necessary, however, to provide a procedural precis of this dispute to put plaintiffs' petition in the proper perspective.

[Seven plaintiffs sued Equitable Trust Co. in the U.S. District Court for the District of Delaware for violations of the federal securities laws. Portions of the complaint were dismissed. After additional discovery, the plaintiffs filed an amended complaint. Portions of this amended complaint were also dismissed. Meanwhile, several actions commenced by Equitable against the plaintiffs in the District of Maryland were transferred to the District of Delaware and consolidated with the plaintiffs' actions against Equitable. One of these transferred actions contained a RICO counterclaim.

The district court in Delaware set June 14, 1985, as the cut-off date for amending the pleadings. On September 10, 1985, plaintiffs filed a motion to amend to add a RICO count to the their complaint. Equitable opposed the amendment. At a subsequent conference between the court and opposing counsel on October 10, 1985, the court extended the time for the defendant to complete discovery until January 31, 1986, and postponed the trial date indefinitely.]

Plaintiffs ... seek to add a new count to their complaint alleging violations of 18 U.S.C. § 1962. Plaintiffs present four points in support of their motion for leave to amend. First, the Court should grant motions to amend freely as justice requires. Second, justice requires that this motion be granted because the availability of a private RICO cause of action in these circumstances was made clear only after the U.S. Supreme Court decision in *Sedima, S.P.R.L. v. Imrex Co.*, 473 U.S. 479 (1985), issued after the deadline to file motions to amend in this case. Third, plaintiffs assert that defendant will not be prejudiced by the amendment because it already had been put on notice of the facts comprising the RICO claim. In particular, the predicate offenses needed to support a RICO claim were alleged in the existing complaint, and a RICO claim already was present in the case through the Stritzinger counterclaim. Finally, plaintiffs argue that they will suffer great prejudice if their motion is denied.

In response, Equitable makes three arguments. First, it argues that filing a motion to amend three years after the case was brought originally constitutes undue delay, especially since no adverse precedent prevented plaintiffs from seeking the RICO amendment much earlier. Second, Equitable argues that the facts on which plaintiffs base their RICO claim have been known to them for several years. Finally, Equitable argues that it will be prejudiced unduly if plaintiffs are allowed to amend. The particular types of prejudice claimed by Equitable include the necessity of facing a novel legal claim close to trial, the great increase in its potential liability because of RICO's provisions for treble damages and attorneys' fees, the tactical advantage conferred on plaintiffs, and the possibility that the RICO count would require Equitable to file a motion to dismiss and conduct additional discovery.

Having considered the parties' arguments and the relevant authorities, the Court will grant plaintiffs' motion for leave to amend their complaint.

. . . .

Leave to amend pleadings under Fed. R. Civ. P. 15(a) is at the discretion of the district court, *Foman v. Davis*, 371 U.S. 178, 182 (1962). Courts "have shown a strong liberality ... in allowing amendments under Rule 15(a)." ... In *Foman*, the Supreme Court identified a number of factors governing motions to amend under Rule 15(a):

> Rule 15(a) declares that leave to amend "shall be freely given when justice so requires";[a] this mandate is to be heeded.... If the underlying facts or circumstances relied upon by a plaintiff may be a proper subject of relief, he ought to be afforded

---

a. [Eds. Note. Restyled Rule 15(a)(2) now reads: "The court should freely give leave when justice so requires." The substitution of the word "should" for "shall" in the restyled version is intended to be stylistic only and is not intended to effect any substantive change in the application of the rule or the court's obligation under the rule to freely grant leave when justice so requires.]

an opportunity to test his claim on the merits. In the absence of any apparent or declared reason—such as undue delay, bad faith or dilatory motive on the part of the movant, repeated failure to cure deficiencies by amendments previously allowed, undue prejudice to the opposing party by virtue of allowance of the amendment, futility of amendment, etc.—the leave sought should, as the rules require, be "freely given." ...

The Third Circuit has interpreted these factors to emphasize that "prejudice to the non-moving party is the touchstone for the denial of an amendment." . A party's delay in moving to amend a pleading generally is an insufficient ground to deny an amendment, unless that delay unduly prejudices an opposing party. In addition, the non-moving party must do more than simply claim prejudice; it must show that it will be unfairly disadvantaged or deprived of the opportunity to present facts or evidence which it otherwise could have offered had the amendment been timely. Where substantial prejudice is not proven, a court may deny leave to amend only where the non-moving party shows bad faith, dilatory motive, truly undue or unexplained delay, futility, or repeated failure to cure deficiencies by amendment.

In accordance with these principles, the Court first must consider the extent to which granting plaintiffs' motion will prejudice Equitable. As discussed above, Equitable claims several ways in which it will be prejudiced: the proximity of trial, the great increase in its potential liability, the tactical advantage conferred on plaintiffs, and the necessity of filing a motion to dismiss and additional discovery requests. The Court finds none of these arguments persuasive.

Equitable's most compelling argument is that plaintiffs' motion was filed only four months before the scheduled trial date and less than a month before the discovery cutoff date.... The subsequent indefinite postponement of the trial and extension of the discovery period have vitiated considerably the force of this argument, because defendant now has time to complete any additional preparation.

Indeed, it is unclear that Equitable will have to undertake substantial additional work to meet plaintiffs' RICO claim. The RICO allegations are based on the same facts as the existing claims. RICO is not a new issue in the litigation, given the RICO counterclaim present in the *Stritzinger* case transferred from Maryland and consolidated with the instant case. Equitable presumably has been on notice all along to defend against that claim.

Equitable's claim of prejudice based on its need to move for summary judgment and conduct additional discovery similarly must fail. There are no pressing time constraints now that the trial has been postponed. Moreover, in moving to dismiss plaintiffs' RICO count, Equitable can draw on the research used to prepare the briefs seeking to dismiss the RICO counterclaim filed in the *Stritzinger* case. Regarding discovery, Equitable's counsel acknowledged at oral argument that he did not expect that substantial new discovery would be required if the RICO count were added.

Equitable simply cannot claim prejudice based on its increased exposure to liability if RICO claims are part of the case. First, a RICO claim already is present in the case through the *Stritzinger* counterclaim, so that Equitable already faces potential liability for treble damages and attorneys' fees. In addition, the mere fact that the defendant may be held liable as a result of an amendment should not prevent the Court from granting an amendment that otherwise is valid. ...

Equitable's argument that it will be prejudiced through some tactical advantage plaintiffs will gain if the amendment is granted is simply beside the point. Equitable would gain a similar advantage if plaintiffs' motion were denied. Practically any decision by a court

in the progress of litigation conveys a tactical advantage on one side and presumably prejudices the other. This fact does not prevent the court from making decisions; it is the
normal state of affairs.[4]

Given that Equitable has failed to convince the Court that it will be substantially prejudiced by the proposed amendment, the Court must consider other factors which might
allow the amendment to be denied. Equitable does not suggest that plaintiffs' motion is
a futile gesture or stems from bad faith or dilatory motive. Equitable, however, does claim
that plaintiffs delayed unduly in seeking amendment. It points out that plaintiffs could
have filed their amendment years before they actually did, because the proposed RICO
count is not based on hitherto unknown facts or legal theories.

Plaintiffs seek to justify this delay by arguing that the law on civil RICO was unclear
until the Supreme Court handed down its decision in *Sedima*....[5] This proffered justification is not particularly convincing. Certainly, courts in the Third Circuit and elsewhere
had reached vastly different conclusions about the circumstances in which RICO was
available to civil litigants.... No decision binding on a district court in Delaware existed,
however, to preclude plaintiffs from asserting a RICO claim previously. Many other litigants, including plaintiff-counterclaimant Stritzinger, did not feel similarly inhibited and
took the gamble of asserting RICO claims.

Nevertheless, the Court cannot conclude that plaintiffs delayed unduly in seeking
amendment. Because Equitable has failed to show significant prejudice, plaintiffs will be
allowed, despite delay, to amend their complaint to assert a RICO claim against Equitable. An Order will enter in accordance with this Opinion.

Notes and Questions

1. *Hill* is typical in noting that "prejudice to the non-moving party is the touchstone
for the denial of an amendment." As the court explained, "[a] party's delay in moving to
amend a pleading generally is an insufficient ground to deny an amendment, unless that
delay unduly prejudices an opposing party." But can undue delay, without more, ever be
a sufficient basis for denying an amendment? In *Hill*, the court noted that "[w]here substantial prejudice is not proven, a court may deny leave to amend only where the non-moving
party shows bad faith, dilatory motive, truly undue or unexplained delay, futility, or repeated failure to cure deficiencies by amendment." The court did not find undue delay
in *Hill*, but sometimes the courts do. *See, e.g., Leary v. Daeschner,* 349 F.3d 888 (6th Cir.
2003) (trial court did not abuse its discretion in denying leave to amend complaint after
time for amendment in scheduling order had expired); *FGS Constructors, Inc. v. Carlow,*
64 F.3d 1230 (8th Cir. 1995) (the passage of extensive time coupled with the need to reopen discovery justified denial of leave to amend).

---

4. *Komie v. Buehler Corp.,* 449 F.2d 644 (9th Cir. 1971), the only case cited by defendant in its discussion of the prejudice issue, is readily distinguishable. In *Komie*, the defendants sought to amend
their answer and pretrial order a month before trial in order to deny material facts which they had previously admitted. In this case, on the other hand, the trial date is not yet on the horizon, and plaintiffs are basing the RICO count on the same facts as their original claims.

5. Plaintiffs also assert that the only period of delay to be considered is the time between June 14,
1985—the cut-off date for filing amendments to the pleadings—and the date the motion to amend
was filed, because plaintiffs could have filed any amendment prior to June 14, 1985, without leave of
the Court. This assertion is incorrect. The Court would have had to approve any motion to amend,
regardless of whether it was filed before the cut-off date.

2. Should the court be able to impose conditions on a party seeking leave of court to serve an amended complaint? For example, should the party seeking to amend be forced to agree to pay to the defendant the reasonable cost of preparing a new answer? Or should the court be allowed to condition amendment of a complaint on the plaintiff not seeking a jury trial when the claim in the original complaint would have been tried by the court without a jury?

2. Trial of Issues by Consent and Amendments at Trial: Rule 15(b)

Federal Rule 15(b)(1) and (2) permit amendments of the pleadings at trial with respect to new matter not raised in the pleadings. The distinction between the two provisions depends on whether or not an objection is made to the new matter at trial. Rule 15(b)(1) provides that if a party objects that evidence is not "within the issues raised in the pleadings," the court may permit the pleadings to be amended. The court is directed to "freely permit an amendment when doing so will aid in presenting the merits and the objecting party fails to satisfy the court that the evidence would prejudice that party's action or defense on the merits." The court is authorized to grant a continuance to enable the objecting party to meet the evidence.

Rule 15(b)(2) applies when no objection is made and the issue is tried by consent. This provision states that when an issue not raised by the pleadings "is tried by the parties' express or implied consent," the issue "must be treated in all respects as if raised in the pleadings." Rule 15(b)(2) provides that a party may move at any time, even after judgment, to amend the pleadings to conform to the evidence. Even if no formal amendment is made, Rule 15(b)(2) states that "the failure to amend does not affect the result of the trial of that issue."

Comparison to Common-Law and Code Pleading. Federal Rule 15(b) substantially liberalizes the common-law and code practice regarding amendments at trial. Traditionally, evidence offered to prove a matter outside the issues formed by the pleadings and not directed to a proposition of consequence in the action could be objected to as irrelevant or immaterial. It was held that such evidence produced a "variance" between the issues framed by the pleadings and the proof. At common law, a variance was fatal, even if the evidence in question disclosed a meritorious claim outside the pleadings. Proof without allegation was as ineffective as allegation without proof. *See* Teply & Whitten at 579, 1003.

The codes permitted liberal amendment of pleadings, including the discretion to deal with variances by ruling on amendments to the pleadings after an objection had occurred. However, the codes did not permit amendments substantially changing the cause of action, and this restriction also applied to amendments at trial, which significantly limited the court's discretion to allow amendments. *See id.* at 1003; Clark § 115.

At common law, under the doctrine of "aider by verdict," if a party introduced evidence on an issue outside the pleadings that the opposing party did not object to and the verdict was in favor of the party offering the evidence, the court would presume that any fact necessary to sustain the verdict was sufficiently proved even if it was ill-pleaded. However, aider by verdict only applied when the party offering the evidence had pleaded something concerning the ultimate fact required to establish the pleader's case, but not when the party's pleadings contained no allegation at all concerning the matter. *See* Koffler

& REPPY § 299, at 556–57. In code and Federal Rule practice, the doctrine of aider by verdict has been replaced by the doctrine of trial by consent as illustrated by Rule 15(b)(2).

Problems

Problem 6-10. Assume that *P* sues *Dr. D* for malpractice. At trial, *P* attempts to offer evidence that *D* had held herself out as a specialist, but *P's* complaint only alleges that *D* was a general practitioner. Under the substantive law, *D* would be charged with a higher standard of care if she had held herself out as a specialist. *D* objects to the evidence on the ground of variance and *P* seeks to amend. What factors should determine whether the court allows the amendment under Federal Rule 15(b)?

Problem 6-11. Reconsider the facts stated in *Problem 6-10*, but assume that *D* did not object to the admission of evidence that she had held herself out as a specialist. Before the case goes to the jury, *P* seeks to amend the complaint to conform it to the evidence pursuant to Federal Rule 15(b). Did *D* consent to the trial of the issue? Should *D's* failure to object, in and of itself, constitute consent? If not, what other factors should be considered in deciding whether the issue was tried by consent?

3. Relation Back of Amendments: Rule 15(c)

Federal Rule 15(c)(1) provides that "[a]n amendment to a pleading *relates back* to the date of the original pleading" when the requirements of (c)(1)(A), (B) or (C) are met. Relation back is important when the statute of limitations has expired on a claim. Statutes of limitations provide that actions must be commenced within a specified period of time after the accrual of a substantive cause of action. The troublesome problem is how to deal with amendments made to the party's pleading that assert new claims that are otherwise barred by the applicable statute of limitations. If an amendment is permitted to "relate back" to the date of the original pleading, the statute of limitations will not bar the amended claim, provided the original pleading was filed within the time allowed by the statute of limitations applicable to the amended claim.

For example, assume the plaintiff's cause of action against the defendant accrues on Jan.1, 2010. If the applicable statute of limitations is two years, the plaintiff must commence an action by Jan. 1, 2012. Assume that the plaintiff timely commences the action on Dec. 1, 2011. Thereafter, on Jan. 1, 2013, the plaintiff seeks to amend the complaint to add a related claim also covered by the two-year statute of limitations. In this situation, under Rule 15(c)(1)(B), plaintiff's amended claim on Jan. 1, 2013, would "relate back" to the date of the original pleading, Dec. 1, 2011, and be treated as timely filed within the two-year limitations period. Assume, however, that plaintiff's amended claim is governed by a one-year statute of limitations. Now, even if the amended claim relates back under Rule 15(c)(1)(B) to the date of the original pleading, Dec. 1, 2011, the amended claim would still have been untimely on that date and would remain time barred under the applicable statute of limitations.

Different procedural systems address the relation back problem in different ways. Traditional code-pleading systems allowed amendments to relate back whenever the amendments were permitted. However, the code-pleading systems would not permit amendments "changing the cause of action." This restriction effectively subjected amendments changing the cause of action to the bar of the statute of limitations. Under the Federal Rules, relation back is permitted even though the amendment may assert a new claim or defense or change the party against whom a claim is asserted, provided the requirements of Rule 15(c) are satisfied.

(a) Relation Back of Amendments in Federal Court Based on State "Relation Back" Law Under Rule 15(c)(1)(A)

Rule 15(c)(1)(A) provides that an amendment shall relate back when "the law that provides the applicable statute of limitations allows relation back." In situations in which Rule 15(c)(1)(A) is applicable, therefore, relation back is permitted irrespective of whether relation back would otherwise be permitted under 15(c)(1)(B) or (C). As explained in the Advisory Committee's Note to the 1991 amendment to Rule 15(c) which added this provision, "[w]hatever may be the controlling body of limitations law, if that law affords a more forgiving principle of relation back than the one provided in this rule, it should be available to save the claim."

This provision incorporates *state* "relation back" law whenever a *state* statute of limitations is applicable in a federal court action. This would occur in two situations. First, in all situations in which the federal court is adjudicating a state law claim, *i.e.*, diversity of citizenship actions and supplemental jurisdiction claims, the *Erie* doctrine, as held in *Guaranty Trust Co. v. York,* 326 U.S. 99 (1945), reprinted in Chapter 5, requires that the federal court apply the applicable state statute of limitations as a substantive law.

The second situation is when the federal court is adjudicating a federal law claim that is governed by a *state* statute of limitations. This situation occurs because Congress frequently enacts federal statutory rights of action without providing an applicable statute of limitations for the federal action. When this occurs, federal courts usually adopt the statute of limitations of the state in which they are sitting governing the most analogous state right of action.

The availability of state "relation back" rules can be significant, especially on amendments changing a party, as some states have more generous rules than Rule 15(c)(1)(C) for relation back when changing a party. *See, e.g.,* N.J. Ct. Rule 4:26-4 (fictitious party practice) permitting substitution of the actual defendant for a "John Doe" defendant after the expiration of the statute of limitations without the need to also satisfy the New Jersey equivalent of Federal Rule 15(c)(1)(C); *See also Derienzo v. Harvard Indus., Inc.,* 357 F.3d 348 (3d Cir. 2004) (upholding use of New Jersey "John Doe" relation back rule to change party under Rule 15(c)(1)(A) in federal diversity action applying New Jersey statute of limitations).

(b) Amendments Asserting a Claim or Defense Under Rule 15(c)(1)(B)

Rule 15(c)(1)(B) allows relation back of amendments asserting a new claim or defense when the claim or defense in the amended pleading arises out of the "conduct, transaction, or occurrence set out—or attempted to be set out—in the original pleading." This provision reflects the basic philosophy of the federal rules to provide maximum opportunity for parties to fairly present their claims and defenses. The theory underlying relation back in Rule 15(c)(1)(B) is that an opposing party should not generally be surprised or prejudiced when the amended claim or defense arises out of the conduct, transaction, or occurrence set out in the original pleading. Rule 15(c)(1)(B), however, only addresses whether an amendment relates back, and not whether the amendment itself is allowable. Whether an amendment is permissible is governed by Rule 15(a) and (b).

(c) Amendments Changing the Party Under Rule 15(c)(1)(C)

Rule 15(c)(1)(C) specifically applies to amendments changing "the party or the naming of the party against whom a claim is asserted." Thus, the rule explicitly deals with both misnomers and changes in parties. An amendment to which Rule 15(c)(1)(C) applies will relate back if the same "conduct, transaction, or occurrence" test of Rule 15(c)(1)(B) is satisfied and, within the period provided by Rule 4(m) for service of the summons and complaint, the party to be brought in by amendment has "(i) received such notice of the action that it will not be prejudiced in defending on the merits; and (ii) knew or should have known that the action would have been brought against it, but for a mistake concerning the proper party's identity."

The notice requirement of Rule 15(c)(1)(C) has two aspects—the timing of the notice and the nature of the notice. With respect to the timing requirement, the rule borrows the 120-day time period under Rule 4(m) for the service of a summons and complaint on a defendant. Rule 15(c)(1)(C) only *borrows* this time period under Rule 4(m) and does not require that the new party be actually served with the summons and complaint within this time period or that the amending party file its motion to amend within this time period. Rule 15(c)(1)(C) only requires that the party to be brought in by amendment receive "notice" of the action within the 120-day time period, not that the party be officially served with process within this period or that the motion be filed within this period.

As to the nature of the notice, Rule 15(c)(1)(C)(i) only requires that it be "such notice of the action that [the party] will not be prejudiced in defending on the merits." The 1966 Advisory Committee's Note explained that "the notice need not be formal." *See, e.g., Loveall v. Employer Health Servs., Inc.*, 196 F.R.D. 399 (D. Kan. 2000) (letter from company originally named as defendant in products liability action advising other company, that in opinion of its attorneys, the other company "would likely find itself drawn into this lawsuit" was sufficient to place other company on notice of action).

The proper application of the Rule 15(c)(1)(C) raises various interpretive questions which are addressed in the following case.

Krupski v. Costa Crociere S.p.A.

United States Supreme Court, 2010
560 U.S. ___, 130 S. Ct. 2485, 177 L. Ed. 2d 48

Justice Sotomayor delivered the opinion of the Court.

. . . .

I

On February 21, 2007, petitioner, Wanda Krupski, tripped over a cable and fractured her femur while she was on board the cruise ship Costa Magica. Upon her return home, she acquired counsel and began the process of seeking compensation for her injuries. Krupski's passenger ticket—which explained that it was the sole contract between each passenger and the carrier ...—included a variety of requirements for obtaining damages for an injury suffered on board one of the carrier's ships. The ticket identified the carrier as

> Costa Crociere S.p.A., an Italian corporation, and all Vessels and other ships owned, chartered, operated, marketed or provided by Costa Crociere, S.p.A., and all officers, staff members, crew members, independent contractors, med-

ical providers, concessionaires, pilots, suppliers, agents and assigns onboard said Vessels, and the manufacturers of said Vessels and all their component parts....

The ticket required an injured party to submit "written notice of the claim with full particulars ... to the carrier or its duly authorized agent within 185 days after the date of injury." ... The ticket further required any lawsuit to be "filed within one year after the date of injury" and to be "served upon the carrier within 120 days after filing." ... For cases arising from voyages departing from or returning to a United States port in which the amount in controversy exceeded $75,000, the ticket designated the United States District Court for the Southern District of Florida in Broward County, Florida, as the exclusive forum for a lawsuit.... The ticket extended the "defenses, limitations and exceptions ... that may be invoked by the CARRIER" to "all persons who may act on behalf of the CARRIER or on whose behalf the CARRIER may act," including "the CARRIER's parents, subsidiaries, affiliates, successors, assigns, representatives, agents, employees, servants, concessionaires and contractors" as well as "Costa Cruise Lines N. V.," identified as the "sales and marketing agent for the CARRIER and the issuer of this Passage Ticket Contract." ... The front of the ticket listed Costa Cruise Lines' address in Florida and stated that an entity called "Costa Cruises" was "the first cruise company in the world" to obtain a certain certification of quality....

On July 2, 2007, Krupski's counsel notified Costa Cruise Lines of Krupski's claims.... On July 9, 2007, the claims administrator for Costa Cruise requested additional information from Krupski "[i]n order to facilitate our future attempts to achieve a pre-litigation settlement." ... The parties were unable to reach a settlement, however, and on February 1, 2008—three weeks before the 1-year limitations period expired—Krupski filed a negligence action against Costa Cruise, invoking the diversity jurisdiction of the Federal District Court for the Southern District of Florida. The complaint alleged that Costa Cruise "owned, operated, managed, supervised and controlled" the ship on which Krupski had injured herself; that Costa Cruise had extended to its passengers an invitation to enter onto the ship; and that Costa Cruise owed Krupski a duty of care, which it breached by failing to take steps that would have prevented her accident.... The complaint further stated that venue was proper under the passenger ticket's forum selection clause and averred that, by the July 2007 notice of her claims, Krupski had complied with the ticket's presuit requirements.... Krupski served Costa Cruise on February 4, 2008.

Over the next several months—after the limitations period had expired—Costa Cruise brought Costa Crociere's existence to Krupski's attention three times. First, on February 25, 2008, Costa Cruise filed its answer, asserting that it was not the proper defendant, as it was merely the North American sales and marketing agent for Costa Crociere, which was the actual carrier and vessel operator.... Second, on March 20, 2008, Costa Cruise listed Costa Crociere as an interested party in its corporate disclosure statement.... Finally, on May 6, 2008, Costa Cruise moved for summary judgment, again stating that Costa Crociere was the proper defendant....

On June 13, 2008, Krupski responded to Costa Cruise's motion for summary judgment, arguing for limited discovery to determine whether Costa Cruise should be dismissed. According to Krupski, the following sources of information led her to believe Costa Cruise was the responsible party: The travel documents prominently identified Costa Cruise and gave its Florida address; Costa Cruise's Web site listed Costa Cruise in Florida as the United States office for the Italian company Costa Crociere; and the Web site of the Florida Department of State listed Costa Cruise as the only "Costa" company registered to do business in that State.... Krupski also observed that Costa Cruise's claims administrator had responded to her claims notification without indicating that Costa

Cruise was not a responsible party.... With her response, Krupski simultaneously moved to amend her complaint to add Costa Crociere as a defendant....

On July 2, 2008, after oral argument, the District Court denied Costa Cruise's motion for summary judgment without prejudice and granted Krupski leave to amend, ordering that Krupski effect proper service on Costa Crociere by September 16, 2008.... Complying with the court's deadline, Krupski filed an amended complaint on July 11, 2008, and served Costa Crociere on August 21, 2008.... On that same date, the District Court issued an order dismissing Costa Cruise from the case pursuant to the parties' joint stipulation, Krupski apparently having concluded that Costa Cruise was correct that it bore no responsibility for her injuries....

Shortly thereafter, Costa Crociere — represented by the same counsel who had represented Costa Cruise, ... moved to dismiss, contending that the amended complaint did not relate back under Rule 15(c) and was therefore untimely. The District Court agreed.... Rule 15(c), the court explained, imposes three requirements before an amended complaint against a newly named defendant can relate back to the original complaint. First, the claim against the newly named defendant must have arisen "out of the conduct, transaction, or occurrence set out — or attempted to be set out — in the original pleading." Fed. R. Civ. P. 15(c)(1)(B), (C). Second, "within the period provided by Rule 4(m) for serving the summons and complaint" (which is ordinarily 120 days from when the complaint is filed, *see* Rule 4(m)), the newly named defendant must have "received such notice of the action that it will not be prejudiced in defending on the merits." Rule 15(c)(1)(C)(i). Finally, the plaintiff must show that, within the Rule 4(m) period, the newly named defendant "knew or should have known that the action would have been brought against it, but for a mistake concerning the proper party's identity." Rule 15(c)(1)(C)(ii).

The first two conditions posed no problem, the court explained: The claim against Costa Crociere clearly involved the same occurrence as the original claim against Costa Cruise, and Costa Crociere had constructive notice of the action and had not shown that any unfair prejudice would result from relation back.... But the court found the third condition fatal to Krupski's attempt to relate back, concluding that Krupski had not made a mistake concerning the identity of the proper party.... Relying on Eleventh Circuit precedent, the court explained that the word "mistake" should not be construed to encompass a deliberate decision not to sue a party whose identity the plaintiff knew before the statute of limitations had run. Because Costa Cruise informed Krupski that Costa Crociere was the proper defendant in its answer, corporate disclosure statement, and motion for summary judgment, and yet Krupski delayed for months in moving to amend and then in filing an amended complaint, the court concluded that Krupski knew of the proper defendant and made no mistake.

The Eleventh Circuit affirmed in an unpublished *per curiam* opinion.... Rather than relying on the information contained in Costa Cruise's filings, all of which were made after the statute of limitations had expired, as evidence that Krupski did not make a mistake, the Court of Appeals noted that the relevant information was located within Krupski's passenger ticket, which she had furnished to her counsel well before the end of the limitations period. Because the ticket clearly identified Costa Crociere as the carrier, the court stated, Krupski either knew or should have known of Costa Crociere's identity as a potential party. It was therefore appropriate to treat Krupski as having chosen to sue one potential party over another. Alternatively, even assuming that she first learned of Costa Crociere's identity as the correct party from Costa Cruise's answer, the Court of Appeals observed that Krupski waited 133 days from the time she filed her original complaint to seek leave to amend and did not file an amended complaint for another month after that.

In light of this delay, the Court of Appeals concluded that the District Court did not abuse its discretion in denying relation back.

We granted certiorari to resolve tension among the Circuits over the breadth of Rule 15(c)(1)(C)(ii)..., and we now reverse.

II

....

In our view, neither of the Court of Appeals' reasons for denying relation back under Rule 15(c)(1)(C)(ii) finds support in the text of the Rule. We consider each reason in turn.

A

The Court of Appeals first decided that Krupski either knew or should have known of the proper party's identity and thus determined that she had made a deliberate choice instead of a mistake in not naming Costa Crociere as a party in her original pleading.... By focusing on Krupski's knowledge, the Court of Appeals chose the wrong starting point. The question under Rule 15(c)(1)(C)(ii) is not whether Krupski knew or should have known the identity of Costa Crociere as the proper defendant, but whether Costa Crociere knew or should have known that it would have been named as a defendant but for an error. Rule 15(c)(1)(C)(ii) asks what the prospective *defendant* knew or should have known during the Rule 4(m) period, not what the *plaintiff* knew or should have known at the time of filing her original complaint.

Information in the plaintiff's possession is relevant only if it bears on the defendant's understanding of whether the plaintiff made a mistake regarding the proper party's identity. For purposes of that inquiry, it would be error to conflate knowledge of a party's existence with the absence of mistake. A mistake is "[a]n error, misconception, or misunderstanding; an erroneous belief." *Black's Law Dictionary* 1092 (9th ed. 2009); *see also Webster's Third New International Dictionary* 1446 (2002) (defining "mistake" as "a misunderstanding of the meaning or implication of something"; "a wrong action or statement proceeding from faulty judgment, inadequate knowledge, or inattention"; "an erroneous belief"; or "a state of mind not in accordance with the facts"). That a plaintiff knows of a party's existence does not preclude her from making a mistake with respect to that party's identity. A plaintiff may know that a prospective defendant—call him party A—exists, while erroneously believing him to have the status of party B. Similarly, a plaintiff may know generally what party A does while misunderstanding the roles that party A and party B played in the "conduct, transaction, or occurrence" giving rise to her claim. If the plaintiff sues party B instead of party A under these circumstances, she has made a "mistake concerning the proper party's identity" notwithstanding her knowledge of the existence of both parties. The only question under Rule 15(c)(1)(C)(ii), then, is whether party A knew or should have known that, absent some mistake, the action would have been brought against him.

Respondent urges that the key issue under Rule 15(c)(1)(C)(ii) is whether the plaintiff made a deliberate choice to sue one party over another.... We agree that making a deliberate choice to sue one party instead of another while fully understanding the factual and legal differences between the two parties is the antithesis of making a mistake concerning the proper party's identity. We disagree, however, with respondent's position that any time a plaintiff is aware of the existence of two parties and chooses to sue the wrong one, the proper defendant could reasonably believe that the plaintiff made no mistake. The reasonableness of the mistake is not itself at issue. As noted, a plaintiff might know that the prospective defendant exists but nonetheless harbor a misunderstanding about his status or role in the events giving rise to the claim at issue, and she may mistakenly choose to sue a different defendant based on that misimpression. That kind of deliberate but mistaken choice does not foreclose a finding that Rule 15(c)(1)(C)(ii) has been satisfied.

This reading is consistent with the purpose of relation back: to balance the interests of the defendant protected by the statute of limitations with the preference expressed in the Federal Rules of Civil Procedure in general, and Rule 15 in particular, for resolving disputes on their merits. *See, e.g.,* Advisory Committee's 1966 Notes 122.... A prospective defendant who legitimately believed that the limitations period had passed without any attempt to sue him has a strong interest in repose. But repose would be a windfall for a prospective defendant who understood, or who should have understood, that he escaped suit during the limitations period only because the plaintiff misunderstood a crucial fact about his identity. Because a plaintiff's knowledge of the existence of a party does not foreclose the possibility that she has made a mistake of identity about which that party should have been aware, such knowledge does not support that party's interest in repose.

Our reading is also consistent with the history of Rule 15(c)(1)(C). That provision was added in 1966 to respond to a recurring problem in suits against the Federal Government, particularly in the Social Security context. Advisory Committee's 1966 Notes 122. Individuals who had filed timely lawsuits challenging the administrative denial of benefits often failed to name the party identified in the statute as the proper defendant—the current Secretary of what was then the Department of Health, Education, and Welfare—and named instead the United States; the Department of Health, Education, and Welfare itself; the nonexistent "Federal Security Administration"; or a Secretary who had recently retired from office. *Id.* By the time the plaintiffs discovered their mistakes, the statute of limitations in many cases had expired, and the district courts denied the plaintiffs leave to amend on the ground that the amended complaints would not relate back. Rule 15(c) was therefore "amplified to provide a general solution" to this problem. *Id.* It is conceivable that the Social Security litigants knew or reasonably should have known the identity of the proper defendant either because of documents in their administrative cases or by dint of the statute setting forth the filing requirements.... Nonetheless, the Advisory Committee clearly meant their filings to qualify as mistakes under the Rule.

....

B

The Court of Appeals offered a second reason why Krupski's amended complaint did not relate back: Krupski had unduly delayed in seeking to file, and in eventually filing, an amended complaint.... The Court of Appeals offered no support for its view that a plaintiff's dilatory conduct can justify the denial of relation back under Rule 15(c)(1)(C), and we find none. The Rule plainly sets forth an exclusive list of requirements for relation back, and the amending party's diligence is not among them. Moreover, the Rule mandates relation back once the Rule's requirements are satisfied; it does not leave the decision whether to grant relation back to the district court's equitable discretion. *See* Rule 15(c)(1) ("An amendment ... *relates back* ... when" the three listed requirements are met (emphasis added)).

The mandatory nature of the inquiry for relation back under Rule 15(c) is particularly striking in contrast to the inquiry under Rule 15(a), which sets forth the circumstances in which a party may amend its pleading before trial. By its terms, Rule 15(a) gives discretion to the district court in deciding whether to grant a motion to amend a pleading to add a party or a claim. Following an initial period after filing a pleading during which a party may amend once "as a matter of course," "a party may amend its pleading only with the opposing party's written consent or the court's leave," which the court "should freely give ... when justice so requires." Rules 15(a)(1)–(2). We have previously explained that a court may consider a movant's "undue delay" or "dilatory motive" in deciding whether to grant leave to amend under Rule 15(a).... As the contrast between Rule 15(a) and Rule 15(c) makes clear, however, the speed with which a plaintiff moves to amend her complaint or files an amended complaint after obtaining leave to do so has no bearing on whether the amended complaint relates back....

Rule 15(c)(1)(C) does permit a court to examine a plaintiff's conduct during the Rule 4(m) period, but not in the way or for the purpose respondent or the Court of Appeals suggests. As we have explained, the question under Rule 15(c)(1)(C)(ii) is what the prospective defendant reasonably should have understood about the plaintiff's intent in filing the original complaint against the first defendant. To the extent the plaintiff's post-filing conduct informs the prospective defendant's understanding of whether the plaintiff initially made a "mistake concerning the proper party's identity," a court may consider the conduct. *Cf. Leonard v. Parry*, 219 F.3d 25, 29 (1st Cir. 2000) ("[P]ost-filing events occasionally can shed light on the plaintiff's state of mind at an earlier time" and "can inform *a defendant's* reasonable beliefs concerning whether her omission from the original complaint represented a mistake (as opposed to a conscious choice)"). The plaintiff's postfiling conduct is otherwise immaterial to the question whether an amended complaint relates back.[5]

C

Applying these principles to the facts of this case, we think it clear that the courts below erred in denying relation back under Rule 15(c)(1)(C)(ii). The District Court held that Costa Crociere had "constructive notice" of Krupski's complaint within the Rule 4(m) period.... Costa Crociere has not challenged this finding. Because the complaint made clear that Krupski meant to sue the company that "owned, operated, managed, supervised and controlled" the ship on which she was injured, ... and also indicated (mistakenly) that Costa Cruise performed those roles, ... Costa Crociere should have known, within the Rule 4(m) period, that it was not named as a defendant in that complaint only because of Krupski's misunderstanding about which "Costa" entity was in charge of the ship-clearly a "mistake concerning the proper party's identity."

....

It is also worth noting that Costa Cruise and Costa Crociere are related corporate entities with very similar names; "crociera" even means "cruise" in Italian.... This interrelationship and similarity heighten the expectation that Costa Crociere should suspect a mistake has been made when Costa Cruise is named in a complaint that actually describes Costa Crociere's activities....

....

---

5. Similarly, we reject respondent's suggestion that Rule 15(c) requires a plaintiff to move to amend her complaint or to file and serve an amended complaint within the Rule 4(m) period. Rule 15(c)(1)(C)(i) simply requires that the prospective defendant has received sufficient "notice of the action" within the Rule 4(m) period that he will not be prejudiced in defending the case on the merits. The Advisory Committee Notes to the 1966 Amendment clarify that "the notice need not be formal." ...

In light of these facts, Costa Crociere should have known that Krupski's failure to name it as a defendant in her original complaint was due to a mistake concerning the proper party's identity. We therefore reverse the judgment of the Court of Appeals for the Eleventh Circuit and remand the case for further proceedings consistent with this opinion.

It is so ordered.

[JUSTICE SCALIA concurred in part and concurred in the judgment. He objected to the Court's reliance on the Notes of the Advisory Committee as establishing the meaning of the rule. According to JUSTICE SCALIA, it is the text of the rule that controls, not the intention of the Committee.]

Question

Was *Krupski* a case that was appropriate for the application of Rule 15(c) at all? If not, how should it have been analyzed?

Figure 6-4 summarizes the various "relation back" provisions of Rule 15(c)(1)(A)-(C).

Problems

Problem 6-12. P, a citizen of State X, wants to sue D, a citizen of State Y, in the U.S. District Court for the District of State Y. P seeks $100,000 for personal injuries received in an accident suffered on property owned by D in State Y. P's complaint mistakenly names C, a citizen of State Y, as the defendant in the action. C is served two days after the action is commenced. Six months after the complaint is filed and the statute of limitations applicable to P's claim has run, P discovers that P has mistakenly named and served C, rather than D. P amends the complaint to drop C and substitute D as the correct defendant. When D is served with process, it is the first time that D becomes aware of the action. Should the amendment relate back under Rule 15(c)(1)(C)?

Problem 6-13. On the facts of *Problem 6-12*, assume that D became aware of P's claim at the time the accident occurred. D also became aware that P had mistakenly sued C a week after P commenced the action against C, which was still within the limitations period. Should P's amendment adding D relate back under Rule 15(c)(1)(C)?

Problem 6-14. On the facts of *Problem 6-12*, assume that D became aware of P's claim at the time of the accident, but was not aware that P had filed suit on the claim until D was served with process six months after commencement of the original action. Should the amendment relate back under Rule 15(c)(1)(C)?

Problem 6-15. P, a citizen of State X, and D, a citizen of State Y, have a two-car automobile accident in State Y. P sues D in the U.S. District Court for the District of State Y. P seeks $100,000 in damages for personal injuries received in the accident. D answers the complaint before the State Y statute of limitations runs. After the expiration of the period prescribed by the statute of limitations, D moves to amend the answer to include a counterclaim against P for $100,000 in damages for personal injuries received by D in the accident with P. Is D's counterclaim timely? If the counterclaim had been for breach of a contract that was factually and legally unrelated to the automobile accident between P and D, would it be timely? Does your answer to either of these questions have anything to do with the concept of relation back?

Problem 6-16. P-1, a citizen of State X, D, a citizen of State Y, and P-2, a citizen of State Z, are involved in a three-car collision in which P-1 and P-2 were injured. Presuit

OPERATION OF FEDERAL RULE 15(c)

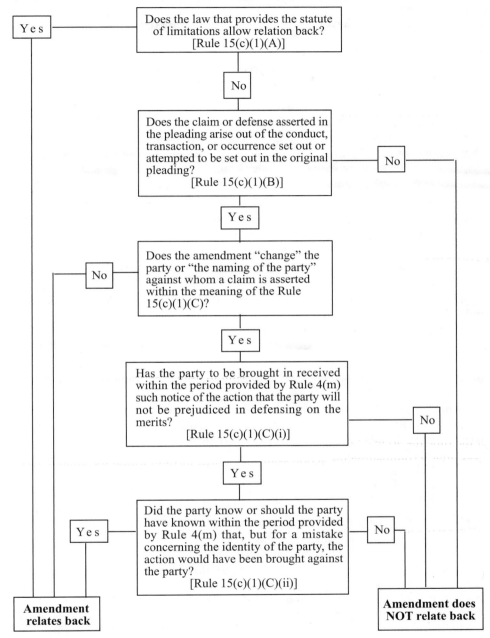

Figure 6-4

investigation by all three parties indicates that *D* and *P-2* were driving in excess of the speed limit at the time of the accident. *P-1* sues *D* for personal injuries resulting from the accident in a U.S. District Court based on diversity of citizenship and more than the requisite amount in controversy. After the applicable statute of limitations and the 120-day period for service of process under Rule 4(m) expire, *P-1* moves to amend the complaint to add *P-2* as a plaintiff. Should the amendment relate back to avoid the bar of the statute of limitations? Why or why not?

Section F. Supplemental Pleadings

Amendments of pleadings pursuant to Federal Rule 15(a) should be distinguished from "supplemental pleadings" authorized by Federal Rule 15(d). Rule 15(d) allows a supplemental pleading "setting out any transaction, occurrence, or event that happened after the date of the pleading to be supplemented." A party seeking to serve a supplemental pleading must first seek the permission of the court by motion. The court may grant such a motion "on just terms."

A typical use of a supplemental pleading would be to raise new defenses or new damages occurring after commencement of the action. For example, a defendant might be permitted to raise a res judicata defense by supplemental answer if another pending action against the defendant based on the same claim reaches final judgment after the original answer is served. Or a plaintiff suing for breach of contract might be allowed to serve a supplemental complaint asserting additional breaches that occurred after the original complaint was filed. Note also that Rule 15(d) expressly permits "supplementation even though the original pleading is defective in stating a claim or defense." For example, when events occurring after the filing of the original complaint make clear the plaintiff's right to relief, a supplemental pleading may be used to cure the defects in the original complaint.

Notes and Questions

1. One question that sometimes arises is whether some relationship should be required between the matters set forth in the original pleading and the supplemental pleading. In particular, should a "same transaction or occurrence" or other relationship test be required? Is the failure to specify the relationship that supplemental pleadings should have to original pleadings an oversight of Rule 15(d)'s drafters? Or did the drafters likely assume the relationship problem would be handled through the court's exercise of discretion in deciding whether or not to allow the filing of the supplemental pleading?

2. Assume that the plaintiff's original complaint contains a breach-of-contract claim against the defendant. After the original complaint is filed and served, the plaintiff and defendant have an automobile accident. The plaintiff then moves under Rule 15(d) for permission to serve a supplemental complaint on the defendant asserting a negligence claim arising out of the automobile accident. It is clear that the supplemental complaint does not arise out of the same transaction or occurrence as the breach-of-contract claim in the original complaint. It is also clear that the original complaint and supplemental complaint do not involve common questions of law or fact. Nevertheless, if the automobile accident had occurred prior to the filing of the original complaint, the tort claim could have been joined in that complaint with the contract claim under the normal rules of claim joinder, even though the claims are unrelated. *See* Fed. R. Civ. P. 18(a). On the other hand, if the plaintiff had sued on the contract and tort claims in separate actions, the actions could not be consolidated because they do not share a common question of law or fact as required for consolidation under Rule 42(a). Does any of this help you decide the issue raised in Note 1?

3. Does Rule 15(c)(1) have any application to supplemental pleadings under Rule 15(d)? Under a plain reading of Rule 15(c)(1), the rule only applies to "an amendment to a pleading," and not to the assertion of a supplemental pleading. Because supplemental pleadings, by definition, assert claims based on events occurring since the original pleading, the filing of such claims would not normally present a statute-of-limitations problem. In rare circumstances, however, a limitations problem may arise. *See, e.g., Bromley v. Michigan Educ. Ass'n-NEA*, 178 F.R.D. 148 (E.D. Mich. 1998), in which the plaintiffs sought to serve a supplemental complaint after remand to the district court from the court of appeals. The supplemental complaint asserted some claims barred by the statute of limitations that the plaintiffs had not previously had a chance to assert because the case was on appeal. The district court held that Rule 15(c) applied to supplemental pleadings and allowed relation back. Given the plain language of Rule 15(c), was the court correct?

Problem

Problem 6-17. *P* sues *D* in federal district court for breach of contract for $100,000. *D* serves an answer admitting the existence of the contract, but denying *D* breached. During discovery, *D* learns that *P* may have induced *D* to enter into the contract by fraud. How should *D* raise this defense? Assume also that after *D* has served the answer, *P* has been found to have committed fraud in related litigation between *P* and other parties. *D* wants to assert issue preclusion against *P* on the fraud issue. How should *D* raise this matter?

Section G. Good-Faith Pleading

Verification. Verification is a statement under oath that the facts alleged in a pleading are true. The original Field Code contained a verification requirement. It required that the complaint, answer, and reply had to be verified in most circumstances. Act of Apr. 12, 1848, ch. 379, § 133, 1848 N.Y. Laws 497, 523. Subsequently, the Field Code was modified to give the option to the plaintiff of verifying and to give any party the power, by verifying, to force the opposing party to verify subsequent pleadings, subject to certain exceptions. Act of Apr. 11, 1849, ch. 438, § 157, 1849 N.Y. Laws 613, 648. Other code states adopted versions of these two New York provisions. When verification was required, an unverified pleading could be treated as a nullity. *See* CLARK § 36, at 216–20. In the federal system, verification is required only in a few circumstances. *See, e.g.,* 28 U.S.C. § 1734(b) ("Court Record Lost or Destroyed"); FED. R. CIV. P. 23.1 ("Derivative Actions"), 65(b) ("Temporary Restraining Order").

History and Amendment of Federal Rule 11. Instead of verification, Federal Rule 11 is the primary source for regulating truthful pleading and other abuses of the litigation process in the U.S. District Courts. Original Rule 11, in part, provided that the attorney's signature on a pleading constituted a certification that the attorney had "read the pleading; that to the best of [the attorney's] knowledge, information, and belief there is good ground to support it; and that it is not interposed for delay." The rule provided that a pleading violation of the rule could be stricken as sham and false. In addition, willful violations could result in disciplinary action being taken against the offending attorney.

Since its original adoption in 1938, Rule 11 has been significantly amended twice, once in 1983 and once in 1993. The 1983 amendments (1) clarified that Rule 11 applied to papers other than pleadings, (2) made the certification requirements of the rule applicable to pro se litigants as well as attorneys, (3) clarified the duty of a person signing a litigation paper to investigate the facts and the law, (4) mandated sanctions for violations of the rule, and (5) strengthened the sanctions that could be imposed on an attorney or party who signed a litigation paper in violation of the rule. The strengthened sanction provisions of Rule 11 included a specific reference to the award of reasonable expenses, including attorney's fees, to the party harmed by the Rule 11 violation. By far the most frequent sanction under the 1983 version of Rule 11 was an order requiring the violator to pay attorney's fees to the opposing party. The 1983 amendments produced a large amount of satellite litigation. Undoubtedly, the provisions allowing the court to award the opposing party a sanction that would include attorney's fees contributed to this litigation.

Dissatisfaction with some of the 1983 amendments produced another significant set of amendments in 1993. The 1993 amendments now comprise the current version of Rule 11. The 1993 amendments expanded the certification requirements of Rule 11(b) by (1) applying them to any presentation of a litigation paper to the court (as opposed to signing a paper only), (2) extending them to individual claims, defenses and other legal contentions (as opposed to entire litigation papers that were unfounded), (3) requiring that allegations and other factual contentions either have evidentiary support or be identified as likely to have evidentiary support after further investigation or discovery, and (4) requiring that denials of factual allegations be warranted on the evidence or else identified as based on belief or a lack of information.

The 1993 amendments to Rule 11(c) now make it discretionary with the court whether to impose sanctions for a violation of the rule. Rule 11(c)(2) was also added to introduce a so-called "safe harbor" provision, which requires a party moving for sanctions to serve the motion for sanctions on the opposing party, but prohibits the movant from presenting the motion to the court for 21 days to give the offending party time to withdraw or correct the offensive matter. Rule 11(c)(1) was also amended to allow sanctions to be imposed on law firms as well as attorneys working for the firms who violate the rule. Rule 11(c)(4) also makes it clear that sanctions should be limited to what is necessary to deter the offending conduct. Significantly, Rule 11(c)(4) provides that the sanctions may consist of "nonmonetary directives; an order to pay a penalty into court; or, if imposed on motion and warranted for effective deterrence, an order directing payment to the movant of part or all of the reasonable attorney's fees and other expenses directly resulting from the violation." The 1993 Advisory Committee's Note states that, although it will sometimes be appropriate to award fees and expenses to the opposing party, monetary sanctions should ordinarily be paid into court as a penalty, rather than to the opposing party.

The 1993 amendments were the last amendments to Rule 11, other than the nonsubstantive, restyling amendments of 2007 and a separate 2007 amendment to Rule 11(a) requiring that all papers must now include, in addition to the signer's address and telephone number, the signer's email address.

Rule 11 Inapplicable to Discovery. Rule 11(d) expressly provides that Rule 11 "does not apply to disclosures and discovery requests, responses, objections and motions under Rules 26 through 37." Certification requirements for discovery documents and sanctions for discovery-related conduct are governed by Rules 26(g) and 37. Discovery is examined in depth in Chapter 8.

Rule 11 Sanctions on Court's Motion. Rule 11(c)(3) permits the court "[o]n its own" to order an attorney, law firm, or party to show cause why it has not violated a specified provision of Rule 11(b). The court's right under Rule 11(c)(3) to institute sanction proceedings *sua sponte* is distinct from a party's right to file a motion for sanctions under

Rule11(c)(2). Unlike Rule 11(c)(2), Rule 11(c)(3) does not contain a "safe harbor" provision. Thus, withdrawal of an offending paper does not insulate a party from sanctions on the court's own motion. The 1993 Advisory Committee's Note indicates that "corrective action" by a violator "should be taken into account in deciding what, if any, sanction to impose."

Inherent Power of Court. As explained in the discussion of the *Chambers* case in Chapter 5, the federal courts have inherent power to impose sanctions for bad-faith litigation misconduct, in addition to the court's express power under Rule 11.

Attorney Sanctions Authorized by 28 U.S.C. § 1927. In addition to Rule 11 and the court's inherent power, 28 U.S.C. § 1927 provides that district courts may impose sanctions upon any attorney who "multiplies the proceedings in any case unreasonably and vexatiously." The sanctions authorized are the payment of "the excess costs, expenses, and attorney's fees reasonably incurred" because of the offending attorney's conduct.

Rules of Professional Conduct. Aside from the requirements of Rule 11 and the other provisions above, attorneys are also subject to the governing Rules of Professional Conduct (RPC) in each jurisdiction. Specifically, RPC 3.1 of the *ABA Model Rules of Professional Conduct* (2012) provides that "[a] lawyer shall not bring or defend a proceeding, or assert or controvert an issue therein, unless there is a basis in law and fact for doing so that is not frivolous, which includes a good faith argument for an extension, modification or reversal of existing law." Be aware that even though Rule 11(c)(2) provides a 21-day "safe harbor" for the withdrawal of any offending matter, an attorney submitting an offending matter may still be subject to discipline under the Rules of Professional Conduct by the appropriate attorney disciplinary authority.

Notes and Questions

1. One of the most difficult problems under Rule 11 is coordinating the notice pleading provisions of the Federal Rules with the 1993 amendments to the rule. Clearly, the amendments do not repeal the notice pleading provisions of the rules. Nor does Rule 11 repeal Rule 8(d)(2) or (3), which allow alternative, hypothetical, and inconsistent pleading. Just as clearly, however, Rule 11 requires the attorney or party presenting a claim or defense to make a reasonable investigation of the facts and the law before presenting the claim or defense. With regard to the provisions of Rule 11(b)(3), the Advisory Committee stated:

> The certification with respect to allegations and other factual contentions is revised in recognition that sometimes a litigant may have good reason to believe that a fact is true or false but may need discovery, formal or informal, from opposing parties or third persons to gather and confirm the evidentiary basis for the allegation. Tolerance of factual contentions in initial pleadings by plaintiffs or defendants when specifically identified as made on information and belief does not relieve litigants from the obligation to conduct an appropriate investigation into the facts that is reasonable under the circumstances; it is not a license to join parties, make claims, or present defenses without any factual basis or justification.

Recall the discussion in Note 8 following *Iqbal* which raised the issue of Rule 11(b)(3). Do you think this provision may have been helpful to the plaintiffs in *Twombly* or *Iqbal*?

2. Assume that a plaintiff's attorney commences an action in federal court when the court clearly does not have subject-matter jurisdiction. Has the attorney violated Rule 11 in filing the action? *See Walker ex rel. Walker v. Norwest Corp.*, 108 F.3d 158 (8th Cir.

1997) (sanctioning an attorney for commencing a federal court action in violation of the "complete diversity" rule for subject-matter jurisdiction under 28 U.S.C. § 1332).

3. Assume that a plaintiff's attorney commences an action in federal court that the plaintiff's attorney knows is subject to a conclusive, but waivable, affirmative defense. Does this action violate Rule 11? *See Zuk v. Eastern Pa. Psychiatric Inst. of the Med. Coll.*, 103 F.3d 294 (3d Cir. 1996) (Rule 11 sanctions appropriate for failure of attorney to investigate facts that would indicate statute of limitations had expired). Is this situation different than that in Note 2, above?

4. What kind of "nonmonetary sanctions" might be appropriate under the amended rule? Do you think a court could order an attorney to write out the provisions of Rule 11 one hundred times in the attorney's own handwriting as a sanction? *See, e.g., Curran v. Price*, 150 F.R.D. 85 (D. Md. 1993) (attorney who filed groundless notice for removal in federal court ordered to copy "in his own handwriting" the jurisdiction section from a federal practice treatise).

Problems

Problem 6-18. P would like to commence an action against D in a U.S. District Court. P believes that D negligently ran P down with a motor vehicle on a certain date, at a certain time, while P was crossing a specific street. However, P has not been able to develop any evidence that D was negligent because P has, despite reasonable efforts, been unable to interview W, who was a witness to the accident. However, P believes that W will be available for an interview at a future date, but fears that the statute of limitations may run before P can conduct the interview. Under these circumstances, can P file a complaint in federal court without violating Rule 11? If so, what must P do to comply with Rule 11? Do the answers to these questions depend on why P does not have personal knowledge of D's behavior leading to the accident?

Problem 6-19. P sues D in a U.S. District Court. P alleges that E, D's employee, negligently ran P down while P was crossing a certain highway. Shortly after the alleged accident, E was killed in a motor vehicle accident with another party. Therefore, there is no witness to the alleged accident other than P. D has no direct evidence whether E ran P down or not, but believes P may have faked the accident after P learned that E had been killed. D provides D's attorney with information that P is not a credible witness and can be effectively impeached at trial. In D's answer, can D's attorney deny the allegation that E ran P down consistently with Federal Rule 11? If so, what must D's attorney do to comply with Rule 11?

Problem 6-20. On the facts of *Problem 6-19*, assume that D's attorney denied the facts of the accident in D's answer in an appropriate fashion. At a later date, however, D's attorney finds a neutral witness who saw E run D down as alleged by P. What are the attorney's obligations under Rule 11 after discovery of the witness?

Problem 6-21. Assume that the plaintiff has commenced an action in federal court by filing a complaint against D-1 and D-2 similar to Federal Form 12 ("Complaint for Negligence When the Plaintiff Does Not Know Who is Responsible"). The plaintiff must prove who was driving the motor vehicle that hit the plaintiff in order to recover. Defendant D-1 tells D-1's attorney that D-1, and not defendant D-2, was driving the motor vehicle that hit the plaintiff. However, D-1 is pretty sure that the plaintiff cannot prove that D-1 was driving. May D-1's attorney answer the complaint by denying that D-1 was driving?

Problem 6-22. On the facts of *Problem 6-21*, assume instead that *D-1* tells the attorney that *D-1* cannot remember who was driving the car. What must the attorney do before signing and serving an answer that denies *D-1* was driving? Does it matter whether the attorney thinks the client is lying about not knowing who was driving? Would your answer be different if a disinterested witness to the accident was available to be asked who was driving?

Problem 6-23. Assume that in an action brought in federal court the plaintiff alleges that the plaintiff loaned the defendant a car, and that contrary to the defendant's promise to take good care of the car, the defendant damaged it in a drag race. The plaintiff sues for damages. Is there any way that the defendant, given Rule 11, can properly plead in the answer that (1) the plaintiff did not loan the defendant the car, (2) the defendant returned the car undamaged, and (3) the car already was damaged when the plaintiff loaned it to the defendant? Consider both Federal Rule 11 and Federal Rule 8(b) and (d)(2) & (3), as well as the circumstances the defendant might face at trial, in answering this question.

Chapter 7

Joinder of Claims and Parties

Civil actions in modern procedural systems can involve a complex configuration of claims and parties. A variety of procedural rules define the permissible boundaries of claim and party joinder, and these rules are explored in depth in this chapter. The particular focus will be on the claim and party joinder provisions of the Federal Rules of Civil Procedure, which have served as models for many state provisions. As you begin to study these rules, it is helpful to keep several points in mind.

First, all procedural systems begin with a basic litigation formula of one plaintiff suing one defendant on one claim. Beyond this basic configuration, specific rules of claim and party joinder establish the procedural circumstances under which additional claims and parties may be joined. If the requirements of these claim and party joinder rules are not met, it is procedurally impermissible for the additional claim or party to be joined.

Second, the rules of claim and party joinder only define when it is *procedurally permissible* to join an additional claim or party. They do not establish *jurisdictional authority* for the joinder of an additional claim or party. For example, simply because a procedural rule of party joinder may permit the plaintiff to join an additional party on the complaint, the plaintiff must still establish that proper subject-matter and personal jurisdiction exists as to this additional party and that proper venue exists in the action. Indeed, Federal Rule 82 expressly provides that "[t]hese rules do not extend or limit the jurisdiction of the [federal] district courts or the venue of actions in those courts." The requirements of subject-matter jurisdiction, personal jurisdiction, and venue, which are examined in depth in Chapters 2, 3, and 4, must be satisfied independently of the claim and party joinder rules.

Third, the ability to join an additional claim in a pending action can affect the extent to which a final judgment precludes litigation of the nonjoined claim in a subsequent action. A decision not to join a factually related claim in a pending action, when it is procedurally and jurisdictionally permissible to do so, usually will preclude a party from litigating that claim in a subsequent action under the doctrine of "claim preclusion." You should keep in mind, therefore, that even though a particular *procedural* rule of claim joinder states that a party "may" join a particular claim, the doctrine of "claim preclusion" sometimes converts a *may* to a *must* as a matter of practical consequence. The doctrine of "claim preclusion" will be fully examined in Chapter 12.

Finally, in examining the materials in this chapter, you should inquire whether the federal claim and party joinder rules are configured in the way that best assures the "just, speedy, and inexpensive determination of every action and proceeding," as required by Federal Rule 1. Your inquiry should include an examination of whether any rules should be liberalized to permit broader claim and party joinder as well as an examination of whether certain rules should be framed more restrictively to narrow claim or party joinder. You may even conclude that some rules should be abolished altogether. The federal claim and party joinder rules are summarized in Figure 7-1 on the next page.

JOINDER OF ADDITIONAL CLAIMS OR PARTIES UNDER THE FEDERAL RULES		
The plaintiff (or another party asserting a claim) wants to assert multiple claims	**Rule18(a)**	May join as many claims as the party has against an opposing party
The defendant wants to assert a claim ("counterclaim") against the plaintiff	**Rules 13(a), 13(b)**	Compulsory: A pleading must state as a counterclaim any claim that, at the time of service of the pleading, the pleader has against any opposing party if it arises out of the transaction or occurrence that is the subject matter of the opposing party's claim. Permissive: Any other claims against an opposing party that are not compulsory counterclaims
The defendant wants to assert a claim ("cross-claim") against another defendant ("coparty")	**Rule 13(g)**	The crossclaim must arise out of the transaction or occurrence that is the transaction or occurrence that is the subject matter either of the original action or a counterclaim or it must relate to property that is the subject matter of the original action
The plaintiff (or a party asserting a counterclaim or a crossclaim) wants to join with other plaintiffs	**Rules 20(a)(1), 13(h)**	(1) All plaintiffs must be asserting a right to relief jointly, severally, or in the alternative with respect to or arising out of the same transaction, occurrence, or series of transactions or occurrences and (2) any question of law or fact common to all plaintiffs will arise in the action
The plaintiff (or a party asserting a counterclaim or a crossclaim) wants to join more than one defendant	**Rules 20(a)(2), 13(h)**	The defendants may be joined (1) if the plaintiff is asserting against them jointly, severally, or in the alternative, any right to relief with respect to or arising out of the same transaction, occurrence, or series of transactions or occurrences and (2) any question of law or fact common to all defendants will arise in the action
A defending party wants to bring into the lawsuit ("implead") someone that the defending party believes is or may be liable for all or part of any amount that the defending party might have to pay an opposing party	**Rule 14**	Any time after commencement of an action, a defending party ("third-party plaintiff") may serve a summons and "third-party complaint" on a person not a party to the action ("third-party defendant") for this purpose
Someone in possession of money or other property is faced with claims by several parties and a potential danger of double or multiple liability	**Rule 22 or 28 U.S.C. § 1335**	The "stakeholder" can bring all the adverse claimants to the property before the court to resolve their claim in a single proceeding ("interpleader"), the stakeholder can do so pursuant to Federal Rule 22 or special federal interpleader statutory provisions (28 U.S.C. §§ 1335, 1397, and 2361)
A "required" ("necessary") party has been left out of the action	**Rule19**	If the plaintiff has inadvertently or intentionally left someone out of the action but the joinder of that absent party is needed to accord complete relief among the existing parties, to protect the absent party's interests, or to prevent an existing party from being subject to the risk of incurring double, multiple, or otherwise inconsistent obligations, the plaintiff can be forced to join such a party
Someone outside of the lawsuit voluntarily wants to become a party in the lawsuit	**Rule 24**	May be able to intervene "of right" under certain circumstances; otherwise, the court may allow intervention permissibly

Figure 7-1

Section A. The "Real Party in Interest" Requirement

Historical Background: Real Party in Interest at Common Law, in Equity, and Under the Codes. At common law, civil actions had to be brought in the name of the person who owned the legal right being asserted. Although this requirement may seem straightforward enough, restrictive rules governing matters such as the assignment of legal rights would often prevent persons who had only "equitable or beneficial interests" from suing in their own name. *See* 6A WRIGHT ET AL. § 1541, at 461. Thus, if the legal owner of a right assigned the right to another party, the assignee could not sue to vindicate the right. Rather, the assignor had to sue for the benefit of the assignee, even though the latter was the functional owner of the right after the assignment and the assignor was only a nominal party. In contrast, equity courts would permit the assignee to sue in the assignee's own name. *Id.* The New York Field Code adopted the equity practice and provided that every action had to be prosecuted in the name of the "real party in interest." *See* Act of Apr. 12, 1848, ch. 379, § 91, 1848 N.Y. Laws 497, 515; CLARK § 21, at 155.

Real Party in Interest Under the Federal Rules of Civil Procedure. The codes were the model for former Equity Rule 37, which governed practice in the federal courts before the Federal Rules of Civil Procedure. Federal Rule 17(a) was derived from code and federal equity practice. *See* 6A WRIGHT ET AL. § 1541, at 462.

In federal practice, it is important to distinguish between two similar, but functionally very different doctrines. One doctrine is the doctrine of real party in interest, which is the subject of this subsection. The other doctrine is the doctrine of standing. These doctrines sometimes overlap, but they differ in their scope and consequences. The "real party in interest" is the person to whom the substantive law gives the right to bring and control the action. In contrast, "standing" is a concept in the area of public law that serves a function similar to the real-party-in-interest doctrine. Standing is used to determine the proper party to challenge governmental action on constitutional or other grounds. An issue of standing typically arises when the plaintiff files an action challenging the validity of a statute or an administrative or executive decision by a governmental agency. Standing resembles real party in interest to the extent that both doctrines require the party bringing an action to have suffered an injury by the defendant's action. However, standing is a much broader concept than real party in interest, because it contains discretionary elements that are employed to ensure that the exercise of the power of judicial review over legislative and executive decisions will be confined to proper cases. *See generally* 6A WRIGHT ET AL. § 1542, at 468–69.

As the following case illustrates, in order to determine whether a party is the real party in interest, one must consult the applicable substantive law. If the substantive law does not create a right of action on behalf of a person, that person cannot be the real party in interest. On the facts of the following case, the substantive law conferred the right of action on the corporation, not the shareholders who sued as plaintiffs. Thus, the shareholders could not be considered the real parties in interest. As the notes following the case indicate, the real party in interest doctrine may overlap with other procedural objections, such as a motion to dismiss for failure to state a claim upon which relief can be granted under Federal Rule 12(b)(6), a motion for failure to join a required party under Federal Rule 19, and, sometimes, a motion to dismiss for lack of subject-matter jurisdiction (in a diversity case where a real party in interest is of the same citizenship as the defendant). You should ask whether any of these alternative objections were available to the defendants in the case and, if so, why they were not raised.

Schrag v. Dinges

United States District Court, District of Kansas, 1993
825 F. Supp. 954

Theis, District Judge.

This is a civil action brought under the Racketeering Influenced and Corrupt Organizations Act ("RICO"), 18 U.S.C. §1961 *et seq.* The plaintiffs allege that the defendants were involved, in various combinations, in four separate fraudulent schemes concerning development of a real estate investment firm called Rexmoor Properties, Inc. ("Rexmoor"). The matter is before the court on motions for summary judgment filed by defendant Mark Youngers..., defendant Robert Simpson..., and defendant Fred Shaffer.... These defendants were officers and/or directors of financial institutions which participated in the financing of the Rexmoor projects. Defendant Youngers was also a director of Paganica, Inc., one of the real estate development firms involved.

Although the defendants have presented arguments relating to each claim against them, this Memorandum and Order deals only with Count I. The court reserves ruling as to the other claims. Defendant Simpson is named only in Count I of the Third Amended Complaint.

[Count I of the complaint alleged that one of the defendants, Gary Dinges, owned a country club complex through his company, Paganica. Plaintiffs Schwartz and Meier operated a pro shop and supper club within the country club complex under a lease between Paganica and their corporation, S & M, Inc. Paganica and S & M contracted to allow S & M to take over operations of the entire country club complex, with an option to purchase the complex and golf course for $1,000,000. An EPA order resulted in unexpected development costs, and these costs brought Paganica to the verge of bankruptcy. Dinges and Ewing devised a plan to return the corporation to profitability by transferring Paganica's assets to a new corporation (Rexmoor) and refinancing the corporation's debt. Various financial machinations then ensued, involving several fraudulent loans and a violation by Dinges of a management agreement not to further encumber the property subject to the option to purchase agreement, but Rexmoor eventually failed.]

The plaintiffs allege that the defendants committed mail fraud on various specified occasions in using the United States Postal Service to deliver correspondence, loan documents, mortgages, and other materials in connection with the fraudulent Paganica Supper Club scheme.

Defendants Shaffer, Simpson and Youngers argue that they should be granted summary judgment as to Count I of the Third Amended Complaint, which is brought by plaintiffs Schwartz and Meier. Defendants present several arguments in favor of summary judgment. However, the court will consider only the issue of whether plaintiffs are the proper parties to assert the RICO claim as it is dispositive of Count I. The allegations set forth above are uncontested for purposes of resolving this issue.

Schwartz and Meier were the major shareholders of S & M. Although plaintiffs were parties to the Management Agreement, it was S & M, not Schwartz and Meier as individuals, who had the option to purchase the Paganica property. The agreement that the property would not be further encumbered related to the option to purchase. Defendants argue, therefore, that the injury alleged is actually an injury to the corporation and not to the individual shareholders, and that Schwartz and Meier do not have standing to bring an action for such injury.

As a matter of general corporation law, an action for damages to a corporation may be brought either by the corporation or, in some circumstances, as a derivative action by the shareholders. Generally, the shareholders cannot sue directly for corporate injuries, including diminution in the value of their stock.... The general rule does not apply when the shareholder plaintiff alleges either a distinct injury that other shareholders in the corporation did not suffer or a breach of a special duty between the plaintiff shareholder and the defendant.... Where the general corporation law would prohibit nonderivative suits by shareholders, the prohibition also applies in civil RICO actions....

Plaintiffs contest neither the facts nor the rules of law set forth above. However, plaintiffs contend that because they were parties to the Management Agreement as well as shareholders in S & M, the defendants breached a special duty to them, which makes them proper parties to bring this action. The court disagrees. The Management Agreement gave plaintiffs the option to sell their S & M stock to Paganica, Inc., under specified circumstances, but it did not provide plaintiffs any rights respecting the option to purchase the Paganica property. Plaintiffs make unsupported and conclusory statements that defendants violated their contractual rights, but they do not demonstrate any duty owed specifically to them which was violated. Plaintiffs were not injured in their "business or property" except through the alleged injury to their corporation.

It appears that Schwartz and Meier assume they were owed a special duty as individuals because they conducted the negotiations for S & M. That assumption is erroneous. It is hardly remarkable that in forming the Management Agreement defendants spoke to and through the natural persons who controlled the corporation. Corporations, although legal persons, are obviously incapable of conducting their own affairs. They must rely on the input of natural persons. This does not enable those natural persons to bring lawsuits to assert the rights of the corporation. To hold otherwise would create an exception that nearly swallows the rule.

Moreover, plaintiffs do not allege, nor could they show under the facts of this case, that their losses were distinct from those of the other S & M shareholders. The only damages claimed derive from the violation of the promise to the corporation that the Paganica property would not be further encumbered. Any losses plaintiffs suffered, therefore, were shared proportionally by the other S & M shareholders. It is clear, then, that Schwartz and Meier are not the proper parties to assert the RICO claim set forth in Count I of the Third Amended Complaint.

Defendants have argued that Schwartz and Meier lack standing to assert the RICO claim. In fact, many courts have held that shareholders lack standing to sue for injuries to the corporation.... However, there is some indication that the issue is actually one of real party in interest and should be handled according to Federal Rule of Civil Procedure 17(a)....

    ....

The Tenth Circuit has stated in a case in which the defendants challenged the joinder of a shareholder-plaintiff both under Rule 17(a) and the standing doctrine:

> [T]he standing challenge is not properly raised in connection with real party interest analysis under Rule 17(a). Professor Wright has explained that "[t]he concept of real party in interest should not be confused with the concept of standing. The standing question arises in the realm of public law, when gov-

ernmental action is attacked on the ground that it violates private rights or some constitutional principle.... 'Real party in interest' is very different from standing." ...

Defendants Youngers, Shaffer and Simpson are the only defendants who seek summary judgment. Whether the matter is one of standing or real party in interest, it is clear that plaintiffs do not have the right to bring the Count I RICO claim. Accordingly, Youngers, Shaffer and Simpson are entitled to judgment as a matter of law on Count I.

The court must decide how to proceed with respect to the remaining defendants, Ted and Gary Dinges, who did not file motions for summary judgment. If the plaintiffs lack standing, then the court does not have subject matter jurisdiction over Count I and must dismiss the claim *sua sponte* pursuant to Fed. R. Civ. P. 12(h)(3)....

On the other hand, Rule 17(a) provides that dismissal of a claim not brought in the name of the real party in interest is proper only after a reasonable time for substitution or ratification. In this case substitution and ratification are not feasible because plaintiffs sold their stock in the corporation to a third party, after which the corporation, the real party in interest, dissolved. Another distinction is that a real party in interest defense is not jurisdictional and is waived if not timely raised. There is no issue of waiver in this case because defendants Ted and Gary Dinges raised the standing/real party in interest defense both in their answer and in the pretrial order.

It appears, therefore, that the distinction between standing and real party in interest is of no significance under the facts of this case. Plaintiffs have had three opportunities to address the issue of their right to bring this action. The issue is the same regarding the remaining defendants. Therefore, there seems to be no reason why summary judgment should not be granted as to defendants Ted and Gary Dinges. However, the court will grant plaintiffs thirty (30) days in which to show cause why this court's real party in interest analysis should not apply to those defendants. Summary judgment is at this time granted to defendants Youngers, Shaffer and Simpson as to Count I.

....

Notes and Questions

1. Under the Federal Rules of Civil Procedure, how is an objection raised when the plaintiff is not the real party in interest? *Schrag* stated that if the objection is not "timely raised," it is waived. If this statement is correct, what is the time period within which the objection must be raised? Can you make an argument that the objection should not be waivable at all, at least in some circumstances?

2. The real-party-in-interest doctrine has come under vigorous criticism in recent years. It has been argued that Rule 17(a) serves no function that cannot better be served by other procedural devices such as a motion to dismiss for failure to state a claim upon which relief can be granted under Rule 12(b)(6), a motion to join a required party under Rule 19(a), or a motion to dismiss under Rule 12(b)(7) for failure to join a Rule 19 required party. Do you agree? Can you think of a function that the real-party-in-interest objection serves that is not served by one of the other motions listed above?

3. Manipulation of Rule 17(a) or confusion produced by its overlap with other rules may result in evasion of the subject-matter jurisdiction requirement of "complete diversity" in diversity of citizenship cases, which requires that all named plaintiffs be citizens of different states than all named defendants. Do you understand how such manipulation or confusion might occur? *See* TEPLY & WHITTEN at 738–39.

4. Given the language in Rule 17(a) requiring that the action be prosecuted in the *name* of the real party in interest, should it ever be permissible under the Federal Rules of Civil Procedure for a plaintiff to sue under a fictitious name? *See Doe v. FBI*, 218 F.R.D. (D. Colo. 2003) (a plaintiff should be able to proceed anonymously only in exceptional cases involving matter of a highly sensitive and personal nature, real danger of physical harm, or when the injury litigated against would be incurred as a result of the disclosure of the plaintiff's identity).

Problems

Problem 7-1. I, an insurer, agreed to insure *P* against all property damage *P* might suffer in automobile accidents. Subsequently, *P* and *D* are involved in an automobile accident and *P's* car is damaged. In a suit against *D* for the damage to *P's* automobile, who is the real party in interest if (1) *I* has paid *P's* entire claim; (2) *I* has not paid any of *P's* claim; or (3) *I* has paid part, but not all, of *P's* claim? Do you need additional information to answer any part of this question? If so, what?

Problem 7-2. In *Problem 7-1*, suppose *I* is the real party in interest under Rule 17(a) in one of the situations described, but mistakenly brings suit in the name of *P*. Suppose the mistake is not discovered until the statute of limitations has run on *P's* claim. Can *I* be substituted as the plaintiff in the action after the statute has run?

Section B. The "Capacity to Sue or Be Sued" Requirement

Every legal system has rules governing who has the capacity to sue and be sued in civil actions. For example, a person who is *legally incapacitated* by reason of age or mental infirmity may not be named as the plaintiff or the defendant in a lawsuit. This requirement does not necessarily mean, however, that legally incapacitated persons cannot sue or be sued. Instead, a representative will have to sue or defend on their behalf. Capacity rules in modern times also concern the ability of certain institutional litigants, such as corporations, to sue and be sued. The issue of a corporation's capacity to sue and be sued is addressed in the following case.

Joseph Muller Corp. Zurich v.
Societe Anonyme de Gerance et D'Armement
United States District Court, Southern District, 1970
314 F. Supp. 439

MacMahon, District Judge.

Defendant Societe Anonyme De Gerance Et D'Armement moves, pursuant to Rule 12(b), Fed. R. Civ. P., to dismiss the complaints in two separate but related actions....

Plaintiff is a corporation organized under the laws of Switzerland with its principal place of business in Zurich. The moving defendant is a corporation organized under the laws of France with its principal place of business in Paris.

In the first of the two actions, plaintiff claims defendant breached a written charter party agreement with plaintiff to transport by ship a chemical product, vinyl chloride monomer (VCM) from the United States to Europe....

In the second action, plaintiff claims defendant violated the federal antitrust statutes by monopolizing the transportation of VCM and conspiring to fix transportation charges.

Defendant's motions to dismiss the complaints in both actions on the ground of lack of subject matter jurisdiction ... raise the same question: plaintiff's legal capacity to sue defendant in the United States. Defendant contends that the Swiss laws under which plaintiff was organized prohibit plaintiff from suing defendant anywhere except in France.

Specifically, defendant relies on a Convention on Jurisdiction and Enforcement of Judgments in Civil Matters entered into by France and Switzerland in 1869. This treaty provides in substance that in all disputes of a civil or commercial nature between French and Swiss nationals, the plaintiff is required to institute the action in the courts of the nation of the defendant.

The Federal Rules of Civil Procedure provide that "the capacity of a corporation to sue or be sued [in a federal court] shall be determined by the law under which it was organized." Fed. R. Civ. P. 17(b).[a]

At first glance, Rule 17 would appear to allow the state or nation under whose laws a corporation is organized to grant the corporation the capacity to sue and immunize it from being sued anywhere except in the state or nation of incorporation. "Capacity to sue or be sued," however, as used in the Rule was, in order to obviate this problem of creating immunity, intended to mean the general capacity to sue or be sued. The laws under which a corporation is organized either grant or withhold the capacity to sue or be sued, and the Federal Rules look to the laws under which a corporation is organized to determine if a corporation has been granted this general capacity.

Once it is determined that a corporation has the general capacity "to sue or be sued," the Rule is satisfied and the federal statutes governing venue will determine the place of trial, regardless of whether or not the laws under which the corporation was organized limit the places where a corporation can sue or be sued....

Defendant does not claim that either it or plaintiff lacks the general capacity to sue or be sued. Both parties have been granted by the laws under which they are organized the

---

a. [Eds. Note. Restyled Rule 17(b) now reads in relevant part: "Capacity to sue or be sued is determined ... (2) for a corporation, by the law under which it was organized."]

capacity to sue or be sued, and the venue limitations imposed by the treaty do not inca-pacitate plaintiff from suing defendant, nor do they affect our subject matter jurisdiction.

. . . .

Accordingly, defendant's motion to dismiss both complaints is denied. . . .

So ordered.

Notes and Questions

1. In *Muller*, the defendant moved to dismiss the two actions on the ground that the court lacked subject-matter jurisdiction over the actions. Was this method the procedu-rally correct way to raise the capacity issue? *See* Fed. R. Civ. P. 9(a)(2). Some commen-tators have argued that lack of capacity "should be considered as waived under Rule 12(h)(1) if not raised by a preliminary motion before trial." *See* 6A Wright et al. § 1559, at 605. Assume that capacity is not properly classified as a subject-matter jurisdiction ob-jection. Assume further that it is not properly classified as an objection of failure to state a claim upon which relief can be granted, a failure to state a legal defense to a claim, or a failure to join a person required by Rule 19(b). *See* Fed. R. Civ. P. 12(h)(2). Can you make an argument that it should be considered improper to raise it by motion at all?

2. Despite the general provision of Rule 17(b)(2) that the capacity of a corporation to sue and be sued in federal court is determined by the law under which the corporation was organized, the Supreme Court in *Woods v. Interstate Realty Co.*, 337 U.S. 535 (1949), held that the law of the forum state must also be considered when the corporation is suing in federal court on a state law claim. In *Woods*, the Court held that a state statute that closed the doors of the state's courts to foreign corporations that failed to qualify under state law to do business within the state must be followed by the federal courts located in that state when the corporation is suing on a state law claim. Thus, even though a cor-poration may have the capacity to sue under the law of the state where the corporation was organized, if the law of the forum state bars the corporation from suing in its state courts, the corporation will also be barred from suing in a federal court in that state on a state law claim. The issue of when a federal court must apply state law in adjudicating a state law claim is examined in depth in Chapter 5.

Section C. Basic Joinder of Claims by Plaintiffs

Historical Background: Claim Joinder at Common Law, in Equity, and Under the Codes. Under the common-law system of procedure, joinder of claims was highly restricted. Plain-tiffs could only join claims falling within the same form of action. However, when this re-quirement was met, the claims did not have to be factually related. In addition, misjoinder of causes of action was considered very serious and impeached the validity of the plaintiff's entire declaration. *See* Teply & Whitten at 685. Joinder in equity was more flexible than at common law. The policy of equity was to determine in a single action as many factually re-lated claims concerning a particular subject matter as was convenient. In addition, the "eq-uitable clean-up" doctrine would, in certain cases, allow an equity court to take jurisdiction of a legal claim and award damages in addition to equitable relief in order to prevent a mul-tiplicity of suits. Thus, the "equitable clean-up" doctrine effectively permitted joinder of legal and equitable claims, which was impossible in the common-law courts. *See id.* at 685–86.

The New York Field Code of 1848 attempted to liberalize claim joinder as it had existed at common law, but the codes retained various restrictions on claim joinder that produced substantial rigidity and inefficiency in joinder practice. Although the courts might have mitigated this rigidity with enlightened construction, they did not always, or even often, do so. *See id.* at 686.

Joinder of Claims Under the Federal Rules of Civil Procedure. In contrast to the restrictive approach at common law and under the codes, the Federal Rules eliminate these former procedural barriers to joinder and expressly authorize unrestricted claim joinder in a single action. Rule 18(a) applies not only to plaintiffs, but to *any* "party asserting a claim, counterclaim, crossclaim, or third-party claim." The Rule provides that such a party "may join, as independent or alternative claims, as many claims as it has against an opposing party."

In terms of claim joinder, Rule 18 could not be any broader. The rationale is to give maximum *procedural* flexibility to the parties in shaping the action, while reserving to the court the right to order separate trials if the joinder of multiple claims becomes confusing or unwieldy. *See* Fed. R. Civ. P. 42(b) ("For convenience, to avoid prejudice, or to expedite and economize, the court may order a separate trial of one or more separate issues, claims, crossclaims, counterclaims, or third-party claims.").

Claim joinder under Rule 18(a) is not compulsory, only permissive. Rule 18(a), of its own terms, does not obligate a party to join claims against an opposing party on pain of later preclusion. As noted in the introductory text of this chapter, however, the separate judicial doctrine of "claim preclusion" generally requires a party asserting a claim in an action to join all other claims that the party possesses against that opposing party which arise out of the same transaction or occurrence. As also noted in the introductory text, Rule 18(a) only establishes *procedural* authority for the joinder of additional claims. As with all of the joinder rules discussed in this chapter, *jurisdictional* requirements must be separately satisfied.

Prior to restyling, Federal Rule 18(b) stated that "[w]henever a claim is one heretofore cognizable only after another claim has been prosecuted to a conclusion, the two claims may be joined in a single action." The purpose of this provision was to remove any doubt whether past practices requiring separate suits for *contingent* claims were still valid. The problem was produced because, although Rule 18(a) permits a party to join as many claims as the party *has* against an opposing party, it is possible to argue that a party does not *have* a claim that is contingent for its existence on the prosecution of another claim to a successful conclusion. Restyled Rule 18(b) deleted the reference to claims "heretofore cognizable only after another claim has been prosecuted to a conclusion" to make clear that the rule is not tied to some meaning "fixed by [a] retrospective inquiry from some particular date." Fed. R. Civ. P. 18(b) advisory committee's note to the 2007 amendment. As restyled, Rule 18(b) now simply states that "[a] party may join two claims even though one of them is contingent on the disposition of the other."

Notes and Questions

1. Prior to the restyling of the Federal Rules in 2007, Rules 8(a), 12(b), and 18(a) each contained a list of all the possible claims that could be asserted under the rules. Rule 8(a) referred to an "original claim, counterclaim, cross-claim, or third-party claim." Rule 12(b) referred to a "claim, counterclaim, crossclaims, or third-party claim." Finally, Rule 18(a) referred to an "original claim, counterclaim, crossclaim, or third-party claim." Except for

the omission of the word "original" before the word "claim" in Rule 12(b), these lists were identical. Rules 41(c) and 42(b) contained a similar listing of individually identified claims. Rule 41(c) referred to "counterclaim, crossclaim, or third-party claim" and Rule 42(b) referred to any "claim, crossclaim, counterclaim, or third-party claim."

2. Under the restyled rules, the lists have been deleted from Rules 8(a) and 12(b), but retained in the others. These two rules now simply speak of "claim[s] for relief," thus presumably intending to include all the claims in the former lists under the general label, "claim for relief." The 2007 Advisory Committee's Note does not explain the reason for this difference. Given that one of the express purposes of the restyling of the rules was "to make them more easily understood and to make style and terminology consistent throughout the rules," see See FED. R. CIV. P. 1 advisory committee's note to the 2007 restyling amendment, do you think that the rulemakers should have made all references to "claims" consistent? Or is there some reason for the retention of the list in some, but not other rules?

Section D. Basic Joinder of Claims by Defendants: Counterclaims and Crossclaims

Modern pleading systems permit a party who is defending a claim to also assert a claim against the opposing party. Such a claim is called a *counterclaim*. Modern pleading systems also permit co-parties (parties aligned on the same side of the action) to assert claims against each other. Such claims are normally called *crossclaims*.

Joinder by Defendants at Common Law. Under the common-law system of procedure, nothing like the modern counterclaim or crossclaim rules existed to allow defendants to assert claims against plaintiffs or other defendants joined in the action. The device of *recoupment* allowed a defendant to assert a claim arising out of the same transaction as the plaintiff's claim in order to diminish or defeat the plaintiff's recovery. A claim in recoupment could only be used defensively and thus could not be used to obtain an affirmative judgment against the plaintiff. *See* TEPLY & WHITTEN at 700.

Joinder by Defendants in Equity. Equity allowed the defendant to *set-off* a claim against the plaintiff's claim under certain circumstances. Unlike common-law recoupment, a set-off claim did not have to arise out of the same transaction or occurrence as the plaintiff's claim. In addition, a defendant could obtain an affirmative judgment against the plaintiff by means of a set-off. Equity also permitted *cross-bills*, which allowed the defendant to assert claims against the plaintiff or other co-defendants. Cross-bills were available to (1) obtain discovery, (2) secure full relief among all the parties to the action, (3) bring a new matter before the court in aid of a defense that could not be raised by answer, and (4) to obtain affirmative relief against the plaintiff that was within the jurisdiction of an equity court. *See id.* at 701–02.

Joinder by Defendants Under the Codes. The 1852 amendments to the Field Code provided for counterclaims, but on a limited basis. The Field Code provision included the former devices of both recoupment and set-off. However, it was broader than common-law recoupment because it permitted an affirmative judgment against the plaintiff. In addition, it was broader than traditional set-off because the defendant's claim did not have to be liquidated. Nevertheless, as with joinder of plaintiffs' claims, the drafters of the Field Code were unable to free themselves entirely from prior practice and authorize unlimited joinder of claims by defendants.

Under the Codes, a counterclaim had to arise out of the same transaction as the plaintiff's claim. If it did not, but was asserted in a contract action, the counterclaim had to be based on a contract theory. These requirements posed interpretive obstacles similar to those experienced with the basic claim joinder provisions of the Code. When defendants sought to use the "same transaction" clause of the counterclaim provision to join claims against plaintiffs, the issue frequently arose whether the defendants' claims were sufficiently related to the plaintiffs' claims to permit the joinder. Similarly, when defendants wanted to use the "contracts provision" to join counterclaims against plaintiffs, difficulties sometimes arose concerning the proper categorization of the counterclaims. Counterclaims under the codes were also not compulsory. *See generally* Teply & Whitten at 703.

The codes also provided for crossclaims against co-parties. However, in some codes, such claims were called "counterclaims," just like claims against opposing parties, and in others they were called "cross-complaints." *See* Clark § 105. Code crossclaims were permissive in nature, and they had to arise out of the same transaction or occurrence as the principal claim in the action. *See id.*

Counterclaims Under the Federal Rules of Civil Procedure. Unlike the practice under the codes, the joinder of counterclaims under the Federal Rules of Civil Procedure, like claim joinder, is unlimited. However, Federal Rule 13(a) makes certain counterclaims *compulsory*. A counterclaim that "arises out of the transaction or occurrence that is the subject matter of the opposing party's claim" is compulsory under Rule 13(a), subject to certain exceptions specified in the rule. Any counterclaims that do not qualify as compulsory counterclaims under Rule 13(a) may be asserted under Rule 13(b). Such counterclaims are called *permissive* counterclaims.

Crossclaims under the Federal Rules of Civil Procedure. Rule 13(g) authorizes a crossclaim against a coparty "if the claim arises out of the transaction or occurrence that is the subject matter of the original action or of a counterclaim, or if the claim relates to any property that is the subject matter of the original action."

Distinguishing Counterclaims and Crossclaims. There are several important distinctions to keep in mind in studying the above rules. First, a counterclaim is asserted against an *opposing party, i.e.,* a party who has asserted a claim against the counterclaiming party. A crossclaim is asserted against a *coparty, i.e.,* a party on the same side of the action as the crossclaiming party, for example a co-defendant. Second, the defining requirement to qualify as a "compulsory counterclaim" under Rule 13(a) or a "crossclaim" under Rule 13(g) rests in both instances on a "transaction or occurrence" relatedness test. Despite this common relatedness requirement, Rule 13(a) counterclaims are *compulsory* and must be asserted under pain of later preclusion, while Rule 13(g) crossclaims are *permissive* and may be asserted in a separate action at the option of the pleader.

Third, Rule 13(b) authorizes, but does not require, the assertion of unrelated counterclaims, *i.e.,* counterclaims that do not arise out of the transaction or occurrence that is the subject matter of the opposing party's claim. However, there is no analogous provision under Rule 13(g) for the assertion of "unrelated" crossclaims. To qualify as a crossclaim under Rule 13(g), the claim must meet the rule's relatedness requirement. However, if a defendant possesses a related claim against a coparty that qualifies under Rule 13(g), the defendant is then eligible to invoke the claim joinder provisions of Rule 18(a) to join a separate unrelated claim.

"Transaction or Occurrence" Test. As noted in the historical section above, the courts experienced difficulty under the codes in determining when a claim arose from the same transaction or occurrence that is the subject matter of the opposing party's claim. The precise dividing line between transactionally related and unrelated claims will always present some interpretive questions, but the following standard is representative of the approach of the federal courts.

> A counterclaim is compulsory if it "arises out of the transaction or occurrence that is the subject matter of the opposing party's claim." Fed. R. Civ. P. 13(a)(1). In interpreting this Rule, the Third Circuit has stated that the "operative question in determining if a claim is a compulsory counterclaim is whether it bears a logical relationship to an opposing party's claim." ... Such a relationship will be found if "separate trials of the claims would involve a substantial duplication of effort and time by the parties and the courts;" the claims "involve many of the same factual and legal issues or the same factual and legal issues;" and the claims "are offshoots of the same basic controversy between the parties."

Geisinger Med. Ctr. v. Gough, 160 F.R.D. 467 (M.D. Pa. 1994).

Considering that the penalty for failing to assert a compulsory counterclaim is preclusion in a later action, and that the assessment of whether a claim was sufficiently "related" to have qualified as a compulsory counterclaim will be done in hindsight by a second court, it is wise for a pleader to always err on the side of caution in deciding whether to assert a counterclaim.

Scope of Rules 13(a), (b), and (g). The wording of these Rules expressly use the generic terms "pleader" and "party" to make clear that their provisions apply not only to defendants, but to *any* party in the action who meets the rule requirements. Thus, the compulsory counterclaim requirements of Rule 13(a) apply to *any* party who has a related claim against any *opposing party*. Similarly, Rule 13(g) applies to the related claim of any party against a *coparty*, irrespective of whether the coparties are plaintiffs, defendants, or third-party defendants. Sometimes, a *coparty* can convert to an *opposing party* triggering operation of the compulsory counterclaim rule, as the following case explores.

1. Who Is an "Opposing Party"?

Rainbow Management Group, Ltd. v. Atlantis Submarines Hawaii, L.P.

United States District Court, District of Hawaii, 1994
158 F.R.D. 656

FONG, DISTRICT JUDGE.

On November 7, 1994, the court heard defendant Atlantis Submarines Hawaii, L.P.'s motion for summary judgment. For the reasons detailed below, the court GRANTS the motion.

....

Plaintiff Rainbow Management Group ("RMG") has sued defendants Atlantis Submarines Hawaii, L.P. ("Atlantis") and George A. Haydu ("Haydu") for damages to and loss of use of RMG's vessel *Elua*, sustained when the *Elua* collided with Haydu's vessel. Defendant Atlantis has filed the instant motion for summary judgment. Atlantis argues that RMG's claims are barred because they were compulsory counterclaims not pleaded in previous litigation regarding the collision.

....

Defendant Atlantis operates commercial submarine tours off-shore at Waikiki Beach. At the time of the accident, RMG was under contract with Atlantis to transport passengers back and forth from the shore to the submarine.

On January 27, 1992, RMG's vessel *Elua* was ferrying passengers from the shore to Atlantis' submarine *Atlantis X*. The exchange of passengers required the *Elua* and *Atlantis X* to come alongside each other to allow their respective crews to secure the two vessels with lines. After the vessels were tied together, a ramp was placed between the two vessels for the passengers to walk on.

That same day, Haydu and four passengers were aboard Haydu's vessel, the *Boston Whaler*, preparing to scuba dive. The *Boston Whaler* was moored at an Atlantis reef approximately 200 yards from where *Elua* and *Atlantis X* were beginning to transfer passengers.

The *Elua* collided with the *Boston Whaler*. The *Boston Whaler* was destroyed, and several of its passengers suffered personal injuries. The *Elua* was damaged and repaired.

Plaintiff RMG now seeks recovery against Atlantis for damages to *Elua's* hull and the resultant loss of use of the vessel. In response, Atlantis asserts that RMG's claim is a compulsory counterclaim that RMG should have asserted in a previous lawsuit by one of the injured *Boston Whaler* passengers against Atlantis, RMG, and Haydu....

....

George Martin Berry, a passenger on the *Boston Whaler* on June 27, 1992, was injured as a result of the collision. Berry and his wife sued Atlantis and RMG as co-defendants on July 22, 1993. The complaint alleged that both Atlantis and RMG were negligent in the operation of their vessels.

On August 23, 1993 Atlantis filed a cross-claim against RMG and a third-party complaint against Haydu. Its cross-claim against RMG stated two counts, one for breach of contract, and the second for contribution and indemnity.

On September 3, 1993, RMG filed a cross-claim against Atlantis and a third-party complaint against Haydu.[1] RMG sought contribution and indemnity, denied any wrongdoing, and prayed for joint and several liability against Atlantis and Haydu. However, RMG did not assert its claim for damage to or loss of use of the *Elua* resulting from the January 27, 1992 collision.

On April 19, 1994, Haydu filed an amended answer and counterclaim against Atlantis and RMG. Haydu claimed that Atlantis and RMG had been negligent and were responsible for damage to his vessel. Haydu also denied responsibility for plaintiff Berry's claims. On April 28, 1994, RMG answered Haydu's counterclaim, denying liability for Haydu's losses and asserting the right to contribution and indemnity. However, RMG again failed to assert its *Elua* damage claim.

In June 1994, RMG filed a second suit (the subject of the instant summary judgment motion). In this suit, RMG sought recovery for damage to the *Elua* and loss of its use resulting from the collision of June 27, 1992. On August 30, 1994, RMG moved to consolidate its suit with the still-pending *Berry* case. However, Magistrate Judge Barry Kurren denied the motion, because of delay and prejudice to the opposing parties.[2]

---

1. In its pleadings, RMG incorrectly identified its claim against Haydu as a counterclaim.
2. RMG filed its motion for consolidation several months after the deadline for amended pleadings set by the Rule 16 scheduling order, after discovery was closed and approximately one and one-half months before the trial date.

Atlantis and RMG have settled with the parties in the *Berry* case. In addition, RMG has settled with Haydu in the instant case. Thus, the only remaining controversy is between RMG and Atlantis.

. . . .

In support of the instant motion [for summary judgment], Atlantis argues that RMG's claims are compulsory counterclaims, barred by Fed. R. Civ. P. 13(a) because RMG failed to assert them in the *Berry* case. Rule 13(a) provides in pertinent part:

> ... A pleading must state as a counterclaim any claim that — at the time of its service — the pleader has against an opposing party if the claim: (A) arises out of the transaction or occurrence that is the subject matter of the opposing party's claim...."[a]

Fed. R. Civ. P. 13(a). Atlantis argues that, after it filed its initial cross-claim against RMG, RMG became an "opposing party" within the meaning of Rule 13(a), and thereafter was required to plead any claims against Atlantis that arose out of the same transaction or occurrence as the initial cross-claims.

In response, RMG argues that its *Elua* claim is not a compulsory counterclaim, but is instead a permissive cross-claim pursuant to Fed. R. Civ. P. 13(g). Rule 13(g) provides in pertinent part:

> ... A pleading may state as a crossclaim any claim by one party against a co-party arising out of the transaction or occurrence that is the subject matter of the original action or of a counterclaim....[b]

Fed. R. Civ. P. 13(g). RMG argues that Atlantis was a co-party in the *Berry* case, not an opposing party. Thus, RMG could have asserted its *Elua* claim in the *Berry* case, but it was not required to do so.[3]

This issue appears to be an open question in the Ninth Circuit, and the case law from other circuits is limited and contradictory....

Professor James W. Moore addresses this problem in his treatise, and concludes that co-parties become opposing parties within the meaning of Rule 13(a) after one party pleads a cross-claim against the other:

> [A]ssume that A and B sue X on a contract claim; and X pleads a permissive counterclaim for damages caused by the negligence of A and B. A may plead a cross-claim against B to the effect that B is liable to A for all or part of X's claim. A's claim is related to X's counterclaim, but it has certain characteristics of an independent claim, since it in no way affects X. If B, now an *opposing party* to A on the cross-claim also has a claim against A, which arises out of the same transaction or occurrence that is the subject matter of A's cross-claim against

---

a. [Eds. Note. The above quoted passage was edited to reflect the current language of Rule 13(a) following the 2007 restyling amendments.]

b. [Eds. Note. The above quoted passage was edited to reflect the current language of Rule 13(g) following the 2007 restyling amendments. Note that the restyled rules no longer hyphenate "crossclaim" and "coparty."]

3. Alternatively, RMG argues that its *Elua* damage claim does not arise from the same transaction or occurrence as the *Berry* case. This contention is without merit. Both lawsuits resulted from the June 27, 1992 collision involving the three vessels, *Elua*, *Boston Whaler*, and *Atlantis X*. Moreover, in its motion for consolidation, RMG itself claimed that "[b]oth lawsuits arise out of the same occurrence, with the underlying facts identical and common fact witnesses."

him, such a claim is a counterclaim within subdivision (a) and must be pleaded, unless within an exception thereto....

. . . .

... [T]his approach is consistent with the goal of judicial economy and reducing unnecessary litigation, because it encourages parties to plead all claims arising out of a single incident and to resolve such claims in a single lawsuit.

The court finds Professor Moore's approach to this issue to be persuasive, and, accordingly, adopts the following rule: Co-parties become opposing parties within the meaning of Fed. R. Civ. P. 13(a) after one such party pleads an initial cross-claim against the other. The court holds, however, that this rule should be limited to situations in which the initial cross-claim includes a substantive claim (as opposed to merely a claim for contribution and indemnity). The reason for this modification is that an unlimited rule may actually increase the amount or complexity of litigation.

For example, assume in the instant case that Atlantis' initial cross-claim did not include a substantive claim for breach of contract, but merely a claim for contribution and indemnity. In the typical case, RMG would respond with a cross-claim of its own for contribution and indemnity. Such cross-claims would not introduce new issues into the case, and could, in all likelihood, be litigated without substantially increasing the cost or complexity of the litigation.

If the court were to adopt Professor Moore's approach without the limitation discussed above, however, RMG would be forced to file all additional claims against Atlantis arising from the same transaction or occurrence underlying the initial cross-claim. RMG might therefore choose to file claims it might otherwise have chosen *not* to litigate, such as claims for minor damages or other claims for small dollar amounts. The court's modified approach eliminates this problem, because claims against the initial cross-claimant only become compulsory when the initial cross-claim itself includes substantive claims.

. . . .

In the instant case, Atlantis' initial cross-claim included a claim for contribution and indemnity, as well as an additional substantive claim for breach of contract. RMG was therefore on notice that it would have to defend against claims other than its own original claim. Accordingly, under the rule adopted today, the court GRANTS Atlantis' motion for summary judgment.

. . . .

For the foregoing reasons, defendant's motion for summary judgment is GRANTED.

IT IS SO ORDERED.

Notes and Questions

1. In *Rainbow Management*, the court limited its holding to situations in which "substantive claims," as opposed to crossclaims for contribution, are asserted in the action. Does the language of Federal Rule 13(a) justify this limitation? Does the policy of the compulsory counterclaim rule justify it? Would you feel secure in relying on the limitation in a district or circuit in which that distinction had not yet been recognized in precedent?

2. The wording of Federal Rule 13(a) makes it imperative in every action to determine when a person upon whom a pleading is being served is an "opposing party" within the meaning of the rule. Consider the following situations:

(a) *P*, *D*, and *T* have a three-car automobile accident. *P* sues *D* in a federal diversity action for $120,000 in damages for personal injuries. *D* impleads *T* under Federal Rule 14. *D* asserts that if *D* is liable to *P*, *T* is liable to *D* for 50% of any amount *D* must pay to *P*. *T* suffered property damage in the accident of $85,000. When *T* serves the third-party answer on *D*, must *T* include a counterclaim against *D* for the $85,000? Does the answer depend upon whether the district in question has adopted the limitation on Rule 13(a) articulated in *Rainbow Management*?

(b) On the facts of question 2(a), above, must *T* include a claim for the $85,000 in property damage against *P* in the third-party answer? If not, may *T* do so? If *T* may do so, what is *T*'s claim called and what rule authorizes *T* to assert it?

(c) In *Rainbow Management*, the court states that RMG filed a third-party complaint against Haydu, but RMG did not join a claim for damages to the *Elua* in the third-party complaint. Should RMG's claim against Haydu for damages to the *Elua* have been precluded by the failure to assert that claim in the third-party complaint? If so, on what theory?

3. Having studied both joinder of claims practice under Federal Rule 18 and counterclaim practice under Federal Rule 13, can you explain why the drafters of Federal Rule 18 did not *require* the plaintiff to join all claims that arise out of the same transaction or occurrence?

Problems

Problem 7-3. *P*, *D-1*, and *D-2* have a three-car automobile accident in which all the parties suffer personal injuries. *P* sues *D-1* and *D-2* in a U.S. District Court to recover for *P*'s personal injuries received in the accident, alleging that either *D-1* or *D-2* or both were negligent and caused *P*'s injuries. *D-1* believes that either *P* or *D-2* or both were negligent and inflicted *D-1*'s injuries. In addition, *D-1* possesses a breach of contract claim against *P* that is factually and legally unrelated to the automobile accident. *D-2* believes that *D-1* was negligent and caused *D-2*'s injuries. Determine whether *D-1* and *D-2* may assert the claims described above in *P*'s action against them and, if so, how. Determine also whether each of the claims is permissive or compulsory and, if so, under what circumstances.

Problem 7-4. *P*, a citizen of State *X*, sues *D*, a citizen of State *Y*, in a state court in State *Y*. *P* seeks $150,000 in property damage from *D* arising out of an automobile accident. Subsequently, *D* files a federal diversity action against *P* in State *Y*, in which *D* seeks $100,000 in damages for personal injuries suffered in the same accident. Based on the language of Federal Rule 13, must *P* plead the claim for property damages as a counterclaim in the federal action?

Problem 7-5. *P* sues *D* in a federal court. *D* does not appear or answer in the action, and a default judgment is entered against *D* under Federal Rule 55. *D* subsequently sues *P* on a claim arising out of the same transaction as *P*'s claim in the federal action. Based on the language of Federal Rule 13, is *D* barred from asserting this claim by Federal Rule 13(a)?

Problem 7-6. *P*, *D-1*, and *D-2* have a three-car automobile accident. *P* sues *D-1* and *D-2* in a U.S. District Court to recover damages for personal injuries received in the accident. *D-1* was also injured in the accident. In addition, *D-1* has a breach of contract claim against *D-2* that is factually and legally unrelated to the automobile accident. Can *D-1* assert the breach of contract claim against *D-2* in the action? If so, under what circumstances?

Problem 7-7. *D* is involved in an automobile accident with a vehicle owned by *P*. *I* is *P's* insurance company. *I* sues *P* and *D* in a U.S. District Court for a declaratory judgment that the automobile insurance policy issued by *I* to *P* does not cover the accident. *D's* answer contains a crossclaim against *P* for *D's* personal injuries received in the accident. Should *D* be able to join this crossclaim against *P* in the action under Federal Rule 13(g)? Should it matter whether *I* is contending that the policy does not cover the accident because the automobile was not being driven with *P's* permission and *P* is defending against the claim asserted by *D* on the same grounds?

2. Claims Not Coming into Existence Until a Judgment Is Rendered

In addition to problems of administering the same "transaction or occurrence" test under Federal Rule 13, several other problems of administration exist under the rule. The following case discusses two of those problems: (1) whether a claim that does not come into existence until a judgment is rendered can be joined at all under Rule 13; and (2) if so, whether it is a compulsory counterclaim.

Tenneco Oil Co. v. Templin
Court of Appeals of Georgia, 1991
201 Ga. App. 30, 410 S.E.2d 154

POPE, JUDGE.

The issues presented in this appeal appear to be issues of first impression in this state. The first is whether a claim by a defendant in a tort action against a plaintiff for contribution for damages awarded in favor of a co-plaintiff is a compulsory counterclaim so that the defendant is barred by the doctrine of res judicata from pursuing the claim for contribution in a separate action after judgment has been rendered. The other is whether a claim by one defendant in a tort action against a co-defendant for contribution is barred by the doctrine of res judicata if it was not brought as a cross-claim in the original action.

In the previous action on which the claim in this appeal was brought (hereinafter, the "tort action"), appellee Douglas Lynn Bullman and the woman who later became his wife, who were injured in a multi-car collision, sued appellant Tenneco Oil Company, the Tenneco employee who was driving Tenneco's vehicle and four others, including appellee Barbara Gay Templin. Two of the defendants in the tort action were dismissed and the trial proceeded against Tenneco and its employee and Templin. Templin filed a counterclaim against Mr. Bullman, who was the driver of the plaintiffs' automobile, alleging he was liable to Templin for contribution if she was found liable for his wife's injuries. The jury returned a verdict in favor of plaintiffs against both Tenneco and Templin and awarded damages to the wife in the amount of $400,000 but awarded no damages to Mr. Bullman. Finding that Mr. Bullman's negligence contributed to his wife's injuries, the jury returned a verdict in favor of Templin on her counterclaim for contribution. The verdict was reduced as a result of the settlement with the other defendants and judgment was entered in favor of the wife in the amount of $393,000. Both Tenneco and Templin satisfied one-half of this judgment and Templin was awarded a judgment of $98,250 against Mr. Bullman on her claim for contribution. In effect, Tenneco satisfied one-half of the judgment and Templin and Mr. Bullman each satisfied one-fourth of the judgment.

Shortly after judgment was entered in the tort action, Tenneco filed the case now before us on appeal—a claim against Templin and Bullman for contribution (hereinafter, the "contribution action"). In the contribution action Tenneco argues that because all three parties were found to be joint tortfeasors then all three parties should bear a pro rata share of the total judgment in the tort action. The trial court granted summary judgment to Templin and Bullman and denied Tenneco's motion for summary judgment. Tenneco appeals.

1. We first address the claim against appellee Bullman, which Bullman argues is barred because it was a compulsory counterclaim in the tort action. "A pleading shall state as a counterclaim any claim which at the time of serving the pleading the pleader has against any opposing party, if it arises out of the transaction or occurrence that is the subject matter of the opposing party's claim and does not require for its adjudication the presence of third parties of whom the court cannot acquire jurisdiction." Ga. Code Ann. § 9-11-13(a).[a] Essentially, a compulsory counterclaim is one which: 1) arises out of the same transaction or occurrence as the main claim; and 2) has matured at the time the answer is filed. Tenneco argues its claim for contribution against Mr. Bullman meets neither of these requirements and was, therefore, not a compulsory counterclaim in the original tort action.

We reject Tenneco's argument that its claim against Mr. Bullman for contribution to the judgment entered on the claim of his co-plaintiff wife did not arise out of the same transaction as Mr. Bullman's claim against Tenneco. While Mr. Bullman's claim and his wife's claim may have stated two separate causes of action, both claims undeniably arose out of the same transaction or occurrence. "The key phrase is that the claim 'arises out of the transaction or occurrence that is the subject-matter of the opposing party's claim.' Cause of action has no express bearing on the issue." ...

Whether the claim for contribution existed at the time Tenneco's answer in the tort action was served is the more complicated issue. Because a claim for contribution to a judgment award is contingent upon a judgment being entered against the party claiming a right to contribution, it can be argued that such a claim has not matured and therefore cannot be brought as a compulsory counterclaim.

Section 13(a) of the Georgia Civil Practice Act is, in all relevant respects, identical to Rule 13(a) of the Federal Rules of Civil Procedure, so it is instructive to look to the interpretation of the federal rule. The two leading commentaries on the Federal Rules of Civil Procedure agree that a claim for contribution cannot be a compulsory counterclaim because it has not yet matured. According to *Moore's Federal Practice*, because a claim for contribution does not mature until a judgment is entered in the case and is satisfied, a claim for contribution cannot be brought as a counterclaim.... The authors of *Federal Practice and Procedure* agree that Rule 13(a) of the Federal Rules of Civil Procedure

---

a. [Eds. Note. The language of Federal Rule 13(a), upon which the above quoted Georgia version of Rule 13(a) was based, was restyled in 2007, but this restyling effected no substantive change in the application or interpretation of Rule 13(a) and does not affect the court's analysis of Rule 13(a) in *Tenneco*. Restyled Federal Rule 13(a) now reads: "(1) *In General*. A pleading must state as a counterclaim any claim that—at the time of its service—the pleader has against an opposing party if the claim: (A) arises out of the transaction or occurrence that is the subject matter of the opposing party's claim; and (B) does not require adding another party over whom the court cannot acquire jurisdiction. (2) *Exceptions*. The pleader need not state the claim if: (A) when the action was commenced, the claim was the subject of another pending action; or (B) the opposing party sued on its claim by attachment or other process that did not establish personal jurisdiction over the pleader on that claim, and the pleader does not assert any counterclaim under this rule."]

may not be employed to bring a claim for contribution because it is not a matured claim.... *But* ... the authors state "a counterclaim will not be denied treatment as a compulsory counterclaim solely because recovery on it depends on the outcome of the main action."

The federal courts which have considered whether a contingent claim may be brought as a counterclaim are split on the issue. "While it is true that courts have held that, the right to contribution does not mature unless and until one has been compelled to pay damages in excess of his proportionate share under a comparative negligence theory, ... the recent trend, and the more pragmatic approach, has been to permit counterclaims for contribution...." In a Georgia case, the Eleventh Circuit Court of Appeals ruled that a claim for contribution against a joint tortfeasor does not accrue at the time of the commission of the tort but at the time a judgment is entered on the injured party's claim against one of the joint tortfeasors and, therefore, such a claim may not be brought as a counterclaim because it has not matured.... We note, however, that appellees have cited no cases, and we have found none, in which a separate suit for contribution was barred for failure to bring the claim as a compulsory counterclaim in the underlying tort action.

    ....

In fact, this court has ruled that the right to contribution to a judgment by a joint tortfeasor does not accrue until after judgment is entered or a compromise settlement is made, although a third-party action ... may be brought prior to obtaining a judgment.... Likewise, the statute of limitation on a claim for contribution does not begin to run until a judgment is rendered, although, again, a third party action may be brought as part of the main claim before a judgment is obtained.... The statute permitting third-party claims expressly permits a defendant to serve a third-party complaint upon a person "who is or may be liable to him for all or part of the plaintiff's claim against him." ... By contrast, the statute permitting counterclaims describes a compulsory counterclaim as a claim which the pleader has against an opposing party "at the time of serving the pleading" in answer to the opposing party.... Thus, even though a third-party complaint may be served before the claim has accrued and ... such claims have been brought as permissive counterclaims, a claim which has not yet accrued cannot be treated as a *compulsory* counterclaim.

One rather cumbersome solution to the problem which would permit a claim for contribution to be tried in the same action as the main tort action is to sever the claims of the two plaintiffs, thereby permitting the plaintiff against whom the claim for contribution is made to be named as a third party to the claim of the other plaintiff, and then to consolidate the two actions for trial.... Perhaps the better practice for allowing a claim for contribution to be tried together with the main claim is to allow such a claim to be brought as a permissive counterclaim,[b] with or without the formality of severance and re-consolidation after the addition of a third-party defendant.... A party may choose to pursue a claim for contribution in the underlying tort action but may not be limited to bringing it in that manner because "'the permission to have contribution ... is absolutely unrestricted.'" ... We cannot say that a party who chooses not to assert his or her claim for contribution as a counterclaim is barred from bringing a separate suit for contribution after a judgment has been entered in the original tort action.

---

    b. [Eds. Note. Following the 2007 restyling amendments, Federal Rule 13(b), which permits permissive counterclaims, was restyled to provide that: "[a] pleading may state as a counterclaim against an opposing party any claim that is not compulsory." Prior to restyling, Rule 13(b) provided that "[a] pleading may state as a counterclaim any claim against an opposing party not arising out of the transaction or occurrence that is the subject matter of the opposing party's claim."]

2. Next, we address the claim against appellee Templin, which Templin argues is barred because it was a matter which could have been raised in the tort action as a cross-claim. "A judgment of a court of competent jurisdiction shall be conclusive between the same parties and their privies as to all matters put in issue or which under the rules of law might have been put in issue in the cause wherein the judgment was rendered...." ... In the tort action appellant Tenneco and appellee Templin were co-defendants and Tenneco could have brought its claim for contribution as a cross-claim against a co-party. The statute authorizing cross-claims expressly authorizes the bringing of a cross-claim for contribution. "The cross-claim may include a claim that the party against whom it is asserted is or may be liable to the cross-claimant for all or part of a claim asserted in the action against the cross-claimant." ... The language of the statute, however, is permissive and in no way makes a cross-claim arising out of the same transaction or occurrence as the main claim compulsory.

....

The trial court erred in ruling Tenneco's contribution action against appellees was barred.

Judgment reversed.

BIRDSONG, P.J., and COOPER, J., concur.

Notes and Questions

1. The *Tenneco* case concludes that "contingent" counterclaims are permissive in nature and can be joined, though they need not be. Consider, first, the question whether a contingent counterclaim like the one in *Tenneco* can be joined at all in an action. The problem concerns the word "has" in the text of Rule 13(a). Technically, a defendant does not "have" a claim for contribution against another tortfeasor until such time as the judgment is rendered holding the defendant liable to the injured party. Thus, peculiar as it may seem, Tenneco's claim for contribution against Mr. Bullman did not come into existence until Mrs. Bullman won her claim against Tenneco.

Note also that Rule 13(a) does not contain a provision like Rule 18(b), which would have allowed Tenneco to assert a contingent counterclaim against Mr. Bullman arising out of the accident. Do you understand why Rule 18(b) would not, of its own force, authorize the joinder of such a contingent claim in a case like *Tenneco*? Would Federal Rule 13(e) allow Tenneco to assert a counterclaim for contribution against Mr. Bullman in the first action? Are there any problems with using Rule 13(e) as authority for joining the counterclaim for contribution? In *Ohio Cellular Products Corp. v. Adams USA, Inc.*, 175 F.3d 1343 (Fed. Cir. 1999), the court held that a third-party complaint may be amended after judgment to add a new third-party defendant who will be personally liable for the judgment. Does this suggest an answer to the problems of contingent counterclaims under Rule 13(a)?

2. The court concluded that Tenneco's counterclaim against Mr. Bullman was permissive and could have been joined in the initial action under Rule 13(b). Was this conclusion correct? Unlike Rule 13(a), neither the original nor the restyled language of Rule 13(b) contains the word "has." Thus, Rule 13(b) might be read as indicating that contingent, permissive counterclaims are authorized under this rule. With respect to cross-claims, note that the last sentence of Rule 13(g) expressly avoids this problem by authorizing permissive, contingent crossclaims for contribution or indemnification against a coparty. Thus, Tenneco's contingent crossclaim against Templin for contribution could have been

properly asserted in the original action under Rule 13(g). Unlike Rule 13(a), however, crossclaims under Rule 13(g) are permissive and thus Rule 13(g) did not prevent Tenneco from asserting its claim for contribution against Templin in the second action. Given the debate in *Tenneco* as to whether a contingent claim for contribution may be asserted as a counterclaim, do you think it curious that no one seemed to question Templin's assertion of such a counterclaim for contribution against Mr. Bullman in the first action?

3. Consider restyled Federal Rule 13(b). Although the restyling of the rules was not supposed to effect "substantive" changes in the application or interpretation of the rules, the language of the restyled Rule 13(b) no longer states, as it formerly did, that a permissive counterclaim is one "*not* arising out of the transaction or occurrence that is the subject matter of the opposing party's claim." The restyled version simply states that a "pleading may state as a counterclaim against an opposing party any claim that is not compulsory." Note that this language, had it been in effect in the *Tenneco* case, could have been more easily interpreted than former Rule 13(b) to authorize the joinder of unmatured (including contingent) counterclaims. Given that there were numerous lower federal court decisions under the former Rule 13(b) holding that unmatured counterclaims may not be asserted in an action, *see* 6 WRIGHT ET AL. § 1411, what should a federal court do with such a counterclaim if it is asserted under restyled Rule 13(b)?

4. If, before the restyling of the Federal Rules, there were lower federal court decisions on a specific issue that were conflicting and a restyled rule seems verbally to embrace one of the conflicting positions and to prohibit the other, what should the lower federal courts do in districts and circuits in which (a) the new language seems to confirm the courts' prior decisions on the issue; (b) the new language seems to prohibit the courts' prior decisions on the issue; or (c) the issue arises for the first time?

5. Does the continued presence of Rule 13(e) in restyled Rule 13 help you arrive at the "correct" conclusion about how unmatured counterclaims should be treated? Are there different kinds of premature claims, some of which might rationally be included in restyled Rule 13(b) and others which might have to be asserted by the procedure in Rule 13(e)?

6. The 2007 restyling amendments of the Federal Rules apply, of course, only in federal court actions. State courts with rules patterned after the federal rules may or may not adopt the restyled language of the federal rules. In state courts still adhering to the original language of Rule 13(b), is the presence or absence of the word "has" the only textual obstacle a defendant must overcome in order to be able to join a contingent counterclaim for contribution of the kind involved in *Tenneco*? (Recall the court's other conclusion about the nature of the counterclaim in *Tenneco*.)

7. We saw earlier that it is important to define who is an "opposing party" at the time of serving a pleading in order to determine whether a counterclaim is compulsory under Rule 13(a). Defining who is an opposing party is also important under Rules 13(a) & (b) for the purpose of determining whether counterclaims can be joined at all. For example, if a plaintiff brings suit in one capacity against the defendant, the defendant may not be able to join a counterclaim under which the plaintiff is liable only in another capacity. *See* TEPLY & WHITTEN at 713–16. Does this problem still exist under the restyled Rule 13?

8. The beginning language of Federal Rule 13(a) provides that "[a] *pleading* must state as a counterclaim...." Thus, by its express terms, the compulsory counterclaim requirement of Rule 13(a) is triggered only when a pleader serves a "pleading" that omits claims arising out of the transaction or occurrence that is the subject matter of the opposing party's claim. The restrictions of Rule 13(a), therefore, should not preclude a later action on a defendant's potential claims against the plaintiff when the defendant defaults or

only files a preanswer motion in the original action and never files an answer to the plaintiff's complaint. Nonetheless, some cases have held otherwise. *See* Todd David Petersen, *The Misguided Law of Compulsory Counterclaims in Default Cases*, 50 Ariz. L. Rev. 1107 (2008) (discussing and criticizing these cases).

Problems

Problem 7-8. P *Insurance Co.* sues D, its insured, for a declaratory judgment that a policy issued by P to D does not cover a certain loss. D's answer contains a counterclaim against P under a statute that provides for recovery of attorney's fees and expenses in actions between insurance companies and insured parties over policy coverage, when such actions terminate in favor of the insured. The counterclaim seeks to recover such fees and expenses for the action filed by the company. Is the counterclaim proper under Federal Rule 13?

Problem 7-9. P *and* W, who are respectively, husband and wife, set out on an automobile trip with P driving. They are involved in an accident with a car driven by D, and W is killed. P, as administrator of W's estate, sues D for the wrongful death of W. P alleges that D's negligence caused the accident. D counterclaims against P for injuries D received in the same accident. D alleges that P's negligence was the sole cause of the accident. Is the counterclaim proper under Federal Rule 13?

Section E. Permissive Joinder of Plaintiffs and Defendants

Joinder at Common Law, in Equity, and Under the Codes. At common law, multiple plaintiffs had to be equally entitled to the recovery before they could join in an action. Likewise, multiple defendants had to be equally subject to a common liability before they could be joined. Equity recognized "proper" parties, who could be joined in an action, but did not have to be because their interests were "separable." In addition, equity recognized certain parties, called "formal" parties, who had a general interest in the subject matter of the action that could be settled conveniently in the suit, but who had no interest in the particular question being litigated. Like proper parties, formal parties could be joined in the action, but did not have to be. *See* Teply & Whitten at 731–33.

Under the codes, three main restrictions existed. First, the restrictions on claim joinder required that the causes of action joined by or against multiple parties had to "affect all the parties to the action." This restriction effectively limited joinder of plaintiffs to cases in which each plaintiff would share in the recovery of the other. Similarly, it restricted joinder of defendants to cases in which each defendant would be obligated on all the claims joined against the defendants. Second, under some codes, it was impossible to join defendants in the alternative—alleging that one or the other was liable for the plaintiff's injuries. A complaint alleging liability in the alternative would be considered defective for failure to state facts sufficient to constitute a cause of action. Finally, some code courts restrictively interpreted the requirement that all persons joined as plaintiffs had to have an interest in the subject of the action "and" in obtaining the relief demanded. Act of Apr. 12, 1848, ch. 379, §97, 1848 N.Y. Laws 497, 516. These courts interpreted the word "and" to require that each plaintiff had to be interested in all the relief demanded. *See* Teply & Whitten at 735.

Permissive Joinder of Parties Under the Federal Rules. Modern permissive joinder practice is exemplified by Federal Rule 20, which expressly eliminates the three main restrictions, described above, on party joinder under the codes. Specifically, Rule 20(a) expressly authorizes multiple party joinder even though the right to relief is asserted "jointly, severally, *or in the alternative.*" In addition, Rule 20(a)(3) expressly provides that "[n]either a plaintiff nor a defendant need be interested in obtaining or defending against *all* the relief demanded" and that judgment may be granted "to one or more plaintiffs *according to their rights,* and against one or more defendants *according to their liabilities.*"

Rule 20(a) contains two main requirements for multiple party joinder. First, the claims asserted by multiple plaintiffs or against multiple defendants must arise "out of the same transaction, occurrence, or series of transactions or occurrences." Second, there must be a "question of law or fact common to" all plaintiffs or all defendants that will arise in the action. Consistent with Rule 18(a)'s liberal claim joinder philosophy, Rule 20(a) is designed to afford broad flexibility to plaintiffs in shaping an action free from unnecessary *procedural* impediments. Provided its requirements are met, Rule 20(a) allows plaintiffs to decide, based on litigation strategy and efficiency, whom to voluntarily join together with as plaintiffs and whom to join as defendants.

As a balance on this right of party joinder, and similar to the court's right with respect to claim joinder, Rule 20(b) preserves the right of the court to order separate trials "to protect a party against embarrassment, delay, expense, or other prejudice." Similarly, Rule 21 provides that "[o]n motion or on its own, the court may at any time, on just terms, add or drop a party [and] ... may also sever any claim against a party." Rule 21 further specifies that "[m]isjoinder of parties is not a ground for dismissing an action."

Joinder of Additional Parties by Defendants Under Rule 13(h). In addition to the separate right of a defending party to join a new party to the action under the impleader provisions of Rule 14(a), discussed in section F, below, Rule 13(h) authorizes a party asserting a counterclaim or crossclaim to also join additional parties to those claims in accordance with Rule 20(a). For example, suppose in the *Tenneco* case, reprinted in section D(2), above, Mr. and Mrs. Bullman only sued Templin in the first action, and not Tenneco. Suppose that Templin had suffered personal injuries in the accident and claimed that Mr. Bullman and Tenneco were the cause of her injuries. If Templin then filed a counterclaim against Mr. Bullman seeking recovery for her injuries, she could now join Tenneco to the action on her counterclaim using Rule 13(h) and Rule 20(a) because Templin would be asserting that both Mr. Bullman and Tenneco were liable to her on her counterclaim. Similarly, suppose that Mrs. Bullman sued both Templin and Tenneco in the first action, but Mr. Bullman was not a party. If Templin then filed a crossclaim against Tenneco seeking recovery for her injuries, Templin could now join Mr. Bullman to the action on her crossclaim using Rule 13(h) and Rule 20(a).

The following materials explore practice under Rule 20 in the federal courts and in states following the Federal Rules of Civil Procedure.

Lucas v. City of Juneau

District Court for the Territory of Alaska, 1955
127 F. Supp. 730

FOLTA, DISTRICT JUDGE.

The plaintiff seeks damages in the amount of $90,000 for personal injuries sustained as the result of the alleged negligence of the defendants. It appears that while in the order office of Sears, Roebuck & Co., at Juneau, as an invitee, he stepped on a round pencil on the floor, which, rolling under his weight, caused him to fall and injure his back. After confinement in the local hospital for some time it was decided that he should enter the Veterans' Hospital at Seattle for further treatment. Pursuant to this decision he commenced his journey to the airport in the defendant city's ambulance, 18 days after the injury. En route the driver was seized with an epileptic fit, according to plaintiff's brief, as a result of which the ambulance went out of control and off the highway, the plaintiff was thrown to the floor of the ambulance, and his original injury aggravated.

Alleging that the extent of the injury caused by each of these acts of alleged negligence is indeterminable, plaintiff has joined the defendants in this action. His claim is based on the allegation that Sears, Roebuck & Co., hereinafter called Sears, was negligent in allowing the pencil to remain on the floor, and that the city was negligent in employing an epileptic driver. The defendants have countered with motions to dismiss for misjoinder.

Two interrelated questions are presented—1, whether Sears may be held liable for both injuries, and, 2, whether the parties may be joined under Rule 20(a), Fed. R. Civ. P....

. . . .

Turning to the question of joinder, it seems clear that Sears is liable for the aggravation, as is, of course, the city. Plaintiff may assert against them severally a right to relief, and the facts and circumstances of the aggravation will present questions of fact common to both causes of action arising out of a single occurrence. Hence the defendants may be joined under Rule 20, Fed. R. Civ. P. It follows, therefore, that the motion of the city..., and the motion of Sears ... should be denied....

. . . .

Notes and Questions

1. In *Lucas*, the court held that the defendants were not joint tortfeasors. The significance of this holding was that the city could not be held liable for the original injury to the plaintiff's back. The reason for the court's conclusion was that "the negligent acts of the defendants did not set in motion forces which united to produce a single injury but did produce two successive and separate injuries to the plaintiff's back." However, the court did hold Sears liable both for the original injury and for the aggravation of the injury resulting from the ambulance accident. This was done by analogy to a rule that the "original wrongdoer" (Sears) is liable for aggravation to the injury caused by reasonably foreseeable intervening forces, or "which is a normal incident of the risk created," such as negligent medical treatment. Given this substantive context, can you identify how each portion of Rule 20 was satisfied?

2. Suppose that the substantive law applicable to the facts of *Lucas* provided that Sears was liable only for the original injury and the city was liable only for the aggravation. Would joinder still be proper under Rule 20?

3. Why do you suppose the drafters of Rule 20 required that claims for relief arising out of the same transaction or occurrence and raising common questions of law or fact be present before parties could join or be joined in an action? Should any two parties be able to join or be joined in an action regardless of the relationship between their claims, subject only to the court's power to order separate trials where inconvenience would result from trying unrelated matters together?

4. On the other hand, why is joinder of parties under Rule 20 not made compulsory? Should all parties asserting claims arising out of the same transaction or occurrence and

raising common questions of law or fact be forced to join as plaintiffs? Should plaintiffs be forced to join all defendants against whom such claims are asserted?

Problems

Problem 7-10. P sued *D-1* and *D-2* for breach of a contract made with *D-1* and *D-2*. P joined with this breach of contract claim a separate factually unrelated contract claim with *D-2*. Can the claim against *D-2* properly be joined under the Federal Rules of Civil Procedure?

Problem 7-11. *P-1* and *P-2* join in an action against the City of *D*. *P-1* and *P-2* seek an order requiring the city to issue them licenses to sell alcoholic beverages in their restaurants. The city had refused licenses to *P-1* and *P-2* on the same grounds, but on different occasions. Both *P-1* and *P-2* contend that the grounds for refusing them licenses are invalid for the same legal reasons. There is no other relationship between *P-1* and *P-2*. What argument can be made that *P-1* and *P-2* are properly joined as plaintiffs under Rule 20? Regardless of these arguments, do you believe joinder is proper under Rule 20? If *P-1* and *P-2* must bring separate actions against the city, is there any way that they could have their claims tried together? If *P-1* and *P-2* are properly joined, is there any way in which the city can have their claims tried separately?

Problem 7-12. *P-1* and *P-2* join in an action against *D*. *P-1* and *P-2* allege that *D* fraudulently induced both of them to invest in a sham corporation by issuing a false prospectus. Other than the fact that they were defrauded by the same (allegedly) false prospectus, no relationship exists between *P-1* and *P-2*. Are *P-1* and *P-2* properly joined under Rule 20?

Problem 7-13. How and when should a misjoinder of plaintiffs or defendants under Rule 20 be raised? Can such an objection be waived? Consider the following situations: *P-1* and *P-2* join in a suit against *D* for fraud. Both plaintiffs allege that *D* defrauded them on a separate occasion, but by an identical fraudulent statement. Except that they were both allegedly defrauded by the defendant, the plaintiffs are unrelated. After extensive discovery, there is a trial in which *D* is held liable to both plaintiffs for the separate acts of fraud. On appeal, *D* raises the objection for the first time that the plaintiffs were not joined properly in the action, in addition to contending, as *D* always has, that the statements made to the plaintiffs were not fraudulent. May *D* raise the misjoinder objection for the first time on appeal? If the appellate court believes there was a misjoinder at the trial level, what should it do?

Section F. Impleader

Impleader, also known as *third-party practice*, is a procedure that allows a defending party, as a *third-party plaintiff*, to join a person to an action who is or may be liable to the *defending party* for all or part of the claim asserted against the defending party. Impleader is initiated by serving a *third-party complaint* upon the impleaded party, known as a *third-party defendant*. Because the third-party defendant is a new party being involuntarily joined to action, all of the normal rules and requirements for acquiring personal jurisdiction over a defendant fully apply. The requirements of personal jurisdiction are examined in Chapter 2.

Impleader is an extremely useful device for a defendant. Not only does impleader save the defendant the time and expense of filing a separate action against the third-party defendant, but most importantly impleader eliminates the risk that the defendant will be faced with inconsistent judgments. For example, suppose *P* is injured in a car accident following a rupture in the brake system of *P's* car. *P* sues *D*, the car manufacturer, on a products liability claim alleging that the brakes were defectively made. After a full trial, the court finds that the brakes were defective and awards $1 million to *P*. Assume that *D* purchases all of its brakes from *T*, a brake manufacturer, and now wishes to sue *T* on a claim for indemnification to reimburse *D* on the $1 million judgment. Because *T* was not a party to the first action, however, *T* is not bound by the judgment or its finding that the brakes in question were defective. In this new action of *D v. T*, the second court would be free to rule that the brakes manufactured by *T* were not defective and that *T*, therefore, owes no duty to indemnify *D* on the judgment. By using impleader in the first action to join *T* as a third-party defendant, *D* would have avoided this risk of inconsistent judgments. One court would have decided whether the brakes were defective, what amount *D* owed *P*, and what amount *T* owed *D* in indemnification and this *single* judgment would bind all of the affected parties.] Example

Historical Background: Impleader at Common Law and the Conformity Acts. At common law, the procedure known as *vouching to warranty* was the predecessor of modern impleader. In "vouching to warranty," a defendant who was sued for the recovery of land could "vouch in" a person who had given a warranty of title to the defendant. The person "vouched in" then had the opportunity to defend the action. If the person vouched in refused to defend, the defendant could sue the warrantor in a second action on the warranty. In that action, the judgment in the first proceeding would bind the warrantor, provided the defendant proved the attempt to vouch in the warrantor in the first suit, the terms of the warranty, and the judgment in the first suit. *See* 6 WRIGHT ET AL. § 1441, at 336; Note, *Developments in the Law—Multiparty Litigation in the Federal Courts*, 71 HARV. L. REV. 874, 907 (1957).

In the nineteenth century, the "vouching to warranty" practice was expanded in English law to permit a defendant to bring in a third party who was obligated to indemnify the defendant against the plaintiff's claim. Based in part on this expanded English practice, the American states developed their own forms of impleader. *See* 6 WRIGHT ET AL. § 1441, at 336. In the nineteenth century, federal courts recognized a right to impleader in admiralty cases. *See, e.g., The Hudson*, 15 F. 162 (S.D.N.Y. 1883). Further, under the Conformity Acts, the federal courts could employ impleader in actions at law when the state in which the federal court was sitting had adopted an impleader procedure. *See* 6 WRIGHT ET AL. § 1441, at 337.

Impleader Under the Federal Rules of Civil Procedure. Federal Rule 14 ("Third-Party Practice") provides for impleader today in actions brought in the U.S. District Courts. Rule 14 generally exemplifies modern impleader practice in both state and federal courts. Under Rule 14, the right to implead a nonparty as a third-party defendant is expressly limited to a claim by a defending party, as a third-party plaintiff, that the third-party defendant is or may be liable to the defending party for all or part of the claim against the defending party. The basis of the third-party claim may be indemnity, subrogation, contribution, express or implied warranty, or any other legal theory supporting derivative liability. *See* 6 WRIGHT ET AL. § 1446, at 415–21. Unlike a crossclaim under Rule 13(g), however, which need only be transactionally related to the plaintiff's claim or a counterclaim to properly qualify, a claim does not qualify as a Rule 14 impleader claim simply because it is transactionally related to the claim against the third-party plaintiff. An impleader claim under 14(a) must be based on some *substantive legal theory* that requires the third-party defendant to reimburse the third-party plaintiff for all or part of the claim against the third-party plaintiff.

For example, assume that *P, D,* and *T* are involved in a three-car accident. Assume that *D's* car hits *P's* car and that *T's* car hits *D's* car. *P* sues *D* for the damage *D* caused to *P's* car. Can *D* now implead *T* as a third-party defendant under Rule 14(a) to assert a claim for the damage *T* caused to *D's* car? No. Even though this claim arises out of the same accident that gives rise to *P's* claim against *D, D's* claim against *T* does not qualify as an impleader claim. *D* is only seeking to recover for damage to *D's* car and is not claiming that *T* is legally responsible to reimburse *D* for the damage *D* caused to *P's* car. If *P* had sued both *D* and *T* as co-defendants in this action, *D's* claim against *T* would have qualified as a crossclaim under Rule 13(g). If *T* had sued *D, D's* claim against *T* would have qualified as a compulsory counterclaim under Rule 13(a). But it does not qualify as an impleader claim under Rule 14(a).

Suppose, however, that *D* now claims that *T's* negligence was the cause of *D's* car hitting *P's* car. Now an impleader claim joining *T* would be proper. Do you see why? What about *D's* related claim for the damage that *T* caused to *D's* car? Once *D* properly asserts a Rule 14(a) impleader claim, *D* is now entitled to join this claim pursuant to Rule 18(a). The following case further examines the proper basis of a Rule 14(a) impleader claim.

Collini v. Wean United, Inc.

United States District Court, Western District of Pennsylvania, 1983
101 F.R.D. 408

DIAMOND, DISTRICT JUDGE.

Presently before this Court is the defendants' motion for leave to file a third-party complaint....

The present case is a suit by nine individuals under ERISA and the common law of Pennsylvania against two benefit plans and Wean United, Inc. ("Wean"), as sponsor and administrator, to secure plan benefits and cure alleged breaches of certain statutory and fiduciary duties. The plaintiffs allege that they qualified for permanent incapacity pensions and attendant insurance coverage, but that Wean, claiming that the plaintiffs were no longer permanently incapacitated, discontinued these benefits.

Civil Action No. 83-128 was consolidated with the present case for purposes of discovery and trial. It is a suit brought by the International and Local Unions to enforce an arbitration award by a medical arbitrator concerning the issue of the permanent incapacity of the nine individual plaintiffs of the present case.

The defendants seek to implead, under Rule 14 of the Federal Rules of Civil Procedure, the United Steelworkers of America, AFL-CIO-CLC, and the United Steelworkers of America, Local Union No. 1388, both plaintiffs in Civil Action No. 83-128. The defendants seek impleader on the grounds that the United Steelworkers, as exclusive bargaining agent of the plaintiffs, failed to pursue grievance and mandatory arbitration provisions of a collective bargaining agreement, and that such failure caused or exacerbated any harm or damage to the individual plaintiffs in the present action.

The plaintiffs oppose the motion to implead on two grounds. First, the third-party complaint is infirm under Rule 14 because it does not attempt to implead persons who are or may be liable to the defendant for all or part of the plaintiff's claim against him. Second, the third-party complaint fails to state a claim upon which relief can be granted because it fails to allege a bad faith motive on the part of the union. Because of the Court's findings on the first ground for objection, we do not and need not reach the merits of the second.

Rule 14 allows a third-party plaintiff to implead a party "who is or may be liable to him for all or part of the plaintiff's claim against him."[a] Rule 14 only provides the procedural device for impleader. There must be some substantive basis in law for the third-party's liability, and this liability must be in some way dependent on the outcome of the main claim or be in the nature of derivative or secondary liability to the defendant.... The plaintiffs argue that the asserted liability of the third-party defendants, the unions, is not dependent on the outcome of the main claim or in the nature of derivative or secondary liability to the third-party plaintiff....

....

The Court finds that there is no substantive basis in law which supports a motion to implead the unions. First, the Court finds that the impleader claim is not dependent upon the main claim. The main claim is based on ERISA and the common law of Pennsylvania while the liability of the unions is asserted under the National Labor Relations Act. Further, the Court does not believe that ERISA provides a right to contribution. The Court bases its opinion in part on ERISA's silence as to right of contribution, the fact that ERISA sets out a detailed remedial scheme which the Court should not lightly amend or supplement, and that it is uncontroverted by the parties that the legislative history of ERISA does not provide support for a right of contribution. Third, while the union owes a duty of fair representation to its members, ... and while the union is given a specific role in the Pension Plan's arbitration provisions concerning permanent incapacity, such a role does not make the union subject to impleader by the employer-trustee in the present suit.... As *Vaca v. Sipes*, 386 U.S. 171 (1967), and *Bowen v. United States Postal Service*, 459 U.S. 212 (1983) make clear, a union sued by an employee under § 301 of the National Labor Relations Act is liable to an employee for any harm that results from the breach of its duty of fair representation....

These decisions do not provide a basis for impleading a union when an employer has reason to believe that the union has caused or exacerbated the harm. To allow impleader under such circumstances would be to allow a defendant to implead one who is directly (and possibly solely) liable to the plaintiff. This has not been permitted since Rule 14 was amended in 1946....

Rule 14 must be liable to Δ for ...π's claim against Δ

....

Therefore, because the defendants have not provided a basis in law which supports their motion to implead a third-party, their motion for leave to file a third-party complaint will be denied.

Notes and Questions

1. In *Temple v. Synthes, Ltd.*, reproduced in section H, below, the U.S. Supreme Court observed that the defendant had not attempted to implead a third-party defendant who was a joint tortfeasor with the defendant. Do you understand why impleader would be appropriate in the case of joint tortfeasors, but not in *Collini*?

2. Rule 14 permits the construction of a rather complicated lawsuit. After a third-party defendant has been impleaded, Rule 14(a)(2)(A) and (B) require the third-party defendant to assert any defense against the third-party plaintiff's claim and assert any com-

---

a. [Eds. Note. Restyled Rule 14(a)(1) now reads in relevant part: "A defending party may, as third-party plaintiff, serve a summons and complaint on a nonparty who is or may be liable to it for all or part of the claim against it."]

pulsory counterclaim against the third-party plaintiff under Rule 13(a). Under Rule 14(a)(2)(B), the third-party defendant may also assert any permissive counterclaim against the third-party plaintiff under Rule 13(b) and may assert any crossclaim against another third-party defendant under Rule 13(g). In addition, under Rule 14(a)(2)(C), the third-party defendant may assert any defense that the third-party plaintiff has against the plaintiff's claim.

Under Rule 14(a)(2)(D), the third-party defendant may also assert against the plaintiff "any claim arising out of the same transaction or occurrence that is the subject matter of the plaintiff's claim against the third-party plaintiff." Rule 14(a)(3) also allows the plaintiff to assert against the third-party defendant "any claim arising out of the transaction or occurrence that is the subject matter of the plaintiff's claim against the third-party plaintiff." In this latter event, the third-party defendant must assert any defense against the plaintiff's claim under Rule 12 and any counterclaim under Rule 13(a) and may assert any counterclaim under Rule 13(b) or crossclaim under Rule 13(g). As provided in Rule 14(a)(5), third-party defendants may also implead other persons who are liable to the third-party defendant for all or part of any claim asserted against the third-party defendant.

3. Rule 14 does not describe the names of the documents in which all of the claims described in the preceding note may be asserted. It is left to the pleader to deduce the labels from Rule 7(a), which describes the pleadings allowed by the Federal Rules. Some of the documents are clear. For example, the third-party defendant's defenses to the third-party plaintiff's claim should be asserted in "an answer to a third-party complaint." What a pleader decides to call the document will depend, in part, on the order in which the pleadings are served and what seems to be the most reasonable option available. *Cf. Thomas v. Barton Lodge II, Ltd.*, 174 F.3d 636 (5th Cir. 1999) (permitting a third-party defendant to assert a "crossclaim" against an original defendant even if it would be technically inappropriate to classify the third-party defendant and the original defendant as "coparties").

4. Under Rule 14(b), when a counterclaim is asserted against a plaintiff, the plaintiff is entitled to join a third-party defendant under Rule 14(a) to the same extent that a defendant would be allowed to do so. Thus, if *P* sued *D*, and *D*'s answer contained a counterclaim against *P*, *P*, as a "defending party" on the counterclaim, may implead a nonparty, *T*, under Rule 14(a)(1) and (b), and assert a third-party claim against *T* alleging that *T* is or may be liable to *P* for all or part of *P*'s liability to *D*.

5. Although third-party claims are typically asserted by the defendant in response to the plaintiff's claim against the defendant, Rule 14(a) authorizes any defending party to file a third-party claim, irrespective of whether the party is defending a counterclaim, crossclaim, or other claim. As part of the 2007 restyling of Rule 14(a), the ending phrase of the first sentence of the rule was accordingly restyled to read that a defending party may serve a third-party claim on a nonparty who is or may be liable to it "for all or part of the *claim* against it." The former rule used the phrase "for all or part of the *plaintiff's claim* against the third-party plaintiff." Do you think in restyling Rule 14(a)(1) as they did, the rulemakers should have similarly restyled the language of Rule 14(a)(2)(C) & (D) and (3) to more clearly cover third-party claims that are triggered by claims other than the plaintiff's claim against the defendant?

For example, assume *P* sues *D-1* and *D-2* and *D-1* asserts a crossclaim under Rule 13(g) against *D-2*. Under Rule 14(a)(1), *D-2*, as a defending party on the crossclaim, could join a nonparty, *T*, as a third-party defendant alleging that *T* is or may be liable to *D-2* for all or part of *D-2*'s liability to *D-1*. Under the language of Rule 14(a)(2)(C) and

(D), however, the third-party defendant, *T,* is only expressly permitted to assert defenses and counterclaims against *P* and not against *D-1.* But in this situation, it is not *P's* claim against *D-2* that has triggered *D-2's* third-party claim against *T,* but rather *D-1's* claim. The language of Rule 14(a)(3) is similarly drafted from the perspective of a third-party claim triggered by the plaintiff's claim against the defendant. Thus, in the above example, Rule 14(a)(3) would only expressly allow *P,* not *D-1,* to assert claims against *T.* How do you think these provisions could have been restyled to more clearly accommodate these other situations of third-party claims?

Problems

Problem 7-14. P, D, and *T* are involved in a three-car collision. *P* is injured in the accident and sues *D* for $200,000. *P* alleges that *D's* negligence caused the accident. *D* impleads *T,* alleging that *T's* negligence also contributed to the accident and that *T* is obligated to pay *D* one-half of any amount *P* may recover from *D.* Is Rule 14 impleader proper under such circumstances? What do you need to know in order to answer this question?

Problem 7-15. P, D-1, and *D-2* are involved in a three-car automobile accident and *P* is injured. *P* sues *D-1* and *D-2,* alleging that both defendants were negligent and that their negligence jointly caused *P's* injuries. Under the substantive law applicable to *P's* claim, if both defendants were negligent and caused *P's* injuries, *P* may recover his entire damages against either or both of them at *P's* option. If *P* obtains judgment against both defendants, *P* may execute the judgment against whichever one *P* chooses. However, if *P* executes the judgment against only one of them, the defendant who pays has a right to obtain contribution from the other defendant. Assume that *D-1* wishes to assert this right of contribution against *D-2* in *P's* action. What is the proper procedure for *D-1* to use in asserting the right to contribution?

Problem 7-16. P and *T* are involved in a two-car automobile accident. Both parties are injured and both cars are damaged. When the accident occurred, *T,* who is *D's* employee, was driving a car owned by *D* and conducting business for *D.* Under the applicable substantive law, if *T's* negligence caused the accident, *T* is liable to *P* for *P's* personal injuries and property damage, and *D* is also liable to *P.* However, this is true only if *P* was free of contributory negligence. Likewise, if *P's* negligence caused the accident, *P* is liable to *D* for the property damage to *D's* automobile and also is liable to *T* for *T's* personal injuries. This is only true, however, if *T* was free of contributory negligence; if *T* was guilty of contributory negligence, *P* would not be liable to either *D* or *T.* If *D* must pay *P* because of *T's* negligence, *D* is entitled to be indemnified by *T.* Also, if *T's* negligence caused the accident, *D* is entitled to be paid by *T* for the damage to *D's* automobile, even if *P* is also liable to *D* because of *P's* negligence.

(a) If *P* sues *D* in federal court and *D* wishes to assert all defenses and claims that *D* has against everyone involved in the accident, what defenses and claims should *D* assert and what procedure should *D* use to assert the defenses and claims? Which of the defenses and claims are permissive and which are compulsory under the Federal Rules? If *D* possesses a claim for breach of contract against *T* that is factually unrelated to the accident, would any Federal Rule allow *D* to assert that claim against *T* in the action?

(b) Assume that *P* sues *D* in federal court and *D* impleads *T* in the action. Assume further that *T* wishes to assert all defenses and claims that *T* possesses against everyone involved in the case. What defenses and claims should *T* assert and what procedure should *T* use to assert them? Which of *T's* defenses and claims are permissive and which are compulsory under the Federal Rules? If *T* possesses a breach of contract claim against *D* that is factually unrelated to the accident, may *T* assert the claim against *D* in the action? If so, under which Federal Rule? If *T* possesses a breach of contract claim against *P* that is factually unrelated to the accident, may *T* assert that claim against *P* in the action? If so, which Federal Rule authorizes *T* to assert the breach of contract claim?

(c) Assume that *P* sues *D* in federal court and *D* impleads *T* in the action. *P* wants to assert all defenses and claims that *P* possesses against everyone in the action. What defenses and claims should *P* assert, and what procedures should *P* use to assert them? Which of *P*'s defenses and claims are permissive and which are compulsory under the Federal Rules? In answering this last question, does it matter what defenses and claims have been asserted already by *D* and *T* against *P*, by the time *P* acts to assert *P*'s own defenses and claims? If *P* possesses a breach of contract claim against *T* that is factually unrelated to the accident, may *P* assert it against *T* in the action? If so, under what circumstances?

Section G. Interpleader

Interpleader is a procedure that allows a party in possession of money or other property to bring all the adverse claimants to the property before the court to resolve their claims in a single proceeding. The purpose of interpleader is to eliminate the danger of double liability that would exist if the party in possession of the money or property (called the "stakeholder") were to be sued in separate actions by the claimants.

Interpleader at Common Law. The common-law courts recognized interpleader in certain kinds of cases. However, interpleader shifted from the common-law courts to equity over a period of time, and the remedy came to be viewed as exclusively equitable. The reason for the shift may have been the fact that juries in common-law cases required a narrow issue, which made them unsuitable for more complicated proceedings, such as interpleader. *See* Zechariah Chafee, Jr., *Modernizing Interpleader*, 30 YALE L.J. 814, 822 (1921). The shift may also have been due to the fact that interpleader at common law was only available to defendants, whereas equity allowed plaintiffs beset by multiple claimants to seek interpleader. *See* Ralph V. Rogers, *Historical Origins of Interpleader*, 51 YALE L.J. 924, 947–50 (1942).

Interpleader in Equity. Even in equity, strict technical requirements circumscribed interpleader and limited its usefulness. Professor Pomeroy summarized these requirements:

1. The same thing, debt, or duty must be claimed by both or all the parties against whom the relief is demanded;

2. All their adverse titles or claims must be dependent, or be derived from a common source;

3. The person asking the relief—the plaintiff—must not have nor claim any interest in the subject matter;

4. [The person seeking relief] must have incurred no independent liability to either of the claimants; that is, [that person] must stand perfectly indifferent between them, in the position merely of a stakeholder.

4 JOHN N. POMEROY, A TREATISE ON EQUITY JURISPRUDENCE § 1322, at 906 (5th ed. 1941).

The restrictions summarized by Professor Pomeroy applied only to a "strict" bill of interpleader. There was also something known as a bill "in the nature of interpleader," which could be used by a stakeholder who could show an independent basis of equitable jurisdiction other than the need for interpleader. If such a basis could be shown, the requirements of the strict bill of interpleader were not rigidly enforced. However, it was not entirely clear which requirements would be enforced. Thus, substantial confusion existed about the differences between a strict bill and a bill in the nature of interpleader. Some commentators, however, suggested that there was no real difference except as to whether the restrictions of the strict bill would be applied or not. *See* Geoffrey C. Hazard, Jr. & Myron Moskovitz, *An Historical and Critical Analysis of Interpleader*, 52 Cal. L. Rev. 706, 745–49 (1964).

Interpleader Under the Codes. The Field Code, as amended in 1851, provided for interpleader, but, strangely, limited it to defendants only, as at common law. *See* Act of July 10, 1851, ch. 479, § 122, 1851 N.Y. Laws 876, 883. Nevertheless, some states still retain the Field Code provision more or less in its original form, while others have modernized interpleader. Some states still adhere to the traditional interpleader requirements described by Pomeroy.

Development of Federal Statutory Interpleader. In *New York Life Insurance Co. v. Dunlevy*, 241 U.S. 518 (1916), which is discussed in Chapter 2, the Supreme Court held that interpleader proceedings were "in personam" in nature and required personal service of process on the adverse claimants within the state for personal jurisdiction to be validly acquired. After *Dunlevy*, the presence of the property alone would not provide the basis for jurisdiction in an interpleader proceeding brought to settle the adverse claims. When the claimants were citizens of different states and the stakeholder could be sued in the claimants' home states, which was the case with many insurance company defendants, separate actions could be maintained against the stakeholder. This possibility gave rise to the double liability problem that interpleader was designed to solve. In response, Congress enacted interpleader statutes in 1917, 1925, 1926, and 1936. *See* 7 Wright et al. § 1701, at 527–33.

The modern versions of the interpleader statutes are codified in 28 U.S.C. §§ 1335, 1397, and 2361. Section 1335 grants subject-matter jurisdiction to the federal courts when (1) there are two or more adverse claimants of diverse citizenship and (2) an amount in controversy of at least $500. The stakeholder's citizenship is, therefore, irrelevant under § 1335, at least if the stakeholder is not also asserting a claim to the fund. Under § 1397, venue is proper in a judicial district "in which one or more of the claimants reside." Finally, § 2361 grants nationwide long-arm jurisdiction permitting service upon the claimants within any U.S. judicial district.

The Supreme Court sustained the constitutionality of the minimal diversity-of-citizenship requirement of § 1335 in *State Farm Fire & Casualty Co. v. Tashire*, 386 U.S. 523, 530–31 (1967). Actions under the interpleader statute are governed by the *Erie* doctrine like other diversity actions, which means that state substantive law will ordinarily be applied in an interpleader action. *See Griffin v. McCoach*, 313 U.S. 498, 503–04 (1941).

Federal Rule Interpleader. In addition to the special federal "statutory" interpleader, the federal courts also recognize so-called "rule" interpleader under Federal Rule 22. In rule interpleader cases, subject-matter jurisdiction is based on statutes (other than § 1335) granting subject-matter jurisdiction to the federal courts in noninterpleader cases, such as 28 U.S.C. §§ 1331 (federal question) and 1332 (diversity of citizenship). Thus, in rule interpleader based on diversity of citizenship, the citizenship of the stakeholder must be diverse from the citizenship of all of the claimants. Likewise, venue in rule interpleader cases is based on the general venue statutes, such as 28 U.S.C. § 1391. Service of process and long-arm jurisdiction are controlled by Rule 4.

COMPARISION OF POTENTIAL DIFFERENCES BETWEEN "RULE" AND "STATUTORY" INTERPLEADER		
Potential Requirement	**Rule Interpleader**	**Statutory Interpleader**
Diversity of citizenship	Complete diversity required between all plaintiffs and defendants	Only minimal diversity required - two or more claimants of diverse citizenship required
Amount in controversy	More than $75,000	At least $500
Venue	Normal venue provisions of 28 U.S.C. § 1391 apply	In any judicial district where one or more of the claimants reside, 28 U.S.C. § 1397
Service of process	Must serve process pursuant to Rule 4 with normal personal jurisdiction requirements	Nationwide long-arm jurisdiction permitting service upon the claimants within any judicial district, 28 U.S.C. § 2361
Deposit of "stake" with the court	Not required (although the court can so order using its general equitable powers)	Must pay the stake into the registry of the court or post a bond to assure compliance with future court orders
Enjoining claimants	Court can only enjoin the parties over whom it is able to obtain personal jurisdiction in conventional ways; Anti-Injunction Act applies	Court can enjoin the claimants nationwide from commencing or maintaining ongoing actions in any state or federal court concerning the stake

[handwritten annotation: Example of Fed Long Arm Statute]

Figure 7-2

Additional Procedural Differences Between Statutory and Rule Interpleader. The procedures applicable to rule and statutory interpleader differ slightly in other ways. For example, § 1335(a)(2) explicitly requires that the stakeholder either pay the stake into the registry of the court or post a bond to assure compliance with the future orders of the court concerning the stake. There is no such requirement in Rule 22. However, the general equitable powers that the courts possess in interpleader allow them to accept a deposit or even to order the stakeholder to deposit the stake or post a bond.

In addition, 28 U.S.C. § 2361, which is applicable in statutory interpleader cases, permits the court to enjoin the claimants from commencing actions in any state or federal court concerning the property. This authority is important "[b]ecause the injunction power is tied to the nationwide service of process provision [of § 2361]." Thus, a federal court in § 1335 proceedings can stop inconsistent actions nationwide. *See* 7 WRIGHT ET AL. § 1717, at 658–59. However, this broad injunctive power is only available in statutory interpleader actions. In rule interpleader proceedings, the court can only enjoin the parties over whom it is able to obtain personal jurisdiction in conventional ways — *e.g.*, through application of state long-arm statutes under the authority of Rule 4. *See id.* at 660.

With regard to the injunctive power, note also that 28 U.S.C. § 2283, the federal Anti-Injunction Act, prohibits federal courts from enjoining ongoing state-court proceedings "unless expressly authorized by Act of Congress, or where necessary in aid of [their] jurisdiction, or to protect or effectuate [their] judgments." Section 2361 is an expressly authorized congressional exception to § 2283. However, it only applies in statutory, not rule, interpleader cases. *See* 7 WRIGHT ET AL. § 1717, at 660–62.

The differences between statutory and rule interpleader are summarized in Figure 7-2 on the next page. Obviously, the requirements of subject-matter jurisdiction, personal jurisdiction, and venue differ radically between statutory and rule interpleader cases.

These varying requirements may eliminate the possibility of using one or both of the procedures in any given case. The following notes, questions, and problems explore general issues about interpleader under § 1335, Rule 22, and state practice.

Notes and Questions

1. Interpleader is a two-stage process. In the first stage of interpleader, the stakeholder demonstrates that interpleader is proper because multiple claims against the stake pose the threat of double liability. Typically, the stakeholder also deposits the stake into the registry of the court in the first stage of interpleader or posts a bond to assure compliance with the court's future orders concerning the stake. After these steps are taken, the court will discharge the stakeholder in a "pure" interpleader action (*i.e.*, one in which the stakeholder does not make a claim to the stake). The action will then proceed to the second stage, in which the claimants will litigate their rights to the stake. In this second stage of interpleader, the action usually proceeds as in any other case under the procedural rules of the jurisdiction where the action is being conducted. Is interpleader ever proper if the stakeholder cannot demonstrate a danger of double liability, as where, *e.g.*, the stakeholder seeks to assure that a limited "pie" is fairly "sliced" for the claimants? *See Lawhorne v. Employers Ins. Co.*, 680 A.2d 518, 523–24 (Md. 1996) (pie-slicing-interpleader proper).

2. Interpleader can become more complicated than the simple description in the preceding note indicates. For example, suppose one of the claimants asserts a counterclaim against the stakeholder for independent liability. (As we will see below, a counterclaim is possible in federal proceedings as a result of the abolition of some or all of the requirements of the strict bill of interpleader described in the quotation from Professor Pomeroy in the text above.) Thus, if a counterclaim is allowed, the adjudication of the counterclaim may occur in the second stage of interpleader or be pushed to a third stage, after the relative rights of the claimants to the stake have been adjudicated.

3. Federal Rule 22 and 28 U.S.C. § 1335 appear to have abolished at least some of the requirements of the strict bill of interpleader. Examine the text of the rule and the statute carefully. Which of the requirements have been abolished and which ones may still exist under each provision?

4. Recall the discussion of the declaratory judgment remedy in Chapter 1. A declaratory judgment is appropriate in federal and most state courts whenever it will serve a useful purpose in resolving a dispute or controversy between adverse parties. Thus, the declaratory judgment procedure is a possible alternative to interpleader in some circumstances. The stakeholder faced with multiple liability can sue the claimants for a declaratory judgment to determine who is entitled to the stake. Declaratory judgments will rarely be useful as a substitute for interpleader in federal court because statutory and rule interpleader will usually cover all the situations that a declaratory judgment action will encompass. Even if a declaratory judgment is otherwise a viable substitute for federal interpleader, the federal courts will not be able to enjoin state actions brought by the claimants to recover the property that is the subject of the action. However, the procedure might be useful in states in which interpleader is unavailable to the stakeholder because of applicable restrictions on the procedure. For example, a stakeholder claiming an interest in the stake could sue for declaratory relief even though interpleader would be precluded because of the stakeholder's interest.

5. Sometimes, stakeholders will request a declaratory judgment of no liability and interpleader in the alternative. However, the remedy of declaratory judgment is discre-

tionary. If a declaratory judgment is requested from a federal court when there are pending state actions against the stakeholder, the district court can refuse to hear the declaratory judgment action if the controversy can be better settled in the state actions. *See, e.g.,* *Wilton v. Seven Falls Co.*, 515 U.S. 277, 282–83 (1995). The Supreme Court has expressly declined to answer the question whether a federal court might properly dismiss a declaratory judgment action in the absence of a parallel state-court proceeding. *Id.* at 290.

6. How should the principles in the preceding note be applied in interpleader situations where a declaratory judgment action is being used as a substitute for interpleader? If a stakeholder is threatened with double liability by state-court actions brought by the claimants, will the pendency of the state suits require a federal district court to dismiss a federal declaratory judgment action to adjudicate the stakeholder's liability to all claimants? If a declaratory judgment action is brought to determine that the stakeholder has no liability and interpleader is requested in the alternative under the interpleader statute, do you think the district court should abstain from giving both declaratory and interpleader relief?

7. Required party joinder rules, such as Federal Rule 19, might also be useful to a stakeholder threatened with double liability who is sued by one of the claimants and cannot, because of jurisdictional restrictions or otherwise, join the other claimant in the action. Rule 19 is examined in the following section.

Problems

Problem 7-17. Consider Professor Pomeroy's statement of the requirements for the strict bill of interpleader reproduced in the text above. Would any of the following actions qualify under the requirements? If so, explain why. If not, explain why not.

(a) *S*, a student, has been eating at a college boarding house. *S* made no express agreement with anyone, but expected to pay the standard rates. A quarrel breaks out between *C-1*, the cook in the boarding house, and *C-2*, the cook's spouse, as to who owns the house. As a result, *C-1* and *C-2* each claim that *S* should pay them the money due for the meals *S* has eaten, *C-1* claiming the amount due is $75.00 and *C-2* claiming the amount due is $100.00.

(b) *S* is in possession of land. *C-1* claims title to the land under a deed, and asserts that *S* owes *C-1* $1,000 as the value of *S's* use and occupation of the land. *C-2* claims title to the same land by adverse possession and also asserts that *S* owes *C-2* $1,000 as the value of *S's* use and occupation of the land.

(c) *S Insurance Co.* issued a policy of automobile insurance to *A*. Subsequently, *A* is involved in an automobile accident with *C-1* and *C-2*, both of whom are injured in the accident. *C-1* and *C-2* each claim the $100,000 face amount of the policy. *A's* negligence is conceded by everyone, but *S* argues that it owes nothing under the policy because the policy terms did not cover the accident. *S* claims in the alternative that even if it is liable on the policy, *C-1* and *C-2* ought to be forced to interplead because their claims exceed the total amount of its liability under the policy.

(d) *S* issued a fire insurance policy to *A*, covering *A's* property. Subsequently, a fire destroyed the insured property. *C-1 Loan Co.*, a mortgagee of the property, claimed that *S* should pay the proceeds of the policy over to *C-1* and instituted a suit against *S* to recover the proceeds. *S* settled the suit with *C-1* and agreed to pay the proceeds of the policy to *C-1*, provided *C-1's* action against *S* is dismissed on the merits, which was done. *C-2 Loan Co.*, a creditor of *A's*, then claimed the proceeds of the policy as the result of a bankruptcy proceeding involving *A* prior to *S's* settlement with *C-1*. *S*, which had not yet paid over the proceeds of the policy to *C-1*, seeks to interplead *C-1* and *C-2* to determine who is entitled to the proceeds. *C-1* claims that even if *C-2* is entitled to the proceeds because it has priority under the bankruptcy proceedings, *S* is liable to *C-1* for the same amount under the settlement agreement.

Problem 7-18. *S* is in possession of property claimed by *C-1* and *C-2*. *S* also claims ownership of the property. All the parties are citizens of the same state and their claims to the property are all based on state law. *S* would like to interplead *C-1* and *C-2*. However, *S* cannot do so because (1) the state in which all of the parties live follows the traditional restrictions on interpleader and (2) *S* is not a disinterested stakeholder. Is there any procedure other than interpleader that *S* can use to avoid the threat of double liability? Assume that *C-1* sues *S* to recover the property. Outline the possible steps that *S* may be able to take to protect against the threat of double liability in the state action.

Section H. Required Joinder of Parties

Although plaintiffs are given the right under Rule 20(a) to join additional parties to the action, this right of joinder under Rule 20(a) is entirely permissive with the plaintiff. Sometimes plaintiffs fail to join certain persons in an action who nevertheless should be joined because they bear some special relationship to the case. When the nonjoinder of the absent person will prevent the court from granting complete relief to the existing parties or will prejudice the interests of the absent person or the existing parties, the plaintiff is required to join the absent person to the action. Traditionally, such persons were called *necessary* parties. Under restyled Rule 19, these persons are now called *required* parties. This change in labelling is purely stylistic and effects no substantive change in the proper application and interpretation of Rule 19's joinder standards.

If joinder of such a person is impossible because of jurisdictional or other restrictions, some attempt must be made to avoid the prejudice that the person's nonjoinder will cause. If the prejudice can be avoided, the action may continue without joinder of the absent person. If the harm cannot be avoided, the action must be dismissed for refiling in a court where all required persons may be properly joined. In this situation, the absent person was traditionally called an *indispensable* party. Restyled Rule 19(b) no longer uses the label *indispensable* to describe such a person and simply provides that the action should be dismissed.

Common-Law Joinder Practice. At common law, all persons who had joint interests had to be joined in a civil action, while persons who had separate interests had to sue separately. However, if a person who held a joint interest with another refused to join in a common-law action as a plaintiff, nothing could be done about the refusal, and the action would fail. If a plaintiff wanted to sue multiple parties who possessed a joint interest, the plaintiff would simply join them as defendants. Of course, if all the defendants could not be joined (such as when the court could not obtain personal jurisdiction over them), the action would, again, fail. *See* TEPLY & WHITTEN at 731.

Joinder Practice in Equity. Equity possessed more flexible rules of joinder than the common-law courts. However, equitable practice evolved in an unfortunate way that was carried over into American law and made mandatory party joinder more rigid than it needed to be. Until about 1780, equity followed the rule that all persons interested in a controversy should be made parties unless joinder was impossible or inconvenient. *See* Geoffrey C. Hazard, Jr., *Indispensable Party: The Historical Origin of a Procedural Phantom*, 61 COLUM. L. REV. 1254, 1256–71 (1961). This early joinder practice was based on two fundamental ideas: "that a court cannot adjudge the rights of an absent person, and that a court should avoid inconclusive determinations." John W. Reed, *Compulsory Joinder of Parties in Civil Actions*, 55 MICH. L. REV. 327, 332 (1957). If a party whose interests were aligned with those of the plaintiff refused to join with the plaintiff in the action, equity provided for the party to be joined as a defendant. *See* TEPLY & WHITTEN at 733.

After about 1780, equity began to develop the notion that if a party interested in the controversy could not be joined, the action would have to be dismissed, because courts "should do 'complete' justice or none at all." Geoffrey C. Hazard, Jr., *Indispensable Party: The Historical Origin of a Procedural Phantom*, 61 COLUM. L. REV. 1254, 1271 (1961). This led to the traditional distinction in the law between "necessary" and "indispensable" parties. Necessary parties were those who had such an interest in the controversy that they should be joined if possible. If a necessary party could not be joined, as where the party was not subject to personal jurisdiction, the party's presence in the action could be dispensed with, and the court could proceed to judgment against those who were parties. Indispensable parties were those who possessed such an interest in the controversy that the action could not continue without them and would have to be dismissed if they could not be joined. *See id.* at 1254.

It was the development of the indispensable party concept in equity that proved troublesome. The courts sometimes applied the concept of indispensability to deprive the plaintiff of a remedy against defendants who were joined in an action, on the theory that persons who were not joined would be prejudiced by the judgment. However, the courts reached this result without examining whether the absent parties would really be prejudiced in any meaningful way. *See id.* at 1287–89. As a result, the equitable practice was unnecessarily inflexible.

Code Joinder Practice. The New York Field Code of 1848 adopted the equity approach to joinder of parties. Section 98 provided that "[a]ny person may be made a party defendant, who has an interest in the controversy, adverse to the plaintiff." Act of Apr. 12, 1848, ch. 379, §98, 1848 N.Y. Laws 497, 516. Section 99 added that persons who were "united in interest must be joined as plaintiffs or defendants; but if the consent of any one, who should have been joined as plaintiff, cannot be obtained, [that person] may be made a defendant." *Id.* §99, 1848 N.Y. Laws 497, 516. Finally, §102 provided that "[w]hen a complete determination of the controversy cannot be had without the presence of other parties, the court may order them to be brought in, by an amendment of the complaint, or by a supplemental complaint, and a new summons." *Id.* §102, 1848 N.Y. Laws 497, 516. Unfortunately, the decisions in the code states relied on prior equity cases, with the result that the rigidity of the indispensability doctrine (as it had developed after 1780) was carried over into the codes.

Early Joinder Practice in Federal Court: The *Shields* Case. Before the Federal Rules of Civil Procedure, the federal courts followed the equity practice described above. The U.S. Supreme Court's decision in *Shields v. Barrow*, 58 U.S. (17 How.) 130 (1855), typifies early practice. In *Shields*, Barrow had sold plantations located in Louisiana to Shields. Both Barrow and Shields were citizens of Louisiana. The price of the plantations was to be paid in installments evidenced by notes, each of which was endorsed by six persons, two of whom were citizens of Mississippi and four of whom were citizens of Louisiana. After payment of $107,000 in installments, Shields defaulted. Subsequently, the parties entered into a compromise in which Shields and the six endorsers agreed to return the plan-

RULE 19(a) "CATEGORIES" OF "REQUIRED" PARTIES TO BE JOINDED IN AN ACTION IF FEASIBLE	
Rule 19(a)(1)(A)	In the person's absence, **complete relief cannot be accorded** among those who are already parties **or**
Rule 19(a)(1)(B)(i)	The person claims an interest relating to the subject of the action and is so situated that disposing of the action in the person's absence may as a practical matter **impair or impede the person's ability to protect** the interest **or**
Rule 19(a)(1)(B)(ii)	The person claims an interest relating to the subject of the action and is so situated that disposing of the action in the person's absence may leave an existing party subject to a **substantial risk of incurring double, multiple, or otherwise inconsistent obligations** because of the interest

Figure 7-3

tations to Barrow. The endorsers executed new notes in varying amounts to Barrow totaling $32,000, and Barrow retained the $107,000 already paid. In return, Barrow released Shields and the endorsers from their prior liabilities and discontinued state-court litigation commenced against them.

Later, Barrow brought a federal diversity action against the two Mississippi endorsers seeking to rescind this compromise on the ground that he had been persuaded to enter into the compromise by fraud. The U.S. Supreme Court ultimately held that Shields and the four Louisiana endorsers were indispensable parties who had to be joined in the action. The Court was influenced by the fact that if only some of the parties to the compromise were before the court, a decree of rescission would either destroy the rights of the absentees or leave the contract in full force with respect to them, but set aside as to the parties before the court.

Joinder Practice Under Rule 19 of the Federal Rules of Civil Procedure. Probably due to some unfortunate language and analysis in the Supreme Court's decision in *Shields*, the federal courts were plagued with the rigidity of the indispensable party doctrine described above. *See* John W. Reed, *Compulsory Joinder of Parties in Civil Actions*, 55 MICH. L. REV. 327, 340–46 (1957). Original Rule 19, which was derived from the Federal Equity Rules of 1912, was phrased in terms that did not alleviate the inflexibility that attended some of the decisions under the prior joinder practice. *See* 7 WRIGHT ET AL. § 1601, at 7, 9–11. The 1966 amendments to Rule 19 were expressly designed to address the inadequacies of the original rule's terminology and the unilluminating reasoning that sometimes characterized the decisions under the former practice. The 2007 restyling amendments continue that evolution by discarding the traditional term "indispensable" from the language of Rule 19(b).

As amended in 1966, Rule 19 first requires an examination whether an absent person should be joined in the action, if feasible. The various categories of such parties have come to be identified by the subdivisions of the Rule 19(a). Those categories are summarized in Figure 7-3. If such a person cannot be made a party, Rule 19(b) then directs the court to consider whether "in equity and good conscience" the action should proceed among the parties before it or whether the action should be dismissed. Rule 19(b) sets out four factors that should be considered by the court in making this determination. Those factors are summarized in Figure 7-4.

The *Provident Tradesmens* Case. An excellent illustration of how the amended Rule 19 is designed to work is provided in *Provident Tradesmens Bank & Trust Co. v. Patterson*, 390 U.S. 102 (1968). In this case, several tort plaintiffs sought a declaratory judgment action

	THE (NON-EXCLUSIVE) FACTORS LISTED IN RULE 19(b) IN DETERMINING WHETHER THE ACTION SHOULD PROCEED WITHOUT JOINDER OF A RULE 19(a) REQUIRED PARTY OR SHOULD BE DISMISSED
First	The extent to which a judgment rendered in the person's absence might prejudice that person or the existing parties
Second	The extent to which any prejudice could be lessened or avoided by (A) protective provisions in the judgment, (B) shaping the relief, or (C) other measures
Third	Whether a judgment rendered in the person's absence would be adequate
Fourth	Whether the plaintiff would have an adequate remedy if the action were dismissed for nonjoinder

Figure 7-4

in a U.S. District Court in Pennsylvania against an insurance company and the estate of a deceased driver to the effect that the insurance company was obligated to defend and indemnify the estate because the driver was driving the automobile with the owner's permission. The Third Circuit Court of Appeals had held that the action should have been dismissed because the owner of the automobile was an indispensable party to the action who could not be joined without destroying diversity of citizenship. The Supreme Court reversed the Third Circuit on the ground that the analysis employed by the Third Circuit under Rule 19 was faulty.

The Court assumed that the owner of the automobile (Dutcher) was a Rule 19(a) party because he might have judgments against him and want to preserve the insurance fund represented by the insurance policy. At the trial level, he could not have been made a party because he would have destroyed diversity. However the Court said that the case must be evaluated as it stood on appeal, and that it must ask what the effect was of the failure of anyone to raise the Rule 19 objection at the trial level, and also what effect should be given to the fact that by the time of the appeal, a judgment binding on the parties present in the action had been reached after extensive litigation, even though that judgment would not be binding on the owner.

In answering these questions, the Court took into account several interests:

(1) the plaintiffs' interests in a forum, which varies in strength. It is strong at the trial level if no alternative forum exists; however, at the appellate level, if the plaintiffs have won, they have a strong additional interest in preserving their judgment; the Court reasoned that while it was impossible now to tell whether the plaintiffs would have had an adequate forum if the action had been dismissed at the trial level, now that they had won a judgment, the opposing interests must be stronger to overturn the judgment;

(2) the defendant's interests in avoiding multiple litigation or inconsistent judgments, or sole responsibility for liability he shared with another; this interest is waivable if the Rule 19 objection is not raised at trial; in *Provident Tradesmens*, the defendants were foreclosed by the failure to raise the objection about the owner's absence; in addition, the insurance company would have a full opportunity to litigate each claim on the fund by the claimants;

(3) the interest of the outsider (the owner, Dutcher) in avoiding practical adverse impacts that the judgment might have on him; this interest is not waivable, but it must be evaluated when raised for the first time on appeal on the basis of whether the judgment actually rendered affects any interests of the outsider; in *Provident Tradesmens*, the court of appeals erred in holding that the owner had a substantive right to be joined because he was adverse to the estates on the issue of the Dead Man's Statute; the

owner was not harmed by the judgment rendered because (a) if he was bound by the judgment because he had failed to intervene (which the Court did not decide), his interest would be foreclosed by his own inaction, and (b) if he was not bound, he had not been harmed; furthermore, his only interest was in preserving the fund, which may have disappeared by the time litigation against him has been concluded; however, the state actions against him had laid dormant for years, there appeared to be no chance of recovery against him under Pennsylvania vicarious liability law, and he could, if necessary, defend each action on the basis of lack of permission of the driver; in addition, the district court could have required payment to be withheld on the judgment against the driver (Cionci) until the litigation against the owner was complete, and the tort plaintiffs said they would limit all claims to the amount of the policy; and

(4) the interests of the courts and the public in complete, efficient, and consistent settlement of controversies—*i.e.,* whether a judgment rendered in the absence of a Rule 19 party will be adequate; after trial, this must be evaluated in light of the fact that there has been the expense of a trial; at the trial level, it might have been preferable to dismiss if there existed an alternative forum, but even this is doubtful because it depended on the likelihood of judgments against the owner and the amount of the fund, which the district court did not know; by the time of the appeal, this interest had disappeared.

The following materials continue to explore the practice under Rule 19 and its state equivalents. In examining the cases, you should ask yourself whether the existing version of Rule 19 has solved all of the problems it was designed to address.

Temple v. Synthes, Ltd.
United States Supreme Court, 1990
498 U.S. 5, 111 S. Ct. 315, 112 L. Ed. 2d 263

PER CURIAM.

Petitioner Temple, a Mississippi resident, underwent surgery in October 1986 in which a "plate and screw device" was implanted in his lower spine. The device was manufactured by respondent Synthes, Ltd. (U.S.A.) (Synthes), a Pennsylvania corporation. Dr. S. Henry LaRocca performed the surgery at St. Charles General Hospital in New Orleans, Louisiana. Following surgery, the device's screws broke off inside Temple's back.

Temple filed suit against Synthes in the United States District Court for the Eastern District of Louisiana. The suit, which rested on diversity jurisdiction, alleged defective design and manufacture of the device. At the same time, Temple filed a state administrative proceeding against Dr. LaRocca and the hospital for malpractice and negligence. At the conclusion of the administrative proceeding, Temple filed suit against the doctor and the hospital in Louisiana state court.

Synthes did not attempt to bring the doctor and the hospital into the federal action by means of a third-party complaint, as provided in Federal Rule of Civil Procedure 14(a). Instead, Synthes filed a motion to dismiss Temple's federal suit for failure to join necessary parties pursuant to Federal Rule of Civil Procedure 19. Following a hearing, the District Court ordered Temple to join the doctor and the hospital as defendants within twenty days or risk dismissal of the lawsuit. According to the court, the most significant reason for requiring joinder was the interest of judicial economy.... The court relied on this Court's decision in *Provident Tradesmens Bank & Trust Co. v. Patterson*..., wherein we recognized that one focus of Rule 19 is "the interest of the courts and the public in complete, consistent, and efficient settlement of controversies." . . . When Temple failed to join the doctor and the hospital, the court dismissed the suit with prejudice.

Temple appealed, and the United States Court of Appeals for the Fifth Circuit affirmed. . . . The court deemed it "obviously prejudicial to the defendants to have the separate litigations being carried on," because Synthes' defense might be that the plate was not defective but that the doctor and the hospital were negligent, while the doctor and hospital, on the other hand, might claim that they were not negligent but that the plate was defective. . . . The Court of Appeals found that the claims overlapped and that the District Court therefore had not abused its discretion in ordering joinder under Rule 19. A petition for rehearing was denied.

In his petition for certiorari to this Court, Temple contends that it was error to label joint tortfeasors as indispensable parties under Rule 19(b) and to dismiss the lawsuit with prejudice for failure to join those parties. We agree. Synthes does not deny that it, the doctor, and the hospital are potential joint tortfeasors. It has long been the rule that it is not necessary for all joint tortfeasors to be named as defendants in a single lawsuit. . . . Nothing in the 1966 revision of Rule 19 changed that principle. . . . The Advisory Committee's Note to Rule 19(a) explicitly state[s] that "a tortfeasor with the usual 'joint-and-several' liability is merely a permissive party to an action against another with like liability" . . . There is nothing in Louisiana tort law to the contrary. . . .

The opinion in *Provident Bank* does speak of the public interest in limiting multiple litigation, but that case is not controlling here. There, the estate of a tort victim brought a declaratory judgment action against an insurance company. We assumed that the policyholder was a person "who, under § (a), should be joined if 'feasible'" . . . and went on to discuss the appropriate analysis under Rule 19(b), because the policyholder could not be joined without destroying diversity. . . . After examining the factors set forth in Rule 19(b), we determined that the action could proceed without the policyholder; he therefore was not an indispensable party whose absence required dismissal of the suit. . . .

Here, no inquiry under Rule 19(b) is necessary, because the threshold requirements of Rule 19(a) have not been satisfied. As potential joint tortfeasors with Synthes, Dr. LaRocca and the hospital were merely permissive parties. The Court of Appeals erred by failing to hold that the District Court abused its discretion in ordering them joined as defendants and in dismissing the action when Temple failed to comply with the court's order. For these reasons, we grant the petition for certiorari, reverse the judgment of the Court of Appeals for the Fifth Circuit, and remand for further proceedings consistent with this opinion.

It is so ordered.

Notes and Questions

1. Even if, contrary to *Temple*, joint tortfeasors should be considered Rule 19(a) parties, is there any basis for considering them persons whose nonjoinder would require dismissal of the action under Rule 19(b)? Can you think of a way in which the defendant's dilemma in *Temple* can be solved without forcing the *plaintiff* to join the absent joint tortfeasor? In this regard, consider the Court's discussion of Rule 14 in *Temple*.

2. The Court in *Temple* held that joint tortfeasors do not fit within any of the categories of Rule 19(a). However, the Court did not analyze each of the categories separately to see if they fit the circumstances of a joint tortfeasor. Instead, it merely cited a statement from the Advisory Committee's note to the 1966 amendments to the rule. The Advisory Com-

mittee's statement itself was conclusory. Nevertheless, the result in *Temple* is in accord with the overwhelming weight of authority. *See* 7 WRIGHT ET AL. § 1623 (citing authorities).

3. Co-obligors in contract were traditionally held to be "necessary," today Rule 19(a) required parties, but were not held to be "indispensable," today Rule 19(b) parties that require dismissal of the action. *See id.* § 1613. Should such parties even be considered Rule 19(a) parties today? For example, assume that *D-1* and *D-2* co-sign a note for $200,000 in which they jointly and severally obligate themselves to *P*. In other words, *P* can recover the entire sum from either *D-1* or *D-2*. A dispute develops about whether *P* released *D-1* and *D-2* from the obligation to repay. *P* then sues *D-1* to recover the $200,000. Assume that under the applicable substantive law, if *D-1* has to pay the $200,000 to *P* pursuant to the judgment of the court, *D-1* is entitled to recover "contribution" of $100,000 from *D-2*. If *D-2* is not a party to the action between *P* and *D-1*, *D-2* would not be bound by the judgment in that action. Therefore, in *P v. D-1*, if no valid release is found, that determination would not bind *D-2*, who would be entitled to relitigate the release issue in *D-1*'s contribution action.

It is possible that in the action between *D-1* and *D-2*, *P* could be found to have released *D-1* and *D-2*, even though the opposite had been found in *P v. D-1*. Thus, *D-1* would be subject to disproportionate liability. That is, *D-1* would be obligated to pay *P* the entire amount of the note, but *D-1* would be unable to obtain contribution from *D-2*. Should *D-2* be classified as a Rule 19(a)(1)(B)(ii) party and joined as a defendant in *P v. D-1* if feasible? Is *D-1* faced with the possibility of "double," "multiple," or "inconsistent" obligations within the meaning of Rule 19(a)(1)(B)(ii)? If so, how can the situation of joint tortfeasors, dealt with in *Temple* be distinguished from the situation of joint and several contract obligors? Should both be considered Rule 19(a) parties or neither?

Z & B Enterprises, Inc. v. Tastee-Freez International, Inc.

United States Court of Appeals for the First Circuit, 2006
No. 05-1064, 162 Fed. Appx. 16, 2006 WL 123775,
2006 U.S. App. LEXIS 1124 (Jan. 18, 2006)

TORRUELLA, CIRCUIT JUDGE.

In this suit, Plaintiffs are suing Defendant for deceptive and fraudulent conduct in the sale of a Tastee-Freez franchise. The district court granted Defendant's motion to dismiss under Federal Rule of Civil Procedure 12(b)(7) for failure to join [a required party under Rule 19]. Plaintiffs appeal the district court's finding that the missing parties are indispensable. We affirm.

I.

Tastee-Freez is "one of America's favorite establishments for high quality fast food and delicious soft-serve products." ... This case concerns alleged deceptive and fraudulent activities arising from the sale of a Tastee-Freez franchise in Aguadilla, Puerto Rico. Plaintiffs Luis Valle-Figueroa ("Valle-Figueroa") and Luis Valle-Gonzalez ("Valle-Gonzalez") sought to purchase a Tastee-Freez franchise, and they formed Z & B Enterprises, also a Plaintiff, to be the owner of the franchise. Additional Plaintiffs are the spouses of Valle-Figueroa and Valle-Gonzalez and their respective conjugal partnerships. Defendant is Tastee-Freez International ("TFI"), a corporation that grants Tastee-Freez franchises to franchisees.

In April 2001, Plaintiffs commenced negotiations with J.F., Inc., ("JF") to purchase the Tastee-Freez franchise in Aguadilla owned by JF. Plaintiffs and JF entered into a contract where Plaintiffs would be required to pay about $800,000. Plaintiffs paid JF $191,400, although it is not clear if this was an initial installment or payment for an option to purchase. In June 2001, Plaintiffs paid the balance, and JF advised Plaintiffs that they had the rights to operate the Aguadilla Tastee-Freez. Plaintiffs were never presented with and never signed the Restaurant License Agreement that is normally entered into by franchise owners and TFI.

Plaintiffs allege that they were forced to enter into an Account Executive Agreement with Auspiciadora TF, Inc., ("ATF"), but does not state how they were forced. ATF and/or JF also forced Plaintiffs to enter into other agreements and contracts. These agreements and contracts violated TFI's Restaurant License Agreement and rules established by the Federal Trade Commission ("FTC"). It was not until after these agreements and contracts were entered into that TFI, ATF, or JF presented Plaintiffs with the disclosures required by the FTC and/or TFI.

Plaintiffs were hindered in the operation of their Aguadilla Tastee-Freez by a lack of support from TFI, ATF, and JF. TFI did not fulfill its obligations to provide advertising, training programs, and promotions. Although Plaintiffs had never signed a Restaurant License Agreement, TFI cashed checks written by Plaintiffs, and TFI invited Plaintiffs to attend a Tastee-Freez conference. The franchise lost money, and Plaintiffs shut it down on April 30, [2002].

Plaintiffs filed suit in Puerto Rico Commonwealth Court against ATF and JF, and this suit is still pending. Plaintiffs filed another suit in federal district court against TFI, asserting several grounds for TFI's liability. First, Plaintiffs allege that TFI is liable for the actions of ATF and JF because ATF and JF are its agents, and TFI ratified or authorized their actions. Second, Plaintiffs claim that TFI is liable under the indemnity provision of the Restaurant License Agreement that Plaintiffs never signed. Finally, Plaintiffs claim that TFI failed to support the franchise and make required disclosures. In this suit, Plaintiffs seek rescission of the contracts they signed with ATF and JF.

TFI moved to dismiss Plaintiffs' complaint for failure to state a claim and for failure to join indispensable parties ATF and JF. A federal magistrate judge denied TFI's motion to dismiss. The district court rejected the magistrate's recommendation and found that ATF and JF were indispensable parties under Federal Rule of Civil Procedure Rule 19. The district court granted TFI's motion to dismiss under Federal Rule of Civil Procedure 12(b)(7), and Plaintiffs appeal.

II.

The joinder of parties is controlled by Rule 19 of the Federal Rules of Civil Procedure. "The Rule furthers several related policies, including the public interest in preventing multiple and repetitive litigation, the interest of the present parties in obtaining complete and effective relief in a single action, and the interest of absentees in avoiding the possible prejudicial effect of deciding the case without them." *Acton Co. v. Bachman Foods, Inc.*, 668 F.2d 76, 78 (1st Cir.1982). Rule 19 defines a two-step process. In the first step under Rule 19(a), the court determines whether a party is necessary, *i.e.*, one who must be joined if feasible to do so. Joinder is not feasible if it will deprive the court of subject matter jurisdiction. If the party is necessary but joinder is not feasible, the court must then determine under Rule 19(b) whether the party is indispensable or whether "in equity and good conscience, the action should proceed among the existing parties or should be dismissed." Fed. R. Civ. P. 19(b).[a]

---

a. [Eds. Note. The above passage was edited to reflect the current language of Rule 19(b) following the 2007 restyling amendments.]

A.

The parties dispute the standard of review we should apply to the district court's determination that ATF and JF are indispensable parties under Rule 19. Plaintiffs erroneously argue that we should review this determination de novo, because the district court ultimately dismissed the case for lack of subject matter jurisdiction. While a district court's decision to dismiss for lack of subject matter jurisdiction is reviewed de novo, this standard of review clearly does not apply to all determinations by the district court leading up to the dismissal. *See United States v. San Juan Bay Marina*, 239 F.3d 400, 403 (1st Cir.2001).

Defendant correctly notes that our standard of review under Rule 19(b) is abuse of discretion. *Id.* Defendant ignores, however, that a necessary precursor to a decision under Rule 19(b) is a decision under Rule 19(a). *Id.* at 405. We have yet to determine whether abuse of discretion or de novo review is the appropriate standard of review for district court decisions under Rule 19(a). *Id.* at 403. Because we would come to the same conclusion under either standard of review, we need not and do not decide this issue here.

B.

We first consider whether ATF and JF are necessary parties under Rule 19(a). Necessary parties are those "who ought to be made parties, in order that the court may act on that rule which requires it to decide on, and finally determine the entire controversy, and do complete justice, by adjusting all the rights involved in it." *Shields v. Barrow*, 58 U.S. (17 How.) 130, 139 (1854). "[A] court essentially will decide whether considerations of efficiency and fairness, growing out of the particular circumstances of the case, require that a particular person be joined as a party." *Pujol v. Shearson/American Express, Inc.*, 877 F.2d 132, 134 (1st Cir.1989).

In Plaintiffs' vaguely-worded Complaint, they seek recovery from TFI primarily for acts of its alleged agents. The complaint does not identify the agents by name or the basis of the agency relationship, but the parties' briefs identify the alleged agents as ATF and JF. Before turning to the text of Rule 19, it is fruitful to consider the relationships between the present and absent parties, and Plaintiffs' theories for imposing liability upon TFI for the actions of its alleged agents.

First, virtually all of the affirmative acts that caused harm to the Plaintiffs were done by ATF or JF. It was ATF and JF that "provided false and misleading information and representations" and "deceived and misled plaintiffs into signing contracts." In contrast, the alleged involvement by TFI is much less clear and arises from the failure to act and what it should have known. Plaintiffs do allege that TFI failed to comply with FTC rules regulating franchise agreements. Although TFI cashed Plaintiff's checks, Plaintiffs and TFI never entered into an explicit franchise agreement, and thus it is not clear whether TFI was obligated to comply with these FTC rules. Plaintiffs state that TFI should have been aware of the deceptive practices of ATF and JF but never explains why. It appears that the presence of ATF and JF "is critical to the disposition of the important issues in the litigation." *Freeman v. Northwest Acceptance Corp.*, 754 F.2d 553, 559 (5th Cir.1985) (internal quotation marks omitted).

Second, Plaintiffs assert that TFI is liable for the actions of ATF and JF, because ATF and JF were acting as agents on behalf of TFI. TFI denies that ATF and JF were its agents, and even if they were, they were acting outside the scope of the agency relationship. Plaintiff has not put forth any evidence of an agency relationship between TFI and ATF or JF, and the Restaurant License Agreement between TFI and JF explicitly states that JF is not TFI's agent.

Third, Plaintiffs assert that TFI's liability arises from the indemnity provision of the Restaurant License Agreement. The Restaurant License Agreement requires TFI to indemnify a franchisee for "any obligations or liability for damages attributable to agreements, representations or warranties of or authorized by [TFI]" or "caused by the negligence or willful actions of [TFI]." Plaintiffs' argument is difficult to understand because Plaintiffs never state whom TFI is obligated to indemnify and for what reasons. It is undisputed that JF signed a Restaurant License Agreement with TFI. Under certain circumstances, the Restaurant License Agreement could thus require TFI to indemnify JF for damages incurred by JF. In this situation, only JF could invoke the indemnity provision of the contract. It is also undisputed that Plaintiffs did not sign a Restaurant License Agreement with TFI. Even if other circumstances effectively bound TFI and Plaintiffs to the Restaurant License Agreement, most of the acts causing harm to Plaintiffs and requiring indemnification were done by ATF and JF, not TFI. ATF and JF are thus active participants and "more than ... key witness[es] whose testimony would be of inestimable value." *Id.*

Plaintiffs argue that ATF and JF should not be considered necessary parties because TFI could join them as third-party defendants. Plaintiff is correct that TFI could implead ATF and JF as third-party defendants without breaking this court's diversity jurisdiction even though Plaintiffs, ATF, and JF are all citizens of Puerto Rico. *See Owen Equip. & Erection Co. v. Kroger*, 437 U.S. 365, 370 (1978). Disregarding the fact that TFI is by no means required to implead ATF and JF, even if TFI did implead ATF and JF they would be only third-party defendants and not principal defendants in this suit. As a result, Plaintiffs could not assert claims against ATF and JF. *See id.* at 377. If ATF and JF are necessary parties in this suit, then they are necessary as defendants and not as third-party defendants.

We now consider the factors enumerated in Rule 19(a).... To be necessary, a party need only satisfy one of these factors. We find that two of the [Rule 19(a)] factors show that ATF and JF are necessary parties who ought to be joined if feasible.

First, we may not be able to grant complete relief to Plaintiffs in the absence of ATF and JF. Plaintiffs are seeking rescission of contracts they made with ATF and JF. If this case were to proceed without ATF and JF, they would not be bound by a judgment concerning the invalidity or enforceability of the contracts to which they were parties. This would be a waste of judicial resources. "The interests that are being furthered [by Rule 19(a)(1)(A)] are not only those of the parties, but also that of the public in avoiding repeated lawsuits on the same essential subject matter." Fed. R. Civ. P. 19 advisory committee's note [to the 1966 amendment].

[handwritten margin note: Advisory Committee's Note]

Second, TFI could be subject to inconsistent or double obligations. Plaintiffs have filed a suit against ATF and JF in commonwealth court. It is possible that the federal district court could find that TFI is not liable to Plaintiffs, but that the commonwealth court could find that ATF and JF are liable to Plaintiffs. Then TFI might be liable at least to JF because of the indemnity provision in the Restaurant License Agreement. Alternatively, the commonwealth court could find that ATF and JF are liable to Plaintiffs, and the federal court could find that TFI is liable to Plaintiffs. JF could then file suit against TFI for indemnity, thus subjecting TFI to a double obligation.

C.

Under Rule 19(a), a necessary party is to be joined as long as it is feasible to do so. Joinder is not feasible if it would deprive the court of subject matter jurisdiction. Plaintiff is a citizen of Puerto Rico, Defendant TFI is a citizen of Michigan, and the amount in controversy exceeds $75,000. Without ATF and JF, this court thus has diversity jurisdiction under 28 U.S.C. § 1332. ATF and JF are also citizens of Puerto Rico. Joining ATF and JF as defendants in this suit would break complete diversity and thus deprive this court of subject matter jurisdiction. Plaintiffs do not contend that the doctrine of supplemental jurisdiction extends our jurisdiction to include ATF and JF as defendants. *See Acton*, 668 F.2d at 79–80; 28 U.S.C. § 1367(b).

D.

Finally, since ATF and JF are necessary parties but joinder is not feasible, we must "determine whether in equity and good conscience the action should proceed" without ATF and JF as defendants. Fed. R. Civ. P. 19(b). If we cannot proceed without ATF and JF, then they are indispensable parties. Rule 19(b) gives four non-exclusive factors for courts to consider in making this determination.... Applying these four factors, we find that ATF and JF are indispensable parties.

For the first factor [restyled Rule 19(b)(1)], we already discussed above how proceeding to judgment without ATF and JF could be prejudicial to TFI, as TFI could be subjected to double or inconsistent obligations. This factor weighs in favor of finding ATF and JF indispensable. The second factor [restyled Rule 19(b)(2)] is whether this prejudice may somehow be lessened by the court's shaping of the potential verdicts. Plaintiffs proposed a one-sentence solution for shaping relief to lessen the prejudice to TFI:

> [P]ursuant to the indemnity clause of the franchise agreement, [TFI could be made liable] for any damages attributable to the agreements, representations or warranties of or authorized by TFI, specifically providing that ATF and JF are not bound by such a judgment because they cannot be liable under the indemnity clause.

Plaintiffs' proposition does not prevent TFI from being subjected to double or inconsistent obligations, and we do not see any manner of shaping relief that would prevent this from occurring.

The third factor [restyled Rule 19(b)(3)] is whether a judgment rendered in the absence of ATF and JF is likely to be adequate. This factor includes "the interest of the courts and the public in complete, consistent, and efficient settlement of controversies." *Provident Tradesmens Bank & Trust Co. v. Patterson*, 390 U.S. 102, 111 (1968). ATF and JF are the principal actors in this lawsuit and could be the only entities liable to Plaintiffs. Alternatively, if TFI is liable to Plaintiffs, ATF and JF could in turn be liable to TFI. The absence of ATF and JF could thus prevent complete relief to the parties. For the same reasoning, the outcome could be inefficient as a further lawsuit could be necessary that would require relitigating nearly identical issues. Finally, because Plaintiffs are suing ATF and JF in commonwealth court, any judgment made by a federal court could be inconsistent with the outcome in the commonwealth court.

Finally, the last factor [restyled Rule 19(b)(4)] is whether an adequate, alternative forum is available to the Plaintiffs. Plaintiffs can join TFI, ATF, and JF as defendants in a suit in commonwealth court. Plaintiffs have not given any reason as to why the commonwealth court would be an inadequate alternative, and we see no reason to believe that the commonwealth court would be an inadequate forum.

Considering the four factors together, it is clear that ATF and JF are indispensable parties in this lawsuit. A judgment in the absence of ATF and JF could be prejudicial to TFI, relief cannot be shaped to avoid this prejudice, a judgment rendered in the absence of ATF and JF is unlikely to be adequate, and the commonwealth court provides an adequate remedy for Plaintiffs. "Equity and good conscience" require us to dismiss this lawsuit for failure to join indispensable parties ATF and JF.[b]

III.

For the foregoing reasons, the district court's decision is affirmed.

Notes and Questions

1. Did the court's analysis of the Rule 19(a) issue in *Z & B Enterprises* conform to the kind of analysis demanded by the Supreme Court's decisions in *Provident Tradesmens* and *Temple*? In Section I.B of its opinion, the court first considered a number of preliminary factors, such as whether ATF and JF could be joined under Rule 14, in analyzing the Rule 19(a) issue before considering the explicit party categories of Rule 19(a). What was the relevance of these preliminary factors to the Rule 19(a) analysis?

2. Do you agree with the court's ultimate determination in *Z & B Enterprises* that without the joinder of ATF and JF, the problem of inconsistent judgments and potential double liability required dismissal of the action under Rule 19(b)? For example, consider the court's analysis of the ability of TFI to join the absent parties under Rule 14. The court seemed to think that this was an inadequate solution to the Rule 19 problem because the absentees needed to be joined as primary defendants. In determining whether this is true, consider the matters that might be litigated entirely between TFI and the absentees after Rule 14 joinder. Would resolution of those matters have solved the problems of inconsistent judgments and double liability, even if restrictions on supplemental jurisdiction would not have permitted plaintiffs to assert claims against ATF and JF? Assuming that the court was correct that Rule 14 joinder of the absentees would not solve the inconsistent judgment and double liability problems, was there any other alternative open to the court that might have avoided those problems without the need to dismiss the federal action?

3. How should the availability or unavailability of an alternative forum be weighted under Rule 19(b)(4)? That is, if an alternative forum is available, should that weigh in favor of a classification of indispensability and, therefore, in favor of dismissal? Or should the unavailability of an alternative forum be weighed heavily in favor of not dismissing, but the availability of an alternative forum not be given much weight. How did the court evaluate this factor in *Z & B Enterprises*?

4. Should a court be able to deny a Rule 12(b)(7) motion on the ground that it is untimely? If so, should it matter whether the Rule 19(a) party's absence would harm someone in the lawsuit or whether the lawsuit would affect the Rule 19(a) party's interests adversely?

5. As noted in the introductory text of this section, Rule 19 was substantially revised and amended into its current form in 1966. The 1966 Advisory Committee's Note is especially helpful in understanding the proper application of the Rule, particularly the factors of 19(b), and you should study this Note carefully. With respect to the second factor of Rule 19(b), now contained in 19(b)(2)(A)-(C), *i.e.*, protective provisions in the judg-

---

b. [Eds. Note. Restyled Rule 19(b) deleted the former concluding phrase of the first sentence of Rule 19(b), "the absent person being thus regarded as indispensable." The 2007 Advisory Committee's Note indicates, as illustrated by the court's use of the term here, that it was simply "used only to express a conclusion reached by applying the tests of Rule 19(b)." The Advisory Committee's Note explains that the term "indispensable" was therefore discarded from the language of Rule 19(b) "as redundant."]

ment or other measures to avoid or lessen the prejudice, the Note explains that this analysis focuses on (1) what the court can do, such as awarding money damages in lieu of an injunction; (2) what the prejudiced party can do, such as joining the absent person under impleader or interpleader; and (3) what the absent person can do, such as voluntarily intervening in the action. Intervention is examined in the next section.

6. In *Republic of Philippines v. Pimentel*, 553 U.S. 851 (2008), the Supreme Court addressed the application of Rule 19 in the context of parties who cannot be joined because of foreign sovereign immunity. In this case, the holders of assets that were transferred to a Panamanian company by the former President of the Republic of the Philippines brought an interpleader action in federal district court seeking to resolve conflicting claims to the assets. The district court awarded funds to a class of human rights victims of the former Philippine president. On appeal, the Ninth Circuit affirmed, but the Supreme Court reversed.

The Court concluded that action could not proceed without joining the Republic of the Philippines and the Philippine Presidential Commission on Good Governance. These entities could not be joined because of foreign sovereign immunity. The Court held that the district court had been insufficiently attentive to the importance of the sovereign interests of the Republic and the Commission, specifically their interest in not having their claimed governmental assets disposed of by an American proceeding. The Court concluded that those interests warranted dismissal of the action under Rule 19(b).

Problems

Problem 7-19. P, a citizen of State X, sues D-1, a citizen of State Y, in a federal court in State Y. P is a beneficiary of a trust and D-1 is the trustee of the trust. P's suit seeks to have D-1 augment the corpus of the trust by $200,000. P asserts that D-1 breached D-1's fiduciary duty as trustee, resulting in the loss of $200,000 of trust assets. P does not join D-2, who is also a beneficiary of the trust. D-2 is a citizen of State Y. Under the law of State Y, which governs the trust, a cause of action against a trustee to augment the corpus of a trust exists in all the beneficiaries of the trust jointly; no single beneficiary of a multiple beneficiary trust possesses a cause of action against the trustee. Does state law or Federal Rule 19 control the question whether D-2 must be joined in the action? Under Rule 19(a), is D-2 a person whose joinder is necessary for the just adjudication of the action? If so, should the action be dismissed pursuant to Rule 19(b)?

Problem 7-20. P, the executor of a will, sues *D-1 Charity*, to have the residuary clause of the will declared void. Under the residuary clause, D-1 would inherit a substantial sum of money. If the residuary clause is declared void, D-2, another heir under the clause, stands to lose $100,000. P does not join D-2 because D-2's joinder would destroy diversity of citizenship. Is D-2 a Rule 19(a) party? If so, can the court take some kind of action under Rule 19(b) that would allow the action to continue in D-2's absence?

Section I. Intervention

Intervention is a procedure by which a person who is not a party to an action, but whose interests are affected by the action, may become a party. The object of intervention is to allow the nonparty to protect its interest without unduly disrupting the interests of the persons already parties to the action.

Intervention at Common Law and in Equity. Intervention was derived primarily from civil law procedure. It was quite familiar in Roman law. *See* CLARK § 65, at 420. The common-law courts restricted intervention out of concern that it would interfere with the plaintiff's ability to control the action. The English ecclesiastical courts introduced the Roman practice into England, and the admiralty and equity courts also had narrow procedures for intervention. *See* TEPLY & WHITTEN at 808–09.

Intervention Under the Codes. Section 122 of the Field Code, as amended in 1851, provided for a narrow right of intervention that generally corresponded to the pre-code equity practice:

> [W]hen, in an action for the recovery of real or personal property, a person, not a party to the action, but having an interest in the subject thereof, makes application to the court, to be made a party, it may order him to be brought in by the proper amendment.

Act of July 10, 1851, ch. 479, § 122, 1851 N.Y. Laws 876, 883. In some code states, this provision was replaced by more lenient statutes. These statutes allowed nonparties to intervene when they had an interest in the subject matter of the suit or in the success or failure of either or both parties to the action.

Intervention in Federal Court Actions. Prior to the Federal Rules of Civil Procedure, intervention in the federal courts was controlled by Equity Rule 37 in equitable actions and by the Conformity Acts in common-law proceedings. After law and equity were merged by the Federal Rules in 1938, Federal Rule 24 controlled intervention in all cases. Rule 24 made significant changes in federal practice. For example, Rule 24 introduced a distinction between "intervention of right" under Rule 24(a) and "permissive intervention" under Rule 24(b) that had not existed in prior practice. Original Rule 24(a) also contained a distinction between intervenors whose interests might be inadequately represented by the existing parties to an action and intervenors who might be adversely affected by a distribution of property in the action. This distinction was based on the two kinds of intervention statutes existing under the codes. The distinction was abolished by the 1966 amendments to Rule 24. The 1966 amendments attempted to make the right to intervene depend upon general pragmatic considerations. *See* TEPLY & WHITTEN at 809.

The materials below explore intervention practice under Rule 24, as amended in 1966. Rule 24 exemplifies modern intervention practice in the federal courts and in states following the Federal Rules of Civil Procedure.

Sierra Club v. Espy

United States Court of Appeals, Fifth Circuit, 1994
18 F.3d 1202

JERRY E. SMITH, CIRCUIT JUDGE:

Texas Forestry Association ("TFA") and the Southern Timber Purchasers Council ("STPC"), two trade associations representing most of the purchasers of timber from the Texas national forests, appeal the district court's denial of their motion to intervene in this lawsuit between the Sierra Club and the Secretary of Agriculture. Concluding that movants satisfied the requirements of Fed. R. Civ. P. 24(a) for intervention as a matter of right, we reverse.

[Three environmental groups sued the Secretary of Agriculture in 1985. They alleged that the U.S. Forest Service's program for controlling the southern pine beetle violated the Endangered Species Act ("ESA"), the National Environmental Policy Act ("NEPA"), and the National Forest Management Act ("NFMA"). As a result of this litigation, the district court granted a preliminary injunction on May 12, 1993, that, in part, prevented the Forest Service from offering certain planned timber sales challenged by the plaintiffs.] On June 24, 1993, the Forest Service issued a letter advising prospective timber purchasers that, as a result of the injunction, it would refrain from offering not only the planned timber sales challenged by the plaintiffs but also any timber sales with even-aged regeneration cuts. This letter triggered TFA and STPC's motion to intervene on July 9, 1993, which was denied.

....

Movants argue that the district court erred in refusing to allow their intervention as a matter of right under Fed. R. Civ. P. 24(a). A party seeking to intervene as of right must satisfy four requirements: (1) The application must be timely; (2) the applicant must have an interest relating to the property or transaction that is the subject of the action; (3) the applicant must be so situated that the disposition of the action may, as a practical matter, impair or impede its ability to protect its interest; and (4) the applicant's interest must be inadequately represented by the existing parties to the suit.... If a party seeking to intervene fails to meet any one of those requirements, it cannot intervene as a matter of right.... TFA and STPC's right to intervene is a legal issue that we review de novo....

....

Movants argue that their motion to intervene was timely. Determining the timeliness of a motion to intervene entails consideration of four factors: (1) The length of time during which the would-be intervenor actually knew or reasonably should have known of its interest in the case before it petitioned for leave to intervene; (2) the extent of the prejudice that the existing parties to the litigation may suffer as a result of the would-be intervenor's failure to apply for intervention as soon as it knew or reasonably should have known of its interest in the case; (3) the extent of the prejudice that the would-be intervenor may suffer if intervention is denied; and (4) the existence of unusual circumstances militating either for or against a determination that the application is timely....

The analysis is contextual; absolute measures of timeliness should be ignored.... The requirement of timeliness is not a tool of retribution to punish the tardy would-be intervenor, but rather a guard against prejudicing the original parties by the failure to apply sooner.... Federal courts should allow intervention "where no one would be hurt and greater justice could be attained." ...

....

The movants argue that the first factor supports intervention because they promptly moved for intervention once their interest in the case became apparent, i.e., after the preliminary injunction was issued on May 12, 1993. The lawsuit, although pending for eight years, did not raise the NFMA and NEPA claims with regard to the Plan until the fourth amended complaint was filed in May 1992. Even in 1992, movants argue, the TFA and STPC believed that their interests would not be adversely affected, given the magistrate judge's report recommending that the NFMA and NEPA claims be dismissed.

Not until the district court granted the preliminary injunction did the movants become aware that their interests in timber sales were affected. TFA and STPC moved to intervene within two months of the issuance of the preliminary injunction.

The plaintiffs contend that the movants should have become aware in 1987 of any interest they had concerning timber sales because the NFMA and NEPA claims were first raised in the second amended complaint. The district court indicated that it would carry the NFMA and NEPA claims in January 1988, pending exhaustion of administrative remedies. Furthermore, TFA participated as amicus curiae in the 1989 appeal of the decision concerning even-aged management under the ESA. Plaintiffs conclude that the NFMA and NEPA claims have been present for six years and that the movants' interest in these issues has remained unchanged during that time.

Having reviewed the January 1988 district court opinion, we conclude that the status of the NFMA and NEPA claims changed dramatically over the course of the lawsuit. In its January 1988 opinion, the district court dismissed TCONR's claim relating to the land and resource management plan.... Furthermore, the district court denied Sierra Club's motion to amend its complaint to allege noncompliance with NFMA, pending exhaustion of administrative remedies.... Therefore, TFA and STPC had reason to believe that their interests were not adversely affected at that stage.

[W]e [have] rejected the notion that the date on which the would-be intervenor became aware of the pendency of the action should be used to determine whether it acted promptly. Courts should discourage premature intervention that wastes judicial resources... A better gauge of promptness is the speed with which the would-be intervenor acted when it became aware that its interests would no longer be protected by the original parties...

In this case, the movants legitimately believed that the Forest Service would defend its timber sales and planning. When the agency announced on June 24, 1993, that it would apply the preliminary injunction to all timber sales (not merely the nine sales challenged by the plaintiffs), movants became aware that the Forest Service would not protect their interests. Therefore, we conclude that the first factor—the length of time during which the would-be intervenor actually knew or reasonably should have known of its interest in the case before it petitioned for leave to intervene—weighs in favor of the movants.

. . . .

The second factor—the extent of prejudice to the existing parties as a result of the applicant's delay in seeking intervention—also weighs in favor of TFA and STPC. Plaintiffs argue that TFA and STPC's participation in the proceedings would "severely protract the litigation." But prejudice must be measured by the delay in seeking intervention, not the inconvenience to the existing parties of allowing the intervenor to participate in the litigation.... The movants sought intervention less than three weeks after the Forest Service issued its June 24, 1993, letter. We therefore conclude that no prejudice to the existing parties resulted from the delay in seeking intervention.[3]

. . . .

The third factor is the extent of the prejudice the would-be intervenor would suffer if its petition for leave to intervene were denied. Movants argue that the preliminary injunction substantially reduced the acreage available for timber production and foreclosed the agency from offering any more timber sales with even-aged management regeneration cuts in the Texas national forests. The movants' member companies purchase and process timber offered from these forests and have property interests in existing sales contracts.

Plaintiffs claim that TFA and STPC are not prejudiced by denial of intervention because they already have intervened in the Forest Service's appeal of the preliminary injunction,

---

3. Moreover, as movants admit, no prejudice can come from renewed discovery or pretrial proceedings, because an intervenor "must accept the proceedings as he finds them." ... The intervenor has no right to relitigate issues already decided....

and through that appeal movants could argue for their interpretation of NFMA and NEPA. Furthermore, since the movants participated in the development of the Forest Service's land management plan, they can continue to influence the timber industry. Finally, plaintiffs assert that no sales contracts are affected, and movants have failed to show how reduction of acreage adversely affects their interest.

The intervention in the appeal of the district court's preliminary injunction cannot adequately substitute for intervention at the district court level, as many more issues are at stake in the district court than the single issue now on appeal. The claim that the movants' interests are adequately represented by their participation in the development of the Forest Service's land management ignores the legal rights associated with formal intervention, namely the briefing of issues, presentation of evidence, and ability to appeal.

Finally, it is obvious that the economic interests of the movants are at stake. The movants have a financial interest in the ability to use the less expensive even-aged harvesting methods, and they have prospect of injury if the Forest Service cannot deliver constant volumes of timber. Furthermore, the district court's holding that NFMA bars even-aged management could injure movants' member companies in other venues.

. . . .

The final factor in determining timeliness of the intervention is the existence of unusual circumstances militating either for or against a determination that the application is timely. We are aware of no such specific circumstances pertinent to this case. In summary, based upon the brief time that had elapsed between the Forest Service's June 24, 1993, letter and the motion for intervention, the remoteness of prejudice to the existing parties resulting from this delay, and the likelihood of prejudice to the movants if intervention were denied, we conclude that the motion to intervene was timely.

The second requirement for intervention as a matter of right under rule 24(a) is that the applicant have an "interest" in the subject matter of the action. This interest must be "direct, substantial, [and] legally protectable." ... Plaintiffs claim that the movants' interest is too speculative and generalized to satisfy Rule 24. We disagree.

Movants represent the forest products industry, including the major purchasers and processors of Texas national forest timber. These member companies have legally protectable property interests in existing timber contracts that are threatened by the potential bar on even-aged management. Since "the 'interest' test is primarily a practical guide to disposing of lawsuits by involving as many apparently concerned persons as is compatible with efficiency and due process," ... we conclude that movants had an interest sufficient to satisfy rule 24.

. . . .

The third requirement of Rule 24(a) is that the applicant must be so situated that the disposition of the action may, as a practical matter, impair or impede his ability to protect his interest. Plaintiffs argue that adverse *stare decisis* effects will not supply the requisite disadvantage to satisfy this test. As we have stated..., however, an intervenor's interest "is impaired by the *stare decisis* effect of the district court's judgment." The issue of whether the NFMA bars even-aged logging affects the movants and, because of the precedential effect of the district court's decision, an adverse resolution of the action would impair their ability to protect their interest.

. . . .

4rb 24(a) Req

The final requirement for intervention as a matter of right is that the applicant's interest must be inadequately represented by the existing parties to the suit. The applicant has the burden of demonstrating inadequate representation, but this burden is "minimal." ... The applicant need only show that representation "may be" inadequate....

Plaintiffs contend that the government adequately represents the movants' interest because the interests are essentially identical. We cannot agree with this position. The movants have demonstrated, through the June 24, 1993, letter applying the district court's preliminary injunction to all future timber sales, that the government's representation of their interest is inadequate. The government must represent the broad public interest, not just the economic concerns of the timber industry. Given the minimal burden on the movants to satisfy this requirement, we conclude that the government's representation of the intervenors' interest is inadequate.

    ....

Summary of Findings

Applying the four requirements of Rule 24(a), we must conclude that the movants were entitled to intervene as a matter of right. Their motion was timely and indicated a legitimate interest in the subject matter. Moreover, failure to allow intervention would impair TFA and STPC's ability to protect their interest because of the precedential effect of the district court's decisions. We also agree with the movants that the government's representation of their interest is inadequate.

    ....

Because we conclude that the district court, in spite of its diligent and evenhanded effort to manage this difficult and complex case, erred in denying Rule 24(a)(2) intervention, we need not reach the issue of permissive intervention. The order denying intervention is REVERSED.

CIRCUIT JUDGE GARWOOD notes his dissent.

Notes and Questions

1. Rule 24(a)(2) and Rule 19(a)(1)(B)(i) are worded similarly. Thus, a Rule 24(a)(2) party will often be a person whose joinder is required under Rule 19(a). If a Rule 19(a)(1)(B)(i) objection is made in an action, can the objection be obviated by notifying the absent party and giving the party an opportunity to intervene under Rule 24(a)?

2. Rule 24(b)(1)(B) provides for intervention with the permission of the court when the proposed intervenor "has a claim or defense that shares with the main action a common question of law or fact." Because of the absence in Rule 24(b)(1)(B) of an additional same "transaction or occurrence" requirement as in Rule 20(a), this provision could allow a nonparty to intervene on the plaintiff's or defendant's side of the case in circumstances when the party could not have been joined under Rule 20(a) as an original matter. Rule 24(b)(1)(B) is not the only rule that operates in this fashion. Rule 42(a) provides for consolidation of actions that involve a common question of law or fact without an additional same "transaction or occurrence" requirement as in Rule 20(a). Why don't the rulemakers amend Rule 20(a) to allow original joinder of plaintiffs who assert, or defendants who have asserted against them, claims involving common questions of law or fact, without the need for the claims to arise out of the same transaction, occurrence, or series of transactions or occurrences?

3. If a party is permitted to intervene as a matter of right under Rule 24(a), should the court have the power to impose conditions on the party's participation in the action?

The Advisory Committee's Note to the 1966 amendment to Rule 24(a) states that appropriate conditions may be imposed on intervention as a matter of right. If so, how far can a court go in conditioning the intervenor's rights? Rule 24(a) makes no express provision for such restrictions. Can the court refuse to allow the intervenor to assert claims, counterclaims, or crossclaims in the action? Would such a restriction be proper under the plain textual language of Rule 24(a)?

Problems

Problem 7-21. P claims ownership of certain real property. The property is in the possession of D, who P contends is trespassing. P sues D to enjoin D from trespassing. I claims ownership of the same property and seeks to intervene under Federal Rule 24(a) to resist P's claim. I also contends that D is a trespasser. Whether P owns the land depends upon a question of law that will ultimately have to be resolved by an appellate court. Is intervention appropriate under Rule 24(a)? If intervention of right is appropriate, will I be able to assert a counterclaim against P to establish I's own title and a crossclaim against D to enjoin D from trespassing?

Problem 7-22. To secure a debt owed by it to P, D Corp. pledged to P certain stock owned by it in A Corp. Upon default by D, P is permitted to sell the pledged collateral only if it is "commercially reasonable" to do so. D defaults, and P wants to sell the stock to B. However, D contends that it is not commercially reasonable to sell the stock to B under the proposed terms of the sale. P commences an action against D to obtain a declaration that the sale is commercially reasonable. I files a motion to intervene as of right under Rule 24(a), on the grounds that I wants to purchase the stock, and it will pay more than B has agreed to pay. Is intervention proper under Rule 24(a)? Assuming that intervention of right is not available under Rule 24(a), is permissive intervention available under Rule 24(b)?

Section J. Class Actions

A class action is a procedure that allows an action to be brought by or against a party who is a representative of a large number of persons similarly situated to the representative, but who are not formally named as parties in the action. Class actions are designed to avoid multiple litigation over the same basic matter and to permit the vindication of claims that would otherwise be lost due to the impracticability of bringing individual actions by or against the members of the class.

Class Actions at Common Law and in Equity. Class actions were not available in the common-law courts. The class action developed as the "bill of peace" in equity courts. Bills of peace allowed actions by or against representatives of a group when the size of the group was so large that joinder of all its members was impracticable or impossible. *See* ZECHARIAH CHAFEE, JR., SOME PROBLEMS OF EQUITY 149–50, 200–01 (1950).

Class Actions Under the Codes. In the United States, the Field Code provided that "when the question is one of a common or general interest of many persons, or when the parties are very numerous and it may be impracticable to bring them all before the court, one or more may sue or defend for the benefit of the whole." Act of Apr. 11, 1849, ch. 438, § 119, 1849 N.Y. Laws 613, 639. This provision was duplicated widely and still exists in some states. NEB. REV. STAT. § 25-319 (2008).

Reqs:

numerosity

commonality

Typicality

Adequate
protection

BASIC REQUIREMENTS FOR MAINTAINING A CLASS ACTION UNDER RULE 23(a)	
First	The class must be "so numerous" that joinder of all members of the class is "impracticable"
Second	There must be "questions of law or fact common to the class"
Third	The claims or defenses of the representative parties must be "typical" of the claims or defenses of the class members
Fourth	The representative parties must "fairly and adequately protect the interests of the class"

Figure 7-5

Federal Class Action Practice. In the federal courts, the Federal Equity Rules and the Conformity Acts made class actions available before the Federal Rules of Civil Procedure were adopted in 1938. *See* TEPLY & WHITTEN at 829–30. In the Federal Rules of Civil Procedure, Rule 23 made class actions available in a variety of circumstances. However, original Rule 23 was framed in a way that impaired the usefulness of the class action procedure in federal courts. *See id.* The 1966 amendments to Rule 23 corrected many of the problems with the original rule and increased the attractiveness of the class action procedure. The 1966 amendments also added Rules 23.1 and 23.2 to the Federal Rules. Rule 23.1 explicitly deals with derivative actions by shareholders, a special kind of class action that was formerly dealt with by Rule 23. Rule 23.2 deals with actions relating to unincorporated associations, which were also dealt with in the original Rule 23. Federal Rule 23 has been widely adopted in the states and generally exemplifies modern class action practice. Therefore, examination of class action practice under Rule 23 will illustrate the problems that occur in class actions generally.

Rule 23(a) and (b). Federal Rule 23 imposes two sets of requirements on a party who wants to bring a class action. In order to meet the first set of requirements, the party must comply with Rule 23(a). These requirements are summarized in Figure 7-5. Once the requirements of Rule 23(a) have been satisfied, the party bringing the class action must meet the requirements of Rule 23(b). This part of the rule requires the party to demonstrate that the action falls within one of the categories of class actions listed in Rule 23(b), summarized in Figure 7-6 on the next page.

Rule 23(c)-(e). Rule 23(c)(1)(A) provides that "[a]t an early practicable time after a person sues or is sued as a class representative, the court must determine by order whether to *certify* the action as a class action." In making this decision, the court must determine if the action meets the requirements for a class action under Rule 23(a) and (b). Under Rule 23(c)(1)(B), if the court decides to certify the action as a class action, the court "must define the class and the class claims, issues, or defenses, and must appoint class counsel under Rule 23(g)." Judicial certification of the class is thus the first step in the maintenance of a class action.

Wal-Mart Stores, Inc. v. Dukes. In *Wal-Mart Stores, Inc. v. Dukes*, 564 U.S. ___, 131 S. Ct. 2541, 180 L. Ed. 2d 374 (2011), plaintiff female employees commenced a class action alleging that Wal-Mart, the nation's largest private employer, had discriminated against its female employees over many years in violation of Title VII of the Civil Rights Act of 1964, 42 U.S.C. §2000e-2. The plaintiffs relied on the fact that Wal-Mart had given its local managers discretion over pay and promotions, which the employees alleged had been exercised disproportionately in favor of male employees. The district court granted the employee's motion to certify the class under Federal Rule 23(b)(2), which provides for

FOUR "CATEGORIES" OF CLASS ACTIONS PERMITTED BY RULE 23(b)	
Rule 23(b)(1)(A)	Prosecuting separate actions by or against individual class members would create a **risk of inconsistent or varying adjudications** with respect to individual class members that would establish incompatible standards of conduct for the party opposing the class **or**
Rule 23(b)(1)(B)	Prosecuting separate actions by or against individual class members would, as a practical matter, be **dispositive of the interests of the other members not parties to the individual adjudications or would substantially impair or impede their ability to protect their interests or**
Rule 23(b)(2)	The party opposing the class has acted or refused to act on grounds that apply generally to the class, so that final **injunctive relief or corresponding declaratory relief** is appropriate respecting the class as a whole **or**
Rule 23(b)(3)	The court finds that the **questions of law or fact common to class members predominate over any questions affecting only individual members**, and that **a class action is superior to other available methods for fairly and efficiently adjudicating the controversy**. The matters pertinent to these findings include: (A) the class members' interests in individually controlling the prosecution or defense of separate actions; (B) the extent and nature of any litigation concerning the controversy already begun by or against class members; (C) the desirability or undesirability of concentrating the litigation of the claims in the particular forum; and (D) the likely difficulties in managing a class action

Figure 7-6

class actions seeking injunctive or declaratory relief. Incidental to that relief, the action also sought back pay. The certification was substantially affirmed by the Ninth Circuit Court of Appeals. In a 5–4 decision, the U.S. Supreme Court reversed.

The Court held that the plaintiffs' class action failed to meet the general "commonality" requirement of Federal Rule 23(a)(2) (the second requirement stated in Figure 7-5). The Court found that the employees had failed to offer significant proof of a general policy of discrimination. Furthermore, the Court found that the employees' expert testimony failed to show how often the purported company-wide culture, which made the company vulnerable to gender bias, actually played a meaningful role in employment decisions. Nor did the employees' statistical and anecdotal evidence show how any common mode of exercising managerial discretion had operated throughout the entire company. According to the Court, what mattered with regard to commonality in a class certification was not the raising of *common questions*; instead it is the capacity of a class-wide proceeding to generate *common answers* apt to drive the resolution of the litigation. Thus, it is *dissimilarities* within a proposed class that has the potential to impede the generation of common answers.

In addition, the Court held that the employees' back-pay claims were improperly certified under Rule 23(b)(2) because those claims were not incidental to injunctive or declaratory relief. According to the Court, those individualized monetary claims belonged in Rule 23(b)(3), where the procedural protections of the finding of predominance and superiority exist as well as the requirement of mandatory notice and the right to opt out apply.

Comcast Corp. v. Behrend. In *Comcast Corp. v. Behrend*, ___ U.S. ___, 133 S. Ct. 1426, 185 L. Ed. 2d 515 (2013), the Supreme Court again addressed the certification requirements for a Rule 23(b)(3) class action. In this case, the plaintiffs brought an antitrust action against Comcast, alleging that it had engaged in conduct that lessened competition in a particular geographical area and caused the plaintiffs damages through higher prices for cable television services. The plaintiffs sought class certification under Rule 23(b)(3), which requires, among other things, that questions of law or fact predominate over any questions affecting only individual members. To succeed on their antitrust claim, the plaintiffs had to show individual injury based on the antitrust violation, referred to as "antitrust impact." Initially, plaintiffs proposed four theories of antitrust impact, but the district court accepted only one of the theories.

The district court then required the plaintiffs to show class-wide damages resulting from the accepted theory in order to obtain class certification. The plaintiffs did this through expert testimony that addressed damages from anticompetitive impact generally, but concededly did not tie the calculation of the damages to the particular theory of antitrust impact accepted by the district court. Nevertheless, the district court certified the action for class treatment, concluding that the damages could be calculated on a class-wide basis and, therefore, that the predominance requirement of Rule 23(b)(3) would not be violated by the need to engage in damage calculations for individual members of the class.

The Third Circuit Court of Appeals affirmed, but the Supreme Court reversed, holding that the failure to tie the calculation of damages to the particular theory of antitrust impact accepted by the district court made class certification improper. In a 5–4 decision, the Court opined that the failure to tie the calculation to the particular theory of antitrust impact meant that it was not adequately established that damages could be calculated on a class-wide basis and that the predominance requirement of Rule 23(b)(3) was, therefore, not satisfied. Even though an examination of this question would require an inquiry into the merits of the case as part of the class certification process, the majority held that the Court's precedents, including *Wal-Mart*, required such an inquiry.

Administration of Class Actions. The remaining sections of Rule 23 contain provisions governing the administration of class actions, including an important provision in Rule 23(c)(2) requiring that in all class actions brought under Rule 23(b)(3) (*i.e.*, when "the court finds that the questions of law or fact common to the class members predominate over any questions affecting only individual members, and that a class action is superior to other available methods for fairly and efficiently adjudicating the controversy"), the members must be provided (1) notice of the action and (2) an opportunity to be excluded from the action upon request. This mandatory notice provision does not apply to Rule 23(b)(1) or (2) class actions. However, Rule 23(d)(1)(B) gives the court discretion to order notice to the class in any class action.

Notice to the Class. As noted above, in Rule 23(b)(3) class actions, notice to the absent members of the class and an opportunity to opt out of the class is mandatory. This mandatory notice is not required in Rule 23(b)(1) or (2) actions because the class in Rule 23(b)(1) & (2) class actions is supposed to be more closely knit than in Rule 23(b)(3) actions. Therefore, notice to the class in the former actions is not thought to be necessary to satisfy due process on the theory that the adequacy of representation requirements of Rule 23(a) will assure the protection of the absent class members' interests. The lack of this close interest in Rule 23(b)(3) actions was thought to necessitate the notice requirement in Rule 23(b)(3) actions. The U.S. Supreme Court has held that the notice requirement in Rule 23(b)(3) actions is mandatory, even in cases in which the amounts claimed by individual members of the class are so small that individual actions would never be brought by the class members. In the same case, the Court held that the cost of the notice must be paid by the plaintiff, even though the cost of the notice might, as a practical matter, result in termination of the action. *See Eisen v. Carlisle & Jacquelin*, 417 U.S. 156, 177–78 (1974).

Due Process Issues in Class Actions Under Rule 23. There is often overlap between Rule 23(b)(1), (2) and (3) class actions. Therefore, lawyers representing classes often attempt to qualify a class action under Rule 23(b)(1) or (2) in order to avoid the mandatory notice requirement in Rule 23(b)(3) actions. However, because the mandatory notice requirement in Rule 23(b)(3) actions may be a matter of due process, significant constitutional problems may be raised. In *Ticor Title Insurance Co. v. Brown*, 511 U.S. 117 (1994), the Supreme Court recognized the problems, but refused to decide them.

In *Ticor*, a class action was settled under circumstances in which all money damage claims against the defendants were extinguished while injunctive and other non-monetary relief was granted to the members of the class. The district court certified the settlement under Rule 23(b)(1) and (2), rejecting an objection by a member of the class that it was improper to certify the action under these provisions because the relief requested was primarily monetary in nature. Later, a second class action was instituted on behalf of the class in another federal court, and the court granted summary judgment to the defendants in part on the ground that the plaintiffs were bound by the judgment in the prior class action. The court of appeals reversed, holding that it would violate due process to give a binding effect to the judgment in the original class action when the plaintiff bringing the second action had not been permitted to opt out of the first proceeding.

The Supreme Court granted certiorari, but later dismissed the writ as improvidently granted because a majority of the Court felt that the due process issue would not be of consequence if Rule 23 itself required notice and an opportunity to opt out of actions brought for damages. The Rule 23 issue could not be decided in the case because of the doctrine of res judicata (which will be covered in Chapter 12). Consequently, the Court ordered the writ dismissed and reserved judgment on the ultimate question of whether the due process clause requires notice in actions for money damages that can be qualified as class actions under Rule 23(b)(1) or (2). *Id.* at 119–21. However, the due process issue may be broader than this. The question of notice may not depend on whether the action is for money damages, but on whether adequacy of representation and other safeguards protect the absent members of the class sufficiently in Rule 23(b)(1) and (2) actions without notice, or whether due process requires notice even in those kinds of actions.

Class Actions in Mass Tort Cases. In addition to the due process questions discussed above, there are a number of serious management issues with class actions. One of these concerns the propriety of class actions in mass tort suits. In the Advisory Committee's Note to the 1966 amendment to Rule 23, the committee stated that mass torts would ordinarily not be appropriate for class action treatment, because individual issues of damages and defenses would usually be present in such actions, which would mean that the issues common to the class would not predominate. In spite of this statement, however, the Advisory Committee seemed to concede that certain kinds of mass tort cases might be appropriate for class action treatment.

Nevertheless, mass torts present many kinds of management problems that make class certification of the action as a class action difficult, and some federal courts of appeals have begun to scrutinize mass tort class certifications more closely than has been the case in the past. *See, e.g., Castano v. American Tobacco Co.*, 84 F.3d 734 (5th Cir. 1966) (reversing certification of nicotine class action); *In re American Med. Sys.*, 75 F.3d 1084 (6th Cir. 1996) (reversing certification of penile prosthesis class action). Similarly, state courts have also started to scrutinize class actions more carefully under state equivalents of Rule 23 to determine whether class treatment is proper. *See, e.g., Sieglock v. Burlington N. Santa Fe Ry. Co.*, 81 P.3d 495 (Mont. 2003) (common question requirement defeated by fact that class had members from at least 24 states and court would have to apply substantive tort law from multiple jurisdictions).

Settlement Class Actions. In addition to the management issues concerning mass tort class actions, serious questions have arisen in recent years about so-called "settlement class actions." In settlement class actions the parties arrive at a settlement before the action is commenced. The representative party then commences the class action, and the parties ask the court to certify the class as the parties have defined it. The court reviews the settlement before certifying the action. If the court finds the settlement to be fair, it will certify the action as a class action for settlement purposes only. Class counsel will then notify the members of the class simultaneously of the suit, the class certification, and the settlement. Serious questions have been raised about whether settlement class actions are compatible with Rule 23. *See, e.g.,* Teply & Whitten at 846–47 (discussing this issue and citing authorities).

The U.S. Supreme Court has not forbidden settlement class actions, but the Court has placed significant restrictions on them in order to protect the absent members of the class. In *Amchem Products, Inc. v. Windsor*, 521 U.S. 591 (1997), the Court held that the adequate representation requirement of Rule 23(a)(4) and the predominance requirement of Rule 23(b)(3) were not satisfied by the settlement class action certified by the district court. The Court held that settlement is relevant to class certification and that the question whether a trial would produce intractable management problems is not a consideration when settlement-only certification is requested. However, the Court found the adequacy of representation and predominance problems overwhelming in the context of the case. *Id.* at 620, 622–25.

In *Ortiz v. Fibreboard Corp.*, 527 U.S. 815 (1999), the Court reversed another certification of a settlement class action under Rule 23(b)(1)(B). The certification had been predicated on the existence of a limited fund, but the fund had been created by the settlement agreement of the parties. The Court held that in a Rule 23(b)(1)(B) action, there must be a demonstration that the fund in question is limited by more than the agreement of the parties and has been allocated to claimants within the class by a process that addresses any conflicting interests of the class members. The certification of the class in *Ortiz* failed to meet these requirements. In addition to the fact that the fund was limited only by the agreement of the parties, the certification contained exclusions from the class and allocations of assets at odds with the concept of the limited fund treatment and structural protections of Rule 23(a) explained in *Amchem*. *Id.* at 848–61.

In 1996, the Advisory Committee proposed amendments to Rule 23(b), (c), (e) & (f). A new Rule 23(b)(4) would have permitted certification of a class for settlement purposes when

> (4) the parties to a settlement request certification under subdivision (b)(3) for purposes of settlement even though the requirements of subdivision (b)(3) might not be met for trial.

See 167 F.R.D. 523, 559 (1996). This amendment was designed to resolve a conflict in the decisions resulting because some courts refuse to certify a class action for settlement purposes unless it could be certified for trial purposes. *See* Advisory Committee's Note to proposed Fed. R. Civ. P. 23(b)(4), 167 F.R.D. at 563. Recognizing the risks and benefits of the settlement class action, the Advisory Committee stated that the competing forces can be "reconciled by recognizing the legitimacy of settlement classes but increasing the protections afforded to class members." *Id.* at 564.

Note that (b)(4) settlement would only be available when the parties have reached a settlement, not when certification is sought for the purposes of assisting parties who want to explore settlement. *Id.* The Advisory Committee stated that "[n]otice and the right to opt out provide the central means of protecting settlement class members under subdivision (b)(3)," but exhorted the courts (a) to try to do better in framing "clear and succinct" settlement notices that provide the information necessary to determine whether to object to the settlement and (b) to approach the definition of the class with care, so as not to define the class over broadly and thus, *e.g.*, include within it persons with conflicting interests. *Id.*

Before the amendment could be adopted, the Supreme Court decided the *Amchem* and *Ortiz* cases, which restricted the settlement class-action device through interpretation of existing Rule 23. Nevertheless, it is not clear that all the problems with settlement class actions can be solved by a case-by-case interpretative approach. For example, in 2003, Rule 23(e) was amended "to strengthen the process of reviewing proposed class action settlements." *See* Fed. R. Civ. P. 23(e) advisory committee's note to the 2003 amendment. Ultimately, however, additional amendments may be needed to deal with the problems presented by settlement class actions.

Derivative Actions by Shareholders. A derivative action under Rule 23.1 allows a stockholder of a corporation or a member of an unincorporated association to enforce a right of action belonging to the corporation or association. Derivative actions are necessary when the persons in control of the corporation or association will not enforce the claim in question, often because it is a claim against them.

Actions Relating to Unincorporated Associations. Rule 23.2 provides that an action brought by or against the members of an unincorporated association may be brought as a class action by naming as representative parties one or more members of the association who will adequately represent the interests of the association and its members. The provisions of Rule 23(d) and (e), governing management of class actions, are made applicable to class suits relating to unincorporated associations under Rule 23.2.

Class Action Abuse. After the 1966 amendments to Rule 23, a widespread feeling developed that plaintiffs' lawyers were abusing class and derivative actions. The criticisms were many and varied. Some focused on the ease with which, in securities and some other kinds of litigation, plaintiffs could bring weak or even frivolous suits that imposed large defense costs on the party opposing the class even though the suits were not meritorious. Thus, defendants were often inclined to settle class actions for substantial sums in order to avoid the greater litigational costs associated with a full defense of the action.

Private Securities Litigation Reform Act of 1995. In 1995, Congress responded to the criticisms of class action abuse in the securities area by enacting the Private Securities Litigation Reform Act of 1995, 15 U.S.C. §§ 77a *et seq.* The Act amends the Securities Act of 1933 and the Securities and Exchange Act of 1934 to impose special provisions governing class actions under those statutes. In general, the Act adds procedural provisions to the 1933 and 1934 Acts that are designed to discourage frivolous securities litigation. The Act contains, *inter alia*, (1) special certification requirements for securities class actions; (2) special notice requirements to the absent class members designed to allow other members of the class to qualify as lead representative of the class; (3) restrictions on how frequently persons can serve as class representatives in securities actions; (4) proportionate per share restrictions on the amount that the class representative can recover; (5) reasonableness restrictions, keyed to the amount of damages and prejudgment interest paid to the class on the amount that attorneys can be paid; (6) special regulation of class settlements, including specific statements that must be sent to the class concerning proposed settlements; and (7) regulations designed to assure that attorneys representing the class do not have a conflict of interest. In addition, the Act alters the provisions of Federal Rule 11 as to class and non-class actions brought under the Securities Acts.

Class Counsel and Awarding Attorney's Fees in Class Actions. In 2003, Rules 23(g) and (h) were added. Rule 23(g) regulates the appointment of "class counsel" and emphasizes, *inter alia*, "the obligation of class counsel to represent the interest of the class, as opposed to the potentially conflicting interests of individual class members." *See* FED. R. CIV. P. 23(g) advisory committee's note to the 2003 amendment. In addition, Rule 23(h) now regulates class action attorney's fees and nontaxable costs.

Class Action Fairness Act of 2005. Another "reform" of class actions is embodied in the Class Action Fairness Act (CAFA) of 2005, Pub. L. No. 109-2, 119 Stat. 4 (2005), *partially codified as* 28 U.S.C. § 1332(d)(2). The specific provisions of the CAFA are exceedingly complex and are designed to broaden federal jurisdiction over nationwide class actions to prevent the perceived abuses that have occurred in some state courts in these actions. The CAFA confers original jurisdiction on the United States District Courts of class actions in which the amount in controversy exceeds $5,000,000, exclusive of interests and costs, and minimal diversity of citizenship exists. *See* 28 U.S.C. § 1332(d)(2)(A)-(C). In addition, Congress provided special aggregation rules for class actions covered by the Act to allow the claims of the individual class members to be aggregated to meet the amount-in-controversy requirement. *See* 28 U.S.C. § 1332(d)(6).

In *Standard Fire Insurance Co. v. Knowles*, __ U.S. __, 133 S. Ct. 1345, 185 L. Ed. 2d 439 (2013), plaintiff Knowles filed a class action in Arkansas state court, stipulating that he and the class would seek less than the $5,000,000 jurisdictional amount of CAFA. The defendant attempted to remove, but the district court remanded because of the stipulation, even though it admitted that CAFA's amount-in-controversy requirement would have been satisfied in the absence of the stipulation. The Eighth Circuit Court of Appeals refused to hear the defendant's appeal. The U.S. Supreme Court granted certiorari and reversed. The Court held that the stipulation was not binding because Knowles did not have the power to bind the class prior to the certification of the action as a class action. Because the stipulation was not binding, therefore, the amount in controversy was satisfied.

In addition to the above jurisdictional provisions, the CAFA also contains several class action reforms. Section 1712 primarily deals with the awarding of attorney's fees in the context of coupon settlements. For example, § 1712(a) provides that if a proposed settlement in a class action provides recovery of coupons to a class member, the portion of the attorney's fee award that is attributable to the award of the coupons shall be based on the value to the class members of the coupons that are redeemed. This section is obviously designed to prevent class members from being left with relatively trivial recoveries in the form of coupons for a defendant's product while class attorneys collect large monetary fees.

Section 1713 provides that the court may only approve of a proposed class settlement in which a class member is obligated to pay sums to class counsel that would result in a net loss to the class member after making a written finding that nonmonetary benefits to the class member substantially outweigh the monetary loss.

Section 1714 provides that the court may not approve a class settlement that provides for the payment of greater sums to some class members than to others based solely on the basis that the class members receiving the greater sums are located in closer geographic proximity to the court.

Section 1715 contains provisions for notification to appropriate federal and state officials with regulatory responsibility with respect to the defendant in a class action.

Removal of Class Actions. Under 28 U.S.C. § 1453(b), removal of class actions is provided for without regard for the one-year limit on removal of diversity actions found in 28 U.S.C. § 1446. Removal is also allowed under § 1453(b) even if a defendant is a citizen of the state in which the action is brought, thus eliminating the restriction on removal by in-state defendants that exists in other kinds of diversity actions under § 1441(b). Similarly, removal is also allowed under § 1453(b) by a single defendant, without the consent of the other defendants.

Notes and Questions

1. In an action for damages under Rule 23(b)(3), how should the court determine the amount of damages when the class numbers in the hundreds of thousands or millions? Must each class member submit an individual claim, or is there some fair way to estimate the damages without individual submissions? If the damages can be estimated without individual submission, how are they to be distributed? If there is no way to find all the class members and some of them do not claim their shares of the damages, what is to be done with the remainder? Should the representative party be allowed to keep it?

2. In a Rule 23, 23.1, or 23.2 action, how are the attorneys paid? Does the representative party pay all their fees? Can the court order the representative party to be reimbursed for the expenses of litigation, including attorney's fees (a) by the defendant or (b) out of any damages awarded to the class? *See, e.g., Central R.R. & Banking Co. v. Pettus,* 113 U.S. 116, 124 (1885) (allowing "all expenses properly incurred in the preparation and conduct of the suit, including … reasonable attorney's fees," to be paid out of the "common fund" that is created for the satisfaction of the class members' claims when a class action reaches settlement or judgment). If so, would that create any difficulties?

3. Who gets the recovery in a Rule 23.1 derivative action if the plaintiff wins? *See Bangor Punta Operations, Inc. v. Bangor A. & R.R. Co.,* 417 U.S. 703, 721–22 (1974) (pointing out that the recovery belongs to the corporation because "the shareholder in a derivative action enforces not his own individual rights, but rights which the corporation has").

4. In a class action for damages against an association under Rule 23.2, who pays the judgment if the association loses? If the association has no assets, can the judgment be executed against the assets of the individual members? If the state in which the district court is sitting has a statute that forbids execution against the assets of individual association members, does that statute apply? *See* FED. R. CIV. P. 69(a); *see also* RESTATEMENT (SECOND) OF JUDGMENTS § 61 cmts. a & b (1982).

5. Under Rule 42(a), actions involving "a common question of law or fact" pending before a court may be consolidated in the district court's discretion. Could consolidation be used as a substitute for a Rule 23(b)(3) class action? What would the obstacles be to using Rule 42(a) in this fashion?

6. Does the pendency of a class action toll the statute of limitations for members of the class who wish to assert their claims in individual actions? If so, under what circumstances? *See Stutz v. Minnesota Mining & Mfg. Co.,* 947 F. Supp. 399 (S.D. Ind. 1996) (class action tolling does not protect a plaintiff who files an individual action after the statute of limitations has run unless certification of the class has either been granted or denied; if it is denied, the class action will have tolled the statute for purposes of individual actions; if it is granted, the class member may be able to opt out and proceed individually because the class suit will also have tolled the statute for claims identical to the class claims).

7. There has been a certain amount of hostility, especially among academicians, to the congressional modification of practice under the Federal Rules through the Private Securities Litigation Reform Act of 1995, discussed in the text above. One criticism is that the Federal Rules were designed to be "trans-substantive" in nature. The imposition of special procedural requirements in securities cases is thought to undermine this goal. Do you think this criticism is fair? What is Congress supposed to do in the face of class action abuse that is not remedied by the Supreme Court under the Rules Enabling Act? For that matter, are the Court and its various advisory groups really in a position to balance all the interests that may be at stake in a needed law reform effort of the sort undertaken by the Act?

Problems

Problem 7-23. R brings suit as a representative of all poor persons within the state against the state board of education. R alleges the board is denying the members of the class its educational rights on the basis of economic status in violation of the Equal Protection Clause of the Fourteenth Amendment. Is the class action proper under Rule 23?

Problem 7-24. R, a public school pupil, sued the local board of education seeking an order to compel the board to desegregate public school faculties. R seeks to represent a class consisting of the local public school teachers and principals, whose constitutional rights R alleges are infringed by the segregated system being maintained by the board. Is the class action proper under Rule 23?

Problem 7-25. P sues R, the Mayor of City X, as a representative of a defendant class composed of the mayor and seven city councilmen. P seeks to have a city building desegregated. Is the class action proper under Rule 23?

Problem 7-26. R sues as the representative of a class consisting of all persons who had been defrauded by D. R alleges that D defrauded some 3,000 persons over a period of two years by making a variety of misrepresentations. Is the class action proper under Rule 23?

Problem 7-27. R sues as the representative of a class consisting of 3,000 persons who had been defrauded by D over a period of two years. R alleges that R was defrauded because D failed to disclose that a replica of a famous work of art that R purchased from D was made of brass, information that R alleges D was under a legal duty to disclose. R alleges that the other 2,999 members of the class were defrauded when D told them that the replicas of the same work of art that D sold them were gold, when they were really brass. Is the class action proper under Rule 23?

Problem 7-28. R sues D-1 and D-2 on R's own behalf and as the representative of a class of persons who signed certain loan contracts. The contracts contained clauses permitting the lender to confess judgment in a state court against the borrower, without notice to the borrower, upon a default of payment under the contract. D-1 and D-2 are the sheriff and the clerk of the state court in question. R seeks an order restraining the defendants from entering or executing any judgments by confession. R asserts that the practice is unconstitutional under the Due Process Clause of the Fourteenth Amendment because the class members did not knowingly waive their rights to a hearing when they signed the contracts in question. The class is composed of about 2,000 persons, four percent of whom have incomes in excess of $100,000 and the remainder of whom have incomes of less than $10,000. R has an income of less than $10,000. Is R an adequate representative of the class?

Problem 7-29. In each of the following situations determine whether the action described falls within one of the categories of class actions in Rule 23(b), and, if so, which category is most appropriate:

(a) A suit to challenge as unconstitutional a state's one-year residency requirement for welfare payments.

(b) A suit against a local school board seeking an order to require the school board to cease maintaining schools segregated by race.

(c) A suit for damages for fraud, where the fraud was perpetrated on many persons by similar misrepresentations, each victim being damaged in an amount of less than $5.00.

(d) A suit for damages by lakefront property owners brought against a person who allegedly polluted the lake and thus damaged the property.

(e) A mass-disaster tort action in which an airline allegedly was negligent in several respects, thus producing a crash that killed 200 persons.

Problem 7-30. R, a citizen of State X, sues D, an official of a labor union and a citizen of State Y, in a federal court in State X. R's suit is brought against D as a representative of the union, which is an unincorporated association organized under the laws of State X and has members in both State X and State Y. The suit is for $100,000 in damages for personal injuries inflicted on R by union members during a strike. Personal jurisdiction is obtained over D by use of a valid State X long-arm statute. The law of State X provides that associations organized under the laws of the state can be sued only by naming the association as a defendant and suing it as an entity. State X law expressly prohibits suing associations in class action form. Is the federal action proper? Would the result differ if the law of State X permitted actions against associations by joining all their members and did not contain an express prohibition of suits against associations in class action form?

Chapter 8

Discovery

As noted in Chapter 6, modern rules of pleading no longer embrace the detailed fact pleading requirements of the earlier pleading systems. In modern procedural systems, discovery plays a more critical role and acts as a direct complement to these relaxed pleading rules. Modern discovery now serves as the primary mechanism for the exchange of information making it possible for the parties to identify and narrow the issues in the case and to prepare for trial.

The main provisions for discovery under the Federal Rules of Civil Procedure are contained in Rules 26 through 37. As you study this chapter, you should regularly refer to the *specific* text of the current rules. The federal discovery rules are detailed and are difficult to paraphrase with full accuracy. In addition, the rules have been amended significantly in recent years. As you will quickly learn in practice, the specific rules must always be the first resource consulted and must be carefully studied in answering any question of procedure.

The rules of discovery applicable in the state courts vary from state to state. In most states, however, the discovery rules are patterned substantially on the Federal Rules of Civil Procedure. Although many states have not adopted the federal amendments imposing requirements for mandatory disclosure and setting certain limits on discovery, the core concepts concerning the traditional methods of discovery (such as depositions, interrogatories, requests for admission, and requests for the production of documents and tangible things) and the general principles governing the protections of work product and privilege are essentially the same in the state courts. Significantly, the 2006 federal discovery amendments dealing with "electronically stored information" ("e-discovery"), adopted after a meticulous drafting and review process, have become a model for the state courts in this emerging area.

The Federal Rules thus provide a representative format for studying modern discovery. As a practicing attorney in state court, though, you must always carefully research and follow the applicable rules of discovery in the particular jurisdiction in which you are appearing. Chapter 1 provided a brief overview of the various methods of discovery that will be discussed in this chapter. It would be helpful for you to review those general explanations before you begin this reading.

Section A. Basic Discovery Scope and Methods

Historical Overview. At common law, the pleadings were used to narrow the dispute to a single issue of law or fact. Only very limited discovery was available. Bills of particular, discussed in Chapter 6 in the context of code practice, also developed as a means of acquiring more specific information about an opposing party's claim. *See* TEPLY & WHITTEN at 583–84. In contrast, much broader discovery was available in equity actions and, as such, equity practice provided the basis for much of modern discovery. The principal discovery devices in equity were interrogatories, production and inspection of documents, and depositions. Equity also permitted separate actions to secure discovery and ordered discovery in aid of proceedings in other courts, including bills to perpetuate testimony. *See id.* at 580.

The Judiciary Act of 1789 authorized limited use of depositions, interrogatories, and discovery of documents in a pattern similar to traditional equity practice. The states also followed the general pattern of discovery developed in England. The New York Field Code of 1848 specifically provided for pretrial oral depositions. In addition, many states statutorily adopted discovery procedures developed in equity. These discovery procedures included written interrogatories that had to be answered by the adverse party, depositions of certain categories of witnesses related to the parties (such as employees), and production and inspection of documents in a party's possession and control.

Two major restrictions retained from traditional equity practice, however, limited the scope of discovery. First, discovery was limited to facts pertaining to the case of the party seeking discovery. Second, discovery was limited to facts or documents that would be admissible in evidence at trial. *See id.* It was the advent of the Federal Rules of Civil Procedure in 1938 that brought about a dramatic change in discovery practice.

1. The General Scope of Discovery: Rule 26(b)(1)

The Federal Rules of Civil Procedure established a broad scope of discovery and made a wide array of discovery methods available to the parties. The new scope of discovery reflected the underlying philosophy of the Federal Rules: parties should be able to obtain disclosure of all relevant information in the possession of any person before trial, unless the information was privileged. As expressed by the U.S. Supreme Court in the landmark case of *Hickman v. Taylor*, 329 U.S. 495 (1947), reprinted in section C(2)(a), below,

> [n]o longer can the time-honored cry of "fishing expedition" serve to preclude a party from inquiring into the facts underlying his opponent's case. Mutual knowledge of all the relevant facts gathered by both parties is essential to proper litigation. To that end, either party may compel the other to disgorge whatever facts he has in his possession. The deposition-discovery procedure simply advances the stage at which the disclosure can be compelled from the time of trial to the period preceding it, thus reducing the possibility of surprise.

Id. at 507–08.

Consistent with this philosophy, the federal discovery rules eliminated the two major limitations, noted above, on earlier discovery practice. Under Federal Rule 26(b)(1), which defines the general scope of discovery, discovery is permissible whether it relates to the claim or defense of the party seeking discovery or to the claim or defense of any other party. Moreover, under Rule 26(b)(1), discovery is permissible as to matters that would constitute inadmissible evidence at trial provided the information sought "appears reasonably calculated to lead to the discovery of admissible evidence." For instance, if a party in discovery requests information that would be inadmissible hearsay at trial under the Federal Rules of Evidence, the discovery request is, nevertheless, proper, provided disclosure of this information appears reasonably calculated to lead to the discovery of admissible evidence. The discovery standard of "relevance" is, thus, much broader than the evidentiary standard of admissibility under the rules of evidence.

The broad scope of discovery under the Federal Rules of Civil Procedure serves many purposes. Not only does broad discovery help to identify and sharpen the issues in the case, but it also works to eliminate surprise at trial, which hopefully yields a more just result. The parties are afforded the opportunity prior to trial to examine and preserve the testimony of the fact and expert witnesses fully. In addition, the parties are able to review the documentary evidence. As a result, each party can better prepare and present the party's case and counter the case of the opposing party. Finally, the free exchange of information allows the parties to critically assess the relative strengths and weaknesses of their respective cases for the purposes of both trial preparation and the facilitation of settlement.

Until December 1, 2000, the general scope of discovery under Rule 26(b)(1) was always defined as a single standard. Under former Rule 26(b)(1), the parties were entitled to obtain discovery, without the necessity of a court order, "regarding any matter, not privileged, which is *relevant to the subject matter* involved in the pending action." The amendments to the federal rules effective December 1, 2000, however, imposed a new dual standard for discovery differentiating between party-controlled and court-ordered discovery. Under amended Rule 26(b)(1), the parties may obtain discovery without the necessity of a court order "regarding any nonprivileged matter that is relevant to *any party's claim or defense....*" The former standard of "*relevant to the subject matter*" involved in the action was still retained as the overall standard for the scope of discovery, but under amended Rule 26(b)(1), such matters are now only discoverable by court order and only upon a showing of "good cause."

This amendment generated intense debate among members of the bench and bar. Proponents of the amendment argued that narrowing the scope of party-controlled discovery was necessary to curtail burdensome over-discovery and to reduce litigation expense. Opponents argued that discovery operated reasonably well in the overwhelming majority of cases and that instances of discovery abuse were primarily limited to contentious, "high stakes" cases. If a party in a particular case objected to discovery as overbroad or oppressive, relief was available to the aggrieved party by requesting a protective order under Rule 26(c), an order limiting discovery under Rule 26(b)(2), or sanctions under Rule 26(g). (These protective discovery provisions are reviewed in sections 2 and 5, below.)

Opponents also feared that the new dual standard would encourage resistance to discovery and trigger "satellite litigation" as courts and parties struggled to define the dividing line between that which is relevant to a "claim or defense" and that which is only more broadly relevant to the "subject matter involved in the action." Indeed, even the Advisory Committee's Note to amended Rule 26(b)(1) offered no clear guidance as to the distinction between matters relevant to a "claim or defense" and those relevant only to the "subject matter" of the action and conceded that the terms "cannot be defined with precision" and must be evaluated in each individual case "according to the reasonable needs of the action."

As it turned out, however, the new standard did not effect a significant change in discovery practice, and the courts have been able to handle discovery disputes under the dual standard without much difficulty. Although clearly intended to tighten the scope of party-controlled discovery, the new standard ("relevant to any party's claim or defense") is still a very broad standard and has proved sufficient to cover the discovery requests of the parties in the vast majority of cases. Liberal discovery remains the norm under the new standard. *See Breon v. Coca-Cola Bottling Co.,* 232 F.R.D. 49, 53 (D. Conn. 2005) ("The definition of relevance continues to be liberally interpreted even after changes to *Rule 26* in 2000.... Relevancy continues to be 'broadly construed, and a request for discovery should be considered relevant if there is *any possibility* that the information sought may be relevant to the claim or defense of any party'") (emphasis in original).

The breadth of the new standard is further evidenced by the Advisory Committee's Note to amended Rule 26(b)(1), which states that certain matters "not directly pertinent to the incident in suit" can nevertheless be relevant to a claim or defense in a particular case. The Advisory Committee's Note explained that

> other incidents of the same type, or involving the same product, could be properly discoverable under the revised standard. Information about organizational arrangements or filing systems of a party could be discoverable if likely to yield or lead to the discovery of admissible information. Similarly, information that could be used to impeach a witness, although not otherwise relevant to the claims or defenses, might be properly discoverable.

As illustrated by the *Anderson* and *Behler* cases, below, this passage from the Advisory Committee's Note has proved useful to the courts in interpreting the proper scope of the new "claim or defense" standard of Rule 26(b)(1). As you read *Anderson,* look to see which reference in this Note the court was applying. Do the same when you read *Behler.*

It is important to note that the adoption of the new dual standard for the scope of discovery was not intended to alter Rule 26(b)(1)'s longstanding definition of "relevance" for purposes of discovery, which remains broader than the evidentiary standard of admissibility under the rules of evidence. Thus, whether one is deciding if information is "relevant" to a "claim or defense" or "relevant" to the "subject matter," the test for "relevance" is the same. As stated in Rule 26(b)(1), "[r]elevant information need not be admissible at the trial if the discovery appears reasonably calculated to lead to the discovery of admissible evidence."

The *Anderson* case is typical of how the lower federal courts have analyzed the new dual standard of Rule 26(b)(1), especially in relying on the Advisory Committee Note quoted above.

Anderson v. Hale

United States District Court, Northern District of Illinois, 2001
No. 00 C 2021, 2001 WL 641113, 2001 U.S. Dist. LEXIS 7538

Ashman, United States Magistrate Judge.

Plaintiff, Reverend Stephen Tracy Anderson, filed a complaint against Defendants, Matthew F. Hale, the World Church of the Creator, and the Estate of Benjamin Nathaniel Smith, alleging that Defendants conspired to deprive Plaintiff of his federally protected rights by physically injuring him. Presently before this Court is Defendants' Emergency

Motion to Stay Plaintiff's Subpoenas to the Ohio and Wyoming Bars.[1] Defendants contend that state bar investigative files on Hale are not discoverable under amended Federal Rule of Civil Procedure 26(b)(1). For the following reasons, Defendants' motion is denied.

. . . .

The instant dispute mirrors that which we confronted in March 2001. At that time, Plaintiff subpoenaed the State Bar of Montana to obtain its investigative file on Hale. Montana created the file upon receiving Hale's application for admission to the Montana bar. The file contained approximately 2500 pages of information relating to Hale's character and fitness, some of which Plaintiff believed may be helpful to his § 1985(3) claim.

Defendants countered that the information contained in the investigative file was not remotely relevant to the lawsuit and not reasonably calculated to lead to the discovery of admissible evidence. Furthermore, Defendants contended that the subpoena was issued in bad faith to interfere with Hale's endeavor to secure a law license.

On March 29, 2001, this court determined that Plaintiff was entitled to discover state bar investigative files on Hale.... We held that the files were relevant because they may include information relating to the alleged Hale-Smith conspiracy, including communications between Hale and Smith. Additionally, we concluded that any notes taken and documents gathered concerning Hale's character and fitness appeared reasonably calculated to lead to the discovery of admissible evidence. In other words, we concluded that state bar investigative files may hold some information that Plaintiff could use to prove his § 1985(3) claim.

The order lived a short life. On April 11, 2001, Defendants filed a Rule 60(b) motion, alleging that this court erred by applying old Rule 26(b)(1) instead of amended Rule 26(b)(1). Admitting error, this court vacated its March 29, 2001 order on May 18, 2001. In the meantime, however, Plaintiff obtained the entire Montana investigative file and perused the documents contained therein.... Moreover, in reliance on the prospective language in the March order, Plaintiff served subpoenas on three other state bars—Iowa, Ohio, and Wyoming.... Plaintiff has reviewed the Iowa file; the Ohio and Wyoming files remain untouched....

To resolve the issue once and for all, the parties now want a blanket determination of the propriety of Plaintiff serving subpoenas on state bars to obtain investigative files on Hale. Given the timing of this motion and discovery posture of this case, amended Rule 26(b)(1) governs the dispute.

. . . .

Since December 1, 2000, amended Rule 26(b)(1) has applied to federal court proceedings insofar as just and practicable. Amended Rule 26(b)(1) provides that "[p]arties may obtain discovery regarding any matter ... that is relevant to the claim or defense of any party." Fed. R. Civ. P. 26(b)(1). Further, "[r]elevant information need not be admissible at the trial if the discovery appears reasonably calculated to lead to the discovery of admissible evidence." *Id.* Exactly what this means vis-a-vis old Rule 26(b)(1) will be settled over time. *See id.* advisory committee's note ("The dividing line between information relevant to the claims and defenses and that relevant only to the subject matter of the action cannot be defined with precision."). In any event, a narrowing has taken place.

The Committee's note provides some insight on this narrowing. It tells us that information is relevant if it directly involves the claims or defenses of the lawsuit. Moreover,

---

1. This motion is properly brought under Rule 26(c). *See* Fed. R. Civ. P. 26(c).

it tells us that information could be relevant even though it is indirectly related to the claims or defenses of the lawsuit. For example, "other incidents of the same type" could be relevant. Lastly, the note tells us that information, not relevant to the claims or defenses of the lawsuit per se, is discoverable if the information could be used to impeach. This gloss on relevance expands the claim or defense standard.

In terms of admissibility, the Committee's note instructs that only relevant information is discoverable. Similar to old Rule 26(b)(1), the relevant information need not be admissible; it need only be reasonably calculated to lead to the discovery of admissible evidence.

As of this writing, few courts have addressed the scope of amended Rule 26(b)(1). In *Sanchez v. Turner*, the court referenced the "other incidents" language of the Committee's note, but ultimately relied on the subject-matter standard of old Rule 26(b)(1) to allow discovery. 2001 WL 303719, at *2 (S.D.N.Y. Mar. 29, 2001) (applying the "just cause" exception of amended Rule 26(b)(1)). In *Behler v. Hanlon*, 199 F.R.D. 553, 561 (D. Md. 2001), the court allowed discovery for impeachment. Finally, in *McCann v. Bay Ship Management, Inc.*, the court relied on amended Rule 26(b)(1) to deny a motion to compel because the movant did not describe how the information sought was relevant to the claims or defenses of the lawsuit. 2000 WL 1838714, at *1 (E.D. La. Dec. 8, 2000). None of the decisions suggests that amended Rule 26(b)(1) will bring about a dramatic effect on the scope of discovery.

The gravamen of Plaintiff's complaint is a § 1985(3) claim, alleging a conspiracy between Hale and Smith to deprive Plaintiff of his federally protected rights. As explained in the March order, state bar investigative files may contain some information directly pertinent to this claim. For instance, the files may contain communications between Hale and Smith, and perhaps others, evincing an intent to act in concert to injure Plaintiff on the basis of his race.... The files may also contain statements made by Hale that demonstrate to some degree his knowledge of the Smith shootings. After all, any state bar investigation likely probed Hale's prior conduct during the relevant time period.

Additionally, the files may contain discoverable information that is not directly pertinent to Plaintiff's claims or Defendants' defenses. As we also explained in the March order, Hale's prior conduct becomes the topic of study in any state bar investigation. Montana, for example, culled some 2500 pages of information relating to Hale's past behavior. Within this morass of paper, Plaintiff may find evidence linking Hale to violent activity against members of non-White races, again assuming such information exists. State bar investigations aim to establish Hale's character; evidence of Hale engaging in violent activity goes toward determining good character. We need not discuss the ways in which such information might be helpful to Plaintiff's § 1985(3) claim. At this time it is enough to say that Plaintiff is entitled to discover the information because other incidents of the same type are relevant under amended Rule 26(b)(1). *relevant to claim or defense*

The remaining issue involves who should ferret through the voluminous investigative files to ascertain if any relevant information actually exists. As the producing party, a state bar would normally be responsible for sorting through and selecting documents responsive to Plaintiff's subpoena. But because the State Bar of Ohio, Wyoming, and so on, would be unfamiliar with the claims or defenses of this lawsuit, they could not locate and deliver all the relevant documents without undue burden. For this reason, wholesale disclosure of investigative files is warranted. *See, e.g.*, *Gucci Am., Inc. v. Exclusive Imports Int'l*, 2000 WL 1357787, at *2 (S.D.N.Y. Sept. 14, 2000).

. . . .

For the reasons stated, Defendants' motion is denied. Plaintiff is entitled to discover state bar investigative files on Hale.

Notes

1. As noted in the introductory text, the new dual standard did not effect a dramatic change in discovery practice. *Anderson, Behler* (reprinted below), and similar cases demonstrate that the courts have adopted a practical approach to the new standard and continue to permit broad discovery, as was the practice under the old standard, if the request is relevant in any way to a claim or defense in the action. *See, e.g., Klein v. AIG Trading Group Inc.,* 228 F.R.D. 418 (D. Conn. 2005) (defendants' objection that plaintiff's discovery request related only to the subject matter of the action and thus required a showing of good cause is rejected; plaintiff-employee's request for "spreadsheets and accounting records" of defendant-employers was relevant to plaintiff's damage claim for lost wages and wrongful discharge and thus was properly within the new "claim or defense" standard); *Sanyo Laser Prods., Inc. v. Arista Records, Inc.,* 214 F.R.D. 496 (D. Ind. 2003) (request by record companies in copyright infringement action for discovery as to business relationships between the named infringer and its unnamed affiliated companies was relevant to the record companies' copyright claim against the infringer and provided a "solid basis" for discovery under the new "claim or defense" standard because such discovery could reveal whether the infringer engaged in or conspired to engage in copyright infringement with its affiliated companies).

2. In addition, as under the prior practice, courts are continuing to monitor and curtail discovery by using the traditional protective limitations of Rule 26(b)(2)(c) and 26(c) when the discovery requests are deemed overbroad, excessive, or unduly burdensome. *See, e.g., Gill v. Gulfstream Park Racing Ass'n, Inc.,* Civ. No. 03-CV-155-JD, 2005 WL 1711119, 2005 U.S. Dist. LEXIS 14733 (D.N.H. July 21, 2005) (plaintiff-race horse owner's request for confidential information regarding preparation of horse racing investigative report whose publication triggered plaintiff's defamation action against defendants is denied; although the plaintiff "has a relevant interest in the confidential information either as it pertains to his present defamation claim or to the subject matter of that claim," the interests of the other parties, the informants, and the public warrant protection of the information under Rule 26(c)). In denying discovery in these situations, the courts sometimes cite the requester's failure to meet the new "good cause" requirement of Rule 26(b)(1) after deeming the discovery relevant only to the subject matter of the action. *See, e.g., BG Real Estate Servs., Inc. v. American Equity Ins. Co.,* Civ. A. 04-3408, 2005 WL 1309048, 2005 U.S. Dist. LEXIS 10330 (E.D. La. May 18, 2005) (plaintiff-insured's request for information on other claims by other insureds against the defendant-insurers was not related to "claims or defenses" in the case and "at best" was only relevant to the "subject matter" of the action; good cause for discovery was not shown by plaintiffs, especially considering the "tremendous burden and expense faced by defendants if they were required to respond to these requests").

2. Limitations on Discovery Under Rule 26

Even though a matter falls within the general scope of discovery authorized under Rule 26(b)(1), Rule 26, nevertheless, provides that certain matters are exempt from discovery and that, in particular cases, discovery may be limited by court order. In addition to the limit of Rule 26(b)(1) requiring a court order for discovery of matters relevant only to the "subject matter" of the action, the following are the principal limitations on discovery under Rule 26.

Privileged Matter. Rule 26(b)(1) provides that "[p]arties may obtain discovery regarding any nonprivileged matter...." Privileged matter is thus exempt from discovery.

The discovery rules do not define when a matter is "privileged." Instead, the law of privilege derives from other sources. Some privileges, such as the Fifth Amendment privilege against self-incrimination, are based on constitutional authority, while others, such as the attorney-client privilege, are based on statutory or common-law authority. Privilege is discussed in detail in section C(1), below.

Trial Preparation Materials. Rule 26(b)(3) affords special protection from discovery to trial preparation materials, commonly known as "work product." Under Rule 26(b)(3)(A), such material is only discoverable upon a showing of substantial need and undue hardship by the party seeking discovery. Work product protection is discussed in detail in section C(2)(*a*), below.

Protective and other Orders Limiting Discovery. Under Rule 26(c)(1), a party or any person from whom discovery is sought may seek a "protective order" from the court limiting discovery "to protect a party or person from annoyance, embarrassment, oppression, or undue burden or expense." Rule 26(c)(1)(A)-(H) identifies eight discovery limitations that the court may impose "for good cause," including an order "forbidding the disclosure or discovery" or "specifying terms, including time and place, for the disclosure or discovery." In addition to Rule 26(c), Rule 26(b)(2)(C) expressly requires the court to limit the frequency and extent of discovery otherwise allowed under the rules to guard against redundant or disproportionate discovery. As noted by the Advisory Committee in 1983, this limitation was designed "to encourage judges to be more aggressive in identifying and discouraging discovery abuse." Rule 26(b)(1) expressly states that "[a]ll discovery is subject to the limitations imposed by Rule 26(b)(2)(C)."

Rule 26(b)(2)(C) currently provides:

> On motion or on its own, the court must limit the frequency or extent of discovery otherwise allowed by these rules or by local rule if it determines that:
>
> (i) the discovery sought is unreasonably cumulative or duplicative, or can be obtained from some other source that is more convenient, less burdensome, or less expensive;
>
> (ii) the party seeking discovery has had ample opportunity to obtain the information by discovery in the action; or
>
> (iii) the burden or expense of the proposed discovery outweighs its likely benefit, considering the needs of the case, the amount in controversy, the parties' resources, the importance of the issues at stake in the action, and the importance of the discovery in resolving the issues.

The following case illustrates the basic interplay of Rules 26(b)(1), (b)(2)(C), and 26(c). Additional considerations are triggered by these rules in the discovery of electronically stored information because of its potential enormous volume and retrieval cost. These special "e-discovery" issues are treated in section B, below.

Behler v. Hanlon

United States District Court, District of Maryland, 2001
199 F.R.D. 553

GRIMM, UNITED STATES MAGISTRATE JUDGE.

This diversity personal injury case has been assigned to me, with the consent of the parties, for all proceedings. 28 U.S.C. §636(c). The pending dispute involves Mr. Behler's [the plaintiff's] efforts to obtain discovery of facts relating to income earned, and work done, by Robert D. Keehn, M.D., on behalf of insurance companies and defense attorneys in connection with conducting Rule 35 examinations of plaintiffs in personal injury cases. Such examinations, euphemistically referred to by counsel as "independent medical examinations" ("IME"), can be anything but independent, if they are performed by a doctor who has significant financial ties with insurance companies and attorneys assigned to defend personal injury cases. Counsel for Mr. Hanlon, the defendant, vehemently has objected to the discovery that plaintiff seeks....

. . . .

Plaintiff originally served a Rule 34 request on defendant, seeking tax returns, and documents relating to income earned during the last five years by Dr. Keehn from defense attorneys and insurance companies, in connection with performing IME's, and testifying as an expert witness in deposition or at trial. Further, plaintiff sought documents relating to the amount of time Dr. Keehn has spent doing such activities, as well as a list of cases where he has been retained for such services, and attorneys and insurers on whose behalf he has provided forensic services. It is plaintiff's contention that for more than 20 years Dr. Keehn has been a "defense expert for insurance companies," and plaintiff wants to discover information to use at trial to impeach Dr. Keehn's credibility by demonstrating bias.[1] Defendant answered plaintiff's Rule 34 request with a blanket refusal to provide the requested information. Undeterred, plaintiff had a Rule 45 subpoena served on Dr. Keehn, which requested production of the information. In response, defendant filed a torturously titled "motion to strike reply to defendant's response to request for production of documents, to quash subpoena and for injunction," when a simple motion for protective order under Rule 26(c) would have been sufficient. Resolution of this motion turns on whether the information sought by plaintiff is discoverable under Rule 26(b)(1), and, if so, whether it must be produced as requested, *Issue* or in some other manner, after application of the balancing factors of Rule 26(b)(2)[(c)].

The pre-December, 2000 version of Rule 26 governs this dispute, as the scheduling order in this case was issued prior to December 1, 2000. However, under either the "old version" of Rule 26(b)(1), which defined the scope of discovery broadly to include any matter, not privileged, that was relevant to the "subject matter" of the litigation, or the "new version" of Rule 26(b)(1), which defines the scope more narrowly as unprivileged facts relevant to the claims and defenses raised in the litigation, the result would be the same. This is because the information sought relates to the credibility of a witness whose testimony will be directed towards important issues in the case. Such information will fall within the scope of discovery under either version of the rules of procedure because, as will be shown, a witness always may be impeached by evidence that she or he is biased, prejudiced, has a financial interest in the outcome of the case, or a motive to testify in a particular manner.

. . . .

---

1. In support of his request, plaintiff cites *Wrobleski v. Lara*, 727 A.2d 930 (Md. 1999), in which the Maryland Court of Appeals permitted inquiry regarding expert witness income for purposes of developing bias impeachment. While instructive, and consistent with the ruling in this order, it is not binding authority, as this is a diversity case governed by the Federal Rules of Evidence and procedure, not state procedural rules or cases. *See Hottle v. Beech Aircraft Corp.*, 47 F.3d 106, 109 (4th Cir.1995) (*citing Scott v. Sears, Roebuck & Co.*, 789 F.2d 1052, 1054 (4th Cir.1986)) (holding that the Federal Rules of Evidence govern in diversity cases); *Rowland v. Patterson*, 852 F.2d 108, 110 (4th Cir.1988) (*citing Hanna v. Plumer*, 380 U.S. 460 (1965)) (holding that "federal courts apply federal rules of procedure, both those promulgated in the Federal Rules of Civil Procedure as well as wholly judge made procedural rules, unless the *Erie* doctrine commands otherwise"); *Ronk v. Corner Kick, Inc.*, 850 F. Supp. 369, 370, n.2 (D. Md. 1994) (*citing Hanna v. Plumer*, 380 U.S. 460 (1965)) (holding that the Federal Rules of Civil Procedure govern all matters of procedure in a diversity case).

... However, as Rule 26(b)(2) instructs, the mere fact that such information falls within the scope of legitimate discovery does not mean that parties are entitled to unfettered discovery of impeaching information, by whatever means of discovery they seek. Indeed, ... a determination that facts which a party seeks to discover fall within the scope of discovery set out by Rule 26(b)(1) is but the first step in the analysis.... Even if discoverable, the court may, upon a Rule 26(c) motion for protective order, or on its own initiative, restrict or prevent requested discovery if, following an evaluation of the Rule 26(b)(2) factors, it determines that the discovery would be burdensome, duplicative, unnecessarily costly, or insufficiently probative to the issues in the litigation to warrant the expense of production....

In the present case, no intellectually honest argument can be made that the information sought by plaintiff regarding Dr. Keehn's activities as a defense expert witness is not relevant to bias/prejudice impeachment, and, therefore, within the scope of discovery permitted by Rule 26(b)(1). However, legitimate issues are raised regarding the extent of the bias discovery sought, the methods of discovery employed, and possible abuses that could occur if the discovery is permitted without a protective order. For example, plaintiff seeks discovery of the total income earned by Dr. Keehn for the last five years, the amount thereof earned providing defense Rule 35 examinations, records relating to the hours spent by Dr. Keehn in this capacity, copies of his tax returns, and a listing of all insurance companies with whom he is affiliated, as well as a listing of all cases in which he has provided expert services. This is overkill. While there may be cases in which an expert's gross income, and the specific amounts thereof earned by providing services as an expert witness, may be discoverable, this should not be ordered routinely, without a showing, absent here, why less intrusive financial information would not suffice. Most people are sensitive about their income, and who knows the details about it. By their very nature, expert witnesses are knowledgeable of information that is scientific, technical, or specialized, generally acquired by long, hard study and experience. When asked to provide expert testimony, they are in a position to request compensation that matches their qualifications, which can seem shockingly high to those not familiar with the costs of modern litigation. Moreover, ... in light of the Rule 26(a)(2) disclosure requirements and the recent changes to Rules 702 and 703, counsel increasingly are more selective in whom they ask to be expert witnesses, knowing that they will be subject to the utmost scrutiny. Those who pass muster likely will be able to command fees commensurate with their skill and experience, which may, to a lay member of the jury, appear exorbitant, when in fact what was charged is the going rate. Rule 26(a)(2)(B)[(vi)] requires disclosure of the compensation received by a retained expert in the particular case at issue, and counsel routinely bring this out during cross-examination when questioning an opposing expert witness. However, permitting routine disclosure of the expert's gross compensation, from all sources—including those unrelated to litigation activities—would provide the jury with little information relevant to a fair assessment of the expert's credibility, while concomitantly introducing the real possibility of creating confusion, distraction and even prejudice....

Instead, the jury readily should be able to assess possible bias on the part of an expert witness if they are made aware of the total percentage of his or her gross income that is earned from providing expert witness services. Similarly, there is no need for the expert to have to produce his or her tax returns, if the party seeking the discovery has accurate information regarding the percentage of income earned as an expert.

Additionally, while documents relating to all cases within a stated period of time for which an expert was retained are relevant to possible bias impeachment, in this case I do not believe that Dr. Keehn should be required to assemble these records, provided the plaintiff is able to obtain the equivalent information by a more expedient, less costly method. To this end, I will order that Dr. Keehn be produced for questioning at a deposition regarding the information sought by plaintiff. If possible, this deposition will be by telephone, and its scheduling will be expedited. The questioning by plaintiff at the deposition will not last more than 2 hours, provided Dr. Keehn provides complete and unevasive answers to proper questions asked, as is required by Rule 37(a)(3). Further, prior to the deposition, he will make a diligent search of all records in his possession, custody and control, to enable him to provide the following information: (1) The percentage of his gross income earned for each of the preceding five years attributable to performing expert witness services on behalf of insurance companies, and/or attorneys defending personal injury cases; (2) a list of cases in which he has provided such services during the last five years, in sufficient detail to enable the plaintiff to locate the court file, and/or issue a subpoena for it. At a minimum, the name, address and telephone number of the attorney and/or insurance claims representative that engaged Dr. Keehn will be provided; (3) the name of each insurance company for which Dr. Keehn has provided services as an expert witness in personal injury cases, for the preceding ten years.

If, after taking this deposition, plaintiff can demonstrate that additional information is required to enable him to undertake reasonable bias impeachment of Dr. Keehn, he may seek leave from the court to take additional discovery. Further, should the court determine that Dr. Keehn has not provided complete, and unevasive, answers to the discovery herein ordered, or if the court determines that he has not made a good faith, diligent effort to assemble the information for which discovery was ordered, then additional discovery will be ordered, and appropriate sanctions, including not allowing him to testify at trial, if warranted by the level of non-compliance, may be imposed.

Finally, to protect against possible abuse of the sensitive financial information for which discovery has been allowed, it will be subject to a protective order that prohibits dissemination or copying of the information produced for any purpose not directly related to the prosecution of this case, absent the consent of Dr. Keehn, or further order of this Court. This protective order will remain in effect following the conclusion of the pending case, unless withdrawn by order of this Court.

. . . .

For the reasons stated above, the defendant's motion to preclude the plaintiff from discovering information about Dr. Keehn's income in connection with his forensic activities on behalf of personal injury defendants is denied. However, the information sought by plaintiff will not be produced as requested, it will be produced as specified in this Memorandum and Order, and its production will be subject to the protective order imposed.

— 26(c)

Problem

Problem 8-1. Would the following situations be within the scope of discovery as defined by Rule 26(b)(1)? Would discovery in any of these situations be subject to limitation by the court as in the *Behler* case?

(a) Assume that *P*, the plaintiff, is in doubt whether *D*, the defendant, has sufficient assets to satisfy the judgment that *P* hopes to obtain in a pending negligence action. Should *P* be allowed to compel *D* through discovery to provide an estimate of *D*'s net worth?

(b) Assume that *P* and *D* have had an auto accident. *P* alleges that *D* negligently drove *D's* motor vehicle at an excessive rate of speed. In the course of the pending action, *P* seeks through an interrogatory to make *D* state what the weather conditions were for the ten-hour period prior to the accident—the temperature, amount of rainfall, etc. Should it matter that the information sought is equally available to the parties from the weather bureau?

(c) Assume that in a pending negligence action to recover for injuries sustained in a fall on *D's* premises, *P* seeks to discover from *D* what precautions *D* took following the accident to ensure a non-skid surface at the place of the accident. Does Rule 407 of the Federal Rules of Evidence have any bearing on your answer?

(d) Assume that in a pending action, *D* wants to discover *P's* motives for commencing the action, the fee arrangements that *P* has for bearing the costs of the litigation, and *P's* ability to satisfy a judgment for costs should *D* prevail in the action. Should it make any difference if (i) *P* is a government instead of a private party, (ii) the pending action is a stockholders' derivative suit, or (iii) the pending action is a class action? Why or why not?

(e) Assume that *P* had sued *D* for injuries arising out of an automobile accident. *P's* attorney has said that *P* is unable to walk as a result of the accident. *D's* attorney then hires a photographer to videotape *P* surreptitiously. The photographer videotapes *P* playing tennis at a resort. *D's* attorney plans to use these surveillance videotapes to impeach *P's* testimony at trial. Can *P* discover any impeaching information *D* has acquired, such as the videotape?

3. The Mechanics of Discovery Exchange

(a) Introduction

As noted in the overview section on discovery in Chapter 1, the Federal Rules of Civil Procedure provide a wide array of discovery procedures and methods to facilitate the exchange of discovery information. Although the overriding philosophy of the federal discovery rules is to promote the liberal exchange of essential information between the parties, it is important to note that, with limited exceptions, discovery operates within the overall framework of the adversary system. Thus, while the discovery rules provide the structure and means to access essential information, the parties themselves must initiate the discovery process by specifically requesting information from another party or person via one or more of the methods for discovery. Although a party must respond to all proper discovery requests with truthful and accurate information, and supplement those responses when required under Rule 26(e), there is no general requirement that parties disclose information to their adversary that has not been requested. In 1993, this practice was altered slightly with the adoption of the "mandatory disclosure" provisions of Rule 26(a), which provide for the disclosure of certain basic information without the necessity of a discovery request. All other information, however, must be requested by the parties in discovery. To date, many states have not adopted similar provisions for mandatory disclosure and continue to rely on the parties to initiate the discovery process.

Traditional Methods of Discovery. As noted in Chapter 1, the federal rules provide for five traditional methods of discovery: (1) oral depositions and depositions by written questions, Rules 30 and 31; (2) interrogatories, Rule 33; (3) requests for the production of documents and tangible things, Rule 34; (4) physical and mental examinations,

Rule 35; and (5) requests for admission, Rule 36. Although the specific procedures for discovery may vary from state to state, these traditional methods of discovery constitute the essence of discovery practice in the state courts as well. Each method of discovery will be discussed in the subsections following this introduction.

Discovery from Nonparties. As will be explained in greater detail, the above discovery methods generally apply only to discovery sought from another *party* to the action. Interrogatories under Rule 33, requests for the production of documents and tangible things under Rule 34, and requests for admission under Rule 36 may only be sent by one party for response by another party. These discovery procedures may not be used to request information from a person or entity that is *not* a party to the action. Similarly, under Rule 35, a physical or mental examination may only be ordered of a party or "a person who is in [the party's] custody or under [the party's] legal control."

The only discovery device that expressly allows discovery as to nonparties is the oral or written deposition under Rules 30 and 31 ("A party may ... depose *any* person, including a party....") Thus, if a nonparty has information relevant to the action within the scope of Rule 26(b)(1), any party may schedule the deposition of such a person to discover this information. In addition, if the nonparty is in possession of documents or tangible things, including electronically stored information, Rule 45 authorizes a party to serve the nonparty with a _subpoena_ to produce the items for inspection and copying at the deposition or at a separate time and place. Such a subpoena is known as a _subpoena duces tecum_. Through the use of a subpoena duces tecum, therefore, a party is able to effectuate the discovery of documents and tangible things that would otherwise be permitted only against a party under Rule 34. Recall that in the first two cases of this chapter, *Anderson* and *Behler,* the discovery dispute was triggered by a Rule 45 subpoena duces tecum served upon nonparties in the action to produce certain files and records. Subpoenas are examined in greater detail in subsection *(c)*, below.

Other Methods of Discovering Information. Keep in mind that the federal rules do not prohibit the parties from conducting "informal discovery" on their own outside of the structure of the formal discovery rules. Thus, a party or the party's attorney or investigator could interview witnesses in the action, take written statements from the witnesses, review documents in their possession, visit the accident scene, etc. Of course, the individual witnesses would have to be willing to voluntarily meet and speak with the party or the party's attorney or investigator, but such informal discovery often will be less expensive than formal discovery, especially when compared to the alternative of a formal deposition, and it will generally yield the same basic information.

One significant drawback, however, with respect to preserving witness testimony is that only an actual deposition formally preserves a witness' testimony for trial under the provisions of Rule 32(a)(4) if the witness is unavailable to testify at trial. Under the Federal Rules of Evidence, a witness statement, even if given under oath, is considered hearsay if offered for substantive purposes and cannot be used as a substitute for the witness' live testimony if the witness is unavailable to testify at trial.

Police and other governmental reports may also be valuable sources of information concerning the events giving rise to a lawsuit. Nonprivileged government documents may be available through the federal Freedom of Information Act, 5 U.S.C. § 552, or a similar state statute permitting access to public documents.

Party Stipulations Regarding Discovery. Finally, Rule 29 expressly provides that, unless the court orders otherwise, the parties in a particular case may agree to modify the formal procedures governing or limiting discovery under the rules. As explained in the

Advisory Committee's Note to the 1993 amendments to the discovery rules, Rule 29 is designed "to give greater opportunity for litigants … to agree on less expensive and time-consuming methods to obtain information, as through voluntary exchange of documents, use of interviews in lieu of depositions, etc."

Rule 29(a) specifically authorizes the parties to stipulate that "a deposition may be taken before any person, at any time or place, on any notice, and in any manner specified — in which event it may be used in the same way as any other deposition." This provision is especially beneficial because, as will be explained in subsection *(c)*, below, on depositions, depositions are the most effective and valuable discovery device, but they have the disadvantage of being expensive. The ability to modify the formal deposition procedure is particularly useful in smaller value cases because the witness could be deposed in a less expensive manner, for example in a deposition by telephone or other remote means as allowed under Rule 30(b)(4). Valuable information could then be secured from the witness, as would be possible in an informal interview with the witness, but the evidentiary hearsay problem noted in the previous section regarding informal interviews and witness statements is avoided. Because Rule 29(a) states that a "modified" deposition "may be used in the same way as any other deposition," the deposition may be fully used at trial in accordance with the provisions of Rule 32(a)(4) if the witness becomes unavailable to testify at trial.

Under Rule 29, the parties are generally not required to obtain court approval of discovery stipulations. Under Rule 29(b), however, stipulations extending the time for any form of discovery require court approval if the extension "would interfere with the time set for completing discovery, for hearing a motion, or for trial."

(b) Required Disclosures: Rule 26(a)(1)-(3)

As discussed in Chapter 1, Rule 26(a) was amended in 1993 to impose a duty on the parties of mandatory "automatic" disclosure of certain information without the need for any formal discovery request from another party. As expressed in the Advisory Committee's Note to the 1993 amendments, the mandatory disclosure provisions were designed to "accelerate the exchange of basic information about the case and to eliminate the paper work involved in requesting such information." Mandatory disclosures are sequenced in three phases. First, early in the action, the parties must exchange basic information about the case under Rule 26(a)(1) regarding potential witnesses, documentary evidence, damages, and insurance. Second, at a later appropriate time during the discovery period, the parties must exchange information under Rule 26(a)(2) about expert witnesses who may be used at trial. Third, as the trial date approaches, the parties must provide information under Rule 26(a)(3) regarding the evidence they may offer at trial.

Rule 26(e)(1) further requires the parties to supplement these mandatory disclosures "(A) in a timely manner if the party learns that in some material respect the disclosure … is incomplete or incorrect, and if the additional or corrective information has not otherwise been made known to the other parties during the discovery process or in writing; or (B) as ordered by the court." Full compliance with all of the requirements for mandatory disclosure is crucial because of the penalty provisions of Rule 37(c)(1). Under Rule 37(c)(1), if a party fails to provide information or identify a witness as required by Rule 26(a) or 26(e), the information or witness may not be used by the party at a motion, hearing, or trial, "unless the failure was substantially justified or is harmless."

The 1993 amendments requiring mandatory automatic disclosures, particularly the initial disclosure requirements under Rule 26(a)(1), were controversial. Critics of the amended rule raised a number of procedural concerns about implementation, but the overriding argument was that mandatory disclosure was inconsistent with the basic notion of the adversary system in requiring a party to "do the work for" another party. The level of controversy even reached the U.S. Supreme Court, with a majority of the Justices approving the amendments, but with three Justices dissenting. Intense lobbying efforts in Congress narrowly failed to block the new amendments from going into effect and the new requirements became effective on December 1, 1993. After several years of implementation, the decision was made to retain, but refine, the mandatory disclosure requirements, and these changes are reflected in the 2000 amendments.

(i) Initial Disclosures: Rule 26(a)(1)

The initial mandatory disclosures of Federal Rule 26(a)(1)(A) focus on four areas: (i) potential witnesses, (ii) documentary evidence, (iii) damages, and (iv) insurance. When these initial disclosure requirements were first enacted in 1993, the federal district courts were already in the process of establishing civil litigation reform plans pursuant to the Civil Justice Reform Act of 1990. As a consequence, and also because of various concerns raised regarding the implementation of these disclosure requirements, Rule 26(a)(1) permitted a period of local experimentation and authorized individual federal districts to "opt-out" of the requirements for initial disclosure by local rule. Thereafter, approximately half of the federal districts chose to "opt-out" of the requirements for initial disclosure in some fashion. The result was a confusing patchwork of local rules with varying requirements of initial disclosure.

Gradually a general sentiment emerged that, irrespective of the relative pros and cons of initial disclosure, a uniform nationwide standard for all of the federal courts was the better choice. Rule 26(a)(1) was, therefore, amended in 2000 to eliminate this local rule "opt-out" provision and the initial disclosure requirements now have nationwide application in all federal district courts. In exchange for imposing a nationwide standard, Rule 26(a)(1) was correspondingly amended to address some of the earlier concerns regarding the initial disclosure requirements. The scope of the initial disclosure requirements under Rule 26(a)(1)(A)(i) and (ii) regarding witnesses and documents were narrowed substantially. In addition, under Rule 26(a)(1)(B), certain categories of cases in which little or no discovery normally occurs were expressly exempted from the initial disclosure requirements. As under the former rule, the requirements of initial disclosure may still be modified or excused by the court in a particular case or by stipulation of the parties.

Rule 26(a)(1)(A) currently provides:

(A) *In General.* Except as exempted by Rule 26(a)(1)(B) or as otherwise stipulated or ordered by the court, a party must, without awaiting a discovery request, provide to the other parties:

(i) the name and, if known, the address and telephone number of each individual likely to have discoverable information—along with the subjects of that information—that the disclosing party may use to support its claims or defenses, unless the use would be solely for impeachment;

(ii) a copy—or a description by category and location—of all documents, electronically stored information, and tangible things that the disclosing party has in its possession, custody, or control and may use to support its claims or defenses, unless the use would be solely for impeachment;

(iii) a computation of each category of damages claimed by the disclosing party—who must also make available for inspection and copying as under Rule

34 the documents or other evidentiary material, unless privileged or protected from disclosure, on which each computation is based, including materials bearing on the nature and extent of injuries suffered; and

(iv) for inspection and copying as under Rule 34, any insurance agreement under which an insurance business may be liable to satisfy all or part of a possible judgment in the action or to indemnify or reimburse for payments made to satisfy the judgment.

As noted above, the 2000 amendments to Rule 26(a)(1) substantially narrowed the scope of the initial disclosure requirements under Rule 26(a)(1)(A)(i) and (ii). The former Rule 26(a)(1)(A)(i) required a party to identify all individuals likely to have discoverable information "relevant to disputed facts alleged with particularity in the pleadings." Former Rule 26(a)(1)(A)(ii) also required a party to provide a copy or description of all documents in the possession or control of the party based on the same standard of relevance. Current Rule 26(a)(1)(A)(i) and (ii) now limit these disclosure requirements to the identification of those individuals with discoverable information and those documents that the disclosing party "*may use to support its claims or defenses,* unless the use would be solely for impeachment." As explained in the 2000 Advisory Committee's Note, the term "use" includes use at a pretrial conference, deposition, motion, or trial.

Significantly, under current Rule 26(a)(1)(A), a party is no longer required, as part of the initial disclosure requirements, to identify persons or documents that are unfavorable to the party's position. The current rule only requires disclosure as to individuals with information and documents that support a party's position and only then if the party "may use" the information or document to support its case. Matters that will be used solely for impeachment purposes, *i.e.,* to attack the credibility of a witness, are also excluded from the initial disclosure requirements.

As reflected in the public announcement of the proposed 2000 rule amendments, the purpose of this narrower disclosure standard was to present a "less controversial rule for national uniformity" and to address "one of the fundamental objections" to the former rule "that one side should not be forced to work for the other side." Under the revised rule, "a party need only figure out its own positions and disclose the identity of witnesses and documents that support these positions." Reports of the Advisory Committee on Civil Rules, the Honorable V. Neimeyer, Chair, Advisory Committee on Civil Rules, June 30, 1998, *reprinted in* 181 F.R.D. 24, 30 (1998).

Distinguishing Formal Discovery Requests. It must be emphasized that this provision limiting disclosure only to "supporting" matter applies only to the requirements of initial disclosure under Rule 26(a)(1) and does not affect or limit the scope of discovery under the other traditional methods of discovery. Thus, in the absence of privilege or some other special limitation on discovery, a party *must* disclose in response to a proper discovery demand all requested information, irrespective of whether the information is favorable or unfavorable to the party's position and irrespective of whether the party intends to "use" the information at trial.

Liability Insurance Agreements. Because of the practical significance of liability insurance in the resolution of civil cases, Rule 26(a)(1)(A)(iv) requires initial disclosure of any liability insurance agreement that may be applicable for payment of all or part of a judgment in the action. This provision replaced the former Rule 26(b)(2), which was added in 1970 to expressly authorize discovery of such agreements. It is important to note that simply because liability insurance agreements are subject to disclosure under Rule 26(a)(1)(A)(iv), the fact that they must be disclosed does not mean that such agreements are admissible in evidence at trial. Evidence of insurance at trial could improperly influence a jury to find liability where it otherwise would not. Accordingly, Federal Rule of Evidence 411 provides that "[e]vidence that a person was or was not insured against liability is not admissible upon the issue whether the person acted negligently or otherwise wrongfully."

Initial Disclosure Procedures and the Discovery Conference. Except in cases exempt from initial disclosure under Rule 26(a)(1)(B) or when the court orders otherwise, the parties are required under Rule 26(f) to confer in the early stages of the action to "consider the nature and basis of their claims and defenses and the possibilities for promptly settling or resolving the case; make or arrange for the disclosures required by Rule 26(a)(1); discuss any issues about preserving discoverable information; and develop a proposed discovery plan." Rule 26(f)(3) expressly requires that the discovery plan include, among other things, a statement when initial disclosures were or will be made, the subjects on which discovery may be needed and when discovery should be completed, any issues about disclosure or discovery of electronically stored information, and any issues relating to claims of privilege or work product. Requiring the parties to confer early in the action is an important step in facilitating discovery exchange, issue clarification, and early settlement. First added to the rules in 1993, the Advisory Committee noted in its comments to the 2000 rule amendments that the requirement of a discovery conference was praised by the bench and bar as "one of the most successful changes made in the 1993 amendments."

Under Rule 26(a)(1)(c), the initial disclosures required by Rule 26(a)(1)(A) must be made within 14 days after the Rule 26(f) discovery conference, unless a different time is set by stipulation or court order, or unless a party objects during the conference and states the objection in the discovery plan. Under Rule 26(f)(1), the discovery conference must be held "as soon as practicable—and in any event at least 21 days before a scheduling conference is to be held or a scheduling order is due under Rule 16(b)." Rule 16(b)(2) requires the court to enter a scheduling order "as soon as practicable, but in any event within the earlier of 120 days after any defendant has been served with the complaint or 90 days after any defendant has appeared." Under Rule 16(b)(3), a "scheduling order" governs the timing limits for motions, amendments to pleadings, joinder of parties, completion of discovery, and any "other appropriate matters."

Objections to Initial Disclosures. The 2000 amendments to current Rule 26(a)(1)(c) also included a new provision for objection to initial disclosures. Under this rule, if a party believes "that initial disclosures are not appropriate in [the] action," the party must object at the discovery conference and state the objection in the Rule 26(f) discovery plan. The court must then rule on the objection and "determine what disclosures, if any, are to be made, and must set the time for disclosure." As explained in the 2000 Advisory Committee's Note, this provision for objection does not allow a party "to 'opt out' of disclosure unilaterally," but only affords a party the opportunity to present its objection to the court.

When might it be "inappropriate" in the circumstances of the action for initial disclosures to be required? Suppose the defendant, rather than answering the plaintiff's complaint, files one of the pre-answer motions to dismiss under Rule 12(b)? Should the defendant, nevertheless, have to comply with the requirements for initial disclosure if the defendant has filed a motion to dismiss the plaintiff's complaint for lack of subject-matter or personal jurisdiction or for failure to state a claim? As part of the 2000 amendments, the Committee considered postponing initial disclosure pending disposition of such preliminary motions, but ultimately rejected any provision for an automatic stay of disclosure.

Under such circumstances, how should the parties proceed? Under Rule 26(a)(1), the parties could stipulate to postpone initial disclosure. What would the defendant have to do, though, if the plaintiff refused to agree to such a stipulation? Compare the approach taken under the Private Securities Litigation Reform Act of 1995, 15 U.S.C. § 77a *et seq.*, which was enacted, in large part, to reform class-action securities litigation. In response to the concern that the cost of discovery resulting from "fishing expedition" lawsuits often forced innocent parties to settle frivolous securities litigation, Congress sought to limit "abusive" discovery in such cases. The Act provides, *inter alia*, that "all discovery and other proceedings shall be stayed during the pendency of any motion to dismiss, unless the court finds upon the motion of any party that particularized discovery is necessary to preserve evidence or to prevent undue prejudice to that party." 15 U.S.C. § 77z-1(b)(1).

Problems

Problem 8-2. P is a passenger on D's bus and is injured when the bus is involved in an accident. In its investigation of the accident, D discovers the identity of two eyewitnesses to the accident, A and B, and interviews them. A's version of the accident would support D's position, but B's would not. Consequently, D would use A, but not B, in its defense of P's claim. Must D disclose the identity of A or B under Rule 26(a)(1)(A)(i)? Must D disclose the identity of A or B if asked in a formal discovery request, such as an interrogatory, for the names of persons with relevant information about the accident?

Problem 8-3. P sues D for breach of warranty. P's complaint alleges that component parts supplied by D were "defective" in some unspecified manner. In addition to seeking general damages of $200,000, P also asserts a special damage claim for loss of profits of $800,000. With regard to P's damage claims, what would P have to disclose as part of P's initial disclosures under Rule 26(a)(1)(A)(iii)?

Problem 8-4. On the facts of *Problem 8-3*, would D have to disclose the existence of insurance covering the potential claim, including the policy limits?

(ii) Disclosure of Expert Testimony: Rule 26(a)(2)

The second stage of mandatory disclosure involves information concerning expert witnesses. Rule 26(a)(2)(A) and (B) requires the parties to disclose the identity of all expert witnesses who may be used at trial and to provide detailed written reports with respect to retained or specially employed experts and experts who are employees of a party and whose duties "regularly involve giving expert testimony." In the absence of court order or party stipulation, Rule 26(a)(2)(C) states that these disclosures are due "at least 90 days before the date set for trial or for the case to be ready for trial." These disclosure requirements will be discussed more fully in section C(3) on expert discovery, below.

(iii) Pretrial Disclosures: Rule 26(a)(3)

The final stage of mandatory disclosure involves information concerning a party's intended evidence at trial. Rule 26(a)(3)(A)(i), (ii), and (iii) require the parties to identify each witness, document, or other exhibit that they expect to offer or may offer at trial "if the need arises." If a party expects to present a witness' testimony at trial by means of a deposition, rather than through live testimony, the witness must be so designated and, if the deposition was not taken stenographically, "a transcript of the pertinent portions of the deposition" must be provided. Under the express wording of Rule 26(a)(3)(A), the above disclosure requirements do not apply to evidence that the party intends to use "solely for impeachment" purposes.

Unless otherwise ordered by the court, these disclosures must be made "at least 30 days before trial." A party who does not properly comply with these disclosure requirements incurs the risk that any non-disclosed witness, document, or exhibit will be excluded at trial under the penalty provisions of Rule 37(c)(1).

Rule 26(a)(3) also requires the other parties in the action to serve and promptly file a list of any objections to the use of a witness' deposition at trial under Rule 32(a) and any evidentiary objections to the use of the identified documents and exhibits. Failure to properly object as required by this rule constitutes a waiver of the objection, unless the failure is "excused by the court for good cause" or the evidentiary objection is based on Rule 402 ("General Admissibility of Relevant Evidence") or Rule 403 ("Excluding Relevant Evidence for Prejudice, Confusion, Waste of Time, or Other Reasons") of the Federal Rules of Evidence.

(c) *The Traditional Methods of Discovery: Depositions*

As noted in subsection *(a)*, above, there are five traditional methods of discovery: depositions; interrogatories; requests for the production of documents and things; physical and mental examinations; and requests for admissions. Even though the federal discovery rules now provide for the mandatory disclosure of certain information under the provisions of Rule 26(a)(1)-(3), the parties are still authorized to utilize any or all of the traditional methods of discovery to secure additional information. In fact, the 2000 amendment to the initial disclosure requirements of Rule 26(a)(1)(A)(i) and (ii) limiting disclosure solely to information that a party "may use to support its claims or defenses" ensures that the parties must resort to the traditional methods of discovery in order to obtain information unfavorable to another party.

Functions of Depositions. As noted earlier, the deposition is the most effective and valuable method of discovery. Depositions can be taken in two basic forms: (1) oral depositions under Rule 30; and (2) depositions by written questions under Rule 31. Oral depositions are by far the more frequently used and are the "workhorse" of traditional discovery practice. A deposition is a record of testimony of a party or witness, *i.e.*, the deponent, that is taken outside of court. Testimony at a deposition is taken in the same manner that live testimony would be taken at trial. The deponent is placed under oath and is then subject to direct and cross-examination questioning by the parties in the same manner that a witness would be examined at trial. Because deposition testimony is taken under oath and is subject to direct and cross-examination by the parties, the federal discovery rules and the Federal Rules of Evidence afford depositions special evidentiary status. Under Rule 32(a)(4) of the Federal Rules of Civil Procedure, depositions may be used as a substitute for the deponent's live courtroom testimony in the event the deponent becomes legally unavailable to testify at trial within the meaning of Rule 32(a)(4). *See also* FED. R. EVID. 804(b)(1) (providing an exception to the hearsay rule for deposition testimony by a witness who is legally unavailable to testify at trial).

In addition to preserving the testimony of a party or witness for trial, depositions have many other important discovery functions and advantages. Most significantly, the deposition is the broadest and most flexible device for acquiring information about the case. Unlike interrogatories and requests for admissions, which may be served only upon other parties in the action, depositions may be taken of "*any person*," whether a party to the action or not. *See* FED. R. CIV. P. 30(a)(1) & 31(a)(1). Moreover, the oral deposition is superior to all other methods of discovery in allowing the examiner to examine the deponent freely in face-to-face questioning that requires spontaneous responses with the immediate opportunity for follow-up questions. Interrogatories under Rule 33, by comparison, are generally carefully answered by a party in consultation with the party's attorney. Usually, the responses are narrowly drafted to respond only to the precise question asked.

At a deposition, a deponent may also be questioned about documents or other exhibits that the deponent has been requested to bring to the deposition or that are supplied to the deponent by the examiner. As will be explained in later notes, a party may request a party deponent to bring documents to the deposition pursuant to Rule 30(b)(2). Likewise, a nonparty deponent may be similarly requested to produce documents pursuant to a subpoena duces tecum under Rule 45(a)(1)(C).

Through a series of broad, open-ended questions, followed by more specific, probing questions, a skillful examiner at an oral deposition is able to fully explore what the deponent knows and thinks about the relevant matters in the case. Not only will this questioning process reveal valuable information about the case, but the examiner will now be able to better prepare for trial knowing how this deponent will likely testify at trial. Moreover, under Rule 32(a)(2), if the deponent testifies at trial in a manner inconsistent with the deponent's deposition testimony, the deposition may be used at trial to impeach the credibility and trial testimony of the deponent. Most lawyers anticipate that a witness may surprise them at trial with new facts and, therefore, ask the witness at the deposition, "Have you told me everything about … ?" In this way, if the witness adds new facts at trial, the attorney can impeach the witness with this portion of the deposition.

In addition to these important discovery and trial-preparation functions, depositions also play a critical role in the resolution of cases. Oral depositions allow the parties to carefully observe the demeanor of the various deponents and to realistically measure and assess the testimonial strengths and weaknesses of each party's case. For example, assume that the plaintiff or the plaintiff's fact or expert witnesses present themselves at the depositions as strong and persuasive witnesses whose testimony cannot be shaken by the opposing party on cross-examination at the deposition. Such witnesses may encourage the defendant to settle the case with the plaintiff and avoid the risk of a more unfavorable outcome if the case is fully tried to final judgment. Conversely, if the plaintiff or the plaintiff's witnesses present poorly at the depositions, the defendant may be encouraged either to take the case to trial in the hopes of securing a favorable judgment or to settle the case, but on less favorable terms to the plaintiff.

In the reality of litigation practice today with the vast majority of cases being resolved prior to trial (over 95% in the federal courts), the deposition has increasingly become the first, and often the last, opportunity for the parties and their witnesses to testify to their version of the case. Thus, how and on what terms and conditions an action resolves is directly affected by the relative strengths and weaknesses of the testimony presentations at the depositions.

Deposition Expenses. The main disadvantages of depositions are the time and expense necessary to conduct them. Expenses include the fee of the court reporter or other officer who will take the deposition as well as the cost of transcribing the testimony. Usually, court reporters charge an hourly or per diem rate for the deposition and a per page charge for the written transcript. In addition, there is the time and expense for the parties and/ or their attorneys to travel to and attend an oral deposition. Depending on the location and length of the deposition, this expense can be substantial.

In most situations, however, the advantages of depositions far outweigh these considerations of time and expense, and on balance, depositions are viewed as the best and most effective discovery device. Moreover, as previously noted in section A(3)(a), above, Rule 29(a) allows the parties to modify standard deposition procedures by stipulation, and such stipulations can result in cost savings. The parties can agree, for instance, not to transcribe the deposition testimony unless it becomes necessary at a later stage of the proceeding. As a further cost saving measure, Rule 30(b)(4) expressly authorizes the parties to stipulate "that a deposition be taken by telephone or other remote means." Rule 30(c)(3) also allows a party to submit written questions to be posed to the deponent in lieu of participating in the oral deposition. Finally, as explained below, the parties may also use the less expensive "deposition by written questions" under Rule 31 as an effective alternative to an oral deposition in appropriate cases.

Deposition Practice and Procedure. The federal discovery rules establish very specific procedures for the scheduling and conducting of depositions. The best way to understand these deposition procedures is to carefully study Rule 30 and the related deposition rules. When you are in practice, it will be important for you to adhere fully to all applicable court procedures and regular reference to the rules will soon become second nature to you. Most trial judges have little patience for attorneys who fail to follow the rules of procedure. The federal deposition procedures set forth in Rule 30 are representative of general deposition practice. Individual state procedures will vary, however, and you must always familiarize yourself with the rules of practice in the particular jurisdiction and court in which you are appearing.

It should also be emphasized that learning the rules for scheduling and conducting a deposition is only the first step in deposition practice. Actually conducting an effective deposition requires careful planning and preparation as well as skillful use of deposition questioning techniques. Learning how to ask follow-up questions, how to blend open-ended and specific questions, how to ask wrap-up questions that will be useful for impeachment at trial if witnesses alter their testimony, how to control hostile witnesses, etc. are all acquired advocacy skills. Such training is beyond a basic textbook course in civil procedure. It is highly recommended that if you plan to pursue a litigation practice, you take a class in "Pretrial Advocacy" if offered at your school and, in addition, after you enter practice, register for one of the many deposition skills training programs offered to attorneys by bar associations and trial advocacy groups, such as the National Institute of Trial Advocacy.

Oral Depositions Under Rule 30. Federal Rule 30 is the general rule governing oral depositions and the following is an overview of some of the basic deposition requirements. Rule 30(b)(1) authorizes a party to commence the oral deposition process by giving reasonable written notice to all other parties in the action. In most cases, once the parties have met to prepare a discovery plan as required by Rule 26(f), depositions may be freely scheduled, and leave of court is ordinarily not necessary. *See* FED. R. CIV. P. 26(d) ("Timing and Sequence of Discovery"). Under Rule 30(a)(2), however, leave of court is required in certain circumstances, such as when the deponent is in prison or, in absence of a stipulation of the parties, a proposed deposition would exceed the presumptive limit of ten depositions for each side.

The deposition notice must provide the time and place for taking the deposition. As a general rule, the party scheduling the deposition has the right to choose the time and location for the deposition. In addition, the notice must indicate the name and address of each person to be examined. Under Rule 30(b)(6), if the deponent is "a public or private corporation, a partnership, an association, a governmental agency, or other entity," the notice can simply name the organization as the deponent and describe "with reasonable particularity the matters for examination." In turn, the named organization is required to designate appropriate persons to testify on the organization's behalf.

If the deponent is a party, a proper deposition notice is all that is needed to compel the appearance of the party at the deposition. Rule 37(d)(1)(A)(i) provides for sanctions against a party deponent who fails to appear for the party's deposition after being served with a proper notice. If a nonparty is to be the deponent, however, a subpoena must be issued under Rule 45(a) to compel the nonparty's attendance at the deposition. Under Rule 45(b), the subpoena must be properly served and accompanied by the witness attendance fee and mileage allowance set by law. *See* 28 U.S.C. § 1821. Under Rule 30(b)(2), the deposition notice may also request a party deponent to bring documents and tangible things to the deposition. A nonparty deponent may be similarly requested to bring documents and tangible things to the deposition pursuant to a subpoena duces tecum under Rule 45(a)(1)(C).

Finally, under Rule 30(b)(3)(A), the notice must state the method for recording the testimony. Traditionally, a deposition was recorded stenographically, usually by a certified court reporter. However, with the advent of modern technology, other possibilities exist, and Rule 30(b)(3)(A) currently provides that "[u]nless the court orders otherwise, testimony may be recorded by audio, audiovisual, or stenographic means." As a result, video depositions are being used more often, especially if the parties know or anticipate that a key witness will be legally unavailable to testify at trial within the meaning of Rule 32(a)(4). Under these circumstances, a video deposition will be the best method of preserving the witness' testimony for effective presentation at trial.

Depositions By Written Questions Under Rule 31. In addition to choosing the method of recording the testimony at a deposition, a party must choose between an oral deposition and a deposition by written questions. The principal difference between an oral deposition and a deposition by written questions is the questioning procedure. In an oral deposition, the deponent is subject to live direct and cross-examination questioning by the parties in the same manner that a witness would be examined at trial. In a deposition by written questions, a written list of direct and cross-examination questions are prepared in advance by the parties and sent to the designated officer before whom the deposition will be taken. The questions are then read to the deponent at the deposition and are orally answered and recorded in the same manner as at an oral deposition. *See* Fed. R. Civ. P. 31(a) and (b).

As previously noted, oral depositions are clearly the preferred method of discovery and depositions by written questions are used much less frequently. The main drawback of the deposition by written questions is the requirement that all questions be in written form and scripted in advance. This requirement deprives the parties of the important opportunity of asking spontaneous follow-up questions based on the actual responses of the deponent, the primary advantage of the oral deposition. In addition, unless the deposition by written questions is videotaped, the parties have no opportunity to observe the demeanor of the witness, another important feature of the oral deposition.

Nevertheless, under appropriate circumstances, the deposition by written questions can be an effective and affordable alternative to an oral deposition. Depositions by written questions are particularly useful in obtaining discovery from nonparty witnesses who only possess information about certain limited matters. For example, suppose a witness needed to be examined solely to authenticate certain documents or to confirm certain facts necessary in the party's presentation of the case. A deposition by written questions would be an efficient and inexpensive alternative in these situations. The necessary questions to establish the evidentiary points could be framed in written form and the witness could then confirm the information at the deposition. The witness' answers would then be fully preserved for use at trial under Rule 32(a) in the same manner as an oral deposition. However, the additional expense of an oral deposition for the parties and/or their attorneys to attend the deposition is avoided. The cost saving of a deposition by written questions is even more significant when the witness resides outside of the forum and the attorneys would have to incur substantial travel expenses to attend the deposition.

Distinguishing Written Interrogatories. Depositions by written questions under Rule 31 should not be confused with written interrogatories under Rule 33. Although both discovery devices are similar in that each requests answers under oath to written questions, Rule 33 interrogatories may only be served upon another party. Under Rule 31(a), a deposition by written questions may be taken of any person, whether or not a party. In addition, in a deposition by written questions, questions may be posed by all parties to the action in both direct and cross-examination format. Rule 33 interrogatories consist of only a single set of questions posed by one party for answer by another party. Finally, Rule 33 interrogatories do not have the same evidentiary status at trial as depositions. Although answers to interrogatories may be admitted in evidence at trial *against* the answering party, the answers may not be offered as substantive evidence *by* the answering party, as a deposition could under Rule 32(a)(4), if the answering party becomes legally unavailable to testify at trial.

Numerical and Duration Limits on Depositions. As part of an overall tightening of discovery standards under the 1993 amendments to the discovery rules, Rules 30 and 31 were amended to place presumptive limits on the number of oral and written depositions that may be taken in a case. Unless the parties stipulate to the deposition or leave of court is obtained, each side in the litigation, *i.e.*, the plaintiffs, defendants, and the third-party defendants, may take a maximum of ten depositions per side. *See* FED. R. CIV. P. 30(a)(2)(A)(i) and 31(a)(2)(A)(i). In the majority of cases, ten depositions per side is more than adequate. In certain complex, multi-party cases, however, more witnesses may need to be deposed. In the absence of party stipulation, the parties would need to seek leave of court to take additional depositions.

As a further attempt at reducing discovery costs, the federal discovery rules were again amended in 2000 to impose a presumptive time limit on all depositions. Unless otherwise stipulated or ordered by the court, Rule 30(d)(1) provides that "a deposition is limited to 1 day of 7 hours." Although seven hours is generally sufficient for the vast majority of depositions, Rule 30(d)(1) recognizes that exceptions will arise and provides that "[t]he court must allow additional time consistent with Rule 26(b)(2) if needed to fairly examine the deponent or if the deponent, another person, or any other circumstance impedes or delays the examination." The 2000 Advisory Committee's Note outlines a variety of factors that the court should consider in extending the time limit—a deposition in which an interpreter is needed, a deposition covering a long series of events or voluminous documents, multi-party cases in which each party needs to examine the witness, and depositions involving expert witnesses.

Document Production at a Deposition. As previously noted, Rule 30(b)(2) permits a deposition notice to a *party* deponent to be accompanied by a request under Rule 34 for the production of documents and tangible things at the taking of the deposition. Although this provision is useful in situations in which only a few documents are requested from the party at the deposition, it is often better practice to request documents separately under the normal provisions of Rule 34 and to schedule the party's deposition after having an opportunity to thoroughly examine and prepare questions about the documents. When Rule 30(b)(2) is used to compel the party to produce documents at the deposition, the deposing party will lose valuable (and expensive) deposition time reviewing these documents and, in the haste of reviewing unfamiliar documents, important areas of inquiry may be overlooked.

Although Rule 34 only authorizes requests for the production of documents from parties, requests for the production of documents from nonparties can be similarly accomplished through the subpoena provisions of Rule 45. Specifically, Rule 45(a)(1)(C) authorizes a party to serve the nonparty with a *subpoena* "to produce documents, electronically stored information, or tangible things" at a deposition or at a separate time and place. A subpoena commanding the production of documents or tangible things is known as a *subpoena duces tecum*. Through the use of a subpoena duces tecum, therefore, a party is able to effectuate the discovery of documents and tangible things that would otherwise be permitted only against a party under Rule 34. *See* FED. R. CIV. P. 30(b)(2) (first sentence).

Rule 45(a)(1)(C) was amended in 1991 to expressly authorize the issuance of a subpoena duces tecum separate from a scheduled deposition. Rule 45(a)(1)(C) provides that a command to produce documents and tangible things "may be included in a subpoena commanding attendance at a deposition, hearing, or trial, *or may be set out in a separate subpoena.*" This later provision authorizing a separate subpoena was added as a cost and time-saving measure to spare the necessity of a formal deposition when the party issuing the subpoena only desires production of the documents or tangible things and has no need to question the witness. When a deposition of the nonparty is planned, however, Rule 45(a)(1)(C) enables a party to accomplish the above procedure for pre-deposition examination of documents and tangible things by first issuing a separate subpoena to the nonparty for the production of the documents or things at a designated time and place and thereafter issuing a second subpoena to the nonparty to command the nonparty's appearance at the deposition. In order to protect the right of other parties in the action to object to the production of documents or things from a nonparty, Rule 45(b)(1) [revised as Rule 45(a)(4) effective Dec. 1, 2013] requires that notice be served on each party before a subpoena commanding the production of documents and things before trial is served.

Deposing Corporate Employees. Reconsider the process of noticing the deposition of a corporation under Rule 30(b)(6), discussed earlier. Suppose the party taking the deposition wants to depose a particular employee of the corporation rather than requiring the corporation under Rule 30(b)(6) to designate the person(s) who will testify about the matters that will be covered in the deposition. Under these circumstances, an ordinary corporate employee must be subpoenaed under Rule 45 as any other nonparty witness, even if the corporation itself is a party to the action. However, if the corporation is a party and the specific employee to be deposed is an officer, director, or a managing agent of the corporation, the corporation is obligated by virtue of the sanction language of Rule 37(d)(1)(A)(i) to produce the person designated in the notice. *See* 8A WRIGHT ET AL. §2103, at 484–85.

Non-Appearance Sanctions. When either the party scheduling the deposition or the deponent fails to appear at the deposition, the federal discovery rules provide for various sanctions. For instance, assume that under Rule 30(b)(1), a party sends notice of the taking of an oral deposition to the other parties and then fails to attend and proceed with the deposition as scheduled. In this case, Rule 30(g)(1) authorizes the court to order the noticing party to pay the reasonable expenses incurred by the other parties and their attorneys in attending the deposition, including attorney's fees.

What happens if a party schedules the deposition of another party and the party to be deposed fails to appear? Under these circumstances, Rule 37(d)(1)(A)(i) authorizes the court to impose sanctions if a party deponent fails to appear for the party's deposition after being served with a proper deposition notice. Under Rule 37(d)(3), the court may impose such sanctions as are just, including an order dismissing the action or rendering a judgment by default against the non-appearing party.

If the deponent is a nonparty and fails to appear at the deposition after being properly served with a subpoena under Rule 45, the court may hold the nonparty in contempt under Rule 45(e) [revised as Rule 45(g) effective Dec. 1, 2013] if the failure to appear is "without adequate excuse." However, suppose a party gives notice of an oral deposition of a nonparty witness and arranges for the witness to voluntarily attend the deposition without serving a subpoena on the witness. What are the consequences if all the parties attend at the time and place designated in the notice, but the witness fails to appear? Because of the absence of a subpoena, the witness may not be sanctioned under Rule 45. Under Rule 30(g)(2), though, the party scheduling the deposition may be ordered to pay the reasonable expenses incurred by the other parties and their attorneys in attending the deposition, including attorney's fees.

Deposition Objections and Use at Trial. As explained in the introductory section, depositions are not only very effective devices for discovering information prior to trial, but also have significant evidentiary use at trial. Under Rule 32(a)(2), depositions may be used to impeach or contradict the trial testimony of any witness if the witness' trial testimony is inconsistent with the witness' deposition testimony. In addition, under Rule 32(a)(3), the deposition of a party may be used by any adverse party not only to impeach the party, but also as substantive evidence to prove any part of the adverse party's case. Finally, depositions of any witness may be used as substantive evidence in lieu of the witness' live testimony at trial if the witness is legally unavailable to testify at trial within the meaning of Rule 32(a)(4)(A)-(E).

Under Rule 32(a)(1)(B), when depositions are used as evidence at trial, their use is subject to the Federal Rules of Evidence. As Rule 32(a)(1)(B) states, a deposition may be used against a party "to the extent it would be admissible under the Federal Rules of Evidence if the deponent were present and testifying." Recall from section A(1), that the standard for relevance in discovery, *i.e.,* "reasonably calculated to lead to the discovery of admissible evidence," is much broader than the standard for the admission of evidence at trial under the Federal Rules of Evidence. As a result, the examination of a deponent at a deposition may properly inquire into matters that would otherwise be objectionable and inadmissible in evidence at trial. The problem arises when the deposition is then offered in evidence at trial under Rule 32. In order to avoid constant battles at the deposition over anticipated evidentiary objections at trial, Rule 32(b) and (d)(3) wisely provide that evidentiary objections to the admissibility of a deposition at trial are generally not waived by the failure to assert them at the deposition.

Objections as to privilege, however, and certain objections that could be cured if promptly presented are waived if not asserted before or during the deposition. Specifically, Rule 32(d)(3)(A) provides that an "objection to a deponent's competence—or to the competence, relevance, or materiality of testimony—is not waived by a failure to make the objection before or during the deposition, unless the ground for it might have been corrected at that time." *See, e.g., Cronkite v. Fahrbach*, 853 F. Supp. 257 (W.D. Mich. 1994) (objection to testimonial competence of medical expert not waived by failure to object at deposition if competency depends on factors that could not be obviated). Rule 32(d)(3)(B) contains a similar provision governing "errors and irregularities" occurring at an oral deposition relating to "the manner of taking the deposition, the form of a question or answer, the oath or affirmation, a party's conduct, or other matters that might have been corrected at that time." If not timely made during the deposition, such objections are waived. *See, e.g., Cabello v. Fernandez*, 402 F.3d 1148, 1160 (11th Cir. 2005) ("Because the defect in the oath could have been cured at the taking of the deposition," this case falls within Rule 32(d)(3)(B) and "even though [defendant] objected at trial, his failure to object at the taking of the deposition was correctly deemed a waiver"). Rule 32(d)(1) and (2) further provide that objections based on an error or irregularity in the deposition notice or the qualification of the officer taking the deposition are waived unless timely made.

When deposition objections are made, Rule 30(c)(2) requires that all objections "be stated concisely and in a nonargumentative and nonsuggestive manner." Asserting an objection at a deposition preserves the objection on the record, but does not necessarily permit the objecting party to instruct the deponent not to answer. Under Rule 30(c)(2), "[a] person may instruct a deponent not to answer only when necessary to preserve a privilege, to enforce a limitation ordered by the court, or to present a motion under Rule 30(d)(3)" that the deposition is being conducted in bad faith or in an unreasonable manner.

Depositions to Perpetuate Testimony. In most instances, depositions are taken in the context of a pending lawsuit. However, under certain circumstances, depositions to perpetuate testimony for use in a future action may be taken pursuant to Rule 27(a). Under Rule 27(a)(1)(A), a person desiring to perpetuate testimony must file a verified petition showing, *inter alia,* that "the petitioner expects to be a party to an action cognizable in a United States court but cannot presently bring it or cause it to be brought." Rule 27(a)(4) provides that depositions taken to perpetuate testimony may be used under Rule 32(a) in any later-filed action in a United States district court involving the same subject matter.

In what kinds of cases do you think a person might invoke the provisions of Rule 27(a)? Suppose a person expected to be sued as a defendant at some future time, but because of a lengthy statute of limitations, the action may not be filed by the potential plaintiff for many years. For example, in most jurisdictions, the statute of limitations on a tort injury to a minor child does not begin to run until the child reaches the age of majority. Suppose a doctor were to cause injury to a five-year-old child during surgery. Even though the applicable statute of limitations for a medical malpractice claim may normally be two years, the minor child would have two years from the date of majority to commence an action against the doctor. At that time, nurses or other hospital personnel, whose testimony may have exonerated the doctor, may have died or disappeared, lost their memories, or be otherwise unavailable as witnesses.

In order to utilize the provisions of Rule 27(a), the petition to perpetuate testimony must also demonstrate that the future action would be within federal subject-matter jurisdiction. If not, the petitioner would have to seek to perpetuate testimony in state court under an applicable state court rule. *See, e.g.,* N.J. Ct. R. 4:11-1 (authorizing petitions to perpetuate testimony under similar standards to Rule 27(a)).

Problems

Problem 8-5. P was killed in an auto accident. *P* was a passenger in *D's* car. Prior to the accident, *P* and *D* had been alone. The accident occurred late at night when *D's* car crashed over a bridge after making a wrong turn. There were no witnesses to the accident other than *D. D* reported the accident the next morning. Assume that *P's* estate has commenced a civil action against *D.* Assume that the attorney for *P's* estate is taking the oral deposition of *O,* the police officer to whom *D* reported the accident. Based on Rule 32(d), determine whether *D's* failure to object seasonably during the deposition in the following situations results in a waiver of the objection. Assume that the objection is being raised for the first time at trial.

(a) the notice of the deposition is defective;

(b) the witness did not properly take the oath or affirmation;

(c) the witness was incompetent to testify because the witness is too young;

(d) the question was a leading question (which would be impermissible on direct examination under most circumstances);

(e) the question was irrelevant;

(f) the deponent answered a question that calls for an expert opinion about certain complex aspects of automobile accident reconstruction. At trial, an objection is made that the deponent's qualifications to testify as an expert on the question were not sufficiently shown.

Problem 8-6. Assume that the attorney for *P*'s estate also takes *D*'s deposition during the course of the litigation described in *Problem 8-5*. *P*'s attorney asks *D* a question that *D*'s attorney believes is clearly outside the scope of discovery. Based on Rule 30(c)(2), is it proper for *D*'s attorney to direct *D* not to answer the question? If *D* refuses to answer the question, what action, if any, can *P*'s attorney take to obtain an answer to the question?

Problem 8-7. During the deposition described in *Problem 8-5*, assume that *D*'s attorney believes that *P* is unreasonably harassing and embarrassing *D*. Based on Rule 30(d), what, if anything, can *D*'s attorney do to protect *D*?

Special Considerations with Regard to Deposing Nonresident and Foreign Parties or Witnesses. As a general rule, the party scheduling a deposition has the right to select the location where the deposition will be held. This general rule, however, is subject to certain limitations. Upon an appropriate showing of undue burden or expense, the court may enter a protective order under Rule 26(c)(1)(B) changing the location of a deposition. In addition, if a nonparty deponent is subpoenaed to appear at the deposition, Rule 45(c)(3)(A) [revised as Rule 45(c)(1)(A) effective Dec. 1, 2013] provides that a subpoena can only command a nonparty deponent to appear at a deposition within 100 miles of where that person "resides, is employed, or regularly transacts business in person." The issue of where a deposition may be held, therefore, raises special concerns when the party or witness to be deposed is a nonresident of the forum.

Party-Deponents. As previously explained in this subsection, when the person to be deposed is a party, a subpoena is not necessary and a proper deposition notice is all that is required to compel the party's appearance. As the party selecting the forum, a nonresident plaintiff ordinarily must appear for a deposition in the judicial district in which the plaintiff has instituted suit. When the plaintiff is a nonresident corporation, it may similarly be required to produce its officers and agents for depositions in the chosen forum. *See, e.g., Cadent Ltd. v. 3M Unitek Corp.,* 232 F.R.D. 625 (C.D. Cal. 2005) (plaintiff foreign corporation must comply with defendants' request to depose three plaintiff's officers and one employee in California, where plaintiff instituted action, even though corporation's principal place of business was Israel). In a case of undue hardship or other special circumstances, however, the court may grant a protective order allowing depositions to be taken in the plaintiff's home state. *See, e.g., Operative Plasterers' & Cement Masons' Int'l Ass'n v. Benjamin,* 144 F.R.D. 87 (N.D. Ind. 1992) (on balance of equities, depositions of officers of plaintiff-union who had "minimal involvement" in case could be taken at plaintiff's out-of-state headquarters and officers would not be required to appear for depositions in forum where action was pending).

When the nonresident deponent is a defendant, the courts are more willing to enter an order protecting the nonresident from having to appear for a deposition in the forum. *See, e.g., Morin v. Nationwide Fed. Credit Union,* 229 F.R.D. 362 (D. Conn. 2005) (protective order granted allowing defendant corporation's vice-president to be deposed at defendant's principal place of business in Ohio, rather than in forum); *Chris-Craft Indus. Prods., Inc. v. Kuraray Co.,* 184 F.R.D. 605 (N.D. Ill. 1999) (depositions of employees of defendant Japanese corporation who reside in Japan should be held at defendant's principal place of business in Japan; depositions in forum would unduly burden the defendant "in terms of lost executive work time and expenses"). The court has discretion in entering such a protective order, however, and may require a nonresident defendant to appear for depositions in the forum. *See, e.g., M&C Corp. v. Erwin Behr GmbH & Co.,* 165 F.R.D. 65 (E.D. Mich. 1996) (request of defendant German corporation to require plaintiff to conduct corporate depositions in Germany is denied because defendant's "complaints of hardship are exaggerated" and are part of "a calculated strategy to delay payment of this judgment or to increase costs of collection for [plaintiff]").

Nonparty Deponents. Entirely different rules apply when the nonresident deponent is a nonparty. Nonparties are not subject to deposition on notice and, unless the appearance of the nonparty can be secured voluntarily (by offering to pay the travel expenses of the nonparty, for instance), a subpoena must be issued under Rule 45 to compel the nonparty's attendance at the deposition. As noted above, however, a nonparty deponent may only be commanded to appear at a deposition within 100 miles of where that person "resides, is employed, or regularly transacts business in person." Fortunately, litigants in federal court can take special advantage of the nationwide structure of the federal court system and the federal district court can properly issue a deposition subpoena to a nonresident, nonparty deponent to appear at a deposition within 100 miles of where the nonparty resides, is employed, or regularly transacts business in person.

State Court Actions. The above procedure for compelling the attendance of a nonresident, nonparty deponent at a deposition in another jurisdiction is only available for actions pending in federal, not state, court. The subpoena power of a state court is limited to the territorial boundaries of the state where the court is located. Thus, in order to be valid, a state court subpoena must be properly served upon the nonparty within the territorial boundaries of the state, and the subpoena can only order the nonparty to appear within that state. In this sense, the subpoena power of the state courts continues to align with the traditional notions of territorial sovereignty expressed in *Pennoyer v. Neff* and has not experienced a parallel expansion of extraterritorial power commensurate with the exercise of personal jurisdiction under the principles of *International Shoe.*

For example, if an action were pending in New Jersey state court, and a nonparty deponent resided in California, the deposing attorney would have to follow the deposition and subpoena procedures of the appropriate *California* state court that had jurisdiction over the deponent. All states have some procedure for the issuance of subpoenas for depositions to be taken within their borders for use in an action pending in another jurisdiction. The application procedures vary among the states. Some states require formal applications with documents known as "letters rogatory" or "commissions," which must be obtained from the court where the action is pending and formally request the second court to issue a deposition subpoena. The procedures in the particular state where the deposition is to be held must be carefully followed and may sometimes require the retention of local counsel. Nothing would be more frustrating than to travel to a distant state to depose a witness, only to have the witness fail to appear because the proper deposition procedures were not followed. Thus, in the above example, the New Jersey attorney would need to secure the issuance of a California state court subpoena to compel the witness to appear for a deposition in California.

Depositions in Foreign Countries. When the deponent's attendance at a deposition within the United States cannot be accomplished, a deposition in a foreign country may be necessary. Rule 28(b)(1) provides that depositions may be taken in a foreign country (A) under an applicable treaty or convention; (B) under a letter of request, whether or not captioned a "letter rogatory"; (C) on notice before a person authorized to administer oaths under federal or foreign law; or (D) before a person specially commissioned by the court to administer the oath and take testimony. Full understanding of the various procedures and requirements for conducting foreign discovery requires careful study and is beyond the scope of this course. In addition to the practical difficulties of travel and language translation, conducting a deposition in a foreign country requires special recognition and respect of the jurisdictional sovereignty of the other nation, especially if foreign process will be sought to compel the attendance of the proposed deponent. The "Hague Convention on the Taking of Evidence Abroad in Civil or Commercial Matters" is designed to address these concerns. This Hague Convention establishes procedures for obtaining pre-trial discovery in participating nations (currently 72) and may be utilized pursuant to Rule 28(b)(1)(A).

(d) Interrogatories Under Rule 33

Interrogatories are written questions prepared by one party and served upon another party. A party may serve interrogatories upon any other party to the action irrespective of whether the other party is adverse. Under Rule 33(a)(2), interrogatories "may relate to any matter that may be inquired into under Rule 26(b)." The party served must answer the questions "separately and fully in writing under oath." FED. R. CIV. P. 33(b)(3). Under Rule 33(b)(4), if the answering party objects to a question, the answering party must state "with specificity" the reason for the objection.

Functions of Interrogatories. Interrogatories under Rule 33 are a frequently used discovery device because they are simple and inexpensive and can be easily utilized in all types of cases. Other than the expense of preparing the questions, interrogatories are virtually cost free to the propounding party. In smaller cases in which the expense of depositions would be cost inefficient or beyond the financial resources of the parties, interrogatories are an essential discovery device. Even in cases in which depositions will be taken, interrogatories are an important supplement to the mandatory disclosure provisions of Rule 26(a) in securing basic information not covered by these provisions. Recall, for instance, that Rule 26(a)(1)(A)(i) and (ii) only require disclosure of the identity of persons and documents that a party "may use to support its claims or defenses." Interrogatories may properly inquire as to the identity of any person with relevant information or the identity of any relevant document, whether favorable or unfavorable to the responding party. In addition, interrogatories are particularly useful in preparing for depositions. Interrogatories help to identify the witnesses who should be deposed and also help the deposing party to more effectively develop and plan the areas of inquiry that should be explored at the depositions.

Interrogatories do have certain limitations, however. Interrogatories may only be directed to another party and may not be served upon non-parties. In addition, in the absence of a court order or stipulation of the parties, Rule 33(a)(1) limits the number of interrogatories that a party may serve upon another party to 25, "including all discrete subparts." Finally, because interrogatories are posed only in written format, they cannot duplicate the spontaneity and flexibility of an oral deposition examination. Responding parties are given 30 days under Rule 33(b)(2) to answer interrogatories, thus affording a party ample opportunity to carefully draft responses in consultation with the party's attorney.

Answering Interrogatories. A party must answer interrogatories on the basis of all information that is available to the party. Unless the information is privileged or otherwise protected from discovery, responses must be based not only on information of which the party is personally aware, but must also include information possessed by the party's attorney, insurer, employees, investigators, representatives, or other agents. *See* 8B Wright et al. § 2177, at 82 and cases cited therein. When the answering party is an organization, the interrogatories must be answered by an officer or agent who must similarly furnish all information available to the party. Fed. R. Civ. P. 33(b)(1)(B). In this sense, the scope of an interrogatory reply is broader and more demanding than the scope of a deposition reply. Unless a deponent has been specially designated to testify on behalf of an organization under Rule 30(b)(6), a deponent need only answer on the basis of what the deponent personally knows.

When the answer to an interrogatory may be derived or ascertained from the business records, including electronically stored information, of the responding party, Rule 33(d) allows this party to make the business records available to the party serving the interrogatory in lieu of answering it. However, this option is only available when "the burden of deriving or ascertaining the answer will be substantially the same for either party." Under Rule 33(d), the designation of records by the responding party must be "in sufficient detail to enable the interrogating party to locate and identify them as readily as the responding party could."

"Contention" Interrogatories. The two principal types of interrogatories are (1) those seeking basic information, such as the names of witnesses or the existence, location, and contents of documents; and (2) those seeking what a party contends and the factual and legal bases for those contentions. These latter interrogatories, known as "contention" interrogatories, are permissible under Rule 33(a)(2), which provides that an interrogatory "is not objectionable merely because it asks for an opinion or contention that relates to fact or the application of law to fact." An example of such an interrogatory would be, "Explain the basis for your contention that the defendant's product violated the standards of the Federal Consumer Safety Act." While this interrogatory is permissible because it asks for the application of law to fact, interrogatories that "extend to issues of 'pure law,' *i.e.*, legal issues unrelated to the facts of the case" are prohibited under Rule 33(a)(2). *See* Fed. R. Civ. P. 33 advisory committee's note to the 1970 amendment.

Determining when an interrogatory asks a question of "pure law" is often difficult. In *O'Brien v. International Brotherhood of Electrical Workers*, 443 F. Supp. 1182 (N.D. Ga. 1977), for example, the plaintiff had been disciplined by the defendant union for violating certain provisions of the union's constitution. The plaintiff then sued the union. In interrogatories, the plaintiff asked the defendant to explain how the plaintiff's actions violated these provisions of the union's constitution. The plaintiff then asked the defendant to explain why these provisions were "not deprived of force and effect by operation of [the Federal Labor Management Reporting and Disclosure Act.]" While noting that "the line demarcating permissible discovery under Rule 33[(a)(2)] may be obscure," the court held that the first interrogatory was proper, but the second interrogatory was not. *Id.* at 1187–88.

"Contention" interrogatories under Rule 33(a)(2) also raise an issue with respect to "work product" protection. The interplay between these two provisions is discussed in section C(2)(*c*), below.

Objections to Interrogatories and Sanctions. Under Rule 33(b)(4), the grounds for objecting to an interrogatory "must be stated with specificity [and] [a]ny ground not stated in a timely objection is waived unless the court, for good cause, excuses the failure." Objections to interrogatories may be made on a variety of grounds. For example, the answering party may assert that the information requested is outside the scope of discovery, the preparation of the answers would be too burdensome, the questions are too vague or overbroad, the information sought is unnecessary or repetitious, or the information sought is privileged.

Notes and Questions

1. When a party has objected to or otherwise failed to answer a particular interrogatory, how does the requesting party compel an answer? *See* FED. R. CIV. P. 37(a)(3)(B)(iii). What sanctions can be imposed if the court rules in favor of the requesting party and orders the opposing party to answer? *See* FED. R. CIV. P. 37(a)(5)(A).

2. What happens if a party completely fails to serve any answers or objections to an entire set of interrogatories? *See* FED. R. CIV. P. 37(d)(1)(ii) and (d)(3). Why do you think the rules provide for more severe sanctions in this situation? Rule 37(d)(2) further provides that the failure to respond "is not excused on the ground that the discovery sought was objectionable, unless the party failing to act has a pending motion for a protective order under Rule 26(c)."

Duty to Amend. Under Rule 26(e)(1), a party is under a duty to amend a prior interrogatory response "(A) in a timely manner if the party learns that in some material respect the ... response is incomplete or incorrect, and if the additional or corrective information has not otherwise been made known to the other parties during the discovery process or in writing; or (B) as ordered by the court." If a party fails to properly amend an interrogatory response as required by Rule 26(e)(1), the sanction provisions of Rule 37(c)(1) are triggered and may result in exclusion of the undisclosed evidence.

Use at Trial. Rule 33(c) provides that interrogatory answers may be used at trial "to the extent allowed by the Federal Rules of Evidence." As with any prior statement by a witness, interrogatories may be used to impeach or contradict the trial testimony of the answering party if the party's testimony is inconsistent with the party's interrogatory answers. In addition, because interrogatory answers are statements made by a party, they are an exception to the hearsay rule and may be offered as substantive evidence *against* the answering party. *See* FED. R. EVID 801(d)(2)(A). Unlike depositions, however, answers to interrogatories may not be offered as substantive evidence *by* the answering party, as a deposition could be under Rule 32(a)(4), if the answering party becomes legally unavailable to testify at trial. *See* FED. R. EVID. 804(b)(1).

(e) Production of Documents and Tangible Things: Rule 34

Rule 34(a)(1) permits a party to serve upon any other party a request "to produce and permit the requesting party ... to inspect, copy, test, or sample the following items in the responding party's possession, custody, or control: (A) any designated documents or electronically stored information—including writings, drawings, graphs, charts, photographs, sound recordings, images, and other data or data compilations—stored in any medium ...; or (B) any designated tangible things." Rule 34(a)(2) also authorizes a party to serve a request "to permit entry onto designated land or other property possessed or controlled by the responding party, so that the requesting party may inspect, measure, survey, photograph, test, or sample the property or any designated object or operation on it." Under

Rule 34(b)(1), the request (A) must describe with reasonable particularity each item or category of items to be inspected; (B) must specify a reasonable time, place, and manner for the inspection; and (C) and may specify the form or forms in which electronically stored information is to be produced.

Functions of Rule 34 Requests. Depending on the nature and complexity of the case, document production and inspection can be an important part of the discovery process. In many cases, such as securities, antitrust, and other complex actions, document discovery is often the most critical factor in the preparation and resolution of the case. Rule 34 also serves as a necessary supplement to the initial disclosure requirements of Rule 26(a)(1)(A)(ii). Recall that Rule 26(a)(1)(A)(ii) does not automatically mandate the production of documents. A "description by category and location" of the documents is also sufficient to satisfy this rule. In addition, Rule 26(a)(1)(A)(ii) only requires disclosure of documents that the disclosing party "may use to support its claims or defenses." All other documents relevant in the action must be requested under Rule 34. Rule 34 requests may be effectively combined with Rule 33 interrogatories. Interrogatories under Rule 33 can be used to discover if relevant documents exist, and Rule 34 can then be used to request production of the documents.

Party and Nonparty Production. A Rule 34 request may only be served upon another party to the action and only applies to documents and tangible things in the "possession, custody or control" of a party and to designated land or other property "possessed or controlled" by a party. Of these limits, "control" has raised the most difficulties. For example, are requested documents in the "control" of a party when the documents are in the possession of (1) a nonparty corporation that is related to a corporate party or (2) a present or former employee of a corporate party? *See* 8B WRIGHT ET AL. § 2210, at 149 (rather than adopting a blanket rule for such situations, courts tend to focus on specific facts presented in a particular case in determining the issue of "control").

When the desired document or property is in the possession or control of a nonparty, the subpoena provisions of Rule 45 can be effectively used to achieve the functional equivalent of a Rule 34 request to a party. Rule 45(a)(1)(A)(iii) closely aligns with the scope of Rule 34 and provides that a subpoena may command a person to "produce designated documents, electronically stored information, or tangible things in that person's possession, custody or control; or permit the inspection of premises." Rule 45(a)(1)(D) further provides that a subpoena to produce documents, electronically stored information or tangible things requires the responding person "to permit inspection, copying, testing, or sampling of the materials."

As explained in the earlier section on "Document Production at a Deposition," a subpoena to produce documents and tangible things is known as a *subpoena duces tecum*. Under Rule 45(a)(1)(C), it may be issued separately from a subpoena to appear at a trial, hearing, or deposition. As a nonparty, however, the subpeona may only compel the person to produce documents or tangible things at a place within 100 miles of where the person "resides, is employed, or regularly transacts business in person." *See* FED. R. CIV. P. 45(c)(3)(A) [revised as Rule 45(c)(2)(A) effective Dec. 1, 2013].

Production Responses and Sanctions. Under Rule 34(b)(2)(A) and (B), the party served with a Rule 34 request must serve a written response within 30 days and either state that the inspection and related activities will be permitted as requested or state an objection to the request, including the reasons. Under Rule 34(b)(2)(E)(i), a party must produce documents as they are kept "in the usual course of business or must organize and label them to correspond to the categories in the request." If the served party responds and indicates that inspection will not be permitted as requested, the party submitting the request may move for an order under Rule 37(a)(3)(B)(iv) compelling inspection in accordance with the request. Under Rule 37(a)(5), the court may require payment of reasonable expenses incurred in making the motion, including attorney's fees.

What happens, however, if the served party fails to serve any response to the Rule 34 request? What sanctions may the court now impose? *See* FED. R. CIV. P. 37(d)(1)(A)(ii) and (3).

Duty to Amend. Responses to Rule 34 requests must be amended in accordance with the provisions of Rule 26(e)(1) if the party learns that the earlier response is incomplete or incorrect in some material respect or as ordered by the court. Failure to amend triggers the sanction provisions of Rule 37(c)(1).

Electronically Stored Information. The 2006 amendments to Rule 34 expressly added reference to "electronically stored information" in Rule 34(a)(1). As stated in the 2006 Advisory Committee's Note, this inclusion was intended "to confirm that discovery of electronically stored information stands on equal footing with discovery of paper documents." A precise definition of electronically stored information was not used so that the term would be read expansively and understood "to be broad enough to cover all current types of computer-based information and flexible enough to encompass future changes and developments." *See* FED. R. CIV. P. 34 advisory committee's note to the 2006 amendment.

Special provisions for the production of electronically stored information were also added with the 2006 amendments. New Rules 34(b)(2)(D) and (E)(ii) and (iii) provide that a responding party must produce electronically stored information, if the request does not otherwise specify, "in a form or forms in which it is ordinarily maintained or in a reasonably usable form or forms" and "need not produce the same electronically stored information in more than one form." The 2006 amendments also added a parallel provision in Rule 45, with identical language to Rule 34(b)(2)(E)(ii) and (iii), when the discovery of electronically stored information is sought from a nonparty through the service of a subpoena. *See* FED. R. CIV. P. 45(d)(1)(B) and (C) [revised as Rule 45(e)(1)(B) and (C) effective Dec. 1, 2013]. The special considerations relative to the production and discovery of electronically stored information are further analyzed in section B, below.

(f) Requests for Admission: Rule 36

Rule 36(a) allows a party to "serve on any other party a written request to admit, for purposes of the pending action only, the truth of any matters within the scope of Rule 26(b)(1)." The requests may relate to "(A) facts, the application of law to fact, or opinions about either; and (B) the genuineness of any described documents." Matters admitted under Rule 36(a) are admitted only for purposes of the pending action, but all matters so admitted are "conclusively established unless the court, on motion, permits the admission to be withdrawn or amended." *See* FED. R. CIV. P. 36(b). A sample request for admission is contained in Federal Form 51.

Functions of Requests for Admission. Requests for admission are similar in format to interrogatories. Like interrogatories, requests for admission may only be served on another party. Requests for admission, however, serve a different purpose than interrogatories and the other discovery devices. Unlike the other discovery methods, requests for admission are not designed to discover information, but rather to narrow the issues for trial by requesting that certain matters be formally admitted.

Interrogatories and depositions, for example, would pose informational questions, such as: "What did you do immediately after the accident?" "When did you first seek treatment for your injury?" and the like. Requests for admission, by comparison, would request a response as to the genuineness of a specific document or the truth of a specific statement, *e.g.*, "The notice sent to you on [date] complied with the requirements of the Truth in Lending Act." Requests for admission can be particularly useful in securing admissions to minor, but essential, matters that would otherwise require the appearance of a special witness to prove at trial, *e.g.*, "Ace Mortgage Co. conducted business in New York from [date] to [date]."

Requests for admission are thus designed as a time and cost-saving device to expedite the litigation process for the parties and the court. To encourage parties to admit matters for which there is no genuine dispute, Rule 36(b) expressly states that any admission may be used in the pending action only and "is not an admission for any other purpose and cannot be used against the party in any other proceeding."

Admission Responses. In the absence of a court order or proper party stipulation under Rule 29(b), a party must respond to requests for admission within 30 days after service of the requests. Unlike the other discovery methods, if the served party does not respond to the Rule 36 requests within the prescribed time, no enforcement action need be taken by the propounding party to compel a reply because the sanction for non-response is self-executing. Under Rule 36(a)(3), all requests for admission are automatically admitted unless a timely answer or objection is served by the responding party.

If a party objects to a request, the reasons for the objection must be stated. If the party responds to the request, the answer must "specifically deny [the matter] or state in detail why the answering party cannot truthfully admit or deny it." A party may cite lack of information or knowledge as the reason for failure to admit or deny "only if the party states that it has made reasonable inquiry and that the information it knows or can readily obtain is insufficient to enable it to admit or deny."

Under Rule 36(a)(6), the party requesting an admission may move to determine the sufficiency of an answer or objection if the party feels that the response fails to comply with the requirements of the rule. If the objection is unjustified, the court must order an answer. If the answer does not comply with the rule, the court may order (a) that the matter is admitted or (b) that an amended answer be served.

Duty to Amend and Sanctions. Responses to requests for admission must be amended in accordance with the provisions of Rule 26(e)(1) if the party learns that the earlier response is incomplete or incorrect in some material respect or as ordered by the court. Failure to so amend triggers the sanction provisions of Rule 37(c)(1). In addition, if a party in its response refuses to admit the truth of a matter or the genuineness of a document and the requesting party thereafter proves these matters, Rule 37(c)(2) authorizes the party to move for an order "that the party who failed to admit pay the reasonable expenses, including reasonable attorney's fees, incurred in making that proof." Unless the court finds good reason for the failure to admit as set forth in Rule 37(c)(2)(A)-(D), the rule requires the court to enter the order.

Judicial Versus Evidentiary Admissions. The concept of admissions can be confusing because the same term is used in both the rules of civil procedure and the rules of evidence, but with different meanings in both. An admission under Rule 36 is a formal "judicial" admission which, unless amended or withdrawn by permission of the court, conclusively establishes the matter admitted for purposes of the pending litigation and the introduction of contra evidence on the matter is not permitted.

Under the rules of evidence, the term "admission" is also used, but in a different context to signify an exception to the hearsay rule. Under Federal Rule of Evidence 801(d)(2), any statement made by a party is an exception to the hearsay rule and may be offered as substantive evidence *against* that party, assuming the requirements of relevance are otherwise met. Under the rules of evidence, such a statement is also known as an "admission," but it is distinct from a Rule 36 "judicial" admission. An admission under Rule 801(d)(2) is only an "evidentiary" admission and does not conclusively establish the matter contained in the party's statement. A party who has made an "evidentiary" admission may, nevertheless, introduce evidence to contradict the matter contained in the party's statement. A party's answers to interrogatories or at a deposition would be examples of "evidentiary" admissions.

Note that although a party's answer to an interrogatory is treated as an "evidentiary" admission and may normally be countered with contra evidence at trial, a party may, under certain circumstances, be precluded from offering contra evidence to an interrogatory answer as a discovery sanction. Do you recall what rules might trigger such a sanction? Under Rule 26(e)(1)(A), a party has a duty to amend an interrogatory answer if the party learns that "in some material respect the ... response is incomplete or incorrect." What may happen under Rule 37(c)(1) if a party fails to properly amend an interrogatory answer as required under Rule 26(e)(1)?

Problems

Problem 8-8. Determine the specific objection, if any, that could be made to each of the following interrogatories. Assume that they have been served in a personal injury suit commenced by *P* involving an auto accident in which *D* collided with *P's* automobile from the rear. To the extent that it is relevant, assume that no special showing of need has been made with respect to any of these interrogatories.

(a) State in detail all facts in *D's* possession concerning the accident.

(b) State whether or not *D* is a communist.

(c) Summarize the contents of any written or oral statements that *D* has obtained from witnesses to the accident.

(d) State what *D* told the physician who treated *D* immediately after the accident concerning *D's* vision at the time of the accident.

Problem 8-9. Would the following interrogatories be permitted under Rule 33(a)(2)?

(a) State whether the defendant at the time of the accident was engaged in interstate commerce.

(b) With respect to the defense of contributory negligence (raised by the defendant's answer), state upon what specific conduct, acts, or omissions that charge was based.

(c) Assume that the plaintiff in an action in federal court has filed and served a complaint identical to Federal Form 21. The defendant then serves an answer admitting the execution of the note, denying that the defendant owed the amount of the note to the plaintiff, and admitting that the defendant conveyed the property to E.F., but denying the conveyance was fraudulent. The defendant also asserts as an affirmative defense that the plaintiff released the claim on the promissory note for a valuable consideration. Assume that a reply to the defendant's answer has not been ordered and that the defendant serves the following interrogatories. (i) State whether the plaintiff denies that there was such a release. (ii) State whether the release was given in return for a valuable consideration. (iii)

State whether the plaintiff contends that there was fraud in securing the release. (iv) State whether in the plaintiff's opinion there are any other defenses applicable to the release.

Problem 8-10. Assume on the basic facts of *Problem 8-5*, that the attorney representing *P's* estate in a civil action against *D* asks the following question in an interrogatory to *D*: How many drinks did *D* have immediately prior to the accident? Without *D's* attorney's knowledge, *D* answers the question falsely because *D* knows that it will be very difficult for *P's* estate to prove otherwise. Later, while *D's* attorney is preparing for trial, *D* tells the attorney that *D* did not answer the interrogatory truthfully. Does Rule 26(e)(1) require the attorney to advise *D* that *D* must correct the prior response? If so, what happens if *D* refuses to amend the prior response?

Problem 8-11. Assume that *P* receives a Rule 34 request to produce tax returns for the past two years as well as all hospital records relating to an injury. Assume that *P* has neither in *P's* possession. Can *P* legitimately refuse to comply with the discovery request? What is meant by the word "control" in Rule 34(a)(1)?

Problem 8-12. Assume that you represent the executor of *P's* estate in a civil action for negligence against *D* arising out of an automobile accident at a highway intersection. The intersection has stop signs at all access roads. *P* died in the accident, and *B*, a passenger in *P's* car, stated to you in an interview that *P* did not come to a full stop before entering the intersection. *B* has since died from causes unrelated to the accident, and no other witnesses claim to have seen *P* enter the intersection. You have no reason to doubt the accuracy of *B's* statement. *D* has alleged contributory negligence as a defense and has submitted the following Rule 36 request for admission: "*P* did not come to a full stop before entering the intersection where the accident in this suit occurred." What is the proper response to this request? Would it be proper to object to the request on the ground that it presents a genuine issue for trial? Would it be proper to respond that the answering party cannot truthfully admit or deny the matter? If so, what is the reason (required by Rule 36(a)(4) to be "stated in detail")? If the request was denied and the jury found that *P* had been contributorily negligent by failing to come to a complete stop before entering the intersection, should that denial give rise to a Rule 37(c)(2) sanction?

(g) *Compulsory Physical and Mental Examinations: Rule 35*

Rule 35(a) authorizes the court, "on motion for good cause," to order "a party whose mental or physical condition—including blood group—is in controversy to submit to a physical or mental examination by a suitably licensed or certified examiner." Rule 35(a) also gives the court the same authority to order a party to produce for examination a person "who is in [the party's] custody or under its legal control."

Because of the special privacy concerns raised by Rule 35, the requirements of the rule are distinct from the other methods of discovery in several important respects. Most significantly, Rule 35 is the only discovery device that, in the absence of agreement by the parties, must be authorized by a court order upon a special showing of "good cause." With respect to the other methods of discovery, unless the discovery request is outside the "claim or defense" relevancy standard of Rule 26(b)(1) or otherwise restricted by a limitation on discovery, no court order or showing of good cause is necessary to support any discovery request.

In addition, because of these special privacy concerns, the failure to submit to a physical or mental examination ordered under Rule 35 is expressly exempted under Rule 37(b)(2)(A)(vii) from the sanction of contempt of court, a sanction which is otherwise applicable under that provision to the violation of all other discovery orders. Violation of a Rule 35 order by a party, however, is subject to the other sanctions of Rule 37(b)(2)(A)(i)-(vi). Rule 35 also stands alone as the only discovery provision challenged in the Supreme Court as unconstitutional and violative of the Rules Enabling Act, 28 U.S.C. § 2072, because of the privacy and substantive right issues raised by the rule. *See Schlagenhauf v. Holder*, 379 U.S. 104 (1964) ("We hold that Rule 35, as applied to either plaintiffs or defendants to an action, is free from constitutional difficulty and is within the scope of the Enabling Act").

The need to resort to the requirements of Rule 35 is unnecessary if the parties agree to arrange for an examination by stipulation. In cases in which physical or mental condition is clearly in controversy, such as the typical personal injury tort action in which a plaintiff seeks damages for physical and/or psychological injuries, attorneys routinely agree to the scheduling of an appropriate examination(s). Rule 35 is not limited only to personal injury tort actions, however, and is available in any civil action in which the physical or mental condition of any party, or any person in the party's custody or legal control, is in controversy. Rule 35 has been used in a wide range of cases, such as sexual harassment and employment discrimination actions. Resort to the requirements of Rule 35 is necessary whenever the parties disagree on whether an examination is justified.

In *Schlagenhauf v. Holder*, 379 U.S. 104 (1964), the Supreme Court made clear that the "good cause" and "in controversy" requirements of Rule 35 are not a mere formality and must be properly satisfied before an order compelling a physical or mental examination may be entered. The standard enunciated by the Court in *Schlagenhauf* as to the requirements of Rule 35 remains the standard today. In this case, injured bus passengers sued various defendants, including the bus driver, after the bus collided with the rear of a tractor-trailer. The owners of the tractor-trailer, also named as defendants, sought several mental and physical examinations of the bus driver. In holding that a proper showing under Rule 35 had not been made, the Court explained:

> ... [T]he "in controversy" and "good cause" requirements of Rule 35 ... are not met by mere conclusory allegations of the pleadings—nor by mere relevance to the case—but require an affirmative showing by the movant that each condition as to which the examination is sought is really and genuinely in controversy and that good cause exists for ordering each particular examination. Obviously, what may be good cause for one type of examination may not be so for another. The ability of the movant to obtain the desired information by other means is also relevant.

> Rule 35, therefore, requires discriminating application by the trial judge, who must decide, as an initial matter in every case, whether the party requesting a mental or physical examination or examinations has adequately demonstrated the existence of the Rule's requirements of "in controversy" and "good cause," which requirements, as the Court of Appeals in this case itself recognized, are necessarily related.... This does not, of course, mean that the movant must prove his case on the merits in order to meet the requirements for a mental or physical examination. Nor does it mean that an evidentiary hearing is required in all cases. This may be necessary in some cases, but in other cases the showing could be made by affidavits or other usual methods short of a hearing. It does mean, though, that the movant must produce sufficient information, by whatever means, so that the district judge can fulfill his function mandated by the Rule.

> Of course, there are situations where the pleadings alone are sufficient to meet these requirements. A plaintiff in a negligence action who asserts mental or phys-

ical injury ... places that mental or physical injury clearly in controversy and provides the defendant with good cause for an examination to determine the existence and extent of such asserted injury. This is not only true as to a plaintiff, but applies equally to a defendant who asserts his mental or physical condition as a defense to a claim....

Here, however, Schlagenhauf did not assert his mental or physical condition either in support of or in defense of a claim. His condition was sought to be placed in issue by other parties. Thus, under the principles discussed above, Rule 35 required that these parties make an affirmative showing that petitioner's mental or physical condition was in controversy and that there was good cause for the examinations requested. This, the record plainly shows, they failed to do.

379 U.S. at 242–43.

Notes and Questions

1. In its original version, Rule 35 only authorized examinations by a physician. In 1988, Rule 35 was amended to allow mental examinations by a psychologist, and was amended again in 1991 to further expand the range of qualified examiners. Rule 35(a)(1) currently authorizes examination "by a suitably licensed or certified examiner." As explained in the 1991 Advisory Committee's Note, the purpose of the amendment was to extend Rule 35 "to include other certified or licensed professionals, such as dentists or occupational therapists, who are not physicians or clinical psychologists, but who may be well-qualified to give valuable testimony about the physical or mental condition that is the subject of dispute." Some state rules patterned after Rule 35 continue to require examinations only by a physician. *See, e.g., Green ex rel. Green v. Lewis Truck Lines, Inc.*, 443 S.E.2d 906 (S.C. 1994) (under South Carolina Rule 35, examinations are limited to "physicians"; "plain meaning" excludes clinical psychologists).

2. Rule 35(a)(1) provides for physical or mental examinations only of a party or "a person who is in [the party's] custody or under its legal control." In the latter situation, the court does not direct its order to the person to be examined, but rather orders the appropriate party to produce the person for examination. The party's failure to produce the person as ordered may result in sanctions against the party as provided in Rule 37(b)(2)(A)(i)-(vi), "unless the disobedient party shows that it cannot produce the other person" for examination. *See* Fed. R. Civ. P. 37(b)(2)(B).

3. When is a person in the custody or under the legal control of a party for purposes of Rule 35(a)(1)? In a case like *Schlagenhauf*, for example, assume that the bus driver is not named as a party to the action, but is alleged in the pleadings to be the defendant bus company's agent (employee). Even though the bus driver is not a party, would the bus driver, nevertheless, qualify as a person in the custody or under the legal control of a party? Rule 35(a)(1) does not define "custody" or "legal control," but the 1970 Advisory Committee's Note indicates that this provision was added to "settle beyond doubt that a parent or guardian suing to recover for injuries to a minor may be ordered to produce the minor for examination." The 1970 Advisory Committee's Note further indicates that the rule "makes no reference to employees of a party." Rule 35's "custody" or "legal control" provision is, thus, narrowly construed by the courts as only applying to certain persons, such as the minor child of a party, and not to agents or employees of a party who are not themselves parties to the action. *See* 8B Wright et al. § 2233, at 250–51. If a

Rule 35 examination is not available in the above example, what discovery devices can a party use to acquire information as to a nonparty's eyesight or other physical or mental condition?   Depose driver

4. Rule 35(a)(2)(B) provides that an examination order "must specify the time, place, manner, conditions, and scope of the examination, as well as the person or persons who will perform it." The party moving for an order under Rule 35(a) will offer these proposed specifics as to the examination, but the court has final authority in setting the terms and conditions for the examination. In exercising its discretion, the court will consider the scientific acceptance and reliability of the proposed examination method and may refuse to order an examination that would be painful or dangerous to the person to be examined. The court will also determine who may be present at the examination. To avoid potential interference with the examination, the examinee's attorney or physician is generally not allowed to be present, although the court has discretion to allow their presence in an appropriate case. *See* 8B WRIGHT ET AL. §§ 2235–2236.

5. (a) Pursuant to Rule 35(b)(1), the party against whom an examination order is issued or the person examined is entitled to receive on request "a copy of the examiner's report, together with like reports of all earlier examinations of the same condition." Rule 35(b)(2) provides that the report "must set out in detail the examiner's findings, including diagnoses, conclusions, and the results of any tests." Upon delivery of these reports, the party who moved for the examination is entitled on request to receive from the party against whom the examination order was issued "like reports of all earlier or later examinations of the same condition."

(b) What happens under Rule 35(b)(3) if the party against whom the order is made is unable to obtain such reports—for example, a report of a previous examination of a nonparty who qualified under Rule 35(a)(1) as a person under the party's legal control? If a copy of a report is obtained or the examiner's deposition is taken, Rule 35(b)(4) provides that "the party examined waives any privilege it may have—in that action or any other action involving the same controversy—concerning testimony about all examinations of the same condition." Do these exchange and waiver provisions apply only to examinations ordered by the court pursuant to Rule 35? For example, do they apply to examinations arranged by agreement of the parties? *See* FED. R. CIV. P. 35(b)(6).

Problems

Problem 8-13. Assume that *P* sues *D Tire Co.* for personal injuries sustained in an accident. *P* was injured while *P* was mounting a tire on a rim at a service station where *P* worked. *P's* complaint seeks damages for *P's* future lost wages, medical expenses, and disability. During discovery, *D* learns that *P* was a former drug abuser who had shared hypodermic needles. In addition, *P* admits to being bisexual and engaging in unprotected sexual activity. *P* has never taken a test to determine *P's* human immunodeficiency virus (HIV) status. Pursuant to Rule 35, *D* seeks to compel *P* to submit to a blood test to determine whether *P* is HIV positive. *D* asserts that information obtained from the test is essential to its ability to defend against *P's* alleged future damages. *D* further asserts that if *P* is HIV positive, *P's* life expectancy will be dramatically lower than the life expectancy of a person not infected with the virus. In light of *Schlagenhauf*, do you think that *D* has shown that *P's* physical condition is "in controversy"? Do you think *D* has shown "good cause"? If the court ordered *P* to submit to the test, would that order "abridge, enlarge, or modify" *P's* substantive rights within the meaning of 28 U.S.C. § 2072?

Problem 8-14. Assume on the facts of *Problem 8-13* that the court orders *P* to submit to the test, but *P* refuses. Can the court sanction *P* by holding *P* in contempt? Can the court preclude *P* from introducing evidence at trial of *P's* life expectancy? Can the court dismiss *P's* action?

4. Pretrial Conferences and Orders: Rule 16

Rule 16 is designed to improve the quality of justice in the federal courts by ensuring judicial control and monitoring of civil actions throughout the litigation process. Rule 16 expressly provides for a series of pretrial conferences during the action to allow the judge to manage cases effectively and efficiently. These conferences are especially important in monitoring cases through the discovery stage by establishing time limits for the completion of discovery and identifying any special problems, especially with respect to the assertion of privilege and work product claims and the discovery of electronically stored information. As set forth in Rule 16(a)(1)-(5), the focus of such conferences is to establish the judge's control of the litigation early in the action, expedite the disposition of the action, discourage wasteful pretrial activities, facilitate settlement of the case, and improve the quality of trial through more thorough preparation. Rule 16(c)(2) lists sixteen matters for consideration at pretrial conferences. These matters range from formulating and simplifying the issues to adopting special procedures for managing potentially difficult or protracted litigation.

The actions taken at the pretrial conferences result in the issuance of pretrial orders. Under Rule 16(d), a pretrial order "controls the course of the action unless the court modifies it." The order following the final pretrial conference may be modified by the court "only to prevent manifest injustice." *See* Fed. R. Civ. P. 16(e). In effect, these provisions mean that the final pretrial order supersedes the pleadings in the action by eliminating and preserving issues for later adjudication at trial. Claims, defenses, and issues that are not included in the pretrial order are waived, even if asserted in prior pleadings, and conversely, matters included in the pretrial order are preserved for trial, even though never asserted in prior pleadings. *See, e.g., Rockwell Int'l Corp. v. United States,* 549 U.S. 457, 474 (2007) (plaintiffs' statement of claims in final pretrial order "superseded" plaintiff's allegations in original complaint and controlled whether action was properly within federal jurisdiction); *Youren v. Tintic Sch. Dist.,* 343 F.3d 1296, 1304 (10th Cir. 2003) (defendant's failure to preserve statute-of-limitations defense in pretrial order constitutes waiver, even though asserted by defendant in answer); *Studiengesellschaft Kohle, m.b.H. v. Shell Oil Co.,* 112 F.3d 1561, 1566 (Fed. Cir. 1997) (introduction of new claim by plaintiff in pretrial order permissible, even though not asserted by plaintiff in complaint).

In order to reinforce the importance of these pretrial conferences in the litigation process, Rule 16(f) provides for sanctions for non-compliance. Not only may sanctions be imposed if a party or its attorney fails to appear at a scheduling or pretrial conference or fails to obey a scheduling or other pretrial order, but sanctions are also authorized if a party or its attorney "is substantially unprepared to participate—or does not participate in good faith—in the conference." The judge may impose such sanctions as are just, including those authorized in Rule 37(b)(2)(A)(ii)-(vii). These latter provisions permit the court to, among other things, strike the pleadings of the disobedient party, dismiss the action, enter default judgment, and treat the violation as a contempt of court.

5. Discovery Certifications and Sanctions: Rules 26(g) and 37

Throughout the preceding sections, reference to the various sanction provisions of Rule 37 have been interwoven into the discussion as applicable to the particular methods of discovery. This subsection contains a more general overview of Rule 37 as well as the certification requirements of Rule 26(g).

Rule 26(g). Originally adopted in 1983 and amended in 1993, Rule 26(g) was designed "to curb discovery abuse" by imposing "an affirmative duty to engage in pretrial discovery in a responsible manner that is consistent with the spirit and purposes of Rules 26 through 37." *See* FED. R. CIV. P. 26(g) advisory committee's note to the 1983 amendment. Similar to the certification requirements of Rule 11, Rule 26(g)(1) requires that all discovery requests, responses, objections, and mandatory disclosures, other than expert testimony disclosures under Rule 26(a)(2), be signed by the attorney or unrepresented party serving or filing the discovery paper.

Under Rule 26(g)(1)(A), the signature of the attorney or party on an initial or pretrial disclosure constitutes a certification that "to the best of the person's knowledge, information, and belief formed after a reasonable inquiry ... [the disclosure] is complete and correct as of the time it is made." Under Rule 26(g)(1)(B), the signature on a discovery request, response, or objection constitutes a certification, based on this same standard, that the request, response, or objection is (i) consistent with the federal rules and warranted by existing law or by a nonfrivolous argument for extending, modifying, or reversing existing law; (ii) not interposed for any improper purpose; and (iii) neither unreasonable nor unduly burdensome or expensive considering the needs and circumstances of the case.

Because the signer's belief must be "formed after a reasonable inquiry," compliance with Rule 26(g)(1) is assessed, similar to Rule 11, on the basis of an objective standard and the subjective bad faith of the signer is not a prerequisite to a violation. Rule 26(g)(3) further provides that "[i]f a certification violates this rule without substantial justification, the court, on motion or on its own, must impose an appropriate sanction on the signer, the party on whose behalf the signer was acting, or both," which may include an award of reasonable expenses and attorney's fees. What constitutes an "appropriate sanction" in a particular case is within the sound discretion of the court. In one case, the court required the attorney to write an article explaining why the attorney's objections to interrogatories were improper and to submit the article to two bar journals. *See St. Paul Reinsurance Co. v. Commercial Fin. Corp.*, 198 F.R.D. 508 (N.D. Iowa 2000). Depending on how egregious the violation is, the court may impose more severe sanctions, including preclusion of evidence, dismissal of the action, or the entry of default judgment.

Rule 37. Rule 37 is the umbrella rule governing discovery enforcement and sanctions. This rule establishes detailed procedures and standards for a wide range of discovery violations relative to all of the discovery methods studied in this chapter. Careful reading of all of the provisions of Rule 37 is essential to understand the requisite procedures and standards. This discussion only provides a general overview of the enforcement structure of Rule 37.

In most cases, discovery enforcement under Rule 37 proceeds in two stages. First, a motion is brought under Rule 37(a) for an order compelling disclosure or discovery that has been refused by another party. If an order is entered and the party still refuses to comply, the next stage is to seek sanctions under Rule 37(b)(2) for violation of the court's order.

With respect to the first stage, motions to compel under Rule 37(a) apply to specific discovery violations, such as the failure to make a mandatory disclosure, Rule 37(a)(3)(A); failure to answer a deposition question, Rule 37(a)(3)(B)(i); failure to answer an interrogatory, Rule 37(a)(3)(B)(iii); or failure to permit inspection as requested under Rule 34, Rule 37(a)(3)(B)(iv). Although expenses on the motion may be awarded under Rule 37(a)(5), the primary purpose of Rule 37(a) is not to sanction the disobedient party, but to compel disclosure of the requested information. In order to reduce the necessity of a motion, Rule 37(a)(1) provides that a motion to compel must include "a certification that the movant has in good faith conferred or attempted to confer with the person or party failing to make the disclosure or discovery in an effort to obtain it without court action."

If the court enters an order compelling discovery under Rule 37(a) and the party still fails to comply, the court may then impose sanctions under Rule 37(b)(2). The sanction provisions of Rule 37(b)(2) apply to the violation of any order to provide or permit discovery, not only orders entered under Rule 37(a). The sanction provisions of Rule 37(b)(2) also apply to violations of protective orders under Rule 26(c). Under Rule 37(b)(2), the court has discretion to impose such sanctions as the court deems "just" given the circumstances of the case and the seriousness of the violation. Rule 37(b)(2) provides that the court may, among other sanctions, preclude the disobedient party from introducing certain evidence, strike the pleadings of the disobedient party, dismiss the action or enter a default judgment against the disobedient party, or hold the disobedient party in contempt of court.

The dismissal and default judgment sanctions of Rule 37(b)(2)(v) and (vi) are indeed harsh sanctions for discovery abuses and are generally used only as a last resort. Nevertheless, in appropriate cases, the courts have imposed these sanctions. In *National Hockey League v. Metropolitan Hockey Club*, 427 U.S. 639 (1976), a case in which the plaintiffs repeatedly failed to provide answers to interrogatories over a 17-month period, the Court noted that

> here, as in other areas of the law, the most severe in the spectrum of sanctions provided by statute or rule must be available to the district court in appropriate cases, not merely to penalize those whose conduct may be deemed to warrant such a sanction, but to deter those who might be tempted to such conduct in the absence of such a deterrent. If the decision of the Court of Appeals [reversing the order of dismissal] remained undisturbed in this case, it might well be that *these* respondents would faithfully comply with all future discovery orders entered by the District Court in this case. But other parties to other lawsuits would feel freer than we think Rule 37 contemplates they should feel to flout other discovery orders of other district courts. Under the circumstances of this case, we hold that the District Judge did not abuse his discretion in finding bad faith of the part of these respondents, and concluding that the extreme sanction of dismissal was appropriate in this case by reason of respondents' "flagrant bad faith" and their counsel's "callous disregard" of their responsibilities.

Id. at 643.

Under Rule 37(d), certain discovery violations are considered so serious that sanctions may be imposed as authorized under Rule 37(b)(2)(A)(i)-(vi), even though no prior order of discovery has been entered. Compare, for instance, the nature of the discovery violations that trigger sanctions under Rule 37(d) with the violations listed in Rule 37(a)(3)(B)(i)-(iv). As noted above, Rule 37(a)(3)(B) deals with relatively minor violations, such as failing to answer a particular question posed at a deposition or in an interrogatory. The violations of Rule 37(d)(1)(A)(i) and (ii) are more severe and involve (i) the failure of a party, or its designated agent, to appear at the person's scheduled deposition or (ii) the failure of a party to serve any answers or objections to interrogatories or any written response to a Rule 34 request. For these violations, the court may directly impose sanctions as authorized under Rule 37(b)(2)(A)(i)-(vi). The court is similarly empowered under Rule 37(c)(1)(C) to impose such sanctions if a party "fails to provide information or identify a witness as required by Rule 26(a) or 26(e)." The sanctions of Rule 37(c)(1) are not triggered, however, if the party's failure is "substantially justified or is harmless."

The 2006 rule amendments added a special sanction provision, Rule 37(e), to govern the failure to provide electronically stored information. Absent exceptional circumstances, Rule 37(e) specifically exempts from court sanction the failure to provide electronically stored information "lost as a result of the routine, good-faith operation of an electronic information system." Rule 37(e) is discussed in section B, below.

Notes and Questions

1. Assume that a party improperly acquires information from the other party outside the discovery process (*i.e.,* by stealing it). Should the court be able to impose a sanction on the party for this kind of behavior? If so, what Rule, if any, authorizes the sanction? *See Fayemi v. Hambrecht & Quist, Inc.,* 174 F.R.D. 319 (S.D.N.Y. 1997) (Rule 26(c) does not provide authority for regulating the use of information obtained outside discovery, but the court may use its inherent equitable powers to sanction a party that seeks to use in litigation evidence that was wrongfully obtained).

2. In *In re Tutu Wells Contamination Litigation,* 120 F.3d 368 (3d Cir. 1997), the defendant's attorneys suppressed certain information that allegedly increased discovery time and expense significantly. The district court suspended the attorneys from practice before the district court as a sanction, invoking its inherent power under Rule 37. The court of appeals reversed, holding that the district court was obligated to give the attorneys particularized notice that the severe sanction of suspension was being considered. The district court had also ordered a community service fund of $750,000 to be created into which monetary sanctions against the attorneys were deposited. The court of appeals held that the district court's inherent power did not extend to the imposition of sanctions for the benefit of third parties. *Id.* at 379–91.

Section B. Special Considerations in the Discovery of Electronically Stored Information ("E-Discovery")

"Electronically stored information" refers to the enormous range of data that is stored in a computer medium. In the modern information infrastructure, this includes word processing files, databases, e-mails, web pages, and all other forms of information that may be stored in a computer. Discovery of electronically stored information ("e-discovery") raises many issues not presented in traditional discovery of "paper" documents.

Foremost is the sheer volume of such electronic data. Computer networks of large organizations, for instance, store information in "terabytes, each of which represents the equivalent of 500 million typewritten pages." REPORT OF THE JUDICIAL CONFERENCE COMMITTEE ON RULES OF PRACTICE AND PROCEDURE, Sept. 2005, *reprinted in* 234 F.R.D. 269, 272 (2005). As one court explained, electronic data is so voluminous because, unlike paper documents, "the costs of storage are virtually nil. Information is retained not because it is expected to be used, but because there is no compelling reason to discard it." *Rowe Entm't, Inc. v. William Morris Agency, Inc.,* 205 F.R.D. 421, 429 (S.D.N.Y. 2002). Second, the costs of retrieving and producing such information can be excessive. For example, in *Zubulake v. UBS Warburg,* 217 F.R.D. 309 (S.D.N.Y. 2003), a case cited extensively in *Aubuchon,* below, the defendant estimated the cost of producing plaintiff's requested e-mails on backup tapes at $175,000, exclusive of attorney time in reviewing the emails. Third, given the volume of such stored information and the electronic nature of retrieval, legitimate claims of privilege and work product can be easily compromised by inadvertent disclosure more so than with traditional "paper discovery." Finally, the capacity for overwriting or altering stored information in the routine operation of an electronic information system raises special concerns of preservation and spoliation of litigation information.

Prior to December 1, 2006, the courts dealt with these "e-discovery" issues in the context of the existing rules, particularly Rules 26(b)(1), (b)(2), and (c), fashioning reasoned solutions from the existing standards. In fact, the series of well-reasoned opinions by U.S. District Court Judge Sheindlin in the lengthy *Zubulake* litigation became leading precedents on "e-discovery" and heavily influenced the 2006 amendments. On December 1, 2006, the "e-discovery" rule amendments became effective, amending Rules 16, 26, 33, 34, 37, and 45, as well as Form 52 governing Rule 26(f) discovery conferences, to incorporate appropriate references to "e-discovery" issues. The following are the two key provisions of the 2006 amendments.

Rule 26(b)(2)(B) — Electronically stored information that is "not reasonably accessible." Recognizing that some information may be accessible only at substantial burden or expense, new Rule 26(b)(2)(B) creates a so-called "two-tiered system" distinguishing "accessible" and "not reasonably accessible" information. Under this provision, a party need not provide discovery of electronically stored information, even though relevant and otherwise discoverable, if the party identifies the "sources" of information "as not reasonably accessible because of undue burden or cost." The 2006 Advisory Committee's Note gives several examples including back-up tapes intended for disaster recovery, legacy data from obsolete systems unintelligible on successor systems, and "deleted" data in fragmented form requiring a modern version of forensics to restore and retrieve.

If the opposing party moves to compel discovery, however, the rule requires that the *responding* party "show that the information is not reasonably accessible because of undue burden or cost." Even if this showing is made, the court may still order discovery, after considering the limitations of Rule 26(b)(2)(c), if the *requesting* party "shows good cause." The court "may specify conditions for the discovery" and, as stated in the Advisory Committee's Note, in addition to limits on the amount and type of information to be produced, an order shifting all or part of the cost to the requesting party may be a possible condition.

Of necessity, the analysis under Rule 26(b)(2)(B) is extremely "fact specific" and requires the court to conduct an independent analysis in each case. The 2006 amendments also added a provision in Rule 45 containing identical procedures to Rule 26(b)(2)(B). The Rule 45 provisions are applicable when the discovery of electronically stored information is sought from a nonparty through the service of a subpoena. *See* FED. R. CIV. P. 45(d)(1)(D) [revised as Rule 45(e)(1)(D) effective Dec. 1, 2013].

Rule 37(e)—Sanction "safe harbor" for "good-faith" loss of electronically stored information. Recognizing that routine modification, overwriting, and deletion of information is an essential, and sometimes automatic feature of electronic information systems, new Rule 37(e) provides that "[a]bsent exceptional circumstances, a court may not impose sanctions under these rules on a party for failing to provide electronically stored information lost as a result of the routine, good-faith operation of an electronic information system." Rule 37(e)'s "good-faith" standard is intended to prevent the intentional destruction of information by a party. *See* Notes 3–5 following *Aubuchon*.

W.E. Aubuchon Co. v. BeneFirst, LLC

United States District Court, District of Massachusetts, 2007
245 F.R.D. 38

HILLMAN, UNITED STATES MAGISTRATE JUDGE.

INTRODUCTION

By order of this Court dated September 7, 2006, the Defendant, BeneFirst, LLC ("BeneFirst"), was ordered to produce medical claims files, including actual bills in its possession, custody, or control. On September 18, 2006, BeneFirst filed the instant Motion for Reconsideration of Court's Discovery Order Related to Medical Bills, together with an accompanying memorandum and affidavit. BeneFirst claims that the documents are not reasonably accessible because the cost of their production far outweighs their value to the Plaintiffs. For the reasons set forth below, I deny the motion.

BACKGROUND

This case involves the administration of qualified benefits plans under the Employee Retirement Income Security Act of 1974 ("ERISA"), 29 U.S.C. § 1001. W.E. Aubuchon Co., Inc. ("Aubuchon") is the employer, sponsor and administrator of the W.E. Aubuchon Co., Inc. Employee Medical Benefit Plan ("Aubuchon Plan"). Aubuchon is the sponsor and Aubuchon Distribution, Inc. ("Aubuchon Distribution") is the employer and administrator of the W.E. Aubuchon Co., Inc. & Aubuchon Distribution, Inc. Employee Medical Benefit Plan ("Aubuchon Distribution Plan," and, together with the Aubuchon Plan, the "ERISA Plans").

BeneFirst ... entered into a contract with the Plaintiffs pursuant to which BeneFirst assumed the rights, duties and obligations to administer the ERISA Plans, as a third-party administrator. BeneFirst's obligations included "investigating and determining eligibility, payments, co-pays, coinsurance and subrogation claims," for which BeneFirst allegedly "exercised discretion and control over [its] decisions [presumably with respect to payment of claims] and was paid to execute these duties properly." The Plaintiffs charge that BeneFirst failed to perform its duties in a reasonably prudent manner, thereby breaching its fiduciary duty and that it breached the underlying contract by failing to provide services accurately and completely.

In the initial motion to compel, Plaintiffs sought, among other things, to compel BeneFirst to produce all medical claims files, including the actual medical bills in BeneFirst's custody or control. This Court ruled that BeneFirst was to provide those files and bills. It is that ruling that is the subject of this motion for reconsideration.

FACTS

BeneFirst is no longer in operation. Therefore, I will set out a historical summary of the procedures utilized by BeneFirst for processing, storing and retrieving claims at the time it administered the ERISA Plans. In order to comply with this Court's initial ruling, BeneFirst would have to hire personnel to retrieve the claims sought by the Plaintiffs in accordance with the procedures described below.

BeneFirst would typically receive requests for payment from medical providers who had provided covered medical services to Aubuchon/Aubuchon Distribution personnel. These requests for payment were on claim forms. These claims would be sorted or "batched" into client groups for processing. Once processed for payment, the claim forms were retained for a 60 day period. After 60 days, the batch of claim forms would be scanned and stored as electronic images and then destroyed. These scanned forms were stored in groups according to their processing date and the person who processed the claim.

If a claim needed to be retrieved after the 60 day period, the claim number, processor, and date of processing would be needed in order to retrieve the image. If all of this information was available, then the search would take 3–4 minutes. If all of the information was not available, it could take upwards of 7 minutes. It is particularly important to the search process to have the name of the person who processed the claim because on any given day, 3–4 claims examiners would process Plaintiffs' claims and during the relevant period, 14 different examiners were employed. Furthermore, for parts of 2001, 2002 and 2003, BeneFirst utilized an outside vendor to process claims. The outside vendor would scan the claims and return them to BeneFirst on a CD-R for further processing. The images scanned by the outside vendor would then be batched in the same way as was done during in-house processing.

The search process for retrieving claims is further complicated by the fact that there is no index of images per se. The images are stored on BeneFirst's server first, according to year of processing, then by claims examiner, then by the month of processing, and finally by the actual processing date. Inexplicably, BeneFirst's system was not set up to for the wholesale retrieval of claim images on a group by group basis.

During the 3.5 years at issue in this litigation, BeneFirst was administering up to 48 different plans and, by its estimation, processed between 550,000 and 600,000 claims. Of that number, 34,112 claims were submitted for processing under the ERISA Plans. Of that number, the Plaintiffs have narrowed their request, based upon a dollar value, to approximately 3,000 claims. BeneFirst estimates that it would cost approximately $80,000.00 and take almost 4,000 hours to retrieve all 34,112 claims. They have not provided a cost/time estimate for the retrieval of the 3,000 claims.

DISCUSSION

Our courts have repeatedly reiterated that [the federal] "'notice pleading standard relies on liberal discovery rules' ..." and that "it is now beyond dispute that '[b]road discovery is a cornerstone of the litigation process contemplated by the Federal Rules of Civil Procedure.'" *Zubulake v. UBS Warburg*, 217 F.R.D. 309, 311 (2003). While the principle is relatively straightforward, its application is not. This principle of liberal discovery is sorely tested when the object of the discovery is electronic data. As of December 1, 2006, the Federal Rules of Civil Procedure were amended to give greater guidance to courts and litigants in dealing with electronic discovery issues. There are four key areas of change to the Rules that address electronic discovery: early attention to e-discovery issues; the role of accessibility; the form of production; and sanctions under Rule 37. This case squarely presents the question of whether the information sought is reasonably accessible within the meaning of the Rule and if not, whether it still should be produced.

The Recent Amendments

On December 1, 2006, Rule 26 was amended, in relevant part, to provide the following limitation to the general rule that a party may obtain discovery of any matter, not privileged, that is relevant to such party's claim or defenses:

> A party need not provide discovery of electronically stored information from sources that the party identifies as not reasonably accessible because of undue burden or cost. On motion to compel discovery or for a protective order, the party from whom discovery is sought musts show that the information is not reasonably accessible because of undue burden or cost. If that showing is made, the court may nonetheless order discovery from such sources if the requesting party shows good cause, considering the limitations of Rule 26(b)(2)(c). The court may specify conditions for the discovery.

Fed. R. Civ. P. 26(b)(2)(B).

Application of the Rule 26 Amendment

Under Rule 26, as revised, this Court must determine whether the information sought is reasonably accessible. If the information is not reasonably accessible, this Court may still order discovery if Aubuchon shows good cause for requesting the information, taking into consideration the limitations of Rule 26(b)(2)(c).

Is the requested information "reasonably accessible" within the meaning of Fed. R. Civ. P. 26(b)(2)?

BeneFirst asserts that the requested claims forms are not reasonably accessible within the meaning of Fed. R. Civ. P. 26(b)(2)(B) because of the high cost to retrieve such information (both in monetary terms and in terms of the man hours it would require to retrieve the information). BeneFirst contends that the high cost/time to retrieve such data is necessitated by the fact that it is maintained in an inaccessible format.

In *Zubulake*, the court found that the time and expense required to retrieve documents and electronic data depends primarily on whether such information "is kept in an *accessible or inaccessible* format ... [furthermore,] [w]hether electronic data is accessible or inaccessible turns largely on the media on which it is stored." *Zubulake*, 217 F.R.D. at 318. *Zubulake* broke down electronic data into the following five categories, listed in order of most accessible to least accessible: (1) active on-line data (hard drives, for example); (2) near-line data (typically, robotic storage devices such as optical disks); (3) offline storage/archives (removable optical disks or magnetic tape media which can be labeled and stored in a shelf or rack); (4) backup tapes (devices like tape recorders that read data from and write it onto a tape; they are sequential access devices which are typically not organized for retrieval of individual documents or files); and (5) erased, fragmented or damaged data (such data can only be accessed after significant processing).

Generally, the first three categories of data are considered "accessible" and the last two categories are considered "inaccessible". That the data is deemed "accessible" does not mean it is readily obtainable, "the time it takes to actually access [such] data ranges from milliseconds to days, [however] the data does not need to be restored or otherwise manipulated to be usable." *Id.* at 320. "'Inaccessible' data, on the other hand, is not readily usable. Backup tapes must be restored ... fragmented data must be defragmented, and erased data must be reconstructed. That makes such data inaccessible." *Id.*

Because, as noted by Judge Sheindlin, the determination of whether the production of electronic data is expensive or unduly burdensome often depends on whether it is maintained in an "accessible" or "inaccessible" format, I find that it is instructive to apply this media based analytical approach in considering whether electronic data is "reasonably accessible" for purposes of the new Rule 26(b)(2)(B). In this case, the records sought by the Plaintiffs are stored on a server used by BeneFirst in Pembroke Massachusetts, which is clearly an accessible format. However, because of BeneFirst's method of storage and lack of an indexing system, it will be extremely costly to retrieve the requested data. I am hard pressed to understand the rationale behind having a system that is only searchable by year of processing, then claims examiner, then the month of processing, and finally the claims date. None of these search criteria reflect the name of the individual claimant, the date that the claimant received the medical service, who the provider was, or even the company that employed the benefit holder. It would seem that such a system would only serve to discourage audits and the type of inquiries that have led to the instant litigation. Nevertheless, the retrieval of the records will be costly and for the purposes of this decision, I find that such retrieval would involve undue burden or cost. Accordingly, the images are not reasonably accessible within the meaning of Fed. R. Civ. P. 26(b)(2)(B).

Not reasonably Accessible [handwritten margin note]

Since the images are not reasonably accessible is there "good cause" to order their production?

The Plaintiffs argue that the information they have requested goes to the heart of their case and that they have established "good cause" for production of the same. In making a determination of whether the requesting party has established "good cause," this Court must consider whether: "(i) the discovery sought is unreasonably cumulative or duplicative, or is obtainable from some other source that is more convenient, less burdensome, or less expensive; (ii) the party seeking discovery has had ample opportunity by discovery in the action to obtain the information sought; or (iii) the burden or expense of the proposed discovery outweighs its likely benefit, taking into account the needs of the case, the amount in controversy, the parties' resources, the importance of the issues at stake in the litigation, and the importance of the proposed discovery in resolving the issues." Fed. R. Civ. P. 26(b)(2)(c). To the extent not covered by the aforementioned factors, the Court should also consider:

26(B)(2)(c) [handwritten margin note]

> (1) the specificity of the discovery request; (2) the quantity of information available from other and more easily accessed sources; (3) the failure to produce relevant information that seems likely to have existed but is no longer available on more easily accessed sources; (4) the likelihood of finding relevant, responsive information that cannot be obtained from other, more easily accessed sources; (5) predictions as to the importance and usefulness of the further information; (6) the importance of the issues at stake in the litigation; and (7) the parties' resources.

Fed. R. Civ. P. 26 Advisory Committee's note, to 2006 Amendment.

The specificity of the discovery request

BeneFirst's Motion seeks reconsideration of this Court's earlier discovery order which ordered BeneFirst to produce "all claims files, including the actual bills in BeneFirst's possession or control." The parties have responded intelligently and vigorously to this Order and there is no misunderstanding or confusion about the specificity of the information sought by the Plaintiffs.

This factor favors the Plaintiffs.

The quantity of information available from other and more easily accessed sources; The failure to produce relevant information that seems likely to have existed but is no longer available from more easily accessed sources

The gravamen of the Plaintiffs' Amended Complaint is that BeneFirst mishandled their employees' medical claims by failing to determine eligibility for payment, the availability of co-payment and co-insurance, and subrogation. The processing of the claim forms was presumably the mechanism for making these determinations. While the Amended Complaint and subsequent pleadings are silent, the relevant time period appears to be from 2001 to 2004.

According to BeneFirst, the original claim forms and medical bills were processed by hand, kept for 60 days, converted to a digital image and then destroyed. Therefore, digital images which constitute the information requested by the Plaintiffs are in the custody and control of BeneFirst and are not available through any other source.

These factors favor the Plaintiffs.

Predictions as to the importance and usefulness of the further information; the likelihood of finding relevant, responsive information that cannot be obtained from other, more easily accessed sources

I agree with the Plaintiffs that the requested claim forms and medical bills are clearly an integral part of the litigation; the requested information goes not only to BeneFirst's culpability, but also to the amount of damages, if any, to which the Plaintiffs may be entitled. There can be no serious contention that the information is not highly relevant. In fact, it is difficult to imagine how this case could be prosecuted or defended without the claims forms and attendant bills. As previously found, they are not available from any other source (a determination which is uncontroverted).

These factors favor the Plaintiffs.

The importance of the issues at stake in the litigation

While the importance of the claims/issues in this case are real and substantial vis a vis the parties, such claims/issues do not raise any global concerns.

This factor favors the Defendants (if it favors any party at all).

The parties' resources

While the Defendant has understandably engaged in a lengthy discussion of the cost of production, neither party has provided the court with any information about their resources. BeneFirst does represent that they no longer have a full time staff and that in order to retrieve the images that they would have to hire temporary help. At the same time, as previously noted, the Plaintiffs have significantly narrowed the breadth of their request and therefore, the time and cost for BeneFirst to produce the requested information should be significantly reduced.

Given the lack of information available to the Court, this factor is neutral.

Other relevant considerations

In addition to the above 7 factors, it is important to note that a provision in the Service Agreement between the parties provided that: "... The Records are the property of the Plan Sponsor. The Plan Sponsor has the right of continuing access to their records...." In other words, although in the custody and control of BeneFirst, the records at issue are the property of the Plaintiffs.

The Plaintiffs Have Met Their Burden To Establish Good Cause

On balance, I find that the Plaintiffs have clearly established good cause for requiring BeneFirst to produce the requested information. As noted above, the Plaintiffs have significantly narrowed their original request from approximately 34,000 claims to a list of approximately 3,000. This reduction should serve to reduce the time and expense of retrieving the requested information. Under the circumstances, I find that the requested information should be produced by BeneFirst at its own expense.

....

Notes and Questions

1. Under the discovery rules, "the presumption is that the responding party must bear the expense of complying with discovery requests." *Oppenheimer Fund, Inc. v. Sanders*, 437 U.S. 340, 358 (1978). A responding party may, however, invoke the court's discretion under Rule 26(c)(1) to grant an order protecting the party from "undue burden or expense," including "an order conditioning discovery on the requesting party's payment of the costs of discovery." *Id.*

Determining which party should bear the cost of discovery is particularly complicated when electronic data is sought because such data is often only available from expensive-to-restore backup media. As such, the courts in appropriate cases have employed "cost-shifting" to balance the special needs and expenses of electronic discovery. Accordingly, Rule 26(b)(2)(B) provides that "the court may specify conditions for the discovery" if the court, upon the required showing of good cause, orders discovery of electronic data that is "not reasonably accessible." In this regard, the 2006 Advisory Committee's Note to Rule 26(b)(2)(B) expressly states that these conditions may include "payment by the requesting party of part or all of the reasonable costs of obtaining information from sources that are not reasonably accessible."

Why did the court in *Aubuchon* order the defendant to produce the requested information at its own expense and not impose any cost-shifting upon the plaintiff?

2. In the *Zubulake* opinion cited in *Aubuchon*, Judge Scheindlin first ordered production of a sampling of the "not reasonably accessible" data to better inform the court's decision as to the relevance of the requested data and the time and cost required to retrieve it. This approach is expressly adopted in the 2006 Advisory Committee's Note. As stated by the Advisory Committee:

> [t]he good-cause determination ... may be complicated because the court and parties may know little about what information the sources identified as not reasonably accessible might contain, whether it is relevant, or how valuable it may be to the litigation. In such cases, the parties may need some focused discovery, which may include sampling of the sources, to learn more about what burdens and costs are involved in accessing the information, what the information consists of, and how valuable it is for the litigation in light of information that can be obtained by exhausting other opportunities for discovery.

3. As explained in the text immediately preceding the *Aubuchon* opinion, the second key 2006 "e-discovery" amendment was the addition of Rule 37(e) providing a sanction "safe harbor," absent exceptional circumstances, for the loss of electronically stored information "as a result of the routine, good-faith operation of an electronic information system." Rule 37(e)'s "good-faith" standard is intended to prevent the intentional destruction of in-

formation by a party and may require a party's intervention to modify or suspend certain features of a routine system to prevent the loss of information that is subject to a preservation obligation. The Rule itself does not create a preservation obligation, but recognizes that such an obligation may arise from many sources, including a statute, regulation, court order in the case, or the common law doctrine of spoliation of evidence.

4. In *Silvestri v. General Motors Corp.*, 271 F.3d 583 (4th Cir. 2001), the Fourth Circuit Court of Appeals stated that "[s]poliation refers to the destruction or material alteration of evidence or the failure to preserve property for another's use as evidence in pending or reasonably foreseeable litigation.... The duty to preserve material evidence arises not only during litigation but also extends to that period before the litigation when a party reasonably should know that the evidence may be relevant to anticipated litigation." *Id.* at 590–91.

5. A later decision in the *Zubulake* litigation (*Zubulake IV*) involved this very issue of spoliation and sanctions. *Zubulake v. UBS Warburg,* 220 F.R.D. 212 (S.D.N.Y. 2003). In this opinion, Judge Scheindlin found that even though plaintiff's employment discrimination complaint was not filed until August 2001, the duty to preserve evidence attached in April, 2001 because litigation was reasonably anticipated by the defendant-employer at that time. The court imposed sanctions on the defendant finding that its personnel had wilfully destroyed relevant e-mails after that date in defiance of explicit instructions by defendant's counsel not to do so. Given the court's finding that the defendant had wilfully destroyed the e-mail evidence do you think the court's imposition of sanctions would still be proper under new Rule 37(e)?

Section C. Additional Discovery Standards: Privilege, Work Product, and Expert Witnesses

1. Privilege

Rule 26(b)(1) provides that "[p]arties may obtain discovery regarding any nonprivileged matter...." Privileged matter is thus exempt from discovery even though it may otherwise satisfy the relevancy standard of Rule 26(b)(1). The discovery rules do not define when a matter is "privileged," and the law of privilege derives from other sources. Some privileges, such as the Fifth Amendment privilege against self-incrimination, are based on constitutional authority, while others, such as the attorney-client privilege, are based on statutory or common-law authority. The usual view is that the law of privilege applies in discovery in the same way that it applies at trial. *See* 8 Wright et al. § 2016, at 310–11. In federal court actions, Federal Rule of Evidence 501 provides that, except as otherwise required by the Constitution or provided by federal statute or rule, privilege "shall be governed by the principles of the common law as they may be interpreted by the courts of the United States in the light of reason and experience." When a claim or defense in a federal court action is based on state law, Rule 501 provides that privilege is to be determined by state law.

Depending on the jurisdiction, any number of privileges protecting communications within various relationships are recognized, including attorney-client, physician-patient, psychotherapist-patient, husband-wife, priest-penitent, journalist-confidential news source, and government-informer. Special governmental privileges, such as the state secrets privilege and executive privilege, have also been recognized. Except for constitutional privileges, the extent to which a particular privilege is recognized varies between federal and state law and from state to state.

In exempting privileged matter from discovery irrespective of its potential relevance, the federal rules recognize that the general goal of providing access to all relevant information must, at times, yield to competing societal interests in protecting certain information from disclosure. The Fifth Amendment privilege against self-incrimination, for example, reflects the societal value that persons should not be compelled to be witnesses against themselves in criminal cases. Other privileges emanating from certain relationships, such as the attorney-client, priest-penitent, and similar privileges, reflect the societal belief that the confidentiality and privacy of these relationships should be protected. Governmental privileges also recognize that certain information needs to be protected from disclosure for the effective functioning of government.

Assertion and Waiver of Privileges. Although privilege protection is designed to foster societal goals, it is well settled that the holder of a privilege may waive its protections. A privilege is generally waived if the holder of the privilege voluntarily discloses or consents to disclosure of the privileged matter. In the context of discovery, therefore, proper objection must be made on the basis of privilege in order to preserve the protection. Accordingly, Rule 30(c)(2) provides that a deponent may be instructed not to answer a question "when necessary to preserve a privilege."

Rule 26(b)(5)(A) further provides that when a party withholds otherwise discoverable information because of a claim of privilege or work product protection, "the party must: (i) expressly make the claim; and (ii) describe the nature of the documents, communications, or tangible things not produced or disclosed—and do so in a manner that, without revealing information itself privileged or protected, will enable other parties to assess the claim." Rule 45(d)(2)(A) [revised as Rule 45(e)(2)(A) effective Dec. 1, 2013] contains a similar provision for the assertion of privilege protection when the person is a nonparty responding to a subpoena.

Should a party be permitted to refuse to respond in discovery on the ground of privilege if the party intends to use the privileged material as evidence at trial? Most cases hold that discovery is permissible of privileged matter to the extent it is contemplated that the privilege will be waived at trial. *See generally* 8 Wright et al. § 2016.2.

Assertion of Privilege After Disclosure. Special problems can arise with the timely assertion of privilege and work product protection especially when dealing with electronically stored information. Because of the sheer volume of such information, it is often impossible in terms of time, effort, and expense to review all of the information prior to disclosure for potential privilege claims. The 2006 amendments accordingly added new Rules 26(b)(5)(B) and 45(d)(2)(B) [revised as Rule 45(e)(2)(B) effective Dec. 1, 2013] which, in parallel language, provide a procedure for the assertion of privilege or work product claims after production. Under these rules, the producing party must notify the receiving party of the claim and the basis and the receiving party may not thereafter use or disclose the information until the claim has been resolved.

Note that these new provisions merely establish procedures for the assertion of privilege claims after inadvertent disclosure, and as stated in the 2006 Advisory Committee's Note to Rule 26(b)(5)(B), these provisions do "not address whether the privilege or protection that is asserted after production was waived by the production." The courts have developed an extensive body of case law to determine whether, and under what circumstances, waiver results from inadvertent production of privileged or protected information and these new provisions do not affect this case law. For a comprehensive review of this case law, *see* Edna Selan Epstein, The Attorney-Client Privilege and the Work Product Doctrine 433–474, 1085–88 (5th ed. 2007) & 106–27, 241–42 (Supp. 2012).

New Rule 26(b)(5)(B) is meant to operate in tandem with new Rules 26(f)(3)(D) and 16(b)(3)(B)(iv) that were also added in 2006 to encourage the parties to identify and address privilege and work product issues early in the case at the discovery and scheduling conferences, respectively.

Distinguish Work Product Protection. As will be discussed in the next section, Rule 26(b)(3) affords special protection to trial preparation materials, commonly known as "work product." Work product protection, however, is not absolute and such material is discoverable upon a showing of substantial need and undue hardship by the party seeking discovery. Privileged matter, by comparison, is fully protected from discovery. If a matter satisfies the requirements for protection under an applicable privilege, discovery is barred, irrespective of the need of the discovering party for the privileged matter.

Problem

Problem 8-15. Should a privilege be recognized in the following situations? If so, what socially useful purpose would it serve?

(a) Assume the facts of *Problem 8-5* and that *D's* deposition is being taken in a civil action brought by *P's* estate. During the deposition, the attorney representing *P's* estate asks *D* how many drinks *D* had immediately prior to the accident. *D* refuses to answer, claiming privilege.

(b) Assume that *D* tells *D's* wife, *W*, about the accident described in (a) above, later that night. Subsequently, *D* and *W* are divorced. The attorney representing *P's* estate deposes *W* in an effort to learn what *D* said. *W* wants to answer the question, but *D's* attorney objects, claiming privilege.

Effect of Specific Privileges in the Discovery Process. Although full treatment of the law of privilege is beyond the scope of this course, a brief discussion of the following privileges is helpful in understanding the effect of privilege in the discovery process.

(a) Privilege Against Self-Incrimination

The Fifth Amendment to the U.S. Constitution provides that "[n]o person ... shall be compelled in any criminal case to be a witness against himself." This privilege against self-incrimination applies to party and nonparty witnesses alike. The privilege only applies to persons, however, and does not apply to corporations, unincorporated associations, or other entities. Importantly, the Fifth Amendment privilege against self-incrimination only serves to protect a person from *criminal*, not *civil*, liability. No comparable provision protects a person from being compelled to be a witness against himself with respect to a purely civil action. Thus, in discovery and at trial, a party in a civil action must respond fully and honestly to all proper requests for information, irrespective of whether the response is damaging to the party's civil claim or defense.

It is well established, though, that the Fifth Amendment privilege against self-incrimination can be asserted in the *context* of a civil case if a criminal charge is pending or may be filed against a person and the person's responses in the civil action could incriminate the person in the criminal prosecution. A party asserting the Fifth Amendment privilege in a civil action may not simply refuse to participate in any discovery on the basis that incriminating questions might be asked. The party must respond to the discovery and must assert the privilege against self-incrimination as to the specific questions or requests that are objectionable. It is the court's role to then determine the legitimacy of the assertion.

The burden of establishing the propriety of the privilege is on the person asserting it. The assertion will be sustained when it is "evident from the implications of the question, in the setting in which it is asked, that a responsive answer to the question or an explanation of why it cannot be answered might be dangerous because injurious disclosure could result." *Hoffman v. United States*, 341 U.S. 479, 486–87 (1951). As with other privileges, the privilege against self-incrimination can be waived by failure to preserve the protection properly. *See, e.g., SEC v. Parkersburg Wireless Ltd. Liab. Co.*, 156 F.R.D. 529, 536 (D.D.C. 1994) ("The Fifth Amendment cannot be used after later rumination as a sword to sever incriminating statements which were voluntarily made at the time of the deposition.").

Although the assertion of the privilege against self-incrimination is permissible in a civil case, the courts have recognized that this assertion of the privilege creates a special tension in civil litigation in balancing the rights of the other parties to the action. Unlike a criminal proceeding, the parties in a civil case "are on a somewhat equal footing [and] one party's assertion of his constitutional right should not obliterate another party's right to a fair proceeding." *Serafino v. Hasbro, Inc.*, 82 F.3d 515, 518 (1st Cir. 1996).

Sometimes, the tension can be alleviated by the entry of a protective order under Rule 26(c), staying discovery until the conclusion of the criminal matter. Delay, however, may be prejudicial to the other party and prolonged, especially in cases in which a criminal action is only possible and not yet pending. Another remedy is to permit adverse inferences to be drawn by the factfinder based on a party's invocation of the Fifth Amendment privilege in a civil case. *See Baxter v. Palmigiano*, 425 U.S. 308, 318–20 (1976) ("[T]he Fifth Amendment does not forbid adverse inferences against parties in civil actions when they refuse to testify in response to probative evidence offered against them. . . ."). Some courts have imposed more severe sanctions against parties invoking the Fifth Amendment in a civil case, such as dismissing the action or entering an adverse judgment against the party, but the validity of such sanctions has been questioned. *See* 8 Wright et al. § 2018 at 449–55 ("It is difficult to believe that sanctions of this kind [for exercising a constitutional right] can be defended.").

(b) Attorney-Client Privilege

The attorney-client privilege is the oldest of all evidentiary privileges recognized in Anglo-American jurisprudence. Its origins trace to Roman and canon law. As explained by the Supreme Court in *Upjohn*, reprinted below, the purpose of the attorney-client privilege "is to encourage full and frank communication between attorneys and their clients and thereby promote broader public interests in the observance of law and administration of justice." *Upjohn Co. v. United States*, 449 U.S. 383, 389 (1981). Because attorneys are so intimately involved in the litigation process, issues concerning the attorney-client privilege repeatedly arise in determining the proper scope of discovery.

The attorney-client privilege is recognized in all jurisdictions. Although some variations exist among the jurisdictions, four basic elements are required to establish the existence of the privilege: "(1) a communication (2) made between privileged persons (3) in confidence [and] (4) for the purpose of obtaining or providing legal assistance for the client." Restatement (Third) of the Law Governing Lawyers § 68 (2000). Communications between the client and the attorney may be oral or written. However, they must be intended to be confidential. Courts will not normally protect communications that are intended to be disclosed in a non-privileged setting or that are made in the presence of third parties who are unconnected to either the attorney or the client. Although some courts only protect communications from an attorney that reflect confidences conveyed by the client, the attorney-client privilege generally applies symmetrically to protect not only the client's communications to the attorney, but also the attorney's communications to the client. Communications by the client to representatives and agents of the attorney, such as secretaries, paralegals, law clerks, and investigators, are also within the privilege.

To be protected, communications must be for the purpose of seeking, obtaining, or providing legal assistance to the client. The matter need not involve litigation, and the privilege covers all forms of professional legal service and advice. However, the client must consult the attorney primarily for the purpose of obtaining legal advice or service. If the attorney is consulted in a non-legal capacity, for instance, as a business advisor or as a friend, and not as a professional legal advisor, the attorney-client privilege does not attach.

The communication must be made during the course of the attorney-client relationship. In order for an attorney-client relationship to be created, it is not necessary that a formal retainer agreement be entered into or that any fee be paid. All that is required is that a client consult an attorney for the purpose of obtaining legal advice or service, even if the attorney ultimately decides to decline representation in the matter. Once an attorney-client relationship is created, the confidential communications between the attorney and the client during the course of the relationship are protected and remain protected, even after the termination of the relationship and even after the death of the client. *See Swindler & Berlin v. United States*, 524 U.S. 399, 407 (1998) ("Knowing that communications will remain confidential even after death encourages the client to communicate fully and frankly with counsel.... Posthumous disclosure of such communications may be as feared as disclosure during the client's lifetime.").

The attorney-client privilege is for the protection of the client, not the attorney. The client is the holder of the privilege. Unless otherwise instructed by the client, the attorney must assert the privilege on behalf of the client. As with all privileges, however, the privilege may be waived, and the client may do so, even against the advice of the attorney.

Unlike the privilege against self-incrimination, which only applies to persons, the attorney-client privilege fully applies to all clients who seek professional legal services, including corporations, unincorporated associations, and other entities. When a corporation or other organization is the client, the critical issue is determining which members of the organization may properly speak on behalf of the organization so that their communications with the attorney are privileged. The Supreme Court addressed this issue in the *Upjohn* case.

Upjohn Co. v. United States

United States Supreme Court, 1981
449 U.S. 383, 101 S. Ct. 677, 66 L. Ed. 584

Justice Rehnquist delivered the opinion of the Court.

We granted certiorari in this case to address important questions concerning the scope of the attorney-client privilege in the corporate context and the applicability of the work-product doctrine in proceedings to enforce tax summonses.... With respect to the privilege question the parties and various *amici* have described our task as one of choosing between two "tests" which have gained adherents in the courts of appeals. We are acutely aware, however, that we sit to decide concrete cases and not abstract propositions of law. We decline to lay down a broad rule or series of rules to govern all conceivable future questions in this area, even were we able to do so. We can and do, however, conclude that the attorney-client privilege protects the communications involved in this case from compelled disclosure and that the work-product doctrine does apply in tax summons enforcement proceedings.

Held

I

Petitioner Upjohn Co. manufactures and sells pharmaceuticals here and abroad. In January 1976 independent accountants conducting an audit of one of Upjohn's foreign subsidiaries discovered that the subsidiary made payments to or for the benefit of foreign government officials in order to secure government business. The accountants, so informed petitioner, Mr. Gerard Thomas, Upjohn's Vice President, Secretary, and General Counsel. Thomas is a member of the Michigan and New York Bars, and has been Upjohn's General Counsel for 20 years. He consulted with outside counsel and R. T. Parfet, Jr., Upjohn's Chairman of the Board. It was decided that the company would conduct an internal investigation of what were termed "questionable payments." As part of this investigation the attorneys prepared a letter containing a questionnaire which was sent to "All Foreign General and Area Managers" over the Chairman's signature. The letter began by noting recent disclosures that several American companies made "possibly illegal" payments to foreign government officials and emphasized that the management needed full information concerning any such payments made by Upjohn. The letter indicated that the Chairman had asked Thomas, identified as "the company's General Counsel," "to conduct an investigation for the purpose of determining the nature and magnitude of any payments made by the Upjohn Company or any of its subsidiaries to any employee or official of a foreign government." The questionnaire sought detailed information concerning such payments. Managers were instructed to treat the investigation as "highly confidential" and not to discuss it with anyone other than Upjohn employees who might be helpful in providing the requested information. Responses were to be sent directly to Thomas. Thomas and outside counsel also interviewed the recipients of the questionnaire and some 33 other Upjohn officers or employees as part of the investigation.

On March 26, 1976, the company voluntarily submitted a preliminary report to the Securities and Exchange Commission on Form 8-K disclosing certain questionable payments. A copy of the report was simultaneously submitted to the Internal Revenue Service, which immediately began an investigation to determine the tax consequences of the payments. Special agents conducting the investigation were given lists by Upjohn of all those interviewed and all who had responded to the questionnaire. On November 23, 1976, the Service issued a summons pursuant to 26 U.S.C. §7602 demanding production of:

IRS Demanded Production

> All files relative to the investigation conducted under the supervision of Gerard Thomas to identify payments to employees of foreign governments and any political contributions made by the Upjohn Company or any of its affiliates since January 1, 1971 and to determine whether any funds of the Upjohn Company had been improperly accounted for on the corporate books during the same period.

> The records should include but not be limited to written questionnaires sent to managers of the Upjohn Company's foreign affiliates, and memorandums or notes of the interviews conducted in the United States and abroad with officers and employees of the Upjohn Company and its subsidiaries....

The company declined to produce the documents specified in the second paragraph on the grounds that they were protected from disclosure by the attorney-client privilege and constituted the work product of attorneys prepared in anticipation of litigation. On August 31, 1977, the United States filed a petition seeking enforcement of the summons under 26 U.S.C. §§ 7402(b) and 7604(a) in the United States District Court for the Western District of Michigan. That court adopted the recommendation of a Magistrate who concluded that the summons should be enforced. Petitioners appealed to the Court of Appeals for the Sixth Circuit which rejected the Magistrate's finding of a waiver of the attorney-client privilege, 600 F.2d 1223, 1227, n.12, but agreed that the privilege did not apply "[t]o the extent that the communications were made by officers and agents not responsible for directing Upjohn's actions in response to legal advice ... for the simple reason that the communications were not then 'client's.'" *Id.* at 1225. The court reasoned that accepting petitioners' claim for a broader application of the privilege would encourage upper-echelon management to ignore unpleasant facts and create too broad a "zone of silence." Noting that Upjohn's counsel had interviewed officials such as the Chairman and President, the Court of Appeals remanded to the District Court so that a determination of who was within the "control group" could be made.

II

Federal Rule of Evidence 501 provides that "the privilege of a witness ... shall be governed by the principles of the common law as they may be interpreted by the courts of the United States in light of reason and experience." The attorney-client privilege is the oldest of the privileges for confidential communications known to the common law. 8 J. Wigmore, *Evidence* § 2290 (McNaughton rev. 1961). Its purpose is to encourage full and frank communication between attorneys and their clients and thereby promote broader public interests in the observance of law and administration of justice. The privilege recognizes that sound legal advice or advocacy serves public ends and that such advice or advocacy depends upon the lawyer's being fully informed by the client.... Admittedly complications in the application of the privilege arise when the client is a corporation, which in theory is an artificial creature of the law, and not an individual; but this Court has assumed that the privilege applies when the client is a corporation....

The Court of Appeals, however, considered the application of the privilege in the corporate context to present a "different problem," since the client was an inanimate entity and "only the senior management, guiding and integrating the several operations, ... can be said to possess an identity analogous to the corporation as a whole." ... Such a view, we think, overlooks the fact that the privilege exists to protect not only the giving of professional advice to those who can act on it but also the giving of information to the lawyer to enable him to give sound and informed advice.... The first step in the resolution of any legal problem is ascertaining the factual background and sifting through the facts with an eye to the legally relevant....

In the case of the individual client the provider of information and the person who acts on the lawyer's advice are one and the same. In the corporate context, however, it will frequently be employees beyond the control group as defined by the court below—"officers and agents ... responsible for directing [the company's] actions in response to legal advice"—who will possess the information needed by the corporation's lawyers. Middle-level—and indeed lower-level—employees can, by actions within the scope of their employment, embroil the corporation in serious legal difficulties, and it is only natural that these employees would have the relevant information needed by corporate counsel if he is adequately to advise the client with respect to such actual or potential difficulties....

The control group test adopted by the court below thus frustrates the very purpose of the privilege by discouraging the communication of relevant information by employees of the client to attorneys seeking to render legal advice to the client corporation. The attorney's advice will also frequently be more significant to noncontrol group members than to those who officially sanction the advice, and the control group test makes it more difficult to convey full and frank legal advice to the employees who will put into effect the client corporation's policy....

The narrow scope given the attorney-client privilege by the court below not only makes it difficult for corporate attorneys to formulate sound advice when their client is faced with a specific legal problem but also threatens to limit the valuable efforts of corporate counsel to ensure their client's compliance with the law. In light of the vast and complicated array of regulatory legislation confronting the modern corporation, corporations, unlike most individuals, "constantly go to lawyers to find out how to obey the law." ... [I]f the purpose of the attorney-client privilege is to be served, the attorney and client must be able to predict with some degree of certainty whether particular discussions will be protected. An uncertain privilege, or one which purports to be certain but results in widely varying applications by the courts, is little better than no privilege at all. The very terms of the test adopted by the court below suggest the unpredictability of its application. The test restricts the availability of the privilege to those officers who play a "substantial role" in deciding and directing a corporation's legal response....

The communications at issue were made by Upjohn employees to counsel for Upjohn acting as such, at the direction of corporate superiors in order to secure legal advice from counsel.... Information, not available from upper-echelon management, was needed to supply a basis for legal advice concerning compliance with securities and tax laws, foreign laws, currency regulations, duties to shareholders, and potential litigation in each of these areas. The communications concerned matters within the scope of the employees' corporate duties, and the employees themselves were sufficiently aware that they were being questioned in order that the corporation could obtain legal advice.... Pursuant to explicit instructions from the Chairman of the Board, the communications were considered "highly confidential" when made ... and have been kept confidential by the company. Consistent with the underlying purposes of the attorney-client privilege, these communications must be protected against compelled disclosure.

The Court of Appeals declined to extend the attorney-client privilege beyond the limits of the control group test for fear that doing so would entail severe burdens on discovery and create a broad "zone of silence" over corporate affairs. Application of the attorney-client privilege to communications such as those involved here, however, puts the adversary in no worse position than if the communications had never taken place. The privilege only protects disclosure of communications; it does not protect disclosure of the underlying facts by those who communicated with the attorney:

> [T]he protection of the privilege extends only to *communications* and not to facts. A fact is one thing and a communication concerning that fact is an entirely different thing. The client cannot be compelled to answer the question, "What did you say or write to the attorney?" but may not refuse to disclose any relevant fact within his knowledge merely because he incorporated a statement of such fact into his communication to his attorney.

Philadelphia v. Westinghouse Elec. Corp., 205 F. Supp. 830, 831 (E.D. Pa. 1962); *see also ...* *State ex rel. Dudek v. Circuit Court*, 150 N.W.2d 387, 399 (Wis. 1967) ("[T]he courts have noted that a party cannot conceal a fact merely by revealing it to his lawyer."). Here the Government was free to question the employees who communicated with Thomas and outside counsel. Upjohn has provided the IRS with a list of such employees, and the IRS has already interviewed some 25 of them. While it would probably be more convenient for the Government to secure the results of petitioner's internal investigation by simply subpoenaing the questionnaires and notes taken by petitioner's attorneys, such considerations of convenience do not overcome the policies served by the attorney-client privilege. As Justice Jackson noted in his concurring opinion in *Hickman v. Taylor*, 329 U.S. at 516: "Discovery was hardly intended to enable a learned profession to perform its functions ... on wits borrowed from the adversary."

... [W]e conclude that the narrow "control group test" sanctioned by the Court of Appeals, in this case cannot, consistent with "the principles of the common law as ... interpreted ... in the light of reason and experience," Fed. R. Evid. 501, govern the development of the law in this area.

 . . . .

Accordingly, the judgment of the Court of Appeals is reversed, and the case remanded for further proceedings.

It is so ordered.

[The opinion of Chief Justice Burger, who concurred in part and concurred in the judgment, is omitted.]

Notes and Questions

1. (a) Do you understand why the Court stated near the end of its analysis that "application of the attorney-client privilege ... puts the adversary in no worse position than if the communications had never taken place?" What precisely does the attorney-client privilege protect from disclosure? For example, suppose a client is involved in an accident and is asked by the client's attorney to write out for the attorney everything that the client remembers about the accident. At the client's deposition, the opposing attorney asks: "Tell me everything that you remember about the accident?" Can the client refuse to answer this question on the basis of the attorney-client privilege? Can the client be required to produce the written memo prepared for the client's attorney?

(b) As explained by the Court, the privilege only extends to *communications* and does not extend to the underlying facts that may be contained in the communication. Thus, the opposing attorney may not demand production of the actual written memo or ask the client to state what the client told the attorney about the accident. Nevertheless, the client may not refuse to disclose relevant facts about the accident simply because the client previously communicated those facts to the client's attorney. Do you now understand what the Court meant by its statement?

2. On this point, it is important to distinguish the privilege against self-incrimination. Unlike the attorney-client privilege and the other relationship privileges that only protect confidential communications, the privilege against self-incrimination entitles a person to refuse to answer any question or reveal any matter, factual or otherwise, that may incriminate the person in a criminal case. Thus, in the above example, if the facts related to the accident could subject the client to criminal prosecution, the client could refuse to

answer those questions that would be incriminating criminally, not because of the attorney-client privilege, but rather because of the privilege against self-incrimination.

3. It is also important to distinguish the attorney-client privilege from "work product" protection under Rule 26(b)(3). As will be explained in the following section, Rule 26(b)(3) protects certain materials from discovery but only if they are prepared in anticipation of litigation or for trial. In contrast, the attorney-client privilege fully protects confidential communications related to any form of legal service or advice, irrespective of whether the communications are made in anticipation of any litigation. Moreover, work product protection may be pierced upon a showing of substantial need and undue hardship, whereas protected attorney-client communications are fully exempt from discovery, irrespective of the need or hardship of the party seeking discovery.

4. (a) Certain exceptions to the attorney-client privilege are recognized. The most significant is the "crime-fraud" exception. Under this exception, the attorney-client privilege does not apply if the client seeks the attorney's advice or services with respect to an *ongoing* or *future* crime or fraud. Under Rule 1.2(d) of the *ABA Model Rules of Professional Conduct* (2012), it is unethical for an attorney to "counsel a client to engage, or assist a client, in conduct that the lawyer knows is criminal or fraudulent." No societal interest is served in extending confidentiality to enable clients to use attorneys to pursue criminal or fraudulent activity. Applying the attorney-client privilege to communications under these circumstances would violate strong public policy.

(b) A distinction is made, however, as to *past* crimes and frauds. A client may properly seek the advice and services of an attorney with respect to past misconduct. Thus, a person charged with a past crime could properly seek representation from an attorney and the attorney-client privilege would apply, even though the client may admit to the attorney in confidence that the client committed the criminal act. Although the attorney would be allowed to keep the client's communications confidential, the attorney could not allow the client to testify falsely at trial and commit perjury. *See* ABA MODEL RULES OF PROFESSIONAL CONDUCT 3.3(a)(3) (2012) ("A lawyer shall not knowingly ... offer evidence that the lawyer knows to be false. If a lawyer ... has offered material evidence and the lawyer comes to know of its falsity, the lawyer shall take reasonable remedial measures, including, if necessary, disclosure to the tribunal."). Another exception to the attorney-client privilege allows disclosure of communications relevant to a breach of duty by the attorney to the client or by the client to the attorney. For example, if the client sues the attorney for malpractice or the attorney sues the client for non-payment of the fee, disclosure of otherwise confidential communications is permissible to the extent necessary to prosecute or defend the claim. *See id.* 1.6(b)(5).

2. "Work Product" and Trial Preparation Materials: Rule 26(b)(3)

(a) The "Work Product" Doctrine

The attorney-client privilege and the work product doctrine derive from a common principle that certain matters must be protected from disclosure in order for an attorney to properly represent a client in our adversary system of justice. Beyond this basic commonality, the two principles are distinct and their applicability must be carefully distinguished. As explained in *Upjohn,* the attorney-client privilege is designed to encourage full and frank communication between the attorney and the client, whereas work product protection is designed to encourage thorough and careful preparation of the case by the attorney free of intrusion by the adversary. As the Court noted in the *Hickman* case, reprinted below,

> [i]n performing his various duties, ... it is essential that a lawyer work with a certain degree of privacy, free from unnecessary intrusion by opposing parties and their counsel. Proper preparation of a client's case demands that he assemble information, sift what he considers to be the relevant from the irrelevant facts, prepare his legal theories and plan his strategy without undue and needless interference. That is the historical and the necessary way in which lawyers act within the framework of our system of jurisprudence to promote justice and to protect their clients' interests.

Hickman v. Taylor, 329 U.S. 495, 510–11 (1947).

In studying the following materials, it is important to keep in mind several key distinctions between the nature and scope of the attorney-client privilege and the work product doctrine. The attorney-client privilege extends only to confidential communications between the attorney and the client, whereas work product protection broadly applies to all trial preparation materials, irrespective of whether the material contains confidential communications and irrespective of the source of the information. Work product protection, however, only applies to materials prepared in anticipation of litigation or for trial. The attorney-client privilege, on the other hand, extends to confidential communications between the attorney and the client with respect to all forms of legal service or advice, irrespective of whether the matter involves litigation.

Furthermore, work product protection is not absolute and such materials are discoverable upon a showing of substantial need and undue hardship by the party seeking discovery. In contrast, protected attorney-client communications, as with all privileged matters, are fully exempt from discovery, irrespective of the need or hardship of the party seeking discovery. Because privilege protection is absolute and work product protection is only qualified, a work product analysis is only appropriate when a matter is not privileged. Finally, in the federal courts, work product protection is a matter of federal law, even when the federal court is adjudicating a state law claim or defense. In contrast, Federal Rule of Evidence 501 requires the application of state law in determining the issue of privilege when the federal court is adjudicating a state law claim or defense.

When the federal discovery rules were revised in 1970, Rule 26(b)(3) was adopted to set forth express standards for the discovery of trial preparation materials. The standards of Rule 26(b)(3), however, derive from the Supreme Court's seminal decision in *Hickman v. Taylor*, which established the work product doctrine and its special protection for an attorney's mental impressions, thought processes, and trial strategies.

Hickman v. Taylor

United States Supreme Court, 1947
329 U.S. 495, 67 S. Ct. 385, 91 L. Ed. 451

JUSTICE MURPHY delivered the opinion of the Court.

This case presents an important problem under the Federal Rules of Civil Procedure ... as to the extent to which a party may inquire into oral and written statements of witnesses, or other information, secured by an adverse party's counsel in the course of preparation for possible litigation after a claim has arisen. Examination into a person's files and records, including those resulting from the professional activities of an attorney, must be judged with care. It is not without reason that various safeguards have been established to preclude unwarranted excursions into the privacy of a man's work. At the same time, public policy supports reasonable and necessary inquiries. Properly to balance these competing interests is a delicate and difficult task.

On February 7, 1943, the tug "J. M. Taylor" sank while engaged in helping to tow a car float of the Baltimore & Ohio Railroad across the Delaware River at Philadelphia. The accident was apparently unusual in nature, the cause of it still being unknown. Five of the nine crew members were drowned. Three days later the tug owners and the underwriters employed a law firm, of which respondent Fortenbaugh is a member, to defend them against potential suits by representatives of the deceased crew members and to sue the railroad for damages to the tug.

A public hearing was held on March 4, 1943, before the United States Steamboat Inspectors, at which the four survivors were examined. This testimony was recorded and made available to all interested parties. Shortly thereafter, Fortenbaugh privately interviewed the survivors and took statements from them with an eye toward the anticipated litigation; the survivors signed these statements on March 29. Fortenbaugh also interviewed other persons believed to have some information relating to the accident and in some cases he made memoranda of what they told him. At the time when Fortenbaugh secured the statements of the survivors, representatives of two of the deceased crew members had been in communication with him. Ultimately claims were presented by representatives of all five of the deceased; four of the claims, however, were settled without litigation. The fifth claimant, petitioner herein, brought suit in a federal court under the Jones Act on November 26, 1943, naming as defendants the two tug owners, individually and as partners, and the railroad.

One year later, petitioner filed 39 interrogatories directed to the tug owners. The 38th interrogatory read: "State whether any statements of the members of the crews of the Tugs 'J. M. Taylor' and 'Philadelphia' or of any other vessel were taken in connection with the towing of the car float and the sinking of the Tug 'John M. Taylor'. Attach hereto exact copies of all such statements if in writing, and if oral, set forth in detail the exact provisions of any such oral statements or reports."

Supplemental interrogatories asked whether any oral or written statements, records, reports or other memoranda had been made concerning any matter relative to the towing operation, the sinking of the tug, the salvaging and repair of the tug, and the death of the deceased. If the answer was in the affirmative, the tug owners were then requested to set forth the nature of all such records, reports, statements or other memoranda.

The tug owners, through Fortenbaugh, answered all of the interrogatories except No. 38 and the supplemental ones just described. While admitting that statements of the survivors had been taken, they declined to summarize or set forth the contents. They did so on the ground that such requests called "for privileged matter obtained in preparation for litigation" and constituted "an attempt to obtain indirectly counsel's private files." It was claimed that answering these requests "would involve practically turning over not only the complete files, but also the telephone records and, almost, the thoughts of counsel."

In connection with the hearing on these objections, Fortenbaugh made a written statement and gave an informal oral deposition explaining the circumstances under which he had taken the statements. But he was not expressly asked in the deposition to produce the statements. The District Court for the Eastern District of Pennsylvania, sitting *en banc*, held that the requested matters were not privileged.... The court then decreed that the tug owners and Fortenbaugh, as counsel and agent for the tug owners forthwith "Answer Plaintiff's 38th interrogatory and supplemental interrogatories; produce all written statements of witnesses obtained by Mr. Fortenbaugh, as counsel and agent for Defendants; state in substance any fact concerning this case which Defendants learned through oral statements made by witnesses to Mr. Fortenbaugh whether or not included in his private memoranda and produce Mr. Fortenbaugh's memoranda containing statements of fact by witnesses or to submit these memoranda to the Court for determination of those portions which should be revealed to Plaintiff." Upon their refusal, the court adjudged them in contempt and ordered them imprisoned until they complied.

The Third Circuit Court of Appeals, also sitting en banc, reversed the judgment of the District Court.... It held that the information here sought was part of the "work product of the lawyer" and hence privileged from discovery under the Federal Rules of Civil Procedure. The importance of the problem, which has engendered a great divergence of views among district courts, led us to grant certiorari....

The pre-trial deposition-discovery mechanism established by Rules 26 to 37 is one of the most significant innovations of the Federal Rules of Civil Procedure. Under the prior federal practice, the pre-trial functions of notice-giving, issue-formulation, and fact-revelation were performed primarily and inadequately by the pleadings. Inquiry into the issues and the facts before trial was narrowly confined and was often cumbersome in method. The new rules, however, restrict the pleadings to the task of general notice-giving and invest the deposition-discovery process with a vital role in the preparation for trial. The various instruments of discovery now serve (1) as a device, along with the pre-trial hearing under Rule 16, to narrow and clarify the basic issues between the parties, and (2) as a device for ascertaining the facts, or information as to the existence or whereabouts of facts, relative to those issues. Thus civil trials in the federal courts no longer need be carried on in the dark. The way is now clear, consistent with recognized privileges, for the parties to obtain the fullest possible knowledge of the issues and facts before trial.

....

In urging that he has a right to inquire into the materials secured and prepared by Fortenbaugh, petitioner emphasizes that the deposition-discovery portions of the Federal Rules of Civil Procedure are designed to enable the parties to discover the true facts and to compel their disclosure wherever they may be found. It is said that inquiry may be made under these rules, epitomized by Rule 26, as to any relevant matter which is not privileged; and since the discovery provisions are to be applied as broadly and liberally as possible, the privilege limitation must be restricted to its narrowest bounds. On the premise that the attorney-client privilege is the one involved in this case, petitioner argues that it must be strictly confined to confidential communications made by a client to his attorney. And since the materials here in issue were secured by Fortenbaugh from third persons rather than from his clients, the tug owners, the conclusion is reached that these materials are proper subjects for discovery under Rule 26.

As additional support for this result, petitioner claims that to prohibit discovery under these circumstances would give a corporate defendant a tremendous advantage in a suit by an individual plaintiff. Thus in a suit by an injured employee against a railroad or in a suit by an insured person against an insurance company the corporate defendant could pull a dark veil of secrecy over all the pertinent facts it can collect after the claim arises merely on the assertion that such facts were gathered by its large staff of attorneys and claim agents. At the same time, the individual plaintiff, who often has direct knowledge of the matter in issue and has no counsel until some time after his claim arises could be compelled to disclose all the intimate details of his case. By endowing with immunity from disclosure all that a lawyer discovers in the course of his duties, it is said, the rights of individual litigants in such cases are drained of vitality and the lawsuit becomes more of a battle of deception than a search for truth.

But framing the problem in terms of assisting individual plaintiffs in their suits against corporate defendants is unsatisfactory. Discovery concededly may work to the disadvantage as well as to the advantage of individual plaintiffs. Discovery, in other words, is not a one-way proposition. It is available in all types of cases at the behest of any party, individual or corporate, plaintiff or defendant. The problem thus far transcends the situation confronting this petitioner. And we must view that problem in light of the limitless situations where the particular kind of discovery sought by petitioner might be used.

We agree, of course, that the deposition-discovery rules are to be accorded a broad and liberal treatment. No longer can the time-honored cry of "fishing expedition" serve to preclude a party from inquiring into the facts underlying his opponent's case. Mutual knowledge of all the relevant facts gathered by both parties is essential to proper litigation. To that end, either party may compel the other to disgorge whatever facts he has in his possession. The deposition-discovery procedure simply advances the stage at which the disclosure can be compelled from the time of trial to the period preceding it, thus reducing the possibility of surprise. But discovery, like all matters of procedure, has ultimate and necessary boundaries. As indicated by Rules 30(b) and (d) and 31(d), limitations inevitably arise when it can be shown that the examination is being conducted in bad faith or in such a manner as to annoy, embarrass or oppress the person subject to the inquiry.[a] And as Rule 26(b) provides, further limitations come into existence when the inquiry touches upon the irrelevant or encroaches upon the recognized domains of privilege.

We also agree that the memoranda, statements and mental impressions in issue in this case fall outside the scope of the attorney-client privilege and hence are not protected from discovery on that basis. It is unnecessary here to delineate the content and scope of that privilege as recognized in the federal courts. For present purposes, it suffices to note that the protective cloak of this privilege does not extend to information which an attorney secures from a witness while acting for his client in anticipation of litigation. Nor does this privilege concern the memoranda, briefs, communications and other writings prepared by counsel for his own use in prosecuting his client's case; and it is equally unrelated to writings which reflect an attorney's mental impressions, conclusions, opinions or legal theories.

But the impropriety of invoking that privilege does not provide an answer to the problem before us. Petitioner has made more than an ordinary request for relevant, nonprivileged facts in the possession of his adversaries or their counsel. He has sought discovery as of right of oral and written statements of witnesses whose identity is well known and whose availability to petitioner appears unimpaired. He has sought production of these matters after making the most searching inquiries of his opponents as to the circumstances surrounding the fatal accident, which inquiries were sworn to have been answered to the best of their information and belief. Interrogatories were directed toward all the events prior to, during and subsequent to the sinking of the tug. Full and honest answers to such broad inquiries would necessarily have included all pertinent information gleaned by Fortenbaugh through his interviews with the witnesses. Petitioner makes no suggestion, and we cannot assume, that the tug owners or Fortenbaugh were incomplete or dis-

---

a. [Eds. Note. The deposition limitations noted by the Court are now contained in Rule 30(d)(3)(A).]

honest in the framing of their answers. In addition, petitioner was free to examine the public testimony of the witnesses taken before the United States Steamboat Inspectors. We are thus dealing with an attempt to secure the production of written statements and mental impressions contained in the files and the mind of the attorney Fortenbaugh without any showing of necessity or any indication or claim that denial of such production would unduly prejudice the preparation of petitioner's case or cause him any hardship or injustice. For aught that appears, the essence of what petitioner seeks either has been revealed to him already through the interrogatories or is readily available to him direct from the witnesses for the asking.

The District Court, after hearing objections to petitioner's request, commanded Fortenbaugh to produce all written statements of witnesses and to state in substance any facts learned through oral statements of witnesses to him. Fortenbaugh was to submit any memoranda he had made of the oral statements so that the court might determine what portions should be revealed to petitioner. All of this was ordered without any showing by petitioner, or any requirement that he make a proper showing, of the necessity for the production of any of this material or any demonstration that denial of production would cause hardship or injustice. The court simply ordered production on the theory that the facts sought were material and were not privileged as constituting attorney-client communications.

In our opinion, neither Rule 26 nor any other rule dealing with discovery contemplates production under such circumstances. That is not because the subject matter is privileged or irrelevant, as those concepts are used in these rules. Here is simply an attempt, without purported necessity or justification, to secure written statements, private memoranda and personal recollections prepared or formed by an adverse party's counsel in the course of his legal duties. As such, it falls outside the arena of discovery and contravenes the public policy underlying the orderly prosecution and defense of legal claims. Not even the most liberal of discovery theories can justify unwarranted inquiries into the files and the mental impressions of an attorney.

Historically, a lawyer is an officer of the court and is bound to work for the advancement of justice while faithfully protecting the rightful interests of his clients. In performing his various duties, however, it is essential that a lawyer work with a certain degree of privacy, free from unnecessary intrusion by opposing parties and their counsel. Proper preparation of a client's case demands that he assemble information, sift what he considers to be the relevant from the irrelevant facts, prepare his legal theories and plan his strategy without undue and needless interference. That is the historical and the necessary way in which lawyers act within the framework of our system of jurisprudence to promote justice and to protect their clients' interests. This work is reflected, of course, in interviews, statements, memoranda, correspondence, briefs, mental impressions, personal beliefs, and countless other tangible and intangible ways—aptly though roughly termed by the Circuit Court of Appeals in this case as the "Work product of the lawyer." Were such materials open to opposing counsel on mere demand, much of what is now put down in writing would remain unwritten. An attorney's thoughts, heretofore inviolate, would not be his own. Inefficiency, unfairness and sharp practices would inevitably develop in the giving of legal advice and in the preparation of cases for trial. The effect on the legal profession would be demoralizing. And the interests of the clients and the cause of justice would be poorly served.

We do not mean to say that all written materials obtained or prepared by an adversary's counsel with an eye toward litigation are necessarily free from discovery in all cases. Where relevant and non-privileged facts remain hidden in an attorney's file and where production of those facts is essential to the preparation of one's case, discovery may properly be had. Such written statements and documents might, under certain circumstances, be admissible in evidence or give clues as to the existence or location of relevant facts. Or they might be useful for purposes of impeachment or corroboration. And production might be justified where the witnesses are no longer available or can be reached only with difficulty. Were production of written statements and documents to be precluded under such circumstances, the liberal ideals of the deposition-discovery portions of the Federal Rules of Civil Procedure would be stripped of much of their meaning. But the general policy against invading the privacy of an attorney's course of preparation is so well recognized and so essential to an orderly working of our system of legal procedure that a burden rests on the one who would invade that privacy to establish adequate reasons to justify production through a subpoena or court order. That burden, we believe, is necessarily implicit in the rules as now constituted.

Rule 30(b), as presently written, gives the trial judge the requisite discretion to make a judgment as to whether discovery should be allowed as to written statements secured from witnesses.[b] But in the instant case there was no room for that discretion to operate in favor of the petitioner. No attempt was made to establish any reason why Fortenbaugh should be forced to produce the written statements. There was only a naked, general demand for these materials as of right and a finding by the District Court that no recognizable privilege was involved. That was insufficient to justify discovery under these circumstances and the court should have sustained the refusal of the tug owners and Fortenbaugh to produce.

But as to oral statements made by witnesses to Fortenbaugh, whether presently in the form of his mental impressions or memoranda, we do not believe that any showing of necessity can be made under the circumstances of this case so as to justify production. Under ordinary conditions, forcing an attorney to repeat or write out all that witnesses have told him and to deliver the account to his adversary gives rise to grave dangers of inaccuracy and untrustworthiness. No legitimate purpose is served by such production. The practice forces the attorney to testify as to what he remembers or what he saw fit to write down regarding witnesses' remarks. Such testimony could not qualify as evidence; and to use it for impeachment or corroborative purposes would make the attorney much less an officer of the court and much more an ordinary witness. The standards of the profession would thereby suffer.

Denial of production of this nature does not mean that any material, non-privileged facts can be hidden from the petitioner in this case. He need not be unduly hindered in the preparation of his case, in the discovery of facts or in his anticipation of his opponents' position. Searching interrogatories directed to Fortenbaugh and the tug owners, production of written documents and statements upon a proper showing and direct interviews with the witnesses themselves all serve to reveal the facts in Fortenbaugh's possession to the fullest possible extent consistent with public policy. Petitioner's counsel frankly admits that he wants the oral statements only to help prepare himself to examine witnesses and to make sure that he has overlooked nothing. That is insufficient under the circumstances to permit him an exception to the policy underlying the privacy of Fortenbaugh's professional activities. If there should be a rare situation justifying production of these matters, petitioner's case is not of that type.

We fully appreciate the wide-spread controversy among the members of the legal profession over the problem raised by this case. It is a problem that rests on what has been

---

b. [Eds. Note. At the time of the *Hickman* opinion, Rule 30(b) contained provisions authorizing the entry of a protective order. These provisions for protective orders are now contained in Rule 26(c).]

one of the most hazy frontiers of the discovery process. But until some rule or statute definitely prescribes otherwise, we are not justified in permitting discovery in a situation of this nature as a matter of unqualified right. When Rule 26 and the other discovery rules were adopted, this Court and the members of the bar in general certainly did not believe or contemplate that all the files and mental processes of lawyers were thereby opened to the free scrutiny of their adversaries. And we refuse to interpret the rules at this time so as to reach so harsh and unwarranted a result.

We therefore affirm the judgment of the Circuit Court of Appeals.

Affirmed.

Justice Jackson, concurring.

. . . .

Counsel for the petitioner candidly said on argument that he wanted this information to help prepare himself to examine witnesses, to make sure he overlooked nothing. He bases his claim to it in his brief on the view that the Rules were to do away with the old situation where a law suit developed into "a battle of wits between counsel." But a common-law trial is and always should be an adversary proceeding. Discovery was hardly intended to enable a learned profession to perform its functions either without wits or on wits borrowed from the adversary.

. . . .

I agree to the affirmance of the judgment of the Circuit Court of Appeals which reversed the district court.

Justice Frankfurter joins in this opinion.

Notes and Questions

1. In *Hickman*, the work product consisted of the signed written statements that Fortenbaugh took from certain witnesses and his personal notes and mental recollections of his witness interviews. Work product comes in many other forms, however. Rule 26(b)(3)(A) broadly extends work product protection to any "documents and tangible things" that are prepared in anticipation of litigation or for trial and there is no prescribed limit on what may qualify. Work product may consist of written material of all sorts, including memos, reports, studies, letters, and statements as well as other tangible things, including computer-generated data, photographs, diagrams, drawings, surveillance videos, etc. Like privilege, work-product protection can be waived and under Rule 26(b)(5)(A), all claims of work product, as with privilege, must be expressly made.

2. (a) As reflected in *Hickman*, and as carried forward in Rule 26(b)(3)(A) and (B), there are two levels of work product protection depending on the nature of the work product sought. Work product is generally distinguished between so-called "fact" or "ordinary" work product and "opinion" work product. "Ordinary" work product consists of documents or tangible things prepared in anticipation of litigation or for trial that contain general factual information relevant to the case. An example of "ordinary" work product would be the signed written statements of the witnesses in *Hickman*. Under Rule 26(b)(3)(A)(i) and (ii), "ordinary" work product is discoverable only if it is otherwise discoverable under Rule 26(b)(1) and "the party [seeking discovery] shows that it has substantial need for the materials to prepare its case and cannot, without undue hardship, obtain their substantial equivalent by other means."

(b) "Opinion" work product, as set forth in Rule 26(b)(3)(B), consists of the "mental impressions, conclusions, opinions, or legal theories of a party's attorney or other representative concerning the litigation." An example of "opinion" work product would be Fortenbaugh's personal notes and mental recollections of his interviews with the witnesses. "Opinion" work product is entitled to an extremely high level of protection and is not discoverable simply by demonstrating the normal showing of substantial need and undue hardship for "ordinary" work product. As the Court held in *Hickman* with respect to Fortenbaugh's personal notes and recollections, "[i]f there should be a rare situation justifying production of these matters, petitioner's case is not of that type." Why did the Court in *Hickman* hold that Fortenbaugh's personal notes and mental recollections of his interviews with the witnesses were entitled to a higher level of protection than "ordinary" work product, such as the signed witness statements? What would his personal notes and recollections contain that signed witness statements would not? "Opinion" work product is further discussed in subsections *(b)* and *(c)*, below.

3. Rule 26(b)(3) only expressly addresses discovery of "documents and tangible things that are prepared in anticipation of litigation or for trial." *Hickman*, however, made clear that work product protection also applies to "intangible" work product, as the Court fully protected Fortenbaugh's mental impressions of his interviews with the witnesses, even though unwritten and unrecorded in tangible form. ("But as to oral statements made by witnesses to Fortenbaugh, whether presently in the form of his mental impressions or memoranda, we do not believe that any showing of necessity can be made under the circumstances of this case so as to justify production." *Hickman*, 329 U.S. at 512). Under the authority of *Hickman,* therefore, intangible work product remains protected and the special protection for mental impressions and thought processes cannot be circumvented simply by the requesting this information in non-documentary form through deposition or interrogatory questions. As explained in subsection *(c)* below, contention interrogatories under Rule 33(a)(2) provide a limited exception for inquiry into this otherwise protected work product.

4. (a) In understanding the scope of work product protection, it is important to emphasize that not everything that is the product of trial preparation work is protected as work product. If facts relevant to the case are unearthed by one side as a result of its trial preparation work, the facts themselves are not protected under the work product doctrine and are subject to discovery, even though the facts may be contained in a document that is not discoverable. As the Court explained in *Hickman*, "[m]utual knowledge of all the relevant facts gathered by both parties is essential to proper litigation. To that end, either party may compel the other to disgorge whatever facts he has in his possession." *See also* Fed. R. Civ. P. 26(b)(3) advisory committee's note to the 1970 amendment ("No change is made in the existing doctrine, noted in the *Hickman* case, that one party may discover relevant facts known or available to the other party, even though such facts are contained in a document which is not itself discoverable.").

(b) Thus, in *Hickman*, Fortenbaugh may have worked very hard to discover the identity and whereabouts of the various witnesses and expended considerable trial preparation time interviewing them. Nevertheless, the names and addresses of these witnesses, as well as the relevant facts Fortenbaugh now acquired as a result of his interviews with them, are fully discoverable. Fortenbaugh's client need not disclose the work product itself, *i.e.*, the written statements that Fortenbaugh took from the witnesses or his personal notes and recollections of the witness interviews, but must answer honestly when asked in interrogatories or other discovery about relevant facts concerning the accident. As the Court explained, "[i]nterrogatories were directed toward all the events prior to, during and subsequent to the sinking of the tug. Full and honest answers to such broad inquiries would necessarily have included all pertinent information gleaned by Fortenbaugh through his interviews with the witnesses."

5. In *Hickman*, all of the trial preparation work had been performed by attorney Fortenbaugh and the Court's opinion, therefore, only addressed the protection to be afforded the trial preparation work of an attorney. Recognizing that in the reality of trial preparation, many persons may be involved in the investigation of a party's case besides the attorney, Rule 26(b)(3)(A) substantially broadens the scope of work product protection by expressly extending its coverage to trial preparation materials prepared "by or for another party or its *representative* (including the other party's attorney, consultant, surety, indemnitor, insurer, or agent)." Rule 26(b)(3)(B) further protects the mental impressions, conclusions, opinions, or legal theories "of a party's attorney or *other representative*."

6. (a) An essential requirement for work product protection under Rule 26(b)(3)(A) is that the material must be "prepared in anticipation of litigation or for trial." As explained in the 1970 Advisory Committee's Note to Rule 26(b)(3), "[m]aterials assembled in the ordinary course of business, or pursuant to public requirements unrelated to litigation, or for other nonlitigation purposes are not under the qualified immunity provided by this subdivision."

(b) Determining this issue can be difficult, especially in the insurance setting because a normal function of an insurance company is to investigate claims made against its policies. When an insurance company investigates a matter to resolve a direct claim *by* its insured on a so-called "first-party" policy, such as a property or health insurance policy, the resulting investigation as to whether the insurance company will cover the claim is generally considered to be in the ordinary course of business. Once the insurance company rejects coverage, however, litigation between the insured and the insurer is more likely and the courts generally extend work product protection to materials generated after the rejection of coverage. When an insurance company investigates a matter under a "third-party" liability policy in connection with a potential claim by a third party *against* its insured, the prospect of litigation is likely from the start and the courts generally hold that any materials prepared by an insurer in connection with a third-party claim are prepared in anticipation of litigation. *See* Edna Selan Epstein, The Attorney-Client Privilege and the Work Product Doctrine 908–10 (5th ed. 2007) & 206–08, 212–14 (Supp. 2012).

7. In order to pierce the qualified immunity of "ordinary" work product under Rule 26(b)(3)(A), a party must demonstrate "substantial need" for the material and "undue hardship" in obtaining the substantial equivalent by other means. Under what circumstances do you think a party would be able to meet this standard? In *Hickman*, the Court indicated that written witness statements might be discoverable when "the witnesses are no longer available or can be reached only with difficulty." The 1970 Advisory Committee's Note further indicates that the standard may be met when the witness has given "a fresh and contemporaneous account in a written statement" and is only available to the discovering party a substantial time thereafter, or when the witness is "reluctant or hostile" or suffering "a lapse of memory." What about discovering other "tangible things"? What if a party inspects and photographs an accident scene which has since been cleared or otherwise changed?

8. Suppose a party engages in conduct that would be unethical under the rules of professional conduct governing attorneys, such as surreptitiously recording conversations in preparation for litigation. If the recordings would qualify as work product under Rule 26(b)(3), should the work product protection be lost because of the attorney's unethical conduct? *See Sea-Roy Corp. v. Sunbelt Equip. & Rentals, Inc.*, 172 F.R.D. 179 (M.D.N.C. 1997) (yes).

9. With respect to witness statements, Rule 26(b)(3)(C) creates a special exception to the normal work product requirements in allowing the person, whether a party or non-party, who actually made the statement to request a copy of *that* person's own statement without the required showing. This exception does not allow the person to request the statement of any other person in circumvention of the normal work product requirements, only the person's own statement.

10. Does work product protection end after a case is concluded? *See Duplan Corp. v. Moulinage et Retorderie de Chavanoz,* 487 F.2d 480, 483–84 (4th Cir. 1973) ("[W]e find no indication that the [*Hickman*] Court intended to confine the protection of the work product to the litigation in which it was prepared or to make it freely discoverable in a subsequent law suit.... [W]e think the legal profession and the interests of the public are better served by recognizing the qualified immunity of work product materials in a subsequent case as well as that in which they were prepared.").

(b) "Opinion" Work Product

As explained in Note 2 above, "opinion" work product is entitled to an extremely high level of protection. Courts have struggled in determining what circumstances, if any, justify piercing the special protection of "opinion" work product. In *Hickman,* the Court indicated that discovery may be justified in a "rare situation," but gave no further guidance. Similarly, Rule 26(b)(3)(B) states that the court "must protect against disclosure of the mental impressions, conclusions, opinions, or legal theories of a party's attorney or other representative," but does not indicate whether that protection is intended to be absolute or qualified. To date, the Supreme Court has not resolved this issue.

In *Upjohn v. United. States,* 449 U.S. 383 (1981), the Court recognized the issue, but declined to decide the question. In *Upjohn,* reprinted in part in section C(1)*(b),* above, the IRS requested not only the written questionnaires between General Counsel Thomas and the Upjohn managers, which the Court held were protected by the attorney-client privilege, but also Thomas' personal notes from his interviews with Upjohn officers and employees. The Court held that Thomas' interview notes were protected by the attorney-client privilege to the extent they revealed communications between Thomas and the Upjohn officers and employees. To the extent Thomas' notes did not reveal communications, the Court held that the notes were protected as "opinion" work product because "they reveal the attorneys' mental processes in evaluating the communications."

In so finding, the Court emphasized Thomas' description of his notes as containing "what I considered to be the important questions, the substance of the responses to them, my beliefs as to the importance of these, my beliefs as to how they related to the inquiry, my thoughts as to how they related to other questions. In some instances they might even suggest other questions that I would have to ask or things that I needed to find elsewhere." *Id.* at 400, n.8.

Because the lower courts had applied improper standards in deciding the case, the Court remanded the case for further proceedings and declined to decide whether the protection for "opinion" work product was absolute or not. The Court held, however, that a "far stronger showing" was required to discover "opinion" work product.

> As Rule 26 and *Hickman* make clear, such work product cannot be disclosed simply on a showing of substantial need and inability to obtain the equivalent without undue hardship. While we are not prepared at this juncture to say that such material is always protected by the work-product rule, we think a *far stronger*

showing of necessity and unavailability by other means than was made by the Government or applied by the Magistrate in this case would be necessary to compel disclosure.

Id. at 401–02 (emphasis added).

Consistent with *Hickman* and *Upjohn*, the lower federal courts have held that "opinion" work product is entitled to near absolute immunity and is discoverable only in rare circumstances. *See, e.g., Baker v. General Motors Corp.*, 209 F.3d 1051, 1053–54 (8th Cir. 2000) ("Opinion" work product "enjoys almost absolute immunity and can be discovered only in very rare and extraordinary circumstances, such as when the material demonstrates that an attorney engaged in illegal conduct or fraud").

Some courts have allowed the discovery of "opinion" work product when the protected opinions and mental impressions are "central" to a party's substantive claim or defense. For example, in *Holmgren v. State Farm Mutual Automobile Insurance Co.*, 976 F.2d 573 (9th Cir. 1992), a third-party tort victim sued the defendant insurance company for bad faith settlement of her claim. The court held that handwritten memoranda prepared by the defendant's adjuster concerning the plaintiff's claim was discoverable even though it was considered to be "opinion" work product. "In a bad faith insurance claim settlement case, the 'strategy, mental impressions and opinions of [the insurer's] agents concerning the handling of the claim are directly at issue'" and may be discovered when the need is compelling. *Id.* at 577.

In what other kinds of cases might the opinions and mental impressions of a party's attorney or representative also be "directly at issue" and "central" to a party's claim or defense? What about a suit for attorney malpractice or malicious prosecution in which the key issues are how and why the underlying litigation was handled as it was by the attorney? What if a party is sued for misconduct and asserts a "good faith" defense on the basis of "advice of counsel?" Should the plaintiff be allowed to discover the "opinion" work product of the attorney in order to ascertain the validity of the defendant's "good faith" defense? For a further discussion of the limited and exceptional situations in which courts have allowed discovery of "opinion" work product, *see* Edna Selan Epstein, The Attorney-Client Privilege and the Work Product Doctrine 946–93 (5th ed. 2007) & 220–22 (Supp. 2012).

Problems

Problem 8-16. Would the following statements be immune from discovery under Rule 26(b)(3)?

(a) Assume *P* and *D* have had an auto accident. *D* hired *C*, an attorney, to defend any lawsuit *P* might bring. Pursuant to *C's* instructions, *E*, a private investigator, interviewed several witnesses to the accident. *E* obtained signed statements from these witnesses shortly after the accident. One year later, *P* hired an attorney and sued *D*. *P's* attorney wants to obtain the statements. Should it make any difference whether the witnesses were still available to be interviewed or deposed by *P's* attorney? Should it make any difference whether the witnesses were all *D's* employees? Should it make any difference whether *P* claimed that *P* could not afford to interview or depose the witnesses?

(b) Assume that *E* also interviewed *P* the day after the accident and obtained *P's* signed statement. *P's* attorney now wants to obtain *P's* statement. If discovery is permitted, would there be any value to postponing delivery of the statement until after *D* had the opportunity to take *P's* deposition?

Problem 8-17. Assume that *T* consulted an attorney about the tax consequences of a proposed "tax shelter." The attorney drafted an analysis of the various tax aspects of the scheme, including the positions and arguments most favorable to the attorney's client. The attorney also employed an accountant, who prepared a written analysis. The attorney concluded that favorable tax treatment would be "very questionable" and that it was likely that the I.R.S. would challenge the shelter. The client went ahead with the proposed plan and civil litigation ensued. The I.R.S. now seeks to discover the papers, reports, and other materials concerning the tax shelter in the attorney's possession to show that the taxpayer had not acted in good faith. Assume that the good or bad faith of the taxpayer would be relevant to the penalty assessed. Should discovery be permitted under Rule 26(b)(3)?

Problem 8-18. Assume that a law firm prepares various analyses of liability in defending a suit brought by *P* against *D*, who is insured by *I*. *P* wins a judgment substantially in excess of the policy limits. *D* then sues *I* to recover the difference between the judgment and the policy limits based upon *I*'s bad faith refusal to settle the prior lawsuit within the policy limits. *D* seeks to discover the documents that *D*'s former counsel prepared in the prior litigation. Should discovery be permitted under Rule 26(b)(3)?

Problem 8-19. To what extent, if any, would Rule 26(b)(3) protect from discovery the material prepared for litigation described in *Problem 8-1(e)*?

(c) Contention Interrogatories and Work Product Protection

As previously explained in the section on interrogatories, there are two principal types of interrogatories: (1) those seeking basic information, such as the names of witnesses or the existence, location, and contents of documents; and (2) those seeking what a party contends and the factual and legal bases for those contentions. These latter interrogatories, known as "contention" interrogatories, are permissible under Rule 33(a)(2), which provides that "[a]n interrogatory is not objectionable merely because it asks for an opinion or contention that relates to fact or the application of law to fact...." This provision allowing inquiry into the opinions and contentions of another party, however, would seem to conflict with the special protections afforded "opinion" work product. The following case addresses the interplay between Rule 33(a)(2) and work product protection.

Alta Health Strategies, Inc. v. Kennedy

United States District Court, District of Utah, 1992
790 F. Supp. 1085

ANDERSON, SENIOR DISTRICT JUDGE.

This matter is before the court on the motions of Plaintiff ... Alta Health Strategies, Inc. ("Alta") for Partial Summary Judgment and to Compel Discovery....

....

Alta moves the court to compel discovery on the grounds that [defendants] Kennedy and O'Donnell refuse to respond to three interrogatories, numbers eighteen through twenty of Alta's Third Discovery Request. The dispute involves Alta's request for "[e]ach and every basis on which [Kennedy and O'Donnell] claim that [a statement of Alta or its agents] constitutes an admission." Pl. Third Set of Interrogs. Nos. 18–20. Kennedy and O'Donnell object to these interrogatories "because [they intrude] on the thought process of the defendants' attorneys and require them to reveal their strategy ... [and] seek privileged work product."...

....

Kennedy and O'Donnell oppose this motion arguing that interrogatories eighteen through twenty seek undiscoverable attorney work product. Under Rule 26(b)(3) of the Federal Rules of Civil Procedure, "the court shall protect against disclosure of the mental impressions, conclusions, opinions, or legal theories of an attorney or other representative of a party concerning litigation." Underlying this prohibition is the policy articulated by the United States Supreme Court in *Hickman v. Taylor*, 329 U.S. 495 (1947):

> In performing his various duties, however, it is essential that a lawyer work with a certain degree of privacy, free from unnecessary intrusion by opposing parties and their counsel. Proper preparation of a client's case demands that he assemble information, sift what he considers to be relevant from irrelevant facts, prepare his legal theories and plan strategy without undue and needless interference.

Id. at 510–11. "This protection is not limited to documents and tangible things that are protected under Fed. R. Civ. P. 26(b)(3)." *Hoffman v. United Telecommunications, Inc.*, 117 F.R.D. 436, 439 (D. Kan. 1987).

Wright and Miller note that "Rule 26(b)(3)[(B)] must be read in harmony with [Rule 33(a)(2)] ... which ... [allows] interrogatories ... involving opinions or contentions that relate to fact or the application of law to fact." 8 Charles A. Wright & Arthur R. Miller, *Federal Practice and Procedure*, Civil § 2026. "Interrogatories ... of this type do require the attorney to disclose, to some extent, his mental impressions, opinions, and conclusions, but he is entitled to keep confidential documents containing these matters that have been prepared for internal use."[26] *Id.* (footnotes omitted). Generally, interrogatories requiring legal or factual conclusions or opinions are to be answered "when they would serve a substantial purpose in expediting the lawsuit, leading to evidence or narrowing the issues." *Luey v. Sterling Drug, Inc.*, 240 F. Supp. 632, 636 (W.D. Mich. 1965).

Having established the scope of Rule 33 with respect to the mental impressions of attorneys, the court finds that although interrogatories eighteen through twenty seek legal or factual conclusions which constitute mental impressions of Kennedy and O'Donnell's attorneys, they are discoverable under Rule 33. The court further finds that answers to these interrogatories will expedite the litigation and lead to evidence or a narrowing of the issues. Accordingly, Alta's motion to compel discovery of interrogatories eighteen through twenty is granted. Finally, the court denies costs to either party, because the matters at issue in this motion are close legal questions, and there is no showing that either party has acted without substantial justification....

Note

It should be emphasized that Rule 33(a)(2) only authorizes inquiry as to the opinions and contentions of a party through interrogatories. The rule does not authorize the pro-

---

26. This discussion is drawn from the Advisory Committee's Note to Rule 26(b)(3):
Rules 33 and 36 have been revised in order to permit discovery calling for opinions, contentions, and admission relating not only to fact, but also to the application of law to fact. Under those rules, a party and his attorney or other representative may be required to disclose, to some extent, mental impressions, opinions, or conclusions. But documents or parts of documents are protected against discovery by this subdivision. Even though a party may ultimately have to disclose in response to interrogatories or requests to admit, he is entitled to keep confidential documents containing such matters prepared for internal use.

duction of "work product" documents that contain those opinions and contentions. As explained in the 1970 Advisory Committee's Note to Rule 26(b)(3), even though a party "may be required to disclose, to some extent, mental impressions, opinions, or conclusions" in answering interrogatories, the party "is entitled to keep confidential documents containing such matters prepared for internal use."

3. Discovery Concerning Experts

Experts are often essential in establishing necessary elements of the parties' claims and defenses and testify on a host of issues in a wide range of cases from complex antitrust and securities cases to standard tort and contract damage actions. Pretrial discovery from an opposing party's expert is critical in order to conduct an effective cross-examination of the expert at trial and to properly prepare a rebuttal case to counter the expert's testimony. Discovery exchange as to experts also facilitates settlement by exposing the relative strengths and weaknesses of the expert testimony that will likely be presented at trial.

Qualifying as an expert carries evidentiary importance because, under the rules of evidence, experts are allowed, due to their special status, to offer opinion testimony at trial. Opinion testimony by lay witnesses is much more restricted. The federal discovery rules do not define how a person qualifies as an expert. Instead, the rules of evidence govern the qualification of experts. Under Rule 702, a witness may testify as an expert and offer opinion testimony "[i]f scientific, technical, or other specialized knowledge will assist the trier of fact to understand the evidence or to determine a fact in issue...." The witness must demonstrate that he/she qualifies as an expert in the particular specialized area "by knowledge, skill, experience, training, or education."

The key to determining what discovery is allowed or required as to experts under the federal discovery rules depends on whether or not the expert may testify at trial.

(a) Discovery as to Experts Who May Testify at Trial

If a person may be used by a party as an expert witness at trial, full discovery is permitted as to this expert and the pretrial disclosure requirements of Rule 26(a)(2) must be followed. Under Rule 26(a)(2)(A), a party is required to disclose to the other parties "the identity of any witness it may use at trial to present" expert testimony. In addition, Rule 26(b)(4)(A) expressly provides that "[a] party may depose any person who has been identified as an expert whose opinions may be presented at trial." The authority to depose such an expert as of right was added in 1993 to make the right to full discovery from such experts explicit and to eliminate the need to apply to the court for permission to depose such an expert, as required under the former rule. A party may also inquire about such an expert through interrogatories under Rule 33(a) addressed to the party who may use the expert at trial.

Expert Reports and Disclosures. Rule 26(a)(2)(B) further imposes a special written report requirement if the expert "is one retained or specially employed to provide expert testimony in the case or one whose duties as the party's employee regularly involve giving expert testimony." Rule 26(a)(2)(B)(i)-(vi) requires that this report contain: (i) a complete statement of all opinions the witness will express and the basis and reasons for them; (ii) the facts or data considered by the witness in forming the opinions; (iii) any exhibits that will be used to summarize or support the opinions; (iv) the qualifications of the witness, including a list of all publications authored by the witness in the previous ten years;

(v) a list of all other cases in which the witness, during the previous four years, has testified as an expert at trial or by deposition; and (vi) a statement of the compensation to be paid for the study and testimony in the case.

This requirement of a special written report only applies to those experts who meet Rule 26(a)(2)(B)'s criteria of a retained or specially employed or regular employee expert. For other expert witnesses who are not within the definition of Rule 26(a)(2)(B), but are identified under Rule 26(a)(2)(A) as witnesses who may present expert testimony at trial, Rule 26(a)(2)(C), newly added in 2010, requires a summary disclosure of the subject matter, facts, and opinions to be offered by the witness at trial. Examples of such experts would be treating physicians and other health care professionals who acquire their information in the normal course of their duties unconnected to the litigation, or employees of a party who do not regularly provide expert testimony. The 2010 Advisory Committee's Note explains that the disclosure required under new Rule 26(a)(2)(C) "is considerably less extensive than the report required by Rule 26(a)(2)(B)" and that the disclosure obligation "does not include facts unrelated to the expert opinions the witness will present."

Communications with Experts and Work Product Protection. In 2010, new Rule 26(b)(4)(C) was added to explicitly extend ordinary and opinion work product protection to attorney communications with experts required to provide a report under Rule 26(a)(2)(B). As explained in the 2010 Advisory Committee's Note, this new provision is designed to ensure that "lawyers may interact with retained experts without fear of exposing those communications to searching discovery." The 2010 Advisory Committee's Note also emphasizes that the three exceptions of 26(b)(4)(C) are limited. With respect to exception (ii), for instance, the Advisory Committee's Note states that it "applies only to communications 'identifying' the facts or data provided by counsel; further communications about the potential relevance of the facts or data are protected."

Similarly, with respect to exception (iii), the Advisory Committee's Note states that it applies only to assumptions that counsel provides the expert, such as telling the expert to assume the truth of certain testimony or evidence, and only to the extent the expert actually relies on these assumptions in forming the expert's opinion. The Advisory Committee's Note cautions that "[m]ore general attorney-expert discussions about hypotheticals, or exploring possibilities based on hypothetical facts, are outside this exception."

Although new Rule 26(b)(4)(C) expressly applies only to attorney communications with experts required to provide a written report under Rule 26(a)(2)(B), and not with other experts, the Advisory Committee's Note states that the new Rule "does not exclude protection [as to these latter communications] under other doctrines, such as privilege or independent development of the work-product doctrine."

Draft Expert Reports and Disclosures. In 2010, new Rule 26(b)(4)(B) was also added to explicitly extend ordinary and opinion work product protection to drafts of expert reports and disclosures required under Rule 26(a)(2). Prior to this new Rule, some courts held that work product protection did not apply to draft reports prepared by expert witnesses. New Rule 26(b)(4)(B) overrules the result in these cases. Moreover, unlike new Rule 26(b)(4)(C), which extends its protections only as to experts required to provide a report under Rule 26(a)(2)(B), new Rule 26(b)(4)(B) applies to all experts identified under Rule 26(a)(2)(A) who must make a report or disclosure under the Rule.

Timing of Expert Disclosures. Rule 26(a)(2)(D) envisions that a time for the expert disclosures required under Rule 26(a)(2)(A)–(C) will be prescribed in a pretrial scheduling order. Ordinarily, the party with the burden of proof on an issue should be required to disclose its expert testimony before other parties are required to make their disclosures on the issue. *See* FED. R. CIV. P. 26(a)(2) advisory committee's note to the 1993 amendment. In the absence of a stipulation by the parties or other directions from the court, this disclosure must be made at least 90 days before the date set for trial or for the case to be ready for trial. However, evidence intended solely to contradict or rebut evidence identified by another party under this rule must be disclosed within 30 days after the other party's disclosure. *See* FED. R. CIV. P. 26(a)(2)(D)(i) & (ii).

Duty to Supplement. The duty under Rule 26(e)(1) to supplement pretrial disclosures and to supplement or amend other discovery responses fully applies to discovery concerning experts. Rule 26(e)(2) further provides that with respect to an expert whose report must be disclosed under Rule 26(a)(2)(B), the party's duty to supplement "extends both to information included in the report and to information given during the expert's deposition." Failure to properly satisfy the pretrial disclosure requirements of Rule 26(a)(2) or to properly supplement information concerning experts as required under Rule 26(e) may trigger serious sanctions under Rule 37(c)(1). Rule 37(c)(1) provides an "automatic sanction" for failure to make or supplement required disclosures and expert testimony may not be used on direct examination when it has not been properly disclosed, "unless the failure is substantially justified or is harmless."

(b) Discovery as to Experts Who Are Not Expected to Testify at Trial

In contrast to the full discovery allowed as to experts who may testify at trial, discovery as to experts who have been "retained or specially employed by another party in anticipation of litigation or to prepare for trial" and who are not expected to testify at trial is not allowed except under the limited provisions of Rule 26(b)(4)(D). Rule 26(b)(4)(D) provides that "[o]rdinarily, a party may not, by interrogatories or deposition, discover facts known or opinions held by [such] an expert ... [b]ut a party may do so only: (i) as provided in Rule 35(b) [request for report of physical or mental examination]; or (ii) on showing exceptional circumstances under which it is impracticable for the party to obtain facts or opinions on the same subject by other means." Unless these requirements are satisfied, discovery as to this expert is precluded. When these requirements are satisfied and discovery is allowed, Rule 26(b)(4)(E) provides that "[u]nless manifest injustice would result," the party seeking discovery must pay the expert a reasonable fee for the time spent in responding to the discovery and pay the other party a fair portion of the fees and expenses reasonably incurred by the other party in obtaining the expert's facts and opinions.

Rule 26(b)(4)(D) only expressly restricts discovery as to "facts known or opinions held" by a retained or specially employed non-testifying expert. Is a party entitled to obtain the identity of such an expert, who is otherwise protected under Rule 26(b)(4)(D), without meeting the special requirements of the rule? The provisions of Rule 26(b)(4)(D) were first adopted as part of the 1970 amendments to the federal discovery rules and the 1970 Advisory Committee's Note to the Rule states that "a party may *on a proper showing* require the other party to name experts retained or specially employed." (emphasis added). Is this reference to a "proper showing" the same as a showing of "exceptional circumstances"? *See Ager v. Jane C. Stormont Hosp.*, 622 F.2d 496, 503 (10th Cir. 1980) (the protective provisions of Rule 26(b)(4)(D) as to facts known and opinions held by non-testifying experts are "subverted" if the expert's identity is disclosed; requirement of a "proper show-

can't get name either

ing" corresponds to a showing of "exceptional circumstances" and absent exceptional circumstances, expert's identity is protected).

With respect to the protective provisions of Rule 26(b)(4)(D), what is the justification for treating differently, for disclosure and discovery purposes, those experts who are expected to testify from those who are specially retained but who are not expected to testify? What "exceptional circumstances" might make it impracticable for the party seeking discovery to independently obtain facts or opinions from such experts? The following case addresses these issues.

Bank Brussels Lambert v. Chase Manhattan Bank, N.A.

United States District Court, Southern District of New York, 1997
175 F.R.D. 34

[In this case, a group of banks, collectively referred to as the "Bank Group," entered into a revolving credit agreement to fund two entities, AroChem International, Inc. and AroChem Corporation, collectively referred to as "AroChem." Thereafter, the Bank Group discovered significant financial discrepancies in the inventories of AroChem. AroChem then formed a special committee ("Special Committee") to investigate the matter and retained the public accounting firm of Arthur Andersen & Co., "Andersen," to conduct a financial investigation. While this investigation was pending, the Bank Group filed an action against AroChem. As part of their negotiations, the Bank Group and AroChem agreed that they would jointly retain Andersen to continue its investigation of AroChem.

Andersen's investigation lasted over seven months and revealed serious financial misconduct at AroChem. As a result, the Bank Group then filed a number of additional actions against various parties. One of the defendants sued by the Bank Group was Bank Paribas (Suisse) S.A., ("BPS"). BPS then sought to take depositions of the nonparty Andersen and a subpoena was issued to one of Andersen's partners. When objection was made, BPS filed a motion to compel depositions of the nonparty Andersen. The district court affirmed the opinion and order of the U.S. Magistrate Judge.]

ELLIS, UNITED STATES MAGISTRATE JUDGE.

. . . .

This matter is before the court upon the motion of defendant Bank Paribas (Suisse) S.A. ("BPS") to compel depositions of the public accounting firm, Arthur Andersen & Company ("Andersen"), with respect to cases 93 Civ. 6876 and 94 Civ. 1317 ("the CLS/BPS Cases"). [Nonparty] Andersen opposes the motions and cross-moves for a protective order. The Chase Manhattan Bank, N.A. ("Chase") joins in Andersen's opposition and cross-motion. For the following reasons, BPS's motion is GRANTED and Andersen's cross-motion is DENIED.

. . . .

Andersen asserts that it is shielded from discovery by Rule 26(b)(4)([D]) of the Federal Rules of Civil Procedure, which provides in relevant part,

> Ordinarily, a party may not, by interrogatories or deposition, discover facts known or opinions held by an expert who has been retained or specially employed by another party in anticipation of litigation or to prepare for trial and

who is not expected to be called as a witness at trial. But a party may do so only ... (ii) on showing exceptional circumstances under which it is impracticable for the party to obtain facts or opinions on the same subject by other means.[a]

Andersen claims that Rule 26(b)(4)([D]) applies here because it was retained as an expert in anticipation of litigation and will not be called to testify at trial in the CLS/BPS Cases. Andersen contends, however, that BPS has not made the requisite showing of exceptional circumstances.

....

A. Does Rule 26(b)(4)([D]) apply?

1. Is Andersen an ordinary fact witness or an expert?

BPS first argues that Andersen is an ordinary fact witness, not an expert witness, and therefore is subject to discovery under the rules governing ordinary fact witnesses rather than under the rules governing expert witnesses. This argument is without merit. Andersen is clearly an "expert" in that it brought its technical background to bear in examining AroChem's accounts and records and in that it was specifically engaged to so examine AroChem in connection with the alleged discrepancy between the actual and reported value of AroChem's inventory. Andersen does not forfeit its status as an expert merely because it learned "facts" in the course of its investigation in addition to developing expert opinions. *See Chiquita Int'l Ltd. v. M/V Bolero Reefer*, 1994 WL 177785, at *1 (S.D.N.Y. May 6, 1994). For purposes of Rule 26(b)(4)([D]), "the relevant distinction is not between fact and opinion testimony but between those witnesses whose information was obtained in the normal course of business and those who were hired to make an evaluation in connection with expected litigation." *Id.* Thus, the next inquiry is whether Andersen was hired in anticipation of litigation.

2. Was Andersen hired in anticipation of litigation?

In determining whether an expert was hired in anticipation of litigation, the court must examine "the total factual situation in the particular case." *Hartford Fire Ins. v. Pure Air on the Lake Ltd. Partnership*, 154 F.R.D. 202, 207 (N.D. Ind. 1993). To conclude that an expert was hired in anticipation of litigation, a lawsuit need not have been filed, but there must have existed "more than a remote possibility of litigation." *United States v. Bell*, 1994 WL 665295, at *4 (N.D. Cal. Nov. 9, 1994).

The facts surrounding the Special Committee's decision to hire Andersen reflect that there existed more than a remote possibility of litigation and that Andersen was hired in anticipation of litigation. Andersen was hired by AroChem's Special Committee in the wake of the discovery by AroChem's major financier, the Bank Group, that there was a significant discrepancy between the actual value of AroChem's inventory and the value reported to the Bank Group. At least one member of the Bank Group suspected that there had been a "massive fraud" at AroChem, and in response, the Bank Group threatened to terminate further draw downs of capital if AroChem could not satisfactorily explain the discrepancy. AroChem reacted quickly and radically to recent events by empowering a special committee to investigate the discrepancy, investigate AroChem's financial operations generally, and investigate the performance of AroChem's officers. AroChem immediately hired not only Andersen, but also outside legal counsel, and removed Harris and Dispenza as officers and employees. Also, two of AroChem's board members resigned

---

a. [Eds. Note. The above quoted passage was edited to reflect the current language of Rule 26(b)(4)(D) following the 2007 restyling amendments.]

and consulted attorneys in order to protect themselves from liability.

The facts leading up to and surrounding AroChem's decision to hire Andersen demonstrate that litigation was highly likely, "particularly given the immediate involvement of counsel, [an expert], and the enormous [potential] damages involved." *Hartford Fire Ins.*, 154 F.R.D. at 207 n.8. The significant discrepancy reflected the potential that there had been a "massive fraud" at AroChem. Obviously, someone was going to be blamed and [AroChem] had a reasonable expectation that [they] would be a target." *Id.*

. . . .

B. Do exceptional circumstances exist which justify discovery?

Rule 26(b)(4)([D]) "is not an 'impenetrable fortress' against discovery and parties seeking discovery can make a showing of exceptional circumstances when there is no practicable alternative by which they can obtain the information." *Hartford Fire Ins.*, 154 F.R.D. at 207. The party seeking discovery of a non-testifying expert carries the burden of showing exceptional circumstances. *Id.* at 207–08. Courts and commentators have commonly identified two situations where the exceptional circumstances standard has been met. The first situation is where the object or condition observed by the non-testifying expert is no longer "observable by an expert of the party seeking discovery." *See id.*; David S. Day, *Expert Discovery in the Eighth Circuit*, 122 F.R.D. 35, 39 (1988). This situation has been demonstrated where some physical condition has deteriorated enough so that one party's expert may be the only expert who actually could have fairly observed it before its deterioration. *See, e.g., Delcastor, Inc. v. Vail Assoc.*, 108 F.R.D. 405 (D. Colo. 1985) (holding that one party's expert who observed a site one day after a mud slide had knowledge unobtainable through any other source); *Sanford Constr. Co. v. Kaiser Aluminum & Chem. Sales, Inc.*, 45 F.R.D. 465, 466 (E.D. Ky. 1968) (holding that plaintiff's expert had knowledge unobtainable through any other source where plaintiff refused to allow defendant's experts access to site where ruptured sewer pipe was being removed); *MacDonald Sprague Roofing Co. v. USM Weather-Shield Sys. Co.*, 38 Fed. R. Serv. 2d 518 (D. Mass. 1983) (compelling discovery of non-testifying expert's report where defendant was unable to test allegedly defective roof since roof had been replaced).

The second situation commonly recognized as constituting exceptional circumstances is where it is possible to replicate expert discovery on a contested issue, but the costs would be judicially prohibitive. *See In re Agent Orange*, 105 F.R.D. 577, 581 (E.D.N.Y. 1985) (compelling discovery of experts retained in a companion case which was part of the same multidistrict litigation because otherwise plaintiffs would have to devote enormous time and resources to duplicating the experts' efforts).

BPS has made the requisite showing of exceptional circumstances. Andersen was able to observe and analyze AroChem's financial condition as soon as the discrepancy was discovered in December 1991. Andersen apparently had "a broad base charge to just look everywhere and find anything and turn it over twice." The bulk of Andersen's investigation lasted from December 1991 through June 1992, consuming 10,000 hours of time, and involving eight to fifteen people. During this time, numerous other parties were given unlimited access to AroChem's books and records, as well as its personal legal files. Although there is no evidence that any documents were lost during this time, it was not until October 1993, almost two years after Andersen began its investigation, that the files from AroChem's offices were placed in storage and maintained under close supervision. The same month that the documents were placed in storage, the Bank Group sued CLS, and four months later, in February 1994, the Bank Group sued BPS.

*Cond.
may
have
changed*

It would be impracticable for BPS to reconstruct AroChem's financial condition, which Andersen had the opportunity to observe and analyze extensively for several months immediately after the discrepancy was discovered. BPS was sued more than two years after the discrepancy was discovered and more than one year after Andersen and numerous parties had the opportunity to observe, remove, and copy AroChem's files. AroChem's files were placed in storage only after numerous parties had unlimited access to the files over the course of a year or more. It is likely that documents were rearranged and possible that documents were lost or altered over the course of the year that the numerous parties had unlimited, unmonitored access to the files. As noted earlier, at least one of plaintiffs' officers has conceded that it would be more difficult now to reconstruct AroChem's collateral position as of December 1991 than it was for Andersen to reconstruct that collateral position when it conducted its work.

Moreover, even if it were possible to reconstruct [AroChem]'s financial condition, the costs of hiring an expert to reconstruct that situation and then to analyze it would be judicially prohibitive. Andersen itself spent over 10,000 hours over the course of six months, utilizing eight to fifteen people, in investigating AroChem's situation. Given that BPS was sued long after Andersen had already completed the bulk of its investigation, BPS did not have the same opportunity to hire an expert to investigate the situation as the parties who hired Andersen had.

Thus, given the evidence in the record, I conclude that BPS has met its burden of showing exceptional circumstances under which it is impracticable for BPS to obtain facts or opinions on the same subject by other means. This conclusion does not obviate the policy considerations underlying Rule 26(b)(4)([D]). Four commonly articulated policy considerations are: (1) the "interest in allowing counsel to obtain the expert advice they need in order properly to evaluate and present their clients' positions without fear that every consultation with an expert may yield grist for the adversary's mill"; (2) the view that "each side should prepare its own case at its own expense"; (3) the concern that it would be unfair to the expert to compel its testimony and also the concern that experts might become unwilling to serve as consultants if they suspected their testimony would be compelled; and (4) the risk of prejudice to the party who retained the expert as a result of the mere fact of retention. *Rubel v. Eli Lilly & Co.*, 160 F.R.D. 458, 460 (S.D.N.Y. 1995). None of these considerations changes the court's finding of exceptional circumstances.

Firstly, the interest in allowing counsel to obtain expert advice without fear that the consultation might work against them does not apply here where the party now retaining Andersen—the Bank Group—does not join in this motion opposing discovery and where the party who originally retained Andersen—AroChem—agreed to permit parties with potentially adverse interests—the Bank Group and the U.S. Government—to employ Andersen. Secondly, the policy that each side should prepare its own case at its own expense is not neglected, given Rule 26(b)(4)([E]) requiring the moving party to pay the reasonable costs incurred in deposing the expert. Thirdly, the interest in fairness to the expert is not harmed here where there is no evidence that the expert opposed its employment by parties other than AroChem. Fourthly, while there may be some risk of prejudice to AroChem or the Bank Group, the parties who retained Andersen, arising from the mere fact of retention, neither party asserts that there is such risk, since neither party joined in this motion. Also, the risk is minimized by the fact that Andersen has already been employed by more than one party.

. . . .

Defendant BPS's motion to compel depositions of Andersen is GRANTED, and Andersen's cross-motion for a protective order is DENIED. Defendant BPS shall serve a copy of this order on the other parties.

Notes and Questions

1. As noted in the above case, the protections of Rule 26(b)(4)(D) only apply to non-testifying experts who have been "retained or specially employed by another party in anticipation of litigation or to prepare for trial." The provisions of Rule 26(b)(4)(D) were first adopted as part of the 1970 amendments to the federal discovery rules and, as explained in the Advisory Committee's Note to those amendments, the limitations of Rule 26(b)(4)(D) were not intended to apply to experts whose "information was not acquired in preparation for trial." Although the 1993 amendments to Rule 26(b)(4) deleted the introductory language to the original Rule, which expressly contained this limitation, the Rule is still interpreted in the same manner. *See* 8A WRIGHT ET AL. §2033, at 114–15. For certain non-testifying experts, therefore, normal discovery applies, irrespective of whether the special requirements of Rule 26(b)(4)(D) are met. What kinds of experts do you think might acquire information about a case but not in anticipation of litigation?

2. (a) As explained in the 1970 Advisory Committee's Note, sometimes an expert is "an actor or viewer with respect to transactions or occurrences that are part of the subject matter of the lawsuit. Such an expert should be treated as an ordinary witness." Can you think of any examples of such experts? What about a physician in an emergency room who examines and treats an accident victim? The physician will certainly acquire information about the case, but only for purposes of treating the victim and not "in anticipation of litigation." Even though the physician may not be called as a witness at trial, normal discovery would, nevertheless, be allowed as to what the physician did and observed in treating the victim in the emergency room, irrespective of whether the special requirements of Rule 26(b)(4)(D) are met.

(b) What about government experts who are required by law to investigate a variety of matters, such as medical examiners, safety officials, fire marshals, and similar experts? These persons will also acquire information about the case, but as part of their regular business duties as government officials and not "in anticipation of litigation." Normal discovery as to such an expert would similarly be allowed, even though the expert is not expected to be called as a witness at trial. Why did the court in *Bank Brussels* treat Andersen as an expert under Rule 26(b)(4)(D) and not as an ordinary witness as in the above examples?

3. The 1970 Advisory Committee's Note further indicates that the protections of Rule 26(b)(4)(D) only apply to non-testifying experts "retained or specially employed in anticipation of litigation or preparation for trial (thus excluding an expert who is simply a general employee of the party not specially employed on the case)." Regular employees of a party are generally subject to normal discovery. Some courts, however, have extended the protections of Rule 26(b)(4)(D) to non-testifying employee experts who are specially assigned by the party in anticipation of litigation to employ their expertise in the case. *See* 8A WRIGHT ET AL. §2033, at 124–25 (courts are divided on whether a regular employee can be covered by Rule 26(b)(4)(D), although "[i]t would seem that a rigid rule precluding the possibility of such treatment of regular employees is not warranted").

4. What if a non-testifying expert is considered to have been only "informally consulted" and not "retained or specially employed" by a party? The 1970 Advisory Committee's Note states that Rule 26(b)(4)(D) "is concerned only with experts retained or specially consulted in relation to trial preparation. Thus the subdivision precludes discovery against experts who were informally consulted in preparation for trial, but not retained or specially employed." The dividing line between specially retained and informally consulted experts is far from clear. *See Ager v. Jane C. Stormont Hosp.*, 622 F.2d 496, 501 (10th Cir. 1980) ("[T]he status of each expert must be determined on an *ad hoc* basis" considering a variety of factors, including the manner in which the consultation was initiated, the nature and extent of the information provided to or determined by the expert, and the duration, intensity, and terms of the consultative relationship).

Problem

Problem 8-20. For purposes of Rule 26(b)(4)(D), should the experts in the following situations be considered as "retained or specially employed"?

(a) Assume that P sues D to recover for injuries sustained in an automobile accident. D's attorney meets a psychiatrist at a cocktail party and tells the psychiatrist about the facts of the case. D's attorney then asks the psychiatrist for an opinion about the viability of a defense that D is using in the case—that D was overcome by a sudden insane delusion that D's car was being operated by aliens through remote control and that D was therefore powerless to do anything about the collision that ensued.

(b) Assume on the facts of *Problem 8-3* that P's attorney had asked a mechanical engineer regularly employed by the company to examine the damaged component and to give an expert opinion about its functioning in anticipation of litigation that was later filed. P's attorney does not expect to call the employee at trial.

Chapter 9

Disposition of the Action without Trial

This chapter examines the basic methods of disposing of an action without trial: default judgments; judgments on the pleadings; summary judgments; and voluntary and involuntary dismissals. In addition, the chapter examines both procedural rules and alternative methods of dispute resolution that are designed to encourage disposition of an action without trial.

Section A. Default Judgments

In modern procedural systems, failure of the defendant to appear after being served with process can result in a default judgment. Assuming jurisdiction is otherwise proper, such a judgment can be enforced against the defendant to the same extent as a judgment rendered after a full adjudication of the action. The default rules also apply to any other party in the action against whom a claim for affirmative relief has been asserted. Thus, a plaintiff served with a counterclaim by the defendant must properly plead or otherwise defend against the counterclaim or risk the entry of a default judgment.

In addition to the failure to plead or otherwise defend in response to a claim, a default can occur at stages of a civil proceeding after an initial appearance. For example, a default judgment can result when a party fails to comply with court orders or rules or fails to take other action that the procedural system requires. *See, e.g.,* Fed. R. Civ. P. 16(f)(1)(A)-(C) (authorizing entry of a default judgment as a sanction against a party who fails to appear at a scheduling or other pretrial conference, fails to participate in good faith or is substantially unprepared, or fails to obey a scheduling or other pretrial order); 37(b)(2)(A)(vi) (authorizing entry of a default judgment as a sanction for failing to obey an order to provide or permit discovery). Federal courts have also held that they may enter default judgments pursuant to their inherent power to sanction litigation misconduct. A default judgment is thus a way of disposing of an action without trial. This section examines default practice under Rule 55 of the Federal Rules of Civil Procedure. Rule 55 exemplifies default practice in the federal courts and other modern procedural systems.

Historical Background. In the English common-law and equity systems, the defendant's appearance was essential to allow the court to adjudicate the action. As a result, both systems developed methods to compel the defendant's appearance. *See* Teply & Whitten at 338–39, 937. Even before the Federal Rules of Civil Procedure, the federal courts could grant default judgments in common-law cases under the Conformity Acts and in equity cases under the Equity Rules. A default judgment in equity was called a *de-*

cree pro confesso. Federal Rule 55 was largely derived from the prior federal equity practice. *See id.* at 937.

Difference Between "Commission of a Default" and a "Default Judgment." Commission of a "default" by a party is a prerequisite to a default judgment. However, as will be explained, not every default will result in such a judgment. Also, entry of a default in the record and entry of a default judgment are different. Entry of a default, like commission of a default, is a prerequisite to a default judgment, but the provisions governing entry of the judgment are distinct from those governing the entry of the default, and the party seeking the default must comply with both. The classic example of a default is the failure of the defendant to respond to the complaint within the time limits required by the procedural system after being properly served with process in the action. But a default can be triggered by any failure to take action that is required by the rules of the procedural system in which the action is pending, even if the party has initially appeared in the action. A perfect example is the court's entry of default against the defendant in the *Pretzel* case, below, because the defendant's attorney failed to appear at a status hearing scheduled by the court.

Basic Operation of Federal Rule 55. Federal Rule 55 establishes a two-step process for the purpose of securing a default judgment. First, Rule 55(a) allows the clerk to enter default on the record when a party against whom a judgment for affirmative relief is sought fails to plead (*e.g.*, fails to serve an answer to the complaint) or otherwise defend (*e.g.*, fails to serve an appropriate preanswer motion challenging jurisdiction, service, venue, etc.), provided the failure is made to appear by affidavit or otherwise.

Second, depending on the circumstances, the clerk or the court enters the default judgment. Rule 55(b)(1) provides that the clerk, as opposed to the court, may enter a default judgment when (1) the plaintiff's claim is for a sum certain or for a sum that can be made certain by computation. In addition, for the clerk to enter a default judgment, (2) the defendant must have been defaulted for failure to appear, and (3) the defaulting defendant must not be an infant or incompetent person. If any of these requirements is not satisfied, only the court can enter a judgment by default under Rule 55(b)(2).

Under Rule 55(b)(2), the court is required to exercise discretion in determining whether to enter the judgment. In exercising its discretion under Rule 55(b)(2), a court often considers several factors in determining whether to enter or deny a default judgment. These factors include the amount of money involved, whether issues of public importance are involved in the action, whether the default is a technical one, whether the adversary has been prejudiced by the actions of the defaulting party, how harsh the default judgment would be, etc. *See* 10A WRIGHT ET AL. § 2685, at 32–38.

Rule 55(b)(2) states that if the party against whom the default judgment is sought is a minor or incompetent person, no default judgment may be entered unless the person is represented by a general guardian, conservator, or other like fiduciary who has appeared in the action. In other cases, when the party against whom the default judgment is sought has appeared in the action personally or by a representative, written notice of the application for judgment must be given to that party or its representative at least seven days before the hearing of the application. This procedure provides the party time to demonstrate why the court should not enter a default judgment.

In addition, it is standard practice for the court to determine whether the plaintiff's complaint states a claim upon which relief can be granted before granting a default judgment. Rule 55(b)(2)(A)-(D) authorizes, but does not require, the court to conduct a hearing or make a referral when, in order to enter or effectuate judgment, it needs to conduct an accounting, determine the amount of damages, establish the truth of any allegation by evidence, or investigate any other matter.

Limitation on Relief Granted in a Default Judgment. The general standard of Federal Rule 54(c), set forth in the Rule's second sentence, provides that every final judgment, *other* than a default judgment, "should grant the relief to which each party is entitled, even if the party has not demanded that relief in its pleadings." The relief which may be granted in a default judgment, however, is expressly limited by the first sentence of Rule 54(c) which provides that "[a] default judgment must not differ in kind from, or exceed in amount, what is demanded in the pleadings." This restriction in Rule 54(c) as to default judgments is designed to allow a defendant to decide on the basis of the complaint whether an action is worth defending or not. It would be unfair to increase the amount awarded against a defendant over and above the amount requested in the complaint if the defendant has decided, based on a demand for a smaller amount, not to defend the action.

54(c)

Setting Aside Entry of a Default on the Record or a Default Judgment. Federal Rule 55(c) provides that even after a default has been entered on the record, the court may set it aside for good cause shown. Similarly, if a default judgment has been entered, the court may set it aside in accordance with Rule 60(b). Setting aside the entry of a default or a default judgment is within the discretion of the court. However, when the court has entered a default judgment, the court's discretion is confined by the requirements of Rule 60(b). In determining whether good cause has been shown to set aside a default under Rule 55(c), the courts often rely on the list of factors in Rule 60(b), such as mistake, inadvertence, excusable neglect, newly discovered evidence, etc.

55(c)

60(b)

Furthermore, the courts require a party seeking to set aside the entry of a default or a default judgment to demonstrate that a meritorious defense exists to the opposing party's claim. However, a defending party is not required to demonstrate the existence of a meritorious defense as a condition of vacating a default judgment when the judgment is void because the rendering court never possessed or properly acquired personal jurisdiction over the defendant or the defending party failed to receive proper notice of the action. *See Peralta v. Heights Med. Ctr., Inc.*, 485 U.S. 80, 86–87 (1988) (violates due process to require meritorious defense when defendant never properly served).

The operation of these rules is well illustrated in the *Pretzel* case, below. As you read this case, consider whether you think the court properly decided not to set aside the default judgment. What factors seem to have been the most important to the court? What practical lessons does this case provide to lawyers in managing their practice?

Pretzel & Stouffer v. Imperial Adjusters, Inc.

United States Court of Appeals, Seventh Circuit, 1994
28 F.3d 42

KANNE, CIRCUIT JUDGE.

In this case a defendant who was defaulted and had a default judgment entered against it seeks relief. This case began when the law firm of Pretzel & Stouffer, Chartered, filed a complaint against Imperial Adjusters, Inc., on September 23, 1991, alleging that Imperial, and co-defendant Savoy Reinsurance Co., Ltd., owed Pretzel $132,000 in unpaid legal fees. On November 14, 1991, counsel for Imperial, filed his appearance, and on November 19, Imperial filed its answer to Pretzel's complaint.

On January 17, 1992, Imperial filed a motion for judgment on the pleadings pursuant to Fed. R. Civ. P. 12(c). Pretzel responded, on February 11, by filing a motion for leave to file a First Amended Complaint. A copy of the First Amended Complaint was attached to Pretzel's motion.

The First Amended Complaint contained two counts. The first count was a reiteration of the original complaint's claim for legal fees. The second count was new. It was a claim under the Illinois Consumer Fraud and Deceptive Business Practices Act, alleging that Imperial made misrepresentations which induced [Pretzel] to continue to provide legal services which Imperial never intended to pay for.

A hearing was held on February 20, 1992, regarding Pretzel's motion to file its amended complaint. At that time Pretzel filed its amended complaint. The district court ordered Imperial to answer by March 5. A status hearing was set for March 24, 1992.

Imperial did not file an answer by March 5; nor did Imperial's attorney attend the status hearing on March 24. At the time of the hearing, nearly three weeks after it was required to file an answer, Imperial still had not answered Pretzel's First Amended Complaint. At the status hearing the district court entered an order of default against Imperial and set the matter for prove-up on April 7, 1992.

One week after the court entered the default of Imperial, on March 31, 1992, Imperial filed a motion requesting that the default be vacated. Imperial also submitted for filing an answer to the Amended Complaint with the court, but failed to request leave of court for such a filing. Imperial also failed to serve a copy of its answer upon Pretzel.

Imperial's tendered answer contained general denials of the new allegations in the second count of the First Amended Complaint. Imperial's answer also contained an affirmative defense, which stated that it was not liable to Pretzel for any damages because it was merely the agent of Savoy.

Imperial's motion to vacate the default was set for hearing on April 7, 1992, at the same time as Pretzel's prove-up. At the April 7 hearing counsel for Imperial attempted to explain his absence from the March 24 status hearing. He stated that he had failed to properly calendar the date. Also, he said he had not received a minute order from the clerk of the court. The court responded that it does not send out minute orders of status hearing dates; and that counsel must keep track of these dates themselves.

Because Pretzel first saw Imperial's answer to their amended complaint at the hearing, the court continued the hearing until April 9, 1992, giving Pretzel two days to review the answer and to respond.

At the hearing on April 9 the court asked Imperial if it had a meritorious defense to Pretzel's complaint, including the new count under the Consumer Fraud Act. Counsel for Imperial responded by referring to its agency defense. The court concluded that this was not a defense to the consumer fraud claim, and that Imperial had therefore not raised any meritorious defense at all to the second count of Pretzel's First Amended Complaint. The court then denied Imperial's motion to vacate the default and set a new prove-up date of April 23, 1992. On that date the court ordered default judgment entered against Imperial in the amount of $132,408.18.

. . . .

At issue in this case is whether or not the trial court erred when 1) it denied Imperial's motion to vacate the default and 2) subsequently entered default judgment against Imperial.

....

Relief from entry of a default requested prior to entry of judgment is governed by Fed. R. Civ. P. 55(c). A request to set aside a default judgment is controlled by Rule 60(b). However, the standard of review is the same under both Rule 55(c) and Rule 60(b).... Abuse of discretion is the standard we apply when reviewing the denial of a motion to vacate a default order and when reviewing a default judgment. However, the test is more liberally applied in the Rule 55(c) context.... The district court will be found to have abused its discretion only if we conclude that no reasonable person could agree with its judgment....

It is undisputed, and the facts amply demonstrate, that a default was properly entered against Imperial on March 24, 1992. The relevant rule states that default should be entered against any party "against whom a judgment for affirmative relief is sought [who] has failed to plead or otherwise defend as provided" by the Federal Rules. Fed. R. Civ. P. 55(a). Imperial had not filed an answer by the date it was required to do so. In addition, Imperial's attorney failed to attend a status hearing. Imperial therefore failed to "plead or otherwise defend" and was correctly defaulted. Imperial claims, however, that the district court abused its discretion when it denied Imperial's motion to vacate the default.

In order to vacate an entry of default the moving party must show: (1) good cause for default (2) quick action to correct it and (3) meritorious defense to plaintiff's complaint....

....

The defaulting party must show good cause for its default or the default order will not be vacated.... In this case, on the date the court entered the default order Imperial had not yet filed its answer even though three weeks had passed since the deadline for filing. It was not until a week after that, at the prove-up hearing for the default judgment, that Imperial finally submitted an answer for filing. Moreover, even at that late date, Imperial failed to move for leave to file the answer, and failed to provide a copy of the answer to opposing counsel.

Imperial demonstrated no good cause for the late submission of its answer. Imperial's counsel claimed that he had difficulties communicating with his clients. This is not an uncommon problem, but the solution to it is emphatically not to ignore filing deadlines. Imperial's attorney could have requested more time to answer if he was having difficulties, as he was allowed to do under Fed. R. Civ. P. 6(b).

Furthermore, we have previously found specifically that lack of communication between attorney and client was not a basis for showing of good cause in this context.... Maintaining communication during the course of litigation is the responsibility of both attorneys and their clients. Mere lack of communication does not excuse compliance with the rules, or from the penalties for failing to do so.

The failure to file an answer on time was not the only problem faced by counsel for Imperial. He also did not appear at the March 24 status hearing, and he was not able to produce a valid excuse for his absence. He claimed to have mis-calendared the date. Mis-calendaring a date is certainly a plausible mistake, but it is the attorney's mistake and he and his client are responsible for the consequences....

....

We have held that "routine back-office problems ... do not rank high in the list of excuses for default ..." Counsel's mistake regarding the date of the hearing, and communication problems with his clients, were just such "routine" problems. They do not establish good cause for defaulting.

....

The second count of the Amended Complaint charged Imperial with violation of the Illinois Consumer Fraud and Deceptive Business Practices Act.... Generally, the Consumer Fraud count consisted of an accusation that an agent of Imperial misled Pretzel by promising payment when Imperial never intended to pay. Imperial's answer to the Amended Complaint consisted of denials, and a blanket claim that it had a "meritorious defense in this matter because it is only the agent of the disclosed principal who is the other defendant in this matter."

At the hearing on April 9, counsel for Imperial had an opportunity to state a meritorious defense to the Consumer Fraud count. The court told counsel that he had so far failed to do so, and that if he did not then and there articulate a meritorious defense the court would not vacate the default.

Counsel reiterated Imperial's agency defense. The attorney for Pretzel responded that an agency defense is appropriate to the contract claim, but not to the consumer fraud claim in the second count of the amended complaint. The court stated "that's correct," and concluding that no meritorious defense had been presented by Imperial, denied the motion to vacate.

Imperial failed to do more than deny the consumer fraud claim. The assertion that Imperial was an agent of Savoy is irrelevant. Agents are liable for their own torts.... Furthermore, it is generally true under Illinois law that principals are not liable for the torts of their agents, where the agent is not an employee.... Even if Imperial was Savoy's agent, as they claim, they were certainly liable for their own torts.

It is a violation of the Illinois Consumer Fraud Act to make affirmative misrepresentations in the course of business to the detriment of consumers. This is what the second count accused Imperial of doing. Imperial was obliged to offer a meritorious defense to this charge. For whatever reason it offered no cognizable defense to the second count. What remains is Imperial's bare denial of Pretzel's allegations.

[W]e [have] held that a defendant's response to a motion for default judgment [is] insufficient if it [lacks] a grounding in facts which would support a meritorious defense of the action by the non-moving party.... We have also held that a meritorious defense requires more than a "general denial" and "bare legal conclusions." ...

Imperial failed to clear the first hurdle when it did not show good cause for its default. This would have been sufficient basis to refuse to vacate Imperial's default, even if it had a meritorious defense....

We need not analyze the third requirement, *i.e.*, whether or not Imperial's action to correct the default was "quick" enough. Imperial needed to meet all three requirements, and it failed to meet two. Given these failures, the speed with which it may have acted to correct the default cannot change the result.

Imperial did not pass the three part test required to vacate an entry of default. The district court did not abuse its discretion when it denied the motion to vacate the default order.

....

As we stated ... earlier, the elements required for vacating a default judgment are the same as the elements for setting aside an entry of default, but the tests for granting relief are more stringent in the case of a default judgment.... In *Chrysler Credit Corp. v. Macino*, 710 F.2d 363, 368 (7th Cir. 1983), we held that because appellants had "failed to establish good cause for vacating the original entry of default, they clearly cannot satisfy the more stringent requirements for relief from the default judgment...." As shown above, Imperial failed to establish good cause to vacate the entry of default against them. Therefore it cannot meet the higher standard required for relief from the default judgment.

In prior cases the acts or omissions which led to a default judgment may have been more egregious than Imperial's conduct in this case. Nonetheless, the default judgment was within the judge's discretion. It is not an abuse of that discretion if the district court finds that docket conditions require a rigorous application of Rule 55. We have long since moved away from the position of disfavoring default judgments, and we are therefore increasingly reluctant to set them aside....

....

The judgment of default entered in favor of Pretzel & Stouffer Chartered and against Imperial Adjusters, Inc. is *affirmed.*

Notes and Questions

1. In *Pretzel*, the court held a hearing before a default judgment was entered. Assume that events in the *Pretzel* case had developed in a slightly different way. Instead of counsel failing to appear at the status hearing, assume that the defendant had simply failed to serve the second answer, and the defendant's default had been entered by the clerk. Under these circumstances, could the clerk also have entered a judgment under Federal Rule 55(b)(1)? *NO Even though sum certain, appeared*

2. As the court observed in *Pretzel*, usually the factors urged in support of a motion to set aside an entry of default will be the same as those that would be urged to set aside a default judgment. However, as the court also notes, the courts ordinarily require a higher showing to obtain relief from a default judgment than from an entry of default. This higher showing is required because the entry of a default judgment implicates the policy of finality that supports the doctrine of res judicata.

3. When a plaintiff seeks a default judgment, it is standard practice for the court to determine whether the plaintiff's complaint states a claim upon which relief can be granted. Of course, this cannot be done in cases in which the clerk enters judgment for a sum certain when the defendant fails to appear. Appearance is, therefore, an important protection for the defendant, which allows the court to determine the sufficiency of the complaint and otherwise to set aside the default judgment under appropriate circumstances.

Problems

Problem 9-1. P sues D for an injunction in a federal district court. D does not appear in the action. The clerk enters D's default under Federal Rule 55(a) upon the filing of a proper affidavit by P. P then requests the clerk to enter judgment in P's favor under Rule 55(b)(1). Should the clerk do so?

Problem 9-2. P sues D for $200,000 in damages. D moves under Federal Rule 12(b)(6) to dismiss P's complaint for failure to state a claim upon which relief can be granted. D's motion is denied. Thereafter, D fails to answer within the time prescribed by Rule 12(a)(1). Upon the filing of a proper affidavit by P, the clerk enters D's default in the record. P then files another affidavit, which demonstrates that the amount due from D is $200,000. May the clerk enter judgment for the $200,000 against D under Rule 55(b)(1)?

Section B. Judgment on the Pleadings

At common law, a party could challenge the legal sufficiency of the opposing party's pleading at any stage of the pleading process by a demurrer. When the code reforms replaced common-law pleading in the states, the demurrer still performed the function of challenging the legal sufficiency of the opposing party's pleadings. Today, in the federal courts and many states, the motion for judgment on the pleadings is used to test the legal sufficiency of the opposing party's case after the pleadings are closed. If a motion for judgment on the pleadings is granted, the case is terminated without the need for a trial. The following text, notes, questions, and problems explore the general nature of the motion for judgment on the pleadings.

Practice Under Federal Rule 12(c). Federal Rule 12(c) allows either party to move for judgment on the pleadings after the pleadings are closed. In the ordinary case, this requirement will mean that the complaint and answer will have to be served in the action before a party may move for judgment on the pleadings. If the answer contains a counterclaim, the motion for judgment on the pleadings will not be proper until the plaintiff's answer to the counterclaim is served. Likewise, if one defendant's answer contains a cross-claim against a co-defendant, a Rule 12(c) motion will not be proper until an answer to the cross-claim is served, and so forth.

If the *defendant* moves for judgment on the pleadings, the motion serves the same function as a motion to dismiss for failure to state a claim upon which relief can be granted under Rule 12(b)(6), and the same standard is used to determine the validity of the Rule 12(c) motion. If the *plaintiff* moves for judgment on the pleadings, the motion raises the legal sufficiency of the defendant's answer.

Like the Rule 12(b)(6) motion (discussed in Chapter 6), a motion for judgment on the pleadings admits all the well-pleaded allegations in the opposing party's pleading, but only for purposes of the motion. The court may not resolve disputed factual issues in determining a motion for judgment on the pleadings. Similarly, in ruling on a motion to dismiss under Rule 12(b)(6) or a motion for judgment on the pleadings under Rule 12(c), the court may not take into account matter outside the pleadings other than exhibits and matters of public record. Rule 12(d) provides that if matters outside the pleadings are presented to and not excluded by the court on a motion to dismiss under Rule 12(b)(6) or a motion for judgment on the pleadings under Rule 12(c), "the motion must be treated as one for summary judgment under Rule 56 [and] [a]ll parties must be given a reasonable opportunity to present all the material that is pertinent to the motion."

Relationship of Judgment on the Pleadings to a Motion to Strike. Federal Rule 12(f) also allows a motion to strike for the purpose of challenging "an insufficient defense." A motion to strike is proper when one or more legally insufficient defenses appear in a pleading, but a motion for judgment on the pleadings would be improper because other legally sufficient defenses are present in the pleading.

"Searching the Record." At common law, a demurrer was said to "search the record," which meant that, regardless of the stage that the pleading process had reached before the demurrer was made, the court would return to the beginning of the process and begin examining the pleadings in sequence to find the first legally insufficient pleading. Thus, if the defendant's answer contained a plea of confession and avoidance to the plaintiff's declaration and the plaintiff demurred to the plea, the court would return to the declaration and examine it to determine whether it stated a cause of action. If the declaration were found to be legally insufficient, the plaintiff would lose, even though the defendant had not demurred to the declaration.

Like the common-law demurrer, a motion for judgment on the pleadings pursuant to Federal Rule 12(c) will also "search the record." Thus, when a plaintiff moves for judgment *12(c)* on the pleadings, the court will rule against the plaintiff if the complaint fails to state a claim upon which relief may be granted even if the defendant has admitted the facts of the complaint and has not raised its legal sufficiency.

Problems

Problem 9-3. P sues D in a federal district court. P's complaint alleges facts X, Y, and Z. Although facts X, Y, and Z do not state a claim upon which relief can be granted, D does not challenge the legal sufficiency of P's complaint. Instead, D admits facts X, Y, and Z and asserts an affirmative defense. D's affirmative defense, however, is also legally insufficient. P moves for judgment on the pleadings. Should judgment on the pleadings be granted for P under Federal Rule 12(c)?

Problem 9-4. P sues D in a federal district court. P's complaint alleges facts X, Y, and Z. D's answer admits facts X, Y, and Z and alleges an affirmative defense. Both P and D move for judgment on the pleadings. What issues do these motions raise?

Problem 9-5. P sues D in a federal district court. P's complaint alleges facts X, Y, and Z. D's answer admits facts X, Y, and Z and alleges affirmative defenses Q and V. P wants to challenge the legal sufficiency of affirmative defense Q. What should P do?

Section C. Summary Judgment   56

Summary judgment is a procedure that allows a party to demonstrate that the factual disputes in the pleadings are not genuine and that, once the apparent disputes are eliminated, the moving party is entitled to judgment as a matter of law. In federal courts, summary judgment is authorized by Rule 56 of the Federal Rules of Civil Procedure, which was revised in 2010.

Motions for Summary Judgment. As provided in revised Rule 56(a), either party may move for summary judgment on any claim or defense, or any part of a claim or defense. Rule 56(a) provides that "[t]he court shall grant summary judgment if the movant shows that there is *no genuine dispute as to any material fact* and the movant is entitled to *judgment as a matter of law*." (emphasis added). In this situation, there is no need for the court or the parties to incur the burden and expense of a full trial, and the court will therefore grant summary judgment in favor of the moving party. A moving party need not prevail on all issues and may receive "partial" summary judgment. For example, the court may find that the undisputed facts justify the grant summary judgment to the plaintiff on the issue of liability, but that factual disputes as to the proper amount of damages must be decided at trial.

The standard for determining if the moving party is entitled to "judgment as a matter of law" is whether the evidence is such that a judge or jury at trial would _not have a legally sufficient basis_ to find for the *nonmoving* party. In making this determination, the court draws all reasonable inferences in favor of the nonmoving party. This is the same standard as a Rule 50 motion for judgment as a matter of law at trial, which is further discussed in Chapter 11.

When a motion for summary judgment is properly made and supported, an opposing party may not rely merely on allegations or denials in its own pleading; rather, its response must properly demonstrate, as required by Rule 56(c), that a genuine dispute of material fact exists. The *Celotex* case, below, explores how the summary judgment process operates in actual practice. As you will see, in making a summary judgment determination, it is important to know whether the moving party does or does not have the burden of proof at trial.

Supporting Factual Positions. Under Rule 56(c)(1), "[a] party asserting that a fact cannot be or is genuinely disputed must support the assertion" by specific citation to materials in the record. As stated in Rule 56(c)(1)(A), these materials may include "depositions, documents, electronically stored information, affidavits or declarations, stipulations (including those made for purposes of the motion only), admissions, interrogatory answers, or other materials."

Parties typically submit affidavits or declarations from the parties and witnesses to attest to various facts in order to demonstrate the existence or nonexistence of a genuine dispute of material fact. Rule 56(c)(4) requires that these supporting and opposing affidavits or declarations "must be made on personal knowledge, set out facts that would be admissible in evidence, and show that the affiant or declarant is competent to testify on the matters stated." Rule 56(h) further provides that if the court finds that any affidavit or declaration has been submitted "in bad faith or solely for delay, the court ... may order the submitting party to pay the other party the reasonable expenses, including attorney's fees, it incurred as a result." An offending party or attorney may also be held in contempt or subjected to other sanctions.

Rule 56(d) provides that when a party opposing a motion for summary judgment demonstrates that "it cannot present facts essential to justify its opposition, the court may: ① defer considering the motion or deny it; ② allow time to obtain affidavits or declarations or to take discovery; or ③ issue any other appropriate order."

Timing of a Summary Judgment Motion. Rule 56(b) provides that "[u]nless a different time is set by local rule or the court orders otherwise, a party may file a motion for summary judgment at any time until 30 days after the close of all discovery."

2010 Revision of Rule 56. One of the principal amendments to the Federal Rules of Civil Procedure in 2010 was the major revision of the text, organization, and procedures of Rule 56. As explained in the 2010 Advisory Committee's Note to amended Rule 56, the purpose of the revision is "to improve the procedures for presenting and deciding summary-judgment motions and to make the procedures more consistent with those already used in many courts."

Although the 2010 amendment revised and reorganized the text and procedures of Rule 56, the long-established standard for the grant of summary judgment, which is the main focus of the *Celotex* case, remains identical. Although Rule 56(a) changed the traditional term "genuine *issue* of material fact" to "genuine *dispute* of material fact," the 2010 amendment effects no change in Rule 56's well-established standard which remains that summary judgment is only proper if "the movant shows that there is no genuine dispute as to any material fact and the movant is entitled to judgment as a matter of law." As you read the *Celotex* opinion, note that the Court's citations to the provisions of former Rule 56 were adjusted to reflect the current language and subsections of revised Rule

56. All of the holdings in *Celotex*, however, as to the proper application of the Rule 56 remain fully valid under the revised Rule.

Celotex Corp. v. Catrett

United States Supreme Court, 1986
477 U.S. 317, 106 S. Ct. 2548, 91 L. Ed. 2d 265

JUSTICE REHNQUIST delivered the opinion of the Court.

The United States District Court for the District of Columbia granted the motion of petitioner Celotex Corporation for summary judgment against respondent Catrett because the latter was unable to produce evidence in support of her allegation in her wrongful-death complaint that the decedent had been exposed to petitioner's asbestos products. A divided panel of the Court of Appeals for the District of Columbia Circuit reversed, however, holding that petitioner's failure to support its motion with evidence tending to negate such exposure precluded the entry of summary judgment in its favor.... This view conflicted with that of the Third Circuit ... We granted certiorari to resolve the conflict ... and now reverse the decision of the District of Columbia Circuit.

Respondent commenced this lawsuit in September 1980, alleging that the death in 1979 of her husband, Louis H. Catrett, resulted from his exposure to products containing asbestos manufactured or distributed by 15 named corporations. Respondent's complaint sounded in negligence, breach of warranty, and strict liability. Two of the defendants filed motions challenging the District Court's in personam jurisdiction, and the remaining 13, including petitioner, filed motions for summary judgment. Petitioner's motion, which was first filed in September 1981, argued that summary judgment was proper because respondent had "failed to produce evidence that any [Celotex] product ... was the proximate cause of the injuries alleged within the jurisdictional limits of [the District] Court." In particular, petitioner noted that respondent had failed to identify, in answering interrogatories specifically requesting such information, any witnesses who could testify about the decedent's exposure to petitioner's asbestos products. In response to petitioner's summary judgment motion, respondent then produced three documents which she claimed "demonstrate that there is a genuine material factual dispute" as to whether the decedent had ever been exposed to petitioner's asbestos products. The three documents included a transcript of a deposition of the decedent, a letter from an official of one of the decedent's former employers whom petitioner planned to call as a trial witness, and a letter from an insurance company to respondent's attorney, all tending to establish that the decedent had been exposed to petitioner's asbestos products in Chicago during 1970–1971. Petitioner, in turn, argued that the three documents were inadmissible hearsay and thus could not be considered in opposition to the summary judgment motion.

In July 1982, almost two years after the commencement of the lawsuit, the District Court granted all of the motions filed by the various defendants. The court explained that it was granting petitioner's summary judgment motion because "there [was] no showing that the plaintiff was exposed to the defendant Celotex's product in the District of Columbia or elsewhere within the statutory period." ... Respondent appealed only the grant of summary judgment in favor of petitioner, and a divided panel of the District of Columbia Circuit reversed. The majority of the Court of Appeals held that petitioner's summary judgment motion was rendered "fatally defective" by the fact that petitioner "made no effort to adduce *any* evidence, in the form of affidavits or otherwise, to support its motion." 756 F.2d at 184 (emphasis in original). According to the majority, Rule 56 of the Federal Rules of Civil Procedure, and this Court's decision in *Adickes v. S.H. Kress & Co.*, 398 U.S. 144, 159 (1970), establish that "the party opposing the motion for summary judgment bears the burden of responding *only after* the moving party has met its burden of coming forward with proof of the absence of any genuine issues of material fact." ... The majority therefore declined to consider petitioner's argument that none of the evidence produced by respondent in opposition to the motion for summary judgment would have been admissible at trial.... The dissenting judge argued that "[t]he majority errs in supposing that a party seeking summary judgment must always make an affirmative evidentiary showing, even in cases where there is not a triable, factual dispute." ... According to the dissenting judge, the majority's decision "undermines the traditional authority of trial judges to grant summary judgment in meritless cases." ...

We think that the position taken by the majority of the Court of Appeals is inconsistent with the standard for summary judgment set forth in Rule 56([a]) of the Federal Rules of Civil Procedure. Under Rule 56([a]), summary judgment is proper " ... if [the movant shows] that there is no genuine [dispute] as to any material fact and ... the [movant] is entitled to a judgment as a matter of law." In our view, the plain language of Rule 56([a]) mandates the entry of summary judgment, after adequate time for discovery and upon motion, against a party who fails to make a showing sufficient to establish the existence of an element essential to that party's case, and on which that party will bear the burden of proof at trial. In such a situation, there can be "no genuine issue as to any material fact," since a complete failure of proof concerning an essential element of the nonmoving party's case necessarily renders all other facts immaterial. The moving party is "entitled to a judgment as a matter of law" because the nonmoving party has failed to make a sufficient showing on an essential element of her case with respect to which she has the burden of proof. "[T]h[e] standard [for granting summary judgment] mirrors the standard for a directed verdict under Federal Rule of Civil Procedure 50(a)...."

Of course, a party seeking summary judgment always bears the initial responsibility of informing the district court of the basis for its motion, and identifying those portions of "the pleadings, depositions, answers to interrogatories, and admissions on file, together with the affidavits, if any," which it believes demonstrate the absence of a genuine issue of material fact. But unlike the Court of Appeals, we find no express or implied requirement in Rule 56 that the moving party support its motion with affidavits or other similar materials *negating* the opponent's claim.... The import of the [Rule] is that, regardless of whether the moving party accompanies its summary judgment motion with affidavits, the motion may, and should, be granted so long as whatever is before the district court demonstrates that the standard for the entry of summary judgment, as set forth in Rule 56([a]), is satisfied. One of the principal purposes of the summary judgment rule is to isolate and dispose of factually unsupported claims or defenses, and we think it should be interpreted in a way that allows it to accomplish this purpose.

...

[T]he nonmoving party [need not] must produce evidence in a form that would be admissible at trial in order to avoid summary judgment. Obviously, Rule 56 does not require the nonmoving party to depose her own witnesses. Rule 56 permits a proper summary judgment motion to be opposed by any of the kinds of evidentiary materials listed in Rule 56(c)[(1)(A)] ... and it is from this list that one would normally expect the nonmoving party to make the showing to which we have referred.

...

Our conclusion is bolstered by the fact that district courts are widely acknowledged to possess the power to enter summary judgments sua sponte, so long as the losing party was on notice that she had to come forward with all of her evidence.... It would surely defy common sense to hold that the District Court could have entered summary judgment sua sponte in favor of petitioner in the instant case, but that petitioner's filing of a motion requesting such a disposition precluded the District Court from ordering it.

Respondent commenced this action in September 1980, and petitioner's motion was filed in September 1981. The parties had conducted discovery, and no serious claim can be made that respondent was in any sense "railroaded" by a premature motion for summary judgment. Any potential problem with such premature motions can be adequately dealt with under Rule 56([d]), which allows a summary judgment motion to be denied, *56(d)* or the hearing on the motion to be continued, if the nonmoving party has not had an opportunity to make full discovery.

In this Court, respondent's brief and oral argument have been devoted as much to the proposition that an adequate showing of exposure to petitioner's asbestos products was made as to the proposition that no such showing should have been required. But the Court of Appeals declined to address either the adequacy of the showing made by respondent in opposition to petitioner's motion for summary judgment, or the question whether such a showing, if reduced to admissible evidence, would be sufficient to carry respondent's burden of proof at trial. We think the Court of Appeals with its superior knowledge of local law is better suited than we are to make these determinations in the first instance.

The Federal Rules of Civil Procedure have for almost 50 years authorized motions for summary judgment upon proper showings of the lack of a genuine, triable issue of material fact. Summary judgment procedure is properly regarded not as a disfavored procedural shortcut, but rather as an integral part of the Federal Rules as a whole, which are designed "to secure the just, speedy and inexpensive determination of every action." FED. R. | CIV. P. 1. Before the shift to "notice pleading" accomplished by the Federal Rules, motions to dismiss a complaint or to strike a defense were the principal tools by which factually insufficient claims or defenses could be isolated and prevented from going to trial with the attendant unwarranted consumption of public and private resources. But with the advent of "notice pleading," the motion to dismiss seldom fulfills this function any more, and its place has been taken by the motion for summary judgment. Rule 56 must be construed with due regard not only for the rights of persons asserting claims and defenses that are adequately based in fact to have those claims and defenses tried to a jury, but also for the rights of persons opposing such claims and defenses to demonstrate in the manner provided by the Rule, prior to trial, that the claims and defenses have no factual basis.

The judgment of the Court of Appeals is accordingly reversed, and the case is remanded for further proceedings consistent with this opinion.

It is so ordered.

JUSTICE WHITE, concurring.

I agree that the Court of Appeals was wrong in holding that the moving defendant must always support his motion with evidence or affidavits showing the absence of a genuine dispute about a material fact. I also agree that the movant may rely on depositions, answers to interrogatories, and the like, to demonstrate that the plaintiff has no evidence to prove his case and hence that there can be no factual dispute. But the movant must discharge the burden the Rules place upon him: It is not enough to move for summary judgment without supporting the motion in any way or with a conclusory assertion that the plaintiff has no evidence to prove his case.

. . . .

Petitioner Celotex does not dispute that if respondent has named a witness to support her claim, summary judgment should not be granted without Celotex somehow showing that the named witness' possible testimony raises no genuine issue of material fact.... It asserts, however, that respondent has failed on request to produce any basis for her case. Respondent, on the other hand, does not contend that she was not obligated to reveal her witnesses and evidence but insists that she has revealed enough to defeat the motion for summary judgment. Because the Court of Appeals found it unnecessary to address this aspect of the case, I agree that the case should be remanded for further proceedings.

[The dissenting opinion of JUSTICE BRENNAN, with whom CHIEF JUSTICE BURGER and JUSTICE BLACKMUN concurred, is omitted. The dissenting opinion of JUSTICE STEVENS is also omitted.]

Notes and Questions

1. Although Justice White concurred in both the opinion and the judgment of the Court in *Celotex*, is Justice White's concurrence consistent with Justice Rehnquist's opinion? Could Justice Rehnquist's opinion be interpreted to say that a party defending against a claim may, after an adequate opportunity has been afforded for discovery, move for summary judgment without supporting materials? Would this force the party prosecuting the claim to show how that party could meet its burden of proof if the case went to trial? Justice White would clearly require more than this, wouldn't he? However, after sufficient discovery, how hard would it be to meet the burden Justice White would place on the defending party?

2. The Supreme Court in *Celotex* stopped short of actually deciding whether the plaintiff's showing in this case was sufficient to defeat Celotex's motion for summary judgment. The Court instead remanded this issue to the Court of Appeals to make the determination "in the first instance" in light of the clarified standards set by the Court. On remand, the Court of Appeals again held that the district court erred in granting summary judgment in favor of Celotex. The Court of Appeals ruled that Celotex had waived its hearsay objection to the plaintiff's documentary evidence. When considered with Celotex's interrogatory responses and other Celotex documents, a genuine issue of material fact existed as to whether the decedent had been exposed to Celotex products and the issue "was not so one-sided that Celotex was entitled to judgment as a matter of law." *See Catrett v. Johns-Manville Sales Corp.*, 826 F.2d 33 (D.C. Cir. 1987).

3. When the moving party does not have the burden of proof, as in *Celotex*, what more, practically speaking, can the party do than point out to the court that there is no evidence in the record to sustain the nonmoving party's burden of proof at trial? The moving party cannot be expected to prove a negative, can she? On the other hand, when the moving party has the burden of proof (as where a plaintiff moves for summary judgment on a claim for relief), it is clear that the party must support the motion with materials outside the pleadings under Rule 56. Otherwise, if factual disputes exist on the face of the pleadings, it would be impossible to demonstrate that no genuine issue of fact exists within the meaning of the rule. Furthermore, to win, a moving party with the burden of proof must present enough evidence (in quality and quantity) to justify the conclusion that the party

would be entitled to a judgment as a matter of law, formerly a directed verdict, at trial if the opposing party does nothing to resist the motion for summary judgment.

4. *Celotex* is one of several U.S. Supreme Court decisions that seem to encourage the granting of summary judgment motions more than they have been granted in the past. *See Matsushita Elec. Indus. Co. v. Zenith Radio Corp.*, 475 U.S. 574 (1986) (examined in Note 7, below); *Anderson v. Liberty Lobby, Inc.*, 477 U.S. 242 (1986). Do you think that summary judgment practice of the breadth described in *Celotex* is wise? Why or why not? Taking both *Celotex* and the materials in the preceding notes into account, isn't it clear that the party who has the burden of proof on a claim or defense at trial is at a substantial disadvantage under prevailing summary judgment practice, whether the party is a moving or nonmoving party? Is that situation just a normal incident of having the burden of proof, or is it an unwise pretrial impairment of important rights, including the right to trial by jury, that are afforded in the trial process?

5. It is commonplace for the courts to say that on a motion for summary judgment, they must view the evidence in the light most favorable to the nonmoving party and must give the nonmoving party the benefit of all favorable inferences that can be drawn from the evidence. Similarly, it is black letter law that judges are not supposed to resolve factual conflicts or weigh evidence in determining motions for summary judgment. Do you think it is possible to determine whether an issue of fact is "genuine," as Rule 56 requires, without resolving factual disputes or weighing evidence? If not, how would you express what the judge's proper role is in determining a motion for summary judgment? *See* TEPLY & WHITTEN at 944–48.

6. In *Matsushita Electric Industrial Co. v. Zenith Radio Corp.*, 475 U.S. 574 (1986), the plaintiffs brought a federal antitrust action alleging that the defendants had conspired to raise, fix, and maintain artificially high prices for television sets in Japan and to fix artificially low prices for television sets in the United States. After extensive discovery, the defendants moved for summary judgment. The district court found that the admissible evidence submitted by the plaintiffs to defeat the motion did not raise a genuine issue of fact and granted the motion. The court of appeals reversed and was, in turn, reversed by the U.S. Supreme Court.

While paying lip service to the standards described in Note 6, above, the Court stated that a plaintiff seeking recovery under the antitrust laws must present evidence that tends to show the inference of conspiracy is reasonable in light of the competing inferences of (a) independent action by the defendants and (b) collusive action that could not have harmed the plaintiffs. After canvassing the nature of predatory pricing conspiracies and the defendants' behavior over the course of the alleged conspiracy, the Court concluded that the defendants had no plausible motive to engage in the conspiracy with which they were charged. The dissenting Justices stated that the majority was evaluating the persuasiveness of the plaintiffs' evidence, a task that should be reserved for the jury. *See id.* at 598–607 (White, J., with whom Brennan, Blackmun, and Stevens joined, dissenting). After *Matsushita*, is there anything left of the restriction that the court should not weigh evidence or resolve factual disputes on a motion for summary judgment? What about the rule the court should view the evidence in favor of the nonmoving party and that all inferences should be drawn in favor of that party?

7. It is also commonplace to see statements to the effect that summary judgment can rarely be granted in negligence cases because negligence involves a judgment about the reasonableness of the defendant's conduct that must be made by a trier of fact.

Problems

Problem 9-6. P sues D in federal district court. P alleges that D made slanderous utterances about P to W. D's answer denies that the slanderous utterances were ever made. D moves for summary judgment, supporting the motion with affidavits by D and W. D's affidavit denies that D ever made the slanderous utterances. W's affidavit states that W never heard D make the slanderous utterances. P was not present when the slanderous utterances were made. However, P contends that D and W are lying and that, at trial, the jury should be allowed to conclude that (1) they are lying and (2) the truth is the opposite of their denials. Should summary judgment be granted?

Problem 9-7. P sues D for damages in federal district court. P alleges facts X, Y, and Z. D's answer denies facts X, Y, and Z. P and D are the only witnesses to facts X, Y, and Z. P moves for summary judgment against D. P supports the motion with P's own affidavit, which if accepted as true, would demonstrate that facts X, Y, and Z are true. D opposes P's motion with D's own affidavit, which if accepted as true, would demonstrate facts X, Y, and Z to be false. The judge does not believe D's affidavit because the judge thinks D is not a credible witness, so the judge grants P's motion for summary judgment. Was summary judgment properly granted?

Problem 9-8. P and D collide in their automobiles, and P is injured seriously. P sues D in a federal district court. P alleges that D was negligent, in that D was driving faster than reasonably warranted by the conditions. D's answer admits the fact of the collision, but denies that D was negligent. P moves for summary judgment under Federal Rule 56. P supports the motion with affidavits showing that D was driving 45 miles per hour (ten miles per hour under the speed limit) on a highway that was wet from a recent rain. One of the affidavits supplied by P was an affidavit by E, an expert on the causes of highway accidents. E's affidavit opined that a speed of 45 miles per hour was ten miles per hour faster than justified by the conditions of the highway and was unsafe. D failed to oppose P's motion with affidavits or other materials. Should P's motion be granted? Why or why not?

Problem 9-9. P contracts to sell and D to buy a tract of land. The value of the land depends mainly on timber located on it. It turns out that the timber had been destroyed by fire at the time P and D entered into the contract. Giving this reason as an excuse, D refuses to go through with the contract. P sues D for the difference between the contract price and the market value of the land on the date performance was called for. D defends on the sole ground that a mutual mistake of fact rendered the contract voidable at D's option. D's defense is good if both P and D believed that the timber was still on the land at the time they entered into the contract. P moves for summary judgment against D. P supports the motion with an affidavit that states that D must have known the timber was destroyed by fire all along, because the price bargained for was much lower than would have been justified by land with timber on it. D does not oppose the motion with affidavits or other materials outside the pleadings. Should summary judgment be granted? Do you suppose that summary judgment is granted frequently in cases in which a party's state of mind is in issue?

Section D. Voluntary and Involuntary Dismissals

1. Voluntary Dismissals

At common law and equity, the plaintiff could voluntarily dismiss an action at any time prior to judgment. Such dismissals were not considered to be "on the merits" or "with prejudice," which meant that the plaintiff could bring a second action against the defendant on the same claim.

Modern systems of procedure also permit voluntarily dismissals, but usually restrict them in certain ways. Federal Rule 41(a) exemplifies voluntary dismissal practice in the federal courts and the states that have adopted rules patterned after the Federal Rules of Civil Procedure. The following materials explore voluntary dismissal practice under Rule 41(a).

Structure of Federal Rule 41(a). This rule is divided into two subdivisions. The first, Rule 41(a)(1), deals with voluntary dismissals by the plaintiff without court involvement. The second, Rule 41(a)(2), deals with voluntary dismissals pursuant to a court order. As provided in Rule 41(c), the provisions of Rule 41 also apply to dismissals of any counterclaim, crossclaim, or third-party claim.

Voluntary Dismissals Without a Court Order Pursuant to Federal Rule 41(a)(1). Except in a few situations (such as a dismissal of a class action), Rule 41(a)(1)(A) permits the plaintiff to voluntarily dismiss an action without a court order "by filing: (i) a notice of dismissal before the opposing party serves either an answer or a motion for summary judgment; or (ii) a stipulation of dismissal signed by all parties who have appeared."

Effect of a Notice or Stipulation of Voluntary Dismissal on Future Actions. Federal Rule 41(a)(1)(B) provides that "[u]nless the notice or stipulation states otherwise, the dismissal is without prejudice," meaning that the plaintiff can bring another action on the same claim against the defendant. However, the second sentence of Rule 41(a)(1)(B) provides an important exception when the same claim has been previously dismissed by the plaintiff and states that "[i]f the plaintiff previously dismissed any federal- or state-court action based on or including the same claim, a notice of dismissal operates as an adjudication on the merits."

Note that this "two voluntary dismissal" penalty provision of Rule 41(a)(1)(B) expressly applies only when the second voluntary dismissal by the plaintiff is by a *notice of dismissal,* as opposed to a stipulation of voluntary dismissal or a voluntary dismissal by court order. Rule 41(a)(1)(B), though, does not indicate the specific method by which the first voluntary dismissal must have been obtained to implicate the penalty provision. Rule 41(a)(1)(B) only states that this provision applies "if the plaintiff previously dismissed any federal- or state-court action." The courts have generally applied this provision narrowly in determining what type of voluntary dismissal in the first action qualifies. *See, e.g., ASX Inv. Corp. v. Newton,* 183 F.3d 1265 (11th Cir. 1999) ("two voluntary dismissal" rule does not apply when first voluntary dismissal was by court order on plaintiff's motion); *Poloron Prods., Inc. v. Lybrand Ross Bros.,* 534 F.2d 1012 (2d Cir. 1976) ("two voluntary dismissal" rule does not apply when first voluntary dismissal was by stipulation of dismissal signed by all parties).

In addition, for the penalty provision of Rule 41(a)(1)(B) to apply, the second voluntary dismissal must occur in a federal court action. By contrast, under Rule 41(a)(1)(B), the first voluntary dismissal by the plaintiff could have occurred in either an earlier federal or state court action. Note that in the *Lake at Las Vegas* case, below, the first voluntary dismissal by the plaintiff was by a notice of dismissal and occurred in Nevada state court.

Voluntary Dismissals Approved by the Court Pursuant to Federal Rule 41(a)(2). For dismissals not falling within the provisions of Rule 41(a)(1), the plaintiff must seek court approval of a voluntary dismissal. Rule 41(a)(2) directs the court to dismiss the action "on terms that the court considers proper." Such a dismissal is "without prejudice" unless the court states otherwise in its order of voluntary dismissal.

Effect of a Pending Counterclaim. Federal Rule 41(a)(2) provides that "[i]f a defendant has pleaded a counterclaim before being served with the plaintiff's motion to dismiss, the action may be dismissed over the defendant's objection only if the counterclaim can remain pending for independent adjudication."

Costs of a Previously Dismissed Action. Federal Rule 41(d) provides that "[i]f a plaintiff who previously dismissed an action in any court files an action based on or including the same claim against the same defendant, the court: (1) may order the plaintiff to pay all or part of the costs of that previous action; and (2) may stay the proceedings until the plaintiff has complied."

Lake at Las Vegas Investors Group, Inc. v. Pacific Malibu Development Corp.

United States Court of Appeals, Ninth Circuit, 1991
933 F.2d 724

FARRIS, CIRCUIT JUDGE.

. . . .

Lake at Las Vegas Investors Group, Inc. appeals the district court's dismissal of its action for interference with and breach of contract against Transcontinental Corporation, Transneva Corporation, and Transneva Limited Partnership. The dismissal was pursuant to the rule that two voluntary dismissals under Federal Rule of Civil Procedure 41(a) operate as an adjudication on the merits.

. . . .

On October 9, 1987, Investors filed its first complaint against Pacific Malibu Development Corporation, Barry Silverton, and Transcontinental Corporation alleging that Transcontinental had interfered with and induced the breach of an agreement between Investors and Pacific Malibu and Silverton. On October 15, Investors filed a notice of voluntary dismissal of this complaint pursuant to Nevada Rule of Civil Procedure 41(a)(1) and refiled the same complaint immediately thereafter. Pacific Malibu removed to federal court on diversity grounds.

On November 10, 1987, Investors filed a voluntary dismissal of all claims against Transcontinental pursuant to Federal Rule of Civil Procedure 41(a)(1). It also moved to amend its complaint against Pacific Malibu and Silverton. On April 4, 1988, Investors moved for leave to add as parties Transcontinental, Transneva Corporation (a wholly owned subsidiary of Transcontinental), Transneva Limited Partnership (in which Transneva Corporation is a general partner), and Lake at Las Vegas Joint Venture.

On October 28, 1988, the district court granted Transcontinental's motion to dismiss Transcontinental and the two Transneva entities pursuant to the two dismissal rule of

Rule 41(a)(1) and denied Investors's motion for oral argument. Investors's motion for reconsideration was denied.

. . . .

Nevada Revised Statute § 80.210(1) provides that foreign corporations "shall not be allowed to commence, maintain, or defend any action or proceeding in any court of the state" until registered to do business in Nevada. Investors argues that because it was not registered when it filed its first state court complaint, the complaint did not commence an action within the meaning of Rule 41(a), but rather was a "nullity" by operation of section 80.210(1). Therefore, it argues, its motion to dismiss under Rule 41(a) was not a voluntary dismissal of an action since an action never existed.

Nevada law does not provide a clear answer to this ingenious argument.... Lack of capacity to sue is an affirmative defense in other contexts, ... and an "action" is deemed commenced by the filing of a complaint under Nevada Rule of Civil Procedure 3. We reject Investors's argument. We hold that although the complaint may have been subject to dismissal, Investors commenced an "action" that could be and was voluntarily dismissed under Rule 41(a).

. . . .

Investors next argues that, even if it did commence an "action" within the Rule, its first dismissal was not "voluntary." It bases this argument on the fact that its action would have been subject to dismissal under Nevada Revised Statute § 80.210(1). It urges us to hold that voluntary dismissal of a complaint subject to dismissal is no different than having the complaint dismissed by an order of the court.

In *Randall v. Merrill Lynch*, 820 F.2d 1317 (D.C. Cir. 1987)..., the D.C. Circuit explained:

> The term "voluntary" in Rule 41 means that the party is filing the dismissal without being compelled by another party or the court. In other words, it does not mean that other circumstances might not have compelled the dismissal or that the party desired it....

We find the D.C. Circuit's reasoning sound. Rule 41 distinguishes between voluntary, or section (a), dismissals and involuntary, or section (b), dismissals on the basis of which party initiates the dismissal. And, while it delineates the bases upon which the defendant may seek an involuntary dismissal, it does not consider the plaintiff's reasons for seeking a voluntary dismissal.

. . . .

Investors also argues that the two dismissal exception should not be applied if the dismissals were not for the purpose of harassing or abusing the defendants. The Rule does not require an inquiry into the circumstances of the two dismissals. However, a few cases have suggested that, in certain limited circumstances, the Rule will not be literally applied. In *Poloron Products, Inc. v. Lybrand Ross Bros. & Montgomery*, 534 F.2d 1012, 1017–18 (2d Cir. 1976), the Second Circuit held that the two dismissal bar of Rule 41(a) does not apply where one of the prior voluntary dismissals was by stipulation knowingly consented to by all parties. The court acknowledged that Rule 41(a) does not distinguish between unilateral and stipulated voluntary dismissals, but held that a stipulated voluntary dismissal posed little danger of harassment and therefore should not bar an otherwise proper suit.... The court observed that the defendant could have declined to agree to the dismissal or could have insisted that it be with prejudice.... This holding, when followed, has been limited to its facts and does not preclude application of the bar where the voluntary dismissal is unilateral....

Sutton Place Development Co. v. Abacus Mortgage Investment Co., 826 F.2d 637, 640–41 (7th Cir. 1987) ... also cited by Investors, held that a dismissal *by motion* (*i.e.*, a dismissal falling outside of the language of Rule 41(a)(1)) would not be considered for purposes of the two dismissal bar, because to do so would expand the exception to the rule that voluntary dismissals are without prejudice. *Sutton Place* limits an expansion of Rule 41(a)(1), but it hardly suggests that dismissals which fall squarely within the language of the Rule should be read out of it via an intent inquiry.

. . . .

Investors contends that ... its second dismissal was not a dismissal for Rule 41(a)(1) purposes because it dismissed only Transcontinental, and dismissal of an "action" occurs only when all defendants are dismissed.

Rule 41(a) may be invoked to dismiss less than all of the parties.... We need not decide whether a Rule 41(a)(1) dismissal of less than all parties should be sufficient in every instance to trigger the two dismissal bar. We hold only that upon these facts, the Rule applies.

. . . .

Investors argues that even if the dismissal of Transcontinental was proper under the two dismissal bar, Transneva Corporation and Transneva Limited Partnership were never dismissed and therefore can not claim the benefit of the bar. The question is what relationship, if any, is required between the party twice dismissed and a party seeking to enforce the bar against the plaintiff.

Investors argues that Rule 41(a)(1) requires privity. We ... find the argument for a strict privity requirement inapplicable here. We agree with Investors that the weight of authority requires at least a relationship between the dismissed party and the party seeking to claim the benefit of the bar....

The relationship between Transcontinental and the two Transneva defendants is sufficient to render them "substantially the same" for purposes of Rule 41(a)(1).... We need not define the precise parameters of the applicable test. We hold only that the wholly-owned subsidiary and partnership in which that subsidiary is the general partner may invoke the two dismissals of the subsidiary's parent and claim Rule 41(a)(1) res judicata. Investors's error is typical of the type of error motivating voluntary dismissals under Rule 41(a)(1). As a practical matter, the danger of harassment to the parent continued when the closely related Transneva entities were sued.

. . . .

Affirmed.

Notes and Questions

1. Consider the Second Circuit's decision in the *Poloron Products* case, discussed in *Lake at Las Vegas*. In that case, the first action was brought in an Indiana federal court against Poloron-Indiana; Lybrand was added to the action as a defendant by amendment and the action was transferred to the Southern District of New York. After transfer, Poloron, the parent corporation of Poloron-Indiana, was also added to the action as a defendant. Poloron and the plaintiff agreed that the losses that they both had suffered were Lybrand's responsibility, and the plaintiff agreed to dismiss the action voluntarily and assign its right to damages to Poloron. The voluntary dismissal was accomplished by a stipulation of dismissal signed by all parties. Subsequently, Poloron brought an action against Lybrand in the Northern District of Illinois. A later decision of the Seventh Circuit Court

of Appeals caused Poloron to fear that this second action would be held barred by the Illinois statute of limitations, so Poloron filed a notice of dismissal pursuant to Rule 41(a)(1)(A)(i). Poloron then recommenced the same suit against Lybrand in the Southern District of New York. Lybrand moved to dismiss under the "two voluntary dismissal" rule of Rule 41(a)(1)(B).

The district court granted this motion, but the Second Circuit Court of Appeals reversed. The court rejected the argument that the "two voluntary dismissal" rule was inapplicable because Poloron was not the plaintiff in the first action. However, the court agreed that the rule should not be applied when the first voluntary dismissal was by stipulation of the parties, even though the court acknowledged that the language of Rule 41(a)(1)(B), for purposes of the first voluntary dismissal, did not distinguish between voluntary dismissals by stipulation of the parties or by notice of dismissal by the plaintiff.

2. Rule 41(a)(1) provides that the plaintiff's right to dismiss the action voluntarily by filing a notice of dismissal terminates upon the service of an answer or a motion for summary judgment. Why do you think the rule restricts voluntary dismissals in this way?

Problems

Problem 9-10. P sues D in a state court, but dismisses the action voluntarily under a state rule providing for dismissal without prejudice at any time prior to trial. Subsequently, P sues D on the same claim in a federal court, but again dismisses the action; this time the dismissal is accomplished pursuant to Federal Rule 41(a)(1)(A)(i) by filing a notice of dismissal before D serves an answer or motion for summary judgment. Subsequently, P again sues D in a state court on the same claim. D pleads the federal dismissal as a defense to the state action. What should the result be?

Problem 9-11. On the facts of *Problem 9-10*, if the first dismissal had been in federal court under Federal Rule 41(a)(1)(A)(i), the second dismissal had been in state court under state law, and the third action had been in federal court, would the result be different? Do you need additional information to solve this problem?

2. Involuntary Dismissals

Involuntary dismissals occur in a number of circumstances. For example, in Chapter 6, you examined the motion to dismiss for failure to state a claim upon which relief can be granted under Federal Rule 12(b)(6). If such a motion is granted, it results in an involuntary dismissal because, in contrast to the voluntary dismissals discussed in the previous subsection, the plaintiff does not want it to occur. Indeed, all the grounds of dismissal listed in Rule 12(b), as well as the motion for judgment on the pleadings under Rule 12(c), and a motion for summary judgment under Rule 56, can result in involuntary dismissals if they are granted in favor of the defendant.

Federal Rule 41(b) also states that the defendant can move for a dismissal of a claim or the entire action "[f]or failure of the plaintiff to prosecute or to comply with these rules or any order of court." For example, this provision may be used when the plaintiff is not ready for trial, when the plaintiff fails to comply with a pretrial order, etc.

Effect of an Involuntary Dismissal on the Plaintiff's Ability to Commence Another Action on the Same Claim. In addition to the question about when it is proper to grant one, the most important question about an involuntary dismissal is whether the dismissal results in a judgment "on the merits." A judgment on the merits precludes the plaintiff from bringing a second action on the same claim. On the other hand, if an involuntary dismissal is "without prejudice," it does not result in a judgment "on the merits" and the plaintiff can sue again on the dismissed claim.

Traditionally, certain kinds of dismissals on procedural grounds did not result in judgments "on the merits." For example, as we will see in Chapter 12, if a demurrer was granted on the grounds that the plaintiff's complaint did not state facts sufficient to constitute a cause of action, the resulting judgment was not considered "on the merits," and the plaintiff could, by framing a sufficient complaint, sue again on the same claim. Likewise, dismissals for lack of personal jurisdiction, subject-matter jurisdiction, or improper venue, among others, were considered to be on procedural grounds and, therefore, not on the merits.

Federal Rule 41(b) (second sentence) appears to specify the effect of all involuntary dismissals in federal court: "Unless the dismissal order states otherwise, a dismissal under this subdivision (b) and any dismissal not under this rule—except one for lack of jurisdiction, improper venue, or failure to join a party under Rule 19—operates as an adjudication on the merits." The operation of Rule 41(b) is intertwined with the doctrine of claim preclusion examined in Chapter 12 and will be considered again in that chapter. The following material explores some problems of administration under Rule 41(b) and will also provide useful background for the materials in Chapter 12. In particular, it focuses on two key terms used in Rule 41(b). First, what is the meaning of the words "lack of jurisdiction"? Second, what is the meaning of "adjudication on the merits"?

(a) Meaning of "Lack of Jurisdiction" in Rule 41(b)

The following U.S. Supreme Court decision provides an important early interpretation of what is meant by the words "lack of jurisdiction" in Rule 41(b). As you read it, consider whether you think the Court reached the correct result.

Costello v. United States

United States Supreme Court, 1961
365 U.S. 265, 81 S. Ct. 534, 5 L. Ed. 2d 551

JUSTICE BRENNAN delivered the opinion of the Court.

The petitioner became a naturalized citizen on September 10, 1925. The District Court for the Southern District of New York revoked his citizenship on March 9, 1959, in this proceeding brought by the Government under §340(a) of the Immigration and Nation-

---

1. The statute, 66 Stat. 260, as amended, 68 Stat. 1232; 8 U.S.C. §1451, reads in pertinent part as follows:

   (a) *Concealment of material evidence; refusal to testify.*

   It shall be the duty of the United States attorneys for the respective districts, upon affidavit showing good cause therefor, to institute proceedings in any court specified in subsection (a) of section 1421 of this title in the judicial district in which the naturalized citizen may reside at the time of bringing suit, for the purpose of revoking and setting aside the order admitting such person to citizenship and canceling the certificate of naturalization on the ground that such order and certificate of naturalization were procured by concealment of a material fact or by willful misrepresentation, and such revocation and setting aside of the order admitting such person to citizenship and such canceling of certificate of naturalization shall be effective as of the original date of the order and certificate, respectively:....

ality Act of 1952. That Act authorizes revocation of naturalized citizenship "on the ground that such order and certificate of naturalization were procured by concealment of a material fact or by willful misrepresentation...."[1] The petitioner, in 1925, swore in his Preliminary Form for Naturalization, in his Petition for Naturalization, and when he appeared before a Naturalization Examiner, that his occupation was "real estate." The District Court found that this was "willful misrepresentation and fraud" and that "his true occupation was bootlegging".... The Court of Appeals for the Second Circuit affirmed.... We granted certiorari....

An earlier denaturalization complaint brought under 8 U.S.C. (1946 ed.) § 738(a), the predecessor of § 340(a), was dismissed on the ground that wiretapping may have infected both the Government's affidavit of good cause and its evidence.... The Court of Appeals for the Second Circuit reversed on the ground that the Government should have been afforded an opportunity to show that its evidence either was untainted or was admissible in any event.... We granted certiorari and reversed.... on a ground not considered below, namely, that the affidavit of good cause, which is a prerequisite to the initiation of denaturalization proceedings under § 340(a), ... was not filed with the complaint. On remand the District Court declined to enter an order of dismissal "without prejudice" and entered an order which did not specify whether the dismissal was with or without prejudice. The Government did not appeal from that order but brought this new proceeding under § 340(a) by affidavit of good cause and complaint filed on May 1, 1958.

The petitioner argues several grounds for reversal of the order revoking his citizenship. He contends ... (4) that the second denaturalization proceeding was barred under Rule 41(b) of the Federal Rules of Civil Procedure ... by the failure of the District Court on remand of the first proceeding to specify that the dismissal was "without prejudice" to the filing of a new complaint.

We find no merit in any of these contentions. The judgment of the Court of Appeals will be affirmed.

    ....

The petitioner moved for leave to amend his petition for a writ of certiorari to add a question whether the present proceeding was barred by the order of the District Court dismissing the earlier proceeding on remand, without specifying whether the dismissal was with or without prejudice. We deferred decision on the motion pending oral argument. The motion is granted and we proceed to determine the merits of the question.

It is the petitioner's contention that the order dismissing the earlier complaint must be construed to be with prejudice because it did not specify that it was without prejudice, and the ground of dismissal was not within one of the exceptions under Rule 41(b).... That Rule provides:

> If the plaintiff fails to prosecute or to comply with these rules or a court order, a defendant may move to dismiss the action or any claim against it. Unless the dismissal order states otherwise, a dismissal under this subdivision (b) and any dismissal not under this rule — except one for lack of jurisdiction, improper venue, or failure to join a party under Rule 19 — operates as an adjudication on the merits.[a]

We hold that a dismissal for failure to file the affidavit of good cause is a dismissal "for lack of jurisdiction," within the meaning of the exception under Rule 41(b). In arguing contra, the petitioner relies on cases which hold that a judgment of denaturalization re-

---

a. [Eds. Note. The above quoted passage was edited to reflect the current language of Rule 41(b) following the 2007 restyling amendments.]

sulting from a proceeding in which the affidavit of good cause was not filed is not open to collateral attack on that ground.... We think that petitioner misconceives the scope of this exception from the dismissals under Rule 41(b) which operate as adjudications on the merits unless the court specifies otherwise. It is too narrow a reading of the exception to relate the concept of jurisdiction embodied there to the fundamental jurisdictional defects which render a judgment void and subject to collateral attack, such as lack of jurisdiction over the person or subject matter. We regard the exception as encompassing those dismissals which are based on a plaintiff's failure to comply with a precondition requisite to the Court's going forward to determine the merits of his substantive claim. Failure to file the affidavit of good cause in a denaturalization proceeding falls within this category....

At common law dismissal on a ground not going to the merits was not ordinarily a bar to a subsequent action on the same claim. In *Haldeman v. United States*, 91 U.S. 584, 585–86 (1875), which concerned a voluntary nonsuit, this Court said, "there must be at least one decision on a *right* between the parties before there can be said to be a termination of the controversy, and before a judgment can avail as a bar to a subsequent suit.... There must have been a right adjudicated or released in the first suit to make it a bar, and this fact must appear affirmatively." A similar view applied to many dismissals on the motion of a defendant. In *Hughes v. United States*, 71 U.S. (4 Wall.) 232, 237 (1866), it was said "In order that a judgment may constitute a bar to another suit, it must be rendered in a proceeding between the same parties or their privies, and the point of controversy must be the same in both cases, and must be determined on its merits. If the first suit was dismissed for defect of pleadings, or parties, or a misconception of the form of proceeding, or the want of jurisdiction, or was disposed of on any ground which did not go to the merits of the action, the judgment rendered will prove no bar to another suit." ...

We do not discern in Rule 41(b) a purpose to change this common-law principle with respect to dismissals in which the merits could not be reached for failure of the plaintiff to satisfy a precondition. All of the dismissals enumerated in Rule 41(b) which operate as adjudications on the merits — failure of the plaintiff to prosecute, or to comply with the Rules of Civil Procedure, or to comply with an order of the Court, or to present evidence showing a right to the relief on the facts and the law — primarily involve situations in which the defendant must incur the inconvenience of preparing to meet the merits because there is no initial bar to the Court's reaching them. It is therefore logical that a dismissal on one of these grounds should, unless the Court otherwise specifies, bar a subsequent action. In defining the situations where dismissals "not provided for in this rule" also operate as adjudications on the merits, and are not to be deemed jurisdictional, it seems reasonable to confine them to those situations where the policy behind the enumerated grounds is equally applicable. Thus a *sua sponte* dismissal by the Court for failure of the plaintiff to comply with an order of the Court should be governed by the same policy. Although a *sua sponte* dismissal is not an enumerated ground, here too the defendant has been put to the trouble of preparing his defense because there was no initial bar to the Court's reaching the merits....

In contrast, the failure of the Government to file the affidavit of good cause in a denaturalization proceeding does not present a situation calling for the application of the policy making dismissals operative as adjudications on the merits. The defendant is not put to the necessity of preparing a defense because the failure of the Government to file the affidavit with the complaint require the dismissal of the proceeding. Nothing in the term "jurisdiction" requires giving it the limited meaning that the petitioner would ascribe to it. Among the terms of art in the law, "jurisdiction" can hardly be said to have a fixed content. It has been applied to characterize other prerequisites of adjudication which will not be re-examined in subsequent proceedings and must be brought into controversy in the original action if a defendant is to litigate them at all.... Decisions in the lower courts applying the exception construe "jurisdiction" to encompass dismissals on grounds similar to that in the present case.... We therefore hold that the Government was not barred from instituting the present proceeding.

Affirmed.

[The dissenting opinion of JUSTICE DOUGLAS, with whom JUSTICE BLACK concurred, is omitted.]

Notes and Questions

1. Under the "plain meaning" rule of interpretation, how does the Court's opinion in *Costello* fare? Can the term "jurisdiction" bear the weight the Court places on it? What other kinds of cases, not involving pure questions of subject-matter jurisdiction or personal jurisdiction, might fit within the meaning of the term "jurisdiction" after *Costello*?

2. At one point in *Costello*, the Court states that Rule 41(b) does not make dismissals for failure to satisfy preconditions to suit judgments on the merits. At another point, the Court seems to indicate that the significant question in determining the applicability of Rule 41(b) is whether the defendant was put to the necessity of preparing a defense on the merits. Are these the same or different grounds? Are there cases in which dismissal for failure to satisfy a precondition to suit would nevertheless require the defendant to prepare a defense on the merits? If so, what are those cases?

3. What about dismissals for improper venue, which are also not on the merits under Rule 41(b)? Should the term "venue" be interpreted flexibly under the rule? If so, what should it be held to include? Assume that a federal court in a state dismisses an action under the federal doctrine of forum non conveniens in preference to the courts of a foreign nation and the plaintiff later brings an action in a state court of the same state that does not follow the doctrine of forum non conveniens. Do you think that the federal dismissal should be considered "on the merits" under Rule 41(b)? If not, does the dismissal fall within the "jurisdiction" exception to Rule 41(b) as interpreted by *Costello* or within the "improper venue" exception of the rule?

4. Under *Costello's* interpretation of Federal Rule 41(b), should a dismissal for failure to state a claim upon which relief can be granted be considered a dismissal for lack of jurisdiction or a judgment on the merits, assuming that the court does not specify the dismissal to be without prejudice?

Problem

Problem 9-12. P sues D in a federal district court on September 1. P's claim is based on a note that matures on December 1. D moves to dismiss the action on the ground that P's suit is premature. D's motion is granted. After the note matures, P sues again in a federal district court. D pleads the judgment in the first action as a defense. Who should win?

(b) Meaning of "Adjudication on the Merits" in Rule 41(b)

In *Semtek International Inc. v. Lockheed Martin Corp.*, 531 U.S. 497 (2001), discussed in Chapters 5(C) and 12(G)(2), the plaintiff commenced an action in California state court. Recall that the complaint alleged a breach of contract and various business torts. The defendant removed the action to a California federal district court on the basis of diversity. The defendant then moved to dismiss the plaintiff's claims on the ground that they were barred by California's two-year statute of limitations. Adopting language suggested by the defendant, the court ordered the plaintiff's claims dismissed "in [their] entirety on the merits and with prejudice." Without contesting the court's designation of the dismissal as one "on the merits," the plaintiff appealed to the Ninth Circuit Court of Appeals. The Ninth Circuit affirmed the district court's order. *Id.* at 499.

In addition to the appeal, the plaintiff commenced an action in Maryland state court against the defendant. The plaintiff alleged the same causes of action, which were not barred under Maryland's three-year statute of limitations. Eventually, after further legal maneuvering, the Maryland courts were faced with the question whether the defendant's motion to dismiss the action on the ground of res judicata should be granted because the California federal dismissal was on the merits and claim preclusive as a matter of federal law. The Maryland Court of Special Appeals affirmed the trial court's conclusion that the action should be dismissed on this basis. *Id.* at 500.

In the U.S. Supreme Court, the defendant argued that Federal Rule 41(b) controlled the outcome of the case because the dismissal order by the California federal district court did not "state otherwise" and did not pertain to the excepted subjects of jurisdiction, venue, or joinder. Thus, as a result of the operation of Rule 41(b) making all other dismissals operate "as an adjudication on the merits," the defendant asserted that the dismissal by the California federal district court was entitled to claim preclusive effect. *Id.*

In response, the U.S. Supreme Court asserted that the use of the words "on the merits" in Rule 41(b) (and in the California district court's order) did not automatically produce a claim-preclusive effect. *Id.* at 503. Apart from the Rules Enabling Act and *Erie* considerations, the Court offered three principal "interpretative" reasons for its conclusion that "on the merits" language in Rule 41(b) did not dictate the result in the case.

First, the Court asserted that Rule 41(b) was merely a "default rule for determining the import of a dismissal" and was not designed to announce a federally prescribed rule on the complex question of claim preclusion. *Id.*

Second, the Court concluded that the phrase "without prejudice" as used in Rule 41(a) meant that the defendant could return later to the same court with the same underlying claim. It then concluded an "adjudication on the merits," as used in Rule 41(b), was simply meant to establish the opposite of a "dismissal without prejudice," *i.e.*, that the plaintiff could not return to the same court with the same underlying claim when there had been an "adjudication on the merits." *Id.* at 505.

Third, because Rule 41(b) was a rule "governing the internal procedures of the rendering court itself," *id.* at 503, the Court concluded the adjudication-on-the-merits "default provision of Rule 41(b) — and, presumably, of the explicit order in the ... case that used the language of that default provision — [means] simply that, unlike a dismissal 'without prejudice,' [the plaintiff is barred from] refiling the same claim in the United States District Court for the Central District of California." *Id.* at 506.

In addition, the Court went on to hold that a "federal common-law rule" of preclusion that adopted state law as the rule of decision in diversity actions controlled the case, with the result that California preclusion law would determine the effect of the California federal diversity judgment.

Problem

Problem 9-13. P, a citizen of State X, sues D, a citizen of State Y, in a federal district court in State Y. Jurisdiction is based solely on diversity of citizenship between the parties. D moves to dismiss the action on the ground that the complaint fails to state a claim upon which relief may be granted. The motion is granted without specifying that the dismissal was without prejudice. Answer the following questions:

(a) Assume that P attempts to revise the language of the complaint in a way to eliminate the basis of D's objection and commences a new action using the revised complaint in the same federal court. Under Rule 41(b) as interpreted by *Semtek*, was the first dismissal "on the merits"?

(b) If not, does there appear to be any limit on the number of times that P can attempt to "fix" the complaint as long as P changes the complaint each time it is filed?

(c) Assume instead that P commenced the second action by filing the revised complaint in a state court of State Y. Does Rule 41(b) make the first dismissal "on the merits" for purposes of this action?

(d) Does it matter in answering any of the above questions whether the dismissal of a complaint for failure to state a claim upon which relief could be granted would be considered "on the merits" under State Y preclusion law?

Section E. Devices to Encourage Settlement

Federal Rule 68 is designed to encourage settlement by allowing a party defending a claim to offer to have judgment voluntarily entered against the defending party on specified terms. As an inducement to the opposing party to accept the offer of judgment, Rule 68(d) shifts the "costs" of the action accruing after an unaccepted offer to the opposing party if the judgment finally obtained by the opposing party "is not more favorable than the unaccepted offer." This section considers the basic operation of the rule — the timing of the offer, its acceptance or rejection, and its evidentiary effects. It then discusses two difficult interpretative problems: What does it mean to fail to "obtain" a judgment that "is not more favorable than the unaccepted offer"? And what does the term "costs" include?

Timing of the Offer of Judgment. Rule 68(a) provides that "[a]t least 14 days before the date set for trial, a party defending against a claim may serve on an opposing party an offer to allow judgment on specified terms, with the costs then accrued." Under Rule 68(b), an unaccepted offer is considered withdrawn, but this does not preclude a subsequent offer of judgment. In addition, Rule 68(c) provides that "[w]hen one party's liability to another has been determined but the extent of liability remains to be determined by further proceedings, the party held liable may make an offer of judgment" within a reasonable time, but at least 14 days before a hearing to determine the extent of liability.

Acceptance of the Offer. Rule 68(a) provides that "[i]f, within 14 days after being served, the opposing party serves written notice accepting the offer, either party may then file the offer and notice of acceptance, plus proof of service." The clerk must then enter the judgment.

Evidentiary Admissibility of an Unaccepted Offer. Rule 68(b) specifically provides that an unaccepted offer is considered withdrawn and evidence of an unaccepted offer is not admissible in a later proceeding, except a proceeding to determine costs.

Failing to Obtain a Judgment More Favorable than the Offer. Rule 68(d) states that "[i]f the judgment that the offeree finally obtains is not more favorable than the unaccepted offer, the offeree must pay the costs incurred after the offer was made." Does the rule's reference to "the judgment that the offeree finally obtains" mean that the penalty provisions of Rule 68(d) are triggered only when the plaintiff-offeree is awarded some form of judgment, albeit on less favorable terms than the defendant's offer, and not when the defendant completely prevails in the action?

In *Delta Airlines, Inc. v. August*, 450 U.S. 356 (1981), the plaintiff, Rosemary August, sued Delta Air Lines under the Civil Rights Act of 1964. August alleged that Delta had discharged her from her position as a stewardess because of her race. She sought reinstatement and $20,000 in back pay, attorney's fees, and costs. Delta made an offer of judgment pursuant to Rule 68 in the amount of $450.00. August refused the offer. After trial, August lost, and the district court entered judgment in favor of Delta and directed that each party bear its own costs. Delta's motion for costs under Rule 68 was denied on the ground that it had not been made in a good-faith attempt to settle the case. The Court of Appeals for the Seventh Circuit affirmed on the same ground. *Id.* at 348–49.

The Supreme Court affirmed, but instead focused on whether Rule 68 applied at all to this situation. The Court held that Rule 68 does not allow costs to be awarded against a plaintiff-offeree when the defendant obtains a judgment in the case. Instead, Rule 68 applies only to judgments obtained by plaintiffs in an amount less than the defendant offered. The Court reasoned, in part, that Rule 68's reference to the *judgment* obtained by the *offeree* "would not normally be read by a lawyer to describe a judgment in favor of the other party." *Id.* at 350–51. The Court also found this interpretation to be consistent with purpose of the rule.

> The purpose of Rule 68 is to encourage the settlement of litigation. In all litigation, the adverse consequences of potential defeat provide both parties with an incentive to settle in advance of trial. Rule 68 provides an additional inducement to settle in those cases in which there is a strong probability that the plaintiff will obtain a judgment but the amount of recovery is uncertain. Because prevailing plaintiffs presumptively will obtain costs under Rule 54(d), Rule 68 imposes a special burden on the plaintiff to whom a formal settlement offer is made. If a plaintiff rejects a Rule 68 settlement offer, he will lose some of the benefits of victory if his recovery is less than the offer. Because costs are usually assessed against the losing party, liability for costs is a normal incident of defeat. Therefore, a nonsettling plaintiff does not run the risk of suffering additional burdens that do not ordinarily attend a defeat, and Rule 68 would provide little, if any, additional incentive if it were applied when the plaintiff loses.
>
> ....
>
> ... If a plaintiff chooses to reject a reasonable offer, then it is fair that he not be allowed to shift the cost of continuing the litigation to the defendant in the event that his gamble produces an award that is less than or equal to the amount offered. But it is hardly fair or evenhanded to make the plaintiff's rejection of an utterly frivolous settlement offer a watershed event that transforms a prevailing defendant's right to costs in the discretion of the trial judge [under Rule 54(d)]

into an absolute right to recover the costs incurred after the offer was made [under Rule 68].

Id. at 352, 356.

Meaning of "Costs." As explained in the preceding note, a prevailing party is normally entitled to costs under Rule 54(d). Such costs normally include relatively minor items, such as fees of the clerk, marshal, and court reporter; fees for printing and witnesses; docket and copying fees; and fees for court-appointed experts and interpreters. *See* 28 U.S.C. § 1920 ("Taxation of costs"). The penalty provisions of Rule 68(d), however, can affect the award of costs that may otherwise be available to a prevailing party.

In *Marek v. Chesny*, 473 U.S. 1 (1985), for example, a plaintiff in a civil rights action, who had rejected the defendant's offer of judgment under Rule 68, ultimately prevailed in the action, but recovered less than the amount offered by the defendant. The plaintiff moved for an award of attorney's fees under 42 U.S.C. § 1988, which provides that a prevailing plaintiff in a civil rights action under § 1983 may recover attorney's fees as part of the costs of the action. The Supreme Court held, however, that attorney's fees were to be included within the term "costs" in Rule 68(d) whenever attorney's fees were properly awardable as costs under the applicable substantive statute. Because the defendant had made a proper offer of judgment under Rule 68 and the plaintiff had recovered less than the amount offered, it was the plaintiff who was responsible for costs under Rule 68(d) and thus the plaintiff was not entitled to recover attorney's fees against the defendant. The Court in *Marek* also held that it is immaterial whether the offer recites that costs are included, whether it specifies the amount that the defendant is allowing for costs, or whether it refers to costs at all. As long as the offer does not "implicitly or explicitly" provide that the judgment will not include costs, the offer will be valid. *See id.* at 6.

Comparison to State Offer-of-Judgment Rules. As explained in the above notes, Federal Rule 68 only applies to an offer of judgment by a defending party and the only penalty for rejection of an offer is the award of costs. State offer of judgment rules often apply to offers by either a claiming or defending party and may impose more significant sanctions for the rejection of an offer. Under the New Jersey offer of judgment rule, for example, an offer of judgment may be made to either accept a specified monetary judgment in the offeror's favor or to allow such a judgment to be taken against the offeror. If the offer is not accepted and the resulting judgment is either 120% or more of the claimant's offer or 80% or less of the defending party's offer, mandatory sanctions are imposed, which, in addition to costs of suit, include all reasonable litigation expenses and attorney's fees following rejection of the offer. *See* N.J. Ct. R. 4:58.

Section F. Alternative Dispute Resolution

Alternative dispute resolution ("ADR") has caught the attention of policy makers and the public as an efficient and effective means of disposing of legal disputes. Courts have experimented with various forms of ADR for several years. In addition, the Civil Justice Reform Act of 1990, 28 U.S.C. § 1, required every federal district court to develop a "civil justice expense and delay reduction plan." The Act suggested six specific methods for this purpose, including three ADR methods: mediation, mini-trial, and summary jury trial. This section explores these and other ADR methods, with a particular emphasis on when the parties to litigation can be forced to participate in them.

1. Arbitration

Noton EXAM

As explained in Chapter 1, arbitration is the most formalized alternative to litigation of a dispute in court. In arbitration, the disputing parties present their "case" to a neutral third person or persons who are empowered to render a decision. Arbitration may result from a contractual agreement in which the parties have agreed to arbitrate future disputes or, after a dispute has arisen, from an ad hoc agreement to arbitrate in lieu of formal judicial proceedings. Arbitration may also result from a court rule or statute that requires arbitration of certain disputes.

Arbitration Agreements. As noted above, arbitration may result from a private contractual agreement between the parties and this is the most common form of arbitration. Either before or after a controversy arises, the parties may voluntarily agree to submit their dispute to arbitration. Arbitration agreements are fully enforceable, like other contracts, in accordance with their terms. If a party refuses to submit the case to arbitration, the aggrieved party may seek a court order compelling arbitration. When the underlying transaction between the parties giving rise to the dispute involves interstate commerce, the arbitration agreement is governed by the Federal Arbitration Act ("FAA"), 9 U.S.C. §§ 1–16. When interstate commerce is not involved, state arbitration acts, which are typically patterned after the FAA, govern the arbitration process.

The purpose of the FAA, and state acts patterned after it, is to ensure that arbitration can function as an effective and efficient method of dispute resolution. Under the FAA, arbitrators are given the power to summon witnesses in the same manner that a judge would have under the court's subpoena power. Following the decision of the arbitrator, either party may seek to have the arbitrator's award confirmed by the court. Once confirmed, the arbitrator's award is docketed as a judgment and given "the same force and effect, in all respects ... as if it had been rendered in an action in the court in which it is entered." *See* 9 U.S.C. § 13. Unlike a judgment by a trial court, however, an arbitrator's award is subject to very limited judicial review. Under the FAA, an award may be vacated or modified by the court only for specified reasons, such as that the award was "procured by corruption, fraud, or undue means," the arbitrator was "guilty of misconduct," or the arbitrator "exceeded" the scope of the authority granted by the parties in deciding matters not within the arbitration agreement. *See* 9 U.S.C. § 10-11.

Despite the limited judicial review, private arbitration is an accepted and widespread method of dispute resolution in the United States. Arbitration is particularly favored over court litigation in transactions involving international commerce. Unlike U.S. court judgments, arbitration awards are internationally recognized and enforceable under the United Nations Convention on the Recognition and Enforcement of Foreign Arbitral Awards. Under this convention, 146 participating countries, including the United States, agree to recognize and enforce the domestic arbitration awards of the other participating nations, subject to very limited defenses.

Arbitration Proceedings and Hearings. Arbitration proceedings can be flexible and varied depending on the circumstances of the case and the agreement of the parties. In an appropriate case, the parties may agree to an arbitration based entirely on submitted documents and other materials without a hearing. Normally, however, an arbitration hearing is held and resembles an informal nonjury trial. Witnesses testify under direct and cross-examination, documents and other exhibits are submitted, and the parties argue their positions to the arbitrator. After each side has presented its evidence and arguments, the arbitrator renders an award.

Court-Annexed Arbitration. In "court-annexed" arbitration, a court assigns selected cases to arbitration as a precondition to or substitute for trial. Unlike the arbitration process described above, which is the result of the private agreement of the parties, "court-annexed" arbitration programs are established through an applicable court rule or statute. In such programs, court personnel screen cases at the close of the pleading stage to determine whether they fall within the preselected criteria for arbitration. In jurisdictions that do not have an automatic assignment system, the parties have the opportunity to request that the case be assigned to arbitration at this time. If the case is appropriate for diversion, the court clerk will notify the parties, who will have an opportunity to object. The courts establish the arbitrators' qualifications, and, depending on the jurisdiction, the parties are allowed to select from a list of certified arbitrators, or an arbitrator is simply appointed by the court.

Once an arbitrator has been selected, a hearing is held. Although some procedures may vary, "court-annexed" arbitration hearings are similar to the private arbitration hearings described above. After each side has presented its evidence and arguments, the arbitrator submits an "award" to the court. If neither party rejects the award and demands a trial de novo with the court, the court enters the award as the judgment in the action, which becomes a fully enforceable order.

Penalties for Failing to Improve on the Result in Court-Annexed Arbitration. An early leading case involving a challenge to court-annexed arbitration is *Kimbrough v. Holiday Inn*, 478 F. Supp. 566 (E.D. Pa. 1979). In *Kimbrough*, the plaintiffs, husband and wife, brought a diversity action for personal injuries allegedly suffered by the wife during an assault when she was a business visitor at the defendants' hotel. The defendants demanded a jury trial as permitted by Federal Rule 38(b). Pursuant to an experimental local rule, however, the case was referred to compulsory, nonbinding arbitration because it met certain preselected criteria. The defendants moved to prohibit the arbitration and to vacate the order of referral. Under this experimental scheme, a "penalty" was imposed to discourage "frivolous" appeals, *i.e.*, when a party demanded a trial de novo after arbitration but then failed to obtain a more favorable judgment (exclusive of interest and costs). The local rule imposed on such a party the amount of the arbitration fees; it also imposed upon the defendant interest on the award from the time it was filed if the defendant sought the trial de novo. *Id.* at 567.

In *Kimbrough*, the defendants' challenges centered on two principal grounds: by making arbitration a mandatory prerequisite to jury trial, the defendants argued that the local rule violated the parties right to a trial by jury because it imposed a "burdensome, onerous condition." In addition, the defendants argued that the local rule was an inappropriate type of rulemaking that was inconsistent with the Federal Rules of Civil Procedure. *Id.* The court rejected the jury trial challenge because arbitration is a useful tool to promote greater efficiency in litigation and that pretrial review in no way infringes upon constitutional rights of litigants. The court explained:

> ... [A]rbitration provides a valuable service by promoting speedy and inexpensive dispute resolution. Litigants have the opportunity to test the validity of their claims very shortly after they are filed. Certainly, this limits the time and expense of discovery prior to arbitration. In the normal course of trial without arbitration, voluminous resources can be expended in discovery which is of marginal advantage at trial. The pendency of arbitration forces counsel to focus their attention on the basic elements of the case. Aside from the ultimate award, if arbitration reveals that no claim exists, settlement will become a viable possibil-

ity. At the very least, arbitration helps counsel streamline their case and direct their additional discovery in profitable areas.

Id. at 571.

The court also found no inconsistency with the literal language of any Federal Rule or statute (the Rules Enabling Act) nor with the spirit of any specific rule or local rulemaking generally. *Id.* at 572–77.

Note and Questions

Most court-annexed ADR programs, like the program in *Kimbrough*, require that the party demanding a trial de novo improve the party's position or suffer a "penalty" of some sort. Such penalties are designed to serve as disincentives to demanding a trial de novo. Recall that in *Kimbrough*, the penalty was (a) the amount of the arbitration fees and (b) if the party was the defendant, interest on the arbitration award from the date when it was filed. What other kinds of penalties do you think could be imposed? For example, do you think it would be appropriate to require a party who fails to improve the award to pay the prevailing party's attorney's fees incurred subsequent to the arbitration award?

2. Mediation

Mediation is another method of alternative dispute resolution that is increasing in popularity. As discussed in Chapter 1, the role of the mediator is to facilitate the parties in reaching a settlement. The mediator has no authoritative decision-making power, which sharply contracts with the power of a judge, "who is designated by law or contract to make a decision for the parties based on societal norms, laws or contracts rather than the specific interests or personal concepts of justice held by the parties." *Department of Transp. v. City of Atlanta*, 380 S.E.2d 265, 268 (Ga. 1989). In contrast, the mediator works to reconcile the competing interests of the two parties. The mediator's goal is to assist the parties in examining the future and their interests or needs as well as negotiating an exchange of promises and relationships that will be mutually satisfactory and meet their standards of fairness. *Id.*

Court-Annexed Mediation. Like arbitration and other ADR processes, mediation may be "annexed" to a court proceeding. In an early leading case upholding the authority of the courts to order parties to participate in the mediation process during the course of litigation, the Georgia Supreme Court extolled the value of court-annexed mediation:

> A great service a court may provide for litigants is a referral to mediation. There are times when parties have reached a standstill in settlement negotiations such that for either party to suggest mediation is to perhaps admit a weakness or at least suggest he is willing to yield further. At this point a referral to mediation by the court may secretly be welcomed by both sides. Then too, it may be that the parties are simply unaware of the benefit which may flow from mediation and a referral by a court may serve to introduce them to the process. In any event the court should simply make the referral and leave it to the parties from that point. The court may not order them to resolve their differences in mediation nor to yield on any matter they choose not to yield.... [However, [i]t

ON EXAM

[should] be done in a way not to interfere with nor delay the right of the parties to litigate the issues.

Id. at 267.

Hybrid Processes. In addition to pure mediation and arbitration, various "hybrid" alternative dispute resolution processes are possible. For example, in the traditional "med-arb" process, the same person serves as both a mediator and an arbitrator in the dispute. It is regarded as more efficient than pure mediation followed by arbitration with a different person if mediation does not yield a settlement of the dispute.

Notes and Questions

1. Court-annexed mediation involves problems similar to those discussed in the preceding subsection. For example, in a court-annexed mediation, one of the parties may physically appear at the mediation session, but may refuse to participate in good faith. Do you think it would be appropriate for a court to sanction such a party in such circumstances?

2. Can you think of any drawbacks to widespread use of court-annexed mediation? For example, could the process be used as a fishing expedition or simply as a delaying tactic? Could it be unfair to certain types of parties?

3. Summary Jury Trial

Another innovative method of alternative dispute resolution is the summary jury trial. This procedure was pioneered by U.S. District Court Judge Thomas Lambros in the Northern District of Ohio. A summary jury trial usually occurs after discovery has been substantially completed and pending motions have been resolved. The process itself simulates an actual but abbreviated trial from voir dire through jury instruction to a verdict. A summary jury trial is a non-binding proceeding designed to give the attorneys and their clients an indication of what they may expect at a full-blown trial on the merits. The parties exchange evidence before the summary jury trial has commenced and are limited to the evidence thus disclosed. A jury is selected from the regular jury pool. The parties then present opening statements, summarize the evidence that would be presented at a full trial (no live testimony is permitted), and present closing statements. The jury is then charged with the law and asked to respond to a series of interrogatories concerning liability and damages. After the summary jury trial, the parties have an opportunity to debrief the jurors and conduct settlement discussions in light of the jury's verdict.

Mandatory Participation in Summary Jury Trials. Judge Lambros relied on Federal Rule 16 for the authority to convene a summary jury trial. *See generally* Thomas D. Lambros, *Summary Jury Trial—An Alternative Method of Resolving Disputes*, 69 JUDICATURE 286 (1986); Thomas D. Lambros, *The Summary Jury Trial and Other Alternative Methods of Dispute Resolution*, 103 F.R.D. 461 (1984). The summary jury trial was endorsed in the Civil Justice Reform Act of 1990, although its use was not specifically mandated.

In *In re NLO, Inc.*, 5 F.3d 154 (6th Cir. 1993), the trial court had ordered all parties to participate in a summary jury trial, which would be open to the media and the public. This order was enforceable by sanctions against counsel for anything less than full participation. The defendant in the action sought a writ of mandamus to vacate the district court's order. The Sixth Circuit granted the petition and issued the writ vacating the trial court's order. The Sixth Circuit refused to allow forced participation in a summary jury trial pursuant to Federal Rule 16(a) and also rejected the argument that the court has inherent power to force the parties to participate. *Id.* at 157–59.

Notes and Questions

1. What benefits do you see from a summary jury trial procedure? Can you formulate any criticisms of the procedure?

2. The summary jury trial in the *NLO* case was to be open to the media and the public. Do you think that the First Amendment right of access should apply to summary jury trials?

4. Early Neutral Evaluation

Another alternative dispute resolution program in the courts is court-annexed early neutral evaluation. Early neutral evaluation provides the litigants with a neutral evaluation of the case early in the lawsuit. The evaluation is provided by a private lawyer who is experienced in the substantive area of law involved in the case. The first such program was conducted in 1985 in the Northern District of California. It became a permanent program in that district in 1988 and has spread to other jurisdictions.

5. Mini-Trial

Another innovative alternative dispute resolution procedure is the "mini-trial." This procedure blends case presentation, negotiation, and mediation. Mini-trials are initiated by an agreement of the parties. Usually, the agreement requires the selection of a neutral advisor, such as a lawyer or retired judge.

Mini-trials generally involve three phases. (1) During the discovery phase, the parties typically exchange introductory statements, key exhibits, and summaries of testimony. (2) Then a one-day hearing is held in which each side's lawyers present a summary of their "best cases" to persons from each side's organizations, usually senior executives with full settlement authority. During the hearing phase, the neutral advisor may ask questions, make comments on the evidence or arguments, and predict the probable outcome of the case. (3) In the post-hearing phase, the representatives on the mini-trial panel discuss settlement. The neutral advisor may serve as a mediator during these discussions.

NOT ON EXAM

Chapter 10

Trial

If none of the methods previously examined in Chapters 6 and 9 (motions to dismiss, summary judgment, etc.) have resulted in disposition of the action without trial, the case must be set for trial to determine the disputed factual issues and to enter final judgment. This chapter examines the various constitutional and procedural issues related to the trial process, including the right to a trial by jury. This is not a chapter on trial advocacy, however. Trial advocacy, including methods of trial preparation not dealt with in Chapter 8 (discovery) and trial tactics, are reserved for courses on trial practice and pretrial litigation. Section A of this chapter deals with the selection of the trier, judge or jury, while Section B is devoted to various procedural issues and rules related to the trial process and the entry of final judgment.

Section A. Selecting the Trier of Fact

1. Trial by Jury or by the Court

In the American legal system, trials are held to determine disputed issues of fact. As examined in Chapter 9, if no genuine issue of material fact exists in an action, the case will most likely be resolved on a motion for summary judgment under Federal Rule 56. When disputed factual issues exist, however, the case must be tried. Sometimes the trier of fact will be the judge and sometimes a jury. When the case is tried by the court, the trial is called a "bench" trial. In a bench trial, the judge hears the testimony and then issues specific findings of fact and conclusions of law. Judgment is then entered for the prevailing party. *See, e.g.,* FED. R. CIV. P. 52(a)(1).

When the case is tried to a jury, both the judge and the jury are essential players in the trial process. The traditional allocation of decisionmaking authority between the judge and the jury is that the jury decides questions of fact and questions involving the application of law to fact and the judge decides questions of law. For example, in a products liability action, the jury would decide whether the defendant manufactured a particular product (question of fact) and whether the product was unreasonably dangerous under the applicable law (question of application of law to fact). The judge would preside over the trial and decide all questions of law, which would include matters such as ruling on evidentiary objections and instructing the jury on the applicable law.

At the conclusion of the trial, the jury would deliberate in secret and render a *verdict* in the case. The jury verdict is not a *judgment*. After a jury verdict, judgment must be formally entered in the case. Under rules such as Federal Rule 58(b), the clerk, unless the court orders otherwise, enters final judgment based upon the jury's verdict. As will be explained in Chapter 11, jury verdicts are entitled to great deference and are only over-turned by trial and appellate courts when the jury's verdict is seriously flawed.

As discussed in the following subsection, the right to a jury trial generally exists when the plaintiff seeks legal relief, typically money damages, and is not available when the plaintiff seeks only equitable relief, such as an injunction. Even when the right to a jury trial exists, however, the right may be waived by the parties. Thus, in cases in which the right to a jury trial exists, the parties must decide whether a trial by the judge or jury would be preferable. This decision depends upon a number of factors, including the lawyer's knowledge of the trial judge's propensities, the kind of case being tried, the nature of the jury pool from which the individual panel will be drawn, and other factors.

Some attorneys consider the trier of fact, either judge or jury, as critical in the ultimate outcome of the case. How the credibility of various witnesses and the persuasiveness of various positions are viewed can often be a matter of individual perspective, which may differ from a seasoned judge to an average citizen selected only for the particular case. Attorneys frequently make assumptions about the propensity of juries and judges to find for one side or the other in particular cases. Whether these assumptions can be empiri-cally supported, however, is open to question. One study of federal trials over a ten-year period found that plaintiffs won considerably more often before judges than juries in products liability and medical malpractice trials. *See* Kevin M. Clermont & Theodore Eisenberg, *Trial by Jury or Judge: Transcending Empiricism*, 77 CORNELL L. REV. 1124 (1992).

2. The Right to a Trial by Jury in Civil Cases

(a) Introduction

Chapter 1 examined the historical origins of the right to a jury trial in Anglo-American jurisprudence. There, we saw that the constitutional right to trial by jury in American law is generally determined by referring to those cases in which a trial by jury was af-forded in the common-law courts in England. The right to a trial by jury has often been described in glowing terms. Blackstone described it as "the glory of English law." *See* 3 WILLIAM BLACKSTONE, COMMENTARIES ON THE LAWS OF ENGLAND *379 (Chitty ed. 1826). The U.S. Supreme Court has also praised the jury's ability to achieve just results:

> Twelve men of the average of the community, comprising men of education and men of little education, men of learning and men whose learning consists only in what they have themselves seen and heard, the merchant, the mechanic, the farmer, the laborer; these sit together, consult, apply their separate experience of the affairs of life to the facts proven, and draw a unanimous conclusion. This average judgment thus given it is the great effort of the law to obtain. It is assumed that twelve men know more of the common affairs of life than does one man, that they can draw wiser and safer conclusions from admitted facts thus occur-ring than can a single judge.

Railroad Co. v. Stout, 84 U.S. (17 Wall.) 657, 664 (1874).

Nevertheless, the utility of the jury in civil cases has been a continual source of de-bate. For many years, commentators have argued that juries are incompetent fact find-ers, anachronistic, and unnecessarily extend the time required for trial. *See, e.g.*, Fleming James, Jr., *Trial by Jury and the New Federal Rules of Civil Procedure*, 45 YALE L.J. 1022, 1026 (1936); David W. Peck, *Do Juries Delay Justice?* 18 F.R.D. 455 (1956). A number of reforms in the jury system have also been proposed, including raising the fees for parties who demand jury trials, streamlining jury trials with a variety of procedural reforms, restructuring the jury by altering its size or composition, and constraining jury discretion in a variety of ways, such as by use of special verdict forms. *See* Symposium: *The American Civil Jury: Illusion and Reality*, 48 DePaul L. Rev. 197 (1998). The viability of trial by jury has also been caught up in recent criticism of the tort liability systems, which have generated large damage awards in cases considered to be of marginal, if any, merit by large segments of the public. This has resulted in suggestions for reform, such as "damage caps," which would limit the jury's power to render excessive verdicts.

(b) Sources of the Right to a Trial by Jury: Constitutional and Statutory

In the federal courts, the main source of the right to a jury trial in civil cases is the Seventh Amendment to the U.S. Constitution, which guarantees the right to a trial by jury in certain civil actions. The Seventh Amendment provides that "[i]n suits at common law, where the value in controversy shall exceed twenty dollars, the right of trial by jury shall be preserved...." Unlike the Sixth Amendment, which expressly grants to a *criminal* defendant the right to a jury trial in "all criminal prosecutions," the Seventh Amendment does not create a right to trial by jury, but merely "preserves" the right as it existed at common law. At common law, a right to a jury trial generally existed for actions cognizable in the English "law" courts, *i.e.*, "legal" actions, but no right existed for actions brought in the English "equity" courts, *i.e.*, "equitable" actions. As you will see in the following sections, determining when a constitutional right to a trial by jury is available under the Seventh Amendment is often difficult because in modern procedural systems, the separate common-law systems of law and equity have been "merged." This means that a single court can now provide remedies that previously would have been available only from different courts in the common-law system of separate law and equity tribunals.

While preserving a constitutional right to a trial by jury, the Seventh Amendment is not interpreted as the exclusive source of the right to a jury trial. Although Congress cannot restrict jury trial rights otherwise permitted at common law, Congress has the authority to confer a right to a trial by jury by statute. Thus, in enacting a statute creating a substantive cause of action, Congress may provide for a statutory right to a trial by jury. In creating a statutory right to a jury trial, Congress may confer such a right irrespective of whether a right to a jury trial would otherwise exist under the Seventh Amendment and may grant greater jury trial rights than preserved under the Constitution. Consistent with these principles, Federal Rule 38(a) accordingly provides that "[t]he right of trial by jury as declared by the Seventh Amendment to the Constitution—or as provided by a federal statute—is preserved to the parties inviolate."

(c) The Right to a Trial by Jury Under the Seventh Amendment: General Principles

Although Congress has the power to confer a statutory right to a trial by jury, most statutes creating a cause of action are silent as to whether a right to a trial by jury is provided. In most cases, therefore, whether the substantive cause of action is based on statutory or common-law authority, the right to a trial by jury in federal court is determined according to the principles of the Seventh Amendment. In addition, the Seventh Amendment applies to claims asserted in a federal court action, irrespective of whether the claim is a purely state law claim brought under diversity or supplemental jurisdiction or a federal law claim brought under federal question or some other jurisdictional statute. *See Simler v. Conner*, 372 U.S. 221 (1963). The proper interpretation of the Seventh Amendment's right to a trial by jury, however, has been a source of difficulty for the courts.

The difficulty stems from the fact that the right to a jury trial under Seventh Amendment is linked to the existence of such a right under the English common-law system in 1791, the date the Seventh Amendment was ratified by the original states. Not only does such a historical analysis present a significant challenge for modern jurists and lawyers largely unfamiliar with common-law practice, but a question also arises whether the Seventh Amendment right to a jury trial is frozen in time as it existed in 1791 or whether the constitutional right may be interpreted more flexibly today in light of the many advances that have been adopted in modern procedural systems since 1791.

As explained in Chapter 1, the English common-law system was based on a dual court system, containing "law" and "equity" courts. The "law" courts adjudicated claims based on the common-law "forms of action" (trespass, covenant, account, etc.) and the relief provided, typically money damages, was known as "legal" relief. The "equity" courts developed separately from the "law" courts to provide justice when "the remedy at law was inadequate." The relief provided by the "equity" courts became known as "equitable" relief. Coercive remedies such as injunctions and decrees of specific performance are classic examples of equitable relief. The "law" courts allowed for trial by jury (if the appropriate form of action were chosen), but the "equity" courts did not because the plea for the special justice of "equity" was addressed directly to the Chancellor, as the representative of the King.

The complication in applying these common-law standards for purposes of the Seventh Amendment is that many of the ancient distinctions between law and equity are no longer followed in modern procedural systems. The common-law forms of action have been abolished under modern pleading rules, and many new rights and remedies are now recognized in American jurisprudence that were unknown at common law. In addition, the line of demarcation between "law" and "equity" at common law had blurred by 1791 with both systems "borrowing" from each other. *See* FLEMING JAMES, JR. ET AL., CIVIL PROCEDURE § 8.2, at 495 (5th ed. 2001) ("[A]s of 1791, there was no clear division of jurisdiction between law and equity. There were types of suits that once had been maintainable in equity but no longer could be; also, certain types of claims formerly maintainable in equity came to be maintainable also through common-law forms of action").

Most importantly, though, in modern procedural systems, the separate common-law court systems of "law" and "equity" have now been "merged" into a single court system. Liberal joinder rules now allow parties to join both legal and equitable claims in a single action. Because it is now procedurally permissible for parties to freely join legal and equitable claims, counterclaims, cross-claims, and third-party claims in a single action, the question becomes, how should such "mixed" cases be evaluated for purposes of constitutional provisions "preserving" the right to trial by jury. Is the right to a trial by jury determined with respect to an entire action or may it apply to particular claims or issues determined to be "legal"? Further, to what extent may the court consider modern procedural advances in determining whether the remedy sought is "legal"?

Despite these difficulties, the starting point for analysis under the Seventh Amendment continues to be linked to the common-law distinctions of law and equity. As explained by the Supreme Court in *Tull v. United States*, 481 U.S. 412 (1987),

> [t]he Court has construed [the Seventh Amendment] to require a jury trial on the merits in those actions that are analogous to "Suits at common law." Prior to

the Amendment's adoption, a jury trial was customary in suits brought in the English *law* courts. In contrast, those actions that are analogous to 18th-century cases tried in courts of equity or admiralty do not require a jury trial.... This analysis applies not only to common-law forms of action, but also to causes of action created by congressional enactment....

To determine whether a statutory action is more similar to cases that were tried in courts of law than to suits tried in courts of equity or admiralty, the Court must examine both the nature of the action and of the remedy sought. First, we compare the statutory action to 18th-century actions brought in the courts of England prior to the merger of the courts of law and equity.... Second, we examine the remedy sought and determine whether it is legal or equitable in nature....

Id. at 417–18.

In determining whether a right to a jury trial exists, however, the Supreme Court has also made clear that the Seventh Amendment should not be interpreted in a purely "historical" context, but must be interpreted flexibly in light of the many procedural advances resulting from the merger of law and equity in modern American jurisprudence. Historically, equity jurisdiction existed only when the remedy at law was inadequate. Because the adequacy of legal remedies has expanded as a result of modern procedural developments, a right to a jury trial may now exist in actions that historically would have been decided without a jury in a court of equity.

Throughout this chapter, this modified historical approach of the federal courts is referred to as the "modern federal approach" to distinguish it from the strict historical approach which is followed by many states. This latter approach is referred to as the "pure historical approach." Under the "pure historical approach," the right to a jury trial is determined solely by trying to determine whether the issues historically would have been tried in a court of law or equity. The distinction between these two approaches is important because, as will be explained in subsection (e), the right to a jury trial under the Seventh Amendment only applies in federal court actions and the states are free to develop their own approaches with respect to the right to a jury trial in state court proceedings.

(d) Development and Evolution of the Modern Federal Approach

The "modern federal approach" under the Seventh Amendment originated in *Beacon Theatres, Inc. v. Westover.*

Beacon Theatres, Inc. v. Westover

United States Supreme Court 1959
359 U.S. 500, 79 S. Ct. 948, 3 L. Ed. 2d 988

JUSTICE BLACK delivered the opinion of the Court.

Petitioner, Beacon Theatres, Inc., sought by mandamus to require a district judge in the Southern District of California to vacate certain orders alleged to deprive it of a jury trial of issues arising in a suit brought against it by Fox West Coast Theatres, Inc. The Court of Appeals for the Ninth Circuit refused the writ, holding that the trial judge had acted within his proper discretion in denying petitioner's request for a jury.... We granted certiorari ...

Fox had asked for declaratory relief against Beacon alleging a controversy arising under the Sherman Antitrust Act ... and under the Clayton Act, ... which authorizes suits for treble damages against Sherman Act violators. According to the complaint Fox operates a movie theatre in San Bernardino, California, and has long been exhibiting films under contracts with movie distributors. These contracts grant it the exclusive right to show "first run" pictures in the "San Bernardino competitive area" and provide for "clearance" — a period of time during which no other theatre can exhibit the same pictures. After building a drive-in theatre about 11 miles from San Bernardino, Beacon notified Fox that it considered contracts barring simultaneous exhibitions of first-run films in the two theatres to be overt acts in violation of the antitrust laws. Fox's complaint alleged that this notification, together with threats of treble damage suits against Fox and its distributors, gave rise to "duress and coercion" which deprived Fox of a valuable property right, the right to negotiate for exclusive first-run contracts. Unless Beacon was restrained, the complaint continued, irreparable harm would result. Accordingly, while its pleading was styled a "Complaint for Declaratory Relief," Fox prayed both for a declaration that a grant of clearance between the Fox and Beacon theatres is reasonable and not in violation of the antitrust laws, and for an injunction, pending final resolution of the litigation, to prevent Beacon from instituting any action under the antitrust laws against Fox and its distributors arising out of the controversy alleged in the complaint.[2] Beacon filed an answer, a counterclaim against Fox, and a cross-claim against an exhibitor who had intervened. They denied the threats and asserted that there was no substantial competition between the two theatres, that the clearances granted were therefore unreasonable, and that a conspiracy existed between Fox and its distributors to manipulate contracts and clearances so as to restrain trade and monopolize first-run pictures in violation of the antitrust laws. Treble damages were asked.

Beacon demanded a jury trial of the factual issues in the case as provided by Federal Rule of Civil Procedure 38(b). The District Court, however, viewed the issues raised by the "Complaint for Declaratory Relief," including the question of competition between the two theatres, as essentially equitable. Acting under the purported authority of Rules 42(b) and 57, it directed that these issues be tried to the court before jury determination of the validity of the charges of antitrust violations made in the counterclaim and cross-claim.[3] A common issue of the "Complaint for Declaratory Relief," the counterclaim, and the cross-claim was the reasonableness of the clearances granted to Fox, which depended, in part, on the existence of competition between the two theatres. Thus the effect of the action of the District Court could be, as the Court of Appeals believed, "to limit the petitioner's opportunity fully to try to a jury every issue which has a bearing upon its treble damage suit," for determination of the issue of clearances by the judge might "operate either by way of res judicata or collateral estoppel so as to conclude both parties with respect thereto at the subsequent trial of the treble damage claim." ...

The District Court's finding that the Complaint for Declaratory Relief presented basically equitable issues draws no support from the Declaratory Judgment Act, 28 U.S.C. §§ 2201, 2202; ... That statute, while allowing prospective defendants to sue to establish their nonliability, specifically preserves the right to jury trial for both parties. It follows

---

2. Other prayers aside from the general equitable plea for "such further relief as the court deems proper" added nothing material to those set out.

3. [Eds. Note. In this footnote, the Court quoted provisions of Rules 42(b) and 57. Following the 2007 restyling amendments, the relevant provision of Rule 42(b) now reads without any intended substantive change: "For convenience, to avoid prejudice, or to expedite and economize, the court may order a separate trial of one or more separate issues, claims, crossclaims, counterclaims, or third-party claims." Rule 57 now reads in relevant part: "The court may order a speedy hearing of a declaratory-judgment action."]

that if Beacon would have been entitled to a jury trial in a treble damage suit against Fox it cannot be deprived of that right merely because Fox took advantage of the availability of declaratory relief to sue Beacon first. Since the right to trial by jury applies to treble damage suits under the antitrust laws, and is, in fact, an essential part of the congressional plan for making competition rather than monopoly the rule of trade, ... the Sherman and Clayton Act issues on which Fox sought a declaration were essentially jury questions.

Nevertheless the Court of Appeals refused to upset the order of the district judge. It held that the question of whether a right to jury trial existed was to be judged by Fox's complaint read as a whole. In addition to seeking a declaratory judgment, the court said, Fox's complaint can be read as making out a valid plea for injunctive relief, thus stating a claim traditionally cognizable in equity. A party who is entitled to maintain a suit in equity for an injunction, said the court, may have all the issues in his suit determined by the judge without a jury regardless of whether legal rights are involved....

... Assuming that the pleadings can be construed to support [a request for an injunction against threats of lawsuits] and assuming additionally that the complaint can be read as alleging the kind of harassment by a multiplicity of lawsuits which would *traditionally* have justified equity to take jurisdiction and settle the case in one suit, we are nevertheless of the opinion that, under the Declaratory Judgment Act and the Federal Rules of Civil Procedure, neither claim can justify denying Beacon a trial by jury of all the issues in the antitrust controversy.

The basis of injunctive relief in the federal courts has always been irreparable harm and inadequacy of legal remedies. At least as much is required to justify a trial court in using its discretion under the Federal Rules to allow claims of equitable origins to be tried ahead of legal ones, since this has the same effect as an equitable injunction of the legal claims. And it is immaterial, in judging if that discretion is properly employed, that before the Federal Rules and the Declaratory Judgment Act were passed, courts of equity, exercising a jurisdiction separate from courts of law, were, in some cases, allowed to enjoin subsequent legal actions between the same parties involving the same controversy. This was because the subsequent legal action, though providing an opportunity to try the case to a jury, might not protect the right of the equity plaintiff to a fair and orderly adjudication of the controversy.... Under such circumstances the legal remedy could quite naturally be deemed inadequate. Inadequacy of remedy and irreparable harm are practical terms, however. As such their existence today must be determined, not by precedents decided under discarded procedures, but in the light of the remedies now made available by the Declaratory Judgment Act and the Federal Rules.

Viewed in this manner, the use of discretion by the trial court under Rule 42(b) to deprive Beacon of a full jury trial on its counterclaim and cross-claim, as well as on Fox's plea for declaratory relief, cannot be justified. Under the Federal Rules the same court may try both legal and equitable causes in the same action.... Thus any defenses, equitable or legal, Fox may have to charges of antitrust violations can be raised either in its suit for declaratory relief or in answer to Beacon's counterclaim. On proper showing, harassment by threats of other suits, or other suits actually brought, involving the issues being tried in this case, could be temporarily enjoined pending the outcome of this litigation. Whatever permanent injunctive relief Fox might be entitled to on the basis of the decision in this case could, of course, be given by the court after the jury renders its verdict. In this way the issues between these parties could be settled in one suit giving Beacon a full jury trial of every antitrust issue.... By contrast, the holding of the court below while granting Fox no additional protection unless the avoidance of jury trial be considered as such, would compel Beacon to split his antitrust case, trying part to a judge and part to a jury. Such a result, which involves the postponement and subordination of Fox's own legal claim for declaratory relief as well as of the counterclaim which Beacon was compelled by the Federal Rules to bring, is not permissible.

Our decision is consistent with the plan of the Federal Rules and the Declaratory Judgment Act to effect substantial procedural reform while retaining a distinction between jury and nonjury issues and leaving substantive rights unchanged. Since in the federal courts equity has always acted only when legal remedies were inadequate,[13] the expansion of adequate legal remedies provided by the Declaratory Judgment Act and the Federal Rules necessarily affects the scope of equity. Thus, the justification for equity's deciding legal issues once it obtains jurisdiction, and refusing to dismiss a case, merely because subsequently a legal remedy becomes available, must be re-evaluated in the light of the liberal joinder provisions of the Federal Rules which allow legal and equitable causes to be brought and resolved in one civil action. Similarly the need for, and therefore, the availability of such equitable remedies as Bills of Peace, Quia Timet and Injunction must be reconsidered in view of the existence of the Declaratory Judgment Act as well as the liberal joinder provision of the Rules. This is not only in accord with the spirit of the Rules and the Act but is required by the provision in the Rules that "[t]he right of trial by jury as declared by the Seventh Amendment to the Constitution or as given by a statute of the United States shall be preserved ... inviolate."[16]

If there should be cases where the availability of declaratory judgment or joinder in one suit of legal and equitable causes would not in all respects protect the plaintiff seeking equitable relief from irreparable harm while affording a jury trial in the legal cause, the trial court will necessarily have to use its discretion in deciding whether the legal or equitable cause should be tried first. Since the right to jury trial is a constitutional one, however, while no similar requirement protects trials by the court, that discretion is very narrowly limited and must, wherever possible, be exercised to preserve jury trial. As this Court said in *Scott v. Neely*, 140 U.S. 106, 109–10 (1891): "In the Federal courts this [jury] right cannot be dispensed with, except by the assent of the parties entitled to it; nor can it be impaired by any blending with a claim, properly cognizable at law, of a demand for equitable relief in aid of the legal action, or during its pendency." This long-standing principle of equity dictates that only under the most imperative circumstances, circumstances which in view of the flexible procedures of the Federal Rules we cannot now anticipate, can the right to a jury trial of legal issues be lost through prior determination of equitable claims.... We as have shown, this is far from being such a case.

Respondent claims mandamus is not available under the All Writs Act, 28 U.S.C. § 1651. Whatever differences of opinion there may be in other types of cases, we think the right to grant mandamus to require jury trial where it has been improperly denied is settled.

The judgment of the Court of Appeals is reversed.

---

13. *See* 36 Stat. 1163, derived from Act of Sept. 24, 1789, § 16, 1 Stat. 82. This provision ... antedates the Seventh Amendment....

16. Fed. R. Civ. P. 38(a) [Eds. Note. Following the 2007 restyling amendments, this provision now reads: "The right of trial by jury as declared by the Seventh Amendment to the Constitution — or as provided by a federal statute — is preserved to the parties inviolate"]. In delegating to the Supreme Court responsibility for drawing up rules, Congress declared that: "Such rules shall not abridge, enlarge or modify any substantive right and shall preserve the right of trial by jury as at common law and as declared by the Seventh Amendment to the Constitution." 28 U.S.C. § 2072. The Seventh Amendment reads: "In Suits at common law, where the value in controversy shall exceed twenty dollars, the right of trial by jury shall be preserved, and no fact tried by a jury, shall be otherwise reexamined in any Court of the United States, than according to the rules of the common law."

Reversed.

JUSTICE FRANKFURTER took no part in the consideration or decision of this case.

[The dissenting opinion of JUSTICE STEWART, with whom JUSTICES HARLAN and WHITTAKER concurred, is omitted.]

Notes and Questions

1. The *Beacon Theatres* case has been described as "a dramatic re-evaluation of the right to jury trial in the federal courts." 9 WRIGHT & MILLER § 2302.1, at 26. Two important principles are established in *Beacon Theatres*. First, the Court abandoned a "pure historical approach" to determining the right to a trial by jury in holding that the adequacy of legal remedies "must be determined, not by precedents decided under discarded procedures, but in the light of the remedies now made available by the Declaratory Judgment Act and the Federal Rules." Historically, equity jurisdiction existed only when the remedy at law was inadequate. The Court held that by broadening the kinds of claims that could be joined in a civil action, the Declaratory Judgment Act and the Federal Rules of Civil Procedure had increased the adequacy of legal remedies, thus correspondingly contracting the traditional scope of equity. In effect, this results in a greater availability of jury trial than before the merger of law and equity. Nevertheless, even though *Beacon Theatres* abandons a pure historical approach in determining the right to trial by jury, the approach of the case remains partly historical, in that a court determining jury trial rights is still obliged to determine as a preliminary matter whether an issue would have been triable historically in a court of law or equity.

2. The second important principle is the Court's holding that the right to a jury trial under the Seventh Amendment extends to any legal issues properly presented and cannot be defeated simply because equitable issues are also presented in the action. The Court's holding means that the "equitable clean-up doctrine," which is followed in many state courts and allows the court to decide, without a jury, legal claims that are "incidental" to a main equitable claim, is not followed under the Seventh Amendment. Thus, even if Fox had asserted a purely equitable claim, Beacon still would have been entitled to a jury trial on its antitrust counterclaim for treble damages because Beacon's claim was legal. The trial court would not have been permitted to decide the legal counterclaim without a jury as "incidental" to the equitable claim of the plaintiff. Moreover, when legal and equitable claims are asserted in the same action, all issues which are either purely legal or common to both the legal and equitable claims must be first tried to the jury. This is to avoid any problem of issue preclusion as to the legal claim if the trial court determines the equitable issues first. As the Court held, "only under the most imperative circumstances, circumstances which … we cannot now anticipate, can the right to a jury trial of legal issues be lost through the prior determination of equitable claims."

3. (a) In *Dairy Queen, Inc. v. Wood*, 369 U.S. 469 (1962), the Court reaffirmed the principle discussed in Note 2 that the "equitable clean-up doctrine" does not apply under the Seventh Amendment. In *Dairy Queen*, the plaintiffs alleged that the defendant breached a trademark licensing agreement by failing to pay the agreed amount for the use of the plaintiffs' trademark within a certain territory. The plaintiffs also alleged that after they had canceled the agreement, the defendant continued business. The plaintiffs requested temporary and permanent injunctions to restrain the defendant from any future use of the trademark, an accounting to determine the exact amount of money owed by the defendant and a judgment for that amount, and an injunction pending the accounting to

prevent the defendant from collecting any money from stores in the territory using the plaintiffs' trademark.

(b) In response, the defendant, *inter alia*, denied the breach of contract, asserted the affirmative defenses of laches and estoppel because the plaintiffs failed to raise the claim promptly and asserted violations of the federal antitrust laws. The trial court granted a motion to strike the defendant's demand for a jury trial because the action was (1) "purely equitable" or (2) even if it were not, the legal issues were "incidental" to the equitable issues. The defendant sought mandamus in the Court of Appeals for the Third Circuit to compel the judge to vacate this order. The Third Circuit denied this request without opinion. The U.S. Supreme Court granted certiorari and reversed. The Court stated:

> At the outset, we may dispose of one of the grounds upon which the trial court acted in striking the demand for trial by jury — that based upon the view that the right to trial by jury may be lost as to legal issues where those issues are characterized as "incidental" to equitable issues — for our previous decisions make it plain that no such rule may be applied in the federal courts....
>
> ....
>
> The plaintiffs' contention that this money claim is "purely equitable" is based primarily upon the fact that their complaint is cast in terms of an [equitable] "accounting," rather than in terms of an action for "debt" or "damages." But the constitutional right to trial by jury cannot be made to depend upon the choice of words used in the pleadings. The necessary prerequisite to the right to maintain a suit for an equitable accounting, like all other equitable remedies, is, as we pointed out in *Beacon Theatres*, the absence of an adequate remedy at law. Consequently, in order to maintain such a suit on a cause of action cognizable at law, as this one is, the plaintiff must be able to show that the "accounts between the parties" are of such a "complicated nature" that only a court of equity can satisfactorily unravel them. In view of the powers given to District Courts by Federal Rule of Civil Procedure 53(b) to appoint masters to assist the jury in those exceptional cases where the legal issues are too complicated for the jury adequately to handle alone, the burden of such a showing is considerably increased and it will indeed be a rare case in which it can be met. But be that as it may, this is certainly not such a case. A jury, under proper instructions from the court, could readily determine the recovery, if any, to be had here, whether the theory finally settled upon is that of breach of contract, that of trademark infringement, or any combination of the two. The legal remedy cannot be characterized as inadequate merely because the measure of damages may necessitate a look into [the defendant's] business records.
>
> ....
>
> We conclude therefore that the district judge erred in refusing to grant [the defendant's] demand for a trial by jury on the factual issues related to the question of whether there has been a breach of contract. Since these issues are common with those upon which [plaintiffs'] claim to equitable relief is based, the legal claims involved in the action must be determined prior to any final court determination of [the plaintiffs'] equitable claims. The Court of Appeals should have corrected the error of the district judge by granting the petition for mandamus.

Id. at 470, 478–79.

4. (a) Unlike the situations in *Beacon Theatres* and *Dairy Queen* in which the legal and equitable claims were presented in the *same* action, another difficult, but separate, question is whether the right to a jury trial can be affected if the legal and equitable claims are filed in *separate* actions and the equitable action is tried first. Because the first action would be purely equitable, no right to a jury trial would exist, but a right to a jury trial would exist in the second action on the legal claim. The problem in these situations is the danger that jury trial rights on the legal claim will be lost in the second action through the doctrine of *issue preclusion*. The doctrine of issue preclusion, which is examined in depth in Chapter 12, precludes a party who has fully and fairly litigated an issue in an initial action from relitigating the same issue in a subsequent action. When the initial action is brought on an equitable claim and a subsequent action is brought on a legal claim, the normal rules of issue preclusion would preclude the losing party from relitigating in the subsequent legal action the same issues that were fully and fairly litigated in the equitable proceeding. The practical result is that the party does not get a trial by jury on the issues that would have been afforded such a right if the legal claim had been litigated first.

(b) It is important to emphasize that this example of issue preclusion in a *subsequent* action is distinct from the Supreme Court's rule in *Beacon Theatres* that "only under the most imperative circumstances ... can the right to a jury trial of legal issues be lost through the prior determination of equitable claims." The *Beacon Theatres* rule applies when both the legal and equitable claims are asserted in the *same* proceeding and when this occurs, the legal issues must be first tried to a jury before the equitable issues are decided.

(c) An illustration of the problem of issue preclusion in a *subsequent* action is *Parklane Hosiery Co. v. Shore*, 439 U.S. 322 (1979). In this case, Shore sued Parklane in a class action to recover money damages for misleading statements made by Parklane. In a separate equitable action, the Securities and Exchange Commission also sued Parklane to enjoin the same misleading statements. In the SEC action, the court found that the statements were indeed misleading and granted the injunction against Parklane. Based on the court's finding in the SEC action, Shore moved for partial summary judgment in the class action for damages arguing that the doctrine of issue preclusion established that the statements were misleading. Parklane contended that applying issue preclusion in the class action would deprive it of its Seventh Amendment right to a jury trial in that action. The Supreme Court rejected this contention, holding that issue preclusion applied and did not deprive Parklane of its Seventh Amendment rights. The state courts are divided on the *Parklane* rule, though it applies in full force in federal court actions.

Parklane

5. (a) Another difficult question is whether the Seventh Amendment applies to the many new substantive causes of action, unknown at common law, that have been created by congressional statute since the ratification of the Seventh Amendment in 1791. As explained in subsection (b), above, Congress has the power, in creating a substantive cause of action, to confer a *statutory* right to a jury trial, irrespective of whether a right to a jury trial would otherwise exist under the Seventh Amendment. But what if Congress creates a substantive cause of action and the statute, as is most common, is silent as to whether a statutory right to a jury trial exists? Does the Seventh Amendment's guarantee of a constitutional right to a jury trial "[i]n suits at common law" apply in the same manner to these statutory claims?

(b) In *Tull v. United States*, 481 U.S. 412 (1987), the Supreme Court held that the Seventh Amendment right to a jury trial "applies not only to common-law forms of action, but also to causes of action created by congressional enactment." Even though a statutory cause of action may not have existed at the time the Seventh Amendment was ratified in 1791, a constitutional right to a jury trial, nevertheless, exists in statutory actions that are analogous to common law actions ordinarily decided in the English "law" courts in the late eighteenth century. The Court indicated that a two-step analysis must be conducted in determining the right to a jury trial in this statutory context: "First, we compare the statutory action to 18th-century actions brought in the courts of England prior to the merger of the courts of law and equity.... Second, we examine the remedy sought and determine whether it is legal or equitable in nature...." *Id.* at 417–18.

(c) In *Tull*, the government sought injunctive relief and civil penalties against a real estate developer for allegedly violating the federal Clean Water Act. The Court held that the government's claim for civil penalties under the Clean Water Act was analogous to a legal claim for a civil penalty at common law and thus entitled the developer to a right to a jury trial under the Seventh Amendment on the issue of liability. The Court held, however, that the determination of the amount of the penalty, which Congress in the Clean Water Act assigned to the court, was not a "fundamental element of a jury trial" and could properly be determined by the trial judge. As the Court held:

> Congress' assignment of the determination of the amount of civil penalties to trial judges therefore does not infringe on the constitutional right to a jury trial. Since Congress itself may fix the civil penalties, it may delegate that determination to trial judges. In this case, highly discretionary calculations that take into account multiple factors are necessary in order to set civil penalties under the Clean Water Act. These are the kinds of calculations traditionally performed by judges.... We therefore hold that a determination of a civil penalty is not an essential function of a jury trial, and that the Seventh Amendment does not require a jury trial for that purpose in a civil action.

Id. at 426–27.

6. (a) Since *Tull*, the Supreme Court has addressed the issue of statutory causes of action in several other cases. In *City of Monterey v. Del Monte Dunes Ltd.*, 526 U.S. 687 (1999), the plaintiff sued under a federal civil rights statute, 42 U.S.C. § 1983, to obtain compensation from the city for a regulatory taking of property without just compensation. The Supreme Court held that the Seventh Amendment right to jury trial applied on the issue of the plaintiff's regulatory takings claim. The Court reasoned that a suit for just compensation is a compensatory remedy, like ordinary money damages, and is legal in nature. Thus, because the plaintiff's suit sounded in tort and sought legal relief, it was an action at law to which the Seventh Amendment applied, even though there was no equivalent to § 1983 framed in specific terms for "vindicating constitutional rights" at the time the Seventh Amendment was ratified.

(b) Similarly, in *Feltner v. Columbia Pictures Television, Inc.*, 523 U.S. 340 (1998), the plaintiff exercised his right to recover statutory damages under § 504 of the Federal Copyright Act instead of actual damages. The district court denied the defendants' request for a jury trial and ultimately awarded plaintiff $8,800,000. The Supreme Court held that the Seventh Amendment guaranteed the defendants a right to a jury trial under the circumstances. The Court found that before the Seventh Amendment, damage actions for copyright infringement were tried in courts of law before juries. *Tull* was distinguished on the grounds that there was no indication in *Tull* that juries had historically determined the amount of civil penalties to be paid to the government and because an award of civil penalties could be viewed as analogous to sentencing in a criminal proceeding.

(c) Finally, in *Chauffeurs, Teamsters & Helpers, Local No. 391 v. Terry*, 494 U.S. 558 (1990), union members brought an action for back pay and damages alleging that the union breached a duty of fair representation. The Court held that the plaintiff's action was analogous to an 18th-century equitable action by a trust beneficiary against a trustee for breach of fiduciary duty and also analogous to a traditional (legal) breach of contract action, because the employees had to prove both that the employer breached the collective bargaining agreement and that the union breached its duty of fair representation to recover. The Court then analyzed the remedy requested, which it had previously stated was the most important element in the Seventh Amendment inquiry. The Court held that the remedy was purely legal because the employees were seeking compensatory money damages rather than a "restitutionary" award, which would be equitable. Thus, a right to jury trial existed under the Seventh Amendment.

7. What if Congress creates a statutory cause of action but provides that the enforcement of the statutory right is to be handled in a special administrative proceeding in a non-jury setting? Does the Seventh Amendment right to a jury trial apply to such actions? In *Atlas Roofing Co. v. Occupational Safety & Health Review Commission*, 430 U.S. 442 (1977), the Court held that the Seventh Amendment was not violated by the Occupational Safety & Heath Act of 1970 which created a new statutory duty upon employers and allowed the government to seek civil penalties for violations of the Act in an administrative proceeding.

> At least in cases in which "public rights" are being litigated—*e.g.*, cases in which the Government sues in its sovereign capacity to enforce public rights created by statutes within the power of Congress to enact—the Seventh Amendment does not prohibit Congress from assigning the fact finding function and initial adjudication to an administrative forum with which the jury would be incompatible.
>
> ....
>
> ... Congress is not required by the Seventh Amendment to choke the already crowded federal courts with new types of legislation or prevented from committing some new types of litigation to administrative agencies with special competence in the relevant field. This is the case even if the Seventh Amendment would have required a jury where the adjudication of those rights is assigned to a federal court of law instead of an administrative agency.

Id. at 450, 455.

8. When there were separate courts of law and equity, sometimes equity would not give relief until a law court had first acted. For example, if a plaintiff sought an injunction to prevent the defendant from trespassing on the plaintiff's land and the defendant raised the defense that the plaintiff did not have title to the land, the equity courts would not hear the case until the law courts had resolved the title issue. *See* FLEMING JAMES, JR. ET AL., CIVIL PROCEDURE §8.8 (5th ed. 2001). Equity would not try the title to land. Today, what would be the result of such a case under *Beacon Theatres*? *Beacon Theatres* reasoned that the Federal Rules had increased the adequacy of legal remedies by broadening the kinds of claims that could be joined in a civil action thus allowing greater availability to a jury trial than in 1791. Would it also be legitimate to reason that the merger of law and equity by the Federal Rules broadened the scope of equity to enable a single court to both try the title issue and give equity relief, so that no jury trial right exists any longer? Or would it be too great a departure from history to *deny* a jury trial on the title issue when one would have been given in 1791?

Problems

Problem 10-1. *P* and *D* enter into an insurance contract, whereby *D* agrees to insure *P's* property against casualty losses. Subsequently, the property is destroyed by fire. *P* then learns that the property has been misdescribed in the policy. *P* sues in federal court for reformation of the contract and to enforce it against *D* as reformed. Historically, the power to effect reformation exclusively resided in equity courts. Under *Beacon Theatres*, is there a right to trial by jury in this action?

Problem 10-2. Consider Federal Rule 54(c): "A default judgment must not differ in kind from, or exceed in amount, what is demanded in the pleadings. Every other final judgment should grant the relief to which each party is entitled, even if the party has not demanded that relief in its pleadings." Assume that *P* sues *D* for an injunction to prevent *D* from harassing *P* by following *P* and photographing *P*. The injunction is the only remedy *P* requests, but *P's* complaint alleges facts which, if proved at trial, will also entitle *P* to punitive damages because of *D's* past actions in harassing *P*. Based on *Beacon Theatres*, what argument, if any, could *D* make in support a demand for a jury trial in the action?

(e) Comparing the Right to a Trial by Jury in Federal and State Court

All of the cases discussed to this point have dealt with the right to a jury trial in *federal* court under the Seventh Amendment of the U.S. Constitution. Unlike some other amendments in the Bill of Rights, however, the Seventh Amendment has not been held to apply to the states and thus *only* governs the constitutional right to a trial by jury for actions adjudicated in federal court. Nearly all state constitutions, however, contain a similar provision preserving the right to trial by jury in civil cases adjudicated in state court. With regard to state constitutional guarantees, the time reference for preservation of the right to trial by jury is usually the date when the state constitutional provision was adopted. *See, e.g., Housing Fin. & Dev. Corp. v. Ferguson*, 979 P.2d 1107 (Haw. 1999) (Seventh Amendment preserves right to jury trial that existed under English common law when Amendment was adopted in 1791, while state constitution preserves the right to jury trial that existed under the common law of the state at the time the Hawaii Constitution went into effect in 1959); *State v. One 1981 Chevrolet Monte Carlo*, 728 A.2d 1259 (Me. 1999) (Maine constitution guarantees a right to jury trial in all civil cases for which such a right existed under state law in 1820).

As noted above, the Seventh Amendment does not apply to the states and the states are free to interpret their jury trial provisions differently than the U.S. Supreme Court interprets the Seventh Amendment. Although the U.S. Supreme Court cases previously reviewed in this Chapter illustrate the difficult questions presented in modern merged systems, the approach taken by the U.S. Supreme Court under the Seventh Amendment, the "modern federal approach," has not always been followed by the states in interpreting their state constitutional provisions. In determining the right to a trial by jury under state law, many state courts apply the "pure historical approach."

In most cases, where the parties seek relief that is clearly legal, such as compensatory money damages for negligence or breach of contract, or seek relief that is clearly equitable, such as an injunction or specific performance, the result under both approaches is the same. A right to a jury trial will exist as to the legal relief, but not as to the equitable relief. For some cases, however, the result will differ depending on whether the "modern federal approach" or the "pure historical approach" is followed. For example, in *Ross v. Bernhard*, 396 U.S. 531 (1970), the Supreme Court, applying the "modern federal approach," held that a right to a jury trial existed under the Seventh Amendment in a shareholders' derivative action on behalf of the corporation. At common law, such actions could only be brought in an equity court, even though money damages may have been sought. The Court held that because modern rules of procedure had removed the historical impediment to such actions being tried in a court of law, the right to a jury trial now applied because the underlying corporate claim seeking money damages for breach of contract and negligence was legal. *Id.* at 538–43.

By comparison, in *Pelfrey v. Bank of Greer*, 244 S.E.2d 315 (S.C. 1978), the South Carolina Supreme Court, applying the "pure historical approach," held that a right to a jury trial did not exist in a shareholders' derivative action under that state's constitution.

> *Ross* was brought under the Seventh Amendment to the United States Constitution, which governs the right to a trial by jury in Federal courts. This amendment has never been held applicable to the States; and this Court has interpreted Article 1, Section 14, of the South Carolina Constitution, which preserves the right of trial by jury inviolate, to mean that right of jury trial shall be preserved only in those cases in which the parties were entitled to it under the law or practice existing at the time of the adoption of the constitution [in 1868]....

> ....

> Historically, the shareholder's derivative suit has always been tried exclusively in equity. "Even where the only relief allowable is a recovery of damages the suit is nevertheless one in equity and not an action at law." ...

> ....

> Since the shareholder's derivative action has historically been considered as one exclusively in equity, a party is not entitled to a trial by jury as a matter of right. The constitutional provision (Art. 1, Section 14), that the right of jury trial shall remain inviolate, does not apply to cases within the equitable jurisdiction of the court.

244 S.E.2d at 316–17.

As explained earlier in subsection (d) in connection with the *Beacon Theatres* and *Dairy Queen* cases, another important distinction between the "modern federal approach" and the "pure historical approach" is that the common-law "equitable clean-up doctrine" is not followed in the federal courts. Under this doctrine, if an equity court properly assumed jurisdiction over an action that was "essentially equitable," the court had jurisdiction to decide, without a jury, all aspects of the entire case, including any legal claims that were deemed "incidental" to the equitable claim or claims. The Court held in *Beacon Theatres* and *Dairy Queen* that the right to a jury trial under the Seventh Amendment extends to any legal issues properly presented in an action and this right cannot be defeated simply because equitable issues are also presented or the legal issues are characterized by the court as "incidental" to the equitable issues. If legal and equitable claims are presented in the same action, all issues which are either purely legal or common to both the legal and equitable claims must be first tried to the jury.

One final point should be noted on the right to a jury trial in a state court action. As explained above, the *constitutional* right to a trial by jury under the Seventh Amendment does not apply in state court actions. However, if a federal law claim is asserted in a state court action and there is a federal *statutory* right to a trial by jury for this federal claim, this statutory right to a jury trial may be enforceable in the state court action. *See Dice v. Akron, Canton & Youngstown R.R. Co.*, 342 U.S. 359 (1952) (right to a trial by jury is "part and parcel of the remedy" afforded railroad workers under the Federal Employers' Liability Act and a jury trial must be granted under the federal Act in a state court proceeding even though no right to a jury trial exists as to all issues under state law).

(f) Right to a Trial by Jury Versus "Mere Incidents" of the Right

In *Tull v. United States*, 481 U.S. 412 (1987), discussed in subsection (d), Note 5, the Supreme Court held that the Seventh Amendment preserves the right to a jury trial, but not "mere incidents" of the right. As explained by the Court, only those "incidents" that are regarded as "fundamental elements of a jury trial" are protected by the Seventh Amendment. In accordance with this principle, the *Tull* Court held that the right to a jury trial applied to the determination of liability for a civil penalty under the federal Clean Water Act, but not to the determination of the amount of the civil penalty, because the latter function was not an "essential function of a jury trial." *Id.* at 426–27.

The Court also explored this distinction between fundamental elements of the right to a jury trial and mere incidents of the right in <u>*Colgrove v. Battin*</u>, 413 U.S. 149 (1973). In a 5–4 decision, the Court in *Colgrove* held that the Seventh Amendment was not violated by a local federal rule that provided for a jury of six persons in civil cases instead of the common-law tradition of twelve. *Id.* at 159–60. In *Williams v. Florida*, 399 U.S. 78 (1970), the Court had sustained the constitutionality under the Sixth Amendment of a state statute providing for six member juries in certain *criminal* cases. The Court, however, reserved the question of whether six member juries in civil cases were constitutional under the Seventh Amendment. In *Colgrove*, the Court addressed this issue:

> The pertinent words of the Seventh Amendment are: "In Suits at common law … the right of trial by jury shall be preserved".… On its face, this language is not directed to jury characteristics, such as size, but rather defines the kind of cases for which jury trial is preserved, namely, "suits at common law." And while it is true that "[w]e have almost no direct evidence concerning the intention of the framers of the [S]eventh [A]mendment itself," the historical setting in which the Seventh Amendment was adopted highlighted a controversy that was generated, not by concern for preservation of jury characteristics at common law, but by fear that the civil jury itself would be abolished unless protected in express words.… We can only conclude, therefore, that by referring to the "common law," the Framers of the Seventh Amendment were concerned with preserving the *right* of trial by jury in civil cases where it existed at common law, rather than the various incidents of trial by jury.…
>
> Consistently with the historical objective of the Seventh Amendment, our decisions have defined the jury right preserved in cases covered by the Amendment, as "the substance of the common-law right of trial by jury, as distinguished from mere matters of form or procedure." …
>
> Our inquiry turns, then, to whether a jury of 12 is of the substance of the common-law right of trial by jury.… In *Williams*, we rejected the notion that "the reliability of the jury as a factfinder … [is] a function of its size," … and nothing has been suggested to lead us to alter that conclusion. Accordingly, we think it cannot be said that 12 members is a substantive aspect of the right of trial by jury.
>
> ….
>
> … Thus, while we express no view as to whether any number less than six would suffice, we conclude that a jury of six satisfies the Seventh Amendment's guarantee of trial by jury in civil cases.

Colgrove, 413 U.S. at 152–60.

Consistent with *Colgrove*, Federal Rule 48 now expressly authorizes the empaneling of six member juries in all civil actions in which a right to a jury trial exists. In *Colgrove*, the Court indicated that it reached the conclusion that six-member juries are as reliable as twelve-member juries "on the basis of presently available data." *Id.* at 160 n.16. In 1995, the Advisory Committee on Civil Rules recommended that Rule 48 be amended to restore the twelve member jury, because post-*Colgrove* research increasingly demonstrated "[t]he wisdom enshrined in the twelve-member tradition." The Committee noted that twelve member juries "substantially increase the representative quality of most juries" and also enhance the "sociological and psychological dynamics of jury deliberation" because such juries are better able to recall the evidence, more likely to rise above individual prejudices, and provide a broader base of community experience. The proposed amendment, however, was rejected by the Judicial Conference.

With respect to the distinction for purposes of the Seventh Amendment between "fundamental elements" of the right to a jury trial and mere "incidents" of the right, would any of the proposed jury reforms reviewed in subsection *(a)*, violate the right to a jury trial? Recall the proposals for "damage caps," which would limit the amount of damages the jury may award in certain cases. Some scholars have suggested that such recommendations violate the right to a trial by jury under the Seventh Amendment. At least one state has held that its legislature's attempt to place a cap on punitive damages violates the state constitution's guarantee of a right to trial by jury. *See Henderson ex. rel. Hartsfield v. Alabama Power Co.*, 627 So. 2d 878 (Ala. 1993).

(g) *Right to a Trial by Jury in Complex Cases*

In *Ross v. Bernhard*, 396 U.S. 531, 538 n.10 (1970), the Supreme Court stated that the "legal" nature of an issue for purposes of the right to a trial by jury is determined by considering three factors: "first, the pre-merger custom with reference to such questions; second, the remedy sought; and, third, the practical abilities and limitations of juries." This third factor suggested that the Court might restrict the right to a jury trial in cases that are too complex for juries to resolve. Since *Ross*, however, the Supreme Court has not given any further indication that it is prepared to recognize a general "complexity exception" to the Seventh Amendment. Two important court of appeals decisions, though, have considered the issue.

In *In re United States Financial Securities Litigation*, 609 F.2d 411, 424 (9th Cir. 1979), the Ninth Circuit held that *Ross* should not be read as establishing a new test for determining when the Seventh Amendment applies. The court indicated that counsel had an obligation to present the issues in a comprehensible manner and concluded that "we do not believe any case is so overwhelmingly complex that it is beyond the abilities of a jury." *Id.* at 432.

In *In re Japanese Electronics Products Antitrust Litigation*, 631 F.2d 1069 (3d Cir. 1980), *aff'd in part and rev'd in part on other grounds following summary judgment*, 723 F.2d 238, 319 (3d Cir. 1983), *rev'd on other grounds*, 475 U.S. 574 (1986), the Third Circuit agreed with the Ninth Circuit that the Seventh Amendment guaranteed a right to trial by jury in complex cases. However, the court concluded that the Due Process Clause of the Fifth Amendment prohibits a trial by jury in an action that is too complex for a jury to decide. Although the Third Circuit recognized that no specific precedent existed for finding a due process violation in the trial of any case to a jury, the court held that "the primary value promoted by due process in fact-finding procedures is 'to minimize the risk of erroneous decisions' [and] ... [a] jury that cannot understand the evidence and the legal rules to be applied provides no reliable safeguard against erroneous decisions." 631 F.2d at 1084.

The question of the jury's ability to decide complex and technical issues can also arise in the context of determining which issues in a jury trial are questions of law for the court and which are questions of fact for the jury. As noted above, the traditional dividing line between the decisionmaking authority of the judge and jury in a jury trial is that the jury decides questions of fact and questions involving the application of law to fact and the judge decides questions of law. The jury's ability to perform certain functions can be a factor in determining the dividing line between questions of law and fact. For example, in *Markman v. Westview Instruments, Inc.*, 517 U.S. 370 (1996), the Supreme Court held that although a constitutional right to a jury trial exists in a patent infringement case, the construction of claim terms in the patent document is a task for the judge, not the jury. In so holding, the Court noted that "functional considerations" are a factor in determining who should decide an issue and considering "the relative interpretive skills of judges and juries, … judges, not juries, are the better suited to find the acquired meaning of patent terms." *Id.* at 387–91.

3. Requesting a Jury Trial: Rules 38 and 39

In cases in which a right to a trial by jury exists, the right is not automatically granted, but must be properly demanded in accordance with the procedural rules of the system in which the action is being adjudicated. Federal Rule 38 sets out the basic procedures for demanding a jury trial in the federal courts and states following the Federal Rules.

As explained in the previous section, the constitutional right to a trial by jury exists as to any legal issue in the case and may be properly demanded by any party, irrespective of whether the party is the one asserting or defending the issue for which a right to a jury trial exists. For instance, in the *Beacon Theatres* and *Dairy Queen* cases, discussed in subsection 2(d), above, it was the defendants, not the plaintiffs, who requested and were granted a jury trial on the legal issues presented in those cases. Accordingly, Rule 38(b) provides that "[o]n any issue triable of right by a jury, a party may demand a jury trial" by timely service of a proper demand. Thus, even though the plaintiff may object to a jury trial on the legal issues raised by the plaintiff's claim, the defendant may properly demand a trial by jury on these issues. Such a demand is proper because the right to a trial by jury is a constitutional one, "while no similar right protects trials by the court." *Beacon Theatres, Inc. v. Westover*, 359 U.S. 500, 510 (1959).

The procedures for the proper demand of a right to a trial by jury are examined in the following case, notes, and problems.

Burns v. Lawther
United States Court of Appeals, Eleventh Circuit, 1995
53 F.3d 1237

PER CURIAM:

Appellant Robert H. Burns is a federal prisoner. The events giving rise to this action occurred while he was housed at the Federal Correctional Institution at Talladega, Alabama (FCIT).

In the spring and summer of 1988, Appellant suffered from a medical condition known as a fistula, which occurs when an organ's swelling interferes with the operation of another organ. The fistula eventually required surgery and, according to the Appellant, caused him considerable pain from May 1988 until August 1988. Appellant's Bivens[2] claim contends that two physician's assistants at FCIT, Appellees Lawther and Torres, were deliberately indifferent to his known medical needs in violation of the Eighth Amendment. Appellant also brought a Federal Tort Claims Act[3] (FTCA) action against Appellee United States of America alleging negligence arising from the same facts and circumstances.

Appellant filed his original complaint in March 1990, but did not make a demand for jury trial at that time. The original complaint alleged only an Eighth Amendment *Bivens* violation by Appellees Lawther and Torres. In April 1990, the Magistrate Judge managing the case ordered Lawther and Torres to file a "special report" responding to the complaint. The order stated:

> The special report should address each and every allegation made by the plaintiff. If the defendants wish to do so, they may submit a special report under oath or accompanied by affidavits so that the Court may, if appropriate, consider the special report as a motion for summary judgment.... The defendants are not required to file an answer or other responsive pleading (except for the special report requested herein) until this preliminary review has been completed.

Lawther and Torres responded in June 1990, denying Appellant's allegations and submitting affidavits and records disputing Appellant's version of the facts.

In March 1991, nine months after Lawther and Torres filed their special reports, Appellant filed two amended complaints which added the FTCA claims and included a demand for jury trial. Appellees supplemented their special reports in response to [the] amended complaints. In May, the magistrate judge decided to treat the special reports as motions for summary judgment when deciding whether the case should go to trial.

In September 1991, the magistrate recommended that the action proceed to trial against Lawther and Torres on the *Bivens* claim, and against the United States under the FTCA. The district court adopted the magistrate's report and recommendation later that month. Appellees Lawther, Torres, and the United States finally answered Appellant's complaints on September 30, 1991, over six months after the first demand for jury trial was made.

The case was set for a non-jury trial over Appellant's objection. A trial before the district judge was held in June 1993. After the two-day bench trial, the district court ruled for Appellees on all claims. This appeal follows.

....

There is no dispute that Appellant's Eighth Amendment *Bivens* claim for damages is a legal dispute, entitling either party to a jury fact-finder under the Seventh Amendment.... There also is no dispute that Appellant's FTCA action against the United States does not entitle him to a jury fact-finder. 28 U.S.C. § 2402....[a] Thus, the issue to be resolved is

---

2. *Bivens v. Six Unknown Named Agents of the Fed. Bureau of Narcotics*, 403 U.S. 388 (1971).

3. *See* 28 U.S.C. §§ 1346(b), 2674.

a. [Eds. Note. Even though the plaintiff's claim against the United States under the FTCA was a negligence claim for compensatory money damages and would normally qualify as "legal" relief entitling the plaintiff to a jury trial under the Seventh Amendment, no constitutional right to a jury trial exists under the Seventh Amendment for claims asserted against the government. The rationale is that the Seventh Amendment applies only to "suits at common law" and at common law there was no right of action against the sovereign enforceable by jury trial or any other form. Following these principles, a right to a jury trial on a claim against the government only exists if a statute so provides and the Federal Tort Claims Act makes no such provision for a right to a jury trial in actions against the government.]

whether Appellant invoked his right to a jury fact-finder on his *Bivens* claim according to the Federal Rules of Civil Procedure.

. . . .

The Seventh Amendment right to a civil jury is not absolute and may be waived if the request for a jury was not timely. . . . Nevertheless, because the right to a jury trial is fundamental, "courts must indulge every reasonable presumption against waiver." . . .

38(d) The procedure for determining the timeliness of a party's jury demand is contained in Federal Rule of Civil Procedure 38[d], which states that "[a] party waives a jury trial unless its demand is properly served and filed." . . . A party makes a timely demand for jury trial:

> by: (1) serving the other parties with a written demand — which may be included in a pleading — *no later than 14 days after the last pleading directed to the issue is served*; and (2) filing the demand in accordance with Rule 5(d).

Fed. R. Civ. P. 38(b) (emphasis added).[b]

In this case, the district court found that Appellant waived his jury trial right by failing to demand a jury trial within [14] days after service of the last pleading directed to such an issue as required by Rule 38(b)(1). The district court presumably concluded that the special reports responding to Appellant's original complaint constituted the "last pleading directed to [the] issue" within the meaning of the rule. Appellant's demand for jury trial arrived nine months after the special reports and, therefore, the district court found his demand untimely.[5]

Appellant maintains that the district court erred by treating the special reports as a "pleading" within the meaning of Rule 38(b). Appellant points to Appellees' answers, filed six months after his demand for jury trial, as the last pleading. Accordingly, Appellant insists that his demand was timely within the meaning of Rule 38. Thus, the narrow question on appeal is what constitutes a "pleading" within the meaning of Rule 38.

The Federal Rules of Civil Procedure, like any statutory scheme, should be given their plain meaning. . . . In seeking the meaning of "pleading" in Rule 38, we should begin by "looking to the provisions of the whole law . . . ," and should avoid interpretations contrary to the rest of the statutory scheme. . . . In this way, "[a] provision that may seem ambiguous in isolation is often clarified by the remainder of the statutory scheme — because the same terminology is used elsewhere in a context that makes its meaning clear. . . ."

Standing alone, it would be difficult to determine what constitutes a pleading under Rule 38. Fortunately, the Rules themselves provide a clear and precise meaning of "pleadings" in Rule 7. Rule 7(a) states:

7(a)

> Pleadings. Only these pleading are allowed: (1) a complaint; (2) an answer to a complaint; (3) an answer to a counterclaim designated as a counterclaim; (4) an answer to a crossclaim; (5) a third-party complaint; (6) an answer to a third-party complaint; and (7) if the court orders one, a reply to an answer.[c]

The special reports filed in this case do not constitute pleadings within the plain meaning of Rule 7(a). . . . Under the well-settled doctrine of *inclusio unius, exclusio alterius*, the

---

b. [Eds. Note. The above quoted passages were edited to reflect the current language of Rule 38(b) and (d) following the 2007 restyling amendments and the 2009 timing amendments.]

5. Appellant's amended complaint could not revive any waived right to jury trial because it did not raise any new issues which carry a Seventh Amendment right to jury trial. . . .

c. [Eds. Note. The above quoted passage was edited to reflect the current language of Rule 7(a) following the 2007 restyling amendments.]

listing of some things implies that all things not included in the list were purposefully excluded.... More important, Rule 7 explicitly excludes everything else from its definition of pleadings.

....

We hold that the plain text of Rule 7(a) defines what constitutes a pleading for purposes of Rule 38. On remand, the district court should consider Appellees' answer to Appellant's complaint as the "last responsive pleading" and, consequently, treat Appellant's jury demand as timely filed.

....

The district court erred in finding that Appellant waived his right to a jury trial. On remand, Appellant's *Bivens* claim should be tried before a jury.

VACATED and REMANDED.

Notes and Questions

14?

1. Rule 38(b)(1) provides that the demand for a jury trial "may be included in a pleading," and it is commonplace for a party desiring a jury trial to include the demand in a pleading. Note that this was what the plaintiff did in his amended complaints in *Burns*. Suppose the defendants in *Burns* had actually served answers to the complaint, instead of special reports. Suppose further that more than ten days after the answers were served, the plaintiff amended the complaint to insert the FTCA claims into the case and demanded a jury trial on the *Bivens* claims. Would the demand for jury trial have been timely under such circumstances? *See* 9 WRIGHT ET AL. §2320, at 152–54 (noting that an "amendment does not revive a right to jury trial previously waived on the issues already framed by the original pleadings").

14

2. Rule 38(c) allows a party to demand a jury trial on only some of the issues in a case, but provides that "any other party may—within 10 days after being served with the demand or within a shorter time ordered by the court—serve a demand for a jury trial on any other or all factual issues triable by jury." If a demand is general in nature and does not specify the issues upon which the party wishes a jury trial, the request is treated as a demand for a jury trial on all issues. What if a party demands a jury trial on some issues as to which the right to trial by jury exists and others as to which it does not? *See* 9 WRIGHT ET AL. §2320, at 136–37 (demand is only effective as to issues for which a right to a jury trial exists).

3. Rule 38(d) provides that once a demand for a jury trial has been properly made, it cannot be withdrawn without the consent of all the other parties in the action. Why do you think Rule 38(d) has such a requirement?

4. Rule 38(d) further provides that the failure of a party to properly serve and file a demand for a jury trial results in a waiver by the party of a jury trial. Assume that a party entitled to a trial by jury fails to properly demand a jury trial within the time limits prescribed by Rule 38(b). Is a jury trial possible under such circumstances? Rule 39(b) provides that, notwithstanding this failure, "the court may, on motion, order a jury trial on any issue for which a jury might have been demanded." The courts, however, have expressed "a wide divergence of views" on how to exercise their discretion under Rule 39(b) and such motions are generally not treated sympathetically. *See* 9 WRIGHT ET AL. §2334, at 185, 204–06; §2321, at 168 ("[D]istrict judges have been extremely reluctant to exercise [their] discretion" under Rule 39(b)). Given the reality of overcrowded court dock-

39(b)

ets and the increased time required to try a jury case, does it surprise you that courts are reluctant to excuse a party's failure to properly demand a jury trial in accordance with Rule 38?

5. Does Rule 38(d) provide the exclusive means by which a party can waive a right to trial by jury? For example, do you think a party should be able to waive a right to trial by jury in a contract? In general, a prior contractual agreement not to seek a jury trial will be enforced, but will be strictly construed.

Problem

Problem 10-3. P sues D in a federal diversity action. P seeks $600,000 for personal injuries received in an automobile accident due to D's negligence. P's complaint does not contain a demand for a trial by jury. D's answer to the complaint denies negligence and asserts contributory negligence as a defense. In addition, D's answer contains a permissive counterclaim in which D seeks $100,000 for breach of a contract between P and D that is factually and legally unrelated to the automobile accident between the parties. D's answer also does not contain a demand for a trial by jury. P's answer to the counterclaim is served 15 days after D's answer is served on P and demands a trial of all issues raised by P's original claim and D's counterclaim in the action. Under Rule 38(b), is P's demand timely as to all issues — or only as to some of the issues — in the action?

———————

Advisory Juries. As previously explained above, a right to a trial by jury did not exist at common law in the courts of equity. Nevertheless, at common law, an equity court had the right to empanel an "advisory jury" to assist the court in deciding the case. Rule 39(c)(1) preserves this practice in providing that "[i]n an action not triable of right by a jury, the court, on motion or on its own: (1) may try any issue with an advisory jury." There is no right to an advisory jury, however, and the court has full discretion to decide whether to empanel such a jury. Moreover, the function of an advisory jury is only to serve as an aid to the court. The findings of an advisory jury have no binding effect and the court is entirely free to accept or reject, in whole or in part, the jury's findings. The court retains full responsibility for deciding the case and under Rule 52(a), the court must issue findings of fact and conclusions of law as in any other non-jury trial.

Jury Trial by Consent. Rule 39(c)(2) also authorizes the court, with the consent of the parties, to order a trial by jury in an action even though no right to a trial by jury would otherwise exist in the action. The court has discretion in ordering a jury trial under this "consent" provision of Rule 39(c)(2), but if a jury trial is ordered, the jury's verdict, unlike that of an advisory jury, has "the same effect as if a jury trial had been a matter of right, unless the action is against the United States and a federal statute provides for a nonjury trial."

4. Selection of Jurors: Rule 47

If a jury trial is available and has been properly demanded, one of the first steps in the trial will be the selection of the jurors. Every procedural system has provisions governing the qualifications of jurors, the method and procedures for assembling master lists of prospective jurors, and the process for selecting jurors for individual cases. Ordinarily, summonses or notices will be sent to those persons who are randomly selected for jury service during a particular term of court in which jury trials have been scheduled. These persons then comprise the main jury pool from which the individual jurors for particular cases will be selected. In selecting the jurors for a particular case, every system provides for a *voir dire* examination in which the prospective jurors, commonly known as the *venire*, are asked questions in order to determine their fitness to serve in the particular case.

Voir dire

venire

In some systems, the presiding judge asks the questions and in others, the parties or their attorneys either conduct the examination or share the questioning with the judge. Federal Rule 47(a), for instance, gives broad discretion to the presiding judge and provides that "[t]he court may permit the parties or their attorneys to examine prospective jurors or may itself do so." In many federal courts, the usual practice is for the judge to ask the questions and this approach is also the practice in some states. In most state courts, however, the parties or their attorneys play an active role in the *voir dire* examination. The questioning process also varies. In some jurisdictions, the jurors are questioned individually, but in many both group and individual questions are utilized.

47(a)

The purpose of the *voir dire* is to reveal to the attorneys conducting the case whether individual jurors should be challenged. Challenges to jurors are divided into challenges for cause and peremptory challenges. As the name suggests, challenges for cause are challenges based on a juror's inability to serve as a fair and impartial fact finder in the case. The number of challenges for cause is not limited since "cause" has to do with a person's individual fitness to serve as a juror in the particular case. For example, bias or prejudice on the part of a juror, because of the juror's relationship with one of the parties, financial or personal interest in the case, or some other reason, is a valid basis to challenge the juror for cause.

In contrast, peremptory challenges are challenges that a party may exercise without giving a reason. The number of peremptory challenges permitted for each party varies from jurisdiction to jurisdiction. *See, e.g.,* 28 U.S.C. § 1870 (permitting three peremptory challenges for each party, but allowing the court to treat multiple plaintiffs or defendants as a single party or to allow additional challenges); N.J. Ct. R. 1:8-3(c) (six peremptory challenges for each separately represented party). Lawyers use peremptory challenges to eliminate jurors who cannot be challenged for cause, but whom the lawyer feels may, for some reason, be inclined to favor the opponent's side of the case. However, as you will see in subsection (b), below, the U.S. Supreme Court in recent years has imposed constitutional restrictions on the ability to use peremptory challenges.

peremptory challenges

47(b)

§ 1870

3 allowed

NJ: 6

(a) Challenges for Cause

Bell v. Vanlandingham
Supreme Court of Alabama, 1994
633 So. 2d 454

Ingram, Justice.

Hollis Ray Bell and his wife Helen Bell brought a medical malpractice action against Dr. John A. Vanlandingham. The jury returned a verdict for Dr. Vanlandingham. The Bells moved for a new trial on the ground that the trial judge had erred by declining the Bells' request to strike three jurors for cause. The court overruled their motion for new trial, and the Bells appealed.

The dispositive issue is whether the trial court abused its discretion by refusing to dismiss for cause three jurors, Wood, Turk, and Kornegay.

In a recent case this Court reiterated that well-established rule of law "that a trial judge is given broad discretion in regard to sustaining or denying a challenge for cause, and [that] his decision is therefore entitled to great weight and will not be interfered with unless it is clearly erroneous and equivalent to an abuse of discretion." ... We also recognize that a doctor-patient relationship between a potential juror and a party to a lawsuit is prima facie evidence of probable prejudice on the part of the potential juror.... It continues to be the trial court's responsibility to determine whether that presumption can be overcome. "Ultimately the test to be applied is whether the juror can set aside her opinions and try the case fairly and impartially, according to the law and the evidence." ...

According to his voir dire statement, Juror Wood was not then a patient of Dr. Vanlandingham and he had not used Dr. Vanlandingham's services in the past. Wood, a pastor, voiced concern at the conclusion of voir dire as to whether he could be objective, given that many members of his congregation were also patients of Dr. Vanlandingham and that he often visited patients at the hospital where Dr. Vanlandingham worked. Wood merely said that he felt "like I am supposed to know the Bells." The fact that Wood might "feel a little uncomfortable" sitting on the jury was not an adequate ground to support a challenge for cause. We find no error here.

Juror Turk had been a patient of Dr. Vanlandingham in the past, but they had no ongoing doctor-patient relationship; thus, there is no presumption of probable prejudice as to this juror. He had also hunted with Hollis Ray Bell. Although Turk was acquainted with the parties on both sides of the lawsuit, nothing in his voir dire statement indicates that he would not be able to view the evidence fairly and objectively. Turk merely indicated that he did not want to get involved, because he knew the parties. The trial court's decision not to strike Turk from the venire for cause was not an abuse of discretion.

However, we reach a different conclusion as to Juror Kornegay. In *Wright v. Holy Name of Jesus Medical Center*, 628 So. 2d 510 (Ala. 1993), this Court held that probable prejudice existed where a venire member said that she would feel "awkward" returning to her doctor for treatment if she served on the jury in a medical malpractice action against him.... Dr. Vanlandingham was Kornegay's family physician. When asked if this fact would "prevent [him] from giving both sides a fair and equal trial in this case," Kornegay stated that he would feel "awkward" serving on the jury. The trial court erred in not striking Juror Kornegay for cause; therefore, the Bells are entitled to a new trial.

The judgment is reversed and the case is remanded for proceedings consistent with this opinion.

Reversed and remanded.

HORNSBY, C.J., and SHORES and COOK, JJ., concur. STEAGALL, J., concurs specially.

STEAGALL, JUSTICE (concurring specially).

I concur specially to point out that this case is factually distinguishable from *Wright v. Holy Name of Jesus Medical Center*, 628 So. 2d 510 (Ala. 1993). In my dissent in *Wright*, I stated that I would hold that the trial court in that case did not abuse its discretion in denying the plaintiff's motion to strike prospective juror P.C. The plaintiff insisted that P.C. should be subject to a challenge for cause because P.C. had admitted that she would feel awkward on her next visit to the defendant doctor after having served on the jury; but P.C. did not say that she would feel awkward sitting on the jury. In this case, however, the prospective juror, Kornegay, stated that he would feel awkward serving on the jury. Accordingly, I agree with the majority that the trial court in this case erred in not striking juror Kornegay for cause.

Notes and Questions

1. A challenge for cause can be sustained based on relationships that a juror has with the parties in the action. The question explored in *Bell* is how close the relationship must be before the court must draw the conclusion that prejudice will result to a party by not striking the juror. Note that the court seemed to focus on what the jurors in question said about how their relationship with the parties would affect their service on the jury. Do you think it is necessary in all cases to have a statement that the juror would have some kind of problem serving on the jury before a challenge for cause will be granted? Aren't there some situations where the relationship between a juror and a party is so close that prejudice will be presumed? For example, if the defendant moves to strike a juror for cause because the juror is the plaintiff's brother, should there also have to be a statement from the juror indicating bias before the challenge is allowed? In what other kinds of situations do you think prejudice should be presumed? *See, e.g., Getter v. Wal-Mart Stores, Inc.,* 66 F.3d 1119, 1122 (10th Cir. 1995) (despite assurances of impartiality, bias presumed when prospective juror has direct financial interest in the trial's outcome, such as when "juror [is] a stockholder in or an employee of a corporation that [is] a party to the suit").

2. Note the difference between the statements made by Juror Wood and Juror Kornegay. Juror Wood said he would feel a little uncomfortable sitting on the jury because his occupation as a pastor might bring him in regular contact with the defendant. Juror Kornegay said that his ongoing relationship as a patient of the defendant would make him feel awkward in sitting on the jury. The court held that Kornegay should have been stricken, but not Wood. Was it the difference in the two jurors' relationships with the defendant that accounts for the difference in result or what they said about how they would feel about sitting on the jury?

3. Consider the distinction drawn by the concurring justice. Should it really be significant whether a juror says that sitting on the jury will make the juror feel awkward going back to the doctor, or says instead that sitting on a jury in which the juror's doctor is the defendant will be awkward? Do the permissible relationships between jurors and parties differ depending on whether the action is being tried in a small or large community?

Problem

Problem 10-4. P, a former employee of D, sues D for damages for breach of an employment contract. J, another employee of D and a member of the same labor union as P is summoned for jury service in the action. The voir dire examination reveals J's relationship to the parties in the action. What argument could D make that J should be stricken for cause? What argument could P make that J should be stricken for cause? Do you think the court should grant either D's or P's motion to strike in the absence of further evidence of actual bias?

(b) Constitutional Limits on Peremptory Challenges

As explained above, peremptory challenges allow a litigant to remove a juror during the jury selection process, even though the juror is otherwise qualified to serve as a juror and is not subject to disqualification for "cause." Traditionally, litigants were permitted to exercise their allotted number of peremptory challenges as of right without the requirement of reason or explanation. In a series of cases, however, the Supreme Court has imposed constitutional restrictions on the exercise of peremptory challenges. In *Batson v. Kentucky*, 476 U.S. 79 (1986), the Court held that the Equal Protection Clause of the Fourteenth Amendment prohibited the prosecutor in a criminal case from exercising peremptory challenges to exclude jurors on the basis of race. In *Edmonson v. Leesville Concrete Co.*, 500 U.S. 614 (1991), the Court extended the rule of *Batson* to prevent litigants in a private civil action from exercising peremptory challenges to exclude jurors on the basis of race.

Following its previous decision in *Powers v. Ohio*, 499 U.S. 400 (1991), the Court in *Edmonson* held that race-based peremptory challenges violated the equal protection rights of the excluded jurors. As you will learn in Constitutional Law, the protections of the Fourteenth Amendment apply only to actions by the government or its officials that violate a person's constitutional rights. In *Edmonson*, the Court held that even though the peremptory challenges in that case were exercised by a private litigant, and not by the government as in *Batson* and *Powers*, the "significant participation" of the government in authorizing the system of jury selection qualified the action of the private litigant as "state action" for purposes of the Fourteenth Amendment. 500 U.S. at 621–23, 628.

In *J.E.B. v. Alabama ex rel. T.B.*, 511 U.S. 127 (1994), the Court extended *Batson* to peremptory jury strikes of all males from a jury in a civil action by a state to establish paternity and recover child support. The Court observed:

> Failing to provide jurors the same protection against gender discrimination as race discrimination could frustrate the purpose of *Batson* itself. Because gender and race are overlapping categories, gender can be used as a pretext for racial discrimination. Allowing parties to remove racial minorities from the jury not because of their race, but because of their gender, contravenes well-established equal protection principles and could insulate effectively racial discrimination from judicial scrutiny.

Id. at 145. The Court explained the practical operation of the restrictions on peremptory strikes as follows:

> Our conclusion that litigants may not strike potential jurors solely on the basis of gender does not imply the elimination of all peremptory challenges. Neither does it conflict with a State's legitimate interest in using such challenges in its effort to secure a fair and impartial jury. Parties still may remove jurors whom they feel might be less acceptable than others on the panel; gender simply may not serve as a proxy for bias. Parties may also exercise their peremptory challenges to remove from the venire any group or class of individuals normally subject to "rational basis" review.... Even strikes based on characteristics that are disproportionately associated with one gender could be appropriate, absent a showing of pretext.[16]

---

16. For example, challenging all persons who have had military experience would disproportionately affect men at this time, while challenging all persons employed as nurses would disproportionately affect women. Without a showing of pretext, however, these challenges may well not be unconstitutional, since they are not gender- or race-based....

If conducted properly, *voir dire* can inform litigants about potential jurors, making reliance upon stereotypical and pejorative notions about a particular gender or race both unnecessary and unwise. *Voir dire* provides a means of discovering actual or implied bias and a firmer basis upon which the parties may exercise their peremptory challenges intelligently....

The experience in the many jurisdictions that have barred gender-based challenges belies the claim that litigants and trial courts are incapable of complying with a rule barring strikes based on gender.... As with race-based *Batson* claims, a party alleging gender discrimination must make a prima facie showing of intentional discrimination before the party exercising the challenge is required to explain the basis for the strike.... When an explanation is required, it need not rise to the level of a "for cause" challenge; rather, it merely must be based on a juror characteristic other than gender, [or race] and the proffered explanation may not be pretextual....

511 U.S. at 143–44.

Notes and Questions

1. What other extensions of the *Batson* principle might occur? For example, suppose a party to a federal civil action strikes all persons of a particular religion from the jury. Would this violate the Equal Protection Clause? The First Amendment? Consider the following argument:

> Gender-based stereotypes that form the basis of peremptory challenges are often overbroad and archaic. Gender, like race, is an inaccurate predictor of a juror's ability to be impartial....
>
> On the other hand, it does not seem entirely irrational for an attorney, who has had little time and opportunity to learn about prospective jurors in any great detail, to act on the assumption that members of particular religious faiths share similar thoughts and philosophies linked to the particular belief system embraced by these faiths. Religion, unlike race and gender, may in fact be an accurate predictor of the attitudes of prospective jurors.

J. Suzanne Bell Chambers, *Applying the Break: Religion and the Peremptory Challenge*, 70 IND. L.J. 569, 595–96 (1995) (footnotes omitted).

2. In footnote 11 in *J.E.B*, the Court observed that

> [e]ven if a measure of truth can be found in some of the gender stereotypes used to justify gender-based peremptory challenges, that fact alone cannot support discrimination on the basis of gender in jury selection. We have made abundantly clear in past cases that gender classifications that rest on impermissible stereotypes violate the Equal Protection Clause, even when some statistical support can be conjured up for the generalization.... The Equal Protection Clause, as interpreted by decisions of this Court, acknowledges that a shred of truth may be contained in some stereotypes, but requires that state actors look beyond the surface before making judgments about people that are likely to stigmatize as well as to perpetuate historical patterns of discrimination.

J.E.B., 511 U.S. 127, 140 n.11. Doesn't this footnote make it clear that even if gender is a partly accurate predictor of attitudes, gender-based peremptory challenges perpetuate unconstitutional stereotypes? Why should religion be treated differently?

3. Assume that a U.S. District Court erroneously refuses to dismiss a juror for cause on the basis of bias and the party seeking the juror's dismissal uses a peremptory challenge to strike the juror. The party later loses the action and appeals, asserting that it was reversible error to deny the challenge for cause because it forced the party to use a peremptory challenge. If the appellate court concludes that the actual jury that decided the case was comprised wholly of impartial jurors, should it nevertheless reverse on this ground? *See Ross v. Oklahoma*, 487 U.S. 81 (1984) (loss of a peremptory challenge is not reversible error if chosen jury is impartial).

4. If a party exercises a peremptory challenge to strike the only juror of a particular race for a race-neutral, but factually mistaken, reason, who has the burden of showing that the reason is a pretext? *See Hurd v. Pittsburg State Univ.*, 109 F.3d 1540 (10th Cir. 1997) (the party raising a *Batson* challenge bears the burden).

5. Does the controversy over peremptory challenges indicate that they should simply be eliminated?

5. Jury Size and Unanimity: Rule 48

As previously noted above, a jury at common law consisted of twelve persons. In *Colgrove v. Battin*, 413 U.S. 149 (1973), however, the Court held that the Seventh Amendment was not violated by a jury of six persons. Consistent with this ruling, Federal Rule 48 provides that "[a] jury must initially have at least 6 and no more than 12 members, and each juror must participate in the verdict unless excused under Rule 47(c)." Some federal district courts set the number of jurors by local rule, with most setting the jury size at six. Others leave the jury size to the discretion of the court in a particular case.

At common law, a jury was also required to return a unanimous verdict. In *Colgrove*, the Supreme Court only decided that six person juries were permissible under the Seventh Amendment and did not address the separate common-law requirement of unanimity. In the *criminal* context, the Court has held that non-unanimous twelve member jury verdicts are constitutional under the Sixth Amendment, but that non-unanimous six member jury verdicts are not. The Court has not addressed, however, whether unanimous jury verdicts are required in civil cases under the Seventh Amendment. Nevertheless, Federal Rule 48 currently preserves the common-law requirement of unanimity and expressly provides that "[u]nless the parties stipulate otherwise, the verdict must be unanimous and be returned by a jury of at least 6 members."

As previously explained above, the jury trial requirements of the Seventh Amendment do not apply to state court actions and the states may, therefore, establish their own rules for jury size and unanimity free of the requirements of the Seventh Amendment. Many states permit six-person juries in all or some civil cases. *See, e.g.*, N.Y. C.P.L.R. §4104 (McKinney 2007) (six-person juries in all civil cases); ILL. COMP. STAT. ANN. ch.735 §5/2-1105 (West Supp. 2012) (six-person juries in civil cases in which the claim for damages is less than $50,000).

Many states also allow for non-unanimous verdicts in civil cases. *See, e.g.*, N.J. STAT. ANN. 2B:23-17 (West 2006) (five-sixths of the jurors sufficient); CAL. CIV. PROC. CODE§ 220 (West 2006), §613 (West 2011) (three-fourths of jurors sufficient, but twelve-member juries required unless parties agree to smaller number).

Section B. The Trial Process, Jury Verdicts, and Final Judgment

1. Procedure at Trial

(a) Order of Trial

After it has been determined whether the trial will be to a judge or a jury, and after the jury has been empaneled (if there is to be one), the actual trial will begin. The party having the burden of proof on the principal issues in the case, usually the plaintiff, will make an opening statement. After the plaintiff's opening statement, the defendant will be given an opportunity to make an opening statement and may choose to do so at this time or defer the statement to a time just prior to the presentation of the defendant's case. Opening statements generally explain the nature of the party's case and summarize the evidence that will be presented.

Opening statements are quite important, especially in jury trials. Studies have shown that verdicts in a substantial majority of cases are consistent with the initial impressions formed by the jurors during the opening statements. However, an opening statement may not be necessary in a trial before a judge, since the trial judge is usually familiar with the case. There are limits to the propriety of things that can be said in opening statements, and objections can be made by the opposing party to improper matter. Lawyers should not refer to inadmissible evidence, make argumentative statements, state personal beliefs or opinions, ask the jurors to put themselves in the place of a party to the action in deciding the case, make disparaging remarks about the opposing party or counsel, etc.

[handwritten margin note: opening statement) objectionable matter]

After the opening statements, the party having the burden of proof (usually the plaintiff) will then present the party's case in chief. After the plaintiff has completed the presentation of evidence, the defendant will be able to offer rebuttal evidence and present affirmative evidence on issues upon which the defendant has the burden of proof, such as affirmative defenses and counterclaims. The plaintiff will then be allowed to offer further evidence to rebut the defendant's evidence, and the defendant will be allowed to offer surrebuttal evidence. The process will continue until each side rests.

After both sides have rested their cases, they will make closing arguments. Usually the plaintiff proceeds first, followed by the defendant's closing argument and a brief conclusion by the plaintiff. Closing arguments are the last chance that the lawyers have to persuade the trier of fact that their side should win the case. Consequently, lawyers use the closing argument to summarize the evidence and their factual theories about what happened in the case, to explain the significance of the evidence, to draw reasonable inferences from the evidence, to comment on the credibility of the witnesses, to explain the legal theory of the case, and so forth.

After the closing arguments in a jury trial, the judge will instruct the jury. However, in federal court and some states, the judge has the discretion whether to instruct the jury either before or after closing argument. The instructions state the law that applies to the kind of case before the court and set out the rules about how the jury should conduct its deliberations to arrive at a verdict. After the court has instructed the jury, it will retire to deliberate and reach its verdict. In a nonjury trial, the judge will simply take the case under advisement after closing arguments and ultimately decide it by entering findings of fact and conclusions of law.

The decision of the case by a judge or jury will be followed by the entry of judgment. The judgment will embody the remedy to which the plaintiff is entitled if the plaintiff has won the action or will direct that the plaintiff take nothing if the defendant has won. Entry of judgment initiates the running of time periods for making various post-trial motions and for appealing. The entry of a judgment granting a remedy will also bring into play various devices for executing the judgment. As you will see in Chapter 12, the entry of judgment also has important effects on the ability to pursue further litigation on the matter that was the subject of the action leading to the judgment.

(b) Presentation of Evidence

As discussed in the preceding subsection, at trial the parties attempt to meet their respective burdens of proof by presenting evidence. The rules of evidence limit and regulate the parties' ability to do this. Chapter 1 discussed the process of examination and cross-examination by which the testimony of live witnesses is conducted. Likewise, Chapter 1 briefly discussed two of the most important rules of evidence, concerning relevancy and hearsay. A more complete exposition of methods of presenting and objecting to evidence and of the rules of evidence must await courses specifically devoted to those subjects.

(c) Burden of Proof and Mechanisms for Enforcing the Burden

The expression "burden of proof" has two meanings: (1) the burden of production and (2) the burden of persuasion. The burden of production is the duty to produce evidence or go forward with evidence. Unlike the burden of persuasion, which only becomes relevant at the end of the trial, the burden of production is relevant at the outset of the trial and can shift back and forth between the parties during the trial.

To satisfy the burden of production, the plaintiff must introduce some evidence on each fact that must be established as part of the plaintiff's claim to justify a favorable decision. Failure to do so can be raised by a motion for a nonsuit, an involuntary dismissal, a directed verdict, or a judgment as a matter of law. In ruling on one of these motions, the judge will allocate the burden of production and determine whether the party possessing the burden has introduced sufficient evidence to meet the burden.

If a party meets the initial burden of production, however, the party does not necessarily win the action. Rather, the party merely escapes an unfavorable decision on a motion for a nonsuit, involuntary dismissal, directed verdict, or judgment as a matter of law made by the opposing party. At that point, if the party possessing the burden of production has introduced enough evidence so that the trier of fact *may* find in favor of the party on the facts, but not so much that the trier of fact *must* find in the party's favor, the production burden will not shift to the opposing party. However, if the party introduces sufficient evidence so that the trier of fact *must* find in the party's favor in the absence of evidence to the contrary, the burden of production will shift to the opposing party. Under these circumstances, the failure of the opposing party to introduce contrary evidence will result in a ruling against the opposing party on a motion for a directed verdict, judgment as a matter of law, etc.

The burden of persuasion becomes relevant only at the end of the trial when the parties have satisfied their respective burdens of production and the trier must decide the case. If the trier of fact is a jury, the judge will instruct the jury on the burden of persuasion that each party must meet on the factual issues. If the party with the burden of persuasion on an issue fails to meet that burden, the jurors will be instructed by the court that they must find against the party on the issue.

In civil actions, the burden of persuasion is usually described as a requirement that the party with the burden prove the fact in question by a *preponderance of the evidence* or the *greater weight of the evidence.* If the action is to be decided by a judge rather than a jury, the judge will simply decide whether the party with the burden of persuasion has met the burden and will so state in writing.

What determines how the law allocates the burden of production and the burden of persuasion on specific issues to particular parties? It is generally agreed that no single principle controls how the burden of production or persuasion is apportioned between the parties. Rather, allocation of the burden will depend upon the weight given to "any one or more of several factors, including (1) the natural tendency to place the burdens on the party desiring change [normally the plaintiff], (2) special policy considerations such as those disfavoring certain defenses, (3) convenience, (4) fairness, and (5) the judicial estimate of the probabilities." *See* 2 Kenneth S. Broun et al., McCormick on Evidence § 337, at 477 (6th ed. 2006).

There are a variety of mechanisms, both before and after trial, for enforcing a party's burden of proof. Recall, first, that Chapter 9 examined how the motion for summary judgment can be used to enforce the burden of proof against a party asserting a claim for relief. There we saw that a claimant, after an adequate opportunity for discovery, must be able to demonstrate the existence of some evidence with which to satisfy the burden or have summary judgment granted against the claimant. In theory, the motion for summary judgment would also work in the same fashion against a defending party who bears the burden of proof on some issue — for example, an affirmative defense.

At trial, the burden of proof is enforced against the plaintiff through the motion for a directed verdict in a jury trial or a motion for an involuntary dismissal in a nonjury trial. In the federal courts and many states, these motions are now called motions for judgments as a matter of law. *See* Fed. R. Civ. P. 50, 52. After a party has been fully heard at trial, the court may enter judgment as a matter of law against that party if the court finds that the evidence in the case is legally insufficient to support a judgment for that party. As you will see in Chapter 11, the burden of proof can also be enforced after trial through the mechanism of a motion for judgment notwithstanding the verdict (now also called a judgment as a matter of law in federal court). *See* Teply & Whitten at 1010–12.

2. Jury Instructions and Verdicts

(a) Jury Instructions: Rule 51

Jury instructions are the means by which the court informs the jury about the substantive law applicable to the case and tells the jury how to decide the factual issues during its deliberations. This will include information about the burden of proof on each party. In the federal courts and many states, if a party wishes to request that a particular instruction or set of instructions be given, the party must make a request at the close of the evidence or at such earlier reasonable time that the court orders. *See* Fed. R. Civ. P. 51(a)(1). Under Federal Rule 51(a)(2)(A) requests may be made after the close of the evidence "on issues that could not reasonably have been anticipated by an earlier time" set by the court. With the court's permission, untimely requests may also be filed "on any issue." The court is required to inform the parties of its proposed action on requested instructions before arguments to the jury and objections to jury instructions must be made at that time. *See* Fed. R. Civ. P. 51(b) and (c). By statute or rule in some states, as well as by local rule in federal court, each party may be required

to submit a complete, proposed set of jury instructions to the court. *See* Teply & Whitten at 1004–05.

Jury instructions are hard to visualize in the abstract, and the difficulty is com-
pounded by the fact that instructions on the same claim or defense will vary slightly
from state to state. Fortunately, most states have pattern jury instructions to aid the
practitioner, and there are a large number of excellent general works containing pattern instructions. The following are two sample instructions on negligence and burden
of proof:

> A person is "negligent" when the person fails to exercise ordinary care. "Ordinary
> care" is the care a reasonable person would use in similar circumstances. A per-
> son is negligent if the person, without intending to do harm, does something
> (or fails to do something) a reasonable person would recognize as creating an
> unreasonable risk of injury or damage to a person or property.
>
> ....
>
> In order to prove the essential elements of plaintiff's claim, the plaintiff has the
> burden to establish by a preponderance of the evidence the following facts:
>
> First, that defendant was negligent in one or more of the particulars alleged; and
>
> Second, that defendant's negligence was a proximate [*legal*] cause of some in-
> jury and consequent damage sustained by plaintiff.

3 Kevin F. O'Malley et al., Federal Jury Practice and Instructions: Civil §§ 120:02
& 120:03 (6th ed. 2011).

Although this subsection has focused on the jury instructions given at the end of the
trial, you should be aware that the court also gives instructions to the jury at other stages
of the proceeding. For example, the court may give general instructions to the jury at the
beginning of the case to inform the jurors about the nature of the case and their duties
and obligations during the case. Or it may be necessary for the court to instruct the jury
that certain evidence is admissible for one purpose but not another.

(b) General and Special Jury Verdicts: Rule 49

Most jury trials in federal court are resolved by the rendering of a *general verdict* by the
jury. In a general verdict, the jury simply finds for the plaintiff and awards damages in a
specified amount or finds for the defendant. No reason or other explanation of the jury's
verdict is required. A typical general verdict would be: "We, the jury, find ... for [the]
plaintiff and against [the] defendant and fix the damages at $___"; or "We, the jury,
find ... for [the] defendant and against [the] plaintiff."

Sometimes, however, because of the factual or legal complexity of the case, the court
may feel that the jury needs greater guidance in deciding the case and may require the
jury to return a *special verdict* or a *general verdict with answers to written questions* under
Federal Rule 49. The decision to use either of these alternative verdict forms is not a matter of party right, but is solely within the sound discretion of the trial judge.

Although similar, these two verdict forms are distinct. Under Rule 49(a)'s provision for
a *special verdict*, the court is authorized to dispense with the general verdict entirely and
ask the jury to return "only a special verdict in the form of a special written finding on
each issue of fact." When utilizing a special verdict, the jury answers only specific factual
questions. It is the court's function to then apply the law to the jury's answers and enter
judgment accordingly.

The procedure under Rule 49(b) for a *general verdict with answers to written questions* is a "middle ground" between a general and special verdict, combining aspects of both. Under this procedure, the jury returns a general verdict, but is also directed to answer one or more specific factual questions.

These alternative verdict forms are designed to focus the jury's attention on the proper issues in the case and to provide a clearer record of the bases upon which the jury rendered its decision. These features are intended to address the principal drawbacks of the general verdict. Because the jury in rendering a general verdict need not offer any explanation as to how it reached its verdict, it is impossible to know whether the jury properly addressed all of the issues in the case as required by the judge's instructions. When multiple theories of recovery or defense are presented, it is also difficult to know which theories or defenses were accepted by the jury and formed the actual basis of the jury's general verdict. Uncertainty as to the jury's decision can create difficulties for a court reviewing the jury's verdict on post-trial motions or on appeal. Uncertainty as to the jury's decision can also raise problems in determining whether the principles of issue preclusion may be applied to the jury's verdict.

While attempting to address these drawbacks of the general verdict, the alternative verdict forms create problems of their own, in part because of the difficulty in properly drafting clear and unambiguous questions for the jury. The special difficulties that can arise with the alternative verdict forms are illustrated in the following case. Perhaps, the judge's comment in footnote 1 of the opinion explains why, despite its drawbacks, the general verdict remains the most commonly used verdict form among trial judges.

Selgas v. American Airlines, Inc.

United States District Court, District of Puerto Rico, 1994
858 F. Supp. 316, *modified in part*, 69 F.3d 1205 (1st Cir. 1995)

FUSTE, DISTRICT JUDGE.

Defendants, American Airlines, Inc. and Whadzen Carrasquillo, move for judgment as a matter of law and, in the alternative, for remittitur or a new trial in this sexual discrimination and sexual harassment action. The plaintiff, Mary Jane Kerr Selgas, was employed by American for eighteen years, and at the time of her lay-off was working as an account executive in cargo sales. After a three-week trial, the jury awarded Kerr $1,000,000 in compensatory damages (which is automatically doubled under state law), $20,000 under the state unlawful termination statute, and $350,000 in punitive damages under Title VII, for a total of $2.37 Million.

. . . .

American first asserts that the jury's original verdict required an entry of judgment for defendants on the claims of sex discrimination and retaliation. . . .

Defendants'. . . argument requires an analysis of the jury form utilized at trial. See Appendix. The verdict form, agreed upon by both parties,[1] consisted of a number of special interrogatories; the controversy centers around the first four. Questions 1 and 3 reflect a finding by the jury for the plaintiff on the questions of sexual discrimination and retaliation. The answers to questions 2 and 4, however, suggest that the jury found that

---

1. The court's intention was to use a general verdict form. This controversy confirms once again the teaching of experienced judges to never give in to pressure by counsel regarding the use of special verdict forms. Seeking consensus, we did agree to use the special verdict form.

American had valid reasons for the termination of plaintiff. Yet, the jury awarded the plaintiff $1,000,000 in compensatory damages and $350,000 in punitive damages, and made a finding of unlawful termination of employment under local law.

In an attempt to clarify this ambiguity, this court solicited suggestions from counsel on how to proceed. Counsel for defendants and plaintiff agreed that the contradiction could be rectified by submitting the following general questions to the jury: "Please explain to us the meaning of your verdict, Part A (sex discrimination claims) and Part B (retaliation claims). Was it your intention to find in favor of the plaintiff or in favor of the defendants in each of these claims?" The handwritten supplement to the verdict form was sent to the jury, which returned with the following answers: "A. We are in favor of the plaintiff about [sic] sex discrimination. B. Also, we are in favor of the plaintiff about [sic] retaliation claims."

Defendants contend that the original verdict was consistent and that, therefore, there was no reason to propound additional questions to the jury. Defendants further argue that judgment should be entered for them on the issues of sex discrimination and retaliation.[2]

The Supreme Court has instructed that courts must attempt to harmonize answers to special interrogatories if at all possible.... Even keeping this admonishment in mind, we are unable to find that the initial verdict form was consistent.

Several aspects of the initial verdict form support the finding of inconsistency. Although the jury found that defendants would have made the same employment decision concerning plaintiff even if no sexual discrimination or retaliation was involved (Questions 2 and 4), in direct contravention to this finding, in Question No. 8, the jury found that the defendants failed to prove that there was just cause for the layoff of plaintiff. In addition, the jury awarded plaintiff punitive damages, which the court instructed the jury could only be granted upon a finding that the defendants had engaged in discriminatory practices with malice or reckless indifference to the constitutional rights of the plaintiff.[3] In order for the jury to double the amount of the compensatory award, it must have found that the defendants were liable under the Puerto Rico anti-discrimination statute, which provides for doubling of compensatory damages.... Finally, if, as American argues, the jury meant to find for the defendants on the theories of sexual discrimination and retaliation, the entire $2.37 Million award would have to have been premised upon a finding of an invasion of privacy, a scenario which both parties agree is incredible.[4]

---

2. The defendants argue that because the jury found that American would have made the same employment decisions regarding the plaintiff even if her gender was not taken into account, the defendants proved a complete defense to the Title VII claims, citing *Price Waterhouse v. Hopkins*, 490 U.S. 228, 244–45 (1989). However, the Civil Rights Act of 1991 partially overruled *Price Waterhouse*. Title VII now provides that "an unlawful employment practice is established when the complaining party demonstrates that race, color, religion, sex or national origin was a motivating factor for any employment practice, even though other factors also motivated the practice." ... However, when a defendant proves that the same employment decision would have been made even without the discriminatory factor, a plaintiff is only entitled to declaratory relief, injunctive relief, and attorney's fees and costs, not compensatory or punitive damages or reinstatement.... Therefore, even if we were to find that [the jury's] answers to questions 2 and 4 were consistent with the rest of the verdict form, defendants would not have established a complete defense. The result would be that plaintiff could not recover punitive or compensatory damages under the federal claims.

3. Although the jury was unaware of this, punitive damages cannot be awarded under Title VII if the defendants had proved that plaintiff would have been terminated even without the presence of discrimination. In other words, an affirmative answer to questions 2 and 4 on the verdict form legally prohibited the jury from awarding punitive damages in question 10.

4. The situation at hand is different from that in *McVey v. Phillips Petroleum Co.*, 288 F.2d 53 (5th Cir. 1961), relied on by plaintiff. In *McVey*, there was a way to reconcile the jury's finding based on an explanation given by the jury. Here, we see no way to reconcile factual findings that (1) the defendants

Defendants argue that the jury found for defendants on the sexual discrimination and retaliation claims, attributing the hefty recovery given by the jury to the admission at trial of evidence regarding events which took place prior to the statute of limitations period. We disagree with defendants' argument because, even assuming that the jury incorrectly relied upon information which occurred outside of the statute of limitations, this does not establish that the jury meant to find for defendants on the questions of sexual discrimination and retaliation. Rather, it merely underlines the fact that the jury did find evidence of sexual discrimination.

Since we conclude that the initial verdict was inconsistent, we proceed to two remaining issues related to the jury procedure. First, whether it was proper to submit the additional general verdict form to the jury. Second, whether there remained any inconsistency following the second jury submission.

The parties agree that the initial jury verdict form consisted of a special verdict, because it asked the jury for findings of fact without requesting a general finding for one of the parties. Therefore, the analysis should begin with Fed. R. Civ. P. 49(a). The rule does not *49(a)* specify what is to be done in the event of an inconsistency in the written questions on a special verdict form. The First Circuit has held that where the answers on a special verdict form are inconsistent, the attorneys are present, and the jury has not yet been discharged, it is appropriate to resubmit the questions to the jury. *Santiago-Negron v. Castro-Davila*, 865 F.2d 431 (1st Cir. 1989).

In *Santiago-Negron*, this court resubmitted the original jury form with an additional instruction, in order to explain an inconsistency in the first set of answers. The situation here presents a somewhat different context, because following the initial inconsistent jury form, we submitted to the jury a supplemental general verdict form. Defendants allege that this action was impermissible, in that it transformed a special verdict form into a general verdict form. However, defendants cite no support for the proposition that such a solution is prohibited by the Federal Rules or the Seventh Amendment. Initially, the trial court has complete discretion over whether a general or special verdict is to be used.... If the initial choice of the type of form is left to the discretion of the court, and in light of the directive that jury verdicts should be reconciled if at all possible, we cannot find error in the submission of the general verdict form to the jury.

We note also that when resubmitting questions to a jury for clarification, it is imperative that the court refrain from any action which might compel the jury to tailor its findings to any particular outcome.... By requesting the jury to answer simple general questions as to which party they intended to find for on the retaliation and discrimination claims, this court avoided any undue influence on the jury process.

Even if we were to find that the general verdict questions should not have been submitted to the jury, the defendants not only failed to object to the questions, but agreed with the court that such a procedure was the correct path to follow. A party who fails to object to the resubmission of a jury verdict at trial cannot later challenge that action....

Defendants allege that after the general verdict was combined with the special interrogatories on the initial verdict form an inconsistency arose because of the fact that the jury held for the plaintiff, while finding that the defendants had established that American Airlines would have made the same employment decision even if the unlawful motive were not present. We disagree. When faced with an apparent inconsistency between

---

proved that they would have dismissed the plaintiff regardless of discrimination, and (2) the defendants failed to establish that there was just cause for the layoff of plaintiff.

a general verdict and special interrogatory answer, the trial court has a duty to reconcile any such inconsistency.... A court need only resort to the three options for dealing with such a situation provided in Rule 49(b) if it is "not reasonably possible to resolve the apparent inconsistency between the answers and the verdict." ...[6]

We find that the supplemental questions submitted to the jury remedied any inconsistency in the verdict. The jury's holding that it intended to find for the plaintiff on the issue of liability for discrimination and retaliation, combined with the finding of wrongful discharge, the substantial damage award, and the granting of punitive damages, leads to a conclusion that the affirmative answers to questions 2 and 4 on the initial form were not conclusions that the defendants had met their burden of proof on these issues, but rather that the jury found some evidence that the employers had other reasons for the dismissal of plaintiff, in addition to sexual discrimination and retaliation.

Even if there remained any discrepancy in the final combined verdict, defendants failed to voice any objection before the jury was dismissed. Failure to point out an inconsistency in a verdict after the verdict is read and before the jury is dismissed constitutes waiver....

....

To summarize, we DENY defendants' motion for judgment as a matter of law, holding that the clarified verdict form clearly expressed the jury's findings, and that there was sufficient evidence to find for the plaintiff on the issues of sex discrimination, invasion of privacy, and retaliation. As to the damage award, the $20,000 allocated under Puerto Rico Law 80 must be ELIMINATED, as they are duplicative of compensatory damages, the amount of punitive damages under Title VII must be LIMITED to $300,000 to comply with the statute, and finally, we ORDER a remittitur of the compensatory damages to $600,000, to be doubled under state law, for a total damages award of $1,500,000. Plaintiff can either accept the remittitur, or a new trial will be ordered.

IT IS SO ORDERED.

APPENDIX

....

We, the Jury, find as follows:

A. SEX DISCRIMINATION CLAIMS:

1. Has plaintiff Mary Jane Kerr proved that her sex (gender) was, more likely than not, a motivating factor in defendants' employment decisions after July 15, 1991?

YES X NO

If your answer to question number 1 is "YES," please answer question number 2.

If your answer to question number 1 is "NO," do not answer question number 2 and proceed to answer the questions under the heading "Retaliation Claims."

---

6. Rule 49(b)[(3)] provides three options if there is an inconsistency between a general verdict and interrogatories. (1) judgment may be entered in accordance with the answers to the interrogatories, notwithstanding the general verdict; (2) the court may return the jury for further consideration of its answers and verdict; (3) the court may order a new trial. When the answers to the interrogatories are inconsistent with each other and one or more is inconsistent with the general verdict, then judgment may not be entered, but the court can either return the jury for further consideration of its answers and verdict or order a new trial.

2. Have defendants American Airlines and Whadzen Carrasquillo proved, more likely than not, that they would have made the same employment decision(s) concerning plaintiff even if the unlawful motive, namely plaintiff's sex, was not present?

YES X NO

B. RETALIATION CLAIMS:

3. Has plaintiff Mary Jane Kerr proved that her reporting the claim to the employer or her filing of a discrimination charge with the Puerto Rico Department of Labor and the Equal Employment Opportunity Commission was, more likely than not, a motivating factor in defendants' employment decisions to terminate her employment after July 15, 1991?

YES X NO

If your answer to question number 3 is "YES," please answer question number 4.

If your answer to question number 3 is "NO," do not answer question number 4 and proceed to answer the questions under the heading "Sexual Harassment."

4. Have defendants American Airlines and Whadzen Carrasquillo proved, more likely than not, that they would have made the same employment decision concerning plaintiff even if unlawful motive, namely plaintiff's filing of a discrimination charge with the Puerto Rico Department of Labor and the Equal Employment Opportunity Commission, was not present?

YES X NO

. . . .

E. WRONGFUL DISCHARGE CLAIM:

8. Have defendants proved that there was just cause for the layoff of plaintiff Mary Jane Kerr on November 30, 1992?

YES NO X

If your answer to question number 8 was "NO," please indicate the amount of severance pay plaintiff is entitled to in dollars: $20,000.00.

F. DAMAGES:

If your answer to any of the questions numbered 1, 3, 5 or 7 was "YES," then proceed to answer questions numbered 9 and 10. If your answer was "YES" only to question number 8, do not answer the questions numbered 9 and 10 and return your verdict.

Should have said: NO to 2 & 4

9. Under the law given to you in the judge's instructions, state the amount of compensatory damages plaintiff should be awarded.

$1,000,000.00; multiplied by 2 = $2,000,000.00.

10. Under the law as given to you in the instructions, state the amount, if any, of punitive damages that the plaintiff should be awarded. State such award in the space numbered 10B. If you decide not to grant punitive damages, say so by placing an "X" in the space numbered 10A.

10A. _____ Punitive damages should not be awarded.

10B. $350,000.00 in punitive damages should be awarded.

. . . .

Notes and Questions

1. On appeal, the Court of Appeals for the First Circuit affirmed the judgment in *Selgas* with the exception of the portion of the district court's judgment awarding punitive damages on the federal claims, which it vacated. *See Kerr-Selgas v. American Airlines, Inc.*, 69 F.3d 1205 (1st Cir. 1995).

2. In studying the questions submitted to the *Selgas* jury as set forth in the Appendix to the opinion, how do you think the verdict form could have been re-worded to avoid the confusion in the case? Based on the substantive law as the court recites it in footnotes 2 and 3 of the opinion, what was the legal significance of the jury answering YES to questions 2 and 4? In the section marked "F. Damages," were the jurors instructed, consistent with the substantive law recited in footnotes 2 and 3, that they proceeded to damages only if they answered NO to questions 2 and 4? Were the jurors ever instructed what they should do if they answered YES to questions 2 and 4? How do you think the first sentence of the section marked "F. Damages" should have been worded to accurately reflect the substantive law? Do you think the attorneys for the defendants were remiss in failing to clarify the verdict form before it was submitted to the jury?

3. Findings by the Court: Rule 52

In an action tried to the court, findings of fact and conclusions of law by the trial judge are the equivalent of a jury verdict. Some states permit the court to state findings generally, like a general verdict of a jury, at least unless the parties make a request for specific findings. *See* Neb. Rev. Stat. § 25-1127 (2008). Federal Rule 52(a)(1) requires a federal court to "find the facts specially and state its conclusions of law separately." Judgment is then entered on the findings of fact and conclusions of law under Rule 58. Rule 52(a)(1) also provides that "[t]he findings and conclusions may be stated on the record after the close of the evidence or may appear in an opinion or a memorandum of decision filed by the court." Appellate courts must not set aside findings of fact, whether based on oral or other evidence, "unless clearly erroneous, and the reviewing court must give due regard to the trial court's opportunity to judge the witnesses' credibility." *See* Fed. R. Civ. P. 52(a)(6).

Question

In a jury trial in federal court, the jury is permitted to render a general verdict if the court in its discretion so chooses. However, in a trial to the court, the court is *required* to make special findings of fact and conclusions of law. Why the difference in treatment of judges and juries? Are judges considered less trustworthy than juries, so that some means of control must be exerted over them? *See* 9A Wright & Miller § 2571, at 477–80 (purpose of requiring findings by the trial court is "to evoke care on the part of the trial judge in ascertaining the facts" and to have a clear record of the court's decision for purposes of appellate review and the application of res judicata and collateral estoppel).

4. Judgments: Rules 54 and 58

Whether a case is decided in a trial by jury or by the court, the culmination of litigation at the trial level is the entry of *judgment*. A jury verdict is not a judgment and a case is not concluded until judgment has been formally entered. Federal Rule 58 is a typical provision providing for the entry of judgment. Rule 58(b)(1) provides that "unless the court orders otherwise, the clerk must, without awaiting the court's direction, promptly prepare, sign, and enter the judgment when: (A) the jury returns a general verdict; (B) the court awards only costs or a sum certain; or (C) the court denies all relief." If the court grants other relief, or if the jury has returned a special verdict or a general verdict with answers to written questions, "the court must promptly approve the form of the judgment, which the clerk must promptly enter." *See* FED. R. CIV. P. 58(b)(2). Under Rule 58(a), a judgment must be set out in a separate document. The judgment is only effective when entered in the civil docket in accord with Rule 79(a) ("Records Kept by the Clerk"). However, a separate document is not required for an order disposing of certain post-trial motions, such as a motion for a new trial or attorney's fees. *See* FED. R. CIV. P. 58(a)(1)-(5).

When a civil action involves multiple claims or parties, Rule 54(b) permits the court to "direct entry of a final judgment as to one or more, but fewer than all, claims or parties only if the court expressly determines that there is no just reason for delay." When the court does not dispose of all of the claims, the court may stay the enforcement of a judgment entered under Rule 54(b) until a subsequent judgment or judgments are entered.

The final judgment in a civil action has important effects on the ability to appeal and to litigate (in later proceedings) the same subject matter as the action leading to the final judgment. If the plaintiff wins the action, the judgment will also embody the remedy to which the plaintiff is entitled under the applicable substantive law. Local statutes or rules will provide for the taxation of costs against the losing party. In cases where attorneys' fees are allowed to a prevailing party under an exception to the ordinary "American Rule," (that each side bears its own counsel fees), such statutes and rules will also set forth the procedures for recovery of such fees. *See, e.g.,* FED. R. CIV. P. 54(d); *see also* TEPLY & WHITTEN at 1007–08.

If the defendant does not pay a money judgment voluntarily, the plaintiff may use a writ of execution to seize the defendant's assets in satisfaction of the judgment. The plaintiff can use the same discovery mechanisms that are available before trial to locate nonexempt assets of the defendant for purposes of execution. *See* FED. R. CIV. P. 69(a). As discussed in Chapter 1, injunctions can be enforced through the processes of civil and criminal contempt.

Problem

Problem 10-5. P sued D in a federal district court for an injunction to prevent D from taking and carrying away D's property. If the district court grants the injunction, may the clerk prepare, sign, and enter the judgment without any direction from the court? What if the court denies the injunction? Does Rule 58 help you answer this question?

Chapter 11

Post-Trial Motions, Appellate Review, and Extraordinary Relief from Judgments

Section A. Post-Trial Motions

After the trial has been completed and judgment has been entered, the parties are permitted to make a (1) motion for judgment notwithstanding the verdict, which is now called a motion for "judgment as a matter of law" in federal court; (2) motion for a new trial; and (3) motion to alter or amend the judgment. *See* FED. R. CIV. P. 50(b), 59(b) & (e). These motions are principally used to (1) correct errors that occurred during the trial; (2) challenge the sufficiency of the evidence on which the judgment rests; and (3) rectify improper conduct by the parties, their attorneys, or the jury. They give the trial judge a final opportunity to correct these deficiencies before the complaining party is forced to appeal or seek other relief.

1. Motions for Judgment Notwithstanding the Verdict (Judgment as a Matter of Law)

Historical Background. The modern motion for judgment notwithstanding the verdict has no direct analog under common-law practice. Although at common law a *motion for judgment non obstante veredicto* (judgment n.o.v.) was recognized, the common-law motion, unlike the modern motion, was only addressed to the sufficiency of the pleadings and not to the sufficiency of the evidence produced at trial. The common-law courts permitted the plaintiff to move for a judgment n.o.v. after a verdict for the defendant when the defendant's plea was in proper form but failed to demonstrate any valid defense to the merits of the plaintiff's action. Under a similar common-law device, defendants were allowed to move for a *motion to arrest judgment on the verdict* when the plaintiff's pleadings were insufficient to support a judgment in the plaintiff's favor. *See Slocum v. New York Life Ins. Co.*, 228 U.S. 364, 381–82 (1913).

Unlike the common-law practice, the modern motion for judgment notwithstanding the verdict is used to challenge the sufficiency of the evidence to support a verdict. It is, therefore, a complementary mechanism to a motion for a directed verdict that is used to enforce the burden of proof in a civil action.

Judgment as a Matter of Law in Federal Court as the Equivalent of a Motion for Judgment Notwithstanding the Verdict. Under the 1991 amendments to Rule 50(b) of the Federal Rules of Civil Procedure, a motion for judgment notwithstanding the verdict is now called a motion for *judgment as a matter of law*. The motion for a directed verdict is now also called a motion for judgment as a matter of law under Rule 50(a)(1).

Under Rule 50(a)(1), the court may grant a motion for judgment as a matter of law (formerly a motion for a directed verdict) "[i]f a party has been fully heard on an issue during a jury trial and the court finds that a reasonable jury would not have a *legally sufficient* evidentiary basis to find for the party on that issue" and under the controlling law, the party's claim or defense "can be maintained or defeated only with a favorable finding on that issue." A Rule 50(a) motion focuses on the *legal sufficiency* of the evidence, hence the term judgment as a *matter of law*. As examined in Chapter 9, a motion for summary judgment under Rule 56 is also based on this same legal standard and similarly requires a finding under Rule 56(c) that "the movant is entitled to judgment as a matter of law." Under Rule 50(a)(2), the motion may be made "at any time before the case is submitted to the jury" and "must specify the judgment sought and the law and facts that entitle the movant to the judgment." Failure to make the proper specification is a sufficient reason to deny the motion.

Rule 50(b) provides that "[i]f the court does not grant a motion for judgment as a matter of law made under Rule 50(a), the court is considered to have submitted the action to the jury subject to the court's later deciding the legal questions raised by the motion." Rule 50(b) then provides that "[t]he movant may file a renewed motion for judgment as a matter of law and may include an alternate or joint request for a new trial under Rule 59." The renewed motion for judgment as a matter of law must be filed "[n]o later than 28 days after the entry of judgment—or if the motion addresses a jury issue not decided by a verdict, no later than 28 days after the jury was discharged." This provision in Rule 50(b) for a renewed motion for judgment as a matter of law is thus the federal court equivalent of the traditional motion for judgment notwithstanding the verdict.

In many state court systems, a party must move for a directed verdict *at the close of all the evidence* in order to later move for a judgment notwithstanding the verdict. In federal court, however, Rule 50(b) was amended in 2006 to eliminate this timing requirement. A party is now permitted under Rule 50(b) to renew its motion for judgment as a matter of law after the jury verdict provided the party made a motion for judgment as a matter of law under Rule 50(a) at *any time* prior to the submission of the case to the jury, even though the motion was not made at the literal close of all the evidence. The 2006 amendment only changes this timing requirement, however, and makes no change in the long-standing requirement that a Rule 50(a) motion *must* be made in order to preserve the right to later file a *renewed* motion for judgment as a matter of law under Rule 50(b).

Even though the court may be inclined to grant a motion for judgment as a matter of law under Rule 50(a), the court will frequently deny or reserve decision on a Rule 50(a) motion and submit the case to the jury. If the jury returns a verdict in disagreement with the court's assessment of the legal sufficiency of the evidence, the court can then grant a renewed motion for judgment as a matter of law under Rule 50(b). Reserving decision on a Rule 50(a) motion avoids the necessity of a new trial if the appellate court later decides that the trial court improperly granted judgment as a matter of law. In such a case, the appellate court can simply order reinstatement of the jury verdict. In contrast, if the trial court erroneously grants a motion under Rule 50(a) before the jury renders its verdict, the case must now be retried with a new jury.

Necessity of Preserving Record in Trial Court. In *Unitherm Food Systems, Inc. v. Swift*, 546 U.S. 394 (2006), the Supreme Court interpreted Rule 50 in a manner that emphasizes the importance of adherence to the Rule's requirements in order to obtain appellate review of a jury verdict on the ground that the evidence is legally insufficient to support the verdict. In *Unitherm*, the defendant properly moved for judgment as a matter of law under Rule 50(a) before the case was submitted to the jury. The district court denied the motion, and the jury returned a verdict against the defendant. After the verdict, the defendant did not renew its motion for judgment as a matter of law under Rule 50(b), nor did the defendant file a motion for a new trial under Rule 59. Instead, the defendant appealed.

The court of appeals considered and upheld the defendant's argument that the evidence was legally insufficient to support the verdict. The court of appeals did not grant the defendant judgment as a matter of law, but instead remanded the case for a new trial. The Supreme Court granted certiorari and reversed, holding it impermissible for the court of appeals to consider the defendant's objection that the evidence was legally insufficient, even to grant the defendant a new trial, because the defendant did not file the appropriate post-verdict motions in the district court. The defendant did not renew its preverdict Rule 50(a) motion after the verdict as required under Rule 50(b) and had not filed a post-verdict motion for a new trial under Rule 59.

The Court's opinion, written by Justice Thomas, was clearly influenced by the need for the trial judge to be able to exercise the maximum latitude under Rule 50 in determining insufficiency objections. *See id.* at 405–06. To accomplish this, the trial judge must be able to submit a case to the jury and then reconsider the insufficiency objection after the verdict, because if the verdict is in favor of the moving party, the need for the court to rule on the motion becomes moot. The Court further emphasized that the trial judge is in the best position to determine, in the first instance, whether a new trial should be granted or a judgment entered under Rule 50(b) because the trial judge sees and hears the witnesses and develops a feel for the case that a printed trial transcript cannot fully convey to the court of appeals. *See id.* at 401.

The Rule 50(a) motion prior to verdict did not give the trial judge the option to grant a new trial, and the trial judge was "without power to do so under Rule 50(b) absent a post-verdict motion pursuant to that Rule." *Id.* at 405. The denial of the preverdict Rule 50(a) motion could not form the basis of defendant's appeal, because the denial of the motion was not error. It was simply an exercise of the trial court's discretion to make an initial judgment under Rule 50(a) about the sufficiency of the evidence, subject to later revision, if necessary, under Rule 50(b) after the jury verdict. Later revision, however, requires a defendant to renew its objection subsequently to the verdict in order to give the trial judge the maximum latitude in the exercise of its discretion.

Note that the result in *Unitherm* means that the defendant lost a case that it would have won on the merits because of the failure to make an essentially costless Rule 50(b) renewal motion after the verdict or a motion for a new trial under Rule 59.

Judgment in a Bench Trial. When the action is tried to the court without a jury, Rule 52(c) ("Judgment on Partial Findings") serves as the analog of Rule 50(a) in authorizing the entry of judgment after a party has been fully heard on an issue. Rule 52(c) provides that "[i]f a party has been fully heard on an issue during a nonjury trial and the court finds against the party on that issue, the court may enter judgment against the party on a claim or defense that, under the controlling law, can be maintained or defeated only with a favorable finding on that issue."

Deciding a Motion for Judgment as a Matter of Law. In deciding a motion for judgment as a matter of law, the court draws all reasonable inferences in favor of the *nonmoving* party and disregards all evidence favorable to the *moving* party that the jury is not required to believe. (The jury would be required to believe, for instance, conceded or stipulated facts). The court then decides whether the evidence is sufficient as a *matter of law* to sustain a judgment for the *nonmoving* party. If not, the moving party is entitled to judgment as a matter of law. By example, consider a standard negligence action. Four legal elements are required to prevail on a negligence claim: (1) a duty of care owed by the defendant; (2) the defendant's breach of that duty; (3) a direct causal connection between the breach of duty and the infliction of injury; and (4) actual damage to the plaintiff. Assume that in such an action, the plaintiff offers sufficient evidence of the defendant's breach of the duty of care, but fails to offer any proof that the defendant's breach was a proximate cause of the plaintiff's injuries.

Under such circumstances, the judge would grant the defendant's motion for judgment as a matter of law. Granting such a motion in a jury trial does not infringe the plaintiff's right to a jury because the jury could not have properly decided in the plaintiff's favor. "Reasonable minds" could not have differed on the outcome because no proof existed on an essential element of the plaintiff's claim, *i.e.*, causation. The same result would obtain if the plaintiff offered some slight evidence on causation, but the judge, viewing the evidence in the light most favorable to the plaintiff, concluded that as a matter of law a "reasonable" jury would not be justified in finding in favor of the plaintiff.

2. Motions for a New Trial

A motion for a new trial allows the trial judge to correct prejudicial error that has occurred during the trial of the case. In federal court and in states with rules patterned after the Federal Rules of Civil Procedure, the power to grant new trials is governed by Federal Rule 59 or its state equivalent. A motion for a new trial under Rule 59 is one of several motions that are available to a losing party after judgment has been entered and must be "filed no later than 28 days after entry of the judgment."

Grounds for Granting New Trials. Rule 59(a)(1)(A) provides that new trials can be granted by the court in cases tried to a jury "for any reason for which a new trial has heretofore been granted in an action at law in federal court." Some typical reasons include erroneous jury instructions or evidentiary rulings, juror or attorney misconduct, newly discovered evidence, the jury verdict is "against the weight of the evidence," or the damages awarded are excessive or inadequate.

Distinguishing Motions for Judgment as a Matter of Law under Rule 50. Although a motion for a new trial because the jury verdict is "against the weight of the evidence" and a motion for judgment as a matter of law under Rule 50 are similar in that both challenge the evidentiary support for the jury's verdict, the two motions are distinct. On a motion for judgment as a matter of law, the court draws all reasonable inferences in favor of the nonmoving party and decides whether the evidence is sufficient as a *matter of law* for a reasonable jury to find for the nonmoving party. In contrast, the standard on a motion for a new trial is less stringent, and the court may find that although the jury verdict is *legally* sufficient under Rule 50, the verdict is, nevertheless, seriously flawed and clearly against the weight of the evidence.

The difference is one of degree and on a motion for a new trial, unlike a Rule 50 motion, the court may weigh the evidence and consider the credibility of the witnesses. The new trial standard is less stringent than the Rule 50 standard because the grant of a Rule 50 motion results in an immediate judgment for the moving party, whereas the grant of a new trial only leads to a re-trial of all or part of the case.

Remittitur and Additur. When the trial judge feels that the jury's award of damages is excessive, the court may offer the plaintiff the option of accepting a reduction in the amount of damages, known as *remittitur*, in lieu of granting a new trial to the defendant. Remittitur is a useful device because it saves the parties and the court the unnecessary expense and delay of a new trial. In *Hetzel v. Prince William County*, 523 U.S. 208 (1998), however, the Supreme Court held that if a remittitur of damages is ordered on the ground that the evidence does not support such a large award, the Seventh Amendment requires that the plaintiff be allowed the option of a new trial on the damages issue rather than forcing the plaintiff to accept remittitur for the lesser amount.

Conversely, when the trial judge feels that the jury award is inadequate, the court may offer the defendant the option of increasing the amount of damages, known as *additur*, in lieu of granting a new trial to the plaintiff. Although additur is recognized in many state courts, it is not available in the federal courts. In *Dimick v. Schiedt*, 293 U.S. 474 (1935), the Supreme Court held in a 5–4 decision that additur violated the Seventh Amendment because it authorized an award of damages never found by a jury, whereas remittitur involved "merely lopping off" the excess. *Id.* at 486. As explained in Chapter 10(1)(e), the Seventh Amendment does not apply to jury trials in the state courts and thus the states are constitutionally free to authorize additur in state court proceedings.

Bench Trials. In actions tried to the court, Rule 59(a)(1)(B) states that new trials can be granted "for any reason for which a rehearing has heretofore been granted in a suit in equity in federal court." However, in an action tried to the court, the court can simply re-open the judgment, if one has been entered, and take new testimony, or it may amend findings of fact and conclusions of law or make new findings and conclusions and direct the entry of a new judgment. A new trial may be granted on all or part of the issues.

Combining a Motion for a New Trial with a Motion for Judgment as a Matter of Law. Under Rule 50(b), when a motion for judgment as a matter of law is renewed after verdict, the moving party may combine with it a motion for a new trial. Rule 50(c)(1) provides that if a renewed motion for judgment as a matter of law is granted, the court must also conditionally rule on any motion for a new trial that is combined with it and determine whether there should be a new trial if the court is later reversed for granting the motion for judgment as a matter of law.

New Trials Ordered on the Court's Own Initiative. Rule 59(d) also permits the court on its own initiative to order a new trial for any reason that would justify granting a new trial on a party's motion. If the court exercises this power, it must specify the reasons in its order and must make the order no later than 28 days after the entry of the judgment.

3. Motions to Alter or Amend a Judgment

Another post-trial motion is one to alter or amend a judgment. This type of motion is recognized by Federal Rule 59(e) which provides that "[a] motion to alter or amend a judgment must be filed no later than 28 days after the entry of the judgment." This time period aligns with the time period for the other post-trial motions under Rule 50(b) and 59(b).

Grounds for Motions to Alter or Amend a Judgment. Federal Rule 59(e) does not specify the grounds that properly serve as the basis for a motion to alter or amend a judgment. In practice, it is used for a wide variety of matters. Typically, it is used "to correct manifest errors of law or fact upon which the judgment is based." *See* 11 WRIGHT ET AL. § 2810.1, at 127. It is also used to "prevent manifest injustice" resulting from, for example, misconduct of counsel. In addition, it may be used when there has been an intervening change in the controlling law or when newly discovered or previously unavailable evidence comes to light. *Id.*

Motions for "Reconsideration." Although a party may characterize a post-trial motion as one for "reconsideration," the Federal Rules of Civil Procedure do not authorize such a motion. If one is filed no later than 28 days after the entry of the judgment, courts will construe it as seeking to alter or amend a judgment pursuant to Federal Rule 59(e). If the motion for reconsideration is filed more than 28 days after the entry of the judgment, courts will consider the motion as one seeking relief from a judgment under Federal Rule 60(b), discussed in the final section of this chapter. The principal practical consequence of how a motion for "reconsideration" is classified relates to the time periods for initiating an appeal.

Clerical Mistakes. Even when more than 28 days have passed since the entry of a judgment, Federal Rule 60(a) allows "a clerical mistake or a mistake arising from oversight or omission" in a judgment, order, or other part of the record to be corrected by the court on its own initiative or on the motion of any party. After an appeal has been docketed in the appellate court and while it is pending, such mistakes "may be corrected only with the appellate court's leave."

Problems

Problem 11-1. In a trial to the judge in a federal district court, the court granted the defendant's motion for judgment as a matter of law under Federal Rule 50(a) at the close of the plaintiff's evidence. However, the judgment erroneously specified that the dismissal of the action was without prejudice. Which of the following motions, if any, is available to the defendant to correct this error: (1) a motion for judgment as a matter of law; (2) a motion for a new trial; or (3) a motion to alter or amend the judgment?

Problem 11-2. After a trial to a jury in a federal district court, there is a verdict for the defendant and the entry of judgment on the verdict. Two days after the judgment has been entered, the plaintiff discovers new evidence that was in existence at time of the trial but of which the plaintiff was excusably unaware. This evidence, if introduced at the time of the trial, would almost certainly have changed the result of the case. Which of the following motions, if any, may the plaintiff use to ask the court for relief on the basis of the newly discovered evidence: (1) a motion for judgment as a matter of law; (2) a motion for a new trial; or (3) a motion to alter or amend the judgment?

Section B. Appellate Review

1. Right to Appeal

Several fundamental rules limit the right to appeal: (1) a prevailing party cannot appeal a judgment; (2) a nonparty cannot appeal a judgment in an action between others; and (3) a party cannot appeal a judgment against another party. As you read the following case, *Walker v. Kazi*, determine which of these rules applied.

Walker v. Kazi

Supreme Court of Arkansas, 1994
316 Ark. 616, 875 S.W.2d 47

DUDLEY, JUSTICE.

Because of traffic, plaintiff Jenoddin Kazi stopped his pickup truck on State Highway 14. His truck was hit from behind by a second car. A third vehicle, another pickup truck, struck the second car from behind and pushed it into plaintiff's pickup truck. Plaintiff alleges he suffered injury in the accident. The police report shows that the third vehicle was driven by Gary Walker, Route 2, Weiner, Arkansas 72479. Plaintiff filed suit and caused summons to be served on Gary Walker, Route 2, Weiner, Arkansas 72479. Gary L. Walker of Route 2, Weiner was served. Gary L. Walker filed an answer denying that he was the driver of the third vehicle, and averred that his son, Gary D. Walker, also of Route 2, Weiner, was the driver of the vehicle at the time of the accident.

Gary L. Walker then filed a motion for summary judgment. Plaintiff responded with a motion asking that he be allowed to amend his complaint to name Gary D. Walker as the defendant and that the amendment relate back to the filing of the complaint. The trial court granted Gary L. Walker's motion for summary judgment. At the same time, the trial court granted plaintiff's motion to amend his complaint to name Gary D. Walker as the defendant and allowed the amendment to relate back to the date of filing the complaint. The notice of appeal and appellant's brief are both in the name of "Gary Walker" only. We dismiss the appeal.

The trial court granted Gary L. Walker's motion for summary judgment. If Gary L. Walker is the appellant, we dismiss the appeal because he was the prevailing party, and a prevailing party cannot appeal.... Further, Gary L. Walker has no standing to appeal for Gary D. Walker....

If Gary D. Walker is the appellant, the order allowing the amendment to relate back to the date of filing is not a final order and is not an appealable order.... The issue of a final order is a jurisdictional issue which the appellate court has the duty to determine.... We raise the issue and dismiss the appeal regardless of which Gary Walker is attempting to appeal.

Appeal dismissed.

Notes and Questions

1. In addition to the rules set out immediately before the *Walker* case, another rule was involved in the *Walker* case. That rule requires that a judgment be "final" before an appeal can be taken from the judgment. As you will see, if Gary D. Walker had been the appellant, the judgment would not have been "final" as to him because the order allowing the plaintiff to amend the complaint and allowing the complaint to relate back did not finally dispose of the action against Gary D. Walker. The "final judgment" rule is examined in section B(3)(a), below.

2. If the losing party in an action appeals, the prevailing party may rely on any matter in the record that will sustain the lower court's decision without the necessity of taking a cross appeal. However, if the prevailing party is dissatisfied with the judgment, the party will have to appeal, (or cross-appeal if the losing party appeals) in order to obtain correction of the error that leads to the dissatisfaction. For example, the plaintiff may win a judgment, but the court may erroneously not grant all the relief to which the plain-

tiff is entitled. Thus, the plaintiff may wish to appeal to correct the error and obtain complete relief. This situation is not really an exception to the rule against a prevailing party appealing because the plaintiff in this situation has "lost" relative to what the plaintiff sought by way of relief.

3. Should a nonparty to an action ever be allowed to appeal? For example, assume in a class action that the plaintiff class loses the action and the representative party decides not to appeal. Should a member of the class who has not intervened in the action be allowed to appeal? *See, e.g., Rosenbaum v. MacAllister*, 64 F.3d 1439 (10th Cir. 1995) (unnamed class member has standing to appeal award of attorney's fees to plaintiff's counsel without intervening). Should a nonparty who is adversely affected by a decision be allowed to intervene for the sole purpose of participating in an appeal? *See, e.g., Felzen v. Andreas*, 134 F.3d 873 (7th Cir. 1998) (nonparties may not appeal from a decision of any kind in a class action).

4. Closely related to the rules discussed above governing the right to appeal are certain rules that preclude parties from appealing based on their behavior in the action or in relation to the judgment. Certain kinds of orders, such as orders voluntarily dismissing claims against the defendant, are not appealable by the plaintiff, since they are not considered adverse to the plaintiff and do not have the effect of determining the case against the plaintiff. In addition, a party may not, pursuant to the doctrine of "invited error," ask the court to make a ruling in its favor and then complain on appeal about the ruling. Also, a party may not accept the benefits of a judgment and then appeal from the judgment. Finally, a party who voluntarily complies with a judgment "acquiesces" in it and cannot appeal the judgment.

Problem

Problem 11-3. P sues D, asserting multiple claims against D in the complaint. Subsequently, P voluntarily dismisses one of the multiple claims, and the trial court grants summary judgment on the other claims in favor of D. P seeks to appeal on the claims as to which summary judgment was granted and also on the claim that was voluntarily dismissed. Does P have the right to appeal on all of these claims?

2. Steps, Scope, and Standards of Review, the "Harmless Error" Doctrine, and Timing of the Appeal

Steps of an Appeal with Respect to "Error." The basic function of appellate courts is to review and correct "errors" made in lower court proceedings. However, not all errors will result in a reversal. Figure 11-1 on the next page highlights the four basic questions that must be considered as part of an appeal.

Review Generally Limited to Matters Contained in the Trial-Court Record. It is important for a lawyer to "make the record" in the trial court to preserve an error for appeal. Appellate courts will ordinarily reverse only on the basis of errors that have been properly raised below and presented to the trial court. The purpose of this rule is to allow the trial court to do something about the error while there is time to correct or avoid it. *See, e.g.,* Fed. R. Civ. P. 51(c)(1) ("A party who objects to an instruction [to the jury] or the failure to give an instruction must do so on the record, stating distinctly the matter objected to and the grounds for the objection").

BASIC QUESTIONS WITH RESPECT TO AN APPEAL	
Question 1	Was the alleged error **properly preserved** for appeal in the trial court?
Question 2	Assuming the error was properly preserved for appeal, does the challenged action constitute **error under the appropriate standard of review**?
Question 3	Assuming error was committed and properly preserved for appeal, was the error **"prejudicial" or "reversible"** error?
Question 4	Did the party seeking the appeal meet the **time limits** set for bringing an appeal?

Figure 11-1

"Plain Error" Exception. Even when the basis for error was not properly raised and preserved in the trial court, an appellate court may, nevertheless, reverse in cases of "plain error"—error which, if left uncorrected, would result in a manifest miscarriage of justice. Reversal based on "plain error" is rare and reserved for cases in which fundamental rights or the public interest is affected by the error.

Raising Matters on the Appellate Court's Own Motion. In addition, as discussed in Chapter 4, appellate courts will raise certain kind of errors, such as lack of subject-matter jurisdiction, on their own motion. Likewise, as discussed in Chapter 7, appellate courts will sometimes raise the lack of joinder of a Rule 19 required party on their own motion.

Standards of Appellate Review. The standard of review used by the appellate court depends on the type of matter that is being reviewed. Trial error may be predicated on the basis of a legal ruling, a discretionary ruling, or a factual finding. Each of these three types of potential error is examined under a separate standard of appellate review. Legal rulings by the trial judge, such as the judge's determination of the law applicable to the case, the judge's instructions to the jury, or the judge's decision on a motion to dismiss for failure to state a claim, summary judgment, or judgment as a matter of law under Rule 50, are examined by the appellate court under a "de novo" standard of review. No deference is given by the appellate court to legal rulings by the trial judge and the appellate court is free to decide the matter anew.

In contrast, factual findings by the trial judge are examined under a deferential standard of review. Under Rule 52(a)(6), factual findings must not be set aside unless they are "clearly erroneous" and the appellate court must give "due regard" to the trial court's opportunity to judge the credibility of the witnesses. Finally, discretionary rulings by the trial judge, such as granting or denying a motion for a new trial, permitting amendment of pleadings, limiting the extent of discovery, imposing discovery sanctions, or severing or consolidating issues for trial, are also reviewed under a deferential standard of review and are only considered error if the appellate court finds an "abuse of discretion" by the trial court.

"Harmless Error" Doctrine. Even when an error has been found under one of the above standards of review, the appellant must further demonstrate that the error is "prejudicial" to obtain reversal, *i.e.*, the error probably affected the outcome of the case. Appellate courts will not reverse on the basis of "harmless error." *See* 28 U.S.C. § 2111. Indeed, appeals are often not successful. In the federal courts, for example, the reversal rate is very low—less than 15% annually for private civil cases. *See* Administrative Office of the United States Courts, Statistical Tables for the Federal Judiciary, Table B-5, 2007–2012 (annual reversal rate in private civil cases for all circuits from 2007 through 2012 ranged from a low of 10.4% to a high of 13.6%).

Availability of Other Grounds. Finally, appellate courts will uphold judgments of trial courts if they are correct for any reason, even if the actual reasons given by a lower court for its conclusions are erroneous.

Timing of the Appeal. An appeal is initiated by filing a notice of appeal with the district court. The filing of a timely notice of appeal is jurisdictional. Thus, failure to file a notice of appeal with the clerk of the district court within 30 days after the date of entry of the judgment or order appealed from (60 days if the U.S. or an officer or agency thereof is a party) will result in dismissal of the appeal. *See* Fed. R. App. P. 3(a), 4(a)(1). The specific process for computing the time periods is set out in Rule 26(a) of the Federal Rules of Appellate Procedure.

Effect of Post-Trial Motions on the Timing of the Appeal. If a party files certain post-trial motions, the time for appeal under Rule 4(a)(4)(A) of the Federal Rules of Appellate Procedure "runs for all parties from the entry of the order disposing of the last such remaining motion." As set forth in Federal Rule of Appellate Procedure 4(a)(4)(A)(i)–(iv), these motions are (i) for judgment under Federal Rule 50(b); (ii) to amend or make additional findings of fact under Federal Rule 52(b), "whether or not granting the motion would alter the judgment"; (iii) for attorney's fees under Federal Rule 54 "if the district court extends the time to appeal" under Federal Rule 58; (iv) to alter or amend the judgment under Federal Rule 59; (v) for a new trial under Federal Rule 59; or (vi) for relief under Federal Rule 60 "if the motion is filed no later than 28 days after the judgment is entered."

3. The "Final Judgment" Rule and Its Exceptions

The" *final judgment" rule* limits appeals to situations in which the court has rendered a "final judgment" in the case. However, several exceptions provide opportunities for appellate review of lower court rulings and decisions prior to a final judgment.

(a) The "Final Judgment" Rule

An important aspect of applying the "final judgment" rule is determining when such a judgment has in fact been rendered. This aspect of the rule is explored in the *Gagnon* case, below. As you read this case, see if you can formulate a working definition of a "final judgment."

Gagnon v. Allstate Insurance Co.

Supreme Judicial Court of Maine, 1994
635 A.2d 1312

Clifford, Justice.

The defendant, Allstate Insurance Company, appeals from a judgment entered in the Superior Court (Aroostook County, Pierson, J.) vacating a judgment entered in the District Court (Madawaska, Daigle, J.) in favor of Allstate in an action filed by Daniel and Mona Gagnon, and remanding to the District Court for a determination of damages. Because the Superior Court's action does not constitute a final judgment, we dismiss the appeal.

On May 29, 1989, the Gagnons returned to their home in Van Buren after a weekend trip to discover extensive damage to the interior of the house. It is alleged that the hot water hose from the Gagnons' washing machine had ruptured during their absence, resulting in the escape of hot water and steam.

At the time of the incident, the Gagnons' home was insured against loss by a homeowner's policy issued by Allstate. The policy, by its terms, excluded coverage for water damage, but covered direct losses resulting from explosion. The Gagnons claim to have sustained a loss in the amount of $10,964.04. Allstate declined to honor the claim. The Gagnons then filed suit in the District Court, alleging Allstate's breach of the insurance contract.

After trial, the District Court entered judgment for Allstate, finding that the "sudden release of water" from the washing machine was an explosion within the meaning of the policy, but that most of the property loss was not covered because it was caused by the flow of water and steam subsequent to the explosion. The court held that the Gagnons failed to meet their burden of proof as to any damages resulting directly from the explosion and directed entry of judgment for Allstate. The Gagnons then filed an appeal with the Superior Court. The Superior Court determined that the District Court erred in applying the "water damage" exclusion to the Gagnons' loss, and that the provision covering direct loss from an explosion was applicable. The Superior Court then remanded the case to the District Court for a determination of damages. Allstate then filed this appeal.

Generally, as an appellate court, we do not entertain for review judgments that are not final.... A judgment is final as opposed to interlocutory when "1) the trial court's action fully decides and disposes of the whole matter leaving nothing further for the consideration and judgment of the trial court, and 2) no subsequent proceedings in the case will render the appellate court's decision immaterial." ... When the Superior Court remands a matter to the District Court, the nature of the remand order determines if the order constitutes a final judgment.... If the issue or issues that the parties seek to present to this court might be affected by actions taken pursuant to the remand order, we will generally decline to entertain the appeal.... In this case, the remand was for a determination of the damages that the Gagnons were to recover pursuant to the insurance policy as construed by the Superior Court. Although the parties stipulated that the Gagnons suffered "substantial damages," the nature and extent of those damages has not been fully and finally determined. That determination could well affect the construction of the insurance contract, which is the issue on which the appeal to this court is based. The damages determination is not a "procedural or ancillary matter," distinct from the construction of the contract, that would allow us to entertain the appeal....

Accordingly, because the Superior Court order is not a final judgment, we dismiss Allstate's appeal.

....

Notes and Questions

1. The "final judgment" rule applied in *Gagnon* is the basic rule governing appeals in American judicial systems. The rule is prescribed by statute in every procedural system. It is designed to (1) prevent multiple appeals in the same case; (2) avoid appeals that might turn out to be unnecessary if the complaining party wins the action or the ruling complained of otherwise turns out to be harmless; and (3) avoid disruption of proceedings at the trial-court level that would be caused by the periodic appeal of the trial court's rulings during the pre-trial and trial stages of the litigation.

2. With regard to the federal court system, the "final judgment" rule is found in § 1291 of Title 28, which provides that "[t]he courts of appeals … shall have jurisdiction of appeals from all *final decisions* of the district courts … except where a direct review may be had in the Supreme Court."

Problem

Problem 11-4. *P* sues *D* for $100,000 for breach of contract. *D* moves to dismiss the complaint on the ground that it fails to state a claim upon which relief can be granted. The motion is denied by the trial court. Is the denial of *D's* motion to dismiss a final decision from which *D* can appeal?

(b) Cases Involving Multiple Claims or Parties

Certain kinds of final decisions of matters in multiple-claim, multiple-party actions are made specially appealable by court rule or statute upon special certification by the trial court. Generally, these decisions are appealable only if the trial court directs the entry of a final judgment as to one or more (but fewer than all) of the claims or parties upon an express determination that there is no just reason for delay in the entry of judgment. In the federal courts, Federal Rule 54(b) follows this approach.

Notes and Questions

1. Original Rule 54(b) did not authorize the district courts to certify that a determination of less than all of the claims in a multiple claim action was final and appealable. *See* 10 WRIGHT ET AL. § 2653, at 19–24. The rule was amended to permit this certification in 1948 and was amended again in 1961 to make it expressly applicable to judgments for or against one or more but fewer than all the parties in a multiple party action. *See id.* at 24–29. Did the amendments to Rule 54(b) invalidly enlarge the jurisdiction of the courts of appeals? More specifically, if a particular order would not have been appealable before the advent of the rules, does making it appealable solely because of the trial judge's certification under the amended rule enlarge the jurisdiction of the appellate courts by operation of the rule? If not, by what process of reasoning could one conclude that the amendments to Rule 54(b) did not expand the jurisdiction of the courts of appeals?

2. In *Sears Roebuck & Co. v. Mackey*, 351 U.S. 427 (1956), the Supreme Court stated that Rule 54(b) "does not relax the finality required of each decision, as an individual claim, to render it appealable, but it does provide a practical means of permitting an appeal to be taken from one or more final decision on individual claims, in multiple claims action, without waiting for final decisions to be rendered on *all* the claims in the case." *Id.* at 435. The Court carefully noted that "[t]he District Court *cannot*, in the exercise of its discretion, treat as 'final' that which is not 'final' with the meaning of § 1291." *Id.* at 437. Recall that § 1291 provides that "[t]he courts of appeals … shall have jurisdiction of appeals from all *final decisions* of the districts courts … except where a direct review may be had in the Supreme Court." However, the Court concluded that a "District Court *may*, by the exercise of its discretion in the interest of sound judicial administration, release for appeal final decisions upon one or more, but less than all, claims in multiple claims actions." *Id.*; *accord Cold Metal Process Co. v. United Eng'g & Foundry Co.*, 351 U.S. 445 (1956).

3. How does a court determine whether a case presents more than one claim or only a single claim supported by multiple grounds? For example, for more than one claim to

be presented, do the claims have to arise out of different factual occurrences? *See* 10 Wright et al. § 2657, at 67–72 (pointing out that *Mackey* and *Cold Metal Process* do not require that the a "separate claim" for purposes of Rule 54(b) be one that is entirely distinct from all other claims in the action nor do they require that it arise from a different transaction or occurrence). On the other hand, should every variation in a claim be treated as a separate claim? *See id.* at 70–71 (suggesting the decided cases do not support such a position).

4. The district court must finally decide at least one claim in a multiple claim action or finally decide the rights and liabilities of at least one party before a proper certification and direction of entry of judgment can be made under Rule 54(b). For example, assume that *P* sues *D* in a U.S. District Court, asserting a claim for personal injuries against *D* and a factually unrelated claim for breach of contract. On *P's* motion, the court grants a partial summary judgment for *P* on the personal injury claim. A partial summary judgment deciding some of the issues relevant to a claim is not a final decision. Therefore, the court could not properly make a certification and direction of entry of judgment under the rule.

5. In *Curtiss-Wright v. General Electric Co.*, 446 U.S. 1, 12 (1980), the U.S. Supreme Court indicated that a district court's determination that there is no just reason for delay in entering judgment should be given substantial deference. Do you think that this same standard of review should apply to the other matters discussed in the preceding notes — *i.e.,* to the question whether the action involves multiple claims or to the question whether the district court has finally disposed of a claim? *See* 10 Wright et al. § 2655, at 39–42 (indicating that some deference is paid to the district court's determination that the Rule 54(b) requirements are satisfied, but, for example, the abuse of discretion standard is not applied to review of whether the district court's decision on the multiple claim is "final" in the sense discussed in Note 4, above).

Problem

Problem 11-5. *P* sues *D* in U.S. District court within the diversity jurisdiction. *P* asserts a claim against *D* for personal injuries and a factually unrelated claim for breach of contract. On *D's* motion, the court dismisses the breach of contract claim for failure to state a claim upon which relief can be granted, with leave to amend. Should the court certify this claim as appropriate for appellate review under Rule 54(b)? Suppose the court had dismissed the claim for lack of personal jurisdiction. Could a certification be made then?

(c) The "Collateral Order" Exception

A decision of a trial court is clearly final when all proceedings have been concluded at the trial-court level and a final judgment has been entered. This "pure" type of final decision is the model against which all other decisions are measured in determining finality. However, there are other circumstances in which a decision will be deemed final for purposes of appeal, even though the entire action has not been terminated. One of those circumstances involves "collateral orders."

The collateral order exception originated in *Cohen v. Beneficial Industrial Loan Corp.*, 337 U.S. 541 (1949). In *Cohen*, the defendant argued that the plaintiff was obligated by a state statute to provide security for the defendant's expenses and attorneys' fees in a stockholders' derivative action brought in a federal court based on diversity of citizenship between the parties. The district court held that the state statute was not applicable in diversity actions. The court of appeals reversed. The Supreme Court affirmed the court of appeals. In considering whether the district court's decision denying the defendant's request for security was appealable, the Court stated:

> This decision appears to fall in that small class which finally determine claims of right separable from, and collateral to, rights asserted in the action, too important to be denied review and too independent of the cause itself to require that appellate consideration be deferred until the whole case is adjudicated. . . .

> We hold this order appealable because it is a final disposition of a claimed right which is not an ingredient of the cause of action and does not require consideration with it. But we do not mean that every order fixing security is subject to appeal. Here it is the right to security that presents a serious and unsettled question. If the right were admitted or clear and the order involved only an exercise of discretion as to the amount of security, a matter the statute makes subject to reconsideration from time to time, appealability would present a different question.

Id. at 546–47; *see also Will v. Hallock*, 546 U.S. 345 (2006) (order denying application of a judgment bar contained in the Federal Tort Claims Act not an appealable collateral order).

As it has been developed by the courts, the "collateral order" doctrine provides that appeals can be taken from certain kinds of decisions made by trial courts when the decisions are (1) final determinations by the trial court (2) of matters separate from and collateral to the merits of the claims pursued in the litigation, (a) if the matters are too important to be denied immediate review by an appellate court, (b) if delay in appellate review may result in the matter being effectively unreviewable after termination of the entire action, and, perhaps, (c) if the matter involves a serious, unsettled question of law.

Most of the time, these requirements are unlikely to be satisfied. *See, e.g., Cunningham v. Hamilton County*, 527 U.S. 198, 209 (1999) (holding that an order imposing sanctions on an attorney pursuant to Rule 37(a)(4) is not an appealable final judgment under the collateral order rule even where the attorney no longer represents the party in the case; the Court's decision was influenced in part by the fear that permitting an immediate appeal from a Rule 37 sanctions order would undermine the purposes of Rule 37(a), which was designed to prevent delay or harassing tactics during the discovery process; "[i]mmediate appeals of such orders would undermine the trial judges' discretion to structure a sanction in the most effective manner."); *Digital Equip. Corp. v. Desktop Direct, Inc.*, 511 U.S. 863 (1994) (holding that a refusal to enforce a settlement agreement claimed to shelter a party from suit altogether was not a basis for immediate appeal as a collateral order).

Problems

Problem 11-6. P, a citizen of State *X*, sues *D*, a citizen of State *Y*, in a U.S. District Court in State *Y*. *D* moves to transfer the action to the U.S. District Court for the District of State *Z* under 28 U.S.C. § 1404(a) for the convenience of the parties and the witnesses and in the interests of justice. Assume that the district court denies transfer. What argument could be made that the denial of this order meets the requirements of an appealable collateral order? Does it matter whether *P* is complaining that the transfer was erroneous because the District of State *Z* is not a place where the action "might have been brought" within the meaning of § 1404(a) or because, even though it is, the district court in State *Y* did not properly weigh the public and private interest factors governing transfer?

Problem 11-7. P, a citizen of State *X*, and *D*, a citizen of State *Y*, enter into a contract containing a forum selection clause. The clause requires that suits on any controversies arising out of the contract be brought in a state court in State *X*. Subsequently, a controversy arises under the contract and *P* sues *D* in a state court in State *X*. *D* removes the action to the U.S. District Court for State *X* on the basis of diversity of citizenship. *P* moves to remand on the basis of the forum selection clause, and the district court grants *P's* motion. What argument could be made that this order should be appealable under the collateral order doctrine?

(d) Pendent Appellate Jurisdiction

Several federal courts of appeals have recognized the existence of this power to assert "pendent appellate jurisdiction," which involves the assertion of jurisdiction over a non-appealable order because of its relationship to another order over which the appellate court has jurisdiction. However, the courts of appeals have indicated that pendent appellate jurisdiction should be exercised "rarely" and only in "exceptional circumstances." *See, e.g., Natale v. Town of Ridgefield*, 927 F.2d 101 (2d Cir. 1991) (holding pendent party appellate jurisdiction improper on the facts of the case). In *Swint v. Chambers County Commission*, 514 U.S. 35, 50–51 (1995), the Supreme Court refused to "definitively or preemptively settle here whether or when it may be proper for a court of appeals with jurisdiction over one ruling to review, conjunctively, related rulings that are not themselves independently appealable." Thus, the propriety of pendent appellate jurisdiction is currently unsettled.

(e) The Rejected "Death Knell" Doctrine

In *Coopers & Lybrand v. Livesay*, 437 U.S. 463 (1978), the Supreme Court rejected the doctrine that had been recognized by several federal courts of appeals as another exception to the "final judgment" rule. This rejected exception was known as the "death knell" doctrine, which allowed a party to appeal a non-final order when the order sounded the "death knell" of the action.

(f) Interlocutory Appeals

Interlocutory appeals usually involve decisions about matters that may involve serious harm to a party before the entire action can be concluded, even though the matter may not qualify as a final disposition in other respects. In addition, statutes may authorize discretionary review of certain kinds of trial-court determinations when review could ultimately lead to the termination of the action at an early stage. Interlocutory appeals in the federal court system are governed by 28 U.S.C. § 1292.

Section 1292 of Title 28 authorizes two kinds of interlocutory appeals. First, § 1292(a) authorizes appeal from certain interlocutory orders of the district courts as a matter of right. The most important part of the statute is § 1292(a)(1), which provides jurisdiction in the courts of appeals to review "[i]nterlocutory orders ... granting, continuing, modifying, refusing, or dissolving injunctions, or refusing to dissolve or modify injunctions, except where a direct review can be had in the Supreme Court."

Second, § 1292(b) authorizes appeal from certain interlocutory orders (not covered by § 1292(a)) when the district judge certifies in writing that the order involves a controlling question of law as to which there is a substantial ground for difference of opinion and that an immediate appeal from the order may materially advance the ultimate termination of the litigation. When such a certification is made, § 1292(b) provides that the court of appeals may "in its discretion" permit an appeal to be taken from the order "if application is made to it within ten days after the entry of the order." The statute further provides that an "application" for an appeal under § 1292(b) "shall not stay proceedings in the district court unless the district judge or the Court of Appeals or a judge thereof shall so order."

Notes and Questions

1. Consider § 1292(b). Should § 1292(b) be used only in "exceptional cases" or is it permissible to use it in any case in which a good reason can be given why the final judgment rule should not be applied? *See* 16 WRIGHT ET AL. § 3929, at 433–35 (indicating that the legislative history and early case law under the statute support its use only in exceptional cases). Personal jurisdiction questions in the federal courts are normally reviewed after final judgment. Are such questions ever appropriate for review under § 1292(b)? If so, are there any conditions on the review of personal jurisdiction questions that the courts of appeals should recognize? *See* TEPLY & WHITTEN at 1019 (asserting that personal jurisdiction questions should be certifiable only if they pose truly difficult and unresolved questions).

2. Consider § 1292(a)(1), which provides jurisdiction in the courts of appeals to review "[i]nterlocutory orders … granting, continuing, modifying, refusing, or dissolving injunctions, or refusing to dissolve or modify injunctions, except where a direct review can be had in the Supreme Court." Why is there a need for a special statute authorizing appeals from interlocutory orders granting, denying, etc. injunctions? *See* 16 WRIGHT ET AL. § 3921, at 19–21 (indicating that the purpose of allowing interlocutory appeals from injunctive orders is based on the notion that these orders can involve serious consequences).

3. What kinds of interlocutory orders involve the grant or denial of "injunctions" under § 1292(a)(1)? Do grants or denials of temporary restraining orders qualify? If not, what is there about the policies supporting the statute that causes them to be excluded from its reach? *See* 16 WRIGHT ET AL. § 3922.1, at 92 (indicating that temporary restraining orders do not fit within the policy of the statute because their brief duration lessens the chance that they will involve irreparable injury).

4. Although grants of temporary restraining orders are not appealable under 28 U.S.C. § 1292(a)(1), grants of preliminary injunctions are. Assume that a district court grants a "mandatory" temporary restraining order against a party — *i.e.,* a temporary restraining order that requires the party to undertake affirmative action, rather than simply to refrain from acting in a certain way. Suppose further that the affirmative action will require an outlay of substantial funds by the party "restrained." Should such an order be appealable in spite of the general unappealability of temporary restraining orders? If not, how will the restrained party be able to recoup the amounts expended if the temporary restraining order is later held to be erroneous?

Problems

Problem 11-8. In an action in a federal district court, the defendant moves to dismiss the action on the ground that subject-matter jurisdiction is lacking. The question of subject-matter jurisdiction concerns the proper standard for determining the jurisdictional amount in controversy. The district court denies the motion. The defendant moves to have the district court certify the question of subject-matter jurisdiction for an interlocutory appeal under 28 U.S.C. § 1292(b). What standard has to be met to justify such an appeal? Do you think this kind of question is appropriate for certification under § 1292(b)?

(g) Review by Extraordinary Writs

Review by extraordinary writ — usually mandamus or prohibition — is available for certain kinds of nonfinal matters that are considered important enough to warrant review prior to the final termination of the entire action. Such review is normally limited to cases involving serious abuses of power by the trial court in withholding action it is obligated to take or in acting beyond its jurisdiction.

This "extraordinary writ" exception to the "final judgment" rule in the federal system is authorized by 28 U.S.C. § 1651(a). This section allows the court of appeals to issue an extraordinary writ of mandamus, prohibition, or certiorari to review actions taken by the trial court. This extraordinary authority permits intervention when the orders or judgments issued by the trial courts are not otherwise appealable or reviewable.

Notes and Questions

1. A petition for an extraordinary writ technically commences an original action in the appellate court. A typical example of the use of a writ of mandamus has been to protect the Seventh Amendment right to a jury trial. A typical example of the use of a writ of prohibition is to assert sovereign immunity from suit.

2. As indicated in the text above, the statute governing review by extraordinary writ in the federal courts is 28 U.S.C. § 1651. This statute only permits federal courts to issue writs "in aid of their respective jurisdictions." In the context of "potential appellate jurisdiction," what does the requirement that the writ be "in aid of" the court's jurisdiction mean? Does it mean that extraordinary writ review is available only when some matter would be unreviewable by appeal after final judgment? If not, what restrictions should be placed on review by extraordinary writ in order to protect the policies embodied in the final judgment rule and the interlocutory appeals statutes examined in the preceding subsections?

Section C. Extraordinary Relief from a Judgment

"Extraordinary" relief from a judgment is sometimes sought when the time for ordinary post-verdict motions and appeal has expired. As discussed in Chapter 12, it is also sometimes sought when the effect of the judgment is questioned in a later action.

Historical Background. Common-law courts could modify, reopen, or vacate a judgment during the term of the court in which it was rendered. Furthermore, the common-law writ of "error coram nobis" was addressed to the rendering court was available both during and after expiration of the term. This writ was used to set aside a judgment for clerical errors in fact. It was not available for errors of judgment. *See* ROBERT W. MILLAR, CIVIL PROCEDURE OF THE TRIAL COURT IN HISTORICAL PERSPECTIVE 390–95 (1952).

Another possible way to obtain "extraordinary" relief from a common-law proceeding was to bring an independent suit in equity, provided a party had grounds for relief that could not have been pleaded in the action at law, such as fraud or mistake. Equity court decrees were challenged by a bill or petition to reopen the decree. Furthermore, a plea of invalidity could be asserted against a judgment set up by an adverse party in a subsequent action. *See id.* at 386, 396–401.

Relationship of Federal Rule 60(b) on Earlier Methods of Obtaining Extraordinary Relief from a Judgment. Except for an independent suit in equity to set aside a judgment or the attempt to avoid the judgment in a subsequent action, Rule 60(b) of the Federal Rules of Civil Procedure supersedes all of the above-described devices for extraordinary relief from a judgment.

Bases for Relief Under Federal Rule 60(b). Rule 60(b) authorizes post-judgment motions addressed to the judgment-rendering court on six grounds:

(1) mistake, inadvertence, surprise, or excusable neglect;

(2) newly discovered evidence that, with reasonable diligence, could not have been discovered in time to move for a new trial under Rule 59(b);

(3) fraud (whether previously called intrinsic or extrinsic), misrepresentation, or misconduct by an opposing party;

(4) the judgment is void;

(5) the judgment has been satisfied, released, or discharged; it is based on an earlier judgment that has been reversed or vacated; or applying it prospectively is no longer equitable; or

(6) any other reason that justifies relief.

Time Limits on Rule 60(b) Motions. Federal Rule 60(c)(1) requires that the motion "must be made within a reasonable time—and for reasons (1), (2), and (3) no more than a year after the entry of the judgment or order or the date of the proceeding."

Notes and Questions

1. Under Rule 60(c)(1), a motion for relief from a judgment must be made within a "reasonable time." How much time do you think is reasonable? What factors do you think the court should take into account?

2. Federal Rule 59(e) provides for motions to alter or amend a judgment, Federal Rule 60(a) provides for correction of "clerical mistakes," and Rule 60(b)(1) provides for relief from judgments based on "mistakes." Do you understand the differences of when and how these rules might be used? To what extent do they overlap and to what extent does their coverage differ?

3. More specifically, what kinds of "mistakes" do you think should be covered by Rule 60(b)(1)? For example, is the language broad enough to cover "erroneous applications of law"?

Problem

Problem 11-9. After a trial to a jury in a federal district court, there is a verdict for the defendant and the entry of judgment on the verdict. Several months after the judgment has been entered, the plaintiff discovers new evidence that was in existence at time of the trial but of which the plaintiff was unaware. This evidence, if introduced at the time of the trial, would almost certainly have changed the result of the case. What specific requirements would the plaintiff have to meet in order to secure relief under Federal Rule 60(b)(2)?

11/27/13

12:43 am

Chapter 12

Finality in Litigation

Chapter 1 briefly explored the principle of finality in litigation. The principle of finality concerns the effect that a final judgment rendered in one action is to be accorded in a subsequent action with respect to claims and issues adjudicated in the first action. This chapter explores the doctrines of claim and issue preclusion as well as other aspects of finality in greater depth.

Section A. Introduction

Basic Terminology. Legal systems in the United States group the main rules embodying the principle of finality under the label "res judicata." Within the doctrine of res judicata, finality rules are further subdivided into two basic categories: (1) rules of "claim preclusion" and (2) rules of "issue preclusion."

An important point about terminology concerns the relationship of the phrase "res judicata" to the doctrines of claim and issue preclusion. Basically, "claim preclusion" prevents a party, after final judgment has been entered, from litigating any part of the same *claim* in another action, whereas issue preclusion prevents a party from relitigating in another action an *issue* of fact or law determined in the first action. Some courts use the label "res judicata" to refer only to claim preclusion. These courts use the label "collateral estoppel" to refer to issue preclusion. However, under the influence of the RESTATEMENT (SECOND) OF JUDGMENTS (1982), this terminology is slowly disappearing. The RESTATEMENT (SECOND) uses the label "res judicata" to encompass both claim and issue preclusion and refers to claim and issue preclusion by name to designate which doctrine the drafters of the RESTATEMENT (SECOND) are discussing at any particular point in their text.

For present purposes, the lesson is that you must read judicial opinions dealing with preclusion, in this casebook and elsewhere, carefully to determine how the courts are using the expression "res judicata." The notes and other text created by the authors of this book use the terminology of the RESTATEMENT (SECOND), but the cases reproduced in this chapter do not always do so.

Pervasive Features of "Res Judicata." In studying the materials that follow, you should keep in mind four pervasive features of the doctrine of res judicata. These four features fundamentally affect the administration of the doctrine in particular cases.

First, the doctrine of res judicata, as expressed in both claim and issue preclusion, is designed to operate even if error has been committed by a court in the proceeding leading to the judgment pleaded as "res judicata." Error, even error of a constitutional magnitude, must ordinarily be corrected by "direct attack" on the erroneous judgment, as opposed to "collateral attack" in a subsequent action. Direct attack is usually by means of an appeal. Collateral attack occurs in an action separate from the one leading to the judgment that is pleaded as res judicata. This aspect of finality is designed both to conserve judicial resources and to prevent vexation of parties by multiple litigation over the same matter.

Second, the extent to which the doctrine of res judicata prevents litigation, or relitigation, in a subsequent action will depend upon the nature of the procedural system leading to the judgment pleaded as "res judicata." Generally speaking, the more liberal the rules governing pleading, amendment, and joinder in a procedural system are, the broader the scope of a judgment rendered within the system will be. The reason for this variance in the scope of judgments between different procedural systems is the policy which insists that every litigant receive a full and fair opportunity to have the litigant's claims or defenses heard. Obviously, a procedural system that liberally allows claims and defenses to be pleaded, amendments to be made, parties to be joined, and so forth, will afford better opportunities to be heard than procedural systems that restrict a party's options in litigation. Such "liberal" systems will, therefore, usually produce judgments in initial litigation that preclude more matters from subsequent litigation than do more restrictive systems. The policy of affording every party a full and fair opportunity to litigate also supports many of the exceptions to the doctrines of claim and issue preclusion examined in later sections.

Third, the doctrine of res judicata usually only comes into play when someone attempts to use a judgment in one action to establish a claim or defense in *another* action. The doctrine does not prevent continued litigation over a claim or issue at a different stage of the action in which an original judgment is rendered. Thus, res judicata does not prevent review of claims or issues on appeal of a judgment in the original action. As stated above, traditionally courts have expressed this difference between the applicability of res judicata in original and subsequent proceedings in terms of "direct attack" and "collateral attack" on judgments. That is, res judicata does not apply to direct attacks on judgments, such as appeals, but only to collateral attacks on judgments made by a party in a different action.

Fourth, in most states, res judicata is a defense that can be waived if not raised in a proper and timely fashion. In procedural systems modeled on Federal Rule 8(c), res judicata is an affirmative defense. As an affirmative defense, it should ordinarily be raised in the defendant's answer. However, some courts have permitted the defense to be raised at later stages of a civil action, and a few states even treat the defense as nonwaivable. *See, e.g.,* *Swift v. Dairyland Ins. Co.*, 547 N.W.2d 147 (Neb. 1996) (appellate court may raise res judicata *sua sponte*).

Related Doctrines of "Law of the Case," "Stare Decisis," and "Judicial Estoppel." Two discretionary doctrines, the "law of the case" and "stare decisis," operate to prevent litigation of issues of law previously determined by a court. In addition, the doctrine of "judicial estoppel" sometimes precludes a party from taking inconsistent positions in successive judicial proceedings. These three doctrines sometimes overlap with the doctrines of claim and issue preclusion. When they do, claim and issue preclusion will normally control because they are not as subject to relaxation in the courts' discretion as are the other doctrines. Thus, law of the case, stare decisis, and judicial estoppel are most useful when, for some reason, claim and issue preclusion do not operate in a second action.

The doctrine of law of the case prevents relitigation of issues of law decided at successive stages of the same case. The doctrine is designed to maintain consistency, to terminate litigation over particular matters, and to maintain the prestige of courts. Like res judicata, law of the case involves costs. When the doctrine is applied without regard to whether the earlier ruling was correct, the benefits of the rule will be obtained at the expense of justice to the parties. This cost may be too great to pay within the confines of a single case than it is between different proceedings.

The doctrine of law of the case can operate differently depending on whether (a) a single court is attempting to decide whether to adhere to its own previous rulings on an issue in the same case, (b) a court is attempting to decide whether to adhere to the previous rulings in the same case of a court higher than itself in the judicial structure, or (c) a judge of a court is trying to decide whether to adhere to the prior rulings of another judge of the same court in the same case. Law of the case can also operate between successive stages of litigation in transferred and consolidated cases, as well as in multi-district litigation. Furthermore, courts and litigants sometimes become confused about whether claim preclusion or issue preclusion is the appropriate doctrine to apply in a given situation. Likewise, litigants sometimes confuse law of the case with claim and issue preclusion. Note that if a party argues law of the case when res judicata is the appropriate doctrine, the res judicata defense may be waived.

The doctrine of stare decisis requires that once a court has established a principle of law, the court will follow that principle in all future cases in which the facts are substantially the same. Thus, even if no other preclusion doctrine operates to prevent relitigation of an issue of law, an attempt to relitigate the issue may be futile because of *stare decisis*. Note also that *stare decisis* binds nonparties as well as parties to the action in which the principle of law was announced. In this respect, it is a broader doctrine than res judicata and law of the case.

Stare decisis is based on policies of security and certainty. Because people rely on decisions of courts in ordering their day-to-day affairs, departure from the principles of law announced in decisions should not be undertaken lightly. However, *stare decisis* is a doctrine of discretion. Courts can and often do depart from established principles when sufficiently weighty reasons exist for doing so, and sometimes even when they do not.

The policy supporting the doctrine of judicial estoppel is the protection of the integrity of the judicial process. This would be undermined if a party could take a position in litigation that produces a favorable result for the party and then take an inconsistent position in later litigation in order to obtain another favorable judgment. The issue arises often in disability cases when a party first obtains an award of disability benefits and later commences an action based on the premise that the party is not disabled.

In *Cleveland v. Policy Management Systems Corp.*, 526 U.S. 795 (1999), the U.S. Supreme Court held that a person who seeks and receives Social Security Disability Insurance ("SSDI") benefits cannot automatically be precluded from pursuing a claim against her employer under the Americans with Disabilities Act ("ADA"). SSDI benefits are available only to people who are unable to engage in an substantial gainful activity by reason of a disability. The ADA prohibits covered employers from discriminating against disabled individuals who can perform the essential functions of their jobs, including those who can do so only after receiving reasonable accommodations. The Court held that judicial estoppel could not be applied to prevent a claimant of SSDI benefits from asserting that she is a qualified individual under the ADA, because there are situations in which a person may qualify for SSDI benefits and still be capable of performing the essential functions of her job. However, the Court emphasized that its holding did not change the rules of judicial estoppel applicable to directly conflicting statements about purely factual matters. In addition, the Court indicated that in order to avoid summary judgment, the plaintiff in the

ADA action must explain any apparent discrepancies between her SSDI statements that she is totally disabled and her ADA claim that she can perform the essential functions of her job.

Not all courts follow the doctrine of judicial estoppel. Some reject the doctrine as inconsistent with modern pleading rules, which allow inconsistent and alternative pleading. Others refuse to follow the doctrine because they feel that it is an unnecessarily costly interference with the truth-finding function of courts. The Supreme Court has not yet indicated whether the *Erie* doctrine requires federal courts in diversity actions to follow state law on matters of judicial estoppel when it differs from the judicial estoppel doctrine that the federal courts would otherwise follow in federal question cases.

Section B. Claim Preclusion

1. Basic Principles

Claim Preclusion Generally. Claim preclusion rules are concerned with the effect that a final judgment in one action is to be accorded in a subsequent action on the "cause of action" or "claim" adjudicated in the first action. Generally, claim preclusion rules prevent a party from relitigating against the same party any matter that was a part of the same claim or cause of action adjudicated in the first action. In the second action, the party is prevented from litigating not only that which was actually litigated and decided in the first action, but also that which *might* have been litigated in the first action.

For example, assume *P* sues *D* for damages to *P's* arm resulting from an assault committed by *D* and recovers a judgment. *P* may not later sue *D* for damages to *P's* leg inflicted by the same assault. For reasons examined below, the doctrine of claim preclusion treats the injuries to *P's* arm and leg as a single claim or cause of action. Consequently, *P* is obligated to ask for both elements of damages in the first action that *P* brings against *D*. *P's* failure to do so precludes *P* from seeking the omitted element of damages in a second action against *D*. The same would be true if *P* brought the first action on a theory of negligence and the second action on a theory of intentional tort or for punitive instead of compensatory damages.

It is irrelevant that "new" matters presented in the second action were not actually litigated in the first action because the test for claim preclusion is not whether the matter was actually litigated in the first action, but whether it *might* have been. As noted in § 25(1) & (2) of the RESTATEMENT (SECOND) OF JUDGMENTS, the judgment in the first action precludes relitigation of the plaintiff's claim "even though the plaintiff is prepared in the second action (1) to present evidence or grounds or theories of the case not presented in the first action, or (2) to seek remedies or forms of relief not demanded in the first action."

Merger and Bar; Rule Against Splitting a Claim. Rules of claim preclusion are sometimes expressed in terms of "merger" and "bar." When a plaintiff sues a defendant on a claim and *wins*, it is said that the plaintiff's claim is "merged" in the judgment. As a result, the original claim no longer exists and has been replaced by the judgment, which the plaintiff can enforce against the defendant. Merger is the correct term to apply to the judgment described in the preceding paragraph because *P* won the first action leading to the judgment. If a plaintiff *loses* the initial action, it is said that the plaintiff is "barred" from bringing a second action on the same claim. Merger and bar are components of a more general principle governing claim preclusion: a party asserting a claim may not "split" the claim into separate parts and sue on the parts in separate actions.

Defining the Scope of a Claim — Traditional Approach. Obviously, in determining whether a party has split a "claim" or "cause of action," it is quite important to determine what constitutes part of a single claim or a single cause of action and what should be considered parts of different claims or causes of action. Comment a to § 24 of the RESTATEMENT (SECOND) points out that

> in the days when civil procedure still bore the imprint of the forms of action and the division between law and equity, the courts were prone to associate claim with a single theory of recovery, so that, with respect to one transaction, a plaintiff might have as many claims as there were theories of the substantive law upon which he could seek relief against the defendant. Thus, defeated in an action based on one theory, the plaintiff might be able to maintain another action based on a different theory, even though both actions were grounded upon the defendant's identical act or connected acts forming a single life-situation.

Under this older way of defining the scope of a claim or cause of action, a plaintiff might well have multiple claims or "causes of action" arising from a single transaction or occurrence. For example, in a case in which a person contracts to perform services for another and actually performs the services, the person might have a claim for breach of contract if the other contracting party does not pay for the services and also a claim for quantum meruit for restitution if the contract claim fails.

The Modern Transactional Test. The modern view, embodied in § 24(1) of the RESTATEMENT (SECOND) is to treat the scope of a claim as coextensive with the "transaction, or series of connected transactions, out of which the action [leading to the judgment] arose." This rule is based on the ability of a plaintiff, in modern procedural systems, to plead and join claims liberally against the defendant in the first action brought by the plaintiff. For example, Federal Rule 18(a) provides that a "party asserting a claim ... may join, as independent or alternative claims, as many claims as it has against an opposing party." Under the modern transactional test, however, the "may" of Rule 18(a) converts to a "must" under the common-law rules of claim preclusion if the additional claims are transactionally related to the plaintiff's original claim.

When the ability to join claims liberally is absent, of course, the scope of claim preclusion narrows accordingly. For example, if jurisdictional or other restrictions prevent a party from joining a claim seeking a certain remedy with a claim seeking other relief, claim preclusion will not prevent the party from bringing a second action for the additional remedy. *See* § 26(1)(c) of the RESTATEMENT (SECOND), discussed in subsection 3, below.

Under the modern rule, it therefore becomes important for purposes of claim preclusion to define what constitutes a single "transaction," or a "series of connected transactions." Section 24(2) of the RESTATEMENT (SECOND) sets forth a pragmatic approach to making this determination,

> giving weight to such considerations as whether the facts are related in time, space, origin, or motivation, whether they form a convenient trial unit, and whether their treatment as a unit conforms to the parties' expectations or business understanding or usage.

Scope of a Claim — Multiple Parties. The doctrine of claim preclusion does not require the joinder of additional *parties,* only the joinder of additional claims, and the failure to join an additional party does not violate the rule against "claim-splitting." For example, assume that *P* sues *D-1*. Assume that *P* also possesses a transactionally related claim against *D-2* and that it would be procedurally permissible for *P* to join *D-2* to the first action as an additional defendant under Federal Rule 20(a)(2) or an analogous state rule. Nevertheless, *P* is not required under the doctrine of claim preclusion to join *D-2* to the action and *P* is free to sue *D-2* in a separate action.

Similarly, assume that *P-2* possessed a transactionally related claim against *D-1,* such that it would be procedurally permissible for *P-2* to join with *P-1* in the pending action as an additional plaintiff under Federal Rule 20(a)(1) or an analogous state rule. *P-2* is not required under the doctrine of claim preclusion to join as an additional plaintiff and *P-2* is free to sue *D-1* in a separate action. Thus, for purposes of claim preclusion, the "may" in Federal Rule 20(a)(1) and (2) that "persons *may join*" or "*may* be joined" in one action remains a "may" and does not convert to a "must" under the common-law rules of claim preclusion, even though the claims involving the additional parties are transactionally related.

Nonparties in Privity with Parties. The rules of claim preclusion apply to both the parties and their "privies." Courts use the term "privity" to describe a number of special relationships and this concept is examined more fully in section D, below.

Judgments on the Merits. For the doctrine of claim preclusion to operate, the judgment in an initial action traditionally had to be "on the merits." Thus, if a plaintiff lost the initial action due to a dismissal on a "procedural" ground, the plaintiff could ordinarily bring a second action on the dismissed claim because the judgment was not "on the merits." Recall from Chapter 9 that the expression "on the merits" is the same as the expression "with prejudice," and the expression "not on the merits" is the same as the expression "without prejudice." For example, if an action is dismissed for improper venue, the dismissal is universally considered to be "without prejudice," or "not on the merits," and the plaintiff can bring a second action on the same claim in a court that has proper venue.

Under the traditional rule, a judgment was not considered to be rendered "on the merits" when it was rendered on some "procedural" ground unrelated to the merits. Thus, if an action were dismissed on the ground that the court lacked personal or subject-matter jurisdiction over the defendant, the plaintiff could bring a second action on the same claim in a court with jurisdiction. One area in which the operation of the "on the merits" rule has become controversial in modern times occurs when the plaintiff's first action is dismissed on the ground that the complaint is legally insufficient (*e.g.*, fails to state facts sufficient to constitute a cause of action). Traditionally, such a dismissal would not have been considered "on the merits" so as to preclude a second action on the same claim. However, comment d to § 19 of the RESTATEMENT (SECOND) articulates the modern rule that the general rule of bar should be applicable to judgments rendered against the plaintiff on the ground of legal insufficiency. The view of the RESTATEMENT (SECOND) is predicated on the liberal pleading and amendment rules available in modern procedural systems as well as on the availability of appellate review to correct erroneous dismissals.

Even under the traditional rule, there were restrictions on the ability of a plaintiff to bring successive actions on the same claim after a dismissal for legal insufficiency. For example, if the plaintiff's complaint were dismissed for failure to state a cause of action and the plaintiff brought a second action with an unchanged complaint, the doctrine of issue preclusion—here called "direct estoppel"—would preclude the second action.

Final and Valid Judgments. In addition, for claim preclusion to operate, a judgment must be *final*, and the judgment must be *valid*. With regard to finality, a claim usually cannot "merge" into or be "barred" by anything less than the final disposition of the claim in the initial action. The plaintiff must either have won or lost on the claim for merger and bar to be relevant. As a result, finality for purposes of claim preclusion will ordinarily coincide closely with finality for purposes of appeal. The validity requirement obviously necessitates that a judgment on a claim be rendered with personal jurisdiction over the defendant and subject-matter jurisdiction over the action. However, as you will see below, it is also possible for questions of subject-matter and personal jurisdiction to be foreclosed by a judgment in an initial action, so that the validity of the judgment cannot be challenged in a subsequent action seeking to enforce the judgment.

Res Judicata From the Defendant's Perspective. Claim preclusion effectively operates against defendants as well as plaintiffs. A defendant must assert all the defenses that the defendant possesses against the claim adjudicated in the original action. If the defendant fails to assert a defense, the defendant will be precluded from doing so in any subsequent proceeding to collect on the judgment. Thus, similar to the preclusive effect on the plaintiff, the defendant is precluded in a subsequent collection action from asserting not only those defenses that were asserted and actually litigated in the first action, but also any defenses that *might* have been asserted in that action. The ability of a defendant to withhold a claim against the plaintiff is determined by the rules governing counterclaim practice, which is examined in subsection 4, below.

2. Applying the Requirements of Claim Preclusion

Powder Basin Psychiatric Associates, Inc. v. Ullrich

Court of Appeals of Idaho, 1996
129 Idaho 658, 931 P.2d 652

WALTERS, CHIEF JUDGE.

After Powder Basin Psychiatric Associates, Inc. (Powder Basin) terminated George J. Ullrich's employment contract, Powder Basin filed two actions against Ullrich. In the first action, Powder Basin claimed that Ullrich was in wrongful possession of the corporation's personal property, and it sought recovery of the property pursuant to the claim and delivery statutes, *Idaho Code* §§ 8-301 through 8-312. The parties later negotiated a settlement, and that action was dismissed. In the second action, which is now before this Court, Powder Basin claimed that Ullrich wrongfully retained monies that belonged to Powder Basin and that were earned through services Ullrich rendered before being terminated. The district court granted summary judgment in favor of Ullrich on the ground that the claim was barred by res judicata resulting from the earlier action. Powder Basin now appeals from this order. For the reasons set forth below, we affirm.

I. FACTUAL AND PROCEDURAL BACKGROUND

Drs. Billy O. Barclay and George J. Ullrich, both psychiatrists, were employees of Powder Basin.[1] During Ullrich's employment, Powder Basin maintained offices in Coeur d'Alene and Spokane. On November 30, 1994, Powder Basin and Ullrich terminated their business relationship which had extended over a period of approximately seven months. They agreed to settle accounts between themselves and to establish separate practices.

---

1. For the purposes of this action, Barclay and Powder Basin are considered one and the same since Barclay owned all of the corporation's stock during the time of the events at issue.

Powder Basin subsequently sued Ullrich, alleging that Ullrich had taken some office furniture and office equipment from the corporation's office in Spokane in order to furnish the office for his new practice. Powder Basin claimed that Ullrich, as its employee, came into possession of these corporate assets which did not become Ullrich's personal property upon his termination. Pursuant to the claim and delivery statutes, Powder Basin alleged that Ullrich wrongfully retained these assets, and it requested an expedited hearing for return of the property. Ullrich responded that he was entitled to certain financial offsets from Powder Basin as a result of his employment agreement.

In a letter to Ullrich dated January 11, 1995, Powder Basin claimed that Ullrich was in possession of more corporate property than alleged in the complaint, which he was also wrongfully retaining. The assets described in the letter were monies arguably received by Ullrich for "services [Ullrich] performed at Pine Crest Hospital for Washington Medicaid patients and as Director of the Children's Unit...." Powder Basin stated in the letter that before the lawsuit could be settled, a complete accounting must be made of these monies. In its second letter to Ullrich, dated February 10, 1995, Powder Basin stated in pertinent part that:

> Any and all earnings generated after November 30, 1994[,] belong to Dr. Ullrich, without exception. Any earnings generated before November 30, 1994[,] belong to Powder Basin. In this regard we have reason to believe that DSHS income generated before November 30 is regularly paid within 30 or 60 days thereafter. We require that those sums be accounted to and paid to Powder Basin. We believe that this directorship fee for the [C]hildren's [U]nit for period of service ending November 30 is an asset of and must be paid to Powder Basin.

Powder Basin did not amend its complaint to either seek an accounting or to recover the money referenced in these letters. The record shows, however, that the parties later negotiated a settlement. Powder Basin subsequently drafted a stipulation to dismiss the lawsuit with prejudice which the district court granted in February of 1995.

On March 23, 1995, Powder Basin filed a second action, alleging that Ullrich wrongfully retained monies in excess of $10,000 for services rendered during his employment. Ullrich responded that this second action was barred by the doctrine of res judicata because Powder Basin's claim arose from the same transaction as the first action. Ullrich also counterclaimed that Powder Basin was unjustly enriched by wrongfully retaining accrued profits in excess of $10,000 because Ullrich had detrimentally relied upon representations by Powder Basin that Ullrich would either receive a cash bonus or be allowed to purchase a fifty percent interest in the corporation.

After a hearing on the motion for summary judgment, the district court granted a partial summary judgment in favor of Ullrich, and later upheld its ruling on a motion to reconsider. The court then certified the order as a final judgment pursuant to Idaho R. Civ.P. 54(b). In an order amending the judgment, the district court stated that "upon final affirmance by the appellate Court ... the Counterclaim shall be dismissed with prejudice...." Powder Basin now appeals from the court's order granting partial summary judgment and its order denying its motion to reconsider.

. . . .

III. DISCUSSION

Powder Basin claims that the district court erred in applying res judicata principles in this case to support an award of a partial summary judgment in favor of Ullrich. In determining whether the district court erred in granting summary judgment on the basis that the claim was barred by the doctrine of res judicata, we note that this doctrine precludes the relitigation of a matter previously adjudicated. *Ernst v. Hemenway & Moser Co.*, 895 P.2d 581, 585 (Idaho Ct. App.1995); *Aldape v. Akins*, 668 P.2d 130, 132 (Idaho Ct. App. 1983). Functionally, the doctrine has two components—claim preclusion and issue preclusion. *Aldape*, 668 P.2d at 132.

> "[C]laim preclusion," or true res judicata … treats a judgment, once rendered, as the full measure of relief to be accorded between the same parties on the same "claim" or "cause of action." … When the plaintiff obtains a judgment in his favor, his claim "merges" in the judgment; he may seek no further relief on that claim in a separate action. Conversely, when a judgment is rendered for a defendant, the plaintiff's claim is extinguished; the judgment then acts as a "bar." … Under these rules of claim preclusion, the effect of a judgment extends to the litigation of all issues relevant to the same claim between the same parties, whether or not raised at trial.… [C]ollateral estoppel or "issue preclusion" … bars relitigation of issues actually adjudicated, and essential to the judgment, in a prior litigation between the same parties.… [T]he contested issue must have been litigated and necessary to the judgment earlier rendered.

Roselle v. Heirs & Devisees of Grover, 789 P.2d 526, 528–29 (Idaho Ct. App. 1990); *Aldape*, 668 P.2d at 132–33.

Claim preclusion "[preserves] the acceptability of judicial dispute resolution against the corrosive disrespect that would follow if the same matter were twice litigated to inconsistent results." … *Aldape*, 668 P.2d at 133. Second, it serves the public interest in protecting the courts against the burdens of repetitious litigation and third, it advances the private interest in repose from the harassment of repetitive claims.…

A. Expedited Settings of *Idaho Code* § 8-312 and *Idaho Code* § 6-310 Are Not Analogous.

By use of an analogy to the procedure for an unlawful detainer action, Powder Basin argues that its claim should not be barred by res judicata as a result of the earlier action. It asserts that the earlier action was brought to obtain an expedited setting before the trial court for the determination of the right to possession of personal property, a situation which is similar to the statutory procedure in unlawful detainer actions allowing for an expedited hearing to determine the right to possession of real property.

Powder Basin points out that the unlawful detainer statute, *Idaho Code* § 6-310, provides that the right to an expedited trial setting (within twelve days from the filing of the complaint and service of the summons) is available only if the action is exclusively for the possession of a tract of land of five acres or less after nonpayment of rent. As a result, a claimant is precluded from obtaining an expedited setting where the complaint seeks relief on any other claims. Powder Basin argues that the same process should be applied to an action for claim and delivery with respect to personal property. In short, Powder Basin contends that in order to obtain an expedited setting on its claim for possession of the property in the earlier action, it could not also assert a claim for any other form of relief.

We disagree. Both the unlawful detainer process and the claim and delivery process are statutorily controlled. The claim and delivery statute, *Idaho Code* § 8-312, provides that while such actions generally may be given precedence over other pending civil actions insofar as setting the same for hearing or trial, the statutes relating to claim and delivery process do not require, as does the unlawful detainer action, that the action for recovery of personal property be an "exclusive" claim.

This method is not based on the uniqueness of real property for which the unlawful detainer statutes were established. We believe that a closer analogy can be found in the processes for either a writ of attachment or for injunctive relief accompanied by a temporary restraining order. In either case, the underlying cause of action triggering the right to claim and delivery continues to exist, and the claim remains subject to defenses and to counterclaims which may compel various processes requiring time and more involvement, such as discovery. We are not persuaded that—by judicial interpretation—we should engraft the "exclusiveness" requirement of the unlawful detainer action on to the statutes governing claim and delivery.

We reject Powder Basin's argument and hold that the ancillary claim presented in this case could have been pursued in conjunction with the claim and delivery process filed in the first action.

B. Transactional Facts for Both Cases Are Similar.

Next, Powder Basin argues that its claim should not be barred by res judicata because the transactional facts required in the first action, where the issue was wrongful detainment of personal property, differ from the transactional facts in this action, where the issue is the accounting of the earnings from Ullrich's service as an employee of Powder Basin. Powder Basin contends that as a result, the claim in this action is neither one that should have been decided in the first action nor was it necessary to the resolution of the claim in the first action.

A valid and final judgment rendered in an action extinguishes all claims arising out of the same transaction or series of transactions out of which the cause of action arose. *Bell Rapids Mut. Irrigation Co. v. Hausner*, 890 P.2d 338, 339 (Idaho 1995); *Diamond v. Farmers Group, Inc.*, 804 P.2d 319, 323 (Idaho 1990). In *Diamond*, the Court applied the formulation of the *Restatement (Second) of Judgments* § 24, for determining the scope of a "transaction":

> What factual grouping constitutes a "transaction" … [is] to be determined pragmatically, giving weight to such considerations as whether the facts are related in time, space, origin, or motivation, whether they form a convenient trial unit, and whether their treatment as a unit conforms to the parties' expectations or business understanding or usage.

804 P.2d at 323 n.4. However, claim preclusion is not applicable where matters raised in the second suit were not ripe for adjudication in the prior case. *Bell Rapids*, 890 P.2d at 338–39.

. . . .

The essence of the claims in both actions is that, upon the termination of his employment, Ullrich converted property belonging to Powder Basin. The record clearly shows that Powder Basin terminated Ullrich on November 30, 1994, that several business accounts were to be settled thereafter, and that Ullrich retained office equipment and office furniture belonging to Powder Basin. No other events occurred upon which either the claim in the first action or the claim in this action could have been based. We therefore agree with the district court that the claims in both cases are based upon the same transactional facts. We uphold the district court's determination that this second action was barred on claim preclusion grounds.

C. District Court's Application of Res Judicata Was Not Inequitable.

Finally, Powder Basin argues that its claim should not be barred by res judicata because the district court's application of this doctrine was inequitable inasmuch as the court failed to dismiss Ullrich's counterclaim which arose from the same transaction. Powder Basin asserts that such inequity arises because Ullrich's counterclaim can be resurrected and available to him if the district court's order for partial summary judgment is affirmed on appeal. Powder Basin further asserts that if Ullrich pursues his counterclaim, it would have no viable defenses available.

This argument is illogical and contrary to the record. The record does not support the assertion that upon affirmance of the court's order, Ullrich's counterclaim can be resurrected. In the district court's order amending its final judgment, the court stated that "upon final affirmance by the appellate Court[,] ... the Counterclaim shall be dismissed *with* prejudice." (emphasis added.) Because we affirm the court's order, Ullrich's counterclaim must be dismissed and it cannot be refiled.

IV. CONCLUSION

We conclude that the district court did not err in applying the doctrine of res judicata to the claim in this case. We affirm the court's order granting partial summary judgment and its order denying the motion to reconsider. Costs on appeal are awarded to the respondent, George Ullrich....

LANSING and PERRY, JJ., concur.

Thibeault v. Brackett

Supreme Judicial Court of Maine, 2007
2007 ME 154, 938 A.2d 27

GORMAN, JUDGE.

Steven A. Brackett appeals from a judgment of the Superior Court ... finding in favor of Shari Thibeault on her claim of unjust enrichment and awarding her $40,617 in damages. Brackett argues that ... a previous small claims judgment Thibeault obtained bars the present action under the doctrine of *res judicata*....

....

Shari Thibeault and Steven A. Brackett began a relationship in New Hampshire in 1996. In June 1998, Thibeault and Brackett moved together to Temple, to property Brackett purchased for $24,000. The deed was in Brackett's name only and both parties testified that the property was intended to belong solely to Brackett. Thibeault's two daughters lived with the couple in Temple until the couple separated in June 2004.

During the six years that Thibeault lived with Brackett in his home, both parties put money into converting the hunting shack that existed on the property at the time of purchase into a three or four bedroom home worth, in Brackett's estimation, about $150,000. Thibeault was anxious to build a bathroom and equip the shack with basic facilities for her two daughters. Brackett testified that they added two upstairs bedrooms and a bathroom for Thibeault's daughters. Improvements continued gradually as the parties, who worked rarely or not at all, periodically had money available. The improvements were finally finished in 2004 with the completion of a deck.

After the couple's separation in June 2004, Thibeault filed and received a judgment in a small claims action to recover certain items of her personal property from Brackett. Shortly thereafter, Thibeault filed a complaint in the Superior Court against Brackett alleging (1) breach of contract, and (2) unjust enrichment arising out of her contributions to the improvement and rehabilitation of the home, and claiming $100,000 in damages. Brackett moved to dismiss, arguing that the small claims judgment Thibeault received bars her present action under the doctrine of *res judicata*. The court denied Brackett's motion to dismiss. Brackett then counterclaimed for rent and for repayment of a $1000 loan he made to Thibeault.

At a one-day jury-waived trial in October 2006, the court ... found for Brackett on the breach of contract claim, but found that Brackett had been unjustly enriched and awarded Thibeault $40,617 in damages. The court also found for Brackett on his counterclaim for repayment of a $1000 loan, but found for Thibeault on Brackett's claim for rent. Brackett filed this appeal.

   ....

Brackett's first argument on appeal is that Thibeault's action is barred, under the doctrine of *res judicata,* in particular the doctrine of "bar and merger," by the small claims judgment and should have been dismissed. We disagree.

We review decisions regarding the effect of a prior judgment on a present action, which is a question of law, de novo. *Currier v. Cyr,* 570 A.2d 1205, 1207–08 (Me. 1990). Pursuant to 14 Me. Rev. Stat. § 7485 (2006), which deals with the effect of a small claims judgment on later actions:

> [a]ny fact found or issue adjudicated in a proceeding under this chapter, may not be deemed found or adjudicated for the purpose of *any other cause of action.* The judgment obtained shall be res judicata as to the amount in controversy. The only recourse from an adverse decision shall be by appeal.

(emphasis added.) This Court has found that the doctrine of bar and merger applies to section 7485, and held that a small claims judgment does bar relitigation of the *same cause of action. Caporino v. Lacasse,* 511 A.2d 445, 447 (Me.1986). Under the doctrine of bar and merger, relitigation of the same claim, even when different relief is sought and different theories are advanced, is precluded if "(1) the same parties or their privies are involved in both actions; (2) a valid final judgment was entered in the prior action; and (3) the matters presented for decision in the second action were, or might have been litigated in the first action." *Johnson v. Samson Constr. Corp.,* 1997 ME 220, ¶6, 704 A.2d 866, 868 (quotation marks omitted). We apply the transactional test to define "cause of action" and determine whether the matters presented could have been litigated in the first action. *Id.* Pursuant to the transactional test:

> [T]he measure of a cause of action is the aggregate of connected operative facts that can be handled together conveniently for purposes of trial. A prior judgment bars a later suit arising out [of] the same aggregate of operative facts even though the second suit relies on a legal theory not advanced in the first case, seeks different relief than that sought in the first case, and involves evidence different from the evidence relevant to the first case.

Id. (citation omitted).

Here, the two matters do not involve the same cause of action. The first case involved the factual question of what items of Thibeault's personal property Brackett had in his home. Conversely, the second involved the factual question of what contributions Thibeault made to improvements to real property and what she was entitled to in return. Although the two cases may have arisen as a result of the couple's separation, they do not involve the same operative facts and, therefore, are not one cause of action. For this reason, the doctrine of bar and merger does not bar Thibeault's current action.

   ....

Judgment affirmed....

Notes and Questions

1. In *Powder Basin*, the first action was for return of personal property, and the second action was for money wrongfully retained. The court held that claim preclusion prevented the second action. In *Thibeault*, the first action was for return of personal property, and the second action was for $100,000 in damages for unjust enrichment. The *Thibeault* court held that claim preclusion did not prevent the second action. Do you see a distinction between the two cases that justifies the difference in result? Does it matter that *Powder Basin* involved a commercial relationship while the actions in *Thibeault* both arose out of a personal relationship?

2. In *Thibeault*, the court held that it was not an obstacle to claim preclusion that the first action was in a small claims court. Was this holding correct? Consider the exceptions to claim preclusion examined in the next subsection and *Problem 12-4*.

Problems

Problem 12-1. P and D were involved in an automobile accident due to D's negligence. Immediately after the accident D jumped from D's car, punched P in the nose, and stated falsely to a bystander that P was an alcoholic. P sues D for personal injuries received in the automobile accident and recovers a judgment. P then sues D for the assault and battery occurring immediately after the accident. May P bring this second action? Why or why not? Could P have sued in a second action for slander based on D's statement to the bystander? Why or why not? Do you need additional information to answer either of these questions?

Problem 12-2. P pays state income taxes for the years 20xx and 20xx+1. In 20xx+2, P sues the state for a refund of the 20xx taxes and recovers. P then sues the state for a refund of the 20xx+1 taxes. May P bring this second action? Why or why not?

Problem 12-3. P leases land to D for the years 20xx and 20xx+1, beginning January 1st of the first year and ending December 31st of the following year. A dispute arises between P and D over the amount of land leased. As a result, D occupies a larger portion of the land during the lease period than P allegedly leased to D. P contends that the fair rental value of this extra land is $1,000 per year, but D refuses to pay either the $1,000 allegedly due for the first year or the $1,000 allegedly due for the second year. In 20xx+2, P sues D for the $1,000 allegedly due for the first year (20xx) and recovers. P then sues D for the $1,000 allegedly due for the second year (20xx+1). May P bring this second suit? Why or why not? If your answer to this problem is different than your answer to *Problem 12-2*, what distinction do you see between the facts of the two problems?

3. Exceptions to the General Rule of Claim Preclusion

The general rule of claim preclusion has numerous exceptions. Under § 20(1) of the RESTATEMENT (SECOND) OF JUDGMENTS, a valid and final judgment for the defendant will not bar another action by the plaintiff on the same claim when the judgment is for lack of jurisdiction, improper venue, or nonjoinder or misjoinder of parties, or when the plaintiff elects to take a voluntary dismissal without prejudice or the court specifies that the dismissal is without prejudice, or when a statute or rule of court otherwise makes the dismissal without prejudice.

Likewise, under § 20(2) of the RESTATEMENT (SECOND), a judgment that is based on the prematurity of the action or on the plaintiff's failure to satisfy a precondition to suit does not preclude another action on the same claim once the claim has matured or the precondition has been satisfied "unless a second action is precluded by the operation of the substantive law." The latter circumstance might occur, for example, if a party has failed to render substantial performance under a contract at the time of an original suit for nonpayment against the other party to the contract and later tries to recover in a second suit after rendering or offering to render the remaining services under the contract.

The rule of § 20 of the RESTATEMENT (SECOND) is very similar to the result that the U.S. Supreme Court reached under Federal Rule 41(b) in the *Costello* case, discussed in Chapter 9. However, it should not be assumed that every court operating under a rule identical to Rule 41(b) would reach the same result as *Costello*. It is quite possible that a court operating in a procedural system containing a rule identical to Rule 41(b) might hold that the rule is all-encompassing and that no exceptions to the rule of bar exist other than those recognized in the rule. A court operating within such a system might also refuse to construe the lack of jurisdiction exception of Rule 41(b) to include a failure to satisfy a precondition of suit. Thus, the presence of a rule like Rule 41(b) could render the doctrine of bar substantially more rigid than it would be under § 20.

In addition to the exceptions recognized in § 20, § 26 of the RESTATEMENT (SECOND) also recognizes exceptions to the general rule against splitting a claim. The exceptions in § 26 deal with situations in which there has been "partial merger or bar," with the plaintiff losing some of the freedom the plaintiff originally had to present the case. In contrast, the exceptions under § 20 involve situations in which the general rule of bar does not apply at all. In addition, the § 20 exceptions do not deal with situations in which "policy reasons favoring the maintenance of the second action come to light only after the first action is completed." The exceptions recognized under § 26 are as follows:

(1) Because res judicata is a defense that can be waived, the parties can agree that a claim can be split, or the defendant can acquiesce in the splitting of the claim;

(2) a court can reserve the right of the plaintiff in an initial action to bring a second action on the same claim;

(3) if the plaintiff is unable to rely on a certain theory of the case in the first action or is restricted by jurisdictional or other rules from seeking complete relief in the initial action, the plaintiff can bring a second suit on the same claim;

(4) an exception exists if the judgment in the first action was inconsistent with the fair and equitable implementation of a statutory or constitutional scheme;

(5) for reasons of substantive policy in a case involving a continuing or recurrent wrong, a plaintiff may be given the option to sue once for the total harm or to sue from time to time for the damages incurred to the date of suit; and

(6) an exception exists when it is shown that policies favoring preclusion of a second action are overcome for an extraordinary reason having to do with personal liberty or the failure of the prior litigation to yield a coherent disposition of the controversy.

Problems

Problem 12-4. P sues *D* for negligently causing *P* personal injury. Instead of suing in a court of general jurisdiction within the state as *P* could have done, *P* brings suit in a court that has no jurisdiction to give judgments in excess of $500. At trial *P*'s damages are assessed at $2,000, and *P* obtains a $500 judgment. *P* then sues *D* in a second action in a court of general jurisdiction to recover the remainder of the $1,500. May *P* maintain this action? Why or why not?

Problem 12-5. *P* suffers personal injuries resulting from *D's* negligence. Under the applicable substantive law, if *P* was *D's* employee at the time of the accident, *P's* sole remedy is under worker's compensation law. If *P* was not an employee, then *P* only has a common-law action for negligence. *P* files an action before the state worker's compensation commission, which has jurisdiction only to hear worker's compensation claims, but loses because he is found not to have been *D's* employee. Does the doctrine of res judicata preclude *P* from maintaining a second action for common-law negligence? Why or why not?

Problem 12-6. *P* sues *D* for personal injuries and the action is dismissed on the ground of improper venue. *P* then files a second action in the same court. *P* asserts the same claim, alleging that error was committed in the first action when the judge dismissed the action for improper venue. May *P* maintain this second action? Why or why not? May *P* maintain an action on the claim in any court?

Problem 12-7. *P* sues *D* in a United States District Court in California. *D* moves to dismiss the action for improper venue and *D's* motion is granted, the court specifying the dismissal to be with prejudice. *P* then sues *D* in a United States District Court in New York, where venue is proper. *D* asserts that the judgment of dismissal in the first action is res judicata because the court specified the dismissal to be with prejudice. How should the court rule on *D's* defense?

Problem 12-8. On January 1st, *P* sues *D* alleging that in consideration for the payment of $100 by *P*, *D* agreed to deliver certain goods to *P* and that *D* has failed to deliver the goods. At the trial it appears the goods were not to be delivered until June 1st. As a result, the court renders judgment as a matter of law for *D*. If *D* has failed to deliver the goods by June 1st, may *P* maintain a second action for breach of contract against *D*? Why or why not? If the jurisdiction in question has a procedural rule identical to Federal Rule 41(b), could *P* maintain the second action?

Problem 12-9. *P* and *D* are involved in an automobile accident. *P* files two actions in the same jurisdiction against *D*, one for personal injuries resulting from the automobile accident and one for property damage resulting from the accident. *D* could have filed an objection in the second action on grounds that there was another action pending concerning the same subject matter, but did not do so. Had *D* objected, *D* would have been entitled to have the second action consolidated with the first. After a judgment in *P's* favor, in the personal injury action, *D* requests dismissal of the second action for property damage on grounds that the judgment in the personal injury action is res judicata. Should the court grant *D's* request? Why or why not?

Problem 12-10. *P*, a citizen of Oregon, sued *D*, a citizen of Nebraska, in the U.S. District Court for the District of Nebraska. *P* asserted claims against *D* under the federal antitrust laws, claims over which the federal courts have exclusive jurisdiction. Subsequently, *P* also sued *D* in a state court of Oregon, asserting a number of state claims that arise out of the same facts as *P's* antitrust claims. The U.S. District Court ultimately dismissed *P's* antitrust suit with prejudice. After this dismissal occurred, *D* moved for summary judgment in the state court action on ground of res judicata, arguing that *P* split *P's* claim for relief. Should *D* win?

Problem 12-11. *P* sues *P's* spouse, *D*, for separate maintenance on the basis of desertion by *D* and obtains a judgment. Subsequently, *P* sues *D* for a divorce on the same grounds (desertion). May *P* maintain the second action? Why or why not?

4. Counterclaims, Crossclaims, Third-Party Claims, and Claims by Intervenors and Rule 19 Parties

The requirements of claim preclusion apply not only to the claims asserted by the plaintiff, but to all claims asserted by any party in the action. Thus, counterclaims under Federal Rule 13(a) and (b), crossclaims under Federal Rule 13(g), third-party claims under Federal Rule 14(a), and claims by parties who intervene under Federal Rule 24(a) and (b) or are joined under Rule 19 are fully subject to the same requirements of claim preclusion discussed earlier. For example, if a party in the action asserts a claim and omits an element of damages, the party has "split" the claim and cannot bring a subsequent action to recover the element of damages omitted. In addition, under the modern transactional test, once a party asserts a claim, the party is required to also assert all other claims that the party has against the opposing party that arise from the same transaction or series of connected transactions as the first claim.

The key for triggering the application of claim preclusion, however, is the assertion of an initial claim. As discussed in Chapter 7, counterclaims under Rule 13(b), crossclaims under Rule 13(g), and third-party plaintiff complaints under Rule 14(a) are all *permissive* in an initial sense. A party is not required to assert any of these claims under federal principles of claim preclusion or under the express wording of the Federal Rules themselves. For example, even though a crossclaim under Rule 13(g) must be transactionally related to either the original claim or a counterclaim in the action to qualify for joinder, it is not mandatory that a party assert a crossclaim under Rule 13(g). Similarly, even though a person must have some connection to an action to qualify as an intervenor under Rule 24(a) or (b), a person is not required to intervene under Rule 24.

Nevertheless, once a party joins or is joined in an action and chooses to assert a claim, then the prohibitions against claim splitting fully apply and require that all transactionally related claims also be asserted under penalty of claim preclusion. For example, even though a party is not required to assert a crossclaim under Rule 13(g), once a party chooses to asserts a crossclaim against a coparty, the party must then assert under penalty of claim preclusion all other transactionally related claims that the party has against that coparty. Thus, the "may" of Federal Rule 18(a), which provides that a party "asserting a claim, counterclaim, crossclaim, or third-party claim *may* join, as independent or alternate claims, as many claims as it has against an opposing party," converts to a "must" for purposes of claim preclusion if the additional claims are transactionally related to the party's initially asserted claim.

This general principle that claim preclusion ~~does not apply~~ is inapplicable until a party has first asserted an initial claim does not apply, of course, to *compulsory* counterclaims. Compulsory counterclaim rules, such as Federal Rule 13(a) require a party to assert any claim that the party possesses against an opposing party arising out of the same transaction or occurrence that is the subject-matter of the opposing party's claim. If a claim qualifies as a compulsory counterclaim under such a rule, the counterclaim must be asserted in the current action under penalty of preclusion in a subsequent action, even though the party never asserts any claim in the first action.

The following materials examine the operation of the "same transaction or occurrence" test in compulsory counterclaim rules. One interesting question is whether the "same transaction occurrence" test used in a compulsory counterclaim rule, such as Federal Rule 13(a), is broader or narrower than the "same transaction or occurrence" test used for purposes of claim preclusion. This question is explored in Note 2, below.

United-Bilt Homes, Inc. v. Sampson

Supreme Court of Arkansas, 1993
315 Ark. 156, 864 S.W.2d 861

CORBIN, JUSTICE.

Appellant, United-Bilt Homes, Incorporated, appeals a judgment of the Pulaski Chancery Court finding that appellant's complaint for foreclosure against appellee, Charles Sampson, was a compulsory counterclaim that should have been filed in a previous suit between the same parties. For reversal appellant relies on Ark. R. Civ. P. Rule 13(a) and (d) and asserts two points of error. We find merit to the first point of error and therefore reverse and remand.

This is the second appeal we have heard involving the same parties. In *United-Bilt Homes, Inc. v. Sampson*, 832 S.W.2d 502 (Ark. 1992) (*Sampson I*), we affirmed Sampson's judgment for compensatory and punitive damages against United-Bilt. In that case, we held that United-Bilt, who was the loss-payee on Sampson's homeowner's policy, had wrongly refused to release insurance proceeds to the contractor who repaired Sampson's home following a fire. The instant case was initiated on July 23, 1992, the day after we delivered our decision in *Sampson I*, when United-Bilt filed a complaint for foreclosure against Sampson. Sampson answered and filed a motion to dismiss claiming the foreclosure action was a compulsory counterclaim under Ark. R. Civ. P. Rule 13 which should have been asserted in *Sampson I*. After a hearing on the motion, the chancery court found the action for foreclosure was a compulsory counterclaim which should have been brought in the previous lawsuit and granted the dismissal.

On appeal, United-Bilt asserts two reasons the chancellor's ruling was in error. First, United-Bilt argues the foreclosure action did not "arise[ ] out of the transaction or occurrence" litigated in the previous suit as that phrase is used in Rule 13(a). Second, United-Bilt argues that according to Rule 13(d), its cause of action did not mature until after the issues were joined because it did not exercise its option to accelerate the entire indebtedness until after it had filed its answer.

Initially, we observe that issues are joined when a fact or conclusion of law is asserted in one party's pleading and is admitted or denied in the responding party's pleading.... We also observe that a cause of action on an entire debt owed under an installment sales contract with an optional acceleration clause does not arise until the option is exercised.... The issues in *Sampson I* were joined on December 5, 1990, when United-Bilt filed its answer to Sampson's third-party complaint. As of that point in time, the record reveals that Sampson was at most two payments behind, but that United-Bilt had not exercised its option to accelerate the debt. Thus, we are inclined to agree with United-Bilt's second argument. However, because we conclude the trial court erred in determining the two cases arose out of the same transaction or occurrence, we need not analyze the merits of United-Bilt's second argument.

From the bench, the trial court stated its reasoning for granting the dismissal. The chancellor reasoned that the two cases arose from the mortgage and thus from the "same transaction or occurrence." In order to decide whether appellant's foreclosure action arose out of the same transaction or occurrence litigated in *Sampson I*, we must look to the facts surrounding that case. There was a fire at Sampson's home. United-Bilt was the loss-payee on Sampson's homeowner's insurance policy. Consequently, the insurance company issued a check payable to both United-Bilt and Sampson. Sampson and United-Bilt agreed the insurance proceeds would be used to repair the home. On that promise, Sampson endorsed the check and contracted with a contractor to complete the repairs. United-Bilt held the funds in escrow, but refused to pay out approximately $12,000.00 of the funds when the repairs were finished. Sampson was unable to pay the contractor who had completed the work. The contractor sued Sampson for the balance due on the contract and Sampson impleaded United-Bilt alleging tortious interference with his contract with the contractor.

Sampson I involved two contracts. First, there was the contract between Sampson and the contractor who made the repairs. Second, there was the contract between Sampson and United-Bilt, whereby Sampson agreed to have the property repaired and United-Bilt agreed to use the insurance proceeds to pay for the repairs. While the relationship of mortgagor and mortgagee between Sampson and United-Bilt existed at the time of the contract regarding the insurance proceeds and was the reason the proceeds were payable to Sampson and United-Bilt jointly, neither this relationship nor the mortgage itself was at issue in *Sampson I*. To the contrary, it is precisely the mortgage and the mortgagee-mortgagor relationship that is at issue in the instant case.

[The court here quoted Rule 13(a) and (b) of the Arkansas Rules of Civil Procedure, which are in all essential respects the same as Federal Rule 13(a) and (b).]

The transaction or occurrence at issue in *Sampson I* was the disbursement of insurance proceeds for a repair contract. The execution of the mortgage and subsequent default thereof that is at issue in the instant foreclosure action is a separate "transaction or occurrence." Thus, according to Rule 13(a), the chancellor erred in dismissing the suit.

This court has previously held that one document may be the source of two independent claims, one of which is not necessarily a compulsory counterclaim to be asserted with the other. *Baltz v. Security Bank*, 613 S.W.2d 833 (Ark. 1981). Our holding today is consistent with *Baltz*. Moreover, as Sampson at most was two payments behind at the time the issues were joined in *Sampson I*, our holding is consistent with the principle of permitting equity courts to protect a debtor against an inequitable acceleration of the maturity of a debt....

The judgment dismissing the foreclosure action is reversed and remanded for further proceedings consistent with this decision.

Notes and Questions

1. One commentator has concluded that the Arkansas Supreme Court unjustifiably abandoned the "logical relationship" test for determining whether counterclaims are compulsory in favor of a version of the "same evidence" standard. *See* Rebecca D. Hattabaugh, Case Note, United-Bilt Homes, Inc. v. Sampson: *A New Standard for Compulsory Counterclaims?* 48 Ark. L. Rev. 1009, 1024–25 (1995). Do you agree? Both tests are ways of determining whether the same transaction or occurrence test of the compulsory counterclaim rule has been satisfied. Based on your recollection from earlier chapters of how the same transaction or occurrence test is administered in different contexts, do you see a good reason for not holding the counterclaim in *United-Bilt* compulsory?

2. (a) All counterclaim rules patterned on Federal Rule 13(a) use the "same transaction or occurrence" test to determine whether a counterclaim is compulsory and should have been asserted in a prior action. As illustrated by the *Powder Basin* case above, §24 of the Restatement (Second) also employs a transactional approach to determine the scope of a claim for the purposes of determining when a plaintiff has impermissibly split a claim between two (or more) actions. In addition, §22(2)(a) of the Restatement (Second) provides that a defendant who fails to interpose a counterclaim in an action is precluded from maintaining an action on the claim if the counterclaim was required to be interposed by a compulsory counterclaim statute or court rule.

(b) The Restatement (Second) does not indicate explicitly how to determine when a compulsory counterclaim rule employing the same transaction or occurrence standard should be considered violated by an *omitted* counterclaim in an initial action. In other respects, as indicated by §§ 21 and 24 of the Restatement (Second), the general rules governing merger and bar of plaintiff's claims are also applicable to counterclaims. Thus, if a party interposes a counterclaim, the usual rules of merger or bar governing original claims apply to extinguish the right of the party to remedies against the opposing party with respect to all or any part of the transaction, or series of connected transactions, out of which the counterclaim arose. However, if a party fails to assert any counterclaim at all and the jurisdiction has a rule identical to Federal Rule 13(a), the counterclaim will only be precluded if it satisfies the same transaction or occurrence test of the compulsory counterclaim rule.

(c) This difference gives rise to the possibility that a claim which would be precluded under the normal rules of claim preclusion if it had been omitted by a plaintiff may not be precluded if it is omitted by a defendant under Rule 13(a) if the "same transaction" test of Rule 13(a) is interpreted to be narrower than the "same transaction" test of the Restatement (Second). Should the transactional test of the Restatement (Second) and Rule 13(a) be administered identically, or is there a good reason to have a narrower test for determining when a counterclaim is compulsory? Is there a good reason to require a plaintiff in an initial action to bring forward more elements arising out of a general series of events (or a relationship) than there is for requiring a defendant (or a third-party defendant, as in the *Sampson* case) to assert a factually related claim against an opposing party under a compulsory counterclaim rule?

3. If the transactional test of the Restatement (Second) had been used to determine whether the counterclaim in *United-Bilt* was compulsory, would the result in the case have been the same?

4. Like plaintiff's claims, omitted counterclaims are not precluded if the defendant cannot assert them in the initial action because of restrictions on the subject-matter jurisdiction of the court and the unavailability of devices such as removal to another court or consolidation that might allow the defendant to assert the counterclaim. *See* Restatement (Second) of Judgments § 21(2) (1982).

5. Compulsory counterclaim rules like Federal Rule 13(a) also do not apply to a defendant's potential claims against the plaintiff when the defendant defaults before serving an answer. As discussed in Chapter 7(D)(2), the compulsory counterclaim requirement is triggered only when a pleader serves a "pleading" that omits claims arising out of the transaction or occurrence that is the subject matter of the opposing party's claim.

6. Nevertheless, in addition to formal compulsory counterclaim rules or statutes, a well-accepted, common-law rule exists that sometimes prohibits a defendant who loses an initial action from maintaining a claim against the plaintiff in a subsequent proceeding even in the absence or nonapplicability of a compulsory counterclaim provision. This result occurs when allowing the defendant to assert the claim will "nullify the initial judgment or would impair rights established in the initial action." Restatement (Second) of Judgments § 22(2)(b) (1982). Thus, if *P* sues *D* to quiet title to Blackacre and obtains a judgment by default, *D* may not bring a subsequent action to quiet title to the same property even in the absence or nonapplicability of a compulsory counterclaim provision. Allowing a second action by *D* would completely undermine the judgment obtained by *P* in the initial action.

It is important to remember that this rule operates only when the second action would completely undermine or nullify the judgment in the first. It would not operate, for example, if *P* sued *D* for personal injuries arising out of an automobile accident and won and then *D* sued *P* for personal injuries arising out of the same accident. Although, as we will see below, issue preclusion might well prevent *D* from maintaining this second action, in the absence of a compulsory counterclaim rule, no common-law rule of claim preclusion would do so. Technically, *P's* judgment and *D's* judgment can coexist without either nullifying or completely undermining the other. However, it would not be surprising to find that a state would allow *P* in the second action to set-off any amount that *D* owed *P* under the first judgment.

Problems

Problem 12-12. *P* sued *D* for the contract price for goods sold and delivered to *D* and recovered a judgment. Subsequently, *D* sued *P* for an assault and battery that occurred when *P* came to *D's* home prior to the initial action by *P* and sought to collect the money owed from *D*. If the jurisdiction in question possesses a compulsory counterclaim rule, may *D* maintain the action for assault and battery?

Problem 12-13. *D* is the editor of a newspaper who wrote an allegedly libelous article about *P*. After the article was published, *P* and *D* met on the street and got into an argument about the article, whereupon *P* allegedly assaulted *D*. *P* sued *D* for libel and won. Subsequently, *D* sued *P* for the assault and battery. If the jurisdiction in question possesses a compulsory counterclaim rule, may *D* maintain the action for the assault?

Problem 12-14. On the facts of each of the preceding two problems, assume that both claims are possessed by *P* and are asserted in successive actions by *P*. Would *P* be permitted to maintain an action on the second (assault and battery) claim in either of the two problems under the test of the RESTATEMENT (SECOND) for determining the scope of a claim, examined in the preceding subsection, assuming that the assault and battery had occurred in both cases by the time the first action for libel was brought?

Problem 12-15. *P* sued *D* in a state court for breach of contract. *D* defends on the ground that the contract is illegal under state and federal antitrust laws and pleads a counterclaim under the state antitrust laws against *P*. Judgment in the action goes against *P* on *P's* contract claim and for *D* on *D's* counterclaim. Subsequently, *D* sued *P* in federal court asserting a claim under the federal antitrust laws for additional relief obtainable only under those laws, a claim over which the federal courts have exclusive jurisdiction. May *D* maintain this action? Why or why not? Do you need additional information to solve this problem?

Problem 12-16. *P* brings an action against *D* for failure to pay the contract price for goods sold and delivered and recovers judgment by default. After entry of final judgment and payment of the price, *D* brings an action against *P* to rescind the contract for mutual mistake, seeking restitution of the contract price and offering to return the goods. Even though in a default situation, a compulsory counterclaim rule is not applicable, is there any other rule that would prevent *D's* action against *P*?

Section C. Issue Preclusion

1. Basic Principles

The Context in Which Issue Preclusion Arises. Issue preclusion rules concern the effect that a judgment entered in a first action is to be accorded in a second action with respect to *issues* of fact or law that were actually litigated and determined in the first action. The policy underlying issue preclusion is that a party who has had a full and fair opportunity to litigate an issue in an initial action should be precluded from relitigating the same issue again in a subsequent action. Analytically, issue preclusion usually becomes relevant only when a subsequent action is brought on a *different* claim or cause of action than the one involved in the initial action in which the issue was determined. If the second action is brought on the *same* claim as the first action, the second action will usually be barred by *claim* preclusion, and the question of *issue* preclusion would never be reached. So if the claims are different, how can an underlying issue be the same? Consider the following example.

Assume that in Year 1, *P* and *D* enter into a five-year contract for the delivery of goods. In Year 2, *P* sues *D* for breach of contract claiming that in June of Year 2, *D* failed to deliver goods in conformance with the contract. Two issues are disputed and fully litigated by *P* and *D* in the case — (1) is the contract valid and if so, (2) did *D's* conduct in June of Year 2 constitute a breach of the contract. The court specifically finds that contract was valid and that *D's* conduct in June of Year 2 constituted a breach of the contract. Judgment is entered in favor of *P*. Assume that after the first action concludes, the parties continue in their contractual relationship under the original contract. In May of Year 4, *P* again sues *D* claiming that in Year 4, *D* failed to deliver goods in conformance with the contract.

Although *P's* second action against *D* is also for breach of the same contract that *P* sued *D* on in the first action, *P's* second action against *D* is not barred by claim preclusion. The claim that *D's* conduct in May of Year 4 breached the contract is a *different* claim than the claim asserted in the first action, *i.e.*, that *D's* conduct in June of Year 2 breached the contract. Even though *P's* second action against *D* based on *D's* conduct in May of Year 4 is not barred by claim preclusion, issue preclusion would apply. Assume that in the second action, *D* wants to again argue that the Year 1 contract is invalid under the same legal theory presented in the first action.

Because the identical issue was fully litigated by *D* in the first action and *D* was the losing party in that action, *D* is now precluded from relitigating this identical issue again in this second action. As the losing party, if *D* felt that the first court's ruling on the validity of the contract was erroneous, *D* should have appealed. However, *D* is not precluded from litigating the issue of whether *D's* conduct in May of Year 4 violated the contract. The issue litigated in the first action was *D's* conduct in June of Year 2, not May of Year 4. Because this new issue has never been litigated by *D*, issue preclusion does not apply.

Preclusion Operates Against Losing Party. Issue preclusion ordinarily only prevents relitigation of issues that are decided against the *losing party* in the first action because of the right to appeal. Prevailing parties cannot appeal, only losing parties. Thus, if an issue has been decided against a party, but the party ultimately prevails on the final judgment, the party cannot have any error made in adjudicating the issue corrected by a higher court because the party would not be able to appeal. *See* Chapter 11(B)(1), above.

For example, assume that in the case described above, the first court ruled against *D* on the issue of the contract's validity, but ruled in favor of *D* on the second issue finding that *D's* conduct in June of Year 2 did not violate the contract. Based on these findings, the court enters judgment in favor of *D*. In the second action, *D* would not be precluded from relitigating the issue of the validity of the Year 1 contract. Indeed, as you will see in section C, below, the right to appeal a judgment in an initial action is also an important consideration in determining whether a party has had a full and fair opportunity to litigate in the action for all issue preclusion purposes.

Issue Preclusion on "Procedural" Determinations. A judgment does not have to be "on the merits" before issue preclusion can operate. Thus, a judgment can have an issue preclusion effect on procedural issues. For example, if an action is dismissed for improper venue and the plaintiff recommences a second action on the same claim in the same venue, claim preclusion would not operate because the first judgment was not on the merits, but issue preclusion would prevent the plaintiff from relitigating the issue of venue in the second action. If the plaintiff believes the trial court's determination of the issue of venue is incorrect in the first action, the remedy is to appeal the judgment.

Finality for Issue Preclusion Purposes. As in the case of claim preclusion, a judgment must be final to have an issue preclusion effect. However, finality for issue preclusion purposes is not as rigid as for claim preclusion purposes or appellate review. For issue preclusion to operate, it is not necessary for the final judgment to be rendered in an action. Instead, issue preclusion can be applied to "any prior adjudication of an issue in another action that is determined to be sufficiently firm to be accorded conclusive effect." *See* RESTATEMENT (SECOND) OF JUDGMENTS § 13 (1982). For example, if there is a split trial of liability and damages in a personal injury action based on negligence, a determination that the defendant is negligent in the liability portion of the trial will have an issue preclusion effect in any other action pending between the parties, even though the judgment cannot be appealed by the defendant until damages have been assessed.

Validity of Judgments. Also as with claim preclusion, a judgment must be *valid* to have an issue preclusion effect. This requirement of validity ordinarily means that a judgment must be rendered with subject-matter and personal jurisdiction in order to have an issue preclusion effect. However, as noted above in conjunction with claim preclusion, defects of subject-matter and personal jurisdiction that might otherwise render a judgment invalid for issue preclusion purposes can be foreclosed by a judgment under appropriate circumstances. Preclusion of jurisdictional matters is examined in section F, below.

Mutual and Nonmutual Estoppel. Traditionally, courts limited issue preclusion to actions between the same two parties: the winner of an initial action could preclude the loser from relitigating issues determined in the action in any subsequent proceeding between the parties on a different claim. However, a person who was not a party to the initial action could not use issue preclusion against the loser of the action in any subsequent proceeding between the nonparty and the loser. This rule was called "mutuality of estoppel." As the rule was stated, "estoppel had to be mutual," which meant that both parties to an action ordinarily had to be bound by a judgment in a prior action for issue preclusion to apply in a subsequent action. A nonparty to an action usually cannot be bound by the judgment in the action as a matter of due process. As a result, under the rule of mutuality of estoppel, a nonparty to the initial action could not use issue preclusion against the loser of that action in any subsequent proceeding between the nonparty and the loser.

The "mutuality of estoppel" rule made little sense, and courts in the United States have largely abandoned it. The modern approach is to allow nonparties to the initial action to assert issue preclusion in all cases, subject to a number of exceptions to issue preclusion designed to take into account the problems that can occur when a stranger to an initial action attempts to use the judgment against the losing party in the action. *See* RESTATEMENT (SECOND) OF JUDGMENTS § 29 (1982). Nonmutual estoppel is examined in section C(3), below.

Preclusion of Nonparties. Although, as stated above, nonparties to an action ordinarily are not bound by a judgment in the action, there are exceptions to this rule. Generally, these exceptions exist in circumstances in which special substantive relationships exist between a nonparty and a party to an initial action, or in which a nonparty's interests are represented in the initial action. Preclusion of nonparties is examined in section D, below.

2. The Essential Elements of Issue Preclusion

As indicated in the preceding subsection, issue preclusion, unlike claim preclusion, does not focus on what might have been litigated in an initial action, but on what was actually litigated and determined. The general rule governing issue preclusion is stated by § 27 of the RESTATEMENT (SECOND) OF JUDGMENTS:

> When an issue of fact or law is actually litigated and determined by a valid and final judgment, and the determination is essential to the judgment, the determination is conclusive in a subsequent action between the parties, whether on the same or a different claim.

Several discrete requirements appear within this rule. The issue litigated in the first action must be the same as the one involved in the second. The issue must be determined in the first action. And the determination of the issue must support the judgment in the first action. These requirements are explored in the following cases, notes, and questions.

Cycles, Ltd. v. Navistar Financial Corp.
United States Court of Appeals, Fifth Circuit, 1994
37 F.3d 1088

PATRICK E. HIGGINBOTHAM, CIRCUIT JUDGE.

Cycles challenges the district court's decision to reverse its original ruling in Cycles' favor. We are persuaded that although the district court had the power to revise its original decision, it wrongly believed itself bound by the contrary findings of a later court. We vacate and remand.

Cycles leased certain truck trailers to W.J. Digby. In August 1980, their deal collapsed, Digby refused to return the trailers to Cycles, and a complicated chain of lawsuits followed. First, Cycles sued Digby for conversion (*Digby I*). The Southern District of Mississippi ruled for Cycles, finding that the lease agreement required Digby to return the trailers to Cycles.

Second, Cycles sued Navistar in the Southern District of Mississippi. In this second suit, the present action, Cycles claims that three years after Digby's conversion of Cycles' trailers, Navistar also converted Cycles' trailers. Navistar had financed Cycles' original purchase of the trailers and held Cycles' installment payment note and certificates of title for the trailers. In early 1983, Navistar transferred the certificates of title to Digby in exchange for full payment of the installment payment note.

At first, the district court agreed that Navistar converted the trailers by transferring the certificates to Digby. It held that delivering the certificates of title to Digby put the trailers further out of Cycles' reach, and Navistar at least should have known at the time that the trailers belonged to Cycles, not to Digby. As the district court then saw it, Navistar's action both aided Digby's conversion, and itself converted property. The court on June

30, 1989, filed a "Final Judgment" and awarded damages to Cycles. Navistar filed post-judgment motions to amend the findings of fact and conclusions of law under Rule 52(b) and to alter or amend the judgment under Rule 59(e).

Cycles, however, could not persuade the court to cement this judgment into a final, appealable order. Instead of resolving the post-judgment motions, the court waited four years for the resolution of a third suit: *Digby II*.

Digby II grew out of the demise of *Digby I*. In 1989, we vacated *Digby I* for lack of jurisdiction over Digby.... Cycles then filed *Digby II*, an action against Digby in federal district court for the Eastern District of Arkansas. The Arkansas federal court ruled for Digby. It determined that Cycles had agreed to Digby's disposition of the trailers and that Digby had a qualified right of refusal to return them to Cycles.

After *Digby II*, the court below revised its original opinion and entered judgment for Navistar, explaining that principles of res judicata and collateral estoppel compelled it to reverse its original judgment for Cycles and to render judgment for Navistar. Cycles appeals this ruling.

The district court's concern with the Arkansas judgment is understandable. The premise of its original opinion finding Navistar liable was that Digby's possession of the trailers was tortious. From that premise, it originally concluded that Navistar's later delivery of the trailers' certificates of title to Digby was also tortious, since it aided Digby's wrongful possession of the trailers and made it harder for Cycles to get the trailers back.

The Arkansas judgment denied the premise of the Mississippi court's conclusion. The Arkansas court ruled that Digby did not convert Cycles' property. If Digby did not, Navistar's transfer of the certificates to Digby could not. The two acts of claimed conversion were separate, but logically dependent.

In reviewing its original opinion on Navistar's motions, the district court did not rest its decision on the persuasive force of the Arkansas court's reasoning. Rather, it revised its original opinion, persuaded that the Arkansas judgment compelled it to do so.

This was error. The Arkansas judgment had no preclusive effect upon decisions already reached after full litigation, like the original ruling. Judgments are final for purposes of issue preclusion when fully litigated, even if not yet appealable.... Such fully litigated judgments, strong enough to preclude later inconsistent judgments, are *a fortiori* strong enough to withstand preclusion by inconsistent later judgments.

Case law supports our conclusion that a court is not compelled to revise its fully litigated decision by later inconsistent decisions of other courts. In *American Postal Workers Union v. United States Postal Service*, 736 F.2d 317, 319 (6th Cir. 1984) (*APWU*), the Sixth Circuit found no preclusion in a similar case. There, an action by a Columbus, Ohio local union survived the Postal Service's motion to dismiss. Later, another local union filed a similar suit in Dallas, Texas. A federal district court in Dallas granted the Postal Service's motion to dismiss, and we affirmed. Armed with our decision, the Postal Service moved for summary judgment in the Ohio court, arguing that the preclusive force of its Dallas victory compelled the Ohio district court to revise its original ruling on the motion to dismiss. The Ohio district court agreed and granted summary judgment for the Postal Service.

The Sixth Circuit disagreed. In dicta, the court stated that the preclusive force of the Dallas decision did not compel the Ohio court to revise its prior opinion.... The Dallas decision would preclude contrary determinations in all subsequent cases, but not issues already decided.... The fact that the Ohio ruling was not final for purposes of appeal made no difference. The Sixth Circuit acknowledged that even though the Ohio court's ruling was not yet appealable, it had preclusive force. Indeed, the Sixth Circuit noted that the ruling "should have been given preclusive effect in the Dallas case." ...

In this respect, *APWU* differs from this case. In *APWU*, the first decision should have precluded the second. Because two plaintiffs were bringing separate actions against the same defendant, the first plaintiff's victory in Ohio could have enjoyed issue-preclusive effect in the second case in Dallas.... Here, by contrast, the first decision could not have precluded the second. One plaintiff, Cycles, had been pursuing two actions against two defendants: first Navistar, then Digby. Cycles could not have used its victory against Navistar to win the case against Digby, since in the prior case Digby neither had a chance to contest its liability nor was in privity with a party that did....

Yet the mark of a decision's maturity for the purposes of issue preclusion is whether the decision was fully litigated. If the first decision had the power to preclude relitigation of the same issues, for our purposes it does not matter if a later case ignores the opinion's preclusive power, as in *APWU*, or if no later case had the opportunity to consider its preclusive power, as here. In either event, the fully litigated opinion stands unaffected by a later inconsistent judgment.

. . . .

Navistar's proposed rule would unfairly force plaintiffs like Cycles, who must pursue defendants in separate jurisdictions, to play for all or nothing, recovering only with an uninterrupted stream of victories. If, like Cycles, they won one fully litigated judgment against one defendant but lost a second case to a second defendant, they would lose everything. The second adverse judgment would undo their prior, fully litigated victory. Our rejection of this backward reach lies with the longstanding rule that plaintiffs who lose against one defendant are collaterally estopped from prevailing on the same issue in future cases against other defendants....

We are persuaded that the district court's original decision was final for purposes of issue preclusion, and the district court erred in concluding that it was bound by the later decision of the Arkansas federal court to reverse its original ruling. We vacate the decision below and remand to the district court for decision of Navistar's post-judgment motions to amend the original findings of fact and conclusions of law and to alter or amend the original judgment, free of any binding effect of the ruling by the Arkansas court.

VACATED and REMANDED.

Notes and Questions

1. The opinion in *Cycles* illustrates the statement made in section C(1) that finality for purposes of res judicata is not exactly the same as finality for purposes of appellate review. In the issue preclusion context, it is settled that finality means any prior adjudication of an issue that is "sufficiently firm to be accorded conclusive effect." *See* Restatement (Second) of Judgments § 13 & cmts. a & g (1982).

2. As *Cycles* also indicates, this concept of finality can cause problems. As the court noted, if Digby did not convert the trailers, Navistar could not. Yet Navistar may now be bound by a judgment for damages rendered on the factual premise that Digby did convert the trailers. Is there anything in the court's opinion that suggests whether, and if so how, Navistar might be able to win on remand?

3. As examined further below in subsection 3, under the doctrine of nonmutual estoppel, nonparties to an action can often benefit by a judgment against a party. This point is illustrated by the court's discussion in *Cycles* of the *American Postal Workers* case. The court indicated that the judgment in the first action in Ohio should have had an issue preclusion effect against the defendant when the defendant was sued by a different plaintiff in the second action. However, the court went on to observe that the plaintiff in *Cycles* could not use its judgment against Navistar to preclude Digby in the second action. As you will see in subsection 3, below, the court is correct on both points. Do you understand the difference between the two cases?

Holtman v. 4-G's Plumbing & Heating, Inc.

Supreme Court of Montana, 1994
264 Mont. 432, 872 P.2d 318

GRAY, JUSTICE.

Roger Holtman (Holtman) appeals from an order entered by the Fourth Judicial District Court, Missoula County, granting summary judgment in favor of 4-G's Plumbing and Heating, Inc. (4-G's Plumbing). The court determined that dismissal with prejudice of Holtman's counterclaim in a previous lawsuit barred his trespass, invasion of privacy and asbestos contamination claims against 4-G's Plumbing under the doctrines of *res judicata* and collateral estoppel. Holtman asserts error only in the court's application of the doctrines to his asbestos contamination claim. Because all of the elements of *res judicata* and collateral estoppel are not met, we reverse the court's grant of summary judgment in favor of 4-G's Plumbing on that claim.

Holtman owned a condominium located in the Edgewater Townhouse Complex in Missoula, Montana. In February of 1989, the Edgewater Townhouse Homeowner's Association (the Association) authorized an employee of 4-G's Plumbing to enter Holtman's condominium, in his absence, to repair a leak and install a new heating system. When Holtman returned to his condominium, he discovered a partially installed heating system and alleged asbestos contamination. Holtman refused to allow further installation of the system.

The Association filed a complaint seeking an injunction to require the installation of the heating system. Holtman responded by generally denying the Association's allegations. Nearly two years later, Holtman filed a counterclaim without leave of court. He alleged that the Association had deprived him of property rights, invaded his privacy, and contaminated his condominium with asbestos. In addition to other rulings, the court dismissed the counterclaim with prejudice because the compulsory counterclaim was not timely filed under Rule 13(a), Mont. R. Civ. P., and Holtman had failed to obtain leave of court pursuant to Rule 13(f), Mont. R. Civ. P. Both Holtman and the Association appealed. We affirmed the dismissal of Holtman's counterclaim....

In January of 1992, Holtman filed the present action against the Association and 4-G's Plumbing, asserting claims of invasion of privacy, trespass, and asbestos contamination. The Association moved for summary judgment, arguing that the claims were barred by *res judicata*. 4-G's Plumbing joined in the Association's motion and filed a separate motion for summary judgment relying on both *res judicata* and collateral estoppel. The District Court granted summary judgment for each defendant by separate order, dismissing the claims against the Association under *res judicata* and the claims against 4-G's Plumbing under *res judicata* and collateral estoppel. Holtman appeals only from the summary adjudication in favor of 4-G's Plumbing.

[In this portion of its opinion, the court reversed the trial court's ruling that the plaintiff was precluded by the doctrine of *res judicata* (claim preclusion) from suing 4-G's Plumbing in this second action. While the plaintiff was barred by *res judicata* from refiling his claims against the Association, 4-G's Plumbing was neither a party nor in privity with a party from the first action and therefore the plaintiff was not barred from filing his action against this new defendant. The court held that simply because the Association hired 4-G's Plumbing to perform work in plaintiff's condominium did not make 4-G's Plumbing the legal "privy" of the Association for purposes of *res judicata*.(The concept of legal representation and privity is further examined in section D, below.)]

Again focusing entirely on the asbestos contamination claim, Holtman asserts that the District Court erred in concluding that 4-G's Plumbing was entitled to summary judgment under the doctrine of collateral estoppel. He contends that collateral estoppel does not bar the claim because the issue of 4-G's Plumbing's negligence was not raised in his prior counterclaim.

Collateral estoppel, sometimes referred to as issue preclusion, is a form of *res judicata*. While *res judicata* bars parties from relitigating claims in subsequent proceedings based on the same cause of action, collateral estoppel bars the reopening of an issue ... that has been litigated and determined in a prior suit. ... The doctrine has three elements:

1) the identical issue raised has been previously decided in a prior adjudication;

2) a final judgment on the merits was issued in the prior adjudication; and

3) the party against whom the plea is now asserted was a party or in privity with a party to the prior adjudication. ...

Our analysis need not proceed beyond the first element.

Identity of issues is the most crucial element of collateral estoppel. ... In order to satisfy this element, the identical issue or "precise question" must have been litigated in the prior action. ... To determine whether the issue raised is identical, we compare the pleadings, evidence and circumstances surrounding the two actions. ... We note that we have only the asbestos-related allegations to examine from the previous litigation since Holtman's counterclaim was dismissed on legal grounds prior to the receipt of any evidence on the claim.

It is true that Holtman's prior counterclaim against the Association arose from the same events as his claim against 4-G's Plumbing and, like his present claim, sought damages for the alleged asbestos contamination. Holtman's asbestos-related contamination claim against the Association in the prior litigation was as follows:

> [The Association] did, without the knowledge or consent of [Holtman], terminate the heating service to [Holtman's] unit sometime between March, 1988 and February 5, 1989, which resulted in certain waterlines freezing, breaking and creating water leaks in [Holtman's] unit and subsequently therewith caused the asbestos covering of certain pipes to be removed and generally distributed throughout the unit, all of which rendered [Holtman's] unit damaged, unsafe and uninhabitable.

When this claim is compared to Holtman's asbestos contamination claim against 4-G's Plumbing set forth above, it is clear that the identical issue, or precise question, raised in the present case was not raised and decided in the earlier litigation involving the Association.

Holtman's prior asbestos-related claim can be read as alleging an intentional wrongful act by the Association—the unauthorized termination of heat to the condominium—

followed by all the damage that flowed therefrom, including broken waterlines and asbestos disturbance and distribution. To the extent the prior claim is read in this fashion, it is clear that the issue of the alleged negligence of 4-G's Plumbing in the present case is not identical.

Furthermore, to the extent the prior asbestos-related claim is read as an allegation of negligence against the Association resulting in asbestos contamination, that claim did not raise the issue of 4-G's Plumbing's negligent workmanship in the installation of the new heating system. A negligence action is premised, first, on the existence of a duty.... 4-G's Plumbing has not established that its legal duties to Holtman in installing the new heating system were co-extensive with the duties owed him by the Association.

We conclude that the "identical issue" element of collateral estoppel is not met under the circumstances before us. Therefore, we hold that the District Court erred in concluding that Holtman is collaterally estopped from asserting the asbestos contamination claim and in granting summary judgment in favor of 4-G's Plumbing on that claim.

Reversed and remanded for further proceedings consistent with this opinion.

TURNAGE, C.J., HARRISON, HUNT, TRIEWEILER, NELSON and WEBER, JJ., concur.

Hebden v. Workmen's Compensation Appeal Board

Supreme Court of Pennsylvania, 1993
534 Pa. 327, 632 A.2d 1302

PAPADAKOS, JUSTICE.

Appellant, Thomas Hebden, a coal miner for over thirty years, was awarded workmen's compensation partial disability benefits for an occupationally acquired pulmonary lung disease (coal worker's pneumoconiosis) by order of a referee dated July 19, 1985. Effective as of August 25, 1983, Appellant was ordered to receive $227.40 per week as compensation. Neither Appellant nor his employer appealed this award. It thereby became a final determination not subject to future attack collaterally or by relitigation. On October 30, 1987, the employer (Bethenergy Mines, Inc.) filed a petition for modification—treated as a petition to terminate—alleging that Appellant's disability had changed and that he was no longer disabled from occupational pulmonary disease. The matter came before a new referee who conducted several hearings. At a hearing on March 9, 1988, Dr. George W. Ketter testified on behalf of the employer. On August 3, 1988, Dr. Robert K. Klemens testified on behalf of Appellant.

When Dr. Ketter testified, he expressed the opinion that Appellant had neither pneumoconiosis nor any impairment as a result thereby. On cross-examination, Dr. Ketter admitted that if Appellant had no pneumoconiosis in 1988, then he would not have had it in 1983 either.... The employer also offered the testimony of Dr. Robert G. Pickerill by way of deposition. Dr. Pickerill also contended that Appellant did not have pneumoconiosis, but stated the opinion that Appellant had a mild functional respiratory impairment due to chronic bronchial asthma, a non-occupational condition. This was, in effect, an opening of the original, unappealed determination that Appellant suffered from work-related pneumoconiosis and, thus, constituted impermissible relitigation.

Appellant was deemed by these two doctors to be fit to return to work at his last job as a shuttle car operator in the mines. The employer further offered medical evidence by way of a written report of Dr. Gregory Fino. Dr. Fino concluded that even if Appellant was disabled in 1983, he was not disabled currently.... Dr. Fino also concluded that Appellant was suffering from non-occupational bronchial asthma and that he was fit to return to work.

Appellant's medical witness, Dr. Robert F. Klemens, testified to the contrary that he had examined Appellant in October, 1987, and that Appellant continued to suffer from pneumoconiosis, that he remained partially disabled and was unable to return to work. The only evidence in the record dealing with the reversibility of pneumoconiosis was offered by Dr. Klemens. He clearly testified that once a person has pneumoconiosis, he has it for the rest of his life and that once he has that disability, he cannot recover from it. Moreover, the disease is a progressive disorder and only tends to get worse with time....

The referee resolved the conflict in the medical evidence in favor of the employer, finding that Appellant's disability has ceased to exist. She held that Appellant was neither partially nor totally disabled as a result of coal worker's pneumoconiosis nor any occupationally acquired lung disease. She adopted the opinion of the employer's doctors holding that Appellant suffered from a non-occupational disease, bronchial asthma. She ordered that Appellant's benefits should cease and terminate, and she specifically found that there was no *res judicata* issue in the case ... because the prior award of benefits merely addressed Appellant's disability status at an earlier and different point in time. The Workmen's Compensation Appeal Board affirmed the holding that the employer had sustained its burden of proof on the medical issues. The Commonwealth Court, *en banc*, also affirmed.... We granted Appellant's petition for review because we were alarmed by the decision's revisitation and reopening of a disability issue that had long been settled. If such issues can be retried at will, the statutory system of workmen's compensation would be seriously undermined. Our alarm was well founded, and for the reasons set forth below, we reverse.

The Commonwealth Court's decision is centered on a lengthy and erudite discussion of the doctrine of *res judicata*. We acknowledge that the term "res judicata" is a somewhat sloppy term and that it is sometimes used to cover both *res judicata* itself (claim preclusion) as well as collateral estoppel ("broad" *res judicata* or issue preclusion). Collateral estoppel, broad *res judicata* or issue preclusion "forecloses re-litigation in a later action, of an issue of fact or law which was actually litigated and which was necessary to the original judgment." ... It is admitted in the Commonwealth Court opinion itself that res judicata or issue preclusion prevents an employer from relitigating, by way of a petition to modify or terminate benefits, the original medical diagnosis underlying a referee's finding of a claimant's disability as of the date of the compensation award.... Yet, that is, in essence, what happened here. It is no mystery why res judicata or issue preclusion applies to these situations. If it did not, disability victims could be continually harassed with petitions and hearings where they would be repeatedly forced to redemonstrate or redefend their claim of occupational disease and consequent disability. Such a system would be intolerable. We do not lose sight of the fact that the Workmen's Compensation Act ... expressly provides that an award may be terminated based upon *changes* in the employee's disability. But that raises the logical question of whether an employee's disability is *changeable* in a given case. If it is, an employee's condition may be re-examined at a later time to see if he is still disabled or not. If it is not, an attempt to re-examine the employee's condition is merely a disguised attempt to relitigate what has already been settled. We think that the latter is what occurred here.

In the instant case, logically, the employer should first have addressed the issue of whether pneumoconiosis is reversible or not. On this record, the issue was first raised by Dr. Klemens' testimony for Appellant! He testified clearly that the disease is irreversible and progressive, that is, it only gets worse over time....[1] This testimony, at a minimum, shifts the burden of production to the employer to present rebuttal evidence. Nowhere in this record or in the briefs filed with this Court does it do so. Indeed, Dr. Ketter's testimony for the employer, set forth above, reinforces Appellant's argument. Appellant's brief points out, moreover, that the U.S. Supreme Court has held that coal worker's pneumoconiosis is "irreversible in both its simple and complicated stages. No therapy has been developed." ... We find that the employer here did not meet its burden of producing evidence to rebut Appellant's contention that pneumoconiosis is not reversible.

Unable to show the disease's reversibility, the employer here is precluded from trying to show that the disease has, in fact, been reversed in the case of Appellant. To allow the employer to do so would simply be allowing it to revisit the initial finding of Appellant's disability and, in a disguised way, to relitigate that issue. Sound principles of res judicata, collateral estoppel and issue preclusion bar such an attempt. Proof of a miracle cure must be left to theologians.

The order of the Commonwealth Court is reversed.

LARSEN, J., did not participate in the decision of this case.

CAPPY, J., joins the Majority Opinion and files a Concurring Opinion in which NIX, C.J., and FLAHERTY and MONTEMURO, JJ., join.

ZAPPALA, J., concurs in the result.

[The concurring opinion of JUSTICE CAPPY is omitted.]

Notes and Questions

1. Although the court in *Holtman* held that issue preclusion was inappropriate because the "identical issue" requirement was not met, another fundamental requirement of issue preclusion is that the identical issue must have been *actually* litigated and determined in the first action. In *Holtman*, the plaintiff's counterclaim in the first action alleging asbestos contamination was dismissed with prejudice for procedural violations, and the issue of asbestos contamination was never actually litigated by the parties or decided by the court. As such, although this dismissal with prejudice precluded the plaintiff from refiling his claim against the Association under claim preclusion, the dismissal would not have precluded the plaintiff under issue preclusion from litigating the issue of asbestos contamination in his new action against 4-G Plumbing. *See* Notes 7–9, below.

2. *Holtman* demonstrates the importance of the requirement that the identical issue must be involved in both the prior and subsequent litigation for issue preclusion to operate. *Hebden* further illustrates the ways in which parties can attempt to relitigate issues that have already been litigated and determined against them. Note that even if the initial determination in *Hebden* that the employee was suffering from pneumoconiosis was incorrect, that would not have changed the result in the second action. The whole point of the doctrine of finality, including the issue preclusion component of the doctrine, is to foreclose relitigation even when error infects the original judgment. However, is it clear that the burden should be placed upon the employer to demonstrate the reversibility of the condition established by the initial judgment? If the burden had been placed on the employee to

---

1. The Commonwealth Court distinguishes disease from disability. Dr. Klemens' testimony clearly states that not only is the disease here irreversible, but it is also progressive, that is, the disability resulting from the disease can only get worse.

demonstrate irreversibility, would the result in the case have changed? If not, can you envision cases in which it would change?

3. In *Holtman*, the Montana Supreme Court first construed Holtman's claim against the Association as an intentional tort claim, but then stated that even if it was construed as a negligence claim, issue preclusion did not apply. This was because the *plumbing company* did not establish that its duties to Holtman were coextensive with the association's duty to Holtman. Do you agree with the court's analysis? In what way could the duty of the plumbing company differ from the duty of the Association not to contaminate Holtman's premises with asbestos? Was it because Holtman might have proceeded against the association on a different theory of negligence than he asserted against the plumbing company? If so, what might that theory be?

4. (a) A common problem in determining the scope of the issue determined in an initial action is that a party may bring forward in successive actions different grounds or evidence upon which the party wishes the trier of fact to reach its decision. Thus, a total identity between the matters involved between two actions may not exist. Comment c for § 27 of the RESTATEMENT (SECOND) states that several factors should be considered in determining whether the issues in the two proceedings are the same: (i) whether substantial overlap exists between the evidence or arguments made in the first and second actions; (ii) whether the new evidence or argument involves the same rule of law as that involved in the first proceeding; (iii) whether pre-trial preparation and discovery in the first action could reasonably be expected to have embraced the matters presented in the second proceeding; and (iv) whether a close relationship exists between the claims in the two proceedings.

(b) An example of how these factors apply to a specific case is found in Illustration 4 to § 27 of the RESTATEMENT (SECOND). Assume that *P* sues *D* to recover for personal injuries received in an automobile accident, alleging that *D* was negligent in driving at an excessive rate of speed. After trial, verdict and judgment are given for *D* on the ground that *D* was not negligent. Subsequently, *D* sues *P* for personal injuries in the same accident. Assume that *D's* action is permitted because the jurisdiction has no compulsory counterclaim rule. *P* is precluded from defending the second action on the grounds that *D* was guilty of contributory negligence in failing to keep a proper lookout. According to the RESTATEMENT (SECOND), it is reasonable to require *P* to bring forward all evidence in support of *D's* alleged negligence in the first action.

5. Illustration 4 seems straightforward enough, and it is clear how the RESTATEMENT (SECOND) drafters envision that the factors bearing on the identity of the issue between successive actions apply to preclude *P* from relitigating the issue of negligence in the second proceeding. However, consider Illustration 6 of the RESTATEMENT (SECOND): *P* sues *D* to recover an installment payment due under an oral contract between *P* and *D*. *D's* only defense is that the contract is unenforceable under the statute of frauds. The court enters judgment for *P* based on a specific finding that the oral contract is enforceable. Subsequently, *P* sues *D* to recover a second installment payment that came due after the first action was completed. Although *D* is precluded from raising the statute of frauds as a defense, even if *D* is prepared to make arguments about the applicability of the statute that were not made in the first action, *D* is not, according to the RESTATEMENT (SECOND), precluded from asserting that the contract is unenforceable on any other ground. For example, *D* is not precluded from asserting that the contract violated the state's usury statute. Thus, in Illustration 4, the RESTATEMENT (SECOND) considers the issue in both actions to be *D's* negligence, while in Illustration 6, the issue is considered to be the statute of frauds.

6. It seems obvious, however, that the issue in Illustration 6 could be stated at a higher level of generality — *i.e.*, the issue could be considered to be "the enforceability of the contract." If it were so stated, *D* would be unable to raise usury, or any other defense bearing on enforceability, in the second action. The apparent difference in result between the two illustrations is due to the application of the four factors listed by the RESTATEMENT (SECOND) in comment c to § 27. In Illustration 4, all of the factors point toward determining that the issue in both actions is negligence and should be precluded. In contrast, in Illustration 6, only the third and fourth factors would point toward considering the issue to be "the enforceability of the contract," as opposed to the "statute of frauds" (in the first action) and "usury" (in the second action). Nevertheless, are you convinced that *D* should be able to bring forward additional grounds of unenforceability in the second action in Illustration 6? Do you think most courts would be convinced that *D* should be able to do so? If not, and you were the lawyer representing *D* in a similar situation, what would you do to preserve all of your client's defenses?

7. One of the other requirements stated in § 27 of the RESTATEMENT (SECOND) is that the issue of fact or law to be precluded must actually have been litigated and determined in the first action. Comment d states that this requirement is fulfilled when the issue "is properly raised, by the pleadings or otherwise, and is submitted for determination, and is determined." For example, the actual litigation requirement is satisfied if an issue is determined on a motion for summary judgment. In contrast, however, issue preclusion should not operate when the plaintiff wins a default judgment after the defendant fails to appear. Similarly, an issue is not actually litigated if it is admitted, stipulated, or conceded in an action.

8. Why should it matter whether an issue is litigated or not? Why should issue preclusion not operate like claim preclusion to prevent litigation of all issues that *might have been* litigated in a prior action? *See* RESTATEMENT (SECOND) OF JUDGMENTS § 29 cmt. e (1982) ("The action may involve so small an amount that litigation of the issue may cost more than the value of the lawsuit. Or the forum may be an inconvenient one in which to produce the necessary evidence or in which to litigate at all. The interests of conserving judicial resources, of maintaining consistency, and of avoiding oppression or harassment of the adverse party are less compelling when the issue on which preclusion is sought has not actually been litigated before. And if preclusive effect were given to issues not litigated, the result might serve to discourage compromise, to decrease the likelihood that the issues in an action would be narrowed by stipulation, and thus to intensify litigation.").

9. Following its position on identity and scope of issue problems, the RESTATEMENT (SECOND) also takes the position that an issue is not actually litigated if it is an affirmative defense that the defendant chose not to raise. *See id.* This position would presumably mean, as in Illustration 6 (discussed in Note 4, above), that if a party chooses to raise one affirmative defense to a claim, such as the statute of frauds, but not another, such as usury, the party could raise the omitted defense in a second action on a separate claim. Again, however, the problem of determining the identity and scope of the issue litigated in the initial action can be tricky. Caution therefore dictates that a defendant who chooses to raise one affirmative defense should carefully consider whether there is a danger that other affirmative defenses omitted will also be considered precluded by an adverse determination against the defendant on the issue raised.

10. Obviously, if issue preclusion only applies to matters actually litigated and determined, it must be possible to see what was decided in the initial action for the doctrine to apply. This is sometimes impossible. For example, when an action involves multiple issues and terminates with a general verdict by a jury, it is not always evident what issues

the jury determined or how they were determined. Evidence extrinsic to the record can sometimes be introduced to establish what issues were litigated and determined, but even this is not always possible.

11. Issue preclusion operates only when issues determined in an action support the judgment. For example, assume that P sues D for negligence and D defends by denying negligence and pleading P's contributory negligence as a defense. After a trial, a jury specifically finds that D was negligent and that P was guilty of contributory negligence and renders a verdict for D (contributory negligence being an absolute bar to a recovery in the state). The court enters a judgment on the verdict for D. Under these circumstances, the issue of D's negligence may be relitigated in a subsequent action between the parties, because the determination of the issue against D did not support the judgment. This is because it was decided against the winning party, D. As indicated in subsection 1, above, this rule is essential to protect a person in D's position, because winning parties cannot ordinarily appeal. Thus, D would be unable to obtain correction of any error that infected the finding of negligence from an appellate court.

12. In addition to supporting the judgment, the modern rule, reflected in § 27 of the RESTATEMENT (SECOND), is that a determination must be *essential* to the judgment to be precluded in subsequent litigation. This gives rise to a distinction between determinations that are "essential" to the judgment and "alternative" determinations. This issue is explored in the next case and the notes that follow it.

Malloy v. Trombley

Court of Appeals of New York, 1990
50 N.Y.2d 46, 405 N.E.2d 213, 427 N.Y.S.2d 969

JONES, JUDGE.

. . . .

On the evening of October 13, 1974, Douglas A. Trombley, defendant herein, was driving north on Purdy Road, a two-lane, unlighted rural highway in Niagara County, New York. At about 10:30 p.m. he stopped his automobile either on the easterly shoulder of the road or partially on the shoulder and partially in the northbound lane, turned off the lights and began a conversation with his passenger who later became his wife. Shortly thereafter, Trooper Britt, on routine patrol traveling south on Purdy Road, noticed the unlit vehicle and brought his patrol car to a stop opposite the Trombley car, partially on the highway. The trooper left his headlights on and may have activated his emergency lights. He left the patrol car, approached the Trombley car and began questioning its occupants. He then observed an automobile, driven by Thomas E. Malloy, plaintiff herein, approaching from the south in the northbound lane at what he later testified was a normal, although constant, rate of speed, apparently not going to stop or otherwise avoid a collision with the Trombley automobile. The trooper shouted to the passengers in the Trombley car to "get down" and ran for cover behind his patrol car. The Malloy vehicle continued in the northbound lane, its driver unaware of the presence of the Trombley car, and struck the rear of the Trombley car. Both Trombley and Malloy suffered serious injuries.

Malloy and Trombley sued each other in Supreme Court and both filed claims against the State of New York in the Court of Claims, based on alleged negligence on the part of Trooper Britt. The two claims against the State were tried jointly, and after a five-day trial before The Honorable Jeremiah J. Moriarty, the court, which was aware of the pending Supreme Court actions, held both that each claimant had failed to prove negligence on the part of the State and that each was guilty of contributory negligence barring recovery against the State. No appeal was taken by either claimant from the decision of the Court of Claims.

Defendant Trombley thereafter served a supplemental answer in the Supreme Court action against him and moved for summary judgment on the ground that the finding of contributory negligence on the part of Malloy by Judge Moriarty barred recovery by him as plaintiff in his Supreme Court action. Supreme Court denied the motion, but the Appellate Division unanimously reversed and granted summary judgment dismissing the complaint. We now affirm that disposition.

The question before us is one of issue preclusion, sometimes referred to as collateral estoppel, inasmuch as the disposition in the Court of Claims was not made in the course of prior litigation between the same parties but in prior litigation between one of those parties, Malloy, and a third party, the State of New York. The critical question is what effect should be given in the present action to the finding in the Court of Claims action of contributory negligence on the part of Malloy.

Appellant Malloy and the dissenters would invoke the recognized principle that conclusive effect is not to be accorded a finding which is but an alternative ground for the prior court's decision because it cannot be said to have been essential to the judgment rendered ... and would apply that principle rigidly to deny issue preclusion in the present instance. We are persuaded that to do so would be improperly to ignore the substantive worth of the finding of the Court of Claims in this instance.

It is entirely accurate to observe that the disposition in the Court of Claims was predicated both on its conclusion that there had been no proof of negligence on the part of the State of New York and on its further finding that claimant Malloy had been contributorily negligent. Indeed in introducing that portion of his decision dealing with contributory negligence on the part of the two claimants, Judge Moriarty forthrightly noted that he proceeded to those issues, "[a]lthough unnecessary to a decision herein." Under a strict application of the alternative determination exception to the rule of issue preclusion, neither the finding of no negligence on the part of the State nor the finding of contributory negligence on the part of the claimant would subsequently be given conclusive effect, for in a logical analysis either finding standing independently would have been sufficient to support the decision of the court; each was a literal alternative. Mechanical application on the basis of such analysis would fail to take into account the vitality of the rationale behind the doctrine of issue preclusion.

There can be no doubt in this instance that the issue of Malloy's contributory negligence was actually and fully litigated. Although it is true that Malloy and Trombley did not stand toe-to-toe in the Court of Claims, Malloy's incentive vigorously to oppose a finding of contributory negligence was no less there than it would be in the present Supreme Court action. No suggestion is now advanced that he was in any way handicapped or inhibited in his address to the issue in the Court of Claims; he had full opportunity there and no heavier burden to establish his freedom from contributory negligence with respect to defendant State in that action than with respect to defendant Trombley in the present action. None of the grounds recognized for other exceptions to the general rule of issue preclusion are to be found in this case.

The justification for the alternative determination exception to the general rule is said to be that "the determination in the alternative may not have been as carefully or as rigorously considered as it would have been if it had been necessary to the result, and in that sense it has some of the characteristics of dicta." The care and attention devoted to the issue by Judge Moriarty in this instance saps such a contention of any vitality. "Although unnecessary to a decision herein, we note that, based upon the evidence presented at trial, neither claimant appears to have established the requisite freedom from culpable conduct necessary for success in a cause of action for negligence which accrued prior to September, 1975.... Insofar as the conduct of Mr. Malloy is concerned, there is little direct evidence, apart from the testimony of Trooper Britt as to his brief observations of the approaching vehicle just prior to the collision and the demonstrative photos of the condition of the vehicles thereafter, from which we can infer what observations Mr. Malloy made or actions he took as he approached the scene. Mr. Malloy did not testify at the trial since he is a man of advanced years and has been institutionalized continually since the accident. We are aware that ... while the burden of proof does not shift on the issue of contributory negligence, the degree of proof necessary to make out a prima facie case on that issue is diminished in a situation such as the one at bar. Nevertheless, it is clear that the tremendous impact with which Mr. Malloy collided with the Trombley vehicle indicates that he proceeded at a high rate of speed towards the scene despite the warning lights from Trooper Britt's car which should have prompted Mr. Malloy to proceed with caution. Therefore, Mr. Malloy's conduct on the night of October 13, 1974, can hardly be characterized as reasonable, and he also was chargeable with contributory negligence which bars recovery."

No persuasive argument is now put forward to support the relevance to this case of the suggestion in the *Restatement* [*(Second)*] that, inasmuch as a losing party might be dissuaded from taking an appeal because of the likelihood that an appellate court would sustain at least one of two or more alternative grounds on which the decision below had been predicated, such alternative determinations might not be exposed to appellate review (a safeguard as to their correctness), and therefore the rule of issue preclusion should not be applied to them. Nor is any argument now based on the related notion that there might similarly be little motivation to take an appeal from an alleged error which had no effect on the judgment. Indeed in the context of negligence litigation involving interrelated fact situations these suppositions may be unrealistic. As to the suggestion that to require Malloy to have appealed would be to waste judicial time, it appears that an appeal would be less time consuming and at a less beleaguered level of our court system than would be true in consequence of the new trial which the dissenters would grant.

But there is another element of validating authenticity to Judge Moriarty's alternative finding of contributory negligence on the part of each claimant. It is accurate to observe, of course, that the dismissal of the claims could have been upheld on appeal had the appellate court affirmed the trial court's finding of no negligence on the part of the State. That, however, in the circumstances presented could not be considered a foregone conclusion, especially in view of the broader authority of the Appellate Division to substitute its view of the facts on an appeal from a decision of the court following a nonjury trial in the Court of Claims than would be true on appeal from the verdict of a jury. From all that appears, it seems likely that Judge Moriarty thought it prudent in the discharge of his judicial responsibility, following the five-day trial, to make full-blown findings both on the issue of negligence and on the issue of contributory negligence. In the event that the Appellate Division were to disagree on the finding of no negligence, the appeal could still be properly disposed on the basis of the court's finding of contributory negligence, without the necessity of remittal for a new trial.

For the reasons stated, and without intending to enunciate any broad rule, we hold in this instance that the rule of issue preclusion is applicable notwithstanding that in a precise sense the issue precluded was the subject of only an alternative determination by the trial court. The issue was fully litigated, and the party precluded had full opportunity to be heard and was in no way, motivationally or procedurally, restricted or inhibited in the presentation of his position. Additionally, and critically in our view, the decision of the trial court gives significant internal evidence of the thorough and careful deliberation by that court, both in its consideration of the proof introduced and of the applicable law, and the determination made, although recognized to be an alternative, served a substantial operational purpose in the judicial process, thus negativing any conclusion that the trial court's resolution was casual or of any lesser quality than had the outcome of the trial depended solely on this issue....

Accordingly, the order of the Appellate Division should be affirmed, with costs.

[The concurring opinion of JUDGE FUSCHSBERG and the dissenting opinion of JUDGE GABRIELLI are omitted.]

MEYER, JUDGE (dissenting).

Precedent long established gives conclusive effect to prior judgments only where the issue of fact as to which preclusion is sought was essential to the judgment.... On the basis of precedent alone, therefore, reversal is in order.

Reversal is, however, required by logic as well. What the majority is saying, in essence, is that Judge Moriarty's finding of contributory negligence was essential to the judgment in the sense that it was in the interest of both the parties and the judicial system for him to pass upon the contributory negligence issue even though he could have dismissed the claim solely on the ground that the State was not negligent. Deciding both issues saves the parties and the State the time and money waste of a new trial if the determination on appeal is that he was wrong on the negligence issue. If the only basis for the requirement of essentiality is that dictum may not be carefully considered there is logic in saying that a Judge conscientious enough to decide both issues (and careful enough to label his decision of the contributory negligence issue "unnecessary to a decision herein") will give no one short shrift.

But the matter does not end there. If well-considered dictum is to be accorded the status of a conclusive finding, then there are here alternate findings of nonnegligence and contributory negligence. The majority, however, rejects the *Restatement* view ... that neither alternative finding can be conclusive, reasoning that its predicate, the practical unavailability of an appeal, is "unrealistic" supposition. To me the shoe is on the other foot; it is the majority which indulges unrealistic supposition.

Rules of preclusion, by whatever name, are essentially rules "of justice and fairness" ... adopted in furtherance of the policy of conserving judicial resources and protecting the winning litigant against the expense and harassment of relitigating a question already decided. They are, however, a means to an end, not an end in themselves. And because they are rules of policy predicated on fairness, the absence of a right to appeal is held to proscribe preclusion.... It is the absence of a meaningful appeal upon which the *Restatement* relies in denying preclusive effect to alternative determinations, reasoning that when the record strongly supports the lower court's finding on one issue, the losing party will be dissuaded, if not foreclosed, from appealing in order to preserve his position on the (to him) wrongly decided second issue.

Far from being unrealistic, that "supposition" is more than likely why the Court of Claims judgment was not appealed by Malloy, for it was essentially Trombley's negligence, not any act of the State, which caused Malloy's injuries. To require Malloy to appeal is [1] to impose upon the court system an appeal destined to failure as to Malloy's claim against the State, [2] to waste judicial time[3] and [3] to mandate what appellate counsel generally would consider "unrealistic" action, the deck being as strongly stacked against Malloy as it would be on such an appeal.

Professor Maurice Rosenberg noted in 1969 that "the New York courts have set a hectic pace in expanding the applicability of collateral estoppel (Rosenberg, *Collateral Estoppel in New York*, 44 St. John's L. Rev. 165, 171). In my view our recent decisions have accelerated that expansion until the means threatens to become the end, to the detriment of litigants foreclosed by it, and without reasonable relation to the policy factors giving rise to the doctrine in the first instance.

Whether because the contributory negligence finding was dictum or because it was an alternative finding, I would deny it preclusive effect. I, therefore, vote to reverse and remit for further proceedings.

Notes and Questions

1. In order to understand the debate over alternative determinations, it is first necessary to distinguish between determinations that are essential to the judgment and those that support the judgment, but which are not essential. The latter are classified as alternative determinations. For example, assume that *P* sues *D* to recover for damages for personal injuries received in an automobile accident. *D* denies negligence and asserts *P's* contributory negligence as a defense. After trial, a verdict and judgment are rendered for *P*, the jury specifically finding that *D* was negligent and that *P* was not guilty of contributory negligence. Under these circumstances, the findings in favor of *P* on the issues of negligence and contributory negligence are essential to the judgment. *P* had to win on both issues to win at all. Suppose, however, that the verdict and judgment had been for *D*, the jury specifically finding that *D* was not negligent and that *P* was guilty of contributory negligence. Under these circumstances, the findings in favor of *D* both support the judgment, but both findings are not essential to the judgment. They are alternative determinations because *D* could have won on either issue, lost on the other, and still won the action.

2. Essential determinations are always precluded in subsequent litigation, but there is a question about the propriety of precluding alternative determinations in a second action. The first RESTATEMENT OF JUDGMENTS stated that alternative determinations would be precluded in subsequent litigation. *See* RESTATEMENT OF JUDGMENTS §68 cmt. n (1942). However, as *Malloy* indicates, the RESTATEMENT (SECOND) OF JUDGMENTS takes the position that neither of the alternative determinations should be precluded in subsequent litigation. *See* RESTATEMENT (SECOND) OF JUDGMENTS §27 cmt. i (1982). The RESTATEMENT (SECOND) gives two reasons for this rule of nonpreclusion. First, neither determination in the alternative may have been considered as carefully or as rigorously as if it were an essential determination. Second, the losing party may be dissuaded from appealing because of the likelihood that at least one of the determinations might be upheld and the judgment sustained against the appellant even if there were error in the other determination.

3. Note that *Malloy* takes an intermediate position. Instead of preclusion always or never applying, the New York courts will take a discretionary, case-by-case approach to determining the preclusive effect of alternative determinations. In *Malloy*, this approach

---

3. As noted in *Halpern v. Schwartz*, 426 F.2d 102, 106 (2d Cir. 1970), a rule according estoppel effect to alternative findings "at best would preclude some future trial litigation at the expense of currently creating extra appellate litigation."

resulted in the alternative determinations being precluded. However, wasn't *Malloy* a particularly strong case for nonpreclusion under the Restatement (Second) rationale?

4. Even under the Restatement (Second), however, comment i to § 27 indicates that alternative findings can result in preclusion when they constitute "alternative bases for a determination that is essential to the judgment." Do you find it hard to understand what kind of case would involve "alternative bases" in support of a determination that is essential to the judgment? Do you understand why the Restatement (Second) would not apply the rationale discussed in Note 2, above, to this kind of case in order to preclude relitigation of the "alternative bases"?

Problems

Problem 12-17. P sues D to recover for personal injuries received in an automobile accident, alleging that D was negligent in driving at an excessive rate of speed. After trial, verdict and judgment are given for D on the ground that D was not negligent. Subsequently, D sues P for personal injuries received in the same accident. D's action is permitted because the state in question has no compulsory counterclaim rule. May P defend this action on the ground that D was negligent in failing to keep a proper lookout?

Problem 12-18. P sues D for personal injuries received in an automobile accident, alleging that D was negligent. D admits D's own negligence in the answer and asserts contributory negligence as a defense. After trial, verdict and judgment are given for D on the ground that P was guilty of contributory negligence. Subsequently, D sues P for personal injuries received in the accident. D's action is permitted because the state has no compulsory counterclaim rule. P contends that the prior judgment establishes that D was negligent and that, as a result, D's suit must fail on P's defense that D was guilty of contributory negligence. Does the doctrine of issue preclusion operate on these facts to make P's defense good? Why or why not?

Problem 12-19. P sues D for personal injuries received in an automobile accident, alleging that D was negligent. D denies negligence and asserts contributory negligence as a defense. After trial a general verdict is returned for D and judgment is entered on the verdict. Subsequently, D sues P for personal injuries received in the same accident; D's action is permitted because the jurisdiction has no compulsory counterclaim rule. P defends by denying P's own negligence and asserting D's contributory negligence. D contends that the judgment in the first action establishes conclusively that P was negligent and D was not negligent. Are D's arguments sound? Why or why not? Do you need any further information to answer this problem?

Problem 12-20. P sues D to recover interest on a promissory note payable to P, the principal not yet being due. D defends by alleging that D was induced by the fraud of P to execute the note, and further alleges that P gave D a release of the obligation to pay interest. After a trial, a general verdict is returned in favor of P. After the note matures, P brings an action for the principal of the note. P contends in this suit that the judgment in the first action is conclusive that D was not induced by P's fraud to execute the note. Is P's argument sound, or may D raise fraud as a defense? Why or why not?

Problem 12-21. P sues D to recover interest on a note, the principal not yet being due. D alleges that D was induced by P's fraud to execute the note and that P gave D a binding release of the obligation to pay interest. After a trial, the court sitting without a jury finds that D was not induced by P's fraud to execute the note, but that P had given D a binding release of the obligation to pay interest and enters judgment for D. After the note matures,

P sues *D* for the principal. Is *D* precluded by the first judgment from defending the action on the ground that *D* was induced by *P's* fraud to execute the note? Why or why not?

Problem 12-22. On the facts of *Problem 12-21*, if the court in the first action had found that *D* was induced by *P's* fraud to execute the note and that *P* had given *D* a binding release of the obligation to pay interest, would the judgment have established *P's* fraud conclusively for the purpose of the second action for the principal? Why or why not? Would it matter whether *P* had (a) not appealed the judgment for *D* in the first action or (b) appealed and the appellate court had upheld both determinations by the trial court?

Problem 12-23. On the facts of *Problem 12-22*, if the second action had been for a second installment of interest rather than the principal of the note, would the result be the same? The drafters of the RESTATEMENT (SECOND) see an important difference between this situation and that in *Problem 12-22*. What is that difference?

3. Exceptions to Issue Preclusion

The basic rule of issue preclusion examined in subsection 1, above, has numerous exceptions. These exceptions are described in § 28 of the RESTATEMENT (SECOND) OF JUDGMENTS. Many of the exceptions focus on the adequacy of the opportunity to litigate afforded the party to be bound in the first litigation. Others focus on the fundamental fairness of binding a party in other respects. In examining the exceptions, you should attempt to determine what the policy basis of each one is and how that policy basis should affect the administration of the exception.

Inability to Obtain Appellate Review. One important exception exists when the losing party in the initial action cannot, as a matter of law, obtain appellate review of the judgment in order to obtain correction of errors that may infect the determinations made against the party. Of course, if appellate review is available but not sought by the party, this exception does not apply. RESTATEMENT (SECOND) OF JUDGMENTS § 28(1) cmt. a (1982).

Issues of Law. Issue preclusion applies to issues of law as well as to issues of fact. However, it is sometimes considered unfair to bind parties for all time on determinations against them on issues of law. For example, when the claims between the parties are substantially unrelated, it may be unfair to prevent the losing party from relitigating an issue of law decided against the party in the initial action when other persons who were not parties to that action are free to argue for a change in the applicable law. In addition, even when the claims in the two actions are substantially related, it is sometimes appropriate to permit a new determination of an issue of law in order to take account of an intervening change of law or to prevent "inequitable administration of the laws." *See id.* § 28(2) cmts. b & c.

For example, assume that the government litigates the question of the rate at which a party is liable to pay a tax and loses — with the party prevailing against the government establishing that the lower of two rates is the appropriate one. Subsequently, in an action between the government and a second party in identical circumstances, the highest court in the state overrules the precedent that caused the first party to win. Under such circumstances, it would be inappropriate to allow the party to the first action to pay the lower tax rate for all time because of issue preclusion, when others in identical circumstances, but who litigated later, will now be have to pay at a higher rate.

Actions in Different Courts with Qualitatively Different Procedures. A third exception to the general rules of issue preclusion exists when the initial and the subsequent actions take place in different courts. When this occurs, there may be differences in the quality of the procedures followed in the two courts that make issue preclusion inappropriate. Also, there may be situations in which the legislative allocation of jurisdiction between the two courts indicates that the determination by the first court should not be given preclusive effect. Under either circumstance, issue preclusion will not operate. *See id.* § 28(3) cmts. d & e.

Shifts in Burden of Proof. The burden of proof placed on a party or the party's adversary in an action has a potentially significant effect on the outcome of the action. As a result, an exception to issue preclusion is recognized when a party has a heavier burden of proof in the first action than in the second action, when the burden of proof has shifted to the party's adversary in the second action, or when the party's adversary has a significantly heavier burden of proof in the second action than in the first. *See id.* § 28(4).

Foreseeability that an Issue Would Be Important in a Subsequent Action. Traditionally, the courts drew a distinction between the preclusive effect of a determination on matters of "ultimate fact" as opposed to "mediate data." Findings on "ultimate facts" in the first action could be used to establish "ultimate facts" or "mediate data" in a subsequent action. However, determinations of "mediate data" could not be used at all in subsequent proceedings. *See id.* § 68 cmt. p. An "ultimate fact" is the logical conclusion that is drawn from the evidence produced in the action, while "mediate data," or "evidentiary facts," are the steps leading to the "ultimate fact." For example, in a negligence action, negligence is the "ultimate fact," while evidence that the defendant was driving at excessive speed is a "mediate datum," or "evidentiary fact." To put it mildly, the distinction between "ultimate facts" and "mediate data" was unclear. The distinction seemed really to be directed at assuring that the issue in question was litigated with a full awareness of its implications for future proceedings. Thus, the modern rule simply asks directly whether it was sufficiently foreseeable at the time of the first action that the issue would arise in a subsequent proceeding. *See id.* § 28(5)(b).

Impact of a Determination on Nonparties. Sometimes litigation can have an impact on persons who are not parties to the litigation. For example, a class may be represented in a class action by a member of the class. The representative party may be satisfactory to the class as far as the claim being asserted in the class action is concerned. However, issues may be determined in the class action that would have a bearing on an unrelated claim in which members of the class have an interest. Under such circumstances "due consideration of the interests of persons not themselves before the court in the prior action may justify relitigation of an issue actually litigated and determined in that action." *Id.* § 28(5)(a) cmt. h.

Inability or Lack of Incentive to Obtain a Full and Fair Adjudication. Finally, modern practice supports an exception to the operation of issue preclusion whenever the circumstances surrounding the first action did not afford "an adequate opportunity or incentive to obtain a full and fair adjudication in the initial action." *Id.* § 28(5)(c). Can you think of circumstances in which it would be appropriate to apply this last exception? Do you see any problems with an exception expressed this broadly? *See id.* cmt. j ("In an action in which an issue is litigated and determined, one party may conceal from the other information that would materially affect the outcome of the case. Such concealment may be of particular concern if there is a fiduciary relationship between the parties. Or one of the parties may have been laboring under a mental or physical disability that impeded effective litigation and that has since been removed. Or it may be evident from the jury's verdict that the verdict was the result of compromise. Or the amount in controversy in the first action may have been so small in relation to the amount in controversy in the second that preclusion would be plainly unfair.").

Problems

Problem 12-24. P sues D for a declaratory judgment that a statute being enforced by D against P is unconstitutional. The trial court finds the statute constitutional as applied and enters judgment for D. P appeals, but the appeal is dismissed for mootness because P has ceased the activities prohibited by the statute; however, the judgment of the trial court is not vacated. Subsequently, P again undertakes activities prohibited by the statute and sues D again for a declaratory judgment that the statute is unconstitutional. Does the judgment in the first action preclude P from relitigating the constitutional issue? Why or why not?

Problem 12-25. P sues D for property damage arising out of an automobile accident. P's suit is brought in a small claims court that has a jurisdictional ceiling on its competence of $500 and operates informally without pleadings, counsel, or rules of evidence. The court finds D was negligent and a judgment is rendered for P. In a subsequent action by D against P for personal injuries received in the same accident, brought in the state court of general jurisdiction, does the judgment in the small claims court establish conclusively that D was guilty of contributory negligence, thus precluding the action?

Problem 12-26. P sues D for personal injuries resulting from an automobile accident, alleging that D was negligent. In the state in which P brings the action, the plaintiff in a negligence suit is required to plead and prove the plaintiff's freedom from contributory negligence. After a trial, the court holds that P has failed to discharge this burden and finds P guilty of contributory negligence. A judgment is entered for D based on this finding. Subsequently, D sues P for personal injuries received in the same accident. D's action is permitted because the state has no compulsory counterclaim rule. D contends that the judgment in the first action conclusively establishes P's negligence in the second action. Is D's argument sound? Why or why not?

Problem 12-27. P sues D for $50.00 in property damage resulting from an automobile accident. P alleges that D was negligent, which is denied by D. After a trial to the court without a jury, D is found negligent, and judgment is entered for P. Subsequently, D sues P for $100,000 in damages for personal injuries received in the same accident. D's action is permitted because the jurisdiction does not have a compulsory counterclaim rule. P contends that the judgment in the first action establishes D's contributory negligence conclusively for purposes of the second action. Is P's argument sound? Why or why not?

4. Nonmutual Preclusion

Traditionally, a nonparty to a prior action who was not bound by the judgment could not assert issue preclusion against another party who was bound by the judgment. As discussed briefly in subsection 1, above, this was the result of the rule of "mutuality of estoppel." Only a party bound by the judgment could assert issue preclusion against another party bound by the judgment. Thus, assume that P, D-1, and D-2 collided in their automobiles and each of them suffered personal injuries. P sued D-1 and lost, the jury finding that P was contributorily negligent. If P then sued D-2, D-2 would have to relitigate the issue of P's contributory negligence. In this and similar situations, it was said that "estoppel must be mutual." That is, all the parties to the second action had to be bound by the prior judgment or none of them were bound. D-2 could not be bound by the first judgment, because D-2 was not a party to the first action. Therefore, P could not be bound either, even though P had a full and fair opportunity to litigate the issue of contributory negligence in the first proceeding.

In 1942, in *Bernhard v. Bank of America National Trust & Savings Association*, 122 P.2d 892 (Cal. 1942), the California Supreme Court abolished the mutuality rule in its courts and allowed the defendant in the second action to use the judgment in the first action defensively against the person who was the plaintiff in the first action. This nonmutual defensive use of issue preclusion against the party who was the plaintiff in the first action is the strongest case in which to do away with the mutuality rule. The plaintiff controlled the timing of the action, the selection of the forum, and the opponent in the first action and is just trying again against a different adversary.

Eventually, the doctrine of mutuality was abolished or relaxed in many other courts, including the federal courts and many state courts, not only in the *Bernhard* situation, but also in other, more questionable, kinds of cases. The following materials explore the modern rule in the variety of situations in which it is applied.

Hunter v. City of Des Moines

Supreme Court of Iowa, 1981
300 N.W.2d 121

ALLBEE, JUSTICE.

The important question which we confront in this appeal is whether offensive use of issue preclusion can be invoked where mutuality of the parties is lacking. The sole assignment of error here is predicated upon trial court's denial of plaintiffs' application for separate adjudication of law points; in that application they asserted defendant City of Des Moines should be precluded from relitigating the issues of its negligence and of proximate cause in this action due to a judgment obtained against it by a different plaintiff in a prior negligence action which arose from the same factual background.

On January 18, 1978, plaintiff Michael J. Hunter was involved in a collision in Des Moines with another vehicle while operating an automobile owned by plaintiff Becky Mc-Murry. At the time of the mishap, Karen Wadle was a passenger in the automobile driven by Hunter. Following the accident, separate lawsuits were filed by Wadle and the plaintiffs. In addition to the driver of the other car,[1] both actions named the City of Des Moines as a defendant. The cause of action against the city in both cases was based upon its purportedly negligent failure to remove a snow pile in the vicinity of the intersection where the accident took place which allegedly obstructed the vision of the drivers involved. Plaintiffs did not attempt to join the Wadle lawsuit. Pursuant to Iowa R. Civ. P. 185, the city filed a motion to consolidate the two actions for trial, which was overruled. It then made application to this court for permission to appeal that ruling. The application, resisted by both Wadle and plaintiffs, was denied and the two actions proceeded separately. The *Wadle* case was the first to be tried, and resulted in a judgment against the city.

Plaintiffs then filed an amendment to their petition, in which they asserted that the judgment in the *Wadle* action precluded the city from relitigating the issues of its negligence and of proximate cause in this action. Plaintiffs followed with the application for separate adjudication of law points, in which, as before indicated, they requested a trial court ruling barring the city from contesting its negligence due to the prior adverse judgment in the *Wadle* case. Trial court denied this application, and the action proceeded to trial. Following submission of the case, the jury returned a verdict for the city. This appeal followed.

---

1. The driver of the other car settled at an early stage of the proceedings and is not involved in this appeal.

I. In general, the doctrine of issue preclusion prevents parties to a prior action in which judgment has been entered from relitigating in a subsequent action issues raised and resolved in the previous action. "When an issue of fact or law is actually litigated and determined by a valid and final judgment, and the determination is essential to the judgment, the determination is conclusive in a subsequent action between the parties, whether on the same or a different claim." ... As we have noted in prior cases, the doctrine may be utilized in either a defensive or an offensive manner.

> The phrase "defensive use" of the doctrine of collateral estoppel is used here to mean that a stranger to the judgment, ordinarily the defendant in the second action, relies upon a former judgment as conclusively establishing in his favor an issue which he must prove as an element of his defense.

> On the other hand, the phrase "offensive use" or "affirmative use" of the doctrine is used to mean that a stranger to the judgment, ordinarily the plaintiff in the second action, relies upon a former judgment as conclusively establishing in his favor an issue which he must prove as an essential element of his cause of action or claim.

> In other words, defensively a judgment is used as a "shield" and offensively as a "sword." ...

Traditionally, the presence of three prerequisites was required before the doctrine of issue preclusion could properly be applied in any given case: (1) identity of issues raised in the successive proceedings; (2) determination of these issues by a valid final judgment to which such determination is necessary; and (3) identity of the parties or privity[3] (mutuality of estoppel).... Subsequent cases developed from these traditional prerequisites a four-factor standard to be utilized in determining the applicability of the doctrine.... Before issue preclusion may now be employed in any case, these four prerequisites must be established: (1) the issue concluded must be identical; (2) the issue must have been raised and litigated in the prior action; (3) the issue must have been material and relevant to the disposition of the prior action; and (4) the determination made of the issue in the prior action must have been necessary and essential to the resulting judgment....

In addition to elaborating on the prerequisites to issue preclusion, this court has modified the traditional requirement of privity where the doctrine is invoked in a defensive manner.... Issue preclusion may properly be applied in that fashion as between nonmutual parties where the four prerequisites delineated above are satisfied and where the party against whom the doctrine is invoked defensively "was so connected in interest with one of the parties in the former action as to have had a full and fair opportunity to litigate the relevant claim or issue and be properly bound by its resolution." ... However, until now we have declined to modify the traditional requirement of mutuality with respect to offensive use of issue preclusion.... In this case, we must again consider whether the requirement of mutuality should in all instances remain a bar to the offensive use of issue preclusion by a litigant not a party or in privity with a party to the prior adjudication relied upon. This is because plaintiffs, non-parties to the *Wadle* judgment, seek to invoke the doctrine offensively, and it is undisputed that they fall outside the traditional definition of privity.

As is true where the doctrine is employed defensively, offensive use of issue preclusion may prevent needless relitigation and therefore promote judicial economy in some cases.

---

3. A "privity" in this context has been defined as "one who, after rendition of the judgment, has acquired an interest in the subject matter affected by the judgment through or under one of the parties, as by inheritance, succession, or purchase." ...

Thus, strict adherence to the traditional requirement of mutuality in connection with the offensive use of issue preclusion may be unwarranted in appropriate circumstances. Nonetheless, other considerations support the adoption of a more restrictive modification of that rule than that which has been approved where the doctrine is invoked in a defensive manner. Two sound reasons for distinguishing between these applications of issue preclusion were noted by the United States Supreme Court:

> First, offensive use of collateral estoppel does not promote judicial economy in the same manner as defensive use does. Defensive use of collateral estoppel precludes a plaintiff from relitigating identical issues by merely "switching adversaries." (Citation omitted.) Thus defensive collateral estoppel gives a plaintiff a strong incentive to join all potential defendants in the first action if possible. Offensive use of collateral estoppel, on the other hand, creates precisely the opposite incentive. Since a plaintiff will be able to rely on a previous judgment against a defendant but will not be bound by that judgment if the defendant wins, the plaintiff has every incentive to adopt a "wait and see" attitude, in the hope that the first action by another plaintiff will result in a favorable judgment. (Citations omitted.) Thus offensive use of collateral estoppel will likely increase rather than decrease the total amount of litigation, since potential plaintiffs will have everything to gain and nothing to lose by not intervening in the first action.

> A second argument against offensive use of collateral estoppel is that it may be unfair to a defendant. If a defendant in the first action is sued for small or nominal damages, he may have little incentive to defend vigorously, particularly if future suits are not foreseeable. (Citations omitted.) Allowing offensive collateral estoppel may also be unfair to a defendant if the judgment relied upon as a basis for the estoppel is itself inconsistent with one or more previous judgments in favor of the defendant. Still another situation where it might be unfair to apply offensive estoppel is where the second action affords the defendant procedural opportunities unavailable in the first action that could readily cause a different result.

Parklane Hosiery [*v. Shore*], 439 U.S. [322], 329–30 [(1979)]. While cognizant of these distinguishing factors, the Supreme Court nonetheless concluded that the preferable approach in the federal courts would be to grant trial courts broad discretion in permitting offensive use of the doctrine, as opposed to precluding such application. Under the general rule adopted by the Supreme Court, offensive use of issue preclusion would not be allowed in cases where a plaintiff could easily have joined in the earlier action or where offensive application would be unfair to a defendant....

A similar position was taken by the *Restatement (Second) of Judgments* [§ 29]....

....

Mindful of the foregoing, we conclude that offensive application of the doctrine of issue preclusion should not invariably be precluded where mutuality of parties is lacking. Rather, we adopt as ours the position taken by *Restatement (Second) of Judgments* § [29] with respect to the use of issue preclusion in this context.

II. In determining whether the doctrine of issue preclusion could properly have been applied offensively in this case, we must first consider whether the four prerequisites necessary for utilization of the doctrine were sufficiently established....

....

We ... conclude that the four general prerequisites for the application of issue preclusion are satisfied in this case. However, because plaintiffs seek to invoke the doctrine of-

Non - Mutual offensive CE Additional Factors

fensively where mutuality is lacking, we must additionally consider whether it may be utilized in that fashion here, guided by the *Restatement* position which we have today adopted. Under that approach, the questions which must next be answered are (1) whether the city was afforded a full and fair opportunity to litigate the issues of its negligence and of proximate cause in the *Wadle* action, and (2) whether any other circumstances are present which would justify granting the city occasion to relitigate those issues....

The record discloses nothing from which it could be inferred that the city lacked a full and fair opportunity in the prior action to litigate the issues in question. Indeed, there is no indication that a vigorous defense was not undertaken with respect to those issues. Thus, this aspect of the *Restatement* approach affords no basis for declining to apply issue preclusion offensively in this case.

However, among those circumstances delineated by the *Restatement* which may justify affording a party an opportunity to relitigate issues sought to be precluded is the situation where, as in this case, "the person seeking to invoke favorable preclusion ... could have effected joinder in the first action between himself and his present adversary." *Restatement (Second) of Judgments* § [29(3)].... Plaintiffs here could easily have effected joinder in the *Wadle* action, but failed to do so. That fact provides the basis for denying offensive application of issue preclusion in this case. Consequently, [the] trial court's denial of plaintiffs' application for separate adjudication of law points, although premised upon other grounds, must be affirmed....

In summary, we decide today that the absence of mutuality will no longer invariably bar the offensive application of issue preclusion. In cases where the four general prerequisites of the doctrine are satisfied, issue preclusion may be applied offensively where mutuality is lacking if it is determined that the party sought to be precluded was afforded a full and fair opportunity to litigate the issue in the action relied upon and that no other circumstances justify affording him an opportunity to relitigate that issue.

AFFIRMED.

Notes and Questions

1. As explained in the introductory text and in *Hunter,* nonmutual issue preclusion is now authorized in those jurisdictions that have abolished or relaxed the doctrine of mutuality. This relaxation of mutuality, however, only means that a nonparty (stranger) to the first action can take *advantage* of issue preclusion and assert it against a party who is bound by the judgment. It does *not* mean that a bound party can now assert issue preclusion against a nonparty (stranger) to the first action. Unless a person is a party to an action or in "privity" with a party to the action (see section D, below), a nonparty to the first action cannot be bound by the judgment in terms of issue preclusion.

2. As indicated in *Hunter* and the text preceding it, nonmutual preclusion has been approved in a number of situations that pose difficult problems. In many states and the federal courts, judgments can be given a defensive issue preclusion effect against persons who were defendants in the first action, an offensive issue preclusion effect against persons who were plaintiffs in the first action, and an offensive issue preclusion effect against persons who were defendants in the first action. Do you understand why these situations are more controversial than the *Bernhard* situation (defensive use of preclusion against the plaintiff in the prior action) in which to abolish the mutuality rule? Which of the situations poses the most difficult questions about nonmutual preclusion?

3. As *Hunter* also indicates, the modern approach, exemplified by § 29 of the RE-STATEMENT (SECOND), is to permit nonmutual preclusion in all cases, subject to a number of exceptions designed to assure that the person precluded by the judgment in the first action had a full and fair opportunity to litigate the issues on which preclusion will operate. Of course, all of the basic rules of issue preclusion examined above must be satisfied, and none of the exceptions to the basic rule must be applicable. If the basic rules are satisfied and no exceptions to the basic rules exist, nonmutual preclusion will operate subject to the exceptions in § 29.

4. In *Hunter*, the Iowa Supreme Court approved of nonmutual offensive issue preclusion, but then found one of the exceptions in § 29 to be applicable. Because the plaintiff in the second action did not effectuate joinder of the plaintiff's claim in the initial action brought against the defendants by another plaintiff, preclusive effect was denied to the first judgment. *See* RESTATEMENT (SECOND) OF JUDGMENTS § 29(3) (1982). Does this exception always require parties injured in the same event to join in suing the allegedly responsible party, or were there special considerations in *Hunter* that made application of this exception appropriate? Would it be a stronger or weaker case for the application of the exception if a plaintiff failed to join multiple defendants in an action whom the plaintiff believed were jointly or alternatively liable to the plaintiff? In this regard, consider Comment e to § 29 of the RESTATEMENT (SECOND):

> A person in such a position that he might ordinarily have been expected to join as plaintiff in the first action, but who did not do so, may be refused the benefits of "offensive" issue preclusion where the circumstances suggest that he wished to avail himself of the benefits of a favorable outcome without incurring the risk of an unfavorable one. Such a refusal may be appropriate where the person could reasonably have been expected to intervene in the prior action, and ordinarily is appropriate where he withdrew from an action to which he had been a party.... Due recognition should be given, however, to the normally available option of a plaintiff to prosecute his claim without the encumbrance of joining with others whose situation does not substantially coincide with his own. On the other hand, where a plaintiff brings a subsequent action involving the same issues against a person whom he could appropriately have joined as a co-defendant in the first action, only strongly compelling circumstances justify withholding preclusion.

5. In addition to the exception to nonmutual preclusion applied in *Hunter*, § 29 of the RESTATEMENT (SECOND) also recognizes seven other exceptions. Nonmutual preclusion is not appropriate when

(a) treating the issue as conclusively determined would be incompatible with an applicable scheme of administering the remedies in the successive actions (§ 29(1));

(b) the forum in the second action affords the party to be precluded procedural opportunities in litigating the issue that were not present in the first action and that might produce a different result on the issue (§ 29(2));

(c) the determination relied on as preclusive was inconsistent with another determination of the same issue (§ 29(4));

(d) the prior determination may have been affected by relationships between the parties to the first action that are not present in the second action, or the determination was apparently based on a compromise verdict or finding (§ 29(5));

(e) precluding the issue from relitigation may complicate determination of the issues in the subsequent proceeding or prejudice the interests of a party to that proceeding (§ 29(6));

(f) the issue is one of law and treating it as conclusively determined would inappropriately foreclose the opportunity to obtain reconsideration of the legal rule upon which the determination was based (§ 29(7)); or

(g) other compelling circumstances make it appropriate that the party be permitted to relitigate the issue (§ 29(8)).

Note that this last exception may pose even worse problems of over breadth than the broad "full and fair opportunity to litigate" exception to the basic rule of issue preclusion found in § 28(5)(c) of the RESTATEMENT (SECOND), discussed in the preceding subsection. Indeed, since the proper analysis of issue preclusion questions necessitates that the requirements of the basic rule be satisfied and that none of the exceptions to the basic rule be applicable before considering the exceptions in § 29, it would have to be the case that the exception in § 29(8) would be applicable in a situation in which, concededly, the party to be precluded had been afforded a "full and fair opportunity to litigate" the issue within the meaning of § 28(5)(c). Does this make sense?

6. In *Garcia v. General Motors Corp.*, 990 P.2d 1069 (Ariz. Ct. App. 1999), the plaintiffs were injured in a single-car accident in Idaho while riding in a General Motors van. One of the plaintiffs sued General Motors in the U.S. District Court for Idaho. Idaho state law provided that the failure to use a seat beat was inadmissible as evidence of contributory or comparative negligence. Applying this law, the court ruled in a pretrial motion that all evidence that plaintiff was not wearing her seatbelt would be excluded at trial. After this ruling, but before trial, plaintiff settled with General Motors. Subsequently, other plaintiffs sued General Motors in Arizona state court to recover for their injuries received in the same accident. General Motors again raised the seatbelt defense. The plaintiffs argued that the Idaho federal court's ruling on the defense bound General Motors in the second action.

The Arizona Court of Appeals held that issue preclusion did not apply for several reasons. First, the court held that because the Idaho action was settled after the evidentiary ruling, the seat-belt ruling was not essential to the judgment. Second, the court held that the ruling did not possess the requisite finality for issue preclusion because of the lack of opportunity for appellate review of the ruling. Finally, the court stated that it was "troubled" by the application of issue preclusion to the case because of the possibility that one plaintiff in a multiple plaintiff case could bring suit in the forum most likely to give a favorable choice-of-law ruling against the defendants in a subsequent action. The court ultimately held that Arizona law should be applied to the seatbelt issue and that the jury should be allowed to consider seatbelt nonuse in determining damages.

Problems

Problem 12-28. P-1 sues D in a small claims court for $100 in property damage arising from an automobile accident. After a trial, the court finds D negligent and enters judgment for P-1. Subsequently, P-2 sues D for $50,000 for personal injuries arising out of the same automobile accident. Is D precluded from relitigating the issue of negligence determined against D in *P-1 v. D*, assuming that the RESTATEMENT (SECOND) approach is followed in the state?

Problem 12-29. P-1 sues D for the wrongful death of P-1's spouse allegedly caused by D's negligence. After a trial, the court finds D negligent and enters judgment for P-1. The wrongful death statute provides that judgments in wrongful death actions are entitled to be treated as prima facie correct in subsequent actions. P-2 then sues D for the wrongful death of *P-2's* spouse allegedly caused by the same act of negligence. If the Restatement (Second) approach is followed generally in the state, is *D* precluded from relitigating the issue of negligence in the action with *P-2*?

Problem 12-30. *P-1*, the administrator of *T's* estate, sues *D* for wrongful death, alleging that *T* was killed in a three-car automobile accident due to *D's* negligence. At trial, *D* is prevented from testifying because of the state's "Dead Man's Statute," which prevents a person from testifying in civil actions about the events giving rise to the suit, when the opposing party is the administrator of a deceased individual who was a participant in the events. After trial, the jury finds *D* negligent and a judgment is entered against *D*. Subsequently, *P-2* sues *D* for personal injuries received in the same accident. *P-2* moves for summary judgment in the action on the grounds that the prior judgment conclusively establishes *D's* negligence. Should summary judgment be granted? Why or why not?

Problem 12-31. *P-1* sues *D* in a federal court for an injunction to prevent *D* from engaging in illegal activities under a federal statute. After trial, the court finds that *D* indeed did engage in the activities alleged and that the activities were illegal and grants the injunction. In a subsequent action, *P-2* sues *D* in another federal court for damages resulting from the same activities. *P-2* contends that the prior judgment is conclusive that *D* engaged in the illegal activities. Is there any effective argument that *D* can make to avoid issue preclusion in this situation, assuming that the federal courts refuse to apply the mutuality rule as a general matter?

Problem 12-32. *P-1* stores goods in *P-2's* warehouse. The warehouse is destroyed by a fire allegedly caused by *D's* negligence. *P-1* sues *D* for the loss of *P-1's* property. After a trial, *P-1* recovers a judgment based on a finding of *D's* negligence. Subsequently, *P-2* sues *D* for the destruction of the warehouse. *P-2* contends that the prior judgment is conclusive on the issue of *D's* negligence, the rule of mutuality having been abolished generally by the jurisdiction. Is there any argument that *D* can make that preclusion should not apply in this situation? Are there additional facts you would like to know before answering this question?

Problem 12-33. After the wreck of a passenger train, *P-1*, a passenger on the train, sues *D Railroad* for personal injuries, alleging that *D's* negligence caused the accident. After a trial, verdict and judgment are given for *D* on the ground that it was not negligent. Subsequently, *P-2*, another passenger on the wrecked train, sues *D* for personal injuries arising out of the same wreck, again alleging negligence. This time, verdict and judgment are given for *P-2* after a finding that *D* was negligent. Subsequently, *P-3*, a third passenger on the train, sues *D* for personal injuries received in the accident. *P-3* contends that *D's* negligence is conclusively established by the judgment in *P-2 v. D*, the jurisdiction in question having abolished the mutuality rule. Is *P-3's* contention sound? If *P-2 v. D* had been the first suit brought and concluded and *P-1 v. D* had not yet been brought, would the result in *P-3 v. D* be different? Does this last possibility indicate any problem with abolition of the mutuality rule in mass disaster cases?

Problem 12-34. *P-1* and *P-2* are killed in the wreck of *D's* car. *P-1's* personal representative sues *D* for $70,000 for wrongful death. At trial the evidence of *D's* negligence is minimal, but the jury returns a verdict in favor of *P-1's Rep.* for $35,000. Subsequently, *P-2's* representative sues *D* for $100,000 for wrongful death. Assuming that the state in question does not adhere generally to the mutuality rule, should the issue of *D's* negligence be deemed precluded by the judgment in *P-1's Rep. v. D*?

Problem 12-35. *P* sued *D-1 Bank* for damages, alleging that the bank breached a loan contract with her by charging a higher annual interest rate than that permitted by a state statute, and alleging further that the bank's method of computing interest rates was illegal. There being no genuine issue of fact, the court granted a motion for summary judgment against *P* on the grounds that the rates charged by the bank were permissible under the statute and that the bank's method of computing interest was also lawful. *P* subsequently sued *D-2 Bank* raising the identical issues. Assuming that the state follows the approach of §§ 27–29 of the RESTATEMENT (SECOND), should *P* be permitted to relitigate the issues of law decided against her in the first action? Do you understand what kind of case might involve an issue of law that would be precluded despite § 28(2) in a subsequent suit between the same parties, but would be relitigatable under § 29(7) in a suit between different parties?

Problem 12-36. *D* damages property that is owned by *P-1* and *P-2* and is stored in the same location. *P-1* sues *D* for damages, alleging that *D's* negligence caused the destruction of *P-1's* property. After trial, verdict and judgment are rendered for *P-1* based on a finding that *D* was negligent. *W*, a key witness on *D's* behalf, was unable to testify at the trial. Subsequently, *P-2* sues *D* for the damage to *P-1's* property. If *D* is able to produce *W* to testify in *P-2 v. D*, should *D* be permitted to relitigate the issue of negligence if the state has generally abolished the mutuality rule?

Section D. Preclusion of Nonparties

General Principles. Because nonparties have not been afforded their "day in court" to litigate a claim or issue, the rules of claim and issue preclusion do not ordinarily operate against nonparties to a judgment. In *Taylor v. Sturgell*, 553 U.S. 880 (2008), the Supreme Court reaffirmed that "'[i]t is a principle of general application in Anglo-American jurisprudence that one is not bound by a judgment *in personam* in a litigation in which he is not designated as a party or to which he has not been made a party by service of process.'... A person who was not a party to a suit generally has not had a 'full and fair opportunity to litigate' the claims and issues settled in that suit. The application of claim and issue preclusion to nonparties thus runs up against the 'deep-rooted historic tradition that everyone should have his own day in court.'" *Id.* at 884, 892.

The Court noted, however, that "[s]everal exceptions, recognized in this Court's decisions, temper this basic rule." *Id.* at 884. Specifically, the Court identified six exceptions to the general rule that nonparties to an action are not bound by the judgment:

(1) if the nonparty agrees to be bound by the judgment;

(2) if the nonparty has a pre-existing substantive legal relationship with a party to the judgment, such as preceding and succeeding owners of property, bailee and bailor, and assignee and assignor;

(3) if the nonparty was formally and adequately represented by someone who was a party to the judgment, such as properly conducted class actions and suits brought by trustees, guardians, and other fiduciaries on behalf of the nonparty;

(4) if the nonparty assumed control over the litigation in which the judgment was rendered;

(5) if the nonparty later brings suit as the designated representative or agent of a party to the judgment; and

(6) if a special statutory scheme expressly forecloses successive litigation by non-parties, provided the scheme is otherwise consistent with due process—such as bankruptcy and probate proceedings, or other actions that under governing law may be brought only on behalf of the public at large.

Id. at 893–95.

In *Taylor*, the Court found that none of the above exceptions applied and refused to recognize a "virtual representation" exception that some lower federal courts had adopted when there were, among other factors, an identity of interests and a "close relationship" between the party and the nonparty. In this case, plaintiff, Brent Taylor, filed a lawsuit under the Freedom of Information Act seeking certain documents from the Federal Aviation Administration. A friend of the plaintiff, Greg Herrick, had previously brought an unsuccessful suit seeking the same records. The Court noted that the two friends had "no legal relationship," and there was "no evidence that Taylor controlled, financed, participated in, or even had notice of Herrick's earlier suit." *Id.* at 884. As such, the earlier judgment against Herrick did not bar the plaintiff's current action.

Distinguish Nonparties with Factually Similar Claims. As held by the Court in *Taylor*, a nonparty must have some special relationship with a party to be bound by an earlier judgment and not simply possess a factually similar claim. Thus, if one passenger on a bus sues the bus company for negligence after an accident and loses, this judgment does not bind the other bus passengers in terms of either claim or issue preclusion. Although each passenger on the bus would have the same negligence claim arising from the same accident, this alone is insufficient to establish a legal relationship among the passengers. Unless the first passenger sues in a representative capacity on behalf of the other passengers or the passengers formally join the action, the nonparty passengers are not bound by the first judgment and are entitled to their "day in court" on their claims.

Transformational Effects. Certain judgments may also have "transformational effects," *i.e.*, judgments can sometimes transform relationships between parties in ways that nonparties will be unable to contest. For example, when a couple is validly divorced, nonparties may not ordinarily dispute whether the couple is married. This result is not based on the doctrine of res judicata, but instead reflects the change in the couple's relationship produced by the judgment of divorce. *See* Geoffrey C. Hazard, Jr. et al., Civil Procedure § 14.24, at 646–47 (6th ed. 2011).

Notes and Questions

1. A person appearing in one capacity in litigation is not normally bound by or entitled to the benefits of res judicata in another capacity. Thus, a person appearing in a purely representative capacity, and not in an individual capacity, is ordinarily treated as a completely different person for purposes of res judicata if the person brings a second action in an individual capacity. The reason for such treatment is that a person suing in a representative capacity binds the legal interests of the persons represented and must act with complete fidelity to the interests of those persons "uninfluenced by consideration of his own interest or advantage." *See* Restatement (Second) of Judgments § 36 cmt. a (1982). On the other hand, when a person appears in an action in both an individual and representative capacity, such as the representative in a class action who sues on behalf of himself and all members of the class, the person will be bound by the judgment in the class action both as an individual and as a member of the class. *See id.* § 41.

2. Even when a person appears in a purely representative capacity, representatives who are also beneficiaries are bound by judgments as beneficiaries. For example, a state may authorize a wrongful death action to be brought by the representative of a decedent's estate or by certain of the decedent's survivors who are also beneficiaries of the estate. If the representative brings the wrongful death action and loses, the survivor-beneficiaries would be bound by the judgment and precluded from bringing a second action. The judgment would similarly preclude the representative from bringing a second action in his capacity as a survivor-beneficiary.

3. Under the general rule, a person who sues in a representative capacity will be able to obtain the benefit of issue preclusion where the mutuality rule has been abolished, if the representative wins the first action and is later allowed to sue on a claim possessed in an individual capacity. However, all things being equal, issue preclusion would not *bind* the person suing in a subsequent action in an individual capacity when the person has previously lost an action against the same defendant brought in a representative capacity. Is this fair?

4. As noted by the Court in *Taylor* (exception 2), one recognized exception in which a nonparty can be bound by a judgment is when the nonparty has a pre-existing legal relationship with a party to the judgment. One example involves successors in interest in property, either through purchase or inheritance. Thus, assume that the owner of Blackacre sues the owner of Whiteacre to establish an easement over Whiteacre on the basis of a conveyance by the owner of Whiteacre and loses, the court finding that the conveyance did not give the owner of Blackacre an easement. If the owner of Blackacre later sells the property to another person, the buyer will be bound by the judgment in the action and precluded from relitigating the issue of the easement. *See* RESTATEMENT (SECOND) OF JUDGMENTS §§ 43–44.

5. Organizational relationships can also result in preclusion against nonparties. For example, if a corporation sues one of its officers for breach of a fiduciary relationship to the corporation, the action will preclude a subsequent derivative action on the same claim against the officer by a shareholder. *See id.* § 59(2). Likewise, if a corporation brings an action for injunctive relief and loses, a shareholder cannot bring a subsequent derivative action against the same defendant for damages due to the same activity by the defendant but accruing after the first action terminated.

6. Indemnitee-indemnitor relationships can also result in judgments binding on nonparties. For example, assume that a party possesses an insurance policy indemnifying the party against certain judgments that may be rendered against the party and requiring the insurance company to defend actions against the insured. If an injured party sues the insured, the insured can notify the insurance company of the action and call upon it to defend. If the company defends, it will be bound under rules providing that parties who control actions are bound by the judgments in the actions. *See id.* § 39. However, even if the company does not defend, it can be precluded from relitigating the issue of the insured's liability to the injured party, although it can still dispute its obligation to indemnify. *See id.* §§ 57–58.

Problems

Problem 12-37. P is injured severely in an automobile accident with *D*. *P* sues *D* for damages received in the accident, but after a trial a verdict and judgment are rendered for *D*. Subsequently, *P* dies from the injuries received in the accident. *R*, the representative of *P*'s estate, sues D for the wrongful death of P. D pleads res judicata in defense. Should D's defense be good? Why or why not?

Problem 12-38. R and P are traveling in an automobile when D collides with them, causing personal injuries to both. P dies from the injuries received in the accident. R is appointed representative of P's estate and brings a wrongful death action against D. After a trial, a verdict and judgment are rendered for D, the jury finding specifically that D was not negligent. Subsequently, R brings an action against D for R's own personal injuries. D defends on grounds of issue preclusion, arguing that R is bound by the finding that D was not negligent in the prior action. Is D's defense good?

Section E. Preclusion of Coparties

Traditionally, rules of res judicata have only applied to determinations between persons in an adversary relationship because, ordinarily, only persons aligned on opposite sides of an action will have a full and fair opportunity to litigate matters determined in the action. *See* RESTATEMENT (SECOND) OF JUDGMENTS § 38 cmt. a (1982). Sometimes, however, coparties may find themselves in an adversary relationship on some matters, while remaining aligned against the opposing party on other matters. That adverse relationship will always occur when the coparties are asserting claims, such as crossclaims, against one another. However, it can occur even in the absence of such claims.

Problem

Problem 12-39. P, the owner of an apartment building, sues D-1, a gas utility company, and D-2, a contractor working on the building. P claims that a gas line was ruptured through the negligence of both defendants, which resulted in an explosion that destroyed the building. D-1 and D-2 each defend on the ground that they were not negligent but the other defendant was. After trial, a judgment is rendered in favor of P against D-2, but in favor of D-1. Subsequently, D-2 sues D-1 for damage to D-2's equipment caused by the explosion. D-1 contends the prior judgment in P v. D-1 and D-2 precludes this action. Are D-1's contentions sound? Why or why not?

Section F. Preclusion of Subject-Matter and Personal Jurisdiction Questions

Rules of claim and issue preclusion operate only when a valid judgment is rendered in an action. Whether the judgment is valid or not depends on whether the plaintiff has complied with the rules of subject-matter and personal jurisdiction examined in previous chapters. However, questions of subject-matter and personal jurisdiction can themselves be foreclosed by the judgment in a prior action.

Personal Jurisdiction — Preclusion When Defendants Appear. Chapter 2 examined the concepts of general and special appearance and waiver of personal jurisdiction objections. These concepts play a critical role in determining whether a judgment can be "collaterally attacked" in another proceeding on the ground that it was rendered without personal jurisdiction over the defendant. A defendant who appears for the purpose of challenging personal jurisdiction in a court will be bound by a determination that personal jurisdiction exists, even if the determination is erroneous, and the defendant will not be able to collaterally attack an adverse judgment on personal jurisdiction grounds in a subsequent proceeding.

The defendant's remedy for an erroneous determination of a personal jurisdiction question is the same as the remedy for other erroneous determinations — direct attack on the judgment by appeal within the court system in which the judgment is rendered. In the absence of an appeal, or in the event of an unsuccessful appeal, the defendant will be bound by the ordinary rules of issue preclusion on the question of personal jurisdiction. In addition, a defendant who "waives" personal jurisdiction objections will be prevented from litigating them in a subsequent proceeding as well as in a direct attack on appeal.

Subject-Matter Jurisdiction — Preclusion When Defendants Appear. Issue preclusion can also operate on issues of subject-matter jurisdiction. In the ordinary case, when subject-matter jurisdiction is determined to exist in an initial proceeding, the determination will bind the parties in subsequent litigation, thus insulating the judgment from collateral attack. *See* Restatement (Second) of Judgments § 12 cmt. c (1982). Waiver does not apply to subject-matter jurisdiction objections. However, when a subject-matter jurisdiction objection exists, but it is not raised in an initial action that is litigated, the objection is normally foreclosed by the principles of claim preclusion from being raised by way of collateral attack on the judgment in a later action. *See id.* cmt. d.

Nevertheless, because of the reverence with which judicial systems in the United States view subject-matter-jurisdiction restriction, there are exceptions to the rules of preclusion that apply whether the issue of subject-matter jurisdiction has been litigated or not. The Restatement (Second) recognizes three situations in which subject-matter jurisdiction can be raised in subsequent litigation after an initial proceeding in which the issue was raised and determined, or in which the merits were litigated without raising and determining the subject-matter jurisdiction issue:

(1) when the subject-matter of the initial action was so plainly beyond the court's jurisdiction that entertaining the action was a manifest abuse of authority;

(2) when allowing the judgment to stand would substantially infringe the authority of another tribunal or agency of government; or

(3) when the judgment was rendered by a court lacking the capability to make an adequately informed determination of its own subject-matter authority and procedural fairness dictates that the party challenging the judgment be given a "belated opportunity" to attack the court's subject-matter jurisdiction. *See id.* § 12(1)-(3).

Nonlitigated Cases. The above discussion has assumed that the issues of personal and subject-matter jurisdiction have either been litigated and determined in the initial litigation, or that the merits of the action have been litigated while the issues of personal and subject-matter jurisdiction have been ignored. This leaves one further situation for discussion. Traditionally, a party who possesses a personal or subject-matter jurisdiction objection has been allowed to raise these objections in a subsequent proceeding after a default judgment has been rendered against the party for failure to appear at all. *See id.* § 65. Obviously, a party who never appears in an action and litigates cannot be bound by issue preclusion on either personal or subject-matter jurisdiction questions. Similarly, if there is no appearance at all, there can be no waiver of personal jurisdiction objections. Although claim preclusion rules do bind parties who default for failure to appear as far as the merits of an action are concerned, those rules have not traditionally prevented the party from raising personal or subject-matter jurisdiction challenges to a judgment in a later proceeding.

As far as subject-matter jurisdiction is concerned, however, states have the constitutional power to restrict defendants to an application for relief in the court where the original judgment was rendered. *See id.* § 12 cmt. f. Likewise, a state may be able to limit collateral attack on the judgments of its courts for lack of subject-matter jurisdiction, since subject-matter jurisdiction rules purely concern the domestic law of each state. The same cannot be said about the ability of a state to limit collateral attack on a default judgment rendered in violation of personal jurisdiction restrictions imposed by the U.S. Constitution. Finally, in the case of both personal and subject-matter jurisdiction, a defaulting party wishing to collaterally attack a judgment can be prevented from doing so if the party, after having actual notice of the judgment, "manifest[s] an intention to treat the judgment as valid" and granting relief from the default "would impair another person's substantial interest of reliance on the judgment." *See id.* § 66.

Notes and Questions

1. In *Dennis Garberg & Associates v. Pack-Tech International Corp.*, 115 F.3d 767 (10th Cir. 1997), the court held that a district court should not enter a default judgment without first determining that it has personal jurisdiction over the defendant. If the court determines that it does have personal jurisdiction, will the nonappearing defendant still be able to collaterally attack the judgment on the ground of lack of personal jurisdiction? If so, what is the purpose of making the court determine the jurisdictional issue before entering the default judgment?

2. A significant number of courts persist in stating that issue preclusion only applies when there is a final judgment "on the merits." As the preceding discussion has indicated, this statement is simply untrue. If it were true, there could never be issue preclusion on a question of personal or subject-matter jurisdiction, among other "procedural" grounds of dismissal. The courts stating that issue preclusion requires a judgment on the merits seem really to be confusing the "on the merits" requirement of claim preclusion with the requirement of issue preclusion that an issue actually have been litigated and determined in the first action. Other courts correctly recognize that the "on the merits" requirement does not apply to issue preclusion. Usually, courts stating that the "on the merits" requirement applies to issue preclusion do not actually reach incorrect results, but occasionally they write truly confused opinions. See Teply & Whitten at 1041.

3. It is true, however, that issue preclusion on questions of personal jurisdiction must be approached with caution. In *Pohlmann v. Bil-Jax, Inc.*, 176 F.3d 1110 (8th Cir. 1999), the court stated that prior decisions on personal jurisdiction issues have an issue preclusive effect, but only if the second action involves the identical issue as the first. Because personal jurisdiction is, to an extent, time sensitive, a dismissal on the ground of personal jurisdiction at one point in time on the ground that the defendant does not have minimum contacts with the state may not be the same question as whether the defendant has minimum contacts at a later point in time with the same state. But note that this approach raises important questions. If a state attempts to assert specific jurisdiction over a defendant and the court dismisses for inadequate contacts, should a later assertion of general jurisdiction on the same claim be allowed, assuming that the defendant has increased its activities in the state between the first and second actions? If the first assertion of personal jurisdiction is general, must the defendant have "systematic and continuous" contacts with the state within some time period relative to the time that the claim arose outside the state?

Problems

Problem 12-40. P, a citizen of State X, sues D, a citizen of State Y, in a state court in State X. D receives adequate notice of the action and specially appears in accordance with State X procedure to object both to the State X court's personal jurisdiction under the Due Process Clause of the Fourteenth Amendment and its subject-matter jurisdiction under State X law. The State X court holds that it has personal jurisdiction over D, but that it lacks subject-matter jurisdiction over the action and dismisses P's suit. Subsequently, P sues D in a State X court of proper subject-matter jurisdiction. D again receives adequate notice of the action and specially appears to contest the State X court's personal jurisdiction under the Due Process Clause of the Fourteenth Amendment. P contends that D is precluded from relitigating the personal jurisdiction issue by virtue of the finding on that issue in the first proceeding. What should be the result and why?

Problem 12-41. On the facts of *Problem 12-40,* assume that D defaulted in the first action, that P then sued D on the State X default judgment in a State Y court, and that D then raised the objections to the State X court's personal and subject-matter jurisdiction in the State Y action. If under the law of State X objections to personal and subject-matter jurisdiction can be raised only on direct attack of a judgment, can D raise either objection in the State Y proceeding? Why or why not?

Section G. Complications of the Federal System

1. Enforcement of State Judgments

The effect to be given to state judgments in the courts of other states and in the federal courts is governed by 28 U.S.C. § 1738, the full-faith-and-credit-implementing statute. As observed in Chapter 2, ever since the Supreme Court decided *Mills v. Duryee,* 11 U.S. (7 Cranch) 481 (1813), the implementing statute has been interpreted to require that the same effect be given to state-court judgments as those judgments would receive in the courts of the state that rendered them. In essence, this rule requires the judgment-enforcing state to use the rules of res judicata that would be used by the judgment-rendering state to determine what matters are precluded by the judgment.

[handwritten margin note: 28 USC §§ 1738 FF&C stat.]

Although the rule of § 1738 has been established since 1813, several issues have arisen concerning the administration of the statute in recent years. One issue concerns the effect to be given to a state court judgment when it adjudicates matters that later become pertinent in an action within the exclusive jurisdiction of the federal courts. The RE-STATEMENT (SECOND) OF JUDGMENTS took the position that if a plaintiff brought a state claim in state court and subsequently brought a federal claim in federal court over which the federal courts had exclusive jurisdiction, there would be no claim preclusion effect, even if the two claims arose out of the same facts. *See* RESTATEMENT (SECOND) OF JUDGMENTS 26(1)(c) cmt. 1, illus. 2 (1982). Two Supreme Court decisions have cast substantial doubt about whether § 1738 will be interpreted in the manner proposed by the RESTATEMENT (SECOND).

In *Marrese v. American Academy of Orthopaedic Surgeons,* 470 U.S. 373 (1985), the Court held that the first inquiry in such a case must be whether the state law of claim preclusion would prohibit a second action. Only if state law would preclude the suit in federal court is it necessary to determine whether an exception should be created to § 1738 on the ground that the policy of Congress in granting exclusive jurisdiction to the federal courts demands it. *See id.* at 382–86. In addition, the Court stated that once the question of an exception under § 1738 is presented, the answer will depend "on the particular federal statute as well as the nature of the claim or issue involved in the subsequent federal action [and in making that determination,] the primary consideration must be the intent of Congress." *Id.* at 386.

In *Matsushita Electric Industrial Co. v. Epstein*, 516 U.S. 367 (1996), a class action was brought in a Delaware state court in which state law claims were asserted arising out of a tender offer made by Matsushita for the common stock of a Delaware corporation. While the state court action was pending, a federal class action was commenced in a California federal district court based on alleged violations of the federal securities laws (over which the federal courts have exclusive jurisdiction). The federal class action was based on the same facts as the pending Delaware action. The California federal district court refused to certify the action as a class action and dismissed the case. After the federal plaintiffs appealed the dismissal, the state class action in Delaware settled. The Delaware settlement released all claims arising out of the tender offer, including the federal claims that had been asserted in the federal class action in California. Class members were notified and could have opted out of the settlement class or could have appeared at the hearing to contest the settlement, but they did not. Matsushita then invoked the Delaware judgment as a bar to further prosecution of the ongoing appeal in the federal action pursuant to § 1738. The Ninth Circuit rejected this argument by holding that the preclusive effect of the Delaware judgment was limited to the state claims involved in the action. The U.S. Supreme Court reversed. *Id.* at 369–72.

Adhering to *Marrese*, the Supreme Court first found that general Delaware preclusion principles as well as particular Delaware decisions involving the preclusive force of class action settlement in federal court indicated that Delaware would give a preclusive effect to the judgment. *Id.* at 375–79. The Court then examined whether the exclusive grant of jurisdiction to the federal courts for violations of the federal securities law should be interpreted to create an exception to § 1738. The Court recognized that the Exchange Act "contain[ed] no express language regarding its relationship with § 1738 or the preclusive effect of related state court proceedings [and that] any modification of § 1738 [would have to be] implied." *Id.* at 380. Focusing primarily on the intent of Congress, the Court concluded that there was no evidence in the federal statutory grant of exclusive jurisdiction "evinc[ing] any intent to prevent litigants in state court—whether suing as individuals or part of a class—from voluntarily releasing Exchange Act claims in judicially approved settlements." *Id.* at 381. The Court also found nothing in the legislative history of the grant of exclusive jurisdiction or other parts of the securities laws that would indicate that Congress intended to create an exception. In addition, the Court found support in its own decisions that state court judgments could have an issue-preclusive effect in subsequent federal actions and that parties can waive the right to have federal securities claims litigated in federal court by agreeing to arbitration. *Id.* at 383–86.

Another issue that has arisen concerning the administration of § 1738 concerns the effect that should be given to state court judgments that adjudicate federal claims or issues. Section 1738 does not distinguish between the effect to be given state judgments based on the law being applied by the court that rendered the judgment. At one time, the argument was made that state judgments determining issues or claims that are the subject of later civil rights actions in the federal courts should be given a limited claim and issue preclusion effect. However, the U.S. Supreme Court has made it clear that state court judgments should be given both a claim and an issue preclusion effect on federal matters that are later raised as part of a civil rights action in federal court. *See Haring v. Prosise*, 462 U.S. 306 (1983); *Kremer v. Chemical Constr. Corp.*, 456 U.S. 461 (1982); *Migra v. Warren City Sch. Dist. Bd. of Educ.*, 465 U.S. 75 (1984); *Allen v. McCurry*, 449 U.S. 90 (1980). So long as the party to be precluded had a full and fair opportunity to litigate in the state action, the state judgment must be given a preclusive effect in the subsequent federal action if it would have a preclusive effect in a subsequent state action.

Finally, a dispute exists whether a state court judgment may ever be given a greater or lesser (as opposed to the same) effect than it would receive in the courts of the state that rendered the judgment, when the judgment is brought into issue in a subsequent action in the courts of another state or a federal court. Arguably, a lesser effect may sometimes be given to other state's judgments if the preclusion rules of the judgment-rendering state are based on narrow procedural policies that are applicable exclusively to subsequent litigation in the courts of that state. If these rules would impinge upon important interests of the judgment-enforcing state, it should be within the power of the latter state to disregard the rules and determine the effect of the other state's judgment under its own rules. *See* TEPLY & WHITTEN at 1093–94.

The harder question is whether a state court should *ever be permitted* to give a greater effect to the judgment of another state's courts than would be given to the judgment in the judgment-rendering state. The problem with giving a greater effect to another state's judgments is that it poses a potential danger of unfair surprise to the parties to the initial action. Whether the party to be precluded is the plaintiff or defendant, the party may plan the initial litigation on the basis of the res judicata rules prevalent in the court in which the litigation is taking place. Thus, a plaintiff may assert some claims in the initial action and reserve others that the forum court's res judicata rules would allow to be asserted in subsequent litigation. If the broader rules of claim preclusion in another state are applied instead, the plaintiff may find the reserved claims have been lost. Similarly, a defending party may decide to litigate the initial action less vigorously on the basis of the forum's issue preclusion rules, only to find the rules of another state applied to preclude relitigation of more matters than the defendant originally expected. Because of these perils, it seems wiser to interpret § 1738 to preclude greater effects from ever being given to a judgment than it would receive under the res judicata rules of the judgment-rendering state unless some device, such as a dismissal without prejudice, can be employed to avoid unfair surprise to the parties. *See id.* at 1095–96.

Notes and Questions

1. Issue preclusion applies to determinations by state courts of questions of historical fact, mixed issues of fact and "legal evaluation," and application of state law to fact, when such determinations are later relevant to the adjudication of claims within the exclusive jurisdiction of the federal courts. However, whether direct determination of issues of federal law that are later pertinent in actions within exclusive federal jurisdiction is more difficult. If the approach of comment e of § 28(3) of the RESTATEMENT (SECOND) is taken to this problem, "[t]he question in each such case would be resolved in the light of the legislative purpose in vesting exclusive jurisdiction in a particular court." Do you think it will be possible to find in the federal statutes granting exclusive jurisdiction to the federal courts over certain kinds of cases or the legislative history of those statutes any concrete evidence that bears on this problem of issue preclusion? After *Matsushita*, discussed above, do you think the position of the RESTATEMENT (SECOND) is viable, or will all determinations of issues of federal law by state courts later be precluded?

2. In *Baker ex rel. Thomas v. General Motors Corp.*, 522 U.S. 222 (1998), the Supreme Court held that § 1738 does not absolutely require that state and federal courts employ the same enforcement mechanisms that would be employed by the courts of the state that rendered the judgment. In *Baker*, a Michigan court had granted an injunction to prevent a former General Motors employee from testifying against G.M. as an expert witness. Subsequently, G.M. was sued by another party in Missouri federal court in a wrongful death and products liability action and sought to depose the employee and use him as a witness. G.M. resisted the employee's appearance on the basis of the Michigan injunction, but the federal district court allowed the employee to testify. The court of appeals reversed, holding that the Missouri federal court was obligated to give effect to the Michigan injunction.

The U.S. Supreme Court, in turn, reversed the court of appeals, holding that Michigan had no power to control courts and parties in other states by precluding them from determining what witnesses could testify. The Court made it clear, however, that it was not creating a broad exception to the full faith and credit command that would allow state courts to refuse to honor sister state judgments based on the forum's choice of law or policy preferences. Rather, the Court merely held that the states need not "adopt the practices of other States regarding the time, manner, and mechanisms for enforcing judgments." *Id.* at 235. In addition, the Court observed that "[o]rders commanding action or inaction have been denied enforcement in a sister State when they purported to accomplish an official act within the exclusive province of that other State or interfered with litigation over which the ordering State had no authority." *Id.* Did General Motors just mistake its remedy? Should it have (a) sued the employee in a separate proceeding in Missouri to enforce the injunction against him or (b) sought to enforce the injunction in Michigan by bringing contempt proceedings against the employee? *See* TEPLY & WHITTEN at 1089–90.

3. In *Haring v. Prosise*, 462 U.S. 306, 313–14 (1983), the Supreme Court stated that "additional exceptions to collateral estoppel may be warranted in [42 U.S.C.] § 1983 actions in light of the 'understanding of § 1983' that 'the federal courts could step in where the state courts [are] unable or unwilling to protect federal rights.'" Would this mean that, if a constitutional issue is adjudicated in a state court that is "unable or unwilling" to protect federal rights, and if a § 1983 action is commenced in the courts of another *state*, the other state likewise can refuse to give the same effect to the judgment that would be given to it in the judgment-rendering state? If so, would the other state be obliged to follow the federal exceptions to § 1738 or could it create its own exceptions?

4. In *San Remo Hotel, L.P. v. City of San Francisco*, 545 U.S. 323 (2005), the Supreme Court continued its strict interpretation of § 1738 in an unusual case involving the federal doctrine of abstention. In *San Remo,* hotel owners brought a § 1983 action against the city to challenge the constitutionality of an ordinance on the ground that it effectuated a taking of property without due process. The Ninth Circuit Court of Appeals ordered the district court to abstain from decision while the plaintiffs sought compensation in state court. Abstention was ordered under the doctrine of *Railroad Commission v. Pullman Co.*, 312 U.S. 496 (1941), because a decision of the state court might make the federal constitutional question unnecessary. Under *Pullman*, litigants forced into the state courts may reserve their federal constitutional issues for later decision by a federal court if the state proceeding does not make decision of those issues unnecessary. *See England v. Louisiana Bd. of Med. Exam's*, 375 U.S. 411 (1964). The plaintiffs attempted to do so in the state proceeding in *San Remo*.

After the state court denied the plaintiffs' relief, they returned to federal court to litigate their federal constitutional questions. However, the plaintiffs' federal constitutional claims depended upon a number of issues that were identical to issues decided in the state court (because the state court had interpreted the relevant state takings law coextensively with federal law), and the district court held that relitigation of those issues was precluded by § 1738. The court of appeals affirmed, and the Supreme Court granted certiorari and affirmed the court of appeals. Because the plaintiffs had not simply reserved the federal constitutional question they sought to litigate in federal court, but had, in the state proceeding, broadened the litigation in a manner that effectively asked that court to resolve the same federal issue they sought to reserve for federal court, they were not able to use the reservation procedure of the abstention doctrine to avoid the force of § 1738. Other issues litigated in state court had not been the subject of the abstention order and could not, therefore, be saved by a reservation of rights to litigate in federal court. In addition, the Supreme Court continued its refusal to allow federal courts to create exceptions to § 1738 when no subsequent federal statute contains an express or implied partial repeal of the provision and Congress had not clearly manifested its intent to depart from § 1738.

5. How does a plaintiff who recovers a judgment against a defendant in one state seek full-faith-and-credit enforcement of the judgment in another state? Such enforcement is often necessary when the defendant has insufficient or no assets in the judgment-rendering state to satisfy the judgment and the plaintiff wishes to enforce the judgment against assets of the defendant in another state. The process of full-faith-and-credit enforcement has been greatly simplified by the adoption in nearly every state of the Uniform Enforcement of Foreign Judgments Act, 13 (pt. 1) U.L.A. §§ 1–10 (2002).

Under this Act, the plaintiff may simply file an authenticated copy of the first state's judgment with the appropriate court clerk in the second state. The clerk will then docket the judgment as any other judgment rendered in that state and the plaintiff may then commence execution on the judgment against the defendant. The defendant may challenge the jurisdictional validity of the first state's judgment as permitted under the full-faith-and-credit clause. The restrictions on these jurisdictional challenges were examined in Section F. If the judgment is valid, however, § 1738 requires the second state to enforce the judgment. The defendant is prohibited from raising any challenges to the substantive merits of the first state's judgment and must return to the first state to raise such challenges. *See Milliken v. Meyer*, 311 U.S. 457, 462 (1940) ("[T]he full faith and credit clause of the Constitution precludes any inquiry into the merits of the cause of action, the logic or consistency of the decision, or the validity of the legal principles on which the judgment is based. Whatever mistakes of law may underlie the judgment it is 'conclusive as to all the media concludendi.'").

Problems

Problem 12-42. P and D are involved in an automobile accident in State X. P sues D in a state court of State X for personal injuries and wins a substantial judgment. P did not sue for damages to P's automobile in this action. Under the res judicata law of State X, damages to person and property arising from the same event are part of the same claim; thus, failure to sue for property damage in the personal injury action would preclude P from suing separately for the damage to the automobile in State X. P brings a second action against D in a state court of State Y for property damage. Under the res judicata rules of State Y, damages to person and property arising from the same accident constitute different claims and can be sued on separately. If D pleads res judicata in the State Y action, does 28 U.S.C. § 1738 require State Y to enforce the res judicata rules of State X?

Problem 12-43. Assume the same facts as stated in *Problem 12-42*, except that State *X* has a compulsory counterclaim rule identical to Rule 13(a) of the Federal Rules of Civil Procedure. In *P's* suit in State *X*, *D* fails to plead a counterclaim for personal injuries received in the accident. If *D* sues *P* for personal injuries in State *Y* and *P* pleads res judicata, does § 1738 require State *Y* to give effect to State *X's* counterclaim rule?

Problem 12-44. *P* and *D* are involved in an automobile accident in State *X*. State *X* considers damage to person and damage to property in the same accident to constitute separate claims. Furthermore, if an action is brought for damage to property or person, but not both, State *X* does not give issue preclusion effect to the judgment in any later action on the omitted claim. *P* sues *D* for property damage in a State *X* state court. After a trial, a verdict and a judgment are entered for *D*—the jury specifically finding that *D* was not negligent. *P* then sues *D* for personal injuries in State *Y*. State *Y* also considers property damage and personal injury arising from the same accident to constitute different claims. However, State *Y* gives issue preclusion effect to judgments in such actions. Can State *Y* give the finding of no negligence a preclusive effect in the action in its courts and dismiss the action, even though State *X* would not do so? If so, should State *Y's* ability to do so be qualified in any respect?

Problem 12-45. *P*, a citizen of State *X*, sues *D Corp.*, a corporation incorporated in State *Y* with its principal place of business there, in a state court in State *X* for $5,000,000 in damages under the State *X* antitrust laws. *D* removes the action to the State *X* United States District Court on the basis of diversity of citizenship. After trial, a verdict and judgment are entered for *D*. Subsequently, *P* commences a federal antitrust action in the United States District Court in State *X* against *D*. This action is within the exclusive jurisdiction of the federal courts and arises out of the same facts as *P's* previous action against *D* in State *X* state court. *D* pleads res judicata. Is the plea good? Why or why not? Are there additional facts you would like to have before answering this question?

Problem 12-46. On the facts of *Problem 12-45*, suppose *P's* action had been for breach of contract under state law and *D* had possessed a defense that the contract was illegal under the federal antitrust laws. Despite the existence of diversity of citizenship, *D* did *not* remove, however. After trial, a verdict and judgment are entered against *D*, the State *X* court having found that the federal antitrust laws did not invalidate the contract. *D* then commenced a federal antitrust action in United States District Court against *P*. *P* contends that the State *X* court's determination of the federal issue is res judicata. Is this plea good? Why or why not? Are there additional facts you would like to have before answering this question?

2. Enforcement of Federal Judgments

The full faith and credit implementing statute does not control the effect of federal judgments. However, this does not mean that federal judgments can be disregarded by state courts or other federal courts. The implications of Article III of the Constitution and the Supremacy Clause of Article VI of the Constitution require that federal judgments receive a binding effect in later proceedings. *See* TEPLY & WHITTEN at 1105–06. The more difficult question is how to determine what rules govern the effect to be given a federal judgment. Section 87 of the RESTATEMENT (SECOND) provides that "[f]ederal law determines the effects under the rules of res judicata of a judgment of a federal court." However, as you will recall from Chapter 5, the U.S. Supreme Court in *Semtek International, Inc. v. Lockheed Martin Corp.*, 531 U.S. 497 (2001), indicated that federal law will adopt state law to govern most res judicata questions when a federal court renders a judgment in a diversity action.

Prior to *Semtek*, the federal courts were divided on whether the scope of federal judgments in diversity actions should be determined by the res judicata rules of the state in which the judgment-rendering district court was sitting or by an independent federal rule. The courts holding that an independent federal res judicata rule should control were following the approach of § 87 of the RESTATEMENT (SECOND). However, this fact did not mean that the rule set out in § 87 was necessarily an accurate restatement. Before *Semtek*, the U.S. Supreme Court accepted the proposition that federal common law should define the scope of a federal judgment rendered in federal question cases. *See, e.g., Parklane Hosiery Co. v. Shore*, 439 U.S. 322 (1979); *Blonder-Tongue Labs., Inc. v. University of Ill. Found.*, 402 U.S. 313 (1971); *see* TEPLY & WHITTEN at 1106. But the Court had reserved judgment on whether the *Erie* doctrine requires state law to define the scope of a federal judgment in a diversity action. *See Heiser v. Woodruff*, 327 U.S. 726, 731–32 (1946). Thus, as far as judgments rendered in diversity cases were concerned, the question upon which § 87 of the RESTATEMENT (SECOND) pronounced was technically open. *Semtek* resolved the question of what law controls a federal diversity judgment by indicating that the scope of most federal diversity judgments would be determined by state law.

Recall that in *Semtek*, the plaintiff brought an action in California state court for breach of contract and various business torts, and the defendant removed the action to federal court on the basis of diversity of citizenship. The defendant then moved to dismiss the action on the ground that the plaintiff's claims were barred by the California statute of limitations. The federal court dismissed the action on this ground "on the merits and with prejudice." The plaintiff commenced a second action in Maryland state court against the defendant on the same claims, which were not barred under Maryland's three-year statute of limitations. However, the Maryland courts concluded that the California federal judgment precluded the action.

The U.S. Supreme Court granted certiorari and reversed. Although the defendant argued that Federal Rule 41(b) made the federal judgment "on the merits" and thus claim preclusive, the Court first held that Federal Rule 41(b) was inapplicable to the case. The result of this was that Rule 41(b) did not make the statute of limitations dismissal by the California federal court a judgment "on the merits" that would have a claim preclusive effect in an action in Maryland. The difficulty with this part of the *Semtek* holding for purposes of this subsection is that the Court spoke in terms that could be applicable to other situations in which a claim-preclusive effect of a federal diversity judgment had been thought settled.

For example, the Court, speaking of Rule 41(b), stated that "it would be peculiar to find a rule governing the effect that must be accorded federal judgments by other courts ensconced in rules governing the internal procedures of the rendering court itself." *Semtek*, 531 U.S. at 503. But other Federal Rules that govern "the internal procedures of the rendering court" have been thought to have a preclusive effect in subsequent actions in other courts. *See* FED. R. CIV. P. 13(a), 41(a)(1)(B). And Rule 41(b) itself has also been viewed as providing for a claim preclusive effect in other courts in situations other than the one in *Semtek*. For example, Chapter 9 discussed the effect of Rule 41(b) in producing a judgment on the merits in cases in which the plaintiff's complaint has been dismissed for failure to state a claim upon which relief can be granted. *Semtek* has now thrown considerable doubt upon the preclusive effect of a federal judgment in this latter situation and under the other Federal Rules of Civil Procedure providing for preclusion.

In addition, *Semtek* held that federal law would control the effect of a federal judgment in a diversity action, but that federal law would adopt the state law of the state in which a federal judgment-rendering court is sitting as the proper rule of decision on questions of res judicata unless "the state law is incompatible with federal interests." *Semtek*, 531 U.S. at 509. As discussed in the notes below, this part of the Court's holding resembles the approach of the RESTATEMENT (SECOND). However, it does not exactly correspond to the approach of the RESTATEMENT (SECOND), and it also resembles some decisions in the substantive federal common-law area that you studied in Chapter 5. Recall that the Supreme Court in that area has sometimes held that federal common law will govern an area, but that state law will be adopted as federal common law. It is impossible to tell from the opinion whether the Court is attempting to follow one approach or the other or, perhaps, an approach completely different from either.

Notes and Questions

1. The position taken by the drafters of the RESTATEMENT (SECOND) was attributable to an influential article by Professor Ronan Degnan. *See* Ronan E. Degnan, *Federalized Res Judicata*, 85 YALE L.J. 741 (1976). Professor Degnan argued that early decisions of the Supreme Court applying state law to determine the scope of a federal judgment were based on the command of the Conformity Acts that federal courts should apply state procedure in actions at law. Therefore, with the adoption of the Federal Rules of Civil Procedure and the end of federal conformity to state procedure, the law governing the scope of federal judgments should have changed accordingly, because the law of res judicata is heavily dependent on the procedural context in which a judgment is rendered. However, Professor Stephen Burbank's examination of the same early decisions discussed by Professor Degnan has created serious doubt whether those decisions were really based on the Conformity Acts. Instead,

> long before *Erie* and the Federal Rules, the Supreme Court had held that federal preclusion law governs at least some questions of the effects to be accorded federal judgments on matters of federal substantive law. During the same period, the Court required that the preclusive effects of federal alienage and diversity judgment on matters of state substantive law follow state law. The Court's articulated concern in both contexts was to protect rights conferred by the substantive law.

Stephen B. Burbank, *Interjurisdictional Preclusion, Full Faith and Credit and Federal Common Law: A General Approach*, 71 CORNELL L. REV. 733, 752 (1986). Recall that Justice Scalia's opinion for the Court in *Semtek* bowed to Professor Degnan's position by observing that the *Dupasseur* case was decided under the Conformity Act of 1872, which required federal courts to follow state procedural law in common-law cases, a fact that the opinion indicated "arguably affected the outcome of the case." *See Semtek*, 531 U.S. at 507–08. Shouldn't Justice Scalia have paid more attention to the historical materials bearing on the effect of diversity judgments?

2. (a) In addition to Professor Burbank's historical proof, it should be observed more generally that the rationale of the RESTATEMENT (SECOND) is questionable. The doctrine of res judicata receives support from multiple sources. The procedural context in which a judgment is rendered is indeed an important source of claim and issue preclusion rules. Thus, when it can be seen that the major contributing factors to a preclusion question are the pleading, joinder, and other "housekeeping rules" of the federal courts, a strong argument can be made that federal law should define the scope of the judgment independent of state law, even in a diversity action.

(b) However, substantive policies can also support res judicata rules. When state law provides the substantive rule of decision and the state possesses related substantive policies that shape its law of res judicata, it would seem that independent federal law should not define the scope of a federal diversity judgment. The RESTATEMENT (SECOND) attempts to walk the substance-procedure line by stating that, while federal law should always determine the effect of a federal judgment, federal law sometimes should incorporate state law to protect state substantive policies. Nevertheless, the RESTATEMENT (SECOND) advocates the adoption of state law only in areas covered by §§ 43 to 61 of its provisions, which deal with substantive legal relationships resulting in preclusion. *See* RESTATEMENT (SECOND) OF JUDGMENTS § 87 cmt. b. (1982). Thus, the drafters of the RESTATEMENT (SECOND) seem to assume that there are no other areas in which substantive law can contribute to rules of res judicata. This position is demonstrably false, as basic rules of claim and issue preclusion can also be supported by substantive policies. *See* 18B WRIGHT ET AL. § 4472, at 377–79 (providing other examples of basic claim and issue preclusion rules supported by substantive policies).

3. Note that Justice Scalia's approach to diversity judgments in *Semtek* resembles, but is not identical to, that of the RESTATEMENT (SECOND). Part III of the opinion states that "federal common law governs the claim-preclusive effect of a dismissal by a federal court sitting in diversity." This, in the abstract, agrees with the RESTATEMENT (SECOND). However, the opinion then goes on to hold that

> [s]ince state, rather than federal, substantive law is at issue there is no need for a uniform federal rule. And indeed, nationwide uniformity is in the substance of the matter is better served by having the same claim-preclusive rule (the state rule) apply whether the dismissal has been ordered by a federal or state court. This is, it seems to us, a classic case for adopting, as the federally prescribed rule of decision, the law that would be applied by state courts in the State in which the federal diversity court sits.

Semtek, 531 U.S. at 508. Although this passage could be interpreted as applying only to the facts of *Semtek*, it was followed by a string citation to a large number of cases under the general *Erie* doctrine. Thus, the most plausible way to interpret the statement is that the scope of federal diversity judgments will usually be governed by state law. The statement was qualified only by Justice Scalia's later indication that state law would not control when it was incompatible with federal interests, as when state law would not accord a claim-preclusive effect to dismissals for willful violation of discovery orders. On the whole, therefore, *Semtek* seems to provide for far broader application of state law to define the scope of federal diversity judgments than does the rule of § 87 of the *Resatement (Second)*.

4. How easy will it be to determine when state law is incompatible with federal interests in a way that demands an independent federal rule of res judicata? Isn't this standard likely to provoke a substantial amount of litigation over whether state or federal law controls the scope of a federal diversity judgment?

5. How does the process of incorporation of state substantive law described in comment b to § 87 of the RESTATEMENT (SECOND) differ from a straightforward application of the *Erie* doctrine to the scope of judgment problems in diversity cases? Comment b states that "[t]he underlying distinction [between situations in which state law should be incorporated and those in which it should not] parallels, and indeed may correspond to, the distinction drawn between 'procedure' and 'substance' under the Rules of Decision Act and the doctrine of *Erie R.R. v. Tompkins*...." Do you understand this statement? The

statement only mentions the Rules of Decision Act. Does that mean that the substance-procedure distinction of the Rules Enabling Act is irrelevant to the incorporation process under § 87? Does *Semtek* clarify or further confuse the answers to these questions?

Problems

Problem 12-47. P brings a federal diversity action against D. D moves to dismiss the action for failure to state a claim upon which relief can be granted. This motion is granted, and judgment is rendered for D after P fails to amend the complaint. P then brings a second action in state court based on the same transaction, but relying on a different state legal theory. Under the law of the state where the federal court that entered judgment in the first action was sitting, P's second suit would not be precluded by the judgment if it had been rendered by a state court. Should P's claim be deemed precluded by the federal judgment? Do you need additional information to answer this question?

Problem 12-48. P sues D in a federal court for violation of the federal antitrust laws, a claim over which the federal courts have exclusive jurisdiction. After trial, judgment is entered for D. P then sues D in a state court under the state antitrust laws on a claim based on the same events that were the subject of P's federal action against D. Assuming that the federal court would have had supplemental jurisdiction of P's state antitrust claim had P chosen to assert it in the federal action, may P maintain the state action? Why or why not? Assume the state claim would normally be precluded by the federal judgment. Can you nevertheless think of circumstances in which it should not be precluded?

Problem 12-49. *D Airways* is incorporated with its principal place of business in State Y. *P-1* sues D in a federal diversity action in a U.S. District Court in State Y. *P-1* asserts a claim for the wrongful death of *P-1's* spouse in the crash of a D aircraft in State Y. After a trial, a verdict and judgment are entered for *P-1*, the jury specifically finding that D was negligent. Under the res judicata law of State Y, the finding of negligence against D does not have issue preclusion effect in a later action by a different plaintiff, because the state legislature has enacted a statute so providing. The express object of the statute is to prevent massive liability from attaching to defendants based on a single judgment in mass disaster cases. (The substantive negligence law of State Y was applied by the district court under the *Klaxon* doctrine to determine B's liability.) Under the federal law of issue preclusion developed in federal question cases, nonmutual estoppel would apply to prevent relitigation by D of its negligence, because it had a full and fair opportunity to litigate in the first proceeding. If a second suit is brought in a state or federal court of State Y by *P-2* to recover for the wrongful death of *P-2's* spouse in the same crash, should the state or federal rule of issue preclusion be applied?

Problem 12-50. P sues D in a federal diversity action, asserting a state claim for personal injuries. D's answer omits a counterclaim that D possesses for D's own personal injuries arising out of the same accident. After a trial to a jury, a verdict and judgment is rendered for D on an express finding that D was not negligent. Subsequently, D brings an action against P for the personal injuries that D received in the accident. P pleads res judicata, on the grounds that the failure of D to assert D's claim as a counterclaim in P's action precludes D from asserting it in a subsequent proceeding because it was a compulsory counterclaim under Federal Rule 13(a). The state in which the federal court in *P v. D* was sitting when it rendered the judgment in the first action does not have a compulsory counterclaim rule. Therefore, if the first action had been in a state court of that state, D's action would not be precluded. Does the federal judgment in *P v. D* preclude D's action because of Rule 13(a)?

3. Enforcement of Foreign Nation Judgments

Neither the Full Faith and Credit Clause nor its general implementing statute, 28 U.S.C. § 1738, requires state or federal courts to give any effect to the judgments of foreign nations. Nevertheless, it is well accepted that these judgments will be enforced by courts within the United States.

The traditional rule in the United States was articulated by the U.S. Supreme Court in *Hilton v. Guyot*, 159 U.S. 113 (1895). In *Hilton*, the Court held that the judgments of foreign courts rendered with jurisdiction would be given effect only to the extent that United States' judgments would be given effect in the courts of the judgment-rendering nation. Most state courts in the United States give the same effect to foreign nation judgments that they would give to the judgments of other state courts. For foreign nation money judgments, many states have adopted the Uniform Foreign-Money Judgments Recognition Act, 13 (pt. 2) U.L.A. §§ 1–13 (Supp. 2012). This Act applies to foreign nation judgments that grant or deny recovery of a sum of money and provides that recognized judgments shall be enforceable in the state "to the same extent as the judgment of a sister state entitled to full faith and credit." *See* §§ 3 & 7. The Act establishes standards for the recognition of the foreign judgment and provides that a state need not recognize a judgment if, among things, the judgment is incompatible "with the requirements of due process of law." *See* § 4.

Adoption of this Uniform Act, however, is purely voluntary with the states and, if adopted by a particular state, it is adopted only as a matter of state law. A serious question remains, therefore, whether the U.S. Supreme Court should create a preemptive *federal* common-law standard to govern the effect that should be given to the judgments of foreign courts. The argument is that such a federal common-law standard would be justifiable because of the difficulties of dealing with foreign judgments under the "potentially divergent law of fifty states and federal courts" and the fact that "recognition of foreign judgments at least touches concerns of foreign relations in which the national government has paramount interests." *See* 18B Wright et al. § 4473, at 403. As yet, however, the Court has not created such a federal common-law standard, and the balance of authority seems to favor control of the effect of foreign judgments by state law. Restatement (Third) of the Foreign Relations Law of the United States § 481 cmt. a (1987). In federal diversity actions, federal courts follow state law on the recognition of foreign nation judgments. However, in federal question cases, independent federal preclusion law determines the effect of foreign nation judgments.

Note

In 2006, the American Law Institute proposed draft legislation that would uniformly regulate the reception and enforcement of foreign nation judgments for both state and federal courts. *See* ALI Recognition and Enforcement of Foreign Judgments: Analysis and Proposed Federal Statute (2006). The ALI legislation is designed to operate even in the absence of a general treaty between the United States and other nations governing judgment enforcement. To date, this proposed legislation has not been enacted.

At the federal level, attempts to negotiate a general treaty under the auspices of the Hague Conference on Private International Law continue to encounter obstacles. Other nations have difficulties with the U.S. concepts of general jurisdiction and jurisdiction based on transient presence as well as U.S. judgments awarding noncompensatory and punitive damages. *Cf.* § 6(a)(iv), cmt. b, & § 7(d).

Problems

Problem 12-51. Assume that an action is brought in federal court and that the judgment of a court of a foreign nation is brought into issue to establish either the claim or a defense. Should federal common law or the law of the state in which the district court sits govern the issue? Should the answer depend upon whether

(a) the action is based on federal question jurisdiction?

(b) the action is based on diversity jurisdiction and the applicable substantive law controlling the action is the law of the state in which the district court sits?

(c) the action is based on diversity jurisdiction and the applicable substantive law controlling the action is the law of the foreign nation from which the judgment is taken?

(d) the action is based on alienage jurisdiction and the applicable substantive law controlling the action is (i) the law of the state in which the district court sits or (ii) the law of the foreign nation from which the judgment is taken?

Problem 12-52. Should the answer to any part of *Problem 12-51* change if the action were brought in a state court?

Index

References are to pages of the casebook where discussion begins.